■ THE RESOURCE FOR THE INDEPENDENT TRAVELER

"The guides are aimed not only at young budget travelers but at the indepedent traveler; a sort of streetwise cookbook for traveling alone."

—The New York Times

"Unbeatable; good sight-seeing advice; up-to-date info on restaurants, hotels, and inns; a commitment to money-saving travel; and a wry style that brightens nearly every page."

—The Washington Post

"Lighthearted and sophisticated, informative and fun to read. [Let's Go] helps the novice traveler navigate like a knowledgeable old hand."

—Atlanta Journal-Constitution

"A world-wise traveling companion—always ready with friendly advice and helpful hints, all sprinkled with a bit of wit."

—The Philadelphia Inquirer

■ THE BEST TRAVEL BARGAINS IN YOUR PRICE RANGE

"All the dirt, dirt cheap."

—People

"Anything you need to know about budget traveling is detailed in this book."

—The Chicago Sun-Times

"Let's Go follows the creed that you don't have to toss your life's savings to the wind to travel—unless you want to."

—The Salt Lake Tribune

■ REAL ADVICE FOR REAL EXPERIENCES

"The writers seem to have experienced every rooster-packed bus and lunar-surfaced mattress about which they write."

—The New York Times

"A guide should tell you what to expect from a destination. Here Let's Go shines."

—The Chicago Tribune

LET'S GO PUBLICATIONS

TRAVEL GUIDES

Alaska & the Pacific Northwest 2003
Australia 2003
Austria & Switzerland 2003
Britain & Ireland 2003
California 2003
Central America 8th edition
Chile 1st edition **NEW TITLE**
China 4th edition
Costa Rica 1st edition **NEW TITLE**
Eastern Europe 2003
Egypt 2nd edition
Europe 2003
France 2003
Germany 2003
Greece 2003
Hawaii 2003 **NEW TITLE**
India & Nepal 7th edition
Ireland 2003
Israel 4th edition
Italy 2003
Mexico 19th edition
Middle East 4th edition
New Zealand 6th edition
Peru, Ecuador & Bolivia 3rd edition
South Africa 5th edition
Southeast Asia 8th edition
Southwest USA 2003
Spain & Portugal 2003
Thailand 1st edition **NEW TITLE**
Turkey 5th edition
USA 2003
Western Europe 2003

CITY GUIDES

Amsterdam 2003
Barcelona 2003
Boston 2003
London 2003
New York City 2003
Paris 2003
Rome 2003
San Francisco 2003
Washington, D.C. 2003

MAP GUIDES

Amsterdam
Berlin
Boston
Chicago
Dublin
Florence
Hong Kong
London
Los Angeles
Madrid
New Orleans
New York City
Paris
Prague
Rome
San Francisco
Seattle
Sydney
Venice
Washington, D.C.

LET'S GO

AUSTRIA & SWITZERLAND 2003

JOANNA SHAWN BRIGID O'LEARY EDITOR
DEBORAH HARRISON ASSOCIATE EDITOR

RESEARCHER-WRITERS
JOCELYN BEH
ALINNA CHUNG
TOM MILLER
CHRISTINE PETERSON
LORA SWEENEY

MATTHEW HARTZELL MAP EDITOR
CELESTE NG MANAGING EDITOR
EDUARDO L. MONTOYA TYPESETTER

ST. MARTIN'S PRESS ✖ NEW YORK

HELPING LET'S GO If you want to share your discoveries, suggestions, or corrections, please drop us a line. We read every piece of correspondence, whether a postcard, a 10-page email, or a coconut. Please note that mail received after May 2003 may be too late for the 2004 book, but will be kept for future editions. **Address mail to:**

> Let's Go: Austria & Switzerland
> 67 Mount Auburn Street
> Cambridge, MA 02138
> USA

Visit Let's Go at **http://www.letsgo.com,** or send email to:

> **feedback@letsgo.com**
> **Subject: "Let's Go: Austria & Switzerland"**

In addition to the invaluable travel advice our readers share with us, many are kind enough to offer their services as researchers or editors. Unfortunately, our charter enables us to employ only currently enrolled Harvard students.

HOW TO USE THIS BOOK

ORGANIZATION. Welcome to Let's Go: Austria and Switzerland 2003! We'll be your guide to to all things Austrian and Swiss, from castles and cheese to mountains and music. The black tabs on the side of the book should help you navigate your way through.

PRICE RANGES AND RANKINGS. Our researchers list establishments in order of value from best to worst. Our absolute favorites are denoted by the Let's Go thumbs-up (👍). Since the best value does not always mean the cheapest price, we have incorporated a system of price ranges in the guide. The table below lists how prices fall within each bracket.

AUSTRIA	❶	❷	❸	❹	❺
ACCOMMODATIONS	€1-8	€9-15	€16-30	€31-70	€71+
FOOD	€1-4	€5-10	€11-16	€17-25	€26+
SWITZERLAND	❶	❷	❸	❹	❺
ACCOMMODATIONS	1-15SFr	16-35SFr	36-60SFr	61-120SFr	121SFr+
FOOD	1-8SFr	9-14SFr	16-24SFr	25-34SFr	35SFr+

PHONE CODES AND TELEPHONE NUMBERS. Area codes for each region appear opposite the name of the region and are denoted by the ☎ icon. Phone numbers in text are also preceded by the ☎ icon.

WHEN TO USE IT

TWO MONTHS BEFORE. The first chapter, **Discover** Austria and Switzerland, contains highlights of the region, including Suggested Itineraries (see p. 4) that can help you plan your trip. The **Essentials** (see p. 7) section contains practical information on planning a budget, making reservations, renewing a passport, and has other useful tips about traveling in.

ONE MONTH BEFORE. Take care of insurance, and write down a list of emergency numbers and hotlines. Make a list of packing essentials (see **Packing**, p. 23) and shop for anything you are missing. Read through the coverage and make sure you understand the logistics of your itinerary (catching trains, ferries, etc.). Make any reservations necessary.

2 WEEKS BEFORE. Leave an itinerary and a photocopy of important documents with someone at home. Take some time to peruse the **Life and Times** (see p. 64), which has info on history, culture, recent political events, and more.

ON THE ROAD. The **Appendix** contains a glossary of phrases, to help you with directions, restaurant menus and conversations with spicy locals. Now, arm yourself with a travel journal and hit the road.

A NOTE TO OUR READERS The information for this book was gathered by *Let's Go* researchers from May through August of 2002. Each listing is based on one researcher's opinion, formed during his or her visit at a particular time. Those traveling at other times may have different experiences since prices, dates, hours, and conditions are always subject to change. You are urged to check the facts presented in this book beforehand to avoid inconvenience and surprises.

CONTENTS

MAPS

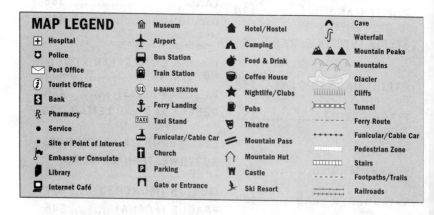

MAP LEGEND

⊞ Hospital	🏛 Museum
✪ Police	✈ Airport
✉ Post Office	🚌 Bus Station
ⓘ Tourist Office	🚆 Train Station
S Bank	Ⓤ U-BAHN STATION
℞ Pharmacy	⚓ Ferry Landing
● Service	TAXI Taxi Stand
■ Site or Point of Interest	🚡 Funicular/Cable Car
⚑ Embassy or Consulate	✝ Church
📕 Library	P Parking
💻 Internet Café	⊓ Gate or Entrance

● Hotel/Hostel	⌃ Cave
⛺ Camping	∫ Waterfall
🍎 Food & Drink	▲▲▲ Mountain Peaks
☕ Coffee House	Mountains
★ Nightlife/Clubs	Glacier
🍺 Pubs	Cliffs
♨ Theatre	Tunnel
⇄ Mountain Pass	Ferry Route
⌂ Mountain Hut	Funicular/Cable Car
♜ Castle	Pedestrian Zone
⛷ Ski Resort	Stairs
	Footpaths/Trails
	Railroads

Austria and Switzerland: Map of Chapter Divisions

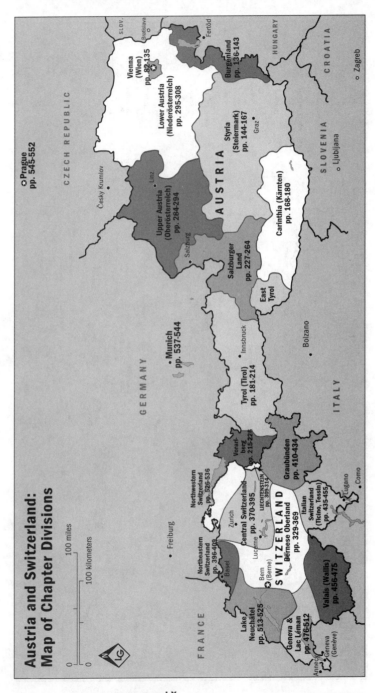

CZECH REPUBLIC

GERMANY

AUSTRIA

SWITZERLAND

FRANCE

ITALY

SLOVENIA

CROATIA

HUNGARY

SLOV.

LIECHTENSTEIN
pp. 309-314

Bratislava

Fertöd

Graz

Ljubljana

Zagreb

Salzburg

Linz

Český Krumlov

Innsbruck

Bolzano

Como

Lugano

Zürich

Luzern

Bern
(Berne)

Basel

Freiburg

Annecy

Geneva
(Genève)

100 miles

100 kilometers

IX

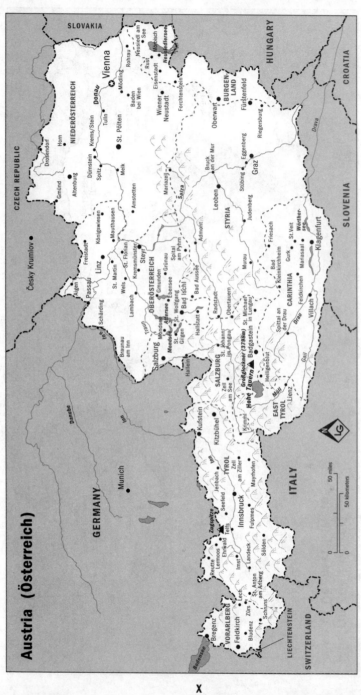

Austria (Österreich)

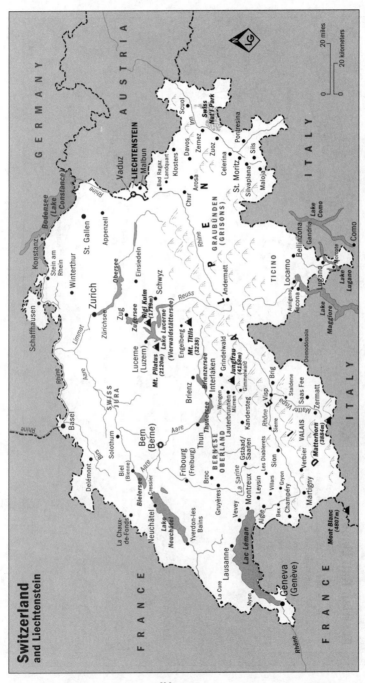

Switzerland
and Liechtenstein

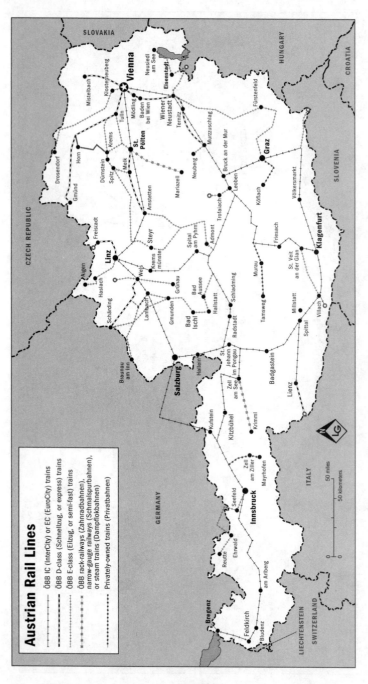

Austrian Rail Lines

ÖBB IC (InterCity) or EC (EuroCity) trains

ÖBB D-class (Schnellzug, or express) trains

ÖBB E-class (Eilzug, or semi-fast) trains

ÖBB rack-railways (Zahnradbahnen),
narrow-gauge railways (Schmalspurbahnen),
or steam trains (Dampflokbahnen)

Privately-owned trains (Privatbahnen)

SLOVAKIA

HUNGARY

CROATIA

SLOVENIA

ITALY

LIECHTENSTEIN

SWITZERLAND

GERMANY

CZECH REPUBLIC

Vienna

Mistelbach
Klosterneuburg
Tulln
Mödling
Baden bei Wien
Wiener Neustadt
Eisenstadt
Neusiedl am See
Fürstenfeld
Ternitz
Mürzzuschlag
Neuberg
Bruck an der Mur
Graz
Köflach
Völkermarkt
Leoben
Trofaiach
Admont
Friesach
Klagenfurt
St. Veit an der Glan
Murau
Tamsweg
Millstatt
Spittal
Villach
St. Pölten
Krems
Dürnstein
Spitz
Melk
Amstetten
Mariazell
Horn
Drosendorf
Gmünd
Freistadt
Aigen
Haslach
Linz
Wels
Krems münster
Steyr
Spital am Pyhrn
Grünau
Bad Aussee
Hallstatt
Schladming
Radstadt
Schärding
Lambach
Gmunden
Bad Ischl
Braunau am Inn
Salzburg
Hallein
St. Johann im Pongau
Zell am See
Badgastein
Lienz
Krimml
Kufstein
Kitzbühel
Zell am Ziller
Mayrhofen
Seefeld
Innsbruck
Reutte
Ehrwald
am Arlberg
Bregenz
Feldkirch
Bludenz

50 miles
50 kilometers
0
0

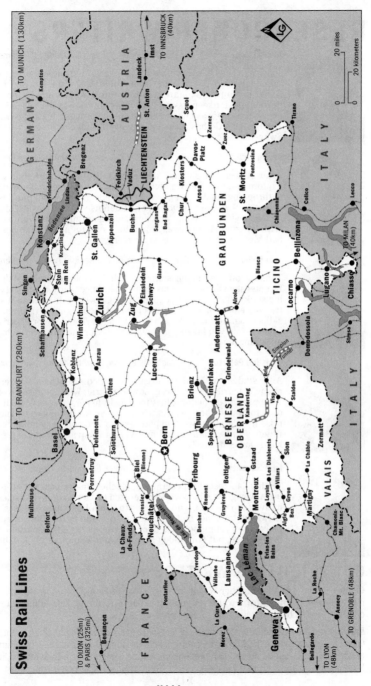

Swiss Rail Lines

RESEARCHER-WRITERS

Jocelyn Beh *Bernese Oberland, Italian Switzerland, Lucerne*

Jocelyn joined Let's Go with skills in German and outdoor orientation leadership. A native of Greenville, PA, she spent a year in Basel although ultimately studied non-Western religions. Befriending innkeepers and canyoning guides was her specialty on the road, as was uncovering brothels masquerading as hotels. Though Let's Go has ceased to pay her, Jocelyn refuses to leave Switzerland.

Alinna Chung *Zurich, Basel, Bern, Geneva, Northern Switzerland*

After 20 years in Boston, Alinna ran out of neighborhoods to explore and took her wandering tendencies overseas. Studying anthropology and singing in an a cappella group round out this expert in Swiss nightclubs and self-defense. In her travels, she mixed English, French, Cantonese, and a sprinkling of German. With discriminating taste, Alinna took careful note of the best bathrooms and chocolatiers in Switzerland.

Tom Miller *Carinthia, Hohe Tauern Region, Tyrol, Vorarlberg*

Tom was off to a running start as he climbed the mountains of the Liechtenstein marathon. This alpine endurance (and a trusty walking stick) allowed him to expand hiking coverage in central Austria. A member of a comedy troupe, Tom used his improvisational skills when he was mistaken for an Italian. Tom left for Austria asking, "Can you hike uphill both ways"—for the answer, see his upcoming novel.

Christine Peterson *Niederösterreich, Salzburgerland, and Styria*

After studying in Munich, Christine satisfied a penchant for Germanic countries by exploring Lower Austria. With the resolve of an applied math major, Christine fought hyperactive schoolchildren to find the best Styrian wine. Her eye for detail was no surprise in light of her work in photography and college admissions. Fluency in German served her well in Austria, though is less handy in her native Texas.

Lora Sweeney *Vienna, Burgenland, Oberösterreich*

Trading lab-coats for Lederhosen, biochem major Lora set off to learn why great minds were so devoted to Vienna. A Los Angeles native (and therefore no stranger to convoluted metropolises), Lora took the Inner and Outer Rings by storm to find the perfect place to get your groove on. Her preferred mode of transportation is the horse, but Lora didn't seem to mind exploring the city by *Straßenbahn*.

CONTRIBUTING WRITERS

Charles Ehrlich was a Researcher-Writer for *Let's Go: Spain & Portugal*. He is formerly a Senior Staff Attorney at the Claims Resolution Tribunal that adjudicates claims to Swiss bank accounts from the Nazi era.

Kata Gellen was a Researcher-Writer for *Let's Go: Germany 1999*. She lived in Austria for the past two years, first on a Fulbright scholarship studying at the University of Vienna, and then as an English-language teaching assistant at a high school in Vienna. She is now a Ph.D. candidate in German literature at Princeton University.

ACKNOWLEDGMENTS

Team A&S thanks: Celeste, your eye for microscopic detail and bolded commas will take you far. Mapper Matt, for cartography extraordinaire. Prod, for bailing us out on a bi-hourly basis. The Axis pod, for laughs and love.

Joanna Shawn Brigid O'Leary thanks: Debbie, with an "e", for editing the appendix while I was working on my own. Scott, for Guffman and the mid-afternoon show. Betsy, your satellite advice is indespensable and for being my first editor. Margaret and Jackie, keep the Boo Radley stories coming. To the pod: Amber, I cherish your groans and moans; Jesse, remember to pick up the dream team at McDonald's; Karoun, let the massage train trek on; and Thea, your one-liners are a joy forever. I adore you guys.

Deborah Harrison thanks: Joanna for refusing to let medical emergencies interfere with more important paper edits; Leichtman, thanks for keeping an eye on our bookteam in times of minor crisis. Jesse, you are the Bringer of Funk to the Germanic people. Ariel, roommates will never get weirder. We, on the other hand, are perfectly normal. Marla, this job was just another step on the road to becoming you; thanks for making me apply. Thank you, Kevin, for chocolate support and endless encouragement.

Matthew Hartzell thanks: Austria and Switzerland, with the highest land:topography ratios in Europe, are a mapper's dream. Thanks to Debbie and Joanna, the friendliest bookteam, mapland, my family, and Ma Go.

Editor
Joanna Shawn Brigid O'Leary
Associate Editors
Deborah Harrison
Managing Editor
Celeste Ng
Map Editor
Matthew Hartzell

Publishing Director
Matthew Gibson
Editor-in-Chief
Brian R. Walsh
Production Manager
C. Winslow Clayton
Cartography Manager
Julie Stephens
Design Manager
Amy Cain
Editorial Managers
Christopher Blazejewski,
Abigail Burger, D. Cody Dydek,
Harriett Green, Angela Mi Young Hur,
Marla Kaplan, Celeste Ng
Financial Manager
Noah Askin
Marketing & Publicity Managers
Michelle Bowman, Adam M. Grant
New Media Managers
Jesse Tov, Kevin Yip
Online Manager
Amélie Cherlin
Personnel Managers
Alex Leichtman, Owen Robinson
Production Associates
Caleb Epps, David Muehlke
Network Administrators
Steven Aponte, Eduardo Montoya
Design Associate
Juice Fong
Financial Assistant
Suzanne Siu
Office Coordinators
Alex Ewing, Adam Kline,
Efrat Kussel

Director of Advertising Sales
Erik Patton
Senior Advertising Associates
Patrick Donovan, Barbara Eghan,
Fernanda Winthrop
Advertising Artwork Editor
Leif Holtzman
Cover Photo Research
Laura Wyss
President
Bradley J. Olson
General Manager
Robert B. Rombauer
Assistant General Manager
Anne E. Chisholm

DISCOVER AUSTRIA AND SWITZERLAND

Austria and Switzerland are the adventurer's paradise, with infinite opportunities for pulse-quickening exploits. Mountain climbing, paragliding, and canyoning, along with the more traditional natural highs of hiking and skiing, provide glimpses of the astonishing outdoor aesthetics that have awed visitors for centuries. Though unparalleled scenic beauty is ample explanation as to why Austria and Switzerland draw millions of tourists each year, it would be a spurious assumption to believe that this alone accounts for their popularity. Between each glorious summit and breathtaking alpine trail are world-class cities such as Vienna, Salzburg, and Zurich, which showcase many of Europe's most prized artistic, musical, and architectural treasures. Their smaller urban counterparts, towns such as Klagenfurt, Hallstatt, and Montreux, add to the countries' allure with their charming *Altstädte* and unique peculiarities. Linking mountain with metropolis is a dense network of carefully coordinated trains and well-tended budget accommodations, allowing the thrifty traveler to travel on schedule and in comfort.

FACTS AND FIGURES

CAPITAL OF AUSTRIA: Vienna	**CAPITAL OF SWITZERLAND:** Bern
POPULATION: 8,120,000	**POPULATION:** 7,444,000
LIFE EXPECTANCY: Men 75, women 81	**LIFE EXPECTANCY:** Men 77, women 83
LAND AREA: 83,857km² (32,377 sq. mi.)	**LAND AREA:** 41,285km² (15,941 sq. mi.)
LANGUAGE: German	**LANGUAGES:** German, French, Italian, and Romansch
RELIGION: 78% Catholic, 5% Protestant, 17% Muslim and other	**RELIGION:** 46% Catholic, 40% Protestant, 14% other

WHEN TO GO

To everything its season in Austria and Switzerland, so determine what your primary interests are when deciding when to travel. Outdoor enthusiasts should know that November to March is peak ski season, while July and August are ideal for hiking. Lodgings tend to be slightly more expensive during these times, and rooms can be harder to come by if you don't have a reservation. The cheapest time to go is in the shoulder season (May-June, September-October) when there is the added benefit of milder weather. However, many mountain towns in Graubünden and Valais in Switzerland, and a few towns in the Tyrol in Austria, shut down in May and June between skiing and hiking seasons so that the hostel owners can take a break from providing vacations for others. Christmastime is particularly

DISCOVER

magical in Austria, where entire towns are decorated for the holidays and *Kristkindlmarkts* selling handmade ornaments, toys, and nutcrackers are held in the central squares. If you're a music or theater fan, be aware that the Vienna State Opera, the Vienna Boys' Choir, and major theaters throughout Austria and Switzerland don't have any performances during July and August.

A LEGACY OF CULTURE

Thanks to the imperious Habsburgs and the smart banking of the savvy Swiss, the two nations have amassed an impressive collection of masterpieces in their museums. **Vienna** has classically reigned supreme on the two-dimensional front: one of the four largest art collections in the world, collected and commissioned by the Habsburgs, is now stored in the **Kunsthistorisches Museum** (p. 124). The **Österreichische Galerie** assembles, among other pieces, great works from the Viennese artistic explosion at the beginning of the 20th century, including Klimt's *The Kiss* (p. 123). The hip, contemporary side of Viennese culture is stored in the MuseumsQuartier, a massive complex of museums and restaurants that opened its doors to rave reviews in 2001. Housing the **ZOOM Kindermuseum** for the under-12 set, as well as a dance performance center, gardens, and a pedestrian mall, this giant arena explores culture in all directions. To see where art was made—rather than stored—head to the under-touristed **Mozarts Wohnhaus** (p. 243) in **Salzburg**. On the way to Salzburg take a virtual flight at the **Ars Electronica** in **Linz** (p. 289).

In Switzerland, don't miss the **Kunsthaus Zürich** (p. 381), which juxtaposes well-known masterpieces with cutting-edge art, or the **Oskar Reinhart Collections** in **Winterthur** (p. 385), where the buildings are as beautiful as the works by Daumier and Picasso within. A trip to **Lausanne** is worthwhile in part because of the haunting works in the **Collection de l'Art Brut** (p. 496) which reveal the unexpected wells of artistic potential locked in the minds of the peasant, the criminal, and the insane. For the young and noisy at heart, the clanging, hands-on, futuristic sculptures in the **Museum Jean Tinguely** will prove an irresistible draw to **Basel** (p. 532).

RELIVING HISTORY

Centuries of serfdom, feudalism, and imperial power-mongering have left their mark on the landscapes of Austria and Switzerland. Crumbling castles, elaborate palaces, and medieval inner cities will transport you back in time. In Austria, explore the ruins of **Burg Dürnstein** (p. 300), where Richard the Lionheart was held for ransom; hike up to **Burg Hochosterwitz** (p. 175) along spiraling outer fortifications; or shiver in the *Hexenzimmer* (Witches' Room) of **Burg Kronegg** in Riegersburg (p. 158), built on a barren cliff of volcanic rock. If you're looking for something a little more ornate, the **Benediktinerstift** of Melk (p. 302) takes the prize for ecclesiastical Baroque splendor. Vienna and Salzburg hold the lion's share of Austria's palaces—among the most impressive are **Lustschloß Hellbrunn** (p. 247), which boasts hilarious *Wasserspiele* (water games) in its gardens, and the delicate, mirrored **Schloß Schönbrunn** (p. 118).

In Switzerland, the **Château de Chillon** in Montreux (p. 502) is the subject of a famous poem by Lord Byron, while the **Castello di Montebello** in Bellinzona (p. 438) boasts a working drawbridge. The lavishly carved, gilt-wood library of the Benedictine monks in **St. Gallen** (p. 403) is also a masterpiece. To complete the medieval experience on a sub-royal level, visit the towns of **Stein** (p. 296) and **Rust** (p. 141) in Austria, or wander the labyrinthine streets of Switzerland's **Bern** (p. 329). Then, relive country life at the **Freilichtmuseum Ballenburg,** a park and open-air museum where over 100 historic homes from across Switzerland have been transported to recreate 13 different villages, on this terrific daytrip from **Brienz** (p. 343).

THE BEATEN PATH...

You'll discover pretty quickly that the backpacker's world is a small one, with large, centrally located hostels in strategic locations throughout Austria and Switzerland. If you want to follow the beaten path and go with the partying crowd, Switzerland's backpacker mecca is in **Interlaken** (p. 345), which year-round boasts a dizzying aggregation of hostels and young, English-speaking travelers seeking adrenaline rushes of every sort imaginable. Other Swiss hot spots are **Zermatt** (p. 456), **Zurich** (p. 370), **Montreux** (p. 499), and **Geneva** (p. 476). In Austria, nothing can touch **Vienna** and its vast array of accommodations (p. 82) for backpacker-congregating, though **Innsbruck** (p. 181) and **Salzburg** (p. 227) put up a good fight.

...AND THE ROAD LESS TRAVELED

If you didn't come to hang out with the same English-speaking backpackers every night, head for the handful of smaller backpacker resorts/hostels hidden in the hills. Switzerland has a number of these getaways, including the **Swiss Alps Retreat** in Gryon (p. 511), the ultra-friendly **Hiking Sheep Guesthouse** in Leysin (p. 509), and the adventure-oriented **Swiss Adventure Hostel** in Boltigen (p. 347). Austria has the **Treehouse** hostel in Grünau (p. 259) and the gorgeous **Schloß Röthelstein** in Admont (p. 158). More comfortable and service-oriented than mainstream hostels, they offer the opportunity to get to know both the owners and the countryside well. *Privatzimmer* are a widespread option for experiencing Austrian and Swiss hospitality (often in the form of a down comforter) away from the crowds of travelers.

▨ LET'S GO PICKS

BEST PLACE TO THROW YOURSELF OFF A CLIFF: If the bungee options in Interlaken (p. 350) don't cut it, head to **Val Verzasca** (p. 445) near Locarno for the highest bungee jump in the world.

NICEST PEOPLE THIS SIDE OF THE ALPS: Andi and Joy, owners of **Pension Sinilill** (p. 274), tell stories of Austrian swimming championships and Filipino cock-fighting on their warm hearth. If you need more love, go to **Haus Wolf** (p. 185), where Frau Wolf charms guests with motherly advice, smiles, and baskets and baskets of bread.

BEST MEETING OF MATTER AND ENERGY: Brush up on quantum mechanics at **Einstein's House** (p. 312).

BEST PLACE TO WARM YOUR BELLY: Be dazzled by the extravagant decor and magnificent views at **Café Tomaselli** while soothing your body with a hot chocolate and rum (p. 238).

MOST FRAGRANT TIMEPIECE: Smell the roses and check the time at the flower clock in the **Theresiengarten** (p. 308).

BEST PLACE TO FRESHEN UP: Cleanse yourself at the **Museum of Historical Sanitary Objects** (p. 215), host to assorted bathtubs and toilets.

BEST OPERA WITHOUT RED VELVET: Every July and August the **Bregenzer Festspiel** (p. 223) stages world-class opera, floating on the Bodensee.

BEST LIGHTING EFFECTS IN A BATHROOM: The pissoir at the **Hotel Goldener Löwe** (p. 166) illuminates (so that you can let the waterfall on the wall inspire you). You get less help in the bathroom at the **Funny Farm** (p. 321), where the only light is a blacklight (wear lots of white—the only other light comes from the disco ball on the ceiling).

BEST PLACE TO WATCH MEN IN TIGHTS: The **Vienna Staatsoper ballet** (p. 126), home to one the world's most prestigious companies, performs a repertoire of classical and modern pieces.

BEST BUS RIDE ON EARTH: Spend five hours gawking from a bus on the ride down the **Großglocknerstraße** (p. 267).

DISCOVER

SUGGESTED ITINERARIES

BEST OF AUSTRIA

quarters of romance. The magic of Strauss's waltzes and the thunder of Beethoven's symphonies resonate through Vienna's Baroque buildings. From the stately Staatsoper to the glittering Musikverein, the majestic Hofburg to Otto Wagner's simple Kirche am Steinhof, Vienna's attractions will leave you with enough sensory stimulation to last until your next vacation, at least.

BEST OF AUSTRIA (MIN. 2 WEEKS)

For the best nature and culture Austria has to offer start your journey in **Bregenz** (p. 218), capital city of Vorarlberg, and spend two days poking around the rolling hills of the Bregenzerwald. Take a train ride through gorgeous Alpine scenery on the way to **Innsbruck** (p. 181). Wander through the imperial palace and gardens in the morning and take a daytrip to Schloß Ambras in the afternoon. After that, explore the Hohe Tauern National Park from **Zell am See** (p. 273). Take one day to visit the Krimml Waterfalls, and another to wind down the serpentine Großglocknerstraße. Descend from the mountains and head north to the hills of the Salzkammergut—the getaway for Austrians in the know. While it may be crowded, the **Salzburg** (p. 227) of Maria von Trapp and Mozart is not to be missed. Spend a day exploring streets preserved in much the same condition as when these two luminaries were around. **Hallstatt** (p. 249), balanced between cliffs and a lake, is of historical interest as a cradle of European civilization, and of immediate interest for its stunning hiking and ice caves. Don't forget to sneak down to **Graz** (p. 285), Austria's second-largest city. This vibrant university town hosts a variety of entertainment venues from opera to musical festivals. Don't miss the Schloßberg (castle mountain) for a bird's-eye view of the city. Make your way up to **Melk** (p. 301) with its unmistakable yellow abbey perched high on a hill. Save an afternoon for the Renaissance courtyard, Romanesque fortress, and Gothic chapel at Schloß Schallaburg, only 5km away. The imposing ruins of Schloß Dürnstein loom over the valley as you make your way along the Danube river, past **Krems** and **Stein**, to **Vienna** (p. 82) itself, the imperial head-

BEST OF SWITZERLAND

BEST OF SWITZERLAND (MIN. 2 WEEKS)

Spend your first day strolling the quiet squares around John Calvin's Cathédrale de St. Pierre in **Geneva** (p. 476), acquainting yourself with this international city and symbol of diversity for a quadrilingual, tri-ethnic nation. To be inspired like T.S. Eliot and Charles Dickens, scoot around the lake to **Lausanne** (p. 490) and recline on the waterfront after a chilling look at the exhibits in the *Collection de l'Art Brut*. Now move north to another lake and enjoy **Neuchâtel** (p. 513), as a stepping-off for wine-tasting in tiny **Cressier** (p. 518). Next, the compact capital city of **Bern** (p. 329) should take at least two days to unravel. Move at a leisurely pace while window-shopping along arcaded streets, buying farm-grown produce at the open market outside the Parliament, and feeding the bears in the *Bärengraben*. Take a break from the city scene with a few days in the **Bernese Oberland.** Skydive, bungee-jump, and river raft your way to adrenalized happiness in **Interlaken** (p. 345), the adventure capital of the world. For a quieter day, take the cable car to charming, car-free **Mürren** (p. 361). Make the expensive-but-worth-it daytrip to the **Jungfraujoch** (p. 354), appropriately dubbed the "top of Europe." After your mountain high, let nearby **Luc-**

erne (p. 386) intrigue you with its Altstadt, museums, and looming twin peaks. Now take the train to **Zurich** (p. 370), where Ulrich Zwingli and the Dadaists fomented revolutions. Then get into hiking mode as you approach **Appenzell** (p. 405). To warm up from the crisp mountain air, head for the Mediterranean climate of **Locarno** (p. 439). The calm waters of warm Lago Maggiore suffuse the *città vecchia* with tranquility (head to one of two sprawling, villa-cum-hostels in Lugano for the night). Now head west to the mighty Alps in **Zermatt** (p. 456). The number of hikes and ski trails within walking distance of the town is unparalleled. Finish it off at the annual Jazz Festival from late July to early August in **Montreux** (p. 499). The festival attracts headlining acts and street-corner musicians from all over the world, ensuring that wherever you go, music will follow.

HIKING THE ALPS (MIN. 2 WEEKS)
Though you can't climb every mountain, you've got a lot of options in Austria and Switzerland. Trace the following route, or carve your own path through the Alps.

Test out your trail legs on the paths that extend from **Zermatt** (p. 456). The carless town's most exciting hikes lead to spectacular views of the Matterhorn. In central Switzerland, unspoiled **Kandersteg** (p. 364) has hikes to glaciers and high-lying glacial lakes like Öschinensee. In Lauterbrunnen, a bit northeast, are great hostels to crash in after days in the **Jungfrau region** (p. 352). The cliff-walled valleys allow for both level and extremely steep hikes, but little in between. These hikes tend to be more social than in other areas, thanks to the villages peppering the region. To get away

from any hint of a resort, head for rustic **Appenzell** (p. 405). The hikes, a short train ride away, are more consistently difficult, but the promise of a warm, wooden guest house at the end of almost every trail will pull you along. Heading south to the wildest canton in the country, Graubünden, will bring more splendid isolation in the **Swiss National Park** (p. 422). There is more wildlife and unbroken silence than almost anywhere in the two countries combined (it is one of few Swiss areas where cows are not allowed). Also in Graubünden is the **Upper Engadine Valley** (p. 429). While chic towns like St. Moritz are more famous for skiing, there is easy access to flat, meandering trails along the valley.

Just over the border in Austria, **Bregenz** (p. 218) provides fantastic walks through rolling hills and rustic towns where wooden shingles never went out of style. Things get more dramatic as you enter the mountainous Alpine territory of the **Ötztal** (p. 212), whose trails up the silent valley above are accessible from Sölden. As you move eastward, you'll run into the **Hohe Tauern National Park** (p. 265), home to 246 glaciers and 304 mountains over 3000m. The largest national park in Europe has countless paths leading through meadows, along glaciers, and up to the roaring *Wasserfallwinkel*. The towns of **Zell am See** (p. 273) and **Lienz** (p. 278) serve as larger bases for exploring the park, or you can stay in Heiligenblut, which lies in the shadow of the Großglockner, Austria's highest mountain. Finish in the **Salzkammergut's** Hallstatt (p. 249); these routes lead past waterfalls, and lush foliage that sometimes looks more tropical than Alpine.

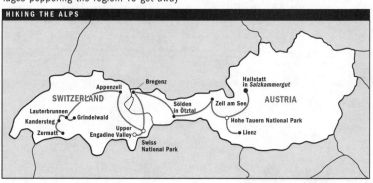

HIKING THE ALPS

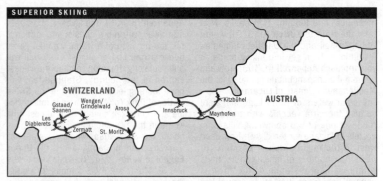

SUPERIOR SKIING

SUPERIOR SKIING (MIN. 3 WEEKS)

You could land just about anywhere in Switzerland or western Austria in the winter and have a fabulous skiing experience. (There are fewer places where you could do the same thing in summer, but it's possible.) It's important to differentiate between the snowbound hot spots—discerning travelers will find great deals for their money *and* the chance to glimpse some famous faces. One good place to start is **Kitzbühel** (p. 197), where downhill skiing was actually invented in 1892—plan carefully to avoid, view, or participate in the gigantic, annual Hahnenkamm World Cup race. On your way west stop in **Mayrhofen** (p. 207), where even August finds skiers on the glacier. Medieval **Innsbruck** (p. 181), home of the 1964 and 1976 Winter Olympics, hosted the games for good reason: shuttles take you to snow-covered mountains, even in the summer. If you're looking to party *après-ski*, hightail it over to happening **Arosa** (p. 414) in eastern Switzerland, where hostel beds come complete with affordable ski passes at a disco-inclusive hostel. Glitzy **St. Moritz** (p. 432) is a familiar name in any skiing household, particularly the royal families of Britain and Hollywood. Take the cog railway up to **Zermatt** (p. 456), the hedonistic ski paradise in southwestern Switzerland. French Switzerland does its best to compete, with **Les Diablerets** (p. 506), where snowboarders and younger crowds flock. As you move north back into German Switzerland, you'll run across thriving **Gstaad** and **Saanen** (p. 366), an international jet-set magnet. The tiny towns of **Wengen** (p. 359) and **Grindelwald** (p. 353) serve as gateways to some of the finest powder and the most breathtaking panoramas known to humankind.

ESSENTIALS

FACTS FOR THE TRAVELER

ENTRANCE REQUIREMENTS.
Passport (p. 9). Required for all foreign visitors.
Visa (p. 10). Required only for a continuous stay of more than three months.
Work Permit (p. 10). Required to work in Austria or Switzerland.
Driving Permit (p. 46). Required for all those planning to drive.

EMBASSIES AND CONSULATES

All diplomatic missions are embassies unless otherwise indicated.

AUSTRIAN CONSULAR SERVICES ABROAD

Australia: 12 Talbot St., Forrest, Canberra ACT 2603 (☎00 6295 1533; fax 0639 6751; austria@dynamite.com.au). **Consulates** in Adelaide, Brisbane, Melbourne, Sydney.

Canada: 445 Wilbrod St., Ottawa, ON K1N 6M7 (☎613-789-1444; fax 789-3431; embassy@austro.org; www.austro.org). **Consulates** in Montreal, Toronto, Vancouver.

Ireland: 15 Ailesbury Court, 93 Ailesbury Rd., Dublin 4 (☎(01) 269 45 77 or 269 14 51; fax 283 08 60; dublin-ob@bmaa.gv.at).

New Zealand: Level 2, Willbank House, 57 Willis St., Wellington (☎04 499 63 93).

South Africa: 1109 Duncan St., Momentum Office Park, Brooklyn, Pretoria 0011 (☎(012) 45 29 155; fax 46 01 151; autemb@mweb.co.az); during sessions of Parliament (Jan.-June), embassy is based in Cape Town, Standard Bank Centre, 1001 Main Tower, Hertzog Blvd., Cape Town 8001. **Consulates** in Cape Town and Johannesburg.

UK: 18 Belgrave Mews West, London SW1 X 8HU (☎020 7235 3731; embassy@austria.org.uk; www.austria.org.uk). **Consulates** in Birmingham, Edinburgh, Hamilton.

US: 3524 International Ct. NW, Washington, D.C. 20008-3035 (☎202-895-6700; fax 895-6750). **Consulates** in Chicago, Los Angeles, and New York.

SWISS CONSULAR SERVICES ABROAD

Australia: 7 Melbourne Ave., Forrest, Canberra ACT 2603 (☎(02) 6273 3977; fax 6273 3428; vertretung@can.rep.admin.ch). **Consulates** in Adelaide, Brisbane, Darwin, Hobart, Melbourne, Perth, and Sydney.

Canada: 5 Marlborough Ave., Ottawa, ON K1N 8E6 (☎613-235-1837; fax 563-1394; vertretung@ott.rep.admin.ch). **Consulates** in Calgary, Edmonton, Montréal, Québec, Toronto, Vancouver and Winnipeg.

Ireland: 6 Ailesbury Rd., Ballsbridge, Dublin 4 (☎(01) 218 63 82 or 218 63 83; fax 283 03 44; vertretung@dub.rep.admin.ch).

New Zealand: Consulate, 22 Panama St., Wellington (☎(04) 472 15 93 or 472 15 94; fax 499 63 02); also a **consulate** in Auckland.

South Africa: P818 George Ave., Arcadia 0083, 0001 Pretoria (☎(012) 430 67 07; fax 430 67 71; vertretung@pre.rep.admin.ch); during sessions of Parliament (Jan.-June), the embassy is based in Cape Town, P.O. Box 1546, Cape Town 8000 (☎(021) 418 36 69; fax 418 15 69). **Consulates** in Cape Town, Durban, and Johannesburg.

UK: 16-18 Montague Pl., London W1H 2BQ (☎(020) 76 16 60 00; fax 77 24 70 01; swissembassy@lon.rep.admin.ch). **Consulates** in Belfast, Edinburgh, Manchester, and Warwick/Bermuda.

US: 2900 Cathedral Ave. NW, Washington, D.C. 20008-3499 (☎202-745-7900; fax 387-2564; vertretung@was.rep.admin.ch; www.swissemb.org). **Consulates** in Atlanta, Boston, Chicago, Houston, Los Angeles, New York, and San Francisco.

CONSULAR SERVICES IN AUSTRIA

Foreign embassies are based in Vienna. Look in the Vienna telephone book under *Botschaften* (embassies) or *Konsulate* (consulates). For more info, see p. 89.

Australia: IV, Mattiellistr. 2 (☎(01) 513 16 56; austemb@aon.at; www.australian-embassy.at).

Canada: I, Laurenzerberg 2 (☎(01) 531 38 30 00; fax 531 38 39 05; vienn@dfait-maeci.gc.ca; www.dfait-maeci.gc.ca).

Ireland: I, Rotenturmstr. 16-18 5th Floor (☎(01) 71 54 24 60; vienna@iveath.irlgov.ie).

New Zealand: The New Zealand embassy in **Berlin,** Germany has responsibility for Austria. Friedrichstr. 60, 10117 Berlin (☎(030) 20 62 10; fax 20 62 11 14; nzemb@t-online.de). **Consulate: Vienna,** XIX, Springsiedelg. 28 (☎(01) 318 85 05; basil.bolt@aon.at).

South Africa: XIX, Sandg. 33 (☎(01) 320 64 93; fax 320 64 93 51; saembvie@aon.at; www.southafrican-embassy.at).

UK: III, Jauresg. 10 (☎(01) 716 13 51 51; fax 716 1359 00; vcenquiries@britishembassy.at; www.britishembassy.at).

US: IX, Boltzmanng. 16 (☎(01) 313 39; fax 512 58 35; embassy@usembassy.at; www.usembassy-vienna.at).

CONSULAR SERVICES IN SWITZERLAND

Nearly all foreign embassies in Switzerland are located in Bern.

Australia: Consulate: Geneva, Chemin des Fins 2, Case Postale 172, Geneva 1211 (☎(022) 799 91 00; fax 799 91 78; australian.consulate-geneva@dfat.gov.au).

Canada: Kirchenfeldstr. 88 (☎(031) 357 32 00; fax 357 32 10; bern@dfait-maeci.gc.ca).

Ireland: Kirchenfeldstr. 68 (☎(031) 352 14 42; fax 352 14 55; irlemb@bluewin.ch).

New Zealand: The New Zealand embassy in **Berlin,** Germany has responsibility for Switzerland. Friedrichstr. 60, 10117 Berlin (☎(030) 20 62 10; fax 20 62 11 14; nzemb@t-online.de). **Consulate: Geneva,** Chemin des Fins 2, 1218 Grand Saconnex (☎(022) 929 03 50; fax 929 03 77; mission.nz@itu.ch; www.nzembassy.com).

South Africa: Alpenstr. 29 (☎(031) 350 13 13; fax 350 13 11; ambassador@southafrica.ch; www.southafrica.ch).

UK: Thunstr. 50 (☎(031) 359 77 00; fax 359 77 01).

US: Jubiläumstr. 93 (☎(031) 357 70 11; fax 351 73 44; www.usembassy.ch).

NATIONAL TOURIST OFFICES ABROAD

AUSTRIAN NATIONAL TOURIST OFFICES

Australia and New Zealand: Sydney, 1st Floor, 36 Carrington St., Sydney NSW 2000 (☎(02) 92 99 36 21; fax 92 99 38 08; oewsyd@world.net).

UK and Ireland: London, 14 Cork St. GB-London W1X 1PF (☎(020) 76 29 04 61; fax 74 99 60 38; info@anto.co.uk).

US and Canada: New York, 500 Fifth Ave., Suite 800, P.O. Box 1142, New York, NY 10110 (☎212-944-6880; fax 730-4568).

SWISS NATIONAL TOURIST OFFICES

UK: London, Swiss Centre, Swiss Court, London W1V 8EE (☎0171 734 1921).

US and Canada: New York, 608 Fifth Ave., New York, NY 10020 (☎877-794-8034; 212-757-5944; fax 262-6116; info.usa@switzerland.com); additional offices in San Francisco (☎415-362-2260) and Los Angeles (☎310-640-8900). In **Canada** call toll free (☎800-002-0030) to be transferred to New York.

DOCUMENTS AND FORMALITIES

PASSPORTS

REQUIREMENTS. Citizens of Australia, Canada, New Zealand, South Africa, the UK, and the US need valid passports to enter Austria or Switzerland and to re-enter their own country, and can stay three months without a visa. If you apply for a visa, make sure your passport is valid for at least three months longer than the visa, or you could face a fine upon returning with an expired passport.

NEW PASSPORTS. File any new passport or renewal applications well in advance of your departure date. Citizens living abroad who need a passport or renewal should contact the nearest consular service of their home country.

Australia: Info ☎ 13 12 32; passports.australia@dfat.gov.au; www.dfat.gov.au/passports. Apply for a passport at a post office, passport office (in Adelaide, Brisbane, Canberra, Darwin, Hobart, Melbourne, Newcastle, Perth, or Sydney), or overseas diplomatic mission. Passports AUS$136 (36-page) or AUS$204 (64-page); valid for 10 years. Children AUS$68 (36-page) or AUS$102 (64-page); valid for 5 years.

Canada: Canadian Passport Office, Department of Foreign Affairs and International Trade, Ottawa, ON K1A 0G3 (☎800-267-8376 or 613-994-4000; www.dfait-maeci.gc.ca/passport). Applications available at passport offices, Canadian missions, post offices, and on the Internet. Passports CDN$65; valid for 5 years (non-renewable). Children age 3-15 CDN$35; valid for 5 years; under age 3 CDN$20; valid for 3 years.

Ireland: Pick up an application at a *Garda* station, post office, Irish embassy or consulate, or request one from a passport office. Then apply by mail to the Department of Foreign Affairs, Passport Office, Setanta Centre, Molesworth St., Dublin 2 (☎(01) 671 16 33; fax 671 10 92; www.irlgov.ie/iveagh), or the Passport Office, Irish Life Building, 1A South Mall, Cork (☎(021) 27 25 25; fax 27 57 70). Passports €57 (32-page) or €69 (48-page); valid for 10 years. Under 16 or over 65 €12; valid for 3 years.

New Zealand: Applications available at the Passport Office or on the Internet; mail completed passport applications to Passport Office, Level 3 Boulcott House, 47 Boulcott St., Wellington (☎(0800) 22 50 50; fax (04) 474 80 10; passports@dia.govt.nz; www.passports.govt.nz) or to the nearest embassy or consulate. Standard processing time is 10 working days. Passports NZ$80; valid for 10 years. Children under 16 NZ$40; valid for 5 years. 3 day "urgent service" NZ$160; children NZ$120.

South Africa: Consult the Department of Home Affairs. Passports are issued only in Pretoria, but all applications must still be submitted or forwarded to the nearest South African consulate. Processing time is 3 months or more. Passports around ZAR110; valid for 10 years. Children under 16 around ZAR120; valid for 5 years. Check out http://usaembassy.southafrica.net/VisaForms/Passport/Passport2000.html.

UK: Info ☎(0870) 521 04 10; www.open.gov.uk/ukpass/ukpass.htm. Get an application from a passport office, main post office, travel agent, or online at www.ukpa.gov.uk/forms/f_app_pack.htm. Then apply by mail or in person at a passport office. Passports UK£28 (32-page) or UK£38 (48-page); valid for 10 years. Children under 15 UK£14.80; valid for 5 years. Processing time about 4 weeks; faster service (by personal visit to the offices listed above) costs an additional £12.

US: Info ☎202-647-0518; www.travel.state.gov/passport_services.html. Apply at any federal or state courthouse, authorized post office, or US Passport Agency (in most major cities); see the "US Government, State Department" section of the telephone book or a post office for addresses. Processing takes 3-4 weeks. New passports US$60; valid for 10 years. Children under 15 US$40; valid for 5 years. Passports may be renewed by mail or in person for US$40. Add US$35 for 2-week expedited service.

PASSPORT MAINTENANCE. Photocopy the page of your passport with your photo, passport number, and other identifying information, as well as any visas, travel insurance policies, plane tickets, or traveler's check serial numbers. Carry one set of copies in a safe place, apart from the originals, and leave another set at home.

If you lose your passport, notify the local police and the nearest embassy or consulate of your home government immediately. In an emergency, ask for immediate temporary traveling papers that will permit you to re-enter your home country. Your passport is a public document belonging to your nation's government. You may have to surrender it to a foreign government official, but if you don't get it back, inform the nearest diplomatic mission of your home country.

VISAS, INVITATIONS, AND WORK PERMITS

VISAS. Citizens of Australia, Canada, Ireland, New Zealand, South Africa, the UK, and the US do not need visas to visit Austria or Switzerland. For more detailed information about which nationalities require visas, visit either the Austrian Embassy web site (www.bmaa.gv.at/embassy/uk/index.html.en) or the Swiss Embassy web site (www.swissemb.org).

WORK PERMITS. Admission to Austria or Switzerland as a visitor does not include the right to work, which is authorized only by a work permit. Studying in either country requires a special visa. For more information, see the Alternatives to Tourism chapter (p. 58).

IDENTIFICATION

When you travel, always carry two or more forms of identification on your person, including at least one photo ID; a passport combined with a driver's license or birth certificate is usually adequate. Many establishments, especially banks, require several IDs in order to cash traveler's checks. Never carry all your forms of ID together; split them up in case of theft or loss.

TEACHER, STUDENT, AND YOUTH IDENTIFICATION. The **International Student Identity Card (ISIC),** provides discounts on transport and accommodations, access to a 24hr. emergency helpline for medical, legal, and financial emergencies (in North America call ☎877-370-ISIC (877-370-4742), elsewhere call US collect +1 715-345 0505), and insurance benefits for holders of US-issued cards. Many student travel

ONE EUROPE. The idea of European unity has come a long way since 1958, when the European Economic Community (EEC) was created to promote solidarity and cooperation between founding states. The EEC has become the European Union (EU), with political, legal, and economic institutions spanning 15 member states: Austria, Belgium, Denmark, Finland, France, Germany, Greece, Ireland, Italy, Luxembourg, The Netherlands, Portugal, Spain, Sweden, and the UK.

What does this have to do with the non-EU tourist? Well, 1999 saw **freedom of movement** established across 14 European countries—the entire EU minus Denmark, Ireland, and the UK, but plus Iceland and Norway. This means that border controls between participating countries have been abolished and visa policies harmonized. While you're still required to carry a passport (or government-issued ID card for EU citizens) when crossing a border, once you've been admitted into one country, you're free to travel to all participating states. Britain and Ireland have also formed a **common travel area,** abolishing passport controls between the UK and the Republic of Ireland, meaning that the only times you'll see a border guard within the EU are traveling between the British Isles and the Continent—and of course, in and out of Denmark. For more important consequences of the EU for travelers, see **The Euro** (p. 14) and **European Customs** (p. 12).

agencies issue ISICs, including STA Travel in Australia and New Zealand; Travel CUTS in Canada; USIT in the Republic of Ireland and Northern Ireland; SASTS in South Africa; Campus Travel and STA Travel in the UK; and Council Travel (www.counciltravel.com/idcards/default.asp) and STA Travel in the US (see Budget and Student Travel Agencies, p. 35). The card is valid from September of one year to December of the following year and costs US$22. Applicants must be degree-seeking students of a secondary or post-secondary school and must be at least age 12. Because of the proliferation of fake ISICs, some services (particularly airlines) require additional proof of identity, such as a school ID or a letter attesting to your student status, signed by your registrar and stamped with your school seal.

The **International Teacher Identity Card (ITIC)** offers the same insurance coverage and similar but limited discounts. The fee is AUS$13, UK£6.50, or US$22. For more info, contact the **International Student Travel Confederation (ISTC),** Herengracht 479, 1017 BS Amsterdam, Netherlands (☎31 (20) 421 28 00; fax 421 28 10; istcinfo@istc.org; www.istc.org). The **ISTC** issues a discount card to travelers who are 26 or under, but are not students. This one-year **International Youth Travel Card** (IYTC; formerly the GO 25 Card) offers many of the same benefits as the ISIC (US$22).

If you are an ISIC card carrier, you can activate your ISIC's ISIConnect service, a new integrated communications service (powered by eKit.com). With ISIConnect, one toll-free access number (in Austria ☎0800 29 10 18, in Switzerland 0800 89 73 06) gives you access to several different methods of keeping in touch via phone and Internet, including a reduced-rate international calling plan that treats your ISIC card as a universal **calling card;** a personalized **voicemail** box accessible from pay phones anywhere in the world or for free via Internet; **faxmail** service for sending and receiving faxes via email, fax machines, or pay phones; various **email** capabilities, including a service that reads your email to you over the phone; an online **"travel safe"** for storing (and faxing) important documents and numbers; and a 24hr. **help line** (via phone or email at ISIConnect@ekit.com) offering assistance and medical and legal referrals. To activate your ISIConnect account, visit the service's web site (www.isiconnect.ekit.com) or call the customer service number of your home country: in Australia ☎800 11 44 78, in Canada 877-635-3575, in Ireland 800 55 51 80 or 800 57 79 80, in New Zealand 0800 00 67 31, in South Africa 0800 99 29 21 or 0800 99 72 85, in the UK 0800 376 23 66 or 0800 731 56 64, and in the US 800-706-1333.

CUSTOMS

Austria and Switzerland prohibit or restrict the importation of firearms, explosives, ammunition, fireworks, booby traps, controlled drugs, most plants, lottery tickets, most animals, pornography, and items manufactured from protected species (e.g. ivory or fur). To avoid hassles about prescription drugs, ensure that your bottles are clearly marked and carry a copy of the prescription. Duty-free allowances were abolished for travel between EU member states on July 1, 1999, but still exist for those arriving from outside the EU. Keeping receipts for purchases made abroad will help establish values when you return.

EUROPEAN CUSTOMS. Goods, as well as people, are permitted freedom of movement in the EU. This means that there are no customs controls at internal EU borders (i.e., you can take the blue customs channel at the airport), and travelers are free to transport whatever legal substances they like as long as it is for their own personal (non-commercial) use—up to 800 cigarettes, 10L of spirits, 90L of wine (60L of sparkling wine), and 110L of beer. You should also be aware that duty-free was abolished on June 30, 1999, for travel between EU member states; however, travelers between the EU and the rest of the world still get a duty-free allowance when passing through customs.

ADDITIONAL CUSTOMS RESOURCES:
Australia: Australian Customs National Information Line (in Australia call ☎(01) 30 03 63, from elsewhere call ☎+61 (02) 6275 6666; www.customs.gov.au).
Canada: Canadian Customs, 2265 St. Laurent Blvd., Ottawa, ON K1G 4K3 (☎800-461-9999 (24hr.) or 613-993-0534; www.revcan.ca).
Ireland: Customs Information Office, Irish Life Centre, Lower Abbey St., Dublin 1 (☎(01) 878 8811; fax 878 0836; taxes@revenue.iol.ie; www.revenue.ie).
New Zealand: New Zealand Customhouse, 17-21 Whitmore St., Box 2218, Wellington (☎(04) 473 6099; fax 473 7370; www.customs.govt.nz).
South Africa: Commissioner for Customs and Excise, Private Bag X47, Pretoria 0001 (☎(012) 314 9911; fax 328 6478; www.gov.za).
United Kingdom: Her Majesty's Customs and Excise, Passenger Enquiry Team, Wayfarer House, Great South West Rd., Feltham, Middlesex TW14 8NP (☎(020) 8910 3744; fax 8910 3933; www.hmce.gov.uk).
United States: US Customs Service, 1330 Pennsylvania Ave. NW, Washington, D.C. 20229 (☎202-354-1000; fax 354-1010; www.customs.gov).

MONEY

CURRENCY AND EXCHANGE

Austria formerly used the *Schilling* as its unit of currency; now, as a member of the European Union, it has completely switched over the euro. The **euro (EUR, €)** is divided into 100 cents. Denominations for coins are 1, 2, 5, 10, 20 and 50 cents and 1 and 2 euros, while bills are available in 5, 10, 20, 50, 100, 200 and 500 euros. In Austria, railroad stations, airports, hotels, and most travel agencies offer exchange services, as do banks and currency exchanges.

The Swiss monetary unit is the **Swiss Franc (SFr),** which is divided into 100 *centimes* (called *Rappen* in German Switzerland). Coins are issued in 5, 10, 20, and 50 centimes and 1, 2, and 5SFr; bills come in 10, 20, 50, 100, 500, and 1000SFr denominations. Currency exchange is easiest at ATMs, train stations, and post offices, where rates are close to bank rates but commissions are smaller.

The currency chart below is based on August 2002 exchange rates between local currency and US dollars (US$), Canadian dollars (CDN$), British pounds (UK£), Australian dollars (AUS$), New Zealand dollars (NZ$), South African Rand (ZAR), Czech crowns (Kč), Hungarian forints (FT), and European Union euros (€). Check a large newspaper or the web (e.g. http://finance.yahoo.com or www.bloomberg.com) for the latest exchange rates.

As a general rule, it's cheaper to convert money in Austria or Switzerland than at home. Bring an ATM card—you'll be able to start your vacation without languishing in lines. Travelers from the US can get foreign currency from the comfort of home: **International Currency Express** (☎ 888-278-6628) delivers foreign currency or traveler's checks 2nd-day (US$12) at competitive exchange rates.

Currency exchange kiosks and change machines should be your last resort when you need local funds. Most have unfavorable rates and charge hefty commissions. Banks, post offices, and small train stations often have better rates, but ATMs and credit cards are your best bet, since you'll profit from their low corporate rates (see p. 14). The only drawback to ATMs is the transaction fee that some banks charge—be sure to check what the fee is with your bank at home. If you need to change cash or traveler's checks, take the time to compare the rates offered by different banks and kiosks (*Wechselstube* in German, *bureau de change* in French, *cambio* in Italian). A good rule of thumb is only to go to banks or kiosks with at most a 5% margin between their buy and sell prices. Since you lose money with each transaction, convert in large sums (unless the rate is unfavorable).

EURO		
US$1 = €1.06		€1 = US$0.43
CDN$1 = €0.691		€1 = CDN$1.45
AUS$1 = €0.607		€1 = AUS$1.65
NZ$1 = €0.517		€1 = NZ$1.53
ZAR1 = €.107		€1 = ZAR9.33
10Kč = €0.32		€1 = Kč30.7
100FT = € 0.4123		€1 = 242.56FT

SWISS FRANC		
US$1 = 1.66 (SFR/CHF)		1SFR = US$0.60
€1 = 1.52SFR		1SFR = €.66
CDN$1 = 1.09SFR		1SFR = CDN$0.92
AUS$1 = 0.88SFR		1SFR = AUS$1.14
NZ$1 = 0.72SFR		1SFR = NZ$1.38
ZAR1 = 0.20SFR		1SFR = ZAR4.94
10Kč = 0.45SFR		1SFR = Kč22.31
100FT = 0.61SFR		1SFR = 164.98FT

TRAVELER'S CHECKS

Traveler's checks (American Express and Visa are the most recognized) are one of the safest means of carrying funds. Several agencies and banks sell them for a small commission. Each agency provides refunds if checks are lost or stolen, and

THE EURO. Since 1999, the official currency of 11 members of the European Union—Austria, Belgium, Finland, France, Germany, Ireland, Italy, Luxembourg, The Netherlands, Portugal, and Spain—has been the **euro**. (In January 2001, Greece was admitted as well.)

The exchange rate between euro-zone currencies was permanently fixed on January 1, 1999 at 1 EUR = 1.96DM (German marks) = 6.56F (French francs) = 1936.27L (Italian lire) = 13.76AS (Austrian Schillings). For more info, see www.europa.eu.int.

many provide other services, such as toll-free refund hotlines, emergency message services, and stolen credit card assistance. If you're ordering checks, do so well in advance, especially when requesting large sums. You can get traveler's checks in most currencies, including Swiss Francs and euros.

In order to collect a **refund for lost or stolen checks,** keep your check receipts separate from your checks and store them in a safe place or with a traveling companion. Record check numbers when you cash them, leave a list of check numbers with someone at home, and ask for a list of refund centers when you buy your checks. Never countersign your checks until you are ready to cash them, and always bring your passport with you when you plan to use the checks.

American Express: Call ☎(800) 25 19 02 in Australia, in New Zealand (0800) 44 10 68, in the UK (0800) 52 13 13, in the US and Canada 800-221-7282. In Austria, call (0800) 20 68 40, in Switzerland (0800) 55 01 00; elsewhere call US collect ☎+1 801-964-6665. www.aexp.com. American Express Traveler's Cheques are available in 10 currencies, including Swiss Francs and euros. Cheques can be purchased for a small fee (1-4%) at American Express Travel Service Offices, banks, and American Automobile Association (AAA) offices (see p. 47). American Express offices cash their cheques commission-free, but often at slightly poorer rates than banks. *Cheques for Two* can be signed by either of 2 people.

Thomas Cook MasterCard: In the US and Canada call ☎800-223-7373, in the UK (0800) 62 21 01, in Austria (0800) 29 62 66, in Switzerland (0800) 55 01 30. Checks available in 13 currencies, including Swiss Francs, at 2% commission. Thomas Cook offices and *Sparkasse* banks in Austria cash Thomas Cook traveler's checks commission-free.

Visa: For the location of the nearest office, in the US call ☎800-227-6811, in the UK (0800) 89 50 78, in Austria 0800) 29 61 02, in Switzerland (0800) 55 84 50, elsewhere call UK collect (44) (20) 79 37 80 91.

CREDIT, DEBIT, AND ATM CARDS

Major credit cards such as **MasterCard** (a.k.a. EuroCard or Access in Europe) and **Visa** (a.k.a. Carte Bleue or Barclaycard) are the most welcomed, and can be used to obtain advances in euros or Swiss Francs from some banks and teller machines. **American Express** cards also work in some ATMs, as well as at AmEx offices and major airports. Many credit cards offer insurance or emergency assistance.

Transaction fees for all credit card advances (up to US$10 per advance, plus 2-3% extra on foreign transactions after conversion) tend to make credit cards a more costly way of withdrawing cash than ATMs or traveler's checks, and not all banks will be willing to let you buy euros or Swiss Francs on credit. In an emergency, however, the transaction fee may be worth it. To be eligible for an advance, you'll need to get a **Personal Identification Number (PIN)** from your credit card company (see **ATMs and Pin Numbers,** p. 15). It's also a good idea to call your credit card company and let them know you'll be using your card abroad, as some companies initiate security measures, such as freezing cards, when spending patterns change.

ATMS AND PIN NUMBERS. All automatic teller machines require a 4-digit **Personal Identification Number (PIN).** You must ask your credit card company to assign you one before you leave. Without a PIN, you will be unable to withdraw cash with your credit card abroad. There are no letters on the keypads of European ATMs, so work out your PIN numerically: ABC correspond to 2, DEF to 3, GHI to 4, JKL to 5, MNO to 6, PQRS to 7, TUV to 8, and WXYZ to 9. If you lose your card, call for help at the following toll-free numbers, all of which have English-speaking operators: **MasterCard** (Austria ☎(0800) 21 82 35, Switzerland (0800) 89 70 92); **Visa** (Austria ☎(0600) 67 04, Switzerland (0800) 89 27 33); **American Express** (call the US collect ☎+1 301-731-5724).

CREDIT CARD COMPANIES. Visa (US ☎800-336-8472) and **MasterCard** (US ☎800-307-7309) are issued in cooperation with banks and other organizations. **American Express** (US ☎800-843-2273) has an annual fee of up to US$55. AmEx cardholders may cash personal checks at AmEx offices abroad, access an emergency medical and legal assistance hotline (24hr.; in North America call ☎800-554-2639, elsewhere call US collect ☎+1 715-343-7977), and enjoy American Express Travel Service benefits (including plane, hotel, and car rental reservation changes; baggage loss and flight insurance; mailgram and international cable services; and held mail). The **Discover Card** (US ☎800-347-2683, elsewhere call US ☎+1 801-902-3100) offers small cashback bonuses, but it may not be readily accepted in Austria and Switzerland.

CASH CARDS AND ATM CARDS. Cash or debit cards—often called ATM (Automated Teller Machine) cards—can be used throughout Austria and Switzerland. ATMs get the same wholesale exchange rate as credit cards, but there is often a limit on the amount of money you can withdraw per day (usually about US$500), and computer networks sometimes fail. There is typically also a surcharge of $1-5 for each withdrawal. The two major international money networks are **Cirrus** (US ☎800-424-7787) and **PLUS** (US ☎800-843-7587). Look for signs reading "Bankomat" with a green or blue "B," and compare the symbols on the back of your card with those above the machine to find out which machines your card will work in. **Visa TravelMoney** is a system allowing you to access money from any Visa ATM, common throughout Austria and Switzerland. You deposit an amount before you travel (plus a small administration fee), and you can withdraw up to that sum. The cards, which give you the same favorable exchange rate for withdrawals as a regular Visa, are especially useful if you plan to travel through many countries. Obtain a card by either visiting a nearby Thomas Cook or Citicorp office, or by calling toll-free (US ☎877-762-3227; minimum US$300 deposit, US$15 activation fee).

GETTING MONEY FROM HOME

If you run out of money, the easiest solution is to have someone make a deposit to your credit card or cash (ATM) card. Or consider one of the following options.

WIRING MONEY. It is possible to arrange a **bank money transfer,** which means asking a bank back home to wire money to a bank in Austria and Switzerland. This is the cheapest way to transfer cash, but it's also the slowest, usually taking several days or more. Travelers from the US, Canada, and the UK can wire money abroad through **Western Union**'s international money transfer services. In the US call ☎800-325-6000, in Canada ☎800-235 0000, in the UK (0800) 83 38 33. In Austria call ☎(01) 514 00 29 86; in Switzerland call the office in Zurich at (041) 761 89 55. The rates for sending cash are generally US$10-11 cheaper than with a credit card, and the money is usually available at the place you're sending it to within an hour. To locate the nearest Western Union location, consult www.westernunion.com.

Some people choose to send money abroad in cash via **Federal Express** to avoid taxes. While FedEx is reasonably reliable, note that this method is illegal.

US STATE DEPARTMENT (US CITIZENS ONLY). In emergencies, the US State Department will forward money within hours to the nearest consular office, which will disburse it according to instructions for a US$15 fee. If you wish to use this service, contact the Overseas Citizens Service division of the US State Department (☎202-647-5225; nights, Sundays, and holidays 202-647-4000).

COSTS

If you stay in hostels and prepare most of your own food, expect to spend anywhere from US$45 to US$75 (70-117SFr; €48-80) per person per day in Switzerland, slightly less in Austria. **Accommodations** start at about US$16 (25SFr) per night for a hostel in Switzerland and US$10 (€12) in Austria, while a basic sitdown meal usually costs around US$12 (19SFr; €14).

TIPPING AND BARGAINING

There is technically no need for **tipping** in Switzerland, as gratuities are already automatically factored into prices; in Austria, menus will say whether service is included (*Preise inclusive* or *Bedienung inclusiv*); if it is, you don't have to tip. If it's not, leave a tip up to about 10%. It is considered polite, however, in both Austria and Switzerland to round up your bill to the nearest euro or 1 or 2 Francs as a nod of approval for good service; tell the waiter or waitress how much you want back from the money you give. If you just say *"Danke,"* the waiter/waitress will most likely assume that you intend for him/her to keep the change. Austrian restaurants expect you to seat yourself, and servers will not bring the bill until you ask them to do so. Say *"Zahlen bitte"* (TSAHL-en BIT-uh) to settle your accounts. Don't leave tips on the table. Be aware that some restaurants charge for each piece of bread that you eat during your meal.

TAXES

No taxes are added to purchases made in **Switzerland.** In **Austria,** there is a 10% to 20% value added tax (VAT) on all books, clothing, souvenir items, art items, jewelry, perfume, cigarettes, alcohol, etc. Tourists must pay this tax at the time of purchase, but may get the tax refunded later if the amount of purchase is €75 (about US$70) or greater at a particular store. To get the refund, fill out the Austrian Form U-34, available at most stores, and an ÖAMTC quick refund form to get a check at the airport or train station. Make sure the store affixes their store identification stamp to the forms at the time of purchase. When you leave the country, go to the VAT or Customs office (located in the airport or train station) to get your form validated for the amount of the refund, which can be cashed in the airport or station.

 Make sure you have your unused purchases and the Austrian form U-34 on your person at the airport or train station so you can get the form validated and get your taxes back!

SAFETY AND SECURITY

PERSONAL SAFETY

EXPLORING. Austria and Switzerland are relatively safe countries, so most safety and security concerns can be resolved by using common sense. In general, safety means not looking like a target. The gawking camera-toter is a more obvious target than the low-profile traveler, so avoid unwanted attention by trying to blend in. Familiarize yourself with your surroundings before setting out; if you must check a map on the street, duck into a cafe or shop. If you are traveling alone, be sure that someone at home knows your itinerary, and never admit that you're traveling alone. When you arrive in a new city, find out what areas to avoid from tourist information or the manager of your hostel. Stick to busy, well-lit streets. Whenever possible, *Let's Go* warns of unsafe neighborhoods and areas, such as drug hangouts. The American Society of Travel Agents provides extensive information at their web site (www.astanet.com), including a section on *Travel Safety*.

EMERGENCY TELEPHONE NUMBERS	**Police:** Austria, ☎133. Switzerland, ☎117. **Ambulance:** Austria and Switzerland, ☎144. **Fire:** Austria, ☎122. Switzerland, ☎118.

SELF DEFENSE. There is no sure-fire way to avoid all the threatening situations you might encounter when you travel, but a good self-defense course will give you concrete ways to react to unwanted advances. **Impact, Prepare,** and **Model Mugging** can refer you to local self-defense courses in the US (☎800-345-5425). Visit the web site at www.impactsafety.org/chapters for a list of nearby chapters. Workshops (2-3hr.) start at US$50; full courses run US$350-500.

DRIVING. Driving in Austria and Switzerland is a pleasant but expensive proposition. The roads are well maintained with the money drivers pay for the right to drive here (they won't even let you on the Autobahn in Switzerland without a permit sticker). Be sure to observe the speed limit and don't drive drunk—the Austrian and Swiss police will not hesitate to take away your license and your car if you have any alcohol in your blood. Study route maps before you hit the road; depending on the region, some roads have poor (or nonexistent) shoulders, few gas stations, and roaming animals. Twisting mountain roads may be closed in winter but, when open, require particular caution. Learn the **Alpine honk:** when going blind around an abrupt turn, stop and give the horn a toot before proceeding. Shift to low gear, drive slowly, brake occasionally, and **never pass anyone.**

For long drives in desolate areas, invest in a cellular phone and a roadside assistance program (see p. 46). Park your vehicle in a garage or well-traveled area, and use a steering wheel locking device in larger cities. Hide baggage in the trunk, and if the tape deck or radio is removable, hide it in the trunk as well, or take it with you. **Sleeping in your car** is one of the most dangerous (and often illegal) ways to get your rest, second only to sleeping in the open. If your car breaks down, wait for the police to assist you. *Let's Go* does not recommend **hitchhiking,** particularly for women—see **By Thumb,** p. 49, for more information.

TERRORISM. In light of the September 11, 2001 attacks on the United States, awareness of terrorist threat has heightened across Europe. Austria and Switzerland enjoy a relatively safe existence, but it is important to remain alert to potential dangers, particularly in major cities and tourist destinations. Report suspicious persons and unattended luggage or packages to proper authorities.

TRAVEL ADVISORIES. The following government offices provide travel information and advisories by telephone, by fax, or via the web:

Australian Department of Foreign Affairs and Trade: ☎(02) 6261 1111 or toll-free within Australia (1300) 55 51 35; fax 6261 3111; www.dfat.gov.au.

Canadian Department of Foreign Affairs and International Trade (DFAIT): In Canada call ☎800-267-8376, elsewhere call +1 613-944-4000; www.dfait-maeci.gc.ca. Call for their free booklet, *Bon Voyage...But.*

New Zealand Ministry of Foreign Affairs: ☎(04) 494 85 00; fax 494 85 06; cons@mft.govt.nz; www.mft.govt.nz/trav.html.

United Kingdom Foreign and Commonwealth Office: ☎(020) 70 08 02 32; fax 72 38 45 45; www.fco.gov.uk.

US Department of State: ☎202-647-5225; http://travel.state.gov. For *A Safe Trip Abroad,* call 202-512-1800.

Always familiarize yourself with the exits in crowded and public locations, such as in theaters, stadiums, and museums. Be patient with security-related transportation delays when flying in and out of the United States and in train stations. Do not talk about bombs or terrorism in airports, even in jest or casual conversation, as airport security have been instructed to question and detain such individuals.

FINANCIAL SECURITY

PROTECTING YOUR VALUABLES. Although Austria and Switzerland have low crime rates, thieves are happy to relieve ignorant tourists of their money. Be on the alert, particularly in crowds. Beware of classic scams: sob stories that require money, distractions that allow enough time to steal your bag, and little kids with big newspapers. To prevent easy theft, don't keep all your valuables (money, important documents, etc.) in one place. **Photocopies** of important documents allow you to recover them in case they are lost or filched. **Don't carry your wallet or money in your back pocket.** Never count your money in public and carry as little as possible. If you go ATMs, avoid those in poorly lit or deserted areas and don't go at night. If you carry a purse, buy a sturdy one with a secure clasp, and carry it crosswise on the side, away from the street with the clasp against you. Secure packs with small combination padlocks that slip through the two zippers. A **money belt** is the best way to carry cash; you can buy one at most camping supply stores. A nylon, zippered pouch with a belt that sits inside the waist of your pants or skirt combines convenience and security. A **neck pouch** is an equally safe way to carry money, though less accessible. Refrain from pulling it out in public; if you must, be very discreet. Avoid keeping anything precious in a waist-pack: your valuables will be highly visible and easy to steal. Keep some money separate from the rest to use for emergencies or in case of theft.

In public, watch your belongings at all times. Beware of con artists and **pickpockets** on the street and on public transportation (although neither Austria nor Switzerland has a big problem with street crime). On buses and trains, keep your bag close to you: don't check your baggage on trains, don't trust anyone to "watch your bag for a second," and don't ever put it under your seat in train compartments. If you take a **night train,** either lock your bag to the luggage rack or use it as a pillow. In your hostel, if you can't lock your room, lock your bag in lockers or at the train station (you'll need your own **padlock**).

DRUGS AND ALCOHOL. Drugs can easily ruin a trip. Every year thousands of travelers are arrested for trafficking or possession of drugs or for simply being in the company of a suspected user. Marijuana, hashish, cocaine, and narcotics are illegal in Austria and Switzerland, and the penalties for illegal possession of drugs, especially for foreigners, range from stern to severe. You may be imprisoned or deported, and a meek "I didn't know it was illegal" will not suffice. It is not unknown for a dealer to increase profits by first selling drugs to tourists and then turning them in to the authorities for a reward. Even such reputedly liberal cities as Vienna, Salzburg, and Zurich take an officially dim view of mussed-up tourists. The worst thing you can possibly do is carry drugs across an international border—you could not only end up in prison but also be hounded by a "Drug Trafficker" stamp on your passport for the rest of your life. If you are arrested, all your home country's consulate can do is visit, provide a list of attorneys, and inform family and friends. Remember that you are subject to the laws of the country in which you travel, not to those of your home country, and it is your responsibility to familiarize yourself with these laws before leaving. Police officers, members of the *Polizei* or *Gendarmerie*, typically speak little English.

Imbibing **alcohol** in Austria and Switzerland is generally trouble-free—beer is more common than soda, and a lunch without wine or beer is unusual. In both Austria and Switzerland, you must be 16 to drink legally. In Switzerland you can only be arrested for being drunk in public if you cause harm to others.

HEALTH

Common sense is the simplest prescription for good health while you travel. Travelers complain most often about their feet and guts, so take precautionary measures: drink lots of fluids to prevent dehydration and constipation, wear sturdy, broken-in shoes and clean socks, and use talcum powder to keep your feet dry.

BEFORE YOU GO

In your **passport,** write the names of any people you wish to be contacted in case of a medical emergency, and also list any **allergies** or medical conditions you would want doctors to be aware of. Allergy sufferers might want to obtain a full supply of any necessary medication before the trip. Matching a prescription to a foreign equivalent is not always easy, safe, or possible. Carry up-to-date, legible prescriptions or a statement from your doctor stating the medication's trade name, manufacturer, chemical name, and dosage. While traveling, be sure to keep all medication with you in your carry-on luggage. Preparation can help minimize the likelihood of contracting a disease and maximize the chances of receiving effective health care in the event of an emergency. Leave all medication in original, labeled containers. What is legal at home may not be legal abroad; check with your doctor or the appropriate foreign consulate to avoid nasty surprises. For tips on packing a basic **first-aid kit,** and other health essentials, see p. 23.

IMMUNIZATIONS AND PRECAUTIONS. Take a look at your immunization records before you go. Travelers over two years old should be sure that the following vaccines are up to date: MMR (for measles, mumps, and rubella); DTaP or Td (for diphtheria, tetanus, and pertussis); OPV (for polio); HbCV (for haemophilus influenza B); and HBV (for hepatitis B). For recommendations on immunizations and prophylaxis, consult with the CDC (see below) in the US or the equivalent in your home country, and ask a doctor for guidance.

USEFUL ORGANIZATIONS AND PUBLICATIONS. The US **Centers for Disease Control and Prevention** (CDC; ☎877-FYI-TRIP (877-394-8747); www.cdc.gov/travel) maintains an international fax information service and an international travelers' hotline (☎ 404-332-4559). The CDC's comprehensive booklet *Health Information for International Travel*, an annual rundown of disease, immunization, and general health advice, is free online or US$25 via the Public Health Foundation (☎ 877-252-1200). Consult the appropriate government agency of your home country for consular information sheets on health, entry requirements, and other issues for various countries (see **Travel Advisories**, p. 18). For quick information on health and other travel warnings, call the **Overseas Citizens Services** (US ☎ 202-647-5225; after-hours 647-4000) or contact a passport agency or diplomatic mission abroad. US citizens can send a self-addressed, stamped envelope to the Overseas Citizens Services, Bureau of Consular Affairs, #4811, US Department of State, Washington, D.C. 20520. For information on medical evacuation services and travel insurance firms, see the US government's web site at http://travel.state.gov/medical.html or the **British Foreign and Commonwealth Office** (www.fco.gov.uk).

For detailed information on travel health, including a country-by-country overview of diseases, try the **International Travel Health Guide,** by Stuart Rose, MD (Travel Medicine, US$24.95; www.travmed.com). For general health info, contact the **American Red Cross** (☎ 800-564-1234). A good book to pick up is *Doctor's Guide to Protecting Your Health Before, During, and After International Travel*. Pilot Books (US$10).

MEDICAL ASSISTANCE ON THE ROAD. Medical care in Austria and Switzerland is generally excellent. Most doctors and pharmacists speak at least some English. If you are concerned about being able to access medical support while traveling, there are special support services you may employ. The *MedPass* from **GlobalCare, Inc.,** 2001 Westside Pkwy., #120, Alpharetta, GA 30004, USA (☎ 800-860-1111; fax 770-475-0058; www.globalems.com), provides 24hr. international medical assistance, support, and medical evacuation resources. The **International Association for Medical Assistance to Travelers** (**IAMAT;** US ☎ 716-754-4883, Canada 416-652-0137, New Zealand (03) 352 20 53; www.sentex.net/~iamat) has free membership, lists English-speaking doctors worldwide, and offers detailed info on immunization requirements and sanitation. If your regular **insurance** policy does not cover travel abroad, you may wish to purchase additional coverage.

Those with medical conditions (diabetes, allergies to antibiotics, epilepsy, heart conditions) may want to obtain a stainless-steel **Medic Alert** ID tag (first year US$35, annually thereafter US$20), which identifies the condition and gives a 24hr. collect-call number. Contact the Medic Alert Foundation, 2323 Colorado Ave., Turlock, CA 95382, USA (☎ 888-633-4298; www.medicalert.org).

ONCE IN AUSTRIA AND SWITZERLAND

ENVIRONMENTAL HAZARDS

Heat exhaustion and dehydration: Heat exhaustion can lead to fatigue, headaches, and wooziness. Avoid it by drinking plenty of fluids, eating salty foods (e.g. crackers), and avoiding dehydrating beverages (e.g. alcohol, coffee, tea, and caffeinated soda). Continuous heat stress can eventually lead to heatstroke, signaled by a rising temperature, severe headache, and cessation of sweating. Victims should be cooled off with wet towels and taken to a doctor.

Sunburn: If you're prone to sunburn, bring sunscreen with you (it's often more expensive and hard to find when traveling), and apply it liberally and often to avoid burns and reduce risk of skin cancer. If you are planning on spending time near water, in the mountains, or in the snow, you risk getting burned, even through clouds. If you get sunburned, drink more fluids than usual and apply calamine or an aloe-based lotion.

Hypothermia and frostbite: A rapid drop in body temperature is the clearest sign of overexposure to cold. Victims may also shiver, feel exhausted, have poor coordination or slurred speech, hallucinate, or suffer amnesia. *Do not let hypothermia victims fall asleep,* or their body temperature will continue to drop and they may die. To avoid hypothermia, keep dry, wear layers, and stay out of the wind. When the temperature is below freezing, watch out for frostbite. If skin turns white, waxy, and cold, do not rub the area. Drink warm beverages, get dry, and slowly warm the area with dry fabric or steady body contact until a doctor can be found.

High altitude: Allow your body a couple of days to adjust to less oxygen before exerting yourself. Note that alcohol is more potent and UV rays are stronger at high elevations.

INSECT-BORNE DISEASES

Many diseases are transmitted by insect (mainly mosquitoes, fleas, ticks, and lice.) Be aware of insects in wet or forested areas, especially while hiking and camping; wear long pants and long sleeves, tuck your pants into your socks, and buy a mosquito net. Use insect repellents such as DEET and soak or spray your gear with permethrin (licensed in the US for use on clothing). **Ticks**—responsible for Lyme and other diseases—can be particularly dangerous in rural and forested regions.

Tick-borne encephalitis: A viral infection of the central nervous system transmitted during the summer by tick bites (primarily in wooded areas) or by consumption of unpasteurized dairy products. Symptoms range from nothing at all to headaches and flu-like symptoms to swelling of the brain (encephalitis). The risk of contracting the disease is relatively low, especially if precautions are taken against tick bites.

Lyme disease: A bacterial infection carried by ticks and marked by a circular bull's-eye rash of 2 in. or more. Later symptons include fever, headache, fatigue, and aches and pains. Antibiotics are effective if administered early. Left untreated, Lyme can cause problems in joints, the heart, and the nervous system. If you find a tick attached to your skin, grasp the head with tweezers as close to your skin as possible and apply slow, steady traction. Removing a tick within 24 hours greatly reduces the risk of infection. Do not try to remove ticks by burning them or coating them with nail polish remover or petroleum jelly.

FOOD- AND WATER-BORNE DISEASES

Prevention is the best cure: be sure that your food is properly cooked and the water you drink is clean. Watch out for food from markets or street vendors that may have been cooked in unhygienic conditions. Other culprits are raw shellfish, unpasteurized milk, and sauces containing raw eggs. Buy bottled water, or purify your own water by bringing it to a rolling boil or treating it with **iodine tablets;** note, however, that some parasites such as *giardia* have exteriors that resist iodine treatment, so boiling is more reliable. Always wash your hands before eating or bring a quick-drying purifying liquid hand cleaner.

Mad Cow Disease: Bovine spongiform encephalopathy (BSE), better known as Mad Cow Disease, is a chronic degenerative disease affecting the central nervous system of cattle that broke out in alarming numbers of cattle in 2001 and 2002. The human variant is called Cruetzfeldt-Jakob disease (nvCJD), and both forms of the disease involve invariably fatal brain diseases. Information on nvCJD is not conclusive, but the disease is supposedly caused by consuming infected beef; however, the risk is very small (around 1 case per 10 billion servings of meat). It is believed that consuming milk and milk products does not pose a risk.

Traveler's diarrhea: Results from drinking untreated water or eating uncooked foods; a temporary (and fairly common) reaction to the bacteria in new food ingredients. Symptoms include nausea, bloating, urgency, and malaise. Try quick-energy, non-sugary foods with protein and carbohydrates to keep your strength up. Over-the-counter anti-diarrheals (e.g. Imodium) may counteract the problems, but can complicate serious infections. The most dangerous side effect is dehydration; drink 8 oz. of water with ½ tsp. of sugar or honey and a pinch of salt, try uncaffeinated soft drinks, or munch on salted crackers. If you develop a fever or your symptoms don't go away after 4-5 days, consult a doctor. Consult a doctor for treatment of diarrhea in children.

Parasites: Microbes, tapeworms, etc. that hide in unsafe water and food. **Giardiasis,** for example, is acquired by drinking untreated water from streams or lakes all over the world. Symptoms include swollen glands or lymph nodes, fever, rashes or itchiness, digestive problems, eye problems, and anemia. Boil water, wear shoes, avoid bugs, and eat only cooked food.

OTHER INFECTIOUS DISEASES

Rabies: Transmitted through the saliva of infected animals; fatal if untreated. By the time symptoms appear (thirst and muscle spasms), the disease is in its terminal stage. If you are bitten, wash the wound thoroughly, seek immediate medical care, and try to have the animal located. A rabies vaccine, which consists of 3 shots given over a 21-day period, is available but is only semi-effective.

Hepatitis B: A viral infection of the liver transmitted via bodily fluids or needle-sharing. Symptoms may not surface until years after infection. Vaccinations are recommended for health-care workers, sexually-active travelers, and anyone planning to seek medical treatment abroad. The 3-shot vaccination series must begin 6 mo. before traveling.

Hepatitis C: Like Hep B, but the mode of transmission differs. IV drug users, those with occupational exposure to blood, hemodialysis patients, and recipients of blood transfusions are at the highest risk, but the disease can also be spread through sexual contact or sharing items like razors and toothbrushes that may have traces of blood on them.

AIDS, HIV, AND STDS

AIDS and HIV are as common in Austria and Switzerland as in the rest of Western Europe. For more detailed information on **Acquired Immune Deficiency Syndrome (AIDS)** in the two countries, call the **US Centers for Disease Control**'s 24hr. hotline at ☎ 800-342-2437, or contact the **Joint United Nations Programme on HIV/AIDS (UNAIDS),** 20 Av. Appia 20, CH-1211 Geneva 27, Switzerland (☎ +41 (22) 791 36 66, fax 791 41 87). The Council on International Educational Exchange's pamphlet, *Travel Safe: AIDS and International Travel,* is posted on their web site (www.ciee.org/Isp/safety/travelsafe.htm), along with links to other online and phone resources.

Sexually transmitted diseases (STDs) such as gonorrhea, chlamydia, genital warts, syphilis, and herpes are easier to catch than HIV and can be just as deadly. **Hepatitis B** and **C** are also serious STDs (see **Other Infectious Diseases,** above). Though condoms may protect you from some STDs, oral or even tactile contact can lead to transmission.

WOMEN'S HEALTH

Women traveling in unsanitary conditions are vulnerable to **urinary tract** and **bladder infections,** common bacterial diseases that cause a burning sensation and painful and sometimes frequent urination. To try to avoid these infections, drink plenty of vitamin-C-rich juice and plenty of clean water, and urinate frequently, especially right after intercourse. If symptoms persist, see a doctor.

Vaginal yeast infections may flare up in hot and humid climates. Wearing loosely fitting trousers or a skirt and cotton underwear will help, as will over-the-counter remedies like Monostat or Gynelotrimin. Bring supplies from home if you are prone to infection, as they may be difficult to find on the road.

Since **tampons, pads,** and reliable **contraceptive devices** are sometimes hard to find when traveling and your preferred brand will rarely be available, bring supplies with you.

 FURTHER READING: WOMEN'S HEALTH.
Adventures in Good Company: The Complete Guide to Women's Tours and Outdoor Trips, by Thalia Zepatos (US$17).
Handbook for Women Travellers, by Maggie and Gemma Moss (US$15).

PACKING

Pack lightly: lay out only what you absolutely need, then take half as many clothes and twice as much money. If you plan to do a lot of hiking, also see the section on **Camping and the Outdoors,** p. 28.

LUGGAGE. If you plan to cover most of your itinerary by foot, a sturdy **frame backpack** is unbeatable. (For the basics on buying a pack, see p. 30.) Toting a **suitcase** or **trunk** is fine if you plan to live in one or two cities and explore from there, but not a good idea if you're going to be moving around a lot. In addition to your main piece of luggage, a **daypack** (a small backpack or courier bag) is a must.

CLOTHING. No matter when you're traveling, it's always a good idea to bring a **warm jacket** or wool sweater, a **rain jacket** (Gore-Tex® is both waterproof and breathable), sturdy shoes or **hiking boots,** and **thick socks. Flip-flops** or waterproof sandals are must-haves for grubby hostel showers. You may also want to add one outfit beyond the jeans and t-shirt uniform, and maybe a nicer pair of shoes if you have the room. If you plan to visit any religious or cultural sites, remember that you'll need something besides tank tops and shorts to be respectful.

SLEEPSACK. Some hostels require that you provide your own linen or rent sheets from them. Save cash by making your own sleepsack: fold a full-size sheet in half the long way, then sew it closed along the long side and one of the short sides.

CONVERTERS & ADAPTORS. In Austria and Switzerland electricity is 220V AC (240V in Britain and Ireland), enough to fry any 110V North American appliance. You can get an **adapter** (which changes the shape of the plug) and a **converter** (which changes the voltage) at a hardware store. **Americans** and **Canadians** should buy an adapter and a converter. Don't make the mistake of using only an adapter. **New Zealanders** and **South Africans** (who both use 220V at home) as well as **Australians** (who use 240/250V) won't need a converter, but will need a set of adapters to use anything electrical.

FIRST-AID KIT. For a basic first-aid kit, pack: bandages, pain reliever, antibiotic cream, a thermometer, a Swiss Army knife, tweezers, moleskin, decongestant,

PACKING LIGHT, THE AUSTRIAN WAY In the
summer of 1870, Austrian climbing legend Hermann von Barth took to the hills of the Karwendel Range in Tyrol and climbed no fewer than 88 peaks, 12 of which were first-ever ascents. His luggage consisted simply of a drinking cup, binoculars, smelling salts, a lighter, a can of paint and a paintbrush to paint his name on each peak, and a bottle of poison in case he fell and wasn't able to rescue himself. He never fell.

motion-sickness remedy, diarrhea or upset-stomach medication (Imodium or Pepto Bismol), an antihistamine, sunscreen, insect repellent, burn ointment, and a syringe for emergencies (get an explanatory letter from your doctor).

IMPORTANT DOCUMENTS. Don't forget your passport, traveler's checks, ATM and/or credit cards, and adequate ID (see p. 10). Also check that you have any of the following that apply to you: a hosteling membership card (see p. 26); driver's license (see p. 10); travel insurance forms; and/or rail or bus pass (see p. 39).

> **USEFUL THINGS TO BRING:**
> **First-aid kit:** (see p. 23), medications, vitamins (see **Health**, p. 19)
> **Laundry supplies:** travel clothesline and small carton of detergent.
> **Shower supplies:** towel, shampoo, slippers for the shower, soap.
> **Personal hygiene supplies:** deodorant, tampons, razors, tweezers, condoms.
> **Sealable plastic bags** for damp clothes, food, shampoo, and other spillables.
> **Money belt** for carrying valuables; small calculator for currency conversion
> **Useful items:** travel alarm clock, water bottle, needle and thread, safety pins, umbrella, sunscreen, sunglasses, sun hat, insect repellent, padlock, earplugs, flashlight, compass, string, electrical tape (for repairing tears).

ACCOMMODATIONS

Accommodations in Austria and Switzerland are usually clean, orderly, and expensive. Always ask if your lodging provides a **guest card** *(Gästekarte)*. Guest cards grant discounts on local sports facilities, hiking excursions, town museums, and public transportation. In Austria, the tax that most accommodations slap on bills funds these discounts—take advantage of them to get your money's worth.

Most local tourist offices distribute extensive listings (the *Gastgeberverzeichnis*), and many will reserve a room for a small fee. National tourist offices can also supply more complete lists of campsites and hotels. Be aware that *Privatzimmer* and *Pensionen* may close their doors without notice; it's best to call ahead.

HOSTELS

> **A HOSTELER'S BILL OF RIGHTS.** Unless we state otherwise, you can expect that every hostel has: no lockout, no curfew, free hot showers, secure luggage storage, and no key deposit.

Hostels (*Jugendherbergen* in German, *Auberges de Jeunesse* in French, *Ostelli* in Italian) are the hubs of the gigantic backpacker subculture that rumbles through Europe every summer, providing innumerable opportunities to meet travelers from all over the world. Hostels generally offer dorm-style accommodations, often in single-sex large rooms with bunk beds, although some hostels do offer private rooms for families and couples. They sometimes have kitchens and utensils for your use, bike or moped rentals, storage areas, and laundry facilities. There can be drawbacks: some hostels close during certain daytime "lockout" hours, have a curfew, don't accept reservations, impose a maximum stay, or, less frequently, require that you do chores. In Austria and Switzerland, a dorm bed in a hostel averages around US$12-20. Check out the **Internet Guide to Hostelling** (www.hostels.com), which provides a directory of hostels from around the world in addition to oodles of information about hosteling and backpacking worldwide. **Eurotrip** (www.eurotrip.com/accommodation/accommodation.html) has information and reviews on budget hostels and several international hostel associations.

ESSENTIALS

LOCAL HI ORGANIZATIONS. To join HI, contact:

Australian Youth Hostels Association (AYHA), Level 3, 10 Mallett St., Camperdown NSW 2050 (☎(02) 95 65 16 99; fax 95 65 13 25; www.yha.org.au). AUS$52, under 18 AUS$16.

Hostelling International-Canada (HI-C), 400-205 Catherine St., Ottawa, ON K2P 1C3 (☎800-663-5777 or 613-237-7884; fax 237-7868; info@hostellingintl.ca; www.hostellingintl.ca). CDN$35, under 18 free.

Youth Hostels Association of New Zealand (YHANZ), P.O. Box 436, 193 Cashel St., 3rd Floor Union House, Christchurch 1 (☎(03) 379 99 70; fax 365 44 76; info@yha.org.nz; www.yha.org.nz). NZ$40, under 17 free.

Hostels Association of South Africa, 3rd fl. 73 St. George's St. Mall, P.O. Box 4402, Cape Town 8000 (☎(021) 424 25 11; fax 424 41 19; info@hisa.org.za; www.hisa.org.za). ZAR45.

Youth Hostels Association (England and Wales) Ltd., Trevelyan House, 8 St. Stephen's Hill, St. Albans, Hertfordshire AL1 2DY, UK (☎(0870) 870 88 08; fax (01727) 84 41 26; www.yha.org.uk). UK£12.50, under 18 UK£6.25.

Hostelling International Northern Ireland (HINI), 22-32 Donegall Rd., Belfast BT12 5JN, Northern Ireland (☎(02890) 31 54 35; fax 43 96 99; info@hini.org.uk; www.hini.org.uk). UK£10, under 18 UK£6.

An Óige (Irish Youth Hostel Association), 61 Mountjoy St., Dublin 7 (☎(01) 830 45 55; fax 830 58 08; anoige@iol.ie; www.irelandyha.org). €13, under 18 €5.

Scottish Youth Hostels Association (SYHA), 7 Glebe Crescent, Stirling FK8 2JA (☎(870) 155 32 55; fax (1786) 89 13 50; reservations@syha.org.uk; www.syha.org.uk). UK£6.

Hostelling International-American Youth Hostels (HI-AYH), 733 15th St. NW, #840, Washington, D.C. 20005 (☎202-783-6161; fax 783-6171; hostels@hiayh.org; www.hiayh.org). US$25, under 18 free.

Both Austria and Switzerland have branches of **Hostelling International (HI).** *Schweizer Jugendherbergen* (SJH or Swiss Youth Hostels) runs HI hostels in Switzerland and has a web site containing contact information for member hostels (www.youthhostel.ch). Austria has two HI organizations that operate together as the *Österreicher Jugendherbergsverband-Hauptverband* (ÖJH). Because of the rigorous standards of the national organizations, the SJH and ÖJH hostels are usually as clean as any hotel. While the clientele of the hostels varies, HI hostels tend to be oriented toward families and school groups.

Many HI hostels also accept reservations via the **International Booking Network** (IBN; Australia ☎(02) 92 61 11 11, Canada 800-663-5777, England and Wales ☎(1629) 58 14 18, Northern Ireland (1232) 32 47 33, Republic of Ireland (01) 830 17 66, New Zealand (09) 379 98 08, Scotland (8701) 55 32 55, US 800-909-4776) for a nominal fee. The HI webpage (www.iyhf.org) has information on the IBN as well as the web addresses and phone numbers of all national associations and can be a great place to begin researching hosteling in a specific region. Other comprehensive hosteling web sites include www.hostels.com and www.eurotrip.com.

Switzerland also has the smaller, more informal **Swiss Backpackers (SB)** organization. SB is an organization of 26 hostels that appeal to the young, foreign traveler interested in socializing. The neon-colored, all-English web site lists the hostels and also has a wealth of general information on backpacking, and specific information on adventure activities in Switzerland (www.backpacker.ch).

OTHER ACCOMMODATIONS

YMCA AND YWCAS. Not all **Young Men's Christian Association (YMCA)** locations offer lodging; those that do are often located in urban downtowns, which can be convenient but a little gritty. YMCA rates are usually lower than hotel rates but higher than hostel rates and may include the use of TV, air conditioning, pools, gyms, access to public transportation, tourist information, safe deposit boxes, luggage storage, daily housekeeping, multilingual staff, and 24hr. security. Many YMCAs accept women and families (group rates often available), but some will not lodge people under 18 without parental permission. There are several ways to make a reservation, all of which must be made at least two weeks in advance and paid for in advance with a traveler's check, US money order, certified check, Visa, or Mastercard in US dollars. Visit www.ymca.net.

HOTELS. Hotels are expensive in Austria (singles €40-100; doubles €70-250) and exorbitant in Switzerland (singles 50-75SFr; doubles 80-150SFr). Switzerland has set the international standard for hotels; even 1-, 2-, and 3-star accommodations tend to be nicer than their counterparts in other countries. The cheapest hotel-style accommodations have **Gasthof** or **Gästehaus** in the name; **Hotel-Garni** also means cheap. Continental breakfast *(Frühstück)* is almost always included.

PRIVATE ROOMS AND PENSIONS. Renting a **private room** *(Privatzimmer)* in a family home is an inexpensive and friendly way to house yourself. Such rooms generally include a sink and use of a toilet and shower. Many places rent private rooms only for longer stays, or they may levy a surcharge (10-20%) for stays of less than 3 nights. *Privatzimmer* start at 25 to 60SFr per person in Switzerland. In Austria, rooms range from €18-30 a night. Slightly more expensive, **pensions** *(Pensionen)* are similar to the American and British notion of a bed-and-breakfast. Generally, finding rooms for only one person might be difficult, especially for one-night stays, as most lodgings have rooms with double beds *(Doppelzimmer);* single travelers can get these rooms if they pay a bit more. Continental breakfast is *de rigueur;* in classier places, meat, cheese, and an egg will grace your plate and palate. Contact the local tourist office for a list of private rooms and pensionen.

UNIVERSITY DORMS. Some **colleges and universities** (see **Vienna: Accommodations,** p. 98), open their residence halls to travelers when school is not in session—some do so even during term-time. Rates tend to be low, and many offer free local calls. *Let's Go* lists colleges that rent dorm rooms among the accommodations for appropriate cities. College dorms are popular with many travelers, especially those looking for long-term lodging, so reserve ahead.

HOME EXCHANGE AND RENTALS. Home exchange offers travelers various types of homes (houses, apartments, condominiums, villas, even castles in some cases), plus the opportunity to live like a native and cut down on accommodation fees. For more information, contact **HomeExchange.com** (US ☎310-798-3864; www.homeexchange.com), **Intervac International Home Exchange** (in **Austria,** call Hans and Ingeborg Winkler (☎/fax (0423) 238 38; intervac.at@utanet.at); in **Switzerland,** call Claudia and Iso Niedermann (☎/fax (071) 944 27 79; intervac@bluewin.ch; www.intervac.com), or **The Invented City: International Home Exchange** (US ☎800-788-CITY (1489), elsewhere US +1 415-252-1141; www.invented-city.com). **Home rentals** are more expensive than exchanges, but can be cheaper than comparably serviced hotels. Both home exchanges and rentals, often including kitchen, maid service, TV, and telephones, are ideal for families or travelers with special dietary needs.

ESSENTIALS

> **FURTHER READING: ACCOMMODATIONS**
> *Europe the European Way: A Traveler's Guide to Living Affordably in the World's Great Cities.* Globe Pequot Press (US$14).

CAMPING AND THE OUTDOORS

CAMPING

Camping can be one of the most inexpensive ways to tour Austria and Switzerland. Be prepared, though, as most campsites are not isolated areas; they are large plots with many vans and cars. Camping in Austria and Switzerland is less about getting out into nature and more about having a cheap place to sleep. Most sites are open in the summer only, but some sites are specifically set aside for winter camping. In Switzerland, prices average 6-9SFr per person, 4-10SFr per tent site. In Austria, prices run €4-6 per person and €4-8 per tent (plus tax if you're over 15), making camping only sometimes cheaper than hosteling.

HIKING

Austria and Switzerland are renowned for their hiking, with paths ranging from simple hikes in the foothills of the Swiss Jura and Carinthia to ice-axe-wielding expeditions through the glaciers of the Berner Oberland and the Zillertal Alps. Nearly every town and city in the two countries has a series of trails in its vicinity which the tourist office will be able to tell you about.

Hiking trails are marked by signs indicating the time to nearby destinations, which may not bear any relation to your own expertise and endurance. ("Std." is short for *Stunden*, or hours.) Usually trails will also be marked with either a red-white-red marker, or a blue-white-blue marker. The blue marker, or any trail marked *"Für Geübte,"* means that mountaineering equipment is needed, while the red markers line paths that require no more than sturdy boots and hiking poles. Most mountain hiking trails and mountain huts are open only from late June to early September because of snow in the higher passes.

Free hiking **maps** are available from even the most basic tourist offices, but for lengthy hikes every hiker should have a topographic map of no more than 1:50,000 scale. In Austria and Switzerland two companies make these maps: **Freytag-Berndt** and **Kümmerly-Frey** (maps about US$10). These maps are available in kiosks, book-

> **OVERNIGHT HIKING IN AUSTRIA AND SWITZERLAND.** Be aware that camping in the back country is not standard practice in Austria and Switzerland as it is in America; in fact, camping overnight in public areas is forbidden in both countries. Travelers planning **overnight hikes** will have to stay in the mountain huts that abound in Swiss and Austrian outdoor areas. Mountain huts, which are run by the alpine clubs in both countries, are quite developed, and many have simple mattresses and hot water. Swiss and Austrian Alpine Club huts are open to all, but members get discounts. Prices are usually 25-35SFr in Switzerland and €15-22 in Austria. Sleeping in one of these huts is safer for the environment than camping out, and it is generally safer for you—when you leave, you are expected to list your next destination in the hut book, thus alerting search-and-rescue teams if a problem should occur.

stores, and tourist offices all over Austria and Switzerland, and from **Pacific Travellers Supply**, 12 W. Anapamu St., Santa Barbara, CA 93101, USA (☎805-963 4438). The Austrian National Tourist Office publishes the pamphlet *Hiking and Backpacking in Austria*, with a complete list of Freytag-Berndt maps and more tips.

Contact the following organizations for information on hiking and the mountain huts which they administrate:

Swiss Alpine Club (SAC), Sektion Bern, Monbijoustr. 61, CH 3007, Bern (☎(031) 370 18 18; fax 370 18 00). Membership 126SFr.

Österreichischer Alpenverein (ÖAV) (Österreichischer Alpenverein, Willhelm-Greil-Str. 15, A-6010 Innsbruck (☎(0512) 595 47; fax 57 55 28). Maintains most mountain huts across Tyrol and throughout Austria. Third-party insurance, accident provision, travel discounts, and a wealth of maps and mountain information are also included with membership. US$55, students under 25 US$40; one-time fee US$10 also includes use of some of the huts operated by the Deutscher Alpenverein (German Alpine Club).

Touristenverein "Die Naturfreunde," Viktoriag. 6, A-1150 Vienna (☎(01) 892 35 34), also operates a network of cottages in rural and mountain areas.

FURTHER READING: HIKING.
100 Hikes in the Alps, by Vicky Spring (US$15).
Walking Austria's Alps, by Jonathan Hurdle (US$11).
Walking Switzerland the Swiss Way, by Marcia and Philip Lieberman (US$13). The "Swiss Way" refers to hiking hut-to-hut.
Downhill Walking in Switzerland, by Richard and Linda Williams (US$12).
Swiss-Bernese Oberland, by Philip and Loretta Alspach (US$17).
Walking Easy in the Austrian Alps and *Walking Easy in the Swiss Alps,* by Chet and Carolee Lipton (US$11).

WILDERNESS SAFETY

Stay warm, stay dry, and stay hydrated. On any hike, you should pack enough equipment to keep you alive should disaster strike. This includes raingear, hat and mittens, a first-aid kit, a reflector, a whistle, high energy food, and extra water. Dress in layers of **synthetic materials** designed for the outdoors, or **wool.** Pile fleece jackets and Gore-Tex raingear are good choices. Never rely on cotton for warmth. Make sure to check all equipment for any defects before setting out, and see **Camping and Hiking Equipment,** below, for more information.

Check **weather forecasts** and pay attention to the skies when hiking. Don't hike when visibility is low. Whenever possible, let someone know when and where you are going hiking. Do not attempt a hike beyond your ability—you may be endangering your life. Of particular concern in Austria and Switzerland is **glacier hiking.** Never hike over glaciers alone. Snow-covered crevasses in glaciers have swallowed many an unsuspecting hiker. See **Health,** p. 19, for information about outdoor ailments such as heatstroke, hypothermia, rabies, and insects, as well as basic medical concerns and first-aid. For more information, consult *How to Stay Alive in the Woods*, by Bradford Angier (Macmillan, US$8).

CAMPING AND HIKING EQUIPMENT

WHAT TO GET...

Purchase equipment before you leave so that you'll know exactly what you have and how much it weighs. Spend some time examining catalogs and talking to knowledgeable salespeople. Camping equipment is generally more expensive in Australia, New Zealand, and the UK than in North America.

Sleeping Bag: Most good sleeping bags are rated by "season," or the lowest outdoor temperature at which they will keep you warm ("summer" means 30-40°F at night and "four-season" or "winter" often means below 0°F). Sleeping bags are made either of down (warmer and lighter, but more expensive, and miserable when wet) or of synthetic material (heavier, more durable, and warmer when wet). Prices vary, but might range from US$80-210 for a summer synthetic to US$250-300 for a good down winter bag. For **sleeping bag pads** you can choose from foam pads (US$10-20) or air mattresses (US$15-50). Both types cushion your back and neck and insulate you from the ground. Therm-A-Rest brand self-inflating sleeping pads are part foam and part air-mattress that partially inflate upon unrolling (US$45-80). Bring a **"stuff sack"** or plastic bag to store your sleeping bag and keep it dry.

Backpack: If you intend to do a lot of hiking, you should have a frame backpack. **Internal-frame packs** mold better to your back, keep a lower center of gravity, and can flex to allow you to hike difficult trails. Make sure your pack has a strong, padded hip belt, which transfers the weight from the shoulders to the legs. Any serious backpacking requires a pack of at least 3000 cubic in. (12,000cc). Sturdy backpacks cost anywhere from US$125-420. Before you buy any pack, try it on and imagine carrying it full; fill it with something heavy and walk around the store to get a sense of how it distributes weight. A **waterproof backpack cover** will prove invaluable. Otherwise, plan to store all of your belongings in plastic bags inside your backpack.

Boots: Be sure to wear hiking boots with good **ankle support** regardless of the terrain you are hiking in. Your boots should fit snugly and comfortably over a pair of wool socks and a thin liner sock. Break in boots for several weeks before setting out to avoid painful and debilitating blisters. If you're planning on doing any serious hiking your boots should be waterproof, with Gore-Tex or a similar fabric. In addition, the fewer seams a boot has the more waterproof it will be—the best hiking boots are solid leather.

Tent: The best tents are free-standing (with their own frames and suspension systems), set up quickly, and require staking only in high winds. Low-profile dome tents are the best all-around. Good 2-person tents start at US$90, 4-person at US$300. Seal the seams of your tent with waterproofer, and make sure it has a rain fly. A **battery-operated lantern**, a **plastic groundcloth,** and a **nylon tarp** are also useful.

Other Necessities: Raingear in two pieces, a top and pants, is far superior to a poncho. Three-layer Gore-Tex is more waterproof and breathable than 2-layer, but the difference will be negligible for casual hikers. **Synthetic materials,** like polypropylene tops, socks, and long underwear, along with a pile jacket, will keep you warm even when wet. When camping in autumn, winter, or spring, bring along a **"space blanket,"** which helps you retain your body heat and doubles as a groundcloth (US$5-15). Plastic **canteens** or water bottles keep water cooler than metal ones do, and are virtually shatter-and leak-proof. Large, collapsible **water sacks** will significantly improve your lot in primitive campgrounds and weigh practically nothing when empty. Bring **water-purification tablets** (iodine) for when you can't boil water, unless you are willing to shell out money for a portable water-purification system. Though most campgrounds provide campfire sites, you may want to bring a small metal grate or grill of your own. For those places that forbid fires or the gathering of firewood (virtually every organized campground in Europe), you'll need a **camp stove.** The classic Coleman stove starts at about US$40. Purchase a fuel bottle and fill it with propane to operate it. A **first aid kit, Swiss Army knife, insect repellent, calamine lotion,** and **waterproof matches** or a **lighter** are other essential camping items.

ESSENTIALS

...AND WHERE TO BUY IT

The mail-order/online companies listed below offer lower prices than many retail stores, but a visit to a local camping or outdoors store will give you a good sense of the look and weight of certain items.

Campmor, P.O. Box 700, Upper Saddle River, NJ 07458, USA (☎888-226-7667; elsewhere call US +1 201-825-8300; www.campmor.com).

Discount Camping, 880 Main North Rd., Pooraka, South Australia 5095, Australia (☎(08) 82 62 33 99; www.discountcamping.com.au).

Eastern Mountain Sports (EMS), 327 Jaffrey Rd., Peterborough, NH 03458, USA (☎888-463-6367 or 603-924-7231; www.shopems.com).

L.L. Bean, Freeport, ME 04033, USA (US and Canada ☎800-441-5713; UK (0800) 89 12 97; elsewhere, call US +1 207-552-3028; www.llbean.com).

Mountain Designs, P.O. Box 1472, Fortitude Valley, Queensland 4006, Australia (☎(07) 32 52 88 94; www.mountaindesign.com.au).

Recreational Equipment, Inc. (REI), Sumner, WA 98352, USA (☎800-426-4840 or 253-891-2500; www.rei.com).

YHA Adventure Shop, 14 Southampton St., London WC2E 7HA, UK (☎(020) 78 36 85 41; www.yhaadventure.com). The main branch of one of Britain's largest outdoor equipment suppliers.

SKIING

Western **Austria** is one of the world's best skiing regions. The areas around Innsbruck and Kitzbühel in Tyrol are saturated with lifts and runs. Skiers swoosh down some glaciers into the summer in the Ötztal, the Dachstein in the Salzkammergut, and Hintertux near Mayrhofen, among other places. High season normally runs from mid-December to mid-January and from February to March. Tourist offices provide information on regional skiing and can suggest budget travel agencies that offer ski packages.

Contrary to popular belief, skiing in **Switzerland** is often less expensive than in the US if you avoid the pricey resorts. Ski passes (valid for transportation to, from, and on lifts) run 30-50SFr per day and 100-300SFr per week. A week of lift tickets, equipment rental, lessons, lodging, and *demi-pension* (half-board—breakfast plus one other meal, usually dinner) averages 475SFr. Summer skiing is no longer as prevalent as it once was, but it's still available in a few towns like Zermatt, Saas Fee, and Les Diablerets.

With peaks above 3000m, the Alpine vertical drop is ample—1000 to 2000m at all major resorts. For mountain country, winter **weather** in the Austrian Alps is moderate, thanks to lower elevation and distance from the ocean. Daytime temperatures in the coldest months (Jan. and Feb.) measure around -7°C (20°F). Humidity is low, so snow on the ground stays powdery longer.

KEEPING IN TOUCH

BY MAIL

The postal systems of Austria and Switzerland are quick and efficient. Letters take one to three days within Switzerland and one to two days within Austria. Mark all letters and packages "mit flugpost" or "par avion." In all cases, include the postal code if you know it; those of Swiss cities begin with "CH," Austrian with "A."

SENDING MAIL HOME FROM AUSTRIA AND SWITZERLAND

For **airmail** transit times, see **Sending Mail to Austria and Switzerland,** below. To send a postcard or letter under 250g from **Switzerland** to an international destination within Europe costs 1.10SFr 1st class and 0.90SFr 2nd class, and to any other international destination via airmail costs 1.80SFr 1st class and 1.20SFr 2nd class. Domestically, postcards require 0.90SFr 1st class and 0.70SFr 2nd class. To send a postcard or letter under 50g from **Austria** to an international destination within Europe costs €0.73, and to any other international destination via airmail costs €1.02. Aerogrammes, printed sheets that fold into envelopes and travel via airmail, are available at post offices. It helps to mark "mit luftpost" if possible, though "par avion" is universally understood. Most post offices will charge exorbitant fees or simply refuse to send aerogrammes with enclosures.

SENDING MAIL TO AUSTRIA AND SWITZERLAND

Mark envelopes "airmail" or "par avion" to avoid having letters sent by sea.

Australia: Allow 4-7 days for regular airmail to Austria and Switzerland. Postcards cost AUS$1, letters up to 50g cost AUS$1.50; packages up to 0.5kg AUS$13, up to 2kg AUS$46. **EMS** will deliver in 3-5 days for AUS$32. www.auspost.com.au/pac.

Canada: Allow 4-7 days for regular airmail to Austria and Switzerland. Postcards and letters up to 20g cost CDN$1.05; packages up to 0.5kg CDN$10.20, up to 2kg CDN$34.00. www.canadapost.ca/CPC2/common/rates/ratesgen.html#international.

Ireland: Allow 3-4 days for regular airmail to Austria and Switzerland. Postcards and letters up to 25g cost €0.41. Add €2.92 for **Swiftpost International**. www.letterpost.ie.

New Zealand: Allow 5-9 days for regular airmail to Austria and Switzerland. Postcards NZ$1.50. Letters up to 20g cost NZ$2.00; small parcels up to 0.5kg NZ$16.41, up to 2kg NZ$52.61. www.nzpost.co.nz/nzpost/inrates.

UK: Allow 3-5 days for airmail to Austria and Switzerland. Letters up to 20g cost UK£0.36; packages up to 0.5kg UK£2.67, up to 2kg UK£9.42. **UK Swiftair** delivers letters a day faster for UK£2.85 more. www.royalmail.com/default.htm.

US: Allow 4-8 days for regular airmail to Austria and Switzerland. Postcards/aerogrammes cost US$0.70; letters under 1 oz. US$0.80. Packages under 1 lb. cost US$8-16; larger packages cost a variable amount (around US$15). **US Express Mail** takes 2-3 days and costs US$23/26 (0.5/1 lb.). **US Global Priority Mail** delivers small/large flat-rate envelopes in 3-5 days for US$5/9. www.usps.gov.

RECEIVING MAIL IN AUSTRIA AND SWITZERLAND

There are a few ways to arrange pick-up of letters sent to you by friends and relatives while you are abroad:

General Delivery: Mail can be sent to Austria and Switzerland through **Poste Restante** (the international phrase for General Delivery; in German *Postlagernde Briefe*) to almost any city or town with a post office. Address *Poste Restante* letters to: Napoleon BONAPARTE, *Postlagernde Briefe*, A-1010 Vienna, Austria. In Switzerland use the same formula, though the postal code will be preceded by a CH. The mail will go to a special desk in the central post office, unless you specify a post office by street address or postal code. As a rule, it is best to use the largest post office in the area, and mail may be sent there regardless of what is written on the envelope. It is usually safer and quicker to send mail express or registered. When picking up your mail, bring a form of photo ID, preferably a passport. There is generally no surcharge; if there is a charge, it usually does not exceed the cost of domestic postage. If the clerks insist that there is nothing for you, have them check under your first name as well. *Let's Go* lists post offices in the **Practical Information** section for each city and most towns.

American Express: AmEx's travel offices throughout the world offer a free **Client Letter Service** (mail held up to 30 days and forwarded upon request) for cardholders who contact them in advance. Address the letter in the same way shown above. Some offices will offer these services to non-cardholders (especially AmEx Traveler's Cheque holders), but call ahead to make sure. *Let's Go* lists AmEx office locations for most large cities in **Practical Information** sections; for a complete, free list, call US ☎800-528-4800.

Surface mail is by far the cheapest and slowest way to send mail. It takes one to three months to cross the Atlantic and two to four to cross the Pacific, appropriate for sending large quantities of items you won't need to see for a while. When ordering books and materials from abroad, always include one or two **International Reply Coupons (IRCs),** a way of providing the postage to cover delivery. IRCs should be available from your local post office and those abroad (US$1.05).

BY TELEPHONE

CALLING HOME FROM AUSTRIA OR SWITZERLAND

A **calling card** is probably your best and cheapest bet. Calls are billed either collect or to your account. **To obtain a calling card** from your national telecommunications service before you leave home, contact the appropriate company below. Ask your calling card provider for directions on calling home with their calling card.

Australia: Telstra Australia (☎ 13 22 00).
Canada: Canada Direct (☎800-668-6878).
Ireland: Ireland Direct (☎(800) 40 00 00).
New Zealand: New Zealand Direct (☎(0800) 00 00 00).
South Africa: Telkom South Africa (☎ 102 19).
UK: British Telecom Direct (☎(800) 34 51 44).
US: AT&T (☎800-222-0300), **Sprint** (800-877-4646), or **MCI** (800-444-3333).

To **call home with a calling card** or to make a **collect call,** contact your service provider in Austria and Switzerland by dialing the appropriate toll-free access number:

AT&T: in Austria ☎(0800) 20 02 88, in Switzerland (0800) 89 00 11.
BT Direct: in Austria ☎(0800) 20 02 09, in Switzerland (0800) 55 25 44.
Canada Direct: in Austria ☎(0800) 20 02 17, in Switzerland (0800) 55 83 30.
MCI WorldPhone Direct: in Austria ☎(0800) 20 02 35, in Switzerland (0800) 89 02 22.
Sprint: in Austria ☎(0800) 20 02 36, in Switzerland (0800) 89 97 77.
Telecom New Zealand Direct: in Austria ☎(0800) 20 02 22, in Switzerland (0800) 55 64 11.
Telkom South Africa Direct: Austria ☎(0800) 20 02 30, Switzerland (0800) 55 85 35.

Wherever possible, use a calling card for international phone calls, as the long-distance rates for national phone services are often exorbitant. You can usually make direct international calls from pay phones, but if you aren't using a calling card you may spend a ridiculous amount in coins. Where available, **prepaid phone cards and** occasionally **major credit cards** can be used for direct international calls, but they are still less cost-efficient.

If you dial direct, first insert the appropriate amount of money or a prepaid card, then dial the country code and number you want to call. The expensive alternative to dialing direct or using a calling card is using an international operator to place a **collect call.** An English-speaking operator from your home nation can be reached by dialing the provider for your country with the phone numbers listed above.

CALLING WITHIN AUSTRIA AND SWITZERLAND

The simplest way to call within the country is to use a pay phone. Most pay phones in Switzerland, and many in Austria, accept only **prepaid phone cards,** not coins. Phone cards are available at kiosks, post offices, or train stations. Rates are highest in the morning, lower in the evening, and lowest on Sunday and late at night. Dial the city code (refer to the phone code box in each city's **Practical Information**) before each number when calling from outside the city; within the city, dial only the actual number.

PLACING INTERNATIONAL CALLS. To call Austria or Switzerland from home or to call home from Austria or Switzerland, dial:

1. The **international dialing prefix.** To dial out of **Australia,** dial 0011; **Canada** or the **US,** 011; the **Republic of Ireland, New Zealand,** or the **UK,** 00; **South Africa,** 09; out of Austria or Switzerland, 00.
2. The **country code** of the country you want to call. To call **Australia,** dial 61; **Canada** or the **US,** 1; the **Republic of Ireland,** 353; **New Zealand,** 64; **South Africa,** 27; the **UK,** 44; Austria, 43; Switzerland, 41.
3. The **city/area code.** *Let's Go* lists the city/area codes for cities and towns in Austria and Switzerland opposite the city or town name, next to a ☎. If the first digit is a zero (e.g., 020 for London), omit the zero when calling from abroad (e.g., dial 20 from Canada to reach London).
4. The **local number.**

TIME DIFFERENCES

Austria and Switzerland are one hour ahead of Greenwich Mean Time (GMT). Both observe daylight savings time.

2 AM	5 AM	10AM	11AM	12 PM	8 PM	10PM
Vancouver Seattle San Francisco Los Angeles	New York Boston	London (GMT)	Austria Switzerland	Johannesburg	Sydney	Auckland

EMAIL AND INTERNET

Internet access is widespread in Austria and Switzerland. You can check your email from cybercafes, which *Let's Go* lists in the Practical Information section for each city, and sometimes from universities, libraries, and hostels. Though limited free access is sometimes available in bookstores and libraries, regular Internet access isn't cheap; there is no standard price, but it tends to range from 10-15SFr per hour in Switzerland, and €2-5 per hour in Austria. For a complete listing of cybercafes in Austria and Switzerland, visit either www.cybercaptive.com, www.netcafeguide.com, or www.cyberiacafe.net/cyberia/guide/ccafe.htm.

GETTING TO AUSTRIA AND SWITZERLAND

BY PLANE

When it comes to airfare, a little effort can save you a bundle. If your plans are flexible enough to accommodate restrictions, courier fares are the cheapest. Tickets bought from consolidators and standby seating are also good deals, but last-minute specials, airfare wars, and charter flights often beat these fares. The key is to hunt around, to be flexible, and to ask persistently about discounts. Students, seniors, and those under 26 should never pay full price for a ticket.

AIRFARES

Airfares to Austria and Switzerland peak between June and August; holidays are also expensive. The cheapest times to travel are fall and spring, post-ski-season. Midweek (M-Th morning) round-trip flights run US$40-50 cheaper than weekend flights, but they are generally more crowded and less likely to permit frequent-flier upgrades. Student tickets will also frequently allow free, lengthy layovers in hub cities (Paris, London, Frankfurt). Traveling with an "open return" ticket can be pricier than fixing a return date when buying the ticket. Round-trip flights are by far the cheapest; "open-jaw" (arriving in and departing from different cities, e.g. Paris-Zurich and Geneva-Rome) tickets tend to be pricier. Patching one-way flights together is the most expensive way to travel. Flights between capitals or regional hubs will tend to be cheaper.

If Austria or Switzerland is only one stop on a more extensive globe-hop, consider a round-the-world (RTW) ticket. Tickets usually include at least five stops and are valid for about a year; prices run US$1200-5000. Try **Northwest Airlines/KLM** (US ☎800-447-4747; www.nwa.com) or **Star Alliance**, a consortium of 22 airlines including United Airlines (US ☎800-241-6522; www.star-alliance.com).

Fares from the US to Austria and Switzerland vary tremendously depending on airfare wars and special deals. For a round-trip ticket during peak season, expect to spend anywhere from US$500-1000 versus US$300-500 during off-season.

BUDGET AND STUDENT TRAVEL AGENCIES

A good agent can make your life easy and help you save, but agents may not spend the time to find you the lowest fare—they get paid on commission. Students and under-26ers holding **ISIC and IYTC cards** (see **identification**, p. 10), respectively, qualify for big discounts from student agencies. Most flights from budget agencies are on major airlines, but in peak season some sell seats on chartered aircraft.

usit world (www.usitworld.com). Over 50 **usit campus** branches in the UK (www.usitcampus.co.uk), including 52 Grosvenor Gardens, **London** SW1W 0AG (☎(0870) 240 10 10); **Manchester** (☎(0161) 273 18 80); and **Edinburgh** (☎(0131) 668 33 03). Nearly 20 **usit NOW** offices in Ireland, including 19-21 Aston Quay, O'Connell Bridge, **Dublin** 2 (☎(01) 602 16 00; www.usitnow.ie), and **Belfast** (☎(02) 890 32 71 11; www.usit-now.com). Offices also in Athens, Auckland, Brussels, Frankfurt, Johannesburg, Lisbon, Luxembourg, Madrid, Paris, Sofia, and Warsaw.

Council Travel (www.counciltravel.com). Countless US offices, including branches in Atlanta, Boston, Chicago, L.A., New York, San Francisco, Seattle, and Washington, D.C. Check the web site or call ☎800-2-COUNCIL (226-8624) for the office nearest you.

CTS Travel, 44 Goodge St., **London** W1T 2AD (☎(0207) 636 00 31; fax 637 53 28; ctsinfo@ctstravel.co.uk).

STA Travel, 7890 S. Hardy Dr., Ste. 110, Tempe, AZ 85284, USA (24hr. reservations and info ☎800-777-0112; fax 480-592-0876; www.sta-travel.com). A student and youth travel organization with countless offices worldwide (check their web site for a listing of all their offices), including US offices in Boston, Chicago, L.A., New York, San Francisco, Seattle, and Washington, D.C. Ticket booking, travel insurance, railpasses, and more. In the UK, walk-in office at 11 Goodge St., **London** W1T 2PF, or call ☎(0870) 160 60 70. In New Zealand, 10 High St., **Auckland** (☎(09) 309 04 58). In Australia, 366 Lygon St., **Melbourne** VIC 3053 (☎(03) 93 49 43 44).

StudentUniverse, 545 Fifth Ave., Suite 640, New York, NY 10017 (toll-free customer service ☎800-272-9676, outside the US 212-986-8420; help@studentuniverse.com; www.studentuniverse.com), is an online student travel service offering discount ticket booking, travel insurance, railpasses, destination guides, and much more. Customer service line open M-F 9am-8pm and Sa noon-5pm EST.

Travel CUTS (Canadian Universities Travel Services Limited), 187 College St., **Toronto,** ON M5T 1P7 (☎416-979-2406; fax 979-8167; www.travelcuts.com). 60 offices across Canada. Also in the UK, 295-A Regent St., **London** W1R 7YA (☎(0207) 255 19 44)

Wasteels, Skoubogade 6, 1158 Copenhagen K, (☎3314 4633; fax 7630 0865; www.wasteels.dk/uk). Huge chain with 203 locations across Europe. Sells Wasteels BIJ tickets—2nd-class international point-to-point train tickets with unlimited stopovers for those under 26 sold only in Europe—discounted 30-45% off regular fare (see p. 40)..

FLIGHT PLANNING ON THE INTERNET. The Internet is one of the best places to look for travel bargains. Many airline sites offer special last-minute deals on the Web. Austrian Airlines lists specials at http://airnet.aua.com/leisure/AT/framesnew/booking.htm. Other sites do the legwork and compile the deals for you—try www.bestfares.com, www.onetravel.com, www.lowestfare.com, www.orbitz.com, and www.travelzoo.com.

STA (www.statravel.com), **Council** (www.counciltravel.com), and **StudentUniverse** (www.studentuniverse.com) provide quotes on student tickets, while **Expedia** (msn.expedia.com) and **Travelocity** (www.travelocity.com) offer full travel services. **Priceline** (www.priceline.com) allows you to specify a price, and obligates you to buy any ticket that meets or beats it; be prepared for antisocial hours and odd routes. **Skyauction** (www.skyauction.com) allows you to bid on both last-minute and advance-purchase tickets.

An indispensable resource on the Internet is the *Air Traveler's Handbook* (www.cs.cmu.edu/afs/cs/user/mkant/Public/Travel/airfare.html), a comprehensive listing of links to everything you need to know before you board a plane. To protect yourself, make sure that the site you use has a secure server before handing over any credit card details. Happy hunting!

COMMERCIAL AIRLINES

The commercial airlines' lowest regular offer is the **APEX** (Advance Purchase Excursion) fare, which provides confirmed reservations and allows "open-jaw" tickets. Generally, reservations must be made seven to 21 days ahead of departure, with seven- to 14-day minimum-stay and up to 90-day maximum-stay restrictions. These fares carry hefty cancellation and change penalties (fees rise in summer). Book peak-season APEX fares early; by May you will have a hard time getting your desired departure date. Use **Microsoft Expedia** (msn.expedia.com) or **Travelocity** (www.travelocity.com) to get an idea of the lowest published fares, then use the resources outlined here to try and beat those fares.

Specials advertised in newspapers may be cheaper but have more restrictions and fewer seats. For cheap commercial flights in the **US**, check **Icelandair** (☎ 800-223-5500; www.icelandair.com). They have stopovers in Iceland for no extra cost on most transatlantic flights. New York to Frankfurt from May to September is US$470-710; from October to April it's US$370-$425. For last-minute offers, subscribe to their email Lucky Fares. In the **UK**, check **buzz** (☎ (0870) 240 70 70; www.buzzaway.com), a subsidiary of KLM. Tickets from London to Vienna run from UK£50-80 but cannot be changed or refunded. Also try **EasyJet** (☎ (0870) 600 00 00; www.easyjet.com), which has flights from London to Geneva and Zurich from UK£47-136; online tickets are available. **Aer Lingus** in Ireland (☎ (01) 886 88 88; www.aerlingus.ie) has return tickets from Dublin, Cork, Galway, Kerry, and Shannon to Munich and Zürich from €105-300. The most popular carriers to Austria and Switzerland are **Lufthansa** and **Austrian Air**. The European Airpass offers good deals to Vienna with coupons for transfer flights to other countries (www.austrianair.com).

AIR COURIER FLIGHTS

Those who travel light should consider courier flights. Couriers help transport cargo on international flights by using their checked luggage space for freight. Generally, couriers travel with carry-ons only and deal with complex flight restrictions. Most flights are round-trip only, with short fixed-length stays (usually 1 week) and a limit of a one ticket per issue. Most of these flights also operate only out of major gateway cities, mostly in North America. Generally, you must be over 21 (in some cases 18). In summer, the most popular destinations usually require a reservation about two weeks in advance (you can usually book up to two months ahead). Super-discounted fares are common for "last-minute" flights (3-14 days ahead).

FROM NORTH AMERICA

Round-trip courier fares from North America to Western Europe run about US$200-500. Most flights leave from Los Angeles, Miami, Montreal, New York, San Francisco, Toronto, or Vancouver. The organizations below provide their members with lists of opportunities and courier brokers worldwide for an annual fee. While no courier companies fly to Austria or Switzerland, the following are the largest companies with flights to Western Europe: **Air Courier Association** (US ☎ 800-282-1202; www.aircourier.org); one-year membership is US$39. **Global Courier Travel** has a searchable online database (www.globalcouriertravel.com); one year membership is US$40, two people US$55. **International Association of Air Travel Couriers (IAATC;** US ☎ 352-475-1584; fax 582-1581; www.iaatc.com) membership is US$45-50. **NOW Voyager** (US ☎ 212-459-1616; fax 262-7407) costs US$50.

FROM THE UK, IRELAND, AUSTRALIA, AND NEW ZEALAND

Although the courier industry is most developed from North America, there are limited courier flights in other areas. The minimum age for couriers from the **UK** is usually 18. **Brave New World Enterprises**, P.O. Box 22212, London SE5 8WB (www.nry.co.uk/bnw), publishes a directory of all the companies offering courier flights in the UK (UK£10, in electronic form UK£8). The **International Association of Air Travel Couriers** (see above) often offers courier flights from London to Budapest. **Global Courier Travel** (see above) also offers flights from London and Dublin to continental Europe. **British Airways Travel Shop** (☎ (0870) 606 11 33; www.british-airways.com/travelqa/booking/travshop/travshop.shtml) arranges some flights from London to destinations in continental Europe (specials may be as low as UK£60). From **Australia** and **New Zealand, Global Courier Travel** (see above) often has listings from Sydney and Auckland to London and occasionally Frankfurt.

TICKET CONSOLIDATORS

Ticket consolidators, or **"bucket shops,"** buy unsold tickets in bulk from commercial airlines and sell them at discounted rates. The best place to look is in the Sunday travel section of any major newspaper (such as the *New York Times*), where many bucket shops place tiny ads. Call quickly, as availability is typically extremely limited. Not all bucket shops are reliable, so insist on a receipt that gives full details of restrictions, refunds, and tickets, and pay by credit card (in spite of the 2-5% fee) so you can stop payment if you never receive your tickets. For more info, see www.travel-library.com/air-travel/consolidators.html. Also check the book *Consolidators: Air Travel's Bargain Basement*, by Kelly Monaghan (Intrepid Traveler, US$8).

TRAVELING FROM THE US AND CANADA

Travel Avenue (☎800-333-3335; www.travelavenue.com) looks for the best published fares, then uses several consolidators to try to beat that fare. Other services worth trying are **Traveleader** (☎305-443-4929; fax 444-1293); **Pennsylvania Travel** (☎800-331-0947; fax 610-644-2150); **Cheap Tickets** (☎800-377-1000; www.cheaptickets.com); and **Travac** (☎800-872-8800; fax 212-563-3631; www.travac.com). Other consolidators on the web include the **Internet Travel Network** (www.itn.com); **Travel Information Services** (www.tiss.com); **TravelHUB** (www.travelhub.com); and **The Travel Site** (www.thetravelsite.com). Keep in mind that these are just suggestions to get you started; *Let's Go* does not endorse any of these agencies. As always, be cautious, and research companies before you hand over your credit card number.

TRAVELING FROM THE UK, AUSTRALIA, AND NEW ZEALAND

In London, the **Air Travel Advisory Bureau** (☎(0207) 636 5000; www.atab.co.uk) can provide names of reliable consolidators and discount flight specialists. From Australia and New Zealand, look for consolidator ads in the travel section of the *Sydney Morning Herald* and other papers.

CHARTER FLIGHTS

Charters are flights a tour operator contracts with an airline to fly extra passengers during peak season. Charters can be cheaper than flights on scheduled airlines, some operate nonstop, and restrictions on minimum advance-purchase and minimum stay are more lenient. However, charter flights fly less frequently than major airlines, make refunds particularly difficult, and are almost always fully booked. Schedules and itineraries may also change or be cancelled at the last moment (as late as 48hr. before the trip, and without a full refund), and check-in, boarding, and baggage claim are often much slower. As always, pay with a credit card if you can, and consider traveler's insurance against trip interruption.

Discount clubs and **fare brokers** offer members savings on last-minute charter and tour deals. Study their contracts closely; you don't want to end up with an unwanted overnight layover. In the US, **Travelers Advantage** specializes in European travel and tour packages (☎203-365-2000; www.travelersadvantage.com; US$60 annual fee includes discounts and cheap flight directories.)

GETTING AROUND AUSTRIA AND SWITZERLAND

Fares on all modes of transportation are either one-way ("single") or round-trip ("return"). "Period returns" require you to return within a specific number of days; "day return" means you must return on the same day. Unless stated otherwise, *Let's Go* always lists one-way fares.

BY TRAIN

European trains are generally comfortable, convenient, and reasonably swift. In fact, the train can get you places throughout Austria and Switzerland a car cannot. Second-class travel is pleasant, and compartments, which seat two to six, are excellent places to meet fellow travelers. Trains, however, are not always safe; lock your compartment door (if possible) and keep your valuables on your person at all times. Non-smokers probably won't be comfortable in smoking compartments, which tend to be very, very smoky. Get your stuff together a few stops before you want to get off, since trains pause only a few minutes before zipping off. For longer trips, make sure that you are on the correct car, as trains sometimes split at crossroads. Towns in parentheses on schedules require a train switch at the town listed immediately before the parenthesis. You might want to ask if your route requires changing trains, as the schedules are confusing.

The **Österreichische Bundesbahn** (ÖBB), **Austria's** federal railroad, is one of Europe's most thorough and efficient. The ÖBB prints the yearly *Fahrpläne Kursbuch Bahn-Inland*, a compilation of all rail, ferry, and cable-car schedules in Austria. The massive schedule is available at any large train station, along with its companion guides, the *Kursbuch Bahn-Ausland* for international trains, and the *Internationales Schlafwagenkursbuch* for sleeping cars. Getting around **Switzerland** is also a snap. Federal **(SBB, CFF)** and private railways connect most towns and villages, with trains running frequently. The national phone number for **rail information** is ☎ (0900) 30 03 00 and has operators who speak English, German, French, and Italian, but it costs 1.19SFr per minute. Check the web site for the federal railway system at www.sbb.ch (available in French, German, Italian, and English versions), or email them at railinfo@sbb.ch (answered only M-F). Be aware that sometimes only private train lines go to remote tourist spots; therefore, Eurail and SwissPass may not be valid. Yellow signs announce departure times *(Ausfahrt, départ, partenze)* and platforms *(Gleis, quai, binario)*. White signs are for arrivals *(Ankunft, arrivé, arrivo)*. On major Austrian lines, make reservations at least a few hours in advance.

Even with a railpass, you are not guaranteed a seat unless you make a **reservation** (US$11); they are advisable during the holiday seasons and often required on major lines. Also, while many high-speed or quality trains (e.g., EuroCity and InterCity) are included in a railpass, certain international trains require a **supplement** (US$11). For overnight travel, a tight, open bunk called a **couchette** is an affordable luxury (about US$28). Both seat and couchette reservations can be made by your local travel agent or in person at the train station (reserve at least a few hours in advance for seats, at least a few days for couchettes).

RAIL TICKETS AND DISCOUNTS

You can purchase **individual tickets** at every train station in Austria and Switzerland, at Bahn-Total service stations, at the occasional automat, most *Tabak* stands, and from the conductor for a small surcharge. Over 130 stations accept major credit cards as well as American Express Traveler's Cheques and Eurocheques. Most ticket validation is based on the honor system, but *Schwarzfahren* (i.e. riding without a ticket) can result in big fines, and playing "dumb tourist" probably won't work.

In Austria, children under 6 travel free, while children ages 6-12 receive a 50% discount. In Switzerland, travelers under 16 travel free with a parent with the Swiss Family Card. When traveling without a parent, children up to 16 have a 50% discount on all the offers of the Swiss Travel System.

For tourists under 26, **BIJ** tickets (Billets Internationals de Jeunesse; a.k.a. **Wasteels, Eurotrain,** and **Route 26**) are a great alternative to railpasses. Available for international trips within Europe as well as most ferry services, they knock 20-40% off regular 2nd-class fares. Tickets are good for 60 days after purchase and allow a number of stopovers along the normal direct route of the train journey. Issued for a specific international route between two points, they must be used in the direction and order of the designated route and must be bought in Europe. The equivalent for those over 26, **BIGT** tickets provide a 20-30% discount on 1st- and 2nd-class international tickets for business travelers, temporary residents of Europe, and their families. Both types of tickets are available from European travel agents, at Wasteels or Eurotrain offices (usually in or near train stations), or directly at the ticket counter. For more info, contact **Wasteels,** Laupenstr. 19, Bern 3008 (☎ (031) 381 15 55; fax 381 32 30; or check www.wasteels.dk/uk for the Wasteels nearest you).

RAILPASSES

Ideally, a railpass allows you to jump on any train in the specified zone, go wherever you want whenever you want, and change your plans at will. In practice, it's not so simple; you must still wait to pay for supplements, seat reservations, and couchette reservations, as well as have your pass validated when you first use it. More importantly, railpasses don't always pay off. For ballpark estimates, consult the **DERTravel** or **RailEurope** railpass brochure for prices of point-to-point tickets. The brochures should be available in most travel agencies. DERTravel brochures can be also ordered online at www.dertravel.com. You can also get prices of point-to-point tickets from the federal railways themselves (see p. 40). Add them up and compare with railpass prices.

SINGLE-NATION RAILPASSES

NATIONAL RAILPASSES. The domestic analogs of the Eurailpass (see p. 43), national railpasses are valid either for a given number of consecutive days or for a specific number of days within a given time period. National railpasses are the way to go if you're going to be covering long distances within Austria or Switzerland. Nearly all are sold either through RailEurope or at local train stations (contact www.raileurope.com for more info, or dial ☎ 1-800-4EURAIL (438-7245). Consider the following options:

Austrian Railpass: Sold worldwide, this pass is valid for 3 days of unlimited train travel in a 15-day period on all Austrian Federal Railway lines, state, and private rail lines in Austria. Also grants a 40% discount on bicycle rental in over 130 railway stations and 50% discount on DDSG steamers between Passau and Linz and 20% on steamers between Melk, Krems, and Vienna. You can purchase up to 5 additional rail days. 2nd-class $107, each additional day $15. Travelers ages 6-12 travel at half price. The card itself has no photo, so you must carry a valid ID in case of inspections.

VORTEILScard Senior: The ÖBB offers a discount card for women over 60 and men over 65 called the VORTEILScard Senior, available in train stations and most travel agencies. Holders get 45% off train fares, 50% if booked on the web (www.oebb.at), at ticket vending machines, or by phone (☎ 05 17 17). The card is also valid for 25% off selected steamers, currency exchange at half the charge, and various other benefits. Good in Austria for 1 year. €25.44, requires a photo and proof of age. Call ☎ (01) 93 00 03 64 57 for more information. Operators speak German only.

VORTEILScard: Offers similar benefits as the VORTEILScard Senior for students under 26. Good in Austria for 1 year. €18.17, requires a photo and ISIC card for non-Austrian students. Call ☎ (01) 93 00 03 64 57 for more information. Operators speak German.

VORTEILScard Behinderte: Offers similar benefits as the VORTEILScard Senior for travelers with disabilities. Good in Austria for 1 year. €18.17, requires ID and proof of status. Call ☎ (01) 93 00 03 64 57 for information. Operators speak German only.

Swiss Transfer Ticket: Good for a 1-day trip from any entry point (airport or border crossing) to any single destination within Switzerland, and the return trip to the border, within a period of 1 month. 2nd-class US$76.

Swiss Card: Same round-trip as the Swiss Transfer Ticket, plus 50% off unlimited rail and bus tickets within the month period between your entry and departure. 2nd-class $110.

SwissPass: Offers unlimited rail travel for a certain number of consecutive days: choose between 4, 8, 15, 22 days, or 1 month, 1st- or 2nd-class. It also entitles you to unlimited urban transportation in 36 cities, unlimited travel on certain private railways and lake steamers, and 25% discounts on excursions to most mountaintops. 2nd-class 4-day passes start at US$160, 8 days at $225, 15 days at $270, 21 days at $315, and 1 month at $350.

Swiss Saver Pass: Offers the same benefits as the SwissPass at a 15% discount for groups of 2 or more adults traveling together.

Swiss Flexipass: Entitles you to 3, 4, 5, 6, or 8 days of unlimited rail travel within a 1-month period, 1st- or 2nd-class, with the same benefits as the SwissPass. 2nd-class adult passes for 3 days start at US$156, 4 days at $184, 5 days at $212, 6 days at $240, 8 days at $282.

Swiss Saver Flexipass: Offers the same benefits as the Swiss Flexipass at a 15% discount for groups of 2 or more adults traveling together.

EURO DOMINO. Like the Interrail Pass (see p. 44), the Euro Domino pass is available to anyone who has lived in Europe for at least six months, but is only valid in one country (which you designate upon buying the pass). It is available for 1st- and 2nd-class travel (with a special rate for under 26ers), for three to eight days of unlimited travel within a one-month period. It is not valid on Eurostar or Thalys trains. **Supplements** for many high-speed trains are included, though you must still pay for **reservations** where they are compulsory. The pass must be bought within your country of residence and can be found at travel agents and major train stations. Below is a sample of prices for Austria and Switzerland:

EURO-DOMINO PASS (SWITZ.)	3 days	5 days	8 days
2nd class	€101	€123	€156
2nd class youth (under 26)	€80	€100	€130

EURO-DOMINO PASS (AUSTRIA)	3 days	5 days	8 days
2nd class	€104	€130	€169
2nd class youth (under 26)	€76	€94	€112

MULTINATIONAL RAILPASSES

EURAILPASS. Eurail is **valid** in most of Western Europe: Austria, Belgium, Denmark, Finland, France, Germany, Greece, Hungary, Italy, Luxembourg, The Netherlands, Norway, Portugal, the Republic of Ireland, Spain, Sweden, and Switzerland. It is **not valid** in the UK. Standard **Eurailpasses,** valid for a consecutive given number of days, are best for those planning on spending extensive time on trains every few days. **Flexipasses,** valid for any 10 or 15 (not necessarily consecutive) days in a two-month period, are more cost-effective for those traveling longer distances less frequently. **Saverpasses** provide 1st-class travel for travelers in groups of two to five (prices are per person). **Youthpasses** and **Youth Flexipasses** provide parallel 2nd-class perks for those under 26. For more information, visit www.raileurope.com.

EURAILPASSES	15 days	21 days	1 month	2 months	3 months
1st class Eurailpass	US$572	US$740	US$918	US$1298	US$1606
Eurail Saverpass	US$486	US$630	US$780	US$1106	US$1366
Eurail Youthpass	US$401	US$518	US$644	US$910	US$1126

EURAIL FLEXIPASSES	10 days in 2 months	15 days in 2 months
1st class Eurail Flexipass	US$674	US$888
Eurail Saver Flexipass	US$574	US$756
Eurail Youth Flexipass	US$473	US$622

Passholders receive a timetable for major routes and a map with details on possible ferry, steamer, bus, car rental, hotel, and Eurostar discounts. Passholders often also receive reduced fares or free passage on many bus and boat lines.

EUROPASS. The Europass is a slimmed-down version of the Eurailpass: it allows five to 15 days of unlimited travel in any two-month period within France, Germany, Italy, Spain, and Switzerland. **First-Class Europasses** (for individuals) and **Saverpasses** (for people traveling in groups of 2-5) range from US$360/306 per person (5 days) to US$710/604 (15 days). **Second-Class Youthpasses** for those ages 12-25 cost US$253-497. For a fee, you can add **additional zones** (including Austria/Hungary): $62 for one associated zone, $102 for two. Plan your itinerary before buying a Europass: it will save you money if your travels are confined to three to five adjacent Western European countries, or if you only want to go to large cities, but would be a waste if you plan to make lots of side trips. If you're tempted to add many rail days and associated countries, consider a Eurailpass.

SHOPPING AROUND FOR A EURAIL OR EUROPASS. Eurailpasses and Europasses are designed by the EU itself and are purchasable only by non-Europeans almost exclusively from non-European distributors. These passes must be sold at uniform prices determined by the EU. Keep in mind that pass prices go up each year, so if you're planning to travel early in the year, save by purchasing before January 1 (you have 3 months from the purchase to validate your pass in Europe).

It is best to buy your Eurailpass or Europass before leaving; only a few places in major European cities sell them, and at a marked-up price. Eurailpasses are nonrefundable once validated; if your pass is completely unused and invalidated and you have the original purchase documents, you can get an 85% refund from the place of purchase. You can get a replacement for a lost pass only if you have purchased insurance on it under the Pass Protection Plan (US$10). Eurailpasses are available through travel agents, student travel agencies like STA and Council (see p. 35), and **Rail Europe,** 500 Mamaroneck Ave., Harrison, NY 10528 (US ☎ 888-382-7245, fax 800-432-1329; Canada 800-361-7245, fax 905-602-4198; UK (08705) 84 88 48; www.raileurope.com) or **DERTravel Services,** 9501 W. Devon Ave. #301, Rosemont, IL 60018 (US ☎ 888-337-7350; fax 800-282-7474; www.dertravel.com).

INTERRAIL PASS. If you have lived for at least six months in one of the European countries where InterRail Passes are valid, they prove an economical option. There are eight InterRail **zones:** A (Great Britain, Northern Ireland, Republic of Ireland), B (Norway, Sweden, and Finland), C (Germany, Austria, Denmark, and Switzerland), D (Croatia, Czech Republic, Hungary, Poland, and Slovakia), E (France, Belgium, The Netherlands, and Luxembourg), F (Spain, Portugal, and Morocco), G (Greece, Italy, Slovenia, and Turkey, including a Greece-Italy ferry), and H (Bulgaria, Romania, Yugoslavia, and Macedonia).

InterRail Card: allows either 14 or 22 days or 1 month of unlimited travel within 1, 2, 3, or all of the 8 zones; the cost is determined by the number of zones the pass covers

(UK£169-355; £114-249 under 26). If you buy a ticket including the zone in which you have claimed residence, you must still pay 50% fare for tickets inside your own country. Purchase at www.railchoise.co.uk/interrail/information.html.

Passholders receive **discounts** on rail travel, Eurostar journeys, and most ferries to Ireland, Scandinavia, and the rest of Europe. Most exclude **supplements** for high-speed trains. For info and ticket sales in Europe contact **Student Travel Center,** 24 Rupert St., 1st floor, London W1V 7FN (☎(020) 74 37 81 01; fax 77 34 38 36; www.student-travel-centre.com). Tickets are also available from travel agents or main train stations throughout Europe.

EUROPEAN EAST PASS. This pass is good for five days of 1st or 2nd-class, unlimited travel in a one-month period, as well as discounts on steamers and private railways within Austria, the Czech Republic, Hungary, Poland, and Slovakia. It also includes a 40% discount on bike rentals in over 130 rail stations. You can purchase up to five days additional travel. The pass costs $220/154, additional days $25/18.

FURTHER READING AND RESOURCES ON TRAIN TRAVEL
Rail schedules: http://bahn.hafas.de/bin/db.w97/query.exe/en. A testament to German efficiency, with minute-by-minute itineraries and connection info.
Point-to-point fares: www.raileurope.com/us/rail/fares_schedules/index.htm. Allows you to calculate whether buying a railpass would save you money.
European Railway Servers: http://home.wxs.nl/~grijns/timetables/time.html and http://mercurio.iet.unipi.it/home.html. Links to rail servers in Europe.
Info on rail travel and railpasses: www.eurorail.com; www.raileuro.com.
Thomas Cook European Timetable, updated monthly, covers all major and most minor train routes in Europe. In the US, order it from Forsyth Travel Library (US$28; ☎800-367-7984; order@forsyth.com; www.forsyth.com). In Europe, find it at any Thomas Cook Money Exchange Center. Alternatively, buy directly from Thomas Cook (www.thomascook.com).
Guide to European Railpasses, by Rick Steves. Available online and by mail (US ☎425-771-8303; fax 771-0833; www.ricksteves.com). Delivery $8.
On the Rails Around Europe: A Comprehensive Guide to Travel by Train, by Melissa Shales. Thomas Cook (US$18.95).
Europe By Eurail 2000, by Laverne Ferguson-Kosinski. Globe Pequot Press (US$16.95).

BY BUS

Just like the railroads, the bus networks of Austria and Switzerland are extensive, efficient, and comfortable; it may be difficult to negotiate the route you need, but short-haul buses can reach rural areas inaccessible by train. Bus stations are usually adjacent to the train station. The efficient **Austrian system** consists mainly of orange BundesBuses that serve mountain areas inaccessible by train. Buy tickets at the station or from the driver. For buses in heavily touristed areas during high season (such as the Großglocknerstraße in summer), you should probably make reservations. Anyone can buy discounted tickets, valid for one week, for any particular route. Trips can be interrupted under certain conditions, depending on your ticket—be sure to ask. Small, regional bus schedules are available for free at most post offices. For more bus information, call ☎(0222) 711 01 within Austria (from outside Austria dial 1 instead of 0222) from 7am to 8pm Austrian time.

In **Switzerland,** PTT Post Buses connect rural villages and towns. SwissPasses are valid on many buses; Eurailpasses are not. Even with the SwissPass, you might have to pay extra (5-10SFr) if you're riding one of the direct, faster buses. In cities, public buses transport commuters and shoppers alike to outlying areas. Buy tickets in advance at automatic machines, found at most bus stops. The system works on an honor code and inspections are infrequent, but expect to be hit for 50-60SFr if you're caught riding without a valid ticket. *Tageskarten*, valid for 24hr. of free travel, run around 7.50SFr, but most Swiss cities are walkable.

BY CAR

Cars offer speed, freedom, access to the countryside, and an escape from the town-to-town mentality of trains. Unfortunately, they also insulate you from the esprit de corps of rail traveling. Although a single traveler won't save by renting or leasing a car, three or four usually will. Before setting off, know the laws of the countries in which you'll be driving (e.g., no right turn on red allowed anywhere in Austria or Switzerland). The **speed limit** in Austria is 50kph (31mph) within cities unless otherwise indicated; outside towns, the limit is 130kph (81mph) on highways and 100kph (62mph) on all other roads. The speed limits are 50kph in cities, 80kph on open roads, and 120kph on highways in Switzerland. In Austria and Switzerland, all people in every car must wear **seat belts** or face heavy fines. Children under 12 may not sit in the front passenger seat unless a child's seat belt or a special seat is installed. Driving under the influence of alcohol is a serious offense—fines begin at €400 and violators may also lose their licenses.

The **Association for Safe International Road Travel** (**ASIRT**; 11769 Gainsborough Rd., Potomac, MD 20854, USA; ☎301-983-5252; fax 983-3663; asirt@erols.com; www.asirt.org) can provide more specific information about road conditions. ASIRT considers road travel (by car or bus) to be relatively safe in both Austria and Switzerland. With armies of mechanized road crews ready to remove snow at a moment's notice, roads at altitudes of up to 1500m generally remain open throughout winter. (Mountain driving does present special challenges, however; see p. 17). Many small Austrian and Swiss towns forbid cars entirely; others forbid only visitors' cars, require special permits, or restrict driving hours. EU citizens driving in Austria and Switzerland don't need special documentation—registration and license will suffice. All cars must carry a first-aid kit and a red emergency triangle. Emergency phones are located along all major highways. The Austrian Automobile, Motorcycle, and Touring Club (ÖAMTC; ☎(01) 71 19 97) provides an English-language service and sells a set of eight detailed road maps, far superior to the tourist office's map. The Swiss Touring Club, 4 Chemin de Blandonnet, 1214 Vernier, Case Postale 820 (☎(022) 417 27 27; fax (022) 417 20 20; www.tcs.ch) operates road patrols that assist motorists in need.

DRIVING PERMITS: INTERNATIONAL DRIVING PERMIT (IDP). If you plan to drive a car while in **Austria,** and are not a citizen of an EU country, you must have an International Driving Permit (IDP) in addition to your driver's license. Most car rental agencies in **Switzerland** don't require the permit, but it may be a good idea to get one anyway, in case you're in a situation (e.g. an accident or stranded in a smaller town) where the police do not know English.

Your IDP is valid for one year, and it must be issued in your own country before you depart. A valid driver's license from kyour own country must always accompany the IDP. To apply, you must be at least 18 and include one or two passport photos, a current local license, additional ID, and a fee.

Australia: Contact your local Royal Automobile Club (RAC) or the National Royal Motorist Association (NRMA) if in NSW or the ACT (☎(08) 94 21 44 44; www.rac.com.au/travel). AUS$15.

Canada: Contact any Canadian Automobile Association (CAA) branch office or write to CAA, 1145 Hunt Club Rd., #200, K1V 0Y3. (☎613-247-0117; www.caa.ca. CDN$10.

Ireland: Contact the nearest Automobile Association (AA) office or write to the UK address below. Permits €5. AA 23 Suffolk St., Rockhill, Blackrock, Co. Dublin (☎(01) 617 99 50), honors most foreign automobile memberships.

New Zealand: Contact your local Automobile Association (AA) or the main office: 99 Albert St., Auckland City, Auckland (☎09 377 46 60; www.nzaa.co.nz). Permits NZ$10.

South Africa: Contact the Travel Services Department of the Automobile Association of South Africa at P.O. Box 596, Johannesburg, 2121 (☎(11) 799 14 00; www.aasa.co.za). ZAR28.50.

UK: To visit your local AA Shop, contact the AA Headquarters (☎(08705) 44 88 66), or write to: The Automobile Association, International Documents, Fanum House, Erskine, Renfrewshire PA8 6BW. For more info, see www.theaa.co.uk/motoringandtravel/idp/index.asp. Permits UK£4.

US: Visit any American Automobile Association (AAA) office or write to AAA Florida, Travel Related Services, 1000 AAA Drive (mail stop 100), Heathrow, FL 32746 (☎407-444-7000; fax 444-8329). You don't have to be a member to buy a permit ($10). AAA Travel Related Services (☎800-222-4357) provides road maps, travel guides, emergency road services, travel services, and auto insurance.

CAR INSURANCE. Some credit cards cover standard insurance allowing their customers to decline the collision damage waiver for a rental car. If you have car insurance on your own car, have your insurance applied to your rental car. Non-Europeans should check with their national motoring organization (like AAA or CAA) for international coverage. If you rent, lease, or borrow a car, you will need an **International Insurance Certificate (green card)** to prove that you have liability insurance at home. Obtain it through the car rental agency.

RENTING A CAR. To rent a car in **Austria,** you must be at least 21 for most companies (and 23 or 25 for others) and carry both an International Driver's Permit and a valid driver's license that you have had for at least one year (see p. 46). Most Austrian companies restrict travel into Hungary, the Czech Republic, Poland, and Slovakia. Rental taxes are high (21%). In **Switzerland,** the minimum rental age is 21 but also varies by company. You must possess a valid driver's license that you have had for at least one year (foreign licenses are valid). In both countries, drivers under 25 must often pay a daily "young driver" fee. Rates for all cars rented in Switzerland and Austria include an obligatory annual road toll, called a *vignette* (40SFr per year in Switzerland, €7.60 per ten days, €72.60 per year in Austria.)

It is significantly less expensive to reserve a car from the US than from Europe. Expect to pay US$200-300 per week, plus tax, for a very small car. Reserve ahead and pay in advance if at all possible. Always check if prices quoted include tax, unlimited mileage, and collision insurance. Ask about discounts and check the terms of insurance, particularly the size of the deductible. Ask airlines about special fly-and-drive packages; you may get up to a week of free or discounted rental.

Auto Europe, 39 Commercial St., P.O. Box 7006, Portland, ME 04112, USA (US and Canada ☎888-223-5555 or 207-842-2000; fax 842-2222; www.autoeurope.com).

Avis, US and Canada ☎800-331-1084; UK (08705) 90 05 00; Australia (800) 22 55 33; New Zealand (0800) 65 51 11; www.avis.com.

Budget, US ☎800-472-3325; Canada 800-527-0700; UK (0800) 18 11 81; Australia ☎13 27 27; www.budgetrentacar.com.

Europe by Car, One Rockefeller Plaza, New York, NY 10020, USA (☎800-223-1516 or 212- 581-3040; fax 246-1458; info@europebycar.com; www.europebycar.com).

Europcar, 145 av. Malekoff, 75016 Paris (☎(01) 45 00 08 06); US ☎877-946-6900; www.europcar.com).

Hertz, US ☎800-654-3001; Canada 800-263-0600; UK (08705) 99 66 99; Australia 96 98 25 55; www.hertz.com.

Kemwel Holiday Autos, (US ☎800-576-1590; www.kemwel.com).

LEASING. For longer than 17 days, leasing can be cheaper than renting; it is often the only option for those ages 18 to 21. The cheapest leases are agreements to buy the car and then sell it back to the manufacturer at a prearranged price. As far as you're concerned, though, it's a lease and doesn't entail enormous financial transactions. Leases generally include insurance coverage and are not taxed. The most affordable ones usually originate in Belgium, France, or Germany. Expect to pay around US$1100-1800 (depending on size of car) for 60 days. Contact **Auto Europe, Europe by Car,** or **Kemwel Holiday Autos** (see above) before you go.

ROADSIDE ASSISTANCE
In **Austria,** call ☎**120.**
In **Switzerland,** call ☎**140.**

BY AIR

Flying across Europe on regularly scheduled flights can devour your budget, but if you are short on time you might consider it. Student travel agencies sell cheap tickets, and budget fares are frequently available in the spring and summer on high-volume routes between northern Europe and resort areas in Italy, Greece, and Spain; consult budget travel agents and local newspapers. The Air Travel Advisory Bureau in London (www.atab.co.uk) allows users to search for agencies that provide discount tickets to many Austrian and Swiss cities. In addition, several European airlines offer coupon packets that discount the cost of each flight leg. Most are only available as tack-ons to their transatlantic passengers, but some are available as stand-alone offers. Most must be purchased before departure.

Europe by Air: US ☎888-387-2479; Australia (02) 92 21 99 88; New Zealand (09) 309 52 06; www.europebyair.com. Coupons good on 16 partner airlines to 130 European cities in 27 countries. Must be purchased prior to departure; available only to non-European residents. US$99 each, excluding airport tax.

Alitalia: US ☎800-223-5730; www.alitaliausa.com. "Europlus," available to North Americans who fly into Milan or Rome on Alitalia, allows passengers to tack on 3 coupons good for flights to 48 airports in Europe. US$299; each additional ticket US$100.

Austrian Airlines: US ☎800-843-0002; www.austrianair.com/specials/visit-europe-fares.html. "Visit Europe," good to cities served by AA and partner airlines, is available in the US to Austrian Airlines transatlantic passengers (3 min., 6 max.). US$100 each.

Lufthansa: US ☎800-399-5838; www.lufthansa-usa.com. "Discover Europe" is available to US travelers booked on transatlantic Lufthansa flights. Special deals vary but usually include up to 6 flights to 100 cities within Europe for around $89 each.

SAS: US ☎800-221-2350; www.flysas.com/airpass.html. One-way coupons for travel within Scandinavia, the Baltics, or all of Europe US$75-225. Most are available only to transatlantic SAS passengers, but some United and Lufthansa passengers also qualify.

GET CARD.

TRAVEL HARD.

There's only one way to max out your travel experience and make the most of your time on the road: The International Student Identity Card.

Packed with travel discounts, benefits and services, this card will keep your travel days and your wallet full. Get it before you hit it!

Visit **ISICUS.com** to get the full story on the benefits of carrying the ISIC.

90 minutes, wash & dry (one sock missing).
5 minutes to book online (Detroit to Mom's)

Save money & time on student and faculty
travel at **StudentUniverse.com**

BY BICYCLE

Many airlines will count your bike as your second free piece of luggage; a few charge extra (US$60-110 one-way). Many airlines sell bike boxes at the airport (US$10). Most ferries let you take your bike for free or for a nominal fee, and you can always ship your bike on trains. For more info, see the Swiss Federal Railway's web site (http://s26282.sbb.ch/pv/velobahn_e.htm). *Let's Go* lists bike rental shops in the Practical Information for most cities and towns.

For info about touring routes, consult national or local tourist offices. The **Touring Club Suisse**, chemin de Blandonnet 4, Case Postale 820, 1214 Vernier (☎ (022) 417 27 27; fax 417 20 20), is a good source of information, maps, route descriptions, and mileage charts. Also check out www.cycling-in-switzerland.ch for routes and travel advisory for cyclists. In Austria, **www.radtouren.at** maintains a list of long-distance bike routes (many not open to cars) throughout Austria.

If you're planning on doing long distance touring, you'll need **panniers** in which you can pack your luggage, a good **helmet** (US$25-50) and a good U-shaped **Citadel** or **Kryptonite lock** (from US$30). For equipment, **Bike Nashbar**, 4111 Simon Rd., Youngstown, OH 44512 (US ☎ (800) 627-4227; www.nashbar.com), beats all competitors' offers and ships anywhere in the US or Canada. To purchase *Europe by Bike*, by Karen and Terry Whitehall (US$15), try **Mountaineers Books**, 1001 S.W. Klickitat Way #201, Seattle, WA 98134 (US ☎800-553-4453 or 800-568-7604; www.mountaineers.org). Know how to change a tire; practice on your own bike. A few simple tools and a good bike manual will be invaluable.

If you are nervous about striking out on your own, **Blue Marble Travel** (US ☎800-258-8689 or 973-326-9533; Canada 519-624-2494; France 01 42 36 02 34; www.bluemarble.org) offers bike tours for small groups for those ages 20 to 50 through Austria. **CBT Tours,** 415 W. Fullerton #1003, Chicago, IL 60614 (US ☎800-736-2453; www.cbttours.com), offers full-package 7- to 12- day biking, mountain biking, and hiking tours (around US$100 per day) to Switzerland.

BY MOPED AND MOTORCYCLE

If you've never been on a **moped** before, twisting alpine roads are not the place to start. However, mopeds can be put on trains and ferries, and are a good compromise between the high cost of car travel and the limited range of bicycles. Always wear a helmet and never ride with a backpack. Expect to pay about US$20-35 per day; try auto repair shops and remember to bargain. **Motorcycles** are more expensive and normally require a license, but are better for long distances. **Bosenberg Motorcycle Excursions**, Mainzer Str. 54, 55545 Bad Kreuznach, Germany (☎(49) 67 16 73 12; www.bosenberg.com) arranges tours in Austria and Switzerland and rents motorcycles (Apr.-Oct.); they have gateways in Zurich and Bern (contact the German office). Before renting, ask if the price includes tax and insurance, or you. Avoid handing your passport over as a deposit; pay ahead of time instead. *Europe by Motorcycle*, by Gregory Frazier (Arrowstar Publishing; US$20), is helpful for planning your itinerary and making arrangements.

BY THUMB

Hitching means entrusting your life to a random person who stops beside you on the road and risking theft, assault, sexual harassment, and unsafe driving. In Austria and Switzerland, men and women traveling in groups and men traveling alone might consider hitching (called "autostop") beyond the range of bus or train routes. If you're a woman traveling alone or even with another woman, don't hitch. It's just too dangerous. If you do decide to hitch, consider where you are; where one stands is vital. Hitching (or even standing) on super-highways is usually illegal: one may only thumb at rest stops or at the entrance ramps to highways. Most Europeans signal with an open hand, rather than a thumb; many write their destination on a sign in large, bold letters. Safety-minded hitchers avoid getting in the back of a two-door car and never let go of their backpacks. They will not get into a car that they can't get out of again in a hurry. If they ever feel threatened, they insist on being let off, regardless of where they are. Acting as if they are going to open the car door or vomit on the upholstery will usually get a driver to stop.

Most large cities in Austria and Switzerland offer a **ride service** (listed as *Mitfahrzentrale* in the **Practical Information**), a cross between hitchhiking and the ride boards common at many universities, which pairs drivers with riders. The fee varies according to destination. Riders and drivers can enter their names on the Internet through the Taxistop web site (www.taxistop.be), but be aware that not all of these organizations screen drivers and riders; ask in advance.

 HITCHHIKERS BEWARE. *Let's Go* strongly urges you to seriously consider the risks before hitching. We do not recommend it as a safe means of transportation, and none of the information presented here is intended to do so.

SPECIFIC CONCERNS

WOMEN TRAVELERS

Women travelers will likely feel safer in Austria and Switzerland than just about anywhere in the world—violent crime is rare and catcalls is not acceptable behavior. It's easy to be adventurous without taking undue risks. If you are concerned, you might consider staying in hostels which offer single rooms that lock from the inside or in religious organizations that offer rooms for women only. Stick to centrally located accommodations and avoid solitary late-night treks or metro rides. Dress conservatively, especially in rural areas. Wearing a conspicuous wedding band may help prevent unwanted overtures. Some travelers report that carrying pictures of a "husband" or "children" is extremely useful to help document marriage status. A mention of a husband waiting at the hotel may be enough in some places to discount your potentially vulnerable, unattached appearance.

In cities, you may be harassed no matter how you're dressed. Your best answer to verbal harassment is no answer at all; feigned deafness, sitting motionless and staring straight ahead at nothing in particular will do a world of good that reactions usually don't achieve. The extremely persistent can sometimes be dissuaded by a firm, loud, and very public "Go away!"

 FURTHER READING: WOMEN TRAVELERS

A Journey of One's Own: Uncommon Advice for the Independent Woman Traveler, by Thalia Zepatos. Eighth Mountain Press (US$17).

Travelers' Tales: Gutsy Women, Travel Tips and Wisdom for the Road, by Marybeth Bond. Traveler's Tales (US$8).

A Foxy Old Woman's Guide to Traveling Alone, by Jay Ben-Lesser. Crossing Press. (US$11).

More Women Travel: Adventures, Advice & Experience, by Miranda Davies and Natania Jansz. Penguin Books (US$16.95).

When traveling, always carry extra money for a phone call, bus, or taxi. Choose train compartments occupied by other women or couples. Look as if you know where you're going (even when you don't) and consider approaching older women or couples for directions if you're lost or feel uncomfortable. Don't hesitate to seek out a police officer or a passerby if you are being harassed. *Let's Go: Austria & Switzerland* lists emergency numbers (including rape crisis lines) in the **Practical Information** listings of most cities. An IMPACT Model Mugging self-defense course prepare you for a potential attack and raise your level of awareness of your surroundings as well as your confidence (see p. 17). Women also face special health concerns when traveling (see **Women's Health,** p. 22).

SOLO TRAVELERS

There are many benefits to traveling alone, including independence and greater interaction with locals. On the other hand, any solo traveler is a more vulnerable target of harassment and street theft. Lone travelers need to be well-organized and look confident at all times. Try not to stand out as a tourist and be especially careful in deserted or very crowded areas. If questioned, never admit you are traveling alone. Maintain regular contact with someone at home who knows your itinerary. For more tips, pick up *Traveling Solo* by Eleanor Berman (Globe Pequot Press, US$17) or subscribe to **Connecting: Solo Travel Network,** 689 Park Road, Unit 6, Gibsons, BC V0N 1V7 (Canada ☎604-886-9099; www.cstn.org; membership US$28).

Several services link solo travelers with companions who have similar travel habits and interests; for a bi-monthly newsletter for single travelers seeking a travel partner, contact **Travel Companion Exchange,** P.O. Box 833, Amityville, NY 11701 (US ☎631-454-0880 or 800-392-1256; www.whytravelalone.com; subscription US$48).

OLDER TRAVELERS

Seniors often qualify for hotel and restaurant discounts as well as discounted admission to many tourist attractions. If you don't see a senior citizen price listed, ask and you may be pleasantly surprised. In Switzerland, women over 62 and men over 65 qualify as seniors, and women over 60 and men over 65 get senior status in Austria. A **Seniorenausweis** (Senior Citizen Identification Card) entitles holders to a 50% discount on all Austrian federal trains and BundesBuses, and the card works as an ID for discounted museum admissions. The card costs about €25, requires a passport photo and proof of age, and is valid for one calendar year. It is available in Austria at railroad stations. Both National Tourist Offices offer guides for senior citizens. Many discounts require proof of status, so prepare to be carded. Agencies for senior group travel are growing in enrollment and popularity. Here are a few:

Elderhostel, 11 Ave. de Lafayette, Boston, MA 02110, USA (☎877-426-8056; www.elderhostel.org). Organizes 1- to 4-week "educational adventures" in Austria and Switzerland on varied subjects for those 55+.

The Mature Traveler, P.O. Box 15791, Sacramento, CA 95852, USA (☎800-460-6676). Deals, discounts, and travel packages for the 50+ traveler. Subscription $30.

Walking the World, P.O. Box 1186, Fort Collins, CO 80522, USA (☎800-340-9255; www.walkingtheworld.com), organizes trips for 50+ travelers to Switzerland.

GAY AND LESBIAN TRAVELERS

As Austria and Switzerland are conservative countries with limited tolerance for homosexuality, public displays of affection can attract unfriendly attention. On

> **FURTHER READING: OLDER TRAVELERS**
>
> *No Problem! Worldwise Tips for Mature Adventurers,* by Janice Kenyon. Orca Book Publishers (US$16).
>
> *A Senior's Guide to Healthy Travel,* by Donald L. Sullivan. Career Press. (US$15).
>
> *Unbelievably Good Deals and Great Adventures That You Absolutely Can't Get Unless You're Over 50,* by Joan Rattner Heilman. Contemporary Books (US$13).
>
> *Have Grandchildren, Will Travel.* Pilot Books (US$10).

the other hand, Geneva, Zurich, and Vienna have a wide variety of homosexual organizations and establishments, from biker and Christian groups to bars and barber shops. The German word for gay is *schwul* (sh-VOOL); for lesbian, *lesben* (LEZ-ben) or *lesbisch* (LEZ-bisch). Bisexual is *bisexual* or simply *bi* (bee). In French, *homosexuelle* can be used for both men and women, but the preferred terms are *gai* (geh) and *lesbienne* (les-bee-YENN).

The age of consent in **Austria** is 18 for gay men, 14 for lesbians. **Homosexuelle Initiative (HOSI)** is a nationwide organization with offices in most cities that provides information on gay and lesbian establishments, resources, and supports as well as publishing warnings about aggressively intolerant areas and establishments. HOSI Wien, II, Novarag. 40, Vienna (☎/fax (01) 216 66 04; www.hosiwien.at), publishes Austria's leading gay and lesbian magazine, the *Lambda-Nachrichten,* quarterly. A number of smaller and alternative organizations operate throughout the country. The age of consent in **Switzerland** is 16. Switzerland's nationwide lesbian, gay, and bisexual information hotline, the **Rainbowline** (☎ (084) 880 50 80) is in German, French, English, and Italian. There are several gay working groups in the larger cities. **Homosexuelle Arbeitsgruppe Dialogai,** headquartered in Geneva at 11-13 r. de la Navigation (mailing address Case Postale 69, 1201, Geneva 21; ☎ (022) 906 40 40; fax 906 40 44; dialogai@hivnet.ch), has a partnership with l'Aide Suisse contre le Sida (ASS), an organization that works against AIDS. Several gay publications are available in centers and bookshops. **Dialogai Info** provides information on French Switzerland, articles, interviews, and more.

Gay's the Word, 66 Marchmont St., London WC1N 1AB (☎(+44) 20 72 78 76 54; www.gaystheword.co.uk). The largest gay and lesbian bookstore in the UK, with both fiction and non-fiction titles. Mail-order service available.

Giovanni's Room, 1145 Pine St., Philadelphia, PA 19107 US (☎215-923-2960; www.queerbooks.com). An international lesbian/feminist and gay bookstore with mail-order service (carries many of the publications listed below).

International Gay and Lesbian Travel Association, 4331 N. Federal Hwy., #304, Fort Lauderdale, FL 33308, USA (☎800-448-8550 or 954-776-2626; fax 776-3303; www.iglta.com). An organization of over 1350 companies that serves homosexual travelers worldwide; web site lists gay-friendly establishments in Austria and Switzerland.

International Lesbian and Gay Association (ILGA), 81 r. Marché-au-Charbon, B-1000 Brussels, Belgium (☎/fax +32 (2) 502 24 71; www.ilga.org). Not a travel service; provides political information, including homosexuality laws of individual countries.

TRAVELERS WITH DISABILITIES

Austria and Switzerland are relatively accessible to travelers with disabilities (*behinderte Reisende*). Disabled visitors to **Austria** may want to contact the Vienna Tourist Board, Obere Augartenstr. 40, A-1025 Vienna (☎(01) 211 14; fax

FURTHER READING: GAY AND LESBIAN TRAVELERS

Spartacus International Gay Guide. Bruno Gmunder Verlag. (US$33).

Damron Men's Guide, Damron Road Atlas, Damron's Accommodations, and *The Women's Traveller.* Damron Travel Guides (US$14-19). Call US ☎415-255-0404 or 800-462-6654, or check their web site (www.damron.com).

Ferrari Guides' Gay Travel A to Z, Ferrari Guides' Men's Travel in Your Pocket, Ferrari Guides' Women's Travel in Your Pocket, and *Ferrari Guides' Inn Places.* Ferrari Guides (US$14-16). For more info, call ☎602-863-2408 or 800-962-2912 or visit www.q-net.com.

The Gay Vacation Guide: The Best Trips and How to Plan Them, by Mark Chesnut. Citadel Press (US$15).

216 84 92; www.info.wien.at), which offers booklets on accessible Vienna hotels and a guide to the city for the disabled. The Austrian National Tourist Offices in New York and Vienna offer many pages of listings for wheelchair-accessible sights, museums, and lodgings in Vienna. With three days' notice, the Austrian railways will provide a wheelchair for the train. The international wheelchair icon indicates access. In **Switzerland,** disabled travelers can contact Mobility International Schweiz, Frogurbstr. 4, 4600 Olten (☎(062) 206 88 35; fax 206 88 39; www.mis-infothek.ch). Most Swiss buildings and restrooms have ramps. The Swiss Federal Railways have wheelchair access for most of their cars, and Inter-City and long-distance express trains have wheelchair compartments. The Swiss National Tourist Office publishes a fact sheet of "Travel Tips for the Disabled." The Green Book (http://members.nbci.com/thegreenbook/home.html) has a partial listing of disabled-access lodgings and sights in Austria and Switzerland.

Rail is probably the most convenient form of travel for disabled travelers in Austria and Switzerland, but you have to be willing to ask for assistance. Many trains have a special compartment reserved for disabled travelers. Guide-dog owners should inquire as to the specific quarantine policies of each destination country. At the very least, they will need to provide a certificate of immunization against rabies. Hertz, Avis, and National car rental agencies have hand-controlled vehicles at some locations. The following organizations might be of assistance:

USEFUL ORGANIZATIONS

Mobility International USA (MIUSA), P.O. Box 10767, Eugene, OR 97440, USA (☎541-343-1284 voice and TDD; fax 343-6812; info@miusa.org; www.miusa.org). Sells *A World of Options: A Guide to International Educational Exchange, Community Service, and Travel for Persons with Disabilities* (US$35).

Moss Rehab Hospital Travel Information Service (US ☎215-456-9600); www.mossresourcenet.org). An information center on travel concerns for those with disabilities.

Society for the Advancement of Travel and Hospitality (SATH), 347 Fifth Ave., #610, New York, NY 10016 (☎212-447-7284; www.sath.org). An advocacy group that publishes the quarterly travel magazine *OPEN WORLD* (free for members, US$13 for nonmembers). Also publishes a wide range of info sheets on disability travel facilitation and destinations. Annual membership US$45, students and seniors US$30.

TOUR AGENCIES

Directions Unlimited, 123 Green Ln., Bedford Hills, NY 10507, US (☎914-241-1700 or 800-533-5343; www.travel-cruises.com). Specializes in arranging individual and group vacations, tours, and cruises for the physically disabled.

FURTHER READING: DISABLED TRAVELERS.
Resource Directory for the Disabled, by Richard Neil Shrout. Facts on file (US$45).
Wheelchair Through Europe, by Annie Mackin. Graphic Language Press (☎760-944-9594; http://wheelchairtravel.tripod.com; booklets US$13; on CD $20).
Global Access (www.geocities.com/Paris/1502/disabilitylinks.html) has specific links for disabled travelers in Switzerland, as well as general links.

Flying Wheels Travel Service, 143 W. Bridge St., Owatonne, MN 55060, US (☎507-451-5005; fax 451-1685); www.flyingwheelstravel.com. Arranges trips for groups and individuals in wheelchairs or with other sorts of limited mobility.

MINORITY TRAVELERS

Although Austria and Switzerland are predominantly white, they are quite tolerant of minority travelers. Most minority travelers will not have difficulty, though the farther you venture into the countryside, the more likely it is that you will encounter the occasional odd stare. Villagers are notoriously curious, so don't be surprised or offended if old women linger in their windows to catch a glimpse of you. In recent years, a growing population of foreign workers (particularly Turks) has felt the sting of Swiss anxiety about economic recession, but physical confrontations are rare. Anti-Semitism is not a large problem in either country. For more information on the concerning political developments in each country see "Haider and Austria's Swing to the Right," p. 71, and "Switzerland Today," p. 319.

TRAVELERS WITH CHILDREN

Family vacations often require a slower pace and prior planning, but that doesn't mean they can't be done cheaply. Austria and Switzerland are decidedly family-friendly, offering transportation discounts and a plethora of attractions. Children under 6 travel free on Austrian trains and children 6-12 for half-price. The **Swiss Family Card** (see **Railpasses,** p. 41) lets children under 16 travel free with at least one parent holding a valid ticket. Children under 16 travel alone at half price. Make sure car rental companies provide a car seat for younger children. Children under 2 generally fly for 10% of adult airfare on international flights (does not necessarily include a seat). International fares are usually discounted 25% for children 2-11.

Young children's needs can limit your choice of lodging; call ahead to make sure *Pensionen* are child-friendly. *Let's Go* notes particularly family-oriented accommodations. Make sure each child, no matter how young, has a valid passport. Be sure that your child carries some sort of ID in case of an emergency or if he/she gets lost, and arrange a reunion spot in case of separation when sightseeing.

FURTHER READING: TRAVELERS WITH CHILDREN.
Backpacking with Babies and Small Children, by Goldie Silverman. Wilderness Press (US$10).
Take Your Kids to Europe, by Cynthia W. Harriman. Globe Pequot (US$17).
Have Kid, Will Travel: 101 Survival Strategies for Vacationing With Babies and Young Children, by Claire and Lucille Tristram. Andrews and McMeel (US$9).
Trouble Free Travel with Children, by Vicki Lansky. Book Peddlers (US$9).

RELIGIOUS CONCERNS

The predominance of Catholics and Protestant churches make it simple for anyone of those faiths to find a place to worship, the same task can be challenging for those of other faiths.

Buddhist communities have centers in **Vienna** (Fleischmarkt 16, 1st fl., A-1010 Vienna; ☎(01) 513 38 80; bodhidharma.zendo@blackbox.at); **Innsbruck** (An der Furt 18, II., A-6020 Innsbruck; ☎/fax (0512) 36 71 13; aldo.deutsch@uibk.ac.at); and **Salzburg** (Schloßstr. 38, A-5020 Salzburg; ☎/fax (62) 74 75 16; sunyata@magnet.at).

Jehovah's Witnesses can check www.watchtower.org for more information.

Jewish visitors to Vienna can contact **The Jewish Welcome Service** (☎(01) 533 27 30). **The Jewish Community Center** (Seitenstetteng. 4, Postfach 145, A-1010 Vienna, ☎(01) 53 10 40; fax 533 15 17) is a good resource for information elsewhere in Austria. Open M-Th 8am-5pm, F 8am-2pm. Switzerland has its own version, the Federation of **Swiss Jewish Communities** (Gotthardstr. 65, 8002 Zurich; ☎(01) 201 55 83; fax (01) 202 16 72.) Or consult *The Jewish Travel Guide*, which lists synagogues, kosher restaurants, and Jewish institutions in over 100 countries, available in Europe from Vallentine Mitchell Publishers, Crown House, 47 Chase Side, Southgate, London N14 5BP, UK (☎(020) 89 20 21 00; fax (020) 844 85 48) and in the US ($16.95 + $4 S&H) from ISBS, 5824 NE Hassallo St., Portland, OR 97213 (☎800-944-6190).

Mormons in Switzerland can visit the temple in Zollikofen, near Bern (Templestr. 2, CH-3052 Zollikofen; ☎(031) 915-5252). For Austria, www.ettl.co.at/mormon/english.

Muslims can turn to www.islam.ch (available in German, French, or Italian) for information and addresses throughout Switzerland.

DIETARY CONCERNS

Vegans will likely have difficulty outside of large cities, but **ovo-lacto vegetarians** can enjoy many traditional meatless dishes. *Let's Go* lists vegetarian and vegetarian-friendly restaurants under Food listings. Travelers who keep **kosher** should contact synagogues in larger cities for information on kosher restaurants. The Swiss National Tourist Office distributes the pamphlet *The Jewish City Guide to Basel*. Also see **Religious Concerns**, above. **Diabetic travelers** can pick up *The Diabetic Traveler* by Davida F. Kruger. American Diabetes Association ($14.95).

FURTHER RESOURCES

TRAVEL BOOK PUBLISHERS AND BOOKSTORES

Hippocrene Books, Inc., 171 Madison Ave., New York, NY 10016 (☎212-685-4371; orders 718 454-2366; www.hippocrenebooks.com). Free catalog. Publishes foreign language dictionaries and foreign language guides.

Adventurous Traveler Bookstore, P.O. Box 2221, Williston, VT 05495, USA (☎800-282-3963 or 802-860-6776; www.adventuroustraveler.com).

Bon Voyage!, 2069 W. Bullard Ave., Fresno, CA 93711, USA (☎800-995-9716, from abroad 559-447-8441; www.bon-voyage-travel.com). They specialize in Europe but have titles pertaining to other regions as well. Free catalog.

Travel Books & Language Center, Inc., 4437 Wisconsin Ave. NW, Washington, D.C. 20016 (☎800-220-2665 or 202-237-1322; travelbooks@aol.com; www.bookweb.org). Over 60,000 titles from around the world.

THE INTERNET

> **WWW TIPS.**
> The **domain** for many Swiss web sites is .ch; Austria's is .at.
> Search for Swiss sites at **www.search.ch** and Austrian sites at **www.search.at.**

LEARNING THE ART OF BUDGET TRAVEL

How to See the World: www.artoftravel.com. A compendium of great travel tips, from cheap flights to self defense to interacting with local culture.

Rec. Travel Library: www.travel-library.com. A fantastic set of links for general information and personal travelogues.

Backpacker's Ultimate Guide: www.bugeurope.com. Tips on packing, transportation, and where to go. Also tons of country-specific travel information.

INFORMATION ON AUSTRIA AND SWITZERLAND

Foreign Language for Travelers: www.travlang.com. Provides free online translating dictionaries and lists of phrases in French, German, and Italian (among others).

Atevo Travel: www.atevo.com/guides/destinations. Detailed introductions, travel tips, and suggested itineraries.

Youth Hostel Listings: The official hostel web pages for Austria (www.jgh.at) and Switzerland (www.jugendherberge.ch) give an overview of all hostels at a glance.

Swiss Introduction: www.myswitzerland.com. Tourism highlights, including virtual tours, hotel booking, and weather report in Switzerland.

Austrian Introduction: www.austria.org. Official American web site for Austria with information on visas, tourism, business, and culture.

AND OUR PERSONAL FAVORITE...

Let's Go: www.letsgo.com. Our constantly expanding web site features photos and streaming video, online ordering of all our titles, info about our books, a travel forum buzzing with stories and tips, and links that will help you find everything you could ever want to know about Austria and Switzerland.

ALTERNATIVES TO TOURISM

While traversing the globe via hostel and hotel is undoubtedly a memorable and worthwhile way to experience a foreign country, foreign travel does not necessarily mean being a perennial tourist. There are a plethora of ways to experience both Austria and Switzerland without conventional sight-seeing. Working, volunteering, or studying for an extended period of time offers an opportunity for a deeper understanding of life in both countries. Often erroneously pigeonholed as solely a backpacker mecca and a resort for the rich and famous, Austria and Switzerland have much to be discovered beyond these stereotypes. Picking grapes in Austria's Styrian wine country teaches more about the trade and the people than a tour of the vineyard; similarly, teaching English in St. Gallen will show you Switzerland beyond skiing and hiking. This chapter outlines some of the different ways to explore Austria and Switzerland on the nontourist ticket. The alternatives below can garner you a more meaningful and educational experience—something that the average budget traveler often misses out on.

STUDYING AND WORKING IN AUSTRIA AND SWITZER-LAND. A residency permit is required to study or to work in **Austria.** Work restrictions are strict, and while citizens of EU countries do not need a work permit for employment, all others must obtain a work permit before leaving their country of origin. Work and residency permits can be obtained from the Austrian consulate or embassy in your country. If you plan to study abroad in **Switzerland** for more than three months, you need to fill out a residency permit and receive authorization from Swiss authorities. Most US universities will arrange permits for students. Working in Switzerland is even more difficult than in Austria; its equally strict immigration policies that can make it very hard for foreigners to find work. The required "work permit" is both a residence and an employment permit, entitling the holder to live in a particular canton and work for a specified employer. Fees and requirements for the permit vary according to your country of origin and the duration of employment. Also, since Switzerland is not a member of the EU, free movement of labor and individuals does not apply as it does in other EU countries. For more information on Swiss permits, contact any Swiss embassy for the free booklet *Living and Working in Switzerland* or download it from www.eda.admin.ch/london-emb/e/home/trach/resid.html.

STUDYING ABROAD

Study abroad programs range from basic language and culture courses to college-level classes, often for credit. Therefore, you should fully research a program in order to choose one that best fits your needs. Find out what kind of students participate in the program and what sort of accommodations are provided. You may feel more comfortable with large groups of students who speak your native language, but you will not have as many opportunities to practice a foreign language or to befriend other international students. Accommodations also impose a trade-off: dorm life makes it easier to mingle with fellow students, while living off-campus allows for you to experience the local scene. If you live with a family, there is the potential to build lifelong friendships and experience day-to-day life. However, conditions vary greatly from family to family and there is no "typical" experience.

Those relatively fluent in German, French, or Italian may find it cheaper to enroll directly in a university abroad, although earning college credit may be difficult. Some American schools still require students to pay them for credits they obtain elsewhere. Most university-level study-abroad programs in Austria and Switzerland are meant as language and culture enrichment opportunities and are conducted in German or French, but many offer classes in English and beginner- and lower-level language courses. A good resource is **www.studyabroad.com,** which has links to semester abroad programs based on a variety of critera, including desired location and focus of study.

In **Austria,** summer or year-long academic programs associated with American universities are based in Vienna, Salzburg, Innsbruck, and Bregenz. In **Switzerland,** there are summer and winter sessions for universities in Geneva and Zurich. Some American universities conduct their own programs, such as the University of Delaware, which organizes a summer-long Swiss Hospitality Program. German language programs are also available in both Austria and Switzerland. In addition, there are walking, bicycling, and hiking programs that can be arranged for students visiting both countries.

American Institute for Foreign Study, College Division, River Plaza, 9 West Broad St., Stamford, CT 06902, USA (☎800-727-2437, ext. 5163; www.aifsabroad.com). Organizes programs for high school and college study in universities in Austria.

Central College Abroad, Office of International Education, 812 University, Pella, IA 50219, USA (☎800-831-3629 or 641-628-5284; www.central.edu/abroad). Offers internships, as well as summer, semester, and year-long programs in Austria. US$25 application fee.

International Association for the Exchange of Students for Technical Experience (IAESTE), 10400 Little Patuxent Pkwy. Suite 250, Columbia, MD 21044, USA (☎410-997-2200; www.aipt.org). 8- to 12-week programs in Austria and Switzerland for students who have completed 2 yr. of college technical study. US$25 application fee.

School for International Training, College Semester Abroad, Admissions, Kipling Rd., P.O. Box 676, Brattleboro, VT 05302, USA (☎800-336-1616 or 802-257-7751; www.sit.edu). Semester- and year-long programs in Switzerland run US$10,600-13,700. Also runs the **Experiment in International Living** (☎800-345-2929; fax 802-258-3428; www.usexperiment.org), 3- to 5-week summer programs that offer high-school students cross-cultural homestays, community service, ecological adventure, and language training in Switzerland and cost US$1900-5000.

Webster University in Geneva and Vienna, Study Abroad Office, Webster University, 470 E. Lockwood, St. Louis, MO, 63119, USA (☎800-984-6857 or 314-968-6900; fax 968-7119; worldview@webster.edu; www.webster.edu/worldwide_locations.html). International students come here to pursue full-degree programs or summer and semester sessions. All courses are taught in English and are fully accredited.

LANGUAGE SCHOOLS

Unlike American universities, language schools are frequently independently-run international or local organizations or divisions of foreign universities that rarely offer college credit. Language schools are a good alternative to university study if you desire a deeper focus on the language or a slightly less rigorous courseload. These programs are also good for high school students that might not feel comfortable with older students in a university program. Some good programs include:

Eurocentres, 101 N. Union St. Suite 300, Alexandria, VA 22314, USA (☎703-684-1494; www.eurocentres.com) or in Europe: Head Office, Seestr. 247, CH-8038 Zurich, Switzerland (☎+41 1 485 50 40; fax 481 61 24). Language programs for beginning to advanced students with homestays in Switzerland.

University of Geneva Summer Courses, contact: Mr. Gerard Benz, University of Geneva, summer courses, r. de Candolle 3, CH-1211 Geneva 4, Switzerland (☎(22) 750 74 34; fax 750 74 39; elcfete@uni2a.unige.ch). Teaches French language and civilization at all levels and offers excursions to Geneva and its surroundings. Tuition for a 3-week summer course 500SFr. Min. age 17.

Wiener Internationale Hochschulkurse, contact: Magister Sigrun Anmann-Trojer, Wiener Internationale Hochschulkurse, Universität, Ebendorserstr. 10, A-1010 Vienna, Austria (☎(01) 405 12 54; fax 405 12 54 10; www.univie.ac.at/wihok). Offers German courses for beginners and advanced students, as well as lectures on German and Austrian literature, music, linguistics, and Austrian culture, including exposure to the Vienna waltz and choir singing. Tuition for a 4-week summer course €338, accommodations €736. Longer courses (trimesters and semesters) are also offered.

FURTHER READING: STUDYING ABROAD.

Academic Year Abroad. Institute of International Education Books (US$45).
Vacation Study Abroad. Institute of International Education Books (US$40).
Peterson's Study Abroad Guide. Peterson's (US$30).
Also see www.language-learning.net.

WORKING

Some travelers desire long-term jobs (e.g. teaching English, working for the Peace Corps) that will allow them to get to know another part of the world in depth. Others work only long enough to finance their travel. Such jobs usually lie in the service sector or in agriculture. In this section are both short-term and long-term opportunities for working in Austria and Switzerland. Before beginning your job hunt, be sure to review the **visa requirements** for working abroad, p. 10.

As stated previously, **Austria** requires a work permit from all non EU citizens, but a stroke of bureaucratic genius has rendered this virtually impossible for casual and seasonal work. Expect to pay 16% of your salary to mandatory health and Social Security programs (except for au pairs). While there are no private employment offices in Austria, German-speakers can contact the state-run employment office *Arbeitmarktservice.* The easiest jobs for foreigners to find are in the hotel and agriculture industries.

Finding employment in **Switzerland** is even more difficult than it is in Austria. The Swiss embassy and consulates will not assist anyone in seeking employment and there are no lists of Swiss or foreign companies, agencies, or organizations available. Do not attempt to find employment without a permit, as ski resorts have been known to hire police solely for the purpose of checking visas. Employers may be fined 3000SFr for hiring illegal workers. One job you don't (usually) need a permit for is busking—street musicians in Bern can do quite well by the end of the day—but check with the local police for authorized areas.

LONG-TERM WORK

If you're planning on spending a substantial amount of time (more than three months) working in Austria or Switzerland, search for a job well in advance. International placement agencies are often the easiest way to find employment abroad, especially for teaching English. **Internships,** usually for college students, are a good way to segue into working abroad; although they are often unpaid or poorly paid, many say the experience is well worth it. Be wary of advertisements or companies that claim to get you a job abroad for a fee—often times the same listings are available online or in newspapers, or even out of date. One reputable organization is:

International Co-operative Education, 15 Spiros Way, Menlo Park, CA 94025, USA (☎ 650-323-4944; www.icemenlo.com). Finds summer jobs for students in Switzerland. Costs include a $200 application fee and a $600 fee for placement.

TEACHING ENGLISH

While English teachers are almost always in demand in Austria and Switzerland, such jobs are rarely well-paid, although some elite private American schools can pay competitive salaries. In most cases, you must have at least a bachelor's degree to be a full-fledged teacher, although usually college undergraduates can get summer positions teaching or tutoring. Many schools require teachers to have a **Teaching English as a Foreign Language (TEFL)** certificate. This does not necessarily exclude you from finding a teaching job, but certified teachers often find higher paying jobs. Native English speakers working in private schools are often hired for English-immersion classrooms where no German, French, or Italian is spoken.

Placement agencies or university fellowship programs are the best resources for finding teaching jobs in Austria and Switzerland. The alternative is to make contacts directly with schools or to try your luck once you get there. If you are going to try the latter, the best time of the year is several weeks before the start of the school year. The following organizations are extremely helpful in placing teachers in Austria and Switzerland.

Fulbright English Teaching Assistantship, U.S. Student Programs Division, Institute of International Education, 809 United Nations Plaza, New York, NY 10017-3580, USA (☎ 212-984-5330; www.iie.org). Competitive program sends college graduates to teach in Austria and Switzerland.

International Schools Services (ISS), 15 Roszel Rd., Box 5910, Princeton, NJ 08543-5910, USA (☎ 609-452-0990; fax 452-2690; www.iss.edu). Hires teachers for more than 200 overseas schools Austria and Switzerland; candidates should have experience teaching or with international affairs. Two year committment expected.

Office of Overseas Schools, US Dpt. of State, Rm. H328, SA-1, Washington, DC 20522 (☎ 202-261-8200; fax 261-8224; www.state.gov/www/about_state/schools/). Keeps a comprehensive list of schools abroad and agencies that arrange placement for Americans to teach abroad.

AU PAIR WORK

Au pairs are typically women, aged 18-27, who work as live-in nannies, caring for children and doing light housework in foreign countries in exchange for room, board, and a small spending allowance or stipend. Most former au pairs speak favorably of their experience and of how it allowed them to get to know the country without the high expenses of traveling. Drawbacks, however, often include long hours of constantly being on-duty and the somewhat low pay. In Austria and Switzerland wages range from €75-120 per week, and much of the au pair experience really does depend on the family you're placed with. The agencies below are a good starting point for looking for employment as an au pair.

Accord Cultural Exchange, 750 La Playa, San Francisco, CA 94121, USA (☎ 415-386-6203; www.cognitext.com/accord).

Au Pair in Europe, P.O. Box 68056, Blakely Postal Outlet, Hamilton, Ontario, L8M 3M7 Canada (☎ 905-545-6305; fax 544-4121; www.princeent.com).

Childcare International, Ltd., Trafalgar House, Grenville Pl., London NW7 3SA, UK
(☎+44 020 8906 3116; fax 8906-3461; www.childint.co.uk).

InterExchange, 161 Sixth Ave., New York, NY 10013, USA (☎212-924-0446; fax 924-
0575; www.interexchange.org).

SHORT-TERM WORK

Traveling for long periods of time is expensive; therefore, many travelers take odd
jobs for a few weeks at a time for extra cash to carry them through another month
or two of touring. In Switzerland hotels hire foreign workers for their summer and
winter tourist seasons. Start your job search early in April or May for the summer
season and September or October for the winter season. Fluency in German will
be helpful, often necessary, in finding a job. Tourist offices may also be of help.

If you are more interested in a rural experience than in making money, a job in
the Swiss agriculture industry might suit you better. One-third of summer farm
hands are foreign workers. Room and board is generally included but free-loaders
beware: expect to work very hard, long hours. The Swiss hold very high standards
for cleanliness and productivity but are willing to pay high wages in return.

Another popular option in both Austria and Switzerland is to work several hours
a day at a hostel in exchange for free or discounted room and/or board. Most
often, these short-term jobs are found by word of mouth, or simply by talking to
the owner of a hostel or restaurant. Many places, especially due to the high turnover in the tourism industry, are always eager for help, even if only temporary.
Let's Go tries to list temporary jobs like these whenever possible; check the practical information sections in larger cities.

VOLUNTEERING

Volunteer work can become even more fulling in conjunction with travel to a foreign country. Be forewarned, though, that your unselfish gesture may actually cost
you—many volunteer services charge you a fee to participate in the program.
These fees can be surprisingly hefty (although they frequently cover airfare and
most, if not all, living expenses). Research a program before committing—talk to
people who have previously participated and find out exactly what you're getting
into, as living and working conditions can vary greatly. Different programs are
geared toward different ages and levels of experience, so be sure that you are not
taking on too much or too little.

Most people choose to go through a parent organization that takes care of logistical details and provides a group environment and support system. There are two
main types of organizations, religous (often Catholic), and secular, although there
are rarely restrictions on participation for either.

Elderhostel, Inc., 11 Avenue de Lafayette, Boston, MA 92111-1746, USA (☎877-426-
8056; fax 426-2166; www.elderhostel.org). Sends volunteers age 55 and over around
the world to work in construction, research, teaching, and many other projects. Costs
average $100 per day plus airfare.

International Cultural Youth Exchange (ICYE), Große Hamburger Str. 30, D-10115 Berlin, Germany (☎28 390 550; fax 28 390 552; www.icye.org). Students 18-25 participate in short or long-term service during a homestay.

Service Civil International Voluntary Service (SCI-IVS), SCI USA, 3213 W. Wheeler St.,
Seattle, WA 98199, USA (☎/fax 206-350-6585; www.sci-ivs.org). Arranges placement
in work sites in Austria and Switzerland for those 18+. Registration fee US$65-125.

Volunteers for Peace, 1034 Tiffany Rd., Belmont, VT 05730, USA (☎ 802-259-2759; www.vfp.org). 2-3 week community service projects with international volunteers 18+ (some 15+). May-Sept., US$200 registration fee.

FURTHER READING: ALTERNATIVES TO TOURISM.

Alternatives to the Peace Corps: A Directory of Third World and U.S. Volunteer Opportunities, by Joan Powell. Food First Books, 2000 (US$10).

How to Get a Job in Europe, by Sanborn and Matherly. Surrey Books, 1999 (US$22).

How to Live Your Dream of Volunteering Overseas, by Collins, DeZerega, and Heckscher. Penguin Books, 2002 (US$17).

International Directory of Voluntary Work, by Whetter and Pybus. Peterson's Guides and Vacation Work, 2000 (US$16).

International Jobs, by Kocher and Segal. Perseus Books, 1999 (US$18).

Overseas Summer Jobs 2002, by Collier and Woodworth. Peterson's Guides and Vacation Work, 2002 (US$18).

Work Abroad: The Complete Guide to Finding a Job Overseas, by Hubbs, Griffith, and Nolting. Transitions Abroad Publishing, 2000 (US$16).

Work Your Way Around the World, by Susan Griffith. Worldview Publishing Services, 2001 (US$18).

AUSTRIA

The shape and size of Austria has changed so many times in its history that Oskar Bender once said, "To be Austrian is not a geographical concept but a spiritual idea." At the peak of Habsburg megalomania, the Austrian Empire was one of the largest in history, encompassing much of Europe from Poland and Hungary in the east to The Netherlands in the west. Today it is approximately the size of Maine. Although the mighty empire crumbled during World War I, Austria remains a complex, multiethnic country with a unique political and cultural history. The wide range of identities within the empire continues today in the diversity of the nine provinces, or *Bundesländer*, of present-day Austria. Clockwise from the northeast, Austria's provinces are Vienna *(Wien)*, Burgenland, Styria *(Steiermark)*, Carinthia *(Kärnten)*, Tyrol *(Tirol)*, Vorarlberg, Salzburg, Upper Austria *(Oberösterreich)*, and Lower Austria *(Niederösterreich)*. At one time each province was an independent region but later became part of the Habsburg lands by marriage, treaty, or trade. Today, each retains a deep-rooted character and unique dialect. The mention of Austria evokes images of onion-domed churches set against snow-capped alpine peaks, castles rising from lush meadows of golden flowers, and 10th-century monasteries towering over the majestic Danube. The mountains see tourists year-round; alpine sports dominate the winter scene, while lakeside visitors flock in the warmer months.

LAND

Austria is a landlocked nation that shares its borders with no fewer than eight countries. It has long been a crucial cog in the wheel of commerce, thanks to the navigable Danube, the only major European river that flows east. The blue-green river has always been central to Austrian industry and aristocracy: both ruling families of early Austria, the Babenbergs and the Habsburgs, set up residences on its shores. Now, river cruises showcase their ruined castles as well as the vineyards whose fruit sweetened the Middle Ages. The Danube's trade capabilities were enhanced in 1992 with the completion of a canal connecting the Danube to the Rhine and Main rivers, allowing the movement of barges from the North Sea to the Black Sea.

Forests and meadows cover two-thirds of Austria's total land area, and much of the land is studded with mountains. The Alps span the South and western regions of the country, while the flatter North and East are home to most of the population. The highest point—the *Großglockner*—looms at 3797m (12,457 ft.) in the central Alps, drawing sightseers and adventure seekers. The mining of salt from vast underground deposits has also proved a valuable industry. From the Celts in 500 BC to many contemporary towns today, this "white gold" has established itself as an invaluable resource on which many Austrians depend.

FLORA & FAUNA

Since much of Austria remains densely forested, you won't have to go far off the beaten path to discover the rich woodland life. The flowers aren't going anywhere, but wildlife tend to be shy, so keep voices low when you walk or hike. Though you're unlikely to see **ibex** unless you're hiking at high elevations, **red deer, roe deer, hare, fox, badger, marten,** and **pheasant** are common to the country and Central Europe in general. A small bear population lives in the southern mountainous and deeply wooded regions. Lake Neusiedl, Austria's only steppe lake, hosts hundreds of bird species on its reed-fringed waters. Austria's national parks, which comprise 3% of the land, are also good places to spot protected wildlife.

Oak and beech trees predominate in Austria's vast forests, with fir trees at higher elevation and stone pines in the mountain regions. The diverse and colorful alpine flora blanket meadows and mountains alike, so look out for **Edelweiss** (sing the song, if you must), **heather, alpine rose,** and **blue gentian** (on the back of the Austrian five-cent euro piece). As a courtesy to those come after you, take only photographs and leave only footprints.

HISTORY

IN THE BEGINNING

The first prehistoric tourists descended on Austria in the form of nomadic hunter-gathers in about 80,000 BC, initiating the region as a popular and welcoming destination. As the nomads settled, mining salt, farming and domesticating livestock, 6km-thick glaciers crawled north, carving out the alpine valleys of postcard fame today and making room for greater habitation of Austrian lands. The 25,000-year-old carved-stone fertility goddess Venus of Willendorf (so valuable that the Natural History Museum in Vienna displays only a copy) reflects the artistic prowess of this early civilization. By 6000 BC, even the remotest areas of Austria were part of a vigorous commercial network that linked mining centers and agricultural communities, as the recent discovery of the 5,300-year-old hunter-trader Ötzi proved.

As economic opportunities moved beyond salt, aggressive peoples fought for a share of wealth. In 500 BC, the **Celts** took control of the salt mines and established the kingdom of **Noricum,** which developed a relatively affluent economy based on a thriving salt and iron trade. In turn, the **Romans** conquered their Austrian neighbors to secure the Danube frontier against marauding Germanic tribes in 15 BC. One of the first Roman military posts was Vindobona, present-day Vienna.

Germanic raids finally forced the Romans to retreat from Noricum in the 5th century. Over the next three centuries, various peoples, including the Huns, Ostrogoths, and Lombards, roamed through the Austrian territories, but none established a lasting settlement. Eventually, three groups divided the region, with **Slavs** in the southwest, **Bavarians** in the north, and **Alemanni** in the south. Bavarian nobles converted peasants to Christianity in an attempt to establish law and order and create a power-base. The Archbishopric of Salzburg, created through their efforts, has remained Austria's ecclesiastical center.

HOLY ROMANS AND HABSBURGS (800-1740)

Charlemagne was the first to make Austria the barrier and meeting point between Eastern and Western Europe by conquering Bavaria in 787. After his death, the German King Otto regained control of the Holy Roman Empire, naming Margrave Liutpoldus (a.k.a. **Leopold of Babenberg**) duke of the Empire's eastern territories in 976. Leopold, a Bavarian lord, was the first ruler Austria called its own. During his reign, Austria gained its name: *Ostarrichi* (Old High German for *Österreich*), which meant "Eastern Realm" of the Empire.

The **Babenbergs,** who served as the Dukes of the Eastern Realm for the next 270 years, claimed Vienna as their home, extending their protectorate through strategic marriages. The Babenburgs made a tidy profit off of international bargains. When Duke Leopold V captured **Richard the Lionheart** on his way home from the Crusades, he chose not to give Richard over to the Holy Roman Emperor, who had put a price on the head of the English king, and instead returned Richard to England for cold, hard cash.

To the detriment of the dynasty, the last Babenberg died childless, leaving the country fragmented for 19 years. Bohemian King Ottokar II, the new Holy Roman Emperor, and the Swiss nobleman **Rudolf of Habsburg** emerged as the major contestants for the Austrian lands. Rudolf had only a small plot of land in Switzerland before he beat out Ottokar in the Battle of Marchfeld in 1278, thereby claiming all of Austria and laying the foundation for six centuries of Habsburg rule. Like their Babenberg predecessors, the Habsburgs made every effort to increase their property through treaties and marriages, with memorable success (though they lost their original Swiss holdings after a farmers' revolution). Gradually, the Habsburgs accumulated the various regions that make up modern Austria plus a few others. The Imperial Crown was passed down through the Hapsburg line until the collapse of the empire in the 19th century. Friedrich expanded the direct claims of the Hapsburg family by strategically betrothing his son, **Maximilian I,** to the heiress of the powerful Burgundian kingdom, giving the Hapsburgs control of much of western Europe, including The Netherlands.

Maximilian is credited with the adaptation of Ovid's couplet: *"Bella gerant alii, tu felix Austria nube."* ("Let other nations go to war; you, lucky Austria, marry"—an early riff on "Make love, not war.") Maximilian's son **Philip** married into the Spanish royal house, endowing his son, **Charles V,** with a vast empire that encompassed Austria, The Netherlands, Spain, Burgundy, Spanish America, and Italian and Mediterranean possessions. It was during Charles' reign that the Habsburg Empire reached its height of power. However, it appears that the power was too much for Charles, who gave the Austrian empire and the crown to his brother **Ferdinand** (and the Spanish possessions to his son Philip) before retiring to the woods to become a monk in 1556. Ferdinand, despite not knowing German, Czech, or Hungarian, managed to add Bohemia and Hungary to the Hapsburg possessions, thanks to another marriage planned earlier by Maximilian.

PROTESTING CHANGE

The massive Habsburg ship hit rough waters in the 16th and 17th centuries, when Martin Luther's Protestant Reformation swept through the Empire. By the time Ferdinand II assumed control of the Habsburg empire in 1619, nearly nine-tenths of the population of Austria had been converted to Protestantism. But Ferdinand II, inspired by his Jesuit education, made Austria the first battleground of the Catholic Counter-Reformation. Resistance by Protestant Bohemian nobles in Prague to Ferdinand's plans sparked Europe's **Thirty Years War** (1618-1648). The Austrian imperial troops promptly (and forcibly) converted most of the peasants back to Catholicism and chased Protestants in the upper classes off to a sympathetic Protestant Germany. This victory was followed by a greater setback at the end of the war with the **Treaty of Westphalia,** in which the Habsburgs forfeited vast tracts of territory. While Austria recuperated, the Ottoman Turks repeatedly besieged Vienna until the French Prince Franz Eugene drove them out with a Christian relief army. In thanks for his assistance, Eugene was given Schloß Belvedere (see p. 118). Eugene again came through for the Habsburgs when he led their troops to victory over the French in the **War of Spanish Succession,** which ended with a treaty giving Belgium, Sardinia, and parts of Italy to the Habsburgs.

CASTLES CRUMBLE (1740-1900)

What the Habsburgs gained in land they sacrificed in stability. Lacking a dominant ethnic group and having had a series of foreign leaders, the empire began to crumble in the 18th century. When **Maria Theresia** ascended the throne in 1740, her neighbor King Friedrich the Great of Prussia seized Silesia (now southwest Poland); she spent the rest of her life unsuccessfully maneuvering to reclaim it. In the **War of Austrian Succession** (1740-1748), Maria Theresia came to be known as *Landesmutter* (mother of the people). Ironically, her relations with her own progency weren't as successful. She married her daughter **Marie Antoinette** to the French Prince Louis XVI, a marriage that ended under the guillotine during the French Revolution. The French revolutionaries who killed her daughter soon declared war on Maria Theresia's son, **Joseph II,** who by 1792 was ruling Austria. Under the military genius of young General Napoleon Bonaparte, the Republic of France wrested Belgium and most of Austria's remaining Italian territories from the Habsburgs. His troops even invaded Vienna, where Napoleon took up residence in Maria Theresia's favorite palace, Schönbrunn (p. 118).

Napoleon's success led to the establishment of a consolidated Habsburg empire. In 1804, **Franz II** renounced his claim to the now-defunct Holy Roman crown and proclaimed himself Franz I, Emperor of Austria. During the Congress of Vienna, which redrew the map of Europe after Napoleon's defeat, Austrian Chancellor **Clemens Wenzel Lothar von Metternich** masterfully re-unified Austrian power. For the rest of the century, Metternich's foreign policy for Austria was dictated by a desire to maintain monarchic stability throughout Europe. Austria feared the crumbling of the Ottoman Empire to the south and the resulting creation of the new independent Slavic states in the Balkans. Metternich rightly believed that the independence of these states would encourage the Slavic people that comprised half the population of the Habsburg Empire to fight for their own independence. In order to maintain stability within Austria, Metternich introduced harshly repressive social policies. Austria, however, like much of Europe in the first half of the 19th century, is remembered more for its age of technological progress. This progress led to the rise of a stereotypically uninspired middle class, satirized in the character Papa Biedermeier by poet Ludwig Eichrocht. The term **Biedermeier** came to label the bourgeois domestic culture that flourished in this time (see p. 76).

As the Ottoman Empire disintegrated, domestic resistance to Austria's repressive social policies increased, as Metternich had feared. In 1848, students and workers built barricades, took control of the imperial palace, and demanded a constitution and freedom of the press. The revolutionary forces were divided, however, and the government was able to suppress the workers' revolution and a Hungarian rebellion. Epileptic emperor **Ferdinand I,** however, was pressured to abdicate in favor of his nephew, **Franz Josef I,** who ruled for 68 years.

Under **Otto von Bismarck,** Prussia dominated European politics and defeated Austria in 1866. The Austrian fall from power continued in 1867, when the Hungarian parliament voted to end the Austrian Empire, and form the dual **Austro-Hungarian Empire** over which Franz Josef was a figurehead. Still, non-German speakers were marginalized within the new empire until 1907, when the government ceded basic civil rights to all peoples in the Empire and accepted universal male suffrage. These concessions to the Slavic peoples of the Empire came too late. Burgeoning nationalist sentiments, especially among the Serbia-inspired South Slavs, led to severe divisions within the multinational Austro-Hungarian Empire.

THE RISE OF THE REPUBLIC (1900-2000)

As the now-free Slavic states of the Ottoman Empire—particularly Serbia—agitated the Slavic elements within the Austro-Hungarian Empire, Franz Josef had to either quiet these forces or relinquish claims to the Slavic half of his empire. When Franz Ferdinand, the heir to the imperial throne, and his wife, Sophie, were assassinated by a young Serbian nationalist in Sarajevo in 1914, Franz Josef finally had an excuse to attack the Serbs. Austria's declaration of war set the dominos falling, and Europe tumbled into **WWI.** Franz Josef died during the war in 1916, leaving the throne to his reluctant grandnephew Charles I. Despite his valiant efforts and those of the army, declarations of independence by the Empire's non-German peoples and the desperate maneuvering of Viennese intellectuals ensured the demise of the monarchy. On November 11, 1918, Charles finally got the peace he had striven for, but only after liberals declared the first **Republic of Austria,** ending the 640-year-old Habsburg dynasty.

Between 1918 and 1938, Austria had its first bitter taste of parliamentary democracy. After the Treaty of Versailles that ended the first World War forbade a unified *Deutsch-Österreich,* the **First Republic** suffered massive inflation and unemployment, but by the mid-1920s the Austrian government had stabilized the currency and established economic relations with neighboring states. Nonetheless, violent internal strife between political parties weakened the Republic's already shaky democratic foundation. In 1933, the weak coalition government gave way to **Engelbert Dollfuss'** declaration of martial law. In order to protect Austria from Hitler, Dollfuss entered an ill-fated alliance with fascist Italy. Two years later, just as Mussolini and Hitler made peace, Austrian Nazis assassinated Dollfuss. His successor, **Kurt Schuschnigg,** was also ultimately unable to maintain Austrian independence in the face of Nazi pressure.

WORLD WAR II AND THE SECOND REPUBLIC

The First Republic ended with the Nazi annexation of Austria. On March 9, 1938, hoping to stave off a Nazi invasion, Schuschnigg called a referendum against unity with Germany, but Hitler demanded Schuschnigg's resignation. On March 12, the new Nazi chancellor invited German troops into Austria, where they met no resistance. Many Austrians believed the *Anschluß* (union with Germany) would improve their future. When the Nazis marched into Vienna on March 14, thousands cheered them on. Austria lost both its name (it became the "Ostmark," merely the "alpine district") and its self-respect. With the exception of individual resistance fighters, cooperation with the Nazis and anti-Semitism (long an Austrian tradition) became the rule, and a failing Austrian economy began to prosper. While **WWII** raged, Austrian and German Nazis directed the construction of Mauthausen, Austria's main concentration camp, and its 49 sub-camps. An estimated 150,000 Jews, along with leading intellectuals, dissidents, handicapped persons, Gypsies, and homosexuals, were systematically tortured and murdered. One-third of the Jewish population was exterminated, and most others fled the country.

After Soviet troops brutally "liberated" Vienna in 1945, Allied troops divided Austria into 4 zones of occupation to re-establish an Austrian government. By April 1945, a provisional government was established with 75-year old **Karl Renner** as president. In November, the National Assembly declared Austria's independence from Germany. Despite Russian plundering and severe famines in the late 1940s, the Marshall Plan helped to jump-start the Austrian economy, laying the foundation for Austria's present prosperity. In 1955, after **Joseph Stalin** died, Austria signed the State Treaty, under which the four powers granted Austria complete sovereignty on the condition that it remain neutral.

The State Treaty, along with the Federal Constitution of the First Republic, which was restored in 1945, formed the basis of the **Second Republic.** These documents provide for a president (head of state) who is elected to a six-year term, a chancellor (head of government), usually the leader of the strongest party, a bicameral parliamentary legislature, and powerful provincial governments. Until recently the government has been dominated by two parties, the Social Democratic Party (SPÖ), and the People's Party (ÖVP). The two parties have built up

THE FAILURE OF MEMORY
Manipulation and Eradication of Austrian Nazi Guilt

It is tragically ironic that Sigmund Freud, perhaps the greatest mind of fin-de-siècle Austria, opened our eyes to humanity's pressing need to repress those facts about ourselves that are most shameful and most traumatizing. Freud, along with 120,000 Austrian Jews, was expelled from the country in 1938, following the *Anschluß* with Germany. Austria's remaining 80,000 Jews were not as lucky: they were sent to concentration and exterminations camps, where 65,000 of them were killed.

But the Austrians did not just send off their nation's Jews to their deaths; many participated actively and vigorously in carrying out Hitler's policies. They staffed concentration camps, carried out programs on Austrian and foreign soil, enacted euthanasia programs against the old, the young, and the mentally and physically disabled, and took part in mass shootings. And the most ambitious of Austrians became higher-ups in Hitler's cabinet—they were the ones giving the orders.

So wherein lies the irony of Freud's insight? He did, after all, escape from the Nazi regime; he was neither a witness to nor a victim of its practices. The twist is that despite Austria's undeniable complicity in the crimes of the Third Reich, its people failed, for over four decades, to accept the burden of guilt. Freud had been sending out a prophetic warning: it is indeed far easier to repress the incriminating facts of our history than it is to confront them.

In the 40s, 50s, 60s, 70s, and well into the 80s, most Austrians smugly embraced what has alternately been called the "foundational myth," the "first-victim theory," and the "historical lie." At the heart of this position is the claim that Austria was annexed by force, and not by choice, by Hitler in 1938. Far from being perpetrators, the Austrians were—according to this version of the story—Hitler's first victims. These theories conveniently ignore the fact that a month after the arrival of the German troops, the Austrians voted overwhelmingly to join their country to Germany.

This stance was not just popular invention; it was the official line of the government, the position adopted by all political parties, the history that was taught in Austrian schools. Propped up by the Moscow Declaration of 1943, Austria defined itself as the first victim of Germany's international aggressions. An international treaty in 1955 was meant to include a passage about Austria's complicity in Nazi crimes, but the passage was deleted shortly before ratification.

The result of this thoroughgoing denial of guilt forged a significant gap between the Austrian varieties of *Vergangenheitsbewältigung* (coming to terms with the past). The Germans confronted their crimes openly and responsibly—perhaps because their guilt was so undeniable. They did this, among other ways, by building monuments and Holocaust museums for the victims of the Nazi regime. Needless to say, the Austrians, who had never admitted to the world or to themselves that they were also to blame for the deaths of Jews and members of other marginalized groups during WWII, did not build monuments or museums to honor these victims. The world did not challenge Austrians to accept their guilt, and the Austrians certainly did not challenge themselves. But then—by a strange twist of fate that might suggest that truth prevails in the end—the Austrians unwittingly forced themselves into a direct confrontation with their Nazi past.

Enter Kurt Waldheim, 1986 presidential nominee of the Austrian People's Party. During the campaign Waldheim's Nazi past was exposed: an investigation by the U.S. Justice Department revealed that he had been a *Wehrmacht* officer in a unit that committed atrocities in Yugoslavia and Greece, which meant he must have known about the war crimes his unit committed—a fact he had denied earlier. Unfortunately, the sheer facts and the exposure of Waldheim's life did not cause a revolution in Austria's self-perception with regard to their guilt. Rather, the older Austrian generation supported him even more fervently; they were proud of Waldheim (who had been U.N. Secretary-General for 10 years), and they refused to let some self-righteous Ameri-

cans who didn't know a thing about Austria ruin their future president. [
Continued on the next page]

Waldheim continued to betray a stance of helplessness and ignorance.He also apologized to the Austrian people for having lied to them; notably, he did not express remorse or regret for his actions. His constituents accepted his facile excuses and empty apologies and elected him president.

The Waldheim Affair did, however, catalyze a change in attitude in many younger Austrians, who did not cling as tightly to the "victim mentality" of the post-war generation. They not only saw the legitimacy of the accusations made against Waldheim personally, but were also beginning to understand the larger significance of these revelations: that the ongoing national denial of guilt and refusal to take responsibility for Austria's Nazi past was an immoral and cowardly lie. This acknowledgment was helped along by the United States' severe reproach of Waldheim. In 1987 the U.S. put him on the Watch List. Though he refused to step down from office, Waldheim's presidency was marked by international isolation, and he did not run for a second term in 1992.

Austria has finally set itself on the slow path towards remembering and taking responsibility. A 1988 act of state openly confessed Austria's complicity in Nazi crimes; at the same time, Waldheim himself admitted that many of the worst perpetrators of National Socialism were Austrians and apologized for the crimes committed by his people. The political climate has indeed undergone a change: there is a sense that remembering the persecution of Jews is important and necessary. With some notable exceptions (like Jörg Haider, who caused a scandal of his own with his pro-Hitler remarks), the political scene in Austria is moving toward greater openness and honesty in dealing with the nation's Nazi past.

One important signal of this came in 1994, when Simon Wiesenthal, a campaigner for the recognition and rights of Holocaust victims, pointed out to the mayor of Vienna that the city still had no memorial dedicated to the 65,000 Austrian Jews killed by Nazis. The mayor responded immediately, organizing an international competition for the design of a statue of remembrance to be erected in a central location in the first district, the ancient *Judenplatz* (Jews' square). Rachel Whiteread's memorial was unveiled in 2000: a concrete cube with a base of 10m by 7m and a height of nearly 4m, an inside-out library with the spines of the books facing inward, the doors locked, and the handles missing. Viewers see only the cold, white stone in which the cut pages of thousands of volumes are depicted, but they cannot get inside to see the titles or read the books. The world of knowledge is accessible only to those in the sealed-off void within the library—that is to say, to no one at all. The base of the monument is engraved with a dedication and the names of all the places where Austrian Jews were killed during the Nazi regime.

The meaning of Whiteread's memorial has been linked to the fact that the Jews are also called, in Hebrew, "the people of the book." It is significant that the memorial was erected on the site of a medieval synagogue, a place of prayer and study, that was built by the Viennese Jewish community in the 13th and 14th centuries and burned down in 1421. (The foundations of the synagogue have been excavated and can be seen in a museum underneath the *Judenplatz*). A library filled with unreadable books suggests the perversity of possessing a wealth of knowledge but expelling and exterminating the people who wrote, read, and used this wisdom.

But the books can also be seen as the history that Austria had failed to read in the 55 years following the end of WWII. Austrians kept themselves blind to the difficult and shameful reality of their participation in Nazi atrocities; they willed their own ignorance, not realizing that this denial was a deepening of already horrific crimes. Whiteread's memorial is not only a tribute to the Austrian Jews who died under Nazis; it is also a tribute to memory itself.

Kata Gellen was a Researcher-Writer for Let's Go: Germany, 1999. *She lived in Austria for the past two years, first on a Fulbright scholarship studying at the University of Vienna, and then as an English-language teaching assistant at a high school in Vienna. She is now a Ph.D. candidate in German literature at Princeton University.*

one of the world's most successful industrial economies, with enviably low unemployment and inflation rates as well as a generous, progressive welfare state.

During the 1990s, Austria moved toward closer European integration. In 1994 **Thomas Klestil** was elected on a platform of integration. In 1995 the country was accepted into the **European Union (EU)**, and the Austrians accepted membership through a national referendum. Unlike some EU countries, Austria also joined the **Economic and Monetary Union (EMU)**, and replaced its currency, the Austrian Schilling, with the euro in 2002.

TODAY

HAIDER AND AUSTRIA'S SWING TO THE RIGHT

Austria has recently been plastered over front pages internationally, thanks to the gains made by the far-right **Freedom Party** in 1999's elections. This party is infamous primarily for its leader **Jörg Haider,** who assumed the reigns of the then-powerless party in 1986. Haider entered the public eye for his anti-immigrant stance and his numerous remarks that were sympathetic to the Nazis. He has demanded a complete ban on immigration, playing off Austrian fears of the influx of immigrants from Eastern Europe. In the November 1999 elections, Haider's party claimed 27% of the vote, second among all parties, effectively breaking up the traditional two-party lock that the Social Democratic Party and People's Party had held on the country's politics since WWII. The Social Democratic Party, which has ruled the country for decades, came in first with 33% of the vote but refused to form a coalition with Haider's party; consequently, Haider's Freedom Party formed a coalition government with the conservative People's Party in February 2000. **Wolfgang Schlüssel** of the People's Party is the chancellor of the new government, while six of the government's 12 cabinet posts are held by Freedom Party members. In Vienna, 100,000 protestors turned out on the day that the Freedom Party government was sworn in. At the same time, the 14 other nations of the **European Union** simultaneously levied unprecedented political sanctions against Austria that essentially cut off official political contact; in addition, the United States recalled its ambassador for "consultation," while the Belgian Foreign Minister called traveling to Austria "immoral." Still, when the new government was entering office, Haider and the new chancellor Wolfgang Schlüssel signed the declaration "Responsibility for Austria," which stated that the new government would work "for an Austria in which xenophobia, anti-Semitism, and racism have no place." In addition, Haider resigned from his post as president of the Freedom Party three weeks after the new government took power in February to dispel questions about his role in the government, though many have called this a purely political move.

These developments led many of the European nations to reconsider their sanctions against Austria, which were all dropped in September 2000. Many critical of the European response to the Austrian situation have claimed that the sanctions were only pushed through in the first place because the liberal Social Democratic parties that rule in a majority of the European nations wanted to protect themselves from challenges by right wing parties in their own countries.

Regardless of the E.U.'s motives or actions, Haider's popularity in Austria itself waned in 2001, with the Freedom Party losing 8% of the vote despite Haider's active campaigning, giving Social Democrats an absolute majority. Haider himself was found guilty of defamation in Austrian court for various offensive comments he'd made.

PEOPLE

DEMOGRAPHICS

Austrians are fiercely proud of their culture, history, and principles. Following the longevity pattern established by Emperor Franz Joseph, Austrians enjoy a life expectancy of 78 years. The great emphasis they place on education is responsible for the literacy rate of over 98% throughout the country. Social welfare is comprehensive, and unemployment hovers at around 4%. Ethnically, the Austrian people embody the idea of the "melting pot," for although 98% of Austria's 8 million people call themselves German, nearly every Austrian has genealogical ties to at least one of the many ethnic groups once within the Habsburg empire. As befits the erstwhile stronghold of the Counter-Reformation, 78% of Austrians are Roman Catholic, 5% are Protestant, while 17% belong to Muslim, Jewish, Baptist, and other religious denominations.

Austrians are as impressed as any tourist by the beauty of their country, and they actively appreciate it by taking extensive *Wanderungen* (hikes). Popular vacation destinations in summer include the lakes of Carinthia and the Salzkammergut and in winter, the Tirol and Vorarlberg. In fact, it was a Moravian Austrian, Matthias Zdarsky, who invented skiing near the end of the 19th century.

LANGUAGE

Although German is the official language of Austria, common borders with the Czech Republic, Slovakia, Hungary, Italy, Slovenia, Liechtenstein, and Switzerland make multilingualism imperative for most Austrians. Even outside German speakers sometimes have difficulty understanding them, as the German spoken in Austria differentiates itself by accent and vocabulary from that of other German-speaking countries. Tourists eager to try out their *Deutsch* don't need to be too worried about being understood, as nearly all Austrians understand High German, but as the inhabitants of each region speak a particular dialect, it is helpful to know some general peculiarities of Austrian German. As a result of the international connections of the Habsburg Empire, many French, Italian, Czech, Hebrew, and Hungarian words have slipped into the language (e.g. *Babuschka* for old woman). Austrians don't greet each other with the standard *Guten Tag,* opting instead for *Servus* or *Grüss Gott.* One easy way to recognize familiar words in Austrian German is to remember that Austrians add a diminutive "*erl*" (instead of the High German "*chen*" or "*lein*") to a lot of words; store clerks may ask if you want a *Sackerl* (a small bag), waiters might inquire if you would like a *Bisserl* (a little bit) more of this or that, and a young girl is called a *Mäderl.* Many vegetables have unique names in Austrian German: the German *Kartoffel* (potato) becomes *Erdapfel;* tomatoes are *Paradeiser;* corn is not *Mais* but *Kukuruz;* and green beans are *Fisoln.* Austrians mean "this year" when they say *heuer* and January when they say *Jänner.* If you get to know an Austrian well, chances are they'll say *Ferti!* for goodbye.

CULTURE

FOOD AND DRINK

Just as the Austrians and their language are ethnically jumbled, many of the most famous Austrian dishes are foreign in origin: *Gulasch* (stewed meat and vegetables with paprika) is Hungarian; *Knödel* (dumplings) are Bohemian; and the archetypal Austrian dish, Wienerschnitzel, probably originated in Milan. Immigrants continue to influence Austrian cooking; Turkish dishes like *Dönerkebab* are on their way to becoming an integral part of Austrian cuisine. In addition, each region of Austria contributes its own particular traditional dishes, such as Carinthian *Kasnudeln* (large cheese- or meat-filled pasta squares) or Salzburger *Nockerl* (a mountain of sweetened, baked egg whites).

Loaded with fat, salt, and cholesterol, traditional Austrian cuisine is a nightmare to a cardiologist but a delight to everyone else. **Staple foods** are simple and hearty, centering around *Schweinefleisch* (pork), *Kalbsfleisch* (veal), *Wurst* (sausage), *Eier* (eggs), *Käse* (cheese), *Brot* (bread), and *Kartoffeln* (potatoes). Austria's most renowned dish, Wienerschnitzel, is a meat cutlet (usually veal or pork) fried in butter with bread crumbs and often served with french fries. Although schnitzel is Austria's most famous meat dish, its most scrumptious variety is *Tafelspitz*, beautifully cooked boiled beef. Soups are also an Austrian speciality; try *Gulaschsuppe* (gulasch soup) and *Frittatensuppe* (pancake strips in broth).

Most of Austria's culinary inventions appear on the **dessert** cart. *Tortes* commonly contain *Erdbeeren* (strawberries) and *Himbeeren* (raspberries). Don't miss *Marillen Palatschinken*, a crepe with apricot jam, or *Kaiserschmarrn*, the Kaiser's favorite (pancake bits with a plum compote). Austrians adore the sweet dessert *Knödeln*, especially *Marillenknödel* (sweet dumplings with a whole apricot in the middle), though the typical street-stand dessert is the *Krapfn*, a holeless doughnut usually filled with jam. The pinnacles of Austrian baking, however, are the twin delights of *Sacher Torte* (a rich chocolate cake layered with marmalade) and *Linzer Torte* (a light yellow cake with currant jam).

Recently, **vegetarianism** has gained popularity in Vienna, and even meaty dishes are showing the influence of a lighter, vegetable-reliant style. Vegetarians should look for *Spätzle* (a homemade noodle often served with melted cheese), *Steinpilze* (enormous mushrooms native to the area), *Eierschwammerl* (tiny yellow mushrooms), or anything with the word "Vegi" in it. Supermarket connoisseurs should have a blast with Austrian staples: yogurt (rich, almost dessert-like), the cult favorite Nutella (a chocolate-hazelnut spread), *Almdudler* (a lemonade-like soft drink), *Semmeln* (very cheap, very fresh rolls), the original *Müsli* (granola of the gods), and all kinds of chocolate, including Milka and Ritter Sport.

In the afternoon, Austrians flock to *Café-Konditoreien* (cafe-confectioners) to nurse the national sweet tooth with *Kaffee und Kuchen* (coffee and cake). While drinking a *Mélange*, the classic Viennese coffee with frothed cream and a hint of cinnamon, nibble on a heavenly *Mohr im Hemd*, a chocolate sponge cake topped with hot whipped chocolate, or just about anything with *Mohn* (poppy seed) in it. If you get the chance, try some steam-cooked *Buchteln* with vanilla sauce or poppy seeds.

To wash it all down, try any variety of Austrian alcoholic beverage. The most famous Austrian **wine** is probably *Gumpoldskirchen* from Lower Austria, the largest wine-producing province. *Klosterneuburger*, named for the district near Vienna where it's produced, is both reasonably priced and dry. Austrian **beers** are outstanding. *Ottakringer* and *Gold Fassl* flow from Vienna's taps, *Stiegl Bier* and *Augustiner Bräu* from Salzburg's, *Zipfer Bier* from Upper Austria's, and *Gösser Bier* from Styria's. Austria imports a great deal of Budweiser beer, but theirs is *Budvar*—the original Bohemian variety, not the chintzy American imitation. If you're looking for something to keep you up rather than put you to sleep, try a Red Bull in its country of origin.

CUSTOMS AND ETIQUETTE

In general, following good manners from your own country will take you far in German-speaking ones. The rules aren't too different in Austria, although there are a few ways you can disguise your tourist-side and impress the locals. For instance, most Germans and Austrians hold their fork in their left hand and knife in their right, but don't switch them after cutting something. While fork-ing left-handed is really hard, you can impress the natives (but not if your schnitzel lands in your lap.) Elbows on the table is fine. In fact they'll look at you a little funny if you have your hands under the table or in your lap. As always, seat yourself in cafes and most restaurants. Meals in Europe are placed a bit slower, so take in the atmosphere and take your time.

THE ARTS

The hills literally are alive with the vibrance of Austria's artistic influence. Beyond the natural majesty of the Alps, Austrians themselves have long sought to create beauty, challenge thought, and recreate life through personal expression. Classical music—today often dismissed by the young as stuffy and constrictive—evolved, devolved, and continually exploded around fresh talent in Vienna across three centuries. Visually, Austria's span of architectural advancements from Romanesque ruins to Habsburg decadence to the postmodern Haas House is a continual reminder of the local innovation that has long characterized Austria.

HISTORY

Landlocked in the middle of Europe and rolling with cash, the Habsburgs married into power and bought into art. In keeping with the cosmopolitan nature of their empire and outlook, the imperial family pursued a cultural policy that decidedly favored foreign artists over their own native sons and daughters. With the popularity of Baroque palaces and churches in the 17th and 18th centuries, the Empire's artists began to develop a distinct, graceful architectural style that still dominates the old centers of former Habsburg towns across Central and Eastern Europe. Around the turn of the 20th century, Austrian artists finally got fed up with traditionalism and foreign decadence and decided to stir up the coals a bit.

ARCHITECTURE

GOLDEN ARCHES. Austria's past as an outpost of the Roman empire is still visible in the ruins of **Carnuntum** and **Vindobona** (Vienna). The influence of such classical remains can be seen in the Romanesque art and architecture of the early Middle Ages throughout Austria: for example, in the Riesentor of Vienna's **Stephansdom** (see p. 107) and the cycle of frescoes in the **Nonnberg Abbey** near Salzburg (see p. 240). Ordinarily this influence takes the form of semi-circular arches, columns, and delicate metalwork, but the builders of the 8th-century **Martinskirche** of Linz actually "borrowed" Roman tombstones to fill in the walls (see p. 289). The elaborate enamel **Verduner Altar,** by the master Nicholas of Verdun, at Stift Klosterneuberg (see p. 133), is witness to the richness of art under the Babenburgs, but if it isn't rich enough for your blood, check out the 10th-century **Imperial Crown** of the Holy Roman Emperor, encrusted with cabochons and gold filigree, its shape echoing those Roman arches.

GOTHIC TRANSCENDENCE. The invention of flying buttresses, pointed arches, and groin vaults that came with the French Gothic style all meant that walls could be thinner, vaults could be higher, and windows could flood the whole space with light. The vast 14th-century additions to the **Stephansdom** in Vienna also show the delicate tracery and stained glass work typical of the period. Sculpture reached new heights with the intricate carvings of **Anton Pilgram** (see p. 107) and the altarpieces of **Albrecht Altdorfer** (see p. 291). Don't miss Austria's castles—these magnificent fortress-palaces, exemplified by **Festung Hohensalzburg** (see p. 240) and **Burg Hochosterwitz** (see p. 175), combined the medieval desire for imposing beauty with the practical goal of imposing power.

BAROQUE EXTRAVAGANCE. Austria's preeminent Baroque architects were Johann Bernhard Fischer von Erlach, Lukas von Hildebrandt and Johann Prandtauer. **Von Erlach,** born in Graz to a sculptor father, drew up the plans for Vienna's Schönbrunn (see p. 118) and Hofburg palaces (see p. 111). His best works, however, were ecclesiastical, including the ornate **Karlskirche** in Vienna. **Von Hildebrandt** shaped Austria's more secular side. His penchant for theatricality shows up in the palace's succession of pavilions and grand views of Vienna; stone sphinxes dotting his ornamental gardens allude to Eugene's victory over the Ottomans. **Prandtauer** was a favorite of the Church. His yellow Benedictine abbey at **Melk** peers over the Danube. After beating the Turks, Prince Eugène of Savoy (see p. 65) got Prandtauer to revamp the **Belvedere palace** (see p. 118).

JUGENDSTIL (A.K.A. ART NOUVEAU). The early 20th century brought the streamlining of ornamentation and a new ethic of function over form gripped Vienna's artistic elite. Vienna's guru of architectural modernism, **Otto Wagner,** cured the city of its "artistic hangover." His Kirche am Steinhof (see p. 120) and Postsparkasse (see p. 116) enclose fluid *Jugendstil* interiors within stark, delineated structures. Wagner frequently collaborated with his student **Josef Maria Olbrich,** notably on the Majolicahaus (see p. 117) and the Karlspl. Stadtbahn (see p. 117). Wagner's admirer **Josef Hoffmann** founded the **Wiener Werkstätte** in 1903, drawing on Ruskin's English art and crafts movement and Vienna's new brand of streamlined simplicity. Its influence later resonated in the **Bauhaus** of Weimar Germany. **Adolf Loos,** Hoffmann's principal antagonist, strongly opposed such attention to luxury. Loos once said, "Ornamentation is criminal," setting himself against the Baroque grandeur that Imperial Vienna supported. Few examples of his work reside in his native city, but his notorious **Goldman and Salatsch building** (1909-1911) in the Michaelerpl. went a step beyond its aesthetic toward a more starkly functional architecture.

URBAN SOCIALISM. In the 1920s and early 1930s, the **Social Democratic** administration built thousands of apartments in large **municipal projects,** their style reflecting the newfound assertiveness of the workers' movement. The most outstanding project of the era is the **Karl-Marx-Hof** (see p. 119). The huge structure, completed in 1930, extends over 1km and consists of 1600 apartments clustered around several courtyards. The Austrian Socialist party fought a pitched battle with rightist rioters in this apartment complex before the outbreak of World War II.

The structures created by American-trained architect **Hans Hollein** recall the sprawling abandon of his training ground while maintaining the Secessionists' attention to craftsmanship and elegant detail. His exemplary contribution to Viennese **postmodern** architecture is the **Haas House** (see p. 108), completed in 1990. Controversy has surrounded the building ever since sketches were published in the mid-80s, mainly because it stands opposite Vienna's landmark Stephansdom. Examples of modern interior design include the **Restaurant Salzamt** (I, Ruprechtspl. 1) and **Kleines Café** (see p. 103), both by Hermann Czech.

AUSTRIA

FINE ARTS

BIEDERMEIER. Between Napoleon and the foundation of the Republic, Austria developed a large, restless middle class. Since political expression and social critique were virtually impossible during this era, artistic expression was funneled into a narrow channel of naturalistic and applied art centered around the family circle and domestic ideals, dominated by genre, landscape, and portrait painting. The *Biedermeier* period (see p. 66) is remembered today primarily as a furniture style, but it was also an artistic movement with limited crossover into literature, characterized by a predilection for symmetries, naturalism, and harmonious detail. *Biedermeier* architecture is exemplified by the well-ordered dignity of the **Dreimäderlhaus** at Schreyvogelg. 10 in Vienna, and the best of the period's furniture is on view in the **Biedermeier Room** of the Österreichisches Museum für Angewandte Kunst (see p. 124).

JUGENDSTIL (A.K.A. ART NOUVEAU). In 1897, the "young" artists split from the "old," as proponents of *Jugendstil* modernism took issue with the Viennese Academy's rigid conservatism and traditional symbolism. The idea was to leave the prevailing artistic conventions behind and formulate a new way of seeing the world. **Gustav Klimt** (1862-1918) and his followers founded what is known as the **Secession** movement. They aimed to provide the nascent Viennese avant-garde with a forum in which to show their work and to make contact with foreign artists. In their revolt against the old-guard Künstlerhaus, Secessionists sought to create space and appreciation for new artistic styles, particularly their own trademark style, Art Nouveau. The effect of this freedom is apparent in Klimt's own later paintings (such as *The Kiss*), which integrate naturalistic portraits into abstractly patterned backgrounds.

EXPRESSIONISM. **Oskar Kokoschka** and **Egon Schiele** revolted against art in the early 20th century, seeking to present the frailty, neuroses, and sexual energy formerly concealed behind the Secession's aesthetic surface. Kokoschka is often considered the founder of Viennese **Expressionism.** Renowned as a portraitist, he was known to scratch the canvas with his fingernails in his efforts to capture the "essence" of his subject. Schiele, like the young Kokoschka, painted with a feverish intensity in line and color. His paintings are controversial even today, for their depictions of tortured figures seemingly destroyed by their own bodies or by debilitating sexuality. His figures are twisted, gnarled, and yet oddly erotic.

MUSIC

THE CLASSICAL ERA. Toward the end of the 18th century, Vienna was a musical colony. Composers hung out in salons, making fun of each other and listening to themselves play music they wrote. The popular style, now described as "Viennese Classicism," fed on itself: the more music was written, the more people wanted to write music. The first master musician of Viennese Classicism was **Josef Haydn** (1732-1809). Working for the princes of Esterhazy, Haydn created a variety of new musical forms that led to the shaping of the sonata and the symphony, structures that dominated music throughout the 19th century. Fifty-two piano sonatas, 24 piano and organ concertos, 104 symphonies, and 83 string quartets provide rich and abundant proof of his pioneering productivity. He wrote the imperial anthem, *Gott erhalte Franz den Kaiser*, in order to rouse patriotic feeling during the Napoleonic wars. After WWI, Germany adopted the melody of *Gott erhalte* for its national anthem.

The work of **Wolfgang Amadeus Mozart** (1756-1791) represents the pinnacle of Viennese Classicism. Born in Salzburg, Mozart was a child prodigy, playing violin and piano by age four, composing simple pieces by five, and performing at

Europe's imperial courts by age six. In 1781 the *Wunderkind* left Salzburg for Vienna, where he produced his first mature concerti, his best-known Italian operas (including *Don Giovanni* and *La Nozze di Figaro*), and the beloved string show-piece, *Eine kleine Nachtmusik*. Throughout his life, Mozart wrote with unprecedented speed, creating 626 works of all kinds during his 35 years, always jotting down music without preliminary sketches or revisions. Unfortunately, what he produced didn't always sell. Mozart's overwhelming emotional power found full expression in his final work, the (unfinished) *Requiem*, which he continued composing until the last hours before his death, fulfilling his bitter aside to favorite student Franz Süssmayr: "You see, I *have* been writing this Requiem for myself." He was buried in an unmarked pauper's grave. Within a few decades of his death, however, Mozart was recognized once more as a master, who in Tchaikovsky's words was "the culmination of all beauty in music."

Only **Ludwig van Beethoven** (1770-1827) could compete with Mozart for the devotion of the Viennese. Born into a family of Flemish musicians in Bonn, he lived and died in Vienna. Beethoven's gifts were manifest in his piano sonatas, string quartets, overtures, and concertos, but shone most intensely in his nine symphonies, today at the core of the orchestral repertoire. His *Ninth Symphony* had an enormous cultural impact, in part because of his introduction of singers to the symphonic form—a chorus and four soloists sing the text to Friedrich Schiller's *Ode to Joy*. Beethoven's *Fidelio*, which premiered May 23, 1814, at the Kärntertortheater in Vienna, is regarded as one of the greatest German operas. Due to increasing deafness, the composer could maintain contact with the world only through a series of conversational notebooks, which provide an extremely thorough, though one-sided, record of his conversations (including his famous emotional outpouring, the *Heiligenstadt Testament*, written in Vienna's 19th district). Music historians place Beethoven between Viennese Classicism and Romanticism.

THE ROMANTIC ERA AND LATE NINETEENTH CENTURY. The music of **Franz Schubert** (1797-1828) is the lifeblood of Romanticism, a movement characterized by swelling emotion, larger orchestras, interest in the natural world, and storytelling. Born in the Viennese suburb of Lichtenthal in 1797, Schubert began his career as a chorister in the royal imperial Hofkapelle and later made his living teaching music. Mainly self-taught, he composed the *Unfinished Symphony* and the *Symphony in C Major*, which are now considered masterpieces but were virtually unknown during his lifetime. His lyrical genius was more readily recognized in his *Lieder*, musical setting of poems by Goethe, Schiller, and Heine. These great song cycles were made famous during musical soirées called *Schubertiaden*, which spawned a new trend of social gatherings in *Biedermeier* Vienna, featuring chamber music, readings, and alcohol. This burst of creativity was cut short by his early death from syphilis at the age of 32—he was buried next to Beethoven. Schubert's genius for pure melody lived on and was a catalyst for later musical innovations.

Like Beethoven, **Johannes Brahms** (1833-1897) straddled musical traditions. In his home near the Karlskirche in Vienna, Brahms composed his Hungarian Dances, piano concerti, and numerous symphonies, all of which were first performed by the Vienna Philharmonic. Despite his own Romantic compositions, Brahms is often regarded as a classicist who used his status and position in the Viennese *Musikverein* to oppose Romanticism and the musical experiments of his arch-rival, Wagner. His artistic credo, "If we cannot compose as beautifully as Mozart or Haydn, let us at least try to compose as purely," emphasized his devotion to the classical style and disinterest in modern music.

Orchestral music had a mass-appeal side as well. Beginning with **Johann Strauss the Elder** (1804-1849), the Strauss family kept Vienna dancing for much of the 19th century. Johann Sr. composed mostly waltzes and showy pieces, including the

AUSTRIA

famous *Radetzkymarsch*, which is still played every New Year by the Vienna Philharmonic. Largely responsible for the "Viennese Waltz," **Johann Strauss the Younger** (1825-1899) shone in his youth as a brilliant violinist and savvy cultural entrepreneur. The waltz became popular during the Congress of Vienna, offering a fresh exhilaration that broke free from older, more stiffly formal dances. Richard Wagner, Strauss' most famous rival, noted admiringly on a visit to the city that Viennese waltzing was "more potent than alcohol." Sensing the trend, Strauss became its master, eventually writing the *Blue Danube* and *Tales from the Vienna Woods*, two of the most recognized waltzes of all time, thereby earning the title "King of the Waltz." In his spare time he managed to produce some popular operas as well, *Die Fledermaus* being his most celebrated.

Gustav Mahler's (1860-1911) music, as a direct precursor to the Second Viennese experiments of Arnold Schönberg, incorporates fragments and deliberately inconclusive musical segments. Like modern literature, these compositions read like nostalgic remnants of a once certain and orderly world. Mahler employed unusual instrumentation and startling harmonic juxtapositions. His Eighth Symphony, called *Symphony of a Thousand*, requires an orchestra and two full choruses. Mahler's music hides formalist experimentation beneath a rich emotional beauty. His works form an integral part of the *fin de siècle* Viennese avant-garde.

THE MODERN ERA. While Mahler destabilized the conventions of composition, **Arnold Schönberg** (1874-1951) broke away from traditional harmony altogether. Originally a devotee of Richard Wagner, Schönberg rejected compositional rules that require music to be set in a tonal key, and with his 12-tone system pursued what is generally called atonality. Some of Schönberg's most famous works are *Pierre Lunaire* and the string piece *Verklärte Nacht*. **Anton von Webern** (1883-1945) studied under Schönberg, eventually adopting and expanding his 12-tone system in music that is incredibly sparse, a sharp contrast to the lush, opulent, often overwritten music of his contemporaries. Webern drifted into obscurity and depression as the Nazis took over. While fleeing the Nazis, he was accidentally shot by U.S. troops in Salzburg. **Alban Berg** (1885-1935), another student of Schönberg's who used a modified version of the 12-tone system, completed few works because of his obsession with ideal expression. Like Schönberg and Webern, he suffered under the Nazis as a creator of "degenerate art" and died young, in 1935.

LITERATURE

EARLY EXAMPLES. A collection of poetry dating from around 1150 and preserved in the abbey of Vorau in Styria marks the earliest known Austrian literature in German. Apart from sacred poetry, the courtly style known as *Minnesang* developed in the 12th and 13th centuries, culminated in the lyrical works of minstrel **Walther von der Vogelweide**. On a more epic scale, the **Nibelungenlied**, which dates from around 1200, is one of the most impressive heroic epics in German (it is also the primary source for Richard Wagner's *Ring of the Nibelungen* opera cycle). **Emperor Maximilian I** (1459-1519), nicknamed "The Last Knight," provided special support for theater and the dramatic arts during his reign. Splendid operas and pageants frequently involved the whole imperial court and led to popular religious drama that has survived in the form of rural **Passionspiele** (passion plays).

THE CLASSICAL WRITERS. Born in Vienna in 1801, **Johann Nestroy** wrote biting comedies and satires lampooning social follies. Although his name is not readily recognized by Anglophones, Nestroy is one of the canonical figures of German drama, famous for such plays as *Der Talisman* and *Liebesgeschichten und Heiratssachen*, as well as the *Tannhäuser* on which Wagner based his famous opera. Often called Austria's greatest novelist, **Adalbert Stifter** wrote around the same time period as Nestroy but concerned himself much more with classical *Bildungsroman* themes and descriptions of nature. Many of his short stories and novels, such as *Der Condor* (1840), *Die Mappe meines Urgroßvaters* (1841), and *Der Nachsommer* (1857), belong to the canon of German literature.

A classicist with a more lyrical style, **Franz Grillparzer** penned plays about the conflict between a life of thought and a life of action. Grillparzer worked as a clerk in the Austrian bureaucracy and wrote some of his most critically acclaimed plays, such as *Des Meeres und Der Liebe Wellen* (1831), in his spare time. Most of Grillparzer's fame came posthumously, when interest grew in his published work and the beautifully composed *Der arme Spielmann* was discovered.

FIN DE SIÈCLE. Around 1890, Austrian literature rapidly transformed in the heat of the "merry apocalypse" atmosphere that permeated society. The satires of **Karl Kraus** tried to awaken the collapsing empire's conscience, while **Sigmund Freud** analyzed its dreams. **Arthur Schnitzler** heated up the Empire's stage with bedroom scenes, while **Hugo von Hofmannsthal** staged its death with reconceptualizations of medieval and Baroque tragedies. At the Cafe Griensteidl, lyric poet, critic, and one-time director of the *Burgtheater* **Hermann Bahr** loosely presided over a pioneer group known as **Jung Wien** (Young Vienna), aimed at capturing the subtlest nuances of the Viennese atmosphere. Hofmannsthal walked a tightrope between Impressionism and verbal decadence, creating such exquisite pieces of drama as *Yesterday* (1891) and *Everyman* (1911) while at the same time collaborating with Richard Strauss to write librettos for, among other things, *Der Rosenkavalier*. Schnitzler, a playwright and colleague of Freud, was the first German to write stream-of-consciousness prose. He skewered Viennese decadence in dramas and essays, and shocked contemporaries by portraying the complexities of erotic relationships in many of his plays, including his famous *Merry-Go-Round* (1897).

Many of Austria's literary titans, such as **Marie von Ebner-Eschenbach** and **Franz Kafka,** lived within the Habsburg protectorate of Bohemia. Ebner-Eschenbach is often called the greatest female Austrian writer, known for her vivid individual portraits and defense of women's rights. Kafka often traveled to Vienna to drink coffee at the Herrenhof Café and swap ideas with other writers. No one else could master the surrealism of Kafka's writing, however, most famously demonstrated in *Die Verhandlung (The Metamorphosis)*, a bizarre, disorienting tale in which the narrator comes to terms with his unexpected transformation into a beetle.

The collapse of the Austro-Hungarian monarchy marked a major turning point in the intellectual and literary life of Austria. Novelists **Robert Musil** and **Joseph Roth** concerned themselves with the consequences of the empire's breakdown. Roth's novels, *Radetzkymarsch* and *Die Kapuzinergruft*, romanticize the former empire. He is most famous for his unfinished work in 3 volumes *Der Mann Ohne Eigenschaften (The Man Without Qualities)*.

THE 20TH CENTURY. **Georg Trakl's** Expressionist works epitomize the early 20th-century fascination with death and dissolution; "All roads empty into black putrefaction" is his most frequently quoted line.

Other Prague-born greats such as **Franz Werfel** and **Rainer Maria Rilke** shaped Austrian literature between the wars. Werfel's works investigate the dark side of the human psyche. In addition to his essays and stories, Rilke is most famous for his lyric poetry cycles the *Duino Elegies* and *Sonnets to Orpheus*. After WWII, Rilke's poetry and Kafka's oppressive parables of a cold world became the models for a new generation of writers. These artistic movements owe their fascination with the unconscious to the new science of psychoanalysis and its most famous proponent, **Sigmund Freud.** Freud is best known for his theories of sexual repression, particularly applicable to bourgeois society, and his theories of the unconscious, which recast the literary world forever.

Contemporary Austrian literature is still affected and informed by its dark, dramatic literary tradition, but there is plenty of modern innovation as well. **Ingeborg Bachman's** stories and novels left an important legacy for Austrian feminism. One of the stalwarts of modern Austrian writing, **Thomas Bernhard** wrote *Holzfäller* (Woodcutters) and *Wittgenstein's Nephew*.

FILM

While most English speakers might not be able to name more than one Austrian actor (Arnold Schwarzenegger is easy), national filmmaking has endured a rocky tradition, alternatively thriving and waning. Emperor Franz Josef himself attended a screening in April 1896 of a short film created by the French Lumière brothers in Vienna. Inspired by Cecil B. DeMille in the U.S., the Kolowrat created the massive *Sodom und Gomorrha* in 1922. The addition of sound to movies allowed for W. Forst's 1933 invention of the Viennese musical film in *Leise flehen meine Lieder*. Anschluss in 1938 brought about the end of independent domestic film production and the consolidation of filmmakers under the Wien-Film corporation. Wien-Film was confiscated by Allied forces in 1945 and the tradition was reborn in 1946. Austrian films moved in a variety of directions, from the "woods and mountain" genre of films like *Echo der Berge* to operettas and works addressing contemporary social problems. Beginning in 1954, the illustrious Goldene Feder ("Golden Feather") has been bestowed upon the director of the "Best Film of the Year."

SPORTS AND RECREATION

Austrians take their recreation seriously; provisions for athletic funding are even written into the national constitution. The Alps are not just a playground for foreign adventure-seekers, either. Over 450,000 Austrians belong to the Austrian Union of Alpine Associations and other mountaineering clubs. The first slalom competition ever was held in Austria in 1905, and since then, Austria has hosted two Winter Olympics and millions of visiting skiiers. Thanks to improved lift facilities, summer skiing is now possible on eight glaciers as well. Other popular recreational sporta are soccer, curling, and cycling, while top spectator sports include Formula One racing and soccer. National fitness campaigns are not uncommon, and the Fitness March and Fitness Run are part of the Austrian National Day.

CURRENT SCENE

Austria's rich culture history has made it a draw for tourists and scholars alike, but it can also be an oppressive force, hindering the exploration of modern art and expression. Tired of Lippizaner, chocolate and Mozart, individuals and the government alike are working to showcase the new, progressive culture and innovative art that is slowly emerging. A new exhibition in Manhattan displays the work of 100 living artists, while a brand-new Jewish theater troupe and contemporary music scene are shedding new light on creativity within Austria's borders.

HOLIDAYS AND FESTIVALS

Shops and businesses are closed on national and most religious holidays. The dates for 2003 include New Year's Day (January 1st) and Epiphany (6th), Good Friday (April 18th), Easter Monday (21st), Labor Day (May 1), Ascension Day (29th), Whitmonday (June 9th), Corpus Christi (June 19th), Assumption Day (August 15), National Day (October 26), All Saint's Day (November 1), Immaculate Conception (December 8), Christmas (25th) and Boxing Day (26th). As Austria is a Catholic country, religious holidays are observed nearly everywhere, and towns and cities essentially shut down. Below are a list of holidays and festivals you'll want to join if you're in the neighborhood.

AUSTRIAN FESTIVALS (2003)

DATE	NAME & LOCATION	DESCRIPTION
February	Fasching, Vienna	"Carnival Season" brings waltzes, parties, and a parade the day before Lent.
mid-April to mid-May	Donau Festival, Krems, Tulnn, Korneuburg	A celebration of art, music, and theater along the Donau River.
mid-May to mid-June	Vienna Festival	Thousands descend upon the city for a celebration with theater, exhibits, and renowned orchestras.
early July	Love Parade, Vienna	Begun after the fall of the Berlin Wall, the annual festive parade celebrates love, respect and tolerance for all people.
late July to late Aug.	Salzburg Music Festival	A summer series of concerts by the Vienna Philharmonic and others.
August	Eisenstadt Fest	Freeflowing music and wine. What could be better?
Oct. 26	Austrian National Day	Commemorates formation of Austria as new independent nation after WWII
mid-Nov. to Dec. 24th	Salzburg Christmas Market (also in Vienna)	Festive cabin-like booths are erected in front of the baroque cathedral.
December 6	Krampus (everywhere, especially small towns)	Watch out as St. Nicholas and his mischievous companion Krampus wander the streets.
December 31	New Year's, everywhere	The top draw is Vienna for the annual performance of "Die Fledermaus" at the opera.

AUSTRIA

ADDITIONAL RESOURCES

GENERAL HISTORY

The Class Art of Viennese Pastry (1997). Christine Berl.

Vienna and its Jews: The Tragedy of Success, 1880s-1980s (1988). Charles E. Berkley.

Vienna: Its Musical Heritage (1968). Egon Gartenberg.

The Fall of the House of Habsburg (1963). Edward Crankshaw.

Fin-de-Siècle Vienna (1961). Carl Schorske.

FICTION

The World of Yesterday (De Welt von Gestern; 1943). Stefan Zweig.

The Metamorphosis (Die Verwandlung; 1915). Franz Kafka.

Eyes Wide Shut (Die Traumspiele; 1900). Arthur Schnitzler.

TRAVEL BOOKS

Hostels Austria & Switzerland: The Only Comprehensive, Unofficial, Opinionated Guide (2002). Paul Karr.

Karen Brown's Austria: Charming Inns & Itineraries (2002). Karen Brown.

German Survival Guide: The Language and Culture You Need to Travel With Confidence in Germany and Austria (2001). Elizabeth Bingham.

The Wines of Austria (2000). Philip Blom.

Walking Austria's Alps: Hut-to-Hut (1999). Jonathan Hurdle.

VIENNA (WIEN)

Vienna is a cultural monument, a living memorial to the geniuses of music, art, and academia who once walked its streets. Here is where Freud struggled with the human psyche, Mozart found his inspiration for symphonies, and Kafka crafted his masterpieces. At the height of its artistic foment at the turn of the century, during the smoky days of the great cafe culture, the Viennese were already self-mockingly referring to their city as the "merry apocalypse." From its humble origins as a Roman camp along the Danube, Vienna became not just the cultural heart of Europe, but the setting for politicians to achieve greatness, or at least infamy. From the glory days of the Habsburg dynasty under Maximilian I and Maria Theresia to *fin-de-siècle* fever, Vienna has rivaled Paris, London, and Berlin in significance, thanks to its imperial wealth and pivotal placement between Eastern and Western Europe.

Although the darker ghosts of Austria's past still lurk in the *Judenplatz*, location of war-time Jewish ghetto, the city shows signs of more recent brighter developments in its postmodern architecture and Friedensreich Hundertwasser's ecological fantasies. A recently opened *MuseumsQuartier*, an ultra-modern venue for various displays further proves Vienna is a city just coming of age.

> **PHONE CODES** — The **city code** for Vienna is 0222 for calls placed from within Austria, 1 for calls from abroad.

⊠ INTERCITY TRANSPORTATION

BY PLANE. Vienna's airport is the **Wien-Schwechat Flughafen** (☎ 700 72 22 33), home of **Austrian Airlines.** (☎ 517 89; www.aua.com. Open M-F 7am-10pm, Sa-Su 8am-8pm.) A daily flight to and from **New York** and frequent flights to **Berlin, London,** and **Rome,** among other places, are available. Travelers under 25 and students under 27 qualify for discounts if they purchase tickets two weeks in advance.

The airport is far from the city center (18km), but easily accessible by public transportation. The cheapest way to reach the city is to take train S7 "Flughafen/Wolfsthal" which stops at **Wien Mitte** (30min., every 30min. 5:03am-9:36pm, €3; Eurail not valid). There is also daily train service between **Wien Nord** or Wien Mitte and the airport (every 30min. 5:03am-10:24pm, €3). The heart of the city, Stephanspl., is a short metro ride from Wien Mitte on the U3 line.

A more convenient option is taking the **Vienna Airport Lines Shuttle Bus** (☎ 93 00 00 23 00; www.oebb.at/regional/wien/wien4.html). Buses leave the airport for the **City Air Terminal** at the Hilton opposite Wien Mitte (every 20min. 6:30am-11:10pm, every 30min. midnight-6am; €5.80). Buses leave from the airport for **Südbahnhof** and **Westbahnhof** (every 30min. 8:55am-7:25pm, every hr. 8:20pm-8:25am). Similarly, buses travel to the airport from the city stations. By far the easiest (and most expensive) way to and from the airport is by private airport shuttle services, such as **JetBus** (☎ 700 73 87 79), which are located just outside the baggage claim and deliver passengers to any address in the city for €12 per person. Call one day in advance to arrange pickup for a return trip. Parties of three or more get discounts when booking a return trip.

BY TRAIN. Vienna has two main train stations with international departures. For general train information, call ☎ 17 17 (24hr.) or check www.bahn.at.

Greater Vienna

VIENNA

Westbahnhof, XV, Mariahilferstr. 132. Trains from here run primarily **west.** Domestically to: **Bregenz** (8hr., 9 per day, €57.41); **Innsbruck** (5-6hr., every 2hr., €48); **Linz** (2hr., every hr., €21.80); **Salzburg** (3½hr., every hr., €33.43). Internationally to: **Amsterdam** (14½hr., 7:17pm, €165.70); **Hamburg** (9½hr., 10:17am, 7:45pm; €175.15); **Munich** (4½hr., 5 per day, €60); **Paris** (14hr., 8:47am, 8:21pm; €155.52); **Zurich** (9¼hr., 3 per day, €80.23). Trains also run to: **Berlin Zoo** (11hr., 9:19pm, €122.24). The **information counter** is open daily 7:30am-8:40pm.

Südbahnhof, X, Wiedner Gürtel 1a. On the D tram. To get to the city take the tram (dir. Nußdorf) to "Opera/Karlspl." From the station, trains leave for destinations **south** and **east.** Domestically to: **Graz** (2¾hr., every hr. 6:04am-10:34pm, €22.53) and **Villach** (5hr., every hr. 6:04am-10:34pm, €34.16). Internationally to: **Budapest** (3-4hr., 6 per day, 6:17am-7:36pm); **Berlin Zoo** (9¼hr., 10:25am, €84.30); **Bratislava** (1hr., 13 per day, €12); **Krakow** (7-8hr., 3 per day, €36); **Prague** (4½hr., 5 per day, €38); **Rome** (14hr., 7:29am); **Venice** (9-10hr., 4 per day, €64); and other European cities. The **information counter** is open daily 6:30am-9:20pm.

Three stations handle mostly commuter trains. The largest is **Franz-Josefs Bahnhof,** IX, Althamstr. 10, on the D tram. There are also two smaller stations: **Bahnhof Wien Mitte,** in the center of town, and **Bahnhof Wien Nord,** by the Prater on the north side of the Danube Canal. Bahnhof Wien Nord is the main S-Bahn and U-Bahn link for trains heading north, but most Bundesbahn trains go through the

VIENNA

Vienna

▲ ACCOMMODATIONS

Believe It Or Not, **20**
Hostel Panda and Lauria Apartments, **18**
Hostel Ruthensteiner (HI), **30**
Jugendgästehaus Wien Brigitenau
  (HI), **1**
Katholisches Studentenhaus, **2**
Myrthne./Neustiftg. (HI), **19**
Pension Falstaff, **6**
Pension Hargita, **25**
Pension Kraml, **26**
Pension Reimer, **23**
Pension Wild, **16**
Porzellaneum der Wiener Universität, **4**
Westend City Hostel, **31**
Wombats City Hostel, **29**

VIENNA

FOOD
Blue Box, 24
Café Nil, 21
Café Willendorf, 33
Elsäßer Bistro, 7
Fischerbräu, 3
OH Pot, OH Pot, 8
Stomach, 5
Vegetasia, 34

COFFEEHOUSES
Berg das Café, 9
Café Rüdigerhof, 32
Café Savoy, 28
Café Stein, 12
Kunsthaus Wien Café, 13

BARS
Alsergrunder Kulturpark, 11
Blue Box, 24
Chelsea, 15
Eagle Bar, 27
Europa, 22
Loop, 14
Miles Smiles, 17

DISCOS
Flex, 10
U-4, 35

Ⓤ③ U-Bahn Ⓢ S-Bahn

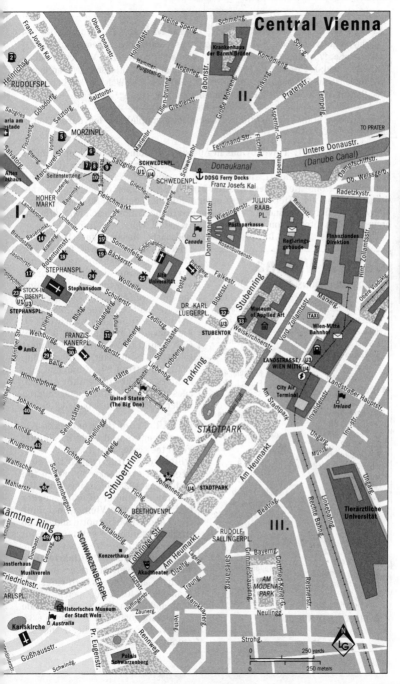

Central Vienna

VIENNA

> **DISTRICT NAMES AND NUMBERS:** Moving in a roughly clockwise direction, Vienna's 23 districts are: I, **Innenstadt;** II, **Leopoldstadt;** III, **Landstraße;** IV, **Wieden;** V, **Margareten;** VI, **Mariahilf;** VII, **Neubau;** VIII, **Josefstadt;** IX, **Alsergrund;** X, **Favoriten;** XI, **Simmering;** XII, **Meidling;** XIII, **Hietzing;** XIV, **Penzing;** XV, **Rudolfsheim Fünfhaus;** XVI, **Ottakring;** XVII, **Hernals;** XVIII, **Währing;** XIX, **Döbling;** XX, **Brigittenau;** XXI, **Floridsdorf;** XXII, **Donaustadt;** XXIII, **Liesing.**

other stations. Some regional trains (Krems, for example) also leave from **Spittelau,** located on the U4 and U6 subway lines.

BY BUS AND BOAT. Travel by bus in Austria is seldom cheaper than travel by train; compare prices before buying a ticket. **City bus terminals** are located at Wien Mitte/Landstr., Hütteldorf, Heiligenstadt, Floridsdorf, Kagran, Erdberg, and Reumannpl. Domestic **BundesBuses** run from these stations to local and international destinations. (Ticket counter open M-F 6am-5:50pm, Sa-Su 6am-3:50pm.) Many international bus lines also have agencies in the stations, each with different hours. For bus information, call BundesBus (☎711 01. Open 7am-7pm).

The famous **Donau Dampfschiffahrtsgesellschaft Donaureisen** (DDSG), I, Friedrichstr. 7 (☎58 88 00; fax 58 88 04 40; info@ddsg-blue-danube.at; www.ddsg-blue-danube.at), organizes cruises on the Danube, hitting the cities of Melk, Spitz, Dürnstein, and Krems/Stein (see p. 296). The DDSG also operates hydrofoils to **Bratislava** (1½hr., Apr.-Oct. 9:30am; €19, round-trip €29) and **Budapest** (5½hr., June-July 8am, Aug. 9am, 1pm; €65, round-trip €89). Eurail and ISIC holders get 20% off within Austria, ages 10-15 are half-price, and children under 10 are free with parent.

BY CAR. From the **west,** take A1, which begins and ends in Vienna. From the **south,** take A2, or A3 to A2, which runs directly into the city. From the **east,** take A4. From the **north,** take A22, which runs along the Danube. A number of much smaller highways lead to Vienna, including Rte. 7 and 8 from the north and Rte. 10 from the south. An economical but less predictable alternative to the train is **ride-sharing. Mitfahrzentrale Wien** pairs drivers and riders over the phone. Call to see which rides are available. (☎408 22 10. Open M-F 8am-noon and 2-7pm, Sa-Su 1-3pm.) A ride to **Salzburg** costs €16, to **Prague** €33. Reservations two days in advance are recommended.

Central Vienna

🏠 ACCOMMODATIONS
Hotel Am Stephansplatz, **17**
Hotel Imperial, **49**
Hotel Zur Wiener Staatsoper, **43**
Studenten Wohnheim der Hochschule für Musik, **40**

🍎 FOOD
Amerlingbeisl, **37**
Bizi Pizza, **18**
Centimeter, **38**
La Crêperie, **25**
DO&CO, **23**
Hunger Künstler, **52**
Inigo, **24**
Korso, **44**
Levante, **16**
Margaritaville, **20**
Maschu Maschu, **9**
Rosenberger Markt, **41**
Smutny, **47**
Trzesniewski, **22**
Wrenkh, **14**
University Mensa, **1**
Yugetsu Saryo, **39**
Zimolo, **29**
Zum Mogulhof, **35**

☕ COFFEEHOUSES
Café Alt Wien, **19**
Café Bräunerhof, **27**
Café Central, **11**
Café Drechsler, **53**
Café Griensteidl, **21**
Café Hawelka, **28**
Café MAK, **33**
Café Museum, **48**
Café Prückel, **32**
Café Sperl, **50**
Demel, **13**
Hotel Imperial, **49**
Hotel Sacher, **42**
Kleines Café, **30**

🍸 BARS
Benjamin, **5**
Cato, **3**
Centro, **15**
Club Berlin, **2**
Das Möbel, **36**
Esterházykeller, **12**
First Floor Bar, **10**
Jazzland, **6**
Kaktus, **8**
Kunsthalle Café, **51**
Mapitom der Bierlokal, **7**
Objectiv, **34**
Santo Spirito, **31**

⭐ DISCOS & DANCE CLUBS
Club Meierei, **46**   Volksgarten Disco, **26**
Havana Club, **45**   Why Not, **4**

While *Let's Go* does not recommend hitching, **hitchhikers** headed for Salzburg have been seen taking U4 to "Hütteldorf"; the highway leading to the Autobahn is 10km farther. Hitchers traveling south often ride tram #67 to the last stop and wait at the rotary near Laaerberg.

⚡ ORIENTATION

Vienna is divided into 23 **districts** *(Bezirke)*. The first is the *innere Stadt*, or *Innenstadt* (city center), and the other districts spiral out from it in a clockwise direction. The *Innenstadt* is defined by the **Ringstraße** on three sides and the Danube Canal on the fourth. The Ringstraße (or "Ring") consists of various segments, each with its own name: Opernring, Kärntner Ring, Dr.-Karl-Lüger-Ring, etc.

Many of Vienna's major attractions are in District I (the *innere Stadt*) and immediately around the Ringstraße, including the **Kunsthistorisches Museum,** the **Rathaus,** and the **Burggarten.** At the intersection of the **Opernring, Kärntner Ring,** and **Kärntnerstraße** stands the **Staatsoper** (Opera House), near the **tourist office** and the **Karlsplatz** U-Bahn stop. Districts II-IX spread out from the city center. The remaining districts expand from yet another ring, the **Gürtel** ("belt"). Like the Ring, this major two-way thoroughfare has numerous segments, including Margaretengürtel, Währinger Gürtel, and Neubaugürtel. Street signs indicate the district number in Roman or Arabic numerals *before* the street and number, and postal codes correspond to the district number: 1010 for the first district, 1020 for the second, 1110 for the eleventh, etc. *Let's Go* includes district numbers for establishments before the street address.

▣ LOCAL TRANSPORTATION

Public transportation in Vienna is extensive and dependable; call ☎ 580 00 for general info. The **subway** (U-Bahn), **tram** (Straßenbahn), **elevated train** (S-Bahn), and **bus** systems operate under one ticket system. A single fare is €1.80 if purchased from a machine on a bus, €1.50 if purchased in advance from a machine in a station, ticket office, or tobacco shop *(Tabak* or *Trafik)*. This ticket permits you to travel to any single destination in the city and switch from bus to U-Bahn to tram to S-Bahn, as long as your travel is uninterrupted. This part is tricky: to validate a ticket, punch it in the machine immediately upon entering the first vehicle. Do not stamp the ticket again when you switch trains. A ticket stamped twice or not stamped at all is invalid, and plainclothes inspectors may fine you €40 plus the ticket price. Other ticket options (available at the same places as pre-purchased single tickets) are a **24hr. pass** (€5), a **3-day "rover" ticket** (€12), a **7-day pass** (€11.20; valid M 9am to M 9am), or an **8-day pass** (€24; valid any 8 days, not necessarily consecutive; valid also for several people traveling together). The **Vienna Card** (€16.90) offers free travel for 72hr., as well as substantial discounts at museums, sights, and events, and is especially useful for non-students. If you are traveling with a child over 6, a bicycle, or a dog, you must buy a half-price ticket (€0.80). Children under 6 always ride free, as does anyone under 15 on Sundays and school holidays. (The pocket map available at the tourist offices lists official holidays.) You can take bicycles on all underground trains; each train restricts bikes to certain cars, marked with a bicycle symbol.

Regular trams and subway cars stop running between midnight and 5am. **Night-buses** run (every 30min.) along most tram, subway, and major bus routes beginning around 12:30am. In major hubs like Schottentor, some buses leave from slightly different areas than their daytime counterparts. "N" signs with yellow cat eyes designate night bus stops. A complete schedule is available at bus counters in U-Bahn stations. (€1 per ride or 4 for €3.27; day transport passes not valid.)

VIENNA

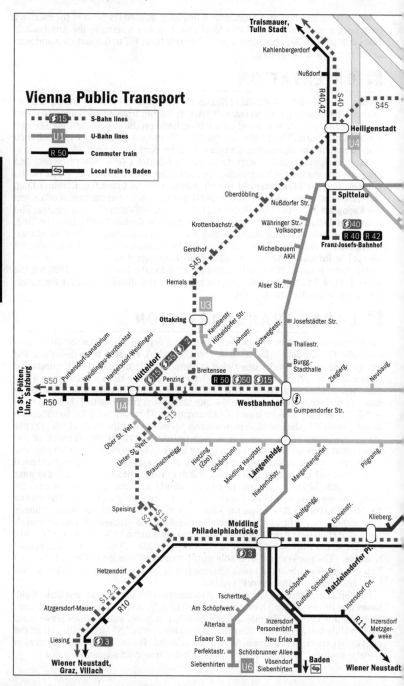

Vienna Public Transport

●S15●■■■	**S-Bahn lines**
U1	**U-Bahn lines**
R 50	**Commuter train**
⇆	**Local train to Baden**

Traismauer,
Tulln Stadt

Kahlenbergerdorf

Nußdorf

R40, 42

S40

S45

Heiligenstadt

U4

Oberdöbling

Nußdorfer Str.

Spittelau

Krottenbachstr.

Währinger Str.-
Volksoper

●S40
R 40 R 42

Gersthof

Michelbeuern
AKH

Franz-Josefs-Bahnhof

S45

Hernals

Alser Str.

Ottakring

U3

Kendlerstr.
Hütteldorfer Str.

Johnstr.

Schweglerstr.

Josefstädter Str.

Thaliastr.

●S15●●45●●2

Purkersdorf-Sanatorium

Weidlingau-Wurzbachtal

Hardersdorf-Weidlingau

Hütteldorf

●S15●●45●

Penzing

Breitensee

R 50 ●S50●S15

Burgg.-
Stadthalle

Ziegierg.

Neubaug.

S50

S15

To St. Pölten,
Linz, Salzburg

R50

U4

S15

Westbahnhof

ⓘ

Gumpendorfer Str.

Ober St. Veit

Unter St. Veit

Braunschweigg.

Hietzing
(Zoo)

Schönbrunn

Meidling Hauptstr.

Längenfeld

Niederhofstr.

Margaretengürtel

Pilgramg.

Speising

S15

S2

Wolfgangg.

Eichenstr.

Klieberg.

Meidling
Philadelphiabrücke

●S3

Matzleinsdorfer Pl.

Hetzendorf

Schöpfwerk

Gutheil-Schoder-G.

Inzersdorf Ort.

R11

Inzersdorf
Metzger-
weke

S1,2,3

R10

Tschertteg.

Am Schöpfwerk

Inzersdorf
Personenbhf.

Atzgersdorf-Mauer

Alterlaa

Neu Erlaa

Liesing ●S3

Erlaaer Str.

Perfektastr.

Schönbrunner Allee

Baden
⇆

Wiener Neustadt,
Graz, Villach

Siebenhirten

U6

Vösendorf
Siebenhirten

Wiener Neustadt

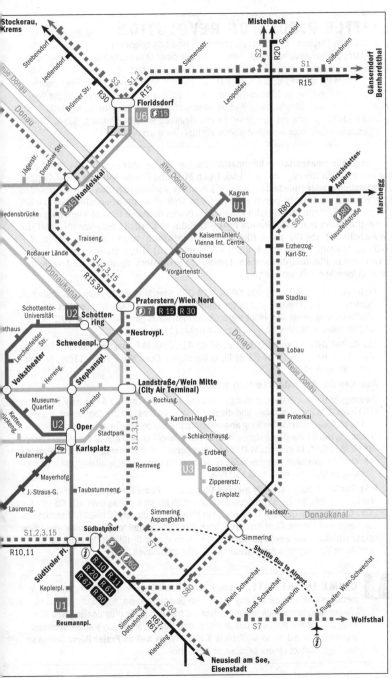

VIENNA

VIENNA

LITTLE PIECES OF REVOLUTION Some weary travelers may be perplexed by the little paper strips taped on columns in train stations, subway stops, and crowded streets. These are none other than *Pflücktexte* (from the verb *pflücken*, to pick flowers). The slips of paper, containing short poems with vaguely anti-establishment messages, are meant to be "picked" from the columns. They inspire, provoke thought, or, as is often the case, are crumpled up and discarded on the floor of Westbahnhof, Stephanspl., and Schwedenpl. stations, only to be mysteriously replaced. The poems are composed by one Helmut Seethaler, Wasnerg. 43/8, 1200 Wien, who offers more insurgent poems via mail "for a small bill."

The **public transportation information line** has live operators who give directions to any point in the city. (☎ 790 91 05. Open M-W and F 8am-3pm, Th 8am-5:30pm.) **Information stands** (marked with an "i") in many stations can also provide detailed instructions on how to purchase tickets, as well as an indispensable free pocket map of the U-Bahn and S-Bahn systems. A comprehensive map of Vienna's public transportation is €1.40. Stands in the U-Bahn at Karlspl., Stephanspl., and the Westbahnhof are the most likely to have information in English. (Open M-F 6:30am-6:30pm, Sa-Su and holidays 8:30am-4pm.) Other stands are located at Praterstern, Philadelphiabrücke, Landstr., Floridsdorf, Spittelau, and Volkstheater. (Open M-F 6:30am-6:30pm.)

Taxis: (☎ 313 00, 401 00, 601 60, or 814 00). Stands at Westbahnhof, Südbahnhof, Karlspl. in the city center, and by the Bermuda Dreiecke for late-night revelers. Accredited taxis have yellow and black signs on the roof. Rates generally €2 plus €0.2 per km; slightly more expensive on holidays, and nights (11pm-6am).

Car Rental: Avis, I, Opernring 3-5 (☎ 587 62 41). Open M-F 7am-8pm, Sa 8am-2pm, Su 8am-1pm. **Hertz,** (☎ 70 07 32 661), at the airport. Open M-F 7:15am-11pm, Sa 8am-8pm, Su 8am-11pm.

Auto Repairs: Call **ÖAMTC** (☎ 120) or **ARBÖ** (☎ 123).

Parking: In the 1st district, parking is allowed M-F 9am-7pm for 1½hr. Buy a voucher (€40 per 30min.) at a *Tabak* and display it, with the time, on the dashboard. It's easiest to park cars outside the Ring and walk into the city center. Garages line the Ringstr., including two by the Opera House, one at Franz-Josef Kai, and one at the Marek-Garage at Messepalast. In districts VI-IX, parking is permitted M-F 9am-8pm for 2hr. **Parking cards** (€5), available at either a *Tabak* or street machine, enable all-day parking there. Parking illegally garners a €25-150 fine.

Bike Rental: Rentals generally average €5 per hour. **Pedal Power,** II, Ausstellungsstr. 3 (☎ 729 72 34; fax 72 35; office@pedalpower.co.at; www.pedalpower.at). €5 per hr., €32 for 24hr. with delivery. They also offer bike tours of the city (€19-23). Discounts for students and Vienna Card holders. Check Wombats Hostel for cheap bike and inline skate rentals. Open May-Sept. 8am-8pm. Pick up *Vienna By Bike* at the tourist office for details on the bicycle scene, including city bike information.

 CRIME IN THE CITY. Vienna is considered to be quite safe, but it is a metropolis with crime like any other. Use common sense, especially after dark. Women should not walk alone. **Karlspl.,** is home to many drug dealers, who also hang around the train stations at night. Also beware of the city's small skinhead population. Avoid areas in districts **X** and **XIV,** as well as **Prater Park.** Vienna's Red Light District covers sections of the Gürtel.

⁊ PRACTICAL INFORMATION

TOURIST AND FINANCIAL SERVICES

Main Tourist Office: I, Albertinapl. (www.info.wien.at). Follow Operng. up 1 block from the Opera House. The newly enlarged tourist office still serves hordes with an assortment of brochures, including a free map of the city. The brochure *Youth Scene* provides vital information for young travelers. The office books rooms for a €3 fee plus a 1-night deposit. Open 9am-7pm.

Branch Offices:

Westbahnhof. Open 7:30am-8:40pm daily.

Highway exit "Wien Auhof," off A1. Open Easter-Oct. daily 8am-10pm, Nov.-Mar. 10am-6pm.

Highway exit "Zentrum," off A2; XI, Trierstr. 149. Open July-Sept. daily 8am-10pm; Oct. and Easter Week to June 9am-7pm.

North Danube Island. Open May-Sept. 10am-6pm.

Vienna International Airport, in arrival hall. Open 8:30am-9pm.

Jugend-Info Wien (Vienna Youth Information Service): I, Bellaria-Passage (☎17 99; jiw@blackbox.at), in the underground passage at the Bellaria intersection. Enter at the "Dr.-Karl-Renner-Ring/Bellaria" stop (trams #1, 2, 46, 49, D, or J) or at the "Volkstheater" U-Bahn station. Hip staff has information on cultural events, housing, and employment opportunities and sells discount youth concert and theater tickets. Get the indispensable *Jugend in Wien* brochure here. Open M-Sa noon-7pm.

Österreichisches Verkehrsbüro (Austrian National Travel Office): IV, Margaretenstr. 1 (☎587 20 00; www.austria-tourism.at.). Open M-W, F 10am-5pm, Th 10am-6pm.

Ökista, IX, Türkenstr. 6 (☎40 14 80), specializes in student travel, tickets, and passes. Open M-F 9am-5:30pm.

Embassies: Generally, each country's embassy and consulate are located in the same building, listed under *"Botschaften"* or *"Konsulate"* in the phone book. Contact consulates for assistance with visas and passports and in emergencies.

Australia: IV, Mattiellistr. 2 (☎50 674; austemb@xpoint.at; www.australian-embassy.at).

Canada: I, Laurenzerberg 2 (☎531 38 30 00; fax 38 33 21; enqserv@dfait-maeci.gc.ca; www.dfait-maeci.gc.ca).

Ireland: I, Rotenturmstr. 16-18, 5th Floor (☎71 54 24 60; vienna@iveath.irlgov.ie).

New Zealand: Consulate, XIX, Karl-Tornay-g. 34 (☎318 85 05; p.sunley@demmer.at).

South Africa: XIX, Sandg. 33 (☎320 64 93; fax 64 93 51; saembvie@aon.at; www.southafrican-embassy.at).

UK: III, Jauresg. 12 (☎716 13 51 51; fax 13 59 00; vcenquiries@britishembassy.at; www.britishembassy.at).

US: IX, Boltzmanng. 16 (☎313 39; fax 310 06 82; www.usembassy-vienna.at).

Currency Exchange: ATMs are your best bet. Nearly all accept Cirrus, DC, MC, V (see p. 15). **Banks** and **airport exchanges** use the same official rates. Minimum commission €5 for traveler's checks, €1 for cash. Most are open M-W and F 8am-12:30pm and 1:30-3pm, Th 8am-12:30pm and 1:30-5:30pm. **Train station** exchanges offer long hours and a €5 fee for changing up to US$700 of traveler's checks. The 24hr. exchange at the **main post office** has excellent rates and charges an €8 fee to change up to US$1100 in traveler's checks. The **24hr. bill exchange** machines in the *Innenstadt* have atrocious rates. The **casino,** I, Kärntnerstr. 41, has better rates. Open 3pm-4am.

American Express: I, Kärntnerstr. 21-23, P.O. Box 28, A-1015 (☎515 40), down the street from Stephanspl. Cashes AmEx and Thomas Cook (min €5 commission) cheques, sells theater, concert, and other tickets, and holds mail for 4 weeks for AmEx members. Open M-F 9am-5:30pm, Sa 9am-noon. For 24hr. refund service, call ☎0800 20 68 40.

LOCAL SERVICES

Luggage Storage: Lockers are €5 per 24hr. at all train stations.

Lost Property: Fundbüro, IX, Wasag. 22 (☎313 44 92 11 or 92 17). For items lost on public transportation, call ☎790 94 35 00. Open M-F 8am-noon. For items lost on trains, call ☎580 03 29 96 (Westbahnhof) or 580 03 56 56 (Südbahnhof).

Bookstores: Shakespeare & Company, I, Sterng. 2 (☎535 50 53; fax 50 53 16). Eclectic and intelligent. Great British magazine selection. Open M-Sa 9am-7pm. The **British Bookshop,** I, Weihburgg. 24 (☎512 19 45; fax 10 26), has an extensive travel section. Open M-F 9am-6:30pm, Sa 9:30am-5pm. New branch at VI, Mariahilferstr. 4. **Comic-Treff Steiner,** VI, Barnabiteng. 12 (☎586 76 27). One of Vienna's best comic book stores. Open M-F 10am-7pm, Sa 10am-2pm.

Radio: FM4, 103.8FM. Mixes classical, oldies, and mainstream music with news updates every hr. until 7pm in English, French, and German, including the BBC World Service. "What's on in Vienna" airs at 1pm. **Radio 03,** 99.9FM Pop and rock. **Energy,** 104.2FM, and **TheMusic,** 88.6FM, both play mainstream pop.

Bi-Gay-Lesbian Organizations: The bisexual, gay, and lesbian community in Vienna is more integrated than in other Austrian cities. The term gay refers strictly to men. For the gay goings-on about town, pick up the *Vienna Gay Guide* from the tourist office, the monthly Viennese magazine (in German) called *Extra Connect,* or the free monthly publication *Bussi* at any gay bar, cafe, or club. *Falter* newspaper lists gay events in a special heading. The following organizations also sponsor events and offer help in Vienna:

Rosa Lila Villa, VI, Linke Wienzeile 102 (gay men: ☎586 43 43; lesbians: ☎586 81 50), is a favored resource and social center for Viennese homosexuals and visitors to the city. Friendly staff speaks English and provides counseling, information, a library, and nightclub listings (see Nightlife, p. 130). Open M-F 5-8pm, gay info closed F.

Homosexuelle Initiative Wien (HOSI), II, Novarag. 40 (☎216 66 04; fax 585 41 59; www.hosi.at). Lesbian group and phone network F at 7pm. Prints a political newspaper, *Lambda Nachrichten.* Open Tu 7-10pm (includes phone counseling). Youth Th 5pm (coming out), 7-9pm (general).

Lesbischwul und Transgender Referat (☎588 01 58 90). Gay student counseling group. F 4-6pm.

Laundromat: Most hostels offer laundry service for €4. **Schnell und Sauber,** VII, Westbahnhofstr. 60 (☎524 64 60); From Westbahnhof, take tram #18 to "Urban-Loritzpl." 6kg wash €4.50, dry €1 per 20min. Soap included. Open 24hr. **Münz-wäscherei Karlberger & Co.,** III, Schlachthausg. 19 (☎798 81 91). 7kg wash €6.50, dry €1. Soap €1. Open M-F 7:30am-6:30pm, Sa 7:30am-1pm.

Public Showers and Toilets: At Westbahnhof, in Friseursalon Navratil downstairs from subway passage. Well maintained. 30min. shower €4, with soap and towel €5.60 (extra for either on Su). Showers are also available at **Jörgerbad,** XVII, Jörgerstr. 42-44, and at the airport. There are cheap pay toilets in most U-bahn stations and a special *Jugendstil* toilet in Graben (9am-7pm, requires coins).

Snow Reports: In German for Vienna, Lower Austria, and Styria ☎15 83; for Salzburg, Upper Austria, and Carinthia ☎15 84; for Tyrol and Voralberg ☎15 85.

EMERGENCY AND COMMUNICATION

Emergencies: Police, ☎133. **Ambulance,** ☎144. **Fire,** ☎122.

Poison Control: ☎406 43 43. Open 24hr.

Crisis Hotlines: All hotlines locate English speakers. **Rape Crisis Hotline:** ☎523 22 22. M 10am-6pm, Tu 2-6pm, W 10am-2pm, Th 5-9pm. **24hr. immediate help:** ☎717 19. **Psychological Counsel Hotline:** ☎319 3566 or 402 7838. M-F 8pm-8am, Sa-Su 24hr.

Medical Assistance: Allgemeines Krankenhaus, IX, Währinger Gürtel 18-20 (☎404 00 19 64). **Emergency care,** ☎141. **24hr. pharmacy,** ☎15 50. Consulates offer lists of English-speaking physicians, or call **Fachärzte Zugeck** (☎512 18 18; open 24hr.). Also **Wolfgang Molnar,** ☎330 34 68.

Internet Access: bigNET.internet.cafe, I, Karntnerstr. 61 (☎503 98 44); I, Hoher markt 8-9 (☎533 29 39); and the recently-opened largest Internet cafe in Austria, Mariahilfer-str. €3.50 per 30min. Hip English-speaking "crew." **Cafe Stein,** IX, Wahringerstr. 6-8 (☎31 97 24 19). €4 per 30min. **Cafe Einstein,** VIII, Rathauspl. 4 (☎405 26 26). M-F 7am-2am, Sa 10am-2am, Su 10am-midnight. **Libro,** XXII, Donauzentrum (☎202 52 55), provides free access at 6 terminals. Open M-F 7am-7pm, Sa 9am-5pm. **Jugend-Info des Bundesministeriums,** I, Franz-Josefs-Kai 51 (☎533 70 30). Free access at 2 PCs. Open M-F 11am-6pm.

Post Offices: Hauptpostamt, I, Fleischmarkt 19. Vast structure contains exchange, phone, fax, and mail services. Open 24hr. Address *Poste Restante* to "LASTNAME, First-name; *Postlagernde Briefe;* Hauptpostamt; Fleischmarkt 19; A-1010 Wien." Branches throughout the city and at the train stations; look for yellow signs with the trumpet logo. **Postal Codes:** 1st district A-1010, 2nd A-1020, 3rd A-1030, etc., to the 23rd A-1230.

⛏ ☎ ACCOMMODATIONS AND CAMPING

Hunting for cheap rooms in Vienna during peak tourist season (June-Sept.) can be unpleasant; write or call for reservations at least 5 days in advance. Otherwise, plan on calling from the train station between 6 and 9am to put your name down for a reservation. If there are no vacancies, ask to be put on a waiting list, and for suggestions. Those unable to find a hostel bed should consider a *Pension.* One-star establishments are usually adequate and are most common in districts VII, VIII, and IX. Singles start around €30, doubles around €40.

If you're staying a longer period of time, try **Odyssee Reisen und Mitwohnzentrale,** VIII, Laudong. 7. They find apartments for €17-25 per person per night. A week costs about €90, and a month starts at €150, but a 20% commission is charged on each month's rent. Bring your passport to register. (☎402 60 61. Open M-F 10am-2pm and 3-6pm.) **Arwag** offers similar services via the web (www.arwag.at) or their 24hr. hotline (☎79 70 01 18). Otherwise, visit either Österreichische Hochschüler-schaft at Rooseveltpl. 5 or the bulletin boards on the first floor of the Neues Insti-tut Gebäude (NIG building) on Universitätstr. 7 near the Votivkirche.

HOSTELS AND DORMITORIES

▧ **Hostel Ruthensteiner (HI),** XV, Robert-Hamerlingg. 24 (☎893 42 02; fax 27 96; info@hostelruthensteiner.com; www.hostelruthensteiner.com). Exit Westbahnhof at the main entrance and turn right onto Mariahilferstr. and continue until Haidmannsg. Turn left, then take the first right on Robert-Hammerlingg.; continue to the middle of the block. This top-notch hostel is an exceptional value and has extremely knowledgeable, English-speaking staff, spotless rooms, snack bar, sunny, rose-filled courtyard, and a down-home feel. Breakfast €2.50. Showers and sheets (except for 10-bed rooms) included. Lockers included and kitchen available. **Internet** €2. 4-night max. stay. Reception 24hr. Reservations recommended, but owners often hold beds for spontane-ous travelers. "The Outback" summer dorm €10.50; 3- to 10-bed dorms €12-13.50; singles and doubles from €20-22. AmEx/MC/V. ❷

Wombats City Hostel, XIV, Grang. 6 (☎897 23 36; fax 25 77; www.wombats.at). From Westbahnhof, take the main exit and turn right onto Mariahilferstr. Continue until 152 (corner Rosinag.). Turn right onto Rosinag. and continue until Grang. (2nd left). While right next to the train tracks and near a number of auto-body shops, this superb modern

hostel compensates with a pub (8am-2am; bar closes at 11pm) and various perks, including movie screenings. New renovations of beautiful loft-like rooms with views of surrounding Vienna complete the scene. Breakfast €3. Shower in room. Laundry €4.50. **Internet** €1 for 12 min. Bike or in-line skate rental €8 per day. 2-, 4-, and 6-bed rooms €14-36 per person. ❷

Westend City Hostel, VI, Fugerg. 3 (☎597 67 29; fax 597 672 927; westendcityhostel@aon.at; www.westendcityhostel.at). Located right near Westbahnhof. Exit Mariahilferstr. and cross the large intersection, make a right on Mullerg. and a left on Fugerg. Look for the bright purple exterior. This new, large hostel lacks community flavor but has comfortable beds and an ideal location. **Internet** €2.60 per 30min. Laundry €5.50. Breakfast and sheets included. Reception 24hr. Check-out 10:30am. Curfew 11:30pm. 12-bed dorms €15; 8-10 bed €16; 4-6 bed €17; singles €35; doubles €38. ❷

Believe It Or Not, VII, Myrtheng. 10, Apt. #14 (☎526 46 58). From Westbahnhof, take U6 (dir.: Floridsdorf) to "Burgg./Stadthalle," then bus #48A (dir.: Ring) to "Neubaug." Walk back on Burgg. 1 block and take the first right on Myrtheng. Ring the bell. A converted apartment on the second floor, this sociable hostel has a kitchen and 2 coed bunkrooms. Reception 8am until early afternoon—call early. Lockout 10:30am-12:30pm. Reservations recommended. €12 per person; Nov.-Easter €8. ❷

Myrthengasse (HI), VII, Myrtheng. 7, across the street from Believe It or Not, and **Neustiftgasse (HI)**, VII, Neustiftg. 85 (☎523 63 16; fax 58 49; hostel@chello.at). These simple, modern hostels, under the same management, are a 20min. walk from the Innenstadt. Breakfast and sheets included. Lunch or dinner €5. Locks €3.65. Laundry €3.50. **Internet** access €4.36 per 30min. Reception at Myrtheng. 24hr. Lockout 9am-2pm. Rooms separated by sex (except for families). Curfew 1am. Reservations recommended; arrive by 4pm. 5-day max. stay. Jan. 7-Mar. 17 and Nov. 11-Dec. 22, 4- to 6-bed dorms with shower €14; 2-bed dorms with shower €16. Rest of the year €15, €17. Non-members add €3.50. AmEx/MC/V. ❷

Hostel Panda, VII, Kaiserstr. 77, 3rd fl. (☎522 53 53). From Westbahnhof take U6 (dir.: Floridsdorf.) to "Burg/Stadthalle." Take second left on Kaiserstrab. From Sudbahnhof, take tram #18 to "Westbahnhof," and follow directions from Westbahnhof. Housed in an old-fashioned, semi-Jugendstil Austrian apartment building, this eclectic hostel has 18 mattresses packed into 2 coed dorms with high ceilings and Chinese lanterns. While cramped, the rooms have access to kitchen and TV. Bring lock for lockers. Dorms €12.50; Nov.-Easter €9. €3.50 surcharge for 1-night stays. ❷

Kolpinghaus Wien-Meidling, XIII, Bendlg. 10-12 (☎813 54 87; fax 812 21 30; www.kolpinghaus-wien.at). Take U6 to "Niederhofstr." Head right on Niederhofstr. and take the 4th right onto Bendlg. This well-lit, institutional hostel has 202 beds and is close to the U-bahn. Breakfast €3.80. Showers in all rooms, bathtubs in some. Sheets included. Reception 24hr. Check-out 9am. 8- and 10-bed dorms €11.30; 4- and 6-bed dorms €13.35-14.50. AmEx/MC/V. ❷

Jugendgästehaus Wien Brigittenau (HI), XX, Friedrich-Engels-Pl. 24 (☎332 82 94 or 330 05 98; fax 330 83 79; oejhv-wien-jgh-brigiltneu@oejhv.or.at). 25min. from city center. Take U1 or U4 to "Schwedenpl.," then tram N to "Floridsdorferbrücke/Friedrich-Engels-Pl." Follow the signs. It's the green building behind the tram stop, across the street and to the left of the tracks. This roomy hostel with excellent facilities for the disabled is unfortunately far from the city center. Breakfast, lockers, and sheets included. Lunch and dinner €5. **Free Internet** access. 5-night max. stay. Reception 24hr. Lockout 9am-1pm. Reservations recommended. 24-bed dorms (men only) €12.15; 4-bed dorms €13; doubles with bath €30-34. Non-members add €3.50. ❷

Turmherberge Don Bosco (HI), III, Lechnerstr. 12 (☎713 14 94). Take U3 to "Kardinal-Nagl-Pl.," then take the Kardinal-Nagl-Pl. exit facing the park. Walk to the other side of the park and turn right on Erdbergstr. Lechnerstr. is the 2nd left. The cheapest beds in

town, in a former bell tower (ca.1950s). Single-sex 6- to 8-bed rooms. Stove in common room. Curfew 11:45pm. Open Mar.-Nov. €6. ❶

Jugendgästehaus Hütteldorf-Hacking (HI), XIII, Schloßbergg. 8 (☎877 02 63; fax 87 70 26 32). From Karlspl., take U4 to "Hütteldorf," take the Hadikg. exit, cross the footbridge, and follow signs to the hostel (10min.). Or take bus #53B from the side of the footbridge opposite the station to the hostel. From Westbahnhof, take S50 to "Hütteldorf." This secluded hostel has great views and is popular with school groups. Breakfast included. Lunch and dinner €5.45 each. Free luggage storage. Keycard €1.82. Reception 7am-11:45pm. Lockout 9:30am-3:30pm. Curfew 11:45pm. Discounts for groups of 18 or more. 6- and 8-bed rooms, and one 22-bed room, €13.50. Add €2.50 per person for 4-bed rooms or €5 for doubles. Non-members add €3.50. MC/V. ❷

HOTELS AND PENSIONS

Check the hostels section for good singles deals as well. The prices are higher here, but you pay for convenient reception hours, no curfews, and no lockouts.

Lauria Apartments, VII, Kaiserstr. 77, Apt. #8 (☎522 25 55). From Westbahnhof, take tram #5 to "Burgg." Find solace among backpackers of all sorts. Fully equipped kitchens. Sheets and TV included. 2-night min. Reception 8am-noon. Dorms €12.50; singles and student-bunk twins €35; doubles €40, with shower €60; student-bunk triples €45; triples €75-120. AmEx/MC/V, except for dorm beds. ❷

Pension Kraml, VI, Brauerg. 5 (☎587 85 88; fax 586 75 73). Take U3 to "Zieierg.," exit onto Otto-Bauerg., take the 1st left, then 1st right. From Südbahnhof, take bus #13A to Esterhazyg. and walk up Brauerg. Near the Innenstadt and the Naschmarkt, Kraml has large airy rooms, a lounge, cable TV, and kind staff. Breakfast buffet €3. 38 beds. Singles €26; doubles €43, with shower or bath €55; triples €65, with shower €70. Apartment with bath €100-115 for 3-5 people. MC/V. ❸

Pension Hargita, VII, Andreasg. (☎526 19 28; fax 04 92). Take U3 to "Zieglerg." and take Andreasg. exit. This quiet *Pension* offers amicable service at a great location. Breakfast €3. Reception 8am-10pm. Singles €31, with shower €50; doubles €43, with shower €52, with bath €53-60. ❹

Pension Reimer, IV, Kircheng. 18 (☎523 61 62; fax 524 37 82; pension.reimer@aon.at), is centrally located and has huge, comfortable rooms that are cleaned continually. Breakfast included. Singles €38, in winter €31. Doubles €56, with bath €64; in winter €25, €30. MC/V for long stays only. ❹

Pension Falstaff, IX, Müllnerg. 5 (☎317 91 27; fax 31 79 18 64). Take U4 to "Roßauer Lände." Cross Roßauer Lände, head down Grünentorg., and take the 3rd left onto Müllnerg. Breakfast included. Reception 7:30am-9pm. Singles €33, with shower €40; doubles €51-66. Reduced rate for stays of 1 week or more in off-season. MC/V. ❹

Pension Wild, VIII, Langeg. 10 (☎406 51 74; fax 402 21 68; info@Pension-wild.com). Take U2 to "Lerchenfelderstr." and take the 1st right onto Langeg. Calls itself "Vienna's only gay hotel," and boasts a gay sauna in the basement. Rooms are rather expensive, but a friendly, English-speaking staff and bright decorations make up for it. Breakfast and shower included. Kitchen access. Reception 6am-10pm. Reservations recommended. 35 beds. Singles €35-64; doubles €45-85; triples €75-100. AmEx/MC/V. ❹

Hotel Zur Wiener Staatsoper, I, Krugerstr. 11 (☎513 12 74 75; fax 12 74 15; office@zurwienerstaatsoper.at; www.zurwienerstaatsoper.at). From Karlspl., exit Oper and follow Kartnerstr. towards the city center. Turn right on Krugerstr. Behind the world-famous Wiener Staatsoper, this hotel offers simple elegance and a prime location in the Inner Ring. Singles with shower €76-88; doubles with shower €109-124; triples with shower €131-146. All prices include breakfast buffet. AmEx/MC/V. ❺

Hotel Am Stephansplatz, I, Stephanspl. 9 (☎53 4050; fax 405 710; office@hotelam-stephansplatz.at.; www.hotelsmstephansplatz.at). Take U3 to "Stephansplatz." Located maximally close to the St. Stephan's cathedral, this comfortable and elegant hotel has central Vienna right outside. On the inside, classy chestnut wood is complimented by oriental rugs and colorful splendor. Breakfast buffet included. Single with bath €105-140; double with bath €130-210. Extra person €35. AmEx/MC/V. ❺

Hotel Imperial, I, Karntner Ring 16 (☎501 10 0; fax 10 0410; Hotel.Imperial@luxurycollection.com; www.luxurycollection.com/imperial). This extravagant hotel has only the finest rooms and the most expensive prices in Vienna. Located right downtown, it has everything from a breathtaking exterior and interior to all the luxury amenities you can imagine. Classic-Royal suites €425-465. ❺

UNIVERSITY DORMITORIES

From July through September, many university dorms become hotels, usually with singles, doubles, and a few triples and quads. Rooms don't have much in the way of character, but showers and sheets are standard, and their cleanliness and relatively low cost suffice for most budget travelers.

Porzellaneum der Wiener Universität, IX, Porzellang. 30 (☎317 72 82; fax 72 82; www.neuhotels.com). From Südbahnhof, take tram D (dir.: Nußdorf) to "Fürsteng." From Westbahnhof, take tram #5 to "Franz-Josefs Bahnhof," then tram D (dir.: Südbahnhof) to "Fürsteng." Great location in the student district. No lockers. Reception 24hr. Call ahead. Singles €16-18; doubles €30-35; quads €56-64. ❸

Studentenwohnheim der Hochschule für Musik, I, Johannesg. 8 (☎514 84; fax 84 49). Three blocks down Kärnterstr. away from Stephansdom and left onto Johannesg. Unbeatable location and cheap meals. Breakfast included. Reception 24hr. Discount for groups larger than 20. Reserve well in advance. Singles €33-36; doubles 58-70; triples €66; quads €80; quints €100. Apartment (includes 2 double rooms, bathroom, kitchen, living room) €28.50 per person; entire apartment €90. ❸

Katholisches Studentenhaus, XIX, Peter-Jordanstr. 29 (☎369 55 85; fax 55 85 12). From Westbahnhof, take U6 (dir.: Heiligenstadt) to "Nußdorferstr.," then bus #35A or tram #38 to "Hardtg." and turn left. From Südbahnhof, take tram D to "Schottentor," then tram #38 to "Hardtg." Enjoy the calm setting of district XIX. Reception closes at 10pm. Free **Internet** access. Call ahead. Close to Fischerbrau (see p. 101). Singles €18; doubles €30. Discounts for more than 1 month stays. ❸

CAMPING

Wien-West, Hüttelbergstr. 80 (☎914 23 14; fax 911 35 94). Take U4 to "Hütteldorf," then bus #14B or 152 (dir.: Campingpl.) to "Wien West." This convenient campground, 8km from the city center, is crowded but grassy and pleasant. Laundry, grocery stores, wheelchair access, and cooking facilities. Reception 7:30am-9:30pm. Closed Feb. €6 per person in July-Aug., €5 rest of the year; ages 4-15 €3, tent €3, camper €5. July-Aug. 2- and 4-person cabins available for €18 and €30-32. Electricity €3. ❶

Aktiv Camping Neue Donau, XXII, Am Kleehäufel 119 (☎/fax 202 40 10, www.wien-camping.at), is 4km from the city center and adjacent to Neue Donau beaches. Take U1 to "Kaisermühlen" then bus #91a to "Kleehäufel." Laundry, supermarket, wheelchair access, and kitchen. Open May 14-Sept. 10. July-Aug. 7 €5.50, children €3; May, June, and Sept. €3.50/€3. Camper €5, tent €3. Electricity €3. Showers included. ❶

Campingplatz Schloß Laxenburg (☎02236 713 33; fax 739 66; www.wiencamping.at), at Münchendorfer Str., Laxenburg, is 15km from Vienna, but popular and near the Gumpoldskirchen vineyards. Restaurant, boat rental, heated pool, kiddie pool, and supermarket. €6 per person, ages 4-15 €3, tents €3, caravans €5. Electricity €3. ❶

☐ FOOD

"Here the people think only of sensual gratifications."
—Washington Irving, 1822

For the Viennese, food is not mere fuel for the body; it is an aesthetic, even philosophical, experience that begins when you wish someone *"Mahlzeit"* and ends with one of Vienna's renowned pastries or sublime chocolates—unbelievably rich, and priced for patrons who are likewise blessed. Unless you buy your sin wholesale at a local bakery, *Sacher Torte, Imperial Torte,* and even *Apfelstrudel* can cost up to €5.

Vienna's restaurants are as varied as its cuisine. *Gästehäuser, Imbiße* (food stands), and *Beisln* (small taverns or restaurants) serve inexpensive meals that stick to your ribs and are best washed down with copious amounts of beer. *Würstelstände,* found on almost every corner, provide a quick, cheap lunch (a sausage runs €2.20 or so). The restaurants downtown near **Graben** and **Kärntnerstraße** are generally expensive—a cheaper bet is the neighborhood north of the university and near the *Votivkirche* (take U2 to "Schottentor"), where **Universitätsstraße** and **Währingerstraße** meet. Cafes with cheap meals also line **Burggasse** in district VI. The area radiating from the **Rechte** and **Linke Wienzeile** near Naschmarkt (take U4 to "Kettenbrückeg.") houses a range of cheap restaurants, and the **Naschmarkt** itself contains open-air stands where you can purchase fresh fruits and vegetables, bread, and a variety of ethnic food to sample while shopping at Vienna's premier flea market (weekends only; see p. 117).

At Christmas time, **Christkindlmarkt** offers hot food and spiked punch amid vendors of Christmas charms, ornaments, and candles. From late June through July, the film festival, **Festwochen,** brings international foodstuffs to the stands set up behind the seats (stands open 11am-11pm). The open-air **Brunnenmarkt** (take U6 to "Josefstädterstr." then walk up Veronikag. 1 block and turn right) is cheap and cheerful. *Bäckereien* (bakeries) are everywhere (common chains include **Anker** and **Der Mann**). To join the legions of Viennese combatting the summer heat, look around for gelato shops that sit at almost every corner (see **Austrian Gelato** p. 101).

As for grocery stores, the lowest prices are on the shelves of **Zielpunkt, Hofer,** and **Spar.** More pricey chains include **Ledi, Mondo,** and **Renner.** Kosher groceries are available at **Kosher Supermarket,** II, Hollandstr. 10 (☎ 216 96 75).

 Most places close earlier on Saturday afternoons and all day Sunday. In general, restaurants stop serving after 11pm.

RESTAURANTS

INSIDE THE RING

- **DO&CO,** I, Stephanspl. 12 (☎ 535 39 69). Set above the Stephanspl. cathedral, this modern gourmet restaurant offers both traditional Austrian as well as other international specialties like Thai noodles and Uruguay beef (main course €18.50-21.50). Prices are high, but so is the quality and location. Reservations recommended. Open daily noon-3pm and 6-midnight. ❺

- **Smutny,** I, Elisabethstr. 8 (☎ 587 13 56; www.smutny.com). Exit Karlspl. on Elizabethstr. and it is directly on the right. A delicious traditional Austrian restaurant offering schnitzel and gulasch with a green-tiled, modern feel. Try the *Menü* (€7; veggie €6.50). ❸

- **Trzesniewski,** I, Dorotheerg. 1 (☎ 512 32 91; fax 513 95 65), 3 blocks down the Graben from the Stephansdom. A famous stand-up restaurant, this unpronounceable establishment has been serving petite open-faced sandwiches for over 80 years. A filling lunch—

6 sandwiches and a mini-beer—costs about €5. Favorite toppings include salmon, onion, paprika, and egg. Open M-F 8:30am-7:30pm, Sa 9am-5pm. **Branches** at VI, Mariahilferstr. 95 (☎596 42 91); and III, Hauptstr. 97 (☎712 99 64) in Galleria. ❷

Levante, I, Wallnerstr. 2 (☎533 23 26; fax 535 54 85; www.levante.at). Walk down Graben away from the Stephansdom, turn left onto Kohlmarkt, and right onto Wallnerstr. This Greek-Turkish franchise features street-side dining with generic fare and some vegetarian dishes. Entrees €7-12, sandwiches €3.60. **Branches** at I, Wollzeilestr. 19 (off Rotenturm, take U3 or U1 to "Stephanspl."); Mariahilferstr. 88a; and VIII, Josefstädterstr. 14 (take U2 to "Rathaus"). All open 11:00am-11:00pm. ❷

Margaritaville, I, Bartensteing. 3 (☎405 47 86). Take U2 to "Lerchenfelderstr." exit onto Museumstr. and cut across the triangular green to Bartensteing. Offers authentic Tex-Mex food among Spanish speakers. Entrees €8-20. Open M-F 4pm-midnight, Sa-Su 11am-midnight and Su 4pm-midnight. MC/V. ❸

Korso, I, Mahlerstr. 2 (☎ 515 16 546). Upon entering this restaurant, you will find yourself overcome with gold and crystal opulence—as if you had been dropped directly into Rococo Vienna. The food mirrors the surroundings—classic Viennese cuisine from schnitzel to gulasch (€25-33). Open daily 12-3pm and 7pm-1am. ❹

Yugetsu Saryo, I, Fuhrichg. 10 (☎ 512 84 70). This place caters to your raw fish needs. At the sushi bar, have a complete lunch (€23-35) or sample individual sushi items (€3.60-5.40). Upstairs, full menu of Japanese cuisine €30-63. Open noon-2:30pm and 6-11pm daily. ❹

Wrenkh, I, Bauernmarkt 10 (☎ 533 15 26). This strictly vegetarian mid-priced restaurant offers deliciously creative cuisine in a relaxed and upscale atmosphere. Main courses from vegetable stews to spinach gnocchi (€7-12). Try the fresh squeezed juices to complement your meal (€3). Open daily 11:30am-11pm. ❷

Maschu Maschu, I, Rabensteig 8 (☎533 29 04). In Bermuda Dreiecke. This hole-in-the-wall-in-a-good-way serves filling and cheap Middle Eastern falafel and schwarma (each €4.10), outdoors in summer. Open M-W 11:30am-12am, Th-Sa 11:30am-3am. ❶

Bizi Pizza, I, Rotenturmstr. 4 (☎513 37 05). One block up Rotenturmstr. from Stephanspl. The best deal in the city center, Bizi will whip up fresh food cafeteria-style for a pittance. Pasta €5.23-6, whole pizza €4.15-5.70, salad bar €2.83-5.01. Open daily 10am-11:30pm. **Branches** with same hours at I, Franz-Josefs-Kai 21 (☎535 79 13), Mariahilferstr. 22-24 (☎523 16 58), and X, Favoritenstr. 105 (☎600 50 10). ❷

La Crêperie, I, Grünangerg. 10 (☎512 56 87; www.lacreperie.at), off Singerstr. near Stephanspl. The sensual decor of this restaurant complements the scrumptious crepes, both sweet and savory (€3.49-18.17). Try the *Himbeer* (raspberry) soda. Open M-Th 11:30am-midnight, F-Su 11am-midnight. AmEx/MC/V. ❷

Inigo, I, Bäckerstr. 18 (☎512 74 51). This popular dining spot, across from Vienna's Jesuit church, was founded by a Jesuit priest as part of a socio-economic reintegration program. It provides employment, training, and social work for 17 people who are long-term unemployed. Menu includes eclectic international dishes, many whole wheat and vegetarian options, and a salad bar. Entrees €5-10, salad €3-7. Open M-Su 8:30am-11:30pm. July-Aug. closed Sa-Su. MC/V. ❷

Zimolo, I, Ballg. 5 (☎513 17 54; fax 99 78), near Stephanspl. off Weihburgg. This charming cafe has candlelit tables and friendly staff. Opera music soothes the ears and accompanies Italian dishes with an Austrian touch. Meals average €8-18. Open M-Sa 11:30am-2:30pm and 6:30pm-midnight. V. ❸

Rosenberger Markt, I, Mayserderg. 2 (☎512 34 58), off Kärntnerstr. This subterranean buffet offers a gargantuan selection of salad, fruit salad, waffle, antipasto, potato, and pasta bars. You pay by the size of your plate, not by weight, so pile high. Salads €2.40-5.80, waffles €4, vegetable dishes €1.80-5.80. Open 11am-11pm. AmEx/MC/V. ❶

OUTSIDE THE RING

🔲 **Centimeter,** IX, Liechtensteinstr. 42 (☎319 84 04). Take tram D to "Bauernfeldpl." This chain offers huge portions of greasy Austrian fare and an unbelievable beer selection. Pay by the centimeter. Schnitzel with salad and fries €5.80. *Maß* (1L) €6. Meter (8.33L beers) €17.60. Other **branches** at VIII, Lenaug. 11 (☎405 78 08), and VII, Stiftg. 4 (☎524 33 29). Open M-F 10am-2am, Sa 11am-2am, Su 11am-12am. AmEx/MC/V. ❷

Elsäßer Bistro, IX, Währingerstr. 32 (☎319 76 89; elaesser.bistro@aon.at). U2 to "Schottentor." In the palace that houses the French Cultural Institute—walk into the garden and follow your nose for an extravagant meal. Wonderful food, with prices hovering around €14, and beautiful French wines. Open M-F 11:30am-3pm and 6:30-11pm. Kitchen closes 1hr. earlier. ❸

Café Nil, VII, Siebensterng. 39 (☎526 61 65). Take tram #49 from the Volksgarten to Siebensterng. to reach this low-key Middle Eastern cafe. Enjoy pork-free and many vegetarian dishes with tortured writers and philosophers (€6.20-11.20). Breakfast until 3pm. Open daily 10am-midnight. ❷

OH Pot, OH Pot, IX, Währingerstr. 22 (☎319 42 59). Take U2 to "Schottentor." This adorable joint serves amazingly good fusion fare. Try one of their filling namesake "pots" (€7.80-8.60), stew-like concoctions in veggie and meat varieties (try the leek soup). Terrific *empanadas* (€5.20). Open M-F, Su 11:30am-12pm, Sa noon-midnight. AmEx/MC/V. ❷

Blue Box, VII, Richterg. 8 (☎523 26 82). Take U3 to "Neubaug.," turn onto Neubaug., and take your 1st left onto Richterg. Blue Box leads a double life, restaurant by day, club by night, as indicated by the decor—an orange-filtered chandelier, black leather couches, and a distinct lack of light. Dishes are fresh and original. DJs spin the latest trance and trip-hop. A great place to come for a late (or really late) breakfast (until 5pm). Choose from Viennese, French, or vegetarian cuisine. Entrees €3.50-7.10. Open M 6pm-2am, Tu, Su 10am-2am. V. ❷

Zum Mogulhof, VII, Burgg. 12 (☎526 28 64). Ample portions of delicious Indian food served by candlelight amidst crimson carpets and velvet wallpaper—indulgence that won't strain your wallet. Vegetarian and meat dishes average €8-12. Open daily 11:30am-2:30pm and 6-11:30pm. AmEx/MC/V. ❸

Fischerbräu, XIX, Billrothstr. 17 (☎369 59 41). Take U6 to "Nußdorfer Str.," follow the exit sign to Wahringer Gurtel. Continue until you reach Döblinger Hauptpt. and take a left, then left again onto Billrothstr. Popular spot for young locals. The leafy courtyard and music create pleasant ambiance for home-brewed beer (large €3-5), delicious veal sausage (€4.65), and chicken salad (€6.54). Open M-F 4pm-1am, Sa-Su 11am-1am. Blues brunch Sa noon-3pm. Jazz brunch Su noon-3pm. ❷

Amerlingbeisl, VII, Stiftg. 8 (☎526 16 60). Take U3 to "Neubaug." and take the "Stiftg." exit. After a couple of blocks on Stiftg. enter courtyard covered with grape vines. Occasional live music. Entrees (including vegetarian offerings) average €6-8, late breakfast (until 3pm) €4-9.50. Open daily 9am-2am (hot food served until 1am). ❷

SWEET TOOTH IN THE CITY
In a city of schnitzel, wurst, and strudel, it's surprising that Italian gelato would find such a popular home. Unbeknownst to many travelers, Vienna is teeming with gelato parlors offering this distinctive, mouth-watering ice cream. Look for an "Eis" shop on practically ever corner, with flavors as exotic and delicious as marscapone and mango or the more traditional chocolate (small cone €1.50; large €5). Try **Eis Garda,** XII, Mariahilferstr. (☎892 34 30), for artistic sundaes and some of the best cones in Vienna. Open 9:30am-11:30pm.

Stomach, IX, Seeg. 26 (☎310 20 99). Take tram D to "Seeg." This sophisticated establishment features first-rate Austrian cooking with a Styrian kick (entrees average €14). Eat your meal inside or outside in a lovely courtyard. 20-something crowd. Open W-Sa 4pm-midnight, Su 10am-10pm. Reservations recommended. ❹

Hunger Künstler, VI, Gumpendorferstr. 48 (☎587 92 10). Take U3 to "Neubaug." for a quiet, candlelit restaurant with outstanding food. Try the Spinatstrudel (spinach quiche with yogurt sauce). Entrees average €8. Open Su-Sa 11am-2am. AmEx/MC/V. ❷

Café Willendorf, VI, Linke Wienzeile 102 (☎587 17 89). Take U4 to "Pilgramg." and look for the big pink building which also houses the Rosa Lila Villa, Vienna's gay and lesbian center. This cafe, bar, and restaurant with a leafy outdoor terrace serves creative vegetarian fare costing between €7.20-8, meat dishes €7.50-12. *Menü* €18.20. Relaxed atmosphere. Open 6pm-2am; meals until midnight. ❸

Vegetasia, III, Ungarg. 57 (☎713 83 32). Take the O tram to "Neulingg." A vegetarian nirvana, this cozy Taiwanese vegetarian restaurant offers tofu, *seitan,* and soy delights artfully disguised as beef, chicken, and fish. Lunch buffet M-Sa €6.50. Open 11:30am-3pm and 5:30-11:30pm. Closed Tu evenings. AmEx/MC/V. ❷

University Mensa, IX, Universitätsstr. 7 (☎42 77 29, ext. 841), on the 7th floor of the university building, between U2 stops "Rathaus" and "Schottentor." Visitors can ride the old-fashioned *Pater Noster* elevator (no doors and it never stops; you have to jump in and out, so say your prayers) to the 6th floor and take the stairs up. Typical cafeteria meals €3.85. Open M-F 11am-2pm. Closed July-Aug. but snack bar open 8am-3pm. ❶

Other inexpensive student cafeterias include **Afro-Asia Mensa,** IX, Türkenstr. 3, near Schottentor (open M-F 11:30am-2:30pm); **Vienna Technical University,** IV, Wiedner Hauptstr. 8-10 (☎586 65 02; open M-F 1pm-5:30pm); **Economics University,** IX, Augasse 2-6 (☎310 57 18; open M-Th 7:30am-7:30pm, F 7:30am-6:30pm; July-Aug. M-F 8am-3pm); or **Catholic University Students' Community,** I, Ebendorferstr. 8 (☎408 35 85; open M-F 11:30am-2pm).

☕ COFFEEHOUSES AND KONDITOREIEN

"Who's going to start a revolution? Herr Trotsky from Café Central?"
—Austrian general quoted on the eve of the Russian Revolution

In Vienna, the coffeehouse is not simply the place to resolve your midday caffeine deficit. For years these establishments were havens artists, writers, and thinkers who flocked to the brooding interiors to exchange ideas and jabs at each other's work. Surrounded with dark wood and dusty velvet, they drank coffee, and stayed into the night composing operettas, writing books, and shaping modern thought. The bourgeoisie followed suit, and the coffeehouse became the city's living room, giving rise to a grand coffeehouse culture. Peter Altenberg, "the café writer," scrib-

---

ONE MORE CUP OF COFFEE... Here is a quick reference guide to some of the most tempting Viennese coffees:

Melange: espresso-like coffee with hot milk, optional whipped cream or cinnamon
Mokka: strong black coffee, much like espresso
Kapuziner: small *Mokka* with cream, sprinkled with cocoa, chocolate, or cinnamon
Verlängerte: weak coffee with cream
Fiaker: black coffee with rum
Pharisär: black coffee with rum, sugar, and whipped cream
Wiener Eiskaffee: chilled black coffee and vanilla ice cream, with whipped cream
Maria Theresia: black coffee with orange liqueur and whipped cream

bled lines, Oskar Kokoschka grumbled alone, and exiles Lenin and Trotsky played chess. Theodor Herzl made plans here for a Zionist Israel, and Kafka came to visit the Herrenhof. The original literary cafe was **Café Griensteidl**, but after it was demolished in 1897, the torch passed to **Café Central** and then to **Café Herrenhof**. Cafes still exist under all these names, but only Café Central looks like it used to; tourists visit it as if it were a museum.

The quintessential Viennese coffee is the *Melange*, and you can order every kind of coffee as a *Kleiner* (small) or *Grosser* (large), *Brauner* (brown, with a little milk) or *Schwarzer* (black). Whipped cream is *Schlag*; if you don't like it, say *"ohne Schlag, bitte."* Choosing your coffee in Vienna requires careful study (see **One More Cup Of Coffee...** p. 102). Decadent pastries complete the picture: *Apfelstrudl*, cheesecakes, tortes, *Buchteln* (warm cake with jam in the middle), *Palatschinken*, *Krapfen*, and *Mohr im Hemd* have all helped place Vienna on the culinary map. The *Konditoreien*, no less traditional, focus their attention on delectables rather than coffee. To see a menu, ask for a *Karte*.

INSIDE THE RING

⬕ Kleines Café, I, Franziskanerpl. 3. Turn off Kärtnerstr. onto Weihburg. and follow it to the Franziskanerkirche. This tiny, cozy cafe, designed by architect Hermann Czech, features green paneling, low, vaulted ceiling, art exhibits, nightclub posters, and tables spilling out into the courtyard. The salads are minor works of art, averaging €6.50. Open M-Sa 10am-2am, Su 1pm-2am.

⬕ Café Central, I (☎533 37 63 24), at the corner of Herreng. and Strauchg. inside Palais Fers. Café Central has surrendered to tourists because of its fame, but this mecca of the café world with arched ceilings and frescoes is definitely worth a visit. Oh, and they serve coffee, too, at elegant tables in a spectacular arcaded court. Occasional live music. Open M-Sa 8am-10pm, Su 10am-6pm. AmEx/MC/V.

⬕ Demel, I, Kohlmarkt 14 (☎535 17 17; ademel@demel.at), 5min. from the Stephansdom down Graben. The most luxurious Viennese *Konditorei*, Demel's was confectioner to the imperial court until the empire dissolved. All of the chocolate is made fresh every morning. A fantasy of mirrored rooms, cream walls, and a display case of legendary desserts. Waitresses in convent-black serve divine confections (€5) that every visit to Vienna should include. Don't miss the *crème-du-jour*. Open daily 10am-7pm. AmEx/MC/V.

Café MAK, I, Stubenring 3-5 (☎714 01 21), inside the Museum für Angewandte Kunst. Take tram #1 or 2 to "Stubenring." Light, bright, white, and very tight at

THE HIDDEN DEAL

STOP AND SMELL THE COFFEE

Three or four euros might seem like a lot for coffee, but it may seem more reasonable when you realize what's included. Sit back and relax in a trendily threadbare atmosphere or in a living, still-serving slice of history. Vienna in the 1890s faced a severe firewood shortage, leaving cafes as some of the only places where many people could enjoy relative comfort and warmth. Some even had their mail addressed to them at their habitual cafe. The literary landscape grew around steaming cups of *Melange* and good conversation.

Today, you probably should keep your own mailing address, but no one minds if you take root in a cafe for the afternoon. In fact, you're actually encouraged to stay and read newspapers. The strictest dictate of coffeehouse etiquette is that you linger. The waiter (known as *Herr Ober*) will serve you as soon as you sit down, then leave you to sip, brood, and read your *Let's Go*. Newspapers and magazines, many in English, are neatly racked for patrons. Most cafes also serve hot food, but don't order food and coffee together (except pastries), unless you want to be really gauche. When you are ready to leave, just ask to pay: "Zahlen bitte!"

night, this cafe feels like a museum display case, but the people are stunning and the furniture is funky Bauhaus. Peek through glass walls into the museum, or dine outside among sunflowers. The cafe gets rowdy with students after 10pm and hosts techno-rave parties on Sa in July. Open Tu-Su 10am-2am (hot food until midnight €8-15).

Café Hawelka, I, Dorotheerg. 6 (☎512 82 30), off Graben, 3 blocks down from the Stephansdom. Dusty wallpaper, dark wood, and old red-striped velvet sofas make Hawelka shabby and glorious. Josephine and Leopold Hawelka put this legendary cafe on the map in 1937—Leopold received an award from the Austrian government and Josephine a visit from Falco. *Buchteln* (fresh from the oven at 10pm) €2. *Melange* €2.80. Open M and W-Sa 8am-2am, Su and holidays 4pm-2am.

Café Alt Wien, I, Bäckerg. 9 (☎512 52 22), is a bohemian joint behind the Stephansdom. Red sofas and walls with concert posters set the mood. Open daily 10am-2am.

Café Prückel, I, Stubenring 24 (☎ 512 61 15). High-ceilinged and spacious, this artsy cafe has developed a noble slouch over time. Prückel hosts numerous readings and performances, and is patronized by art students from the Kunsthochschule (art institute) down the street. Open daily 9am-10pm, kitchen open 10am-9:30pm.

Café Bräunerhof, I, Stallburgg. 2 (☎512 38 93). A delightfully shabby cafe in a small alley near the Hofburg with an excellent selection of newspapers. You can order bread, *Käse* and *Schinken* (cheese and cold cuts), and Austrian salad (€5.60-10). *Melange* €2.80. Open M-F 7:30am-8:30pm, Sa 7:30am-6pm, Su 10am-6pm.

Café Museum, I, Operng. 7 (☎586 52 02), near the Opera. Head away from the *Innenstadt* to the corner of Operng. and Friedrichstr. Built in 1899 by Adolf Loos, in a plain, spacious style with striking curves, this cafe attracts a mixed bag of artists, lawyers, students, and chess players. Open 8am-midnight.

Hotel Sacher, I, Philharmonikerstr. 4 (☎514 560; wien@sacher.com; www.sacher.com). Behind the opera house. This historic site has served world-famous *Sacher Torte* (€4.30) in red velvet opulence for years. While it's still exceedingly elegant, casual clothing is fine—you won't be the only tourist there. Cafe open 11am-11:30pm; bakery open 9am-11:00pm. AmEx/MC/V. (Also see **Sights: Hotel Sacher,** p. 114.)

Café Griensteidl, I, Michaelerpl. 6 (☎535 26 93). Down the street from Café Central toward the Hofburg right in the heart of downtown. Vienna's first literary cafe tries hard to recover its roots, with bookshelves and a variety of international newspapers. Sample a wide array of ice cream such as *Griensteidl Eiszauber* (vanilla ice cream with walnuts, apricots, chocolate, and gingerbread spices; €4.72). Open daily 8am-11:30pm.

Hotel Imperial, I, Kärnter Ring 16 (☎501 10 31 89; fax 50 11 03 55). From the opera, turn left onto the Ring and walk 5min. This elegant, chandeliered cafe, with a lovely flower-hung courtyard, serves its own insignia-stamped, marzipan-filled *Imperial Torte* (€5) to wealthy tourists. Open daily 7am-11pm. AmEx/MC/V.

OUTSIDE THE RING

■ **Café Sperl,** VI, Gumpendorferstr. 11 (☎586 41 58). Take U2 to "Museumsquartier," exit to Mariahilferstr., walk 1 block on Getreidemarkt, and turn right onto Gumpendorferstr. Built in 1880, Sperl is one of Vienna's oldest and most beautiful cafes. Though renovations saw some original trappings removed, the *fin de siècle* atmosphere remains, complimented by modern billiards tables. Coffee €2-4.50; cake €2.54-3.85. Live music Sa after 3pm. Open M-Sa 7am-11pm, Su 11am-8pm; July-Aug. closed Su.

Café Stein, IX, Währingerstr. 6 (☎31 97 24 19; fax 97 24 12), near Schottentor., has chrome seats outside (allowing you to see and be seen) and clustered tables indoors in the smoky red-brown and metallic interior. Intimate, lively, and hip, at night it transforms into "Stein's Diner," when DJs appear. **Internet** access €3.50 per 30min. 5-11pm. Breakfast until 8pm. Open M-Sa 7am-1am, Su 9am-1am. **Stein's Diner** in the basement open M-Sa 7pm-1am.

Café Rüdigerhof, V, Hamburgerstr. 20 (☎586 31 38). Take U4 to "Kettenbrückeng.";
Hamburgerstr. branches off from Rechte Wienzeile. In a 1902 building designed by students of Otto Wagner, this *Jugendstil* cafe is adorned with floral patterns and leather
couches (a gift from King Hussein to the owner), with a large, leaf-covered garden outside. Traditional meat and fish dishes (€5.10-7.10). Delicious iced coffee €3.50. Open
daily 10am-2am; garden open for drinks until 1:45am.

Café Drechsler, VI, Linke Wienzeile 22 (☎587 85 80). From Karlspl., head down
Operng. and continue on Linke Wienzeile, or take U4 to "Kettenbrückeng." This is *the*
place to be the morning after. Early birds and night owls roost in this cafe over pungent
cups of *Mokka*. Great lunch menu (€4.70-7.50). Open M-F 3am-8pm, Sa 3am-6pm.

Café Savoy, VI, Linke Wienzeile 36 (☎786 73 48), is a scruffy cafe with dark wood and
decrepit gold trim. Check yourself out in the gigantic mirror as you step inside. A large
gay and lesbian crowd moves in to make this a lively nightspot on weekends. Open M-F
5pm-2am, Sa 9am-2am.

Kunsthaus Wien Café, III, Untere Weißgerberstr. 14 (☎712 04 97). In a courtyard filled
with hanging plants in Hundertwasser's Kunsthaus museum (see p. 119), the floor in
this cafe waves—literally. Be glad you're not a waiter here. Open daily 10am-midnight.

Berg das Café, IX, Bergg. 8 (☎319 57 20). Take U2 to "Schottentor" and take a right off
Währingerstr. onto Bergg. A casual hang-out by day and super-swank gay cafe/bar by
night, this place is always crowded. Wonderful food, desserts, and music in a relaxed
atmosphere make this place delightful. It recently merged with nearby gay and lesbian
bookstore **Das Löwenherz** (☎317 29 82), so you can browse during the day while you
drink your *Melange* (€2.40). Plenty of English titles. Open 10am-1am.

⬛ HEURIGEN (WINE TAVERNS)

Heurigen, marked by a hanging branch of evergreen at the door, sell new wine
and savory Austrian buffet-style delicacies. The wine, also called *Heuriger*, is
from the most recent harvest and has typically been grown and pressed by the
owner himself. Good *Heuriger* wine is generally white, fruity, and full of body.
Try *Grüner Veltliner* (white) or *Riesling* (red). *Heuriger* is ordered by the *Achtel* or the *Viertel* (eighth or quarter liter, respectively; about €2 per *Viertel*).
G'spritzer (wine and soda water, served separately, then mixed) is a popular way
of enjoying heuriger.

Half of the pleasure of visiting a *Heuriger*, however, comes from the atmosphere. Worn picnic benches and old shade trees provide an ideal spot to converse, or listen to *Schrammelmusik* (sentimental folk songs played by elderly
musicians who inhabit *Heurigen*). A *Heuriger* generally serves simple buffets
(grilled chicken and pork, cabbage or corn, pickles) that make for inexpensive
meals. Order your food inside and sit down outside; a waitress will come around
to serve the wine. Those looking for some traditional fare should order *Brattfett*
or *Liptauer*, a spicy soft paprika-flavored cheese for your homemade bread.

Heurigen cluster together in the northern, western, and southern Viennese suburbs, where the grapes grow. The *Heurigen* are open for the summer months—
stroll along the street and look for the evergreen branches—they indicate which
Heurigen are *ausg'steckt* (serving wine). The most famous region, **Grinzing**, in
district XIX, produces strong wine, perhaps to distract the touristy clientele from
the high prices. Those in Grinzing (incidentally Beethoven's favorite neighborhood) are unfortunately well known to tour bus operators. You'll find better atmosphere and prices among the hills of **Sievering**, **Neustift am Walde** (both in district
XIX), and **Neuwaldegg** (in XVII). Authentic, charming, and jolly *Heurigen* abound
on Hochstr. in **Perchtoldsdorf**, just southwest of the city. To reach Perchtoldsdorf,
take U4 to "Hietzing" and tram #6 to "Rodaun." Walk down Ketzerg. until Hochstr.

and continue for a few minutes to reach the *Heurigen* area. True *Heuriger* devotees should make the trip to **Gumpoldskirchen**, a celebrated vineyard village with bus and train connections to Vienna and Mödling, and on the S-bahn line from Südbahnhof. Most vineyard taverns are open from 4pm to midnight; a particularly good option for a Sunday afternoon when everything else is closed.

■ **Buschenschank Heinrich Niersche,** XIX, Strehlg. 21 (☎440 21 46). Take U6 to "Währingerstr./Volksoper" then tram #41 to "Pötzleing." or bus #41A to "Pötzleindorfer Höhe." Walk up Poltzleing. until it becomes Khevenhuller Str. and turn right onto Strehlg. On the left side street hidden from tourists in the backyard of a house, the beautiful garden overlooks the fields of Grinzing—an oasis of green grass, cheerful voices, and relaxation in a neighborhood atmosphere. *Weiße G'spritzter* (white wine spritzer) €1.45, 0.25L €1.89-2.03. Open W-M 3pm-midnight.

■ **Zum Krottenbach'l,** XIX, Krottenbachstr. 148 (☎440 12 40). Take U6 to "Nußdorferstr." then bus #35A (dir.: Salmannsdorf) to "Kleingartenverein/Hackenberg." With a terraced garden on this Untersievering, this *Heuriger* offers a comfortable spot for savoring the fruit of the vine in a very traditional atmosphere with everything (including the lights) made of gnarled wood. Larger but more touristy and family-oriented than Buschenshank. 0.25L about €2. Open daily 3pm-midnight.

Weingut Heuriger Reinprecht, XIX, Cobenzlg. 22 (☎32 01 47 10; reinprecht@grinzing.net). Take U4 to "Heiligenstadt" then bus #38A to "Grinzing." This place fits the stereotype on a larger scale, with endless picnic tables under an ivy-laden trellis, and *Schrammel* musicians strolling from table to table. Despite many tourists, don't be surprised to hear whole tables of Austrians break into song. There's quite a bottle opener collection near the entryway. In early June, try *Frische Erdbeerbowle*—a delectable mix of sparkling wine and strawberries (€2.20). Open Mar.-Nov. daily 3:30pm-midnight.

Weingut Helm, XXI, Stammersdorferstr. 121 (☎292 12 44). Take tram #31 from Schottenring to the last stop, turn right by the *Würstelstand*, then left. The family who owns and operates this establishment keeps it low-key and friendly. Enjoy the shady garden tables. Open Tu-Sa 3pm-midnight.

Franz Mayer am Pfarrplatz Beethovenhaus, XIX, Pfarrpl. 2 (☎370 12 87). Take U4 to "Heiligenstadt," then bus #38A to "Fernsprechamt/Heiligenstadt." Walk uphill and head right onto Nestelbachg. Beethoven used to stay here when it offered guest quarters. Festive patios with options for all from bustling noise to quite seclusioin. Touristy. Pricey food but reasonable drinks at €2.20 per 0.25L. Live music 7pm-midnight. Open M-F 4pm-midnight, Su and holidays 11am-midnight.

◎ SIGHTS

Vienna's streets are by turns startling, scuzzy, and grandiose. Expect contrasts around every corner: the expanse of the Ringstraße and the narrow confines of a cobblestone courtyard, the curling flourishes of a Baroque palace and the spare lines of Socialist public housing. Grab the brochure *Vienna from A to Z* (with Vienna Card discount €4; at the tourist office). Don't miss the **Hofburg, Schloß Schönbrunn, Schloß Belvedere,** or any of the buildings along the **Ringstraße.** Those ensnared by the flowing tendrils of *Jugendstil* architecture can find many examples of it in Vienna—ask the tourist office for the *Art Nouveau in Vienna* pamphlet, which contains photos and addresses of *Jugendstil* treasures all over town.

The range of available **tours** is overwhelming—walking tours, ship tours, bike tours, tram tours, and more. There are 42 themed walking tours alone, detailed in the brochure *Walks in Vienna* (free at the tourist office). Tours run about €11; some require admission fees to sites. All are worthwhile, but "Vienna in the Footsteps of *The Third Man*," which takes you into the sewers and the graffiti-covered catacomb world of the Wien River's underground canals, is one of the most unusual and exciting (bring your own flashlight). Tours on *fin de siècle* "old-timer" **trams** run May to October. (☎790 94 40 26. 1½hr. €15. Departs from Karlspl. near the Otto Wagner Pavilion Sa-Su 9:30, 11:30am, 1:30pm.) The drivers of legendary **Fiaker** (horse-drawn carriages) are happy to taxi you wherever your heart desires, but be sure to agree on the price before you set out (usually €30-35 per 20min.). There are official *Fiaker* stands in Stephanspl., Albertinapl., Heldenpl., and at the corner of Graben and Kohlmarkt. **Vienna-Bike,** IX, Wasag. (☎319 12 58), **rents bikes** (€5) and conducts 2-3hr. **cycling tours** (€20). **Bus tours** are given by **Vienna Sight-seeing Tours,** III, Stelzhamerg. 4/11 (☎712 46 83) and **Cityrama,** I, Börgeg. 1 (☎534 13). Tours start at €30. For a quick, do-it-yourself tour, take tram #1 or 2 around the Ring. For longer tours, walk by the grouped listings below.

INSIDE THE RING

District I, *die Innenstadt* or *innere Stadt* (Inner city), Vienna's social and geographical epicenter, is enclosed on three sides by the massive Ringstraße and on the northern side by the **Danube Canal.** With the mark of master architects on everything from palaces and theaters to tenements and toilet bowls, the *innere Stadt* is a gallery of the history of aesthetics, from Romanesque to *Jugendstil*.

V I E N N A

STEPHANSPLATZ

Take U1 or U3 to "Stephansplatz."

Right at the heart of Vienna, this square in the shadow of the massive **Stephansdom** teems with activity. It is a prime location for people-watching—suited professionals, political demonstrators, and camera-toting tourists all throng the square, while students in period costumes sell tickets to Strauss or Mozart concerts.

STEPHANSDOM. Affectionately known as "Der Steffl," Stephansdom (St. Stephen's Cathedral) is Vienna's most treasured symbol, fascinating viewers with its Gothic intensity and tapered **South Tower.** The **North Tower** was originally intended to be as high and graceful as the South, but construction ceased after a spooky tragedy (see **A Bad Pact with the Devil,** below). Take the elevator up the North Tower (open Apr.-June and Sept.-Oct. daily 8:30am-4pm; elevator ride €3.50) for a view of Vienna, or climb the 343 steps of the South Tower for a 360° view, and a close encounter with the gargoyles (open 9am-5:30pm, €2.50).

Important pieces inside include the early 14th-century Albertine choir and the Gothic organ loft by **Anton Pilgram,** so delicate that Pilgram's contemporaries warned him that it would never bear the organ's weight. Pilgram replied that he would hold it up himself and carved a self-portrait at the bottom, bearing the entire burden on his back. The **high altarpiece** of the Stoning of St. Stephen is just as stunning. (Cathedral tours M-Sa 10:30am, 3pm; Su and holidays 3pm. €3; in English at 3:45pm. Spectacular evening tour June-Sept. Sa 7pm; €14.)

A BAD PACT WITH THE DEVIL In the 16th century, during the construction of the North Tower of the Stephansdom, a young builder named Hans Puchsbaum wished to marry his master's daughter. The master, jealous of Hans's skill, agreed on one condition: Hans had to finish the entire North Tower on his own within a year. Faced with this impossible task, Hans despaired until a stranger offered to help him. The stranger required only that Hans abstain from saying the name of God or any other holy name. Hans agreed, and the tower grew by leaps and bounds. One day the young mason spotted his love in the midst of his labor, and called out her name, "Maria!" With this invocation of the Blessed Virgin, the scaffolding collapsed and Hans plummeted to his death. Rumors of a satanic pact spread, and work on the tower ceased, leaving it in its present condition.

Downstairs, skeletons of thousands of plague victims fill the **catacombs**. The lovely **Gruft** (vault) stores all of the Habsburg innards. (Tours M-Sa 10-11:30am and 1-4:30pm every 30 min.; Su and holidays 1:30, 4:30pm every 30 min. €3.) Everyone wanted a piece of the rulers—the Stephansdom got the entrails, the Augustinerkirche got the hearts, and the Kapuzinergruft (on Neuer Markt) got the remainder. High above it all hangs the **bell** of the Stephansdom, the world's heaviest free-ringing bell (the whole bell moves, not just the clapper). The original bell, cast in 1711 from the metal of captured Turkish cannons, was smashed during WWII, much to the grief of the Viennese. A series of photographs inside chronicles the process of reconstruction. The new bell has rung in the New Year since 1957.

HAAS HAUS. This controversial modern building, just opposite the cathedral at Stephanspl. 12, reflects the Stephansdom in its post-modern facade of glass and aluminum. The view is even better from inside the Haus, which has a restaurant on the top floor. Primarily a shopping center, the Haus, which opened in 1990 amid rumors of bureaucratic bribery, is considered something of an eyesore by most Viennese (much to the dismay of postmodern architect Hans Hollein).

NEAR PETERSPLATZ

From Stephanspl., take Graben 2 blocks from Stephansdom. Peterspl. is on the right.

This tiny square off Graben is home to the Peterskirche and a good landmark from which to explore the *Fußgängerzone* that spreads from the intersection of Graben and Kohlmarkt off the southwest corner of Peterskirche.

GRABEN. Now closed to all traffic except feet and hooves, this boulevard was once a moat surrounding the Roman camp that became Vienna. The landscape of Graben today shows the debris of Baroque, *Biedermeier*, and *Jugendstil* efforts, which include **Ankerhaus** (#10) and the red-marble **Grabenhof** by Otto Wagner. One of the most interesting (and interactive) sights is the underground *Jugendstil* public toilet complex, designed by Adolf Loos. The **Pestsäule** (Plague Column) in the square was built in 1693, in gratitude for the passing of the Black Death.

PETERSKIRCHE. Charlemagne founded the first version of this church in the 8th century. Town architects just couldn't resist tinkering with the structure: the Baroque ornamentation was completed in 1733, with Rottmayer on fresco duty.

KOHLMARKT. This second leg of the *Fußgängerzone* starts at the end of Graben, just past Peterskirche, and is home to upscale shops marked "K.U.K." (Kaiserlich und Königlich), indicating that they once earned the Habsburg seal of approval.

HOHER MARKT, RUPRECHTSPLATZ, MORZINPLATZ

From Stephanspl., walk down Rotenturmstr. and turn left onto Lichtenst., which runs into Hoher Markt. Or, take Milchg. out of Peterspl., turn right, and go about 3 blocks on Tuchlauben. Hoher Markt is on the right, just after the intersection with Wipplingerstr. Judeng. runs from Hoher Markt to Ruprechtspl. and Morzinpl.

These three squares lie just north of Peterspl. Hoher Markt is the oldest square in town, offering largely historical attractions, while Ruprechtspl. is home to Vienna's oldest church as well as a slew of cafes and bars in Vienna's hottest nightlife district, known as the **Bermuda Dreiecke** (see Nightlife, p. 130). Morzinpl. is a grassy plot along the Danube with a dark history of its own.

HOHER MARKT. Once both market and execution site, Hoher Markt was the heart of the Roman encampment, Vindobona. It boasts **Roman ruins** beneath the shopping arcade on its south side (open Tu-Su 9am-12:15pm and 1pm-4:40pm; €1.82, students €0.73). Fischer von Erlach's **Vermählungsbrunnen** (Marriage

AUSTRIAN GRAFFITI Scratched into the stones near the entrance of the Stephansdom is the mysterious abbreviation "O5." It's not a sign of hoodlums up to no good, but rather a reminder of a different kind of subversive activity. During WWII, "O5" was the secret symbol of Austria's resistance movement against the Nazis. The capital letter "O" and the number "5," for the fifth letter of the alphabet, form the first two letters of "Oesterreich"—meaning Austria. Recently the monogram has received new life. Every time alleged Nazi collaborator and ex-president of Austria Kurt Waldheim attends mass, the symbol is highlighted in chalk. Throughout the city, "O5" has also been appearing on the sides of buildings and on flyers, protesting Jörg Haider's Freedom Party and its anti-immigrant policies.

Fountain), depicting the union of Mary and Joseph, is now the square's centerpiece. The biggest draw, however, is the corporate-sponsored *Jugendstil* **Ankeruhr** (clock). Built in 1914 by Franz Matsch, the magnificent timepiece has twelve 3-m tall historical figures, ranging from Emperor Marcus Aurelius to Maria Theresia to Joseph Haydn, which rotate past the Viennese coat of arms, accompanied by music of their respective eras. (One figure every hr. At noon, all the figures appear.) Take a peek under the bridge to see depictions of Adam, Eve, an angel, and the Devil.

RUPRECHTSKIRCHE. Overlooking the Danube on Ruprechtspl., the Romanesque Ruprechtskirche is the oldest church in Vienna. The present church, dating from the 13th century, was built on the site of a Carolingian church of AD 740 and one of the gates of the Roman settlement. Maria Theresia donated the well-clad skeleton of an early Christian martyr that lives in a glass case in the corner.

STADTTEMPEL. Almost hidden away in Ruprechtspl. at Seitenstetteng. 2-4, the Stadttempel (City Temple) was built in 1826 following an imperial regulation that Jewish and Protestant places of worship should not have conspicuous street fronts. A sign of intolerance at the time, the regulation saved the synagogue from greater persecution. The *Stadttempel* was the only one of Vienna's 94 synagogues to escape Nazi destruction during *Kristallnacht* on November 9-10, 1938. The temple was spared because it stood on a residential block, concealed from the street. The torching of neighboring buildings damaged the synagogue, but it has been restored to its original *Biedermeier* elegance. Today, an armed guard patrols the synagogue as a precaution against repeats of a 1983 terrorist attack. (Bring your passport. Open Su-F. Free.)

MORZINPLATZ. This now quiet, residential square once held the Hotel Metropole, headquarters of the Gestapo, where numerous Viennese were tortured for speaking against the *Anschluß*. The hotel was demolished in 1945 and in its place stands **The Monument to the Victims of Fascism.**

NEAR JUDENPLATZ

From Stephanspl., walk down Graben. When Graben ends, go right and continue in the same direction on Bognerg. Turn right onto Seitzerg. and continue in the same direction on Kurrentg. Or, from Hoher Markt, walk down Wipplingerstr. and turn left onto Jordang.

Judenpl. was the site of the city's first Jewish ghetto, established in the Middle Ages. Wipplingerstr., which runs east-west along this pretty square's north side, offers a number of architectural sights.

JUDENPLATZ. The focal point of the square is Rachel Whiteread's **Memorial to the Victims of the Holocaust,** a giant inverted library made of concrete that was unveiled in 2000. For more on the memorial, see **The Failure of Memory,** p. 69.)

VIENNA

Also in the square is a statue of Jewish playwright Gotthold Ephraim Lessing (1729-81). Originally erected in 1935, the statue was torn down by the Nazis; a new model was returned to the spot in 1982. The square has an outdoor exhibit about the *Stadttempel* (see **Ruprechtsplatz,** above) and viewable excavations of a synagogue built in 1294 and burned down in 1421. House #2, **Zum grossen Jordan,** bears a 16th-century relief and inscription commemorating this medieval purge of Vienna's Jews.

MARIA AM GESTADE. A short stroll down Schwertg., right off Wipplingerstr., passing Judenpl. on the left. This church's cramped position on the very edge of the old medieval town caused the nave's crookedness. The steep steps from the west door leading to **Tiefergraben,** a former tributary of the Danube, explain the name "Am Gestade," meaning "by the riverbank."

ALTES RATHAUS. The *Altes Rathaus* (Old Town Hall), Wipplingerstr. 8, was occupied from 1316 to 1885, when the government moved to the Ringstr. The building is graced by a Donner fountain depicting the myth of Andromeda and Perseus. The *Altes Rathaus* is also home to the Austrian Resistance Museum, chronicling anti-Nazi activity during World War II (see **Austrian Graffiti,** below), and temporary exhibits. An exterior lined with Austrian flags encloses courtyards used for parties and festivals. (☎ 53 43 61 07 79; docarch@email.adis.at; www.doew.at. Open M and W-Th 9am-5pm. Free. Tours by appointment. Archive/library open 9am-5pm.)

AM HOF, FREYUNG, MINORITENPLATZ

From Stepahnspl., walk down Graben. When Graben ends, go right and then continue in the same direction on Bognerg. Am Hof will be on the right, Freyung straight ahead, and Minoritenpl. to the left (take Strauchg. off Freyung). Or, from Judenpl., take Drahtg., which runs into Am Hof.

AM HOF. The grand courtyard, Am Hof, hosts a weekend **market** (open Sa-Su 11am-1pm). What was once a medieval jousting square now houses the **Kirche am Hof** (Church of the Nine Choirs of Angels; built 1386-1662). In the middle of the square looms the black **Mariensäule** (Column to Mary), erected by Emperor Ferdinand III to thank the Virgin Mary for her protection when the Protestant Swedes threatened Vienna during the Thirty Years' War. More **Roman ruins** reveal, however, that Am Hof was in use long before the Habsburgs.

FREYUNG. Just west of Am Hof, Freyung is an uneven square with the **Austriabrunnen** (Austria fountain) in the center. Freyung (meaning "sanctuary") got its name from the **Schottenstift** (Monastery of the Scots) just behind the fountain, where fugitives could claim asylum in medieval times. Freyung was also used for public executions in the Middle Ages, but now, the annual **Christkindl markt** held here each year before Christmas blots out such unpleasant memories. Three art galleries flank Freyung: the **museum in Schottenstift,** the **Kunstforum,** and **Palais Harrach.** A glass-roofed passage leads from Freyung to the Italianate **Palais Ferstel,** which houses one of Vienna's most cherished coffee houses, **Café Central.**

MINORITENPLATZ. Go down Herreng. from Freyung and take a right on Landhausg. to reach this peaceful square, which shelters the 14th-century **Minoritenkirche.** The church's tower was destroyed during the Turkish siege of Vienna in 1529. A mosaic copy of da Vinci's *Last Supper,* commissioned by Napoleon and purchased by Franz I, adorns the north wall of the church. On the north side of the square stands the **Bundeskanzleramt** (Federal Chancery), where the Congress of Vienna met in 1815 and where Chancellor Engelbert Dollfuss was assassinated in 1934 (see p. 67).

UNFORGETTABLE EMPRESS Murdered by an anarchist in 1898, Empress Elisabeth (better known as Sisi) is remembered not for her untimely death, but for her legendary beauty. When she married Franz Josef in 1854, the 16-year-old Bavarian princess was considered by some to be the most gorgeous woman in Europe. Love did not flourish even in the hundreds of rooms of the Hofburg and Schönbrunn palaces—the imperial couple could not get far enough away from each other. Franz Josef built the Hermes Villa in the Wienerwald (Vienna Woods) for his wife's private residence. There, she unhappily wrote: "Love is not for me. Wine is not for me. The first makes me ill. The second makes me sick." In other poems, she complained about her duties as Empress, disparaged her husband, and labeled her children bristle-haired pigs. Over a century later, images of this melancholy, beautiful woman are plastered on postcards and guide books, and immortalized in various musicals and plays. A plaque on a statue of her in the Volksgarten dubs her the "unforgettable Empress Elisabeth."

MICHAELERPLATZ

Take U3 to "Herreng." Take a left onto Herreng., which leads into Michaelerpl. Or, from Minoritenpl., go back up Landhausg., and take a right onto Herreng.

Herreng., Kohlmarkt, and Schauflerg. all meet in this prominent square, which is dominated by the neo-Baroque, half-moon-shaped **Michaelertor,** the spectacular main gate of the Hofburg (see below). In the middle of Michaelerpl. lie more excavated foundations of the Roman military camp called **Vindobona,** where Marcus Aurelius penned his *Meditations.*

MICHAELERKIRCHE. Michaelerpl. is named for this church, which occupies the block between Kohlmarkt and Habsburgerg. The church's Romanesque foundation dates back to the early 13th century, but construction continued until 1792—note the Baroque embellishment over the Neoclassical doorway. (Open May-Oct. M-F 11am-5pm; €1.82, students €0.73.)

LOOSHAUS. On the corner of Kohlmarkt and Herreng. stands the *Looshaus,* constructed by Adolf Loos in 1910-11. Emperor Franz Josef branded it "the house without eyebrows," as a result of the shocking lack of window pediments customary on Viennese buildings. Offended by the building's modernity, the old emperor never again used the Michaelerpl. entrance to the Hofburg.

HOFBURG

Take tram #1 or 2 anywhere on the Ringstr. to Heldenpl., or enter through the Michaelertor, which is in Michaelerpl.

A massive reminder of the Habsburgs' 700-year reign, the sprawling, grandiose **Hofburg** was the imperial winter residence. Construction on the original fortress began in 1279, but it didn't become the official dynastic seat until the mid-16th century. As few Habsburgs were willing to live in their predecessors' quarters, hodgepodge additions and renovations continued until the end of the family's reign in 1918. Today, the complex houses several museums, the **Österreichische Nationalbibliothek** (Austrian National Library), the performance halls of the **Lippizaner stallions** and the **Vienna Boys' Choir,** a convention center, and the offices of the Austrian President. It also includes the **Burggarten** and the **Volksgarten** (see **Gardens and Parks,** p. 120). The Hofburg is divided into several sections, including **In der Burg,** the **Alte Burg, Heldenplatz, Neue Burg, Stallburg, Josefsplatz,** and **Albertina.** The museums, libraries, and apartments within the Hofburg may suit some people's tastes, but the best way to see this palatial cluster is to walk around and look up.

IN DER BURG. If you come through the Michaelertor, you'll first enter the courtyard called In der Burg (within the fortress). The central monument to Emperor Franz II isn't too exciting, but on your left you'll find the more visually stimulating red- and black-striped **Schweizertor** (Swiss Gate), erected in 1552 and named for the Swiss mercenaries who guarded it under Empress Maria Theresia. Street musicians take advantage of the wonderful acoustics here to play melodies of the old Empire, adding to the personal soundtrack of your visit in the hope of a few euros in return. This section of the Hofburg contains the entrances to the **Kaiserappartements** and the **Hofsilber und Tafelkammer.** (Combined admission €6.90, students €5.45. Open daily 9am-4:30pm.)

Kaiserappartements (Imperial Apartments). On the right side of the Michaelertor is the entrance to the imperial apartments. Once the private quarters of Emperor Franz Josef (1830-1916) and Empress Elisabeth (1838-1898). Neither of them spent much time in the Hofburg (or with each other, for that matter), so the rooms are disappointingly lifeless. Amid all the Baroque trappings, the 2 most personal items seem painfully out of place: Emperor Franz Josef's military field bed and Empress Elisabeth's wooden gym bear mute testimony to their lonely lives (see **Unforgettable Empress,** p. 111).

Hofsilber und Tafelkammer (Court Silver and Porcelain Collection), on the ground floor opposite the ticket office, displays examples of the outrageously ornate cutlery that once adorned the imperial table.

ALTE BURG. Behind the Schweizertor lies the **Schweizerhof,** the inner courtyard of the Alte Burg (Old Fortress), which stands on the same site as the original 13th-century palace. The Alte Burg houses the **Burgkapelle** and the **Weltliche und Geistliche Schatzkammer** (Secular and Sacred Treasury).

Burgkapelle, at the top of the stairs on the right of the Schweizertor. This Gothic chapel is where the heavenly voices of the **Wiener Sängerknaben** (Vienna Boys' Choir) sound on Sundays (except in July-Aug.; see p. 127).

Weltliche und Geistliche Schatzkammer, entrance beneath the steps to Burgkapelle, right of the Schweizertor. Stashed within are the Habsburg jewels, the crowns of the Holy Roman and Austrian Empires, imperial christening robes, and an elaborate cradle presented by the city of Paris in 1811 to Napoleon's infant son. The treasury also contains a "horn of a unicorn" (really an 8ft. long narwhal's horn) and a tooth reported to have belonged to John the Baptist. Open W-M 10am-6pm. €7, seniors and students €5. Free audio guide available in English.

HELDENPLATZ. Through the arches in the far side of In der Burg (opposite the Michaelertor), Heldenpl. (Heroes' Square) is an enormous park/parking lot at the feet of the Neue Burg, the large semi-circular wing attached to the southwest side of Alte Burg. On March 15, 1938, the square was filled with a jubilant crowd cheering Adolf Hitler's proclamation of the *Anschluß*. The equestrian statues (both by Anton Fernkorn) depict two of Austria's great military commanders: Prince Eugene of Savoy and Archduke Charles, whose horse rears triumphantly on its hind legs with no other support, a feat of sculpting never again duplicated. Poor Fernkorn went insane, supposedly due to his inability to recreate the effect.

NEUE BURG. Built between 1881 and 1926, the Neue Burg (New Fortress) is the youngest wing of the palace, but as the Empire ended in 1918, no Habsburg ever inhabited the place. The double-headed golden eagle crowning the roof symbolized the double empire of Austria-Hungary. Planned in 1869, the Neue Burg's design called for twin palaces across Heldenpl., both connected to the Kunsthistorisches and Naturhistorisches Museums by arches spanning the Ringstr., but WWI put an end to its grand designs. Today, the Neue Burg houses Austria's largest working library, the **Österreichische Nationalbibliothek** (Austrian National Library), and the **Reichskanzleitrakt,** plus the fantastic **Völkerkunde Museum,** and three branches of the **Kunsthistorisches Museum** (see **Museums,** p. 123).

Österreichische Nationalbibliothek contains millions of books and an outstanding little museum of papyrus, scriptures, and musical manuscripts. The main reading room is open to the public; anyone can request books for in-library use with a picture ID. Entrance on Heldenpl. ☎ 53 41 03 97. Open Oct.-June M-F 9am-7pm, Sa 9am-12:45pm; July-Aug. and Sept. 23-30 M-F 9am-3:45pm, Sa 9am-12:45pm; closed Sept. 1-22. Museum admission €7.30, students €5.

Reichskanzleitrakt (State Chancellery Wing), the building attached to the Neue Burg, opposite the Alte Burg. The architecture is perhaps most notable for a group of buff statues representing the labors of Hercules, said to have inspired the 11-year-old Arnold Schwarzenegger, then on his first visit to Vienna, to pump up.

STALLBURG (PALACE STABLES). Attached to the northeast side of the Alte Burg (to the left of the Michaelertor, if you are facing it from the outside) is the Renaissance Stallburg, the home base of the Royal Lipizzaner stallions and the **Spanische Reitschule** (Spanish Riding School). The cheapest way to get a glimpse of the famous steeds is to watch them train. (From mid-Feb. to June and from late Aug. to early Nov. Tu-F 10am-noon, except when the horses tour. Tickets sold at the door at Josefspl., Gate 2, from about 8:30am. €11.60, children €5. No reservations.) For a more impressive (and more expensive) display, you can try to attend a **Reitschule performance,** but sold-out performances require you to reserve tickets months in advance. Tickets cannot be reserved by phone, only in writing. (☎ 533 90 32; fax 535 01 86; tickets@srs.at; www.spanische-reitschule.com. Write to: Spanische Reitschule, Michaelerpl. 1, A-1010 Wien. Mar.-June and from Sept. to early Nov. Su 10:45am, Apr.-June and Sept.-Oct. Sa 10am; 1½hr. If you reserve through a travel agency, expect at least a 22% surcharge. Reservations only; no money accepted by mail. Tickets €35-150, standing room €22.) You can also learn about Lipizzaner history and training at the **Lipizzaner Museum** (see **Museums,** p. 123).

JOSEFSPLATZ. Just south of Stallburg, this courtyard is named after the statue of Emperor Josef II in the center. The modest emperor would doubtless be appalled at his statue's chest-baring Roman garb, but the sculptor probably couldn't bring himself to depict the decrepit hat and patched frock coat the emperor favored. The square contains the ticket entrance for the Stallburg and the entrance to the **Prunksaal** (Grand Hall). Begun in 1723, the Prunksaal glitters with gilded wood, frescoes, and marble pillars, and is the secular counterpart of Fischer von Erlach's magnificent Karlskirche (see p. 116). Though just a part of the Nationalbibliothek, this is the largest Baroque library in Europe. Multi-media exhibits in the free, functional part of the library on Heldenpl. give three-dimensional tours of the hall. Wander through the floor-to-ceiling bookcases that house over 200,000 leather-bound books and pay your respects to the 16 marble statues of various Habsburg rulers, including Charles VI, the library's founder. (☎ 53 41 00. Prunksaal open from mid-May to mid-Oct. F-W 10am-4pm, Th 10am-7pm; mid-Oct. to mid-May M-Sa 10am-2pm. Closed first 3 weeks of Sept. €5, students €3.)

AUGUSTINERKIRCHE. High masses are held each Sunday in this 14th-century Gothic church, located in a wing attached to the Prunksaal's south side, and on the left side of Josefspl. when viewed from the outside. Eighteenth-century renovations (and Napoleonic flourishes) have altered the interior. The Augustinerkirche held the wedding of Maria Theresia and Franz Stephan and is now the final resting place of the hearts of the Habsburgs, which are stored in the **Herzgrüftel** (Little Heart Crypt). (Mass 11am. Church open M-Sa 10am-6pm, Su 11am-6pm. Free.)

ALBERTINA. Originally part Augustinian monastery, part 18th-century palace, the Albertina (☎53 483), which houses the celebrated **Collection of Graphic Arts,** is closed until spring 2003.

NEAR NEUER MARKT

Take U1 or U3 to "Stephanspl." Walk down Kärntnerstr., away from the Stephansdom. Turn right on Donnerg., which leads into Neuer Markt. Or, from Albertina, walk down Tegetthoffstr., which runs into Neuer Markt.

The spectacular Neuer Markt is centered around George Raphael Donner's **Donnerbrunnen,** a graceful embodiment of the Danube surrounded by four gods who represent her tributaries. The streets radiating from it connect pedestrians to some of the most famous sights in Vienna. Parallel to Neuer Markt and running south into that giant of a **Staatsoper** on Ringstraße, Kärntnerstraße is one of Vienna's grand boulevards, lined with chic cafes and boutiques. Street musicians play everything from Peruvian folk to Neil Diamond.

KAPUZINERKIRCHE (CHURCH OF THE CAPUCHIN FRIARS). On the southwest corner of Neuer Markt. Behind its pale orange, 17th-century facade lies the **Kaisergruft** (Imperial Vault), a series of subterranean rooms filled with coffins, including remains (minus heart and entrails—see **Augustinerkirche** above, and **Stephansdom,** p. 107) of all Habsburg rulers since 1633. Empress Maria Theresia rests next to husband Franz Stephan of Lorraine in a Rococo sepulcher surrounded by cherubim. (Open 9:30am-4pm; entrance until 3:40pm. Imperial Vault €4, students €3.)

HOTEL SACHER. At the end of Kärntnerstr., across from the rear of the Opera, stands the flag-bedecked Hotel Sacher. This legendary institution once served magnificent dinners over which the elite discussed affairs of state, while its *chambres separées* provided discreet locations for affairs of another sort. In one of its elegant suites, John Lennon and Yoko Ono awed the public by holding a press conference while naked in bed—all, of course, in the name of peace. Most tourists today flock here for its renowned chocolate dessert, the *Sacher Torte.*

MONUMENT GEGEN KRIEG UND FASCHISMUS. This "Memorial Against War and Fascism," sculpted by Alfred Hrdlicka in 1988 and located behind Hotel Sacher on Albertinapl., commemorates the suffering caused by WWII.

THE RINGSTRAßE

Trams #1 and 2 run along the Ringstr., and the U-bahn stops on opposite sides of the Ring at U2: "Schottentor" and U3: "Stubentor." From Neuer Markt, take Donnerg. out of the Markt and turn right onto Kärnterstr., which leads roughly to the middle of the Ring.

The Ringstraße defines the boundaries of the inner city, and is an attraction in itself. This 57m-wide, 4km-long boulevard was commissioned by Emperor Franz Josef in 1857 to replace the city fortifications that had encircled Vienna's medieval center since the last siege by the Ottoman Turks in 1683, separating the old town from the suburban districts. The military, still uneasy in the wake of the revolution attempted nine years earlier, demanded that District I be surrounded by fortifications; the emerging bourgeoisie, however, argued for the removal of all formal barriers and for open space within the city. Imperial designers reached a compromise: the walls would be razed to make way for the Ringstraße, a peace-loving, tree-studded spread of boulevard and, at the same time, a sweeping circle designed for the efficient transport of troops. Urban planners from all over Europe put together a group of monuments dedicated to staples of Western culture: religion, scholarship, commerce, politics, and art. In total, 12 giant public buildings were erected along the Ring; counter-clockwise from Schottenring, they are the **Börse,** the **Votivkirche,** the **Universität,** the **Rathaus,** the **Burgtheater,** the **Parliament,** the **Kunsthistorisches Museum** and

Naturhisorisches Museum, the **Staatsoper,** the **Museum für angewandte Kunst,** and the **Postsparkasse,** each built in the appropriate Historicist style (see **Architecture,** p. 74).

SCHOTTENRING. The first stretch of the Ring extending south from the Danube Canal, called Schottenring, leads past the Italianate **Börse** (stock exchange) to Schottentor, which is surrounded by university cafes, bookstores, and bars. Across Universitätsstr. rise the twin spires of the **Votivkirche,** a neo-Gothic wonder surrounded by rose gardens that is home to a number of expatriate religious communities. Franz Josef's brother Maximilian commissioned the church as a gesture of gratitude after the Emperor survived an assassination attempt in 1853.

KARL-LUEGER RING. The next stretch of the Ring runs from the university to Rathauspl. **Universität Wien** was founded in 1365, but by the 19th century, the original building had become far too small. The massive new building was built in the Italian Renaissance style which celebrated the beginning of the "Golden Age" of science. The professors, however, had hoped for a more modern building which would suggest the continuance of that Golden Age. Inside the university is a tranquil courtyard lined with busts of famous departed professors.

DR. KARL-RENNER RING. Rathauspl. and Parliament mark this section of the Ring. The **Rathaus** (town hall), with fluted arches and geraniums in the windows, is meant to honor the Flemish burghers who pioneered the idea of town halls and civic government in Europe. Opera buffs will enjoy the free nightly **Music Film Festival** in July and August (see p. 129). (Free tours M, W, F 1pm; meet at the blue Information booth outside.) Across the street from the *Rathaus* is the **Burgtheater** (Imperial Court Theater), which has seen the premieres of some of the most famous operas and plays by Austrians, including Mozart's *La Nozze di Figaro* ("The Marriage of Figaro"). Inside are frescoes by Gustav Klimt, his brother, and his partner Matsch. (Performance season Sept.-June. Tours July-Aug. M, W, and F 2 and 3pm in English; Sept.-June M, W, and F 3pm in English. €4, students €2.) Next to Rathauspl. is the **Parliament.** Decked out with winged chariots, a grand ramp leading to its columned facade and an imposing statue of wise Athena, the Parliament tries to invoke the great democracies of ancient Greece. (Tours mid-Sept. to mid-July M-F 11am, 3pm; from mid-July to mid-Sept. M-F 9, 10, 11am, 1, 2, 3pm; Easter holidays 11am, 3pm. €3.)

BURGRING. On Burgring, opposite the Hofburg on either side of Maria-Theresien-Pl., stand two of Vienna's largest and most comprehensive museums, the **Kunsthistorisches Museum** (Museum of Art History; p. 123) and the **Naturhistorisches Museum** (Museum of Natural History; p. 125). When construction was complete, the builders realized with horror that Apollo, patron deity of art, stood atop the Naturhistorisches Museum, and Athena, goddess of science, atop the Kunsthistorisches. Also note the statue of Empress Maria Theresia, surrounded by key statesmen and advisers. She holds the Pragmatic Sanction, which granted women the right to succeed to the throne (see p. 66).

OPERNRING/KÄRNTNERRING. Opernring runs from the Burggarten (see **Gardens and Parks,** p. 120) to Schwarzenbergstr., marked by an equestrian statue, the **Schwarzenberg Denkmal.** The largest feature of Opernring is the **Staatsoper** (State Opera). Built in 1869 by and for the opera-adoring public, the Staatsoper had first priority during the construction of the Ringstraße. After its destruction by Allied bombs in 1945, Vienna meticulously restored the exterior and re-opened the building in 1955. Today, the Staatsoper is still at the heart of Viennese culture. You can **tour** the gold, crystal, and red velvet interior (tours in English July-Aug. daily 10, 11am, 1, 2, 3, 4pm; Sept.-Oct. and May-June 1, 2, 3pm; Nov.-Apr. 2, 3pm. €5, students €2), but seeing an opera may be cheaper (see Staatsoper, p. 126).

VIENNA

IN RECENT NEWS

A MUSEUM EXPLOSION

It's one of the ten largest cultural complexes in the world. What does that mean to you? It means it's worth setting aside at least a day for the brand-new **MuseumsQuartier** in Vienna. With over 1.5 million visitors since its opening in June 2001, the complex that links new construction and preexisting royal palaces is an artistic overload.

The **Leopold Collection,** which consists of 5000 paintings from the 19th and early 20th centuries, contrasts the **Museum of Modern Art (MOMUK)** in a 60,000 sq. m venue self-described as "Baroque meets Cyberspace." The MuseumsQuartier also boasts the TanzQuartier, an international dance studio, as well as a "mall" of contemporary artisans creating and selling their work. The ZOOM Kindermuseum (an interactive children's museum) and Electric Avenue for electronic art are just two more facets of the largest cultural project in the history of Austria. Rotating temporary exhibits and featured visiting artists, as well as film and dance festivals, will ensure that the museum remains fresh and cutting-edge.

(☎ 523 58 81 1730. www.mqw.at. Take the U-bahn (U2) or city bus 2a to "MuseumsPlatz." Ticket and Visitor Centers open daily 10am-7pm. Individual attractions priced separately; combination ticket to most sights €26.)

SCHUBERTRING/STUBENRING. From Schwarzenbergstr. to the Danube Canal, Schubertring borders the **Stadtpark** (see **Gardens and Parks,** p. 120). The **Postsparkasse** (Post Office Savings Bank), near the end of Stubenring, at George-Coch-Pl. 2, is Otto Wagner's greatest triumph of function over form, and the most contemporary of the Ringstraße monuments. A bulwark of modernist architecture, the building raises formerly concealed elements of construction, like the thousands of metallic bolts, to an art. The art nouveau interior is open during banking hours. (Open M-W and F 8am-3pm, Th 8am-5:30pm.)

OUTSIDE THE RING

As the city expands beyond the Ring in all directions, the distance between notable sights also expands. But what the area outside the Ring gives up in accessibility, it makes up for in its varied attractions. Some of Vienna's most famous modern architecture is outside the Ring, where 20th-century designers found more space to build. At the same time, this modern sprawl is also home to a number of startlingly beautiful Baroque palaces and parks that were once beyond the city limits.

NEAR KARLSPLATZ

Take U1, U2, or U4 to "Karlspl." Or, from the Staatsoper walk 2 blocks down Kärntnerstr. away from the city center. Karlspl. is left after Rechte Weinzeile intersection.

Once a central gathering place for the Viennese, Karlspl. is now isolated behind a major traffic artery. It is still, however, home to Vienna's most impressive Baroque church, the **Karlskirche,** and is surrounded by the ornate **Musikverein** and several major museums, including the **Secession,** the **Künstlerhaus,** and the **Kunsthalle.**

KARLSKIRCHE. Situated in the center of the gardens, the Karlskirche is an eclectic masterpiece, combining a Neoclassical portico with a Baroque dome and towers on either side. Two massive columns, covered with spiraling reliefs depicting the life of St. Carlo Borromeo ("Karl"), frame the central portion of the church. The interior is beautiful, with colorful ceiling frescoes and a golden sunburst altar. Designed by Fischer von Erlach and completed by his son, Johann Michael, this imposing edifice was constructed in 1793 to fulfill a vow Emperor Charles VI made during a plague epidemic in 1713. In front of the church, a reflecting pool and modern sculpture designed by Henry Moore connect it to the 20th century. (Open M-F 7:30am-7pm, Sa 8:30am-7pm, Su 9am-7pm. Free.)

RESSELPARK. The park opposite Karlskirche, named for Josef Ressel (the Czech gentleman who invented the propeller), is peaceful, shady, and ringed by museums. The **Historisches Museum der Stadt Wien** is to the left of the Karlskirche (see **Museums,** p. 123), while the blocky yellow and blue **Kunsthalle** stands out at the opposite end of the park (see p. 124). Above one side of the park, a terrace links the *Jugendstil* **Karlsplatz Stadtbahn Pavilions,** designed in 1899 by Otto Wagner.

SECESSION BUILDING. Northwest of Resselpark, across Friedrichstr. at #12, is the Secession Building. Its white walls, subtle decoration, and gilded dome (hence the nickname the "Golden Cabbage") are meant to clash with the Historicist Ringstraße. Otto Wagner's pupil Josef Olbrich built this *fin de siècle* monument to accommodate artists who broke with the rigid, state-sponsored Künstlerhaus. The inscription above the door reads: *"Der Zeit, ihre Kunst; der Kunst, ihre Freiheit"* ("To the age, its art; to art, its freedom"). The Secession exhibits of 1898-1903 were led by Gustav Klimt and drew cutting-edge European artists. The exhibitions remain firmly dedicated to avant-garde art (see **Museums,** p. 124).

MAJOLICAHAUS. This colorful wonder of an apartment building, at Linke Wienzeile 40, is steps away from the Kettenbrückeng. (U4) station, but a bit of a hike from Karlspl. From the Secession Building, head away from Karlspl. down Friedrichstr., which runs into Linke Wienzeile. The acclaimed *Jugendstil* Majolicahaus was a collaborative effort by Wagner and Olbrich. The wrought-iron spiral staircase is by Josef Hoffmann, founder of the Wiener Werkstätte, a communal arts-and-crafts workshop and key force in the momentum of *Jugendstil*. The Majolicahaus's golden neighbor, the **Goldammer** building, is another Wagnerian mecca.

NASCHMARKT. West of Karlspl., along Linke Wienzeile, is the beginning of the Naschmarkt, a colorful food bazaar that moved from Karlspl. to its present location in the 1890s. During the week, the Naschmarkt, which derives its name from the German verb *naschen* (to nibble), presents a smorgasbord of fruits and vegetables laid out in front of bakeries, cafes, wurst vendors, and cheese and spice shops. On Saturdays, it becomes a giant **flea market,** selling anything from loose junk to traditional Austrian clothing. Come before 11am to find the cheapest prices from local farmers. (Open M-F 7am-6pm, Sa 7am-5pm.)

THEATER AN DER WIEN. Further down Linke Wienzeile, opposite the Naschmarkt, stands the theater that hosted the premiere of Mozart's *Die Zauberflöte* ("The Magic Flute") once upon a time (see p. 128). The names of the street and the theater commemorate the Wien river, which used to flow freely through Vienna, but which is now almost completely buried under city streets.

MUSIKVEREIN. Step across Lothringerstr. opposite Karlspl. to view the Musikverein, home of the Wiener Philharmoniker. The building's modest exterior conceals the sublime **Grosser Saal,** where the crème de la crème of the international music world performs. Standing-room concert tickets offer an inexpensive way to admire both the music and the golden caryatids that line the hall (see p. 127).

SCHWARZENBERGPLATZ

Take tram #1, 2, D, or 71 to "Schwarzenbergplatz." Or, facing the Künstlerhaus on Karlspl., turn right on Friedrichstr., which leads into the middle of Schwarzenbergpl.

Schwarzenbergpl., marked by the illuminated **Hochstrahlbrunnen** (Tall Fountain), is an elongated square with an unsavory military history. During the Nazi era, the occupied city renamed the square "Hitlerplatz"; when the Russians brutally liberated Vienna, they renamed it "Stalinplatz" and erected an enormous **Russen Heldendenkmal** (Russian Heroes' Monument), a concrete colonnade behind a column bearing the figure of a Russian soldier, with a quotation from Stalin inscribed in the base. The Viennese have attempted to destroy the monstrosity three times, but

VIENNA

the product of sturdy Soviet engineering refuses to be demolished. Vienna's disgust with its Soviet occupiers is further evident in their nickname for an anonymous Soviet soldier's grave: "Tomb of the Unknown Plunderer." Across from Schwarzenbergpl., on the Ring, **Café Schwarzenberg** is a posh meeting-place.

PALAIS SCHWARZENBERG. Its present location on a traffic island behind the Hochstrahlbrunnen makes it hard to believe that Palais Schwarzenberg, designed in 1697 by Fischer von Erlach's rival architect, Lukas von Hildebrandt, was once the center of a neighborhood preferred by Vienna's nobility. The palace is a swank hotel, where daughters of the super-rich gather annually to meet Austrian noblemen at the grand debutante ball. If you're not a hotel guest, the palace is off-limits.

SCHLOß BELVEDERE

Take tram D or tram #71 one stop past Schwarzenbergpl., or walk up Prinz-Eugen-Str. from Südbahnhof. Walking southeast from Schwarzenbergpl. (away from the city center), you'll find Belvedere just beyond the Schwarzenberggarten, which is next to Beleevedere's own gardens.

Designed by Lukas von Hildebrandt, Belvedere was originally the summer residence of **Prince Eugène of Savoy,** Austria's greatest military hero (see **Unpopular Hero,** below). His distinguished career began when he routed the Ottomans in the late 17th century. After Eugene's heirless death in 1736, his cousin sold off his possessions and Empress Maria Theresia snatched up the palace as a showroom for the Habsburgs' art collection, opening the extensive formal gardens to the public. Though the imperial art moved to the Kunsthistorisches Museum in the 1890s, Archduke Franz Ferdinand lived in the Belvedere until his 1914 assassination. The grounds of the Belvedere, stretching from the Palais Schwarzenberg to the Südbahnhof, now contain three spectacular sphinx-filled gardens (see p. 120) and an equal number of excellent museums (see p. 123).

SCHLOß SCHÖNBRUNN

Take U4 to "Schönbrunn."

From its humble beginnings as a hunting lodge, Schönbrunn, named after a "beautiful brook" on the property, was destroyed twice before Fischer von Erlach conceived a plan for a palace that would make Versailles look like a gilded outhouse. Construction began in 1696, but the cost was so prohibitive that the project slowed considerably until, three emperors later in 1740, Maria Theresia inherited the project and created the Rococo palace that became her favorite residence. Its cheery yellow color has been named *"Maria Theresien gelb"* after her. When Napoleon conquered Vienna, he acquired Maria Theresia's fondness for the place and promptly moved in. Tours of some of the palace's 1500 rooms reveal the elaborate and lavish taste of her era. Both the Grand (44 rooms) and the Imperial (22 rooms) tours pass through the **Great Gallery,** where the Congress of Vienna danced the night away after a day of dividing up the continent, and the **Hall of Mirrors,** where the 6-year-old Mozart played. After reaching the **Ceremonial Hall** and its paintings of Joseph II's wedding to Isabella of Parma, however, only those with Grand Tour tickets can enjoy the more sumptuous pleasures of the palace, like the **Millions Room** with Oriental miniatures and rosewood paneling, and Maria Theresia's bedroom, with original red velvet bed cover. The Habsburgs' suites are exquisite, trimmed in gold and silver. (Apartments open Apr.-June and Sept.-Oct. daily 8:30am-5pm; Nov.-Mar. 8:30am-4:30pm; July-Aug. 8:30am-7pm. Imperial Tour €7.50, students €7. Grand Tour €10/€8. Audio-guides included.)

THE GARDENS. At least as impressive as the palace itself are the classical gardens behind it. Designed by Emperor Josef II, the gardens extend nearly four times the length of the palace. They include a wild panoply of elements, ranging from ordered forests with trees planted in lines to geometric flower designs. In some areas, the trees have even been carefully pruned to create the effect of a vaulted arch. Also featured is the massive stone **Neptunbrunnen** (Neptune fountain), with Romanesque sculptures.

While the gardens themselves are the best deal—free and priceless—other sights are worth paying for. At one end of the garden is the **Palmenhaus**, an enormous greenhouse of tropical plants, and the **Schmetterlinghaus** (Butterfly House), an enclosure where soft-winged beauties fly free in the tropical environment. There is also a **maze** in whose center two stones, activated by a master of Feng Shui, emanate energy-giving harmony. To enter this domain of power you must make an offering (€2.90, students €2.05). The compendium is crowned by the **Gloriette,** an ornamental temple serenely perched upon a hill with a beautiful view. If you're feeling indulgent, drink a *Melange* in the temple's new cafe. In summer, open-air opera is performed in the park. (Park open 6am-dusk. Free.) Built to amuse Maria Theresia's husband in 1752, the **Schönbrunn Tiergarten** (zoo) is the world's oldest menagerie, but as the oldest it's not necessarily the best. (Zoo open daily May-Sept. 9am-6:30pm; Feb. and Oct. 9am-5pm; Nov.-Jan. 9am-4:30pm; Mar. and Oct. 9am-5:30pm; Apr. 9am-6pm. €6.90, students €3.27, children €2.18.)

ALONG THE DONAUKANAL

*The Danube Canal cuts a semi-circle into the city south of the river, extending beyond the innere Stadt. Much of the area inside of the semi-circle is now taken up by parks (see **Gardens and Parks,** p. 120), but the outside edge of the canal provided building space for some of Vienna's great 20th-century architects to experiment with populist architecture.*

KARL-MARX-HOF. The most famous example of public housing built during the interwar years by the Austrian Social Democratic Republic set, Karl-Marx-Hof, Heiligenstadterstr. 82-92, illustrates the ideology and aesthetic of *"Rot Wien"* (Red Vienna, the socialist republic from 1918 until the *Anschluß*). The "palace for the people" stretches out for a full kilometer and encompasses more than 1600 identical orange-and-pink apartments, with common space and courtyards to garnish the urban-commune atmosphere. The Social Democrats used this structure as their stronghold during the civil war of 1934, until army artillery shelled the place and broke down the resistance. (Take U4 to "Heiligenstadt.")

HUNDERTWASSER HAUS. Friedensreich Hundertwasser (translation: Peace-filled Hundredwaters; given name: Friedrich Stowasser), a Fantastic Realist and environmental activist, designed Hundertwasser Haus at the corner of Löweng. and Kegelg. in opposition to the aesthetic of *Rot Wien* (see **Karl-Marx-Hof,** above). Completed in 1985, the multi-colored building with 50 apartments makes both an artistic and a political statement. Hundertwasser included trees and grass in the undulating balconies as a means of bringing life back to the urban "desert" the city had become; oblique tile columns and free-form color patterns also contribute to this flamboyant rejection of architectural orthodoxy. Despite hordes of visitors, Hundertwasser Haus remains a private residence, where tenants decorate their window spaces as they see fit. (Take tram N from Schwedenpl. to "Hetzg.")

KUNST HAUS WIEN. Another Hundertwasser project, three blocks away at Untere Weißgerberstr. 13, the Kunst Haus is a museum devoted to the architect's graphic art (see **Museums,** p. 123) on the lower floors and controversial contemporary artists above (Robert Mapplethorpe and Annie Lennox have both exhibited here). A cafe built along the lines of a Hundertwasser blueprint is inside (see **Cafes,** p. 105).

MÜLLBRENNEREI (GARBAGE INCINERATOR). Behind the "Spittelau" U-Bahn station. Hundertwasser fans should check out his jack-in-the-box of a trash dump. It has a smokestack topped by a golden disco ball. Hundertwasser also designed a ferry that cruises the Danube under the auspices of the DDSG (see p. 88).

OTHER SIGHTS

KIRCHE AM STEINHOF. On a hill in northwest Vienna, at XIV, Baumgartner Höhe 1, Wagner's church embodies another approach to architecture for the people. Commissioned for the inmates of the state mental hospital in 1907, this cheerful church unites streamlined symmetry and Wagner's signature functionalism with a Byzantine influence. The white walls are tiled for easy cleaning, the holy water in the basins by the door runs continuously for maximum hygiene, all corners are rounded to avoid injuries, and the pews are widely spaced to give nurses easy access to unruly patients. The stained-glass windows were designed by Koloman Moser, a vanguard member of the Secession. (Take U2 or U3 to "Volkstheater," then bus #48A to "Otto Wagner-Spital/Psychiatriches Zentrum." ☎910 60 11 204. Open M-F 8am-3pm, Sa 3-4pm. Guided tours in German only, Sa 3pm. €4.)

THE ZENTRALFRIEDHOF. The Viennese like to describe the **Zentralfriedhof** (Central Cemetery) as half the size of Geneva but twice as lively. **Tor II** (2nd gate) is the main gate to the cemetery, and the place to pay respects to your favorite Viennese decomposer: beyond it are Beethoven, Wolf, Strauss, Schönberg, Moser, and an honorary monument to Mozart, whose true resting place is an unmarked paupers' grave in the **Cemetery of St. Mark,** III, Leberstr. 6-8. St. Mark's deserves a visit not just for sheltering Mozart's dust, but also for its *Biedermeier* tombstones and the wild profusion of lilac blossoms that flower everywhere for two weeks in spring.

Tor I leads to the **Jewish Cemetery** and Arthur Schnitzler's burial plot. Sadly, the state of the Jewish Cemetery mirrors the fate of Vienna's Jewish population—many of the headstones are cracked, broken, lying prone, or neglected because the families of most of the dead are gone from Austria. Various structures throughout this portion of the burial grounds memorialize the millions murdered in Nazi death camps.

Tor III leads to the Protestant section and the new Jewish cemetery. To the east of the Zentralfriedhof is the melancholy **Friedhof der Namenlosen** on Alberner Hafen, where the nameless corpses of people fished out of the Danube are buried. (Tor II, the main entrance, is at XI, Simmeringer Hauptstr. 234. Take tram #71 from Schwarzenbergpl., or tram #72 from Schlachthausg. The tram stops 3 times, at each of the gates. Bus #6A also serves the other gates. You can also take S-7 to "Zentralfriedhof," which stops along the southwest wall of the cemetery.)

🏛 GARDENS AND PARKS

The Viennese have gone to great lengths to brighten the urban landscape with patches of green. The Habsburgs opened and maintained the city's primary public gardens throughout the last four centuries; the areas became public property after WWII. There are several parks along the Ring, including the **Stadtpark, Resselpark, Burggarten,** and **Volksgarten,** and in nearly every suburb of the city. The gardens of **Schloß Schönbrunn** and **Schloß Belvedere** (see p. 118) are particularly beautiful.

ALONG THE RING. Established in 1862, the **Stadtpark** (City Park) was the first municipal park outside the former city walls. One of Vienna's most photogenic monuments, the gilded **Johann-Strauss-Denkmal,** stands in the center, provides a soothing counterpoint to the central bus station and nearby Bahnhof Wien-Mitte/Landstr. (Take U4 to "Stadtpark.")

Clockwise up the Ring, past the Staatsoper, lie the **Burggarten** (Palace Gardens), a quiet park with monuments to such Austrian notables as Mozart, Emperor Franz Josef, and Emperor Franz I, Maria Theresia's husband. The **Babenberger Passage** leads from the Ring to the marble **Mozart Denkmal** (1896). Reserved for the imperial family and members of the court until 1918, the Burggarten is now a favorite for lounging students, young lovers, and hyperactive dogs.

The Burggarten borders Heldenpl., across from the Kunsthistorisches Museum and behind the Hofburg, which abuts the **Volksgarten** (People's Garden), once the site of a defensive bastion destroyed by Napoleon's troops. In the center of the park, the **Temple of Theseus** sits in the midst of the formal arrangement of roses and trees. At the north end of the garden a stark, white statue of Empress Elisabeth rests on a throne. The statue was erected after her assassination, with the plaque "The people of Austria erected this monument to their unforgettable Empress Elisabeth in steadfast love and loyalty" (see **Unforgettable Empress,** p. 111).

AUGARTEN. The Augarten, on Obere Augartenstr., northeast of downtown Vienna in Leopoldstadt, is Vienna's oldest public park. Originally a formal French garden, the Augarten was given a Baroque face-lift and opened to the public by Kaiser Josef II in 1775. Today, the Augarten is no longer as fashionable as it was in the days of Mozart and Strauss, due primarily to the solemn WWII **Flaktürme** (concrete anti-aircraft towers) that dominate the center of the park. Buildings located within the Augarten include the headquarters for the **Wiener Porzellanmanufaktur** (Vienna China Factory), founded in 1718, and the **Augartenpalais,** now a boarding school for the Vienna Boys' Choir. (To reach the park, take tram #31 up from Schottenring or tram N to "Obere Augartenstr." and head left down Taborstr.)

PRATER. For many nostalgic Viennese, the symbol of their city is the **Prater,** a park extending southeast from the Wien Nord Bahnhof/Praterstern. The park was a private game reserve for the Imperial Family until 1766 and the site of the World Expo in 1873. Squeezed into a riverside woodland between the Donaukanal and the river proper, the park is surrounded by ponds, meadows, and stretches of forest. The Prater is most famous for its old-school amusement park, with the stately wooden 65m-tall **Riesenrad** (Giant Ferris Wheel; €4 for a 10min. ride). Locals cherish this wheel of fortune, and when it was destroyed in WWII, the city built an exact replica, which has been turning since 1947. The area near U1: "Praterstern" is the actual amusement park, which contains rides, arcades, restaurants, and casinos. Entry to the complex is free, but each attraction charges admission (generally €3). The garish thrill machines and wonderfully campy spook-house rides are packed with children during the day, but the Prater becomes less wholesome after sundown due to the proliferation of peep shows. (Open May-Sept. daily 9am-midnight; Oct.-Nov. 3 10am-10pm; Nov. 4-Dec. 1 10am-6pm.)

ON THE DANUBE. The Danube's spring floods were problematic once settlers moved outside the city walls, so the Viennese stretch of the Danube was diverted into canals from 1870 to 1875 and again from 1972 to 1987. One of the side benefits of this restructuring was the creation of new recreational areas, ranging from new tributaries (including the **Alte Donau** and the **Donaukanal**) to the **Donauinsel,** a narrow island stretching for kilometers. The Donauinsel is devoted to bike paths, soccer fields, swimming areas, barbecue plots, boats, discos, and summer restaurants. The northern shore of the island, along the Alte Donau, is lined with beaches and bathing areas. (Take U1 (dir.: Kagran) to "Donauinsel" or "Alte Donau." Open May-Sept. M-F 9am-8pm, Sa-Su 8am-8pm. Beach admission is roughly €4.) To catch a view of Vienna at its best, go after sundown to **Donaupark** and take the elevator up to the revolving restaurant in the **Donauturm** (Danube Tower), near the UN complex. (Take the U1 to "Kaisermühlen/Vienna International Center," exit towards Schüttaustr., and follow signs to the park. Tower open Apr.-Sept. daily 10am-midnight; Oct.-Mar. 10am-10pm. €5, students €4.) On weekends, the brave can also bungee-jump from 150m up the tower. (☎269 62 47; www.jochen.schweizer.at. €100-150. Order tickets ahead to get a better rate.) The area celebrates during the annual open-air **Donauinsel Fest,** which stages jazz and rock concerts and fireworks displays in late June (see **Festivals,** p. 129).

IN THE SUBURBS. Vienna's outlying suburbs shelter parks somewhat wilder than the tame enclaves in the center of the city. Nearly every district has public gardens tucked away somewhere, like the **Türkenschanz Park** in district XVIII. The garden is famous for its Turkish fountain, its pools, and its peacocks. In summer, feed ducks or gaze rapturously at the water lilies. In winter, come for sledding or ice skating. (Take bus #40A or #10A, and enter the park anywhere along Gregor-Mendel-Str., Hasenauerstr., or Max-Emmanuelstr.)

West of district XIII is the **Lainzer Tiergarten** (Lainz Game Preserve). Once an exclusive hunting preserve for the royals, this enclosure has been a nature park and reserve since 1941. Along with paths, restaurants, and spectacular vistas, the park holds the **Hermes Villa.** This erstwhile retreat for Empress Elisabeth houses exhibitions by the Historical Museum of Vienna, most recently one about Viennese fashion from the 18th century to the present. (Take U4 (dir.: Hütteldorf) to "Hietzing"; change to streetcar #60 to "Hermesstr." At the intersection, take a sharp right and walk a block to the bus stop. Take bus #60B to "Lainzer Tor." Open Tu-Su and holidays 10am-6pm; Oct.-Mar. 9am-4:30pm. Villa admission €4, students €1.50, seniors €2, family €6. F mornings free.)

Districts XIV, XVII, XIX, and XX peter off into well-tended forests that invite *Spaziergänger* (people out for a stroll) and hikers alike. The **Pötzleindorfer Park,** at the end of tram line #41 (dir.: Pötzleindorfer Höhe) from Schottentor, overlaps the lower end of the Wienerwald (Vienna Woods).

WIENERWALD. Far to the north and west of Vienna sprawl the forested hills of the Wienerwald (Vienna Forest), which extends past Baden bei Wien to the first foothills of the Alps. The woods are known for their excellent *Heuriger* and divine new wines (see p. 105). One of the most famous and most easily accessible routes to the Wienerwald is via **Kahlenberg** and **Leopoldsberg,** two hills north of Vienna which provide a great view of the city and direct entrance to the woods. **Kahlenberg** (484m) is the highest point of the rolling Wienerwald, and affords spectacular views of Vienna, the Danube, and distant Alps. The Turks besieged Vienna from here in 1683, and Polish king Jan Sobieski celebrated his liberation of the city from Saracen infidels in the small **Church of St. Joseph.** (Open daily 10am-noon and 2-5pm. To get to the Wienerwald on the tram, take tram #38 to "Grinzing," tram D to "Nußdorf," or tram #43 to "Neuwaldegg.") Just off the central square of Kahlenberg stands the trusty **Stefania Warte** tower (open May-Oct. Sa noon-6pm, Su and holidays 10am-6pm); catch the views from part of the river valley's old fortifications. (Take U4 to "Heiligenstadt" then bus #38A to "Kahlenberg," or hike up the steep 1km long Nasen Weg from the Kahlenberg-dorf S-Bahn station.)

The area around Kahlenberg, Cobenzl, and Leopoldstadt is criss-crossed with hiking paths marked by colored bars on trees. Kahlenberg and its country cemetery are within easy walking distance of the wine-growing districts of **Nußdorf** and **Grinzing.** You can follow in an early Pope's footsteps and hike over to the **Leopoldskirche,** a renowned pilgrimage site, located 1km east of Kahlenberg on **Leopoldsberg** (425m), site of a Babenberg fortress destroyed by the Turks in 1529. (Bus #38A also runs from Kahlenberg to Leopoldsberg; 20min.) **Kloster-neuburg,** a Baroque monastery founded by Leopold (see p. 133), is a 1½hr. hike from Leopoldsberg.

🏛 MUSEUMS

All museums run by the city of Vienna are **free Friday before noon** (except on public holidays); they are marked in the tourist office's free *Museums* brochure with a coat of arms. Individual museum tickets usually cost €1.50-7 less with the **Vienna Card,** though student or senior discounts are comparable, see p. 89. If you're in town for a long time, invest in the **Museum Card** (issued through the *Verein der Museumsfreunde*) to save a bundle on entrance fees (ask at a museum ticket window). The newest additions to the museum circuit is the **MuseumsQuartier** (☎523 58 81; www.mqw.at). Originally the imperial barracks, the **Messepalast,** Museum-spl., was transformed in 2001 into the MuseumsQuartier, a modern complex combining several collections previously scattered in different venues (see p. 116).

ART MUSEUMS

▧ **Österreichische Galerie** (Austrian Gallery), III, Prinz-Eugen-Str. 27 (☎79 55 72 61; recorded info ☎79 55 73 33; fax 79 55 71 34; www.belvedere.at), in the Belvedere Palace behind Schwarzenbergpl. (see p. 118). Walk up from the Südbahnhof, take tram D to "Schloß Belvedere," or tram #71 to "Unteres Belvedere." The collection is in 2 parts. The **Upper Belvedere** (built in 1721-22 by Hildebrandt) houses Austrian and European art of the 19th and 20th centuries. Work through the crowds to catch a glimpse of Klimt's *The Kiss* in all its golden decadence. In the less trafficked areas of the museum, linger in front of the violent portraits by Expressionists Kokoschka and Schiele as well as a variety of paintings from the Baroque, Romantic, and Austrian "Ringstraße" periods, such as the impressive *Ariadne* by Makart. Use the same ticket to enter the **Lower Belvedere,** which contains the **Baroque Museum**'s extensive collection of sculptures by Donnere and Maulbertsch, as well as Messerschmidt's busts. David's majestic portrait of Napoleon on horseback is here, as is the **Museum of Medieval Austrian Art,** showcasing Romanesque and Gothic sculptures and altarpieces. Both Belvederes are open Tu-Su 10am-6pm, Upper Belvedere until 9pm on Th. Last admission 30min. before closing. €7.50, students €5. Audio guide in Upper Belvedere €4.

▧ **Kunsthistorisches Museum** (Museum of Fine Arts; ☎52 52 44 03; fax 525 24 371; info.pr@khm.at; www.khm.at). Take U2 to Museumsquartier, U2/U3 to Volkstheater, or tram 1, 2, D, or J. Across from the Burgring and Heldenpl. on Maria Theresia's right. Houses the world's 4th-largest art collection, including vast numbers of 15th to 18th-century Venetian and Flemish paintings. Must-sees include Vermeer's *Art of Painting* (room 24) and Raphael's *Madonna in the Meadow* (room 4). Ancient and classical art, including an Egyptian burial chamber, are also well represented. Open Tu-Su 10am-6pm. Picture gallery also open Th until 10pm. Tickets €9, students and seniors €6.50. Audio guides available for €2. Small **branches** reside in the Neue Burg (M-W, Su 10-6pm).

  Ephesos Museum exhibits the massive findings of an Austrian excavation of classical ruins from Ephesus in Turkey, including an ancient Greek temple and statues.

  Hofjagd- und Rustkammer (Arms and Armor Collection), the 2nd-largest collection of arms and armor in the world.

  Sammlung alter Musikinstrumente (Ancient Musical Instrument Collection). Includes Beethoven's harpsichord and Mozart's piano with a double keyboard.

  MuseumsQuartier (☎523 58 51; fax 58 86; office@mqw.at; www.mqw.at) is 60,000 sq. m of culture and one of the ten largest art districts in the world. Take U2 to "Museumsquartier," or U2/U3 or tram 1, 2, D, or J to "Volkstheater." Uniting Baroque architecture with ultra-modern film, visual art, and performance spaces, the sector offers a spectrum of large museums, including:

  Leopold Museum (☎52 57 00; fax 525 70 15 00; www.leopoldmuseum.org). The world's largest Schiele collection, plus works by Klimt, Kokoschka, Gerstl, and Egger-Lienz. Open M, W-Th, Sa-Su 10am-7pm, F 10am-9pm. €9.

Kunsthalle Wien (☎521 89 33; office@kunsthallewien.at; www.kunsthallewien.at). Themed exhibits of international contemporary artists, from sculptors to filmmakers. Open daily 10am-7pm, Th 10am-10pm. Exhibition Hall 1 €6.50, students €5; Exhibition Hall 2 €5/€3.50; both €8/€6.50.

Museum Moderner Kunst (Museum of Modern Art; ☎525 00; info@mumok.at; www.mumok.at). Holds Central Europe's largest collection of modern art in a brand-new building made from basalt lava. Highlights include Classical Modernism, Pop Art, Photo Realism, Fluxus, and Viennese Actionism. 20th-century masters include Magritte, Motherwell, Picasso, Miró, Kandinsky, Pollock, Warhol, and Klee. Open Tu-Su 10am-7pm; until 9pm on Th. €8, students €6.50.

Kunst Haus Wien, III, Untere Weißgerberstr. 13 (☎712 04 95; fax 77 12 04 96; www.kunsthauswien.com; see p. 119). Take U1 or U4 to "Schwedenpl.," then tram N to "Hetzg." This museum, built by Hundertwasser, displays much of his work, including his environmental machines. The building lacks straight lines, which Hundertwasser called "the Devil's work." The floor bends and swells, creating "a melody for the feet." The Kunst Haus also hosts exhibits of contemporary art from around the world. Open daily 10am-7pm. €8, students €6; M half-price.

Österreichisches Museum für Angewandte Kunst (MAK; Austrian Museum of Applied Art), I, Stubenring 5 (☎71 13 60; fax 713 10 26; office@mak.at; www.mak.at). Take U3, or trams 1 or 2 to "Stubentor." A museum dedicated to the beauty and ingenuity of design, from the smooth curves of Thonet bentwood chairs to the intricate detail of Venetian glass. Recent exhibits have included photography and film by Dennis Hopper and an Andy Warhol retrospective. For Klimt lovers, *The Embrace* is a special highlight. Open W-Su 10am-6pm, Tu 10am-midnight. €6.60, students €3.30. Tours by appointment; call ☎71 13 62 98.

Akademie der Bildende Kunst (Academy of Fine Arts), I, Schillerpl. 3 (☎588 162 25 or 588 162 28). From Karlspl. turn left onto Friedrichstr., right onto Operng., and left on Lungeng. Famous for having rejected Hitler's application, the Academy holds an excellent collection that includes impressive works by Peter Paul Rubens. The centerpiece is Hieronymus Bosch's *The Last Judgment,* placed in a dim room to amplify its effect on the viewer. Open Tu-Su 10am-4pm. €3.50, students €1.50.

Secession Building, I, Friedrichstr. 12 (☎587 53 07; fax 53 07 34; www.secession.at), on the western side of Karlspl. (see p. 117), easily distinguished by its dome of 3000 gilt laurel leaves (once derided as a "head of cabbage"). Although the commitment to new art is evident here, and the museum continually changes its exhibits of contemporary artists, the main attraction, Klimt's controversial *Beethoven Frieze,* is almost 100 years old: this 30m long work is Klimt's visual interpretation of Beethoven's *Ninth Symphony.* Pick up the English brochure for excellent commentary on the work's symbolism. Open Tu-Su 10am-6pm, Th until 8pm. €5.50, students €3.

Palais Surreal, Josefspl. 5 (☎512 25 49; www.dali-wien.at). By the Hofburg; take U3 to "Herreng." The Baroque palace of the Pallavicini family now houses a small but renowned collection of Surrealist sculptures by Dalí, including a wobbly work called "Space Elephant," and ethereal glass sculptures. Open daily 10am-6pm. €6.50, students and seniors €3.60. AmEx/MC/V.

OTHER MUSEUMS

▨ **Haus der Musik,** I, Seilerstatte 30 (☎516 48; fax 512 03 15; info@house-of-music-vienna.at; www.hdm.at). Near the Opera House and the Musikverein, this new, interactive science-meets-music museum easily captures the fancy of adults and children for a day. On four different floors, experience the physics of sound, learn about famous Viennese composers (each has his own room) and play with a neat invention called the Brain Opera. Open daily 10am-10pm. Adults €8.50, students €6.50. Combined admission including Philharmonic exhibit, add €2.

Historisches Museum der Stadt Wien (Historical Museum of the City of Vienna), IV, Karlspl. (☎50 58 74 70; www.museum.vienna.at), to the left of the Karlskirche (see p.

116). This amazing collection of historical artifacts and paintings documents Vienna's evolution from a Roman encampment through the Turkish siege of Vienna to the subsequent 640 years of Habsburg rule. Don't miss the memorial rooms to Loos and Grillparzer, the fin de siècle art, or the 19th century Biedermeier collection. Open Tu-Su 9am-6pm. €3.50, students €1.50.

Jüdisches Museum (Jewish Museum), I, Dorotheerg. 11 (☎535 04 31; www.jmw.at). From Stephanspl., off Graben. Jewish culture and history told through various media, including fragments of text stamped into the walls, holograms, and the traditional objects-in-a-glass-case. Temporary exhibits focus on prominent Jewish figures and contemporary Jewish art. Open Su-F 10am-6pm, Th until 8pm. €5, students €2.90.

Bestattungsmuseum (Undertaker's Museum), IV, Goldegg. 19 (☎501 95 42 27). Take tram D to "Schloß Belvedere" or U1 to Südtirolerpl. This museum displays a morbidly fascinating (if somewhat comical) exhibit, including coffins with alarms (should the body decide to rejoin the living) and Josef II's proposed reusable coffin. Open M-F noon-3pm by appointment only. Free.

Sigmund Freud Haus, IX, Bergg. 19 (☎319 15 96; www.freud-museum.at). Take U2 to "Schottentor," then walk up Währingerstr. to Bergg or take tram D to "Schlickg." The famed couch is not here, but this former Freud home provides lots of photos and documents, including the young Freud's report cards and circumcision certificate. Open July-Sept. 9am-6pm; Oct.-June daily 9am-4pm. €5, students €3.

Lipizzaner Museum, I, Reitschulg. 2 (☎533 78 11; fax 533 38 53; www.lipizzaner.at). Horse-lovers unite in what used to be the imperial pharmacy, now a museum dedicated to the imperial horses, featuring paintings, harnesses, video clips, and a small viewing window through which you can glimpse the stables. Open daily 9am-6pm. €5.09, students €3.63, tour €1.45. Call ahead to arrange a tour in English.

Naturhistorisches Museum (Natural History Museum; ☎52 17 70), opposite the Kunsthistorisches Museum. A substantial collection of dinosaur skeletons, meteorites and giant South American beetles on display. Two of its star attractions are man-made: a spectacular floral bouquet comprised of gemstones and a copy of the fascinating Stone-Age beauty *Venus of Willendorf* (the original is locked in a vault). Open W 9am-9pm, Th-M 9am-6:30pm, last admission 30min. before close; in winter, 1st floor only 9am-3pm. €3.50, students €1.80.

🎵 ENTERTAINMENT

While Vienna offers all the standard entertainment in the way of theater, film, and festivals, the heart of the city beats to music. All but a few of classical music's marquee names lived, composed, and performed in Vienna. Mozart, Beethoven, and Haydn wrote their greatest masterpieces in Vienna, creating the **First Viennese School;** a century later, Schönberg, Webern, and Berg teamed up to form the **Second Viennese School.** Every Austrian child must learn to play an instrument during school, and the Vienna **Konservatorium** and **Hochschule** are world-renowned conservatories. Also not to be missed are the various modern and classical dance groups of Vienna, in particular, the **Vienna Staatsoper Ballet.** Vienna has performances ranging from the above-average to the sublime all year long, and many are accessible to the budget traveler.

TO EVERYTHING THERE IS A SEASON. Beware that Vienna's biggest cultural draws, the **Staatsoper** (State Opera), the **Wiener Philharmoniker** (Vienna Philharmonic), the **Wiener Sängerknaben** (Vienna Boys' Choir), and the **Lipizzaner Stallions** don't perform in Vienna during July and August.

FROM THE ROAD

A NIGHT (STANDING) AT THE OPERA

The clubs aren't hopping on a Monday night in Vienna, but I had a hunch I could find some excitement somewhere else. I decided to go to the famous Staatsoper Opera House to see the ballet. Not knowing quite what to expect, I rounded up some friends from the hostel to join me. After all, for only €2 you can see the ballet if you don't mind standing. Even better, the ballet was *Sleeping Beauty*—a favorite from my childhood. As we switched from U-Bahn (the underground train system), I had romantic visions of prima ballerinas, a live orchestra—and of standing for three hours. Still, *Sleeping Beauty* called, and how could I possibly visit Vienna and skip the ballet?

We decided to divide and conquer to figure out where to purchase tickets. Finally, *Karten* in hand, we ran up the stairs. There were already a bunch of young tourists dressed in jeans, ladies dressed in evening wear, and even a grandfather-type in a suit, all rushing to get in line. Then, we waited. Before too long the stationary line became a mad rush of people hurrying towards the entrance to the Gallery. When we got in, a little flustered, I wasn't sure which way to turn. Everyone had already claimed most of the spots that had two leaning bars, so I darted for the ones with one leaning bar. I had heard that wrapping scarves was the only way to claim and save your space. Scarfless, but unwilling to lose the spot I had fought for, I quickly grabbed my sweater and wrapped it around the bar. With an

OPERA

Staatsoper, Opernring 2 (www.wiener-staatsoper.at), Vienna's premier opera, performs about 300 times a year, nearly every night from Sept. to June. There are three ways to get tickets:

Standing-room tickets: The cheapest way to enjoy the opera. 500 are available for every performance, though you can only buy 1 per person, right before the performance. The tickets aren't bad, but your feet can get a bit sore after 4hr. of Wagner. While the box office opens 1hr. before curtain, those with the desire (and the stamina) should start lining up at least 1½hr. before curtain (2-3hr. in tourist season and for more popular productions) in order to get orchestra tickets. The standing line forms inside the side door on the side of the Opera by Operng. After procuring your precious ticket, hurry to a space on the rail and tie a scarf around it to reserve your spot. Balcony €2, orchestra €3.50. Formal dress unnecessary, but no shorts.

Box office tickets in advance: The more secure ticket option is to purchase tickets through the official ticket offices by fax, phone, or in person; they charge no fees above the ticket price. The main ticket office is the Bundestheaterkasse, I, Hanuschg. 3, around the corner from the opera. (☎514 44 78 80; fax 514 44 29 69. Open M-F 8am-6pm, Sa-Su 9am-noon; first Sa of each month 9am-5pm.) There is also a ticket office inside the Staatsoper with the same hours (though closed Su and holidays), which also offers tours of the building year-round. Tickets may be purchased 1 month before performance. Seats €10-178, depending on location.

Internet: The Bundestheaterkasse maintains a multi-lingual website (www.bundestheater.at; see also www.wiener-staatsoper.st or www.culturall.com) that allows you to purchase tickets in advance, view the seating plan, and check out the season schedule. The web is better used as a source of information than as a means of buying your tickets, however, because it charges a hefty commission (20%).

Volksoper, IX, Währingerstr. 78, specializes (not exclusively) in lighter comedic opera, operettas, and occasional musicals. As the Staatsoper was once for royalty, the "people's opera" is for the commoners. While the theater itself is less elaborate, the music is fantastic and the diversity of performances makes it a lively arts center. Especially for students, this opera is a perfect choice—go 45 minutes before the show to get the best seats in the house for €7. Repertoire is diverse and includes modern operas, musicals, and dance troupes such as Alvin Ailey. Box office tickets are available at the theatre and through Bundestheaterkasse and its website (see **Staatsoper,** above; www.culturall.com). Tickets range from €7-250 depending on performance and location.

Wiener Kammeroper (Chamber Opera; ☎513 60 72; fax 512 01 00 30; ticket@wienerkammeroper.at; www.wienerkammeroper.at) does performances of

Mozart's operas in an open-air theater in the Schönbrunner Schloßpark during the summer as part of the **Klangbogen** festival (☎427 17). Pick up a brochure at the tourist office.

ORCHESTRAS

Wiener Philharmoniker (Vienna Philharmonic Orchestra; www.musikverein.at); performances in the **Musikverein,** Bösendorferstr. 12, on the northeast side of Karlspl. It is Austria's—perhaps the world's—premier concert hall. Constructed in 1867, the building allows for unmatched acoustic perfection. The *Musikverein's* program is essentially conservative, although it occasionally includes contemporary classical music. Tickets to Philharmoniker concerts are mostly on a subscription basis and tend to sell out well in advance, but there are 3 ways to get them (it's worth the trouble):

Musikverein box office tickets in advance: Contact the box office of the Musikverein in person or by letter. Ask about special concerts for teenagers as well. **Standing room tickets** are available from the Musikverein, but even they must be bought in advance, just like a seat. Open Sept.-June M-F 9am-7:30pm, Sa 9am-5pm. Write Gesellschaft der Musikfreunde, Bösendorferstr. 12, A-1010 Wien for more info.

Bundestheaterkasse tickets in advance: As with the Staatsoper, tickets to the Philharmoniker are offered through the Bundestheaterkasse (see **Staatsoper,** above).

Internet: The Philharmoniker maintains its own website (www.wienerphilharmoniker.at), which provides a full schedule, sells tickets, and provides links to sites selling tickets to Philharmoniker performances on tour and at festivals throughout the country. Beware of commissions!

Wiener Symphoniker (Vienna Symphony Orchestra), Vienna's second fiddle, is frequently on tour, but plays some concerts at the grand, late-19th-century Konzerthaus, III, Lothringerstr. 20, just around the corner and across the river Wien from the Musikverein. They focus on 20th-century classical music, including some ultramodern, experimental works. The season runs Sept.-June. Get tickets and information from the Konzerthaus box office. (☎24 20 02; fax 24 20 01 10; wiener@konzerthaus.at; www.konzerthaus.at. Open M-F 9am-7:45pm, Sa 9am-1pm; June 10-Sept. 2 9am-1pm. Tickets €15-100.)

CHORAL MUSIC

Wiener Sängerknaben (Vienna Boys' Choir). Main showcase is mass every Sunday at 9:15am (from mid-Sept. to late June only) in the **Hofburgkapelle** (U3 "Herreng."). Contact hofmusikkapelle@asn-wien.ac.at for info; for more on the boys' daily lives, see www.wsk.at. To get tickets to these masses:

Reserve tickets (€6-30) at least 2 months in advance; write to Hofmusikkapelle, Hofburg, A-1010 Wien, but do not

hour until showtime, the upper gallery looked like a festive gala with different colored scarves lining the two bars.

I poked around the Opera House for a little while until the shrill bell reminded us that the ballet was about to start. I found my sweater and even managed to get comfortable leaning on the brass bar in front of me. The orchestra began to play and the house resonated with Tchaikovsky. The ballet was simply beautiful—rigid bodies, soft music, flowing graceful leaps and spins.

Even though we were leaning for the entire time, I was content, and hardly even noticed when my foot fell fast asleep. The end was spectacular—gold flecks streamed down as Sleeping Beauty and her prince embraced. Her night was a success, and so was mine.

—Lora Sweeney, Researcher-Writer, *Let's Go: Austria & Switzerland 2003.*

enclose money. You will be sent a slip and can pick up tickets at the Burgkapelle on the Friday before mass 11am-1pm or 3-5pm, or before Su mass 8:15-9am.

Unreserved seats are sold in small quantity the Friday before mass 11am-1pm and 3-5pm (get in line 30min.-1hr. early), max. 2 per person. Some tickets sold early Sunday morning.

Standing room is free, despite rumors to the contrary, but arrive before Su 8am to have a chance.

The lads also perform every Friday at 3:30pm at the **Konzerthaus** (see **Wiener Symphoniker,** above) May, June, Sept., and Oct. For tickets (€28.50-32), contact *Reisebüro Mondial,* Faulmanng. 4, A-1040 Wien (☎58 80 41 41; fax 587 12 68; ticket@mondial.at).

Sunday High Masses also occur in the major churches of the city (Augustinerkirche, Michaelerkirche, Stephansdom) and, while they don't include the Boys' Choir, they are glorious—and free—musical experiences (beginning at 10 or 11am, year-round). They are also, of course, services for worshipers, so be respectful.

Wiener Singakademie bills itself as the oldest concert choir in Europe. Brahms was their director for the 1863-1864 season, and they have worked with some of the greatest conductors of choral music, including Mahler, Strauss, Solti, Furtwängler, and Gardiner. They perform in the Konzerthaus. See **Wiener Symphoniker,** above, for ticket info.

PREPUBESCENT PRODIGIES

The 500-year-old **Wiener Sängerknaben (Vienna Boys' Choir)** functions as Austria's "ambassador of song" on its extensive international tours. Dressed in sailor suits, the boys export great works of music to the entire world. Emperor Maximilian I founded the group in 1498, Franz Schubert was a chorister, and Anton Bruckner held the post of organist and music teacher. Today, the choral music of Mozart, Hadyn, Schubert, Bruckner, and Beethoven can be heard as it was originally meant to be sung—by the clear sweet voices of a boys' choir.

THEATRE

In the past few years, Vienna has made a name for itself as a city of musicals, with productions of such Broadway and West End favorites as *Les Misérables.* A recent fad has been creative interpretations of famous Austrians' lives, including *Elisabeth, Mozart!,* and, the "cyber show" *Falco.* Take U1, U2, or U4 to "Karlspl." and you'll find the **Theater an der Wien,** VI, Linke Wienzeile 6, Vienna's top venue for musicals. The nearby **Raimund Theater** also shows popular musicals. Tickets can be bought at the box offices or by phone. (☎588 85; wienticket@vbw.at; www.musicalvienna.at. Box office open 10am-1pm and 2-6pm. Call in advance. €10-180.)

Vienna's English Theatre, VIII, Josefsg. 12, presents drama in English. (☎40 21 26 00; fax 402 12 60 40; www.englishtheatre.at. Box office M-F 10am-6pm. Tickets €15-40, student rush €9.) The **International Theater,** IX, Porzellang. 8, is also an English-language venue (☎319 62 72; tickets €18-25, under 26 €10). **WUK,** IX, Währingerstr. 59, is a center for dance and concerts (☎40 12 10). Two German-language theaters are **Burgtheater** and **Akademietheater** (tickets at the **Bundestheaterkasse;** see **Opera,** p. 126).

FILM

Though not on the same level as Berlin or Paris, Vienna's film scene has much to offer. Serious *cinéastes* should check out the new arenas for experimental film at the Museumsquartier. **Films** in English usually play at **Burgkino,** I, Opernring 19 (☎587 84 06; last show around 9:15pm, Sa around 11pm; also shows *The Third Man* every other Sa), **Top Kino,** VI, Rahlg. 1 (☎587 55 57; films 5:30-10pm), at the intersection of Gumpendorferstr., and **Haydnkino,** VI, Mariahilferstr. 57, near the U3 stop "Neubaug." (☎587 22 62; www.haydnkino.at. Last show usually around 9:30pm.) In the newspaper, films listed with "OF" after the title are shown in the original language; films listed as "OmU" are shown in the original language with subtitles. **Votivkino,** IX, Währingerstr. 12 (☎317 35 71; www.votivkino.at), near Schottentor, is an art house popular with the university crowd and shows all films in the original language with German subtitles. **Artis Kino, Filmcasino,** and **Stadtkino** also show subtitled art and foreign films. **Künstlerhauskino,** I, Karlspl. 5 (☎505 43 28; www.k-haus.at/kino), hosts art-house film festivals (except in July). Movie tickets cost €5-10. In most Austrian cinemas you pay for an assigned seat (middle seats are most expensive.) In summer, there are several **open-air cinemas** in the *Augarten* park. (Take tram #31 to "Obere Augartenstr." Shows at 7pm and 9:30pm. €6.50.) Ask at the tourist office for details on occasional free movies in the *Volksgarten*. While Vienna hosts a full-sized film festival in August (see **Festivals,** below), the rest of the year the Austrian **Filmmuseum,** I, Augustinerstr. 1 (☎533 70 54), shows a program of classic and avant-garde films.

FESTIVALS

Vienna hosts an array of important annual festivals, mostly musical. The **Vienna Festival** (mid-May to mid-June) has a diverse program of exhibitions, plays, and concerts. (☎58 92 20; fax 589 2249; kartenbuero@festwochen.at; www.festwochen.or.at.) The Staatsoper and Volkstheater host the annual **Jazzfest Wien** during the first weeks of July, featuring many famous acts. For information, contact Jazzfest Wien (☎503 56 47; fax 503 55 44; www.viennajazz.org). In addition, on the first weekend in June, most clubs and bars in Vienna host bands and DJs for **Lange Nacht der Musik** (€15 for entrance to all events. Tickets can be purchased at any participating location or at www.events.ORF.at/langenachtdermusik.) While other big guns take a summer siesta, Vienna has held the **Klangbogen** (☎427 17; fax 40 00 99 84 10; tickets@klangbogen.at; www.klangbogen.at) every summer since 1952, featuring excellent concerts across Vienna, including **Wiener Kammeroper** (Chamber Opera; ☎/fax 513 60 72; information@wienerkammeroper.at; www.wienerkammeroper.at) and performances of Mozart's operas in an open-air theater in the Schönbrunner Schloßpark. Pick up a brochure at the tourist office. From mid-July to mid-Aug., the **Im-Puls Dance Festival** (☎523 55 58; www.impuls-tanz.com) attracts some of the world's great dance troupes and offers seminars to enthusiasts. Some of Vienna's best parties are thrown by the parties (political, that is). The Social Democrats host the late-June **Danube Island Festival,** which draws millions of party-goers annually, while the Communist Party holds a **Volksstimme Festival** in mid-August. Both cater to impressionable youngsters with free rock, jazz, and folk concerts. In mid-October, the annual city-wide film festival, the **Viennale,** kicks off (for tickets call ☎526 59 47; www.viennale.at). In past years, the program has featured over 150 movies from 25 countries. Finally, Vienna's **Rathausplatz Music Film Festival,** July-August, in the Rathauspl. at dusk, is actually in part a culinary display from all over the world. Meanwhile, a huge screen broadcasts operas, ballets and concerts from around the world. Come here for atmosphere and tasty treats. Also of interest to free-thinking *Let's Go* readers are two colorful parades in summer. During the first weekend of July is the **Regenbogenparade**--a predominantly gay and lesbian celebration of free love. The following weekend is another **Love Parade,** modeled after the one in Berlin, in which over 400,000 people gather around the Prater and Donau to hear over 20 DJs spin their stuff from techno to trance. It's a crazy party where people are literally dancing in the streets—with clothing, without clothing, and somewhere in between.

VIENNA

WINTER FESTIVITIES

The Viennese don't let long winter nights go to waste. Christmas festivities begin in December with **Krampus** parties. Krampus (Black Peter) is a hairy devil that accompanies St. Nicholas on his rounds and gives bad children coal and sticks. On December 5, people in Krampus suits lurk everywhere, rattling their chains and chasing passersby, while small children nibble marzipan Krampus effigies.

As the weather gets sharper, huts of professional *Maroni-* (chestnut) roasters and *Bratkartoffeln-* (potato pancake) toasters pop up everywhere. Cider, punch, red noses, and *Glühwein* (a hot, spicy mulled wine) become ubiquitous. **Christmas markets** *(Christkindlmärkte)* open around the city; the best-known is probably the somewhat tacky **Rathausplatz Christkindlmarkt,** which offers, among other things, excellent *Lebkuchen* (a soft gingerbread-like cookie), *Langos* (a Hungarian round bread soaked in hot oil, garlic, and onions), and beeswax candles. (Open 9am-9pm.) **Schloß Schönbrunn's** *Weihnachtsmarkt* offers old-fashioned Christmas decorations. (Open M-F noon-8pm, Sa-Su 10am-8pm.) Visit the happy **Spittelberg** market, where artists and university kids hawk offbeat creations (open M-F 2-9pm, Sa-Su and holidays 10am-9pm), or the **Weihnachtsdorf im Unicampus** (at the university campus; daily 1-10pm). The **Trachtenmarkt** shop in Schotteng. near Schottentor offers atmospheric Christmas shopping. Most theaters, opera houses, and concert halls have Christmas programs (see p. 125). The city also turns Rathauspl. into an enormous outdoor skating rink in January and February.

The climax of the New Year's season is the **Neujahrskonzert** (New Year's concert) by the Viennese Philharmonic, broadcast worldwide. The refrain of the *Radetzky-marsch* by Strauss signals that the new year has truly begun. New Year's also brings a famously flashy **Imperial Ball** in the Hofburg. For those lacking 7-digit incomes, the City of Vienna organizes a huge chain of *Silvester* (New Year's) parties in the *Innenstadt.* Follow the **Silvesterpfad,** marked by lights hung over the street, for outdoor karaoke, sidewalk waltzing, firecrackers, and hundreds of people drinking champagne in the streets. At midnight, the St. Stephen's giant bell rings across the country, broadcast by public radio stations.

New Year's is barely over before **Fasching** (Carnival season) arrives in February and spins the city into bubbly bedlam. These are the weeks of the Viennese waltzing balls, the most famous of which, the **Wiener Opernball** (Viennese Opera Ball), draws the world's Princess Stephanies and Donald Trumps. Tickets must be reserved years in advance. For a free *Fasching* celebration, join the **carnival parade** that winds its way around the Ring, stopping traffic before Lent.

◪ NIGHTLIFE

With one of the highest bar-to-cobblestone ratios in the world, Vienna is a great place to party. The *Heurigen* on the outskirts of Vienna provide an old-world Austrian way to spend an evening (see p. 105), but for a more urban night, head downtown. Take the subway (U1 or U4) to "Schwedenplatz," within blocks of the **Bermuda Dreiecke** (Bermuda Triangle), so called both for the three-block triangle it covers and for the tipsy revelers who never make it home. Or, head down **Rotenturmstrasse** toward Stephansdom or walk around the areas bounded by the Jewish synagogue and Ruprechtskirche. Another good zone for nightlife in the inner city is the **Bäckerstraße,** with its cellar bars. Slightly outside the Ring, the streets off Burgg. and Stiftg. in district VII and the university quarter (districts XIII and IX) have tables in outdoor courtyards and loud, hip bars. Along the Danube is the **Donauinsel,** a boardwalk filled with cafes and clubs. Drinks are pricey but the atmosphere is consistently lively in warm weather.

Vienna's kinetic club scene rages every night of the week, later than most bars. DJs spin until dawn, and some clubs keep it going until 11am the next morning.

One fact of Viennese nightlife: it starts late. Don't arrive until after 11pm. The best nights are Friday and Saturday, beginning around 1am or so. For the scoop on raves, concerts, and parties, grab the fliers at swank cafes like MAK or Berg das Café, or pick up a copy of the indispensable **Falter** (€2)—it lists concerts, updates on the gay and lesbian scenes, and places that have sprung up too recently for *Let's Go* to review (Vienna's club turnover is too rapid to keep up with even in a guide updated every year). Also, grab a schedule for the **Nightbus** system (see p. 89), which runs across Vienna all night after regular public transportation stops.

BARS

The term "bar" has a loose definition in Vienna. Many restaurants (see **Restaurants**, p. 99) live a Dr. Jekyll-Mr. Hyde existence as a place both to eat and to party.

INSIDE THE RING

Mapitom der Bierlokal, I, Seitenstetteng. 1 (☎535 43 13). Located right in the center of the Bermuda Triangle, this bar has the feeling of a wine Heurigen–with large tables clustered into the warehouse-style interior. A great place to chat after work F nights and be blasted by music. Beer and Bacardi Breezers about €3. Open daily 5pm-3am, F and Sa till 4am.

First Floor Bar, I, Seitstentteng. 5 (☎535 41 06). Somewhat hidden in the Bermuda Triangle, this swanky upstairs martini bar offers an array of mixed cocktails (€6-7), including eight different kinds of martinis, but no beer. Enter the big wooden door and walk upstairs. Open Su-Th 8pm-4am, F-Sa 7pm-4am.

Cato, I, Tiefer Graben 19 (☎533 47 90). Take U3 to "Herreng.," walk down to Strauchg., turn right, and continue on to Tiefer Graben; the bar will be on your left. By the end of the night, you'll be singing with the friendly clientele in this tiny, excessively comfortable bar, thanks to warm hostess Anna Maria. Try the Sekte Cuvee, an Austrian dry spirit from Burgenland (0.1L €4). Open Su-Th 6pm-2am, F-Sa 6pm-4am.

Benjamin, I, Salzgries 11-13 (☎533 33 49). Outside the Triangle area, down the steps from Ruprechtskirche, left onto Josefs Kai, and left onto Salzgries. Dark and rickety, this is a punk-rocker's heaven. Candles tilt in wax-covered wine bottles while a student crowd parties on. Tequila shot €1.53. Open daily 7pm-2am.

Club Berlin, I, Gonzagag. 12 (☎533 04 79). Near the Bermuda Triangle. Go downstairs in this house of swank to see Vienna's upper-crust wind their way around partitions of a former wine cellar with great music. Open Su-Tu 6pm-2am, F-Sa 6pm-4am.

Kaktus, I, Seitenstetteng. 5 (☎533 19 38), in the heart of the Bermuda Triangle. Packed with the bombed and the beautiful, this bar offers mainstream music and well-oiled bartenders. Beer (0.5L) €3.49. Open Su-Th 6pm-2am, F-Sa 6pm-4am.

Centro, I, Bäckerstr. 1. Behind the Stephansdom, turn right off Rotenturmstr. onto Lugeck, which leads to Bäckerstr. Come and chill among colorful posters in this mellow joint. Chianti €2.50. Open M-Su 11-4am.

Jazzland, I, Franz-Josefs-Kai 29 (☎533 25 75). Near U1/U4 "Schwedenpl." Excellent live jazz of all styles and regions filters through the soothing brick environs for a slightly older clientele. Music 9pm-1am. €3.63 cover. Open Tu-Sa 7pm-2am.

Santo Spirito, I, Kumpfg. 7 (☎512 99 98). From Stephanspl., walk down Singerstr. and turn left onto Kumpfg. (5min.). Opera freaks unite to the sound of classical concerti. Welschresiling €3. Busts on the wall pay homage to famous baton-wavers. M-F 6pm-2am, F-Sa 11am-3am, Su 10am-2am.

Esterházykeller, I, Haarhofg. 1 (☎533 34 82), off Naglerg. (U3 to "Herrengasse.") One of Vienna's least expensive, most relaxed *Weinkeller*, popular with 20- and 30-somethings. *Grüner Veltliner* wine is €2.10 for 0.25L. Open in summer M-F 4pm-11pm. Open in winter M-F 11am-11pm, Sa-Su 4-11pm.

OUTSIDE THE RING

■ **Objektiv,** VII, Kirchbergg. 26 (☎522 70 42). Take U2 or U3 to "Volkstheater," walk down Burgg. 2 blocks, and turn right onto Kirchbergg. With old stoves and sewing machines as tables and cowboy boots as decorations, this small bar offers funky local flavor. A mellow atmosphere and cheap drinks. Happy Hour daily 11pm-1am. Daily discounted drink special €2.50. Open 6pm-2am; closed Sun.

■ **Das Möbel,** VII, Burgg. 10 (☎524 94 97; www.dasmoebel.at). U2/U3 to "Volkstheater." This high-ceilinged cafe functions as a showcase for furniture designers. The metal couches, car seat chairs, and Swiss-army tables—which rotate every 6 weeks—are in full use by a trendy crowd. *Melange* €2.25. Open M-F noon-1am, Sa-Su 10-1am.

Chelsea, VIII, (☎407 93 09), Lerchenfeldergürtel under the U-Bahn between Thaliastr. and Josefstädterstr. The best place in Vienna for underground music: bands from all over Europe come to play this joint (except in summer). Techno-pop atmosphere with dancing. Cover €5-12 if band is playing. Open daily 7pm-4am.

Loop, VII (☎402 41 95; www.loop.co.at). Lerchenfeldgürtel under the U-Bahn, down the street from Chelsea. While slightly more expensive, this modern swanky bar offers a more polished atmosphere.

Alsergrunder Kulturpark, IX, Alserstr. 4. Take U2 to "Schottentor." In the courtyard of a turn-of-the-18th-century university building, the Kulturpark features not only beautifully landscaped grounds, but also a series of beer gardens, *Heurigen*, and bars. Mostly late-20-somethings. Drinks around €3. Open Apr.-Oct. daily 4pm-2am.

Kunsthalle Café, IV, Treitlstr. 2 (☎586 98 64). Exit Karlspl. via "Secession/Giribaldi Park." Inside the bright yellow contemporary art museum, as well as outside on its large rocky terrace, this chill cafe-by-day is filled nightly with students and the bright sounds of funk/jazz/blues. A great place for a chat on a warm summer night. Beer €3. Open 10-2am or whenever the last person leaves.

Europa, VII, Zollerg. 8 (☎526 33 83). Buy a drink and strike a pose. Surrounded by concert posters and funky light fixtures, the hip 20-something crowd hangs out late, especially after a long night of clubbing. Open daily 9am-5am.

Blue Box, VII, Richterg. 8 (☎523 26 82). Take U3 to "Neubaug.," turn onto Neubaug., and take the 1st left onto Richterg. Clouds of smoke, blue leather couches, and deafening bass define this popular bar. No DJs (thus quieter) in July. Elephant beer €3. M 6pm-2am, Tu-Th and Su 10-2am, F-Sa 10-4am. V.

Miles Smiles, VIII, Lange G. 51 (☎405 95 17). Take U2 to "Lerchenfelderstr." Head down Lerchenfelderstr. and take the 1st right. This place has a cool, if somewhat touristy, atmosphere. The music is post-1955 jazz. Open Su-Th 8pm-2am, F-Sa 8pm-4am.

Eagle Bar, VI, Blümelg. 1 (☎587 26 61). Come to scope and be scoped. Gay men only. The young clientele is of the leather and/or denim set. Open 9pm-4am.

DISCOS AND DANCE CLUBS

Flyers advertise "Clubbings"—huge, organized parties throughout the city. They're a bit like raves, only more widely attended. More information is listed in *Falter*.

■ **U-4,** XII, Schönbrunnerstr. 222 (☎815 83 07). Take U4 to "Meidling Hauptstr." In the late 80s, U-4 hosted Nirvana, Mudhoney, and Hole before they were huge. These days the joint is hit-or-miss—check in advance to find out the theme night. 2 dance areas, multiple bars. Th Heaven Gay Night. Cover €8. Open daily 10pm-5am.

Volksgarten Disco, I, Volksgarten (☎533 05 18). Take U2 or U3 to "Volkstheater." Hip-hop/R&B and an adolescent crowd on F nights; house and a somewhat older crowd Sa. A mellower option is the adjoining **Volksgarten Pavillon,** a garden bar with trip-hop, trance, lounge, or house, depending on DJ and night. Cover €6-13. Open Th-Su 10pm-5am. (Pavillon open daily in the summer, usually without cover.)

THE REGENBOGENPARADE
At the end of June or beginning of July every year, Austrians gather for an afternoon and evening of gay pride in Vienna at the Rainbow Parade. The mobile rage consists of over 40 floats sponsored by social, political, and commercial organizations from around Austria, as well as from the Czech Republic and Slovakia. Everyone from Dykes on Bikes and the Rosa Lila Villa to Jewish Homosexuals and AIDS awareness organizations takes part. The effervescent parade parties its way along the Ringstraße down to Karlspl., where the public celebration concludes—to be continued privately in bars the rest of the night. The Viennese gay community also hosts the annual "Life Ball," the only charity event held in Vienna's *Rathaus,* which raises money for people with AIDS and HIV.

Flex, I, Donaulände/Augartenbrücke (☎ 533 75 25), around the corner from the Schottenring U-Bahn station. Head toward the river and down a narrow staircase. This on-the-water club is a paradise for those sick of the Bermuda Triangle crowd. Dance (cover €6-10, free after 3am), grab a beer (€4) and a spot at one of the many outdoor benches filled with young locals, or bring your own fun-in-a-bottle and sit by the river like everyone else. DJs start spinning at 10pm. Open daily 8pm-4am May-Sept.

Havana Club, I, Mahlerstr. 11 (☎ 513 20 75; www.clubhavana.at). This basement salsa fest will put the rumba and latin fire into pretty much anyone. Great on Saturday nights. Salsa dancers and aspirers of all levels welcome—professionals hit center stage and amateurs line the interior. Delicious Brazilian cocktails (€8).

Club Meierei, III, Stadtpark (☎ 710 84 00). Take U4 to Stadtpark, "Heumarkt" exit. Located in the Stadtpark with no neighbors and, thus, more freedom to party loudly. Actually rented to different owners and renamed each night. Particularly good Thursday nights as Club Afterwork when it pumps with both house and dance music. Beer €3.50. Cover €10. Open W-Sa 10pm-late.

Why Not, I, Tiefer Graben 22 (☎ 535 11 58). The neon interior of this relaxed gay and lesbian bar/disco holds both a chill chatting venue and a hip-hop subterranean blackbox dance floor. Sa is the night to be here, with drink specials for €3.50. Cover €8. Open F-Sa from 11pm. Women-only 1 Th per month.

V I E N N A

▶ DAYTRIPS FROM VIENNA

STIFT KLOSTERNEUBURG

Take S-40 from Heiligenstadt (U4) or Spittelau (U4/U6) to "Klosterneuburg-Kierling" (15min., every 30min., €1.53), or walk 1½hr. from Leopoldsberg.

Founded by the Babenberg Leopold III in 1114, the **Chorherrenstift (monastery)** put the small town of Klosterneuburg on the map as the center of medieval Austrian art and culture. In 1133, Leopold elevated the institute to its present monastic status as **Stift Klosterneuburg,** making it one of the most powerful monasteries in the country. In 1730, Emperor Karl IV, Maria Theresia's father, moved into Klosterneuburg and began expanding the complex with a **palace** intended to match the grand scale of the monastery and thus symbolize the importance of the *Kaiserreich* (Emperor's kingdom) to the *Gottesreich* (God's kingdom). Only two of the nine projected domes were completed, but they're still pretty darn impressive. Today, the monastery is still functional, but most parts are open to the public. The ornate church contains the renowned late-Romanesque Verduner Altar, with its elaborate wood and gold detail. (Stiftspl. 1.) To quench your thirst for knowledge, visit the **museum.** (Open May-Nov. Tu-Su 10am-5pm. €4.50.) Call ahead for a guided tour of the complex in English. (☎ 02243 41 12 12; fax 411 31. Tours every hr. 10am-5pm. €5. Tour and museum combo-ticket €6.50.)

MÖDLING AND HEILIGENKREUZ

Trains and S-1 and 2 make the short journey from Vienna Südbahnhof to Mödling all day long (25min., every hr., €3; Eurail valid). Buses depart Südtirolerpl. in Vienna. In Mödling, bus #365 connects to Heiligenkreuz (30min. every 2hr., €3).

"Poor I am, and miserable," Beethoven wrote before his arrival in **Mödling.** Seeking physical and psychological rehabilitation, he schlepped all the way to this tranquil "cradle of ideas." Within Mödling's embrace, he finished *Missa Solemnis*, and his spirits improved. A victim of industrialization, Mödling is slowly regaining the charm that also enchanted Schubert, Wagner, Strauss, Schönberg, and Klimt. From the station, turn right up the small hill and left down Hauptstr. for delightful cafes, and shops. Follow the Hauptstr. to Freiheitspl. and continue straight on Herzogg. to Schrannenpl. (a 10min. walk through town). The **tourist office,** Elizabethstr. 2, is next to the *Rathaus.* (☎ 02236 267 27. Open M-F 9am-5pm.) Pick up some picnic supplies and catch Bus #365 into the countryside near Heiligenkreuz.

Heiligenkreuz itself is a both a peaceful village and a harmonious Cistercian monastery in this remote corner of the Austrian countryside. The bus stops twice in Heiligenkreuz; get off at the second stop (in a cul-de-sac with a gate) to visit the 700-year-old monastic retreat that bears the same name as the village. It was founded by Leopold V, notorious for holding Richard the Lionheart for ransom (see **Holding a Grudge,** p. 299). Life at Heiligenkreuz has never been particularly austere, however—visit the *Weinkeller* where the monks still press their own grapes, enjoy beer and bratwurst in the shade of the *Stiftsgasthaus Heiligenkreuz*, or simply stand in the quiet of the monastery's blooming central courtyard. The chapel has magnificent stained-glass windows, still intact despite threats from stern church elders that they would put the abbot on a fast of bread and water until they were removed. Visitors can enter the abbey only on a tour. (☎ 02258 87 03; www.stift-heiligenkreuz.at. Open daily 9-11:30am and 1:30-5pm. Tours daily 10, 11am, 2, 3, 4pm; no 10am tour on Su. €5, senior citizens €4.50, students €2.50.)

CARNUNTUM

Carnuntum is accessible by S7 from Wien Sudbahnhof (1hr., every 30min., €6.10). The park is a well-marked 10min. walk from the station. You'll pass a little tourist info booth on the way to the park on Hauptstr. By car from Vienna, take highway A4, exit at Fischamend, and follow road B9 to Petronell-Carnuntum.

By 15 BC, Romans had conquered the Alps, Dolomites, and Danube river valleys, using the river to transport soldiers, slaves, and goods through the empire. Of their many outposts, which included Vindobona (Vienna), Iuavum (Salzburg), and Brigantium (Bregenz), Carnuntum was the largest and most impressive until it was conquered by the Germanic Alemanni tribe in the 3rd century. Archaeological digs have uncovered houses, public baths, canals, and a temple to the goddess Diana, all dating from the 1st to 3rd centuries. Most artifacts are on display in the **Archäologischer Park Carnuntum,** Hauptstr. 296, where you can tour the place or take part in the digging. (☎ 02163 337 70; fax 337 75; info@carnuntum.co.at; www.carnuntum.co.at. Open Apr.-Nov. daily 9am-5pm. €4, students €3; guided tours €3.)

Twenty kilometers of bike paths lead through the Heidentor ruins (from 300 BC), an amphitheater, an ancient military camp, and in nearby Bad Deutsch-Altenburg's **Archäologisches Museum Carnuntum.** (Open Jan. 13-Mar. 25 and Nov. 10-Dec. 9 Sa-Su 10am-5pm; Mar. 31-Nov. 9 Tu-Su 10am-5pm. €4, students €3; guided tours €3. Combo museum/park ticket €8, students €6.50.) Carnuntum hosts annual Roman festivals, including the **Roman Athletic Competition** in April, the **Art Carnuntum** fest from July to August, with open-air cinema, theater, and concerts (for information, call ☎ 02163 34 00), and a **Roman Christmas market** in December.

STIFT ALTENBURG

Stift Altenburg can be reached by bus from Südtirolerpl. directly (7am) or via Horn (5 per day, €12). A pleasant option in good weather is to walk the picturesque 6km path from Horn to the Stift (follow the green signs).

The Benedictine abbey **Stift Altenburg**, founded in 1144 by Countess Hildburg von Poigen-Rebgau in memory of her deceased husband, swells with Baroque paintings and sculpture. The abbey was frequently attacked by Hussites and Swedes during the Thirty Years' War, and most of what is visible now dates from after Swedish soldiers sacked the monastery in 1645. Altenburg was subsequently rebuilt under the architect Joseph Munggenast, who replaced most of the Gothic cloister, although remnants of it have been excavated and are visible today. Stift Altenburg is famous for its magnificent church buildings and the **library** within the abbey. Much of the art in the church and library, as well as the ceremonial staircase and intriguing **crypt**, was done by Paul Troger. Sculptures, paintings, and frescoes depict Biblical scenes and mythological divinities. The abbey hosts annual art exhibits and summer concerts given by the **Stift Altenburger Musikakademie.** *(Open Apr.-Nov. daily 10am-5pm, last admission 4pm; mid-June to early Sept. 10am-6pm, last admission 5pm. To see the crypt and library, you must take a guided tour (11am, 2, 4pm, each tour has a different theme). €7.50, students €6. Admission to the art exhibit €6, students €3. Add €1.50 for tours 9:30am, 1, 3pm. For more info contact the Stift at ☎02982 34 51; fax 34 51 13; kultur.tourismus@stift-altenburg.at; www.stift-altenburg.at. For concert tickets, call ☎02982 530 80, in winter 586 19 00; freunde.der.claviermusik@vienna.at.)*

FARTHER AFIELD

The following cities are a bit farther away and offer more than the average tourist can absorb in a single day, but if your time or money are short, it may make sense to tackle them using Vienna as a base. Times listed below are for train travel.

EISENSTADT, BURGENLAND. Fans of Haydn and the powerful Esterházy princes won't want to miss this pleasantly provincial capital of Burgenland, with palaces, concerts, and composer memorabilia (1hr., p. 136).

BADEN BEI WEIN, NIEDERÖSTERREICH. This perennial spa town has been pampering the rich and famous since Caesar Augustus with its sulfur baths, casino, and rosarium (1hr., p. 306).

MELK, NIEDERÖSTERREICH. Jutting from the steep green hills along the Danube, the Benedictine monastery of Melk is a must-see, not only for its architecture, but also for the views of the valley below. Melk's slow pace and quiet charm make it an ideal daytrip (1½hr., p. 301).

KREMS AND STEIN, NIEDERÖSTERREICH. Krems captivates with its pastel Baroque splendor, while Stein charms with its twisting medieval byways—and both are wrapped in vineyard-covered hills that offer wine-tasting cellars and breathtaking views (1hr. by train, but consider taking the DDSG ferry, p. 296).

BURGENLAND

Just southeast of Vienna is Burgenland, Austria's most scarcely populated province (pop. 270,000) and one of Austria's last territorial acquisitions. Until Burgenland was ceded to Austria in 1921, it was part of Hungary; in fact, it owes its name to three castles that now lie beyond its borders in Hungary. Given its history, it is not surprising that Burgenland has a Hungarian-influenced cuisine and pockets of Hungarian speakers in the more rural parts of the province. Burgenland is geographically diverse, with rolling hills and dense woodlands in the west, the Neusiedlersee in the northeast, and the peaks of the Rosaliengebirge on the present Hungarian border. Burgenland's gentle hills and lush river valleys give it the rich wines and *Heurigen* (cozy, vine-hung taverns) that make it world-famous. Because of the seasonal nature of many of Burgenland's delights, it's best to coordinate your visit with one of many festivals that liven up the sleepy towns.

HIGHLIGHTS OF BURGENLAND

Walk in Haydn's footsteps through the sumptuous apartments of the Hungarian Esterházy family in **Eisenstadt** (see p. 136).

Sample rich new wines in the vineyards of **Rust** (see p. 143).

Take a dip in the *Neusiedlersee,* then watch a floating opera in **Mörbisch**.

EISENSTADT ☎ 02682

Where I wish to live and die.
— Josef Haydn

Haydn, *Heurigen*, and Huns are the three cultural pillars of Burgenland's tiny provincial capital (pop. 13,280). As court composer for the **Esterházy** princes, **Josef Haydn** composed some of his greatest melodies here, and the town still basks in his glory. The Esterházy princes, powerful Hungarian landholders claiming descent from Attila the Hun, are to this day one of the wealthiest families in Europe. The Esterházys first settled in Eisenstadt when it was part of Hungary and decided to remain there after the change in borders. Today they own many of the region's famed vineyards, whose new wines rival those produced in Bordeaux.

▐ TRANSPORTATION

Eisenstadt is southeast of Vienna and west of Neusiedler See. The easiest way to get there is by direct bus from **Südtirolerplatz** (U1) (1½hr., every 30min. 6am-8:45pm, fewer on weekends, €6). **Buses** run from Eisenstadt to **Rust, Mörbisch,** and **Wiener Neustadt.** The **bus station** (☎ 623 60) is on Dompl. next to the cathedral. Buy your ticket on the bus and tell the driver where you're going. Getting there by train is a bit complicated: from the Südbahnhof take a *Regionalzug* toward Deutschkreutz and change trains in tiny Wulkaprodersdorf (1¼hr., 2 per hr., €8). Another option is to take the S-bahn from the Südbahnhof (1½hr., every hr., €8) and switch trains in **Neusiedl am See,** but sit in the correct section of the train, since the train splits on its way to Neusiedl am See; one section heads to Hungary.

To get to Eisenstadt by **car,** take Bundesstr. 16 or Autobahn A3 south from Vienna (50km). From Wiener Neustadt, take Bundesstr. 53 or Autobahn S4 east. There is an underground parking garage outside the Esterházy Palace.

◆❼ ORIENTATION AND PRACTICAL INFORMATION

Eisenstadt is centered around Hauptstr., the city's *Fußgängerzone* (pedestrian zone). From the train station, follow Bahnstr. (which becomes St. Martinstr. then Fanny Eißlerg.) to the middle of this central area (20min.). From the bus stop, walk half a block to the church. With your back to the church, cross Pfarrg. and walk down tiny Marckingstr. to Hauptstr. Turn left and walk to the end, where Schloß Esterházy is on your right. The **tourist office** is in the right wing of the castle. The staff has information on accommodations, musical events, guided tours, and *Heurigen* in Eisenstadt and surroundings. For a rural living experience, ask about *Beim Bauern Zur Gast*, which lists winegrowers who rent rooms in their houses. (☎673 90; fax 673 91; tve.info@bnet.at. M-Sa 9am-5pm, Su 9am-1pm.) Services in Eisenstadt include: **currency exchange** at the post office or at **Creditanstalt Bankverein** on the corner of St. Martinstr. and Dompl. (open M-Th 8am-1pm and 2-4pm, F 8am-3pm); and **public bathrooms** at Dompl. and Esterházy Palace. The **post office,** on the corner of Pfarrg. and Semmelweise, has good rates for traveler's checks (☎622 71; open M-F 7am-6pm, Sa 8am-12:30pm). **Postal code:** A-7000.

❒❒ ACCOMMODATIONS AND FOOD

With no youth hostel in the vicinity, *Privatzimmer* are the only budget option. Most are on the outer city limits and rent only during July and August. The hostels in **Vienna** (see p. 95) and **Neusiedl am See** (see p. 140) are cheaper and only 1hr. away. What accommodations do exist are packed in July and August; reservations are a must. At **Gasthaus Kutsenits ❸**, Mattersburgerstr. 30, a clean room is yours at a reasonable price if you're willing to walk 2km down a busy four-lane highway. From Schloß Esterházy, head down Rusterstr. to Mattersburgerstr. (☎635 11. Breakfast included. Rooms €20-28; discounts for multiple-night stays.)

The many **Heurigen** in Eisenstadt offer modest, affordable meals with their wines. Another good bet is to wander along Hauptstr., following your nose. **Café Central ❶**, Hauptstr. 40, is an unassuming cafe popular with young people in a shady courtyard, where a crowd consumes scrumptious baguette sandwiches (€3.30) and strudel (€1.80). (☎752 34. Open M-Th 7am-midnight, F-Sa 7am-2am, Su 9am-midnight.) **Fischhandlung Golosetti ❶**, Joseph-Stanislaus-Albachg. 4 off Hauptpl., offers big, cheap *Schnitzelsemmeln* and other meat sand-

Burgenland

BURGENLAND

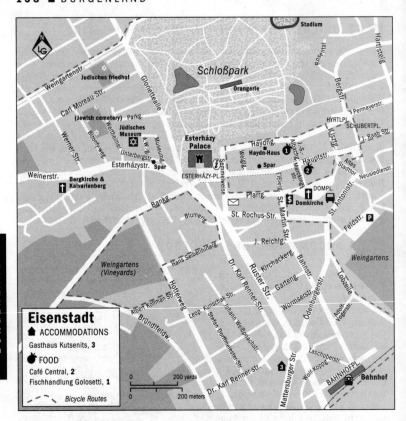

Eisenstadt

▲ ACCOMMODATIONS

Gasthaus Kutsenits, **3**

🍴 FOOD

Café Central, **2**
Fischhandlung Golosetti, **1**

- - - ⌐ *Bicycle Routes*

0 _____ 200 yards
0 _____ 200 meters

wiches for €4-5 (☎629 37. Open M-Th 8am-6pm, F 7:30am-6pm, Sa 8am-1pm.) There are **Spar Markts** at Bahnstr. 16-18 (open M-F 6:45am-12:30pm and 2:30-6pm, Sa 6:45am-12pm) and Hauptstr. 13 (open M-F 7:30am-6:30pm, Sa 7:30am-5pm).

👁 🎵 SIGHTS AND ENTERTAINMENT

THE ESTERHÁZY PALACE. Built on the footings of the Kanizsai family's 14th-century fortress, the castle-turned-palace now known as **Schloß Esterházy** acquired its cheerful hue when the Hungarian Esterházy family showed allegiance to the great Austrian Empress in the 18th century by painting the building *Maria Theresien gelb* (Maria Theresien yellow). More recently, the fabulously wealthy Esterházys, who still own the building, leased the family home to the Austrian provincial government, allowing the bureaucrats to occupy 40% of the castle while the family retrenched itself in the remaining 60%. When it bought its portion for 125,000AS, the government apparently overlooked the Esterházys' clause that made the government responsible for renovation and maintenance costs. Rumor has it the government has spent millions on the upkeep of the Red Salon's silk tapestry alone. In the magnificent **Haydnsaal** (Haydn Hall), the composer conducted the court orchestra almost every night from 1761 to 1790. Since the government removed the marble floor and replaced it with a wooden one, the room is so acoustically perfect that seats for concerts in the room are not numbered—supposedly every seat provides the same magnificent sound. During tours of the Schloß, tourists are encouraged to lift their voices in song in order to test out the hall's sound properties. The room is a visual symphony of red velvet, gold, monumental oil paintings, and woodwork. *(At the end of Hauptstr. ☎ 719 30 00; fax 32 23; management@schloss-ester-hazy.at; www.schloss-esterhazy.at. 50min. tours Easter-Oct. daily every hr. on the hr. 9am-5pm; Nov.-Easter M-F at 10am and 2pm. €4.50, students and seniors €3.)*

HAYDN EVENTS. Catering to the town's Haydn obsession, **Haydnmatinees,** held from May to August, feature revolving groups of chamber musicians, who play 30min. of impeccable Haydn. *(☎ 719 30 00. Th-Sa 11am in the palace. €7.50; students €5.)* The palace also hosts **Haydnkonzerte.** *(July-Aug. Th at 8pm; May-June and Sept.-Oct. Sa 7:30pm. €17-21.)* True Haydn enthusiasts can wait for The Big One: the **Internationale Haydntage,** featuring concerts, operas, and large free video screenings of the best of past festival concerts outdoors near the Schloß in September. *(Festival office ☎ 618 66; fax 618 05; office@haydnfestival.at; www.haydnfestival.at. Tickets €37-780.)*

THE OLD TOWN. The *Kapellmeister* had a short commute to the concert hall each day: he lived just around the corner. His modest residence is now the **Haydn-Haus,** Haydng. 21, which exhibits original manuscripts and other memorabilia. *(☎ 719 39 00. www.haydn-zentrum.at. Open Easter-Oct. daily 9am-5pm. Guided tours by appointment. €3, students €2.)* The *maestro* lies buried in the **Bergkirche.** From the palace, make a right on to Esterházystr. and walk two blocks. Haydn's remains were placed there in 1932 after phrenologists removed his head to search for signs of musical genius on the skull's surface. After being displayed at the Vienna Music Museum for years, Haydn's head was reunited with his body in 1954. Entrance to the *Bergkirche* includes admission to the **Kalvarienberg,** a pilgrimage annex to the church, which illustrates the 14 Stations of the Cross with hand-carved biblical figures. Stand in the central nave and try to distinguish the real Doric columns from the *trompe l'oeil* paintings. The rooftop stations provide a view of Burgenland. *(☎ 626 38. Open Easter-Oct. daily 9am-noon and 1-5pm. €2.50, students €1.50.)*

JEWISH MUSEUM. Eisenstadt's **Jüdisches Museum** presents a history of Jewish life in Eisenstadt and the Burgenland region. The Esterházys were known for their hospitality toward Jews, who played a major part in their rise to power. The museum's display is organized according to Jewish holidays and contains religious items dating from the 17th century. The building contains an original private synagogue with a beautiful ark in the style of Empress Josephine as well as Gothic and Oriental murals from the early 1800s. *(Unterbergstr. 6. From the palace, make a right and then another right onto Glorietteallee, then take the first left to Unterbergstr. ☎ 651 45; info@oejudmus.or.at; www.oejudmus.or.at/oejudmus. Open May-Oct. T-Su 10am-5pm. €3.63, students €2.91.)* Around the corner on Wertheimerstr., near the hospital, is a **Jewish cemetery** dating back several centuries.

> # EISENSTADT'S JEWISH COMMUNITY The history
> of Jews in Eisenstadt is an extraordinary tale of growth and tragic downfall. As early as 1675, Prince Paul Esterházy was moved by the plight of the persecuted Jews and decided to shelter them as "Schutzjuden" (protected Jews) on his estates. From 1732 on, the Jewish quarter of Eisenstadt formed the prosperous independent community of "Unterberg-Eisenstadt," which remained unique in Europe until 1938. In that year, the Jews of the Burgenland were among the first to be affected by the deportation orders of the Nazis. Today, only a few Jewish families remain in Eisenstadt.

FESTIVALS. Leaving Eisenstadt without sampling the wine would be like leaving Vienna without tasting *Sacher Torte*. In early July the **Winzerkirtag Kleinhöflein** floods Hauptpl. with kegs, flasks, and bottles as local wineries attempt to sell their goods. Early August brings the **Festival of 1000 Wines**, when wineries from all over Burgenland crowd the palace's *Orangerie* with their Dionysian delicacies. If you like music with your wine, visit at the end of May when the free, outdoor **Eisenstadt Fest** provides all kinds of music. At any other time of the year, fresh wine is available straight from the source in the wineries themselves. Most are small and aren't allowed to open for more than three weeks per year to sell their wine. Fear not—the wineries stagger their opening times so that wine is always available. To find out which *Buschenschenken*, or *Schenkhäuser* (wine taverns), are open, ask the tourist office for the schedule or look in the local newspaper. Most of the *Buschenschenken* are clustered in Kleinhöfler-Hauptstr.

THE NEUSIEDLERSEE REGION

Burgenland's major lake, the Neusiedlersee, is but a vestige (320 sq. km) of the water that once blanketed the whole Pannenian Plain. It is so big you can barely see the opposite shore, but with no outlets or inlets save underground springs, Austria's only steppe lake never gets deeper than 2m. The water line recedes periodically, exposing thousands of square meters of dry land; from 1868 to 1872, the lake dried up entirely. Warm and salty, the lake is a haven for more than 250 species of waterfowl. The tall marsh reeds that surround the lake shelter many rare plants and animals, including bugs, which can make it unpleasant to swim anywhere other than designated areas. **Storks** thrive—see if you spot their chimneynests, believed to bring good luck. In 1992, the lake and surrounding area were incorporated into the national park **Neusiedlersee-Seewinkel.**

Cruises on the Neusiedlersee allow you to travel between Rust, Illmitz, and Mörbisch with your bike for €4.36, round-trip €7.27. **Gangl** runs boats every hr. from Illmitz to Mörbisch (☎ 02175 21 58 or 27 94; May-Sept. daily 9am-6pm). In Mörbisch, **Schifffahrt Weiss** cruises to Illmitz (☎ 02685 83 24; May-Sept. every 30min. 9am-6pm). For more information about the region, contact the **Neusiedlersee Tourismusbüro** at Peter-Floridang. 4, A-7100 Neusiedl am See (☎ 86 00; fax 86 00 20; info@neusiedlersee.com; www.neusiedlersee.com).

NEUSIEDL AM SEE ☎ 02167

Less than 1hr. from Vienna by train, Neusiedl am See is the gateway to the Neusiedlersee region. The principal attraction is the lake, not the town, so consider Neusiedl a day at the beach. Proximity to the lake, sundry water sports, and affordable accommodations make Neusiedl a popular destination for families.

⊟ TRANSPORTATION. Trains from Vienna (Südbahnhof) and Eisenstadt arrive at Neusiedl am See's **Hauptbahnhof** every hour, 15min. by foot (or a 2min. bus ride) from the town center. (Information and ticket window open 5am-9pm. From Eisenstadt €1.53; Vienna €6.10.) To town, follow Bahnstr. right onto Eisenstädterstr. (which becomes Obere Hauptstr.) and into Hauptpl. By **car** from Vienna, take A4 or Rte. 10 east. From Eisenstadt, take Rte. 50 north and Rte. 51 east.

◪ PRACTICAL INFORMATION. The tourist office is in the *Rathaus* on Hauptpl. (☎ 22 29; fax 26 37; info@neusiedlamsee.at; www.neusiedlamsee.at). Open July-Aug. M-F 8am-7pm, Sa 10am-noon and 2-6pm, Su 4-7pm; May-June and Sept. M-F 8am-noon and 1-4:30pm; Oct.-Apr. M-Th 8am-noon and 1-4:30pm, F 8am-1pm.) **Raiffeisenbank,** Untere Hauptstr. 3, has the best **currency exchange** rates. (☎ 25 64. Open M-Th 8am-12:30pm and 1:30-4pm, F 8am-noon and 1:30-4:30pm.) **Luggage**

storage at the train station (€2); and **emergency help** (☎144). The **post office,** Untere Hauptstr. 53, is on the corner of Untere Hauptstr. and Lisztg. (Open M-F 8am-noon and 2-6pm.) **Postal code:** A-7100.

◪◫ ACCOMMODATIONS AND FOOD. Heavy tourist activity, partly generated by Neusiedl's proximity to Vienna, makes finding accommodations tough. **Jugendherberge Neusiedl am See (HI) ❷,** Herbergg. 1, sports 86 beds in 21 quads and one double. Follow Wienerstr. and turn left onto Goldbergg. The hostel is on the corner at Herbergg. It's an uphill walk, but don't get discouraged—renovations have equipped the hostel with a sauna and winter greenhouse. There are showers in every room, but bathrooms are in the hall. (☎/fax 22 52. Breakfast included. Sheets €1.80. Reception 8am-2pm and 5-8pm. Reservations recommended. Open Mar.-Oct. €13-20, under 19 €11.73.) **Gasthof zur Traube ❸,** Hauptpl. 9, has a cordial staff and pretty pink rooms, and is family-friendly. (☎24 23; fax 242 36; zurtraube@aon.at; www.members.aon.at/traube. Breakfast included. €25.50-27.50 per person.) **Rathausstüberl ❸,** around the corner from the *Rathaus* on Kircheng. 2, is a sunny pension with two singles and 13 doubles. (☎28 83; fax 288 37; rathausstueberl@netway.at; www.rathausstueberl.at. Breakfast buffet included. Reservations recommended. €26.16-50.87 per person.) The pension also has a restaurant with a lovely shaded courtyard, great wine, and plenty of fresh fish and vegetarian dishes. The *Menü* includes soup and an entree, about €5. (Restaurant open Mar.-Dec. daily 10am-10pm.)

If the weather's nice, you can grab a picnic for the beach at the **Billa** grocery store on Seestr. (Open M-Th 7:30am-6:30pm, F 7:30am-8pm, Sa 7am-5pm.) **Rauchkuchl ❷,** Obere Hauptstr. 57, offers *Blaufränker* red wine or other homemade specialties as well as the opportunity to hear local dialect (☎25 85. Open Tu-Sa 5-11pm). Towards the Rauchkuchl on Obere Hauptstr. 9-11 is the small wine cellar **Weinbau Mullner** (☎/fax 33 95) with a cheap and wide selection of wines, including the famous sweet **Eiswein** (€9 per bottle) made from frozen grapes. A bit difficult to find; follow the driveway up and wait for service.

◪◫ OUTDOOR ACTIVITIES AND ENTERTAINMENT. To get to the **beach,** go to the end of Seestr. (1km), or catch the bus from the Hauptbahnhof or Hauptpl. (every hr. until 6pm, €1.50). The beach is rocky but pleasant (beach entrance €2, kids €1.50). The **Segelschule Neusiedl am See** (☎34 00 44; office@segelschule-neusiedl.at; www.segelschule-neusiedl.at), at the docks on the far right, **rents** sailboards (1hr. €11.63, half-day €34.88, full-day €58.14), dinghies (3- to 4-person boat €14.53 per hr., €43.60 per half-day, €72.67 per day), or standard surfboards (from €10.90 per hr.; open daily 8:30am-6pm). Close by on Seestr., find **paddleboats** (€5.81 per hr.) and **rowboats** (€2.91 per hr.) at **Bootsvermietung Leban.**

In early August, Neusiedl hosts a **Stadtfest.** The *Fußgängerzone* comes to life with food booths and music. Admission is free; contact the festival office for more information. (☎32 93; www.impulse-neusiedl.at. Open W and F 10am-noon.)

RUST   ☎02685

During the summer, tourists inundate this tiny wine capital of Austria. Ever since 1524, when the Emperor granted the wine-growers of Rust the exclusive right to mark the letter "R" on wine barrels, Rust has been synonymous with good—really good—wine. The town is known for sweet dessert wines, called *Ausbruch.* The quantity of desiccated grapes needed for a bottle is astounding, and consequently, so is the price. Wine isn't Rust's only attraction, however. The unspoiled town center with medieval houses and nesting storks, as well as Rust's location on the Neusiedlersee, give you something to appreciate while enjoying your buzz.

BURGENLAND

LOOK WHAT THE STORK BROUGHT Since 1910,

Rust's storks have been attracted to the high chimneys of the *Bürger* houses, and by 1960 nearly 40 pairs were nesting in the old city. Soon, however, locals noticed a decline and voiced their concern over these endangered birds. In 1987, Rust and the World Wildlife Federation initiated a special program to protect and reestablish the birds by importing cattle to cut down the overgrown marshes that were preventing them from finding their meals. Blue placards now mark the houses with chimneys in which the storks habitually nest. The storks come to Rust at the end of March, and from the end of May you can see their offspring in the nests. The storks have also hatched a post office, the **Storks' Post Office**, A-7071 Rust, at the *Rathaus*. Its stork postmark provides funds to support the birds.

▮ TRANSPORTATION

Rust lies 17km east of Eisenstadt on the Neusiedlersee. It does not have a train station, but **Post Buses** run from **Eisenstadt** (30min, several per day, €3) and **Vienna** Südtirolerpl. (1½hr., 5 per day, €9). The **bus station** is a glorified stop behind the post office at Franz-Josef-Pl. 14. By **car** from Vienna, take Autobahn A3 to Eisenstadt and then Bundesstr. 52 straight into Rust.

▮ ORIENTATION AND PRACTICAL INFORMATION

The **tourist office,** Conradpl. 1, hands out maps, plans bicycle tours, and gives information on wine tastings, the beach, and *Privatzimmer*. (☎502; fax 502 10; info@rust.or.at. Open Nov.-Mar. M-Th 9am-noon and 1-4pm, F 9am-noon; Apr. M-F 9am-noon and 1-4pm, Sa 9am-noon; May-Sept. M-F 9am-noon and 1-5pm, Sa-Su 9am-noon; Oct. M-F 9am-noon and 1-4pm.) The **Raiffeisenkasse Rust,** Rathauspl. 5, is the best place to **exchange money.** (☎607 05. Open M-F 8am-noon and 1:30-4pm.) There's also a 24hr. **ATM. Reisebüro Blaguss** in the *Rathaus* and **Ruster Freizeit-center** (☎595) by the beach are open late and provide emergency currency exchange. Call **taxis** at ☎65 76. The **post office** exchanges money but not traveler's checks. (Open M-F 8am-noon and 2-6pm.) **Postal code:** A-7071.

▮ ACCOMMODATIONS AND FOOD

If you want to stay in Rust, a *Privatzimmer* is the way to go. Reservations are strongly recommended during July and August. Be warned: prices may rise in the high season. You'll receive a warm welcome at **Gästehaus Ruth ❸,** Dr. Alfred-Ratzg. 1 (☎/fax 68 28), where rooms run €17.80-19.25. Rust's new **Jugendgästehaus ❷,** administered from Conradpl. 1, but located ½mi. away at Ruster Bucht 2, sits on the beachfront near tennis courts and bike paths. (☎591; fax 59 14; jgh_rust@yahoo.de; www.tiscover.com/jugendgasthaus.rust. Dorms €13-27.50.) As a luxury, the four-star **Seehotel Rust ❹,** Am Seekanal 2-4, will take care of your needs on the lake. (☎38 10; fax 381 419; seehotel@austria-trend.at; www.austria-trend.at/rus. Doubles €62-104.) From April to October, tent-dwellers use **Ruster Freizeitcenter ❶,** which offers showers, laundry, a game room, a playground, and a grocery store. (☎595 or 59 52; office@gmeiner.co.at; www.gmeiner.co.at. Reception 7:30am-10pm. €4.40-5.10, children €1.50-2.20; tent €2.40-3.20. 5min. from the beach; guests receive free entrance. Showers included.)

Vineyard-restaurants called *Buschenschenken* offer cheap snacks and superb wine; the tourist office has a complete list. Many of these are only open in the evenings. Good eating options line Rathausstr., though the ravenous should seek out

Zum Alten Haus ❷, on the corner of Feldg. and Franz-Josef-Pl., which serves up enormous portions of schnitzel and salad for only €6.50. (☎230. Open Tu-Su 9am-10pm.) **Alte Schmiede ❸**, Seezeile 24, roofed with grape vines, serves traditional Austrian food with a Hungarian twist in a lively, friendly atmosphere. (☎64 18. Live music at lunch and dinner. Reservations recommended. Open daily 11:30am-2pm and 5:30-10pm.) The **A & O Markt Dreyseitel** is on Weinbergg. between Mitterg. and Schubertg. (☎238. Open M-F 7am-noon and 3-6pm, Sa 7am-noon.)

🔲 🏞 SIGHTS AND OUTDOOR ACTIVITIES

WINE ACADEMY. Rust is home to Austria's only **Weinakademie**, at Hauptstr. 31. The institution offers courses ranging from wine cultivation to basic bartending, and holds wine tours and tastings. *(☎64 51 or 68 53; fax 64 31. Open for wine tastings F-Su 2-6pm; daily in Sept. €11 for 10 tastes.)* Many vintners *(Weinbauern)* offer wine tastings and tours of their own cellars. **Rudolf Beilschmidt,** Weinbergg. 1, has tours *(☎326. May-Sept. F 5pm),* as does **Weingut Marienhof,** Weinbergg. 16 *(☎251. June-Sept. Tu 6pm, €4.50).*

FISCHERKIRCHE. Rust's **Fischerkirche,** around the corner from the tourist office, begun in the 12th century, is the oldest church in Burgenland. In the 13th century, Queen Mary of Hungary donated the Marienkapelle after being rescued from the Mongols by fishermen. This interior chapel contains lovely 15th-century sculptures of the Madonna. The Romanesque and Gothic sections have also survived the Baroque remodeling fervor. *(Open Apr. M-Sa 11am-noon and 2-3pm, Su 11am-noon and 2-4pm; May-Sept. M-Sa 10am-noon and 2:30-6pm, Su 2-4pm. Tours by appointment. Call Frau Kaiser at ☎64 81. €0.73, students €0.36.)*

LAKE ACCESS AND ACTIVITIES. Sun worshipers can sit and splash on the south shore of the **Neusiedlersee.** There is a **public beach** with showers, lockers, restrooms, phones, water slide, and a snack bar. Walk down Hauptstr., take a left onto Am Seekanal, then right onto Seepromenade, which cuts through the marsh lands (about 7km) surrounding the lake. The murky waters of the lake daunt some swimmers, but have no fear—the muddy color comes from the shallow, easily disturbed clay bottom. The beach also has a chlorine pool. Keep your entrance card to exit the park. *(☎501. €3.70 per person, after 11am €3, after 4pm €2.50.)*

Rent a **boat** from **Family Gmeiner,** next to the beach on the water's edge. *(Sailboats €5 per hr., €20 per 5hr; paddleboats €6/€18; electric boats €9/€27.)* The same company runs **Schiffrundfahrten** (boat tours) that can transport you to Illmitz on the opposite shore. *(☎493 or 62683 55 38. Boats leave Rust Apr.-Oct. Th-Su and holidays 10am, 4pm and return from Illmitz 11am, 5pm. 4-person minimum, €19 per person.)* The area is lined with **bike** trails. Many follow the lake shore or wind between towns on the Austro-Hungarian border. The routes cover 170km, but you can take a bus back, or take the Illmitz boat to the opposite shore and bike back.

STYRIA (STEIERMARK)

Styria, promoted by tourist offices as "the Green Heart of Austria," is the country's second largest province. Styria has been spared the brunt of the tourist invasion, which has allowed for the preservation of many of Austria's folk traditions and ancient forests. Even its gem-like city, Graz, remains relatively untarnished by tourists. The crumbling medieval strongholds and stud farm for Austria's Lipizzaner stallions are among the region's most notable attractions. Famous also for its libations, Styrian vineyards are essential to any wine tour of Europe. Styrians are notorious for stubborn individuality and provincial pride; they speak a dialect few outsiders can understand and have gruff senses of humor.

HIGHLIGHTS OF STYRIA

Peruse the collected treasures of **Graz**'s Landesmuseum Joanneum (see p. 152).
Marvel at a glass-blowing demonstration in **Bärnbach** (see p. 138).
Discover hidden staircases in **Admont**'s Benediktinerstift (see p. 142).

GRAZ ☎ 0316

You'll definitely feel like you're in Austria's second largest city when you leave the train station and enter a mob of buses, streetcars, and busy locals. For a more relaxed pace, walk just a few minutes to the pedestrian district of the old city, where locals linger over coffee in one of the many cafes lining the Herreng. or the narrow cobblestone Sporg. Graz's Altstadt, with winding streets, museums, and steep red-tiled roofs, is relatively tourist-free.

The two towers rising from the small mountain in the center of town commemorate the mighty fortress that withstood centuries of attacks. The mountain continued to be a refuge during war in the 20th century—the citizens of Graz hid in the air-raid tunnels deep inside. The eastern slope of the mountain leads down into the calm Stadtpark full of sunbathers and frisbee-throwers. In the evening, the areas around the park become a center for hip nightlife, thanks to the 42,000 students at nearby Karl-Franzens University.

◾ INTERCITY TRANSPORTATION

Flights: Flughafen Graz, Flughafenstr. 51 (☎29 02 0), 9km from the city center. Take bus #631 from the airport into town (20min., every hr. 6:13am-11:30pm, €1.60); taxis into town cost about €14.

Trains: Trains arrive at the **Hauptbahnhof,** on Europapl., west of city center. (☎05 17 17 12, open 7am-8:45pm.) To: **Innsbruck** (6hr., 4 per day 8:23am-10pm, €41.40); **Linz** (3½hr., every 2hr. 6:32am-6:23pm, €27.60); **Munich** (6¼hr., €56.10) via Salzburg; **Salzburg** (4¼hr., 4 per day 6:32am-8:23pm, €33.40); **Vienna Südbahnhof** (2½hr., 9 per day 5:30am-9:23pm, €24.70); **Zurich** (8½hr., 1 per day 10pm, €108).

Buses: Graz-Köflach Bus (GKB), Köflacherg. 35-41 (☎59 87), runs 24hr. Buses leave from Griespl. for western Styria. The **Post Bus** office, Andreas-Hofer-Pl. 17 (☎81 18 18). Open M-F 7am-5pm; customer service M-Th 9:30am-noon and 1-4pm, F 9:30am-noon and 1-3pm. There is a **branch** at the Hauptbahnhof as well. **Bundesbus** lines depart from Europapl. 5 (next to the train station) and from Andreas-Hofer-Pl.

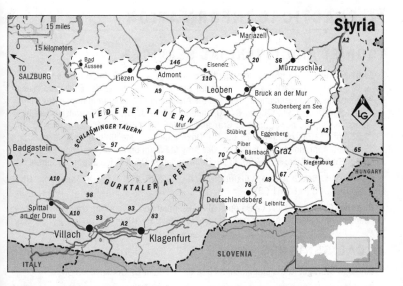

✈ ORIENTATION

Graz spreads across the Mur River in the southeast corner of Austria. The city is a gateway to Slovenia (50km south) and Hungary (70km east). Two-thirds of Graz's area consists of beautiful parks, earning it the nickname "Garden City." **Hauptplatz,** directly in front of the *Rathaus,* is the city center. **Jakominiplatz,** 5min. from Hauptpl., is the hub of the city's bus and streetcar system. **Herrengasse,** a pedestrian street lined with cafes and boutiques, connects Hauptpl. to Jakominipl., forming the heart of the *Fußgängerzone.* The **Universität** is tucked away past the Stadtpark, in the northeast part of Graz. The **Hauptbahnhof** lies on the other side of the river, a short ride from Hauptpl. on tram #3 or 6. To get to the city center by foot from the train station, follow Annenstr. up and over Hauptbrücke (20min.).

▨ LOCAL TRANSPORTATION

Public Transportation: For information on all local buses, trams, and trains, call **Mobil Zentrale,** Schönaug. 6 (☎82 06 06). Open M-F 7am-7pm, Sa 9am-1pm. Purchase single tickets (€1.60) and 24hr. tickets (€3.20) from the driver, booklets of 10 tickets (€12.40) or week-tickets (€7.90) from any *Tabak.* Children half-price. Tickets are valid for all trams, buses, and the cable car and elevator that ascend the Schloßberg; validate them at the orange stamp box. Most trams run until 11pm, most buses until 9pm.

Taxi: Funktaxi, ☎983. **City-Funk,** ☎878.

Car Rental: Budget, Europapl. 12 (☎71 69 66; fax 722 07 64; airport ☎29 02 342).

Automobile Clubs: ÖAMTC, Conrad-von-Hötzendorf-str. 127 (☎120). **ARBÖ,** Kappellenstr. 45 (☎123).

Bicycle Rental: Bicycle Graz, Körösistr. 5 (☎/fax 82 13 57 16). Seven-speed bikes €7 per day, trekking bikes €9, mountain bikes €11. Open M-F 7am-1pm and 2-6pm.

⏾ PRACTICAL INFORMATION

TOURIST AND FINANCIAL SERVICES

Tourist Office: Main office, Herreng. 16 (☎807 50; fax 75 15; info@graztourismus.at; www.graztourismus.at), has free city maps and a city walking guide. English-speaking staff makes room reservations. **Tours** of the Altstadt in English start in front of the office (2hr., Apr.-Oct. Tu, W 2:30pm; €7.50, children 6-15 €3.75). The office also offers bus tours visiting the newer parts of Graz and Schloß Eggenberg (2½hr., Apr.-Oct. M, Th 2:30pm; €11.50, children 6-15 €5.75). Open June-Sept. M-F 9am-7pm, Sa 9am-6pm, Su 10am-4pm, holidays 10am-3pm; Oct.-May M-F 9am-6pm, Sa 9am-3pm, Su 10am-3pm. **Branch office:** ☎807 50, in the Hauptbahnhof. Open M-F 8:30am-5:30pm.

Consulates: South Africa, Villefortg. 13/II (☎32 25 48). Open M 8am-noon. **UK,** Schmiedg. 10 (☎82 61 05).

Currency Exchange: Most banks open M-F 8am-noon and 2-4pm. The **train station** ticketing counter also exchanges currency and is open 6am-10pm.

LOCAL SERVICES

Luggage Storage: At the station; small bag €2, medium €2.50, large €3.50.

Bookstores: English Bookshop, Tummelpl. 7 (☎82 62 66), has two vast floors of fiction and nonfiction. Open M-F 9am-6pm, Sa 9am-noon.

Bi-Gay-Lesbian Organizations: Verein Frauenservice Graz (Women's Information Center), Idlhofg. 20 (☎71 60 22). Office open M, W, F 9am-1pm, Tu 5-7pm. Medical help available W 5-7pm. Pick up the "Genuine Gay Guide" to Styria at LOGO (see below).

Youth Organizations: Jugend Informationsservice "LOGO," Schmiedg. 23a, offers free brochures and advice for young people (☎17 99). Open M-F 11am-6pm.

Women's Health Center: Frauengesundheitszentrum Graz, Brockmanng. 48, 3rd floor (☎83 79 98; frauen.gesundheit@fgz.co.at; www.fgz.co.at).

Laundromat: Putzerei Rupp, Jakoministr. 34 (☎82 11 83). 5kg load €6.18, soap €0.73, dryer €0.36 per 3min., centrifuge €0.36. Open M-F 8am-5pm, Sa 8am-noon.

EMERGENCY AND COMMUNICATIONS

Emergencies: Police, ☎133, (office ☎888 27 75). **Ambulance,** ☎144.

AIDS Hotline: Steirische AIDS-Hilfe, Schmiedg. 38 (☎81 50 50; steirische@aids-hilfe.at; www.aids-hilfe.at.) Counseling available W 11am-1pm, F 5-7pm. Blood tests Tu, Th 4:30-7:30pm. Safer Sex Hotline F 7:30-8:30pm.

Pharmacy: Bärenapotheke, Herreng. 11 (☎83 02 67), opposite the tourist office. Open M-F 8am-6pm, Sa 8am-noon. AmEx/MC/V.

Hospital: Krankenhaus der Elisabethinen, Elisabethinerg. 14 (☎706 30).

Internet Access: Jugendgästehaus Graz, Idlhofg. 74 (see **Accommodations**). €1.50 per 20min. Open 7am-10pm. **Café Zentral,** Andreas-Hofer-Pl. 9 (☎83 24 68). €4.50 for 1hr. minimum. Open M-F 6am-midnight, Sa 6am-noon.

Post Office: Main office, Neutorg. 46. Open M-F 7:30am-8pm, Sa 8am-noon. Cashier closes M-F at 5pm. **Branch office,** Europapl. 10, next to the Hauptbahnhof. Open M-F 8am-11pm, Sa 7am-2pm, Su 3-10pm. **Postal code:** A-8010; branch office A-8020.

Graz

🍴 FOOD
Braun der Praun, **12**
China Restaurant Mond, **2**
Gasthaus Alte Münze, **8**
Gastwirtschaft Wartburg, **4**
Kebap Haus, **19**
Restaurant Brandhof, **16**
Stainzerbauer, **11**
University Mensa, **5**
Wintergarten, **9**
Zur Goldenen Pastete, **10**

▲ ACCOMMODATIONS
Camping Central, **17**
Exerzitienhaus der
  Barmherzigen Schwestern, **1**
Hotel Strasser, **13**
Hotel Zum Dom, **15**
Hotel Zur Stadt Feldbach, **20**
Hotel Zur Stadthalle Johannes, **21**
Jugendgästehaus Graz, **18**

★ NIGHTLIFE
Bang-Inside, **14**
Blue Moon, **7**
Café Harrach, **3**
Kulturhauskeller, **6**
Park House, **9**

STYRIA

⚓ ACCOMMODATIONS

Staking out a cheap bed in Graz may require a bit of detective work, as most budget hotels, guest houses, and pensions run from €25, and many are in the boondocks. Luckily, the web of local transport provides a reliable and easy commute to and from the city center. Ask the tourist office about *Privatzimmer* (€15-30 per night), especially in the crowded summer months.

▨ **Jugendgästehaus Graz (HI)**, Idlhofg. 74 (☎48 76; fax 48 76 88; jgh.graz@jgh.at), 20min. from the train station. Exit the station, cross the street, head right on Eggenberger Gürtel, left on Josef-Huber-G. (after the car dealership), and take a right at Idlhofg. The hostel is through a parking lot on your right. Buses #31 and 32 run here from Jakominipl. (last bus around midnight). This hotel-quality hostel has its own cafe, restaurant, and **Internet** access (€1.50 per 20min.). Breakfast included. Laundry €1.45, soap included; dryer €1.45. Key available (€21.80 deposit). Reception 7am-10pm. Doors open every 30min. 10pm-2am. 4-bed dorms €17; singles €24; doubles €40. All rooms with bath. €2.50 surcharge for stays of less than 3 nights. If the hostel is full, you can stay in the "Notlager," basement rooms with hall bath, for €14. MC/V. ❸

Hotel Strasser, Eggenberger Gürtel 11 (☎71 39 77; fax 71 68 56), 5min. from the train station. Exit the station, cross the street, and head right on Eggenberger Gürtel; the hotel is on the left, across from the car repair shop. Bright, airy rooms with colorful rugs. Breakfast included. Free parking. Singles €26, with shower €33; doubles €40/€51; triples with shower €65. AmEx/DC/MC/V. ❸

Hotel Zur Stadt Feldbach, Conrad-von-Hötzendorf-Str. 58 (☎82 94 68; fax 94 68 15), 15min. walk south of Jakominipl. Take tram #4 (dir: Liebnau) or #5 (dir: Puntigam) to "Jakominigürtel." The hotel is on the right. Sensible, clean rooms. Hall bathrooms. Breakfast €5. Reception 24hr. on 2nd floor. Singles €26, with shower €33; doubles €40/€51; triples with shower €65. ❸

Exerzitienhaus der Barmherzigen Schwestern, Marieng. 6a (☎91 60). Walk straight out of the train station onto Keplerstr., then take a left onto Marieng. The convent will be on your right (10min.). Ring the bell marked Exerzitienhaus at the metal gate across from the Kindergarten. As you might expect from a convent, the rooms are plain, clean, and quiet, and with lots of nuns. Dorms €14, with breakfast €17; Singles €21/€25. ❷

Hotel Zum Dom, Burgerg. 14 (☎824 800; fax 824 800 8; domhotel@domhotel.co.at). This stylish hotel in the old city bring luxury up to date—the red carpets and chandeliers are integrated into a hip colorful decor. Every one of the spacious rooms is decorated uniquely and each has a different kind of marble in the bathroom. Breakfast included. All rooms with bathroom. Singles €85; doubles €155, with jacuzzi €160. ❺

Hotel zur Stadthalle "Johannes," Münzgrabenstr. 48 (☎83 77; fax 77 66 18). Take streetcar #6 from the train station or Jakominipl. to "Neue Technik." The hotel is the pale yellow building on the right close to the stop. On foot from Jakominipl., head down Reitschulg., which turns into Münzgrabenstr. (15min.) Wood furniture and down comforters. Rooms include shower, toilet, TV, and breakfast. Singles €45; doubles €67. ❹

Camping Central, Martinhofstr. 3 (☎(0676) 378 51 02, fax (0316) 69 78 24; Freizeit@netway.at). Take bus #32 from Jakomininpl. to "Bad Straßgang" (10min.). Follow signs, taking the next right at the Mondo supermarket, and walk up the road. This clean campground includes admission to public swimming pool. Laundry €3, dryer €2. Reception 7am-10pm. Open Apr.-Oct. €13 per person, includes tent site and shower; car or camper €24 for 2 people, includes shower and electricity; additional adults €7, children 4-15 €5. There is an additional tax of €0.75 per person per night. ❶

◘ FOOD

Graz's student community sustains a bonanza of cheap eateries. On Hauptpl. concession stands sell wurst, ice cream, and other fast food (€1.50-3) until late. Low-priced student hangouts also line Zinzendorfg. near the university. Note that most salads come dressed in the local dark pumpkin-seed oil. At **farmers' markets** on Kaiser-Josef-Pl. and Lendpl. (M-Sa 7am-1pm), and "Standl" on Hauptpl. and on Jakominipl. (M-F 7am-6pm, Sa 7am-12:30pm), vendors hawk various goods. There's a **Merkur** grocery store to your left as you exit the train station. (Open M-Th 8am-7pm, F 7:30am-7:30pm.) There are numerous Billas and Spars around town.

Braun de Praun, Morellenfeldg. 32 (☎32 20 03). With over 30 menu options (€6-12) and just as many daily specials, Braun de Praun is an Austrian restaurant unafraid of a little culinary experimentation. Main dishes include curry veal with glazed banana and almond-raisin rice (€14) and chicken "mexicano" (€12), but the numerous local dishes, beer garden ambience, and Lederhosen-clad waiters keep it firmly rooted in Graz. Open M-Sa 8am-2am. ❸

Gasthaus "Alte Münze," Schloßbergpl. 8 (☎82 91 51). On the tranquil Schloßbergpl., Gasthaus Alte Münze serves scrumptious Styrian specialities in a traditional setting. Excellent *Eierspatzn* (egg noodles) are €6.90 with salad. Try the local dessert *Besoffene Liesl* (Gugelhopf cake in apple wine). Daily *Menü* €6.90. Open Tu-Sa 8am-midnight, Su-M 10am-7pm. ❷

Zur Goldenen Pastete, Sporg. 28 (☎82 34 16), just up the street from the Hauptpl. This deep red Gasthaus is the oldest in the city, having been built in 1575. It serves up-to-date interpretations of Austrian classics. Chicken with apple plum sauce €7, most entrees €9-11.50. Open daily 11am-midnight. ❸

Wintergarten, Sackstr. 3-5 (☎81 16 16), in the sunny glass-topped atrium of the luxurious Erzherzog Johann Hotel, offers excellent service and gourmet entrees (€14-19). If you're ready to pull out all the stops, order their 7-course daily *Menü* (€47). Open W-Su

Stainzerbauer, Burgerg. 4 (☎82 11 06), specializes in Styrian food, but don't expect heavy plain dumplings here. Delicious dishes include Tafelspitz (€15.90), duck breast with ginger sauce (€19.80), and roasted calf's liver with apple pieces, bacon, and polenta (€10.90), all served in the elegant atmosphere of their Renaissance courtyard decked out with fresh flowers. Open M-Sa 11:30am-midnight. ❹

Restaurant Brandhof, at the corner of Gleisdorferstr. and Glacisstr., is nestled just behind the opera house. The simple red tables in its tree-filled garden fill up in the afternoon with chatty locals enjoying its simple cuisine, including asparagus and spinach strudel (€5.90), fried zucchini (€5.80), and *Zwiebelrostbraten* (€8.80). Open M 10am-3pm, Tu-F 10am-midnight, Sa 10am-3pm and 6pm-midnight, and after the opera. ❷

Gastwirtschaft Wartburg, Halbärthg. 4 (☎38 87 50). This smoky cafe/bar features antique posters on the wall, filling dishes, and a student crowd at the tables. Lunch specials (€5.45) and entrees (€4-9). Open M-F 10am-2am, Sa 5pm-2am. ❷

Kebap Haus, Jakominstr. 16 (☎81 10 06), just south of Jakominipl. A superior Turkish restaurant with falafel (€5.90), pita sandwiches (take-out €2.70-3), and delicious pizzas (€5.80-6). Lunch specials include soup, entree, and salad (around €5.50). Open M-Sa 10am-midnight. ❷

China Restaurant Mond, Harrachg. 12a (☎35 69 79), between Cafe Harrach and the park. Keep both tummy and wallet bulging with the all-you-can-eat lunch buffet (M-F 11:30am-2:30pm, €5.10). A €3.80 *Menü* is also available for both lunch and dinner. Open 11:30am-3pm and 5:30-10pm. ❶

STYRIA

**IN
RECENT
NEWS**

IMMIGRANT OUTCRY

Austria received a lot of international attention a few years ago for the anti-immigration stance of its Freedom Party. Although cutting off immigration entirely is no longer considered an option, there are still fierce debates in Austria about how to handle immigrants. Within the past year, a variety of proposals have been made in the Austrian parliament, including suggestions to provide social services to refugees only at the level of their home countries, or to require immigrants to attend German courses where failure to pass final exams would result in sanctions against them. As a tourist, you can get involved in the campaign for minority rights by buying a copy of the non-profit monthly magazine *Das Megaphon*. On sale since 1995 on the streets of Graz and many other cities in Styria, *Das Megaphon* is primarily a forum for immigrant rights, but also serves the handicapped and the homeless. Half of the profits of each €2 issue sold go directly to the sellers, who are often of Nigerian descent, one of the two largest minority groups in Austria (the other is Turkish). After speaking to one seller in Bruck an der Mur, our *Let's Go* researcher learned that although he had been a biologist in his native Nigeria, he was now unemployed because of his inability to speak German. He summed up the inherent problem well in his complaint, "Everyone here, they want you to speak the Deutsch."

University Mensa, Sonnenfelspl. 1 (☎32 33 62; fax 32 33 62 75), just east of the Stadtpark at the intersection of Zinzendorfg. and Leechg. Take bus #39 or 63 to "Uni/Mensa" for the best deal in town. Simple, satisfying *Menüs* €4.35; student discount €0.15. Large *à la carte* selection. Open M-F 8:30am-2:30pm. ❶

👁 SIGHTS

THE OLD TOWN. An entertaining way to explore Graz is to use the tourist office's free brochure, *A Short Tale of Graz*, or to follow the walking-guide. The tourist office is in the **Landhaus,** the seat of the provincial government, and a sight in itself. The building was remodeled by architect Domenico dell'Allio in 1557 in Lombard style. Through the arch to the right is a striking arcaded Renaissance courtyard, where *Classics in the City* is held (see p. 153).

LANDESZEUGHAUS (PROVINCIAL ARSENAL). Anton Solar built the Landeszeughaus between 1642 and 1644. The first floor details the history of the arsenal and the Ottoman attacks in a series of placards and displays with English translations. In 1749, after the Turks had packed their cannon and gone home, the armory was marked for dismantling, but an eloquent protest by Styrian nobles convinced Empress Maria Theresia to preserve it as a symbolic gesture. The building, with its massive collection of arms and armor intact, served as a firehouse until 1882, when it opened as a museum. Today, the four-story collection includes enough spears, muskets, and armor to outfit 28,000 burly mercenaries. *(Herreng. 16, next to the tourist office. ☎80 17 98 10. Open Mar.-Oct. Tu-Su 9am-5pm; Nov.-Dec. Tu-Su 10am-3pm. Tours in German, French, English throughout the day or by appointment. €1.50, students €0.70. Admission with Joanneum ticket.)*

CHURCHES. The 13th-century Gothic **Leechkirche** is the city's oldest structure, having been built (1202), destroyed (1250), and rebuilt (1275-1283). *(Zinzendorfg. 5, between Stadtpark and the university.)* The yellow **Stadtpfarrkirche** was the Abbey Church of the Dominicans in the 16th century. The late Gothic church suffered severe damage in WWII. When Salzburg artist Albert Birkle designed new stained-glass windows for the church in 1953, one made worldwide news: the left panel behind the high altar portrays the scourging of Christ, silently watched over by two figures bearing a marked resemblance to Hitler and Mussolini. The church holds **organ concerts.** *(Herreng. 23. Concerts mid-July to early Sept., Su 8pm. €5, students €3.)*

Nearby stands Graz's **Dom** (cathedral), built in 15th-century Gothic style by Emperor Friedrich III.

In 1485, the church mounted a picture of the "Scourges of God" on the south side of the building to remind Christians of the most palpable trinity of the time—the plague, Ottoman invasions, and locusts—holy terrors that had wiped out 80% of the population five years earlier. *(On Hofg., opposite the Burggarten and Burgtor. Closes 8pm. Impromptu organ music 11am-noon.)*

SCHLOßBERG. The wooded **Schloßberg** rises 123m above Graz. The hill is named for a castle which stood on it from 1125 until 1809, when it was destroyed by Napoleon's troops. Though the castle is mostly gone, the Schloßberg remains a beautiful city park. From Schloßbergpl., visitors can climb the zigzagging stone steps of the **Schloßbergstiege,** built by Russian prisoners during WWI and traditionally known as the *Russenstiege* (Russian steps) or the *Kriegstiege* (war steps). The path continues through the terraced Herberstein Gardens, a lush park with sweeping views surveying the vast Styrian plain surrounding Graz. The **Glockenturm** (bell tower), built in 1588, is one of the few castle structures still standing, having been spared by the little emperor in return for a sizeable ransom from the citizens of Graz. *(Tower open only with Schloßberg tour, see below.)* Its enormous bell ("Liesl") draws a crowd with its 101 clangings daily (supposedly because it was forged from 101 Turkish cannon balls) at 7am, noon, and 7pm. Next to the Liesl, you'll find the **Freilichtbühne in den Kasematten,** an outdoor theater built into the ruins of the castle foreman's massive basement. Events are published in newspapers and pamphlets. The nearby **Uhrturm** (clocktower) dates from 1265 and was rebuilt in 1569. A guided tour of the Schloßberg includes viewing the Uhrturm clockworks, which date from 1712. *(North of Herreng. and Hauptpl. Tours in German or English Apr.-Oct. Tu-Su every hr. 9am-5pm, meet at Glockenturm; €2.15, students and children €1.05.)*

From Schloßbergpl., the **Schloßberg Passage** burrows into the *Berg.* A network of tunnels was blasted into the hill during WWII to serve as a bomb shelter for up to 50,000 civilians. Visitors may walk through the cool, dark main passage and peer down spooky side tunnels. The largest side tunnel opens up into a large chamber, the **Dom im Berg,** which is now a popular venue for all sorts of events. *(Dom im Berg open 8am-8pm, free. The quickest way to the top of the Schloßberg is the Lift im Berg, which takes you up 77m; enter from Schloßbergpl. Or take the historic Schloßbergbahn, in operation since 1894. Both are open Apr.-Sept. daily 9am-11pm; Oct.-Mar. 10am-10pm; fare is a valid public transportation ticket or €1.50, children €0.75.)*

PARKS AND GARDENS. Down the hill on the eastern side near the Uhrturm and through the Paulustor arch is the **Stadtpark.** Graz acquired the ornate central fountain, whose eight mermaids struggle with huge spitting fish, at the 1873 Vienna World's Fair. South of the fish fountain, the Stadtpark blends into the **Burggarten,** a bit of carefully pruned greenery complementing what remains of Emperor Friedrich III's 15th-century *Burg.* His cryptic wall inscription "A.E.I.O.U." remains a mystery, varyingly interpreted as *"Austria Erit In Orbe Ultima,"* (Austria will be the Ultimate on Earth) or *"Alles Erdreich Ist Österreich Untertan"* (All on Earth is Under Austria).

OTHER SIGHTS. The solemn 17th-century Habsburg **Mausoleum,** an elaborate domed tomb, holds the remains of Ferdinand II. Cryptic English signs are pasted to the stone walls. Master architect Fischer von Erlach (responsible for much of Vienna's Baroque grandeur) designed the beautiful frescoes upstairs. *(Around the corner from the Dom, on Burgg.)* The magnificent **Opernhaus** was built in less than two years by Viennese architects Fellner and Helmer. *(At Opernring and Burgg., down the street from the mausoleum. ☎ 80 08.)* The **Glockenspiel** opens its wooden doors daily to reveal life-size wooden figures spinning to an excruciatingly slow folk song. The black-and-gold ball underneath turns to show the phases of the moon. *(Located just off Engeg. in Glockenspielpl. 11am, 3, 6pm.)*

STYRIA

🏛 MUSEUMS

LANDESMUSEUM JOANNEUM. Graz's state museum is Austria's oldest public museum. The holdings are so vast that officials have been forced to keep portions in museums scattered throughout the city. One ticket, purchased at any location, is valid for the Garrisonsmuseum, the Natural History museum, and most art museums in the city. *(€4.30, students and seniors €2.90.)*

ART MUSEUMS. The **Joanneum** includes the **Neue Galerie,** housed in the elegant Palais Herberstein, which showcases offbeat, avant-garde 19th- and 20th-century works and paintings. *(Sackstr. 16, at the foot of the Schloßberg. ☎82 91 55; fax 81 54 01. Tours €1.45, available by appointment over ext. 93 11. Open Tu-Su 10am-6pm, Th 10am-8pm. Admission with Joanneum ticket.)* Its counterpart, the **Alte Galerie,** presents a mid-sized collection of medieval and Baroque art, mostly of Styrian origin. Notable holdings include Lucas Cranach's *Judgment of Paris* and Jan Brueghel's copy of his father's gruesome *Triumph of Death. (Neutorg. 45. ☎17 97 90, fax 80 17 98 47. Open Tu-Su 10am-5pm. Tours Su 3pm, English by appointment. Admission with Joanneum ticket.)* The Künstlerhaus, an independent museum in the Stadtpark, hosts small exhibitions ranging from Tibetan artifacts to Secessionist paintings by Klimt. *(Open M-Sa 9am-6pm, Su 9am-noon. €1.60, students and children free.)*

HISTORY AND SCIENCE MUSEUMS. At the **Stadtmuseum,** temporary exhibits complement the permanent 3rd-floor display, which features 19th-century drawings of the city alongside modern photographs and a large-scale model c.1800. *(Sackstr. 18, next to the Neue Galerie at western foot of the Schloßberg. ☎82 25 80. Open Tu 10am-9pm, W-Sa 10am-6pm, Su 10am-1pm. €3.63, students and children €2.18.)* On the Schloßberg, the **Garrisonsmuseum** exhibits its modest collection of military uniforms and feathered helmets. *(☎82 73 48. Open Tu-Su 10am-5pm. €1.45, students and children €0.73.)* The Joanneum's scientific wing is the **Natural History Museum,** which encompasses geology, paleontology, zoology, and other -ologies. The museum has a specimen of the largest beetle in the world, a collection of minerals and semi-precious stones, and a set of wildlife scenes. From the geology gallery, you can leave the museum through the secret exit of the coal mine, the "Schaubergwerk." *(Rauberg. 10. ☎30 17 47 60. Open Tu-Su 9am-4pm. Admission with Joanneum ticket.)*

🎭 ENTERTAINMENT

The magazine *Was ist Wo?* (in German), free at the tourist office, details current events with prices and locations. Students can check the 2nd floor of the **student administration office** of the university, which has an **Internet** terminal, billboards papered with concert notices, student activity flyers, and carpool advertisements.

OPERA, THEATER, AND DANCE

For professional music and dance performances, Graz's neo-Baroque **Opernhaus,** at Opernring and Burgg. *(☎80 08)*, sells standing-room tickets 1hr. before curtain call. The program includes operas and ballets of worldwide repute; for many young hopefuls, Graz is considered a stepping stone to an international career. One big show comes each July while the regular companies are on vacation. Tickets cost €10-77, but standing-room slots start at €5, and student rush tickets (27 and under) are discounted by €6. Another dance venue is the annual **Tanzsommer Graz** (July 2-21, 2003), featuring a variety of dance groups, including a tango group from Argentina, and the Bahia ballet from Brazil. *(☎80 00. Tickets €10-77).* The **Schauspielhaus** *(☎80 00)*, the theater on Freiheitspl. (entrance on Hofg.), sells bargain seats just before showtime (daily ticket sales 10am-4pm). All tickets and performance schedules are available at the **Theaterkasse,** Kaiser-Josef-Pl. 10, at the tram stop (☎80 00; open M-F 8am-5pm, Sa 8-10am), and the **Zentralkartenbüro,** Herreng. 7, on the left inside the passage (☎83 02 55; bestellung@zkb.at; www.zkb.at; open M-F 9am-1pm and 2-6pm, Sa 9am-noon).

FESTIVALS

Since 1985, the city has hosted its own summer festival, **Styriarte.** Concerts, mostly classical, are held daily from late June to late July in the gardens of Schloß Eggenberg, the large halls of Graz Convention Center, and the squares of the old city. Tickets are available at Palais Attems, Sackstr. 17. (☎82 50 00; fax 877 38 36. Open M-F 8:30am-12:30pm and 2-6pm.) Every summer between July and August, the **American Institute of Musical Studies** transfers to Graz. Students perform works from Broadway to Schönberg on the streets and in concert halls—ask for a schedule at the tourist office. Tickets are available through the Zentralkartenburo or AIMS itself (Elisabethstr. 93; ☎32 70 66; fax 55 74; aims@sime.com; tickets €7-9). From July to mid-August, **organ concerts** are held once a week at the Stadtpfarrkirche (Su 8pm). July and August also bring **Jazz-Sommer Graz,** a festival of free concerts. Previous years have seen jazz legends like Dave Brubek, Slide Hampton, and Dizzy Gillespie. (Contact the tourist office; concerts Th-Sa 8:30pm at Maria Hilferpl.) From July 26 to Aug. 3, 2003, Graz will surrender its streets to **La Strada,** the international festival of puppet and street theatre. From late Sept. to Oct., the **Steierischer Herbst** (Styrian Autumn) festival, Sackstr. 17, celebrates avant-garde art with a month of films, performances, art installations, and parties. Contact the director for details. (☎81 60 70; fax 83 57 88.)

FILM

The award-winning movie theater **Rechbauerkino,** Rechbauerstr. 6 (☎83 05 08), occasionally screens un-dubbed arthouse films in English (€6.50, children €5.50). The **Royal Kino,** Conrad-von-Hötzendorfstr. 10, a few blocks south of Jakominipl., shows new releases in English, without subtitles (€7.20, but there are a variety of discounts—€6.20 if you sit in one of the first three rows; M-W all features €5; Th-Su before 5:45pm €6.20; students Th-F €5.40, Sa-Su €6.70). In July and Aug. the **Classics in the City Festival** shows free films of great opera performances and serves food in the *Landhaus* courtyard next to the tourist office. (Daily at 8:30pm, pick up the brochure at the tourist office or call ☎80 750 for details.)

THE INSIDER'S CITY

OLD- AND NEW-WORLD TREASURES

Ethnic restaurants tucked into courtyards behind Baroque facades are just reminders of Graz's living history.

1 The **tourist office** is a good starting place. Pick up the brochure "A Short Tale of Graz" for a map.

2 Admire the arcaded courtyard of the **Landhaus,** which reflects Italian influences.

3 Poke around the **Alte Galerie** and **Natural History Museum.**

4 For a snack, try crepes or Leberkäse from a vendor on Hauptpl.

5 Check out modern art at the **Neue Galerie** inside Herberstein Palace.

6 Brush up on you Graz history at the **Stadtmusem.**

7 A special path runs along the Mur a full story beneath street level.

8 Enjoy tapas in a cheerful red-and-yellow Spanish eatery.

9 Sip a ginger or hibiscus drink in this batik-draped African restaurant.

10 Secure tickets to a performance at the **Zentralkartenbüro.**

■ NIGHTLIFE

After-hours activity in Graz can be found in the so-called **"Bermuda Dreieck"** (Bermuda triangle), in the old city behind Hauptpl. and bordered by Mehlpl., Färberg., and Prokopig. Dozens of beer gardens and bars are packed all night, every night; standard procedure is to sit outdoors until about 11pm, when ordinance requires festivities move indoors. Most university students prefer to down their beers in the pubs lining Zinzendorfg. and Halbärthg. on the other side of the Stadtpark.

Kulturhauskeller, Elisabethstr. 30, underneath the Kulturhaus. From the Stadtpark, head straight down Elisabethstr. A young crowd demands loud, throbbing dance music, but the partying doesn't get started until 11pm on weekends. *Weißbier* €2.80. No sports or military clothing. 19+. Obligatory coat check and security fee €2. Open Tu-Sa from 9pm until whenever.

Park House (☎ 82 74 34) in the Stadtpark. From the Künstlerhaus, cross Burgg. and follow the stream 70m. An enclosed pavillion pumping music in a dark bar area, frequented by 18- to 30-year olds, night and day. Drinks €2.30-6.50. In-house DJs nightly. Open daily 11am-2am.

Bang-Inside, Dreihackeng. 4-10 (☎ 71 95 49). This neon-lit gay bar turns into a pumping disco on Friday and Saturday nights. Loud music and plenty of drinks, including gin and tonic (€4) and Bacardi cola (€3.60). Bar open W, Th, Su 9pm-2am, no cover; disco Fr-Sa 9pm-4am, after midnight men only, cover €3.60.

Blue Moon, Sackstr. 40 (☎ 82 97 56). This local hangout just south of the Schloßbergbahn attracts an "alternative" crowd of artists, musicians, and gays. Check out its cool architecture—the low curved ceilings aren't just that way for ambience; the bar is actually built back inside the mountain along a tunnel dug as an air raid shelter in WWII. Beer €2.80 and cocktails €5.80-6.90. Open daily 8pm-3am.

Café Harrach, Harrachg. 26 (☎ 32 26 71). A half-liter of *Gösser* costs €2.50 at this grad-student spot, but this is wine-drinking country. Most everyone is tossing back white wine spritzers (€2). Open M-F 9am-midnight, Sa-Su 7pm-midnight.

■ DAYTRIPS FROM GRAZ

BÄRNBACH AND THE STÖLZE GLAS-CENTER

Take the train from Graz (dir: Köflach) to Voitsberg (45min., 11 per day 5:26am-5:59pm, €5.40). From Voitsberg, take the bus to the Hauptpl. in Bärnbach. Buses leave after the arrival of every train, and the bus trip is included in the train ticket as long as the total time of your trip does not exceed 2hr. The train at 9:16am connects to a bus at 10am and arrives the museum for the 11am glass-blowing demonstration. From the Hauptpl., turn back down Piberstr. and cross back over the stream. The center will be on your left (3min.). By car, take A2 to Mooskirchen and follow the signs toward Voitsberg and then Bärnbach.

The sleek glass facade of the Stölze Glas-Center (Hochregisterstr. 1-3) is the first of many examples you'll see of the beautiful glass produced here. The center houses a **glass museum** which traces the development of glass through history and displays many interesting glass pieces, from ancient beads to modern art, as well as work produced in Bärnbach itself, including perfume bottles, lamps, and a special hand-blown 135L bottle of Almdudler. The showroom in the center has items for sale ranging from simple ashtrays (€3.78) to elegant vases (€30). The most exciting thing are the **glass-blowing** demonstrations every weekday at 11am, which are free with ticket to the museum. (☎ 62 950, fax 706 804, glascenter@stoelze.com. Open M-F 9am-5pm, Sa 9am-1pm; May-Oct. M-F 9am-5pm, Sa-Su 9am-1pm. €5.50, children €3.) The Bärnbach **tourist office** is located inside the glass center, but there is also an information computer and reservation phone in front of the **Hundertwasser Church**. Free **public toilets** are on the Hauptpl. and by the church. The **post office** is on the right just up Hauptstr. from the Hauptpl. (☎ 62 949 13. Open M-F 8am-noon and 2-6pm.) **Postal code**: A-8572.

SCHLOß EGGENBERG

Take tram #1 (dir: Eggenberg) to "Schloß Eggenberg" (5am-midnight). Cross the street and backtrack ¼ block, taking the first right onto Schloßstr.

West of Graz, the grandiose **Schloß Eggenberg**, Eggenberger Allee 90, contrasts sharply with its plain suburban surroundings. Built for Prince Ulrich of Eggenberg, this multi-towered palace now holds an exquisite historical coin museum, an exhibition of artifacts from antiquity, and a prehistoric museum (all open Feb.-Nov. Tu-Su 9am-5pm). The resonating bird calls and wandering peacocks give it an exotic feel. Incidentally, the last knights' tournament in Styria took place here in 1777; knights took sides based on the answer to the question "Which are prettier, blondes or brunettes?" (*Really.*) The guided tour of the elegant **Prunkräume**—filled with 17th-century frescoes, tile ovens, and ornate chandeliers—reveals the palace's convoluted design as a microcosm of time. Four towers symbolize the seasons, 12 gates the months, and 365 windows the days. The **Planetensaal**, or Planet Hall, is decorated with illustrations of the days as gods, bearing a suspicious resemblance to the Eggenberger family. Especially striking is the illustration of Monday, with the image of Diana with a crescent moon in her hair. (☎ 58 32 64. Exhibits €4.30; children, students, and seniors €2.90; Prunkräume tour €1.50 extra. Tours in German and English; Apr.-Oct. Tu-Su, every hr. 10am-noon and 2-4pm.) Royal blue peacocks wander freely in the game preserve surrounding the palace. (Gardens free with castle entrance, €0.30 for gardens only. Open Apr.-Sept. daily 8am-7pm, Oct.-Mar. 8am-5pm.) Classical concerts are held in the castle's **Planetensaal** during Styriarte (see **Entertainment**, p. 153). Call ☎ 82 50 00 for tickets.

ÖSTERREICHISCHES FREILICHTMUSEUM

The most convenient way to get to the museum is a bus that runs from Lendpl. in Graz (dir: Gratwein; M-Sa 9am, 12:30pm) straight to the museum (return 1:35, 4:35pm; €3.20.) Trains run to Stübing from Graz every hr. (€3.20); from the Stübing train station, turn onto the main road and walk 25min. to the museum. Buses run irregularly between Stübing and the museum (4 per day, €1.60), so walking is a better bet. Drivers should take the road toward Friesach and then follow signs to Stübing.

The **Österreichisches Freilichtmuseum (Open-Air Museum)**, in the nearby town of **Stübing**, recreates 19th-century Austrian farm life in a quiet wooded valley. The museum consists of 90 farmhouses, barns, mills, and storehouses from all over Austria, transported plank by plank and lovingly restored, arranged into small villages by their region of origin. If you're accustomed to receiving your food in neat supermarket packaging, seeing how grain is farmed, cheese made, and bees kept is an informative experience. A snack bar at the midpoint of the tour serves slices of bread with various spreads, pastries, and apple wine (€1 each), all fresh from the farm. (☎ (03124) 537 00. Open June-Aug. Tu-Su 9am-6:30pm, no entrance after 5pm; Apr.-May and Sept.-Oct. Tu-Su 9am-5pm, no entrance after 4pm. €6.20, students €3.60, children €2.90. Exhibits in German. English guidebook €2.20. Tour in English or German, 2hr., M-F 10:30am, €1.50.)

GESTÜT PIBER (STUD FARM)

The stud farm is a few kilometers outside of the town of Köflach. Train from Graz (45min., 11 per day 5:26am-5:50pm, €5.40), then the bus to Piber (M-F 6 per day 9:03am-

4:25pm, Sa 4 per day 9:30am-2:20pm, €1.60). From the bus stop, follow the sign point-ing to "Bundesgestüt Piber." By car from Graz, take A2 and exit Mooskirchen, then drive through Voitsberg and Bärnbach to Piber. Signing up for the tour from the tourist office in Graz will resolve any transportation worries and guarantee an English tour (leaves Sa 2pm from the Graz tourist office, Herreng. 16. €24, children €9.)

The **Gestüt Piber (Piber Stud Farm)** is the home of the world-famous **Lippizaner** horses, whose delicate footwork and snow white coats are the pride of the Span-ish Riding School in Vienna. Born either solid black or brown, they become pro-gressively paler, reaching the pure white color sometime between the age of five and ten. The rolling green hills of Piber are home to the mares, their foals, and trained stallions in retirement. On a 1hr. tour of the stud farm, you can see the horses up close in the stables and visit the carriage house and the Lippizaner museum in the 300-year-old Piber castle. In 2003 there is also a special exhibit in Piber on the "Myth of the Horse," which addresses the role of the horse in legend, in chivalry, and in war. (☎(03144) 33 23; fax 33 23 23; besichtigung@piber.com; open Apr.-Oct. daily 9am-10:30am and 1:30-3:30pm. €10, students €5.)

TIER-UND NATURPARK SCHLOß HERBERSTEIN

From Graz, take the Post bus from Andreas-Hofer-Pl. to Hartberg (1½hr., 8am, round-trip €18). After a 2hr. wait, continue with the bus from the post office in Hartberg at 11:30am (dir: Anger). Ask the driver to stop at "Buchberg bei Herberstein." (M-Sa, 11:30am, free with round-trip ticket from Graz.) Backtrack just a bit to the intersection where the bus just turned, and continue straight, following the signs toward Herberstein. The park will be on your right after 2km. (20min). To return, take the bus at 5:22pm from the "Buchberg bei Herberstein" stop back to Hartberg, then the 6:15pm bus from Hartberg to Graz. Be care-ful when reading the Post bus schedule, because many of the times that appear on the schedule run only on certain days as specified in the key. By car, take A2 from Graz head-ing east, exit Gleisdorf-West, then drive through Hirnsdorf and St. Johann and follow the signs toward the park (30min). From Vienna, take A2 south, exit Hartberg, then drive through Hartberg, Kaindorf, Hirnsdorf, and St. Johann (1hr.).

Schloß Herberstein and the surrounding estate have been in the possession of the Herberstein family ever since the year 1290. As late as 1900 the family controlled one-fifth of the state of Styria. Today they retain "just" this castle and land around it. Traditionally every Herberstein son is name Johann, and every daughter Johanna; the current generation has two Johanns and a Johanna.

The **Herberstein castle** is a fascinating mish-mash of styles—when viewed from the valley below, it appears as a stern fortress rising from the cliffs, but when approached from the top its delicate Renaissance facade makes it seem like a delightful country palace. Tours (1hr.) begin in the flower-bedecked arcaded courtyard and explore the castle from the cellar built over the original moat to the museum of the Herberstein family. The **animal and nature park** includes a small herd of buffalo, wolves, lions, and many other exotic animals in large outdoor pens. Some animals, including the prairie dogs and monkeys, are free to roam. For kids, there's a petting zoo and a small blue-and-white trolley which circles the park. The **historical garden** next to the castle recreates the gardens, while **Sigmund's Garden** shows the popular style of gardens from the Middle Ages to the present. The 1hr. walk that runs down to the valley past the castle and back around to the gardens is a highlight. (☎(03176) 88 250; fax 87 75 20; office@herberstein.co.at; www.herberstein.co.at. Open mid-Mar. to early Nov. 8am-6pm, early Nov. to mid-Mar. 10am-4pm; tours of the castle available Mar.-Oct. every hr. from 10am-4pm. Call ahead for a tour in winter. €15, students €13, children €7. The ticket includes all the above attractions, including the guided tour of the castle.)

STYRIAN WINE COUNTRY

Dominating the market in Austria and making an impressive showing in Europe, Styrian wine is known for its fruity bouquets and light quality. Sample local varieties in Deutschlandsberg and visit the *Weinbauschulen* where the intoxicating libations are produced.

DEUTSCHLANDSBERG   ☎03462

Deutschlandsberg is a resort town tucked in the rolling hills of western Styria, and its blooming flowers and freely flowing wine make it a great place to relax. With a population of 8000, it's small enough to be quaint but large enough to offer a wealth of eating, drinking, and accommodations options. Sample the local *Schilcher* wine, a dry blush specialty. Easy connections to Graz make it an excellent daytrip, but a night in a winery guesthouses is a wonderful experience.

🖅📱 TRANSPORTATION AND PRACTICAL INFORMATION. Trains run from Graz to Deutschlandsberg (dir: Wies-Eibiswald; 15 per day 4:30am-7:37pm, roundtrip €13). **Buses** also run directly to Deutschlandsberg from Graz Griespl. for the same price (6 per day 6am-5:20pm, round-trip €13). **By car** from Graz, take B76 through Stainz toward Weis/Eibiswald.

To get to the **tourist office**, Hauptpl. 37, from the train station, go right onto Frauentalerstr., then follow the signs. The office is on your left (10min), with a hiking and biking map (€7) for western Styria. (☎75 20; fax 75 55; tourismus.deutschlandsberg@utanet.at. Open Apr.-Oct. M-Tu and Th-Fr 9am-noon and 3-6pm, W 9am-3pm, Sa 10am-1pm; Nov.-Mar. M-F 9am-3pm, Sa 10am-1pm.) There is a free public **bathroom** in the courtyard next to the tourist office, and an **ATM** at the Die Steirmörkische on the far side of the *Rathaus* from the tourist office (open 5am-midnight). The pharmacy **Hirscher Apotheke,** Hauptpl. 5, is in the middle of town. (Open M-F 8am-12:30pm and 3-6pm, Sa 8am-noon.) The **post office** is at the corner of Fabrikstr. and Frauentalerstr. on the way from the train station to the tourist office. (☎46 55 21. Open M-F 8am-12:30pm and 2-5:30pm.) **Postal code:** A-8530.

🖬📱 ACCOMMODATIONS AND FOOD. Pick up the guest information brochure at the tourist office, which includes a list of all rooms. A good choice is **Buschenschank Kästenbauer ❸,** Schloßweg 21a, situated atop a sloping vineyard. From the train station, go right, then right again onto Villenstr., cross the tracks, and go left up the footpath (20min.) Make sure to buy a bottle of the family's wine. Some rooms have balconies, and all have TV, shower, and toilet. (☎/fax 29 13. Singles €30 the first night, €28 subsequent nights; doubles €50/€46.) **Privatzimmer Klug ❸,** Feilhofg. 18, is a one-story building close to the station (10min.). If you're on foot, they'll pick you up from the station and show you around in their car. TV and fridge are available for guests' use. (☎20 12. Plentiful breakfast included. €15-19.)

The best places to eat (and drink) are the *Buschenschanken* along Schloßweg, which runs from the castle to the train station. At the top of the hill is **Stöcklpeter ❷,** Schloßweg 53. A sunny terrace with bright red tablecloths and green and yellow umbrellas offers views of the valley and castle. Traditional food *(Schweinsbraten* €5.50, grill plate €8) is best with a glass of *Schilcher* (€2.40 for 0.25L). (☎28 89. Open Tu-Su 9am-midnight.) A cheap and convenient option in town is **China Restaurant Peking ❷,** Hauptpl. 39, which offers lunch *Menüs* for €4.80-5.10. (☎26 47. Open M-Tu and Th-Sa 11:30am-2:30pm and 5-11pm). **Gasthof Koller ❷,** Hauptpl. 10, offers lunch *Menüs* (€5.80-6.50) which are a great way to experience the local cuisine. (Open Tu-Sa 7am-midnight.) Pick up picnic ingredients at **Merkur** on Frauentalerstr. (Open M-Th 8am-7pm, F 7:30am-7:30pm, Sa 7am-5pm.)

STYRIA

🔲 **SIGHTS.** The main sight in town is the **Burg Deutschlandsberg,** Burgstr. 19, a 12th-century fortress which now houses the ritzy Burghotel and the Burg museum. From the tourist office, go down the Hauptpl., take a right up Burgstr., and follow the signs—it's hard to miss. The museum, which focuses on Celtic artifacts and history of the region, is a bit dry, but is revived by a lively soundtrack of Celtic music and the ambience of the castle. It also hosts special changing exhibits. Take the stairs up to the top of the castle bastion for great views of the town. (☎56 02; stadt@deutschlandsberg.at. Open Mar.-Nov. daily 9:30am-5pm, last entry 4pm. Museum €6, students €5, children €4; museum and special exhibit €9, students €8, children €6.) From the castle, head back to town along the Schloßstr., where a number of wineries provide excellent refreshments and great views of the city.

RIEGERSBURG ☎03153

This sleepy town, buried in the rolling green country east of Graz, would have gone unnoticed if it weren't for the impressive castle overshadowing it. The **Burg Kronegg** balances on the edge of a steep cliff over vast farmland and misty hills.

🔳🔲 **TRANSPORTATION AND PRACTICAL INFORMATION.** Riegersburg is the perfect destination for a leisurely Sunday afternoon, which is a good thing, because Sunday is the only time you can easily get to and from Riegersburg. Take the **bus** leaving at 10:15am from Andreas-Hofer-Pl. in Graz, then the return bus leaving from Riegersburg at 5:35pm (1½hr., €8). If you happen to be in Graz on Friday, reserve a spot on the Graz tourist office's "Castles and Chateaux Tour." (Tour leaves behind the tourist office on Landhausg. Apr.-Oct. F 2pm. €24, children €9; includes transportation, English-speaking tour guide, and entrance fee.) Going on other days is feasible, but requires more precise planning because of the poor bus-train connections. The same bus from Andreas-Hofer-Pl. also runs during the week (M-Sa 12:35pm, M-F 5:30pm); however, the return buses run only at pre-dawn hours (5:40, 6:05am). A train also runs from Graz to Feldbach (1hr., every hr., round-trip €16), where a bus to Riegersburg leaves the bus depot near the train station (20min., 4 per day M-F 6:50am-5:50pm). An €8 ticket purchased on the bus back to Feldbach (M-F 7 per day 6:50am-5:50pm) is valid for train connections back to Graz (every hr. 4:20am-8:22pm). By **car,** Riegersburg is an easy 55 km trip from Graz. Take A-2 and exit at Ilz. The main **tourist office,** at the beginning of the trail to the castle, helps to find *Pensionen* and *Privatzimmer.* (☎86 70; fax 200 70; tourismus@riegers-burg.com; www.riegersburg.com. Open M-F 9am-6pm.) If you are in Riegersburg when the tourist office is closed, pick up brochures and information at the store next door. A free public **toilet** is at the bus lot downhill from Lasslhof. An **ATM** is at Raiffeisenbank, Riegersburg 30. **Postal code:** A-8333.

🔳🔲 **ACCOMMODATIONS AND FOOD.** Guesthouses in town charge €44-52 for doubles, while *Privatzimmer* are around €28-42. Be aware, there is a fee for one-night stays (€2.50-4). **Lasslhof ❸,** at the Riegersburg bus stop, is a yellow hotel with a popular bar/restaurant and an extensive art collection in the halls between the rooms. (☎82 01 or 82 02. Breakfast included. Reception 7am-midnight. €16.50 per person, with bath €23. €4 fee for one-night stays; €4 extra for a single.) Eat some Wienerschnitzel with potatoes and salad (€6.20) at the restaurant downstairs or snack on *Frankfurter mit Gulaschsaft* (€3.30). (Kitchen open 8am-10pm.) Stock up on groceries at **Nah&Frisch,** across from the start of the stone path. (Open M-F 7:30am-12:30pm and 2:30-6:30pm, Sa 7am-12:30pm.)

🖸 **SIGHTS: BURG KRONEGG.** Riegersburg relies heavily on the revenue from tourists awe-struck by the well-preserved remains of **Burg Kronegg.** Attackers never got inside, but tourists can, after tackling the steep, stone-paved path to the castle. Bring sturdy shoes and bottled water. Lush vineyards clothe the castle slopes, while cypresses peek out in the distance. You can circle the castle and climb the *Eselstiege* (donkey stairs) by heading past the turn-off to the tourist office and turning right at the cemetery, and right at the sign to "Seilbahn Garten." On your way up, look for an inconspicuous crescent moon carved into the stone wall to mark the highest point reached by invading Turks.

Take a good look at the elaborate iron pattern covering the well in the castle's second courtyard—it's said that any woman who can spot a horseshoe within the design will find her knight in shining armor within a year. In the shadow of the castle chirps the **Greifvogelwarte Riegersburg,** showcasing birds of prey. *(Shows in German M-Sa 11am and 3pm; Su 11am, 2, 4pm. €6, students €4.)*

The castle houses two museums. The **Burgmuseum** showcases 16 of the castle's rooms, packed with art, reproductions, and self-congratulatory historical notes on the Liechtenstein family (yes, like the country), who bought the castle in 1822. The **Weiße Saal** (White Hall), with its stucco ceiling flourishes and crystal chandeliers, lacks only waltzing dancers in decolleté gowns. The **Hexenzimmer** (Witch Room) contains an eerie collection of portraits of alleged witches (including Katharina "Green Thumb" Pardauff, executed in 1675 for supposedly causing flowers to bloom in the middle of winter) and a real iron maiden. There's also Prince Friedrich's (the current owner of the castle) gallery of amateur travel photography. The **Hexenmuseum** (Witch Museum) spreads over 12 more rooms, with an exhibit on the biggest witch trial in Styrian history (1673-1675). *(☎83 46. Open Apr.-Oct. daily 9am-5pm. Admission to each museum €7; students, children €4.50; combination ticket €10/€6.80. Call ahead for tours, €1.)*

ADMONT ☎03613

Tiny Admont (pop. 2,800), gateway to the Gesäuse alpine region, lies on the border of Styria and Upper Austria, along the Enns River. Although the town is most famous for the library in its Benedictine monastery, the gorgeous mountain scenery around Admont provides plenty of other diversions.

🖪🔃 TRANSPORTATION AND PRACTICAL INFORMATION. Trains run from **Selzthal,** the regional hub, to Admont (15min., 5:45am-6:28pm, €3). Get to Selzthal from **Linz** (2hr., 6:10am-7:35pm, €15.70) or **Bruck an der Mur** (1¾hr., 5:20am-10:35pm, €12.40). **Buses** to Linz depart from the post office and marketplace. For **taxis,** call ☎28 01. The Admont train station desk is open M-Sa 5:30am-7:30pm, Su 7am-7:30pm. To reach the **tourist office** from the train station, head left down Bahnhofstr., then turn right onto Haupstr. The office will be on your left after the church. Staff finds rooms free of charge and offers activity information. They also have a neat free map of Admont made from an aerial photograph of the town. *(☎21 64; fax 36 48. Open June-Aug. M-F 8am-noon and 2-6pm, Sa 9am-noon; Sept.-May M-F 8am-noon and 2-6pm.)* **Currency exchange** and a 24hr. **ATM** are available at Raiffeisenbank, just past the tourist office on Hauptstr. *(☎21 32. Open M-F 8am-noon and 2:30-4:30pm.)* The Stiftsapotheke **pharmacy** is accessible through the abbey courtyard; enter by the church and turn right. (Open M-F 8am-noon and 2:30-6pm, Sa 8am-noon, and for emergencies.) In **medical emergencies** call ☎23 47. To reach the **post office,** head to your left from the train station—it's at the corner of Haupstr. on the way to the tourist office. *(☎22 41 28. Open M-F 8am-noon and 2:30-5:30pm, exchange closes at 5pm.)* **Postal code:** A-8911.

▐▌ ACCOMMODATIONS AND FOOD. The best reason to come to Admont is the youth hostel, **▉Schloß Röthelstein (HI) ❸**, reputedly the most beautiful in Europe. From the train station, turn left down Bahnhofstr. and left again at the post office. Cross the tracks and walk down that road for 20min. (don't turn right at the "Schloßherberge Röthelstein Fußweg" sign pointing to the castle, unless you feel mountain-goatish), past the lumberyard. Turn right at the "Schloßher-berge Röthelstein" sign and follow the road as it curves up and up (about 35min. more). Taxis from the station run about €6. Housed in a 330-year-old castle, it offers a sauna, soccer field, and small track. Inside, the dining area is a hall draped with ivy and chandeliers. An exquisite *Rittersaal* (knights' hall) functions as a concert hall. The "komfort" rooms have bay windows and elegant lamps. The challenge is getting here—yes, it *is* that castle sitting high on the big hill. Call ahead. (☎24 32; fax 27 95 83. Breakfast included. Reception open 7am-midnight. Checkout 9am. Curfew 10pm. 6-bed dorms €17.54; singles €24.80; doubles €49.60. One-time fee of €3 for sheets, which are required. Non-members add €2.91.)

If the trek is intimidating, try a *Privatzimmer*. Several line Paradiesstr., and generally run about €15-25. Closer to the town center is **Frühstückspension Mafalda ❸**, Bachpromenade 75. At the post office, turn left and cross the rail tracks, then make the next two rights and cross the tracks again. Mafalda is right under the tracks. (☎21 88. Breakfast and hall showers included. €20.35 per person; €21.80 for 1-night stays.) To reach **Gästehaus Burghart ❸**, Sonnenweg 272, exit the tourist office and walk left down Hauptstr. At the blue "Hallenbad" sign, turn left, cross the stream, take the second fork from the right, and take a right onto Wagnerstr. after the stream. Continue down Wagnerstr., which turns into Ennsweg, before going right onto Sonnenweg—the house will be down the street on the left. It is a bit out of the way, but the amenities and the warm owners make it worth the trip. (☎22 59. Breakfast included. Bath and TV in rooms. Singles €18.17-21.80; doubles €29.07. €1.45 surcharge in winter, 20% surcharge for stays of less than 3 nights.)

Check out **Gasthof Zeiser ❷**, Hauptstr. 6, for particularly cheap and generous midday *Menüs* at around €5-6.70. (☎21 47. Open daily 8am-midnight.) **Pizzeria Markt Cafe,** on the right side, serves salads (€3-5) and small pizzas (€5-7). (Open W-M from 6pm). For traditional fare (€5-8) or a salad buffet (€4.29), try **Gasthaus Kamper ❷**, right next door. (Open Tu-Su 8:30am-midnight.) For a quick meal, try **Gasthof Traube ❷**, right next to the church on Haupstr. and across from the tourist information office. Main dishes run €8.50-16, such as Stroganoff and Spätzle (€12.50). Cheaper options include Styrian salad plate (€6.30) and sandwiches (€3-6.30). On the higher end is the **Stifstkeller ❸** in the monastery, where for €14.60 you get entrance to the library and a three-course *Menü* consisting of "original Admont monastery soup," choice of schnitzels with rice, and Admonter *Pralinenschnitte* for dessert. (☎33 54; fax 33 54 4; www.stiftskeller-admont.at.) Head down Haupstr. 5min. and you'll find cheaper, modern alternatives. Get groceries at **Mondo-markt.** (Open M-Th 7:45am-7pm, F 7:30am-7pm, Sa 7:30am-5pm.)

◑ ▌ SIGHTS AND OUTDOOR ACTIVITIES. Aside from its hostel, Admont is best known for its **Benediktinerstift** (Benedictine abbey), founded in 1088 and currently staffed by 26 monks. To get there, head to the church, then take a right to the courtyard behind it. The abbey's library, the largest monastic library in the world, contains over 200,000 precious leather-bound volumes as well as 1,400 manuscripts, some dating back to the 8th century. With pink marble, glimmering statues, and frescoed ceilings, the building is a Baroque masterpiece. Be sure to find the stairways up to the balconies; there are four of them hidden behind false fronts. Look for the sections where the book spines are painted with wood relief. One of the books will have a small black knob coming out of it; when this knob is twisted, the fake spine swings out to reveal a keyhole. Turn the key and the whole section swings out on hinges to reveal wooden steps. (Open Apr.-Oct. daily 10am-1pm and 2-5pm; Dec. and Feb. 10am-noon. Guided tours 11am and 3pm, available in English if you call ahead. English info sheets €0.40. €5, students €2.50.)

It would be a sin to visit Admont without trying one of its hikes. An easy walk starting from the train station heads past the swimming pool and down the **Kajetan-Promenade,** where oaks over 400 years old grow, to the nature park **Eichelau** (30min). The **Naturbad,** less than a 5min. walk from the train station, is a great place to swim outdoors. The non-chlorinated pool is refreshingly cool, and includes a diving board, shallow area for kids, and volleyball courts. To get there from the train station, face away from the tracks, turn left, then go right onto Friedhofsweg and follow the signs. (Open 9:30am-7pm in good weather. €2.90).

LEOBEN ☎ 03842

The buckle of Austria's "Iron Belt," Leoben (pop. 30,000) lies between a ring of mountains and the Mur River. No longer a small town but a tiny charmed city, it offers the benefits of both a little urbanity and the splendid outdoors. Streets lead to an ancient church, the Gösser beer brewery, and the idyllic city park, "Am Glacis." The elegant town square is ringed with elaborate (though slightly run-down) buildings. Just past the narrow streets, forest trails lead into the lush, green countryside that won the town its name: *Liubina,* or "lovely region."

☷ TRANSPORTATION. The train station has an **information counter.** (☎425 45, ext. 390. Open M-F 9am-6pm.) **Trains** arrive from: Graz (1hr., every 2hr. 6:36am-8:29pm, €9); Klagenfurt (2hr., every 3hr. 7:10am-9:11pm, €19.60); Salzburg (3½hr., 3am-7:18pm, €26.30); and Vienna Sudbahnhof (2hr., every 2hr. 7:04am-10:34pm, €21.20). From smaller destinations such as Mariazell, take the **bus** to Bruck an der Mur and then take the train to Leoben (15min., 1-2 per hr. 6:30am-1am, €3.60). For local connections, the main **bus station** in Leoben is a 10min. walk from the train station; turn right onto Parkstr. from Franz Josef-Str. just before Hauptpl. Leoben is just minutes from Autobahn A9, which runs south to Graz and northwest to Steyr and Linz; take the Leoben exit.

◨◪ ORIENTATION AND PRACTICAL INFORMATION. Head straight out of the train station and cross the Mur river, and you'll be on **Franz Josef-Straße,** the main traffic artery of Leoben. Continue straight and you'll reach the center of town, the **Hauptplatz.** The **tourist office** will be on the right. (☎440 18; fax 482 18; stadtinformation@leoben.at; www.leoben.at. Open M 7am-5pm, Tu-Th 7am-6:30pm, F 7am-1pm and 3-6:30pm, Sa 9am-12:30pm.) There are **ATMs** at the post office and Raiffeisenbank, Hauptpl. 15. (Open M-Th 8am-noon and 2-4pm, F 8am-noon and 2-3:30pm.) A **parking garage** is under Hauptpl. with an entrance on Langg.; turn left off Franz-Josef-Str. onto Dominikanerg. (€1.40 per hr., all day €13.) Services include: **lockers** in the train station (€2); free **public restroom** in the garage, accessible from the elevator in the center of Hauptpl. (open M-Sa 7am-8pm, Su 8am-6pm); **taxis** at stand by the train station (☎17 18); and **hospital,** ☎401. The **post office** is at Erzherzog-Johann-Str. 17, the last right before Hauptpl. (☎424 74. Open M-F 8am-6:30pm, Sa 8am-5pm.) **Postal code:** A-8701.

⛰ ACCOMMODATIONS. Rooms are sparse in Leoben and budget rooms even sparser. The **Schulverein der Berg-und-Hüttenschule Leoben ❸,** Max-Tendlerstr. 3, rents 47 double rooms, some of which can be rented as singles. Head straight away from the train station down Franz Josef-Str., then turn right down Max Tendler-Str., which will run into the hostel (10min.). Rooms are large and plain. Call ahead.

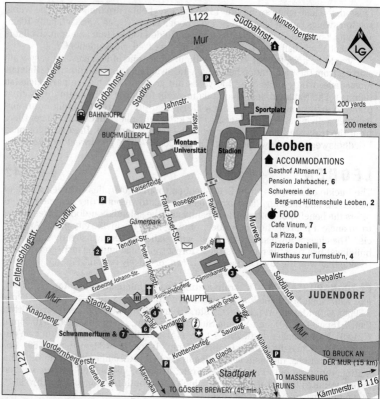

Leoben

⛰ ACCOMMODATIONS
Gasthof Altmann, 1
Pension Jahrbacher, 6
Schulverein der
    Berg-und-Hüttenschule Leoben, 2
🍎 FOOD
Cafe Vinum, 7
La Pizza, 3
Pizzeria Danielli, 5
Wirsthaus zur Turmstub'n, 4

(☎ 448 88; fax 44 88 83. Breakfast included. Singles €16.36; doubles €35.42.) **Gasthof Altmann ❸,** Südbahnhofstr. 32, has 12 doubles and a three-lane bowling alley. Exiting the train station, facing away from the tracks, turn left and walk down Südbahnhofstr. for 10min.; Altmann will be on the right. Private TV sets, showers, and hardwood floors make Altmann more luxurious than most hotels in this price range. The bowling alley and restaurant (meals €7.50-10) fill with locals. (☎/fax 422 16. Bowling alley open Tu-Sa 10am-midnight, Su 10am-3pm; €0.70 for 10min. Free parking. Breakfast included. Closed Aug. Singles €26; doubles €44. MC/V.) **Pension Jahrbacher ❹,** Kirchg. 14, offers bright spacious rooms on the Mur river, just next to the Schwammerlturm. The newly remodeled rooms come with bathroom, TV, and refrigerator. Watch out for the sloping walls and ceilings in some rooms. (☎436 00; fax 253 57. Breakfast €4. Singles €37; doubles €70.)

🗐 FOOD. Kirchg. is home to a number of cheap restaurants. **Wirsthaus zur Turmstub'n ❷,** Kirchg. 7-9, serves reasonably priced Austrian food, with vegetarian meals (€5.50-7) and salads (€4-6), if you can stand a little smoke. (☎426 49. Open M 10am-2pm, Tu-F 10am-10pm, Sa-Su 10am-5pm. English menus available.) Climb the many steps of the Schwammerlturm (named for its mushroom-like shape) to find **Cafe Vinum** at the top of the tower. They serve only drinks, so sip your wine or espresso while watching Leoben below. (Open W-M 10am-1am.) **La Pizza ❷,** Langg.1, has large pizzas for two (€5-9) but only a bar at which to eat—take out a pie to enjoy by the river. (☎453 47. Open M-F 11am-2pm and 5-10pm, Sa-Su 11am-10pm.) **Pizzeria Danielli ❷**, Langg. 8, also offers great Italian meals at reasonable prices (€6-8) with tables outside in the pedestrian zone and indoors in the decorated dining area. (Open M-Sa 10am-midnight, Su 10am-10pm.) Get some edibles at the **markets** along Franz Josef-Str.; **Billa** supermarket in the basement of the shopping arcade, Josef-Grafg. 6 (open M-W 8am-7pm, Th 7:30am-7pm, F 7:30am-7:30pm, Sa 7:30am-5pm); or the **farmers' market** on Kirchpl. (Tu and F 7am-1pm).

☉ ♫ SIGHTS AND ENTERTAINMENT. Most of Leoben's attractions center around **Hauptplatz**, 10min. from the train station (cross the bridge and bear right onto Franz Josef-Str.). Sights are designated by a square sign with an ostrich eating iron horseshoes. This city symbol alludes to Leoben's dependence on the iron trade—in the Middle Ages, ostriches were thought to be capable of eating and digesting iron. It more closely resembles a goose because when the sign was designed no one in Leoben knew what an ostrich looked like.

Most of the buildings on Hauptpl. are former homes of the *Hammerherren* (Hammer men). The most ornate of the bunch is the 1680 **Hacklhaus**, Hauptpl. 9, which bears a dozen statues on its red-and-white facade. Justice holds a sword and a balance, Hope brandishes an anchor, and Wisdom views the world—all backwards—through the mirror in his hand. Standing guard at the center of Hauptpl. is a beautifully crafted monument erected to ward off the fires and plague that devastated much of Styria in the early 18th century. Look for St. Florian the fire-proof and St. Rosalia the plague-resistant. Just outside Hauptpl. is the **Pfarrkirche Franz Xaver,** a rust-colored church whose elaborate interior is dominated by black-and-gold decorations against stark white walls. Go through the Kreuzgang to see 14 paintings showing Christ from condemnation to crucifixion.

Don't miss the chance to inspect the **Gösser brewery,** Brauhausg. 1. To get to Göss, take the bus from Franz Josef-Str., or walk south down Gösser Str. along the Mur in the sun (45min.). The brewery's slogan is *"Gut, Besser, Gösser"* (Good, Better, Gösser). Examine antique brewing machinery and swill down a free stein of fresh brew. (☎209 08 02. Museum open Sa-Su 9am-6pm. €2.60, students €1.80. Tours M-F €4.60, students €2. Arrange ahead.) In Göss, see Styria's oldest abbey, the **Stift Göss,** founded in 1000. (☎221 48 8am-noon. Call ahead for tours.) The **Stadttheater,** Homanng. 5, is the oldest functioning theater in Austria, completed in 1790. (☎406 23 02. Advance tickets at Zentralkartenbüro, and before performances at box office. Theater closed June-Sept.) Summer brings the **Leobener Kultursommer,** a program of theater, concerts, literary readings, and treasure hunts (June-July). Tickets available at Zentralkartenbüro by the tourist office. (Open M 9:30am-12:30pm and 3-5pm, Tu-F 9am-12:30pm, 3-6:30pm and Sa 9am-12:30pm.)

To wander away from Leoben, use hiking maps from the tourist office. A 30min. hike begins at the Stadtpark and leads to the **Massenburg ruins.** The castle was torn down in 1820, but its 13th-century gate building still stands.

◪ DAYTRIP FROM LEOBEN

EISENERZ ☎03848

*Take a **bus** from Leoben (1 hr., 11 per day 6:25am-8:40pm, €5.40). By **car,** take 146 from Liezen or 115 from Leoben.*

The skyline of Eisenerz, a strip-mining town, is dominated by the astounding Erzberg, an orange-and-maroon ziggurat of stone towering above the village. Supposedly, the iron was a gift from a merman who lived in a grotto not far from town. The villagers formed a clever plot to capture him, and as exchange for his release he offered them 10 years of silver, 100 of gold, or iron forever. The men chose iron, and that was the beginning of the prosperous mining center.

STYRIA

FROM THE ROAD

DIVINE TOURISM

I'd been operating under certain assumptions about what people want out of their vacations—relaxation, sightseeing, and adventure. I, too, have these reasons for traveling. But when I went to Mariazell I encountered a different kind of traveler—the religious pilgrim. Riding the bus from Bruck an der Mur, I was surprised by the presence of nuns. Walking about town, I saw even more—in restaurants, at guesthouses, on the streets. I went to the basilica, whose huge towers dominate the Hauptplatz. Usually at a cathedral, there are tourists milling around, but here it was different. I entered into total silence, and was surprised to realize that the pews weren't empty as usual, but rather filled with rows upon rows of people praying. Not only were nuns and elderly people sitting quietly, but so were skinny blond girls, kneeling with their eyes shut and hands clasped before them. Suddenly, I heard a bell ring, and the whole congregation began to sing. I couldn't even tell what language the song was in, but that somehow made it even holier. I leaned over and asked the woman at the desk, and was startled when she replied in a normal tone of "Kroatisch". (Croatian). As I walked through the Schatzkammer, I saw the gifts from those who had made the trip to Mariazell after terrible accidents or family illness. And as I sat quietly, allowing the unfamiliar sermon to swell around me, I felt humbled by the motivations of these other travelers.

—Christine Peterson

The **tourist office,** Freiheitspl. 7, is located in a kiosk on the main square. (☎37 00; fax 21 00; info-buero@eisenerz.steiermark.at; www.eisenerz-heute.at. Open May-Oct. M-F 9am-1pm and 3-5pm, Nov.-Apr. M-F 10:30am-noon and 3-5pm.) A free **public toilet** is next to the fountain in the Bergmannpl. in the low white building with a picture of a man and woman. A youth hostel, **Jugend und Familiengastedorf Eisenerz ❸,** in scheduled to open in summer 2003. Around 5km from the city center, it will offer amenities including a restaurant, sauna, and showers for travelers. (☎70 830; fax 70 83 88; booking-center@jgh.at. €18.50 per person.)

The pyramid of the **Erzberg** is a powerful monument to man's ability to tear apart mountains. (From the tourist office, head straight out across Freiheitspl., turn left onto Hieflauerstr., then left again up to Bergmannpl. Continue across the square to the street branching off at the upper right, then make the next right to the Erzberg (15min.) After donning a yellow helmet and slicker, you'll be ready for action on two tours. The **Schaubergwerk** takes you on a train deep inside the mountain and demonstrates how dynamite is used in mining. You'll also see mining at the entrance to the tunnels, where rock is ground in a huge mortar. The other tour is the **Hauly Abenteuerfahrt,** in which you ride up the mountain in a huge dump truck made for transporting tons of stone, now outfitted with seats. These "largest taxis in the world" fulfill monster truck fantasies. Tours in German. *(☎32 00; fax 32 00 22; erzberg@steirer-oberland.co.at. Open daily May-Oct.; tours 10am-3pm. Fixed tours of the Schaubergwerk 10am, 12:30, and 3pm. Calling ahead for the Hauly ride is recommended. 1½hr. tour of Schaubergwerk or the 1hr. Hauly ride €13, children €6.50; combined ticket €22, children €11. 10% discount for students.)*

MARIAZELL ☎ 03882

The little town of Mariazell, somewhat extravagantly subtitled *Gnadenzentrum Europas* (Europe's Center of Mercy), is both an active resort and pilgrimage site. While many come for lazy walks, hikes, skiing in the Bürgeralpe, or a dip in the nearby Erlaufsee, the faithful and needy come to pay homage to a shrine—the miracle-working Madonna made of linden wood. (See **Legend of Mariazell,** p. 165).

⌐ TRANSPORTATION. Mariazell is accessible from St. Pölten by the mountain train Mariazellerbahn (2½hr., 8 per day 5:28am-6:02pm, €10.90). **Buses** connect Mariazell to Bruck an der Mur (1¾hr., 5:15am-6:15pm, €6); Graz (3hr., 7am-4:50pm,

LEGEND OF MARIAZELL In the year 1157, a monk named Magnus was sent to convert the natives of the region. Magnus rode north through Styria for days without seeing a soul. The only possessions he brought were his horse and a carved wooden statue of the Virgin Mary. When Magnus finally encountered other travelers, he was overjoyed, but later dismayed to find they were thieves. Just past midnight, a vision of the Virgin Mary sitting on the crescent moon holding the infant Jesus appeared to him. She warned that he must go immediately and take with him the statue of her. He raced down the mountain with the robbers hot on his heels, only to be stopped by a wall of stone. Magnus said a prayer, and a crack opened up in the cliff just large enough so that he could slip through to safety. He emerged in a lovely green valley populated by friendly woodsmen and decided to place the miraculous statue on a tree trunk. Thus was the beginning of Mariazell as a center of mercy.

€12.60); and Vienna (4hr., 4 per day 7am-3:50pm, €14.20). The **bus station** is down the steps below the post office, but for bus information, inquire in the post office or ask waiting bus drivers for times and rates. To reach Mariazell **by car** from Graz, take Rte. S-35 north to Bruck an der Mur, then Rte. S-6 to Rte. 20 north over Aflenz-Kurort and Seeberg-Sattel. From Vienna, take Autobahn A-1 west to St. Pölten, and exit onto Rte. 20 south (1hr.), over Lilienberg and Annaberg.

■■ ⁊ **ORIENTATION AND PRACTICAL INFORMATION.** The train station is actually in neighboring St. Sebastian. From the station, face away from the tracks, turn right down Erlaufseestr., and left uphill onto Wiener Str., to the town center, Hauptpl. (20min.) The bus also stops right near the center of town. Face away from the station and head left on Ludwig-Leber-Str., then left again on Grazer Str., and you'll get to the Hauptpl. (5min.). The **tourist office** is at Hauptpl. 13, just uphill from the basilica. (☎23 66; fax 39 45; tvmzl@kom.at; www.mariazell.org. Open May-Sept. M-F 9am-12:30pm and 2-5:30pm, Sa 9am-12:30pm and 2-4pm, Su 10am-12:30pm; Oct.-Apr. M-F 9am-12:30pm and 2-5pm, Sa 9am-12:30pm; closed Sa in Apr. and Nov.) The **train station,** Erlaufseestr. 19 (☎22 30; open M-Sa 5am-6pm, Su 6:15am-6pm), stores **luggage** (€2.50). **Lockers** are available at the bus station (€1). Services include: **currency exchange** and **ATM** at the Raiffeisenbank (turn right from Wienerstr. at Hauptpl.; open M-F 8am-noon and 2-4pm, Sa 8-11am); **pharmacy** Apotheke zur Gnadenmutter at Hauptpl. 4 (☎21 02; open M-F 8am-noon and 2-6pm, Sa 8am-noon, Su 9:30am-12:30pm); St. Sebastian **Hospital,** Spitalg. 4 (☎22 22); **emergency assistance,** ☎144; and **Internet-Cafe,** Hauptpl. 9 (☎37 13; open Sept.-June M-Sa 8am-11pm, Su 10am-11pm; July-Aug. M-Tu and Th-Sa 9am-11pm, W and Su 3-11pm; €1.50 for 15min., €2.50 for 30min., €4 per hr.). The **post office** is downhill from the tourist office; turn right in front of Xing Long and head downhill around the corner. (☎25 51. Open M-F 8am-noon and 2-6pm.) **Postal code:** A-8630.

⌐ **ACCOMMODATIONS**

Sportzentrum-Jugend und Familiaengästedorf (HI), Erlaufseestr. 49 (☎26 69; fax 26 69 88). From the train station, face away from the tracks, turn left, and walk about 5min. 30-40min. from the center of the Mariazell. Amenities include: **Internet** (coin operated), restaurant (8am-11pm), sauna and steam bath (€5.80), squash (M-F €2.90 per 30min.) and tennis courts (M-F €7.30 per hr., Sa-Su €10.90; rackets

€1.50); bike rental (€3 per half day, €5 per whole day); and a fitness studio (€2.20). Room with 2-4 beds €21.50 per person, in winter €23; singles €24.50/€27. Under 3 nights €2.50 fee. MC/V. ❸

Pension Zechner, Wienerstr. 25 (☎60 40; fax 60 40 20), has rooms with bath and many with balconies from which to admire the sunshine spilling through the hills. Common room with TV and small video library. Breakfast included. Singles €21.80, doubles €43.60; €22.53/€45.03 in winter. ❸

Haus Zach, Wiener Neustädter Str. 29 (☎22 72), is a slightly more rustic and lies on the edge of Mariazell. A 10min. walk past the tourist office up Wiener Neustädter Str. leads you to this large white house with red flower window boxes. Breakfast and TV included. Hall bath. €17.60 per person, €0.70 fee for one-night stays. ❸

🔅 FOOD

Wirtshaus Brauerei, Wienerstr. 5 (☎25 23), occupying the oldest building in town, celebrates its age with home-brewed beer (large €2.75, small €2.10) and large pretzels (€1.25). Main dishes of schnitzel and sausage €7-9. Tours of the facilities available F-W, no groups on weekends. Open M-Sa 10am-midnight, Su 10am-2pm. MC/V. ❷

Hotel Goldener Löwe, Hauptpl. 1a (☎24 44), across from the tourist office, lets you sit on the terrace overlooking Hauptpl. while sipping homemade mead ("Met," €1.50), nectar of the gods. Open Tu-Su 9am-7pm. The hotel serves Italian and Austrian dishes, but the real reason to visit is the **1st-floor bathrooms.** A rock- and plant-filled waterfall runs on the wall, a map of constellations lights up as you enter, and each stall is equipped with a 15min. hourglass. ❸

Radlwirt (☎27 31), just up Wiener Neustädter Str. from the tourist office, offers a bit of local color with live music by the owner, whose keyboard is set up in the corner. Pizza €6-8, as well as some Austrian dishes. Open 9am-7pm; hours may vary in winter. ❷

Goldenes Kreuz, Wienerstr. 7 (☎23 09), with its simple but elegant decor, offers a nice break from antlers and heavy wood panelling. Enjoy fresh fish entrees and traditional dishes (€10-14). Open daily 10am-midnight. ❸

Billa Supermarket, Wienerstr. 4. Open M-W 8am-7pm, Th 7:30am-7pm, F 7:30am-7:30pm, Sa 7:30am-6pm, Su 8am-4pm.

👁 🔅 SIGHTS AND OUTDOOR ACTIVITIES

BASILIKA MARIAZELL. Over the years, this town has welcomed millions of devout Christians who come to see the Madonna within the basilica, whose black spires are visible from anywhere in town. Empress Maria Theresia took her first communion in Mariazell and donated the silver and gold grille that encloses the *Gnadenaltar* (Mercy Altar) with the Madonna. There are ten to fifteen services a day for the flock of pilgrims from Austria and eastern Europe. (☎259 50. Open 6am-8pm. Free tours by appointment through the Superiorat, Kardinal-Tisser-ant-Pl. 1.) The church's amazing *Schatzkammer* (treasure chamber) holds former pilgrims' gifts, ranging from paintings and embroidery from the grateful cured to a pearl rosary given by Pope John Paul II upon his pilgrimage to Mariazell in 1983. Behind the church you'll find the *Kerzengrotte* (candle grotto); you can buy a candle there for €0.75. (Open May to late Oct. Tu-Sa 10am-3pm, Su 11am-3pm. €3, students €1.50, children €1.)

OUTDOORS. A cable car at Wienerstr. 24 zips to the top of the Bürgeralpe. (☎ *25 55. Every 20min. Jan.-Mar. 8am-5pm, Apr.-Nov. 9am-5pm, Dec. 8am-4pm. Ascent €6, round-trip €9. Children €4.50, €5.50.)* Ski lifts and trails line the top. *(1-day pass €22, 2-day €40.50, children €21.)* For ski information, call the Mariazell tourist office or contact the **Ski- und Snowboardschule,** Hauptpl. 12. *(☎ 27 20. Courses 10am-noon and 1:30-3:30pm. 1-day course €27.60)* In warmer weather, wander Mariazell's hiking trails or take a swim in the crystal clear **Erlaufsee,** a tiny lake surrounded by a white pebble beach. *(From the town center, take the Hans Wertnek Promenade (5km), or catch the city bus.*

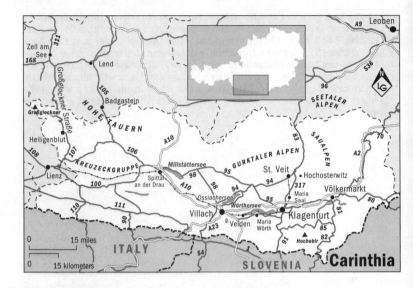

CARINTHIA (KÄRNTEN)

The province of Carinthia covers the southernmost part of Austria, jutting between East Tyrol and Salzburger Land in the west and reaching into the Hohe Tauern National Park and the Glockner mountain range. The peaks that guard the Italian and Slovenian borders in Carinthia may look severe, but they shield the province from cold northern winds. The sunny climate, Italian architecture, and laid-back atmosphere give Carinthia a Mediterranean feel. Natives consider Carinthia a vacation paradise, thanks to its scenic vistas and warm lakesides. There are nearly 200 lakes in Carinthia, including the **Wörthersee, Ossiachersee, Faakersee,** and **Millstättersee.** If your land-legs are surer than your sea-legs, there are rock faces to tackle, and abbeys and castles dot the mountainsides. If you'll be in Carinthia for a while, consider investing in a **Kärnten Card,** good for up to three weeks of unlimited local transportation, free admission to 110 area sights and museums, and discounts on many cable cars, boat cruises, toll roads, stores, and restaurants. The card, available at tourist offices, is a great deal at €32 (ages 5-16 €13).

HIGHLIGHTS OF CARINTHIA

Escape to the warm and seductive **Wörthersee,** home base both to vacationers and an Austrian soap opera (see p. 174).

Travel the (mini-)world in Klagenfurt's **Minimundus** amusement park (see p. 173).

Admire the view from the impressive medieval castle in **Hochosterwitz** (see p. 175).

KLAGENFURT
☎ 0463

On the eastern edge of the idyllic Wörthersee, Klagenfurt (pop. 90,000) is a major summer destination for Austrian travelers. Klagenfurt means "ford of laments," harking back to harsher times when travel across the lake and the surrounding marshes was a matter of life and death. This southernmost provincial capital now attracts thousands of Germanic tourists who unwind in its beachfront suburbs and on the scenic lake. The Wörthersee is the warmest lake in the Alps in summer and serves as Europe's largest skating arena in winter. Strolls through Italian Renaissance courtyards and espressos in outdoor cafes are integral to this tree-lined city.

▐▀ TRANSPORTATION

Trains: Hauptbahnhof (☎ 17 17; open 24hr.) at the intersection of Südbahngürtel and Bahnhofstr. To: **Graz** (3hr., 16 per day 4:15am-8:30pm, €26.10) via **Bruck an der Mur; Lienz** (2½hr., 12 per day 6:24am-8:51pm, €18.10); **Salzburg** (3½hr., 10 per day 5:29am-7:53pm, €26.10); **Vienna Südbahnhof** (4hr., 17 per day 1:48am-8:30pm, €24.80); **Villach** (30min., 2-3 per hr. 12:16am-11:42pm, €5.10).

Buses: Buses depart from the **Autobusbahnhof,** opposite the left end of the train station. **BundesBuses** leave for most destinations in Carinthia. To: **Graz** (2½hr., 3 per day 7:45am-5:05pm, €14.90) and **Villach** (1¼hr., 7 per day 8:10am-6:15pm, €5.96). Ticket window open M-F 7:30-11am and 11:30am-3:30pm. Info line (☎ 543 40) M-F 7am-4:30pm. For info on weekends and after hours call ☎ 017 11 01. Buy tickets either at the Autobusbahnhof ticket window or aboard the bus.

By car: Klagenfurt lies on Autobahn A2 from the west, Rte. 91 from the south, Rte. 70 from the east, and Rte. 317 from the north. From **Vienna** or **Graz,** take Autobahn A2 south to Rte. 70 west.

Public Transportation: Klagenfurt's **bus** system is punctual and comprehensive. The tourist office can provide a *Fahrplan* (bus schedule). The central bus station is at Heiligengeistpl. Buy single tickets (€1.50) or a 24hr. pass (€3.30) from the driver, or a weekly pass (€13) from a bus stop machine. *Tabak* kiosks sell cut-rate blocks of tickets. Illegal riders risk a €40 fine. City bus lines #40-42 leave from the train station.

Car Rental: Hertz, St. Ruprechterstr. 12 (☎ 561 47). Open M-F 8am-5pm, Sa 9am-noon. **Avis,** Villacherstr. 1c (☎ 559 38). Open M-F 7:30am-4:30pm, Sa 9-11am.

Bike Rental: Impulse (☎ 51 63 10) has 6 stations all over town, including the tourist office, across from the train station, and the campground. €4 per 5hr., €8 per day; mountain bikes €8/€14. Helmets €1-2. Discounts for seniors, students, and children. The tourist office distributes the pamphlet *Radwandern,* detailing local bike paths.

▐▛ ▐▌ ORIENTATION AND PRACTICAL INFORMATION

From the station, follow Bahnhofstr. to Paradeiserg. and turn left. Neuer Pl. is two blocks down on the right. **Alterplatz, Neuer Platz,** and **Heiligengeistplatz,** the town's bus center, make up the 3-ring circus of the city. They lie within the **Ring,** the inner district of Klagenfurt, the central commercial activity, bordered by St. Veiter Ring, Völkermarkter Ring, Viktringer Ring, and Villacher Ring. Streets within the Ring generally run in a north-south/east-west grid. The **Lendkanal,** a narrow waterway, and **Villacherstr.** stretch 3.5km from the city center to the Wörthersee.

Tourist Office: Gäste Information is on the 1st floor of the *Rathaus* in Neuer Pl. (☎ 53 72 23; fax 72 95; tourismus@klagenfurt.at; www.info.klagenfurt.at.) From the station,

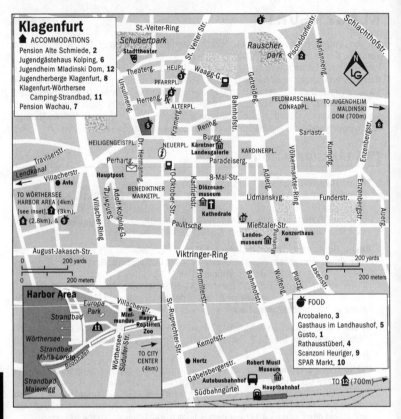

Klagenfurt

♠ **ACCOMMODATIONS**

Pension Alte Schmiede, **2**
Jugendgästehaus Kolping, **6**
Jugendheim Mladinski Dom, **12**
Jugendherberge Klagenfurt, **8**
Klagenfurt-Wörthersee
 Camping-Strandbad, **11**
Pension Wachau, **7**

🍎 **FOOD**

Arcobaleno, **3**
Gasthaus im Landhaushof, **5**
Gusto, **1**
Rathausstüberl, **4**
Scanzoni Heuriger, **9**
SPAR Markt, **10**

Harbor Area

go down Bahnhofstr. and left on Paradeiserg., into Neuer Pl. The staff organizes daily tours of the Altstadt. (1½hr., July-Aug. 10am. Call 2 weeks in advance to arrange a tour in English.) Open May-Sept. M-F 8am-8pm, Sa-Su 10am-5pm; Oct.-Apr. M-F 8am-5pm. The **Jugend Info** office, Fleischbankg. 4 (☎ 17 99), focuses on academic, social, and legal issues and has a knowledgeable staff. Open M-Th 7:30am-4pm, F 7am-12:30pm.

Currency Exchange: Best rates in town are at the main post office (exchange machine 24hr.) and its train station branch.

Luggage Storage: At the train station. **Gepackaufbewahrung,** €2.10 per piece. M-F 7am-6pm, Sa-Su 8am-5pm. 24hr. **Lockers** €2-3.50.

Pharmacy: Landschafts-Apotheke, Alterpl. 32, ☎550 77. Open M-F 8am-6pm, Sa 8am-noon. Check any pharmacy window to find the 24hr. pharmacy on call that night.

Hospital: Klagenfurt Krankenhaus, St.-Veiter-Str. 47 (☎538).

Emergencies: Police, ☎133, 53 33. **Ambulance,** ☎144. **Medical Assistance,** ☎141.

Bi-Gay-Lesbian Organizations: Ask for the pamphlet "Gay Guide" at the tourist office for a list of gay establishments in the city. **Queer Klagenfurt,** Postfach 146 (☎50 46 90). Hotline W 7-9pm. **AIDS-Hilfe Kärnten,** 8-Mai-Str. 19, 4th fl. (☎551 28; fax 51 46 92; www.hiv.at). Open M-Tu and Th 5-7pm.

Internet: Internet Cafe (☎58 88), on the 2nd floor inside the Sparkasse on Neuerpl. €3.70 per 30min. Open M-F 7:45am-3:30pm. **Sir Magic's Internet Pub**, Waagg. 10 (☎59 45 94). €0.10 per min. Open M-Sa 10am-2am, Su 2pm-6pm.

Post Office: Main post office, Dr. Hermann Str. 4, off Neuer Pl. (☎55 65 50). Open M-F 8am-6pm, Sa 7:30am-6pm. **Postal code:** A-9010.

▟ ACCOMMODATIONS AND CAMPING

For budget stays, two student dorms are converted to youth hostels during July and August. Be aware, however, that only Jugendherberge Klagenfurt offers dorm accommodations; for others, you'll pay considerably more for converted student single or double rooms. The tourist office distributes the helpful *Hotel Information* (with a city map) and *You are Welcome* pamphlets, in English, as well as the German lists of private rooms.

▨ **Jugendherberge Klagenfurt,** Neckheimg. 6 (☎23 00 20; fax 00 20 20), at Universität-str., a 20min. walk from the Wörthersee and a 45min. walk from the city center. From the train station, take bus #40, 41, or 42 to "Heiligengeistpl." then bus #10 or 11 to "Neckheimg." from stand #2. Although far from the city center, its proximity to the lake and bars in the nearby university area make it worthwhile. Mostly spacious quads. All rooms have shower and toilet. Breakfast buffet (7-8:30am) and sheets included. Dinner €6. Kitchen, laundry, and sauna available. **Internet** €2.60 per 20min. Reception 7-11am and 5-10pm. Dorms €16.30; doubles €40. Non-members add €3. ❸

Jugendheim Mladinski Dom, Mikschallee 4 (☎356 51; fax 51 11). From the train station, turn right on Südbahngürtel, then right and through the underpass on St.-Peter-Str. Cross Ebentalerstr., follow the road that curves to left and then to the right, and take the 1st left. Or take bus #40, 41, or 42 to "Heiligengeistpl.," then bus #70 or 71 (dir: Ebental) to "Windischkaserne" from stand #13, and walk in the same direction (bus runs M-Sa until 6:57pm). This dorm becomes a bed-and-breakfast in summer with large rooms including shower and bathroom. Parking and televisions available. Breakfast €2.50. Reception 6am-midnight. Open July 10-Aug. Singles €21.50; doubles €35; triples €41. 12 and under €10; 6 and under €7. €1.50 per person per night cheaper for stays of three nights or more. ❸

Jugendgästehaus Kolping (HI), Enzenbergstr. 26 (☎569 65; fax 65 632). From the station, head right down Bahnhofstr., right on Viktringer Ring, left on Völkermarkter Ring, right at Feldmarschall-Conrad-Pl. (which becomes Völkermarkterstr.), and right on Enzenbergstr. (20min.). A student dorm during the year, Kolping welcomes summer travelers, offering singles and doubles with gleaming bathrooms. Breakfast included. Open from early July to early Sept. Reception July-Aug. 24hr. Singles €23; doubles €46. Ages 10-15 €19/€38. €3 surcharge for 1-night stay. Non-members add €3. ❸

Pension Alte Schmiede, Pischeldorferstr. 8 (☎/fax 59 35 59). From the train station, turn right on Südbahngürtel, then left on Lastenstr. Follow Lastenstr. as it becomes Völkermarkter-Ring, then veer left onto Pischeldorferstr. (15min). Singles and doubles, some with living room and couch, all with satellite TV, bathroom, and shower. July-Aug. Singles €28, doubles €60; Sept.-June €26-30/€48-60. ❸

Pension Wachau, Wilfriedg. 19 (☎21 7 17; fax 71 78; office@pension-wachau.at). From Heiligengeistpl., take the #10 or #11 bus to Neckheimg., then walk back two blocks to Wilfriedg. and take a right. Tucked away in a residential neighborhood, but with easy access to the bus, Wachau offers comfortable rooms all with TV, bathroom, and shower. Breakfast included. Reservations recommended. Singles €37-39, doubles €62-64. ❹

Klagenfurt-Wörthersee Camping-Strandbad (☎211 69; fax 69 93), on Metnitzstrand off Universitätsstr. From the train station, take bus #40, 41, or 42 to "Heiligengeistpl.," then bus #12 to "Strandbad Klagenfurter See." Turn left and walk 2min. The busy yet comfortable campsite is on the left, across the street from the Wörthersee. On-site grocery store, mini-golf, and beach. Beach entry included. June 20-Aug. 20 €7 per person, ages 3-14 €2.20. May-June 19 and Aug. 21-Sept. €4.40, €2.20; large caravan site €8; small site €4. Showers included. €1 per person per night tax. AmEx/MC/V. ❶

🍴 FOOD

Warning: With a few notable exceptions, restaurants in Klagenfurt are closed Sundays. The tourist office's *Sonntagsbraten* lists addresses and hours of cafes, restaurants, clubs, and bars that are open on Sundays. Every Thursday and Saturday 8am-noon, the compact **Benediktinerplatz** on the lower west side of the Altstadt welcomes a rickety market of fruits and vegetables. There is a **SPAR** on the corner of Bahnhofstr. and Miesstalerstr. After 5:30pm, breads and sweets in the *Konditorei* are 25% off. (Open M-Th 7:30am-6:30pm, F 7am-7pm, Sa 7am-5pm.) There is a SPAR on Villacherstr., 5min. from Jugendherberge Klagenfurt.

Gasthaus im Landhaushof (☎50 23 63; fax 75 17), inside the courtyard of the *Landhaus* on Ursulineng. Savor hearty, tastefully presented meals in the shadow of the *Landhaus*. Lunch *Menüs* run around €5.80; Wienerschnitzel or *Scheinbraten* dinner, €10. Open daily 10am-midnight, kitchen until 11pm (Su 10pm). AmEx/DC/MC/V. ❷

Rathausstüberl, Pfarrpl. 8 (☎573 47), on a cobblestone street near the *Pfarrkirche*, serves fresh Carinthian specialties like *Marillien-* or *Zweschgenknödeln* (apricots or plums baked into a shell covered in brown sugar and butter, €6.50-7.30) alongside favorites like *Spätzle* (€6.50). Enjoy a couple beers and a full meal with the sociable local crowd. Open M-Sa 9am-11pm. ❷

Gusto, St. Veiter Ring 51a, on the northeast corner of the Altstadt, is a great place for lunch, offering roast chicken, *Käsenudeln*, and other lunchtime *Menüs* for €4.50-5.50 in a location with Van Gogh on the walls. Open M-F 7am-7pm. ❷

Scanzoni Heuriger, 11 Villacherstr, just west of Heiligengeistpl. Under the newly painted ceiling frescoes of common people drinking wine, this restaurant bar offers a range of filling Carinthian dinners (€4.50-5.50), like gulasch and bread or schnitzel and fries. Wine €2-4. Open daily 4pm-2am. ❷

Arcobaleno, Wienerg. 11, at the corner of Heupl., serves a large variety of ice cream for €0.75 a scoop, and sundaes for €4.50-5. Droves of people wait for this tasty treat in almost any weather. Open M-Sa 10:30am-midnight. ❶

🔆 SIGHTS

Klagenfurt and its suburbs are home to no fewer than 23 castles and mansions; the tourist office's English brochure *From Castle to Castle* gives a suggested path. Another brochure, the German *Museumswandern*, gives addresses and hours for the city's 17 art galleries, 18 museums, and other attractions.

THE OLD TOWN. Buildings here display an amalgam of architectural styles: *Biedermeier*, Italian Renaissance, Mannerist, Baroque, and *Jugendstil* facades. At the edge of Alterpl. stands the 16th-century **Landhaus,** originally an arsenal and later the seat of the provincial diet. The symmetrical towers, staircases, and flanking projections create an elegant courtyard sprinkled with umbrellas of outdoor cafes. Inside, 665 brilliant coats of arms blanket the walls. Artist Johann Ferdinand Fromiller took 20 years to complete these pieces. Ask at the ticket counter about guided tours, which are 20min. and include admission to the Provincia congress chambers. (☎57 75 72 15. Open Apr.-Sept. M-F 9am-1pm and 2-5pm. €2, students €1.)

A stroll through Kramerg., one of the oldest streets in Klagenfurt, leads past the bronze statue of the legendary **Wörther-See Manndl,** whose little keg incessantly spills water into the pool below. Continue on Kramerg. directly to **Neuer Platz,** a torrent of motion and activity. Standing proudly over the eastern end, a statue of Empress Maria Theresia glares regally at the occasional skateboarder launching off her pedestal. Compounding the indignity is a 60-ton half-lizard, half-serpent copper creature that spits water in her direction. This fountain depicts the **Lindwurm,** Klagenfurt's heraldic beast.

CATHEDRAL. Rebuilt after Allied bombing in 1944, the modern exterior of the **Kathedrale** renders it almost indistinguishable from its surroundings in the **Domplatz.** The cathedral's interior, however, is awash with high arches, crystal chandeliers, pink and white floral stucco, and a brilliant gold altar. Other ecclesiastical paraphernalia are on display in the tiny **Diözesanmuseum** next door, including the Holleiner Kreuz dating from 1170 and the oldest Austrian stained-glass window—a humble, 800-year-old sliver portraying Mary Magdalene. (Lidmanskyg. 10, 2 blocks south of Neuer Pl., off Karfreitstr. ☎50 24 98. Cathedral open daily 6:30am-7pm. Free. Museum open mid-June to mid-Sept. M-Sa 10am-noon and 3-5pm; mid-Sept. to mid-Oct. and May to mid-June M-Sa 10am-noon. €3, students and children €2.)

LANDESMUSEUM. Klagenfurt's Landesmuseum (Historical Museum), was Emperor Franz Josef's favorite. It houses the *Lindwurmschädel,* the fossilized rhino skull discovered in 1335 that, three centuries later, inspired the *Lindwurm* statue at Neuer Pl. (see "Dragon's Tale" above). Other pieces include 18th-century musical instruments, huge crystals, and ancient Celtic and Roman artifacts. The Medusas at the corners of the fully intact 3rd-century Dionysus mosaic could take on a *Lindwurm* any day. (Museumg. 2. ☎53 63 05 52; fax 63 05 40. Open Tu-Sa 9am-4pm, Su 10am-1pm. €3, students €2.)

AMUSEMENT PARK. Don't miss Klagenfurt's most shameless concession to tourist kitsch, the **Minimundus** park, only minutes from the Wörthersee. If you choose the audio-guide version, Louis Armstrong

IN RECENT NEWS

LOSING GROUND

The posters in Klagenfurt are ominous and uncompromising: "Maria Loretto must not die." They do not refer to a woman, but to one of the most secluded beaches on the Wörthersee, which is now threatened by encroaching housing developments. The near-hysterical response of conservation-minded citizens of the area illustrates the sensitive task of developing the Wörthersee without destroying it. The lake is a true haven—water temperatures hover around 28°C, and the weather is nearly perfect in the summer. Stringent rules have already been put into place to keep the lake in its pristine condition. Rental boats are primarily sailboats or paddleboats, and motorboats are electric. There are virtually no gas-powered boats on the lake, which helps to keep the water clear and emerald green.

But in many ways, the communities around the lake are becoming victims of their own success. The strict environmental protection has resulted in even higher beachfront property values, endangering the very beaches it is meant to protect—resorts and hotels are desperate to snap up whatever beaches can be found.

> **DRAGON'S TALE** Once upon a time, Klagenfurt was harassed by a winged, virgin-consuming lizard—the *Lindwurm* (Dragon). This awful monster terrorized the area, preventing settlers from draining the marshes. Enter Hercules, who quickly dispatched the beast and saved the village. Centuries later, the "skull" of the slain beast was found, proving many an old wives' tale about the heroic founding of the town. The townspeople commissioned sculptor Ulrich Vogelsang to recreate the monster using its "skull" as the model. The statue of the *Lindwurm* on Neuer Platz became the town's symbol, despite the fact that, in 1840, scientists proved the skull belonged not to the beast, but to a prehistoric rhino. Klagenfurt's collective heart broke in 1945 when an Allied soldier climbed onto the *Lindwurm's* sensitive tail, snapping it in two. Today, stuffed animals reminiscent of Puff the Magic Dragon are for sale everywhere.

sings *It's a Wonderful World* as you gaze at the world's most famous buildings and monuments. Artists have created intricate models of over 170 world-famous buildings and sights—all on a 1:25 scale. You'll be on eye level with the Parthenon, Big Ben, the Taj Mahal, and many more; some of the models took over three years to build. At night, the models are illuminated. *(Villacherstr. 241. From the train station, take bus #40, 41 or 42 to "Heiligengeistpl.," then switch to bus #10, 11, 20, 21, or 22 (dir: Strandbad) to "Minimundus."* ☎ *21 19 40; fax 211 94 60. Open Apr., Oct. daily 9am-6pm; May, June, Sept. 9am-7pm; July and Aug. 9am-10pm. €10, students €8.50, ages 6-15 €4.50. English guidebook €3, audioguide €2.*

ZOO. To prevent the persecution of the *Lindwurm's* descendents, the **Happ's Reptilien Zoo** exhibits snake environments. Herr Happ has a loose definition of "reptile"—along with puff adders and iguanas, the reptile zoo features spiders, scorpions, guinea pigs, and fish. The accident-prone should avoid Saturday's 3pm piranha and crocodile feeding. *(Villacherstr. 237, next door to Minimundus.* ☎ *234 25; fax 234 25 14. Open May-Sept. daily 8am-6pm; Oct.-Apr. 9am-5pm. €8.50, students and seniors €7.50, children €4.50.)*

⚑ OUTDOOR ACTIVITIES

On hot spring and summer days, crowds bask in the sun and loll in the clear water of the Wörthersee. This water-sport haven is Carinthia's largest and most popular lake. The two **beaches** closest to Klagenfurt are **Strandbad Klagenfurter See** (open 8am-8pm; €3, children €1.40, family €6.60; locker key deposit €5) and **Strandbad Maria-Loretto.** (Open in good weather May and Sept. 9am-6pm; June 9am-7pm; July and Aug. 9am-8pm. €3.50, ages 6-15 €1.70; after 2pm €2.70, €1.) Both are easily reached by public transportation. From the train station, take bus #40, 41, or 42 to "Heiligengeistpl." then bus #10, 11, or 12 to "Strandbad Klagenfurter See." To get to Maria-Loretto, walk to the end of Metnitz Strand, and turn left onto Lorettoweg. Strandbad Maria-Loretto, around the corner of the lake on the southern side, is quieter than Strandbad Klagenfurter See. The absence of lifeguards means swim at your own risk.

To enjoy the water without getting (too) wet, rent a **rowboat** (€2 per 30min.), **paddle boat** (€3), or **motor boat** (€5.80) from **STW Boote** near the Strandbad Klagenfurter See. A *Radwandern* brochure, free at the tourist office, suggests **bike** tours, including one along a castle-church circuit. The Karawanken mountains to the south, such as the **Hochobir** (2139m) provide good **hiking,** but many are accessible only by car. Ask at the tourist office for details.

NIGHTLIFE

The best of Klagenfurt's nightlife rages in the pubs of **Pfarrplatz** and **Herrengasse.** To maximize your entertainment euro, read the tourist office's *Veranstaltung-Kalender* (calendar of events), available in English. The tourist office has brochures listing concerts, gallery shows, museum exhibits, and plays. Get tickets from **Reisebüro Springer** (☎387 00 55). The *Jugendstil* **Stadttheater** is Klagenfurt's main venue for operas and plays: everything from Christopher Marlowe to Broadway musicals. (Box office ☎540 64. Open from mid-Sept. to mid-June Tu-Sa 9am-noon and 4-6pm. €3-40, students and seniors half-off.)

DAYTRIP FROM KLAGENFURT

BURG HOCHOSTERWITZ

Hochosterwitz is just outside the town of Launsdorf, northeast of Klagenfurt and 10km east of St. Veit. Trains run to Launsdorf from Klagenfurt (30min., 10 per day, fewer on weekends, 3:42am-9:20pm, €9 round-trip). Walk 2km to the base of Hochosterwitz (you can't miss it), and 10min. more to the main parking lot and entrance kiosk. Drivers take Rte. 83 from Klagenfurt to St. Veit and switch to the district road to Hochosterwitz.

Dominating the countryside from the top of a steep hill that seems to rise out of nowhere, **Burg Hochosterwitz** is a striking testament to the erstwhile wealth and power of Carinthia's nobility. This is the stuff that medieval dreams are made of—a fortified wall winds around the hillside, culminating in a stocky castle with turrets and towers. The castle's elevation above pastures and fields of corn and wheat make the sight even more imposing. It's been around since 1571, when German nobleman and governor of Carinthia Georg von Khevenhüller bought the property and made extensive renovations. Irked by marauding Ottoman Turks, Georg constructed the 14 massive gates that guard the road up to the castle, each with its own nickname and strategically designed shooting apertures. The gates alone took 13 years to build; the church was finished in 1586, though later generations of Khevenhüllers tinkered with the walls and fortifications. The path to the top commands postcard-worthy views at every turn, taking in town, country, and mountains beyond. *(Open May-Sept. daily 8am-6pm; Apr. and Oct. 9am-5pm. €7, seniors €5, ages 6-15 €4. English brochure €3.)* A steep, 20min. walk along the outer wall takes you to the top of the hill; a **funicular** also ferries visitors up a nearly vertical track (€3 round-trip). A **restaurant** and a small **museum** filled with old paintings and a collection of medieval arms sits at the top. (Tours in German every 45min. Open same hours as castle. Free with castle admission).

VELDEN ☎4274

Trains run from Klagenfurt to Velden (20min., 1-2 per hr., round-trip €8.40). To reach the town center from the train station, turn right on leaving the station, then left onto Birkenallee, marked with the sign "Zum See."

Dubbed the "Austrian Riviera," the shores of the Wörthersee attract loads of Austrian and German tourists in summer, which is when tiny Velden gears up for action. In mid-July, the town's main street rumbles with race cars. Fireworks fly nightly to the music of Beethoven or the Beatles. The beaches are swamped with sun-worshippers, but the image of Velden wouldn't be complete without the golden *Schloß* (castle) reflecting onto the lake. To many Germans, its fame as the location of the soap opera, "Ein Schloß am Wörthersee" is reason enough to visit.

CARINTHIA

LIGHTS OVER THE LAKE While its location on one of Austria's most picturesque lakes might be enough to attract its share of tourists, Velden isn't taking any chances. They have put the lake to even better use, pumping water straight from the Wörthersee to an area just in front of the castle, where spectacular 25min. light shows are displayed three nights a week. Using an array of lasers, the water is lit and colored into spinning, psychedelic patterns as it shoots and twists into different shapes from the hoses that pump it higher than the *Schloß* itself. Best of all, these "Zauberwelle" (magic waters) are free.

To find the **tourist office,** Villacherstr. 19, turn right at the end of Birkenallee into Am Cerso, then right on Villacherstr. The tourist office is on the left side of the road, in a shiny metal and glass building. A free 24hr. accommodations phone is outside. (☎210 30. Open July-Aug. M-Th 8am-8pm, F-Sa 8am-10pm, Su 9am-5pm; May-June and Sept. M-Th 8am-6pm, F-Sa 8am-8pm, Su 9am-5pm.) **Pension Teppan ❸,** Sternbergstr. 7, has comfy rooms with geranium-covered balconies. From the train station turn right, then left onto Birkenallee (marked with "Zum See" sign). Follow it to the end and turn right onto Am Corso. Turn right onto Kirchenpl., which becomes Kirchenstr. Pension Teppan is at the intersection of Kirchenstr. and Sternbergstr. (15min.) The owners lend **bikes** for free and offer discounted admission to the beach. (☎31 69; pension.teppan@carinthia.com. Call ahead. Breakfast included. Open Apr.-Sept. €23.40, €22 for stays of three nights or more.) Refuel after swimming at **Restaurant Aqua ❷,** with three levels of outdoor seating and deals like bratwurst (€3) or half a grilled chicken and fries (€7.20). Located right on the beach, so most of the clientele wear bathing suits. (Open 8am-1am.)

Beaches line Seepromenade and Seecorso. The chi-chi plant their umbrellas at **Casinobad** (€7), while crowds congregate at **Strandclub** (€5) at the tip of the lake. Smaller beaches include **Strandbad Leopold** (€3.30) and **Strandbad Wrann** (€5, children €3), and **Strandbad Bulfon** (€6, €3). Each beach offers watery fun, but only Leopold gives refunds for bad weather. (Wrann: rowboats €3 per hr., motorboats €13. Strandclub: €11, €14.) There's also windsurfing, waterskiing, and sailing. Beachside activities include volleyball, ping pong, and mini-golf, depending on the beach. On non-beach days, bike along the lake for beautiful views. **Rent bikes** at **Impulse,** Villachstr. 21, at Agip Tankstelle (☎04272 2482).

THE DRAUTAL

Thanks to its moderate climate and proximity to southern Europe, central Carinthia's Drautal (Drau Valley) feels decidedly un-Teutonic, while providing access to alpine activities. Carved by the **Drau river,** the region offers skiing, hiking, and water sports between the Hohe Tauern range and the Villacher Alps. In addition to the transportation hub of Villach and an electronic industry, the Drautal has a handful of beautiful lakes, including the **Millstättersee, Ossiachersee,** and **Faakersee.**

VILLACH ☎04242

Villach (pop. 57,000) is a lively city that quickly fades to grassy, tree-lined suburbs. Italian and Slavic influences keep it multicultural and vibrant, catering to many different types of visitors. An important transportation hub to its southern neighbors, Villach is a pleasant place to spend the day exploring nearby **Mt. Gerlitzen,** the castle **Schloß Landskron,** or the **Ossiachersee** and **Faakersee.**

☞ TRANSPORTATION

Trains run to Graz (3½hr., 13 per day 4:40am-8:05pm, €21); Klagenfurt (35min., 3-5 per day 1:21am-11:55pm, €5.60); and Vienna Südbahnhof (5hr., 12 per day 1:21am-8:05pm, €37). A **free city bus** travels a circuit every 20 min. (M-F 8:40am-6:20pm, Sa 8:40am-12:20pm). **Ferries** cruise up and down the Drau, from Villach in the east to Weinberg-Bad in the west and back again. Boats leave the dock beneath the north end of the main bridge. (1½hr. round-trip. Seasonal schedules are complex, but boats usually leave 10, 11:50am, 2:30, 4:20pm. €10, ages 6-15 €4.) Find **taxis** at the Bahnhof, (☎288 88), or at **Das Radl**, Italienstr. 25 (☎26 954. €10 per day).

◼◼ ◪ ORIENTATION AND PRACTICAL INFORMATION

Villach sprawls on both sides of the Drau River. The train and bus stations are both on Bahnhofspl., north of the town center. Bahnhofstr. leads from the station over a 9th-century bridge to **Hauptplatz**, the commercial heart of the city. Narrow paths weave through this area. Two sweeping arcs of stores flank Hauptpl., enclosed by a towering church at one end and by the Drau at the other.

To get to Villach's **tourist office**, Rathauspl. 1, from the train station, walk out to Bahnhofstr. over the bridge and through Hauptpl. to Rathauspl. The office is at the far end. (☎24 44 40; fax 244 44 17. Open in summer M-F 9am-6pm, Sa 9am-noon; off-season M-F 9am-12:30pm and 1:30-5pm.) The **regional tourist office** in St. Ruprecht (☎420 00; fax 427 77) offers up-to-date ski information. There are **ATMs** throughout the city. The station has 24hr. electronic **lockers** (€2-3). The local **hospital** is on Dreschnidstr. (☎20 80). Call ☎203 30 to reach the **police** headquarters at Tralteng. 34. **Internet** access is available at **Ken-i-di**, Ledererg. 16. (☎213 22. Open Tu-Sa 6pm-2am, Su 3-11pm. €0.10 per min.) The main **post office**, 8-Mai-Pl. 2, also **exchanges currency**. (Open daily 7:30am-noon and 2-5:30pm.) **Postal code:** A-9500.

◪◪ ACCOMMODATIONS AND FOOD

The best priced establishment is **Jugendgästehaus Villach (HI) ❷**, Dinzlweg 34. From the train station, walk up Bahnhofstr., over the bridge, and through Hauptpl. Turn right on Postg., walk through Hans-Gasser-Pl., which merges into Tirolerstr., and bear right at St. Martinstr. Dinzlweg is the first street on the left (30min.), and the hostel is tucked away past the tennis courts. Plastered with 1970s neon, it has 140 beds in spacious 5-bed dorms, each with its own shower. Disco and free sauna are on the premises. (☎563 68. Lunch or dinner €5.81. Breakfast and sheets included. Keys available with ID. Reception 7-10am and 5-10pm. Dorms €14.90; singles €22.17.) **Gästehaus Pirker ❸**, Rennsteinerstr. 21, offers rooms with shower and bath. Turn right out of the station, past the post office, and follow the ramp (Rennsteinerstr.) up to your right, over the train tracks, and around several sharp bends. (☎241 76. Breakfast included. Singles €23.50; doubles €42; triples €63.) In the middle of town is **Hotel Bacchus ❹**, Khevenhüllerg. 13, which lives a double life as a *Weinstübe* and restaurant. From the Hauptpl. facing the bridge on Bahnhofstr., the large park building with turrets is one block to the right. (Rooms with shower and TV. Breakfast included. Singles €30-40; doubles €60-80.)

Lederergasse overflows with small, cheap eateries, while **Hauptplatz** and **Kaiser-Josef-Platz** seat swankier patrons. ▓**Trastevere ❷**, Widmanng. 30 (☎21 56 65), offers fine Italian cuisine in an enclosed courtyard for scores of businessmen and families, may of whom are Italian visitors. For a glass of wine or light lunch with dozens of Villachers away from the crowds, try **Park Cafe ❶**, Moritzstr. 2, across from the post office. Wine and beer (€1.80) and sandwiches (€2-4) are enjoyed in a courtyard off the street. **Konditorei Bernhold ❶**, Nikolaipl. 2, tempts with devilish pastries (€1-2.50), ice cream concoctions, and a river view from a patio worthy of a slowly-sipped cappuccino. (☎254 42. Open M-F 7am-6:30pm, Sa 7am-5pm, Su 9:30am-8pm.) Picnic supplies await at **SPAR Markt**, on Hans-Grasser-Pl. (open M-F 8am-7pm), or at the **farmer's market** in Burgpl. (W and Sa mornings).

🔘 🎵 SIGHTS AND ENTERTAINMENT

DOWNTOWN. Any tour of Villach traverses **Hauptplatz,** the city's 800-year-old commercial center. The southern end of the square lives in the shadow of the mighty Gothic **St. Jakob-Kirche,** one of Villach's 12 churches. Raised on a stone terrace, this 12th-century church was converted during the Reformation in 1526 and became Austria's first Protestant chapel. An ascent up the church's **Stadtpfarrturm,** the tallest steeple in Carinthia (94m), provides a view of Villach and its environs. Squeeze up the narrow spiral staircase and have a look. (☎205 25 40. Open June-Sept. M-Sa 10am-6pm, Su noon-6pm; May and Oct. M-Sa 10am-6pm. €1.82, students €1. Free organ concerts in the church June-Aug. Th 8pm.)

The **Stadtmuseum,** Widmanng. 38, founded in 1873, has archaeological displays spanning six millennia, as well as art from the Middle Ages and the original Villach coat of arms from 1240. Local tradition once required that anyone who wanted to marry had to be able to carry the 90kg statue of Eisner Leonhard around the church. (Many honeymoons were ruined by hernias.) Across from the museum is a glass **Holocaust Memorial** almost hidden by shrubbery. (☎205 35 35 or 205 35 00. Open May-Oct. daily 10am-4:30pm. €2.50, students €1.80, children under 8 free.)

OTHER SIGHTS AND FESTIVALS. Two blocks farther down Peraustr. looms the Baroque **Heilig-Kreuz-Kirche,** the pink edifice visible from the city bridge. Cool for car enthusiasts, the **Villacher Fahrzeugmuseum** is at Draupromenade 12 on the other side of the Drau. Two rooms crammed with vehicles give you a look at some 50s and 60s rides. (☎255 30 or 224 40; fax 30 78; www.oldtimermuseum.com. Open from mid-June to mid-Sept. daily 9am-5pm; mid-Sept. to mid-June M-Su 10am-noon and 2-4pm. €5.45, ages 6-15 €2.90.) On the first Saturday in August, the **Villach Kirchtag** (Church Day), allowed by decree in 1225, helps the town celebrate its "birthday" with raucous revelry. (Admission €6.)

⚑ OUTDOOR ACTIVITIES. Villach lies in a valley between the small but lovely **Ossiachersee** (8km from Villach) and the placid **Faakersee** (10km). Plenty of nearby terrain is ideal for **swimming, boating,** and **cycling.** Trains on the Villach-Rosenbach line stop at Faak am See on the Faakersee, and settlements on the north shore of the Ossiachersee (i.e., Annenheim, Bodensdorf) lie along the Villach-Feldkirchen line. Peaks near Villach make for good **hiking** and **skiing,** with winter resorts near each lake. Buses run to the hills outside Heiligengeist in the Villach Alps. (1-day ticket €21, 15 and under €12.50.) At the corner of Austria and Slovenia, the Drei-Ländereck lifts offer additional slopes. (1-day ticket €22, 15 and under €13.)

SPITTAL AN DER DRAU ☎ 4762

At the foot of the Goldeck Mountain by the Drau river sits the small city once known for its *Spittal* (hospital). People came from far and wide to find cures for their ailments. They still do, only now laughter is the best medicine at the *Komödienspiele* (comedy play festival) held at Schloß Porcia every July and August. Self-dubbed the Komödienstadt ("City of Comedy"), Spittal has seen its share of tragedy too, as the ghost at Schloß Porcia will attest. Along with its mascot, the tragi-comedic clown, Pierrot, Spittal embodies a healthy mixture of Mediterranean gaiety and Central European melancholy.

▉▟ TRANSPORTATION AND PRACTICAL INFORMATION. **Trains** run frequently to Spittal an der Drau from: Klagenfurt (1-1½hr., every hr. 4:44am-11:27pm, €10.20); Lienz (45min.-1hr., every hr. 7:36am-8:42pm, €9.30); and Villach (21-35min., 1-2 per hr. 4:44am-11:27pm, €5.60). **Lockers** are available at the train station (€2). To reach the town center from the train station, walk down Bahnhofstr. and cut diagonally across the park. The creamy white Schloß Porcia is at the end of the park and houses the **tourist office**, Burgpl. 1. (☎ 34 20. Open July-Aug. M-F 9am-8pm, Sa 9am-noon; Sept.-June M-F 9am-6pm, Sa 9am-noon.)

▛▐ ACCOMMODATIONS AND FOOD. The **Jugendherberge Spittal (HI) ❷**, Zur Seilbahn 2, is at the base of Goldeck Mountain. From the train station turn right and walk past the post office. Continue on Körnerstr, turn right on Ortenburgerstr., walk under the train tracks, and make the second right onto Wiesenweg. Take a left through the parking lot and follow the signs to "Goldeck" (20min.). Rooms and hall bathrooms go for function over form. (☎ 32 52; fax 325 24. Restaurant downstairs. Breakfast included. Reception 8-9am and 5-9pm. Call ahead. Dorms €9.50, with all 3 meals €28; singles €13.50, without breakfast €7.30.) For magnificent views try **Jugendherberge Goldeck (HI) ❷.** Follow directions for the first hostel and take the cable car to "Mittelstation." (€5.80, round-trip €6.20 with guest card. Last ascent 5:30pm. ☎ 27 01. Breakfast included. Reception 8-9am and 5-9pm. Open Dec. 26-Easter and from late June to Sept. 20; depends on cable car schedule. Call ahead. Dorms €15.)

Eat like a Countess at **Schloß Café ❸**, Burgpl. 1. A piece of *Spittaler Torte* runs €2.50. For a meal, try *Käsenudeln* or schnitzel. Light lunch entrees are about €7, dinner entrees about €11. (☎ 47 07. Open M-F 7am-9pm, Sa 8:30am-9pm, Su 2pm-8pm; July-Aug. daily until midnight.) Hungrier folks might enjoy the filling food and expansive beer garden at **Das Gösserbrau ❷**, Villacherstr. 5, just on the other side of the river from the center of town. (☎ 23 83; fax 333 31. Wienerschnitzel with salad and fries €9, *Topfenstrudel* for dessert €2.50.) Despite the Donald Duck mascot, **Goldene Ente ❷**, Hauptpl. 20 (351 21) heading toward the river from the town center, offers a wide-ranging Chinese menu. Most meals around €7, with signature duck dishes €8.50-10. (Open daily 11:30am-3pm, 5:30-11pm.) Grab a picnic at **SPAR** supermarket inside the **Gerngroß** store, Neuerpl. 1. (☎ 42 78 70. Open M-F 8:30am-6pm, Sa 9am-5pm. AmEx/DC/MC/V.)

▣ SIGHTS. The rather plain facade of **Schloß Porcia** fails to prepare the eye for the delicate beauty of the Florentine Renaissance courtyard. The arcades serve as a backdrop for the light laughter of Spittal's Komödienspiele in summer (see below). Spanish count Gabriel von Salamanca, who was also the Austrian imperial treasurer, built the castle in the 16th century. It was eventually passed into the hands of the Austro-Italian Porcia family, but at least one Salamanca never left the castle: the ghost of Countess Katherina is said to inhabit its walls to this day. According to one story, the Countess laments the death of her beloved son;

another says she's condemned because of very un-countess-like behavior, such as setting hounds on her subjects and reportedly murdering one of her maidservants for discovering her hidden stash of money. The castle also houses the **Museum für Volkskultur** (Museum of Folk Culture). Through creative displays, including a reconstructed 1900 classroom and rooms devoted to local mining and mountain climbing, this museum recreates Carinthian daily life, with explanations in English. Check out the great collection of carnival masks and *Bartl* costumes: in Carinthia, he's Santa's little helper, only he dresses like a devil, wears a sheep skin, and caries a willow switch to hit bad kids. The first floor ends with the richly decorated living room of Count Salamanca. (☎28 90; fax 5650 61 56. Open May 15-Oct. daily 9am-6pm; Nov.-May 14 M-Th 1-4pm. €4.50, students and seniors €2.25.)

🎭 **ENTERTAINMENT.** During July and August, laughter fills Schloß Porcia's courtyard with the annual 🎭**Komödienspiele** (Comedy Play festival). Europe's greatest comedies are performed by the actors of Spittal's own Komödienschule, or school of comedy. (Tickets €22-29, standing €6.00. Students 40% off. Box office in Schloß Porcia; open every performance day 9am-7pm.) Every odd year on the last weekend in June, Spittal celebrates **Salamancafest**. Sixteenth-century garb becomes standard, drawing the town back to the time of the aristocratic Salamancas who built Schloß Porcia. Food and drink stalls swarm the town center and street musicians add to the merry atmosphere. The highlight of the festivities, however, isn't so merry. The gruesome death of Countess Katherina's son is reenacted in an attempt to somehow appease the Countess.

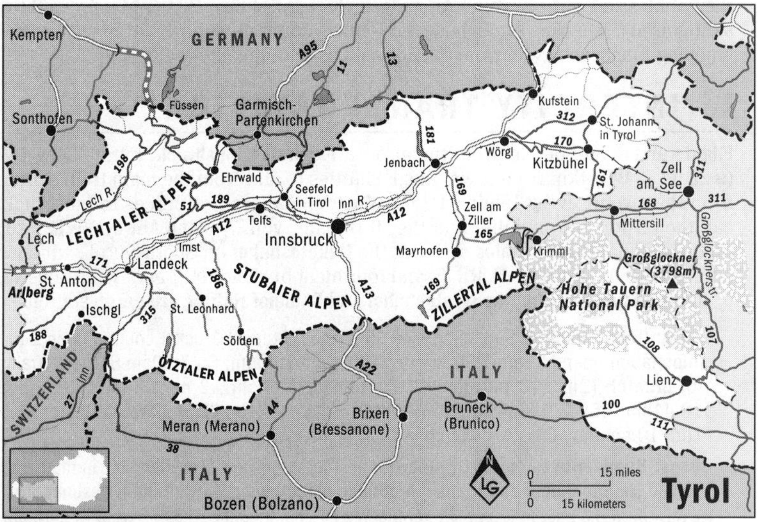
GERMANY
Kempten
Sonthofen
Füssen
Garmisch-
Partenkirchen
Kufstein
St. Johann
in Tyrol
Wörgl
Kitzbühel
Jenbach
Zell
am See
Ehrwald
Seefeld
in Tirol
Inn R.
Lech R.
LECHTALER ALPEN
Telfs
Innsbruck
Zell am
Ziller
Mittersill
Lech
Imst
Mayrhofen
Krimml
Landeck
St. Anton
Arlberg
Großglockner
(3798m)
Großglocknerstr.
STUBAIER ALPEN
ZILLERTAL ALPEN
Hohe Tauern
National Park
Ischgl
St. Leonhard
Sölden
SWITZERLAND
Inn
ÖTZTALER ALPEN
ITALY
Lienz
Meran (Merano)
Brixen
(Bressanone)
Bruneck
(Brunico)
ITALY
Bozen (Bolzano)
A95
A12
A13
A22
15 miles
15 kilometers
Tyrol

TYROL (TIROL)

The Habsburgs fell in love with Tyrol, and it's not hard to see why. Few other regions so effortlessly blend culture, natural spectacle, and ultimate relaxation. Craggy summits rising in the northeast and south cradle four-star resorts and untouched valleys like the Ötzal and Zillertal. In eastern Tyrol, the mighty peaks of the Hohe Tauern range are protected as a national park. In the center of it all, the eternally stylish Innsbruck unabashedly flaunts Baroque facades and bronze statues before an appreciative audience of foreigners. On cobblestone streets gilded houses blend seamlessly with their alpine backgrounds, both reflecting a devilish sparkle that confirms why Tyrol has become the world's mountain playground.

HIGHLIGHTS OF TYROL

Gape at the world's largest jewel in **Innsbruck** (see p. 190).

Relive your Olympic dreams at the ski jump in **Wilten** (see p. 193), or on the slopes in **Seefeld** (see p. 194).

Use **Sölden** as a base for exploring the dramatic **Ötztal Arena** (see p. 212).

INNSBRUCK ☎0512

Although the 1964 and 1976 Winter Olympics brought Innsbruck (pop. 128,000) international recognition, the beautiful mountain city has too rich a history to succumb to ski-resort status. The city boasts numerous intricate Baroque facades, the legacy of the Habsburgs' prolonged stay here; beginning with Maximilian I, many Habsburgs called Innsbruck home. Though the family is gone, the beauty that drew them here remains: the rocky peaks are so close they seem to advance down the cobblestone streets of the Altstadt. If the natural beauty, the history, and the skiing aren't tempting enough, several quiet mountain suburbs offer venues for enjoying Innsbruck away from the normal bustle of the city.

⊠ INTERCITY TRANSPORTATION

Flights arrive and depart from the airport, **Flughafen Innsbruck,** Fürstenweg 180 (☎22 52 53 04), 4km from town. Bus F shuttles to and from the main train station from the airport every 15min. (€1.60). **Austrian Airlines** has offices in Innsbruck; call the airport info number and they'll transfer you. **Tyrolean Airways** (☎222 20) offers regional flights. **Trains** arrive at the **Hauptbahnhof** on Südtirolerpl., which is on bus lines A, DE, F, H, R, RR, S, and four night bus lines NL1 and NL2, trams #3, 6, and the **Stubaitalbahn;** the **Westbahnhof** and **Bahnhof Hötting** are cargo stations.

> **Trains: Hauptbahnhof,** Südtirolerpl. (☎05 17 17). At least 1 ticket counter open 24hr. Information open M 8am-7:30pm, Tu-Sa 7:30am-7:30pm, Su 7:30am-8:40pm. Trains to: **Munich** (2hr., 13 per day, €30); **Rome** (8½-9½hr., 2 per day 11:28am and 10:41pm, €59.20); **Salzburg** (2½hr., 13 per day, €27); **Vienna Westbahnhof** (5½-7hr., 10 per day, €47.90); **Zurich** (4hr., 4 per day, €43.50).
>
> **Buses: BundesBuses** (☎53 07) leave from the station on Sterzingerstr., immediately behind Hauptbahnhof and to the left of the main entrance, for suburban destinations.
>
> **By car:** from the east or west take Autobahn A12. From Vienna, take A1 west to Salzburg, then A8 (in Germany) west to A93, which becomes A12 again in Austria. From the south, take A13 north. From Germany and the north, take A95 to Bundesstr. 2 east, which becomes Bundesstr. 177 east in Austria.

⊞ ORIENTATION

Most of Innsbruck lies between the **Inn River** to the west and the train tracks to the east. The main street is **Maria-Theresien-Straße,** running north and south, at times parallel to both the river and the train tracks. Open only to taxis, buses, and trams, and crowded with tourists and cafes, Maria-Theresien-Str. runs between the Altstadt and **Maximilianstraße,** another big street. Take tram #3 or bus A or H to "Maria-Theresien-Str." to get to the Altstadt from the Hauptbahnhof; or exit the station, turn right onto Südtirolpl. and later Bruneckerstr., then left onto Museumstr. and continue straight ahead for 10min. Most sights are near the Altstadt. To reach the **university district,** near Innrain, continue down Museumstr. toward the river (curving left onto Burggraben, across Maria-Theresien-Str., and onto Marktgraben). The university itself is to the left down Innrain. Though Innsbruck is not particularly confusing (for an old, imperial European city), a color map available at the train station or at tourist offices is useful.

▮ LOCAL TRANSPORTATION

> **Public Transportation:** Head to the **IVB** Office at Stainerstr. 2, near Maria-Theresien-Str., to pick up a local bus schedule. (☎530 17 99; fax 71 10. Open M-F 7:30am-6pm.) The main **bus station** is in front of the main entrance to the train station. Purchase single-ride, 1-zone tickets €1.60, 24hr. tickets €3.20, 4-ride tickets €4.80, and week-long bus passes €10.10, from the office or any driver. Punch your ticket when you board the bus or pay a €30 fine. Most buses stop running around 10:30 or 11:30pm; check each line for specifics. Three *Nachtbus* lines run after-hours every night; NL1 and NL2 go through Maria-Theresien-Str. and Marktpl. (every 30min., 11:39pm-5:09am) on their way to the Hauptbahnhof and beyond.

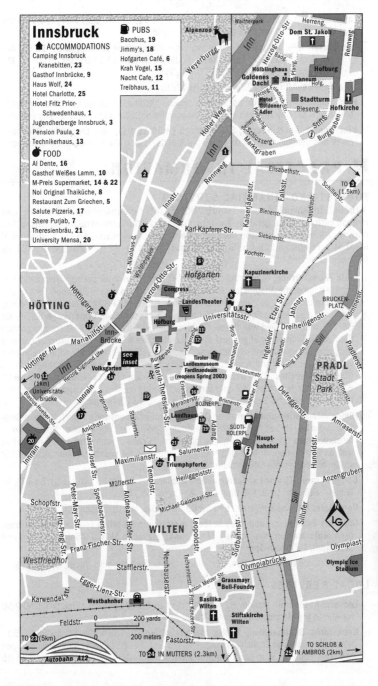

Innsbruck

ACCOMMODATIONS
Camping Innsbruck
  Kranebitten, **23**
Gasthof Innbrücke, **9**
Haus Wolf, **24**
Hotel Charlotte, **25**
Hotel Fritz Prior-
  Schwedenhaus, **1**
Jugendherberge Innsbruck, **3**
Pension Paula, **2**
Technikerhaus, **13**

FOOD
Al Dente, **16**
Gasthof Weißes Lamm, **10**
M-Preis Supermarket, **14 & 22**
Noi Original Thaiküche, **8**
Restaurant Zum Griechen, **5**
Salute Pizzeria, **17**
Shere Purjab, **7**
Theresienbräu, **21**
University Mensa, **20**

PUBS
Bacchus, **19**
Jimmy's, **18**
Hofgarten Café, **6**
Krah Vogel, **15**
Nacht Cafe, **12**
Treibhaus, **11**

TYROL

Taxis: Lined up at the Hauptbahnhof, or call ☎53 11, 17 18, 56 17 17, or 29 29 15. Approximately €10 from the airport to the Altstadt.

Car Rental: Avis, Salurnerstr. 15 in the large yellow office building (☎57 17 54; M-F 7:30am-6pm, Sa-Su 8am-1pm). **Hertz,** Südtirolerpl. 1 (☎58 09 01; fax 09 01 17; M-F 7:30am-6pm, Sa 8am-1pm; AmEx/DC/MC/V).

Auto Repairs: ARBÖ (☎123). **ÖAMTC** (☎120).

Hitchhiking: While *Let's Go* doesn't recommend hitching, thumbers have been known to take bus C to "Geyrstr." and cross the parking lot of DEZ mall to the Shell gas station.

Bike Rental: Sport Neuner, Salurnerstr. 5 (☎56 15 01), near the station. Mountain bikes and helmets €20 per day, €16 per half day. Open M-F 9am-6pm, Sa 9am-noon.

🔁 PRACTICAL INFORMATION

TOURIST AND FINANCIAL SERVICES

Although Innsbruck's myriad tourist offices offer comparable services, the two central offices at Burggraben 3 will probably give the most straightforward information. All offices hawk the **Innsbruck Card,** which gives free access to dozens of local attractions and all public transportation for 24, 48, or 72hr. (€19, €24, or €29; children 50% off).

Main Tourist Office, Burggraben 3 (☎598 50; fax 07; www.tiscover.com/innsbruck), is on the edge of the Altstadt just off the end of Museumstr. on the 3rd floor. Tons of brochures, a city map (€1), and a helpful staff await. Open M-F 8am-6pm, Sa 8am-noon. The large glassed-in office on the ground floor is **Innsbruck-Information** (☎53 56; fax 56 14), which is allied with the tourist office but consists of a profit-maximizing consortium of local hotels; arrange tours and concert tickets here, but don't expect to reserve budget accommodations. Nonetheless, when the tourist office is closed, this can be a valuable source of information. Open daily 9am-6pm. Currency exchange closes 5:30pm. **Branches** at the train station and major motor exits. **Jugendwarteraum** (☎58 63 62), in the Hauptbahnhof near the lockers, hands out free maps and skiing information. Open from mid-Sept. to Juhe M-F 11am-7pm, Sa 10am-1pm.

Hiking information and Insurance: Österreichischer Alpenverein (ÖAV), Wilhelm-Greil-Str. 15 (☎58 78 28; fax 88 42; www.alpenverein-ibk.at). The Austrian Alpine Union's Innsbruck area office provides hiking insurance (in case of Alpine helicopter rescue) as well as information on huts and hiking opportunities for members. Membership €55; students and seniors €40; children 6-18 €10.

Budget Travel: Tiroler Landesreisebüro, Boznerpl. 7, (☎59 88 50; fax 57 54 07), by Wilhelm-Greil-Str. Open M-F 9am-6pm. AmEx/DC/MC/V.

Consulate: UK, Kaiserjägerstr. 1 (☎58 83 20). Open M-F 9am-noon.

Currency Exchange: Good rates at the train station **post office** (see below), and **Innsbruck-Information** (see above). Most **banks** are open M-Th 7:45am-12:30pm and 2:15-4pm, F 7:45am-3pm.

ATMs: Outside the train station, post office, and in front of banks throughout the city.

LOCAL SERVICES

Lockers: At the train station. €2 for 24hr. next to the information office or €1.50-2.50 for 4hr. in the electronic lockers for 4hr.

Bookstores: Buchhandlung Tirolia, Maria-Theresien-Str. 15 (☎596 11; fax 58 20 50). Nineteen shelves of English-language classics and a large table with bestsellers. Open M-F 9am-6pm, Sa 9am-5pm. **Wagner'sche,** Museumstr. 4 (☎59 50 50; fax 595 05

38). Some bestsellers and a respectable collection of classics. Open M-F 9am-6pm, Sa 9am-5pm.

Library: Innsbruck Universität Bibliothek, Innrain 50 (☎ 507 24 31), where it crosses Blasius-Heuber-Str. Take bus O, R, or F to "Klinik." Reading room open July-Aug. M-F 8am-2pm; Sept.-June M-F 8am-8pm, Sa 8am-6pm.

Religious Services: Catholic Mass in English at the church in Karl-Rahnerpl. on Universitätstr. every Sa 6pm. List of services in other languages posted outside of St. Jakob.

Bi-Gay-Lesbian Organizations: Homosexuelle Initiative Tirol, Innrain 100 (☎ 56 24 03; fax 57 45 06). All meetings 8:30-11:30pm: mixed younger crowd M, lesbian night Tu, gay night Th, transgender night every other F. Call ahead to check about meetings. **Frauenzentrum Innsbruck** (Women's Center), Liebeneggstr. 15 (☎ 58 08 39), runs a women's-only cafe for lesbians and straights M, W, F 8pm-midnight, and hosts discotheques and poetry readings. Office hours Tu 10am-1pm, Th 2-5pm.

Laundromat: Bubblepoint Waschsalon (☎ 56 50 07 14; www.bubblepoint.com), with 2 snazzy locations full of English-speakers at Brixnerstr. 1, and Andreas-Hofer-Str. at the corner of Franz-Fischer-Str. 7kg load €4, dryer €1 per 10min. Soap included. **Internet** access €0.10 per min. Open M-F 8am-10pm, Sa-Su 8am-8pm.

EMERGENCY AND COMMUNICATIONS

Emergencies: Police, ☎ 133. Headquarters at Kaiserjägerstr. 8 (☎ 590 00). **Ambulance,** ☎ 144 or 142. **Fire,** ☎ 122. **Mountain Rescue,** ☎ 140.

Pharmacy: Apotheke St. Anna, Maria-Theresien-Str. 4 (☎ 58 58 47; fax 15 67) is open M-F 8am-6pm, Sa 8am-noon. DC/MC/V.

Medical Assistance: Universitätsklink (University Hospital), Anichstr. 35 (☎ 50 40).

Internet Access: International Telephone Discount, Bruneckstr. 12 (☎ 59 42 72 61). Turn right from the Hauptbahnhof; it's on the left just past the end of Südtirolerpl. (€0.11 per min.). Reduced rates on international phone calls. Open daily 9am-11pm.

Post Office: Maximilianstr. 2 (☎ 500 79 00). Open M-F 7am-11pm, Sa 7am-9pm, Su 8am-9pm. Address *Poste Restante* to: Postlagernde Briefe, Hauptpostamt, Maximilianstr. 2, A-6020 Innsbruck. Additional Branch next to the train station. Open M-F 7am-7pm; currency exchange until 5pm. **Postal code:** A-6020.

ﾃ ACCOMMODATIONS

Although 9,000 beds are available in Innsbruck and suburban Igls, cheap accommodations are scarce in June when the only hostels open are Jugendherberge Innsbruck and Youth Hostel St. Niklaus. The opening of student dorms to backpackers in July and August alleviates the crush somewhat. Book in advance if possible. Visitors should join the free **Club Innsbruck** by registering at any Innsbruck accommodation. Membership gives discounts on skiing and ski buses (mid-Dec. to mid-April), bike tours, and the club's hiking program (June-Sept.).

TYROL

🏅 **Haus Wolf,** Dorfstr. 48 (☎ 54 86 73; titti@t-wolf.cc; www.t-wolf.cc), in Mutters. Leave the Hauptbahnhof through the main exit and walk straight to the traffic island with streetcar tracks next to it marked "Stubaitalbahn" (STB). Take the STB to "Mutters," then walk toward the church and turn right onto Dorfstr. (40min.). During the day, you can stay on an extra stop to "Birchfeld" and turn left over the tracks onto Dorfstr. for a shorter walk. (€1.60, week-long ticket €4.80. Last train 10:30pm. Buy tickets from machines on the platform.) Titi and Georg Wolf charm English-speaking visitors with an endless supply of hot bread at breakfast and 30 years of true *Gemütlichkeit*. Call ahead; Titi often provides free breakfast for travelers who arrive before noon. Breakfast, shower, and unlimited mothering included. €12.35-13 per person. ❷

Hostel Fritz Prior-Schwedenhaus (HI), Rennweg 17b (☎58 58 14; fax 58 14 14; www.tirol.com/youth-hostel). Take bus A or tram #4 to "Handelsakademie," continue to the end and straight across Rennweg to the river. This 95-bed hostel in a leafy location offers clean, spacious rooms. On summer weekdays, luggage may be stored at the front desk. Private shower and bathroom included. No door locks, but key for luggage closet available with deposit. Breakfast (7-8am), €4. Sheets €3.10. Laundry €5.50, soap included. Keys with ID deposit. Reception 7-9:30am and 5-10:30pm. Check-in before 6pm. Lockout 9:30am-5pm. Curfew 10:30pm. Open July-Aug. and Dec. 27-Jan. 5. Dorms €10; doubles €28; triples €41.25. ❷

Jugendherberge Innsbruck (HI), Reichenauer Str. 147 (☎34 61 79; fax 61 79 12; info@youth-hostel-innsbruck.at; www.youth-hostel-innsbruck.at). Take tram 3 to "Sill-park" from the train station (6min.) then bus O to "Jugendherberge" (6min.). With sleek glass-and-metal architecture and sliding doors, this 178-bed hostel resembles a high-powered corporation. Rooms with locking closets and shelves for belongings are well-maintained. TV and a small library. **Bicycle rental** €11 per day. Breakfast (7-8am), hall showers, and sheets included. **Internet** access €0.10 per min.; after 9pm €0.05 per min. Laundry (€3.30) until 10pm. Reception daily 5-10pm; July-Aug. 3-10pm. Check-in before 6pm. Lockout 10am-5pm. Curfew 11pm; key available. Quiet time from 10pm. 6-bed dorms €12.05 1st night, then €9.50; 4-bed dorms €14.80, €12.25; singles with shower €28; doubles with shower €40.80. Nonmembers add €3. ❸

Gasthof Innbrücke, Instr. 1 (☎28 19 34; fax 27 84 10; innsbruecke@magnet.at; www.innbruck.nethotels.com/innsbruecke). From the Altstadt, cross the river at Inns-brücke; the Gasthof is at the corner of the intersection. This 575-year-old inn has both a riverside and mountain view, giving it an unbeatable combination of price and location. Head downstairs for a drink at the Innkellner (beer €2-3). Breakfast and shower included. Parking €4. Singles €26, with shower and toilet €33; doubles €44/€49; quads with shower and toilet €109. MC/V. ❸

Hotel Charlotte, Phillipine-Welser-Str. 88a (☎34 02 70; fax 24 83 11; hotel-char-lotte@tirol.com; www.tirol.com/hotel-charlotte-ibk). Take the #3 bus to "Amras," then walk onto the main road and follow the signs. Only 10min. away from the train station, but the chicken-farmer neighbors give this place a country feel. Lushly decorated rooms and shiny bathrooms. TV, shower, and toilet in every room; outdoor swimming pool and parking lot. Breakfast included. Singles €47; doubles €72. MC/V. ❹

Pension Paula, Weiherburgg. 15 (☎29 22 62; fax 29 30 17; office@pensionpaula.at; www.pensionpaula.at). Take bus D to "Schmelzerg." and head uphill. Large, well-fur-nished rooms, many with balconies, for those who wish to escape the city rumble. Beautiful views across the valley. Breakfast included. Reservations recommended. Sin-gles €26, with shower €33; doubles with shower €46; triples €58/€69. ❸

Technikerhaus, Fischnalerstr. 26 (☎282 11 00; fax 110 17). Take bus R to "Unterberg-erstr./Technikerheim." This student housing complex isn't near the train station, but pro-vides clean, well-appointed rooms during the summer crunch. Restaurant and 2 TV rooms. Breakfast and showers included. Reception 24hr.; check-in after noon; check-out 10am. Open from mid-July to late-Aug. Singles €22; doubles €38; triples €52. With student ID, €16, €32, €48. V. ❸

Camping Innsbruck Kranebitten, Kranebitter Allee 214 (☎28 41 80; www.camp-inginnsbruck.com). Take bus O from the "Landesmuseum" stop (near the train station) to "Technik" and then bus LK to "Klammstr." Walk downhill to the right, and follow the road. These pleasant grounds in the shadow of a snow-capped mountain include a play-ground for the young at heart. Restaurant with **free Internet** access open 8-11am and 4pm-midnight. Laundry €4. Reception 8am-9pm; July-Aug. 8am-11pm. If reception is closed, find a site and check in the next morning. €5, children under 15 €3.50, tents €3, cars €3. Tent rental €8. Electricity €3. Showers included. ❶

FOOD

Gawking at the overpriced delis and Konditoreien on glamorous Maria-Theresien-Str. won't fill your stomach, so escape the Altstadt and its profiteers by crossing the river to Innstr., in the university district, where ethnic restaurants and cheap pizzerias proliferate. Those looking for inexpensive or late-night eats may actually find themselves pleased (and filled) by the cheap, large kebab and pizza portions served in and around the Hauptbahnhof. A few more late-night pizza digs are near the station on Ingenieur-Etzol-Str.

Theresianbräu, Maria-Theresienstr. 51 (☎58 75 80), bills itself as the oldest private brewery, and its blacklit bar is built around two giant copper brewing kettles. The microbrew, a pleasant dark lager, is available in glasses sized 0.1 to 2.4L (.5L stein €3) alongside traditional meals such as *Käsespatzl* (cheese with potato noodles, €6) and *Gröstl* (roast potato, beef, and fried egg; €6.50). Chocolate fondue for two or more is available after 6pm (€6 per person). Frequent live music entertains a diverse crowd. Open M-W 10:30am-1am, Th-Sa 10:30am-2am, Su 10:30am-midnight. MC/V. ❷

Salute Pizzeria, Innrain 35 (☎58 58 18), on the side of the street farthest from the river. A popular student hangout with black and white pictures on the wall and what appears to be a tree growing in the middle of the floor. Walk up to the counter to order, then sit back and wait to enjoy some of the best and least expensive pizza in town. Make sure to get a seat quickly though; Salute's is never empty for very long. Pizza €3.05-8, pasta €4.50-6.50, salad €3-4.50. Open 11am-midnight. ❷

Noi Original Thaiküche, Kaiserjägerstr. 1, (☎58 97 77), cooks up a vast array of Thai soups (€4-8.40), and deliciously spiced dishes from the wok (€8-11) ranging from mild to flaming. Most tables are outside and come with umbrellas and neon green chairs. Inhale the sweet aroma drifting out of the kitchen while enjoying your meal. Open M-F 11:30am-3pm and 6-11pm, Sa 6-11pm. ❷

Al Dente, Meraner Str. 7 (☎58 49 47), offers a wide variety of dishes with a hip Italian flair. Watch the food be prepared before your eyes. The young, lively crowd makes this a great place to relax between sightseeing stops. Scrumptious pasta €8-10. Open daily 7am-midnight; kitchen open until 11pm. AmEx/DC/MC/V. ❷

Restaurant zum Griechen, Innstr. 28 (☎29 15 37) is not to be confused with a mere kebab place. Gyros (€8) are on the menu, but suvlaki dishes—grilled meat with tomato sauce, rice and vegetables steal the show. Fasoulada soup (navy bean and tomato; €3), grilled fish (€8-13), and vegetarian options (€5.20-8) round out the menu. Open M-Tu 5pm-midnight, W-Su 11:30am-midnight. ❷

Gasthof Weißes Lamm, Mariahilfstr. 12 (☎28 31 56), on the 2nd floor. A small dining area upstairs decorated with pictures of Greece serves honest fare to a local crowd. Check out the daily *Tagesempfehlungen* (soup, entree, and salad €6.18-14.17). Soups €2.33-3.63, meat dishes €7.63-12. Open F-W noon-2pm and 6pm-midnight; kitchen open until 10pm. MC/V. ❸

Shere Purjab, Innstr. 19 (☎28 27 55), is a small downstairs restaurant with scattered Indian decorations, serving some of the cheapest food around. Of the 3 daily *Menüs*, 1 is always vegetarian (soup, entree with basmati rice, and dessert €5.45), and loads of other vegetarian options are available (€2.18-8.36). Open daily 11:30am-2:30pm and 5:30-11pm. AmEx/DC. ❷

University Mensa, Innrainstr. 52, in the basement of the white building marked "Leopoldino-Francisca." Cheaper eats in Innsbruck are hard to come by. 2 daily *Menüs* (soup, entree, and salad €3.70-4.60). Open M-F 9am-2:30pm; hot lunch 11am-1:30pm.; irregular hours in summer. Closed mid-July to mid-Aug. ❶

IN RECENT NEWS

THE "TEURO"

If everything seems more expensive in Austria than it was a few years ago, it may not be unfavorable exchange rates or faulty memories of the good old days when a Schilling could buy a horse and a tankard of ale. The euro (termed the "Teuro" by many Austrians, punning on *teuer*, German for "expensive") is at least partly to blame. On July 1, 2002, the Schilling offically ceased to exist as currency and all transactions were carried out in euros. Though the transition was without major incident, it hasn't stopped people from grumbling. "It was bloody easy for the shopkeepers to change the prices," complains one Austrian expatriate. "They just rounded everything up." While most people were willing to pay a few extra cents here and there, some increases were harder to swallow. "In many places, they simply divided all the prices by ten and called that price in euros," explained a retired school teacher in Vorarlberg. What initially sounds reaonable seems outrageous once you realize the actual conversion rate was 13.7 Schilllings to a euro. Merchants who chose to divide by ten instead upped prices 37% literally overnight. "I guess we should consider ourselves lucky," a student buying soda said. "In Germany they used to sell Coke for DM1 in some places. Now it's €1, which is twice as much. And it's hurting those who can least afford it the most." Though the runaway inflation of the first few months has come to a halt, the budget traveler will notice that a euro doesn't go as far as it used to.

MARKETS

M-Preis Supermarket has low prices. Branches at Museumstr. 34, Innrain 15, Maximilianstr. by the arch, and across from the train station on the corner of Salurnerstr. and Sterzingerstr. Generally open M-F 7:30am-6:30pm, Sa 7:30am-5pm.

Farmers' Markets at Franziskanerpl. (Th 9am-2pm), Sparkassenpl. (F 8:30am-2:30pm), St. Nikolaus-Brunnenpl. (Sa 8:30-11am), and the *Markthalle* near the river at Innrain and Marktgraben. Food, flowers, fungi, and fun, though the prices on some organically grown produce may cause shoppers to scramble back to the supermarket. Open M-F 7am-6:30pm, Sa 7am-1pm.

◎ 🏛 SIGHTS AND MUSEUMS

Visiting many museums in Innsbruck in a short period is cheapest with the **Innsbruck Card,** available at museums, cable cars, and the tourist office. It allows entry into all museums, cable cars, buses, and trains (24hr. €19, 48hr. €24, 72hr. €29). A 2hr. **bus tour,** including the Altstadt and a visit to the ski jump, leaves from the train station (June-Sept. noon and 2pm, Oct.-May noon; €13, children €6).

THE OLD TOWN. Tourists flood the Altstadt, a cobbled mix of old buildings, churches, and museums on the river. Its centerpiece is the **Goldenes Dachl** (Golden Roof) on Herzog Friedrichstr., a shiny, shingled balcony built to commemorate Maximilian I and Bianca Maria Sforza's marriage. Beneath the 2,657 shimmering gold squares, Maximilian and his wife surveyed a host of jousters and dancers in the square below. Splendid old buildings surround the *Goldenes Dachl.* Facing the *Dachl,* turn around to the left to see the cream facade of the 15th-century **Hölblinghaus,** blanketed with a pale green, 18th-century floral detail and intricate pink stucco work. Climbing the 148 steps in the graffiti-lined staircase of the 15th-century **Stadtturm** (city tower), across from Helbinghaus, yields a modest rooftop view of the city. *(Open daily June-Sept. 10am-8pm; Oct.-May 10am-5pm. €3.50, students and seniors €2, under 15 €1.)* The 15th-century **Hotel Goldener Adler** (Golden Eagle Inn) is a few buildings to the left. A marble slate on the wall informs you that Goethe, Heine, Sartre, Mozart, Wagner, Camus, and Maximilian I ate, drank, and made merry here; you can too if you have €15 to spare.

Innsbruck's most distinctive street is **Maria-Theresien-Straße,** which begins at the edge of the Altstadt and runs south. The street, lined by pastel-colored Baroque buildings, gives a clear view of the snow-capped Nordkette mountains. At the end of the street (away from the Altstadt) stands the **Triumphpforte** (Triumphal Arch), built in 1765 to commemorate the betrothal of Emperor Leopold II. Up the street, the **Annasäule** (Anna Column) commemorates the Tyroleans' victory on St. Anne's Day (July 26, 1703) after a bloody and unsuccessful Bavarian invasion during the War of Spanish Succession.

MAXIMILIANEUM. This small museum commemorates Innsbruck's favorite emperor, Maximilian I, and provides a solid introduction to local history. A 20min. video (in six languages, including English) details Maximilian's conquest of Europe from Portugal to Hungary which shaped the future of Innsbruck and Tyrol. The one-room exhibit next door contains a few artifacts it highlighted. *(Inside the building under the Goldenes Dachl. Open May-Sept. daily 10am-6pm; Oct.-Apr. Tu-Su 10am-12:30pm and 2-5pm. €3.63, students €1.45, seniors €2.91, headphones for commentary included.)*

CATHEDRAL ST. JAKOB. The unassuming gray facade of the Dom St. Jakob (remodeled 1717-1724) conceals a riot of pink and white High Baroque ornamentation within. *Trompe l'oeil* ceiling murals depict the life of St. James. The cathedral's prized possession is the (small) altar painting of "Our Lady of Succor" by Lukas Cranach the Elder. A 1944 air raid destroyed much of the church, but renovations have restored it to its former grandeur. *(One block behind the Goldenes Dachl. Open Apr.-Sept. daily 7:30am-7:30pm; Oct.-Mar. 8am-6:30pm. Free.)*

HOFBURG (IMPERIAL PALACE). The Hofburg was built in 1460 and completely remodeled between 1754 and 1770 under the direction of Maria Theresia. Imposing furniture, large portraits, and elaborate chandeliers fill the sumptuously decorated rooms. The biggest room is the Giants' Hall, a gigantic, two-story space with huge paintings of Maria Theresia and Francis I along the walls, as well as equally gigantic portraits of their 16 children. The White Room contains the portrait of Maria's youngest daughter, Marie Antoinette of France (with head, without cake). Don't miss the gilded "Augusta Family" tableau in the Audience Room, depicting the whole Hapsburg gang in big, round, gold medallions. *(Behind the Dom St. Jakob to the right. ☎ 58 71 86; fax 58 71 86 13. Open daily 9am-5pm. Last entrance 4:30pm. With enough people, English tours at 11am and 2pm. Group tours (limit 35 people) €29.07. English guidebook €1.82. June-Sept. adults €5.45, students €3.63, seniors €4, children 6-14 €1.09.)*

TIROLER VOLKSKUNSTMUSEUM (HANDICRAFTS MUSEUM). Built between 1553 and 1563 as the "New Abbey," the Tiroler Volkskunstmuseum was converted into a school in 1785 and then a museum in 1929. The exhaustive collection of home and farm implements, peasant costumes, and period rooms provides a dusty introduction to Tyrolean culture over the past several centuries. Included are butter churns, playing cards, tobacco pipes, and the *Brotgrammeln* tools used to break bread. Downstairs on the right is a collection of incredibly detailed *Krippen* (nativity scenes) that depict Jesus and the Wise Men. *(At the head of Rennweg. ☎ 58 43 02; fax 02 70. Open M-Sa 9am-5pm, Su 9am-noon. €4.35, students €2.25, ages 7-16 €1.45.)*

HOFKIRCHE (IMPERIAL CHURCH). The Hofkirche houses an intricate sarcophagus decorated with alabaster scenes from Maximilian I's life and the Schwarze Mander. Twenty-eight bronze statues of Habsburg saints and Roman emperors line the nave. Dürer designed the statues of King Arthur, Theodoric the Ostrogoth, and Count Albrecht of Habsburg, who pay their last respects to the emperor. Oddly, Maximilian's resting place is not in the Hofkirche, but in Wiener Neustadt, near Vienna; the elegant Silver Chapel holds the corpse of

Archduke Ferdinand II instead. *(In the same building as the Volkskunstmuseum. Open M-Sa 9am-5pm; Su noon-5pm.)*

HOFGARTEN (IMPERIAL GARDEN). Walk through the lush, manicured grounds of the **Hofgarten** and admire the ponds, elaborately designed flower beds, lofty trees, and concert pavilion. Join the crowd shouting advice at the deep-thinking chess players moving 1m tall pieces. Walk further for a lovely spot to escape the crowds of the Altstadt. *(Walk down Museumstr. toward the river, turning right onto Burggraben and continuing as it becomes Rennweg. Open daily 6am-10:30pm. Free.)*

LANDESMUSEUM (REGIONAL MUSEUM). Closed until Spring 2003.

ALPINE ZOO. The Alpenzoo is the highest-altitude zoo in Europe and houses every vertebrate species indigenous to the Alps, including very sleepy bears, hyperactive *Baummarden* (pine martens), depressed golden eagles, and bearded vulture, the largest bird in the Alps with a 3m wingspan. *(Weherfurgg. 37, near Schwedenhaus hostel, across the covered bridge: follow signs uphill 15min. ☎ 29 23 23; fax 30 89; www.alpenzoo.at. A bus to the zoo leaves from in front of the Landestheater every hr. 10am-5pm in summer; €1.50, students and children €1, round-trip €2.60/€1.60. Open Apr.-Sept. daily 9am-6pm; Oct.-Mar. 9am-5pm. €5.80, students and seniors €4, ages 6-15 €2.90.)*

CRYSTAL MUSEUM. Outside the city is the bizarre **Swarovski Kristallwelten,** an unashamed plug for the decorative crystal figurines made in the nearby factory (the gift shop is nearly as large as the exhibits). Above the underground entrance, the fabulous **Giant,** a vine-covered face on a hillside, spits water and peers through glowing eyes. Inside, the **world's largest jewel** (a hulking 300,000 karat, 125lb. crystal), shares space with 3-D modern art, and weird New Age installation pieces from artists including Salvador Dali, Andy Warhol, and Brian Eno. Make sure to go through the hand-shaped hedge maze in the park behind the Giant's head. *(Take bus #4125 from the bus station to "Wattens Kristallwelten," then walk a little further and take a left. Bus 35min., every 30min. 7:45am-8:22pm, €6.10 round-trip. ☎(05224) 510 80; fax 80 38 30; www.swarovski-crystalworld.com. Open daily 9am-6pm. €5.45, groups €4.72, under 12 free.)*

◪ OUTDOOR ACTIVITIES

HIKING. A ◪**Club Innsbruck** membership lets you in on one of the best deals in Austria (see **Accommodations,** p. 185). The club's excellent and very popular **hiking** program provides guides, transportation, and equipment (including boots) free to hikers of all ages. Participants assemble in front of the Congress Center (June-Sept. daily at 9am), board a bus, and return from the mountain ranges by 4 or 5pm. The hike isn't strenuous, the views are phenomenal, and the English-speaking guides are qualified and friendly. There are a total of 40 different hikes, so many return the next day for new adventures. Free nighttime lantern hikes also leave Tuesday at 7:45pm; the 30min. hike near Igls culminates in a party with traditional Austrian song and dance, in which *everyone* ends up taking part (willing or not).

   If you want to hike on your own, there are several options. For easier hikes, take the J-line bus to "Patscherkofel Seilbahnen" (20min.). The lift provides access to moderate 1½-5hr. hikes near the bald summit of the Patscherkofel, offering vistas of neighboring mountains, Innsbruck, and other towns far below. *(☎37 27 34; fax 37 27 23 15. Open 9am-noon and 12:45-4:30pm. Round-trip €15, ages 16-18 €12, ages 7-15 €8, dogs €1.50).*

For more challenging hikes, head to the lifts ferrying passengers up to the **Nordkette** mountains. The first lift, a short hike from the river and the Schwedenhaus, can also be reached by taking the J bus to "Hungerbergbahn". From here, a second lift leads to the Seegrube, just below the rocky walls of the peaks above. A third and final lift leads to the very top, at the Hafelekarspitze. From both the Seegrube and Hafelekarspitze, several hikes lead up and along the jagged ridges of the Nordkette, but be prepared: they are neither easy, nor particularly well-marked. Even if you don't go hiking, the trip up is worth it for the views. For those more iterested in flying down mountains than climbing up them, Innsbruck Information has a €95 **paragliding** package, including transport, equipment, and photos (or call **Mountain-Fly, ☎** 37 84 88).

WINTER ACTIVITIES. The Club Innsbruck membership also significantly simplifies winter **ski excursions;** hop the complimentary club ski shuttle (schedules at the tourist office) to any suburban cable car (mid-Dec. to mid-Apr.). Membership provides discounts on ski passes. The **Innsbruck Gletscher Ski Pass** (available at all cable cars and at Innsbruck-Information offices) is valid for all 59 lifts in the region (with Club Innsbruck card 3 days €80, teens and seniors €64, children €48; 6 days €141, €113, €85). The tourist office **rents equipment** for the Intersport shop on the mountain (downhill €19-32 per day, children €9; cross-country €9, children €7; snowboarding €15 per day). The bus to **Stubaier Gletscherbahn** for **summer skiing** leaves at 7:20 and 8:30am (☎ (05226) 81 41; fax 814 11 50; www.stubai.gletscher.com). Take the earlier bus—summer snow is slushy by noon. In winter, buses leave at 9:45, 11am, and 5pm (1½hr., last bus back 4:30pm, €10.90 round-trip). One day of winter glacier skiing costs €31.50; summer day passes cost €21, ages 16-19 €14, ages 10-15 €11, under 10 free. Both branches of **Innsbruck-Information** offer summer ski packages (bus, lift, and rental €47).

For a one-minute thrill, summer and winter **bobsled** rides are available at the Olympic bobsled run in Igls (Bus J to "Patscherkofelbahn"; follow the signs). (May-Sept. ☎ (0664) 357 86 07; fax 37 88 43. Rides Th and F after 4pm; the sled has wheels rather than runners. €22. Late Dec. to late Feb. ☎ 37 75 25; fax 33 83 89. Rides Tu 10am-noon and Th at 7pm; €30. Professionals pilot the four-person sleds. Reservations required.)

🎭 ENTERTAINMENT

At a corner of the Hofgarten, the **Congress Center** and **Tiroler Landestheater** (☎ 52 07 44) host various festivals and concert series in Innsbruck. In August, the **Festival of Early Music** features concerts by some of the world's leading soloists on period instruments at Schloß Ambras, Congress Center, and Hofkirche. (For tickets, dial 56 15 61; fax 53 56 14; tickets@altemusik.at; www.altemusik.at. €7.99-102.46.) The **Landestheater** also presents plays, operas, and dance most nights of the year. Recent productions have included Richard Strauss's opera "Der Rosenkavalier," Puccinni's "Turandot," and Theresia Walser's play "King Kong's Daughter." (☎ 52 07 44; fax 52 07 43 38; kassa@landestheater.at; www.landestheater.at. Concerts €6-49, standing room €4; plays €5-40, standing room €3; rush tickets available 30min. before the show to anyone under 21 and students under 27 for a 40% discount.)

The **Tyrol Symphony Orchestra of Innsbruck** plays Brahms, Dvorak, Debussy, and more in the Congress Center from October to May. (☎ 58 00 23. Tickets for symphony concerts €24-37.50, master concerts €27.62-61.77; children and students 26 and younger 30% off.) **Chamber music concerts** (€15-22) are held in the concert hall of the Tyrol Conservatory. (☎ 34 84 46. Same discounts apply.) The Spanish Hall at Schloß Ambras holds **classical music concerts** most Tuesday nights in summer

(€10-44, students and children 30% off). In late June and mid-July world-renowned dancers—everyone from the Alvin Ailey Dance Troupe to the Sydney Ballet—come to the **International Dance Summer** in the Congress Center to perform in a range of styles. Varied workshops are also conducted throughout the three-week festival, held during the last week in June and the first two weeks in July. (☎57 76 77; fax 67 77 30; www.tanzsommer.at. 3-5 days, €130, €95 for each additional course. Tickets for productions at Innsbruck-Information, Burggraben 3; €20-68.)

For something a little more dicey, check out **Casino Innsbruck.** Blackjack, poker, roulette, and much more await in this massive complex in the Hotel Holiday Inn by Landhauspl. Dress nice; the greyhound races this is not. (☎58 70 40; fax 70 40 66; www.casinos.at. Open daily from 3pm. AmEx/DC/MC/V.)

ⓝ NIGHTLIFE

Most visitors collapse after a full day of alpine adventure, but there's action a-plenty to keep party-goers from their pillows. Nightlife revolves around the area between the university quarter and the Altstadt. The **Viaduktbogen,** a stretch of theme bars huddled beneath the arches of the railway on Ingenieur-Etzel-Str., contains animated and un-touristy nightlife. For the very latest club and rave events, stop by Treibhaus (see below) and pick up one of the fliers outside the door.

🏶 **Hofgarten Café** (☎58 88 71; fax 58 99 57; www.hofgarten.at), inside the Hofgarten park. Follow Burggrabenstr. under the arch and past Universitätstr., pass the Landestheater, enter the park through the gate, and follow the path—you'll hear the crowd. By day, diners sip beers beneath a big white tent; by night, it's a relaxed, sprawling outdoor affair with 20- and 30-somethings dressed to the nines. Screened from the noise of the city by the dense trees, it's easy to forget Innsbruck is out there and that there's a world outside the 'garten. In summer, live music most Th. Snacks €2.50-8, beer €2.30, liquor €2.80. Open daily 10am-4am, kitchen until midnight.

Krah Vogel, Anichstr. 12 (☎58 01 49), off Maria-Theresien-Str. Blood-red walls and a student-age crowd at the tables. Small patio in the back. In winter, the upstairs seating area opens up for crowds. Beer €2-3, wraps and sandwiches €5-8. Open daily 10am-2am. Kitchen closes at 11:45pm.

Jimmy's, Wilhelm-Greil-Str. 17 (☎57 04 73), by Landhauspl. East meets West beneath the all-seeing eyes of the fluorescent Buddha (hanging on the wall). Not a nook left un-hip in this trippy world of brushed steel and rough hewn stone. Two bars and a diverse menu, sporting dishes from all over the world. Beer €2-2.80, *Ciabatta* (filled bread pockets) €3.49-5.45, mixed drinks €4-7.20. Open M-Th and Su 11am-1am, F 11am-2am, Sa 7pm-2am. Kitchen 11am-2pm, 6-11pm. DC/MC/V.

Nacht Cafe, Museumstr. 5, near the tourist office. For the night owls who can never get enough partying, the Nacht Cafe offers loud dance music and green and blue lights glowing off the metallic surfaces all night, long after everywhere else is closed. Every night has its own "special" and a 2hr. Happy Hour 10pm-midnight. Beer €2.50-3.50, snacks €3.50-11. Open 10pm-6am, but really stays open until everyone leaves, sometimes as late as noon. AmEx/DC/MC/V.

Treibhaus, Angerzellg. 8 (☎58 68 74). Turn right on Angerzellg. from Museumstr., and right again into the alley next to China Restaurant. Innsbruck's favorite alterna-teen spot has a well-lit indoor cafe and an outdoor tent. Jazz-oriented, with occasional live music. Food €3.50-7, beer €1.80-3.40. Open daily 10am-1am.

Bacchus, 14 Salurnerstr. Across the street from the casino, facing Slumerstr. Open air cafe and discotheque for gays, lesbians, and transvestites. Look for the marble statues of naked Greek gods. Beer €2.20-3.50. Open M-Th 9pm-4am, F-Sa 9pm-6am.

◪ DAYTRIPS FROM INNSBRUCK

SCHLOß AMBRAS

The castle stands southeast of Innsbruck, at Schloßstr. 20. Take tram #6 (dir: Igls) to "Tummelplatz/Schloß Ambras" (20min., €1.60). Follow signs from the stop. Or, take the shuttle bus that leaves every hr. from Maria-Theresien-Str. opposite McDonald's. (Apr.-Oct every hr. 10am-5pm; €1.60, children €0.80; round-trip €2.20, €1.10.) Walk from the city only with a map, as the trail is poorly marked.

One of Innsbruck's most impressive edifices and museums is **Schloß Ambras,** a Renaissance castle built by Archduke Ferdinand II of Tyrol in the 16th century. He acquired vast collections of art, weapons, and trinkets—from Roman busts to the armor of Japanese shoguns (see "Money, " p. 193).

Across the grounds from the museum in the *Hochschloß* is the famous Spanischer Saal (Spanish Room), displaying fresco portraits of Habsburgs along its walls. Upstairs from the Spanish Room are the three floors of the Habsburg Portrait Gallery (only open in summer), showcasing an assortment of famous rulers, including several popes, more Habsburg Kaisers than you can shake a stick at, as well as Napoleon, Catherine the Great, Louis XVI and Marie Antoinette, and Sultan Suleyman II. (☎34 84 46; fax 36 15 42; www.khm.at/ambras. Open Apr.-Oct. daily 10am-5pm; €7.50, students and seniors €5.50, children ages 7-18 €2. Dec.-Mar. closed Tuesday. €4.50, €3, €2. Tours €2; reservations required for English tour.) After several hours in the castle, emerge and take a break in the gardens outside, which vary from manicured shrubs and modern sculptures to shady, forested hillsides. Keep an eye out for the peacocks.

STAMS

Frequent regional trains that head west towards Landeck stop in Stams (35min., €5.70). By car, take Autobahn A12/E60 or highway 171 directly to the abbey.

Stift Stams is a magnificent onion-domed monastery 40km west of Innsbruck. Founded by the Tyrolean Duke Meinhard II in 1273, the cloisters were completely restyled in the 18th century. The 22 Cistercian monks who reside there allow several guided tours per day through the majestic **Basilika** and the heavily frescoed **Fürstensaal.** The frescoes are vulnerable to damage from heat, so the church goes unheated during winter and temperatures can drop to below 20°F (-5°C). The

MONEY CAN'T BUY EVERYTHING. Just how do two-foot wide playing cards get displayed next to mummified sharks, tortoiseshell combs from Goa, and daggers with "animate" blades from Java? It's not madness on the part of the curators of Schloß Ambras but an attempt by 16th century Archduke Ferdinand to own one of, well, everything. It was not originally intended as a museum but rather as a "theatrum mundi" (theater of the world), an encyclopedic collection of all the "miracles of the universe." Such collections were of political importance as nobles tried to outdo each other in their accumulation of exotic and exceptionally beautiful objects. Even if they weren't sure exactly what kind of "miracle" they were getting (16th century audiences marvelled at an intricately carved stone that turned out to be a fossilized fish, and official inventory records misidentify southeast Asian woven baskets as hats), Ferdinand and his descendents put a great deal of time and energy into collecting oddities. While modern scholars can't unravel the mystery of a chessboard with 27 pieces on a side, the remarkably well-preserved pieces in the collection provide rare glimpses into dozens of different cultures across the globe.

basilica, restored for its 700th anniversary in 1974, features the masterwork of local artist Andreas Thamasch. Twelve of his gilded wooden statues line the walls of the basement **crypt** where Meinhard and his wife, among many others, are buried. A little farther down the nave, Thamasch's modest *Madonna* hangs on the wall—its asymmetrical composition makes it unique in its genre. Thamasch died while making it, leaving an empty space for St. John. At the far end of the church, the 14m **tree of life** towers over the altar. Designed by Bartholomäus Steinle in 1613, the tree features 84 golden figures suspended against a blue plaster background, which was added for structural support in the early 1700s. Some 80 flower bulbs, each laboriously carved from a single piece of iron, comprise the **Rose Screen,** which took over six years to complete. (☎ (05263) 569 72 or 62 42; fax 569 74. Entrance to the cloisters only with the tour. Jan.-Apr. and Oct.-Dec. tours every hr. 9-11am and 2-4pm; May also at 5pm; June and Sept. also at 1pm; July-Aug. tours every 30min. 9-11am and 1-5pm. Tours Su only in the afternoon. €3.50, seniors €3, students and children €2.) A **museum,** also within the monastery, has a small collection of religious paraphernalia and art. (Open mid-June to Sept. Tu-Su 10-11:30am and 1:30-5pm. €4, seniors €3, students and children €2.)

NEAR INNSBRUCK

SEEFELD IN TIROL   ☎ 05212

After Innsbruck borrowed its smaller neighbor's terrain for skiing events during the 1964 and 1976 Winter Olympics, Seefeld became famous enough to lure celebrities and charge high prices for its snowy slopes.

■ ▨ **ORIENTATION AND PRACTICAL INFORMATION.** To the the town center, go from the train station down Bahnhofstr., which becomes Klosterstr.; the **tourist office,** Klosterstr. 43, provides a list of accommodations. (☎ 23 13; fax 33 55; info@seefeld.tirol.at; www.seefeld-tirol.com. Open mid-June to mid-Sept. and mid-Dec. to Mar. M-Sa 8:30am-6:30pm; mid-Sept. to mid-Dec. and Apr. to mid-June M-Sa 8:30am-12:15pm and 3-6pm). Seefeld's main square, Dorfpl., and Innsbruckerstr. are on your left coming from the train station; to the right, Münchenstr. forms the other arm of the *Fußgängerzone.* **Mountain bike rental** is available from **Bodenfrost** across from the station (€28 per day). **ATM** at Erstes Bank across from the station. The **post office** is on Klosterstr. one block past the tourist office (open M-F 8am-noon, 2pm-6pm). Leave luggage at the train station for €2.10 per piece (open M-F 8:30am-1:10pm, 2:10-5:10pm). For a **snow report,** call ☎ 37 90.

▐ ▢ **ACCOMMODATIONS AND FOOD.** Seefeld has no hostel, making Pensionen and *Privatzimmer* the best budget options. These rooms average €16-23 in the summer; €4 more in winter. Make reservations. The entire *Fußgängerzone* is stocked with rows of pricey restaurants, outdoor cafes, and bars, but there are a few good deals. **Restaurant Zur Alten Schmiede,** Innsbruckerstr. 18, despite a rather expensive menu, has reasonably priced specials, like delicious Wienerschnitzel with potato salad for €8, posted outside. (☎ 22 53. Open June-Sept. and mid-Dec.-Mar. 11:30am-2pm and 6-9:30pm. AmEx/MC for orders over €10.) One block farther down Innsbruckerstr., next to the Benedictine soap store, **Care Schwartzer Adler** offers bargain priced *Topfenkuchen* and *Apfelstrüdel* (€1.90) as well as a selection of soups, sausages, and sandwhiches (€3.10-5) to revive weary hikers. The **Albrecht Hat's Supermarket,** Innsbruckstr. 24, is located across from Sport Sailer just off Dorfpl. (Open M-Sa 8am-6:30pm, Su 10am-noon.)

⚂ OUTDOOR ACTIVITIES. The tourist office distributes *Seefeld A-Z*, a listing of season-specific activity calendars and local services. The tourist office runs an excellent summer **hiking** program of 5-7hr. hikes that wind through the surrounding countryside. (Hikes leave mid-June to mid-Sept. Tu and F 9:30am, W 8:30am. Register by 5pm the day before. €5 with guest card.) The **Kneipp Association Seefeld** (☎ 22 63) invites guest-card-holders to join its weekly 3-5hr. outings for free, which depart from the train station Thursdays at 9:30am in summer and 11:30am in winter. To wander on your own, pick up hiking or biking maps (€4.50) at the tourist office.

For an impressive hike with several tricky ascents and less uphill hiking than you might expect, try the trails that leave from the **Roßhütte** (1760m) area, accessible with the **Roßhütte Bergbahnen,** including a funicular leading to the hut. Two gondolas climb still higher, to the **Seefelder Joch** (2064m) and the **Härmelekopf** (2045m). To get there, turn right out of the train station, and right again following the sign to "Roßhütte." (15min. walk; round-trip funicular €12, youth €10.50, children €8.50. Funicular and one gondola €14, €12.50, €8.50. Open from late May to mid-Oct. 9am-5pm with rides every 30min. except 12:30pm.) From the Seefelder Joch, it is 30min. to the **Seefelder Spitze** (2220m), with dazzling panoramas on both sides. Continuing farther down the other side of the mountain for about 45min., a narrow trail leads down through tight switchbacks and hugs precipitous limestone cliffs before slowly climbing to the arm below the **Reither Spitze** (2373m), a jagged pile of rock that is the highest mountain in the area. From here, finish the loop back down to the lifts, or undertake another 30min. scramble over steep and sometimes uncertain terrain to the peak, where an unobstructed 360° view of the Tyrolean Alps awaits. Often the "trail" is just a scramble over rock walls with red blazes painted on them. From the summit, there are two options: brave the path a second time or take the trail to the Nördlinger Hütte back towards the lifts. Views of the valley on the second route are tamer, but so is the path (4-5hr.).

Seefeld offers winter tourists two money-saving ski passes. The **Seefeld Card** is valid for Seefeld, Reith, Mösern, and Neuleutasch. (1-day pass €27.50, ages 16-17 €25, ages 5-15 €16.50.) The **Happy Ski Pass** is valid at Seefeld, Reith, Mösern, Neuleutasch, Mittenwald, Garmisch-Zugspitze, Ehrwald, Lermoos, Biberwier, Bichlbach, Berwang, and Heiterwang. (Pass available for 3-20 days and requires a photograph; 3 days €79, ages 5-15 €47.50, ages 16-17 €72.50.) Twelve different **sports equipment rental shops** lease alpine and cross-country skis, snowboards, and toboggans at standard rates. (Downhill skis with poles and boots €7.50-15, snowboards €14-23.) A free **ski bus** runs between town and the **Roßhütte** and **Gschwandtkopf** ski areas (daily, every 20min. 9:20am-4:40pm). For those who prefer their skiing on the level, choose from the 100km of *Langlauf* (cross-country) trails (map available at the tourist office). **Fun Factory,** Riehlweg 492 (☎ 50 90; fax 50 92) offers **snowrafting,** which entails sliding down the side of a mountain in a rubber boat (Tu and Th nights, €9.50 per trip), and tobogganing (W nights 8:30pm-midnight, €20). You can also rent toboggans from any ski shop for €4 per day.

EHRWALD ☎ 05673

Ehrwald (pop. 2,300) is in the Lechtaler Alps, which offer some of the best skiing in the world and the most uninhabited territory in Austria. Other than a few damaged buildings, both World Wars spared the town, and to date nothing has blemished Ehrwald's prized attraction, the majestic **Zugspitze** (2964m, Germany's highest mountain). Despite this tourist magnet, Ehrwald has remained a charmingly sleepy town, carrying on with life in the shadow of its peak.

TRANSPORTATION. All trains to and from Ehrwald pass through Garmisch-Partenkirchen in Germany. **Trains** run to Garmisch-Partenkirchen (26min., 5:46am-7:59pm, €2.80) and Innsbruck (2hr., 5:45am-6:57pm, €9.70) via Garmisch. By **car,** Autobahn A12 follows the Inn from Innsbruck to Mötz. Bundesstr. 314 runs north from Mötz to Ehrwald, close to Germany and Garmisch-Partenkirchen. Bundesstr. 198 runs along the Loesach river.

⁊ PRACTICAL INFORMATION. The **tourist office,** Kirchpl. 1, is in the town center, a few steps beyond the church. (☎200 00; fax 33 14; www.tiscover.com/ehrwald. Open M-F 8am-6pm; July-Sept. and Dec.-Mar. also Sa 9am-4pm). Services include: **currency exchange** at banks (open M-F 8am-noon and 2-4:30pm) and the post office; **ATM** at the **Bank für Tirol und Vorarlberg,** Kirchpl. 21a; **bike rental at Zweirad Zirknitzer,** Zugspitzstr. 16, across the tracks and up the hill. (☎32 19. €9 per day, children €7; mountain bike rentatal €18 per day, children €13. Open M-F 8am-noon and 1-5pm, F until 3pm, Sa 10am-noon.) The **post office,** Hauptstr. 5, is on the right about 100m before the town center coming from the train station. (Open M-F 8am-noon and 2-5:30pm.) **Postal code:** A-6632.

⌂⊞ ACCOMMODATIONS AND FOOD. Ehrwald is filled with fairly inexpensive guest houses. Wherever you stay, pick up a **guest card** for discounts. **Gästehaus Konrad ❸,** Kirweg 10, is only a few minutes from the station. Take the first right onto Kirweg. Each large room has a TV and an alpine painting—step out onto the balcony for the real thing. (☎/fax 27 71. Breakfast included. June-Sept. €16-18 per person; Mid-Dec. to Apr. €20.50.) For more luxurious quarters, try **Hotel Ausfernerhof ❸,** Hauptstr. 85, halfway between the town center and train station. The orange curtains may be right out of the 1970s, but the swimming pool, sauna and elegant breakfast room more than make up for it. All rooms have shower, toilet, phone, and TV. (☎21 08; fax 210 844; ausfernhof@eunet.at. Breakfast, 8-10am, included. May-Oct. €25-27 per person; Dec-Apr. €30.50-46. Add €5.81 for a single.) Camping is available at **Camping Dr. Lauth ❶,** Zugspitzstr. 34—if you're willing to walk about 25min. uphill. Head left out of the train station and immediately turn left. Take the right-hand fork past Zweirad Zirknitzer and continue uphill (ignore the "Leaving Ehrwald" sign). After the road curves left at the Thörleweg intersection, the well-marked campground is on the right. Pitch your tent in the shadow of the Zugspitze. (☎26 66; fax 266 64; www.campingehrwald.at. Restaurant (open 8am-midnight; breakfast €6) and laundry (€5 wash and dry). Reception 8am-midnight. May-Oct. €7.50 per person, tax €1.41 per person; Nov.-Apr. €8, tax €1.80 per person. €7 per child, €4.36 per tent, electricity €2.20.)

The **Metzgerei Restaurant ❷,** Hauptstr. 15, has a surprising number of casual tables beyond its storefront meat counter. The no-brainer choice is fresh wurst with kraut and potatoes (€4-6.40), though other entrees such as smoked bacon with bread and potato salad (€8) show off the local wares equally well. For a lost vegetarian, meatless meals are available for €6.40-7.20. (☎23 41. Open M-Sa 11:30am-8:30pm.) **Al Castagno ❸,** is an outdoor cafe with a penchant for all things yellow and an exhaustive menu. (Pizza €6.50-8, pasta €6-8, fish €10-14, and grilled steak and pork fillets €13-18. Kitchen 11:30am-2pm and 6pm-midnight.) If you're planning a picnic, try the **SPAR supermarket,** Hauptstr. 1, next to the post office. (Open M-Th 8am-7pm, F 8am-7:30pm, Sa 7:30am-5pm.)

◎ ♫ SIGHTS AND ENTERTAINMENT. The **Tiroler Zugspitzbahn** is Ehrwald's leading tourist attraction and an astounding feat of engineering. This cable car climbs to the 2964m summit of the Zugspitze in a hold-your-breath (for some, hold-your-lunch) seven-minute-and-12-second trip. The observation station at the ride's end has what some deem the most breathtaking view in Europe. Bring a sweater; there may be snow on the ground even in summer. (☎23 09. Trains run mid-May to late Oct. and mid-Dec. to Mar. daily every 20min. 8:40am-4:40pm. €31, ages 16-17 €22, ages 5-15 €18.) The **Ehrwalder Almbahn** doesn't climb as high (1510m), but neither do the prices. (☎24 68. May 21-Oct. 18 8:30am-5:40pm; Dec.-Apr. 8:30am-4pm. €10, teens €9, children €5.) Buses leave from Kirchpl. for the Zugspitzbahn (10min., 7 per day 8:15am-5:10pm, €1.50) and the Ehrwalder Almbahn (5min.).

⚠ OUTDOOR ACTIVITIES. Try Bergsport-Total, across the street from the tourist office. (Hikes €13-42, bike tours €14-18, climbing €100-130, rafting from €35.) The tourist office also sells hiking maps for €6.50 and provides information on hiking, fishing, swimming, boating, skating, climbing, tennis, river-rafting, paragliding, and kayaking in Ehrwald and neighboring areas.

For winter guests, Ehrwald offers the **Happy Ski Pass,** the only lift ticket offered for blocks of three days or more. It gives access to 143 lifts, 200km of ski runs, 100km of cross-country trails, and several winter sports arenas (see Seefeld, p. 194). For shorter ski trips, one- and two-day tickets are available for the "Zugspitzarena," the mountains by Ehrwald. (1-day pass €26.60-28, ages 16-17 €24-25.50, ages 5-15 €12.50-13; 2 days €50-52.50, €45-47, €29.50-31.) Shops in the main square and at lift stations rent ski equipment (€23-27 per day, €99-119 per week).

KITZBÜHEL ☎05356

When Franz Reischer arrived in Kitzbühel in 1892, his 2m snowshoes and wild ideas about sliding down mountains stirred up a fair amount of skepticism. Two years later, the town held its first ski championship and everyone wanted a piece of the big-shoe action. The 6 peaks surrounding Kitzbühel were named the "Ski-Circus," and life in town was never the same. Now the annual **International Hahnenkamm Race** (Jan. 23-26 2003), considered the "Wimbeldon of World Cup Skiing," attracts thousands of spectators to watch the world's finest get knocked over by the *Mäusefalle* ("Mousetrap"), the infamous first turn. When the snow melts, opportunities for hiking, cycling and swimming the *Schwartzensee* abound.

▄ TRANSPORTATION

Kitzbühel has 2 **train stations.** The **Hauptbahnhof,** Bahnhofpl. 1 (☎640 55 13 85), and the **Hahnenkamm Bahnhof** are one train stop away from each other. **Buses** stop next to both train stations. Kitzbühel lies on Bundesstr. 161 and is the east terminus of Bundesstr. 170. By **car** from Innsbruck, take Autobahn A12 east to Wörgl and switch to Bundesstr. 170. From Salzburg, take Bundesstr. 21 south to 305 to 178; at St. Johann in Tirol, switch to 161 south, which leads straight to Kitzbühel.

Trains: From Hauptbahnhof to: **Innsbruck** (1hr., every 2hr., €13.40); **Salzburg** (2½hr., 9 per day, €18.90); **Vienna** (6hr., 6:25am-12:47am, €41.50); and **Zell am See** (45min., every 2hr., €8.10).

Buses: Depart regularly from the **Hauptbahnhof,** less frequently from the **Hahnankamm Bahnhof.** Destinations include Lienz, Kufstein and Woergl; for a complete listing of train and bus routes, pick up the free "Fahrpläne Bus und Bahn." A *Stadtbus* local line serves the city (€1.50).

Taxis: In front of the **Hauptbahnhof,** or call ☎69 69, 66 222 or 67 200.

Car Rental: Hertz, Josef-Pirchlstr. 24 (☎648 00; fax 721 44), at the traffic light on the way into town from the main station. Open M-F 9am-6pm, Sa 9am-noon. 20% discount with valid guest card. AmEx/MC/V.

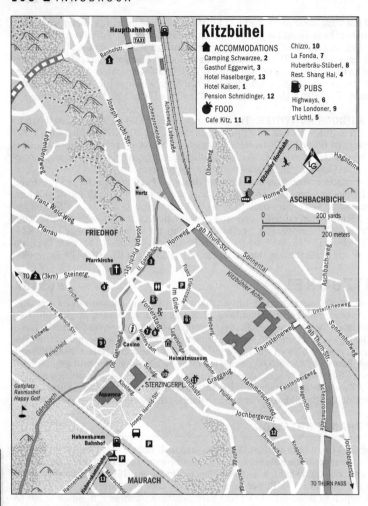

Kitzbühel

ACCOMMODATIONS
Camping Schwarzee, **2**
Gasthof Eggerwirt, **3**
Hotel Haselberger, **13**
Hotel Kaiser, **1**
Pension Schmidinger, **12**

FOOD
Cafe Kitz, **11**

Chizzo, **10**
La Fonda, **7**
Huberbräu-Stüberl, **8**
Rest. Shang Hai, **4**

PUBS
Highways, **6**
The Londoner, **9**
s'Lichtl, **5**

Bike Rental: Mountain bikes at **Stanger Radsport**, Josef-Pirchlstr. 42, for €18 per day. Open M-F 8am-noon and 1:15-6pm, Sa 9am-noon. DC/MC/V. Also at nearly any **Intersport** in town (€20 per day, children €12).

Parking: There are 4 lots in Kitzbühel: **Griesgasse, Pfarrau, Hahnenkamm,** and **Kitzbühlerhorn.** The latter 2 are next to the major ski lifts. In winter a free park-and-ride service operates between the lots and lifts. Free parking at the Fleckalmbahn for the cable car open 8am-6pm. Parking at Hahnekamm is €0.50 per hr. or €3 per day.

⚡ ▶ ORIENTATION AND PRACTICAL INFORMATION

Kitzbühel lies on the hilly banks of the Kitzbüheler Ache River, at the foot of several fair-sized peaks, including the Kitzbüheler Horn (2000m) and the Steinbergkogel (1971m). The tracks connecting the train stations form a sort of U around most of the town, and the stations are on opposite sides of the town. To reach the *Fußgängerzone* (pedestrian zone) from the Hauptbahnhof, head straight out the front door down Bahnhofstr. and turn left at the main road. At the traffic light, turn right and follow the road uphill. The city center is a maze of twisting streets; if you get confused, look for the occasional *Zentrum* (center) signs to point you back to the middle. Be sure to pick up a map at the tourist office as soon as you can; it's easy to get lost at night.

Tourist Office: Hinterstadt 18 (☎62 15 50; fax 623 07; info@kitzbuehel.com; www.kitzbuehel.com), near the *Rathaus* in the *Fußgängerzone*. A **bank** in the office exchanges money in high season. Make sure to pick up a Kitzbühel guest card, which is free upon demand and provides discounts to many shops and services in town. From June-Oct. free **guided hikes** (with guest card, M-F 8:45am and weekends on request) in the country surrounding the city and **guided informative tours** (M 10am) start at the office. Both are available in English. Open July-Aug. and Dec. 25 to mid-March M-F 8:30am-6:30pm, Sa 8:30am-noon and 4-6pm, Su 10am-noon and 4-6pm; Nov.-Dec. 25 and mid-March to June M-F 8:30am-12:30pm and 2:30-6pm, Sa 8:30am-noon.

Budget Travel: Reisebüro Eurotours, Rathauspl. 5 (☎713 04; fax 71 30 44), exchanges currency. Open M-Sa 8:30am-noon and 3-6:30pm, Su 10am-noon.

Alternatives to Tourism: Ask Michael at **Hotel Kaiser** about special offers for short-term backpackers working in the area (**p. 199**).

Currency Exchange: At banks, travel agencies, and the post office. The post office and most banks have **ATMs** outside.

Lost and Found: ☎662 33. In the *Rathaus*, next to the tourist office. Open daily 7:30am-noon and 1:30pm-7pm.

Lockers: At the Hauptbahnhof. Open 5am-1am. €2 for 24hr.

Emergencies: Police, ☎133. **Fire,** ☎122. **Medical,** ☎144. **Auto Repair,** ☎123. **Mountain Rescue,** ☎140.

Ski Conditions: ☎62 15 50 (in English or German). **Road Conditions:** ☎15 86.

Pharmacy: Stadt-Apotheke Vogl, Vorderstadt 15. Open M-F 8am-noon and 2:30-6:15pm, Sa 8am-noon.

Internet: Internet Cafe Videothek, Schloßerg. 10 (724 27). On Jochbergerstr. in the south of the center, head down the stairs in front to Schloßerg. They also rent videos. Internet €1.50 for 10min. (minimum); 30min €3.70. Open daily 11am-9pm.

Post Office: Josef-Pirchlstr. 11 (☎67 21), between the stoplight and the *Fußgängerzone*. Bus schedules, fax, and copier (€0.20) inside. Open M-F 8am-noon and 2-6pm. **Currency exchange** open M-F 8am-noon and 4-5pm. **Postal Code:** A-6370.

▐ ACCOMMODATIONS

Kitzbühel has almost as many guest beds (6159) as inhabitants (8105), but the only youth hostel is far from town and restricted to groups. The cheaper *Privatzimmer* and *Pensionen* generally run €15-22 per person; expect to shell out as much as €8 per person more during the winter. Be sure to call ahead in winter, as the ski races create a huge bed shortage. Cheaper lodging is also available a 6km bus or train ride away in **Kirchberg** (Kirchberg tourist office ☎05357 23 09), or in homes and farms in the country around Kitzbühel.

Hotel Kaiser, Bahnhofstr. 2 (☎647 09; fax: 66213; mikedodemont@hotmail.com). Exit Hauptbahnhof facing away from the tracks and the hotel will be on left at the end of the street. Michael Dodemont (the English-speaking owner) and his staff, all former backpackers, are happy to greet road-weary travelers; if the hotel's 150 beds are full, Michael will try to help you find somewhere else to stay. School groups often book the hotel, and it is occasionally closed off-seasons, so call ahead. There's a terrace, billiards table, and inexpensive bar. Laundry service €5. Parking available. €15 per person in 4-6 bed dorms and doubles, possible winter surcharges. Michael offers a special price Nov.-Dec. for backpackers seeking local work: dorms €9.00. AmEx/DC/MC/V. ❷

Pension Schmidinger, Ehrenbachg. 13 (☎631 34; fax 71994; a.schmidlinger@kitz.net). From the Innenstadt, head south on Bichlerstr., which merges with Ehrenbachg. The rooms are plain and clean, and some include a shower. Almost all are doubles, but if there is space lone travelers can have one to themselves. Reception open about 8am-8pm. Summer €20-23, winter €22-26. Add €4 for in-room bath. ❸

Hotel Haselberger, Maurachfeld 4 (☎62 866; fax. 62 866 14; haselberger@aon.at). Leap from a cable-car gondola directly into your bathroom window! Literally one minute from the bottom station of the Hahmennkammerbahn, with the cables passing just inches from the windows. You can't get any closer to the lift than this full-service hotel decorated like a hunting lodge. Rooms with cable TV, phone and shower/bath. Parking and breakfast included. Summer €31-35 per person, winter €37-44. AmEx/MC/V. ❹

Gasthof Eggerwirt, Gänsbachg. 12 (☎62 455; fax 62 437 22; info@eggerwirt-kizbuehel.at). Approaching town center from the station on Josef-Pirchl-Str., head down the stairs onto Gänsbachg. The crowds at the restaurant here prove the food is good, and so are the rooms. Mostly doubles; all with TV and shower/bath. Summer €31-40 per person; winter €48-55. Add €5 for singles. Breakfast and parking included. MC/V. ❹

Camping Schwarzsee, Reitherstr. 24 (☎62 80 60; fax 644 79 30; hotel.bruggerhof@camping.netwing.at). Take the *Stadtbus* (€1.50), which runs every 30min. until 5pm from the Bahnhof to the campground. Caters more to RVs, but tents are welcome as well. Reception 8am-5pm. €7.50, ages 2-12 €5.60. Showers included. ❶

◘ FOOD

Local specialties include *Tiroler Speckknödel* (bacon-fat dumplings), served either *zu Wasser* (in broth) or *zu Lande* (dry, with salad or sauerkraut), and *Gröstl* (meat and potato hash topped with a fried egg). There is a **SPAR Markt** on the corner of Ehrenbachg. and Bichlstr. (Open M-F 8am-7pm, Sa 7:30am-1pm.)

Huberbräu-Stüberl, Vorderstadt 18 (☎656 77). In the center of town with a terrace that overlooks the street, Huberbräu offers quality Wienerschnitzel (€8.00) and Tyrolian *groestl* (€ 6.20). Or wash a *blutwurst* (blood sausage) down with a Huberbräu and get change back from a ten. Open 9am-midnight. Closed June to mid-July. ❷

Chizzo, Josef Herold-Str. 2 (☎624 75). Skiiers stagger off the Hahnenkammer lift, saying to themselves, "I need *Gulasch* with *Eierspatzl* (€10.20). Give me Tyrol *Bauersalat* (€6.60) and some Preiselberry *Palatschinken* (currant crepes) for dessert (€4.10)!" They find exactly that as they cross the street, in this restaurant-bar filled with posters of every Kitzbühel ski race in the last 40 years. Open year-round daily 11am-11pm. ❸

Cafe Kitz, Bichlstr. 7 (☎753 26). This small cafe boasts excellent *Tiroler Speckbrettl* (bacon, cheese, and pepper platter) and Wienerschnitzel. Enjoy friendly, prompt service while dining on the terrace above the shopping district along Graggaug. Most entrees €7 or under. Reservations recommended in winter. Open 10am-midnight. DC/MC/V. ❷

Restaurant Shang Hai, Kirchg. 5 (☎621 78). Painted dragons and peacocks on the ceiling watch tourists put away fried rice (€7.20), *Verücktes Huhn* (Crazy Chicken; €9.90) and fish with bamboo shoots (€8.70). Chinese harp music reminds you this is a classy establishment. Open daily 11:30am-2:30pm, 5:30pm-11pm. AmEx/MC/V. ❸

La Fonda, Hinterstadt 13 (☎736 73). Straw hats, stucco walls, and Garth Brooks on the stereo: it's Tex-Mex done Austrian-style. Chicken wings, chicken curry, and nachos run €5.50-7. Despite crowds, La Fonda maintains a laid-back atmosphere. Take-out on request. Open June-Sept. 11am-2am, Dec.-Mar. 4pm-2am. Closed late-Mar-May. ❷

🅖 🎵 SIGHTS AND ENTERTAINMENT

Kitzbühel's church steeples define the town's skyline. The **Pfarrkirche** (parish church) and the **Liebfrauenkirche** (Church of Our Lady) lie in an ivy-cloaked courtyard surrounded by an old cemetery. Between the churches stands the **Ölberg Chapel,** dating from 1450, with frescoes from the late 1500s. The town itself is even older, having celebrated its 700th anniversary in 1971. The local **Heimatmuseum** (regional museum), Hinterstadt 34, celebrates this longevity with artifacts in Kitzbühel's oldest house, which dates from the 12th century. Rusty tools from days of yore are displayed, though occasional special exhibits, like "The Magic of Tibet" (the only place in the world Tyroleans are willing to admit has better mountains) move the prehistoric mining equipment and the world's first metal bobsled into storage. (☎672 74. Open M-Sa 10am-11pm; July 10-Sept. 10 10am-4:30pm. €6, ages 12-18 €3, 25% discount with guest card.)

At the free **concerts** in the center of town in July and August, you might find anything from folk harpists to Sousa bands. (F 8:30pm, weather permitting.) **Casino Kitzbühel** is near the tourist office. (☎623 00. W ladies' night, free glass of champagne; Tu men's night, free glass of beer. No cover. 18+. Semi-formal. Open July-Sept. 7pm-late.) At the end of July, the **Austrian Open** Men's Tennis Championship *(Generali Open)* comes to town, drawing such athletes as Austria's own Thomas Muster to the Kitzbühel Tennis Club. (☎633 25; ticket-tennis@kitzbue-hel.netwing.at; www.atp-turnier-kitzbuehel.com. €5-53.)

▮ NIGHTLIFE

During the high tourist season (roughly mid-Dec. to Mar. and July-Sept.), Kitzbühel nightlife comes alive. Particularly during special events like the Hahnenkamm race (Jan. 23-26, 2003) and the Austrian Open tennis tournament (always the last weekend in July), tourists pack the streets, looking for a place to party. With more than 30 bars in town, Kitzbühel is up to the challenge.

The Londoner, Franz-Reichstr. 4 (☎714 28). A staple for 25 years, The Londoner is the place to be. The bar has a huge list of specialities for €3, including the Slippery Nipple, Flugerl, and Kamikazi. Posters and pictures plaster the walls, and the liveliness of both staff and guests makes for an unbeatable party. During the famous Hahnenkamm race, the men's downhill stars take off their shirts and dance on the bar. Dec.-Apr. live bands all week; May-Nov. 3 times per week. Open Dec.-Apr. noon-4am; May-Nov. 6pm-3am.

Highways, Im Gries 20 (☎753 50). From the tourist office, turn right and exit under the arch onto Bichlst., left onto Graggaug., walk two blocks and turn left onto Im Gries. Home to crowds of teenagers in summer and tourists in winter, Highways serves pizza (€5-7) and sandwiches (€3-4), and offers an extensive drink menu (cocktails €7). Their loud music consists of 60s-90s hits, interspersed with occasional live acts. May-Aug. open 8pm-3am; Sept.-Apr. 9pm-4am.

s'Lichtl, Vorderstadt 9. Christmas lights, small disco balls, and blood-red tablecloths give this place a funky feel. DJ plays today's hits. Beer €3, drinks €5. W 60s night. Open June-March 9pm-3am. AmEx/MC/V, for bills over €20.

⚠ OUTDOOR ACTIVITIES

Few visitors to Kitzbühel remain at ground level for long. The Kitzbühel **ski area,** the "Ski Circus," is one of the finest in the world. Every winter since 1931, Kitzbühel has hosted the **Hahnenkamm Ski Competition,** part of the annual World Cup and considered one of the world's most difficult runs. The competition turns the town into a rollicking 7-day party. (☎735 55 for tickets. €4-15 per day.) For summer visitors, 3- or 6-day vacation passes, good for free use of the lifts and Aquarena swimming pool (see below), can save a bundle of money. They are available at all lifts. (3-day pass €35, children €19.50; 6-day €48, €26.50.)

SKIING. The best deal is the **Kitzbüheler Alpen Ski Pass,** which gives access to 260 lifts and 680km of skiing trails. (€155, ages 8-16 €85.50; good for any 6 days of the ski season.) A 1-day ski pass (Dec. 23-Jan. 6 and Feb.-Mar. 10 €33, ages 8-16 €18.50; rest of season €28.50) grants passage on 64 lifts and shuttle buses that connect them. Lift ticket prices drop after the first day. Tickets for anywhere from 2 to 14 days are available, as are tickets for individual lifts, such as the **Gaisberg, Maierl I,** and **Obergaisberg** (€4.50, ages 8-16 €2). Purchase passes at any of the lifts or at the **Kurhaus Aquarena,** which offers a pool, as well as a sauna and solarium at extra fees. (☎643 85; fax 643 85 34. Open daily 9am-8pm. Admission €7.50, children €4.70, with guest card €6.50/€4.50; free entry in winter with ski passes of 2 days or more, in summer with 3- or 6-day vacation pass.)

Rent skis at the Hahnenkamm lift or from a sports shop in the area. Try **Kitzsport Schlechter,** at Jochbergerstr. 7. (☎622 04; fax 622 04. Open M-F 8:30am-noon and 2:30-6pm, Sa 8:30am-12:30pm.) Lessons cost around €35 for a one-day group lesson. Ask at the tourist office about **ski packages:** special low-season deals on lodging, ski passes, and instruction. Week-long packages without instruction start at around €280 per person.

HIKING. More than 70 **hiking trails** snake up the mountains surrounding Kitzbühel and head toward Kirchberg or further. Among these are a variety of pleasurable day hikes, covering a wide range of difficulty levels. To avoid getting lost, pick up a free Hiking Trail Map at the tourist office.

Hausbergweg: trail #36 (5km, 5hr. round-trip). Good for more advanced hikers. A consistently steep trail that tracks straight up the spine of the Hahnenkamm. Be sure to follow the signs to "Hahnenkamm" the whole way up. Grand views almost the entire way, particularly toward the top, make this trail well worth all the sweat. If you go, leave time for some reasonably priced, hearty Tyrolean cuisine at **Gasthaus Seidlalm ❷** (☎631 35; open May-Oct. and Dec.-Easter 9am-6pm), on the side of the Hahnenkamm race trail. The hike finishes at the top of the Hahnenkammbahn (see below) and provides access to other trails that go even farther and higher.

Seidlalmweg: trail #9 (about 10km, 2-5hr.). Slightly less difficult than the Hausbergweg. There are a number of ways to hike this trail without going the whole 10km. The lower parts of the trail generally go through the forest, while the higher part that cuts across the mountains has the best scenery. Starting points are at the Hahnenkammbahn cable car parking lot and the parking lot near the Streifalm chair lift.

Schwarzseerundgang: trail #12 (3.2km, 1½hr.). A great choice for those who don't want to climb a mountain (or even part of one). A generally level, enjoyable hike along the lake on the outskirts of Kitzbühel. Trailhead near "Schwarzee" bus or train stop.

For those with a bit more cash, cable cars do the climbing for you, and give you open vistas during your whole hike. You can take the **Hahnenkammbahn** (8am-5:30pm; €14 up or round-trip, with guest card €13, children €8) to the top of one of the most famous ski runs in the world—during the summer the starting gate is open from 11am-3:30pm daily and visitors can peer down on the course where skiing history is made every January (free). At the top is the **Bergbahn Museum Hahnenkamm,** which gives a history of winter sports in the area, and includes a larger-than-life ski simulator. (☎69 57. Open daily 10am-4pm. Free.) The **Kitzbüheler Hornbahn lift** ascends to the **Alpenblumengarten,** where more than 120 different types of flowers blossom each spring. (Open late-May to mid-Oct. 8:30am-5pm. Same prices as Hahnenkammerlift. Free tours July-Aug. 10am and 1:30pm.) The smaller **Gaisberg, Resterhöhe,** and **Streiteck** lifts also run in summer.

Guest card holders can take advantage of the tourist office's **hiking program.** Daily 3- to 5-hour hikes cover over 100 routes and are easy or moderate. (Mid-May to mid-Oct. M-F at 8:45am from the tourist office; call ahead for weekend hikes, minimum 5 people. Free with guest card, but you pay for cable car rides.)

Contact **Mountain High Adventure Center** (☎/fax 05352 62 101), in neighboring St. Johann, for extreme activities like paragliding (€98, includes lift), skydiving (€180), and rafting (€43).

SWIMMING. The **Schwarzsee,** 2.5km from Kitzbühel, is famed for its healing mud baths. Float in the water and gaze at mountains above. (See directions to Camping Schwarzsee; last bus back at 6pm. ☎623 81. Open 8am-6pm. €3, children €1; after 4pm €1, €0.50. Electric boat rental after 8:30am; €7 per 30min., rowboats €3.70.)

⚡ DAYTRIP FROM KITZBÜHEL

KUFSTEIN ☎05372

Trains run from Kitzbühel with a transfer in Wörgl (1hr., 2 per hr. 5:52am-9:29pm, €7), and from Innsbruck (1hr., 2 per hr., €10.50). The station is on the west bank of the Inn river. (Ticket office open M 5:25am-8pm, Tu-Sa 5:35am-8pm, Su 7:30am-8:30pm.)

A sleepy village along the swift-flowing Inn River, Kufstein retains much of the small-town atmosphere that some of its bigger and glitzier neighbors lack. The impressive 12th-century *Festung* (fortress) on a hill in the middle of town and the mountainous backdrop provide good reasons for a relaxing daytrip. The **tourist office,** Unterer Stadtpl. 8, just across the river from the train station, distributes free hiking, biking, and skiing maps, as well as a complete list of accommodations and restaurants. (☎622 07; fax 614 55; kufstein@netway.at; www.tiscover.com/kufstein. Open M-F 8:30am-6pm, Sa 9am-noon.)

Kufstein's main attraction is the **Festung** (fortress), which towers over the rest of the city. Climb to the fortress grounds via a wooden *Gangsteig* (covered staircase) or take a short cable car ride. Once within the *Festung,* you're free to walk around the stone ramparts and grassy knolls, many of which provide excellent views of the river valley below. At the top of the fortress, the **Heimatmuseum** (regional museum) features an assortment of prehistoric and early modern artifacts, rooms devoted to the lifestyles of locals in previous centuries, and a room with a model of the *Festung* and a history of its construction. Across from the Heimatmuseum is a tower containing the restored former city jail. (☎60 23 50. Open from Palm Sunday to mid-Nov. 9am-5pm; mid-Nov. to Palm Sunday 10am-4pm. Entrance to fortress, museum, and cable-car ride, in summer €8, students €5; in winter €7/€4. 1hr. tours available in summer upon request, €1.50.) The *Festung* also houses the 4037 pipes of the **Heldenorgel** (Heroes' Organ), the world's largest open-air organ, constructed in 1931 in honor of Austrian soldiers

TYROL

who died in WWI. An exhibit in the fortress near the pipes contains WWI artifacts including uniforms and grenades. The organ is played on the keyboard at the base of the fortress every day at noon, and during July and August again at 5pm. (€1 for auditorium seat; cheapskates can stand a bit outside and hear the pipes nearly as well.)

To reach some non-man-made heights, take the **Kaiserlift** into the mountains. Turn left at the end of Unterer Stadtpl., walk a few blocks, and follow the signs to the chairlift parking lot. The first lift goes to Duxeralm, the second to Brentenjoch. (Open daily 9am-4:30pm. Duxeralm ascent €4, children €2, round-trip €6/€3. Brentenjoch ascent €8, children €3, round-trip €10/€4.) There are myriad mid-level **hiking trails** on the mountain. After Unterer Stadtpl., take Georg-Pirmoserstr. to Bachg. (turns into Schutzerstr.) to the trailheads. At the top near the Brentenjoch, the trails open up to breathtaking vistas. It is well worth going above Duxeralm to this point—just follow the signs to Berghaus Aschenbrenner and climb from there. (4-5hr. total hiking time, without any chairlifts.)

THE ZILLERTAL VALLEY

When the fog descends on the small villages of the Zillertal (Ziller Valley) they may as well be cut off from the rest of the world. Squeezed between the Tuxer, Zillertaler, and Kitzbühler Alps, these towns are remote and peaceful year round. Boasting more miles of trails than roads and a larger ski patrol than police force, the Zillertal is the place to come for hiking and skiing away from the masses.

⬢ TRANSPORTATION. Everyone going into the valley must go through **Jenbach**, at the head of the valley. Trains leave Jenbach train station for: **Innsbruck** (20-30min., 2-3 per hr. 5:32am-10:57pm, €5.20); **Vienna** (5hr., 7per day 5:19am-7:50pm, €45.70); **Wörgl** (20min., 2-3 per hr. 5:19am-12:13am, €4.50). Transportation in the region is simple and convenient, thanks to the **Zillertalbahn** (the **Z-bahn**), an efficient network of private buses and trains connecting villages (☎(05244) 60 60; fax (05244) 606 39; office@zillertalbahn.at; www.zillertalbahn.at). The origin of the train line is **Jenbach** and the terminus is **Mayrhofen** (€4.40). Jenbach is accessible from **Innsbruck** (20min., €5.20, Eurail valid). The Z-bahn has 2 types of trains, the **Dampfzug** and the **Triebwagen.** The Dampfzug is a red steam train targeted at tourists; it costs more and moves more slowly. The Triebwagen and the Z-bahn Autobus have the same rates, and one or the other leaves daily every hr. 6am-9pm. Getting into the Tuxertal is done **by bus,** from Mayrhofen. Note that travel on the Z-bahn is not covered by rail passes. Those planning to stay in the region for several days should consider the **Z-ticket,** which covers all train and bus lines from Jenbach to Hintertux (except the Dampfzug), including mountain lifts other than the upper gondolas of the Hintertux glacier (6-day €3, children €19; 9-day €52, €26.10; 12-day €66.20, €32.60).

⬢ ACCOMMODATIONS. Accommodations in the Zillertal Valley are not a problem. Most towns have a variety of inexpensive rooms for rent—look for *Zimmer Frei* signs hanging from houses. Both Mayrhofen and Zell am Ziller are fine bases for exploring the area. Mountain **huts** also litter the area. The **Kreuzjochhütte** (2000m, ☎(0664) 307 54 48) is near Zell am Ziller, while the **Edelhütte** (2238m, ☎(05285) 621 68), **Grüne Wand Hütte** (1440m, ☎(0664) 433 21 07), **Kasseler Hütte** (2177m, ☎(0664) 26 31 94), and the **Greizer-Hütte** (2226m, ☎(0664) 140 50 03) are near Mayrhofen. Call the huts for prices, hours, and trails leading to their doors.

⚠ HIKING AND SKIING. The **Z-Ticket** is valid on all summer lifts in the Zillertal, including those in Zell am Ziller, Fügen, Mayrhofen, Gerlos, and Hintertux Passes are available at tourist offices, lifts, or railway stations in Zell am Ziller and Mayrhofen, and may be used only once at each lift per day. Hiking without cable cars is also possible throughout the valley. Hiking between towns in the Zillertal Valley is an option for the hardy traveler. The Zell am Ziller **ski area**, recently connected to the Gerlos and Königsleiten ski areas, is the **largest ski zone in Tyrol.** The Zillertal Super Skipass, covering this mammoth region, is available at any valley lift station and valid on all of the area's 251 lifts. (☎716 50; www.zillertalski.at. 4 days €97, 7 days €148, 10 days €195; including the Hintertux glacier €114, 176, €235; discounts for children.) The pass includes unlimited use of the Z-bahn network. Free ski shuttles also take skiers around the valley. Head to Hintertux for **summer skiing.**

ZELL AM ZILLER ☎05282

Zell am Ziller (TSELL am TSILLER; pop. 3,500), 20km south of Jenbach, embodies picture-book images of Austrian mountain villages, with fields of tall grass and taller mountains embracing clusters of wood-shuttered alpine houses. Founded by monks in the late 8th century—hence the *Zell*, or chapel— Zell surrendered to materialism in the 1600s when it flourished as a gold-mining town. Today, this idyllic and unassuming village offers skiing and hiking without resort-town hype.

▤ TRANSPORTATION. Zell is at the north central end of the Zillertal, between Jenbach and Mayrhofen. Those taking **ÖBB trains** should get off at **Jenbach** and switch to the private **Zillertalbahn** (Z-bahn; see above), which leaves from the front of the train station. Z-bahn trains and buses leave at least once per hr. from about 6am-8pm for Jenbach or Mayrhofen. Get to Zell am Ziller by **car** from the Inntalautobahn, taking the Zillertal exit and driving 24km on Zillertal-Bundesstr. 109.

▣▨ ORIENTATION AND PRACTICAL INFORMATION. The center of town is **Dorfplatz.** Straight out of the train station down Bahnhofstr., Dorfpl. intersects both of Zell's main streets, Unterdorfstr. next to the river, and Gerlosstr. by the train tracks. The **tourist office** is at Dorfpl. 3a. From the rail station, head right along Bahnhofstr., and turn right at the end—the office is on your left. Pick up a town map, hiking maps (€6.40-7.85), skiing information, and accommodations listings. There's a computer with free reservations telephone on the side of the office. (☎228 10; fax 22 81 80; info@zell.at; www.zell.at. Open M-F 8:30am-12:30pm and 2:30-6pm, Sa 9am-noon and 4-6pm; July-Oct. also Sa 9am-noon and 4-6pm. During peak ski season, Dec-Jan., also Su 4-6pm.) Services include: **luggage storage** at the train station (daily 8am-noon and 2-5pm, €2.10); **taxis** ☎26 25, 23 45, or 22 55; **bike rental** at the train station (€12, children €7.20, with train ticket) or at **SB-Markt Hofer,** Gerlosstr. 30, opposite the campground. (☎22 20. Open M-F 7:15am-noon and 2:30-6:15pm, Sa 7:15am-noon. Mountain bikes €14 per day, road bikes €9, children €5.) In an **emergency,** dial 133 for **mountain rescue** or **police;** for an **ambulance,** dial ☎144. The **post office** at Unterdorf 2 **exchanges** money until 5pm and has an **ATM** in front. (☎23 33 11. Open M-F 8am-noon and 2-6pm.) **Postal code:** A-6280.

▥ ACCOMMODATIONS & CAMPING. Many places offer decent rates, and good accomodations can be found without trekking too far from the town center. To reach **Haus Huditz ❷,** Karl-Platzer-Weg 1, cross the train tracks by the tourist office and continue onto Gerlosstr.; bear left onto Gauderg. (at the Mode Journal building) and look for Karl-Platzer-Weg on the left at the next fork in the road (10min.). The owner provides beverages, TV, down comforters, and balconies with mountain views, all at a reasonable price. (☎22 28. huditz.bern-hard@gutanet.at. Breakfast included. Shower €1. €14.60 per person. In winter €16-17. No credit cards.) **Hotel Rosengarten ❸**, Rosengartenweg 14, is a bit of a misnomer (the window boxes are actually filled with geraniums and marigolds), but offers spacious rooms, all with shower and satellite TV, a sauna, and cafe. (☎24 43; fax 24 434. Double rooms with shower Apr-Oct. €26, Dec-Mar €34.) **Camping Hofer ❶**, at Gerlosstr. 33, offers just enough space for your tent a few blocks from the town center. Barbecues, free bike tours, and weekly hikes are all provided, and there's a grocery store across the street. 'Fritz and Didi,' the house band, performs in the bar adjacent to reception on W nights. (☎22 48; fax 224 88.; office@camping-hofer.at. Laundry €7. Reception Dec. 12 to Jan. 1 and July-Aug. 15 (high season) 8am-10pm; off-season 9am-noon and 3-8pm. Summer €4.50-5.20 per adult, €7-8 per campsite. €1 tax per person per night. Showers included.)

◻ **FOOD.** Local specialties include *Käsespätzle* (baked noodles with cheese and onions, and sometimes wurst or eggs), *Zillertaler Krapfen* (crispy fried shells filled with potato and cheese) and *Tiroler Gröstl* (fried potatoes, onions and bacon wtih a fried egg on top). **SB Restaurant Zeller Stuben ❷**, Unterdorf 11, the cheapest place around, serves big buffet-style portions. Spaghetti (€4.50), *Gulaschsuppe* (€3), and almost nothing over €6.50. The less casual restaurant upstairs features 6-8 daily *Menüs* including soup, entree, and dessert for €6.50-14. (☎22 71. Children's and vegetarian menus available. Both restaurants open July-Oct. and Dec. 20 to mid-Apr. 11am-9pm.) Cross the river to much on pizzas (€6.50-8) at **Pizza Cafe Reiter ❷**, Zelbergr. 4; sit in the atrium and watch the river or sit inside and watch continuous videos of paragliders. The chef also runs **Pizza Air,** the self-proclaimed "World's Smallest Airline" that offers tandem flights from 5-25min. for €70-110. Deliveries by truck, not paraglider. (☎223 90. Pizza Air ☎(0664) 200 4229. Open daily 11am-midnight.) Put the cherry on your night at **Café-Konditorei Gredler ❶**, Unterdorf 10, where 1995 Confectioner of the Year Tobias Gredler whips up desserts for patrons to enjoy on the riverside patio. Banana chocolate torte actually looks like a banana, thanks to the yellow sugar and chocolate shell; the other 17 tortes are no less intricate or delectable (€2.50). (☎248 90; fax 25 16; www.torten.net. Open June-Oct. 10am-11pm; from mid-Dec. to May 10am-6pm.) **SPAR Supermarkt** is around the corner from the tourist office, next to Intersport Strasser. (Open M-F 7:30am-12:30pm and 2-6:30pm, Sa 7:30am-1pm and 2-5pm.)

BRING ON THE BREW The residents of Zell am Ziller celebrate their local brewer with **Gauderfest** on the first weekend in May, when the whole town gets sauced in a 3-day celebration of cold, frothy beverages. The name "Gauderfest" is derived from the estate that owns the local private brewery. The Bräumeister's vats, Tyrol's oldest, concoct the beloved and potent Gauderbock especially for the occasion. The festival even has its own jingle: *Gauderwürst und G'selchts mit Kraut / hei, wia taut dösmunden / und 10 Halbe Bockbier drauf / mehr braucht's nit zum G'sundsein!* ("Gauder sausage and smoked pork with sauerkraut / hey, how good it tastes / and 10 pints of beer to go with it / what more could you need for your health!"). The festival's highlight is the **Ranggeln,** traditional wrestling for the title of "Hogmoar." There are also animal fights (attended by a veterinary surgeon) and customary activities like the **Gra-sausläuten** (ringing bells in order to wake the grass and make it grow). Revelry continues into the night with Tyrolean folk singing and dancing.

⚑ OUTDOOR ACTIVITIES. Zeller **skiing** comes in 2 packages: **day passes** for shorter visits, valid on the **Kreuzjoch-Rosenalm** and **Gerlosstein-Sonnalm** slopes (1 day €28.50, ages 15 and under €23; 2 days €53, €42.50; 3 days €75); and **Super Ski-passes** for longer visits (see p. 209). Single tickets are available for non-skiers who tag along to watch (€5, round-trip €8; children €3, €4.50; discount with guest card). Obtain passes at the **Kreuzjoch** (☎716 50), **Gerlosstein** (☎22 75), or **Ramsberg** (☎27 20) cable car stations (all 3 lifts open 8:30am-5pm). Info from the snowphone (☎71 65 26; fax 71 65 35; www.zillertalarena.at). **Rent skis** at any of Zell's sporting goods stores. Try **Pendl Sport** at Gerlosstr. 3. (☎22 87; fax 39 17. Open M-F 8am-noon and 2:30-6:30pm, Sa 8am-noon; Dec.-Easter also Sa 2-6pm. DC/MC/V.) Prices here average €11-20 for skis and gear, €19-24 for snowboards. **Rent a toboggan** at the Gerlossteinbahn bottom station. (Open M-Sa 7:45am-9:15pm, Su 8:30am-4:30pm. Day rides €5, children €2.50; evening rides same prices.)

Register in any town hotel or Pension to get a **guest card,** which snags you a free hike led by the tourist office. (Register one day in advance at the office; June-Sept. M-W, 2hr. to day-long hikes.) Much hiking around Zell am Ziller is lift-assisted. Two of the three ski lifts in Zell's vicinity offer **alpine hiking:** the **Kreuzjochbahn** (☎716 50; open 8:40am-12:10pm and 1-5:10pm; €13.20, to Rosealm, €8.80 to mid-station (with guest card €12, €8) and the **Gerlossteinbahn** (☎22 75; open 8:30am-12:15pm and 1-5pm; round-trip €8.80, €8 with guest card.) The mountain peak of Karspitz (2264m) provides an ideal hiking goal: on sunny days you can survey the entire valley and the waterfulls on the opposite ridge; on misty ones, hug the trail as the fog seems a living creature, racing towards the paths and the Zill river with tendrils of gray. From the Kreuzjochbahn top station, turn right and follow part #11. At Grindalm, you have the option of heading straight towards Kreuzwiessen-hut, and through fields to the peak, take path #10 back to the lift. If striking out cross country across the steep meadows that lead back to the lifts seems like a good idea, remember the old alpine adage: the shortest path is rarely the best one.

For a down-to-earth look at Zell's history, take a tour of the nearby **gold mine.** The journey begins at a petting zoo and adjacent cheese factory before moving on to a 45min. hike to the mine entrance. (☎48 20; fax 32 72. May-Sept. 2hr. tours every hr. 9am-6pm. €10, ages 3-16 €5.)

MAYRHOFEN ☎05285

At the southernmost end of the Zillertal, Mayrhofen is well-positioned for outdoor recreation. Four valleys (the **Zillergrund, Stillupgrund, Zemgrund,** and **Tuxertal**) stretch south from the town, providing endless opportunities for hikers and skiers. Mayrhofer residents walk the walk: native Peter Habeler and fellow Tyrolean Reinhold Messner completed the first non-oxygen-aided ascent of Mt. Everest. Habeler now runs the town's alpine school. This isn't some rarefied mountaineer's base-camp, though; Mayrhofen is a polished town with a glut of tourists that dwindles away as one leaves the town center for the surrounding mountains.

▣ TRANSPORTATION. Mayrhofen is accessible via the **trains** and **buses** of the Z-Bahn from **Jenbach** (50min.-1hr., 24 per day 6:05am-9:05pm, €5.20) and **Zell am Ziller** (15min., 24 per day 6:38am-9:52pm, €1.80). The **train station** lies slightly northeast of town; to reach the center, walk uphill on the main road and turn left at the intersection. (☎623 62. Open M-Sa 7:30am-6:30pm, Su 7:30am-1pm and 1:30-6:30pm.) For **taxis,** dial 633 64, 638 40, or 622 60. **Bike rental** is available at the train station (€12 per day, €7.20 for a half-day after 1pm).

▨ PRACTICAL INFORMATION. The **tourist office,** Dursterstr. 225, is amidst the hotels in the lower end of town. Enter town from the train station, turn left on

Hauptstr., then right onto Dursterstr. The office leads free **guided hikes and tours,** from town tours to 5hr. hikes; transportation may run €5-10. A 24hr. accommodations board and telephone is outside. (☎67 60; fax 67 60 33; mayrhofen@zillertal.tirol.at; www.mayrhofen.com. Tours mid-May to mid-Oct. M-F, call ahead for times and meeting points. Open M-F 8am-6pm, Sa 9am-noon, Su 10am-noon; July-Aug. also Sa 2-6pm.) Services include: **ATM** at the corner of Einfahrt Mitte and Hauptstr. at **Hypo-Tirol bank; luggage storage** at the train station (M-Su 7am-6:30pm, €2.10 per piece); **Emergency** phone numbers include: **police** ☎133; **fire** ☎122; **mountain rescue** ☎140; and **ambulance** ☎144. There's **Internet** access at **X-dream Net,** Hauptstr. 476 (☎649 36; €2.60 for 15min. minimum, €3.70 per 30min.; open mid-Dec. to mid-Apr. daily 9am-10pm; June-Sept. noon-10pm); The **post office,** Einfahrt Mitte 434, on your right on the way into town, **exchanges currency** until 5pm (☎623 51 11; open M-F 8am-noon and 2-6pm). **Postal code:** A-6290.

🏠🍴 ACCOMMODATIONS AND FOOD. Finding budget accommodations in Mayrhofen can be difficult, since groups tend to book most of the bed-and-breakfasts. Reserve far in advance. Try **Pension Fischnaller ❸,** Hauptstr. 410. Going into town on Einfahrt Mitte, turn left onto Hauptstr. Quiet rooms and cabinets filled with antique china make you feel as if you're at Grandma's for the weekend. The Pension has no sign—ring the doorbell for service. (☎623 47. Breakfast included. €18.20 per person; Dec.-Apr add €0.73 tax.) **Haus Woldrich ❸** is at Brandbergstr. 355. Take Einfahrt Mitte as it turns into Pfarrer-Krapfstr. until a sign for "Brandbergstraße" pointing parallel to the road. Turn right and it's the second house on the left. Spacious rooms, some with balcony. (☎/fax 623 25. Breakfast included, 7:30-9:30am, with TV. Apr.-Oct. €18 per person; Dec.-Easter €20. One bedroom without shower €14, €16.) **Haus Andreas ❸,** Sportplatzstr. 317, a 5min. walk past the tourist office, offers 12 beds in blue and white decorated doubles and triples, all with balconies. (☎/fax 638 45. Breakfast buffet included. €16-22. Closed in May.) **Hotel Pension Sieglerhof ❸,** Durertr. 226, provides a dark wood interior, TV in each room, and a swing set for the kiddies. Bar serves drinks after 5pm. (☎62 493; fax62 49 37; sieglerhof@tirol.com; www.tidiscover.com/sieglerhof. Apr-Nov €17-19 per person, €27-29 for shower; Dec-Mar €20-23, 30-33.)

Mo's Esscafé and Musikroom ❶, Hauptstr. 417, is all about being American, though the menu is heavy on tapas (€4) and much of the decor is borrowed from the Cuban tourist office. Never fear; in spite of the lack of Cajun food to complement the New Orleans artifacts covering the walls, the Mo burger (€4), naches (€3) and "Real American Donuts" (€1.30) will fuel your belly. Live music on weekend nights. (☎634 35; fax 644 94. Open Dec.-Easter Tu-Sa noon-1am, Su-M 4pm-1am; rest of year M-Sa noon-1am.) **Restaurant Manni ❷,** Hauptstr. 439, offers weekly specials (€8-12) like baked potatoes filled with sour cream and chicken strips and veggies, along with pizza (€7-10) and other standards. (☎33 01. Open daily 11am-midnight. AmEx/MC/V. **Café Dengg ❷,** Hauptstr. 412, serves well-prepared dishes beneath an awning just down Hauptstr. (☎648 66. Spaghetti €6.80, pizzas €7-8. Open M-Sa 10am-11pm.) There's a **SPAR Markt** on Hauptstr., right from Einfahrt Mitte. (☎639 10. Open M-F 7:30am-6:30pm, Sa 7:30am-6pm, Su 8am-noon.

🏔 OUTDOOR ACTIVITIES. Hiking and **skiing** trails in the nearby valleys satisfy mountaineers of all levels. Visit the tourist office to pick up a map (€6-8) of routes and mountain huts. Buses and taxis run frequently to and from the valleys. The **Z-Hiking-Ticket** simplifies hiking by providing free portage on all Zillertal cable cars, buses, and trains, and unlimited dips in public swimming pools, as well as reductions on many museums and alpine/paragliding schools (see p. 209).

The **Penkenbahn,** whose dangling gondolas pass directly above the town on their way up the 1850m Penkenberg, is visible on arrival in Mayrhofen, and leads to various paths. (☎626 33 16. Open May 24-Oct. 7 daily 9am-5pm. €12.50, with guest card €11.50, children €7.) The **Ahornbahn** lift takes passengers to the vicinity of both easy and difficult hikes. (☎626 33 16. June 16-Oct. 14 every 30min. 8:30am-noon and 12:30-5pm. Same prices as the Penkenbahn.) Try the **Edelhütte hike** (2-2½hr., moderate). Exit the Ahornbahn, head to the left, and look for trail #42. Winding through scrub meadows and rocky areas before reaching the hut (2238m), this hike offers views of neighboring mountains and their snow aprons. For a slightly less rigorous hike, with panoramic overviews of the entire valley, head to the top of the Penkenbahn, then follow path #23, the widest and best-marked one, uphill to Penkenjoch where photo ops abound. On warm days, watch paragliders launch themselves from the cliff near the chairlift (90min.).

Paragliders catch winds in surrounding valleys, or take a tandem flight with instructors at **Flugtaxi Mayrhofen,** Sportplatzstr. 300 (☎(0664) 205 50 11; from €55), or **Stocky-Air,** in the yellow gondola right next to the Penkenbahn lift (☎(0554) 340 79 76; 7-8min. flight €54.50, 20-30min. €110). Opportunities for **kayaking, rafting,** and **canyoning** and other "don't tell Mom" activities are available; rafting (from €29) and canyoning (from €27); call **Action Club Zillertal,** Hauptstr. 458. (☎629 77).

Come winter, **skiers** and **snowboarders** flock to the Ahorn, Penken, and Horberg ski areas, all of which are covered by the **Ski Zillertal 3000** pass, along with neighboring villages Finkenberg and Tux (1 day €31, children €19; 3-day €82, children €49.50.) The skipass includes free transit on local ski buses. Snow-bunnies can avail themselves of the regional, all-inclusive **Zillertal Super Skipass** (see p. 205). **Rent skis** at **Intersport,** Hauptstr. 415. (☎624 00; fax 624 00 15. Open M-F 8:30am-12:30pm and 2-6:30pm, Sa 8:30am-6pm, Su 8:30am-noon and 3-6pm.

ST. ANTON AM ARLBERG ☎05446

Always one of the world's premier ski towns, St. Anton had the sports world's attention in 2001, when it hosted the world skiing championships. The train station was moved to the other side of the valley for the event, and a glistening new conference center and sports complex were built, giving St. Anton a sleek new look. One thing that hasn't changed is the first snowfall in late autumn, which still brings a cosmopolitan array of Europeans looking to hit the world-class slopes. While summer offers affordable accommodations, you can save a few euros in winter by staying in nearby **St. Jakob** (5min. by bus).

 Be warned that this posh ski town doesn't emerge from hibernation until mid-July. If you visit in May or June, you may feel as if you've entered a ghost town—the majority of the hotels and restaurants will be closed or running on reduced hours.

TYROL

◪ TRANSPORTATION. St. Anton lies at the bottom of a steep, narrow valley, with neighboring **St. Jakob** and **St. Christoph** (both technically part of St. Anton) a few minutes east and west, respectively. Several train and bus routes connect St. Anton with major destinations, including: Feldkirch (45min., every 2hr. 5:15am-11:59pm, €6); Innsbruck (1¼hr., every 2hr. 6:15am-12:44am, €12.40); Vienna Westbahnhof (6½-8½hr., 6 per day 6:15am-11:13pm, €15.40); Zurich (2½-3hr., 4 per day 5:33am-3:57pm, €36.30). From late June to Sept. and Dec.-Apr., **buses** also run to: Lech (30min.; in summer 5 per day 7:48am-4:43pm, in winter every 30min. 7:50am-5:50pm; €3.30); St. Christoph (10min.; in summer 5 per day 7:48am-4:43pm, in winter every 30min. 7:50am-5:50pm; €1.00); St. Jakob (5min;, in summer 9 per day 7:20am-6:45pm; free with town bus, €2.40 with Post Bus). A *Tageskarte* (day pass) allows unlimited bus travel in the Arlberg region, including Lech and Zürs (€7.30). Buses stop at the train station, as well as the "Westterminal," the parking lot by the highway on the east side of town beyond the *Fußgängerzone*.

■**⛷ ORIENTATION AND PRACTICAL INFORMATION.** St. Anton's one main road runs the length of the *Fußgängerzone* (pedestrian zone). The large wooden **tourist office** is across from the train station, and provides information on St. Anton and the Arlberg region. Outside is a 24hr. electronic accommodation board. (☎226 90; fax 25 32; st.anton@netway.at; www.stantonamarlberg.com. Open July to mid-Sept. M-F 8am-noon and 2-6pm, Sa-Su 10am-noon; May to early June and mid-Sept.-Dec. M-F 8am-noon and 2-6pm; Dec.-Apr. M-F 8:30am-6:30pm, Sa 9am-noon and 1-7pm, Su 10am-noon and 3-6pm.) Services include: **currency exchange** at banks and the post office (avoid exchange machines; banking hours M-F 8am-noon and 2-4:30pm); **bike rental** and advice at **Intersport Arlberg** in the pedestrian zone (☎34 53; fax 34 53 25; info@intersport-arlberg.com; 1 day €20; 1 week €99; open M-F 9am-noon and 1-6pm, Sa 9am-noon); **Internet** access at **Mailbox** near Sportcafe Schneider (open July-Aug 10am-2pm and 5-8pm; Dec.-May 10am-10pm; €0.20 per min.); 24hr. **luggage storage** at the station (€2-2.50); and **taxis** (☎231 50, 236 80). For **ski conditions**, dial ☎25 65. **Emergencies: police,** ☎133; **ambulance,** ☎144. To find the **post office**, exit the tourist office, turn right down the main road, right again opposite Hotel Schwarzer Adler, and then take a quick right after the bend to the left. (☎33 80 20. Open M-F 8am-noon and 2-5:30pm; Dec.-Apr. also Sa 9-11am.) **Postal code:** A-6580.

⛷ ACCOMMODATIONS. During the ski season, prices double; make reservations early. **Pension Pepi Eiter ❸,** is a left uphill from the tourist office; after 300m, a green sign points the way up the ramp to the right. Pepi Eiter provides comfy beds and pine-panelled rooms with shower, TV, and a chocolate on the nightstand. (☎25 50 or 23 19. Breakfast and parking included. June-Sept., €18-20 per person; mid-Dec. to Apr. €36 per person.) Four-star accommodations are nearly affordable in the summer: take the **Hotel San Antonio ❸,** Nassereinerstr. 351, for example. From the *Fußgängerzone*, head up Dorfstr. to Nassereiner., then turn left onto Nassereinerstr. The hotel is on the right. Boasting a pizzeria (entrees €6-6.50), candlepin bowling, and huge, sunny rooms with living room, TV, and shower, San Antonio provides luxury for only €21-25 from June-Sept. (€55-60 Dec.-Apr.) Breakfast included. (☎34 74; fax 34 73 15.) Your best bet for an affordable winter lodging is in **St. Jakob** (5min. by free bus). Check the St. Jakob tourist office, or try **Haus Bergwelt ❸,** Römerweg 146, which has spacious, quiet rooms, some with balconies that look out on grazing cows. All rooms come with shower, bathroom, and TV. (☎29 95. Breakfast included. June to mid-Sept. €14-15 per person.; from Dec.-April €30-45 per person. €3 surcharge per night for stays less than three nights.)

⬚ FOOD. For a great meal at a low price, head to **Restaurant Grieswirt ❸,** between the *Fußgängerzone* and the post office. Well-prepared entrees (€6.90-10.61) and two daily *Menüs* including soup, entree, and dessert (€10.54-12, €1.45 more in winter) will leave you fully satisfied. (☎29 65; fax 200 56. Open June-Sept. daily 9am-9pm, Dec. to mid-Apr. 9am-10:30pm. No credit cards.) Though the €25 T-bone at the Schneider steakhouse across the street may not be in your price range, the **SportCafé Schneider ❷,** to the right down the *Fußgängerzone* from the tourist office, is perfect for a quick lunch or late dinner, serving a small selection of soups and sandwiches (€2.60-4.50), spaghetti Bolognese (€6.90), and ice cream desserts for €3-4.70. (☎25 48. Open daily 9am-midnight.) The redesigned train station has been called "The Wall Against Nature," but it's hardly the only wall in town: **Grossmauer China Restaurant ❸,** on the first right from the *Fußgängerzone*, offers *Menüs* from €6.50 including duck, chop suey, and Szechuan beef. Dinners €11-14. Take-out or eat in. (☎39 38. Open daily 11:30am-11pm. MC/V.) The local **SPAR Markt** is down the main road, 10min. away from the tourist office, just past the *Fußgängerzone*. (Open M-F 7am-noon and 2-6pm, Sa 7am-noon.)

 OUTDOOR ACTIVITIES. A century after the Ski Club Arlberg was founded, St. Anton's main draw is still its exceptional slopes. Some 262 trails cover the area, divided into 260km of groomed trails and some 185km of ungroomed or "deep snow" runs. **Ski passes** for the Arlberg region are sold at the larger hotels, but can also be purchased at the ski lift stations (Galzigbahn, Rendlbahn, St. Christophbahn, and Nasserein-Lift), or at the ticket office in the *Fußgänger-zone* behind the Hotel Post. (Half-day pass €28, ages 7-15 €17; 1-day pass €37/ €22.50; week-pass €116/€118. In the first few days of Dec. and the last week of Apr., ticket prices are reduced by 50%.) Those interested in St. Anton's free 4.2km **toboggan run** should call ☎235 20. There are two **ski schools** in St. Anton, **Ski School** (www.skischool-arlberg.com. Open Su-F 8:30am-4:30pm, Sa 9am-noon and 1-5pm. Half-day group lesson €36; private half-day lesson €129) and **Ski and Snowboard School St. Anton** (☎35 63; www.skistanton.com; open Su-F 8:30am-4:30pm, Sa 8am-5pm; half-day group lesson €33; half-day private lesson €94-130; 3-day "Snowboard College" €115).

> **!** On a warm summer night in Austria and Switzerland, you'll realize quickly that window screens haven't caught on everywhere. This means that a whole menagerie of European insects, attracted by the lights, will be moving into your room over the next few hours. Unless you're a fan of bugs, there's no good solution. Closing the window works, unless you happen to have a half-dozen backpackers in bunkbeds as roommates (things get hot and smelly fast). The best thing you can do is keep the windows shut during the day (when no one cares how warm it is indoors anyway), then open them at night after everyone is tucked in and the lights are out. Keep food under wraps. As a last resort, your *Let's Go* book makes a very effective flyswatter.

In the summer, St. Anton is a hiker's haven. Trails lead through the hills around town and the tourist office dispenses maps and directions. Once a week in July, the tourist office sponsors **wildflower hikes.** The easy **Rosannaschlucht hike** (3hr. loop) leads through the Rosanna gorge between St. Anton and Ferwall to the west. Walk on the highway headed towards Lech, leaving St. Anton, and look for the Rendl cable car on the left side of the road, where the trail begins. The first few kilometers follow the Rosanna River, before slowly climbing the sloping walls of the gorge. After soaking your feet in the bright, emerald green Ferwall See, cross the river and head back toward St. Anton; the path is higher in elevation on the far side of the river, providing wonderful views of the roaring river valley below. The **Leutkircher Hütte** mountain hut is a 3hr., moderate hike away. (☎(05448) 82 07. Open early July to late Sept.) For a great view from the roof of the Arlberg, take the series of 3 Galzigbahn lifts starting in St. Anton to the top of the 2811m Valluga. (Lifts daily in summer 9am-4:30pm; round-trip €16.50.) **Biking** in the Arlberg is arduous but rewarding; 60km of marked mountain bike paths await, including the popular Ferwall Valley and Moostal trails.

TYROL

THE ÖTZTAL

Bending its way between hundreds of 3000m peaks on the Italian border, the Ötztal (Ötz valley) offers some of the wildest and most impressive scenery in the Tyrolean Alps. Tiny farms cling impossibly to mountainsides while rivulets carve through the rocks to silt-gray rivers. The 1991 discovery of a frozen man who lived 5000 years ago, nicknamed Ötzi, proves that visitors have been enjoying the breathtaking views for millennia. The area, known as the Ötztal Arena, is Austria's largest skiing and snowboarding center. There is also glacier skiing in summer, as well as some of the most awesome hiking outside of the Hohe Tauern. At the mouth of the valley, **Bahnhof Ötztal** sends trains to **Innsbruck** (40min., 5:27am-1:31am, €6.40) and **St. Anton** (1hr., 9:07am-11:04pm, €7.90). **Buses** pass through the Ötztal's main town of Sölden before forking into the narrow Gurgler and Venter ranges. The region is accessible by public transportation, although buses to the more remote towns run on reduced hours in the summer and fall.

SÖLDEN ☎ 05254

Wedged in the Ötztal valley 40km south of Bahnhof Ötztal, Sölden is an ideal base for exploring surrounding villages. The town is a major ski resort in winter, but the razor-sharp, snow-streaked mountains on either side steal the show. In the summer, these mountains offer of gorgeous hiking trails.

🖳🛈 TRANSPORT AND PRACTICAL INFORMATION. There are several bus stops in town; the most centrally located is "Postamt." **Buses** arrive from Bahnhof Ötztal (1hr., every hr. 7:05am-7:15pm, €6.00) and Innsbruck (2hr., 3 per day 9am-4:15pm, €12.50) before departing for Vent (30min., 5 per day 8:20am-4:45pm, €3.30) and Obergurgl (25min., every hr. 7:45am-7:15pm, €2.30). From the bus stop, turn left and cross the bridge in front of Hotel Tyrolerhof and keep walking straight to the **tourist office,** with two **Internet** terminals (€0.10 per min.). (☎510; fax 51 05 20; info@soelden.com; www.soelden.com. Open M-Sa 8am-6pm, Su 9am-noon; in summer, also Su 2-6pm.) A **24-hour electronic accomodations board** with reservations telephone is across from the "Shell Tankstelle" bus stop. **Rent bikes** at any one of the 5 sports shops in town (full day €16-18, weekend €25-28). The **post office** with **currency exchange** is next to the bus stop. (☎22 66. Open M-F 8am-noon and 2-6pm. From mid-Jan. through Apr., also open Sa 9-11am.) **Postal code:** A-6450.

🖳🖰 ACCOMMODATIONS AND FOOD. Prices rise steeply in winter. To get to **Haus Alpenrose ❸,** take the first right after the "Shell Tankstelle" bus stop at the edge of town. The mounds of skiing trophies in the case downstairs reveal proprietor Reinhard Schöpf's other line of work as a mountain guide and ski instructor; he can tell you what's worth skiing or hiking in the area. All rooms come with TV, shower, and a balcony. (☎23 33. Mid-Dec. to Apr. €30-33 per person; July-Sept. €15-18; Oct. to mid-Dec. €22. Closed May-June. No credit cards.) For a down-home family experience, try **Haus Wachter ❸.** Get off the bus at the beginning of town at "Schmiedhofbrücke," cross the bridge, and turn right. If the Wachters and their two children don't charm you, the gigantic breakfast buffet will. (☎24 23. June-Nov. €20-25; Dec.-Apr. €35-37; Christmas and Mardi Gras holidays €43.) For large quiet rooms that look like they were built yesterday, try **Pension Garni Olympia ❸.** From the Shell Tankstelle, walk back two streets and turn left, following the signs. TV and shower are in every room. Breakfast in a beautiful room with mountain view and free admission to Freizeit Arena pool/sauna in the tourist office complex. June-Nov. singles €22-25; doubles €21-23.50, with balcony and living room €24-28.50. Dec-May. singles €38; doubles €37/€45. (☎24 27; fax: 242 78.)

There are several restaurants in town; many close in summer. One excellent place is **Restaurant-Pizzheria Corso ❷**, across the bridge from the Hotel Liebe Sonne, serving in an elegant, candle-lit atmosphere, with animal skin covers on benches. Pizza is €6.47-10.32, pasta €7.12-10.76. (☎24 98; fax 29 80. Open June-Apr. Th-Tu noon-midnight.) For local fare in a farmhouse-like setting, head to **Die Alm ❷**, on the main road past the post office. House specialties cost €6.58-9.87. (☎24 01; fax 35 35 14. Open daily Oct.-Apr. 11:30am-11pm; May-Sept. 11:30am-2pm and 5-9:30pm. No credit cards.) If the blaring oom-pah music and rustic agricultural implements at **Törggele Stub'n ❷** don't scream "Tyrol," then the menu will. Cheese dumpling soup (€4), and the farmer's plate (roasted meat, veggies, onions, and a fried egg; €8.50) satisfy the hungry. (☎35 35. Cross the bridge toward the tourist office; Törggele is on your right. Open year-round 11am-11:30pm.) Turn left from the post office to **SPAR Supermarkt** (Open M-F 8am-noon and 3-6pm, Sa 8am-noon.)

⚠ OUTDOOR ACTIVITIES. The high altitude of Sölden's skiing areas (1377-3058m) guarantees snow even in the summer. The **Gaislachkoglbahn,** whisking passengers up the 3058m Gaislachkogl in a twin-cable gondola, is the largest of its kind in the world. (Open late June to mid-Sept., and Dec.-Apr., Round-trip €18; ages 8-16 €9.50.) **Lift tickets** for the 32 cable cars and lifts that serve Sölden's slopes are sold at the Gaislachkoglbahn booth at the southern end of town (mid-Dec.-Apr. €33-36; rest of year €28-34). There are ski and snowboard schools in and around Sölden, including **Sölden/Hochsölden** (☎254 66; fax 31 71; www.ski-soelden.com; 4hr. group lesson €45) and **Ötztal 2000** (☎220 35 00; fax 300 10; www.yellowpower.at; 4hr. group lesson €40-45). Ask at the tourist office about toboggan parties on the 5.5km toboggan run, which remains lit in the evening.

The area above Sölden between **Hochsölden** on the right (looking up) and the **Rettenbachalm** on the left is excellent summer hiking ground. To get to Hoch-sölden, the best bet is to use the **Sesselift Hochsölden,** in the parking lot behind the Intersport down the road from the post office. (Open in summer from end of June to mid-Sept. 9am-noon and 1-4:15pm. €6.50 round-trip, ages 8-14 €4.00) If you want to start on the Rettenbachalm side, take the moderate trail to the right of the post office to "Rettenbachalm" (about 2hr. one-way). Plunging through the forest and briefly over a paved road, this trail ends facing the magnificent glacier in the distance beyond the Rettenbachalm. Other good hikes include:

Lehrpfad zur Hochgebirgsökologie (1hr. one-way). Cutting across the face of the mountain between Hochsölden and the Rettenbachalm, this easy trail remains flat the whole way, though never dipping below 2000m. It is mostly on the open mountainside just above tree level, affording uninterrupted, magnificent views of the mountains across the valley. Along the way, colorful signs in German explain the unique ecology of high alpine environments.

Schwarzkogel hike (2½hr. round-trip from the Rotkogelhütte). For those who have always dreamed of climbing a mountain and planting a flag on the top, the 3016m Schwarzkogel will not disappoint. Though fairly difficult, it is a popular climb for intrepid families and adventurous older couples. From the chapel above the Rot-kogelhütte, it leads through a narrow, rocky pass to the Schwartzsee, a tiny, intensely blue glacial lake that remains partly frozen. From there, cross ankle- to knee-deep snowfields and the steep path to the summit. Nearly 2mi. above sea level, the peak holds stunning views of the Urfeld valley, glaciers and mountain faces, including Wildspitze, Tyrol's highest mountain (3774m). Sign the book in the metal stand before heading back.

TYROL

DAYTRIP FROM SÖLDEN

OBERGURGL   ☎ 05256

Buses run from Sölden to Obergurgl (25min., 1-2 per hr. 7:45am-7:15pm, €2.30).

Tiny Obergurgl, Austria's highest village, is little more than a few hotels and guest houses, but you're not likely to stay on the ground long. The **tourist office** is in the same building as the bus stop. (☎64 66; fax 63 53; info@obergurgl.com; www.obergurgl.com. Open July-Sept. M-F 8am-6pm, Sa 8am-4pm, Su 9:30am-noon; Oct. M-F 9am-5pm, Sa 9am-noon; Nov.-Apr. M-Sa 9am-5:30pm, Su 9:30am-noon; May-June M-F 9am-12:30pm and 1:30-5pm, Sa 9am-noon.) When the flakes start falling, **skiing** claims Gurgl's heart and soul, aided by the addition of three new ski lifts for winter 2001-2002. For the hairiest skiing, head to the area above Hochgurgl (3802m), or above Obergurgl to **Hohe Mut** (2670m). Purchase **lift tickets** at lift stations (peak season 1-day pass €35.50, ages 8-16 €23; 1 week €187/€115; off-season €31.50; 10 days €235/€146.50. Children under 8 free.). For **skiing conditions,** call ☎64 69.

In summer, the chair-lift behind the SPAR can carry you, white-knuckled, to the top of **Hohe Mut,** where the stunning view encompasses 21 glaciers and the far-off peaks of Italian Tyrol. (Round-trip €10. Open late July-Sept.; 9am-4:15pm in winter.) The trails beyond the top provide the most gorgeous hiking in all of Austria.

Rotmoosferner hike (2hr.). From Hohe Mut, head straight back along the grassy ridge and follow signs to the "Rotmoosferner" glacier. This easy path remains nearly flat the entire way, keeping an altitude of roughly 2700m. In the summer, hike early in the day, before the snow melts and you find yourself wading knee-deep. On the way back, consider bypassing the chair lift in favor of the trail leading down through the rocky glacial debris field below Hohe Mut and back to Obergurgl via the Zirbenwald (see below; 3hr. from the glacier back to Obergurgl).

Zirbenwald (3hr. round-trip). Walk down the main road in Obergurgl until it becomes gravel at the edge of town, and follow signs to the "Rotmoos Wasserfälle." This moderate hike climbs through a forest of dwarf evergreens that has been declared a "Naturdenkmal" (natural monument) by the province of Tyrol. The deepest and most dramatic gorge is also home to the Rotmoos waterfall, which plummets through a narrow opening to a small pool. After the waterfall, trail #5 leads off to the left and returns to Obergurgl through the higher sections of the Zirbenwald.

VORARLBERG

At the intersection of four nations, the residents of the Vorarlberg speak like the Swiss, eat like Germans, ski with Liechtensteiners, and vote Austrian. Carry a passport at all times, for foreign borders are never more than two hours away, and a daytrip can easily become an international excursion. The Vorarlberg tourist office presents the province as having something for everyone, but it's more than just hype. Bregenz, on the banks of the Bodensee (Lake Constance), is a vacation hotspot, drawing tourists from all over Europe, while Feldkirch on the Ill river is the transfer point for entry into Liechtenstein. As

a result of its international capabilities, Vorarlberg is well-equipped to handle a diverse load of visitors. Since the mountainous terrain precludes any industry other than dairy farming, tourism is the major source of income. Construction everywhere is evidence of the region's success, but the new *Pensions* and hotels have led some denizens to grumble they're ruining the views that garner the tourists in the first place.

The geography offers countless outdoor options. From the tranquil Bodensee in the west, Vorarlberg thrusts increasingly upward as you move south and east, climaxing in the broad Arlberg Alps (passable only through the 10km Arlberg Tunnel) at the boundary to Tyrol. Over 1600km of marked hiking paths from 400m to over 3km in altitude crisscross the region, while hundreds of ski lifts whisk winter slalomers and summer hikers to the mountain peaks. Vorarlberg's 161km network of cycling paths ranges from leisurely tours through the Bodensee plain to challenging climbs in the Alps. Cycling maps are available at bookstores and tourist offices. For more info, contact the **Vorarlberg Information Office** in Bregenz (☎/fax 05574 425 25; www.vorarlberg-tourism.at).

HIGHLIGHTS OF VORARLBERG

Critique the bouquet of an aging red at the **Feldkirch** wine festival (see p. 192).
Admire the works of painter Angelika Kaufmann in **Schwarzenberg** (see p. 195).
Catch a glimpse of the Tyrol's highest peak, the Wildspitze, in **Sölden** (see p. 202).

FELDKIRCH   ☎ 05522

Just minutes from the borders of Switzerland and Liechtenstein, Feldkirch (pop. 28,000) has served as a trade and transportation hub for centuries. More than any other city in Vorarlberg, Feldkirch's history remains vivid today—the triangular Altstadt is a maze of pastel Baroque buildings and medieval towers, lined by arcades that shelter shops and fruit stands. The city itself is compact, quickly fading into shady suburbs with cliffs and mountains rising nearby.

TRANSPORTATION. Trains depart from Feldkirch to: **Bregenz** (45min., 1-2 per hr. 5am-midnight, €4.50); **Innsbruck** (2hr., 5:27am-12:20am, €19.60); **Salzburg** (4¼hr., 7 per day 5:27am-12:20am, €39.20); and **Zurich** (1½-2½hr., 6 per day 4:45am-4:49pm, €24.10). The Liechtenstein bus system runs to **Schaan**, near Vaduz (30min., every 30min. 6:05am-11:05pm, €1.60), with connections to **Buchs** and **Sargans** in Switzerland. **Bus** info at ☎739 74 (M-Th 8am-12:30pm and 2-4:30pm, F 8am-noon), or at the tourist office. **City buses** connect Feldkirch's subdivisions (€1, day pass €2). Buses stop at the train station and at the main bus stop, which can be reached by exiting the train station, walking away from the tracks, and turning left at the intersection. **Taxis** are outside the station, or call for one (☎17 18, 387 00, or 311 50).

PRACTICAL INFORMATION. Primary locations of interest in Feldkirch are clustered on the Ill river in the old city, a confusing warren of streets that makes a map necessary (free at the tourist office). To reach the city center and the **tourist office** at Herreng. 12, walk from the train station to the end of the road, turn left onto Bahnhofstr., and cross the pedestrian underpass in the "Zentrum" direction. Go through the *Bezirkhauptmannschaft* building; it is about 50m ahead on the right. The office distributes walking-tour maps and info about events, and sells hiking maps for €5.74. (☎734 67; fax 798 67; www.tiscover.com/feldkirch. Open May-Sept. M-F 9am-6pm, Sa 9am-noon; Oct.-Apr. M-F 8am-noon and 1-5pm, Sa 9am-noon.) The **Sparkasse** just down the street from the tourist office has a computer kiosk on the first floor providing free **Internet** access. (Open M-Tu and Th 8am-noon and 2-4pm, W 8am-noon and 2-6:30pm, F 8am-4pm.) A **post office** and an **ATM** are on Bahnhofstr., across from the station. (Open M-F 7am-7pm, Sa 7am-noon.) **Postal code:** A-6800.

ACCOMMODATIONS AND CAMPING. Feldkirch's tourist office maintains a short list of *Privatzimmer*, but if you can't find a spot in one of the places listed below, Feldkirch can be best be seen as a daytrip from Bregenz. **Jugendherberge "Altes Siechenhaus" (HI) ❷,** Reichstr. 11, is Feldkirch's lone hostel and might well be the most historic spot on your visit. Buses #1 and 2 run to "Jugendherberge" from the station (5min.), or walk out of the station onto the main road, Bahnhofstr. (which becomes Reichstr.), turn right and walk 15-20min. The hostel is a white, 600-year-old brick-and-wood building that served as an infirmary during several plague epidemics. Today, it serves as a family-oriented hostel with clean rooms and modest beds. (☎731 81; fax 793 99. Wheelchair accessible. Breakfast buffet (€4.07) features pickled fish, homemade sausage, and fresh cherries. Laundry €3. Sheets included, €1.50 discount if you bring your own. Key and key-card available for €20 deposit or ID. Reception M-Sa 7am-10pm, Su 7-11am and 7-10pm. Curfew 10pm. Some bathrooms are co-ed. Dorms €14; doubles €36.) **Gasthof Löwen ❸,** Egelseestr. 20. Take bus #1 or 3 (dir.: Tosters) to "Burgweg," a shady suburb of Feldkirch. From the stop, walk back and take the first right. The hotel has simple, quiet rooms. (☎728 68; fax 378 57; loewen@gmx.at. Breakfast, shower, and TV included. Restaurant meals €9-14. Showers included. Reception Tu-Su 6:30am-noon and 3-11pm, M 6:30am-noon, 3-5pm, and 8-11pm. Singles €30, doubles €48-52, triples €68-72.) For cheap digs in an antique-filled setting, try **Gasthof zum Engel ❸,** 106 Liechtensteinerstr. in nearby Tsis (Liechtenstein Bus 70-75 to Tsis Letzestr.; then walk two blocks). The painstakingly painted flowers on the woodwork make up for the peeling wallpaper, and your dresser just might date from the 19th century. Singles €22, doubles €36. **Waldcamping Feldkirch ❶,** Stadionstr. Take bus #1 (dir.: Gisingen) to "Milchhof," and follow the signs; it lies past the soccer field. Nicer than most, this campground offers camping under the pines, right next to the sprawling town swimming pool (admission included). (☎ 743 08; www.feldkirch.com/kkf/fbg3.htm. Laundry €3.50. Reception 8am-12:30pm and 2-10pm. Sept.-June €4.50, children €2, cars €2.40, tents €2.30-3.50; July-Aug. add €0.50-2. MC/V.)

🖸 **FOOD.** Eateries line the streets of the *Fußgängerzone*, and with the convenient location come high prices. A few budget establishments lurk just outside the pedestrian area. Try **Pizzeria-Trattoria La Taverna ❷,** Vorstadtstr. 18 (☎ 792 93), a busy restaurant near the river. La Taverna offers an extensive menu, including pizza (€4.72-7.27) and many varieties of pasta (€5.09-7.99), all in a candle-lit, wine-cellar interior. (Open 11:30am-2pm and 5pm-midnight.) Probably the only restaurant in all of Vorarlberg to specialize in salads, **Treff ❷** is located just past the end of Vorstadt between the river and the fountain that looks like a cross between a freeway on-ramp and a reflecting pool. Try the *Treffsalat*—beets, radishes, kidney beans, onions, and a half-dozen other veggies give heft and color to standard iceberg lettuce and grilled chicken (€6.50). Mexican, seafood, and other salads by the score (€5-11). Prompt service deliveries. (Open 10am-midnight.) Just across the Illsteg. bridge, **Element ❶,** down Vorstadtstr. and across Illsteg., is a trendy cafe that looks like a postmodern greenhouse. Its drawn shades and soft jazz give it a smooth appeal, and the river rippling outside adds its own music. Small meals and snacks €1.60-7. In summer, ice cream scoops are €0.80. (Open mid-Oct. to mid-Apr. M-F 7:30am-8pm.) An **Inter-SPAR** is on Neustadt, not too far from the Schatterburg, in the same complex as the Holiday Inn. (Open M-F 9am-7:30pm, Sa 8am-5pm.) Marktpl. hosts an **outdoor market** every Saturday morning from March-Nov.

🖸 🖸 **SIGHTS AND ENTERTAINMENT.** Feldkirch's Gothic cathedral, the **St. Nikolaus Kirche,** forms one edge of the Altstadt. The cathedral received a face-lift in 1478 after a series of devastating fires. Frescoes of Feldkirch history and the coats of arms of local potentates adorn the 15th-century **Rathaus** on Schmiedg. At nearby Schloßerg. 8 stands the **Palais Liechtenstein,** completed in 1697. The palace once supported the royal seat of the Prince of Liechtenstein but now houses the town library and city archives.

At the edges of the Altstadt, three towers of the original city wall remain: the **Katzenturm,** the **Pulverturm,** and the **Wasserturm.** Outside the Altstadt, one block toward the station on Bahnhofstr., lies the **Kapuzinerkloster** (Capuchin monastery), built in 1605. Hike up the staircase on Burgg. to reach the **Schattenburg,** Feldkirch's most impressive structure, for a fantastic view of the Altstadt. (Castle and cafe open Tu-Su 10am-midnight.) From the early 1200s until 1390, the castle was the seat of the Counts of Montfort, who dominated the Vorarlberg region. The town purchased the castle in 1825 to save it from demolition and converted it into the **Feldkirch Heimatmuseum,** which now houses sundry objects from the region's history in the remarkably well-preserved castle. The collection includes an 800 year-old fresco, carved wooden furniture, coins from AD 69, and an armory full of old weapons. (☎/fax 719 82. Open Tu-Su 9am-noon and 1-5pm. €2, ages 12-18 €1.)

For those lucky enough to catch one, Feldkirch schedules a number of festivals and special events during the year. Perhaps the biggest is the **Feldkirch Festival,** a music celebration whose program includes music from Monteverdi to jazz (May 30-June 8, 2003). For ticket information, contact the Kulturreferat Feldkirch, Schloßerg. 8 (☎ 304 12 70; fax 12 79; albert.ruetz@feldkirch.at; www.feldkirch.at). From July 11-13, 2003, Feldkirch's annual **wine festival** will intoxicate all those who venture to Marktpl. On the last weekend of July (July 26-27, 2003), the annual **Gauklerfestival** (Jester's Festival) unleashes jugglers, mimes, and clowns from all over the world onto the cobblestone streets. The annual **Christmas bazaar** is from Nov. 28-Dec. 24, 2003 with crafts, candy canes, and carols.

BREGENZ ☎ 05574

Bregenz, the capital city of Vorarlberg, spreads along the eastern coast of the Bodensee (Lake Constance), separated from the different countries by only a few km. If it looks a little tired, it's because it's been hosting a variety of tourists long before the invention of Eurail. First it was the Celts, then the Romans, who established a camp called Brigitania on the site of the present-day city. Later the Irish missionaries Gallus and Columban dropped by and dubbed the shining lake surrounded by mountains "The Golden Bowl" (Bregenz). These days the Bowl plays hosts to hordes wandering along the lakeside or around the historic **Oberstadt**.

☞ TRANSPORTATION

Trains: Bahnhofstr. (☎ 675 50; information ☎ 05 17 17). To: **Feldkirch** (30-45min., 2-4 per day 5:15am-12:01am, €4.50); **Innsbruck** (2¼hr., 8 per day 5am-9:43pm, €23.30); **Munich** (2½hr., 4 per day 9:20am-7:20pm, €31); **St. Gallen** (45min., 4 per day 10:40am-8:40pm, €9.40); **Vienna** (8-10hr., 4 per day 5am-9:43pm, €57.40); **Zurich** (1¾hr., 4 per day 10:40am-8:40pm, €26.60).

Regional Buses: BundesBuses leave from the train station to **Dornbirn** (30min., every 30min. 4:55am-6:55pm, €2.91), **Egg** (1hr., 1-2 per hr. 6:51am-7:44pm, €3.30), and other regional destinations.

Public Transportation: 4 bus lines run through the city. Day pass €1.

Taxis: ☎ 650 00, 866 88, and 718 00. Always several in front of the train station.

Parking: By the *Festspielhaus.* Open 8am-noon and 1-6pm. €0.50 per hr., €3.60 per day; 6pm-midnight €2.20 per hr. Public parking €0.35-0.70 per hr. in the city center and by the Pfänderbahn. Buy parking permits from one of the ubiquitous automats.

▪ PRACTICAL INFORMATION

Tourist Office: Bregenz Tourismus und Stadtmarketing, Bahnhofstr. 14 (☎ 495 90; fax 49 59 59; tourismus@bregenz.at; www.todiscover.at/bregenz). From the train station, face away from the lake, and turn left; it's the glass building with the green "i" sign on the right. The staff makes hotel reservations (€2.20), has *Privatzimmer* lists, hiking and city maps, and provides concert info and free **Internet.** Open M-F 9am-noon and 1-5pm, Sa 9am-noon; during the *Festspiele* M-Sa 9am-7pm, Su 4-7pm.

Consulate: UK, Bundesstr. 110 (☎ 785 86), in neighboring **Lauterach.**

ATM: At the train station.

Lockers: At the train station 6:30am-9:30pm (€1.50-2).

Internet Access: S'Logo, Kirchstr. 47 (☎ 441 91). €0.08 per min. Open 5pm-1am.

Post Office: Seestr. 5 (☎ 437 00; fax 457 57), on Seestr. across from the harbor. Open M-F 8am-7pm (cashier closes at 5pm), Sa 8am-2pm. **Postal code:** A-6900.

▪ ACCOMMODATIONS AND CAMPING

With a half-dozen four-star hotels and fairly reasonable pensions, affluent vacationers, senior citizen's groups, and backpackers should all be able to find something within their price range. When the *Festspiele* come to town during the last week of July and the first three weeks of August, prices rise and reservations become absolutely necessary.

Jugendgästehaus (HI), Mehrerauerstr. 3-5 (☎ 428 67; fax 67 88; bregenz@jgh.at; www.jgh.at), across the bridge that goes over the tracks and out of the train station.

0 200 yards
0 200 meters

Bodensee

Floating Stage

Festival & Congress Hall

TO ② (250m)
Mehreraürstr.

Casino

Kunsthaus
(Art Gallery)

Am Steinenbach

Reichsstr.

Pfänderweg

Schillerstr.

Belruptstr.

Kornmarktstr.

Anton-Schneider-str.

Schäferstr.

Bergstr.

Pfänderbahn
to Pfänder Mtn.

Seestr.

Bahnhofstr.

Montfortstr.

St.-Anna-Str.

Kaiserstr.

Rathausstr.

Weherestr.

Bergmanstr.

Scheibenstr.

Welbensreuteweg

Herz-Jesu
Kirche

Deuringstr.

Maurachg.

OBERSTADT

Kirchstr.

Martinsturm

S'Logo

Deuring
Schlößchen

Ehregutapl.

Berg Isel Weg

Römerstr.

Thalbachg.

Amtstorstr.

Quellenstr.

Vorkloster g.

St. Gallus
Pfarrkirche

Kolumbanstr.

N
L.G.

Sandgrubenweg

Ölrainstr.

Unfallkrankenhaus

Arlbergstr.

Riedergg.

Josef-Huter-Str.

Bregenz

🏠🏔 ACCOMMODATIONS
Camping Lamm, **2**
Kaiser Hotel, **8**
Jugendgästehaus (HI), **3**
Pension Gunz, **4**
Pension Sonne, **7**

🍎 FOOD
China Restaurant Da-Li, **5**
Ikaros, **9**
König Pizza und Kebap, **6**
SB Restaurant, **10**
Wirthaus am See, **1**
Zum Goldenen Hirschen, **11**

🍺 PUBS
Uwe's Bier-Bar, **12**

- - - - Footpath

Facing away from the tracks, walk left through the parking lot and look for the big, yellow-brick building on your left when you come out onto the street. This large, well-staffed hostel offers spic-and-span bunks in 2- to 6-person rooms, all with bathroom and shower. **Internet** access in cafe €3 per hr.; ask for keycard at desk. Breakfast buffet and sheets included. Laundry €4.50. Free bike storage. Reception 7am-10pm. Lockout 10pm, open every half hr. until 2am. Checkout 10am. Dorms Apr.-Sept. €17; Oct.-Mar. €15. Oct.-Apr. €0.51 tax; May-Sept. €1.24. For 1- or 2-night stays, add €3. For singles add €7, for doubles €5. DC/MC/V. ❷

Pension Sonne, Kaiserstr. 8 (☎/fax 425 72; office@bbu.at; www.bbu.at). From the station, go right (facing the lake) on Bahnhofstr., then right on Kaiserstr. Quiet, spacious rooms with wood floors and a sink, conveniently located in the heart of the *Fußgängerzone*. The hallways' colorful rugs give the place an inviting atmosphere. Breakfast included. Reception 7:30am-10pm. Check-in after noon. Singles €28; doubles €52; triples €69; quads €81.4. Add €5-6 for rooms with private shower and toilet. MC/V. ❷

Pension Gunz, Anton-Schneider-Str. 38 (☎/fax 436 57), located 2 blocks behind the post office. This homey *Pension* and restaurant keeps tidy rooms, each with shower. Breakfast included. The restaurant serves fish caught fresh in the Bodensee, as well as daily *Menüs* for €5-10. Restaurant and reception 8am-6pm. Singles €28-31; doubles €54. No credit cards. ❷

FROM THE ROAD

DR.WANDERSTOCK: OR HOW I LEARNED TO STOP WORRYING AND LOVE THE STICK

As a veteran long distance runner and former Boy Scout, I have, at times, felt entitled to break the common sense rules of alpine hiking: I've hiked alone (and felt lonely); I've hiked on glaciers in the afternoon (and sank, getting snow in my underwear); I've hiked in thunderstorms (and made a lot of promises to God I can't possibly keep); I've hiked in sneakers (and turned my ankles). I have, in fact, done about two things right: I always carry a map (nothing can get you lost faster than a good map; on the other hand, nothing can get you un-lost faster than a good map) and I finally broke down and bought a walking stick.

I first saw the things used by an older couple, one in each hand, in the rolling hills outside of Bregenz. I thought perhaps they were ski poles and they were practicing for the winter. Then I saw a few hikers using them in the mountains, and figured they were primarily for older people who need an extra boost to make it up the paths. Then I saw people in their teens and 20s using them, and figured walking sticks were just cool accessories for weekend wanderers. Then I nearly fell off the Rotmoosferner glacier in Obergurgl and decided I needed one.

I bought a close-out, half-price walking stick for €15 and honestly couldn't tell the difference between mine and the model that sold for €50

Kaiser Hotel, Kaiserstr. 2, (☎52 980; fax 982; www.bbn.at/kaiser), slightly uphill from Pension Sonne. If you came to the Bodensee hoping to splurge, this is the place. Marble staircase, oil paintings, and personal attention—it's a hotel fit for a Kaiser. Shower, whirlpool bathtub, satellite TV, VCR, and minibar in each room. It also boasts one of the best cafe-bed ratios in all of Europe, with three different cafes open to the public. Six doubles (€108 Nov.-Apr., €126 May-Oct., €188 Festspiel); rates cheaper if you're staying alone (€65 Nov.-Apr., €80 May-Oct., €123 during Festspiel). ❹

Camping Lamm, Mehrerauerstr. 50-51 (☎71 701 or 745; fax 71 74 54), is 10min. past the youth hostel. Small, economical campground with adjoining restaurant/pension (useful in case of bad weather). Moderate traffic noise. Reception 8-10am, and 5-8pm, or inquire within restaurant. €3.50, ages 6-14 €1.50, tents €2.60-3.30, cars €2.60. ❶

🍴 FOOD

Markets fill up Kornmarktstr. Tuesdays and Fridays; farmer's market Saturday 8am-noon.

Zum Goldenen Hirschen, Kirchstr. 8 (☎428 15). Look for the restaurant with small stained-glass windows and a gold flying reindeer over the door near the *Fußgängerzone*. Dark furniture and a *Fachwerk*-style interior give this place an authentic feel. This building has been dishing up schweinenbraten, sauerkraut, and other hearty local favorites (€7-13), as well as brewing its own beer, for over 300 years. Vegetarian menu available. M and W-Su. Open 10am-midnight. AmEx/DC/MC/V. ❷

Ikaros, Deuringstr. 5 (☎529 54). Look for the blue-and-white-striped awning at the edge of Leutbühel in the *Fußgängerzone*. This exceptional cafe is a little taste of the Mediterranean on the Bodensee. A wide variety of Greek dishes, including lunch *Menüs* (€6 for appetizer and entree), salads, and main dishes (€4.20-7), are served indoors to Greek music or outdoors to the breeze. Open M-Sa 10am-1am. ❶

China Restaurant Da-Li, Anton-Schneider-Str. 34 (☎534 14), near Pension Gunz, serves typical Chinese fare. Stop by weekday afternoons for the *Mittagsmenü* with rice, spring roll, and main dish (€5), or the lunch buffet (€7) to neo-classical Chinese music and a plant-filled interior. Your reward for finishing your meal is a free shot of peach schnapps. Dishes €7-10. Open daily 11:30am-2:30pm and 5:30-11:30pm. MC/V. ❶

König Pizza und Kebap, Rathausstr. 6 (☎538 81), is open late, late, late. Serves some of the cheapest food in town in a squeaky-clean eatery with extensive bar options. Eat-in or take-out pizzas (€3.27-6), *Dönerkebaps* and veggie-*Kebaps* (€3-7). Open M-Th 11am-3am, F-Sa 10am-4am, Su 6pm-4am. ❶

Wirtshaus am See, Seepromenade 2 (422 10; fax 422 10-4 www.wirtshausamsee.at) Walking along the promenade between the harbor and the floating stage, one can't help notice the crowds under the canopy at the Wirtshaus. Serving a variety of Austrian specialties, like gulasch, it attracts a steady dinner crowd as well as those just interested in an ice cream or a beer and waiting for the rows of decorative lights to come on. With a little luck, you can hear the opera at the Seabühne. Open daily 5pm-midnight. V/MC. ❸

SB Restaurant (☎463 59, ext. 15) on the 1st floor of the big "GWL" mall building in the *Fußgängerzone.* If Austrian food makes you daydream about fresh vegetables, the self-serve salad and fruit/dessert bars (€0.90 per 100g) are a godsend. Cafeteria-style and grilled dishes €4-7. Open M-F 8:30am-5:30pm, Sa 8:30am-3pm. ❶ Below the restaurant is a **SPAR** supermarket if you'd rather buy in bulk. Open M-Th 8am-7pm, F 8am-7:30pm, Sa 8am-5pm.

◎ SIGHTS

On the hill above Bregenz looms the **Oberstadt,** or "high city," a once-fortified settlement that contains many of the city's oldest and most attractive buildings. A short hike up Maurachg. from the *Fußgängerzone* are the towering walls, beyond which lie rows of pastel-painted, wood-beamed houses, many hundreds of years old. Some of them have incorporated fragments of the old city walls in their construction; others have extensive rose gardens or are painted with murals. The major landmark of the Oberstadt is the wooden **Martinsturm,** dating from the 13th century, which supports Europe's largest onion dome. The 2nd and 3rd floors of the tower house the **Vorarlberg Militärmuseum,** which chronicles (in German) every war the Vorarlbergers ever fought (including the notorious German Farmer's war of 1525). The 3rd floor, overlooking the Bodensee and beyond, is not to be missed. (☎466 32. Open May to mid-Oct. M-Su 9am-6pm and sporadically in winter. €1, ages 6-14 €0.50.) Next to the tower is the **Martinskirche,** filled with frescoes dating back to the early 14th century. Particularly noteworthy are the depictions of St. Christopher, the Holy Symbol of Grief, and the 18th-century Stations of the Cross. Across Ehregutapl. (with the fountain) from the Martinsturm is **Deuring Schlößchen,** a 17th-century castle that houses a decidedly non-budget hotel.

more (though I'm sure the salesman could have enlightened me). Like most models, the height is adjustable and it collapses to about 18" in length, making it just slightly too long to fit in my pack. As it was explained to me, the correct height for a stick when hiking uphill or over level ground is high enough so that the elbow forms a 90° angle when you hold it in front of you. When descending, add an extra couple of inches, since you'll be reaching forward and down. I only use one stick but it's just as common to see hikers wielding one with both hands.

Does it work? It won't turn you into an *Übermensch,* but it will improve your balance and, especially in hiking uphill, it's nice to swing the stick to help set a cadence. If there is snow, mud, or loose rock on the path, you can prod at it a bit to see if it will hold your weight. A stick will not, however, prevent you from falling on your butt. In fact, the biggest drawback probably is that it will not prevent you from doing stupid stuff (see above) and may even encourage you to do so, since to the outside world you look like an expert. If nothing else, it comes in handy for fending off lovestruck mountain goats and bus drivers.

—Tom Miller

Shaded by overhanging trees and vines, Meißnersteige leads down from the corner of the castle to the bottom of the Oberstadt. Cross Thalbachg. and hike up Schloßbergstr. to reach **St. Gallus Pfarrkirche,** reputedly founded by medieval Irish missionaries, St. Gallus and St. Columban. The white-stucco sanctuary of the 11th-century church now glows with lavish gold ornamentation and a detailed ceiling fresco that dates from 1738. The shepherdess in the altar painting has the face of Maria Theresia, who donated 1500 guilders to the church in 1740. On the opposite side of the Oberstadt at the corner of Am Brand and Bergmannstr., the twin steeples of the imposing **Herz-Jesu Kirche** seem to breach the heavens. Built in 1907 and recently renovated in neo-Gothic style, the huge sanctuary's brick and wood furnishings bring out the Expressionist stained-glass windows.

Walking from the tourist office through the *Fußgängerzone* and away from the train station, you'll come across a large, imposing building covered with translucent gray tiles: the **Kunsthaus Bregenz.** The stark concrete interior, gleaming floor, and subdued lighting are slightly spooky, making this a perfect home for avant-garde exhibits of outlandish modern art. Exhibits rotate approximately every two months and range from installation art—one recent exhibit consisted of an indoor bog and boardwalk—to photographs by Jeff Koons and George & Gilbert. (☎ 48 59 40; fax 48 59 48. Open Tu-W and F-Su 10am-6pm, Th 10am-9pm. €5, students €3.50.)

☒ OUTDOOR ACTIVITIES

There's no better place to stretch your legs and check out the locals than the **Strandweg** and **Seepromenade,** which follow the curve of the Bodensee from one end of town to the other. All along the waterfront, groomed paths, rose gardens, and strategically placed ice-cream stands surround playgrounds, a mini-golf course, and a human-sized chess board. Several companies run **sightseeing cruises** on the Bodensee from the Bregenz Hafen (harbor), Seestr. 4 (☎ 428 68; fax 675 55 20; www.oebb.at), opposite the post office. Ferries run the 2½hr. length of the shimmering lake to the **Blumen Insel Mainau** (Mainau Flower Isle) on the German side, which features a Baroque castle and church, an indoor tropical palm house, a butterfly house, and gardens rife with orchids, tulips, dahlias, and 400 kinds of roses (Admission €6.50. Ferries leave Bregenz July-Aug. 8, at 9:10, 10:20 and 11:25am, return at 2:50, 4:15, and 4:30pm, round-trip and admission €33.20.) An alternative two hour cruise will take you to the **Zepplin Museum** in Friedrichshafen, former home base of round the world Zepplin flights, which provides a fascinating and well-designed look at an era when people thought large balloons filled with volatile gases were a good idea. Along with a (less flammable) mock-up of the Hindenberg's passenger cabin, it hosts a large exhibit of oil paintings and sculpture dating to the 15th century (admission €6.50). Boats leave at 8am and every 70min. following from Bregenz, except Mondays, June-Aug. (€16.80.) For would-be mariners who like to steer themselves, paddle-and motor-boat rentals are available from the "Bootsmeiten" stand near Wirtshaus am See, next to the harbor (10am to twilight; €11-18 per 30min.).

The **Pfänderbahn** cable car leaves the top of Schillerstr., uphill from the post office, and swings up the **Pfänder** mountain (1064m) for a panorama spanning from the Black Forest to Switzerland. (☎ 42 16 00; fax 42 16 04; www.pfaenderbahn.at. Every 30min. 9am-7pm. €5.50, round-trip €9.50. Discounts for seniors and children under 19.) At the top of Pfänderspitze (peak), walk the nature trails in the **Alpine Wildlife Park,** which pass enclosures housing native animals such as boars, mountain goats, and nervous-looking *Murmeltiere* (marmots). They're rightfully nervous, thanks to the heavily advertised **bird flight shows** (May-Oct. daily 11am, 2:30pm. €3.70, children under 16 €1.90), which send birds of prey swooping across the mountainside. If you bought a one-way ticket, the hike back to Bregenz is all downhill and takes a little over an hour.

🎵🎭 ENTERTAINMENT & NIGHTLIFE

The concrete monstrosity on the edge of the lake is not a ski ramp gone awry but rather Europe's largest **floating stage** and the centerpiece for the annual **Bregenzer Festspiele** (☎ 40 76; fax 40 74 00; ticket@bregenzerfestspiele.com; www.bregenzer-festspiele.com; or write to Postfach 311, A-6901 Bregenz). Every year from mid-July to mid-August, the Vienna Symphony Orchestra and other opera, theater, and chamber music groups come to town, bringing some 180,000 tourists with them. The main events are performances on the floating stage, drawing capacity crowds of 6800. In 2003, the floating opera will be Leonard Bernstein's "West Side Story," with German dialogue and English lyrics, premiering on July 17th and running until August 17th. "Das Schlaue Füchslein," a three-act opera by Leos Janacek, will be playing in the *Festspielhaus*, the other main venue, with the score performed by the **Vienna Symphony Orchestra.** Premiere July 16th; runs until Jul. 31. *Festspiele* tickets go on sale in October. Prices depend on the show. Floating stage *(See-bühne)* run €22-124; prices €10-20 higher F-Sa. For the *Festspielhaus*, €40-130. Concerts (depending on the orchestra) run €11-70. Students under 26 get 25% off, except for premieres. Weekday performances rarely sell out more than a few days before the show. Standing room tickets available.

There are several popular late-night student hangouts on and around Kirchstr. **Uwe's Bier-Bar,** Kirchstr. 25, is a popular bar with a young, lively crowd. (Beer €1.70-4. Open daily 7pm-1am, F-Sa until 2am.)

BREGENZERWALD

Spreading out to the south and east of Bregenz, the Bregenzerwald is home to many small towns and villages that preserve the rustic flavor of Vorarlberg's past. The villages are scattered through pastures and copses of pine trees, coddled by the steeply rising mountains, especially toward the southeast. Explore the Bregen-zerwald by taking daytrips into the region from Bregenz or Dornbirn, or by staying in any of the more charming, rural towns in the *Wald* itself.

✳️🚌 ORIENTATION AND TRANSPORTATION

Bundesstr. 200 heads generally southeast from Dornbirn with Egg and Au in its path. Public transportation in the Bregenzerwald is based around a regional net-work of **buses (Netz);** train service in the towns and villages of the Bregenzerwald is rather limited. A few buses to the region depart from lakeside Bregenz, but Dornbirn is a better transportation hub: it's a 15min. train ride from Bregenz, and bus lines lead from Dornbirn to most Bregenzerwald towns. A **Netzticket** allows you unlimited travel by bus and train throughout the Bregenzerwald for a given amount of time: 1 day €7.30, 1 week €14.50. For many single trips into the Bregen-zerwald, a **Tagesticket** (1-day ticket; €3) is the most economical option, but don't buy it unless you plan to take several bus rides in one day. Walking between towns in the Bregenzerwald is not difficult, and signs point the way, but be aware that walking between towns frequently entails strolling next to a road.

🏠 ACCOMMODATIONS

Staying in the Bregenzerwald on the cheap is possible in most small towns. Huts dot the mountains; their telephone numbers are available at the tourist office and in the *Kumpass* Bregenzerwald/Westallgäu map/handbook available at news-stands as well as in the booklet distributed by all Vorarlberg tourist offices.

VORARLBERG

DORNBIRN   ☎ 05572

Dornbirn (pop. 43,000), not actually in Bregenzerwald, is considerably larger and more industrial than its tiny woodland neighbors. It boasts a plethora of shops and cafes in the tiled *Fußgängerzone* and Marktpl. There are limited accommodations, but excellent bus and rail access make Dornbirn more attractive as a transportation hub to hiking in the Bregenzerwald.

🚆 **TRANSPORTATION.** **Trains** to: Bregenz (10-15min., 3-4 per hr. 5:28am-1:08am, €2); Feldkirch (20-30min., 2-3 per hr. 5:09am-12:18am, €3.30); Innsbruck (2¼hr., 7 per day 5:09am-9:52pm, €21.80); Lindau (20min., 11 per day 5:28am-7:07pm, €2.90); St. Anton am Arlberg (1hr., 7 per day 5:09am-9:52pm, €6.60). The station has **lockers** (€2) and **luggage storage** (€2.10; M-Sa 6:30am-8:50pm, Su 7:30am-9pm). Regional **buses** depart from the parking lot at the train station and across the street. Line #38 runs to Schwarzenberg (7:20am-7:35pm) and line #40 to Egg (7:02am-10:35pm). The hub for city buses in Dornbirn is on Riedg.; from the train station, head straight into Marktpl. and turn left onto Riedg. just past the church.

🔃 **PRACTICAL INFORMATION.** Exit the station and walk straight on Bahnhofstr. to reach the town center. The **tourist office,** Rathauspl. 1, is through Marktpl. and across Stadtstr., about 50m to the left. The tourist office has a list of accommodations pasted on the window and sells hiking maps for €3.20 and €5.74. (☎221 88; fax 312 33; www.tiscover.com/dornbirn. Open M-F 9am-noon and 1-6pm, Sa 9am-noon.) **Internet** access is at **Netgate,** on the way to the town center on Bahnhofstr., on the second floor of a shopping center on the left. (€0.08 per min. Open M-Fr 10-7pm.) An **ATM** is located at the post office and across from the tourist office at **Raiffeisenbank,** which also **exchanges currency** for about €2 per $100 (open M-Th 8am-noon and 2-3:30pm, F 8am-noon and 2-4:30pm). The **post office** with **currency exchange** is next to the train station. (Open M-F 8am-noon and 2-6pm; exchange closes at 5pm.) **Postal code:** A-6850.

🏠🍴 **ACCOMMODATIONS AND FOOD.** Most budget accommodations in Dornbirn are a fair distance from town. Try **Haus Ottowitz ❸,** Im Winkel 15. From Riedg., take bus #8 (dir: Messegelände) to "Bürglegasse," walk uphill, and turn left onto Im Winkel. Singles and doubles come at decent prices, with TV, balcony, and views of Dornbirn and the Bodensee beyond. (☎330 25; fax 33 02 54; angelika.ottowitz@vol.at. €20.50-23.70 per person, with discounts on longer stays.) If you'd rather be closer to Dornbirn, **Gasthof zum Grauen Bären ❹,** 17 Dr. Anton-Schneidierstr., offers affordable rooms and a crowd of regulars who down Mohrenbraus in the adjoining Biergartens only minutes away from the train station. From the train station turn left onto Dr. Anton-Schneiderstr. and follow it for 15 minutes. Or take the #3 bus to Eigenheim, then walk two minutes farther. It's a large, yellow building on the left side. (Breakfast included. All rooms with shower and TV. Singles €33; doubles €51.)

While *Menüs* are generally cheap and tasty, 🔲**Extrablatt ❷,** the self-proclaimed cafe-bar at 4 Bahnhofstr. (on the way to Marktpl.) has turned them into an art form, serving €6.25 entrees pleasing to the eye and taste buds long into the night. On Wednesdays carefully grilled pork fillets, stuffed with spinach and covered in a rich, creamy cheese sauce, share a plate with potato croquettes and herb-roasted zucchini; other *Menüs* include tuna steaks and Wienerschnitzel. For those craving pizza, the house pizza is positively crammed full of ham, pepperoni, corn, green peppers, and onions on a thin, chewy crust (€6.80). Sit with the lunchtime and late-night crowds on the geranium-laden terrace or sip on an elaborate mixed drink (€3.20-6.80) while listening to classic American rock in the dimly lit interior. (☎255 68.)

Open daily 8am-1am.) Shoppers, businessmen, and occasional packs of soccer hooligans all converge on **Cafe Steinhauser ❷** and its wicker chairs for a shaded lunch in the Marktpl. Light Italian fare carries the day—mozzarella and tomatoes covered in basil (€6.50) and stuffed zucchini (6.50) make attractive vegetarian options, while chicken Cordon Bleu and pork fillets satisfy carnivorous tastes. Open M-F 9am-midnight, Sa 1pm-midnight.) The huge **EuroSPAR** market, behind the church on Mozartstr., sells everything from bananas to flip-flops. (Open M-F 7am-7pm, Sa 7am-5pm.)

▥ **MUSEUMS.** The **Stadt Museum,** across from the church in the town center, has rotating exhibits on its first floor and historical artifacts on the floors above dating from 800 BC to the 20th century. (☎330 77; fax 77 50. Open Tu-Su 10am-noon and 2-5pm. €2.50, students and children €1.) Take city bus #6 to Gütle to get to the very heavily advertised and unfrequented **Rolls-Royce Museum,** which displays the world's largest exhibit of Rolls-Royce cars, engines, and memorabilia. A local man with a great deal of money to burn "collected" the cars over several decades, which explains what a Rolls is doing 1000km from Great Britain (☎526 52; fax 52 65 26; www.rolls-royce-museum.at. Open Apr.-Oct. Tu-Su 10am-6pm; Nov.-Mar. 10am-5pm. €8, students €4.80.)

◰ **HIKING.** Though Dornbirn itself is mostly devoid of tourist attractions, the hills and forest surrounding it are chock-full of great hiking trails. Be sure to pick up a map from the tourist office, as trails often cross over one another and it is easy to follow the wrong one. Maps also offer suggested routes, many of which leave from the Gütle bus stop (last stop on the #4 line).

For a pleasant view of the town and the valley all the way out to Lake Constance, hop on the cable car at the Karrenseilbahn stop on bus route #3. It runs 9am-11pm in the summer (round-trip €8, children €4.50), depositing riders 1km above sea level. From there, numerous hikes spread out over the countryside—a nature trail (1hr.) begins next to the exit. A particularly nice hike circumnavigates the neighboring peak of Staufenberg, offering views of the mountains and waterfalls from the shade of a pine forest and steps carved into the mountainside. The highlight is crossing the cow pasture near Schuttanen. Hundreds of the curious creatures will stop chewing to stare at you and may start to follow you (American GIs in France had similar problems). They're mainly docile but happen to weigh three times as much as you do, so be polite. (2½hr.) From Karren, follow signs to Kuhberg (10min.), then to Staufenberg and Schuttanen. Exit the pasture through the turnstile, then keep right and follow signs to the Karrenseilbahn. (Moderate.)

SCHWARZENBERG ☎05512

You'll get the impression that not much has changed in Schwartzenberg (pop. 1,700) in the last quarter millennium. Tucked away in meadows surrounded by a ring of mountains, it exemplifies the charms of the Bregenzerwald. Appearing to be clad in pine-colored fish-scale armor, many of the houses are made entirely out of wood from the nearby forests using techniques that are centuries old.

▣◳ **TRANSPORT AND PRACTICAL INFORMATION.** Bus #38 (2 per hr. 7:20am-7:35pm, €2.70) and bus #40 (1-2 per hr. 7:02am-10:35pm, €2.70) both run from Dornbirn. Follow the main road downhill from the church and take the first right to the **tourist office,** which dispenses maps for hikes in and around Schwarzenberg. (☎35 70; fax 29 02. Open M-F 9am-7pm, Sa 10am-noon.) The **Raiffeisenbank,** uphill toward the Heimatsmuseum, has an **ATM.** (Open M, W, F 9am-noon and 3pm-6pm; Tu, Th 9am-noon; Sa 8am-noon) A **post office** with **currency exchange** is near the church. (Open M-F 8am-noon and 1:30-5:30pm; exchange closes at 5pm.) **Postal code:** A-6867.

┌┐ ACCOMMODATIONS AND FOOD. There are dozens of wooden guest houses in Schwarzenberg and the outlying regions. The tourist office can find inexpensive private accommodations. **Haus Feuerstein ❸,** Hof 20, behind the church near the town square, provides five clean doubles and a hearty breakfast in one of the town's older houses. (☎20 39. €20-25 per person. €5.81 surcharge per night for 1-2-night stays and for singles.) For a warm meal, head 50m downhill from the town square to **Mesner Stüble ❷,** with petunias in the window-boxes and tasty Gasthof-style dishes from €6.54-10.54. (☎20 02. Open Dec.-Oct. M-Sa 3pm-midnight, Su 10am-midnight.) Stock up on groceries at the local **SPAR,** downhill from the town square. (Open M-Th 7am-noon and 2:30-6pm, F 7am-6pm, Sa 7am-noon.)

◉ ⚐ SIGHTS AND OUTDOOR ACTIVITIES. The **Pfarrkirche** is an airy church with wrought iron gravestones, unstained carved wood columns, and an altar painting by the town's most famous (sometime) resident, Angelika Kauffmann (1741-1807). Kauffmann was one of the few wealthy female painters of her age, and her work received great acclaim in England and Italy. The **Angelika Kauffmann Museum** (formerly the **Heimatmuseum**), a 300-year-old wooden lodge a few minutes up the main road, houses a small collection of her paintings and memorabilia, as well as rooms displaying woodworking tools and some wildly inflated currency from the Weimar Republic. (☎29 67 or 20 84. Open May-Sept. Tu, Th, and Sa-Su 2-4pm; Oct. Tu and Sa 2-4pm. €2.50, ages 6-14 €0.70.) This year Schwarzenberg will host its eleventh annual **Schubertiade,** a celebration of the composer's works and the creative spirit of local talents (June 7-22 and Aug. 22-Sept. 7, 2003). During the festival, there is at least one performance each night, ranging from chamber concerts to literature readings by Schwartzenberg poets. Purchase tickets at the Angelika-Kauffmann Saal near the tourist office on the day of the events, or in advance. (☎(05576) 729 01; fax 754 50; info@schubertiade.at; www.schubertiade.at.)

Signs in the town center, across from the church, point the way to a variety of well-marked hikes and walks. If you have 3hr. to spare, try the easy-to-moderate loop up to the **Lustenauer Hütte.** When you come to the hillside town of Klausberg, bear right at each fork in the dirt road, and you'll be at the hut within 25min. From there, continue on the other well-marked side of the loop back to Schwarzenberg.

SALZBURGER LAND

The Salzburger Land derives its name from the German *Salz* (salt), and it was this "white gold" that drew Roman Emperor Claudius's attention to the region in the first century, inciting him to unite it for the first time. Although tourism displaced the salt trade long ago, images of St. Barbara, the patron saint of miners, are everywhere. The province itself encompasses a section of the shining lakes and rolling hills of the Salzkammergut, where Hallstatt is among the more enticing destinations. Though mostly in the province of Upper Austria, the Salzkammergut it is accessible primarily through Salzburg.

HIGHLIGHTS OF SALZBURGER LAND

Satiate your sweet tooth with **Mozartkugeln** (see p. 206).
Hobnob with upper echelon musicians at the **Salzburg Festspiele** (see p. 215).
Get in touch with your animal instincts at the **Hellbrunn Zoo** (see p. 218).

SALZBURG   ☎ 0662

Wedged between mountains and graced with Baroque wonders from its position as the ecclesiastical center of Austria, Salzburg offers both spectacular sights and a rich musical culture. Whether it's tourists singing songs, street musicians playing medieval ballads, or a famed soprano bringing the house down with the "Queen of the Night" aria, Salzburg resonates with sound. The city's adulation for homegrown genius Mozart and the arts in general reaches a dizzying climax every summer during the *Salzburger Festspiele* (music festival; p. 245), when wealthy admirers the world over come to pay their respects to the musical elite. The *Festspiele* last for five weeks, during which time hundreds of operas, concerts, plays, and open-air performances dazzle the fawning fans. Salzburg's appeal comes not only from its architectural aesthetics, but also from its deserved reputation as a impeccably clean and very safe city, making it a venerable destination for any tourist—never mind that both Mozart and the von Trapps eventually left.

✈ INTERCITY TRANSPORTATION

Flights: Flughafen Salzburg (☎ 858 00; www.salzburg-airport.com), 4km west of the city center, with frequent connections to **Amsterdam, Innsbruck, Paris, Vienna,** and other major European cities. It is considerably cheaper, however, to fly into **Munich** (see p. 537) and take the train from there. If you do fly into or out of Salzburg, bus #77 (dir: Bahnhof from the airport, Walserfeld from the train station) circles between the train station and the airport (15min., every 15-30min. 5:32am-11pm, €1.60). A taxi from the airport to the train station should cost roughly €11.

Trains: There are 2 train stations in Salzburg; the main passenger hub, the **Hauptbahnhof** on Südtirolerpl., is the 1st Salzburg stop for trains coming from Vienna, while the Salzburg Süd Bahnhof (the 1st stop when coming from Innsbruck) is primarily a cargo station, so don't get off there. Trains from Hauptbahnhof to: **Graz** (4hr., every 2hr. 5:20am-5:13pm, €33.40); **Innsbruck** (2hr., every 2hr. 12:39am-9:19pm, €27.60); **Klagenfurt** (3hr., 7 per day, €26.10); **Munich** (2hr., 27 per day 4:08am-11:35pm, €21.60); **Vienna** (3½hr., 29 per day 2:18am-9:32pm, €33.40); **Zell am See** (1½-2hr., 17 per day 4:48am-10:35pm, €14.80); **Zurich** (6hr., 3 per day, €64.40). For reservations dial ☎ 05 17 17. Regular ticket office open 24hr.

Buses: Leave from the bus depot in front of the train station. Get information at the *Reisebüro am Bahnhof* in the train station (☎05 17 17, 8am-noon and 1-6pm daily). BundesBuses to **Mondsee** (1hr., every hr. 6:35am-8:40pm, €4.50); **St. Wolfgang** (1½hr., every hr. 5:50am-7:15pm, €6.70); **Bad Ischl** (1½-2hr., every hr. 5:50am-9:15pm, €7.40); and throughout Salzburger Land.

By car: From Vienna, exit at any of the Salzburg-West exits off Autobahn A1. Among these, the Salzburg-Nord exit is near Itzling and Kasern, and the Salzburg-Süd exit lies south of the city near Schloß Hellbrunn and Untersberg. A8 and E52 lead from the west into Rosenheim and then branch off to Munich and Innsbruck. A10 heads north from Hallein to Salzburg. From the Salzkammergut area, take Grazer Bundesstr. #158. Since public transportation is efficient within the city limits, consider the **Park and Ride** parking lots—park for free when you get off the highway and take the bus into town. The most convenient lot is **Alpensiedlung Süd** on Alpenstr. (exit: Salzburg-Süd), but a bigger lot is open July-Aug. at the **Salzburger Ausstellungszentrum** (exit: Salzburg-Mitte).

✦ ORIENTATION

Salzburg, just a few kilometers from the German border, covers both banks of the **Salzach River.** Two of Salzburg's three hills loom on the skyline near the river: the

Mönchsberg over the **Altstadt** (old city) on the south side and the **Kapuzinerberg** by the **Neustadt** (new city) on the north side. The Hauptbahnhof is on the northern side of town beyond the Neustadt; buses #1, 5, 6, 51, and 55 connect it to downtown. From the bus, disembark at "Mirabellplatz" in the Neustadt or "Mozartsteg," a footbridge that leads to Mozartpl. in the Altstadt. On foot, from the train station to the Neustadt, turn left out of the station onto Rainerstr. and follow it all the way (under the tunnel) to Mirabellpl.

⊟ LOCAL TRANSPORTATION

Public Transportation: Get information at the **Lokalbahnhof** (☎44 80 61 66), next to the train station. 20 bus lines cut through the city, with central hubs at Hanuschpl. by Makartsteg, Äußerer Stein by Mozartsteg, and the Hauptbahnhof. Single tickets (€1.60) are available at machines or from the drivers; books of 5 (€6.50) are available at *Tabak* (newsstand/tobacco shops) and at the Lokalbahnhof ticket office. *Tageskarte* (€2.90) or *Wochenkarte* (€9) allow travel on buses within the city for a full day or week, and are available at machines, the ticket office, or *Tabak*. Punch your ticket to validate it when you board, or pay a €36 fine. Buses make their last run from downtown to outer destinations at 10:30-11:30pm, earlier for less-frequented routes. Check the schedule posted at stops. **BusTaxi** fills in when the public buses stop running. Meet it at the stop at Hanuschpl. or Theaterg. and tell the driver your destination. S-Th 11:30pm-1:30am, F-Sat 11:30pm-3am. €2.54 for anywhere within the city limits.

Parking: Consider the "Park and Ride" option (see **By car,** above). Otherwise, try 24hr. **Altstadt-Garage** inside the Mönchsberg (€2.40 per hr., €14 per day); **Mirabell-Garage** in Mirabellpl. (open 7am-midnight; €3.20 per hr., €15 per day); or **Parkgarage Linzergasse** at Glockeng. off Linzerg. (open to midnight; €1.80 per hr., €14.40 per day). Other lots are at the airport, Hellbrunn, and Hauptbahnhof. Blue lines on the sidewalk indicate parking is available; buy a ticket for the space from one of the nearby automated machines.

Taxis: (☎81 11). Stands at Hanuschpl., Residenzpl., and the train station.

Car Rental: Avis, Ferdinand-Porsche-Str. 7 (☎87 72 78; fax 88 02 35).

Bike Rental: Top Bike Salzburg, (☎062 72 or 45 56; info@topbike.at; www.topbike.at). at the train station and the Staatsbrücke. €13 per day, €41 per week, 20% off at the train station with valid train ticket. Open May-Jun and Sept. daily 10am-5pm, July-Aug daily 9am-7pm, except in bad weather.

Hitchhiking: While *Let's Go* does not recommend hitching, hitchers headed to Innsbruck, Munich, or Italy have been seen on bus #77 to the German border. Those bound for Vienna have been known to take bus #29 (dir: Forellenwegsiedlung) to the Autobahn at "Schmiedlingerstr." or #15 (dir: Bergheim) to the Autobahn at "Grüner Wald."

⚄ PRACTICAL INFORMATION

TOURIST AND FINANCIAL SERVICES

Tourist Office, Mozartpl. 5 (☎88 98 73 30; fax 889 87 32; tourist@salzburg.or.at; www.salzburg.info.or.at), in the Altstadt. From the train station, take bus #5, 6, 51, or 55 to "Mozartsteg," head away from the river and curve to your right around the building into Mozartpl. On foot from the train station, turn left on Rainerstr., go to the end, cross Staatsbrücke, and continue along the river's south bank upstream to Mozartsteg (20min.). The office has free hotel maps and the **Salzburg Card** (see p. 239). The staff will tell you which hostels have available rooms. Reservation service is €2.18, for 3 or more people €4.40, plus a 12% deposit deductible from the 1st night's stay. There are

SALZBURGER LAND

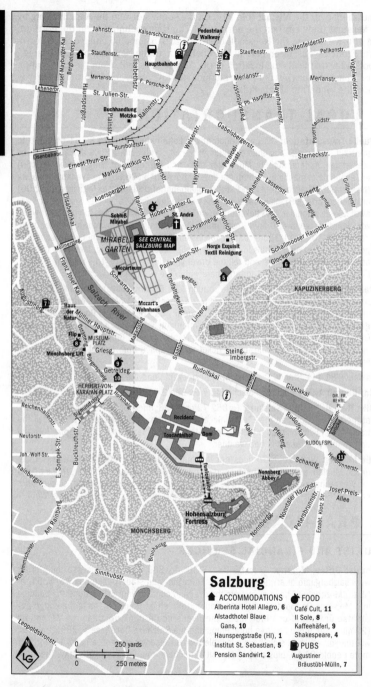

Jahnstr.

Kaiserschützenstr.

Pedestrian Walkway

Stauffenstr.

Breitenfelderstr.

Pelikonstr.

Bergheimerstr.

Josef-Mayburger-Kai

Stauffenstr.

Lastenstr.

1

Hauptbahnhof

2

Merianstr.

Merianstr.

Mertenstr.

F. Porsche-Str.

Ph. Harpfstr.

Bayerhamerstr.

St. Julien-Str.

Paracelsusstr.

Haunspergstr.

Elisabethstr.

Rainerstr.

Plainstr.

Buchhandlung Motzko

Sterneckstr.

Humboldtstr.

Gabelsbergerstr.

Pauernfeindstr.

Eisenbahnbr.

Ernest-Thun-Str.

Weiserstr.

Paracelsusstr.

Vogelweiderstr.

Markus Sittikus-Str.

Faberstr.

Haydnstr.

Steinhauserstr.

Lasserstr.

Rupertg.

Arnog.

Virgilg.

Grillparzerstr.

Auerspergstr.

Franz-Joseph-Str.

Wolf-Dietrich-Str.

Auerspergstr.

4

Hubert-Sattler-G.

St. Andrä

Schranneng.

Schallmooser Hauptstr.

Schloß Mirabell

MIRABELL-GARTEN

SEE CENTRAL SALZBURG MAP

Paris-Lodron-Str.

Dreifaltigkeitsg.

Norge Exquisit Textil Reinigung

Glockeng.

6

Mozarteum

Bergstr.

5

KAPUZINERBERG

Schwarzstr.

Linzerg.

7

Haus der Natur

Mozart's Wohnhaus

Müllner Hauptstr.

Steing.

Imbergstr.

Flip

8

MUSEUM-PLATZ

Griesg.

Gstätteng.

Bürgerspitalg.

Mönchsberg Lift

9

Getreideg.

10

Rudolfskai

i

HERBERT-VON-KARAJAN-PLATZ

Sigmundsplatz

Hofstallg.

Reichenhalerstr.

Neutorstr.

Buckirreuthstr.

Residenz

Toscaninihof

Dom

Kaig.

Pfeilerg.

Rudolfskai

DR. FR. REHRL PL.

RUDOLFSPL.

Joh.-Wolf-Str.

E. Sompek-Str.

Herbrunnerstr.

Rainbergstr.

Am Rainberg

Schanzig.

11

Nonnberg Abbey

Josef-Preis-Allee

funicular

Hohensalzburg Fortress

Nonnbergg.

Nonntaler Hauptstr.

Petersbrunnstr.

Erzabt. Klotz Str.

MÖNCHSBERG

Bruhausg.

Schwimmschulstr.

Sinnhubstr.

Leopoldskronstr.

N

0   250 yards

0   250 meters

Salzburg

🏠 **ACCOMMODATIONS**
Alberinta Hotel Allegro, **6**
Alstadthotel Blaue Gans, **10**
Haunspergstraße (HI), **1**
Institut St. Sebastian, **5**
Pension Sandwirt, **2**

🍴 **FOOD**
Café Cult, **11**
Il Sole, **8**
Kaffeehäferl, **9**
Shakespeare, **4**

🍺 **PUBS**
Augustiner Bräustübl-Mülln, **7**

also guided tours of the city that leave from the tourist office daily at 12:15pm (€8, in German and English). Open daily 9am-6pm. There are other **branches** at the **train station** platform #2a (☎88 98 73 40; open M-Sa 9:15am-8pm), and the Alpensiedlung Süd **"Park and Ride" lot** (☎88 98 73 60; open Easter to early Nov.).

Consulates: South Africa, Buchenweg 14 A-5061 Elsbethen-Glasenbach (☎/fax 62 20 35; dr.r.möbius@elsnet.at; www.srep.südafrika). Open M-Th 3-5:30 pm. **UK,** Alter Markt 4 (☎84 81 33; fax 84 55 63). Open M-F 9am-11:30am. **US,** Alter Markt 1/3 (☎84 87 76; fax 84 97 77), in the Altstadt. Open M, W, and Th 9am-noon.

Currency Exchange: Banks offer better rates for cash than AmEx offices but often charge higher commissions. Banking hours M-F 8am-12:30pm and 2-4:30pm. **Rieger Bank,** Alter Markt 15, has extended exchange hours. Open daily 10am-2:30pm and 3-8pm. The train station's exchange is open 7am-9pm. **Panorama Tours** offers bank rates with no commission; available only to guests taking their tour (see p. 243).

American Express: Mozartpl. 5, A-5020 (☎80 80; fax 808 01 78), near the tourist office. Provides all banking services and charges no commission on AmEx cheques. Holds mail for cheque- or card-holders, books tours. Open M-F 9am-5:30pm, Sa 9am-noon (only for money/traveler's cheque exchange).

LOCAL SERVICES

Luggage Storage: At the train station. Small lockers €2, medium €2.50, large €3.50.

Bookstores: Buchhandlung Motzko (Platz der Bucher), has 2 stores with English-language sections. Elisabethstr. 1 (☎883 31 10), near the train station, has a shelf of English books. Kaig. 11 (☎88 33 11 50), in the Altstadt, has more travel-oriented offerings. Both stores open M-F 9am-6:30pm, Sa 9am-5pm.

Bi-Gay-Lesbian Organizations: Homosexual Initiative of Salzburg (HOSI), Müllner Hauptstr. 11 (☎43 59 27; www.hosi.at), hosts regular workshops and meetings, including a **Café-bar** open from 7, F and S from 8. Other resources include a library and a transgender group.

Laundromat: Norge Exquisit Textil Reinigung, Paris-Lodronstr. 16 (☎87 63 81), on the corner of Wolf-Dietrich-Str. Self-serve wash and dry €9 (including their soap, which patrons must use); open M-F 7:30am-4pm, Sa 8-10am. Full-serve €14.20; clothes ready by 5pm if you bring them in early in the morning, otherwise pick them up the next day. Open M-F 7:30am-6pm, Sa 8am-noon.

Public Toilets: In the Festungsbahn lobby, the Hanuschpl. fish market., and the Altstadt under the archway between Kapitelpl. and Dompl. Although these restrooms are free, it is polite to tip the attendant.

EMERGENCIES AND COMMUNICATIONS

Emergencies: Police, ☎133. Headquarters at Alpenstr. 90 (non-emergency ☎63 83). **Ambulance,** ☎144. **Fire,** ☎122.

Rape Hotline: Frauennotruf (☎88 11 00), lines open M-Tu, 9-11 am.

AIDS Hotline: AIDS-Hilfe Salzburg, Gabelsburgerstr. 20 (☎88 14 88).

Women's Emergencies: Frauenhilfe Salzburg (☎84 09 00), lines open M-F 9am-5pm; ☎43 27 16 or 43 51 28 after hours.

Pharmacies: Elisabeth-Apotheke, Elisabethstr. 1a (☎87 14 84; fax 87 14 84-4), a few blocks south of the train station. Pharmacies in the city center are open M-F 8am-6pm, Sa 8am-noon; outside the center M-F 8am-12:30pm and 2:30-6pm, Sa 8am-noon. There are always 3 pharmacies open; check the door of any closed pharmacy.

Medical Assistance: call the hospital, **St. Johnnspital Landeskrankenanstalten Salzburg,** Müllner Hauptstr. 48 (☎44 820; fax 4482 2020; a.burger@lks.at); or call the **Ärzte Bereitschaftsdienst,** Dr. Franz-Renner-Str. 7 (☎141) F 7pm to M 7am.

Internet Access:

Internet Café, Mozartpl. 5 (☎84 48 22). €0.15 per minute. Open Sept.-June daily 9am-11pm, July-Aug. 9am-midnight.

BIGnet.cafe, Judeng. 5-7(☎84 14 70). 10min. €1.50, 30min. €3.20, and 1hr. €5.90. Snack bar, funky music, and a total of 33 workstations make for great surfing. Open daily 9am-10pm.

Piterfun Internetc@fe, Ferdinand-Porsche-Str. 7 (office@piterfun.at). 15min. €1.80, 30min. €2.90, 60min. €5. Bright colors and loud techno give a rave ambiance. Directly across from the train station. Open daily 10am-10pm.

Post Office: At the Hauptbahnhof (☎88 30 30). Address *Poste Restante* to *Postlagernde Briefe,* Bahnhofspostamt, **A-5020** Salzburg. Open M-F 7am-8:30pm (counter closes at 6pm), Sa 8am-2pm, Su 1-6pm.

♜ ACCOMMODATIONS

Salzburg has a plethora of hostels to host the multitude of tourists that pass through yearly. Most affordable accommodations are on the outskirts of town, easily accessible by local transportation. Ask for the tourist office's list of **private rooms** or the *Hotel Plan* for information on hostels. From mid-May to mid-September, hostels fill by mid-afternoon—call ahead. During the *Festspiele,* hotels fill months in advance, and most hostels and *Gästehäuser* are full days before. At HI hostels there is a €3 surcharge for non-members.

HOSTELS AND DORMITORIES

Stadtalm, Mönchsberg 19c (☎84 17 29; www.stadtalm.com), towers over the Altstadt from atop the Mönchsberg. Take bus #1 (dir: Maxglan) to "Mönchsbergaufzug," then walk down the street a few steps and through the stone arch on the left to the Mönchsberglift (elevator), which takes you to the top of the mountain (9am-11pm; one-way €1.50, round-trip €2.40). At its summit, turn right, climb the steps, and follow signs for "Stadtalm." Or climb the stairs in Toscaninihof after the end of Wiener-Philharmoniker-G., turn right at the top, and look for the "Stadtalm" sign. Get a princely view on a pauper's budget at the most scenic hostel in Salzburg. Holds 26 in small 2- to 6-bed rooms (including a room in the tower), so reserve ahead. Breakfast included. Showers €0.80 per 4min. Sinks in rooms. Reception 9am-9pm. Curfew 1am. Open April-Sept. Dorms €12.50. AmEx/DC/MC/V. ❷

Institut St. Sebastian, Linzerg. 41 (☎87 13 86; fax 87 13 86 85; office@st-sebastian-salzburg.at; www.st-sebastian.at). From the station, take bus #1, 5, 6, 51, or 55 to Mirabellpl. Cross the street and continue in same direction. Turn left onto Bergstr. and left at the end onto Linzerg. The hostel is through the arch on the left before the church. Smack in the middle of the Neustadt on the St. Sebastian church grounds, the buildings are dorms for female students during the school year but accept travelers of either gender year-round. Rooftop terrace with postcard views of the city. Breakfast, kitchen, and lockers included. Laundry €2.90, €3.60 with soap. Reception 8am-noon and 4-9pm. No curfew. Dorms €15, sheets €17; singles €21, with shower €33; doubles €40/€54; triples €60/€69; quads €72/€84. MC/V with €18 per person minimum. ❸

International Youth Hotel (YoHo), Paracelsusstr. 9 (☎87 96 49 or 834 60; fax 87 88 10; www.yoho.at), off Franz-Josef-Str. Exit the train station to the left down Rainerstr.

---

and turn left onto Gabelsbergerstr. through the tunnel. Take the 2nd right onto Paracelsusstr. (7min.). *The Sound of Music* screens daily at 10:30am at the request of tourists. Filled with beer-sipping postcard writers in a frat-party atmosphere, this hostel is a no-frills place to crash. There are no room keys for dorm rooms—lockers in the hall for €0.10-€1. Happy Hour in bar 6-7pm with .5L Stiegl €1.5, other brews €2.50. Breakfast €3-4. Dinner entrees (including veggie options) €5-6. Sheets €5 deposit. Front door locks at 1am, but you can ring the bell anytime. 6-8 bed dorms €14; 4-bed dorms €16; 2-bed dorms €19. ❸

Haunspergstraße (HI), Haunspergstr. 27 (☎87 96 49; fax 88 34 77; office@yoho.at), near the train station. Walk out Kaiserschützenstr., which becomes Jahnstr. Take the 3rd left onto Haunspergstr. and walk one block to the hostel. It will be on the right-hand side on the corner of Stauffernstr. This student dorm becomes a hostel July and August. Houses 90 in surprisingly spacious 2- to 4-bed rooms. Breakfast, shower, and sheets included. All rooms have either a private shower or share it with 1 other room. All guests must leave €10 or other sufficient collateral to obtain their key (including a house key to the main door). Reception 7am-2pm and 5pm-midnight. Open July-Aug. 3. 4-person dorms €14.50; singles €19. MC/V. ❷

Eduard-Heinrich-Haus (HI), Eduard-Heinrich-Str. 2 (☎62 59 76; fax 62 79 80; hostel.eduard-heinrich@salzburg.co.at). Take bus #51 (dir: Salzburg-Süd) to "Polizeidirektion." Cross over Alpenstr., then continue down Billrothstr., turn left on Robert-Stolz-Promenade footpath, walk 200m, and take 1st right; the hostel is the big pink and yellow building up the driveway on the left. Near Salzach Forest with enormous 6- and 7-bed rooms and leather couches in the hallways. Breakfast, lockers, and showers included. **Internet** access: 20min. €2.54, 40min. €4.36, 75min. €7.27. Reception 7-10am and 5-11pm. Lockout 10am-5pm. No curfew, but ask about key deposit. Dorms €14.23; singles €18.59; doubles €36.18; triples €49.23; quads €65.64. ❸

Aigen (HI), Aignerstr. 34 (☎62 32 48; fax 232 48 4; hostel.aigen@salzburg.co.at). From the station, bus #6 or 51 to "Mozartsteg.," then bus #49 (dir: Josef-Käut-Str.) to "Finanzamt" and walk 5min. in the same direction as the bus. It's on the right behind the hedges. Large hostel with clean, large, and simple 2-, 4-, and 6-bed dorms. Breakfast, showers, lockers, and sheets included. Reception 7-10am and 5-11pm. No curfew. Dorms €22.95; singles €27.31. ❸

PRIVATZIMMER AND PENSIONEN

Privatzimmer and *Pension* accommodations in the center of the city can be quite expensive, but better quality and lower prices await on the outskirts, minutes from downtown Salzburg by train. Rooms on **Kasern Berg** are officially out of Salzburg, which means the tourist office can't recommend them, but the personable hosts and bargain prices make these *Privatzimmer* a terrific housing option. These are people's homes, so be on your best behavior. All northbound regional trains run to Kasern Berg (generally 4min.; every 30min. 6:17am-11:17pm; €1.60, Wochenkarte and Eurail valid). Get off at the first stop, "Salzburg-Maria Plain," and take the only road uphill. All the Kasern Berg Pensionen are along this road, whose position on a hill above the city affords marvelous views of the valley below. Alternatively, take bus #15 (dir: Bergheim) from Mirabellpl. to "Kasern," then continue straight up Söllheimerstr. and follow Wickenburgallee up the mountain (15min.). By car, exit A1 on "Salzburg Nord."

📓 **Haus Lindner,** Panoramaweg 5 (☎/fax 45 66 81; www.HouseLindner.at). In her charming house at the top of the hill, friendly owner Matilda offers homey rooms, some with balconies for mountain views. The entire house is warmly decorated, with lots of flowers, vases, and statuettes. Unlimited breakfast served on a sunny terrace and in a room with satellite TV, available for guests' use during the day. Capacity of 15 people

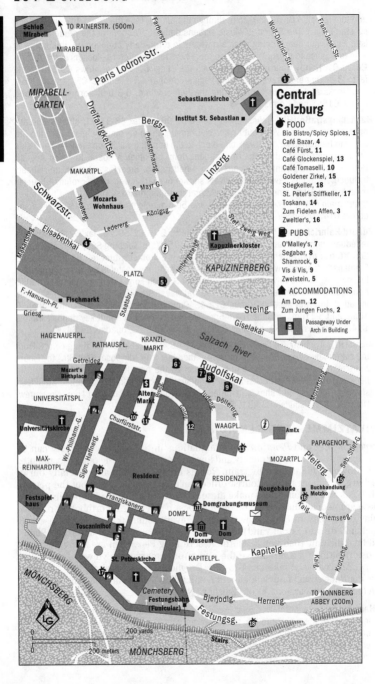

SALZBURGER LAND

TO RAINERSTR. (500m)

Schloß Mirabell

MIRABELLPL.

Paris Lodron-Str.

MIRABELL-GARTEN

Dreifaltigkeitsg.

Bergstr.

Sebastianskirche

Institut St. Sebastian

Schwarzstr.

MAKARTPL.

Theaterg.

Mozarts Wohnhaus

R. Mayr G.

Königsg.

Ledererg.

Elisabethkai

Makartsteg

Kapuzinerkloster

KAPUZINERBERG

PLATZL

F.-Hanusch-Pl.

Fischmarkt

Griesg.

HAGENAUERPL.

RATHAUSPL.

KRANZL-MARKT

Getreideg.

Steing.

Giselakai

Salzach River

Rudolfskai

Mozart's Birthplace

UNIVERSITÄTSPL.

Alter Markt

Churfürststr.

Universitätskirche

Wr.-Philharm.-G.

Sigm. Haffnerg.

MAX-REINHARDTPL.

Residenz

WAAGPL.

AmEx

PAPAGENOPL.

MOZARTPL.

RESIDENZPL.

Neugebäude

Buchhandlung Motzko

Festspielhaus

Franziskanerg.

DOMPL.

Domgrabungsmuseum

Kaig.

Chiemseeg.

Toscaninihof

Dom Museum

Dom

Kapitelg.

St. Peterskirche

KAPITELPL.

MÖNCHSBERG

Cemetery

Festungsbahn (Funicular)

Bjerjodlg.

Herreng.

TO NONNBERG ABBEY (200m)

Festungsg.

Stairs

MÖNCHSBERG

0 — 200 yards
0 — 200 meters

Central Salzburg

FOOD
Bio Bistro/Spicy Spices, **1**
Café Bazar, **4**
Café Fürst, **11**
Café Glockenspiel, **13**
Café Tomaselli, **10**
Goldener Zirkel, **15**
Stiegkeller, **18**
St. Peter's Stiffkeller, **17**
Toskana, **14**
Zum Fidelen Affen, **3**
Zweitler's, **16**

PUBS
O'Malley's, **7**
Segabar, **8**
Shamrock, **6**
Vis á Vis, **9**
Zweistein, **5**

ACCOMMODATIONS
Am Dom, **12**
Zum Jungen Fuchs, **2**

Passageway Under Arch in Building

makes it biggest of Kasern Berg. Matilda will pick you up from the station. Families welcome. €14-15 per person. ❷

Haus Moser, Turnerbühel 1 (☎45 66 76). Climb up the steep hidden stairs on the right side of Kasern Berg road across from Germana Kapeller. If you have a heavy backpack, try the driveway entrance at beginning of Kasern Berg road. Charming, elderly couple offers comfortable rooms in this cozy dark-timbered home. 2 rooms have balconies. Free drinks, unlimited breakfast, shower, and laundry included. Call for pick-up at the train station. €14 for one night, €13.50 for longer stays. ❷

Haus Christine, Panoramaweg 3 (☎/fax 45 67 73; haus.christine@gmx.at). Head five minutes up the road from the train station, and take a left at the top of the hill at the sign. Haus Christine has spacious rooms with a country motif. Friendly family atmosphere and lots of antlers. Generous breakfast (cheese, sausage, Nutella, homemade jam, eggs) included, served on glass-enclosed patio overlooking the countryside. €14-15 per person. MC/V. ❷

Germana Kapeller, Kasern Bergstr. 64 (☎45 66 71). Lively, funny hostess Germana speaks English well and maintains traditional rooms with pleasant, vibrant colors. Some rooms have hand-carved furniture, and others have balconies. Breakfast and showers included. *Sound of Music* screenings for the truly compulsive, and 2 terraces overlooking the valley. €15 per person. No credit cards. ❷

Haus Seigmann, Kasern Bergstr. 66 (☎45 00 01). Clean rooms, some with balconies overlooking the valley, as well as 2 patios on the hillside. Relax on the lounge chairs outside, in the TV room downstairs, or curled up in bed under a delightfully snug comforter. Breakfast included. About €15 per person (negotiable). No credit cards. ❷

The following *Privatzimmer* are on the southern edge of Salzburg, but are easily accessible by car and by public transportation. Take bus #1 to "Hanuschpl.," then bus #60 heading south. For House Ballwein, get off at "Gsengerweg" and for House Bankammer get off at the next stop, "Marienbad."

Haus Ballwein, Moostr. 69a (☎/fax 82 40 29; haus.ballwein@gmx.net). Huge, spotless rooms looking out onto quiet fields and distant mountains, a perfect reprieve from city life. Breakfast room with teapot collection hanging from ceiling. Rooms come with shower (in the hall for singles) and cable TV. Bicycle rental €5 per day. Singles €22; doubles €38-50. ❸

Haus Bankhammer, Moostr. 77 (☎/fax 83 00 67; helga.bankhammer@telering.at). This farmhouse in southern Salzburg has lovely rooms with carved wooden beds and armoires. Doubles with bath. Breakfast of homemade strawberry-rhubarb jam and fresh milk from the family dairy included. Helga speaks English fluently and will happily do laundry for guests. Rooms €19-23 per person. MC/V. ❸

Haus Elisabeth, Rauchenbichlerstr. 18 (☎/fax 45 07 03; info@haus-elizabeth.net). Take bus #51 to "Itzling-Pflanzmann," turn around and walk about 50m back, then head right onto Rauchenbichlerstr., over the footbridge, and continue along the gravel path sloping uphill to your right. Spacious rooms have TVs, balconies, and sweeping views of the city. Breakfast buffet included in newly remodeled room. Refrigerators available for guest use. Singles with shower €26; doubles €44; one quad €80. No credit cards. ❸

Pension Sandwirt, Lastenstr. 6a (☎/fax 87 43 51). Exit the train station from the platform #13 staircase, turn right on the footbridge, and again at the bottom onto Lastenstr., and go behind the building with the Post sign (3min.). This bed-and-breakfast's (not a private home) down-to-earth hosts speak excellent English and will let you do laundry for free. All rooms have TVs. Breakfast included. Surprise: shower is actually *in* the room. Singles €21; doubles €35, with shower €42; triples €50; quads €64. ❸

HOTELS

▨ **Albertina Hotel Allegro,** Glockeng. 4b (☎88 9 60; fax 88 960 404; www.albertina-hotels.at; office@albertina-hotels.at). Turn off Schallmooser Haupstr. where it says Linzer Parkgarage and turn right into Glockeng. This stylish blue building balanced on tall concrete legs is a delightful departure from the staid architecture surrounding it. Hidden behind a row of buildings on the Schallmooser Hauptstr. The interior is well lit and decorated in swaths of bright color. Open July-Sept. Singles €46; doubles €72. ❹

Zum Jungen Fuchs, Linzerg. 54 (☎87 54 96). Just across the street from St. Sebastian, this small hotel is perfect for travelers on a budget who are tired of the bustle of hostels. Don't be discouraged by the tunnel-like hallways and drab reception area—the rooms are pleasant and large. Singles €27; doubles €36; triples €48. ❸

Altstadthotel Blaue Gans, Getreideg. 41-43 (☎84 29 91; fax 24 919; office@blauegans.at; www.blauegans.at). The Blaue Gans dates back hundreds of years, but you can be assured that its decor does not. Each room in this cosmopolitan hotel has sleek furniture and a unique piece of modern art. The hallways and courtyard are home to minimalist sculpture and elaborate wall paintings. Singles €99-115; doubles €109-189. ❺

Am Dom, Goldg. 17 (☎84 27 65; fax 84 27 65-65; bach@salzburg.co.at). This historic wood-panelled hotel great if you are looking for traditional Austrian accommodations in the heart of the Altstadt. As its name implies, it is located just across the square from the *Dom*. Make sure to reserve a room ahead of time in the summer—this small hotel of only 15 rooms fills up fast. Singles €68; doubles €94. ❹

CAMPING

Panorama Camping Stadtblick, Rauchenbichlerstr. 21 (☎45 06 52; fax 45 80 18; info@panorama-camping.at; www.panorama-camping.at). Elisabeth's brother runs this campground next to Haus Elisabeth (see above for directions). By car, take exit "Salzburg-Nord" off A1. Behind a copse of trees with a view of the city. On-site store. Laundry €5. Shower included. Open Mar. 20-Nov. 11. €5.90; *Let's Go* readers €5.30; tent €1.50; bed in a tent €7.27; 2-person RV with fridge and stove €25; 4-person €36. Parking and tent (including electricity) €3.20. ❶

🖸 FOOD AND DRINK

With countless beer gardens and pastry-shop patios, Salzburg is a great place to eat outdoors. The local specialty is **Salzburger Nockerl,** a large soufflé of egg whites, sugar, and raspberry filling baked into three mounds to represent the three hills of Salzburg. If you order one be prepared to wait 20-30min. and pay around €10-12. Also make sure you have a friend to share it with—it's huge. Another regional favorite is **Knoblauchsuppe,** a rich cream soup loaded with croutons and pungent garlic—a potent weapon to be used wisely against pesky bunkmates. During the first two weeks of September, local cafés dispense **Stürm,** a delicious, cloudy cider (reminiscent, aptly enough, of a storm) that hasn't quite finished fermenting.

There are probably more world-famous **Mozartkugeln** (chocolate "Mozart balls," hazelnuts covered with marzipan and nougat and dipped in chocolate) lining cafe windows than notes in all Mozart's works combined. A Salzburg confectioner invented the treats in 1890, but mass production inevitably took over. Although mass-produced *Kugeln* wrapped in gold and red are technically *echt* (authentic), try to find the handmade ones wrapped in blue and silver. Reasonably priced *Kugeln* are sold at the **Holzmayr** confectioners (€0.40 for gold, €0.65 for silver) or at Konditorei **Fürst** (€0.80 for silver), both on Alter Markt. Holzmayr serves many varieties including light and dark chocolate, original recipe, apricot, and diet.

In most cases, markets are open weekdays 8am-7pm, Saturday 8am-noon. Salzburg has many supermarkets on the Mirabellpl. side of the river but few in the Altstadt. **SPAR** is widespread, and a giant **EuroSpar** sprawls next to the train station bus terminal at Sudtirolerp. 11. (Open M-F 8am-7pm, Sa 7:30am-5pm). **Open-air markets** are held on Universitätpl. (M-F 6am-7pm, Sa 6am-1pm) and Mirabellpl. down into Hubert-Sattlerg. (Th 5am-noon).

RESTAURANTS

Zum Fidelen Affen, Priesterhausg. 8 (☎87 73 61), off Linzerg. This wood-paneled restaurant is popular with locals. Hearty, honest Austrian food keeps everyone coming back "At the Faithful Ape." Try the toasted black bread with various toppings or the farmer's salad (€8.50). Meals €8.50-17, beer €3.15. Open M-Sa 5-11pm. ❸

St. Peter's Stiftskeller, St.-Peter-Bezirk 1/4 (☎84 12 680; fax 84 12 68 75; st.peter@haslauer.at; www.haslauer.at). When construction on the fortress began in 1077, this restaurant had already been in business for over 200 years. Tucked away in a courtyard at the foot of the cliffs, St. Peter's Stiftskeller is considered to be the oldest restaurant in central Europe. With traditional Austrian food, old-fashioned decor, and classical music, it is a continuing high-class tradition. Most main dishes are around €18-20, but a few run cheaper, such as asparagus risotto (€10.50). Open M-F 11am-midnight, during the *Festspiele* until 1am. ❹

Zweitler's, Kaig. 3 (☎84 00 44), in the Altstadt. From the tourist office walk straight out to the back left corner of Mozartpl. to Kaig. Cozy wooden interior turns into a lively bar at night. Tasty *Spinatnockerl* (spinach baked into a pan with cheese and parsley) are out of this world at €6.50, or try the *Ofenerdäpf'l* (roast potatoes in sauce with bacon and onions), also €6.50. Standards *Jägerschnitzel* and Styrian fried chicken €9.70. Local customers yell suggestions to the chef on second floor. Open daily 6pm-1am; during the *Festspiele* 11am-2pm and 6pm-1am. AmEx/MC/V. ❷

Shakespeare, Hubert-Sattlerg. 3 (☎87 91 06; fax 87 91 06; office@shakespeare.at; www.shakespeare.at), off Mirabellpl. This artsy, eclectic spot serves a variety of foods, from Italian and Austrian dishes to surprisingly good Chinese dishes. Large, spicy platter of Szechuan pork €8.43, spaghetti alla carbonara €5.96. Art exhibitions about twice every month in the back rooms. **Free Internet.** Open 8am-2am daily. Kitchen open until 11pm. DC/MC/V. ❷

Stiegkeller, Festungsg. 10 (☎84 26 81). When you reach the bottom of the Festungsbahn, don't just automatically continue downhill. It's worth the short walk back up the Festungsg. to the Stiegkeller, a Salzburg tradition ever since 1492. With seating for 1600 there's plenty of room in this restaurant, both outside under shady trees and inside under imposing antlers. Dinner options include the good old standby Wienerschnitzel (€9.60) as well as perch fillet (€13) and salad with strips of roast turkey (€8). Open May-Sept., 10am-10pm. ❸

Il Sole, Gstätteng. 15 (☎84 32 84), just right of the Mönchsberg lift. Enjoy soothing background music and an aromatic setting, along with pizza (€5-10), lasagna (€6.50), or minestrone soup (€2.50). Open 11:30am-2pm and 5:30-11:30pm. ❷

Goldener Zirkel, Papagenopl. (☎/fax 84 11 06). Built in 1647 and rebuilt in 1955, this place has just enough room for a handful of people. Eat hearty food a short way from the frenzy of the Altstadt. English menu available. *Specknödel* (bacon dumplings) €6.18, *Kasnudeln* €6.69, and *Kaiserscharm* €6.50. Open M-F 9:30am-10pm, Sa 10:30am-2pm. ❷

Bio Bistro/Spicy Spices, Wolf-Dietrich-Str. 1 (☎87 07 12). Walk inside this organic eatery and spice store into a world of aromas. Or visit the new and larger location, **Spices**

by Sead, where everyday at lunch there is a different vegetarian *Menü* (€5), soup (€2.50), and 3 kinds of salads (€3). Dinner *Menü* includes appetizer, main course, and dessert (€9.90). Takeout available. Open M-Sa 10:30am-10pm, Su noon-9pm. No credit cards. ❷

Toskana, Sigmund Haffnerg. 11 (☎80 44 69 00), across from Sigmund Haffnerg. 16, through the iron fence and on the right. This college cafeteria is a good deal for penny-pinchers with 2 hot entrees (€3.50-4.25, students €2.50-3.25), served in a courtyard just within the University grounds. Get there early, before ravenous (and smoky) students deplete the food supply. Open M-Th 8:30am-6pm, F 8:30am-3pm. ❶

Stadtalm, Mönchsberg 19c (☎84 17 29). Even if you aren't staying in the Stadtalm youth hostel, you should still make a trip up the Mönchsberg lift to eat at the delightful café of the same name. This casual spot features picnic tables situated under large sun umbrellas, teetering at the brink of the cliff. Enjoy chicken cordon bleu (€9.90), Greek salad (€5.90), or a glass of Stiegl (€2.70) while soaking up the amazing view of the old city. Open Mar.-Oct. daily 10am-10pm. ❷

CAFÉS

Café Tomaselli, Alter Markt 9 (☎80 44 69 00), has been a favorite haunt for wealthier Salzburger clientele since 1705. The interior glows with the light of the crystal chandeliers reflecting off the warm wood panelling and gold trim. Try the hot chocolate with rum (€4.20), guaranteed to warm your belly. Cakes about €3 on a mobile dessert counter. Kick back and sample the *Glühwein* (€4.25), *Grog* (€3.75), or *Tomaselliums Café*, a decadent concoction of mocha, original Mozart liqueur, whipped cream, and almond slivers (€5.70). Newspapers available for leisurely perusal. Open M-Sa 7am-9pm, Su 8am-9pm, during the *Festspiele* until midnight.

Café Bazar, Schwarzstr. 3 (☎87 42 78; fax 87 25 40). Provides a peaceful way to escape the crowds with a terrace behind the shop on the tree-lined footpath on the banks of the Salzach. Indulge in a Kaffee Maria Theresia (espresso with orange liqueur and mocha) for €6.40, or one of their many varieties of cake, including raspberry yogurt, Sachertorte, and Mozarttorte, for around €3. Open M 10am-6pm, Tu-Sa 7:30am-11pm.

Café Cult, Hellbrunnerstr. 3 (☎84 56 01). Go into the Kunstlerhaus building and around to the back on the ground floor. This Mediterranean café is popular with the artistic set of Salzburg, but thankfully less so with tourists. Munch your meal (€6.50-8.40) on the glass terrace overlooking the river or on the trendy orange furniture. Open M-F 9am-11pm, Sa 8am-3pm.

Café Fürst, Brodg. 13 (☎84 37 59). Savor a *Mozartkugel* (€0.73), or any one of a vast selection of candies (try the marzipan potato), chocolates, pastries, *Torte,* strudels, and cakes (around €2). Grab one of the sunny tables outside if you can. Branch in Mirabellpl. Open June-Sept. 8am-9pm; Oct.-May. 8am-8pm. AmEx/DC/MC/V.

Café Glockenspiel, Mozartpl. 1 (☎84 14 03). Near the tourist office, this place serves ice cream concoctions (€4.40-5.80) and cakes (€3.10). Restaurant upstairs serves dishes ranging from bratwurst (€6.60) to duck (€15.90). Vegetarian specials including tortellini and Spinatspätzle. Sit at a table on the square and listen to free concerts of light classical music each evening in July and Aug. Open Easter.-Aug. daily 9am-11pm; Sept.-Easter. 9am-7pm; during the *Festspiele* until midnight. AmEx/DC/MC/V.

Kaffeehäferl, Getreideg. 25 (☎84 32 49), in the passage across from McDonald's. Unpretentious courtyard cafe provides a little piece of serenity in the tourist rush of Getreideg. Coffee around €2.54, strawberry milkshake €2.80, Johannis berry juice €2.10. Open M-Sa 9am-7pm, Su noon-7pm.

BEER GARDENS AND BARS

Salzburg's daytime charm becomes nighttime boogie in its lively and varied nightlife scene. The more boisterous stick to the section of Rudolfskai between the Staatsbrücke and Mozartsteg, where a youthful crowd congregates in the street. Elsewhere, especially along Chiemseeg. and around Anton-Neumayr-Pl., you can throw back a few drinks in a more reserved *Beisl*. More refined, adult bars can be found along Steing. and Giselakai on the other side of the river.

⊠ Augustiner Bräustübl-Mülln, Augustinerg. 4 (☎ 43 12 46). From the Altstadt, follow the footpath from Hanuschpl. downstream along the river, and after the next bridge (the Müllnersteg), take the stairs going up to your left. Cross the street, then continue to your right along the Müllner Hauptstr. Turn left when you get to Augustinerg., and head up under the archway. The entrance will be on your right. Serving home-brewed beer since 1621 in the halls of a former monastery, this gigantic complex seats 2800, split evenly between an outdoor *Biergarten* and 4 gigantic indoor halls. To save a bit of cash, give your mammoth stein directly to the guy standing next to the barrels. The stands outside the beer halls sell snacks to soak up the suds, including sausages, pretzels, and sliced radishes. Open M-F 3-11pm, Sa-Su 2:30-11pm.

Vis à Vis, Rudolfskai 24 (☎ 84 12 90), is cut in the shape of an arched stone tunnel with blacklight and blue neon. Sit in one of the living room areas if you can find space, and lounge with the sharply dressed crowd until the wee hours. Open from 8pm.

Shamrock, Rudolfskai 24 (☎ 84 16 10; www.shamrock.at.tt). Built around part of the old city wall, this relaxed and friendly Irish pub has plenty of room—just keep going until you find a spot you like, or stay by the dance area in front to take in the nightly live music. Also shows sporting events including the Super Bowl. Open Su-M 3pm-2am, Tu-W 3pm-3am, and Th-Sa 3pm-4am.

O'Malley's, Rudolfskai 16 (☎ 84 92 63). Two bars in this establishment ensure that you always have sufficient liquids, while the wall decorations and music transport you to the fair islands of the North. Packed with a mixed crowd of German and English speakers. Happy Hour 8-9pm, all beer half-price. Open June-Aug. F-Sa 6pm-4am, Su-Th 6pm-2:30am; Sept.-May F-Sa 7pm-4am, Su-Th 7pm-2:30am.

Zweistein, Giselakai 9 (☎ 87 71 79). The place to come for Salzburg's gay and lesbian scene. On weekends, this bar becomes crowded, serving liquor for around €4.60-6.40. The wall art changes monthly. Open M-W 8pm-4am, Th 6pm-4am, F-Su 6pm-5am.

Flip, Gstätteng. 17 (☎ 84 36 43). Away from the hectic scene on Rudolfskai, this bar helps keep the Gstätteng. corner of Salzburg alive. The sloping stone roof in the back creates cave-like surroundings while you sip your cocktail (most around €5-6). Side corners allow for greater intimacy. Open nightly 8pm-4am. AmEx/DC/MC/V.

Segabar, Rudolfskai 18 (☎ 84 68 98). This busy bar along the strip on Rudolfskai packs them in on weekends with blasting music and TVs. Creates a body-to-body party scene popular with the younger crowd. Cover €3 F-Sa. Open F-Sa 8pm-4am, Su-Th 8pm-2am.

◎ SIGHTS

Salzburg is a relatively small town with a disproportionate number of *Sehenswürdigkeiten* (points of interest). Whether you're into decadent floral gardens or stoic fortresses, Salzburg's got it. To help bear the financial burden, the tourist office sells the **Salzburg Card,** which grants admission to all museums and sights as well as unlimited use of public transportation, but is really a good deal only if you plan to cram a great deal of sightseeing into a short period of time. (24hr. card €18, 48hr. €26, 72hr. €32; ages 7-15 half-price.)

THE ALTSTADT

THE CITY CENTER. In the shadow of the hill-top fortress, arcade passages open up into tiny courtyards filled with geraniums and creeping ivy that lead, in turn, to the tourist-jammed **Getreidegasse.** The buildings in this area are among the oldest in the city, some dating back to the 12th century. Many of Getreideg.'s shops have wrought-iron signs dating from the Middle Ages, when the illiterate needed pictorial aids to understand which store sold what.

FORTRESS HOHENSALZBURG. Festung Hohensalzburg was built between 1077 and 1681 by the ruling archbishops, who used it as a refuge during religious wars. Looming over Salzburg from atop Mönchsberg, it has never been successfully attacked, making it the largest completely preserved castle in Europe. Nowadays, penetrating the castle walls is simply a matter of forking over a few euros. The trail up to the fortress and the **Festungsbahn** (funicular) can be found at the far end of Kapitelpl. in the Festungsg. The road and stairs require about 20min. of steep uphill walking, while the Festungsbahn takes only a few minutes. Since the ride ends inside the fortress walls, funicular tickets include entrance. *(☎84 26 82. Every 10min. 9am-9pm; Oct.-Apr. 9am-5pm. Ascent €5.55, children €3; round-trip €6.35, €3.50.)* The inner rooms of the castle (Fürstenzimmer) contain formidable Gothic state rooms, the fortress organ (nicknamed the "Bull of Salzburg" for its off-key snorting), and an impregnable watchtower that affords an unmatched view of the city and surrounding mountains. You'll also see the archbishop's medieval indoor toilet—a technological marvel of its day. If you pay close attention to the wall carvings in the state rooms and on the exterior, you'll observe turnips, the symbol of archbishop Leonhard von Keutschach. The origin of this symbol supposedly stems from the fact that as a youth, Leonhard's uncle threw a turnip at him to set his head on straight. The **Burgmuseum** inside the fortress displays findings from 16th-century excavations, stick figures displaying weapons used between 1300 and 1700, and a series of side-by-side timelines depicting the history of the Festung, Salzburg, and the world at large. Also notable is the section on Austrian music inspired by Turkish influences, where you can listen to recordings. Nearby, the **Rainer Museum** contains objects of war from the 17th century to the present, including uniforms, books, weapons, and paintings. Don't miss the life-size model of an Austrian soldier in alpine uniform, complete with ice pick, hiking boots, and knee length pants. The fortress also has a gift shop, cafe, restaurant, and a small marionette museum. *(☎84 24 30. Grounds open mid-June to mid-Sept. daily 8:30am-8pm; mid-Sept. to mid-Mar. 9am-5pm; mid-Mar. to mid-June 9am-6pm. Interior open mid-June to mid-Sept. daily 9am-6pm; mid-Sept. to mid-Mar. 9am-5pm; mid-Mar. to mid-June. 9:30am-5:30pm. If you walk up, entrance to fortress is €3.55, ages 6-15 €2, which allows only access to the perimeter of the castle; combo ticket including fortress, castle interiors, and museums €7.10, €4.)*

From the fortress many footpaths spread out over the Mönchsberg, all providing bird's-eye views of the city below. At times, the paths are framed by damp stone walls on both sides; many were originally parts of the city wall, and some date back as far as the 13th century. After meandering down the leafy trails, hikers can descend the stairs back to the Altstadt or descend via the **Mönchsberglift** (elevator) built into the mountain, which opens on Gstätteng. 13. *(Elevator operates daily 9am-11pm. €1.45, round-trip €2.40.)* Down the hill and to the right of the fortress, **Nonnberg Abbey** (where the real Maria von Trapp lived) is still a private monastic complex, but visitors can tour the church, which has Romanesque wall paintings.

ARCHBISHOP'S RESIDENCE. The square on the far side of the cathedral is **Residenzplatz,** named for the magnificent **Residenz** of Salzburg's powerful Prince Archbishops. The ecclesiastical elite of Austria have resided here, in the heart of the Altstadt, since 1595. A trusty audio-guide leads you through the stunning Baroque

COWED INTO SUMISSION The only time the **Hohen-salzburg** fortress was ever under any kind of siege was during the **Peasant Wars** (see **Holy Romans and Habsburgs,** p. 65), when the peasants surrounded the fortress in an attempt to starve the archbishop out. When the stubborn archbishop had only one cow left, he painted the remaining beast with different spots on both sides and paraded him back and forth along the castle wall in distinct view of the peasants below. Since the peasants, as the saying goes, were simple-minded folk, they believed that the archbishop had a great reserve of food and decided to give up their assault.

Prunkräume (state rooms), once used to host heads of state and for Mozart's concerts. Many rooms are bigger than the average house and contain immense ceiling frescoes and stucco work, gilded furniture, and 17th-century Flemish tapestries. The *Residenz* also houses a gallery (see p. 245). *(☎80 42 26 90. Open 10am-5pm. €7.25, students €5.50, children €2.50, audioguide included.)* Dead-center in Residenzpl. is a 15m **fountain**—the largest Baroque fountain in the world—featuring amphibious horses charging through the water. Appropriately, *Fiaker* (horse-drawn carriages) congregate near the fountain. *(€33 for 25min.)*

MOZART'S BIRTHPLACE AND UNIVERSITY CHURCH. The first Altstadt site most visitors rush to is **Mozart's Geburtshaus.** The long red and white flag suspended from the roof is a beacon for music pilgrims worldwide. Although Mozart eventually settled in Vienna, his birthplace holds the most impressive collection of the child genius' belongings: his first viola and violin, a pair of keyboard instruments, and buttons from his coat. Several rooms also recreate life in Salzburg and Austria during Mozart's time, as well as what Mozart's young years as a traveling virtuoso must have been like. Come before 11am to avoid the tourists who crowd around the exhibits, blocking the prodigy's relics from all but the most persistent. *(On the 2nd floor of Getreideg. 9. ☎84 43 13. Open July-Aug. daily 9am-6:30pm; Sept.-June 9am-5:30pm. €5.50, students and seniors €4.50, children €2.)* Directly in Mozart's backyard stands the **Universitätskirche,** one of the largest Baroque chapels on the continent, and generally considered Fischer von Erlach's masterpiece. Its distinctive dome stands watch over Universitätspl. and the daily farmer's market. Sculpted clouds coat the nave, while pudgy cherubim (lit by pale natural light from the dome) frolic all over the immense apse of the church.

FESTSPIELHAUS. The **Festspielhaus,** once the riding school for the archbishops' horses, now houses many of the big-name events of the annual *Festspiele.* It has three separate performance spaces—the large Opera House, the small Opera House, and an open-air performance space. *(Down Wiener-Philharmonikerg. from Universitätspl. Tours Oct.-May 2pm; June and Sept. 2, 3:30pm; July-Aug. 9:30am, 2, 3:30pm. €5, ages 12 and under €2.90.)* Opposite the *Festspielhaus,* the **Rupertinum Gallery** hosts temporary exhibits of modern painting, sculpture, and photography in a graceful building remodeled by Friedensreich Hundertwasser (see p. 119). *(☎80 42 23 36. Open mid-July to Sept. Tu, Th 9am-5pm; W 10am-9pm; Oct. to mid-July Tu, Th-Su 10am-5pm, W 10am-9pm. €8, students €4.50.)*

ST. PETER'S. The **Toscaninihof,** the courtyard of **St. Peter's Monastery,** hides the stone steps which lead up the Mönchsberg cliffs. The monastery itself, which was already standing when St. Rupert arrived in Salzburg in AD 696, is the oldest monastery north of the Alps. The **Stiftskirche St. Peter,** within the monastery, began as a Romanesque basilica in the 1100s and still features a marble portal from 1244. In the 18th century, the building was remodeled in Rococo style, with green and pink moldings curling delicately across the graceful ceiling and gilded cherubim blowing golden trumpets. *(Open 9am-12:15pm and 2:30-6:30pm.)*

PETERSFRIEDHOF (CEMETERY). Petersfriedhof is one of the most peaceful places in Salzburg, primarily because tour groups are denied entry. The tiny cemetery is filled with delicate flower-covered graves, some dating back to the 1600s. In the middle of the cemetery is St. Margaret's Chapel, built between 1485 and 1491. *(Continue through the arch to the right of the Stiftskirche St. Peter. Open Apr.-Sept. 6:30am-7pm; Oct.-Mar. 6:30am-6pm.)*

KATAKOMBEN (CATACOMBS). The part open to visitors consists of two rooms built into the rock wall above the cemetery. The old stone passageways will make you feel like a medieval monk, minus the robes. In the lower room (St. Gertrude's Chapel), a fresco commemorates the martyrdom of Thomas à Beckett. *(Near the far end of the cemetery, against the Mönchsberg. ☎ 784 74 35. Open May-Sept. Tu-Su 10:30am-5pm; Oct.-Apr. W-Su 10:30am-4pm. €1, students and ages 6-18 €0.60.)*

CATHEDRAL. Archbishop Wolf Dietrich's successor, Markus Sittikus, commissioned the Baroque **Dom** from Italian architect Santino Solari in 1628. Mozart was christened here in 1756 and later worked at the cathedral as *Konzertmeister* and court organist. The cathedral boasts five organs which, when all played at once, create a phenomenal surround-sound experience. The original cupola was destroyed during WWII, but was repaired in 1959 to its previous condition. The square leading out of the cathedral, **Domplatz,** features a statue of the Virgin Mary. Around her swarm four lead figures representing Wisdom, Faith, the Church, and the Devil. *(From the Staatsbr., head through Rathauspl. and take a left on Getreideg., which turns into Judeng. Continue down Judeng. until you reach Residenzpl. The cathedral is the large building with green domes across the square.)*

MOZARTPLATZ. Mozartplatz is dominated by the **Neugebäude,** seat of the city government's bureaucracy. Atop the building, a 35-bell **Glockenspiel** (carillon) rings out a Mozart tune (specified on a notice posted on the corner of the *Residenz*) every day at 7, 11am, and 6pm, and the pipe organ atop the Hohensalzburg fortress bellows a response. *(To the northwest of Residenzpl.)*

THE NEUSTADT

MIRABELL PALACE AND GARDENS. On the bus and walking route into town, **Mirabellplatz** holds the marvelous **Schloß Mirabell.** The supposedly celibate Archbishop Wolf Dietrich had his own place in the *Residenz* (see p. 240), but he also had this Renaissance beauty built for his mistress Salome Alt and their 10 children in 1606. He named the palace "Altenau" in her honor, but when the new archbishop Markus Sittikus imprisoned Wolf Dietrich for arson, Sittikus seized the palace and changed its name to "Mirabell." The castle is now the seat of the city government, and some of the mayor's offices are open for public viewing. The palace hosts classical concerts in the evening, and fans swear that the *Marmorsaal* (Marble Hall) is one of the best concert halls in Europe. *(Open M-F 8am-4pm. Free.)*

Behind the palace, the delicately cultivated **Mirabellgarten** is a maze of flower beds and groomed shrubs. On the left side is a gigantic fountain with four sculptures representing Greek myths, including the rape of Helen and Pluto's abduction of Proserpina. Walk up the staircase by the smaller fountain directly in front of Schloß Mirabell to the **Dwarf Garden,** named for the vertically challenged statues that share the space with playful Salzburg toddlers. The statues' grotesque marble faces were supposedly modeled after the archbishop's court jesters.

From one of the hedge-enclosed clearings in the *Mirabellgarten*, you can see a tiny wooden shack called the **Zauberflötenhäuschen,** where Mozart allegedly composed *The Magic Flute* in just five months. It was transplanted from Vienna as a gift to Salzburg's conservatory for young musicians, the **Mozarteum,** which stands borders the gardens on Schwartzstr. 26-28. The Mozarteum was built for the

Salzburg Academy of Music and Performing Arts, and there are regular performances in its concert hall (see p. 246). It is also known for its enormous **Mozart Archives**. *(☎ 840 62 90; fax 84 06 93; entrance by appointment.)*

MOZART'S WOHNHAUS (RESIDENCE). Mozart moved here at age 17 with his family from their house in the Altstadt, staying from 1773 to 1780. The displays have some original scores from the maestro, as well as old pianos he once played, but audio guides tend to confuse more than they enlighten. *(Makartpl. 8, just down the street from the Mozarteum. ☎ 87 42 27 40; fax 87 29 24. Open daily 9am-6pm; July-Aug. until 7pm. €5.50, students €4.50; audio guide included.)*

KAPUZINBERG AND SEBASTIANSKIRCHE. At Kapuzinerberg's crest stands the simple **Kapuzinerkloster** (Capuchin Monastery) that Wolf Dietrich built in the late 16th century. Stations of the cross are represented by rubbery mannequins locked behind iron gates on the path up from town. Farther down Linzerg. is the 18th-century **Sebastianskirche**. On the far side of the church lies the entrance to its Italian-style cemetery, with overgrown graves and fir trees. In the center, framed by arched walkways, stands the impressive mausoleum of Dietrich, with skylights in the dome allowing light to reflect off the ceramic wall tiles. The tombs of Mozart's wife, Constanze, and father, Leopold, are also here on the path leading to the mausoleum. *(From Mirabellpl., follow Dreifaltigkeitg. south to its intersection Linzerg.; head under the stone arch on right side of Linzerg. 14 and follow the stone staircase up to the monastery.)*

MONK-Y BUSINESS Legend has it that the robes of the *Kapuzinerkloster's* resident monks inspired the world's first cup of cappuccino. A cafe proprietor with an overactive imagination observed the pious gents on a noonday stroll and *voilà*—the world witnessed the birth of a drink with the rich coffee color of the monk's robes topped by white froth hoods. According to this theory, Italy's cappuccino is just a rip-off of the much older *Kapuziner*, still ordered in Austrian cafes today.

THE SOUND OF MUSIC

In 1964, Julie Andrews, Christopher Plummer, and a gaggle of 20th Century Fox crew members arrived in Salzburg to film *The Sound of Music*, based on the true story of the von Trapp family. Salzburg has never been the same. The city encourages the increased tourism due to the film's popularity (although many Salzburgers themselves have never seen the film, and most who have dislike it). Three official companies run **Sound of Music Tours** in Salzburg, and many hostels and pensions work with one of them to offer discounts to guests. **Salzburg Sightseeing Tours** (☎ 88 16 16; fax 87 87 76) and **Panorama Tours** (☎ 87 40 29; fax 16 18) operate rival kiosks on Mirabellpl. and run remarkably similar programs. (Both €33, children €17. Tours leave from Mirabellpl. 9:30am, 2pm.) The renegade **Bob's Special Tours**, Rudolfskai 38, has no high-profile kiosk, but they do have a minibus. The smaller vehicle enables them to tour more of the Altstadt locations that the big tour buses can't reach. (☎ 84 95 11; fax 84 95 12. €35, students €32. Tours in summer daily 9am, 2pm; in winter 10am.) All three companies offer free pick-up from your hotel. Tours last 4hr. and are generally worth the money if you're a big *Sound of Music* fan or if you have a short time in Salzburg and want an overview of the area. Another option is **Fraülein Maria's Bicycle Tours** (☎ 342 62 97), which start at the entrance to the Mirabellgarten behind the Hotel Bristol and cost only €16 for a three-hour trip, including the bike rental. (Mid-May to late Aug daily 9:30am.)

If you have the time and enough interest, you can could rent a bike and do the tour on your own. The film takes a great deal of artistic license with the von Trapps's story—many of the events were fabricated for Tinseltown. Though Maria

IN RECENT NEWS

MAKING MUSEUMS OUT OF MOUNTAINS

You've probably seen the fortress on the top of the Mönchsberg, but have you thought about what's inside that mountain? Salzburgers have been tunneling into it for centuries, starting from the catacombs behind St. Peter's cemetery and continuing into the busy traffic tunnel of the Sigmundstor. A new plan to build a museum of modern art inside the mountain has Salzburgers in a tizzy. The adventurous design first created more than 10 years ago involves a gallery located inside the mountain, lit by skylights from the surface.

Though the idea was rejected in 1990 for financial reasons, the debate is far from over. In 1998, a Europe-wide design competition was held, and the winning museum design was supposed to be finished in 2002. In 2002, however, there was nothing of the museum but a large gravel pit by the top of the Mönchsberg elevator. Dithering by the government and funding concerns have forced the project into limbo for years. The cost of the project has grown 120 million Schillings in 1999 to 300 million Schillings (21.8 million euros, or 21.3 million US dollars). The date of completion has also been pushed back from 2002 to 2003 to 2004.

As a sort of penance for ripping apart the mountain even more, the museum is to incorporate many environmentally friendly features, such as utilization of the warmth coming from the underground garage in the Mönchsberg for heating.

was a nun-apprentice in the film, in reality she merely taught at **Nonnberg Abbey,** high above the city near the Festung (see p. 240). There the crew filmed the nuns singing "How Do You Solve A Problem Like Maria?" The little gazebo where Liesl and Rolf unleashed their youthful passion is on the grounds of **Schloß Hellbrunn** (see p. 247). From the Hellbrun parking lot, head down Hellbrunner Allee. On the way, you'll pass the yellow castle used for the exterior of the von Trapp home (Maria sang "I Have Confidence" in front of the long yellow wall), which is now a dorm for music students at the Mozarteum. Continue along Hellbrunner Allee until it turns into Freisaalweg. At the end of Freisaalweg, turn right on Akadamiestr., which ends at Alpenstr. and the river. The river footpath leads all the way back to Mozartsteg. and Staatsbrücke (1hr.). The back of the von Trapp house (where Maria and the children fell into the water after romping in the city) was filmed at the **Schloß Leopoldskron** behind the Mönchberg, now a center for academic studies. Visitors are not permitted on the grounds, but if you're set on getting a glimpse of the house, take bus #55 to "Pensionistenheim Nonntal," turn left on Sunnhubstr., and left again up Leopoldskroner Allee to the castle. Some of the other filming locations scattered throughout Salzburg include the **Mirabellgarten** (see p. 242) and the **Festspielhaus** (see p. 245).

The von Trapps were married in the church at Nonnberg Abbey, but Hollywood filmed the scene in **Mondsee** instead (see p. 262). The sightseeing tours allow guests to stop in Mondsee for 45min., but the town is really worth a whole daytrip for its pastry shops and beautiful lake. **Buses** leave the Salzburg train station from the main bus depot (45min., every hr., €1).

To squeeze the last few euros out of starry-eyed tourists, the Sternbräu hosts a **Sound of Music Dinner Show.** Performers sing your favorite film songs while servers ply you with soup, schnitzel with noodles, and crisp apple strudel. (☎82 66 17. May-Oct. show starts at 8:30pm. Show and drink €26. Dinner at 7:30pm plus the show €40. 30% student discount, children under 13 free.)

▥ MUSEUMS

Although Salzburg's small, specialized museums often get lost in the shadow of the Festung, *The Sound of Music,* and the *Festspiele,* they are worthwhile attractions. In addition to the art museums, there are also private galleries on Sigmund-Haffnerg. that allow budget art viewing.

ART MUSEUMS. Museum Carolino Augusteum, named after Emperor Franz I's widow, Caroline Augusta, houses local Roman and Celtic artifacts, including mosaics and burial remains, naturally preserved by the region's salt. The upper floors feature Gothic and Baroque art. *(Museumpl. 1. ☎ 62 08 08. Open F-W 9am-5pm, Th until 8pm. €3.27, students €1.09.)* The **Residenz Gallery,** in the *Residenz,* displays 16th-to 19th-century art, much of it religious work. *(Residenzpl. 1. ☎ 84 04 51. Open Apr.-Sept. daily 10am-5pm; Oct.-Mar. closed M. €4.72, students €3.63.)* Finally, the **Barockmuseum,** in the Orangerie of the Mirabellgarten, pays tribute to the aesthetics of 17th-and 18th-century Europe. *(☎ 87 74 32. Open Tu-Sa 9am-noon and 2-5pm, Su 9am-noon. €2.91, students and seniors €1.45, ages 6-14 free.)*

BEER MUSEUM. Stiegl Brauwelt (Brew World) is attached to the Stiegl brewery, close to downtown. Three floors showcase beer-making, its history, and modern beer culture—including the wonder of the *Brauwelt,* a two-story bottle pyramid constructed of 300 beers. Hop on down to the final hands-on exhibit—two glasses of Stiegl beer, a *Brezel* (pretzel), and a souvenir beer glass are included. *(Brauhausstr. 9. Take bus #1 to "Brauhaus" and walk up the street to the giant yellow building. ☎ 83 87 14 92; brau-welt@stiegl.at; www.stiegl.at; Open W-Su 10am-4pm. €9.18, students €8.28.)*

OTHER MUSEUMS. The **Haus der Natur,** opposite the Carolino Augusteum, is an enormous museum (80 rooms) with an eclectic collection—from live alligators and giant snakes to huge rock crystals and spinning planets. *(Museumpl. 5. ☎ 84 26 53 or 84 23 22. Open 9am-5pm. Reptile zoo open 10am-5pm. €4.50, students and children €2.50.)* Inside the main entrance to the *Dom,* the **Dom Museum** houses an unusual collection called the **Kunst- und Wunderkammer** (Art and Curiosity Chamber) that includes jewel-encrusted cups, prayer books bound in gold, and a golden dove made in the 13th century. In the main museum, the gigantic Rupertskreuz guards the back room. *(☎ 84 41 89; dommuseum.salzburg@kirchen.at; www.kirchen.net/dommuseum. Open mid-May to mid-Oct. M-Sa 10am-5pm, Su 1-6pm. €4.50, students €1.50. Guided tours Sa 10:30am, €1.45.)* Down the stairs between Residenzpl. and Dompl., the **Domgrabungsmuseum** provides a near-spelunking experience, displaying excavations of the Roman ruins under the cathedral, some dating back to the 2nd century AD. *(☎ 84 52 95. Open May-Oct. W-Su 9am-5pm. €1.80, students €1.45, children €10.70)* The **Spielzeug Museum,** near the *Festspielhaus,* features three floors of puppets, wooden toys, dolls, electric trains, and nifty pre-Lego castle blocks from 1921. *(Bürgerspitalg. 2. ☎ 62 08 08 320. Open Tu-Su 9am-5pm. Puppet show Tu-W 3pm. €2.53, students €0.73.)*

🎭 ENTERTAINMENT

SALZBURG FESTSPIELE

Max Reinhardt, Richard Strauss, and Hugo von Hofmannsthal founded the renowned **Salzburger Festspiele** (Festival) in 1920. Every year since, Salzburg has become a musical mecca from late July to the end of August. A few weeks before the festival, visitors strolling along Getreideg. may bump into world-class stars taking a break from rehearsal. On the eve of the festival's opening, over 100 dancers don regional costumes, accessorize with torches, and perform a *Fackeltanz* (torchdance) on Residenzpl. During the festivities themselves, operas, plays, films, concerts, and tourists overrun every available public space.

TICKETS. Information and tickets for *Festspiele* events are available through the Festspiele Kartenbüro (ticket office) and Tageskasse (daily box office) in Karajanpl., against the mountain and next to the tunnel. (Open M-F 9:30am-3pm; July 1-July 22 M-Sa until 5pm, and from July 23 through the end of the festival daily until

6:30pm.) The festival prints a complete program of events that lists all concert locations and dates. The booklet is available at any tourist office (€1). Fans snap up the best seats months before the festival begins. To order tickets, contact *Kartenbüro der Salzburger Festspiele*, Postfach 140, A-5010 Salzburg (☎ 804 55 79; fax 804 57 60; info@salzburgfestival.at; www.salzburgfestival.at), no later than the beginning of January. After that, the office publishes a list of remaining seats, which generally include some cheap tickets to the operas, concerts, and plays, as well as standing room places. These tickets, however, are gobbled up quickly by subscribers or student groups, leaving only very expensive tickets and seats at avant-garde modern music concerts. Middle-man ticket distributors sell marked-up cheap tickets, a legal form of scalping—try AmEx or Panorama Tours. Those 26 or younger can try for cheap subscription tickets by writing about eight months in advance to *Direktion der Salzburger Festspiele*, attn: Ulrich Hauschild, Hofstallg. 1, A-5020 Salzburg.

FREE EVENTS. The powers that be have discontinued hawking last-minute tickets for dress rehearsals to the general public—nowadays, you've got to know somebody to get one of these tickets. Those without the necessary connections should take advantage of the Fest zur Eröffungsfest (Opening Day Festival), when concerts, shows, and films are either very cheap or free. Tickets for these events are available on a first-come, first-serve basis during the festival's opening week at the box office in the *Großes Festspielhaus* on Hofstallg. The only other event visitors can always attend without advance tickets is Jedermann. The city stages Hugo von Hofmannsthal's modern morality play about the life, love, and death of an immoral man every year in front of the cathedral. At the end, people placed in strategic locations throughout the city cry out the eerie word "Jedermann," which echoes all over town. Shouting contests determine which locals win the opportunity to be one of the ghostly criers. Standing-room for shows are available at the Festspielhaus.

CONCERTS

Even when the *Festspiele* are not on, Salzburg hosts many other concerts. The **Salzburg Academy of Music and Performing Arts** performs on a rotating schedule in the **Mozarteum** (see p. 243). The school often dedicates one cycle of concerts to students and reduces the ticket price. (For tickets to any of these concerts, contact Kartenbüro Mozarteum, Postfach 156, Theaterg. 2, A-5024 Salzburg. ☎ 87 31 54; fax 87 29 96. Open M-Th 9am-2pm, F 9am-4pm.) The **Dom** also has a concert program in July and August. Five separate organs in the cathedral create a powerful effect. (Concerts Th-F 11:15am. €8.72, students €7.27, children free.) The church has periodic evening concerts; check the door for upcoming programs. Other churches throughout Salzburg perform wonderful music during services and post information on other concerts, particularly near Easter and Christmas. The **5-Uhr Konzerte** (5 o'clock concerts) held at St. Peter's Monastery are performed by young musicians at low prices (€10, students €5).

For a particularly enchanting (and expensive) evening, attend a **Festungskonzert** (Fortress Concert) in the fortress's ornate *Fürstenzimmer* (Prince's chamber) and *Goldener Saal* (Golden Hall). Concerts are year-round, mostly on Fridays and Saturdays, and include dinner at the fortress restaurant for a slight surcharge. Reservations are required for concerts. (For more information, contact Festungskonzerte, Anton-Adlgasserweg 22, A-5020 Salzburg. ☎ 82 58 58; fax 82 58 59; info@mozartfestival.at; www.mozartfestival.at. Open 9am-9pm. Tickets are €29-36, students €20; with dinner €44-48, students €33.) A less tourist-oriented activity is the year-round **Salzburger Schloßkonzerte** in Schloß Mirabell. The box office is in Mozarts Wohnhaus. (☎ 84 85 86; fax 84 85 86

87; info@salzburger-schlosskonzerte.at; www.salzburgerschlosskonzerte.at. Open M-F 9am-5:30pm.) For a bit more money and a lot more kitsch, check out the evening **Mozart Serenaden** (Mozart's Serenades) in the Gothic Hall on Burgerstpitalg. 2. at the end of the Getreideg. Salzburg musicians in knickers and powdered hair perform Mozart favorites. (For information and tickets, contact Konzertdirektion Nerat, A-5013 Salzburg, Postfach 28. ☎43 68 70; fax 69 70; mozart@salzburg.co.at; www.mozartserenaden.at. 7:30pm, June-Aug. 8pm; €26-30.50, students €19.)

In July and August, **outdoor opera** rings out from the historical hedge-theater of Mirabellgarten. Tickets are available from the box office in Schloß Mirabell. (☎84 85 86; fax 84 47 47. Open M-F 9am-5:30pm. Tickets €26-31.) In addition, from May through August there are **outdoor performances,** including concerts, folk-singing, and dancing. The tourist office has leaflets on scheduled events, but an evening stroll through the park might prove just as enlightening. Mozartpl. and Kapitelpl. are also popular stops for talented street musicians and touring school bands, and the well-postered Aicher Passage next to Mirabellpl. is a great source of information for other upcoming musical events.

THEATER, MOVIES, AND GAMBLING

Next to Mirabellgarten, at the **Salzburger Marionettentheater** (☎87 24 06; fax 88 21 41; info@marionetten.at; www.marionetten.at), handmade marionettes perform to recorded *Festspiele* operas. The theater is almost as small as its actors. For information, contact Marionettentheater, Schwarzstr. 24, A-5020 Salzburg. (Box office open days M-Sa 9am-1pm and 2hr. before curtain. €18-33. AmEx/MC/V.) Track down English-language **movies** with the film program in **Das Kino** newspaper. Cinemas rotate a few films each month and often show them in English with German subtitles. Win enough money to pay your concert ticket debt at **Casino Salzburg** in Schloß Klessheim. Slot machines, blackjack, roulette, poker, and much more await you. Ask at the tourist office about the free shuttle service from the city center. (☎85 46 20. Open from 3pm. 19+, semi-formal attire required.)

⚄ OUTDOORS

If you're overwhelmed by Salzburg's culture, you can turn to wonders of a different variety. An adventure tour with **Crocodile Sports,** Gaisbergstr. 34a (☎64 29 07; office@crocodile-sports.com; www.crocodile-sports.com), will get your heart pumping. Owner and operator Wolfgang will pick you up from your hotel for a day (or multiple days) you'll never forget. Adventures include **canyoning** (€44-132), **canoeing** (€40-210), **paragliding** (€105), and **rafting** (€36-124). The lower prices are generally for day or half-day trips; the larger prices correspond to those that are multi-day and include food and accommodations of some kind. Call ahead. You can now also take a 40min. boat trip with **Salzburg City Cruise Line** (☎82 57 69 12; www.salzburgschifffahrt.at; info@salzburgschifffahrt.at) leaving from Makartsteg. The cruise, which runs up the Salzach past the city center and back, is a relaxing way to admire Salzburg's skyline. (Open May-Sept. with boats departing about every hour 8:45am-5pm, Jul.-Aug. until 7pm. €10, €7 for children.)

⚄ DAYTRIPS FROM SALZBURG

HELLBRUNN AND UNTERSBERG

To reach Hellbrun, take bus #55 (dir: Anif) to "Hellbrunn" from the train station, Mirabellpl., or Mozartsteg., 30min. down tree-lined Hellbrunner Allee (see p. 243).

Just south of Salzburg lies the unforgettable **Lustschloß Hellbrunn,** built 1613-1615 at the behest of Archbishop Markus Sittikus. The sprawling estate includes a palace, fish ponds, flower gardens, and tree-lined footpaths through grassy fields. An audio tour leads you through the small yellow palace, which includes a "fish room" and a "bird room" devoted to paintings of the rare and exotic animals the Archbishop had collected at Hellbrunn as a sign of his power. Don't be surprised if you hear screams of surprised laughter from outside. Archbishop Markus amused himself by creating water-powered figurines and a booby-trapped table that could spout water on his guests. The tour of these *Wasserspiele* (water games) is a delight on a warm day. Prepare yourself for an afternoon of wet surprises, including a small crown suspended high in the air on a stream of water and a mechanical demon spouting water from his nose who rolls his eyes and sticks out his tongue at the tourists. (Open after 6pm only. Ticket for castle tour, gardens, *Wasserspiele*, and Volkskundemuseum €7.50, students €5.50. In July and Aug. there is also an evening ticket for the outdoor areas after 6pm, €7.)

On the hill above the manicured grounds sits the tiny hunting lodge **Monatsschlössl** (Little Month Castle). One of the archbishop's many weaknesses was gambling, so when someone bet the archbishop that he couldn't build a castle in a month, he accepted the challenge and began spending church money on architects, engineers, and laborers who toiled around the clock. He won. The castle now houses the **Volkskundemuseum (Folklore and Local History Museum),** whose three floors of exhibits include several *Salzburger Schönperchten*—bizarre 2m hats worn in a traditional Austrian ceremony to scare away the demons of winter. (☎ 82 03 72 49 21. Open Apr.-Oct. daily 9am-5pm.) Continue past the Monatsschlössl to the **Steintheater** where sheer rock faces form a natural theater. The first opera performance in the German-speaking world took place here in 1616. Near the castle also lies the enormous **Hellbrunn Zoo,** the modern-day descendant of the Archbishop's exotic animal collections. Residents include griffin vultures, wolves, leopards, red pandas, emu, and crowned cranes. The zoo prides itself on not caging animals— they put them instead behind fences with cliffs at their backs. Includes a petting zoo for kids. (☎ 82 01 76. Open June-Sept. daily 8:30am-6:30pm, Dec. to mid-Feb. until 4:30pm, Mar.-May until 5:30pm. €6.50, students €4.70, children €3.30.)

Bus #55 continues south from Hellbrunn to the luscious **Untersberg** peak ("St. Leonhard" stop), where **Charlemagne** supposedly rests deep beneath the ground, prepared to return and reign over Europe when he is needed. A **cable car** glides over the rocky cliffs to the summit, and from there hikes lead off into the distance. (☎ (06246) 87 12 17 or 724 77; July-Sept. Th-Tu 8:30am; Mar.-June and Oct. 9am-5pm; Dec.-Feb. 10am-4pm.) The 30min. hike over the alpine ridge out to the Salzburger Hochthron provides unbelievable mountain scenery.

THE SALZKAMMERGUT

Early summer brings tourists, bands of Austrian school children, and groups of elderly Europeans to the smooth lakes and furrowed mountains of the Salzkammergut. The wave of visitors breaks at the resort towns littered across the rolling hills. Though the region takes its name from the salt mines that once financed Salzburg's architectural treasures, today it is the sunshine in summer and the fresh snow in winter that finance an equally profitable industry. Though not technically in Salzburgerland, Salzburg is the hub for all transportation in the area.

If your trip allows only one stop in the Salzkammergut, make it Hallstatt, whose aesthetically striking locale makes it worth more than a day's visit. After Hallstatt, the desirability of other destinations will depend on what you're seeking; you can find everything from posh spas to rustic hostels. For all the best bargains, pick up the ⬛Salzkammergut Card, which provides 30% discounts on countless local sights and attractions (€4.90; available at local tourist offices). For information on the region, contact the **Salzkammergut Regional Tourist Board,** Postfach 65, A-4820 Bad Ischl (☎613 22 86 67; fax 286 67 71; salzkammergut@touristik.at).

▐ **TRANSPORTATION AROUND THE SALZKAMMERGUT.** The Salzkammergut is easily navigable, with 2000km of footpaths, dozens of cable cars and chairlifts, and numerous hostels. Within the region, there is a dense network of **buses** that are the most efficient and reliable method of travel into and through the lake region, since much of the mountainous area is barren of rail tracks. When traveling by bus, be sure to plan your route in advance, as some connections run infrequently (dial ☎05 17 17 from Salzburg for complete schedule information). While *Let's Go* does not recommend it, **hitchers** from Salzburg have been seen taking bus #29 to Gnigl and coming into the Salzkammergut at Bad Ischl. **Bikers** should check out the 280km **Salzkammergut bike path,** which winds through many of the towns in the region. (Contact the Salzkammergut regional tourist office for more information on the route, or consult www.radtouren.at/english.) **Hikers** can capitalize on dozens of **cable cars** in the area to gain altitude before setting out on their own, though there are almost always cheaper hikes that can be made without expensive cable trips. Hiking in this lush area is easier than in many more intense alpine regions. Ask for hiking maps at any tourist office. Reasonably priced **ferries** service each of the larger lakes (railpass discounts available on the **Wolfgangsee, Attersee,** and **Traunsee** lines).

▐ **ACCOMMODATIONS.** Hostels are common throughout the area, but you can often find far superior rooms in private homes and *Pensionen* at just-above-hostel prices. *"Zimmer Frei"* signs peek out from virtually every house (average price is €15-21). **Campgrounds** dot the region, but many are trailer-oriented. Away from large towns, many travelers camp discreetly almost anywhere, generally without trouble. At higher elevations there are **alpine huts,** many of which are accessible on hikes. Contact the **Österreichischer Alpenverein** (Austrian Alpine Club; ☎ (0512) 595 47) for info and rental. Their central office is in Innsbruck, but locally experienced volunteers staff regional branches.

HALLSTATT ☎06134

Teetering on the banks of the **Hallstättersee** in a valley surrounded by the sheer cliffs of the Dachstein mountains, Hallstatt is easily the most striking lakeside village in the Salzkammergut, if not all of Austria. Declared a UNESCO World Cultural Heritage site in 1997, this tiny village of about 960 inhabitants seems to defy gravity, clinging to the face of a stony slope. Its angle on the mountainside assures that the lake dominates the horizon from nearly every vantage point. Hallstatt's salt-rich earth has helped preserve its archaeological treasures, which are so extensive that one era in Celtic studies (800-400BC) is dubbed the "Hallstatt era." The tourists throng the narrow streets, but Hallstatt refuses to be corrupted. The town and area merit more than a daytrip; stay a night (or a week) in a room overlooking the clear blue lake.

▐ **TRANSPORTATION**

From Salzburg, the **bus** (€10.30) is the cheapest way to get to Hallstatt, but it requires layovers in both Bad Ischl and Gosaumühle; buses run from Bad Ischl 6:50am-5:30pm, and the **bus stop** is at the edge of downtown on Seestr. across from the SPAR market. The **train station** is on the other side of the lake, but there is no staffed office to help travelers. A ferry shuttles passengers between the town and the station before and after each train (10min., 7:07am-6:44pm, €1.80). All trains come from Attnang-Puchheim in the north or Stainach-Irdning in the south. Outbound trains run to Attnang-Puchheim (1½hr., every hr., €9.74), Bad Ischl (30min., €2.76), and Salzburg (€17) via Attnang-Puchheim. **By car** from Salzburg or the Salzkammergut towns, take Rte. B-158 to Bad Ischl onto Rte. B-145 to Gosaumühle, then B-166 to Hallstatt. Automobile access to Hallstatt is limited to the town's overnight guests May-October. Ample day **parking** lots are available near the tunnels leading into town (free for guests staying in town).

■ ⚡ ⚡ ORIENTATION AND PRACTICAL INFORMATION

Hallstatt is on the Hallstättersee, a shimmering oasis at the southern tip of the Salzkammergut. Note that street numbers are fairly random. To get to the **tourist office** from the ferry stop, face away from the lake and turn left, walking past the Gemeindeamt until you see the office on your right at Seestr. 169 (7min.). The office offers free maps and finds rooms. (☎82 08; fax 83 52; hallstatt-info@EUnet.at; www.tiscover.com/hallstatt. Open July-Aug. M-F 9am-5pm, Sa 10am-4pm, Su 10am-2pm; Sept.-June M-Tu and Th-F 9am-noon and 2-5pm, W 9am-noon.) When the office is closed, you can always consult the tourist computer at the bus station, which has information on activities and accommodations as well as a free reservations phone. Services include: **ATM** next to the post office; **laundry** at Hotel Grüner Baum, 104 Marktpl. (€11 for washing and drying service, inquire at reception); **public bathrooms** next to the tourist office; and a **doctor** with an in-house **pharmacy** at Baderpl. 108. (Dr. Sonja Gapp, ☎84 01. Walk-in hours M-Tu 8am-noon, Th 10:30am-noon and 5-7pm, F-Sa 8-11am.) **Internet** access at the Hotel Grüner Baum (€5 per 20min.) and **bike rental** (€6 per half day, €11 per whole day). The **post office**, Seestr. 160 (☎82 01), is below the tourist office. (Open M-Tu and Th-F 8am-noon and 2-5:30pm, W 8am-noon.) **Postal code:** A-4830.

⚡ ACCOMMODATIONS AND CAMPING

The tourist office has an extensive list of *Privatzimmer*, but here are a few of the best and cheapest.

Gästehaus Zur Mühle, Kirchenweg 36 (☎/fax 83 18; toeroe.f@magnet.at). Walk uphill to the right of the tourist office, toward the short tunnel at the upper right corner of the square. The hostel is at the end of the tunnel, by the waterfall. Close to the city center with homey, wood-paneled 3- to 20-bed dorms and lots of English-speaking backpackers. Breakfast €2.50. Lunch and dinner available at the restaurant downstairs; see below. Showers included. Lockers with €20 deposit. Sheets €2.50. Reception 10am-2pm and 4-10pm. Closed in Nov. Dorms €10. ❷

Jugendherberge Lahn, Salzbergstr. 50 (☎82 12; fax 200 15). From the bus station, take Malerweg directly away from the lake, then take a left across the stream (5min.); the hostel is the pink-and-white building a little way down the road on the right. Sunny dorms and a small electric oven available for personal use. Breakfast €2.50. Showers included. Sheets €3.30. Call ahead. Open May to mid-Oct. Dorms €9.30. ❷

Frühstückspension Sarstein, Gosaumühlstr. 83 (☎82 17). From the ferry landing, turn right on Seestr. and walk for 10min.; it will be on the right. Although the bathrooms could use some sprucing up, Frau Fischer's *Pension* offers glorious vistas of the lake and village as well as a beachside lawn for sunning and swimming. Carved and painted wardrobes. Breakfast included. Hall bathrooms and showers (showers €1 per 10min.). Singles and doubles €18 per person, without balcony €16. Double with shower, bathroom, and balcony €25. ❸

Seehotel Grüner Baum, Marktpl. 104 (☎82 63; fax 84 20; grünerbaum@magnet.at; www.grünerbaum.at). If you're tired of "water closets" that actually are closets, it's time for a soak in the tub in one of the enormous bathrooms at the Hotel Grüner Baum. This hotel has the best location in town—on the lake at the foot of the quaint old market square. The building was once a salt trader's house and retains much of its historic feel. Pets welcome. Breakfast included. Closed in winter. €50-70; doubles €85-160. ❹

Gasthof Bergfried, Echerntalweg 3 (☎82 48; fax 82 48 33; sharf-bergfried@aon.at; www.interaktive.com/hotels/Bergfried). A convenient, hassle-free stay, and rooms with mountain views. The most hotel-like of the accommodations in Hallstatt, it's between the bus stop and the base of the Salzbergbahn. It's also the easiest to reach by auto—take the first right out of the tunnel. Breakfast included. Singles €35; doubles €56. ❸

Franziska Zimmerman, Gosaumühlstr. 69 (☎868 53), lives slightly closer to town than her sister, Frau Fischer, and offers similar accommodations. Frau Zimmerman rents out 2 doubles and a single, all well-furnished with views of the *Hallstättersee*. Breakfast and showers included. Call ahead. Single €16; doubles €32. ❸

Frühstückspension Seethaler, Dr.-F.-Mortonweg 22 (☎84 21; fax 842 14; pension.seethaler@kronline.at). Turn uphill next to the tourist office and follow the signs; it will be on your right. All rooms have balconies, most with amazing lake views. Breakfast in an antler-studded room included. Shower €1 per 8min. 4-bed dorms €18, with in-room shower and toilet €26; 2- to 4-person apartment with kitchen same price. ❸

Camping Klausner-Höll, Lahnstr. 201 (☎832 24; fax 832 21; camping.klausner@magnet.at). Exit the tourist office and walk past the bus stop on Seestr. for 10min. to this clean campground. Breakfast €3.80-8. Showers included. Laundry service €8. Open mid-Apr. to mid-Oct. Gate closed daily noon-3pm and 10pm-7:30am. €5.80, children 6-14 €3; tent €3.70, car €2.90, camper €4.50, trailer €5.80, electricity €2.90. ❶

▶ FOOD

While rooming in Hallstatt isn't pricey, eating is. The best bet for cheap food is either a pizza restaurant or a wurst stand. Get pizzas (€6.50-6.80), salads (€2.60-6.70), and pasta (€5.50-6.50) at the **pizzeria ❷** in Gästehaus Zur Mühle. (Open W-M 11am-2pm and 5-9:30pm; closed Nov.) **Gästehaus zum Weißen Lamm ❷,** Dr.-F-Mortonweg 166, uphill behind the tourist office, serves large, tasty portions. Head downstairs to the "mountaineer's cellar" or to their outdoor patio for two daily *Menüs* (€7.50-8.50) for lunch and dinner, including soup, entree, and dessert. (☎83 11. Open daily 10am-10pm, closed Tu in winter. Meals 11am-3pm and 5-10pm.) **Restaurant Simony ❷,** Wolfeng. 105, at the foot of the old market square next to the Hotel Grüner Baum, also provides excellent food. Enjoy one of their hearty main dishes on the lakeside patio, but be sure to leave room for the real attraction, dessert. *Marillenknödel,* (apricot dumplings), *Eismohr im Hemd* (spongy chocolate cake with ice cream), *Topfenpalatschinken* (an Austrian specialty), and sundaes, all around €4-5. (☎87 24. Open daily 10am-9pm.) If the weather's nice, you might have to give in to the temptation to splurge a bit and head over to the **Bräugasthof ❸** at Seestr. 120 , about five minutes away from the center of town and the bus stop. Enjoy one of their many fresh fish entrees, appropriate for their lovely lakeside location. Lunch entrees €9-13, dinner €10-16, including Viennese trout strudel for €10.50. (☎82 21. Open 11:30am-3pm and 6-9pm.) For a late-night snack, try homemade pastries and savory treats (around €2.50) at **Bar Zimmermann ❶**, Marktpl. 59. (Open 9am-2am.) **Cafe Derbl ❷**, Marktpl. 61, serves food to tourists at cheap prices. Individual pizzas are €4.10-5; other entrees (including the fascinating "Styrian dumpling secret") are €4-7. (☎82 40. Open 11am-6pm.) For even cheaper, greasier fare, try a frankfurter (€3) at **Imbiß Karl Forstinger ❶** on Seestr. near the bus station. (Open Mar.-Oct. daily 11am-5pm.) The cheapest food is at the **Konsum** supermarket across from the bus stop (open M-Tu and Th-F 7:30am-noon and 3-6pm, W 7:30am-12:30pm, Sa 7:30am-noon); the butcher's counter will prepare simple sandwiches on request.

🔄 🏛 SIGHTS AND MUSEUMS

Hallstatt packs a surprising number of attractions into a very small space. The tourist office sells a €3 English cultural guide, but strolling the steep twisting streets requires no plan. Be sure to get a guest card at your accommodation for discounts at many attractions, as well as entrance to the town by car.

CHURCH AND CHARNEL HOUSE. The charnel house next to St. Michael's Chapel at the **Pfarrkirche** offers a fascinating (if slightly macabre) insight into the burial scene in Hallstatt. Within the parish charnel house (*Beinhaus* in German, literally "bone-house") rest the bones of villagers from the 16th-century onward, the latest added in 1995. The Celts buried their dead high in the mountains, but Christians wanted to rest in the churchyard. Unfortunately, space on the steep hillside soon ran out, so the skulls and femurs of the long deceased were transferred after 10 or 20 years to the charnel house. Each of 610 neatly placed skulls was decorated with a wreath of flowers (for females) or ivy (for males) and inscribed with the name of the deceased and the date of death. The skulls were then stacked neatly on a shelf supported by femurs, tibiae, and fibulae. Today, bones are removed and painted only by special request. *(From the ferry dock, follow the signs reading "K.Kirche." Open June-Sept. daily 10am-6pm, Oct., May until 4pm. In winter, call ☎82 79 for an appointment. €1, students €0.40.)*

HISTORICAL MUSEUMS. In the mid-19th century, archaeologists in Hallstatt unearthed a collection of artifacts, a pauper's grave, and the crypts of the ruling class—all incredibly well-preserved and circa 1000-500BC. The Prähistorisches Museum and Heimatmuseum, across from the tourist office, exhibits some of these treasures, including coiled copper jewelry from the tombs and mines, as well as more modern artifacts such as costumes of the region, modern mining equipment, and local art. Renovations completed in 2002 give amusing multimedia effects to exhibits on the landslide of 350AD and the fire of 1750. *(☎82 20 15; fax 82 80. Open Apr.-June and Sept.-Oct. daily 9am-6pm; July-Aug. daily 10am-7pm; Nov.-Feb. Tu-Su 9am-6pm. €6, students and children €3 .)*

SALT MINES. The 2500-year-old Salzbergwerke, the oldest saltworks in the world, teem with tourists, not miners, these days. The fascinating guided tours *(1hr., in English and German)* include a zip down a wooden mining slide, a visit to a creepy lake deep inside the mountain, and a ride on a miner's train. Be sure to ask for a salt rock as a souvenir, or pick up the photo taken while you sped down the slide. *(To reach the salt mines, turn right at the bus circle. Follow the "Salzbergwerk" signs to the Salzbergbahn. From the end of the line, it's another 15min. uphill. Trains run May-Oct. daily 9am-6pm. For the last tour, take the 4pm train; 2:30pm train in Oct. Runs every 15min. €4.50, round-trip €7.50, children under 15 €2.70/€4.50. Or take the 1hr. hike (see below) to the mines. Salzbergwerke: ☎200 2400; fax 031 22. Open May-Sept. daily 9:30am-4:30pm; Oct. 9:30am-*

3pm. €14; with guest card, students, seniors €9.16; children 5-15 €5.09. Combination train and hike €19.50, students €11.70; children 4 and under not allowed.)

 OUTDOORS

HIKING. Hallstatt offers some of the most spectacular day hikes in the Salzkammergut, through forests where drops of water cling to the pine needles year-round, thanks to a climate very close to that of a temperate rainforest. The tourist office offers an excellent Dachstein hiking guide (€6; in English), which details 38 hikes in the area, as well as bike trail maps (€15). Hike to nearby mountain huts (see guide) or try one of the following shorter hikes:

Salt mine (Salzbergwerk) hike (1hr.). Walk to the Salzbergbahn (see directions above) and take the road upward to the right, turning at the black-and-yellow "Salzwelten" sign. This well-paved, shady, steep hike leads to the salt mine tour, giving you ever more elevated and astonishing views of the Hallstätter See. Halfway up, look for an entrance to the stone tunnel where Emperor Franz Joseph struck the first blow. Follow the same trail back, or take a cable car. Once you get to the top of the Salzbergbahn, it's another 15min. to the entrance to the salt mine. Take the stairs to your left up at the edge of the forest—this archaeological memorial path provides information (in German) about the history of the burial field discovered there.

Waldbachstrub waterfall hike (1½hr.) is a light walk along a crystal stream leading to a spellbinding waterfall. From the bus station, follow the brown signs reading "Malerweg" beginning near the supermarket. The Waldbach river's rush will sound through most of the hike. Follow Malerweg straight, crossing over the various bridges. 40min. later, the "Waldbachstrub" sign appears. If you've got 30min. and strong shoes, make a detour (sticking to the red-white-red Austrian flag markings) to the "Gletschergarten," a fantastic array of riverbed formations and pools created by the glaciers of the last Ice Age. Return and follow the "Waldbachstrub" sign for another 10min. to the magnificent double waterfall. Return by the same trail or turn left when you get to the bridge and follow the main path through an entirely different, un-touristed residential and agricultural area, returning to the bus station in about 40min. Be forewarned: in recent years this trail has been in disrepair.

Gangsteig (45min.-1½hr.), for experienced hikers only, is a primitive stairway carved onto the side of the cliff that is the Echental valley's right wall (the Waldbachstrub waterfall's valley). Completing the trail will take

THE LOCAL STORY

SALT OF THE EARTH

Dr. Fritz Eckart is the head of the archaeological excavations in Hallstatt. He is also the co-author of the books The EU Project Archeo-live *and* Archeological Inheritance of Hallstatt.

Q: How did you choose this career?
A: [At] college 50 years ago.
Q: What kind of [work] do you do?
A: My special area of study is salt mining—Austrian salt mining—and I've been studying the salt mines here in Hallstatt for 40 years.
Q: What would you say is the most important thing that you have found here?
A: Well, it's not just about finding things, but rather about history, interpretation. There are different locations in the mountain where we have found things. For example, there is a place from the 14th century where we can see how they extracted salt from the mountain at that time.
Q: How long has salt mining in Hallstatt been going on?
A: The oldest evidence we have found is from 7000 years ago, so 5000 BC.
Q: And the "man in salt" that was found here—his body is now missing, so how do you know how old he was?
A: Well, the place he was found allows us to say fairly exactly...probably at the time of the Hallstatt grave fields, between 8th century BC and 4th century BC. At that time, the "man in salt" was taken down into the valley and buried.

hiking shoes and a strong will to climb. Follow the Waldbachstrub hike until 2min. before the falls, where "Gangsteig" is marked on the right. It will be about another hour to the top.

WATER SPORTS AND SKIING. For a view of the mountains from below rather than above, try a scenic **boat trip** around the lake, departing from either ferry landing. (Schiffrundfarten Hemetsberger; ☎82 28. 50min.; May to late-Sept. 11am, 1, 2, 3pm, in good weather or by appointment; €6.54.) **Boat rental** for two people costs €5.50 per 30min. for an electric boat, €4.50 for a paddleboat, and €4 for a rowboat from **Hallstatt Schmuck** near the ferry landing by the Marktpl. For **wild water canoeing,** contact Gasthof Zauner "Seewirt" (☎82 46). **Swimming** in the lake is free, but watch out—the water's cold. The best place to swim is the public park, which can be reached from the bus stop by heading away from town along the Seelände, the road closest to the water's edge. There's also a great playground there. Winter visitors can take advantage of Hallstatt's **ski bus** (free with snow gear, contact the tourist office for info), which runs to the Krippenstein and Dachstein-West Ski areas several times a day. The tourist office can provide a map for area skiing.

⚐ DAYTRIP FROM HALLSTATT

OBERTRAUN AND THE DACHSTEIN CAVES ☎06131

To reach Obertraun from Hallstatt, take the bus from the Lahn bus station, on the lake near the Salzbergbahn at the western end of town. (8:35, 9:45, 10:55am, 1, 4:50pm; €1.70.) Stop at the cable car station, "Dachstein," for the caves. Ride the cable car up 1350m to "Schönbergalm" for the ice and mammoth caves (every 15min. 8:40am-5:30pm, last trip for a tour at 4:15pm; €13 round-trip, children €7.50). The Koppenbrüller cave is a 15min. walk from the bus stop in Obertraun. For all cave tours, wear good footwear and something warm—the caves hover near freezing for most of the year.

The magnificent **Dachstein Caves** are one more testament to the region's geological activity. There are three sets of caves: the **Rieseneishöhlen** (Giant Ice Caves) and the **Mammuthöhlen** (Mammoth Caves) are up on the mountain, while the **Koppenbrüllerhöhle,** a giant spring, is in the valley near the village of Obertraun. The Mammoth Cave, as its name implies, is enormous, with an explored length of over 60km. Tours, offered in English and German, are required and last 50min.; you'll be assigned to a group at the Schönbergalm station. (☎84 00. Open May to mid-Oct. 9am-5pm. Admission to each cave €8, children €4.80; for both caves €12.30/€6.80.) The Koppenbrüllerhöhle is more romantic than gigantic, and can be reached without cable car from the Obertraun bus or Koppenbrüllerhöhle train stops. (Tours May-Sept. every hr. 9am-4pm; €6.50, children €3.90.)

For a panoramic **hike,** try the **Karstlehrpfad** (3-4hr., accessible from late June to first snowfall), beginning from **Krippenstein,** the top station of the Dachstein lift. From that station, follow the path below the Schutzhaus restaurant and go left at the split; you'll finish at the bottom of the **Gjaidalm lift** (runs 9am-5pm), which will return you to the Dachsteinbahn (ticket for all three lifts €20, children €12.50.)

The Obertraun **tourist office** is located in the Gemeindeamt, Obertraun 180; turn right onto main road from train station and follow signs. (☎06131 351; fax 342 22. Open M-F 8am-noon and 2-5pm; July-Aug. also Sa 9-11am.) An **ATM** is at the Volksbank directly next to the tourist office. **Post office,** Obertraun 175, is on the way to the tourist office. (☎06131 332. Open M-Tu and Th-F 8am-noon and 2-5pm, W 8am-noon.) Stock up on food at **Konsum market,** at the turn-off for the tourist office. (Open M and W-F 7:30am-noon and 3-6pm, Tu 7:30am-noon.)

BAD ISCHL   ☎ 06132

Bad Ischl (pop. 14,000) was a salt-mining town for centuries, until Dr. Franz Wirer arrived in 1821 to study the curative properties of the heated brine baths in the area. Pleased with his findings, he began to prescribe brine bath vacations in Bad Ischl for his patients in 1822. Archduke Francis Charles and Archduchess Sophia journeyed to Bad Ischl seeking a cure for their infertility and soon managed to produce three sons, the so-called **Salt Princes** (one was Franz Josef I, who made Bad Ischl his annual summer residence).

⌐ TRANSPORTATION

Only one train comes through the **train station** (☎ 24 40 70; desk open M-F 6:30am-6:35pm, Sa 8:05am-5:15pm), running between Attnang-Puchheim in the north (1hr., 4:42am-8:49pm, €6.50) and Hallstatt in the south (30min., 6:17am-8:17pm, €6.50). Trains go through these towns to Linz (€11.60), Vienna (4hr., €30.50), and Zell am See (€24.60). **Buses** leave the station (☎ 231 13; desk open M-F 8am-4pm) for Salzburg (1½hr., every hr. 5am-7:20pm, €7.27) and **St. Wolfgang** (1hr., every hr. 5:47am-9:20pm, €1.40). By **car**, Bad Ischl lies on Rte. 158 and 145. From Innsbruck or Munich, take A-1 East past Salzburg and exit onto Rte. 158 near Thalgau. From Salzburg, take Rte. 158 through St. Gilgen and Fuschl. From Vienna, take A-1 West to Rte. 145 at Regau.

✦❶ ORIENTATION AND PRACTICAL INFORMATION

Though Bad Ischl is one of the only towns in the Salzkammergut not on a lake, it lies at the junction of the **Traun** and **Ischl** rivers, which form a horseshoe around the city. The **tourist office** is on Bahnhofstr. 6. From the station, turn left on Bahnhofstr. The office has lists of *Pensionen* and *Privatzimmer* and an excellent free map—ask for the detailed one. (☎ 277 57. Open M-F 8:30am-noon and 1:30-5pm, Sa 9am-noon.) **Salzkammergut-Touristik,** Götzstr. 12, the regional tourist office, is also great for information and finding a place to stay. Bike rental is €13 per day. From the train station, turn right down Bahnhofstr. and turn left onto Götzstr., just before you get to the river. (☎ 240 000. Open daily 9am-8pm.) Services include: **ATM** at Oberbank on Franz Josef Str.; **lockers** at the train station (€2); **public restrooms** at the train station and under the Parkbad entrance; **Kurapotheke** pharmacy, Kreuzpl. 18 (open 8am-noon, 2-6pm, and for emergencies); **post office,** down Bahnhofstr., on the corner of Auböckpl. (open M-F 8am-6pm, Sa 9am-noon; **Internet** access €2.50 for 30min., €4.50 for 1hr.). **Postal code:** A-4820.

▐ ACCOMMODATIONS

Every guest who stays the night in Bad Ischl pays a *Kurtax*, which entitles you to a guest card (June to mid-Sept. €1.82-2.18 per person per night depending on proximity to city center; Oct.-May €0.94-1.09). Bad Ischl's **Jugendgästehaus (HI) ❸,** Am Rechensteg, is minutes from the *Kaiser*'s summer residence. From the tourist office, walk left on Bahnhofstr., turn right on Franz Josef Str., and keep going until you see the *Jugendgästehaus* sign to the left, after the bend to the right. Head down this street (which looks like it dead ends in a hedge), which curves to the left behind the buildings. The hostel offers mostly quads, each with its own bath. (☎ 265 77; fax 265 77 75. Breakfast included. HI membership required. Reception 10am-1pm and 5-7pm. Quiet hour 10pm. Check-out 9am. Reservations recommended. €15.98 per person; singles €25.43; doubles €18.16.) If the HI hostel is full, try **Haus Stadt Prag ❸,** Eglmoosg. 9. From the

SALZBURGER LAND

train station, go left on Bahnhofstr., right on Franz Josef Str., and left on Kreuzpl. Follow until it becomes Salzburgerstr., and bear left on Stiegeng. at the *Goldschmied* sign. Continue along Stiegeng. and up the steps—Haus Stadt Prag is the building on your right at the top of the hill. It has spacious rooms with balconies decorated in the local style. (☎/fax 236 16. Breakfast included. All rooms with bath and TV. Singles €27; doubles €53.) For a slightly nicer stay, head over to **Villa Dachstein ❹**, Rettenbachweg 3. From the train station, take a right on Bahnhofstr. and head straight. Immediately on the other side of the river, take a right onto the footpath, which heads steeply uphill after going under the railroad bridge. This huge house situated at the top of the hill has great views of Bad Ischl, and its three pointy towers lend it lots of character. (☎23 151; fax 23 151 113; office@villadachstein.at. Breakfast included. €32-34 per person.) At the higher end is **Hotel Stadt Salzburg ❹**, Salzburger Str. 25. From the train station, head left down Bahnhofstr., right on Frnaz Josef Str., and then left through Kreuzpl. to Salzburger Str. This three-star hotel offers many services, and caters especially to fish-lovers with special fly-fishing programs and a restaurant serving up local varieties. (☎235 64; fax 235 64 24; stadt-salzburg@eunet.at. Breakfast included. Singles €42; doubles €70.)

▐ FOOD

Restaurants are tucked into every possible niche in the pedestrian zone. Stop for a kebab (€3.30) at the tiny but modern **Bistro Oriental ❶**, Kreuzpl. 13, near the hostel. (Open daily 10am-10pm.) One of the best deals for a sit-down meal is the **Gasthaus Sandwirt ❷**, Eglmoosg. 4 (☎264 03), just up the street from Haus Stadt Prag. Enjoy one of their cold dishes in the shade of the patio, from bread and sardines for €2.30 to a mixed cold cut platter for €6.80. Other options include ham and cheese sandwiches (€3.80), *Gröstl* (€5), or items from the grill (around €8). Join in Bad Ischl's love for Kaiserin Elizabeth by ordering a Coupe Sisi, a sundae with vanilla, chocolate, and hazelnut ice cream doused in chocolate liqueur. (€4.30). (Open 11am-1:30pm, 5-9pm, closed Th after 2pm.) Probably the most pleasant place to eat outdoors is at the riverside tables at **China Restaurant Happy Dragon ❷**, Pfarrg. 2 (☎234 32), at the intersection of Pfarrg. and Wirestr. Most dishes cost around €7-8, including chicken with pineapple and curry fish. (Open daily 11:30am-3pm and 6-11pm.) If you're really hungry, try out **Gasthaus zu Bürgerstub'n ❷**, Kreuzpl. 7 (☎235 68), just up the street from Bistro Oriental. Their rib dinner (€7.50) is one of the very few "all you can eat" deals you'll see in Austria. (Open 11:30am-3pm and 6-9pm, May-Sept. closed Su.) Cheap eats are also available at the various *Imbiße* in town, particularly the **Börni Börges ❶** stand near the McDonald's on Dr. Franz Wirer Str., which serves various burgers (€2.80-3.40). Almost as famous as the *Kaiser* himself is the **Konditorei Zauner**, Pfarrg. 7 (☎235 22). Established in 1832, this crowded eatery has an international reputation for heavenly sweets and *tortes*. Enjoy the old-fashioned atmosphere and treat yourself to their extravagant desserts (most around €2.80) or gourmet sandwiches (around €3). The **Konsum grocery store** is conveniently located at Auböckpl. 12, behind the Trinkhalle. (Open M-F 7:30am-6:30pm, Sa 7:30am-5pm). Browse at the **open-air market** held every Friday morning on Salinenpl.

▣ SIGHTS

Other than the baths, Bad Ischl's main attractions are the Habsburgs' cultural and architectual legacies, including the Kaiservilla and Pfarrkirche. If you'd rather spend time outdoors, the Siriuskogl hike lets you see it all from above.

VILLAS. In 1854, Austria's last empress, Elisabeth, received the **Kaiservilla** as a wedding present from her mother-in-law. Though she didn't care for the place, her husband Emperor Franz Josef designated it his family's summer getaway. Inside, a vast collection of mounted chamois horns (over 2000!) graces the walls in his wing of the house. Amid the animal remains are many relics of Franz Josef's reign, including the desk where he signed the declaration of war against Serbia that led to WWI. Entrance is allowed only through a guided tour in German, with English text available. *(☎232 41. Open May to mid-Oct. daily 9-11:45am and 1-5:15pm. €9.50, children €4.)* Buy tickets for the tour when you enter the **Kaiserpark.** *(Off Franz Josef Str., after the bend. €3.50, children €2.50.)* Also within the *Kaiserpark*, you'll find the ivy-covered **Marmorschlößl** *(☎244 22),* which houses the **Photo Museum.** Entrance to the Photo Museum requires a pair of fluffy slippers (provided at the front desk) to protect the exquisite wood floors. Habsburg family photos complement temporary exhibitions. *(Open Apr.-Oct. daily 9:30am-5pm. €1.50; students and seniors €0.70; family card €3.)* The **Lehár Villa,** Lehárkai 8, former summer home of composer Franz Lehár, is worth a quick visit. Among Lehár's works is the most popular operetta of all time, *The Merry Widow.* From Bahnhofstr., continue straight until you hit the river and esplanade, then take Grazerstr. across the river and turn left. *(☎269 92. Open May-Sept. 9am-noon and 2-5pm. Obligatory tour €4.40, students and children €1.82.)*

PARISH CHURCH AND ORGAN. The **Stadtpfarrkirche** houses gorgeous wall paintings and the magnificent late-Baroque **Kaiserjubiläumsorgel** (Emperor's Jubilee Organ). To get there, turn left out of the tourist office, then right onto Franz Josef Str.; the church will be on your left. Empress Maria Theresia had it built in place of the original Gothic building, the tower of which still stands. Don't miss the ceiling frescoes (done 1874-1882 by Georg Mader) that depict the life of St. Nicholas. The Latin inscription across the front of the church reads: "Due to the piety and generosity of the empress." Its open, light-flooded interior and acoustics are equally breathtaking. Check in front of the church for organ performance times (free).

SALT BATHS. Regardless of whether or not the **brine baths** that Dr. Wirer promoted really have curative powers, they certainly relieve stress. The bath facilities are mostly in the posh **Kaiser Therme,** a resort across from the tourist office on Bahnhofstr. 1. Splash around in the heated salt baths with whirlpool or consider relaxing in the spacious **sauna.** Massages, mud baths, and other services are more expensive but are sure to soothe both body and soul. *(☎23 32 40. Baths with whirlpool open 9am-10pm; €9, children €5. Sauna open daily 1:30-10pm, Tu men only, Th women only; €13 for 3hr., children €17 for 3hr. Massages, etc., M-Sa 8am-noon or by appointment.)*

🏔 OUTDOOR ACTIVITIES

A free map available at the tourist office shows **local hiking paths;** head to the summit of nearby **Mt. Katrin** (1544m) for a good place to start. Get to the **Katrinseilbahn** (cable car; ☎237 88; 12min.; 9am-5pm; €10.63, children €7.99) by taking a city bus from the train station (€1.31, day pass €2.18, family day pass €2.91) or by walking 15min. on the extension of Bahnhofstr. along the Esplanade, Kaltenbachstr., and Dumbastr. The **Siriuskogl hike** requires no cable car and rewards you with a wondrous panoramic view of Bad Ischl and its environs. To begin the hike from the tourist office, exit the office left, walk toward the train station, and continue over the bridge on the left onto Grazerstr. Turn left onto Siriuskoglg., and follow the sign "Zum Siriuskogl." Stick to the main, trodden trail up to the top, about 30min. from the base, to **Gasthaus Siriuskogl.** *(☎258 36. May-Oct. daily* about 10am-10pm, but be sure to call ahead.) The view from the *Gasthaus* is fantastic and best enjoyed with one of the cheap dishes (averaging €4). **Bikers** can get a small trail map for free at the tourist office or a trail map of the entire region for €10. In winter, Bad Ischl maintains an extensive network of **cross-country skiing** trails (pick up free maps at the tourist office). The **Parkbad Bad Ischl,** located next to the Kaiserpark's entrance, boasts an array of modern outdoor swimming pools on the site of Empress Elizabeth's private pool. (Open May to mid-Sept. daily 9am-7pm; June 15-Aug. 15 9am-8pm. 2hr. €2.20, day pass €3.60, children's day pass €1.80.)

🎵 ENTERTAINMENT

For the low-down around town, pick up the brochure *Bad Ischl Events* from the tourist office. Free outdoor **Kurkonzerte** take place between May and October at the *Kurpark* along Wienerstr. The exact program of performances by the 20-piece *Kurorchestra* or quartet is posted weekly on kiosks, in the hotels, and at the *Kurhaus* itself. Every year in mid-August, the **Bad Ischler Stadtfest** brings a weekend of music—classical, pop, jazz, boogie-woogie, and oom-pah-pah. Just before the *Stadtfest* on August 15, the Bad Ischlers celebrate Franz Josef's birthday with live music on the Esplanade. In July and August, the **Bad Ischl Operetten Festspiele** celebrates the musical talent of operetta composer **Franz Lehár,** who lived in Bad Ischl for 30 years and created *The Merry Widow, Gypsy Love,* and *The Land of Smiles.* Tickets are available from Büro der Operettengemeinde Bad Ischl, Wiesengerstr. 7, A-4820 Bad Ischl. (☎238 39; fax 238 39 39; www.operette.badischl.at. Open Aug.-June daily 9am-3pm, July 9am-6pm.) From May to October, a **flea market** comes to the Esplanade on the first Saturday morning of the month. Bad Ischl indulges in all sorts of Yuletide festivities, including a **Christkindlmarkt** (Christmas market), Advent caroling in the *Kurhaus,* tours of elaborate **Weihnachtskrippen** (nativity scenes) in the area, and horse-drawn sleigh rides *(Pferdeschliffen).*

🚌 DAYTRIP FROM BAD ISCHL

GMUNDEN ☎07612

Only one train goes through Gmunden, running from Attnang-Pucheim in the north to Stainach-Irding in the south. It is best done as a day trip from Bad Ischl (€5) or Hallstatt. Within the city, the street car line (the shortest in Europe) runs from the train station to the lake, with a stop at the ceramics factory. By car from Salzburg, take A1 east and exit onto 145 at Regau. From Vienna, take A1 west and exit onto 144 at Steyermuhl.

Situated at the edge of the clean and cold Traunsee, Gmunden is well known for its ceramics, castles, and beautiful mountain scenery. The city began as a Celtic settlement, and records of it date back to the year 909.

To get to the **tourist office** from the train station, take the street car from the stop to the end of the line from the Esplanade and turn left at the next intersection. The tourist office will be on your right at Am Graben 2. (☎643 05; fax 714 10; info@traunsee.at; www.traunsee.at. Open M-F 8am-1pm and 2-6pm, Sa 9am-1pm.) For overnight stays, pick up a list of *Privatzimmer;* one of the best options is **Haus Hager** (☎/fax 72 775), Pensionatstr. 32. Take bus #2 to "Pensionatstr." It's the house with the beautiful garden right across the street from the stop.

Gmunden is well known in Austria for its ceramics, especially for its green-and-white china pattern. Shops selling dishware and porcelain knick-knacks dot the town. The **ceramics factory** itself also has a large store selling its work and offers guided tours for groups upon request (€3). Take the street car to "Keramik." (☎786. Tours M-Th 9am-2:30pm, F 9am-noon. Store open M-F 9am-6pm, Sa 9am-1pm). Ceramic creations can be seen in many places around town, including the ceramic bells hanging in the town hall and the ceramic fountain in Rinnholz Square. The best place to see true masterpieces, however, is the **Galerie Schloß Weyer**, a museum dedicated to Meissner porcelain inside a small Renaissance castle. It has seven rooms full of delicate figurines, elaborate tables services, and opulent oriental rugs. *(☎650 18; fax 6 56 05 31. Open Tu-F 10am-noon, 2-5:30pm, Sa 10am-1pm.)* The picturesque **Seeschloß Ort** is worth a visit for its unusual location out in the waters of the Traunsee. Walk down the Promenade away from the river, take the first street left, then follow the signs. Don't be surprised by tons of German tourists here—this castle is the location of an extremely popular German television show called "Schloßhotel Ort." Unfortunately, the castle is not actually a hotel, and you can't go inside any of its rooms. Marks on the walls show water levels in various floods. The **▓Museum of Historical Sanitary Objects** (nicknamed "Klo und So") offers a remarkable collection of sinks, toilets, and tubs. Highlights include a collapsible travel bidet and the bidet which belonged to Empress Elizabeth. This museum feeds into the **Volkskundemuseum,** a small exhibit of objects from the past, including umbrellas, pipes, and waffle irons. *(Open May-Oct. Tu-Sa 10am-noon and 2-5pm, Su 10am-noon. €3 for both museums, students under 19 €0.80.)*

There are several places to rent **boats** along the Promenade, including F. Berger Bootverleih or Oberleitner (electric boat €6 for 30min., €10.50 per hr.; pedal boat €4.50 for 30min., €7.50 per hr.; row boat €3 per 30min., €5 per hr.). Be sure to take a ride on Europe's oldest paddle driven **steamer,** *Gisela*. Tours leave from in front of the *Rathaus* and cost between €7.50 and €10.50. The gondola to the top of the Grünberg mountain leads to an excellent **hiking** area. (Gondola open July-Aug. daily 9am-6pm, Apr.-Jun and Sept.-Oct. daily 9am-5pm. Round-trip €10, children €6, ascent only €7/€4.20.)

NEAR BAD ISCHL

GRÜNAU   ☎07616

Sitting in the middle of the **Totes Gebirge** (Dead Mountains), Grünau is a tiny community with an incredible backyard ideal for hiking, skiing, boating, fishing, swimming, and relaxing. A small regional train runs to Grünau from **Wels** (1hr., 6:47am-8:48pm, €6), and a bus runs frequently from near the **Gmunden** post office (45min., 5:35am-5:20pm, €3.60). Grünau is best experienced from ▓**The Treehouse ❷,** Schindlbachstr. 525, a backpacker's dream resort. Each room has its own bathroom with private shower and goose-down blankets. Call ahead and one of the staff will pick you up at the train station free of charge. The easiest way to get there, though, is to take the shuttle directly to the Treehouse from the Yoho hostel in Salzburg (€19; for schedule info call ☎06 64 or 43 51 590). Once you've settled in, take advantage of its many facilities: TV room with hundreds of English-language movies, book-exchange library, sauna, basketball hoop, pool tables, and tennis courts (all free of charge, equipment provided), plus two bars for nighttime revelry. **Internet** access is €0.10 per min. and **mountain bike** rental is €6 per day. (☎(07616) 84 99; treehousehotel@hotmail.com; www.geocities.com/treehousehostel. Breakfast buffet included. 3-course dinner €6.90. 6-bed dorm €13.80 per person; doubles €35; triples €50; quads €61. AmEx/MC/V.)

The staff organizes adventure tours including **canyoning** (€50, not in winter), **bungee jumping** (€95, only on weekends), and **horseback riding** (€9.50 per hr.).

The winter **ski lift** is a 5min. walk from the front door, and snow gear (jackets, snowsuits, gloves, etc.) is free. Day ski-lift passes are €20.50, while ski and snowboard rental runs €13. A free hiking map helps to navigate the mountains and three lakes in the vicinity. For a half-day hike, walk to the Kasberg Mountain (1500m) or the Spitzplaneck Mountain (1617m, 4-5hr.). The more adventurous may try the longer but not-too-difficult hike to Große Priel (2515m). It is often taken as a two-day trek with a mountain hut stay (€10; ask the Treehouse staff for info) along the way.

ST. WOLFGANG ☎ 06138

According to local legend, Bishop Wolfgang of Regensburg hurled his axe into the valley of the Abersee in 976 AD. He built a church where the axe landed, and battled the devil on a rocky outcropping to protect it. Once Wolfgang had been canonized for these miraculous feats, the church on the Abersee (now the **Wolfgangsee**) became the object of mass pilgrimage, although many present-day pilgrims are of the camcorder- and fanny-pack-toting variety. But the tourists are onto something: St. Wolfgang is a great little town to explore.

▐ TRANSPORTATION

The town has no train station, but **buses** run every hour to Bad Ischl (40min., M-F 6:50am-8:13pm, €3) and Salzburg (1½hr., M-F 5:05am-8:13pm, €7.60) via Strobl. The Wolfgangsee **ferry** (☎223 20) runs to nearby St. Gilgen (45min., 9:20am-3:20pm, €4.30) and Strobl (30min., 8:45am-2:47pm, €3.20) and between St. Wolfgang's two ferry landings at St. Wolfgang Markt and the Schafbergbahnhof. (June-Oct., every hr. 9am-7pm. Children half price. Eurail valid.) From Vienna by **car**, take A1 West to Mondsee and head south through St. Lorenz and Scharfling. From Salzburg, take Rte. 158 east through Hof, Fuschl, and St. Gilgen.

❊ ▐ ORIENTATION AND PRACTICAL INFORMATION

St. Wolfgang is a lovely place to get lost, which is fortunate, since street names are difficult to find and maps are as rare as they are indecipherable. There are three bus stops in town—when coming into town, the first stop is "St. Wolfgang Au" at the eastern end; after going through a tunnel, the bus will stop again at "St. Wolfgang Markt," and then at the western end of town at "St. Wolfgang Schafbergbahn." The main **tourist office,** Au 140, is a few steps away from the eastern stop. (☎80 03; fax 80 03 81; info@wolfgangsee.at; www.wolfgangsee.at. Open June-Sept. 9am-8pm; Oct.-May M-F 9am-noon and 2-5pm, Sa 9am-noon.) Services include: **ATMs** in the tourist office; **public bathrooms** near the bus stop "St. Wolfgang Markt" (€0.50); **pharmacy** near Hotel Peter on M. Pacher Str., (☎33 37; open M-F 8am-12:30pm and 2:30-6pm, Sa 8am-noon, Su 9-11am, and anytime for emergencies.) **Post office** around the corner and down Pilgerstr. from the bus stop "St.Wolfgang Markt." (☎22 01; open June-Sept. M-F 8am-noon and 2-5pm; Oct.-May M-Tu and Th-F 8am-noon and 2-5pm, W 8am-noon.) **Postal code:** A-5360.

▐ ACCOMMODATIONS AND CAMPING

Two thousand tourists troop through St. Wolfgang every summer day, and many stay the night. The tourist office's brochure lists hotels, *Pensionen*, and private rooms. Consider staying at the Berghotel Schafbergspitze.

Haus am See, M. Pacher Str. 98 (☎22 24), across the street from the tourist office, next to the bus station, has 50 beds in a sprawling old house on the lake. The bathrooms could use a renovation, but the rooms are clean and the view is fantastic (most rooms with balconies). Breakfast included. Hall showers. Parking available. Open June-Sept. Prices depend on balcony and view. Boathouse 5-person dorm €10.90 per person; singles €14.53-21.80; doubles €29.06-43.60; quads €58.12-87.20. Surcharge for one-night stays. ❷

Haus Reif, Sternalle 143 (☎/fax 22 15; margareta.reif@aon.at). From the bus stop "St. Wolfgang Markt," head downhill and take the first right. Haus Reif will be on your right—its beautifully manicured lawn and the verse painted above the front door make it easy to spot. All rooms with toilet and balcony. Breakfast included. €22-27. ❸

Strandhotel Margaretha, Margarethenstr. 67 (☎23 79; fax 23 79 22; strandhotelf@wolfgangsee.com). Just to the west of the Schafsbergbahn, this luxurious hotel offers great opportunities to enjoy the scenery, including a lakeside deck and free use of the hotel's rowboat and **bicycles.** Receptionist in traditional Austrian costume. Doubles €42-80, depending on view and time of year. ❹

Pension Raudaschl, Deschbühel Au 41 (☎25 61). From the tourist office, continue past the parking lot and turn uphill at Hotel Peter. Climb up the hill, and it's on the left (3min.). This smaller *Pension,* on the way to the major hiking paths, offers 7 rooms with private wooden balconies and baths. Breakfast included. Open May-Oct. Singles €21; doubles €42. Add 20% for one-night stays. ❸

Camping Appesbach, Au 99 (☎22 06), about 1km east of tourist office. Use of the extensive beach and warm showers included. July-Aug. €4-8 for the space per night plus €6 per adult, €3 per child. Rest of year €5.09, €2.91. ❶

◻ FOOD

Most of St. Wolfgang's restaurants and *Imbiße* are rather expensive. Snack shacks selling sausages and hamburgers (€1.40-3.60) line M. Pacher Str. Sit down at **Gasthof Franz Josef ❷,** at the St. Wolfgang Markt ferry landing, for its vegetarian entrees, which run €5.50-6.20. (Open Easter-Sept.) Another good option is the **Zimmerbrau ❷** restaurant (Markt 89, ☎22 04.) just to the east of the Markpl. Most dishes €7-8, but some are less, such as the *Käsespätzle* with caramelized onions (€6.80) and sandwiches from €4.80. *Konditoreien* also serve up a local specialty—**Schafbergkugeln** (about €1.70), a tennis-ball-sized hunk of milk chocolate filled with cream, spongecake, nuts, and marzipan. Pick one up at **Bäckerei Gandl,** Im Stöckl 84. (☎22 94. Open daily 7am-7pm.) The **ADEG** on Pilgerstr. market sells fruits of all kinds and standard groceries. (Open M-Tu and Th-F 7am-noon and 2-6pm, W 7am-noon, Sa 7am-1pm.)

◐ SIGHTS

WALLFAHRTSKIRCHE (PILGRIMAGE CHURCH). St. Wolfgang's main attraction, the **Wallfahrtskirche,** is in the Marktpl. The church's interior is unbelievably ornate. The altarpiece, completed by **Michael Pacher** in 1480 after a decade of labor, opens like a heavenly portal to reveal the coronation of Mary, complete with trumpeting angels. The Baroque Schwanthaler Altar, installed in 1676, was originally made to replace Pacher's, but the sculptor **Thomas Schwanthaler** bravely persuaded the abbot to leave Pacher's masterpiece alone. Together the altars almost overwhelm the church—don't miss smaller treasures like Schwanthaler's *Rosenkranzaltar* (Rose Garland Altar) or the St. Wolfgang memorial room. To see the breadth of St. Wolfgang's attractions in under thirty minutes, take a carriage ride from the church (25min., €19). *(Turn right out of the tourist office and head straight down the road.)*

SCHAFBERGBAHN. St. Wolfgang's other major attraction is the **Schafbergbahn,** a romantic steam engine that slowly ascends to the summit of Schafberg. The railway was built in 1892, and Hollywood found it charming enough to deserve a cameo in *The Sound of Music*, with the Von Trapp children waving from the windows. From the top, dozens of trails wind down the mountain, leading to such nearby towns as St. Gilgen, Ried, and Falkenstein. Tickets for the 30min. ride run as steep as the mountain. *(☎223 20. May-Oct. every hr. 9am-6pm; ascent €12.70, half-way €9.70, round-trip €20.90; children 6-15 half-price; Eurail valid.)* If you must pay full price, you might as well take advantage of the special deal offered by the 🛏 **Berghotel Schafbergspitze ❹** *(☎35 42; fax 354 24)*, a lovely mountain inn peeking over the Schafberg's steepest face. For €44.10 per person, you get a round-trip ticket on the railway, a room (with shower), and breakfast. Reserve in advance.

🔔 🎵 OUTDOORS AND ENTERTAINMENT

The clear and expansive Wolfgangsee guarantees water-sport lovers will be kept busy. Walk east along the lake from Marktpl. for about 10min., to the **public lake-bath's** raft. **Waterskiing** is available through Stadler on the *Seepromenade* near the Schafbergbahn. *(☎(0663) 917 97 53; €10 per circuit.)* Rent **boats** in town at the landing near Marktpl. and at the *Seepromenade.* (Motor boats €8 per 30min., €14 per hr. Pedal boats 30min. €8 per hour.) **Hiking** trails are clearly marked from town, and maps cost €2 (small) and €6.50 (large). Try Vormauerweg ("C," marked near Pension Raudaschl) to **Vormauerstein,** and return over Aschau by Sommerauweg "28" (4-4½hr.). **Bike rentals** are available from Pro Travel Agency by the ferry *(☎252 50. Open daily 9am-6pm. €8.80 per day. Lock and helmet included.)* On a weekend evening in St. Wolfgang, catch a production of local composer Ralph Benatzky's operetta **"White Horse Inn"** *(Im Weißen Rössl).* *(☎80 03. Performed in German May 23-Aug. 23, F 8:30pm; tickets from €18.90 through the Singspielbüro.)*

MONDSEE ☎ 06232

Water sports are raised to a pinnacle in the Salzkammergut's warmest lake, the **Mondsee** (Moon Lake), named for its crescent shape. The town offers hiking and biking opportunities and less strenuous amusement in Schloßgalerie's art exhibits.

📧 TRANSPORTATION. Mondsee has no train station but is accessible by bus from Salzburg's Hauptbahnhof (50min., 1-2 per hr. 6:35am-8:30pm, €4.50) and from Vienna, Wien-Mitte (4hr., M-F 7:30am, Apr.-Oct. M-Sa). Buses run to **St. Gilgen** on the Wolfgangsee (20min., M-F 6:25, 8:40, 11:50am, 6:55, and 7:15pm, Sa 11:50am; €2.60). By **car,** take Autobahn A-1 or the more scenic Rte. 158 from Salzburg to St. Gilgen and then Rte. 154 along the lake to downtown Mondsee.

🔋🛈 ORIENTATION AND PRACTICAL INFORMATION. To reach the **tourist office,** Dr.-Franz-Müllerstr. 3, head up the road from the bus stop, turn right onto Rainerstr., and continue to Marktpl. Turn right again, and the office is on the left. A box in front of the office contains maps of Mondsee. *(☎22 70 or 42 70; info@mondsee.org. Open July-Aug. daily 8am-7pm; June and Sept. M-F 8am-noon and 2-6pm, Sa 9am-noon and 3-6pm; Oct.-May M-F 8am-noon and 1-5pm.)* **ATMs** are at the Volksbank by the tourist office, at the Raiffeisenbank on Rainerstr., which provides tickets to area events, and at the Salzburger Sparkasse on Marktpl. The **post office,** on Franz-Kreuzbergerstr., is across from the bus station. (☎266 50. Open M-F 8am-noon and 2-6pm; exchange closes at 5pm.) **Postal code**: A-5310.

📍 ACCOMMODATIONS. *Gasthöfe* and hotels crowd the area near Marktpl., and *Privatzimmer* hang *"Zimmer Frei"* signs. The tourist office also offers a listings of rooms available. Try the **Jugendgästehaus (HI) ❸,** Krankenhausstr. 9. Go up Kreuzbergerstr. from the bus station, right on Rainerstr., and left onto Steinerbachstr. After 150m, look for a sign on the left and follow Krankenhausstr. (the street most toward the center) around the bend to the left; the hostel is hidden off a driveway to the left and uphill. Guests are asked to take their shoes off in the front hall. The hostel serves lunch and dinner and has reading corners with newspapers and games. It's often filled with groups, so call ahead. (☎24 18; fax 24 18 75; jgh.mondsee@oejhv.or.at. Breakfast buffet included. Reception M-F 8am-1pm and 5-7pm, Sa-Su 5-7pm. Check-in 5-10pm, check-out 9am. Closed Jan. 15-Feb. 15. Dorms €12.35; singles with bath €25.44; doubles €29.06-36.32; quads €58.12-63.92. Non-members pay €2.91 surcharge. MC/V.) To get to **Pension Klimesch ❸,** M. Guggenbichler-str. 13, walk toward the lake from the bus station, take a left onto Atterseestr., then a right onto Guggenbichler-str.; it will be to the left. This well-kept *Pension* has 15 rooms up a steep flight of stairs, common room with TV, and feather comforters.(☎25 63. Breakfast included. Singles from €22; doubles €42-50.) **Hotel Leitnerbräu ❺,** Steinerbachstr. 6, just off of Rainerstr. Friendly staff, soothing pale green decor, and unlimited use of their fitness room, sauna, and steam bath make a stay here truly relaxing. Breakfast included. Parking €8 per day. (☎65 00; fax 65 00 22; hotel@leitnerbräu.at; www.leitnerbräu.at. Singles €67.40-80.50; doubles €109.50-147.30.)

📋 FOOD. Marktpl. is brimming with restaurants and *Gasthöfe* serving Austrian and Italian dishes. **Restaurant Leitnerbräu ❷,** Marktpl. 9, serves regional specialties such as *Kaiserschmarren* (similar to French toast) as well as salads and pasta. Try the salmon filet (€13.50). Cheaper entrees run €6-8. (Open Th-T 8am-midnight. Closed in November. MC/V.) **China Restaurant ❷,** Rainerstr. 13, has a lunch deal for the budget-conscious that includes hot-and-sour soup and an entree for €5. (Open 11:30am-2:30pm and 6-11pm. MC/V.) **Blaue Traube ❸,** Marktpl. 1 (☎22 37), specializes in traditional Austrian food. Most entrees are €10-15 but some, including Mondseer *Kasspatzen* with carmelized onion (€5.96), are less. The **Krone restaurant ❸** (part of Hotel Krone, above) has a lovely patio full of flowers ideal for a leisurely summer meal. They offer local and international food, including fillet of pork with vegetable risotto (€10.20), grilled rumpsteak with spinach croquettes (€15), and Swiss-style sausage salad (€5.60). (Open daily 11am-11pm.) If you just want the ingredients in a bag, the **ADEG Contra Markt & F. Willibald Gmbh,** across from Rainerstr. 15, sells food and develops pictures. (Open M-F 7:30am-7pm, Sa 7:30am-5pm.) A **farmers' market** comes to Marktpl. Saturdays in summer.

🎦 🎿 🎭 SIGHTS, OUTDOOR ACTIVITIES, AND ENTERTAINMENT. Mondsee is the lake resort closest to Salzburg and has remained one of the least touristed, despite tour buses that roll in to see the local **Pfarrkirche,** site of the wedding scene in *The Sound of Music*. The church connects to the remains of a Benedictine monastery dating from AD 748, over which the *Schloß* (castle) was built. The completely-renovated *Schloß* houses businesses, bars, and the **Schloßgalerie,** which displays temporary art exhibits. (Open M-F noon-7pm, Sa-Su 11am-6pm. Free.)

The open-air **Freilichtmuseum,** on Hilfbergstr. (behind the church and uphill to the right), features a 500-year-old smokehouse, dairy, and farmhouse. Play with antique farm tools and utensils. (Open May-Aug. Tu-Su 10am-6pm; Sept.-Oct. Tu-Su 10am-5pm; Apr. and late Oct. Sa-Su only. €2.20, children and students €1.10.)

In summer, the Mondsee waters buzz with activity, but not motor boats—private motors are banned to protect wildlife. The newly renovated **Alpenseebad,** down Kreutzbergerstr. from the bus station, is the main **public beach.** (☎22 91. Open in fair weather May-Sept. 10am-4pm. €2.50, children and students €1.20.) For waterskiiers or wakeboarders, the **Wasserskizentrum** is inside the Seebad. (☎0664 1605 210. €10.20 per circuit, 2-person rafting same price.) Rent a bike at **Velofant,** next to the Seebad (mountain bike €18.17 per day; road bike €13.08 per day). Or, rent a **boat** from Peter Hemetsberger at the **Kaipromenade.** (☎24 60. Rowboats and paddleboats €5.80 per 30min., electric boats €7.25 per 30min.) He also offers *Seerundfahrten,* boat rides around the lake (1hr.; 10:45am, 12:15, 2, and 3:30pm., or as requested; €6.90, children half price). There's also a 2hr. hike around the Mondseeberg: start behind the Pfarrkirche to the right, at the sign for "Hochalm-Oberwang."

Mondsee holds the **Mondseetage,** an annual classical music festival, in early September (tickets €6-36). Tickets can be ordered through the Mondseetage Bestellbüro (☎35 44; karten@mondseetage.com; www.mondseetage.com). Every year **Hugo von Hofmannsthal's** 1922 morality play, *Jedermann,* is performed (in German) at the open-air **Freilichtbühne** theater. (☎(0664) 338 74 97. Performances mid-July to mid-Aug. Sa 8:30pm. Tickets start at €11-13; advance tickets available at Foto Schwaighofer, Rainerstr. 12.)

HOHE TAUERN REGION

The enormous **Hohe Tauern** range extends well into Carinthia, Salzburg, Tyrol, and East Tyrol. As part of the Austrian Central Alps, it boasts 246 glaciers and 304 mountains over 3000m in height. Between 1958 and 1964, large tracts of mountain land in Salzburg and Carinthia were declared preserves. An agreement signed by the governing heads of Tyrol, Salzburg, and Carinthia on October 21, 1971, made **Hohe Tauern National Park** the largest national park in all of Europe. Officially, the park encloses 29 towns and 60,000 residents, though most of the park territory is uninhabited. One of the park's most important goals is preservation, so there are no large campgrounds or recreation areas within its borders. The best way to take advantage of this rare circumstance is by hiking one of the numerous trails, which range from pleasant ambles to mighty summits attempted only by world-class mountaineers. The brochure *Natur Erlebnis* ("An Experience in Nature"), available at any park office and most area tourist offices, plots 84 different hikes and ascents on a map of the park and provides short descriptions of each hike.

Appropriately, the founding papers for the park were signed in **Heiligenblut,** the most central town for visitors. **Zell am See** and **Lienz,** which lie on either end of the **Großglocknerstraße,** are two of the larger towns, while tiny **Krimml** offers famous waterfalls and a few places to crash between strenuous hikes.

> **HIGHLIGHTS OF THE HOHE TAUERN REGION**
>
> Make the trip between Lienz and Zell am See on the **Großglocknerstraße,** the world's most exciting highway (see p. 267).
>
> Sleep in the shadow of Austria's mightiest mountain, the Großglockner, in the tiny mountain town of **Heiligenblut** (see p. 271).
>
> Go skiing in August on the glacier above **Zell am See** (see p. 276).

NATIONAL PARK

Unlike national parks in other countries, the Hohe Tauern National Park is owned not by the government, but by a consortium of private farmers and members of the **Österreichischer Alpenverein** (ÖAV; Austrian Alpine Union). In 1914 the land enclosing the **Glockengruppe** was actually for sale. Just as it was about to be sold to an individual who wanted to turn it into a private hunting ground, wealthy industrialist Albert Wirt bought it instead and donated it to ÖAV so that it could be enjoyed by all. The land remains privately owned and, with the exception of the park's mountainous center, many of its meadows and valleys are used for raising cattle or cutting timber. Farmers still herd their cattle over the same 2500m *Tauern* (ice-free mountain paths) once trod by Celts and Romans. The Glocknergruppe, in the heart of the park, contains Austria's highest peak, the **Großglockner** (3798m), as well as many lakes and glaciers. Besides the omnipresent Edelweiss, the park is also home to dozens of species of endangered alpine flowers (like the fiery *Almsrauch*, or "meadow smoke") as well as armies of marmots. The *Bartgeir* (bearded vulture) and the lyre-horned ibex were recently reintroduced after near extinction throughout Europe. A lazy drive—or a vigorous bike ride—down the Großglocknerstraße offers a beautiful, if summary, look at the peaks and valleys of the park. Rest stops dot the highway, providing vistas of valleys that can be explored only by foot.

ORIENTATION

The center of the park and BundesBus hub, above Heiligenblut, is **Franz-Josefs-Höhe** and the **Pasterze glacier** (see p. 268). Aside from the skiing and hiking opportunities on these mammoths, the main attractions in the park are the **Krimml Waterfalls** (p. 277), just west of Zell am See, and the **Großglocknerstraße** (Bundesstr. 107; see p. 267), a spectacular high mountain road that runs north-south through the center of the park, between Zell am See and Lienz, through the Franz-Josefs-Höhe.

TRANSPORTATION

Two **train** lines service towns near the park: one runs west from Zell am See along the northern border of the park, ending in Krimml (1½hr., 19 per day 6:06am-10:56pm, €6.80); another runs south from Salzburg to Badgastein in the southwest corner (1¾hr., 15 per day 7:13am-9:13pm, €11.10). The park itself is criss-crossed by **bus** lines, which operate on a complicated timetable, with some buses running infrequently and others changing schedules in early summer. Pick up a schedule in one of the tourist offices, then be sure to confirm with your driver (all of whom are experts on schedules) when the next bus to your destination departs. Bus routes from all directions go through the center of the park at Franz-Josefs-Höhe. Buses run to Franz-Josefs-Höhe from Lienz (1½hr., €7.20 total fare) via Heiligenblut, and from Zell am See (2hr., 2 per day 9:20am-12:20pm, €10). Return trips run to: Heiligenblut (30min.; July 7-Oct. 7 M-F 9:30am, 12:06, 3:50pm, Sa 9:30am, 12:06pm, Su 12:06, 4:30pm; €3.60); Lienz (1½hr., 6-8 per day 6:19am-5:15pm, €7.20) via Heiligenblut; and Zell am See (2hr., 2 per day 11:45am-3:50pm, €10). Again, *check with your driver* before getting off the bus. It's either an 8km walk to Heiligenblut or an expensive cab ride if you miss the last ride. By **car** from Kitzbühel, take Bundesstr. 161 south to 108, which leads through the park. From Lienz, take Bundesstr. 107 or 108 north into the park. From Zell am See, take Bundesstr. 311 south to 107. In case of **breakdown,** call the ÖAMTC (☎ 120).

PARK INFORMATION

Because the park is distributed over 3 different provinces, the network of tourist information is decentralized. You can find general information on the park by calling ☎ 04875 51 12, or checking www.hohetauern.org, which has an English page. For more information talk to the park service branch in whichever province of the park you are visiting. All three provinces have a main branch. The **Kärnten (Carinthia) Park Office** is in Großkirchheim (☎ 04825 61 61; fax 61 61 16), the **Tyrol office** is in Matrei (☎ 04875 51 61; fax 51 61 20; npht@tirol.gv.at), and the **Salzburg office** is in Neukirchen (☎ 06565 655 80; fax 65 58 18). There are also small offices scattered throughout the park.

ACCOMMODATIONS

Zell am See and Lienz are larger, city-like bases for exploring the park; Krimml, on the park's northern border, and Heiligenblut, smack in the middle, are smaller and closer to the park. Mountain huts, meanwhile, are excellent places to shed all trappings of civilization. A few are within a day's hike of Heiligenblut and provide intimate views of the Großglockner, including the **Salmhütte** (2644m, 5hr. hike from Heiligenblut; ☎ 04824 20 89; open mid-June to Sept.), and the **Glorerhütte** (2642m, 1½hr. from Salmhütte; ☎ 0664 303 22 00; open late June to late Sept.). The **Erzherzog-Johann-Hütte** is the highest hut in the park, and is nearest the Großglockner peak. (3454m. ☎ 04876 85 00. Open late June to late Sept.; mountaineers only.) For a full list of huts pick up a *Hüttenführer* at any tourist office. For more info on huts, contact the ÖAV in Lienz (see p. 281). Camping in the park is prohibited.

OUTDOOR ACTIVITIES

The best **cycling** in the area is on the **Tauernweg** from Krimml to Zell am See (then on to Salzburg), giving glimpses of the Hohe Tauern to the south. Tourist offices and www.tauernradweg.com have more info on the route. Cyclists can also ride the grueling Großglocknerstraße, but be aware that since the National Park is foremost a preserve, bikes are not always allowed off the main highway.

Hiking trails head into isolated valleys from every road and town. With over 50 mountain huts in or near the park offering overnight stays, serious backpackers can lose themselves in the park for weeks at a time. To do so, pick up the *Hüttenführer* guide at any park office. The park's "An Experience in Nature" brochure suggests good hikes. Also essential are trail maps, which cost around €7.50 at any park office, and give descriptions of popular hikes and cultural attractions along the trails. The National Park also leads daily guided tours along various trails (usually €6-10, depending upon transportation) detailed in its "An Experience in Nature" brochure. The program changes each summer, but includes hikes along the Geotrail Tauernfenster, the Paterze glacier, and a wildlife trek. For anglophones there is a good list and description of hikes on the park's website, but the best idea is to purchase a topographic map of the area and talk to the local tourist office. For safety advice on hiking see **Essentials**, p. 28.

THE GROßGLOCKNERSTRAßE

Each day more than 3000 visitors pack their cars for a full day's ride along the breathtaking **Großglocknerstraße**, one of the most beautiful highways in the world. Skirting Austria's loftiest mountains, Bundesstr. 107 (its less catchy moniker) winds for 50km amid silent valleys, meadows of wildflowers, powerful waterfalls, and giant glaciers between Zell am See and Lienz. It passes its highest point at

DRIVING SAFETY TIPS. Many first-time drivers of the Großglocknerstraße are tempted to lean heavily on the brakes, which can lead to brake failure and overheating. Instead, shift to low gear, drive slowly, and never, ever pass anyone.

A PRIEST, A SLOVENIAN, AND FOUR GUIDES WALK UP A MOUNTAIN...

It's not a joke, but rather the first expedition to reach the summit of the Großglockner, on July 28, 1800. Of the party of more than sixty intellectuals, well-to-do nobles, and locals hired to carry the baggage, only six reached the summit of the peak. At the top, they (and their compatriots at what is today the Kleinglockner peak and the Salmhütte) engaged in cutting-edge scientific research: some measured the blueness of the sky with a device called a cyanometer, others put air into jars for study back at sea level, and a few collected previously undiscovered varieties of moss. Their attempt to measure the elevation was fairly successful—their estimate of 3894m is only 96m higher than today's measurement of 3798m.

Hochtor, 2505m above sea level. The slow, steady climb is choked with rubber-neckers and magnificently conditioned cyclists soaking up the stupefying views.

The trip up to Hochtor takes you from flora and fauna to frigid, Arctic-like environments that never exceed 10°C (50°F) even during the hottest summers. Though the highway is officially only the 6.4km stretch from Bruck an der Großglockner to Heiligenblut, tours generally run from Zell am See or Lienz to Franz-Josefs-Höhe. The full trip on the Großglocknerstr. (with scenic rest stops in between) lasts about 5hr. (2½-3hr. total driving time). Many visitors traverse the Großglocknerstr. in a **tour bus** or **rental car,** neither of which is recommended for those with light wallets or weak stomachs. **Public buses,** with their giant windows, serve as excellent tour buses at much lower prices (see p. 266), although their schedules can be inconvenient. If you only have one day, resist the urge to disembark at any of the cutesy villages along the way; buses come so infrequently that you'll be stuck in Nowheresdorf for hours. Time is better spent at **Franz-Josefs-Höhe** on a clear day, enjoying the magnificent views. Drivers must pay **tolls** at Ferleiten on the Zell am See side, or Roßbach on the Heiligenblut side (€26, €32 for month pass; motorcycles €17/€22). Parking at Franz-Josefs-Höhe is free with your toll receipt. There are also parking and pull-off areas strategically situated at numerous lookout points along the road.

Be aware that the road is open only 5am-10pm mid-June to mid-September and 8:30am-6pm the rest of the year, with last entry 45min. before closing time. Snowfalls, dumping up to 4m of heavy snow on the road, force the Großglocknerstr. to close entirely from October to April. For info on **road conditions** call the Großglockner Hochalpenstraßen Aktiengesellschaft (GROHAG; ☎0662 873 67 30; fax 87 36 73 13; www.grossglockner.at). It is important to note that Großglocknerstr. is not part of the National Park, nor under its auspices. Be aware of this when asking park volunteers about the road, or road officers about the park.

◪ ACTIVITIES ALONG THE GROßGLOCKNERSTRAßE

FRANZ-JOSEFS-HÖHE. Großglocknerstr. buses from Zell am See, Lienz, and Heiligenblut finish their routes at Franz-Josefs-Höhe, a large observation and tourist center stationed above the **Pasterze glacier.** Naturally, Franz-Josefs-Höhe is packed with tour buses and camera-toting visitors spread over two levels of

A word of caution to modern-day would-be mountaineers: unless phrases like "chest and sit harness" and "screwgate carabiners" mean something to you, you have no business attempting the summit (this includes seasoned hikers). To do so risks not only your life, but the lives of experienced mountaineers, whose way you'll get into, and the mountain rescue squad, which is called out as many as two dozen times per summer to pull stranded climbers off the mountains. As an added bonus, if you are the recipient of a really neat helicopter/rope-ladder/St. Bernard-dog-team rescue, under Austrian law, you get to foot the bill (around €50,000). Going with a professional guide is the only way to reach the summit safely. To arrange a guided hike to the Großglockner peak (from €105 per person), call the Bergführerverein in Heiligenblut (☎04824 27 00). Otherwise, content yourself with lots of pictures or a hike to Salmhütte, which is the point where three-quarters of the first expedition up the mountain quit anyway.

HOHE TAUERN

parking lots (with a free bus running between them every 10min.), but even they can't detract from the sight of the glacier's icy tongue extending down the valley. Unless it's shrouded in clouds, you can glimpse the towering summit of the Großglockner (3797m) on the left wall of the valley. Franz-Josefs-Höhe has its own **park office** at the beginning of the parking area, with a free mini-museum and Hohe Tauern information center. The staff also answers questions about availability and opening times of mountain huts in the vicinity. (☎04824 27 27. *Open daily from mid-May to mid-Oct. 10am-4pm; July-Aug. 9am-6pm.*) Several restaurants and snack bars are scattered around Franz-Josefs-Höhe; the larger souvenir shops sell inexpensive sandwiches (€1.50-2.50), but the restaurants tend to have prices as high as the altitude.

GLACIER FUNICULAR AND OBSERVATION CENTER. The **Gletscherbahn funicular** ferries you down from Franz-Josefs-Höhe close to the glacier. (☎04824 25 02. *Runs mid-May to late Sept. daily 9am-4pm. Round-trip €7, children €5.50.*) Alternately, you can hike down to the bottom yourself (see **Hiking,** below). Catch the glacier while you can—it is receding an average of 20m per year, and, given current climate patterns, will continue to do so.

Take the elevator next to the information office or the winding road on the other side of the office and follow it to the **Swarovski Observation Center** at the end for an even better view. This crystal-shaped, many-windowed building houses 3 floors of brief but fun exhibits, including displays on park wildlife and glacier formation. Binoculars are available for viewing the surrounding terrain, allowing you to practice your mountain-wildlife-spotting skills. If you're lucky, you might see some ibex chewing the grass on the mountain behind you. You won't need fancy specs to see the ubiquitous marmots. (*Open daily 10am-4pm. Free.*)

The **visitor center,** near the parking lots, has three floors devoted to the first ascent of the Großglockner, the geology of the mountain, free educational films, and panoramic views with labels on each mountain, an invaluable aid when you develop your pictures. (*Open daily 10am-4pm. Free.*)

HIKING. Although the Gamgrubenweg was closed recently (possibly for good) due to large rock falls, there are still several short, fun hikes right around Franz-Josefs-Höhe, as well as longer and more difficult ones that lead to mountain huts like the Salmhütte or to the tops of mountains themselves. Inquire about these in the park office, and purchase a detailed trail map of the area (try the ÖAV Map #40, €7.19). **Guides** are available for hiking, climbing, or ski touring. (*Call the park office in Heiligenblut. ☎04824 27 00; fax 270 04. Open daily 10am-5pm.*)

HOHE TAUERN

Hohe Tauern Hiking Map

For a moderate hike, try the ■**Gletscherweg** (3hr.). Heading down to the glacier (or coming up from it), follow the "Gletscherweg" sign. This varied trail leads away from the Pasterze through an area that in decades past was covered in ice. The large piles of rock and dust—scree left behind by the glacier—will make you feel like you're walking on the moon. Later highlights include a glacier-fashioned sand lake and the reservoir where runoff from the icy mass still collects. The whole Hohe Tauern panorama comes into view on the descent to the reservoir. The final hour is a stiff climb back to Franz-Josefs-Höhe, so be sure to rest every few minutes, and to drink lots of water.

HEILIGENBLUT ☎04824

The most convenient accommodations for those wishing to explore Franz-Josefs-Höhe and the Hohe Tauern region are in Heiligenblut (pop. 1250), in the middle of the Großglocknerstraße. As the town closest to the highest mountain in Austria, Heiligenblut is a great starting point for many hikes. The center of town is low on a mountainside, with the rest spilling down to the Möll River. Mountains rise sharply on each side of the valley, wedging Heiligenblut into a narrow corridor that looks northward to the Großglockner. The town's name, which means "holy blood," derives from a legend about a Byzantine general named Briccius who died nearby in a snowstorm. He carried with him a vial supposedly containing a few drops of Christ's blood, now kept in a reliquary in the town church.

TRANSPORTATION AND PRACTICAL INFORMATION. Buses run to Heiligenblut from Franz-Josefs-Höhe (30min.; July-Sept. 8:40am-4:05pm, May and Oct. 1 per day 4pm; €3.60), Lienz (1hr., 2-6 per day 6:19am-5:15pm, €5.90), and Zell am See (2½hr., 3 per day 9:20am-12:20pm, €11). The bus stop is in front of Hotel Glocknerhof. The **tourist office**, Hof 4, up the street from the bus stop, dispenses information about accommodations, hiking, sporting activities, and park transportation. (☎20 01 21; fax 20 01 43; www.heiligenblut.at. Open July-Aug. M-F 8:30am-6pm, Sa 9am-noon and 4-6pm; Sept.-June M-F 8:30am-noon and 2:30-6pm, Sa 9am-noon and 4-6pm.) An **ATM** is next to the tourist office at **Raiffeisenbank.** The **post office** with **currency exchange** is below the center of town at the bottom of the hill. Follow the main road past the chair lift. (☎22 01. Open M-F 8am-noon and 1:30-5pm. Exchange closes 4pm.)

ACCOMMODATIONS AND FOOD. ** To reach the **Jugendgästehaus Heiligenblut (HI) ❷, Hof 36, take the path down from the wall behind the bus stop parking lot. Large, pleasant rooms, often with baths and showers, await you. (☎22 59. **HI members** only; exceptions made depending on space. Breakfast included. Key available. Reception July-Aug. 7-10am and 5-10pm; Sept.-June 7-10am and 5-9pm. Curfew 10pm. Dorms €20; ages 19-27 €15, 19 and under €10. Singles €27.27/€22.27/€17.27; doubles €23.63/€18.63/€13.63.) **Pension Bergkristall ❸,** Hof 71, has luxurious rooms, many with balconies and TV; some suites include living room, kitchen, and shower or bathtub. The Pension is near the main lift station. (☎20 05; fax 20 05 33. Breakfast included. Dec.-Easter €28; Easter-Nov. €21.80.) **Nationalpark Camping-Großglockner ❶,** Haderg. 11, across the Möll river, offers scenic campgrounds and a restaurant. (☎20 48; www.heiligenblut.at/nationalpark-camping. Laundry €3.70. Breakfast €8. Reception 8am-midnight. €5.90, children €3, cars and motorcycles €2.20, electricity €2.20. Showers included.)

Cheap eats are tough to come by in the center of town, as most restaurants are run by the big hotels. For affordable grub, head down the hill, cross the river, and turn left (15-20min.). **Gasthof Sonnblick ❷,** Hof 21, offers daily dinner specials for €5.50-6.90. (☎21 31; fax 213 15. Open daily 8am-9pm.) Lodged between the souvenir stores in the square in the center of town is **Dorfstüberl ❷,** Hof 4, an outdoor cafe serving pizzas (€7-9) alongside hearty meat entrees for €9-11. (☎20 19. Open daily 8:30am-midnight.) There is an **ADEG,** Hof 46, just a short ways up the road from the tourist office. (☎22 14. Open M-Sa 8am-6pm, Su 9am-6pm.)

HIKING. The Heiligenblut hiker is a happy one, as almost any hike in the area brings amazing scenery. Before heading out, familiarize yourself with a hiking map, available at the Heiligenblut National Park office, the tourist office, or from many shops nearby. Hohe Tauern National Park officially exists only on the western side of Heiligenblut, across the Möll River from the church and tourist office.

To get there, take the road out of Heiligenblut and descend the hill. Turn right, cross the river, and turn right again. Walk until you see hiking information signs on the left, or walk a bit farther to the parking lot for trails at the end of the road. The **National Park Office,** Hof 8, behind Intersport, can suggest routes and offer advice; they also have a small exhibit on wildlife and geology that will make your hike that much more educational. (Open daily 10am-5pm.)

☒ Wirtsbauer Alm hike (4hr., moderate-difficult). From the parking lot, take the main trail past the signs to the Gössnitzfall. After some steady uphill climbing, the path leads to a meadow and a trail leading up the mountain on the left. Past the initial climb on this trail, the hike is mostly flat, cruising along wooded cliffs above the churning Gössnitz River. The Wirtsbauer Alm boasts magnificent views of the entire alpine valley and all the peaks nearby. The hike to **Elberfelderhütte** (☎ 22 85) is 4½hr. farther and is entirely above the tree line on a path that often skirts the cliff's edge, passing the 3 Langtal Lakes. Both the Wirtsbauer Alm and the Elberfelderhütte accommodate overnight stays (roughly July to mid-Sept.). Call ahead or ask the park office in Heiligenblut.

Salmhütte hike (day hike; moderate to strenuous). This is as close as you can get to the Großglockner peak without a professional guide. Hop on the bus toward FJ Hohe to Glocknerhaus. Proceed downhill, cross the dams across Margaritze Lake, then follow the signs to Salmhütte along trail 741, the "Viennese Highway." The path climbs steadily for the next 1½-2hr. before leveling off at around 2450m, a quarter mile above the valley floor. The three "sword peaks" tower over you; to the left is the fantastically green Leiterbach valley. You'll eventually reach the Salmhütte, which was built in 1799 by the first expedition up Großglockner and was, in fact, where most of them quit walking and went home (see p. 268). If you're more determined, continue another hour over increasingly rugged, difficult terrain past the ruins of the expedition's stone hut, following the cairns uphill to the **Hohenwirt glacier.** This is where you turn around and let the professionals continue on to Erzherzog Johann Hütte (it will take them about 2hr. to cover a quarter mile). Return to the Salmhütte, then take the low road, trail 702b, back to Heiligenblut and enjoy close-ups of the valley and the marmots you towered above on the way out. (Glockneraus to Salmhütte 3hr.; round-trip to glacier 2hr.; return to Heiligenblut 4hr.) ÖAV map #40 (Großglocknergruppe) is extremely useful.

Gössnitzfall hike (1hr., moderate). Hike begins shortly after the parking lot, and continues off the main path, following the sign for "Aussichtspunkt Gössnitzfall." After 10-15min. of steep climbing, an 80m high waterfall appears. Continue to the top of the trail, where you can see the gushing beast in all its glory, as well as the gorge surrounding it, twice as high and just as steep as the waterfall itself. The mist coming off the falls will cool you down, a fitting reward for your effort.

Haritzer Steig (4hr., easy-moderate). Exit the tourist office and turn right, going past the cable car station and bearing right on the road heading up the hill. Follow signs to "Haritzer Steig" or "Briccius Kapelle" to a flat path below the road. This hike leads from Heiligenblut to the Briccius Kapelle, where you can either continue to Franz-Josefs-Höhe, or turn back on the other side of the valley (the Gössnitz side) to complete the 4hr. circuit. Alternately clinging to hillsides and wandering through lush meadows, the Haritzer Steig is long but not terribly difficult. The return loop dips sharply into the ravine that houses the Leiter Fall, a slender waterfall carving its way to the Möll River below. The steep climb from the falls to the Trog Alm (2092m) leads to an almost uniformly downhill path back to town.

◪ OTHER OUTDOOR ACTIVITIES. Two skiing mountains, **Schareck** and **Hochfleiß,** rise from the valley behind Heiligenblut, offering 12 moderately challenging runs and open bowl skiing. (Passes available at the Seilbahn lift station past the tourist office. Access to both mountains €26 per day, youths ages 15-18 €21, ages

6-14 €13. Morning passes valid until 12:30pm €20/€16/€10.) **Bike and ski rental** are available at **Intersport Pichler**, Hof 4, across from the tourist office. (☎22 56 45. Open May-June and Sept.-Nov. M-F 9am-6pm, Sa 9am-4pm; July-Aug. M-F 9am-6pm, Sa 9am-4pm, Su 10am-4pm; Dec.-April M-Sa 9am-12:30pm and 2:30-6pm, Su 9am-noon and 3-6pm. Bikes €18 per day, €25 per weekend; skis €14-24 per day; snowboards €12-18 per day.)

ZELL AM SEE   ☎06542

Surrounded by a ring of snow-capped mountains cradling a broad turquoise lake, Zell am See (TSELL am ZAY; pop. 9700) functions as a year-round resort for mountain-happy European tourists. The town's horizon is dominated by 30 peaks of the Hohe Tauern range, several of which are over 3000m tall. The town is a convenient base from which *Wanderlust*ing tourists explore these on foot or skis. The cool blue lake calls just as enticingly to those who desire summer rest and relaxation, while visitors to the cobblestone town center wind through shops and cafes during the day and a maze of bars and dance clubs at night.

█ TRANSPORTATION

Zell am See lies at the intersection of Bundesstr. 311 from the north and Bundesstr. 168 from the west. It's also accessible by Bundesstr. 107 from the south, which runs into Bundesstr. 311 north. From **Salzburg**, take Bundesstr. 21 south to 305 to 178; at **Lofer**, switch to 311 south.

Trains: The station is at the intersection of Bahnhofstr. and Salzmannstr. (☎73 21 43 57. Ticket counter open M 4:50am-7pm, Tu-Sa 6am-7pm, Su 7:15am-8:20pm.) Trains arrive from: **Innsbruck** (1½-2hr., 3:45am-9:27pm, €19.60); **Kitzbühel** (45min., 7:17am-11:32pm, €8.10); **Salzburg** (1½hr., 1-2 per hr.); and **Vienna** (5hr., 7:47am-6:42pm, €39.40).

Buses: BundesBus station on Postpl., behind the post office and facing Gartenstr. Buy tickets from the driver or the ticket office (☎54 44). Open M-F 7:30am-1:30pm. Buses run to a variety of local destinations, including **Krimml** (1½hr., 6:05am-8:55pm, €7.40) and **Salzburg** (2hr., 6:35am-6:45pm). To **Franz-Josefs-Höhe** (mid-June to Sept. only) 7:20am, 10:45am, 12:20pm; €16.70 round-trip.

Taxis: At the train station, or call ☎680 90 or ☎741 11.

Parking: On Brucker-Bundersstr. between the tourist office and the post office. €1.40 per hr., €11.20 per day. Open 24hr.

Bike Rental: From **Intersport** in the *Fußgängerzone* (pedestrian zone) or at the Schmittenhöhe Talstation. €15 per day, children €8 per day.

█ █ ORIENTATION AND PRACTICAL INFORMATION

Zell am See sits among several towns, all of which are huddled on or near the lake and are connected by bus or bike path. The closest town, Schüttdorf, is only a 15min. walk. Go to the right and up the hill from the train station to reach Zell am See's pedestrian zone.

Tourist Office: Brucker Bundesstr. 3 (☎770; fax 720 32; zell@gold.at; www.zellkaprun.com). From the station, turn right, take the left fork, follow it around the corner, and turn right again. Open July to mid-Sept. and mid-Dec. to Mar. M-F 8am-6pm, Sa 9am-noon and 4-6pm, Su 10am-noon; Apr.-June and Sept. to mid-Dec. M-F 8am-noon and 2-6pm, Sa 9am-noon.

Currency Exchange: At banks or the post office. Almost every bank has an **ATM.**

Luggage Storage: At the train station. €2.10 per piece, in the office next to the ticket window. Open M-Sa 6am-8:30pm. Electronic lockers and ski lockers 24hr., €2.50.

Bookstore: Ellmauer Buchhandlung, Bahnhofstr. 1 (☎473 33; fax 47 33 32), has several racks of novels in the middle of the back room.

Weather conditions: ☎736 94.

Emergencies: Police, ☎133. **Mountain rescue,** ☎140.

Internet: Café Estl, Bahnhofstr. 1 (☎726 10; www.icak.at), has 4 terminals (€0.15 per minute). Open M-Sa 10am-10pm, Su 11am-8pm.

Post Office: Postpl. 4 (☎73 79 10). Open M-F 7:30am-6:30pm, Sa 8-10am; early July to mid-Sept. and Dec. 25 to Easter Sa 8-11am. **Postal Code:** A-5700.

⌂ ACCOMMODATIONS

Zell am See has more than its share of 4-star hotels (and prices), but it has not forgotten the budget traveler. Ask for a free **guest card** at your accommodation, which provides numerous discounts on activities throughout the city.

▨ Pensione Sinilill (Andi's Inn), Thumersbacherstr. 65 (☎735 23). Take the BundesBus (dir.: Thumersbach) to "Krankenhaus" (€1.45, last bus 7:15pm). Turn left after exiting the bus, walk about 200m, and look for an old wooden sign on the left side of the street. If you call ahead, Andi will pick you up. On the north shore of the lake, this Pension features simple furniture and an easy-going environment. The lived-in, down-home feel of the house gives it a charm most Pensions lack. Andi, reared in Zell am See, knows everything about the town and can tell you what's worthwhile. Hall bathrooms and shower. Big breakfast included. Doubles €30, some with balcony. ❷

Haus der Jugend (HI), Seespitzstr. 13 (☎571 85; fax 57 18 54). Exit the station facing the lake ("Zum See"), turn right, and walk along the footpath beside the lake; when the footpath ends, take a left onto Seespitzstr. (15min.). As the footpath is deserted at night, you could also take the Stadtbus to "Alpenblick" (€1.50, last bus 7:45pm). This well-maintained hostel is group-oriented, providing rooms with bath and lakeside terraces. Other amenities include TV room with VCR, foosball table, and snack shop. Breakfast included, 7:30-8:30am. Lunch and dinner €5 each. Key deposit €20 or passport. €1 deposit for locking wardrobes in some rooms. Reception 7-9am and 4-10pm. Check-out 9am. Lockout noon-4pm. Curfew 10pm. Reservations recommended. 6-bed dorms €12.72; 4-bed dorms €13.81; doubles €14.53. One-night stay add €1.45. Tax €0.84. MC/V. ❷

Landesberufschülerheim Zell am See (HI), Schmittenstr. 27 (☎/fax 470 36). From the Bahnhof, go past the tourist office and turn left onto Schmittenstr. just past the post office. Some of the spacious rooms have couches, second showers, or second sinks. Common room with TV and VCR, **free Internet** in the basement, wardrobes that can be locked with room keys, and 3 smaller TVs loaned out to the first people who ask. Breakfast included. Lunch or dinner €5.10. **Bike rental** €10 per day. Reception 8am-10pm. 4-bed dorm €17.24; singles €19; doubles €38. One-night stay add €1.45. ❸

Pension Herzog, Saalfeldnerstr. 20 (☎725 03; fax 745 09; www.members.aon.at/pension.herzog). From the Bahnhof, turn right and go uphill, through and out of the *Fußgängerzone*, past Hotel Grüner Baum. This well-kept Pension sits near the lake and a babbling brook. Plain, clean rooms with wood furniture. Shower and toilet in the hall. Reception 7am-8pm. Check-out 10am. Doubles €13.90-15.90, €22-25 for in-room bathroom and shower. Singles add €2.18. One-night stay add €1.50. ❷

Camping Seecamp, Thumersbacherstr. 34 (☎ 72 11; fax 721 15), in Zell am See/Prielau, can be reached by BundesBus (dir.: Thumersbach) to "Seecamp" (€1.40, last bus 7:15pm). Situated on the lakefront, this campground has a restaurant, a terrace cafe, and a small shopping market. **Bike rental** €11 per day. Showers included. Reception M-Sa 8-11am and 4-6pm, Su 9-11am and 4-6pm. Check-out 11am. Car lockout noon-2pm and 10pm-7am. €7.05, ages 5-15 €3.85, tax €0.90 per person. Tent €3.71, trailer €8. Oct.-Dec. and May-June, prices 20% off. AmEx/MC/V. ❶

◨ FOOD

Zell am See lies in the Pinzgau region, where food is prepared to sustain the strenuous labors of hearty farmers. Try the *Brezensuppe* (a clear soup with cheese cubes) as an appetizer and then *Pinzgauer Käsnocken* (homemade noodles and cheese, onions, and chives). Top it all off with *Lebkuchen Parfait* (spice cake), *Blattlkrapfen* (deep-fried stuffed pancakes), or *Germknödeln* (a steamed sweet roll served with poppy seeds, butter, and sugar). The grocery store **SPAR** is at Brucker Bundesstr. 4. (Open M-Th 8am-7pm, F 8am-7:30pm, Sa 7:30am-5pm.)

Ristorante Pizzeria Giuseppe, Kircheng. 1 (☎ 723 73), in the *Fußgängerzone*. From the station, walk past the church and go straight. Subdued lighting and tasteful decoration give this place a pleasant ambience. Plenty of vegetarian options and an extensive wine list. Pasta dishes €5.45-7.99; pizza €5.67-9.16; salads €3.63-7.19. Open Tu-Su 11:30am-11pm. DC/MC/V. ❷

Fischrestaurant "Moby Dick," Kreuzg. 16 (☎ 733 20). The great white whale—with fries. The restaurant smells like what you'd expect, but no matter. The double fishburger with potatoes and salad is only €6.60. Single fishburger €1.80 or pick out your own fillet and vegetable. Main dishes occasionally feature fish straight from the lake. Open M-F 9am-6pm, Sa 9am-2pm. MC/V. ❶

Euro Kebab 2000, across from the train station. Despite its impressive name, serves up the typical cheap *Döner* fare: spit-roasted turkey in a large roll with spicy sauce (€3.30). Open 9am-9pm. ❶

◉ ▨ SIGHTS AND OUTDOOR ACTIVITIES

HIKING AND ADVENTURE SPORTS. Though expensive, the **Schmittenhöhebahn** leads to many hikes. The BundesBus (dir.: Schmittenhöhebahn/Sonnenalmbahn Talstation; 7min., 7:20am-5:50pm, €1.45 from post office) goes to the lift, about 2km north of town on Schmittenstr. (Lift runs mid-May to late Oct. 8:15am-5pm. €13.81, with guest card €12.35, children €6.54; round-trip €17.44, with guest card €15.99, children €9.08.) The lift station provides several brochures (with English translations) detailing hikes ranging from strolls to cliff-hangers. In the former category, the **Erlebnisweg Höhenpromenade** (1hr.) connects the top stations of the Schmittenhöhe and Sonnkogel lifts. Displays on history, nature, and ecology along the way exercise your mind. Guided hikes, free with a lift ticket, leave from the lower stations and have a variety of themes, including botanical hikes, forest walks, and children's hikes (June-Oct. M-F). Contact the Schmittenhöhebahn Aktiengesellschaft (☎ 78 92 12) or the lower station for details.

Independent of the park, the Zell am See area provides many opportunities to work those calf muscles. Consider the **Pinzgauer Spaziergang**, which begins at the upper terminal of the Schmittenhöhebahn and is marked "Alpenvereinsweg" #19 or 719. It dips and climbs a bit at the beginning, but levels off high in the Kitzbüheler Alps. Most people take an entire day to hike along this trail, eventually taking a side trail leading to one of the valley towns west of Zell am See. From there you can take the bus back. For a shorter hike, walk up Mozartstr. until it ends, and follow the hiking trail. The **Kohlergrabenweg** is a 1hr. hike that gradually ascends through the forest to the Schmittenhohebahn lower station.

For **rafting** (€25-50), **canyoning** (€40-60), **paragliding** (€100), and **climbing** (€36) information, contact **Adventure Service,** Steinerg. 9 (☎735 25; fax 742 80).

SKIING. As you might expect, winter turns Zell am See into a ski resort. The **Zell/ Kaprun Ski Pass** covers both Zell am See and nearby Kaprun; a free bus runs between the two every 45min. from Late-Dec. to late-Mar., as well as every 30min. between Zell am See and the Schmittenhöhebahn from late-Nov. to late-Apr. (Lift passes: 2 days €56.32-60.32, ages 16-18 €50.51-54.14, ages 7-15 €28.34-30.09, under 7 free when accompanied by an adult.) One-day passes are available for Zell's Schmittenhöhe lift (€29.07-32.70, youths €26.53-29.80, children €14.53-16.35). Get a report in German on ski conditions in the Schmittenhöhe area (☎736 94) or the Kitzsteinhorn-Kaprun area (☎(06547) 84 44). The **Kitzsteinhorn** (3203m) and its gla-cier in Kaprun also offer **summer skiing.** Get there early on summer days to avoid skiing in slush. A day pass costs €19.62, children €10.54. Snowboards or skis, boots, and poles run €21.44 per day; all are available at **Intersport Bründl** on the gla-cier. (☎06547 83 88. Open M-F 8am-noon and 2:30pm-6:30pm, Sa 8am-6pm, Su 9am-11am and 3-6pm.) Intersport also has several other shops open in winter, as well as one near the top of Kitzsteinhorn, with a new cross-store return policy that allows you to rent equipment in one store and then return or exchange it at a dif-ferent Intersport store at no extra cost.

OTHER ACTIVITIES. Zell's buildings are clustered in the valley of the Zellersee. Stroll around the lake or get wet at one of the **beaches: Strandbad Zell am See,** near the center of town (walk down Franz-Josef-Str.), complete with platform diving and a waterslide; **Strandbad Seespitz,** by the Haus der Jugend; or **Thumersbacher Strandbad** on the eastern shore. (All open June to early Sept. 9am-7pm; adults €5.09 or €4.72 with guest card; ages 15-18 €3.63, ages 6-15 €2.98, under 6 free.) **Boat tours** depart from the Zell Esplanade, off Salzmannstr. (40min., 8 per day 10am-5:30pm, €5.81, ages 6-14 €2.91.) Visit **Edi's Skischule** near the Strandbad Zell am See for **water skiing** (€7.27 per round) or **sailing** (€8.72 per hr.).

Around the cafes and shops in the middle of the *Fußgängerzone* of Zell stands the *Vogtturm,* Kreuzg. 2, a medieval tower that has housed the funky Heimatmu-seum since 1985. Overflowing with exhibits, highlights include the toilet that Franz Joseph used at the Hotel Schmittenhöhe, an entire room devoted to the history of skiing in the area, stuffed birds, and a history of coinage in the Pinzgau. (☎0664 462 62 53. Open June to mid-Oct. and mid-Dec. to Easter M-F 2-6pm. €2.50, with guest card €2, ages 6-18 €1. English guide €0.50.)

⚑ NIGHTLIFE

Those who want to get really hammered should try the local drinking game **Nageln,** in which drinkers compete to see who can drive a nail into a tree stump first—with the sharp end of a hammer. Somehow, you end up drunk.

Crazy Daisy's Bar, Brucker Bundesstr. 10-12 (☎725 16 59), across from the tourist office, is a fun though touristy joint featuring its own wacky, irreverent t-shirts and the ever-popular aforementioned hammer-in-stump game. Also serves Mexican and Ameri-can food. Hamburgers €6.90, burritos €8.72, salads €2.91-4.36, "breath-killer garlic bread" €2.18. Open in summer 8pm-1am; in winter 4pm-1am. 2-for-1 Happy Hour in summer 8-10pm; in winter 4-6pm. MC/V.

Pinzgauer Diele, Kircheng. 3 (☎21 64), has 2 bars and a small dance area guaranteed to get you moving. A largely under-25 crowd. Mixed drinks €3.63-6.90, beer €4.36-5.45. Cover €6.18. Open Su-M and W-Sa 10pm-3am.

Bierstad'l, Kircheng. 1 (☎72 36 33). 18-to-25-year-olds sample 33 different brews in stock. Creamy, dark *Hirter* €3.49. Open daily 8pm-4am.

▶ DAYTRIP FROM ZELL AM SEE

KRIMML   ☎06564

*The Pinzgauer Lokalbahn **train** comes only from the east, from Zell am See (1¾hr.; 5:47am-6:47pm, €6.80; a steam train runs from July to mid-Sept. Su, €6.80; Eurail valid). **Budesbus** lines run from Zell am See (1½hr., 11 per day 5:47am-8:55pm, €7.50) and Zell am Ziller (1½hr.; 8:52am, 1:32pm; €5.60) to the start of the falls (bus stop: Maustelle Ort).*

Each year, over 400,000 visitors charge up the sloping path from the small mountain town of Krimml to the extraordinary Krimml Waterfalls, a set of three roaring cascades spanning 380m.

The **tourist office** is 2min. from the "Krimml Ort" bus stop at Oberkrimml 37; follow the road by the stop, then turn right down the hill in front of the church. Outside is a free 24hr. accommodation phone and computer. (☎72 39; fax 75 50; krimml.info@aon.at; www.krimml.at. Open M-F 8am-noon and 2:30-5:30pm, Sa 8:30-10:30am.) There is an **ATM** at **Raiffeisenbank** across from the church. The **post office** next door to the tourist office offers good **exchange** rates. (☎72 01. Open M-Tu and Th-F 8am-noon and 2-5pm, W 8am-noon.) **Haus Mühlegg ❸,** Oberkrimmlstr. 24, is 5min. downhill along the road past **ADEG** and the sport shop: it's the brown farmhouse on the right, with flowers on every terrace. Large rooms with mountain views and homey decorations await. (☎73 38. €18.) Buy provisions for the trek up the falls at **ADEG,** just up the hill from the tourist office on Oberkrimmlstr. (Open M-F 7:30am-noon, 3-6pm, Sa 7:30am-noon.)

Parking at the waterfall hike entrance costs €7 per day for cars and €4 for motorcycles. Entrance to the falls costs €1.50 (children €0.50) 8am-6pm. The ÖAV/National Park Information stand, next to the ticket booth, offers maps, pamphlets, and German guides for €3.30-14. (☎72 12. Open May-Oct. M-Sa 11am-4pm. Call for free guided tours of the falls in English for groups of 10 or more.)

Dropping a total of 380m, the Krimml waterfalls, the highest in Europe, are secluded by the spindly pines of the Hohe Tauern National Park. The source of the waterfalls is the Krimml "Kees" (glacier), 20km up the valley above the falls. The upward-sloping trail, **Wasserfallweg** (4km) is a wide hiking path that starts past the entrance booth. The first set of falls are accessible almost directly from the entrance (30min. from the first to the second and an additional 30min. from second to third). A taxi service also runs the length of the falls. (☎72 81 or 72 28. €5.50 to 2nd falls, €7.70 to third falls, €6.50 to Krimml Bahnhof.)

The first and most powerful cascade (65m) is visible almost immediately after the entrance; it kicks up a huge skirt of spray that douses rocks, plants, and tourists who just have to get a liiiitle closer for the perfect picture. The second falls drop from a precipice named **Jagasprung** (Hunter's leap). As legend has it, a poacher once jumped from here to the other side of the falls to elude his pursuers—judge for yourself the likelihood of this feat. The third set of falls (60m) is the most scenic—one long cascade from the upper river valley. The trail continues through the upper Ache valley; a 30min. walk provides views of the towering **Dreiherrenspitze** (3499m) near the source of the waterfalls.

HOHE TAUERN

A little ways before the entrance to the waterfalls lies **WasserWunderWelt,** a new water museum/park with two floors of fun facts about water: everything you ever wanted to know about waterfalls, and the Krimml waterfalls in particular. The Aqua-Park outside has games, including a gauntlet that blasts tourists with water when they step on the wrong tiles. (☎201 13; www.wawuwe.at. €7, children €3.50. Open late Dec. to Easter W-Su 3-7pm; May-Oct. daily 10am-5pm.)

LIENZ ☎ 04852

Lienz is the primary city of East Tyrol *(Osttirol)*, despite a population of only 13,000. The center bustles with businesses and cafes, but walk five minutes and you'd swear you were in a small mountain village. Walk 15 minutes beyond that, and you'll find yourself in a valley surrounded by the Dolomites and the southern reaches of the Hohe Tauern National Park. Its proximity to both mountain ranges makes it a perfect base for exploring the countryside.

▐ TRANSPORTATION

Trains: Hauptbahnhof, Bahnhofpl. (☎660 60; train info ☎017 17). Information booth open M-F 9am-4:45pm; ticket window M-Sa 5:15am-6:40pm, Su 8:20am-7:25pm. Trains to: **Innsbruck** (3hr., 5 per day 4:42am-6:54pm, €17.60); **Spittal-Millstättersee** (Spittal an der Drau) (1hr., 15 per day 5:20am-8:19pm, €10.20); **Villach** (2hr., 5 per day 5:20am-8:14pm, €10.20).

Buses: BundesBuses (☎01 711 01) leave from the Hauptbahnhof (☎649 44) for destinations throughout the region. Open M-F 7:30am-12:30pm and 1:30-4:30pm. To: **Franz-Josefs-Höhe** (in summer 3-4 per day 7:40am-3:05pm); **Heiligenblut** (1hr., 2-8 per day 7:40am-3:05pm, €5.45); **Kitzbühel** (2hr., 1-2 per day 5:45am-5:15pm, €12.40); **Zell am See** (2 per day 10am-2pm) via Franz Josefs-Höhe. July 7-Aug. 23, a **free Stadtbus** circles the city, making 14 stops before returning to station parking lot (every hr. 8am-7pm).

By car: Lienz lies at the junction of Bundesstr. 108 from the northwest, 106 and 107 from the northeast, and 100, which runs east-west. From Innsbruck, take Autobahn A-12 east to 169 south. At Zell am Ziller, switch to 165 east, and at Mittersill take 108 south to Lienz. From Salzburg, take Autobahn A-10 south to 311, and, just before Zell am See, switch to 107 south to Lienz.

Taxi: ☎638 63, 640 64, or 653 65.

Parking: At Europapl. €0.50 per hr.; max. 3hr.

Car Rental: OPEL, Kärntnerstr. 36 (☎623 35; fax 685 91). Open M-F 8am-5:30pm, Sa 8am-noon.

Bike Rental: Trend Sport Wibmer, Egger-Lienz Pl. (☎/fax 69 068).

▐▐ ▐ ORIENTATION AND PRACTICAL INFORMATION

The **Isel River,** which feeds into the Drau, splits Lienz. The Dolomites spread south into Italy, while peaks to the north rise toward the Hohe Tauern range. From the train station, the Hauptpl. and Altstadt are across Tiroler Str. and to the left through Boznerpl.

Tourist Office: Europapl. 1 (☎652 65; fax 65 26 52; tvblienz@aon.at; www.lienz-tourismus.at). From the station, turn left on Tiroler Str. and right on Europapl. **City tours** in German M and F 10am; call ahead for English tours. Open M-F 8am-7pm, Sa 9am-noon

Lienz

♠♠ ACCOMMODATIONS
Bauernhof im Siechenhaus, 1
Brauhaus-Pension Falkenstein, 8
Camping Falken, 9

🍎 FOOD
Batzenhäusl, 6
Café Köstl, 3
Pizza-Spaghetteria
"Da Franco", 4

🍺 PUBS/NIGHTLIFE
Flair-Musik Pub, 5
Odin's Café, 2
Stadtkeller-disco, 7

and 5-7pm, Su 10am-noon. Call **Igelsberg-Stronach Information Center** (☎ 641 17) for info about **national park tours.**

Currency Exchange: Best rates are in the **post office,** which has an **ATM** in front. Exchange open M-F 8am-7pm. ATMs also at the train station and banks.

Luggage Storage: In the train station. Small lockers €2, ski lockers €3. Luggage watch €2.10. Open daily 7:30-11:10am and 1:10-6pm; lockers 6am-9:30pm.

Hospital: Emanuel-von-Hibler-Str. 5 (☎ 60 60).

Emergencies: Police, Hauptpl. 5 (☎ 133). **Fire:** ☎ 122. **Mountain Rescue:** ☎ 140. **Ambulance and water rescue:** ☎ 144. **Road service:** ☎ 120.

Internet Access: Free at the Bücherei (public library; ☎ 639 72), inside the Franziskanerkloster on Mucharg. Open Tu-F 9am-noon and 3-6pm, Sa 9am-noon.

Post Office: Boznerpl. 1, at the beginning of Hauptpl. across from the train station. Open M-F 7:30am-7pm, Sa 8-11am. **Postal code:** A-9900.

FROM THE ROAD

THE UGLY AMERICAN

I took four years of high school German, followed by a year in college, before allowing my command of the language to decay over the next two years. When I dusted off my *Deutsch* for my trip to Austria, I discovered I still have a wonderful accent and that I can remember the word for "gigantic barrel" (*Riesenfaß*), but that I can't read a menu without making a serious error or two, which is why I ended up eating stewed prunes instead of sausage and noodles in a cafe in Klagenfurt. What frightens me even more than the number of words I have forgotten is how many travelers are completely unwilling to make an attempt at speaking German. It is not a trait limited to Americans: I was asked by a group of twenty Italians on bicycles if I knew the way to the lift station. In Italian. I don't speak Italian. I'm also not sure how the tall fellow with a big backpack and a map sticking out of his pocket could have looked like a native when I was, in fact, nearly as lost as they were. I took the map out and we figured out where they wanted to go. The cyclist at the lead of the pack, who had asked me in the first place, said "Grazie," and rode off, but one of the cyclists near the back paused as she rode past and said "Thank you." And here was something about that I deeply appreciated.

There's no shame in speaking imperfect German; most of the people I've dealt with have noticed immediately that I am a foreigner, though most have been polite enough to ask me where I am from, rather than come right out and say, "You're an

▲ ACCOMMODATIONS AND CAMPING

Most *Pensionen* and *Privatzimmer* cost €15-20, and are listed at the tourist office.

Bauernhof im Siechenhaus, Kärtnerstr. 39 (☎621 88). From the station, turn right onto Tiroler Str. and walk across the Isel; take the 1st left and then an immediate right. Walk 1 block to Kärtnerstr. and turn left. This wood-beamed farmhouse was a home for the sick during the Middle Ages and now offers large rooms decorated with jigsaw puzzles. All rooms with radio, most with shower. Doubles €30; triples €45. ❷

Brauhaus-Pension Falkenstein, Pustertalerstr. 40 (☎622 70; fax 704), is run by the same folks who own the Gössler brewery next door, so expect fresh beer at the restaurant/Biergarten downstairs. Take the Lienz-Arnbach bus from the train station to Falkenstein (6:40am-6:10pm) or turn left on Tirolerstr., follow it as it turns into A-Eggerstr., then turn left on Pustertalerstr. and walk 10min. (20min. total). Rooms are large, with TV, couch, and shower. €27.50 per person. ❸

Camping Falken, Eichholz 7 (☎640 22; fax 64 02 26; camping.falken@tirol.com), is across the Drau River. From the station, turn left onto Tiroler Str. and left at the ÖAMTC garage, then pass through the tunnel and over the Drau. Continue past the stadium, then turn left down the asphalt footpath (15min.). This site, encircled by fields and mountains, has a ping-pong table, soccer field, mini-playground, and store. Laundry €3. Car lockout 1-3pm and 10pm-7am in the bigger lot. Reception 8-10am and 4-8pm. Reservations recommended. July-Aug. €5.50, children €3.50, tent site €7, caravan site €9. Sept.-June prices €0.50 less. Showers €1. ❶

◗ FOOD

Calorie-laden delis, bakeries, and cafes lie in wait in Hauptpl. and along Schweizerg. in the heart of the city. A venture through the side streets off Hauptpl. will often unearth more substantial restaurants.

Pizzeria-Spaghetteria "Da Franco," Ägidius Peggerstr. (☎699 69). Head through Hauptpl. to Johannespl., turn left at Zwergerg., and continue down the small alley, then gradually bear right up onto Ägidius Peggerstr. Try terrific stone-oven pizzas (€5.30-9) and pasta (€5.50-9) in this restaurant established by Italians who decided to make it big up north. Open daily 11:30am-2:30pm and 5pm-midnight. AmEx/DC/MC/V. ❷

Batzenhäusl, Zwergg. 1a. The place with the giant coffee pot hanging from the sign offers great deals, like the Wienerschnitzel platter (€6.50), but the real attraction is the outdoor *Gastgarten* next to the old city wall. On weekends, the Batzbar fills with a diverse crowd and frequently has live music. Open M-Sa 10am-2am. ❷

Café Köstl, Kreuzg. 4 (☎620 12). Near the Altstadt, this diner-style restaurant/bakery is good for a light lunch. Ham and eggs or bratwurst run €2.50-4. Delectable ice cream sundaes are around €4. Takeout available. Open M-F 7am-8pm, Sa 7am-12:30pm. ❶

ADEG Aktiv Markt, in Hauptpl. Open M-F 8am-6pm, Sa 8am-noon.

Bauernmarkt (farmer's market), Südtirolerpl. Open Sa 9am-1pm. Also a **Stadtmarkt** with farmers' goods on Messingg. Open F 2:30-7pm.

👁 🏔 SIGHTS AND OUTDOOR ACTIVITIES

On a hill above Lienz, Schloß Bruck houses the **Museum der Stadt Lienz.** From the tourist office, turn right on Tiroler Str., following it as it becomes Albin-Eggerstr. and then Iseltalerstr. (20min.). The castle was built in the mid-13th century as the Count of Gorz's home, and includes a small chapel whose walls and ceiling are adorned with frescoes. It now serves as a museum with rotating exhibits, including a recent one on hometown impressionist painter Albin Eggers-Lienz (whose scenes of farmers at work have been popular in the area for 70 years), along with several sculptures and paintings from Eggers-Lienz's contemporaries Klimt and Rodin. Don't forget to climb the castle's tower for a regal view. (☎/fax 625 80 83. Open Apr.-Nov. daily 10am-6pm. €10, children and students €4.)

HIKING. Outside the National Park, the Dolomites around Lienz afford excellent hikes. For information on hikes and huts, contact either the tourist office or Lienz's chapter of the **Österreichischer Alpenverein (ÖAV),** Franz-von-Defreggerstr. 11. (☎721 05. Open F 3-5pm.) Various day hikes leave from **Schloß Bruck,** round-trips taking 1-7hr. Signs on the trail to the castle give hiking information.

Hochsteinhütte (4hr. to the hut, 7hr. round-trip). From Schloß Bruck, follow signs to "Hochsteinhütte" and keep going. This well-marked hike to the hut maintained by the ÖAV is moderately steep, and suitable for intermediate or seasoned hikers. A climb to the hut

American, aren't you?" (One hiker did say to me, over breakfast one morning, "You're Dutch, aren't you?" I'm not.) Our collective fear of speaking a language that we have not mastered may be rooted in a reluctance to sound stupid and a fear of being mocked. But nobody looks stupider than the guy asking the bus driver if the bus is going to his stop in English, while the driver responds, "I don't understand. I don't understand!" And if your German is shaky, odds are you won't understand the teenager at the back of the bus making fun of you, anyway.

But there are enormous rewards to be reaped by the traveler who is willing to spend a day learning fifty or ten or even two words (*Bitte, Danke*) worth of German. You'll represent yourself and your country as something other than bumbling idiots, and don't be shocked if the service is just a bit friendlier, the bedroom is slightly larger, and the schnitzel arrives faster.

—Tom Miller

(2025m) gives the best views of all, with gorgeous panoramas of the Dolomites to the south and the Hohe Tauern range extending northward. Head for the hut's terrace, sit back, and enjoy the elevation with a glass of beer.

Böses Weibele (1½-2hr. out, 3hr. round-trip). Those with a bit more fortitude can continue past the Hochsteinhütte and head toward this peak, the highest within reach at 2521m. Getting to the "Evil Wench" requires a mostly uphill trek completely above the tree line, making you feel like you're on top of the world. Depending on how late in the summer it is, you may have to ford a few streams of snow. Not for the faint of heart.

Waldehrpfad Hike (45min.). Follow the "Waldehrpfad-Leisach" signs near Schloß Bruck. A level, leisurely forest hike wanders past a number of signs (in German) offering fun facts about the forest or the species of various flora along the way. Most of the hike stays in the woods, but there are occasional views across the valley. Follow the white-and-red blazes and avoid trails that plunge downward. Eventually a sign for "Lienz" appears: follow this path, which ends 20min. out of the town center (otherwise the hike continues, depositing you in nearby Leisach). From the bottom of the path, take a left onto the road, then a right onto Bundesstr. 100, and walk 15min. back to Lienz.

The Tristachersee (5km, 3hr. round-trip). Cross the bridge by the train station and follow Tristacherstr. The sparkling blue lake is at the base of the Rauchkofel mountain. Couch potatoes can enjoy the lake by riding the free **Bäder- und Freizeitbus** (Bath- and Leisure-Bus) from the *Dolomitenstadion* across the Drau to "Parkhotel Tristachersee." (July-Aug. 9 per day 8:53am-6:46pm.)

SKIING. Lienz serves as an excellent base to attack the ski trails of the **Lienzer Dolomiten Complex.** (☎ 639 75; www.lienzerbergbahnen.at. Mid-Dec. to early Jan. and early Feb. to mid-Mar. 1-day pass €25, seniors and youths €21, under 15 €13; half-day tickets €20/€16/€10. Late Nov. to mid-Dec., early Jan. to early Feb., and mid-Mar. to end of season 20-30% off.) The **Skischule Lienzer Dolomiten** (☎ 656 90; fax 67 22 62; www.tirol.com/skischule-lienz) at the Zettersfeld lift offers 1hr. private lessons (€35; €12 for each additional person; group lessons €35 per 4hr.; private snowboard lessons €35 per hr.) **Joachim's Ski Shop** rents **skis** and **snowboards.** (☎ 685 41; fax 642 03. Complete downhill equipment from €15 per day, children €8; snowboard with boots €24/€16.)

OTHER ACTIVITIES. Swimming is at the **Dolomitenbad** waterpark, across the Drau on the way to the campground. (Open mid-June to Aug. 8:30am-7:30pm. €3.50, children €2.) Rookie **paragliders** can call Bruno Girstmair, Beda Weberg. 4, for tandem flights from the nearby peaks. (☎/fax 655 39; Bruno@girstmair.com.)

🎵 🎭 ENTERTAINMENT AND NIGHTLIFE

Disco-lovers get stoked for the **Stadtkeller-disco,** Tiroler Str. 30, near Europapl. (☎ 62 85 24. Two bars and dance floor open daily 9pm-4am; cover €3.50 including one drink. W 9-11pm all drinks €1.60.) Next door to Pizzeria Da Franco is the **Flair Musik-Pub,** with live music every weekend with a range of genres including reggae, jazz, blues, and folk. (Beer €2. Open F-Sa 5pm-6am, Su-Th 5pm-1am.) **Odin's Cafe,** Schweizerg. 3, named after the king of the Viking gods, slams with loud rock and rap, lots of young locals, interesting special events (including a planned boat-burning on the river), and **Internet** access (€0.10 per min.) by the bar. (Wine €1.50-3. Open daily 7pm-2am.) **Cinex Lienz,** Am Markt 2 (☎ 67 111), in the town center, shows mostly recently-released American **films** dubbed into German. (Shows 3pm-midnight. Tickets €5.50-8.)

The third week of July brings out the street artists—musicians, actors, and the finest chalk-drawing guys in the world—for the **Straßentheater Festival** in the city center. Five nights of free performances ensure that accordion players from all over Europe will stay out of trouble. During the second weekend of August, all the local *Musikkappelle* bring out their horns and play the polka from 2pm to 2am, while everyone else makes merry and drinks like crazy—it's Lienz's annual **Stadtfest.** (Admission to town center €4.) The summer months also witness the reaffirmation of Tyrolean culture in a series of *Musiktanzabende*. Watch as local men dust off their old *Lederhosen* and perform the acclaimed shoe-slapping dance. (June-Aug. occasionally F 8pm. Free.)

HOHE TAUERN

UPPER AUSTRIA
(OBERÖSTERREICH)

The province of Oberösterreich (Upper Austria) is comprised of three regions: the **Mühlviertel**, in the northeastern corner; the **Innviertel**, covering the western half; and the **Salzkammergut**, the southwestern corner, encompassing the popular resort area. The charming streets of the provincial capital **Linz** mask the city's industrial soul; it is a major center of iron, steel, and chemical production, and home to many Danube port installations. The relatively flat terrain in Upper Austria makes for wonderful **bicycling** tours. Well-paved paths, suitable for cyclists of any ability, wind throughout the entire province.

HIGHLIGHTS OF UPPER AUSTRIA

Savor a jam-saturated **Linzer Torte** while relaxing in a garden cafe (see p. 288).

Peruse medieval manuscripts at the ornate library in **Kremsmünster** (see p. 291).

Soar like a bird at the Ars Electronica museum in **Linz** (see p. 289).

LINZ AN DER DONAU ☎ 0732

Sandwiched between Vienna to the east and Salzburg to the west, Linz (pop. 106,000) is often overlooked. As a sophisticated yet comfortable old world town, Linz deserves a spot on any Austrian itinerary. The third largest city in the country, Linz was once home to Kepler, Mozart, Beethoven, Bruckner, and Hitler. Technologically, it surpasses Austria's other cities. Its industrial outskirts may not be particularly scenic, but the wealth produced by the factories has been used to modernize and gentrify the central city, with elite shops, modern art galleries, cyber cafes, and a technology museum that will overload your mental circuits. The trams invite passengers to step into the future with "Zukunft. Einsteigen, bitte" written on them. Linz's citizens are friendly and anything but provincial, for its annual festivals—the classy Brucknerfest and the tomfoolery of the *Pflasterspektakel* (street performer's fair)—draw artists and crowds from all over the world.

⊫ TRANSPORTATION

Midway between Salzburg and Vienna, and on the rail line between Prague and Graz, Linz is a transportation hub for Austria and much of Eastern Europe. Frequent **trains** connect to Austrian and European cities. All **buses** arrive and leave from the **Hauptbahnhof**, where schedules are available. (Bus ticket window open M-F 7am-5:50pm, Sa 7am-1:20pm.) **Motorists** arrive via Autobahn West (A1 or E16).

Trains: Hauptbahnhof, Bahnhofpl. (☎ 517 17). To: **Innsbruck** (4hr., every 2hr. 12:19am-11:13pm, €38); **Munich** (3hr., every 1-2hr. 1:37am-10:29pm, €39); **Prague** (6hr., 4 per day 7:16am-5:55pm, €28); **Salzburg** (1½hr., every hr. 1:30am-11:13pm, €16.50); **Vienna** (2hr., every 30min. 3:43am-10:57pm, €25). Not all international trains run daily, so it's better to change trains in Vienna.

Ferries: Wurm & Köck operates boats in **Krems, Linz** (☎ 78 36 07; fax 77 10 909), and **Passau** (☎ (0851) 92 92 92; fax 355 18). To **Passau** (5-7hr.; 2 per day 8am, 2:15pm; €21, round-trip €24) and **Krems** (Sa 9am). Boats dock in Linz at the **Donau Schiffstation,** and stop at a number of Austrian and Bavarian towns along the way including Aschach and Schlogen. Discounts for seniors and children under 15. Ferries run from late Apr. to Oct.

Public Transportation: Linz's public transport system runs to all corners of the city. Trams start at the Hauptbahnhof and run north through the city along Landstr. and Hauptpl. and across Nibelungenbrücke. Several buses traverse Linz, and nearly all pass through **Blumauerplatz,** down the block and to the right from the train station. A hub closer to the city center is **Taubenmarkt,** below Hauptpl. on Landstr. A ticket for 4 stops or fewer ("Mini") costs €0.70; more than 4 ("Midi") €1.40; and a day ticket ("Maxi") €2.90. Buy tickets from any machine at bus or streetcar stops and stamp them before boarding, or face a €30 fine. The tourist office sells a €3.50 combination ticket that includes a day ticket for tram #3 and a round-trip cable car ride to **Pöstlingberg.**

Taxis: At the Hauptbahnhof, Blumauerpl., Bürgerstr., and Hauptpl. (☎ 69 69 or 17 18).

Parking: Free parking at **Urfahrmarkt** and at Stadion Parkpl. Ziegeleistr., beginning directly west from the train station.

◼🛈 ORIENTATION AND PRACTICAL INFORMATION

Linz straddles the **Danube,** which weaves west to east through the city. Most of the Altstadt sights crowd the southern bank, near the **Nibelungenbrücke.** This pedestrian area includes the huge **Hauptplatz,** just south of the bridge, and extends down

UPPER AUSTRIA

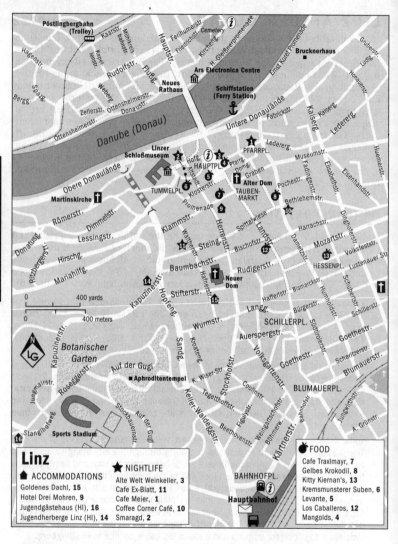

Linz

⌂ ACCOMMODATIONS

Goldenes Dachl, **15**
Hotel Drei Mohren, **9**
Jugendgästehaus (HI), **16**
Jugendherberge Linz (HI), **14**

★ NIGHTLIFE

Alte Welt Weinkeller, **3**
Cafe Ex-Blatt, **11**
Cafe Meier, **1**
Coffee Corner Café, **10**
Smaragd, **2**

🍎 FOOD

Cafe Traxlmayr, **7**
Gelbes Krokodil, **8**
Kitty Kiernan's, **13**
Kremsmunsterer Suben, **6**
Levante, **5**
Los Caballeros, **12**
Mangolds, **4**

Landstraße, which ends near the train station. To get to the center of town from the train station take tram #3 to "Hauptplatz." The tourist office is extremely helpful with detailed pamphlets on dining and hotels in Linz.

Tourist Office: Hauptpl. 1 (☎70 70 17, ext. 77; fax 77 28 73; tourist.info@linz.at; www.linz.at), in the altes *Rathaus* on the left side of the Hauptpl. The multilingual staff helps find rooms. Pick up *A Walk Through the Old Quarter* for a summary of the Altstadt's main attractions. The tourist office sells the **Linz City Ticket** (€20) which provides discounts at various sights around the city, including a voucher for a meal up to €10 at selected restaurants and a free ride on the Linz City Express. Open May-Oct. M-F 8am-7pm, Sa 9am-7pm, Su 10am-7pm; Nov.-Apr. M-F 8am-6pm, Sa-Su 10am-6pm.

Currency Exchange: Banks open M-W 8am-noon and 2-4:30pm, Th 8am-noon and 2-5:30pm, F 8am-2pm. The **post office** offers better rates. Exchange open M-F 7am-5pm, Sa 8am-1pm. €5 commission. **24hr. exchange machine** at the train station.

American Express: Bürgerstr. (☎66 90 13). Only acts as tourist agency; doesn't handle traveler's cheques. Open M-F 9am-5:30pm.

Luggage Storage: At the train station, lockers €2-3.50. At tourist office, €1.

Bi-Gay-Lesbian Organizations: Homosexuelle Initiative Linz (HOSI), Schubertstr. 36 (☎60 98 98; www.hosilinz.at). Open M-F 4-10pm. Counsel M 8-10pm, Th 6:30-10pm.

Internet Access: BIGnet.internet.cafe, Promenade 3 (70 79 68 20 10; fax 79 68 20 20; linzpromenade@bignet.at; www.bignet.at). €3.70 per 30min., students half-price. Open daily 10am-12am. Also **free** at the **Ars Electronica Museum** (see p. 289).

Post Office: Bahnhofpl. 11, next to the train and bus stations. Open M-F 7am-9pm, Sa 9am-6pm, Su 9am-1pm. **Postal code:** A-4020.

ACCOMMODATIONS

Linz suffers from a lack of cheap rooms. The city is just urban enough that locals aren't allowed to rent rooms privately, so it's usually best to stick to the youth hostels and budget hotels. Call ahead everywhere. Note hours for checking in to each hostel because they are rigid.

Jugendherberge Linz (HI), Kapuzinerstr. 14 (☎78 27 20; fax 781 78 94), near Hauptpl. From the train station, take tram #3 to "Taubenmarkt," cross Landstr., walk down Promenade and Klammstr., and turn left onto Kapuzinerstr. This friendly, no-frills hostel offers 36 beds in 4- and 6-bed rooms, the cheapest beds in town in a great location. Breakfast, showers, and sheets included. Laundry €3.27. Reception 8-10am and 6-8pm (at other times hostel is locked). The key to your locker opens the front door. Reservations recommended. Dorms €15, under 19 €12. Non-members add €3. ❷

Goldenes Dachl, Hafnerstr. 27 (☎77 58 97; fax 77 58 97). From the train station, take bus #21 to "Auerspergpl." Continue in the same direction along Herrenstr. for half a block and turn left onto Wurmstr. Hafnerstr. is the 1st right. Large sunny rooms and great location. Courtyard dining area. Only 17 beds. Call ahead. Singles €21.80; doubles €37.80-40.70, with shower €43.60. ❸

Jugendgästehaus Linz (HI), Stanglhofweg 3 (☎66 44 34; fax 44 34 75; jgh.linz@oejhv.or.at). From the train station, take bus #27 (dir.: Schiffswerft) to "Frosch-berg." Walk straight on Ziegeleistr., turn right on Roseggerstr., and continue on to Stanglhofweg. This hostel caters to school groups, and although far from the city center, its rooms are clean and spacious. Parking available. Breakfast and sheets included. Private showers and hall toilets. Reception M-Th 7:30am-4pm and 6-11pm, F 7:30am-12:30pm and 6-9pm, Sa-Su 7:30am-9am and 6-9pm. Curfew 11pm. Call ahead. Singles €26.74; doubles €38.95; triples €43.17; quads €60. MC/V. ❸

Hotel Drei Mohren, Promenade 17 (☎77 26 260; fax 26 266; hotel.drei.mohren@aon.at; www.drei-mohren.at). Ideally located down the Promenade from Hauptpl., this beautiful, historic hotel gleams with chandeliers and oriental carpets. Breakfast included. Singles €95; doubles €124; suite €211; extra bed €22. ❺

Camping Pleschinger See (☎30 53 14; fax 30 53 144; camping-linz@utanet.at). Take tram #1 or 3 to Rudolfstr. and bus #22 to "Pleschinger See." On the Linz-Vienna biking path on Pleschinger Lake. Open May to Nov. €4, children €2.35, RVs/cars €9. ❶

🍴 FOOD

Duck into the alleyway restaurants off Hauptpl. and Landstr. to avoid ridiculously inflated prices, or seek out the supermarkets: **Billa,** Landstr. 44 (open M-W 8am-7pm, Th 7:30am-7pm, F 7:30am-7:30pm, Sa 7:30am-5pm) or **SPAR Markt,** Steing., near the Jugendgästehaus (open M-F 7:30am-7pm). Linz's namesake dessert, the **Linzer Torte,** is rich and worth the price. It's unique for its deceptively dry ingredients—lots of flour and absolutely no cream. The secret is in the red-currant jam filling, which slowly seeps through and moisturizes the crumbly crust. Not all *Linzer Torten* are the same; the best sit out for at least two days after baking for maximum jam saturation. Below is a small cross-section of the eating experiences that Linz has to offer—pick up a *Gastronomie Verzeichnis* from the tourist office for a complete listing.

🍽 **Café Traxlmayr,** Promenadestr. 16 (☎77 33 53). From Hauptpl., head down Schmidttorstr., and turn right onto Promenadestr. Chandeliers and marble tables adorn the elegant interior of this Viennese-style cafe with sprawling patio. For €4.50 you can nibble on rolls and jam, sip coffee from your own little pot, and watch people play chess, cards, and billiards through the afternoon. Try the *Palatschinken* (sweet crepe filled with jam, €1.90) or the *Linzer Torten* (€2.20). Open M-Sa 8am-10pm. ❶

🍽 **Mangolds,** Hauptpl. 3 (☎78 56 88), is a paradise for vegetarians. This cafeteria-style restaurant with a pleasant outdoor space right in the middle of Hauptpl. offers only the freshest stuff. Freshly squeezed fruit and vegetable drinks (€2.11) and an extravagant salad bar with 40 different kinds of salad. Pay by weight: €1.16 per 100g, 30% discount after 6pm. Open M-F 11am-8pm, Sa 11am-5pm. ❶

Gelbes Krokodil, Dametzstr. 30 (☎78 41 82), downstairs in the Moviemento Theater, pleases a young artsy crowd, which relaxes in the beautiful *Gastgarten.* Varying menu includes soups (€2.62), salads (€5.81-6.54), and vegetarian entrees (€5.81-7.27). Open M-F 11am-1am, Sa-Su 5pm-1am. ❷

Kremsmunsterer Suben, Altstadt 10 (☎78 21 22; fax 21 222). This quaint yet luxurious restaurant offers gourmet Austrian cuisine in a delicious environment of ornate carved chairs and oriental rugs. Reservations recommended. Main dishes include gulasch and paella (€20-22). Open M, Sa 6-10:30pm, Tu-F 12-2pm and 6-10:30pm. ❹

Los Caballeros, Landstr. 32 (☎77 89 70), is a Mexican restaurant and bar with a large tequila selection and an excellent all-you-can-eat lunch *Menü* (€6.40) in the commercial district. Drink your Corona (€4.20) indoors or in the courtyard. Daily 11am-2am. ❷

Kitty Kiernan's, Hessenpl. 19 (☎77 34 76). Along Dametzerstr. between Mozartstr. and Bismarckstr. Locals flock for the unique cuisine (Irish cottage pie €7.99) and stay for the mellow hardwood pub, spacious *Gastgarten,* flowing Irish beer (Kilkenny on tap), and friendly atmosphere. Open M-Th 11am-2am, F 11am-4am, Sa-Su 2pm-4am. Kitchen open M-F 11:30am-2pm and 5-11pm, Sa-Su 5-11pm. ❷

Levante, Hauptpl. 13 (☎79 34 30), has crowded outdoor seating on Hauptpl. (look for the bright yellow umbrellas) and authentic Turkish and Greek food at low prices. €3 sandwiches are a great deal. *Menü* €6.20. Open 11:30am-11:30pm. ❷

SIGHTS

THE OLD TOWN. Start your exploration of Linz at **Hauptplatz,** where the green Pöstlingberg rises majestically in the background. The city constructed the enormous plaza in the 14th and 15th centuries when it grew wealthy from taxing all the salt and iron passing through town. The focus of the square is the marble **Trinity column,** commemorating the city's escape from the horrors of war, famine, and the plague. An octagonal tower and an astronomical clock crown the Baroque **Rathaus.** To date, only two people have ever addressed the public from its balcony: Adolf Hitler and Pope John Paul II. Free-spirited stargazer **Johannes Kepler** (the fellow who explained the elliptical orbits of the planets) wrote his major work, *Harmonices Mundi,* while living around the corner at Rathausg. 5. In 1745, Linz's first print shop opened there; today, it houses a pub.

CHURCHES. On nearby Domg. stands Linz's twin-towered **Alter Dom** (Old Cathedral), where symphonic composer **Anton Bruckner** played during his stint as church organist. *(Open daily 7am-noon and 3-7pm.)* To the south, the neo-Gothic **Neuer Dom** (New Cathedral) is the largest house of worship in Austria. Its tower could have been the highest in the country, but regulation decreed no tower could outdo Vienna's Stephansdom. **Martinskirche** is the oldest church in Austria. The central structure, erected during the Carolingian period (in the late 8th century) using debris from Roman ruins, is still intact. *(To the left of the Schloßmuseum on Römerstr.)*

MUSEUMS. The **Ars Electronica** bills itself as the "museum of the future." It's a bird, it's a plane, it's *you* strapped to the ceiling in a full-body flight simulator that sends you soaring over Upper Austria. After this not-so-natural high, head downstairs to the **CAVE,** an interactive 3-D room that sends you even higher to explore the outer reaches of space. Free **Internet** access with entrance. *(Hauptstr. 2, just over the bridge from Hauptpl. ☎727 20. Open W-Su 10am-6pm. €6, students and seniors €3. MC/V.)* The **Neue Galerie** has one of Austria's best modern art collections. Works by Klimt, Kokoschka, Lieberman, and others line the walls. *(Blütenstr. 15, on the 2nd floor of the Lentia 2000 center on the north riverbank. ☎70 70 36 00. Open June-Sept. M-W and F 10am-6pm, Th 10am-10pm, Sa 10am-1pm; Oct.-May M-W and F-Su 10am-6pm, Th 10am-10pm. €5, students €3. In May 2003, it moves across the river to its new location.)* The **Linzer Schloßmuseum** presents an eclectic collection of objects from the Middle Ages to the 20th century including one of Beethoven's pianofortes, and an 18th-century pharmacy. Special exhibits on ground floor. *(Tummelpl. 10. ☎77 44 19. Open Tu-F 9am-5pm, Sa-Su 10am-4pm. €4, students €2.20. English brochure available.)* In 2003, the **Lentos Kunstmuseum Linz** is slated to open in a white rectangular edifice on the Donaulände that locals have already dubbed "the Lego house."

BOTANICAL GARDEN. For sheer olfactory ecstasy, visit the **Botanischer Garten**'s renowned cactus and orchid collections. To visit this hothouse, take bus #27 (dir.: Chemie) from Taubenmarkt to "Botanischer Garten." *(Rosegerstr. 20-22. ☎70 70 18 72. Open May-Aug. daily 7:30am-7:30pm; Sept. and Apr. 8am-7pm; Oct. and Mar. 8am-6pm; Nov.-Feb. 8am-5pm. €2, students and seniors €1, children €0.88.)*

URFAHR AND PÖSTLINGBERG. Cross Nibelungenbrücke to reach the left bank of the Danube. This area, known as **Urfahr,** was a separate city until Linz swallowed it up in the early decades of the 20th century. It boasts some of the oldest buildings in the city and a captivating view of Linz from the apex of the **Pöstlingberg** (537m). To reach the summit, take tram #3 to "Bergbahnhof Urfahr," then either hike .5km up Hagenstr. (off Rudolphstr., which is off Hauptstr. near the bridge) or hop aboard the **Pöstlingbergbahn,** a trolley car that ascends the summit in a scenic 20min. *(☎78 01 70 02 or 78 01 75 45. Every 20min. M-Sa 5:20am-8pm, Su 11:40am-8pm.)*

€2, round-trip €3.20, children €1/€1.60.) The twin-towered **Pöstlingbergkirche**, symbol of the city, stands guard on the crest of the hill. Indulge any lingering childhood fantasies by taking the "magic dragon" train, the **Grottenbahn,** into the fairytale caves of Pöstlingberg. *(☎ 34 00 75 06; www.linzag.at. Open May-Sept. daily 10am-6pm; Apr. and Oct.-Nov. 10am-5pm. €4, under 15 €2.)*

🎵 ENTERTAINMENT

From mid-Sept. to mid-Oct., the **Brucknerfest** brings a rush of concerts paying homage to native son Anton Bruckner at the **Brucknerhaus** concert hall. The opening concerts (the end of the 2nd week in Sept.), billed as *Klangwolken* (sound-clouds), include spectacular outdoor lasers, a children's show, and a classical evening with Bruckner's 7th Symphony broadcast live into the surrounding Donaupark to 50,000 fans. (Tickets €16-80, standing room about €8. Contact *Brucknerhaus-kasse,* Untere Donaulände 7, A-4010 Linz. ☎ 77 52 30; fax 761 22 01; www.brucknerhaus.at.) During the 3rd weekend of July, the city hosts **Pflasterspektakel,** a free, 3-day street performers' festival. Every few steps down Landstr. and Hauptpl., artists from as far away as New Zealand perform Houdini acts, fire-eating, outdoor theater, bongo concerts, and punk rock before a young crowd.

🌙 NIGHTLIFE

The pulse of Linzer nightlife is at the **Bermuda Dreiecke** (Bermuda Triangle), behind the west side of Hauptpl. (head down Hofg. or follow the crowds of decked-out pub crawlers). Frequented by *Linzers* as well as tourists, this area has the highest nightclub-to-square-meter ratio in the city.

Alte Welt Weinkeller, Hauptpl. 4, outside the Dreiecke, (☎ 77 00 53), is an arcaded, Renaissance-era "wine and culture cellar" where you can soak up wine and spirits and enjoy tasteful Latin music. In summer the rows of courtyard benches fill quickly. Tasty salads (€2.50-6). Open M-Sa 5pm-1am; kitchen 5:30pm-11pm.

Smaragd, Altstadt 2, (☎ 79 40 60). From Hauptpl., take Hofg. A cafe, bar, dance floor, and performance space, this complex draws eclectic locals seeking late-night revelry under the moon and stars of its walls. Tu-W live music, Th Fiesta Latina, F-Sa disco and DJs. Open daily 8pm-6am.

Cafe Meier, Pfarrpl. 7, (☎ 77 87 88). From Hauptpl., take Rathausg. This recently-opened mellow cafe serves vegetarian dishes (average €4.36-5.09), coffee (€2.18), and beer (0.5L €2.62) to a 20-something crowd. Open Tu-Th 9am-midnight, F-Sa 9am-1am, Su 10am-midnight. Kitchen until 11pm.

Cafe Ex-Blatt, Waltherstr. 15 (☎ 77 93 19), covered in old Austrian advertisements and movie posters, attracts a hip retro crowd on weekends. Sangria €3.80. Open M-F 10am-2am, Sa-Su 6pm-1am. AmEx/MC/V.

Coffee Corner Cafe, Bethlehemstr. 30 (☎ 77 08 62), draws a sophisticated, mainly gay and lesbian crowd. Open M-Sa 7pm-2am.

🔹 DAYTRIPS FROM LINZ

MAUTHAUSEN

From Linz, take a train to Mauthausen (transfer at St. Valentin, 45min, 4:43am-11:01pm, €5). A special Oberösterreichischer Verkehrsverbund day pass (€7.50) covers the round-trip train ticket from Linz plus all city transportation in Linz and Mauthausen. Beware—the Mauthausen train station is 6km away from the camp, and a bus stops 2km from the camp M-F, only twice a day. To get to the camp, walk through town and turn right after the Freizeitzentrum. Take the signposted (KZ Mauthausen) Fußweg. You'll pass pastures, fields of hay, and orchards before reaching the bleak walls of the camp. Pick up a map from the train station. Alternatively, take a cab (€1.50-2.50 per km). By car, exit Autobahn A1 (Vienna-Linz) at Enns. Camp open Apr.-Sept. daily 8am-6pm; Oct. to mid-Dec. and Feb.-Mar. 8am-4pm. Admission until 1hr. before closing. €1.82, students and seniors €0.73.

About 30min. down the Danube from Linz, the remains of a Nazi *Konzentrationslager* (KZ; concentration camp) stand in silent vigil. Unlike other camps in southern Germany and Austria, Mauthausen remains intact. Built by Dachau prisoners in 1938, Mauthausen was the central camp for all of Austria and administered 49 subcamps throughout the country. More than 200,000 prisoners passed through Mauthausen, mainly Russian, Italian, and Polish POWs, along with Austrian homosexuals and political criminals, Hungarian and Dutch Jews, gypsies, and Communists. Mauthausen was infamous for its **Todesstiege** (Staircase of Death), which led to the stone quarry where inmates were forced to work to exhaustion. The steep, even steps currently in place were added for tourists' safety—when the inmates worked here, there was nothing but a stony drop dotted with boulders and jagged rocks. As the prisoners were going down the path, the guards often shoved the last in line so that the entire group fell down the slope, along with the stones they were carrying on their shoulders. The inner part of the camp is now a **museum** (☎ (07238) 22 69), which displays haunting photographs of the once-packed camps—a striking contrast to the vast, grassy space that remains today. The barracks, roll-call grounds, cremation ovens, and torture rooms are also accessible. A free brochure or audio-tour (in English) walks you through the central camp. There is an exhibit on the history of the camp and video documentaries in various languages.

ST. FLORIAN'S ABBEY

To reach the abbey from Linz Hauptbahnhof, take the bus (dir.: St. Florian Stift) to "Kotzmannstr." in downtown St. Florian or "Lagerhaus" (30min., 6:20am-6:35pm, €2). Both are a 15min. walk from the abbey. The tourist office, Marktpl. 3 (☎/fax (07224) 56 90), has info about the abbey and accommodations (open M-F 9am-1pm). **Tours** *of the abbey minus the Kaiserzimmer leave daily. (☎ (07224) 89 02 10. Abbey open Apr.-Oct. €5, children €1.80. Tours 10, 11am, 12, 2, 3, 4pm. Tour and concert (see below) €6.50.)*

The abbey of St. Florian, 17km from Linz, is Austria's oldest Augustinian monastery. According to legend, the martyr Florian was bound to a millstone and thrown in the Enns river. Although Florian perished, his stone miraculously floated and now serves as the abbey's cornerstone. The complex owes much of its fame to composer Anton Bruckner, who began his career here first as a choirboy, then as a teacher, and finally as a virtuoso organist and composer. His body is interred beneath the organ inside the spectacular, recently renovated church (the only part of the abbey accessible without a tour), allowing him to vibrate in perpetuity to the sound of his dearly-beloved pipes. The abbey contains the **Altdorfer Gallery,** filled with altarpieces by 15th-century artist Albrecht Altdorfer of Regensburg, an Old Master of the Danube school. Although they are works of art with balanced compositions and warm tones, these paintings also contain a political agenda. Notice that Altdorfer paints some of Christ's tormentors as Turks, the sworn enemies of the Austrian Empire. The 14 **Kaiserzimmer** (imperial rooms), built in case of an imperial visit, overwhelm visitors with Baroque splendor. (20min. concerts May-Oct. Su-M and W-F 2:30pm, €2.40.)

KREMSMÜNSTER

Trains go to Kremsmünster from Linz (45min., every hr. 7:40am-7:35pm, €5.60). From the station, follow Bahnhofstr. as it curves left, then right, then left again, and continue

Salzkammergut

on Hauptpl. to Marktpl. The path to the abbey starts at the tourist office, Rathauspl. 1.
(☎(07583) 72 12; fax 70 49; tourismus@kremsmunster.at; www.tiscover.com/
kremsmuenster. Open Tu-F 9am-noon.)

Kremsmünster Abbey (Stift), 32km south of Linz, belongs to Austria's oldest
order and dates from AD 777. Some 75 monks still call the abbey home. The
abbey owns most of the land in the area, including 3800 hectares of woods and a
wine-producing vineyard. Beneath the frescoed ceiling, the Borgesian **library**
flaunts two rows of books on every gold-encrusted shelf, and hidden doors
abound. Visitors are not allowed to handle the books, but guides will take out
any volume and leaf through it on request. The **Kaisersaal,** built to receive imperial visitors, is a Baroque gallery with marble columns and ceiling frescoes. It
feels as if you are being sucked into the scene above. Portraits of the Holy
Roman Emperors (from Rudolf of Habsburg to Charles VI) gaze down at you
from the walls. The abbey's Kunstsammlung (art collection) tour covers the
library, the Kaisersaal, several art galleries, and the **Schatzkammer** (treasury),
which shelters a beautifully engraved golden chalice dating from the time of
Charlemagne. The monks' collection of exotic animal specimens is displayed in
the 7-story **Sternwarte.** Also open is the **Fischkalter,** a series of pools set with

pagan and pastoral statues spouting water. Wooden stag heads with real antlers adorn the room—look for the two with radishes in their mouths. (☎(07583) 527 51 51; www.kremsmuenster.at/stift. Open 9am-noon and 1-6pm. Central chapel free. Fischkalter €1.10—enter through the ticket office. 1hr. Kunstsammlung tours Apr.-Oct. 10, 11am, 3, 4pm; Nov.-Mar. 11am, 2pm. €4.80. 1½hr. Sternwarte tour May-Oct. 10am, 2pm. €5.10. Both tours include the Fischkalter.)

THE MÜHLVIERTEL

Stretching north and west from Linz, the Mühlviertel's shaded woodland paths and pastures are an increasingly popular hiking area. Once this region was the stomping ground of the Celts, but in the Middle Ages Christians constructed churches out of supposedly Celt-proof local granite. This same granite filters mineral-rich waters of the region, considered curative in homeopathic circles.

Along the old **Mühlviertel Weberstraße** (Weaver's Road), textile-oriented towns display their methods of linen preparation. The **Gotischestraße,** which winds past multitudes of High Gothic architectural wonders, and the **Museumstraße,** which boasts more **Freilichtmuseen** (open-air museums) than you can shake a loom at. Poppies are another of the Mühlviertel's big selling points: products range from poppy seed oil to mouth-watering poppy seed strudels. Throughout this pastoral countryside, *Bauernhöfe* (farm houses) open their doors to world-weary travelers. For tourist brochures about trails and *Bauernhöfe*, contact the **Mühlviertel Tourist Office,** Blütenstr. 8 (☎ (0732) 73 50 20; www.tiscover.com/muehlviertel).

FREISTADT ☎07942

Freistadt, the largest town in the Mühlviertel, is an idyllic, compact village at the juncture of the **Jaunitz** and **Feldiast** rivers. Due to its strategic location on the *Pferdeeisenbahn* route that connected the Babenberg and Habsburg lands, Freistadt was a stronghold of the medieval salt and iron trade. In 1985, Freistadt received the International Europa Nostra Prize for the finest restoration of a medieval Altstadt. Freistadt's pride and joy is the **Freistädter Brauerei,** a community-owned brewery that is still in operation but, unfortunately, no longer open to the public.

🖅 TRANSPORTATION AND PRACTICAL INFORMATION. Freistadt is accessible from Linz. The **Post Bus** leaves from Linz's main train station (every 1½hr. 6:20am-8:15pm, €5.80) and arrives at Böhmertor in Freistadt, just outside the old city walls. **Trains** also run from Linz (5:59am-6:59pm, €5.80), but they arrive at the Hauptbahnhof, 3km outside of town, and require a taxi (€10). The tiny **tourist office,** Hauptpl. 14, has a free reservation service and provides info about the surrounding villages (☎/fax 757 00; open May-Sept. M-F 9am-7pm, Sa 9am-noon; Oct.-Apr. M-F 9am-5pm). The **post office,** Promenade 11 at St. Peterstr., exchanges cash only (open M-F 8am-noon and 2-5:30pm, Sa 8-10:30am). **Postal code:** A-4240.

🖪🖸 ACCOMMODATIONS AND FOOD. The **Jugendherberge "Speicher" (HI) ❶,** Schloßhof 3, is a walk around the corner from the tourist office to the red building next to Café Lubinger. Call to let them know you're coming. Hand-painted stripes and silly cartoons decorate the walls, and the rooms are comfortable. There is also a roller skating rink. The proprietress, Margarete Hawel, will wait from 6-8pm to give you a key; if you don't arrive in time, call ☎732 68. (☎743 65. Breakfast and sheets €2.18 each. Hall showers and toilets. Kitchen facilities in youth center below. Dorms €5.80, non-members €7.30.)

There are plenty of inexpensive meals in this budget-friendly town. Enjoy a *tête-à-tête* at **Café Vis à Vis ❷,** Salzg. 13. It offers the local *Mühlviertel Bauernsalat* (farmer's salad, €5.80), and local *Freistädter* beer in a lively garden. (☎ 742 93. Open M-F 9am-2am, Sa 5pm-2am.) Food abounds on the Hauptpl. as well. The best ice cream in all of the Mühlviertel awaits at **Café Lubinger ❶**, Hauptpl. 10 (soft-serve €1, scoops €0.60, less for each additional scoop). Pastries (€1.80) and a great breakfast selection round out the menu. (Open Su-M and W-Sa 8am-5pm.) The most convenient grocery store is **Uni Markt**, Pragerstr. 2, at Froschau behind the Böhmertor side of the *innere Stadt* (open M-F 8am-6:30pm, Sa 7:30am-5pm).

🎦 ♞ **SIGHTS AND HIKING.** Wander around Freistadt's inner and outer fortifications and scan the horizon from its watch tower. The moat is gradually being drained and filled with grass to form a belt-like park around the town. Pick up **A Walk Through the Old Quarter** at the tourist office. The tower of Freistadt's remarkable 14th-century **Bergfried** houses the **Mühlviertler Schloßmuseum Freistadt**, Schloßhof 2, a regional museum that displays traditional tools and period pieces. (☎ 722 74. Admission with tour only. May-Oct. M-F 9, 10:30am, 2, 3:30pm; Sa 10:30am, 2pm; Su 2pm. Nov.-Apr. 30 M-F 10:30am, 2pm; Sa-Su 2pm; €2.40.)

Niederösterreich
(Lower Austria)

LOWER AUSTRIA (NIEDERÖSTERREICH)

The province of Niederösterreich surrounds Vienna, accounting for a quarter of the nation's land mass—and 60% of its wine production. Castle ruins lurk in the hills above medieval towns, while hikers and bikers, enjoying the varied terrain, cruise by on daytrips from Vienna. The region's food provides another motive to visit: one local specialty, the *Wienerwald* cream strudel, a sinful mixture of flaky crust, curds, raisins, and lemon peel, is particularly delicious.

HIGHLIGHTS OF LOWER AUSTRIA

Climb up to the ruins of Richard the Lionheart's prison, **Schloß Dürnstein** (see p. 300).
Marvel at **Melk's** big beautiful yellow Benedictine abbey (see p. 301).
Smell the roses, all 20,000 of them, in **Baden's** rosarium (see p. 306).

DANUBE VALLEY (DONAUTAL)

The "Blue Danube" may largely be the invention of Johann Strauss's imagination, but the valley of this mighty, muddy-green river inspired him to create music for good reason. Glide on a ferry or pedal along its shores to experience the exhilarating beauty of Austria's most famous river. The **Wachau** region holds the most exemplary bends of the river—be sure to catch those between Melk and Krems.

The legendary **Donau Dampfschifffahrts-Gesellschaft** (DDSG—creators of the longest German word in existence, *Donaudampfschifffahrtsgesellschaft-kapitänswitwe*, "the widow of a captain working for the Danube Steamship Company") runs ships daily from May to late October along the Danube. The firm has an office in **Vienna**, I, Friedrichstr. 7. (☎58 88 00; fax 58 88 04 40; www.ddsg-blue-danube.at.) Boats go from Vienna to the Wachau region only on Sundays (May 6-Sept. 30). These trips, complete with didactic commentary, run from Reichsbrücke in Vienna to **Tulln, Krems,** and **Dürnstein** (departing Vienna 8:45am, returning 8:45pm; reservation required; €16.50, round-trip €22)—note that this ship does not make it as far as **Melk,** the site of the fantastic monastery.

In fact, the best trip is not this Sunday cruise from Vienna—instead, take the ferry that runs every day of the week between the most beautiful towns on the river, those in the Wachau region. From April 30 to September 30 boats leave Krems at 10:15am, 1pm, and 3:45pm, and take 2¾hr. to go all the way to Melk, docking at Dürnstein and Spitz on the way (€15.50, round-trip €20.50; bike transport is free but call ahead). **Rail/ferry combinations** are available in Vienna, including train fare to the Wachau region, the ferry within the Wachau valley between Krems and Melk, and entrance to the Benedictine abbey of Melk (€36.20). Eurail and ISIC holders get a 20% discount on travel, and families travel for half-price (min. 1 parent and 1 child ages 6-15; under 6 travel free with a parent). Contact the DDSG or tourist offices for special ship/bus ticket combinations. Specialty tours include the *Nibelungen*, which sails through areas described in the ancient eponymous saga and a *Heurigen* ride with a live *Liederabend* (evening song) trio.

Bicyclists should take advantage of the **Danube Cycle Track,** a cyclist's dream. This 305km riverside bike trail goes from Vienna, through the Wachau Valley and Linz, all the way to Passau, on the German border. It links the Danube villages and offers captivating views of crumbling castles, latticed vineyards, and medieval towns. Area tourist offices carry the route map. There is also information on the route at www.radtouren.at/english. Ask local tourist information for information on renting bikes. One of the most dramatic fortresses on the ride is the 13th-century **Burg Aggstein-Gastein,** formerly inhabited by Scheck von Wald, a robber-baron known to fearful sailors as **Schreckenwalder** (the terror of the woods).

KREMS AND STEIN ☎ 02732

At the head of the Wachau region, the hybrid town of Krems/Stein is surrounded by lush, green hills covered by terraced vineyards. Historically, Krems and Stein have shared a mayor to coordinate trade and military strategy on the Danube trading route, and through the years the towns have grown into each other's territories. Much of the region's wealth came from the tolls on this riverbend's traders—the Kremser Penny was the first coin minted by the Habsburgs.

The stuccoed walls of **Krems** have pastel charm, channeling wanderers to a relatively modern, shop-filled *Fußgängerzone* (when medieval Stein is your neighbor, Baroque *is* modern). Krems holds most of the sights, from art exhibits to sporting events, but **Stein** has a gorgeous Altstadt—its crooked, narrow, cobblestone passages twist and wind back on themselves. In the valley around Krems/Stein, vine-

LITTLE OLD LADIES Lower Austria is packed not only with yellow remnants of the Habsburg days, but also a few reminders of prehistoric times. Krems is one of Austria's top archaeology centers, and its researchers have recently unearthed the remains of a 32,000-year-old hunting community settled in the Danube bend near a place now named Galgenberg. Among the usual shards of bone and clay animal figurines, archaeologists excavated eight pieces of slate that, when fitted together, form a well-endowed female statuette. Fanny von Galgenberg, named for the famous dancer Fanny Elßler, is Austria's oldest known work of art and the world's only known female sculpture from the Aurignae Period. Barely three inches tall and half an inch thick, the figure is engraved with sketches and positioned in a pose that classifies her as part of the archetypal prehistoric Venus figures, like her much younger sister and symbol of fertility, the "Venus of Willendorf," who was found between Krems and Melk.

yards produce 120 different wines. Head for **Steiner Kellergasse,** the high street in Stein that lies next to those hills of plenty, where *Heurigen* offer the fruit of the vines and great views of the **Stift Göttweig** (abbey) across the Danube. Tour buses often block the entrance to this street leading to the *Heurigen*—rich wine and the impressive panorama of the valley make it worthwhile for every tourist.

⬛ TRANSPORTATION

Many visitors arrive on bicycles, but the **train station** is a 5min. walk from Krems's *Fußgängerzone*. To get to the *Fußgängerzone*, exit through the front door of the Bahnhof, cross Ringstr., and follow Dinstlstr. Regional trains connect Krems to **Vienna** (Spittelau station; €11.50, 5:05am-10:05pm) via Tulln. A **bus depot** is in front of the station. Both buses and trains leave every 30min. for routes to Melk and St. Pölten. Krems lies along the **DDSG ferry** route from **Passau** through **Linz** and **Melk** to **Vienna** (see p. 301). The ferry station is on the riverbank close to Stein and the ÖAMTC campground, near the intersection of Donaulände and Dr.-Karl-Dorreck-Str. To reach Krems from the landing, walk down Donaulände, which becomes Ringstr., then left onto Utzstr. To reach Stein, follow Dr.-Karl-Dorreck-Str. and then take a left onto Steiner Landstr.

⬛ ⬛ ORIENTATION AND PRACTICAL INFORMATION

Stein is west of Krems, bracketed by Steiner Kellerg. and Steiner Landstr. The **tourist office** is housed in the Kloster Und at Undstr. 6. From the train station, take a left on Ringstr. and continue (15min.) to Martin-Schmidt-Str. Turn right and follow the street to the end; the office is across the street and to the right. The staff has information on accommodations, sports, and entertainment, as well as the indispensable *Heurigen Kalendar,* which lists the opening times of regional wine taverns. Discmans are provided for self-guided walking tours (€6) and group guided walking tours in several languages leave for Krems or Stein. (1½hr., €52 per group or €2.50 per person for groups larger than 20.) They also book hotel reservations. (☎826 76; fax 700 11; www.tiscover.com/krems. Email austropa.krems@netway.at Open Easter-Oct. M-F 9am-7pm, Sa-Su 10am-noon and 1-7pm; Nov.-Easter M-F 9am-6pm.) **ATMs** are along shopping streets. **Lockers** (€2) are at the train station. **Bike rental** is **Radstudio Krems** (Hafnerpl. 5 ☎/fax 81 880, €11 per day, open M-F 8am-12pm and 1:30-6pm, Sa 8:30am-12pm) and at **R &R** (Steiner Landstr. 103 tel 71 071, €10 per day). **Public toilets** are at the train station, tourist office, and in the *Stadtpark*. **Currency exchange** is at the **post office** right off Ringstr. on Brandströmstr. (☎826 06. Open M-F 8am-noon and 2-6pm, Sa 8-11am.) **Postal code:** A-3500.

FROM THE ROAD

FIND THE RIVER

When I first saw the Danube in Vienna, I was disappointed. The famous blue river I'd heard about so often was just a muddy urban waterway. In some places it hardly even classified as a river and had been separated into industrial canals to prevent flooding. Certain that I was missing something, I went in search of the real river, determined to find whatever it was that had inspired Johann Strauss to write his famous "Blue Danube" waltz. My search began in Krems. I rented a bike with the intention of riding until I found it.

When I first turned the bend of the incredibly flat bike path, it took my breath away. The river was a little muddy and perhaps green at best, but it cut through the valley with a bold and startling force, sharply dividing green terraced vineyards and red roofs. The only noise above it was the occasional cathedral bell.

I rode along, the river on my left encouraging me, the wind in my hair (no one wears helmets here). On the path from Krems to Durnstein, medieval castles rose out of the valley, and I imagined archers perched on stone fortresses, prepared to fight to the death for their mighty river. They, too, would have been encouraged by the same water power that today was making me pedal a little faster. It wasn't blue, but I could see why the Danube was worth fighting for.

—Lora Sweeney

■ ACCOMMODATIONS

No matter where you stay, ask your hosts for a **guest card** that grants a number of discounts. The **Radfahrjugendherberge (HI)** ❷, Ringstr. 77, is a clean, close-quartered hostel accommodating 52 in comfortable 4- and 6-bed rooms. Appropriately, it is packed with strong-calved bicycling enthusiasts. (☎834 52, Fax +4. Email oejhv.noe.krems@aon.at. Breakfast, sheets, and bicycle storage included. **Lockers** included. Reception 7-9:30am and 5-8pm. Open Apr.-Oct. For advance bookings, call the central office in Vienna (☎533 53 53; fax 535 08 61). Dorms€12.20. Non-members pay €3.50 extra. €2.20 surcharge on stays less than 3 nights. Tax included.)

Privatzimmer also abound on Steiner Landstr. Karl and Ingred Hietzgern's **Baroque Bürgerhaus** ❸, Untere Landstr. 53, in Krems's Altstadt, is filled with *Jugendstil* furniture and hand-painted wood. (☎/fax 761 84 or 740 36. Open mid-June to mid-Sept. 2- and 3-bed dorms with shower €20; for stays of 3 nights or more €8. Off-season €11, for stays of 3 nights or more €7.)

Although more costly, Krems's oldest guesthouse, the centrally located **Hotel-Restaurant "Alte Post,"** ❹ Obere Landstr. 32, will host you amid its dark velvet couches, embroidered curtains, and garden cafe. (☎822 76; fax 843 96. Breakfast included. Singles €28, with shower €47; doubles €50-70.)

ÖAMTC Donau Camping ❶, Wiedeng. 7, is on a grassy Danube riverbank near the highway. (☎844 55. Reception 7:30-10am and 4:30-7pm. Facilities for disabled guests. Open Easter to mid-Oct. €3.65 per person plus €0.76 tax, children €2.54; tents €2.18-4.36, bring your own; cars €3.65. Electrical hookup €1.82. Showers included.)

■ FOOD

The area around Krems's pedestrian zone overflows with restaurants and street-side cafes. The famous **Café-Konditorei Hagmann** ❶, Untere Landstr. 8, is known in Krems for its outstanding pastries and chocolates. Try the *Schokotorte* (€2.40) with a *Mokka* (€3) or grab a *Wachauer Kugel* (ball of chocolate and nougat) for the road (€0.80). (☎831 67. Open M-F 7am-7pm, Sa 7am-5pm, Su 1:30-6pm) **Schwarze Kuchl** ❷, in the same building, offers a salad buffet (small €2.76, large €4) and assorted goulashes for €3.56-6.40. (☎831 28. Open M-F 8:30am-7:30pm, Sa 8:30am-5pm.) **Cafe Pizzini** ❶, Spänglerg. 4, a recent addition, serves pizza (€2.10) and other inexpensive Italian delicacies amid funky decor unmatched in the

Wachau region. (M-F 10am-7:30pm, Sa 10am-4pm.) **China Restaurant ❷**, Obere Landstr. 5, offers cheap, filling food at lightning speed. The lunch *Menü* (soup and entree with rice) is only €4.60. (☎841 83. Open 11:30am-2:30pm and 5:30-11:30pm. MC/V/AmEx.) **Heuriger Hamböck ❶**, Steiner Kellerg. 31, has a leafy terrace with a view of the town's spires and a restaurant bedecked with old *Fässchen* (kegs), presses, and other vineyard tools. The owner gives free tours of the cellar, with a tasting. Wine starts at €1.50; snacks are €2.80-4. For a fragrant experience, try the sweet apricot and raspberry wine (€1) (☎845 68. Open daily 3pm until people leave.) The two **SPAR** markets are one block in front of the station on the corner of Sparkasseng. and Obere Landstr. (Open M-F 7:15am-6:30pm, Sa 7:15am-5pm.)

🔊 SIGHTS

THE OLD TOWN. In Stein, medieval buildings line **Steiner Landstraße.** Stone steps tucked between streets and houses lead to impressive views of the town and valley. Krems's *Fußgängerzone*, the center of mercantile activity, consists of Obere and Untere Landstr. The entrance to the pedestrian area is marked by the Steiner Tor. This section of town is a great place to meander past the city's architectural treasures. Markets line Obere Landstr., starting in Dominikanerpl., home of the **Dominikanerkirche,** now the Weinstadt Museum (see below). Farther down the pedestrian zone is **Pfarrkirche Platz,** home of the Renaissance **Rathaus** and the **Pfarrkirche,** with its piecemeal Romanesque, Gothic, and Baroque architecture. Once there, walk up the hill to the **Piaristenkirche** to see life-sized depictions of Jesus' crucifixion. At the end of the pedestrian zone stands the **Simandlbrunnen,** a fountain depicting a husband kneeling in front of his stern wife. The fountain commemorates the power and influence of women in Krems during the Renaissance, when they succeeded in shutting down the Simandl brotherhood, a fraternity of carousing and late-night debauchery.

WEINSTADT MUSEUM. Built in the Dominikanerkloster, the excellent Weinstadt Museum in Krems features a curious combination of paintings by the world-renowned Baroque artist Martin Johann Schmidt and, in the cloister cellars, archaeological treasures from the Paleolithic Era through the Middle Ages. The changing exhibits cover subjects ranging from local folklore to apocalyptic art. *(Körnermarkt 14. ☎80 15 67 or 80 15 72; fax 80 15 76. Open Mar.-Nov. Tu-Su 10am-6pm, closed M. €3.60, students and seniors €2.50.)*

HOLDING A GRUDGE Upon arrival in the Holy Land during the Third Crusade, England's King Richard the Lionheart threw the Austrian flag to the ground, deeply offending Leopold V, Duke of Austria. Needless to say, when the Holy Roman Emperor was short of cash and ordered Richard captured, Leopold was happy to help out. Richard's ship was wrecked en route to England, and he was forced to cross Austria. Despite his clever disguise (as a peasant), Leopold's men recognized him and locked him up in Dürnstein (giving Robin Hood time to flourish under evil Prince John). A legend arose in the 13th century about how Richard was found: Richard's faithful minstrel Blondel wandered through Austria, looking for his master by whistling a tune they had composed together. When the minstrel got to Dürnstein, Richard heard him whistling and whistled back the refrain. England sent representatives with 100,000 Marks for Richard's ransom, of which Leopold garnered 75,000. The pope excommunicated Leopold for imprisoning Richard, but Leopold consoled himself by building (among other things) the town of Wiener Neustadt with his new fortune.

KUNSTHALLE KREMS. Kunsthalle Krems has recently opened a new facility on the corner of Steiner Landstr. and Dr.-Karl-Dorreck-Str. The enormous exhibition hall always has fascinating cultural and historical exhibits, often about postmodern or non-European art. *(Franz-Zeller-Pl. 3. ☎ 90 80 10; fax 90 80 11. Open daily 10am-6pm. €5-7, discounts for students and seniors.)*

WINE CELLARS. The **Heurigen** (wine cellars) are not to be missed. Plan carefully, however—the *Heurigen* are only allowed to stay open for three weeks every two months from April to October. If you don't have time for *Heurigen*, stop by the city-owned **Weingut Stadt Krems**, on the edge of the pedestrian zone. This winery lacks an attached restaurant, but it does offer free tours of the cellar and bottling center. The tastings that follow the tour usually seduce visitors into buying a bottle of wine, which runs €3.90-17.80. *(Stadtgraben 11. Go to the end of Obere Landstr., through the gate, and to the right. ☎ 80 14 40; fax 80 14 42. www.weingutstadtkrems.at Open for tours M-F 8am-noon and 1-5pm, Sa 8am-5pm.)*

🎵 ENTERTAINMENT

Krems is a happening festival town, celebrating everything from apricots to wine. Check with the tourist office for exhaustive info. Each year the **Donaufestival,** from mid-June to early July, brings open-air music and dancing, kicking off a summer of cultural activities including theater, circus, symposia, *Lieder,* folk music, and even Korean drumming. From July 15 to August 15, Krems hosts a **Musikfest,** featuring a number of organ, piano, and quartet concerts in the Kunsthalle and various churches. Tickets are available at the tourist office and *Österreichticket* (☎ 01 536 01). From late August to early September, Krems hosts the **Weinherbst in Krems,** which features wine tastings, culinary specialties, presentations, and folklore. DDSG offers a 40% reduction on ferry rates between Krems and Melk for the occasion. Throughout the year, many **churches** have sacred music and organ concerts, which resonate within Gothic vaults and are usually free.

🏃 DAYTRIP FROM KREMS

DÜRNSTEIN

Trains connect Dürnstein to Krems (every hr. 6am-7pm, €1.89) and Vienna's Franz Josef Bahnhof (every 2hr., €10.68). To reach town, descend the hill, turn right, and pass through the underground walkway (5min.). Boats dock at the DDSG ferry station on the Donaupromenade, a riverside road with beaches and bike paths. To reach town, turn right on Donaupromenade and left on Anzugg., which intersects with Hauptstr.

Located a bend or two down the Danube from Krems, among deep green vineyards, this hilltop medieval village attracts tourists and locals alike with a mythical charm. A main draw is hiking up to the ruined castle where **Richard the Lionheart** was imprisoned after his capture on the way back from the Third Crusade in 1192 (see **Holding a Grudge,** below).

Although Richard's capture was the last big splash for the Kuenninger dynasty, they continued to prosper on their home turf, building the **Augustiner Chorherrenstift.** This Baroque abbey, commissioned by the daughter of the penultimate heir of the family line in 1372, was dedicated to the Virgin Mary. Joseph II dissolved it at the same time he dismantled most of Austria's ecclesiastical institutions, but it has been well maintained nevertheless. You'll get mesmerizing views from the blue and white church steeple. Beware the skeletons that guard the elegant interior of the church from all sides. (☎(02711) 375 (Apr. 1-Oct. 31), 227 (Nov. 1-Mar. 31); fax 432. Open Apr.-Oct. daily 9am-6pm. €2.20, with tour €3.65, tour for students €3.25 including glass of wine on Th.)

The relocated tourist office (www.duernstein.at) is in the same building as the Nah & Frisch grocery store. From the train station take a right at the bottom of the hill; the green "i" is on your right. The office and the local *Rathaus* (on Hauptstr.) provide lists of *Privatzimmer* and open *Heurigen*. (☎02711 200. Tourist office open M-F 8am-noon and 1:30-4pm.)

MELK   ☎ 02752

The yellow mass of Melk's monastery floating over the dark blue makes for one of the most striking vistas you'll find in Austria. The monastery was constructed in AD 994 as a Babenberg residence, until Margrave Leopold II turned it over to Benedictine Abbot Sigibod, thus founding the Benedictine monastery and, subsequently, the village of Melk. The monastery was a renowned ecclesiastical force in the medieval world, famed for its monumental library and learned monks. Today, the abbey wields power as one of few ecclesiastical institutions that report directly to the Pope, with no bishop as middle-man. Below the abbey, the town is a jumble of Renaissance houses, narrow pedestrian zones, cobblestone streets, old towers, and remnants of the medieval city wall.

LOWER AUSTRIA

▮▮ TRANSPORTATION AND PRACTICAL INFORMATION

Trains link Melk to Vienna's Westbahnhof (1½hr., €12) via St. Pölten. Just outside the station's main entrance is the **bus depot.** Bus #1451 runs (slowly) from Melk to Krems (€5.80) and #1538 from Melk to St. Pölten (€3.30). Melk is at the end of the **DDSG ferry** route between Vienna and Passau (from Krems €15.50; round-trip €20.50, see p. 301). The **tourist office,** Babenbergstr. 1, has large **lockers** (€1) and bike racks, and makes free room reservations. (☎523 07 410; fax 523 07 490; melk@smaragd.at; www.tidiscover.com/melk. Open May-June M-F 9am-noon and 2-6pm, Sa-Su 10am-noon and 4-6pm; July-Aug. M-Sa 9am-7pm, Su 10am-noon and 5-7pm; Sept. M-F 9am-noon and 2-6pm, Sa-Su 10am-noon and 4-6pm; Oct. M-F 9am-noon and 2-5pm, Sa 10am-noon.) **Currency exchange** and **luggage storage** (€2) are available at the train station. **Bicycle rental** is at Hotel zur Post, Linzerstr. 1. (☎52 344. €10 per day, €7 after 3pm.) The **pharmacy** Landschaftsapotheke, Rathauspl. 10, is next to the town hall. (☎235 15. Open M-F 8am-noon and 2-6pm, Su 8am-noon.) The **post office** is at Bahnhofstr. 3. (Open M-F 8am-noon and 2-6pm.) **Postal code:** A-3390.

▮▮ ACCOMMODATIONS AND FOOD

To soak up the cozy atmosphere of Melk, stay in a *Privatzimmer* or on a country farm. (List at the tourist office, €13-20.) The recently renovated **Jugendherberge ❷,** Abt-Karl-Str. 42, is 10min. from the train station. This clean hostel offers 104 beds in quads with private showers and hall toilets. Beware of rampant school groups. (☎526 81; fax 542 57. Breakfast and bicycle storage included. Reception 8-10am and 5-9pm. Open Apr.-Oct. Dorms €12.66 including tax; 19 and under €9.90. €3 for non-members. €1.85 extra per night for stays less than 4 nights.) **Gasthof Weißes Lamm ❸,** Linzer Str. 7, offers plain but cheap and convenient rooms, all with bathroom and shower. (☎540 85. Breakfast included. Singles €20, doubles €40). **Camping Melk ❶** overlooks the Danube next to the ferry landing. Stay on Rollfährestr.

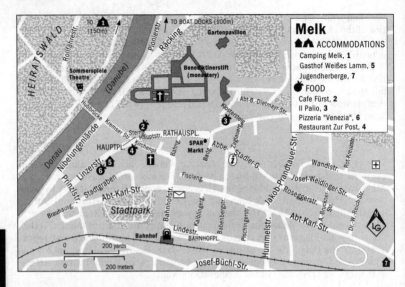

Melk

▲🏠 ACCOMMODATIONS
Camping Melk, 1
Gasthof Weißes Lamm, 5
Jugendherberge, 7

🍴 FOOD
Cafe Fürst, 2
Il Palio, 3
Pizzeria "Venezia", 6
Restaurant Zur Post, 4

(20min.). (☎ 532 91. Reception 8am-midnight. €2.60, children €1.50, tents €2.60, cars €1.90. Showers €1.10. Tax €0.80.)

Restaurants and cafes abound on Rathauspl., but look farther away for less touristed joints. **Pizzeria "Venezia" ❻** Linzerstr. 7, offers 20 lunch *Menüs* €6.17-6.90. (☎ 512 24. Open daily 11am-2:30pm and 5-11pm.) A more substantial traditional meal can be found at **Restaurant Zur Post ❸**, Linzer Str. 1, whose outdoor patio ringed in red geraniums is full of relaxed locals and vacationers. Dishes include fried chicken €10.20, and beef roast with onions €11.20. (☎ 523 45). For an afternoon snack, try **Cafe Fürst ❷**, (☎ 523 43), Rathauspl. 3, for ice cream, pastries, and simple meals such as *Kaiserschmarrn* (€6.50), spaghetti (€5.70), and *Berner Wurstl* (€5.80). Black lacquered wood and faux-Italian decor greet you at **Il Palio ❶**, Wienerstr. 3, home of fantastic ice cream concoctions. (☎ 547 32. Open daily 10am-close.) Stock up on food at **SPAR Markt**, Rathauspl. 9. (Open M-F 7am-6pm, Sa 7am-5pm.) There's a market on Rathauspl. (W 8am-4pm).

👁 🏔 SIGHTS AND OUTDOOR ACTIVITIES

The twin attractions of Melk are the impressive **Benediktinerstift** (Benedictine abbey) and the surrounding Danube countryside, ideal for outdoor activities.

BENEDIKTINERSTIFT. The monastery is huge—the secular wing alone was large enough to house Maria Theresia and her coterie of 300 on visits from Vienna. Today, this wing is filled with exhibits (mostly in German) and various Baroque optical tricks, including a portrait of Leopold II whose eyes follow you around the room and a flat ceiling that appears to be a dome when viewed from the center of the room. The stunning library in the opposite wing is brimming with sacred and secular texts painstakingly hand-copied by monks. The two highest shelves in the gallery are fake—in typical Baroque fashion, the monks sketched book spines onto the wood to make the collection appear even more formidable. The church itself, maintained by 20 monks, is a Baroque masterpiece. Maria Theresia donated the two skeletons that adorn the side altars—unknown refugees from the cata-

HIDDEN TREASURE The crown jewel of Melk's *Benediktinerstift* is unquestionably the *Melker Kreuz*, a bejeweled and gilded cross that contains a splinter believed to be a tiny fragment of the cross upon which Jesus was crucified. Crafted in 1363, the cross is two-faced: the "wealthy" side sparkles with diamonds, rubies, emeralds, and freshwater pearls from the Danube, while the "sacred" side depicts the crucified Christ and the four Evangelists at each of its rounded points. On two occasions, the cross has been stolen from the monastery, but each time has made its way back to the abbey by supernatural means (once by sailing itself back on a boat). Legend has it that anyone who opens the cross to look at the relic will be blinded by the holiness of the sight. For those brave (or foolish) enough to try, the cross can only be opened by simultaneously turning the aquamarine stones at the four corners of the cross.

combs of Rome, lounging in jeweled, embroidered outfits with thin veils over their gaping sockets. The greatest treasure of the monastery is the Melker Kreuz (Melk Cross)—gold, jewels, and the works, all circa 1363 (see "Hidden Treasure," below). The monks curate temporary exhibits of contemporary art and even commissioned artist Peter Bischof to create new murals over weather-ruined frescoes in the interior of the main courtyard. You can also visit the monastery's small garden with its delicate pavillion containing frescoes of imaginary far-off jungles. (☎523 12 52. Open May-Nov. daily 9am-6pm; Nov. to early Apr. daily only with tours at 11am and 2pm. Last entry 1hr. before closing. English guide book €3.50. Guided tours Nov.-Mar. every hr. in German, and every day at 3pm or by arrangement in English. €5.09, students €2.54, tour €1.45 extra, €1.09 extra for garden when combined with Stift.)

SCHLOß SCHALLBURG. Five kilometers out of town is **Schloß Schallaburg,** one of the most magnificent castles in central Europe. Romanesque, Gothic, Renaissance, and Mannerist influences converge in the terracotta arcades of the main courtyard. (☎(02754) 63 17. Open May-Oct. M-F 9am-5pm; Sa, Su, and holidays 9am-6pm. €6.50, students €2.90. Call ahead for a tour.) The castle doubles as the **International Exhibition Center of Lower Austria,** which brings foreign cultures to life. In 2003, the main exhibit will focus on the country of Malaysia. There are also other smaller exhibits (including 100 years of Austrian radio) and a toy museum. (☎63 17. Exhibitions in German. Shuttles leave Melk's train station daily 8:50, 9:40am, 1:15, 4:20pm. Return shuttles run at 9:10, 9:55am, 1:30, and 4:30pm. (15min., €2.50, students €1.50.) You can also hike to the complex; ask the tourist office for a map (2hr.).

OUTDOOR ACTIVITIES. Hikers enjoy the network of trails that winds through tiny villages, farmland, and wooded groves. The tourist office provides a map that lists sights, paths, and information on the 10km Leo Böck trail, 6km Seniorenweg, and 15km Schallburggrundweg. **Cyclists** tour the Danube toward Willendorf on the former canal-towing path. The 30,000-year-old **Venus of Willendorf,** a voluptuous 11cm stone figure and one of the world's most famous fertility symbols, was discovered there in 1908 (see **Little Old Ladies,** p. 297). For a more sedate option, **ferries** travel to the other side of the Danube to **Arnsdorf,** for the local *jause* (an Austrian version of British high tea), here called *Hauerganse* (vintner's special). The ferry returns past the **Heiratswald** (Marriage Woods). Romantic Melk awards couples who marry here a young sapling tree, which the couple tends for the rest of their lives.

▣ ENTERTAINMENT

The **Sommerspiele Melk** (Melk Summer Festival) comes to town in early July. An open-air stage across the arm of the Danube provides the perfect setting for enjoy-

LOWER AUSTRIA

ing world-class theater (in German) on summer nights. Tickets are available at the Melk city hall, travel agencies, and the box office next to the monastery after 7pm. (☎52 30 71 14; fax 52 30 71 40; buero@sommerspiele-melk.at. Performances mid-July to mid-Aug. Th-Sa 8:30pm. Tickets €16-34.)

ST. PÖLTEN   ☎02742

St. Pölten (pop. 50,030) is one of few places in Lower Austria not on the Danube still worth visiting. Its industrial heritage would hamper its present bid for tourism, if not for its shopping-oriented Baroque Altstadt, turn-of-the-century *Jugendstil* buildings, and an architecturally adventurous capital from the 1990s.

⌷ ⁊ TRANSPORTATION AND PRACTICAL INFORMATION. The **train station**, on Bahnhofpl. near the pedestrian zone, sends trains to the Vienna Westbahnhof (3 per hr., €8). The **tourist office** is on Rathauspl. 1 at the end of Rathausg. They provide a room list, lead 1hr. **tours** of the inner city (call up to a week in advance), and rent **cassette tours** in several languages for €1.50. (☎35 33 54; fax 333 28 19; tourismus@st-poelten.gv.at; www.st-poelten.gv.at. Open Nov.-Mar. M-F 8am-5pm; Apr.-Oct. M-F 8am-5pm, Sa 9am-5pm, Su and holidays 10am-5pm.) There is a free reservation phone just across Rathausg. from the tourist office. Other services include: **currency exchange** at **Bank Austria**, Rathausg. 2 (☎549 19; fax 545 75); **bike rental** at the train station for €11, with train ticket €7.50 (☎323 38 74; open daily 5:45am-10pm); and **lockers** at the train station, available 24hr. (€2). **Internet** access is available at **M@trix,** Rennbahnstr. 29, at the edge of the Regierungsviertel. (☎22 640. Open M-Sa 10am-midnight. €0.07 per min.) The main **post office,** Bahnhofpl. 1a, is right by the station. (Open M-F 7am-8pm, Sa 7am-1pm.) **Postal code**: A-3100.

⌷⌷ ACCOMMODATIONS AND FOOD. St. Pölten works well as a day trip, especially since the town lost its only youth hostel a few years ago. You might consider staying in the hostels in **Krems** (☎(02732) 834 52; see p. 296), **Melk** (☎(02752) 26 81; see p. 301), or **Vienna** (see p. 82). The tourist office maintains a list of *Pensionen* and *Privatzimmer*, most of which are outside the city limits.

If you're willing to spend a little money, there are some decent options in town. The **Mariazellerhof ❸,** Mariazellerstr. 6, is just south of the Europapl. The hotel is the pink and blue building at the beginning of Mariazellerstr. (☎769 95; fax 769 958. Breakfast included. Reception M-Th 7am-9pm, F-Su 7-10am and 4-9pm. Singles €30; doubles €50.) **Gasthof Hauster-Eck ❹,** Schulg. 2, in the pedestrian zone, is a green art noveau building erected in 1907 with spacious rooms, floor-to-ceiling curtains, TVs, and sofas. (☎733 36; fax 783 86; m.hauser@eunet.at. Breakfast included. Singles €35-45; doubles €60-74.) The campsite **Megafun ❶,** Am Ratzerdorfer See, is on a small lake outside of town. Take bus #4, which leaves across the street from the train station, to "Unterratzersdorf Schule" (every 30min., 5:45am-6:45pm, €1.50). Go down Ratzersdorfer Hauptstr., take a left onto Fritschstr. As it curves to the left, take a right onto E.-Werk-Weg, continue until you cross the stream, then turn left onto Bimbo-Binder-Promendade. The campground will be on your right (10min.) (☎25 15 10; fax 25 15 10 118. Reception 6am-midnight. €5, children €2, RV €5.50, tent €2.50, car €2. Tax €0.75 per person per night.)

St. Pölten's local specialties include oysters, fried black pudding, and savory Wachau wine. **Pizzerria Maradonna ❷,** Rathauspl./Heitzerlerg. 1, is tucked between the Stadttheater and the Franziskanerkirche. Enjoy one of their pasta dishes (€5.40-7.10) or their pizza *Menü* (€5.80) in a quiet corner of the square. (☎35 21 92. Open M-Tu 11:30am-2pm, W-Su 11:30am-2pm and 5:30-11pm.) The **Landhaus Stüberl ❷,** Landhausstr. 27, is in the heart of the new government quarter and offers a great view of the Landtagschiff from its outdoor patio. Its eclectic menu

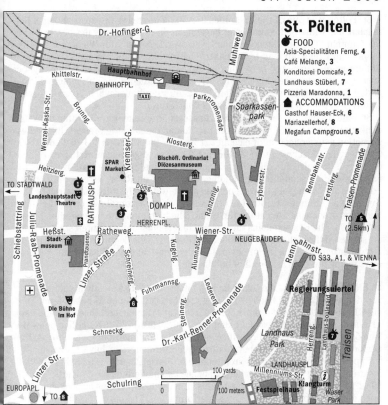

St. Pölten

🍎 FOOD
Asia-Specialitäten Ferng, 4
Café Melange, 3
Konditorei Domcafe, 2
Landhaus Stüberl, 7
Pizzeria Maradonna, 1
🏠 ACCOMMODATIONS
Gasthof Hauser-Eck, 6
Mariazellerhof, 8
Megafun Campground, 5

includes paella (€6.20), tacos (€5.90) and Greek salad (€4.50). (☎ 25 524. Open M-F 8am-10pm, Sa 9am-10pm, Su 9am-3pm.) **Asia-Spezialitaten Ferng ❷**, Wienerstr. 47, cooks up specialties from China, Thailand, and Japan, with lunch *Menüs* M-Sa for €5. (☎ 28 459. Open daily 11am-2:30pm and 5:30-11pm.) A comfortable Viennese-style cafe with newspapers and lingering guests, **Café Melange ❶**, Kremserg. 11, on the second floor, draws a young crowd. They serve a variety of dessert and light snacks, including *Palatschinke*, vegetable strudel, and salami toast, €2.90. (☎ 35 23 93. Open M-F 7:30am-6:30pm, Sa 7:30am-5pm.) **Konditorei Domcafe ❶**, Domg. 8, features fruit frappes (€2.60) and salad buffet (small €2.80, large €4.35) and small pastries (€1.35-2.45), which taste best in the popular outdoor seating area. (☎ 35 23 22. Open M-F 7am-7pm, Sa 7am-6pm.) Cheap and healthy fixings await at the **SPAR** supermarket, Kremserg. 21. (Open M-F 7:30am-6:30pm, Sa 7:30am-5pm.)

🔘 **SIGHTS.** The 13th-century **Rathausplatz** at St. Pölten's core was built on the site of a first-century Roman settlement. The building at Rathausg. 2 earned the name **Schubert Haus** due to Franz's frequent visits to the owners, Baron von Münk and family. A neo-Grecian Schubert (bare-chested, no less) conducts above the window over the door. Pass Dr. Karl-Renner-Promenade to see the only *Jugendstil* (Art Nouveau) **synagogue** in Lower Austria. Architect Joseph Maria Olbrich designed several other *Jugendstil* buildings in St. Pölten's Altstadt.

St. Pölten was one of the first cities in Austria to create a pedestrian zone. **Herrenplatz** has witnessed centuries of haggling at St. Pölten's daily market, inspiring the fountain "The Gossiping Woman." Narrow alleys just after Wienerstr. 29, Herrenpl., and Domg. all lead to **Domplatz**. The remains of the Roman settlement of Aelium were discovered here when sewer installers tripped over Roman hypocausts (ancient floor heating systems). The **Dom** (cathedral) is still intact with the gilded Baroque encrustations added by Jakob Prandtauer when he transformed the original Roman basilica. (Open until 6pm. Free.)

St. Pölten's best museum is the **Stadtmuseum**, Prandtauerstr. 2. with a thorough collection describing St. Pölten from pre-Roman times to the present. Its greatest attraction is its collection of elegant *art noveau* paintings. (☎ 333 26 43 or 333 26 01. Open Tu-Sa 10am-5pm. €2 students €1.) The **Regierungsviertel** (government quarter) is a futuristic collection of minimalistic buildings. Its centerpiece is the Landtagschiff, a semi-circular building on the Traisen River. Its elegantly curved contours are like a giant ship suspended above water. The lofty Klangturm (sound tower) was intended to provide contrast to the horizontal sweep of the other buildings. A viewing area at the top of the 80m high monolith is accessible by elevator (€1). The Festspielhaus theater, Shedhalle museum, and interesting morden art scattered throughout the complex keep it lively. Check out Hans Kupelwieser's *Hohlkopfwand*, an array of several dozen identical silver heads, stacked into rows facing the solid rear wall of building 1a.

🎭 **ENTERTAINMENT. Die Bühne im Hof,** Linzerstr. 18, has mostly modern theater and dance. (☎ 35 22 91; fax 35 22 94; www.bih.at. Office open M-F 9am-5pm. Tickets €19-26; students and seniors 50% off.) **The Landeshauptstadt Theater,** Rathauspl. 11, stages traditional opera and ballet. (☎ 35 20 26; fax 35 20 26 52. Office open M-F 9am-5pm. Tickets €12-32; box office sells a few standing room tickets for €11 on performance evenings.) Neither theater has performances in July or August.

Experience swooping glass architecture at **Festspielhaus,** Franz Schubert-Pl. 2, by attending one of the many classical music and modern dance concerts. (☎ 90 80 80 222; fax 90 80 81; office@festspielhaus.at; www.festspielhaus.at. Ticket counter open M-F 9am-6pm and 1½hr. before performances. Tickets €3.50-43.) More serious bunheads should check out the **Ballettkonservatorium St. Pölten,** the classical ballet school and training ground for the prestigious **Ballett St. Pölten.**

Seasonal festivities include the **St. Pöltner Festwoche,** which brings all kinds of events to local theaters and museums at the end of May. In early July, the **St. Pöltner Hauptstadtfest** pitches its tents and the locals let loose. From late July to early September the **International Culture and Film Festival** screens free flicks weekly. See www.st-poelten.gv.at for more information.

BADEN BEI WIEN   ☎ 02252

Baden is a favorite weekend spot for Viennese and globe-trotters alike to revive their bodies, thanks to the healing effects of its sulfur springs. Under imperial patronage in the 19th century, city notables commissioned magnificent specimens of architecture, turning Baden into a wonderland of pastel buildings. As a tribute to the Emperor, the town created a **rosarium,** with over 20,000 roses, extending $90,000m^2$ from the city center to the **Wienerwald** (Vienna Woods). Baden's prices are, however, the snakes slithering through this idyllic garden; resist temptation by making Baden a daytrip from Vienna, only 26km away.

🚍 **TRANSPORTATION.** The easiest way to get to Baden is by the **Badener Bahn,** a **tram** that runs from **Vienna's Karlspl.,** beneath the Opera House, to Baden's **Josefspl.** (1hr., every 15min. 5am-10:30pm, €3.50 with Vienna U-Bahn pass, €5 without).

Trains also travel frequently between Vienna's **Südbahnhof** and Josefpl. (outbound from Vienna: 4:40am-11:15pm; inbound: 4:16am-11pm, €5). **By car** from the west, take Autobahn West to Bundesstr. 20 at "Alland-Baden-Mödling." From Vienna, take Autobahn South (Süd) and exit at "Baden."

◢ PRACTICAL INFORMATION. Baden's **tourist office,** Brusattipl. 3 at Leopolds-bad, is accessible from the Josefpl. station. Walk toward the fountain, keep right, and follow Erzherzog-Rainer-Ring to the second left (Brusattipl.). The tourist office is at the end of the cul-de-sac. (The staff distributes brochures on request. In the summer, they offer **free tours** of the Altstadt (1½hr.; M 3:30pm, Sa 10am), the wine region (2hr.; W 3pm; make appointments in advance), and guided **hiking** tours (Tu and Sa 2pm). (☎22 60 06 00; fax 807 33; www.baden.at. Open May-Oct. M-Sa 9am-6pm, Su and holidays 9am-noon; Nov.-Apr. M-F 9am-5pm.) Services include: **luggage storage** (at the train station, €1.50); clean, free **public toilets** at Brusattipl., the Rosarium, and the train station; **police,** ☎133; and **medical emergency,** ☎144. **Postal code:** A-2500.

◪◳ ACCOMMODATIONS AND FOOD. The tourist office can give you a list of lodgings in Baden with prices and descriptions. **Pension Steinkellner ❸,** Am Hang 1, offers reasonably priced rooms in a flower-bedecked building. It's a walk from the center of town, up Vöslauerstr. from Josefspl. and right at the fourth stoplight, but the proprietors will pick you up if you call ahead. (☎862 26; fax 228 77; www.baden-bei-wien.at/steinkeller. Breakfast included. Singles €25.50; doubles €52.) Closer to the Altstadt is **Pension Wienerstub'n ❸,** Weilburgstr. 19. (☎481 02; fax 418 35 12; www.members.magnet.at/hotel.artner/page3.html. Breakfast included. Singles €20-37; doubles €35-55.) To enjoy the high life in this small town, the **Grand Hotel Sauerhof ❺** will cater to your every need. This four star hotel is close to the baths and offers luxury (Singles and suites from €124-800). **Café Damals ❷,** Rathausg. 3, in a cool, ivy-hung courtyard, is a popular place for a filling €6 lunch. (☎426 86. Open M-F 10am-midnight, Sa 10am-2pm, Su 10am-7pm.) There are plenty of cafes along Hauptpl. and Pfarrg. If you'd like a side of history with your *Tafelspitz* (boiled beef), head to **Gasthaus zum Reichsapfel ❷,** Spiegelg. 2. Follow Antong. one block from Theaterpl.; the restaurant is on the corner. The oldest guesthouse in Baden, it has served hungry wayfarers since the 13th century. (☎482 05. Dishes €6-12. Open M and W-F 5pm-11:30pm, Sa-Su 11am-2pm and 5pm-11pm.) Try **Restaurant Primavera ❹** for Austrian gourmet treat. **Billa,** Wasserg. 14 (open M-W 8am-7pm, Th 7:30am-7pm, F 7:30am-7:30pm, Sa 7:30am-5pm), and **SPAR,** Rathausg. 7 (open M-F 7:30am-6:30pm, Sa 7:30am-5pm), are grocery stores in the *Fußgängerzone.* A **farmer's market** is at Grüner Markt on Brusattipl. (M-F 8am-6pm, Sa 8am-1pm).

◧ SIGHTS. Centered around Hauptpl., Baden's lovely *Fußgängerzone* features the elaborate Dreifaltigkeitsäule (Trinity Column), erected in 1718. The thermal baths that were Baden's biggest attraction in the days of Caesar Augustus still draw in tourists today. **The Strandbad,** Helenenstr. 19-21, lets you simmer in the hot sulfur thermal pool and cool off in normal chlorinated pools. Kids will go nuts over the huge water slide and pool. A lifeguard is present but not terribly attentive. (☎486 70. Open M-F 8:30am-7:30pm, Sa-Su 8am-6:30pm. M-F €5.40, after 1pm €4.60; Sa-Su €6.30, €5.40; also student rate €2.80) From May to September 28, visit the smaller **pool** at Marchetstr. 13, behind the Kurdirektion (€4.60). The **Kurdi-rektion** itself, Brusattipl. 4 (☎445 31), is the center of all curative spa treatments, housing an indoor thermal pool mainly for patients but open to visitors (€5.50). The spa has underwater massage therapy (€22), sulfur mud baths (€25), and a basic massage, called the *sport und vital* massage (€25). A giant new spa complex, the **Römertherme Baden,** Brusattipl. 4, offers even more soothing luxuries all year long. (☎ 450 30; fax 45 03 03 04; www.roemertherme.at. 2hr. soak €8.20, students €6.30. Open M-Su 10am-10pm.)

If you tire of soaking, north of Hauptpl. via Maria-Theresa-G. lies the **Kurpark.** Set into the southeast edge of the Wienerwald, this carefully landscaped garden is studded with statues, among which the imperial court gamboled during the Congress of Vienna in the early 19th century. The delightful **Theresiengarten** was laid out in 1792 and its flower clock began ticking in 1929. If you're feeling lucky, visit the **Casino** (☎ 444 96. Opens at 3pm. Semi-formal dress required. 19+.).

The **Emperor Franz-Josef Museum,** Hochstr. 51, sits atop the Badener Berg at the end of the park (follow signs through the *Sommerarena* along Zöllner and Suck-füllweg) and holds exhibitions of folk art, weapons, religious pieces, and photography. (☎ 411 00. Open Apr.-Oct. Tu-Su and holidays 2-6pm; Nov.-Mar. Tu-Su 11am-5pm.) The **Beethovenhaus,** at Rathausg. 10, is where the composer spent his summers from 1804 to 1825, banging out part of *Missa Solemnis* and much of his *Ninth Symphony.* The museum features the composer's death mask and locks of his hair. (Open Tu-F 4-6pm, Sa-Su and holidays 9-11am and 4-6pm.)

🎭 **ENTERTAINMENT.** Baden hosts a range of festivals, notably the **Beethoven Festival** in late September, which features performances by famous Austrian musicians and film screenings at the **Stadttheater.** For tickets, contact Kulturamt der Stadtgemeinde Baden, Hauptpl. 1, A-2500 Baden (☎ 86 80 02 31; fax 86 80 02 10); ticket orders by mail must be received by mid-August. From late June to mid-September, the **Sommerarena** in the Kurpark stages open-air performances of classic Viennese operettas. (Tickets available at ☎ 485 47; Stadttheater Baden Kartenbüro, Theaterpl. 7, A-2500 Baden; or stop by the box office in the Stadttheater on Kaiser-Franz-Ring-Str. Open M-F 10am-6:30pm, Sa 10am-1pm and 5-6:30pm, Su and holidays closed; www.stadttheater-baden.at. €13-43, standing room €3.50.) Last-minute tickets, if there are any left, are half-price 1hr. before curtain.

Baden blooms in the beginning of June with the **Badener Rosentage,** a multi-week celebration of roses. Most activities, including children's theater and puppet shows, are free; they take place throughout the *Badener Rosarium.* (Open daily 9am-7pm. €3 per 30min., €5 per hr.) World-class **horse racing** occurs from June to the end of August, primarily on Th and Su and the occasional Sa; dial ☎ 88 77 30 for details. From September to early Oct., Baden hosts the **Grape Cure Weeks,** a bacchanalian gathering of local wineries on Hauptpl. For details, stop by one of the wine taverns. (Stands open daily 8am-6pm. Call 22 60 00 for information.)

LIECHTENSTEIN

FACTS AND FIGURES

CAPITAL: Vaduz

CURRENCY: Swiss Franc (SFr)

POPULATION: 32,000

MAJOR EXPORTS: Dental products

FORM OF GOVERNMENT: Hereditary constitutional monarchy

LAND AREA: 160 sq. km

LANGUAGE: German

RELIGION: 80% Catholic, 7.4% Protestant, 12.6% other

GEOGRAPHY: Flat, river valley in west with two largest towns (Vaduz and Schaan); mountainous terrain in east

PHONE CODE	Country code 0423; **international dialing prefix** 00.

EMERGENCIES	**Police** or **mountain rescue** ☎ 117. **Fire** ☎ 118 **Medical emergency** ☎ 144. **Roadside assistance** ☎ 140.

A recent Liechtenstein tourist brochure unfortunately mislabeled the already tiny 160 sq. km country as an even tinier 160 sq. m. Ironically, this is approximately how much most people see of the world's only German-speaking monarchy, as travelers usually pause only long enough to buy the obligatory postage stamp and hastily record their visit in a passport in the capital city of Vaduz. Most miss the intense alpine beauty of this tiny country altogether. Its ruling monarch, Prince Hans Adam II, is the first ruler to actually live in Liechtenstein since the present dynasty took control of the country in 1699. Before that, the family ruled Liechtenstein from their estates in the former Czechoslovakia. Liechtenstein's ties to Switzerland were established in 1923 with a customs and monetary union, replacing a similar agreement with the Austro-Hungarian empire from 1852 to 1919.

The lack of an army and independent foreign representation does not mean Lichtenstein is weak. The country enjoys great wealth due to the booming industries of dental manufacturing, banking, and tourism. Some locals haven't let it go to their heads, though; a farmer driving an Alfa-Romero will still pick up hitchikers, and old-fashioned huts in the more isolated regions are being built at the same rate as ultra-modern buildings in the capital city of Vaduz. Above the valley towns, cliff-hanging roads are the gateways to those places truly worth visiting—the mountains. Unspoiled and a world away from the tourist traps below, the mountains offer hiking and skiing prospects without the touristy atmosphere infecting some of the alpine resorts of Liechtenstein's neighbors.

VADUZ AND LOWER LIECHTENSTEIN

The hamlet of Vaduz is Liechtenstein's capital and tourist center. It's a town of tourists traveling in packs, furiously scrambling to find something worthy of a photo opportunity, often finding just the *Schloß* looming above town and the high prices looming in town. A handful of museums, but not much else, await the traveler here; Vaduz rarely requires more than one day. While campers and bikers might enjoy the surrounding countryside of Lower Liechtenstein ("lower" referring to the region's 500m elevation), others should consider heading for the hills in Upper Liechtenstein, particularly Malbun.

Liechtenstein

■ TRANSPORTATION. Although trains from Austria and Switzerland pass through the country, Liechtenstein itself has no rail system. Instead, it has a cheap, efficient **Post Bus** system that links all 11 villages (short trips 2.40SFr; long trips 3.60SFr; students and children 16 and under half-price; SwissPass valid). A one-week bus ticket (10SFr; students, seniors, and children 16 and under 5SFr) covers all (and we mean *all*) of Liechtenstein as well as buses to Swiss and Austrian border towns. If you're planning on taking more than two rides, it's the best deal in the country. The principality is a 20-30min. bus ride from **Sargans** or **Buchs** in Switzerland and **Feldkirch** in Austria (3.60SFr). Keep a passport on you when traveling.

■ PRACTICAL INFORMATION. Liechtenstein's **national tourist office,** Städtle 37, one block up the hill from the Vaduz Post Bus stop, will stamp your passport with Liechtenstein's bi-colored seal (2SFr). It also gives advice on hiking, cycling, and skiing in the area, and sells a hiking map for 15.50SFr. (☎232 14 43; fax 392 16 18; touristinfo@liechtenstein.li; www.tourismus.li. Open July-Sept. M-F 8am-5:30pm, Sa-Su 9am-5pm. Oct.-June M-F 8am-noon and 1:30-5:30pm; exceptions: Apr. and Oct. also Sa 9am-noon and 1:30-5pm; May also Sa-Su 9am-noon and 1:30-5pm.) For **currency exchange,** try any **ATM,** the Liechtenstein Landesbank next to the post office and at the post offices in Schaan and Triesenberg. The *Erlebnispass*, available at the tourist office, and post offices (25SFr), offers a variery of discounts for museums and transportation, but is worth it only for an extended stay. **Free Internet** is available at Telecom-Shop, Austr. (bus #1 Richtung Sargans to "Rütti" from Schaan/Vaduz. M-F 9am-noon, 1:30-6:30pm, Sa 9am-1pm. ☎237 74 74.

Rent **bicycles**—a great way to get around the lower country—at **Bike-Garage** in nearby Triesen. (☎390 03 90. 35SFr per day. Open M-F 8am-noon and 1:30-6pm, Sa 8am-2pm.) **Parking** is available on Aulerstr. across from the Old Castle Inn (1SFr per hr.) For a **taxi,** call ☎373 29 52, 392 22 22, or 233 35 35. Liechtenstein's **hospital** can be reached at ☎235 44 11. The main **post office** is near the tourist office and has an amazing selection of postage stamps. (☎239 63 63. Open M-F 7:45am-6pm, Sa 8-11am.) **Postal code:** FL-9490.

■ ACCOMMODATIONS AND FOOD. Budget housing options in Vaduz are few and far between, but nearby **Schaan** is more inviting. Liechtenstein's sole **Jugendherberge (HI) ❷,** Untere Rüttig. 6, is in Schaan. From Vaduz, take bus #1 (dir: Schaan) to "Mühleholz," walk toward the intersection with traffic lights, and turn left down Marianumstr. Walk 4-5min. and follow signs to this spotless pink hostel on the edge of a farm. Clean rooms, a bountiful breakfast buffet, and a game room with a Nintendo make this a great place to stay. (☎232 50 22; fax 58 56; schaan@youthhostel.ch; www.youthhostel.ch. Mountain bike rental 15SFr per day. Dinner 11.50SFr. Laundry 8SFr. Reception 5-10pm, checkout 10am. Curfew 10pm; key code available. Open Feb.-Oct. Dorms 28.60SFr; doubles 37.10SFr.) For convenience, budget-friendly **Hotel Post ❸**, Bahnhofstr. 14, is 10m away from the Schaan Post Bus stop and train station. The down side for light sleepers is that it's 10m away from the noisy bus stop. Rooms are large, carpeted, and reasonably priced. (☎232 17 18. Breakfast included at the restaurant downstairs. Reception 8am-11pm. 40SFr per person, with shower 50SFr. No credit cards.) For a night under the stars, try **Camping Mittagspitze ❶**. Take bus #1 (dir: Sargans) to "Säga," cross the street, and walk toward the mountains on the street near the bus stop, following the signs. Located on a series of hillside terraces at the foot of the redoubtable Mittagspitze, this country campground provides good scenery and a pool. Reception is just past the two babbling brooks; you can check in while the desk is closed and pay later. (☎392 26 86. Laundry 4.50SFr. Shower included. Reception June-Aug. 8-10am and 5-8pm; Sept.-May 7-8am and 5-6pm. 8.50SF, tent 5SFr, electricity 4SFr. 0.30SFr tax.)

If you simply must stay in Vaduz, try the **Landesgasthof Au ❸** (Austr. 2 or #1 bus: Au), which has modern rooms with a view of horses grazing in a lot next door. It's a 5min. from downtown Vaduz and has reasonable prices. (☎423 232 11 17; fax 232 11 68. Breakfast included. Singles 60SFr, with shower 80SFr; doubles 96SFr, 120SFr, each additional person 30SFr. No credit cards.)

Eating cheaply in Liechtenstein is challenging, as most restaurants in the center of town have blood-curdling prices. A basic sit-down meal will easily run 25-30SFr. **Azzuro Pizza ❷**, (Aulestr. 20) sells take-out pizzas for 7-14SFr and kebabs for 9SFr. (☎232 48 18. Open M-Sa 8am-7pm, Su 8am-5pm.) **Kidteuing Thai ❷** (11 Landesstr., #1: Falknis) offers duck curry, pad thai and other pan-asian meals for 10SFr. Though the seasoning may be sharp for some, it won't cut you nearly as badly as the prices at most hotel restaurants in the region. Groceries, another good option, are available at **Migros**, Aulestr. 20, across from the tour bus parking lot in Vaduz. (Open M-F 8am-1pm and 1:30-6:30pm, Sa 8am-4pm. For those staying in or near Schaan, there are several supermarkets and gas stations between Schaan and Vaduz which can provide provisions for a meal or two. (Bus #1 to Mueholz, Falknis, Adler, etc.).

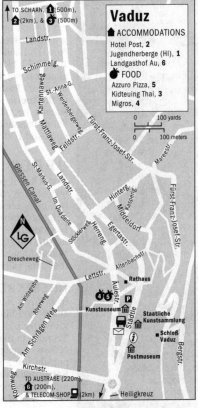

Vaduz

🏠 ACCOMMODATIONS
Hotel Post, 2
Jugendherberge (HI), 1
Landgasthof Au, 6

🍴 FOOD
Azzuro Pizza, 5
Kidteuing Thai, 3
Migros, 4

LIECHTENSTEIN

FROM THE ROAD

A SIX-HOUR TOUR

Let's Go Researcher-Writer Tom Miller volunteered to supplement his job by going for a run—a long one. No stranger to marathons, Tom (having completed the 2001 Bay State marathon in 3hr. 13min. and the 2002 Boston marathon in 3hr. 40min.) was up for the challenge. Though he found it a fantastic way to see the country-side, Let's Go does not necessarily recommend this mode of sightseeing for everyone.

Though we joke about being able to see all of Liechtenstein in a day, it's actually possible to see the entire nation in a little under six hours. The LGT-Alpin marathon runs 42km from Bendern (outside of Schaan) to Malbun, in the southeastern corner of the country. My editor and I rearranged my entire schedule so I could run it.

It was worth it.

The course began in the relatively flat farmland near the Rhine. It was an unseasonably warm day—well over 80 degrees at 9:30am—and the smell of cow manure was overwhelming at times as we ran past farmers harvesting hay. Beginning in the capital city of Vaduz, the next 11km were entirely uphill, rising over 1000m. Most of us slowed to a walk early on, but the enthusiastic Liechtensteiners were out in force chanting, "Haub, haub, haub! Bravo!" as we lumbered past.

The course finally flattened out at about km 22, in the mountains above Gaflei. Coming around a corner I heard dozens of bells tolling and wondered if a local church had decided to ring its bells for us. As I came around the hairpin turn, I found about 400

⑤ SIGHTS. 12th-century **Schloß Vaduz,** the regal home of Hans Adam II, Prince of Liechtenstein, presides over the town. The interior of the ruler's residence is off-limits to the bourgeois masses; only rich politicians, university students with very good final exam grades, and retirees are asked to visit the Prince, usually on New Year's Day. You can hike up to the castle for a closer look; the 15min. trail begins down the street from the tourist office, heading away from the post office. The signs along the path offer a veritable civics lesson on Liechtensteinian government in German, French, and English. Across the street from the tourist office is the large modern building housing the **Kunstmuseum Liechtenstein,** Städtle 32. Showing mostly modern art, this museum opened in November 2000 and boasts works by Dalí, Kandinsky, and Klee, as well as rotating special exhibits. The moderns are a mixed bag, including a few huge installation pieces (like an empty ampitheater and a giant white marble ball enclosed in glass) and are located next door to the prince's collection of Renaissance and Romantic masterpieces, including several by Rubens. (☎ 235 03 00; fax 235 03 29; www.kunstmuseum.li. Open Tu-W and F-Su 10am-5pm, Th 10am-8pm. 8SFr; students, seniors, and ages 10-16 5SFr.) Reproductions of the royal art collection almost inevitably end up on postage stamps in the one-room **Postmuseum,** Städtle 37, on the other side of the tourist office, which has—you guessed it—stamps. (☎ 236 61 05; fax 236 61 09. Open Apr.-Oct. daily 10am-noon and 1:30-5:30pm; Nov.-Mar. 10am-noon and 1:30-5pm. Free.)

UPPER LIECHTENSTEIN

Just when it seems that the roads cannot possibly become any narrower or steeper, they do—welcome to Upper Liechtenstein. It is at these monstrous heights where the real character and beauty of Liechtenstein lies. Even if you're only in the country for one day, take the short bus trip to **Triesenberg** or **Malbun** (30min. from Vaduz) for spectacular views of the Rhine valley below.

TRIESENBERG

Spanning a series of switchbacks and foothills 800m above the Rhine, the first town up the mountain (serviced by bus #10) is Triesenberg (pop 2,600). Founded in the 13th century by the Walsers, a group of Swiss immigrants forced to flee Valais due to overpopulation and religious intolerance, the **Walser Heimatmuseum** chronicles the history of these intrepid people (and of the entire region). With hundreds of artifacts from cowbells to axes to carvings in tree roots, it's worth a quick look. (Behind the post office. ☎262 19 26; fax 19 22. Open Sept.-May Tu-F 1:30-5:30pm, Sa 1:30-5pm; June-Aug. also Su 2-5pm. 2SFr, children 1SFr.) The **tourist office** is in the same building as the museum and has the same hours, phone, and fax.

For aerobic activity, get off a stop or two early and struggle up the steep streets to the tourist office. For a real **hike,** take the #34 bus to Gaflei (dir: Gaflei; 20min., every hr.). Don't panic if the busdriver throws the bus in reverse on one of the hairpin turns; it's because the road is only nine feet wide and he needs to let an oncoming car pass. If you survive the trek up the mountain, stunning views of the **Rhine Valley** await on a 90min., relatively flat hike through alpine meadows and forests. (From the parking lot exit, head toward the gravel path on the left toward "Silum" and then "Ob. Tunnel, Steg." At the end, walk through the tunnel, then down the road to Steg, where bus #10 runs to Vaduz or Schaan every hr.)

For a really challenging hike (5½-6hr.), follow the signs for the **"Drei Schwester" (Three Sisters).** This course will take you uphill, up a couple of ladders and across the craggy peaks that grace postcards in every kiosk in the country. The tourist office specifically suggests those with fear of heights refrain from hiking it (which is probably the best way of getting them to do it). From Drei Schwestern, head toward Sarojasattel and Planken, where you can take the bus back to Vaduz or Schaan. A variety of other shorter hikes (15min.-1hr.) are also marked from Gaflei.

MALBUN

Like a peninsula of green farmland surrounded on three sides by mountains, the mile-high village of Malbun sits in an alpine valley in the southeastern corner of Liechtenstein. It is undoubtedly the hippest place in the principality, harboring approachable people, affordable ski slopes, plenty of hiking, and a **tourist office.** (☎263 65 77; fax 63 73 44; malbuninfo@liechtenstein.li; www.malbun.li. Open June-Oct. and mid-Dec. to mid-Apr. M-Sa 9am-noon and 1:30-5pm.) During the winter two chair lifts, four T-bars, and two ski schools serve you and not too many other people. (Day pass 33SFr; 6-day pass 136SFr, off-season 129SFr.) Right in the middle of town, **Malbun A.G.** (☎263 97 70 or 262 19 15) offers 1-day classes (65SFr), 3-day classes (155SFr), and private lessons (1 day 230SFr). **Malbun Sport** (☎/fax 263 37 55) rents **skis** and snowboards. (35SFr, children 13-18SFr. Cross-country skis 28SFr. Open M-F 8am-6pm, Sa 8am-5pm, Su 9am-5pm.) In summer, Malbun Sport also rents **bikes** (35SFr per day). **Cross-country skiing** is available 2km away in Steg.

cows, all wearing bells. To my left I had a perfect view of the yellow-green rolling hills in the Rhine valley below and of the snow-covered peaks of the Alps straight ahead. A paraglider chose this moment to fly overhead and I wondered if I hadn't stumbled into a picture postcard by mistake.

The euphoria wore off in km 31-35, which were again steep uphills, this time over narrow, rocky paths. As one Liechtensteinian runner stumbled past me, he yelled out, "Hey Meester Meeler!" I had my name written across the back of my shirt, but couldn't figure out how he knew I was American. When I asked him in German how he knew, he said, "Because no one spells Miller with an 'i' around here."

The final 8km were all downhill as we circled the valley that contains Malbun at reckless speeds, winding our way toward the finish line on paths that would have alarmed even downhill skiers. I finished in 5 hours and 40 minutes, about 2.5 hours behind the winner, having crossed the entire country and ascended 1800m in the process. I think the mountain goats were proud of us—they've been doing the same thing for years.

—Tom Miller

PLEASE DON'T EAT THE FLOWERS. Liechten-

stein is particularly protective of its abundant wildflowers. Throughout the area surrounding Malbun and Triesenberg, they are protected by law—picking those violently
purple gentians will result in a 500SFr fine. Cows appear to have legal immunity, as
they munch on hillside flora throughout the spring and summer with impunity. Just in
case pine nuts straight from the tree sound like a good idea, be aware hemlocks are
abundant in alpine regions. The "Tree of Death," as it is referred to on one nature trail,
felled Socrates and will fell you, too, if you indulge in needles, bark, or pinecones.

During the summer the #10 bus from Vaduz (30min., every hr., 2.40SFr) is full of
hikers heading to Malbun. The most worthwhile hike in town is a round-trip hike
to **Pfälzerhütte** (5hr.), the starting point of which is the top of the only chairlift open
in the summer, the **Sareiserjoch**. (7.50SFr one-way, round-trip 11.70SFr; students
5.90SFr/9SFr; ages 5-16 4.30SFr/6.40SFr. Open daily 8-11:50am and 1-4:50pm.) At
the beginning of June, there is snow on one side of the trail, wildflowers on the
other, and *Murmeltiere* (marmots) watching from their burrows. Scramble across
the rocky final ascent to the peak of **Augustenberg** (2359m), Liechtenstein's second
highest mountain, then descend a few hundred meters to the Pfälzerhütte (mountain hut). This is the high point (figuratively and literally) of the country. To get
home, head toward Gritsch and then Tälihöhi, completing three-quarters of a revolution around the entire valley that encloses Malbun.

The best place to stay for hiking and skiing access is **Hotel Alpen** (☎ 263 11 81; fax
263 96 46; alpenhotel@supra.net.), near the bus stop and tourist office. The hotel
has a restaurant, swimming pool, and a large common room with TV. Some rooms
have cable TV, phone, shower, and a stocked fridge, but you'll pay for the luxury.
Open mid-May to Oct. and mid-Dec. to Apr. Reception 8am-10pm. In summer
45SFr per person, with shower 65SFr, with bath 75SFr. In winter, add 20SFr.)

Buses to some of the more remote locations in Liechtenstein (Gaflei, Malbun)
run on a **winter schedule** Nov.-May. During the first two weeks of June, they
switch over to a **summer schedule** with increased service to the mountains. Use
the correct bus schedule (available in post and tourist offices and aboard many
buses) or you may find yourself on an unexpected campout.

SWITZERLAND

Switzerland lures visitors with its breathtaking natural aesthetics. Hikers, skiers, bikers, and paragliders from all over the globe flock to the alpine nation to take advantage of its winding trails, challenging slopes, and illustrious summits. Do not assume, however, that geographic beauty and its corresponding amenities are Switzerland's only virtues, for the urban centers are as fascinating to explore as the Alps that surround them. Besides being international hubs of commerce, trade, and diplomacy, cities such as Zurich, Geneva, and Lucerne are also cultural centers, home to world-famous concert halls, museums, and cathedrals.

Furthermore, even though Switzerland often seems unified behind a front of lederhosen, its segmented ethnic landscape dictates otherwise. These differences fall along the linguistic fault lines that separate the Italian, French, and German regions of the country. These areas retain much of the flavor of their respective national origins, as represented in their varying customs, cuisine, and costume.

The Swiss have raised the hospitality industry to an art: food and accommodations are of consistently high quality. The country's efficient public transportation system makes it an ideal destination for the independent traveler. Though it's not known for being cheap, the thrifty traveler can always find a bargain. And in Switzerland, the best things—sublime vistas—remain priceless.

BUILDING THE SWISS CONFEDERATION:

The Swiss confederation is made up of 23 cantons (states) and 3 half-cantons, having grown from the original three in 1291 (Uri, Schwyz, and Unterwalden). Today, the cantons, clockwise starting with Bern, the capital, are: Bern (incorporated 1353), Lucerne (1332), Obwalden and Nidwalden (1291, originally part of Unterwalden), Zug (1352), Uri (1291), Schwyz (1291), Zurich (1351), Schaffhausen (1501), Thurgau (1803), Appenzell (1501), St. Gallen (1803), Glarus (1352), Graubünden (1803), Ticino (1803), Valais (1815), Geneva (1815), Vaud (1803), Fribourg (1481), Neuchâtel (1815), Jura (1978), Solothurn (1481), Basel (1501), and Aargau (1803).

LAND

The heart of Switzerland (and its major topological feature) is the Alps and the surrounding foothills. Accounting for 60% of Switzerland's total surface area, the Alps have separate characteristic landscapes that can be traced back to the Ice Age. Northern Switzerland is characterized by the Jura (Celtic for wood), the subalpine region comprised primarily of woodland. Thousands of years ago glaciers sculpted the long basin between the Jura and the Alps and created conditions for Switzerland's major lakes: Geneva, Constance, Neuchâtel, Lucerne, Maggiore, and Zurich. As a site of industrialization, the Jura once saw extensive ore mining and metal processing. More recently, the Jura has been promoted as a tourist destination because of its vast opportunities for hiking, riding, and cross-country skiing.

FLORA & FAUNA

With forests still occupying 25% of the countryside, Switzerland is home to a range of plant and animal species that have evolved in accordance to the alpine conditions that surround them. While many of these flora and fauna are common to most of Europe, others are distinctly Swiss, and often times rare.

PLANTS

Much of Switzerland's botanical beauty is found in its large and varied forest. While beech and oak trees predominate the deciduous woods of the Swiss midland and at lower elevations in the alpine valleys, spruce and fir occupy areas of higher altitudes. In the southern and eastern alpine interiors, forests of pine and larch are stark contrast to the palm trees along the shores of Lake Lugano.

Floral beauty abounds even in the harshest and rockiest areas of the Alps, with several species of wildflowers thriving in the midst of snowy conditions. **Edelweiss**, famous for its elusiveness (and for its self-titled song), has a felt stem and leaves, and a distinctive cluster of fuzzy yellowish round balls in the center of its bloom. The **Lady's Slipper** is slightly iris-like in appearance, with a yellow bulb and maroon tendrils coming out from all around it. More conventional flowers such as **daisies, buttercups, bellflowers**, and **dandelions** also abound. Wildflowers begin appearing in late April and disappear at the end of October.

ANIMALS

Many of Switzerland's fauna are of the familiar barnyard and wildlife variety with an alpine twist. **Black squirrels** are plentiful, and **red foxes** and **hedgehogs** make an occasional appearance. Less recognizable animals include the **marmot**, a furry, cat-sized rodent that inhabits the Schilt and upper Sefinen valleys, and **tächis**, large black birds that are swarm around Mürren and Schilthorn. Normal deer abound as well as Switzerland's own variation, the **Gemse**, which tend to be smaller with miniscule horns and roam the Bernese Oberland. Many of these animal populations were once dwindling; the creation of a game preserve in Lower Engadine prevented the extinction of several alpine species.

The cow is somewhat of an institution in Switzerland and one or more bovine encounters during a trip through the Alps is almost guaranteed. Often a herd of them will pass you as you are hiking; simply stand still and let them pass you so that they don't start heading in the wrong direction. Swiss cows can be of the *Simmentaler* (light brown and white), *Brown Swiss* (solid gray-brown), or *Holstein* (black and white) varieties. And, if you decide to approach one for a picture, remember that in Switzerland cows don't have names like "Bessie" or "Daisy," but rather more human titles such as "Claudia" or "Anita."

HISTORY

FROM CAVE MEN TO CELTS

The early Swiss established settlements only 30,000 years ago, after the end of the last glacial period. By 750 BC the Celts dominated Switzerland. The artistic and warlike **Helvetians,** the most prominent Swiss-Celtic tribe, gained notoriety for their (largely unsuccessful) attempts to invade Roman Italy in 222 BC and again as allies of Carthage between 218 and 203 BC (when they assisted Hannibal and his elephants in their famous crossing of the Alps). Julius Caesar halted their attempts to advance into Gaul in 58 BC, crushing and then colonizing the Helvetians. Helvetian lands extended across the alpine valleys of central Switzerland, while **Rhaetians**, an Etruscan people, populated the east (now Graubünden). The language **Rhaeto-Romansch**, a combination of Roman Latin and the Rhaetian Tuscan dialect, is still spoken today in former Rhaetian territories.

As Roman influence waned in the 5th century, the tribes settled permanently. **Burgundians** filled the west, merging peacefully with the Romanized Celts and absorbing their culture and language. The more aggressive **Alemanni,** a Germanic tribe, forced their own culture on the Celts of central and northern Switzerland. They eventually pushed the Burgundians west to the Sarine River, establishing the border between German and French Switzerland that exists today.

ALEMANNI LEGACY (1000-1519)

It was the nonconformist Alemanni who set the stage for centuries of Swiss individualism and decentralized rule. The lack of strong Roman empirical control over the patchwork of states allowed for de facto political autonomy. This growing commitment to democracy caused the descendents of the Alemanni to clash with Holy Roman Emperor **Rudolf of Habsburg** when he attempted to take three of their communities (Uri, Schwyz, and Unterwalden—the "Forest Cantons") under his direct control in the late 13th century (see **Tell-Tale**, p. 317). In a secret pact, the three Forest Cantons decided to rebel and signed the **Everlasting Alliance** in 1291—an agreement that obligated the cantons to defend each other from outside attack. This moment is what the Swiss consider to mark the beginning of the Swiss confederation. The Everlasting Alliance also signaled the beginning of 350 years of struggle against the **Habsburg Empire.** In 1315, the Swiss and the Habsburgs met at the Battle of Morgarten, resulting in Habsburg defeat.

Despite conflict between the Everlasting Alliance and the Habsburg Emperors, the three-canton core of Switzerland expanded over the next several centuries to include Bern, Lucerne, Zurich, Glarus, and Zug. Habsburg emperor Fredrick II allied himself with Zurich, but by force of arms the other cantons forced Zurich to renounce its alliance and rejoin the Confederation. In another attempt to conquer the Swiss, the Habsburgs enlisted the help of the "Swabian League"—a group of Southern German cities whose motto became "the Swiss, too, must have a master." The Swabian War (1499-1500) lasted less than nine months, but strong Swiss efforts engendered independence from the Holy Roman Empire.

TELL-TALE As part of the Holy Roman Empire, the citizens of the first three Swiss cantons–the Forest Cantons–were willing to recognize the emperor as their overlord but refused any other feudal obligations. Legend has it that a particularly haughty Habsburg henchman by the name of Gessler demanded that all freemen bow to his hat in homage. According to the tale, a freeman named William Tell journeyed with his son to the town of Altdorf in canton Uri, where he encountered the knavish Gessler. Tell blatantly ignored Gessler's hallowed hat. Gessler promptly had Tell arrested, and ordered Tell to shoot an arrow through an apple on his son's head. Tell, an expert Swiss marksman, hit the apple and spared his son, then was quick to tell Gessler the next arrow had his name on it. The legend, immortalized in Friedrich Schiller's play in 1804, has come to symbolize the Swiss rough-and-ready mountaineer spirit that vanquishes tyranny in the name of freedom and independence. See Schiller's version of *Wilhelm Tell* during your summer jaunt in Interlaken (p. 351).

REFORMATION TO REVOLUTION (1519-1815)

The lack of a strong central government to settle disputes between cantons of different faiths caused problems for the Swiss during the **Protestant Reformation.** As Lutheranism swept Northern Europe, radical theologian **Ulrich Zwingli** of Zurich spearheaded his own brand of Protestantism that stressed both the importance of lay people reading scripture and a rejection of the symbols and gestures of Catholicism. In 1523, the city government of Zurich sanctioned Zwingli's proposed *Theses* and strengthened Zwingli's influence by banning Anabaptism and harshly punishing its followers. Meanwhile, in Geneva, French-born lawyer and priest **John Calvin** preached a doctrine of predestination: neither God's grace nor good works could get you into heaven, but leading a good life was an indication that you were destined for it. For a time he exercised a theocratic sway over Geneva and instituted moral reforms, turning the city into a shining example of Protestant social control. While Zurich and Geneva became strongholds of the Protestant movement, the Forest Cantons remained loyal to the Catholic Church. Religious differences, combined with tensions between urban and rural cantons, resulted in battle, climaxing with the defeat of the Protestants at Kappel in 1531 and the death of Zwingli. In the mid-16th century the confederation finally interceded, granting Protestants certain freedoms but prohibiting them from imposing their faith on others. The confederation managed to remain neutral during the **Thirty Years War.** In 1648 the **Peace of Westphalia** granted the Swiss official neutrality and a multi-national recognition of their independence from the Austrian Habsburg empire.

In 1798 Swiss independence was challenged when Napoleon's troops invaded Switzerland and established the **Helvetic Republic.** Rebelling against the French puppet government, the Swiss overthrew regime in 1803. Napoleon's **Mediation Act** settled the anarchy that ensued and established Switzerland as a confederation of 19 cantons. After Napoleon's defeat at Waterloo, the Congress of Vienna added Geneva, Neuchâtel, and the Valais to the Confederation and (again) officially recognized Swiss neutrality.

DIPLOMACY: 1815 TO THE 20TH CENTURY

The establishment of neutrality meant Switzerland could turn its attention to domestic issues. Industrial growth brought material prosperity, but the era was far from golden. The **Federal Pact** of 1815 that replaced Napoleon's decrees again established Switzerland as a confederation of sovereign states united only for common defense—united foreign policy was still impossible. Because of logistical barriers (each canton had its own laws, currency, postal service, weights, measures, and army—not to mention language and religion) the inhabitants of different cantons regarded each others as foreigners.

In 1846, continuing religious differences led to the formation of a separatist defense league of Catholic cantons known as the **Sonderbund.** In July 1847, the **Diet,** a parliamentary body representing the other cantons, declared the Sonderbund incompatible with the Federal Pact and demanded its dissolution. A civil war broke out, ending with Protestant victory 25 days later. In 1848, the winning cantons wrote a new constitution, modeled after that of the United States, which guaranteed republican and democratic cantonal constitutions and set up an executive body for the first time. The central government then established a free-trade zone and unified postal, currency, and railway systems across all the cantons.

Now internally stable, Switzerland began to resolve international conflicts. The **Geneva Convention of 1864** established international laws for conduct during war. Geneva also became the **International Red Cross** headquarters. Swiss neutrality was tested in both the **Franco-Prussian War** and **World War I** as French- and German-speaking Switzerland claimed different cultural loyalties. In 1920, Geneva welcomed the headquarters of the ill-fated **League of Nations,** solidifying Switzerland's reputation as the center for international diplomacy. At the onset of **World War II,** Switzerland mobilized 20% of its population for a defensive army. Fortunately, Hitler's plan to invade Switzerland was thwarted by Allied landings, distractions on the North African front, and the protective alpine border. Both sides found it useful to have Switzerland as neutral territory. The

Swiss government, not eager to incur Germany's wrath, officially impeded passage through its territory, while Jews, escaping Allied prisoners, and other refugees from Nazi Germany found secret refuge in Switzerland. Aside from some accidental bombings in 1940, 1944, and 1945, Switzerland survived the war unscathed.

As the rest of Europe cleaned up the rubble of two world wars, Switzerland nurtured its sturdy economy. Zurich emerged as a banking and insurance center, while Geneva housed international organizations. Although Geneva became the focal point of international diplomacy, Switzerland remained independent in its diplomatic relationships, declining offers of membership to the United Nations, NATO, and the European Economic Community.

TODAY

1999 ELECTIONS

While Austria made international headlines when its far-right, anti-immigrant political party made gains in October 1999 elections (see p. 71), no one seemed to notice when a similar thing happened in Switzerland two weeks later. The far-right **Swiss People's Party** (*Schweizerische Volkspartei*) captured 23% of the vote, catapulting from 4th to 2nd among the country's four main parties. The party is strongly anti-immigrant: its members rallied behind the cry "Stop Asylum Abuse," an angry response to the thousands of refugees who poured into Switzerland from Eastern Europe. After the election, Jörg Haider of Austria was one of the first to congratulate fellow business maverick and fast-talking far-right political-leader **Christoph Blocher,** the leader of the People's Party. The People's Party's jump of 7.9 percentage points since the 1995 elections is particularly astounding because the percentage of the vote received by one party has almost never changed more than 1-2% between elections.

One of the primary reasons for the agitation is the Swiss fear that Eastern European refugees are taking their jobs. One in every five people living in Switzerland is foreign, and while Switzerland rarely lets these immigrants become citizens (see **The Swiss Way or the Highway,** below), these extra job-seekers were criticized when unemployment rose in the recent recession. The Swiss panicked when the unemployment rate hit a high of around 5% in the mid-1990s, (a rate still low by most other countries' standards.) This indicated their unrealistically high economic expectations. Recently, the immigration debate was particularly relevant because

> # THE SWISS WAY OR THE HIGHWAY Switzerland is
> beautiful, but don't plan on staying. Rules for citizenship are some of the toughest in the world. The cantons retain the power to grant citizenship, and in most cantons, applicants for citizenship must reside there for twelve years and then be popularly elected by the commune in which they live. The applicant's picture, economic status (including the applicant's yearly wages), and hobbies are distributed in a pamphlet to the voting public. Sometimes officials will even drop by the applicant's house to examine its cleanliness. The world took notice when, in March, 2000 56 candidates applied for citizenship in a small town near Lucerne. Of the 56, only eight were accepted, and none of the eight were from the former Yugoslavia, where a majority of the applicants came from. The popular election of Swiss citizens does not occur in cities, but the newly powerful People's Party is proposing such a procedure.

SWITZERLAND

Switzerland accepted more Kosovar refugees proportional to its population than any other country. The Swiss have never welcomed foreigners, but the recent influx has heightened fears.

SWITZERLAND'S INTERNATIONAL TIES

The People's Party was the only one of the four major parties that did not support Swiss membership in the **EU**; among the requirements for EU membership is that all members accept foreign workers from all other EU nations. Switzerland has historically resisted international organizations primarily because they threaten the Swiss people's fierce sense of independence from outside entanglements. In March 2002, Switzerland finally joined the **United Nations,** an initiative supported by both the people and cantons.

During the Cold War, Switzerland's independence and stability were economically advantageous, helping its people attain one of the highest standards of living in the world. But as the rest of Europe has become more stable and integrated, Switzerland's independence has turned into isolation and has frequently excluded the nation from trade deals. Realizing this, the government offered the people the opportunity to join the **European Economic Area (EEA)**, the economic forerunner to the EU, in 1992. The people rejected the government's plan through a referendum in which 80 percent of the people turned out to vote (usual turnout for referenda is 35 percent). This vote precluded the chance to vote on EU membership.

After the 1992 vote, the government initiated bilateral negotiations with the EU to create closer ties and eventually move Switzerland toward membership. The People's Party was the only political party that did not endorse the new bilateral negotiations. The fear that Switzerland was moving toward isolationism was calmed, however, when in May 2000 two-thirds of the people voted to accept the bilateral negotiations between the EU and the Swiss government in a referendum.

The election results have threatened to shake up the careful political system of consensus that has developed over the last fifty years. The People's Party's gains led Blocher to request a second seat on the seven-seat Federal Council, the cabinet-like board that is the most powerful political body in the country. For the last fifty years the People's Party has held one seat, while the other 3 parties have each held 2 seats, a political arrangement known as the **magic formula.** This formula was carefully crafted so that the Federal Council fairly represented three major languages and two major religions. Blocher's demands for a second seat threaten the political coalition that has kept the divided country stable.

PEOPLE

DEMOGRAPHICS

Switzerland is a culturally diverse nation, with people of German origin making up 65% of the population, French origin 18%, Italian 10%, and Romansch 1%. Other minorities, including mostly foreign workers from Eastern Europe, make up the other 6% of the population. Though heterogeneous in culture, the Swiss are rather homogeneous in character, generally described as gracious, proper, and hardworking. Most Swiss are active people, encouraged to venture outdoors by the alluring mountain landscape. Skiing and hiking are national pastimes, with more than 40% of the population regularly wandering through the countryside. Perhaps this accounts for their high life expectancy rate of 80 years. In general, the Swiss enjoy an incredibly high standard of living due to a strong market economy and a low unemployment rate of 1.9%. Literacy is virtually 100%.

A FAULTY GOLD STANDARD
The Swiss Claims Resolution Tribunal

Unlike most countries, Switzerland did not have banking "dormancy" laws until 2001. Accounts remained open even if clients were not heard from in many years. Indeed, asking around about clients would violate Swiss banking secrecy. Meanwhile, if an heir tried to claim the account, that person would face multiple legal hurdles before the bank could even admit that such an account existed, let alone transfer the balance.

In the period between the two world wars, Switzerland, a stable country amid Europe in turmoil, was a logical safe destination for money. Money could be hidden in Switzerland at a time when other countries were limiting the transfer of money abroad and attempting to repatriate money already abroad back to the home country. With risk of German and French spy infiltration, Switzerland tightened protective secrecy measures in 1934.

The Nazi era turned Europe upside down. If account owners themselves did not survive to collect their assets, the accounts just sat there—or at least those which were not paid out to Nazis (who often coerced their victims to sign over assets) or eaten over time by bank fees. Finally, under increasing international pressure in the mid-1990s, an international tribunal was established in Zurich to deal with accounts left over from before 1945. Between 1998 and 2001, the Tribunal arbitrated over 10,000 claims to nearly 2,500 dormant accounts owned by non-Swiss which had been uncovered by 1997.

The movement was founded on the grounds that many accounts owned by victims of the Holocaust had never found their way to the rightful heirs due to Swiss banking secrecy. However, while many assets did fit this description, about 80% of the dormant assets were not owned by Holocaust victims. Other accounts, owned by wealthy foreigners who had hidden their money from the taxmen by putting it in Switzerland, and then neglected to tell their families how to find it after their deaths, also existed.

The job of the Tribunal was to determine if claimants had plausibly identified account owners as their relatives, who among claimants were entitled, and the amounts to be paid. Most claimants were denied, usually because they did not correctly identify the account owner as their relative, merely as someone with the same or similar name. Accounts belonged to wealthy individuals, as well as people who came to Switzerland on business or to visit their children in boarding school. Lawyers or bankers helped open accounts for foreign clients. Some traveled under great danger from across Europe to deposit their assets in Swiss banks. Accounts were even opened by individuals of seemingly modest means—their heirs had no idea how the account got there.

The work was long and busy and often emotionally draining. In my most rewarding case, I reunited cousins who each had thought no one in their family had survived. One of them submitted photographs she had recovered from Christian neighbors after the war. The photos showed the smiling faces of a happy family living a normal life; shortly after the photos were taken, everyone in them was murdered. For the many claimants who were themselves survivors, it was not about their money. Many of them just wanted the recognition of what they suffered, and they wanted their relatives to be remembered—even if it turned out that their relative was not the same person as the account owner. It was very rewarding to receive thank-you notes even from claimants whose claims were denied. They wrote in, understanding why they were denied, but saying thank you for understanding, for listening, for treating them like human beings when before no one had treated them with dignity. We were not in the reparations business; we only gave money to those to whom it plausibly belonged. No amount of money can put the past right, but we can restore money to entitled heirs and, in all cases, record memories.

Charles Ehrlich has been a Researcher-Writer for Let's Go: Spain & Portugal. *He is formerly a Senior Staff Attorney at the Claims Resolution Tribunal that adjudicates claims to Swiss bank accounts from the Nazi era.*

A CRASH COURSE IN SWISS GERMAN

Though you'll most likely never need to speak Swiss German, it is a charming language that reflects the traditional character of Swiss culture. If you want to pick it up, start with basic practical terms that are nearly the same in all dialects, such as the days of the week: *Mäntig, Zyschtig, Mittwuche, Donschtig, Frytig, Samschtig, Sunntig*. Even if you haven't mastered these tongue-twisters, watch out when buying cereal—be sure to distinguish between *Müsli*, the famous granola, which literally means "little smashed-up things," and *Musli*, the common misspelling, which means "little mice."

LANGUAGE

When in Switzerland, try to speak as the Swiss do (whatever the language happens to be). Fewer people speak English in Switzerland than in many other European countries because of the number of languages that must be learned to get by within Switzerland. Thus, while many do speak English, you're always better off trying one of Switzerland's three and a half official federal languages first: German, French, Italian, or Romansch (which is only partially an official federal language). Each language spans a particular geographic region: **German** is spoken by 64% of the population throughout the bulk of central and eastern Switzerland; in western Switzerland, **French** is the language of choice for 19% of the Swiss, while 8% speak **Italian,** primarily in the southern Ticino region. **Romansch** is spoken by less than 1% of the population, but it has historical and ethnic significance after having survived for hundreds of years in the isolated mountain valleys of Graubünden (see p. 418).

German speakers beware: **Swiss German** (*Schwyzertüütsch*) is unlike any of the dialects spoken in Germany and Austria, nearly unintelligible to a speaker of High German (*Hochdeutsch*). Linguistically, Swiss German more closely resembles Middle High German, spoken in Germany 500 years ago. Geographic isolation led to the development of highly differentiated dialects in each region. *Wallisertütsch*, spoken in the southern Valais region, is one of the oldest Swiss German dialects and hence one of the least comprehensible, even to German-speaking Swiss. On the other hand, *Bärntütsch* and *Züritüütsch*, spoken around Bern and Zurich respectively, are more regular, though there is no written standard of Swiss German. Although words like *chääschüchli* (cheesecake) and *chuchichäschtli* (kitchen cabinets) may sound harsh to Anglophone ears, most German Swiss prefer their dialect to High German. The Swiss will appreciate any effort you make to speak it, so take a breath and practice saying *Ufwiderlüge* (goodbye).

RELIGION

When the dust settled after the Protestant Reformation, Switzerland ended up almost evenly divided between Catholics (46%) and Protestants (40%), though Protestantism has been in slight decline since World War II. Other groups (primarily Jews and Muslims) and agnostics make up the remaining religious preferences. Switzerland has been a welcoming home to many of these religious minorities; Geneva, the "City of Peace," houses various international religious organizations representing 130 faiths, such as the World Council of Churches, the Baha'i International Community, the Lutheran World Federation, the Quaker UN Office, the Christian Children's Fund, and the World Jewish Congress.

CULTURE

FOOD & DRINK

Switzerland is not for the lactose intolerant. The Swiss are serious about dairy products, from rich and varied **cheeses** (see **Say cheese!**, below) to decadent milk chocolate—even the major Swiss soft drink is a dairy-based beverage, *rivella*. These divine bovine goodies are always available at local Migros or Co-op supermarkets. As far as **chocolate** goes, the Swiss have earned bragging rights for their expertise: with the invention of milk chocolate in 1875, Switzerland was poised to rule the world. Today the country is home to some of the world's largest producers: **Lindt, Suchard,** and **Nestlé.** Visit the Lindt factory in Zurich or the Nestlé factory near Bulle to load up on free samples. **Toblerone,** manufactured in Bern, is an international favorite famous for the bits of nougat in creamy milk chocolate, packaged in a nifty triangular box. Chocolate comes in different cocoa concentrations—the higher the concentration, the darker and more bitter the chocolate.

Cheese and chocolate cravings satiated, one might desire a more substantial entree. Not surprisingly, Swiss dishes vary from region to region and what your waiter brings you is most likely related to the language he is speaking. An array of "typical" Swiss dishes might include the Zurich speciality, *Geschnetzeltes* (strips of veal stewed in a thick cream sauce), *Luzerner Chugelipastete* (pâté in a pastry shell), *Papet Vaudois* (leeks with sausage from Vaud), *Churer Fleischtorte* (meat pie from Chur), and Bernese salmon. Each region or town usually has its own specific bread; ask for it by name (e.g. when in St. Gallen, ask for *St. Gallerbrot*) at the local market or bakery.

Switzerland's hearty peasant cooking will keep you warm through those frigid alpine winters. Bernese **Rösti,** a plateful of hash brown potatoes skilleted and occasionally flavored with bacon or cheese, is as prevalent in the German regions as **fondue** (from the French, *fondre,* "to melt") is in the French. Usually a blend of Emmentaler and Gruyère cheeses, white wine, *kirsch,* and spices, fondue is eaten by dunking small cubes of white bread into a *caquelon* (a one-handled pot) kept hot by a small flame. Valaisian **raclette** is made by cutting a special cheese in half and heating it until it melts; the melted cheese is then scraped onto a baked potato and garnished with meat or vegetables.

The world's chocolate experts would never neglect the lingering sweet-tooth. The Swiss are adept at the art of **confectionery.** Among the most tempting cakes are the *Baseler Leckerli* (a kind of gingerbread), *Zuger Kirschtorte* (cherry cake), Engadin nutcakes, the *bagnolet crème* of the Jura (eaten with raspberries and anise seed biscuits), soda rolls, *rissoles* (pear tarts), and the nougat and pralines of Geneva. *Vermicelli* (not the Italian pasta but a dessert made of chestnut mousse) is popular all over Switzerland.

SAY CHEESE! While the words "Swiss cheese" may conjure up images of lunch-boxed sandwiches filled with a hard, oily, holey cheese, Switzerland actually produces innumerable varieties, each made from a particular type of milk. Cheese with holes is usually *Emmentaler,* from the valley of the same name near Bern, but nearly every canton and many towns have specialty cheeses. To name a few of the most well-known: *Gruyère* is a stronger version of *Emmentaler; Appenzeller* is a hard cheese with a sharp tang; *Tome* is a generic term for a soft, uncooked cheese similar to French *Chèvre.* In the Italian regions, cheese often resembles the *Parmigiano* from Italy more than the mountain cheeses of the alpine regions. As Swiss cheese standards are regulated by law, cheese in Switzerland is always of superb quality.

The Romans introduced **wine** to the region, but it was not until the 9th century that beer-drinking laity pried it away from the clergy. Because today there is very little on land available for grape growing, Swiss wines are in short supply and are thus more expensive than most imports. Both whites and reds are very good: the red Dole and the white Aigle are especially fine. A wine statute in 1953 imposed rigorous quality controls, and Swiss wine has retained its reputation.

Each canton has its own local **beer,** a popular beverage in German-speaking Switzerland. Beer is relatively cheap, often less expensive than Coca-Cola. Some notable brands include dry, moderate tasting *Original Quöllfrische*, an organic lager from the Brauerei Locher in Appenzell (formerly the beer of choice on Swiss Air flights), the slightly licorice flavored *Dunkel Lagerbier*, from Stadt Bühler in Gossau, and *Chambière*, a mix of beer and sweet wine from Lucerne.

CUSTOMS & ETIQUETTE

When in Switzerland be punctual and mind your manners; remember to say hello and goodbye to shopkeepers and proprietors of bars and cafés, and always shake hands when being introduced. At mealtime keep both hands above the table at all times, with the knife and fork "open" (apart from one another), unless you are completely finished with your meal. When dining in public, leave your fork and knife crossed in an "X" on your plate if you need to get up and do not want the server to clear your plate; when finished, place the knife and fork together in the lower right hand corner of your plate, pointing towards the center. And, though not uniform across the entire country, it is customary to greet friends or even acquaintances with a kiss on the cheek.

THE ARTS

While Switzerland is not known for erecting great monuments in the artistic canon, it does have a lively arts scene today. This scene is particularly visible in contemporary works by young Swiss artists at Zurich's cutting-edge **Kunsthaus** (see p. 381) or a night spent prowling the city's underground music scene.

ARCHITECTURE

Switzerland is home to a bastion of impressive architecture from every epoch of European history, from Romanesque to Gothic to Baroque. The varying climate and distinctive building materials (stone, timber, clay) have engendered distinctive Swiss styles such as the Bernese farmhouse, the Ticino rustico, and the Engadine house. In recent years world-renowned architects such as Le Corbusier, Peter Zumthor, Maro Botta, and Herzog & de Meuron have given Swiss towns and cities a modern face and villages and bridges a contemporary makeover.

PAINTING AND SCULPTURE

Early greats among Swiss painters include **Urs Graf** (c.1485-1529), a swashbuckling, soldier-artist-poet skilled in court portraiture, and **Ferdinand Hodler** (1853-1918), a Symbolist painter who used Swiss landscapes to convey metaphysical messages. In the 20th century, Switzerland has been a primary space for liberal experimentation exemplified by the work of **Paul Klee,** a member of the Bauhaus faculty, and of *der Blaue Reiter* (The Blue Rider) school led by Kandinsky. Klee's delicate watercolors and paintings helped shape the beginnings of abstraction, calling dominant modes of artistic expression into question.

During the World Wars, Switzerland's art scene was energized by an influx of talented refugees, including **Hans Arp, Richard Hülsenbeck, Janco, Tristan Tzara,** and **Hugo Ball,** some of whom produced the **Dada** explosion in Zurich in 1916. Together they founded the "Cabaret Voltaire" and "Galerie Dada," short-lived centers of Dada activity (see p. 382). The Dada creed was to champion the irrational, by mocking order with chaos. Marginal participants in the Zurich Dada scene later developed into artists in their own right. **Jean Tinguely** created kinetic, mechanized Dada fantasies that celebrated the beauty (and craziness) of motion.

Between and after the wars, Switzerland continued to attract liberal artistic thinkers. The **Zurich School of Concrete Art,** which operated primarily between wars, combined elements of Surrealism with ideas from Russian Constructivism in an attempt to work with objects and environments to explore interactions between humans and space. The school included Paul Klee and **Meret Oppenheim** (a Surrealist famous for her *Fur Cup*), and its philosophy led sculptor **Alberto Giacometti** to play with spatial realities in his creations of the 1930s. Later, Giacometti rejected the premise of Surrealism in order to concentrate on a deep representationalism, creating small, exaggerated, slender figures like *Man Pointing*. After sitting out the Second World War in London and spending time in Prague, Austrian Expressionist painter **Oskar Kokoschka** moved to Switzerland in 1953, settling in Villeneuve. When Kokoschka died in 1980, his widow Olda found herself with an overabundance of pictures and subsequently founded the Foundation Oskar Kokoschka in the Musée Jenisch in Vevey (see p. 504).

LITERATURE

Though not particularly renowned for its native literary traditions, Switzerland has been home to many famous and talented writers. **Jean-Jacques Rousseau,** best known for his *Social Contract* (inspiration for the French Revolution) was born in Geneva in 1712. Rousseau always proudly recognized his Swiss background, despite the facts that he spent most of his time outside the country and that the Swiss burned his books. A more conventional Swiss resident, **Jacob Burckhardt** promoted a new history of culture and art from his Basel home in the late 19th century. His works include *History of the Italian Renaissance* and *Cicerone: A Guide to the Enjoyment of Italian Art.*

The age of Romanticism found **J.J. Bodmer** and **J.J. Breitinger's** advocacy of literature in Swiss German in conflict with many of their German contemporaries who strove to standardize German through literature. The Swiss-born **Madame de Staël** (born Germaine Necker) was an important writer in her own right and the driving force behind Romanticism's spread from Germany to France. Switzerland produced a few Romantic authors as well, most notably **Gottfried Keller,** who penned a classic 19th-century German *Bildungsroman*, entitled *Der Grüne Heinrich.* **Conrad Ferdinand Meyer** was another highly influential Swiss poet, whose writings, which feature individualistic heroes, effectively unite characteristics of Romanticism and Realism.

Only in the 20th century has Swiss literature come into its own with such greats as **Hermann Hesse,** who received the Nobel Prize for literature in 1946 and wrote the masterpiece *Siddhartha.* Hesse's works, including *Steppenwolf* and *Narcissus and Goldmund,* explore the duality of spirit and nature and the protagonist's journey to inner self. Writer and psychologist **Carl Gustav Jung** began as an acolyte of Freud but split off by 1915 when he wrote *Symbols of Transformation;* later he set a growing psychoanalytic practice in Zurich. Critics laud **Max Frisch** for his Brechtian style and thoughtful treatment of Nazi Germany; his most widely known works are the play *Andorra* and the novel *Homo Faber,* which was made into a film in the early 1990s. **Friedrich Dürrenmatt** has written a number of cutting, humorous plays, most notably *Der Besuch der Alten Dame* (The Visit of the Old Lady) and *Die Physiker* (The Physicists). Both Dürrenmatt and Frisch are critical of but loyal to their home country.

EXILES AND EMIGRÉS Ever since **Voltaire** came to Geneva in 1755 to do some heavy-duty philosophizing, Switzerland has been the promised land for intellectuals, artists, and soon-to-be-famous personalities. George Gordon, otherwise known as the opium-smoking Romantic **Lord Byron**, quit England in 1816 for Switzerland. Byron wrote "Sonnet on Chillon" while brooding on Lake Geneva; contemporary **Percy Shelley** crafted "Hymn to Beauty" and "Mont Blanc" in the vale of Chamonix. His wife **Mary Wollstonecraft Shelley** came across some ghost stories while in Switzerland, which, heightened by Switzerland's eternal mist and craggy Alps, inspired *Frankenstein*. Speaking of ghosts, such geniuses as **Gogol, Dostoyevsky, Hugo, Hemingway**, and **Fitzgerald** still haunt the Geneva countryside where they wrote when they were in more solid form. **James Joyce** fled to Zurich during WWI and stayed to scribble the greater part of *Ulysses* between 1915 and 1919.

Other great minds came from Germany, Austria, and Italy. **Johann Wolfgang von Goethe** caught his first distant view of Italy from the top of St. Gotthard Pass in the Swiss Alps. **Friedrich Schiller** wrote about the massive church bell in Schaffhausen before penning *Wilhelm Tell*. While on holiday in the Engadin Valley, **Friedrich Nietzsche** went nuts and produced his mountaintop tome *Thus Spoke Zarathustra*. **Richard Wagner** composed most of his major operas during his years with Nietzsche in verdant Switzerland. **Thomas Mann** also found refuge in Switzerland, using one of the Swiss Alps as the setting for his novel *The Magic Mountain*. More recently Switzerland has harbored writers and scientists from the former Eastern bloc, notably Russian author **Alexander Solzhenitsyn** and Czech novelist **Milan Kundera.**

MUSIC

The subversive artistic spirit of the late 20th century has generated a handful of musical groups that have their pulse on the sound of the twenty-first. Most of them produce alternative music aimed at teenagers and twentysomethings, but their experimentalism extends to all age groups, particularly in the swinging festivals that heat up the summer nights throughout Switzerland.

A sampling of currently popular bands might feature **Chitty Chitty Bang Bang**, a Franco-Swiss rock foursome which has self-produced two CDs. On another note, **Der Klang** has invented a French *chanson* style which has led them far from the well-trodden tracks of the genre. Popular not only in Switzerland but also in Germany and Japan, **Gotthard's** raw, bluesy vocals, hard-rock rhythms and plentiful solos recall the sound of Bon Jovi. A rock band with folk roots, Geneva's **Polar** has performed with the likes of Massive Attack and Fiona Apple. The phrase "Swiss hip-hop" may incur some skepticism, but Switzerland does hold its own with a handful of groups, including Lausanne's **Legal, Rade,** and **Osez**; Geneva's **Fidel'Escro**; Vevey's **CE-2P**; and Neuchâtel's **La Sorcellerie.** Crossing over another genre is the jazz musician **Erik Truffaz,** who learned his trumpet skills from the famed Miles Davis. His sound combines jazz with rap and drum 'n' bass influences.

FILM

As in Austria, the Swiss government subsidizes many film projects in order to encourage the growth of a domestic film industry. Switzerland has produced a handful of pictures that have garnered recognition at various international film festivals. Its own annual Locarno Film Festival, with over 4,000 film professionals representing 20 countries in attendance, is considered to be among the top six film festivals in the world.

The Swiss have also made their mark on American film industry. **Emil Jannings** won the first Academy Awards for Best Actor for his work in *The Way of All*

Flesh (1927) and *The Last Commandment* (1928). Swiss American and Academy Award winner William Wyler directed numerous noteworthy pictures including *Ben Hur*. More recently, H.R. Giger served as art director and set designer for the intense and gripping films *Alien* and *Species*.

SPORTS & RECREATION

The active Swiss spend much of their leisure time doing athletics. Thus, it came as no surprise when in 1972 a federal law ensured government financial support for the promotion of sports. Exercise and sports are regarded as integral parts of life and there are numerous sports organizations throughout the country. Even the headquarters of the **International Olympic Committee** (IOC) are located in Lausanne.

With more than 50,000 kilometers of designated footpaths, **hiking** remains one of the most popular recreational activities. **Skiing** is also extremely popular, for Switzerland is known for having some of the best slopes in the world. Two sports unique to the country are **hornussen** and **schwingen**. **Hornussen** involves an offensive team that uses long metal rods with wooden handles to knock a disc called the *hornuss* as far as possible down the field, while the defensive team uses a wooden shield to prevent the advancement of the disc. If the disc lands on the field without being intercepted, the defense loses a point; if the defense knocks it down, they gain a point. **Schwingen** is a type of Swiss wrestling in which each participant grabs the waistband of his opponent with his right hand and a band on his opponent's leg with his left hand in an attempt to throw him down and hold his back to the ground. The match is over once the wrestler loses both handholds or has both shoulder blades touching the ground.

HOLIDAYS & FESTIVALS

National holidays in Switzerland are almost all of Christian origin. Expect most establishments to be closed on Easter (April 20 in 2003), Christmas (December 25), New Year's Eve (December 31), and Good Friday (April 18), in some areas.

SWITZERLAND'S HOLIDAYS (2003)

DATE	NAME & LOCATION	DESCRIPTION
January 1	New Year's Day	Celebration of the new year
March 1	Unabhängigkeitstag; Neuchâtel	Independence Day
April 30	Walpurgis Nacht	Night before May 1, when witches dance on the Blocksberg in the German Harz mountain range
August 1	Swiss National Day	Commemoration of the agreement made at the beginning of August 1291 between Uri, Schwyz, and Unterwalden
September 16	Bettag/Jeûne	Swiss "Thanksgiving"
October 25	United Nations Day	Commemoration of the ratification of the UN charter in 1994
December 31	Restauration	Celebration of the restauration of the oligarchic Republic after brief French domination

ADDITIONAL RESOURCES

GENERAL HISTORY

Target Switzerland: Swiss Armed Neutrality in World War II (2000). Stephen P. Halbrook.

FESTIVAL FEVER Back in the 70s, a handful of Swiss hipsters put a new spin on the timeworn tradition of celebrating the harvest or honoring a religious holiday with a rip-roaring raucous festival. What started as a small movement has grown to encompass more than a dozen festivals in nearly every part of the Swiss countryside. Thousands of people flock from festival to festival all summer long, following the sounds of jazz, blues, folk, rock, pop, soul, funk, hip-hop, drum 'n bass, house, and techno. Many of the festivals offer free campsites for all-comers, and have cheap tickets. Listed below are the festivals not to be missed.

Bern, *Gurtenfestival.* This 3-day festival in mid-July attracts 15,000 visitors per day to the Gurten hill above Bern (5min. from town center). Features 2 stages, a half-pipe area, and a DJ area. Oasis featured in 2002. (info@gurtenfestival.ch; www.gurtenfestival.ch.)

Winterthur, *Winterthurer Musikfestwochen.* This 17-day festival in late August exhibits over 100 acts of many genres. Open-air festival the last weekend. (☎ (052) 212 61 16; info@musikfestwochen.ch; www.winterthur.musikfestwochen.ch.)

Nyon (near Geneva), *Paléo Festival Nyon.* Switzerland's largest open-air music festival in late July wins the prize for diversity of acts, ranging from electric salsa, hip hop and reggae to trip hop, drum 'n bass, and electronic vibes, as well as rock, pop, blues, and even traditional French *chanson.* A free campsite offers sleeps for thousands of festival-goers. (☎ (022) 365 10 10; paleo@paleo.ch; www.paleo.ch.)

Le Lausanne/Pulley for the Noise, An alternative to alternative music festivals, this 3-day fest in early-August focuses on new up-and-coming groups as well as standbys like Sneaker Pimps and Hillbilly Moon Explosion. (☎ (021) 323 73 30; www.for-noise.ch.)

St. Gallen, *Open-Air St. Gallen.* This weekend festival in late June combines crowd pleasing favorites like the Rage Against the Machine and many less mainstream bands. (☎ (0878) 877 994; contact@openairsg.ch; www.openairsg.ch.)

Zurich, *Streetparade.* For one day in early August more than 400,000 house and techno fans congregate on the streets of Zurich and stay to party afterwards. No invitation necessary. (www.street-parade.ch.)

Gampel (between Sion and Visp), is growing in popularity, attracting 30,000+ visitors each year because of appearances by big names such as The Cure and Papa Roach. (☎ (027) 932 5013; openairgampel@rhone.ch; www.openairgampel.ch.)

Why Switzerland? (1996). Jonathan Steinberg.

Swiss Banks and Jewish Souls (1999). Gregg J. Rickman.

FICTION

Siddhartha (1922) and *Steppenwolf* (1927). Hermann Hesse.

A Tramp Abroad (1879). Mark Twain.

Daisy Miller (1878). Henry James.

Frankenstein (1818). Mary Shelley.

TRAVEL BOOKS

Trekking and Climbing in the Western Alps (2002). Hilary Sharp.

Living and Working in Switzerland: A Survival Guide (2000). David Hampshire.

The German Way: Aspects of Behavior, Attitudes, and Customs in the German-Speaking World (1996). Hyde Flippo.

BERNESE OBERLAND

The Swiss are fiercely proud of the Bernese Oberland. When World War II threatened to engulf the country, the Swiss army resolved to defend the area to the death, and were aided in their endeavor by the natural fortress of savage mountains. The jutting peaks now shelter a pristine and silent wilderness that lends itself to discovery through scenic hikes up the mountains and around the twin lakes, the Thunersee and Brienzersee. Not surprisingly, the area's opportunities for paragliding, mountaineering, and white-water rafting are unparalleled. The lakeside towns attract a young, international, and rowdy crowd. Just north of the mountains and lakes lies exuberant and fun-loving Bern, the metropolitan heartbeat of the region and the Swiss capital. Wide streets buzz with activity, while glowing green hills in the background hint at the splendor of the wilderness just a short train ride south.

The Bernese Oberland provides copious hiking opportunities, but plan your trips wisely; cable cars are expensive. Whenever possible, *Let's Go* lists hikes you can take without mechanical assistance. Try to use a town or village as a hub from which to explore the surrounding area, or buy a regional pass. The 15-day **Berner Oberland Regional Pass** (240SFr; with SwissPass or half-fare card 192SFr) grants 5 days of unlimited regional travel and a 50% discount on the other 10 days. A 7-day pass (195SFr/156SFr with SwissPass) includes 3 days of unlimited travel and a 50% discount on the other 4 days. Both are available at train stations.

HIGHLIGHTS OF THE BERNESE OBERLAND

Climb the Münster for the best view in **Bern** (p. 336).

Hike to **Öschinensee,** then row across the crystal glacial lake (p. 365).

Scream, soar, and hold onto your lunch as you paraglide over **Interlaken** (p. 350).

BERN
☎ 031

Though it borders *Suisse Romande*, the French-speaking part of the country, Bern belongs to the German-speaking *Deutschschweiz*. The Duke of Zähringen founded Bern in 1191, naming it for his mascot, the bear. It's been the capital since 1848, but don't expect fast tracks, power politics, or men in black—Bern prefers to focus on the finer things in life. Endless arcade-lined streets are home to numerous shops and *Weinstubes* filled with intoxicating nectars, inspiring the adage, "Venice is built on water, Bern on wine." The not-to-be-missed Rosengarten peers over the city with its brilliant buds while the lush, green banks of the serpentine Aare provide respite for laid-back locals. Rebuilt in 1405 after a devastating fire, Bern's sandstone and mahogany buildings are dominated by the Bundeshaus and the Gothic Münster's spire. UNESCO named the city a world treasure.

⬛ INTERCITY TRANSPORTATION

Flights: Bern-Belpmoos Airport (☎960 21 11), 20min. from central Bern and is served by Air Engadina (☎084 884 83 28). Direct flights daily to **Amsterdam, Basel, Brussels, London, Lugano, Munich, Paris, Rome, and Vienna.** 50min. before each flight, an airport bus that guarantees you'll make it leaves from the train station in front of the tourist office (10min., 14SFr).

Trains: Bahnhofpl. Rail info: ☎0900 300 300 (24hr., 1.19SFr per min.). **Rail information office** open M-F 8am-7pm, Sa 9am-5pm. Check-in and buses upstairs. Tickets downstairs. To: **Basel** (1¼hr., every hr. 4:33am-11:52pm, 34SFr); **Berlin** (8hr., 14 per

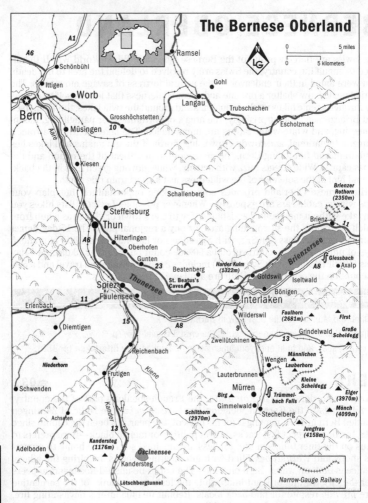

The Bernese Oberland

0 ——— 5 miles
0 ——— 5 kilometers

A1
A6
Schönbühl
Ittigen
Worb
Bern
Aare
Müsingen
Kiesen
Ramsei
Gohl
Langau
Grosshöchstetten
10
Schallenberg
Steffeisburg
Thun
Hilterfingen
Oberhofen
Gunten 23
Beatenberg
St. Beatus's Caves
Spiez
Faulensee
Erlenbach 11
Diemtigen 15
Reichenbach
Niederhorn
Frutigen
Schwenden
Achseten
Adelboden
Kandersteg (1176m)
Kandersteg
Lötschbergtunnel
Trubschachen
Escholzmatt
Brienzer Rothorn (2350m)
Brienz 11
Glessbach
A8 Axalp
Harder Kulm (1322m)
Goldswil
Iseltwald
Bönigen
Interlaken
Wilderswil
Faulhorn (2681m)
First
Grindelwald Große Scheidegg
Zweilütchinen
13
Wengen Männlichen
Lauberhorn
Lauterbrunnen
Kleine Scheidegg
Mürren
Birg
Trümmelbach Falls
Gimmelwald
Stechelberg
Elger (3970m)
Mönch (4099m)
Schilthorn (2970m)
Jungfrau (4158m)
Thunersee
Brienzersee
6
Kiene
Kander
Öscinensee
Narrow-Gauge Railway

BERNESE OBERLAND

day 5:49am-8:49pm, 245SFr); **Geneva** (2hr., every hr. 4:26am-11:24pm, 47SFr); **Interlaken** (50min., every hr. 6:22am-11:26pm, 23SFr); **Lausanne** (1¼hr., every 30min. 4:26am-11:24pm, 30SFr); **Lucerne** (1½hr., every 30min. 5:04am-11:21pm, 30SFr); **Milan** (3½hr., 6 per day 7:34am-4:22pm, 72SFr); **Munich** (6½hr., every hr. 5:49am-7:49pm, 117SFr); **Paris** (4½hr., 3 per day 6:30am-5pm, 109SFr); **Salzburg** (7¼hr., 5 per day 5:47am-9:17pm, 130SFr); **Vienna** (10½hr., 5 per day 5:47am-9:17pm, 157SFr); **Zurich** (1¼hr., every 30min. 5:47am-11:52pm, 45SFr). 25% reduction on all international fares ages 26 and under.

By car: From **Basel** or the **north,** take A2 south to A1. From **Lucerne** or the **east,** take 10 west. From **Geneva** or **Lausanne,** take E62 east to E27/A12 north. From **Thun** or the **southeast,** take A6 north.

✈ ORIENTATION

Most of medieval Bern lies in front of the train station and along the Aare River. It's worth touring even on a rainy day, thanks to the 6km of arcades that cover the streets. Bern's main train station, in front of the tourist office, is a stressful tangle of essential services and extraneous shops. **Warning:** Like many cities, Bern has a drug community; it tends to congregate around the Parliament park and terraces.

⌐ LOCAL TRANSPORTATION

Public Transportation: Bernmobil, Bubenbergpl. 5 (☎321 86 41 or 321 86 31; fax 86 86). A **visitor's card** from the Jurahaus ticket office entitles the holder to unlimited travel on Bernmobil routes and a 10% discount on city tours. 24hr. pass 7SFr; 48hr. 11SFr; 72hr.15SFr. This pass is cheaper than the day pass alone (9SFr), which is dispensed at vending machines along with one-way tickets (1-6 stops 1.70SFr; 7 or more stops 2.60SFr; SwissPass valid). Buses run 5:45am-11:45pm. **Nightbuses** called "Moonliners" leave the train station at 12:45, 2, 3:15am F-Sa nights, covering major bus and tram lines (5-20SFr; no reductions). The Bernmobil office has maps and time-tables. Open M-W and F 6:30am-7:30pm, Th 6:30am-9pm, Sa-Su 7:30am-6:30pm.

Taxis: Bären-Taxi (☎371 11 11). **NovaTaxi** (☎301 11 11 or 0800 879 879). Stands: Bahnhofpl., Waisenhauspl., and Casinopl. 6.80SFr base; 3.10SFr per km; 3.40SFr per km 8pm-6am and Su and holidays.

Car Rental: Avis AG, Wabernstr. 41 (☎378 15 15). **Hertz AG,** Kocherg. 1, Casinopl. (☎318 21 60). **Europcar,** Laupenstr. 22 (☎381 75 55).

Parking: Bahnhof, entrance at Schanzenbr. or Stadtbachstr. **Parking Casino,** Kocherg. **City West,** Belpstr., 1.80-3.60SFr per hr. Day-permit parking discs available at the tourist office. Parking permits (9SFr) available at machines at tram stops.

Bike Rental: The small blue **Bernrollt Kiosk** outside the train station and another in Casinopl. lends for **free.** 20SFr deposit plus ID required. Bikes must be returned on same day. Open daily May-Oct. 7:30am-9:30pm. Otherwise, try **Fly-Gepäck** (☎051 220 23 74) at the station. 30SFr per day. Open daily 7am-9pm.

⁊ PRACTICAL INFORMATION

TOURIST AND FINANCIAL SERVICES

Tourist Office: (☎328 12 12; fax 312 12 33; info@bernetourism.ch; www.bernetourism.ch), on the street level of the station. Distributes maps and *Bern Aktuell,* a bimonthly guide to events in the city, and makes free room reservations. The 24hr. electronic board outside the office has a free phone line to hotels, computerized receipts, and directions in German, French, and English. **City tours** available by bus (25SFr), on foot (8SFr), or by raft (35SFr). Tours daily in summer. Open June-Sept. daily 9am-8:30pm; Oct.-May M-Sa 9am-6:30pm, Su 10am-5pm. **Branch office** at the bear pits (see p. 336) open June-Sept. daily 9am-5pm; Oct. and Mar.-May 10am-4pm; Nov.-Feb. F-Su 10am-4pm.

Budget Travel: STA, Zeughausg. 18 (☎312 07 24; fax 311 28 41; www.statravel.ch). Sells ISICs. Open M-W and F 9:30am-6pm, Th 9:30am-8pm, Sa 10am-1pm. **Hang Loose,** Spitalg. 4 (☎313 18 18; fax 313 18 19; www.hangloose.ch), has student airfares and ISICs. Open M-F 9am-6pm, Th until 8pm, Sa 9am-noon.

Embassies and Consulates: Nearly all foreign embassies in Switzerland are in Bern, southeast of the Kirchenfeldbr. A complete list of consular services can be found in the **Essentials** section (see p. 7).

FANCY FOUNTAINS As if bumpy cobblestone streets and happy-go-lucky pedestrians weren't bad enough, motorists in Bern also have to negotiate their way around the 16th-century fountains that squat squarely in the middle of many of the city's *Straßen*. These creations are all over Switzerland, but the Bernese ones seem especially blinding. Most of the fountains, or *Brunnen*, are attributed to Hans Gieng. The stone fountains have been restored repeatedly since the mid-1500s to maintain their gaudy color schemes (the city mascot, the bear, shows up in fire-engine red). Highlights include the *Gerechtigkeitsbrunnen* on Gerechtigkeitsg., in which Justice stomps on the Pope, Emperor, Sultan, and Mayor, and the *Kindlifresserbrunnen* ("Child-Devourer Fountain") at Kornhauspl., tastefully translated "Ogre Fountain."

Currency Exchange: Downstairs in the station. No commission on traveler's checks. Cash advances on DC/MC/V. Western Union transfers 7am-7pm. Exchange open daily 6:30am-9pm.

ATM: At the train station or at **Credit Suisse** and **Swiss Bank Corp.** Open Tu-F 10am-6:30pm, Sa 9am-3pm.

LOCAL SERVICES

Luggage Storage: Downstairs in the train station. 24hr. Lockers 4-8SFr. **Luggage watch** at the Fly-Gepäck counter upstairs 7SFr. Open daily 8am-10pm.

Lost Property: Downstairs in station and at Zeughausg. 18 (☎220 23 37). Both open M-F 8am-noon and 2-6pm.

Bookstore: JäggiBücher, Spitalg. on Bubenbergpl. 47-51 (☎320 20 20), in Loeb dept. store. Two floors of books including English bestsellers and travel guides. Open M-W and F 9am-6:30pm, Th 9am-9pm, Sa 8am-4pm.

Libraries: Stadtbibliothek (Municipal and University Library), Münsterg. 61 (☎320 32 11), stacks books for the central library of the University of Bern and the city's public library. Open M-F 9am-5pm. **Swiss National Library,** Hallwylstr. 15 (☎332 89 11). Lending library and catalog room open M-Tu and Th-F 9am-6pm, W 9am-8pm, Sa 9am-2pm. Reading room open M-Tu and Th-F 8am-6pm, W 8am-8pm, Sa 9am-4pm.

Bi-Gay-Lesbian Organizations: Homosexuelle Arbeitsgruppe die Schweiz-HACH (Gay Association of Switzerland), c/o Anderland, Mühlenpl. 11, CH-3011. Headquarters of Switzerland's largest gay organization. **Homosexuelle Arbeitsgruppe Bern** (HAB), Mühlenpl. 11, Case Postal 312, CH-3000 Bern 13 (☎311 63 53) in Marzilibad, along the Aare. Hosts get-togethers W evenings, with coffee, drinks, and library access. **Schlub** (Gay Students' Organization), c/o Studentinnenschaft, Lercheweg 32, CH-3000 Bern 9 (☎371 00 87). **Gay Geneva Evenings** (☎022 320 72 65; www.swissgay.ch).

Laundromat: Jet Wash, Dammweg 43 (☎078 743 92 09). Take bus #20 (dir: Wyler) to "Lorraine." Wash 8kg for 6SFr, 5kg 4SFr; dry 4SFr for 1hr. Soap 0.80-1.20SFr. Open M-Sa 7am-9pm, Su 9am-6pm.

Public Toilets and Showers: McClean, at train station. 1-2SFr for toilets, 12SFr for showers. Open daily 6am-midnight.

EMERGENCY AND COMMUNICATIONS

Emergency: Police, ☎117, and downstairs in the station. **Ambulance,** ☎144. **Doctor,** ☎311 22 11. **Rape Crisis Hotline,** ☎332 14 14.

Pharmacy: In the station. Open daily 6:30am-10pm. **Bären Apotheke,** at the clock tower. Open M 1:45-6:30pm, Tu-W and F 7:45am-6:30pm, Th 7:45am-9pm, Sa 8am-4pm. AmEx/DC/MC/V. For the **24hr. pharmacy on duty,** call ☎311 22 11.

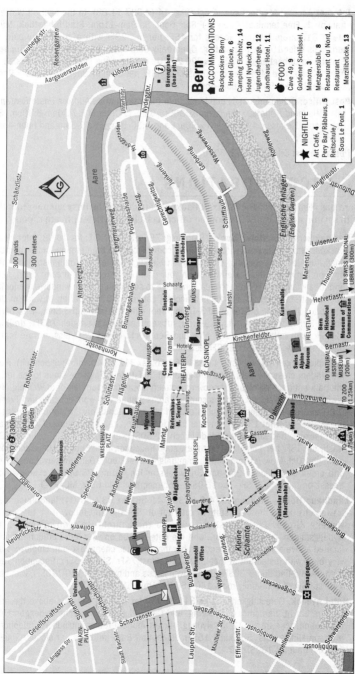

Bern

▲ ACCOMMODATIONS
Backpackers Bern/
Hotel Glocke, **6**
Camping Eicholz, **14**
Hotel Nydeck, **10**
Jugendherberge, **12**
Landhaus Hotel, **11**

● FOOD
Cave 49, **9**
Goldener Schlüssel, **7**
Manora, **3**
Metzgerstübli, **8**
Restaurant du Nord, **2**
Restaurant
Marzilibrücke, **13**

★ NIGHTLIFE
Art Café, **4**
Pery Bar/Räblaus, **5**
Reitschule/
Sous Le Pont, **1**

Internet Access: Medienhaus, Zeughausg. 14 (☎327 11 88), to the right off Waisen-hauspl. 1. Free terminal. Open M-F 8am-6pm, Sa 9am-11pm. **Stadtbibliothek,** Mün-sterg. 61, offers Internet access for 4SFr per hr., 2SFr with a city library card. 2 terminals offer 10min. free surfing. Open daily 9am-5pm. Basement of **JäggiBücher,** Spitalg. on Bubenbergpl. 47-51 (☎320 20 20), in Loeb dept. store. 2 computers allow max. 20min. free, 4 more computers cost 5SFr per 30min. Open M-W and F 9am-6:30pm, Th 9am-9pm, Sa 8am-4pm.

Post Office: Schanzenpost 1, one block from the train station. Address *Poste Restante* to Postlagernde Briefe, Schanzenpost 3000, Bern 1. Open M-F 7:30am-6:30pm, Sa 8am-noon. Express counter M-F 6-7:30am and 6:30-10pm, Sa 7-8am and noon-4pm, Su 3:30-10pm.

Postal codes: CH-3000 to CH-3030.

⚲ ACCOMMODATIONS

Bern has responded to the influx of backpackers during the busy summer months with several new hostels. The tourist office has a list of pricier private rooms.

▨ **Backpackers Bern/Hotel Glocke,** Rathausg. 75 (☎311 37 71; fax 10 08; info@chilis-backpackers.com; www.chilisbackpackers.com). From the train station, cross the tram lines, turn left onto Spitalg., continuing on Marktg. Turn left at Kornhauspl. and then right on Rathausg. The hostel will be on your right. A backpacker's dream: clean, new, and ideally located. TV/lounge area conducive to socializing. Room windows overlook a bustling street. **Internet** and kitchen access. Laundry 3.80SFr per hr. of wash or dry. Reception June-Aug. 8-11am and 3-10pm; Sept.-May 8-11am and 3-8pm. 4- to 6-bed dorms 32SFr for first night, 27SFr for subsequent nights; singles 75SFr; doubles 120SFr, with bath 160SFr. Apr.-May and Sept.-Oct.: dorms 2SFr less, private rooms 5SFr less; Nov.-Mar.: 4SFr/10SFr less. MC/V. ❷

Jugendherberge (HI), Weiherg. 4 (☎311 63 16; fax 312 52 40; info@jugibern.ch). From the station, cross the tram lines and go down Christoffelg. Take the stairs to the left of the park entrance gates and go down the steep slope, then turn left onto Weiherg., fol-lowing the hostel signs. Spacious common areas feature well-worn couches and TV with CNN, and picnic tables to watch life-sized chess matches on the patio. Wheelchair accessible. **Internet** 1SFr for 4min. or 5SFr for 25min., half-price midnight-7am. Break-fast, lockers, and sheets included. Lunch 12.50SFr; dinner 11.50SFr. Laundry 4SFr wash, dry 1SFr per 15min. 3-night max. stay. Reception June-Sept. 7-10am and 3pm-midnight; Oct.-May 7-10am and 5pm-midnight. Check-out 10am. Reservations by fax and email only. Closed 2nd and 3rd weeks in Jan. Dorms 28.50SFr; overflow mat-tresses on the floor 20SFr. Tax 1.30SFr. Non-members add 6SFr. MC/V. ❷

Landhaus Hotel, Altenbergstr. 4-6 (☎331 41 66; fax 332 69 04; landhaus@spec-traweb.ch). From the train station, turn left on Spitalg. and follow it all the way to Nydegg Kirche. Take the stairs down to the church, walk down the hill on Nydeggstalden, cross Untertorbr., and the hotel will be on your left. Partitioned bunks located above a stylish restaurant and bar that provides cheap take-out. Employees are very busy with restaurant at mealtimes. Breakfast 7SFr. Sheets 5SFr. Reception 7am-6pm. 4- to 6-bed dorms 30SFr; double with linens and breakfast 110-120SFr, with bath 140-160SFr; 4-bed family room 140-160SFr. AmEx/DC/MC/V. ❷

Hotel Nydeck, Gerechtigkeitsg. 1 (☎311 86 86; fax 312 20 54), sits above the busy Junkere bar at the corner of Junkerng. and Gerechtigkeitsg., near the Nydeggbr. From the station, take tram #12 to "Nydegg." Bright modern rooms include TV, telephone, and sparkling baths. Breakfast 15SFr. Reception 8am until the bar closes. Singles 110SFr; doubles 160SFr. ❹

Camping Eichholz, Strandweg 49 (☎961 26 02; www.campingeichholz.ch). Take tram #9 to "Wabern," backtrack 50m, and take the 1st right. Walk down Eichholzstr.; signs point the way (10min.). Riverside location opposite the zoo. On-site restaurant. Co-op nearby. Parking 2-3.20SFr. Laundry 5SFr. Reserve ahead. Reception 7am-10pm. Open Apr. 20-Sept. 6.90SFr per person, students 5.50SFr, children 3SFr, tents 5-8.50SFr. Doubles 15SFr; triples 17SFr; quads 22SFr. Electricity 3SFr. Showers 1SFr. MC/V. ❶

🖸 FOOD

Almost every locale ending in "-platz" overflows with cafes and restaurants, though the bigger ones tend to be pricier and more tourist-infested. Try one of Bern's hearty specialties: *Gschnätzlets* (fried veal, beef, or pork), *Suurchabis* (a sauerkraut), or *Gschwellti* (steamed potatoes).

📓 **Restaurant du Nord,** Lorrainestr. 2 (☎332 23 38), right across Lorrainebr. An open and relaxed atmosphere where a diverse, alternative crowd smokes and socializes. Pasta plates from 17SFr; special seasonal menus. Open M-F 8am-12:30am, Sa 9am-12:30am, Su 4-11:30pm. ❸

Cave 49, Gerechtigkeitsg. 49 (☎312 55 92), is a dimly lit Mediterranean underground tavern frequented by rowdy locals. Enjoy tortellini with parmesan (15SFr) or *chorizo* (paprika sausage, 6.50SFr). Beers from 2.70SFr. Open Tu-Su 10am-12:30am. ❷

Manora, Bubenbergpl. 5A (☎311 37 55), over the tramlines from the station, next to the Bernmobil office. This self-service chain tends to be crowded, but sells cheap and healthy meals. Dinner available for as low as 13.90SFr; salad bar 4.40-9.40SFr; fresh squeezed juices 1.90-5.30SFr. 20% discount for students after 5pm. Open M-Sa 6:30am-10:45pm, Su 8:30am-10:45pm. Service ends at 10:30pm. ❶

Metzgerstübli, Münsterg. 60 (☎311 00 45). Charismatic and good-humored waiters serve up well-presented dishes at this chic but cozy restaurant. Provençal specialties from 25SFr, salads 7-27.50SFr. Free-range chicken with cognac chanterelles and sauerkraut 31SFr. Open Tu-F 9am-midnight, Sa 7am-12:30am. MC/V. ❹

Restaurant Marzilibrücke, Gassstr. 8 (☎311 27 80). Turn right from the Jugendherberge onto Aarstr. Divided into a classy restaurant and a not-so-classy pizzeria, this popular joint overflows with people looking to enjoy the outdoor seating. Gourmet pizzas 15.50-25.50SFr; wine 4.20-6.70SFr per glass. Reservations recommended. Open M-Th 11:30am-10:30pm, F 11:30am-11:50am, Sa 4pm-12:30am, Su 10am-10:30pm. Pizzeria open M-F 5:30-11pm, Sa-Su 4-11pm. ❸

Restaurant Goldener Schlüssel, Rathausg. 72 (311 56 88), serves traditional Swiss dishes involving pork and veal. Vegetarian options available for the less carnivorous. A mouthful in every way, the *Kalbeslebegeschnetzeltes,* shredded veal liver in a cognac sauce with *Rösti* (29.80SFr), is truly an experience. Open daily 7am-11:30pm. ❹

MARKETS

Migros, Marktg. 46, also has a restaurant and take-away counters, including one with 4.80SFr sandwiches and a daily *Menü* (10-12SFr). Open M 9am-6:30pm, Tu-W and F 8am-6:30pm, Th 8am-9pm, Sa 7am-4pm.

Reformhaus M. Siegrist, in the Marktg.-Passage (off Marktg.), is a popular health food store. Open Tu-W and F 8am-6:30pm, Th 8am-9pm, Sa 7am-4pm.

Fruit and vegetable markets sell fresh produce daily on Bärenpl. (May-Oct. 8am-6pm) and every Tu and Sa 7am-noon on Bundespl. The off-the-wall **onion market,** which takes the city by storm every 4th M of Nov., is Bern's best-known festival.

🔘 🏛 SIGHTS AND MUSEUMS

Bern is a walkable city, with major sights in a line from the Parliament. Museums ring **Helvetiaplatz** near Kirchenfeldbr. (accessible by tram #3, 5 or 19).

THE OLD TOWN. The solid medieval architecture of Bern's Altstadt glows red with Swiss flags and geraniums. Behind church spires and government domes, the lush hills along the Aare river create a cooling, verdant backdrop. The massive **Bundeshaus,** center of the Swiss national government, dominates the Aare. The politicians hide in the **Parlamentsgebäude.** *(☎322 85 22. 45min. tour every hr. M-Sa 9-11am and 2-4pm, except on holidays and during special parliamentary proceedings. Free.)*

From the state house, Kockerg. and Herreng. lead to the 15th-century Protestant **Münster** (cathedral). The imagination of the late Gothic period runs rampant in the stern portal sculpture of the Last Judgment, left intact during the Reformation, which depicts Dante-esque punishments of sinners, from them hanging by the tongue to throwing them into a fire. Climb the spiral stairs of its spire—one of the tallest in Switzerland at 100m—for amazing area views. *(Open Easter-Oct. Tu-Sa 10am-5pm, Su 11:30am-5pm; Nov.-Easter Tu-F 10am-noon and 2-4pm, Sa 10am-noon and 2-5pm, Su 11am-2pm. Tower closes 30min. before the church. 3SFr. Free concerts June-Sept. Tu 8pm.)*

From the Bundeshaus, turn left off Kocherg. at Theaterpl. to reach the 13th-century **Zytglogge** (clock tower). At 4min. before the hour, figures on the tower creak to life with uneventful clanging and a couple of weak rooster squawks; the oohs and aahs of gathered tourists are more fervent, but quickly die down. *(Tours of the interior May-Oct. daily 4:30pm, also at 11:30am in July-Aug. 8SFr.)*

BEAR PITS. Across the Nydeggbr. lie the **Bärengraben** (bear pits; see **Bären Brain,** p. 336). Descendants of the original Bern bear lounge lazily in stone-lined pits that date back to the 15th century. Tour groups and screaming kids provide the bears with hours of amusement and annoyance. During Easter, newborn cubs are publicly displayed for the first time. *(Open June-Sept. daily 9am-5:30pm; Oct.-May 10am-4pm. 3SFr to feed the bears.)* The tourist office at the pits presents **The Bern Show,** a slickly choreographed multimedia recap of Bernese history that melds into an overly indulgent photo-montage. *(Every 20min. In German and English, alternately. Free.)* The path snaking up the hill to the left leads to the ◩**Rosengarten;** sit among the blooms and admire a stellar view of Bern's Altstadt.

KUNSTMUSEUM. Bern's Klee-crazed Kunstmuseum sprawls over three floors and boasts the world's largest Paul Klee collection: 2500 geometrically dreamy works, from his school exercise-books to puppets made for his son Felix to huge canvases. Works by current artists are displayed next to those of artists who inspired them. A smattering of big names are upstairs: Picasso, Giacometti, Ernst Kirchner, Pollock, and some Dada works by Hans Arp. The museum also has a chic cafe and screens art films. *(Hodlerstr. 8-12, near Lorrainebrücke. ☎328 09 44. Open Tu 10am-9pm, W-*

BÄREN BRAIN Bern's citizens have got bears on the brain. The city's ursine mascot pervades even the most forsaken alleys in the form of statuettes, fountains, flags, stained-glass windows, and matchbox covers. Legend has it that Duke Berchtold V of Zähringen, founder of Bern, wanted to name the city after the first animal he caught when hunting on the site of the planned construction. The animal was a you-know-what, and Bern (from *Bären*, or bears) was born. The *Bärengraben* weren't built until the Bernese victory at the Battle of Nouana in 1513, when soldiers dragged home a live bear as war booty. A hut was erected for the beast in what is now Bärenplatz (Bear Square) and his descendants have been Bern's collective pets ever since.

Su 10am-5pm. Mandatory bag-check 2SFr. Klee collection 7SFr, students and seniors 5SFr. Entire collection 15SFr/10SFr. Under 16 free. Extra fees for temporary exhibitions.)

RIVER AARE. Several walkways lead steeply down from the Bundeshaus to the Aare; a cable car assists passengers on the way up (1.10SFr). The river bank is ideal for shady walks. On hot days, locals dive lemming-style from the bridges and ride its swift currents. (Only experienced swimmers should join in.) Along the banks, numerous stone steps invite you to take the plunge. For a more languid afternoon, the **Marzilibad public pool** lies on the river 3min. to the right of the Jugendherberge. *(Open May-Aug. M-F 8:30am-8pm, Sa-Su 8:30am-7pm; Sept. M-F 8:30am-7pm, Sa-Su 8:30am-6pm. Lockers and showers available.)*

GARDENS AND ZOO. The **Botanical Gardens** of the University of Bern sprawl along the river at Lorrainebrücke. Exotic plants thrive alongside native alpine greenery. *(Take bus #20 to "Gewerbeschule." ☎631 49 44. Park open Mar.-Sept. daily 8am-5:30pm; Oct.-Feb. 8am-5pm. Greenhouse open daily 8am-5pm. Free.)* In a towering forest of cedar and pine, the 24hr. park housing the **Dählhölzli Städtischer Tierpark** (Zoo) gives you the chance to animal-watch at night, too. *(Tierparkweg 1. Walk south along the Aare or take bus #19 to "Tierpark." ☎357 15 15. Open in summer daily 8am-6:30pm; off-season 9am-5pm. 7SFr, students 5SFr. Parking available.)*

BERNISCHES HISTORISCHE MUSEUM. This collection is so big you won't know where to begin, especially after additions in 2002. Luckily, multilingual explanatory notes are available in many rooms of the museum's seven jam-packed levels. Bern's lengthy history is on display, from technology to religious art to 15th-century sculptural finds. The collection of oversized Burgundian tapestries is one of the museum's prized possessions. *(Helvetiapl. 5. ☎350 77 11. Open Tu and Th-Su 10am-5pm, W 10am-8pm. 13SFr, students 8SFr, children under 16 and school groups 4SFr. Tours in German, French, English.)*

SWISS ALPINE MUSEUM. Intricate models of the Alps give a history of Swiss cartography and Alpine exploration. The main floor is an array of topographical models of the country and offers info-stations with innumerable slides. The 2nd-floor exhibit on mountain life may be more interesting—check out the devil masks used to protect against threats from the other world. *(Helvetiapl. 4. ☎351 04 34; www.alpinesmuseum.ch. Open M 2-5pm, Tu-Su 10am-5pm. Signs in German, French, Italian, and English. 7SFr, students and seniors 4SFr. Add 1SFr when there are special exhibits.)*

THE LOCAL STORY

CELEBRITY HOMES

Barbara is a long-time employee of Albert Einstein's House.

Q: What's the best thing about working in Albert Einstein's house?
A: The kind of people that it attracts. People from different countries, backgrounds, and all walks of life. It helps me to look at Einstein from different angles.

Q: What do visitors do inside?
A: Some like to take pictures with his pictures, others take pictures of themselves sitting in his chair or writing at his desk.

Q: What kind of people come in?
A: All different kinds of people—some come because they are physicists and fully appreciate the significance of the place where his theory was developed, while others visit because Einstein is so famous or they saw it in their guidebooks. The discussions are always extremely interesting. I've learned a lot from listening to people. When I first came, I had preconceived ideas of what physicists are like. But I've met so many with such different personalities.

Q: Who are the most interesting people to come in?
A: I remember once a man walked in and stood there for a long time until tears streamed down his face. Afterwards he explained that he was a physicist and taking in where Einstein did his work was so emotional for him.

Q: Any really important visitors?
A: Once Switzerland's only astronaut came in and I got to give him the guided tour of Einstein's house. You get in touch with people way beyond your social sphere.

MUSEUM OF NATURAL HISTORY. Most people come to this bright, colorful museum to see Barry, the now-stuffed St. Bernard who saved over 40 people in his lifetime. Some of the other hyper-realistic dioramas, however, get a bit more intense—hyenas feed on zebra corpses, and more dynamic cousins of the *Bärengraben* bears fight over a recently killed moose. Very family- and school group-friendly. *(Bernastr. 15, off Helvetiapl. ☎ 350 71 11. Open M 2-5pm, Tu and Th-F 9am-5pm, W 9am-6pm, Sa-Su 10am-5pm. 5SFr, students 3SFr, extra for temporary exhibits.)*

ALBERT EINSTEIN'S HOUSE. The humble abode in which Einstein lived during the development of his theory of relativity is now a mecca for physics lovers everywhere. Old pictures, letters, and even a copy of his school records line the walls of the small apartment. *(Kramg. 49. ☎ 312 00 91. Open Feb.-Nov. Tu-F 10am-5pm, Sa 10am-4pm. 3SFr, students and children 2SFr.)*

🎵 ENTERTAINMENT

Bern's cultural tastes run the gamut from classical music concerts to late-night cafe bands. Events are well-publicized on kiosks and bulletin boards. Publications like *Non-Stopp* and *Berner Woche* (the "Going Out" sections of two Bern newspapers) or *Gay Agenda* will be thrust into your hands on street corners.

Operas and ballets are performed at the **Stadttheater,** Kornhauspl. 20. (☎311 07 77. Summer season runs from July to late Aug.; for ticket info, contact Theaterkasse, Kornhauspl. 18, CH-3000 Bern 7.) Bern's **Symphony Orchestra** plays in the fall and winter at the Konservatorium für Musik, Kramg. 36. (Tickets ☎311 62 21.) July's **Gurten Festival** has attracted such luminaries as Bob Dylan, Elvis Costello, Björk, and Sinead O'Connor. (www.gurtenfestival.ch. 1-day ticket 65SFr, 2-day 95SFr, 3-day 135SFr.) Jazz-lovers arrive in early May for the **International Jazz Festival.** (Tickets at any Bankverein Swiss branch; www.jazzfestivalbern.ch. About 16SFr.) Other festivals include the Bernese Easter-egg market in late March and the notorious **onion market** on the fourth Monday in November. The orange grove at Stadgärtnerei Elfnau (take tram #19 to "Elfnau") has free Sunday concerts in summer. Additionally, **Mahogany Hall,** Klösterlistutz 18, (www.mahogany.ch), by the bear pits, is a popular venue for jazz, bluegrass, and folk.

From mid-July to mid-August, **OrangeCinema** (www.orangecinema.ch) screens recently released films, including many American ones, in the open air. Buy tickets at the tourist office in the train station or at the Orange Shop at Spitalg. 14.

🌃 NIGHTLIFE

The fashionable folk linger in the Altstadt's bars and cafes at night. A seedier scene gathers under the gargoyles and graffiti of the Lorrainebr., behind and to the left of the station down Bollwerk.

Pery Bar/Rablaus, Schmiedenpl. 3 (☎311 59 08), off Kornhauspl. A tastefully romantic atmosphere is jolted by incongruent disco music at this local hot spot. The Rablaus Restaurant serves lunch and dinner. Beers from 4.90SFr; wines from 5SFr. Bar open M-W 5pm-1:30am, Th 5pm-2:30am, F-Sa 5pm-3:30am.

Art Cafe, Gurteng. 6 (☎318 20 70). Cafe by day, smoky bar by night. The black-and-white decor sets a casually trendy tone that is overshadowed by neighboring pophouse, Cafe Eclipse. Occasional live acts and DJs. Beers from 5SFr. Open M-W 7pm-12:30am, Th-F 7pm-3:30am, Sa 8pm-3:30am, Su 6pm-12:30am.

Sous le Pont. From Bollwerk, head left before Lorrainebr. through the cement park. A graffiti-covered den of alternative culture serving a colorful and diverse crowd. Occasionally hosts concerts by international indie bands. Beers from 3.50SFr. Open Tu

11:30am-12:30pm, W-Th 11:30am-2:30pm and 6pm-12:30am, F 11:30am-2:30pm and 6pm-2:30am, Sa 6pm-2:30am.

Reitschule, Neubrückstr. 8 (☎302 83 72), left off Bollwerk. This small room painted with bats and buddhas caters to a patchwork crowd of students and loafers. Beers from 3.50SFr; *Menüs* 5SFr. Open daily 8pm-late.

THE THUNERSEE

The Thunersee's diminutive status works to its advantage. The jade-green forests and distant snowcapped Jungfrau peaks seem immediately accessible from the sail-dotted waters of the lake. Its northwestern shores are strewn with castles, enchanting the surrounding towns and cloud-enshrouded peaks. The Thunersee's three significant towns, **Thun, Spiez,** and **Interlaken,** all lie on the main Bern-Interlaken-Lucerne rail line. **Boats** operated by the BLS shipping company (☎334 52 11; www.bls.ch) putter to the smaller villages between the Thun and Interlaken West railway stations (2hr., June 26-Sept. 26 every hr. 8:10am-11:35pm; special evening cruises available June-Dec.; Eurail, SwissPass, and Berner Oberland pass valid). A ferry day-pass good as far as **Brienz** (on the Brienzersee) costs 6.60SFr.

THUN
☎033

Known as the "Gateway to the Bernese Oberland," Thun (pop. 38,000) lies on the banks of the Aare River and the Thunersee. Graced by nearby castles of every imaginable size and color, the quiet town confirms the words of Johannes Brahms, "Relaxing in Thun is delightful, and one day will not be enough." Though picturesque and historic, Thun is not stodgy. The Selve area offers everything from crowded discothèques and bars to a roller skating rink and an indoor racetrack.

▆ TRANSPORTATION

Trains to: **Bern** (every 30min. 5:12am-11:20pm,13.40 SFr); **Interlaken East** (every hr. 7:17am-11:47pm, 15.20SFr); **Interlaken West** (every hr. 6:43am-11:47pm, 14.20SFr);

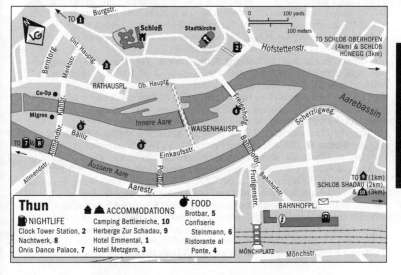

and **Spiez** (every 30min. 6:43am-12:52am, 6.60SFr). There is a rail information desk (open M-F 9am-6:30pm, Sa 9am-4pm). **Boat landing** (☎ 223 53 80) across the street and to the right of the station. Boats depart for: **Faulensee** (11SFr); **Hilterfingen** (5.60SFr); **Interlaken West** (20SFr); **Oberhofen** (6.60SFr); and **Spiez** (10.20SFr).

⚡🏛 ORIENTATION AND PRACTICAL INFORMATION

Thun's main street is the tree-lined boulevard Bälliz. The oldest squares and the castle (all hung with red-and-white flags) lie across the river from the train station on the Aare's north bank. Thun's **tourist office,** Seestr. 2, is outside and to the left of the station. (☎222 23 40; fax 83 23. Open July-Aug. M-F 9am-7pm, Sa 9am-noon and 1-4pm; Sept.-June M-F 9am-noon and 1-6pm, Sa 9am-noon.) Services include: **currency exchange** (open M-Sa 6am-8pm, Su 6:30am-8pm) and **bike rental** (30SFr per day; open M-Sa 8:30am-8pm). **Lockers** (4-6SFr) are at the station. **Free bike rental** at Waisenhauspl. (Open May-Oct. 7:30am-9:30pm, ID and 20SFr deposit required, returned on the same day.) **Taxis** usually wait outside the station, or dial ☎22 22; **parking** is at the Parkhaus Aarestr. on Aarestr. (☎222 78 26; 1.50SFr per hr., half-price nights and weekends). Get **Internet access** at the Sky Bar (Bälliz 25). The **post office** is at Panoramastr. 1a, across from the station. (Open M-F 7:30am-7pm, Sa 8am-noon.) **Postal code:** CH-3601.

🏠🍴 ACCOMMODATIONS AND FOOD

The **Herberge zur Schadau** ❸ packs 30 beds into five small rooms, so close together there's a good chance you'll get to know your fellow hostelers quite well. Exit the train station, turn right, and walk 10min. down Seestr. (☎222 52 22. Breakfast included. Reception 8am-8pm daily, quiet hours 11pm-7am. 39SFr per person. No credit cards.) **Hotel Metzgern** ❸, Untere Hauptg. 2, has simple but sunny rooms equipped with sinks and windows above the popular restaurant downstairs. From the station, veer left on Bahnhofstr. and go straight over two bridges. Signs lead the way. (☎222 21 41; fax 21 82. Breakfast included. Reception Tu-Th and Su 8am-11:30pm, F-Sa 8am-12:30am. Singles, doubles, triples 60 per person; 55SFr for more than 1 night; 50SFr for more than 1 week. Children 7 and under half-price. MC/V.) Spacious and modern rooms with sparkling private bathrooms are hidden within the unique exterior of **Hotel Emmental** ❹, Bernstr. 2. (☎222 01 20. Breakfast and sheets included. Reception 7am-2pm and 4pm-midnight. Apr.-Oct. 80SFr per person; Nov.-Mar. singles 70SFr, doubles 120SFr.)

Campers should head to **Camping Bettlereiche** ❶. Take bus #1 to "Camping" or turn right from the station and walk 45min. down Seestr., which veers sharply left and becomes Gwattstr. The campsite is near water and surrounded by hills. (☎336 40 67; fax 40 17. Showers included. Reception 8:30am-noon and 2-7:30pm, until 8:30pm in July-Aug. July-Aug. 7.40SFr per person, 7SFr per tent; Apr.-June and Sept.-Oct. 5.40SFr per person, 6SFr per tent. AmEx/MC/V.)

Unlike hotel rooms, food in Thun is cheap. Affordable restaurants line Bahnhofstr. The **Brotbar** ❶, Bälliz 11, is equal parts corner bakery and swanky cafe. Cross the river at Allmendbr. and turn right onto Bälliz. Sip exotic teas (3.60SFr), or a creamy smoothie (2.50-3SFr) made from homemade yogurt and fresh fruit, with your meal from the healthy menu. (☎222 22 21. Open M-W 7am-6:30pm, Th-Sa 7am-12:30am.) Dine and feed the waterfowl at **Ristorante Al Ponte** ❸, Freienhofg. 16, at the foot of the Sinnebr. beside the river. For delectable pastries and sandwiches in a comfy corner tea room, try **Confiserie Steinmann** ❶, Bälliz 37, just past Brotbar. Enjoy mouth-watering *Thuner Leckerli* made from honey, lemon rind, and nuts (6SFr for 5 pieces) or strawberry tarts for 3.50SFr. (☎222 20 47. Open M 1-6:30pm, Tu-W and F 6:45am-6:30pm, Sa 6:45am-4pm.) Both **Migros** and **Co-op** have markets and restaurants on Allmendstr. straddling the Kuhbr. (Both open M-W and F 8am-6:30pm, Th 8am-9pm, Sa 7:30am-4pm.) At the **open-air market** in the Altstadt, across the river from the train station, vendors hawk souvenirs, clothes, and produce (Sa 8am-noon). A **food market** covers Bälliz on Wednesdays and Saturdays 8am-2pm.

🄘 SIGHTS

SCHLOß THUN. Thun's centerpiece, this castle presides over the town from the top of the Altstadt. The castle houses a historical museum whose upper floors show off a collection of vicious weaponry, both historic and modern. The tower was the site of a gruesome fratricide in 1322, when Eberhard of Kyburg unsportingly defenestrated his brother Hartmann, but now serves only to give visitors great views of the mountains surrounding Thun. Downstairs in the *Rittersaal* (Knight's Hall) the castle hosts classical music concerts June 7-25. (☎ 223 20 01. *From the station, bear left down Bahnhofstr. and go over 2 bridges, right onto Obere Hauptg., left up the Risgässli steps, and left again at the top; follow the signs to Schloß/Museum. Open Apr.-Oct. daily 10am-5pm. 6SFr, students 4SFr, children 2SFr, children under 6 free, families 12SFr. For concert tickets call ☎ 223 25 30 or contact the tourist office; tickets 30-50SFr.)*

SCHLOß SCHADAU. The pastel pink Schloß Schadau, in the peaceful Walter Hansen Schadaupark by the sea, was built in the style of castles in France's Loire Valley. The castle houses a large gastronomy book collection and a fabulous **restaurant.** Hidden by the foliage, the nearby **Wocher Panorama,** painted by Marquard Wocher of neighboring Basel, recreates the lake and its environs with a room-sized painting of the area. *(Seestr. 45; from the station, turn right and walk about 15min. ☎ 223 24 62. Panorama open May-Oct. 10am-5pm. 4SFr, students 3SFr, under 17 free.)*

SCHLOß HÜNEGG. The most elaborate of the Thunersee castles, Hünegg in the wooded hills of Hilterfingen displays well-preserved lavish furnishings of the later half of the 19th century. Though left unchanged since 1900, the castle is very much in use—it even hosts the occasional birthday party. *(Bus #21 runs to Hilterfingen. Walk 100m back towards Thun; castle will be on the right. ☎ 243 19 82. Open mid-May to mid-Oct. M-Sa 2-5pm, Su 10am-noon and 2-5pm. 8SFr, students 7SFr, children 1.50SFr.)*

🄟 OUTDOOR ACTIVITIES

The popular local **hike** up **Heilingenschwendi,** the hillside above Thun on the lake's north shore, provides a view of the distant Jungfrau mountains (half-day hike). Past the casino and the village of Seematten, turn left, cross the river, and head up through the wooded ridge. Continue farther to the **Dreiländeregg** and **Niesenbänkli** for a panoramic view (3hr.). If you push on to the village of **Schwendi,** near the top, continue hiking a little farther to **Schloß Oberhofen** (see above), where you can catch bus #21 back to town. If the *Schlößer* castles stifle you, hit the water. The tourist office has information on **sailing, wind-surfing, river-rafting,** and **boat rental.**

🄙 🄟 ENTERTAINMENT AND NIGHTLIFE

Bälliz is lined with pricey drinking spots, most with outdoor seating. For a lower-key, cheaper evening, head to **Clock Tower Station,** Obere Hauptg. 89, just a few steps past the Risgässli steps that lead to Schloß Thun. Canadians will feel at home in this canuck-themed sports bar, though a loyal group of Thun locals frequents this small pub most often. Grilled food served until 2am. (☎ 223 57 96. Open Tu-Sa 6pm-3:30am.) The Selvereal part of town provides more lively entertainment and an energetic crowd. From the train station, go down Bahnhofstr., turn left on Aarestr. and keep going until it turns into Schiebenstr. and veers left. This strip is home to the **Thun Indoor Karting,** Scheibenstr. 37, an indoor race track where you can rent a car, safety equipment, and the track for an exhilarating race. (☎222 83 44. Open M 5-10pm, Tu 4-10pm, W-Th 4-11pm, F 4pm-1am, Sa 2pm-1am, Su 2-8pm. All equipment 25SFr, 17SFr for students who arrive before 8pm.) Many bars and clubs lie on the same street, including the very fashionable 20+ **Orvis Dance Palace,** Scheibenstr. 8, which features multiple stages for dancing and DJs spinning techno and house. A separate room has food, beer (5SFr), billiards, and a big-screen TV next to a quiet, cool-down bar. (☎222 27 55. Open Th 9pm-2:30am, F-Sa 9pm-3:30am; cover Th 5SFr, F-Sa 10SFr.) Nearby **Nachtwerk** has a DJ on each floor: techno on the first, hip-hop on the second, and Top 40 on the third.

Thun's outdoor **festivals** are a bit more tame, but the young and energetic are trying to liven things up. Traditional festivals include the **Ausschiesset** (shoot out) among cadets on the last Monday and Tuesday in September and the William Tell shoot honoring the one who takes the best shot at a model of Gessler. The Altstadt rocks with merry music in the **Festival of Barrel Organs and Ballad Singers** every July.

▶ DAYTRIP FROM THUN

SPIEZ
Trains leave every hr. to Bern (30min., 17.20SFr), Thun (10min., 6.60SFr), and Interlaken West (20min., 9.20SFr). Boats to Thun (8.40SFr) and Interlaken (11.40SFr).

Sleepy and silent Spiez overlooks the Thunersee. The **tourist office,** to the left as you exit the train station, sells hiking maps and helps find cheap rooms. Internet access 1SFr per 5min. (☎654 20 20; fax 21 92. Open May M-F 8am-noon and 1-6pm, June M-F 8am-6:30pm and Sa 9am-noon, July-Aug. M-F 8am-6:30pm, Sa 9am-noon and 2-4pm, Sept. M-F 8am-noon and 2-6pm, Sa 9am-noon, Oct.-Apr. M-F 8am-noon and 2-6pm.) If you're not staying in Thun, try ▓**Swiss Adventure Hostel** (see p. 347) in tiny Boltigen, 35min. from Spiez by train (dir: Zweissimen).

Schloß Spiez, its most famous attraction, is a medieval fortress with Romanesque, Gothic, and Renaissance flourishes that attest to its colorful history. To see the castle, bear left on Bahnhofstr. from the station, turn right onto Thunstr., then left onto Seestr., or wander the sloping streets towards it—it's visible from anywhere in town. Stroll through the lovely, walled, lakeside gardens for free. Inside the fortress is a historical museum with enormous bear skins hanging above the mantelpiece, a banquet hall dating from 1614 decorated in Renaissance style, and medieval graffiti. Views of the lake are exquisite from the banquet hall. (☎654 15 06. Open July-Aug. M 2-6pm, Tu-Su 10am-6pm; Apr.-June and Sept.-Oct. M 2-5pm, Tu-Su 10am-5pm. 5SFr, students 4SFr, children 1SFr.) The castle hosts classical music concerts from May to June and live theater in August (☎654 70 18; fax 70 24). Grab a bite at the **Migros** market and restaurant to the right of the station and get a clear view of the castle and the Thunersee. (Open M-Th 8am-6:30pm, F 8am-9pm, Sa 7:30am-4pm.)

The mountain piercing the sky above Spiez is the **Niesenberg** (2363m). Hikes on the mountain, while not for beginners, are accessible and wind through the neighboring towns of Niesen, Kulm, and Schwandegg. Pick up hiking maps at tourist offices in Interlaken, Thun, or Spiez. Hiking all the way up or down the mountain is tough, but a **funicular** chugs to the top, and the **Lötschberg train** towards Reichenbach from Spiez (every hr., 7.20SFr round-trip) connects with the funicular at Mülenen. (June-Nov., 8am-5pm; 43SFr round-trip, 32.30SFr with Swisspass, half price after 4pm.) The funicular's builders pushed the frontiers of human achievement by building steps alongside the track, which became the **longest flight of steps in the world.** Unfortunately, only professional maintenance teams are allowed to use the steps (all 11,674 of them).

BRIENZ AND THE ROTHORN   ☎033

Anachronistic but authentic curiosities, including Switzerland's oldest cog railway, a park of traditional Swiss dwellings, and wood-carvers galore fill the lakeside town of Brienz. The tempo of life here is cued by the opaque green waters of the bordering **Brienzersee**, which move slowly below sharp cliffs and dense forests.

⚏⚐ TRANSPORTATION AND PRACTICAL INFORMATION. Brienz makes an ideal daytrip from Interlaken by **train** (20min., every hr. 6:36am-10:35pm, 6.60SFr) or **boat** (1¼hr., every hr. 8:20am-5:32pm, 15.20SFr). Brienzersee cruises leave Interlaken's Ostbahnhof (June-Sept. every hr. 8:31am-5:40pm; Apr.-May and late Sept.-Oct. 4 per day 9:31am-2:31pm; Eurail and SwissPass valid). The station, dock, and Rothorn cog railway terminus are on the right boundary of the town, flanked on Hauptstr. by the post office, banks, and a supermarket. The Brienz-Dorf wharf bookends the town on the west end. The hostel and campsites lie a short walk along the lake east of the town proper. Brienz's **tourist office,** Hauptstr. 143, is across and left from the train station. (☎952 80 80; fax 80 88. Open M-F 8am-noon and 2-6pm, Sa 9am-noon and 4:30-6pm; July and Aug. M-F 8am-noon and 1-6pm, Sa 9am-12:30pm and 4:30-6pm, Su 4:30-6pm.) The train station **exchanges currency** and has **lockers** (3-5SFr; both open daily 6:30am-9pm). **Police** ☎ 117; **ambulance** 144; **Rotbahn Pharmacy** across from Walz Tea Room (open M-F 8am-12:15pm and 1:30-6:30pm; Sa 8am-4pm; 24hr. emergency ☎951 15 29). **Park** at the Parkhaus Co-op behind the Co-op on Hauptg. (1½hr. limit M-F 7am-7pm, Sa 7am-4pm; unlimited parking M-F 7pm-7am, Sa 4pm-7am.) The **post office** is next to the train station. (☎951 25 05. Open M-F 7:45am-6pm, Sa 8:30-11am.) **Postal code:** CH-3855.

⚏⚐ ACCOMMODATIONS AND FOOD. The **Brienz Jugendherberge (HI) ❷,** Strandweg 10, 400m west (left facing the lake) along the lakeside path from the train station, offers summer-camp-style bunks with doorstep access to the lake. (☎951 11 52; fax 22 60; brienz@youthhostel.ch; www.youthhostel.ch/brienz. Breakfast included. Dinner 11.50SFr. Kitchen facilities. Reception 7:30-10am and 5-10pm. Open mid-Apr. to mid-Oct. Dorms 27SFr; doubles 62SFr.) **Hotel Garni Walz ❹,** Hauptstr. 102, to the left from the station on the main road, offers centrally located rooms overlooking the lake, each with shower. (☎951 14 59; fax 42 26; walz@switzerland-hotel.ch; www.firstweb.ch/walz-brienz. Singles 85SFr; doubles 120-140SFr. AmEx/MC/V.) For a luxurious getaway at a reasonable price, head farther down the street to **Seehotel Bären Brienz ❹.** Wide hallways decorated with old jazz posters lead the way to spacious rooms with balconies overlooking the river. (Breakfast included. Reception 7:30am-9pm. Check-out 11am. Singles 60-75SFr, with shower 65-84SFr; doubles 65-84SFr/84-98SFr; also available with small foreroom. AmEx/DC/MC/V.) Two campgrounds lie past the hostel on the waterfront. **Camping Aaregg ❶,** past the other campsite along the waterfront, has an on-site restaurant. (☎951 18 43; fax 43 24. Reception 8am-noon and 2-8pm. **Bikes** 25SFr per day. Open Apr.-Oct. 14.20SFr per tent.) **Camping Seegärtli ❶** is more secluded and offers free lake swimming and fresh bread at 8am. (☎951 13 51. Parking 15SFr. Reception 8am-7pm. Open Apr.-Oct. 15SFr per 1-person tent.)

Both the Seehotel Bären and Hotel Walz also have worthwhile restaurants. In a quiet dining room decorated with candles the **Bären ❹** offers a vegetarian menu (15.50-23.50SFr), fish options (23.50-36.50SFr), or house specialities such as lamb filet, 32.50-38.50SFr. (Open 7:30am-midnight. AmEx/DC/MC/V.) **Walz Tea Room ❸** has a covered terrace with a view of the lake and the Axalphorn. The welcoming cafe offers a wide variety of salads (14.90-26SFr), omelettes (14-16.50SFr), and pastas (10.50-18.50SFr). Internet access is also available for 5SFr per 15min. (☎951 14 59. Open 8am-10pm. AmEx/MC/V.) **Steinbock Restaurant ❸,** farther along Haupt-

BERNESE OBERLAND

THE ALPHORN TREE If a Swiss pine tree looks suspiciously like an Alphorn, it's with good reason. Instead of growing perpendicular to the ground, the sturdy trees that cover the steep mountain sides of the Alps first grow straight out from the mountain and then curve upward towards the sun. For some, the gentle curve that develops in their trunks becomes the rounded bell of the alphorn. Stripped of its bark, cut in half, and hollowed out, the former tree is bound back together with wicker and fitted with a mouthpiece so traditional musicians can create melodies throughout the hills and valleys. Farmers have been playing Alphorns to call their cattle from the hills since the Middle Ages.

str., provides outside tables and a warm wooden interior. (☎951 40 55. Swiss-style macaroni with apple sauce 18SFr; sausage salad 16SFr; filling house *Rösti* including ham, cheese, tomato, bacon, and eggs 19.50SFr. (Open 8:30am-11:30pm. AmEx/DC/MC/V.) The **Co-op** is on Hauptg. across from the station. (Open M-Th 7:45am-6:30pm, F 7:45am-8pm, Sa 7:45am-4pm.)

▥ **MUSEUMS.** The **Freilichtmuseum Ballenberg** (Open-Air Museum), on Lauenenstr. in the nearby town of Ballenberg, is an 80-hectare country park dedicated to the preservation of Swiss heritage. Authentic rural Swiss houses are clumped by geographical region into 13 villages; most were transplanted from their endangered original locations. Many have live exhibitions of traditional trades, such as iron-smithing or cheese-making. A new addition to the *Schokoladerei* provides **chocolate demonstrations** and **taste-testing**. *(☎952 10 30. Open from mid-Apr. to Oct. 10am-6pm. 16SFr, with visitor's card 10% off. The park is a 1hr. walk from the train station, but a **bus** also connects the two every hr. 6:45am-5pm, round-trip 6SFr.)*

Brienz is also the center of cantonal wood-carving schools. The **Kantonale Schnitzlerschule** (Wood-Carving School; ☎951 17 51) and the **Geigenbauschule** (Violin-Making School; ☎952 18 61) both provide galleries that display their craft. Both centers lie on Schleeg., 400m from the station, in the western end of town. Home to 10 students, the *Geigenbauschule* houses a collection of antique instruments and a showroom of finished violins for a mere 5,000SFr each. *(Wood-carving open M-Th 8-11:30am and 2-5pm, F 8-11:30am and 2-4:15pm; July until mid-Aug. and mid-Sept. until mid-Oct. M-F 8-11:15am. Violin-making open Sept.-May M-F 8-11am and 2-5pm; June-Aug. call for opening hours. Both free.)*

Additionally, the **Jobins Living Woodcarving Museum** lets visitors watch artisans at work, learn about the history of wood-carving, and try their hands at a work-in-progress public display. *(☎952 13 00; info@jobin.ch; www.jobin.ch. Open May-Oct. 8-11:30am and 2-5pm; Nov.-Apr. M-Sa 8-11:30am and 1:30-5pm. Admission 5SFr; guided tour 15SFr.)* Many local wood carvers also let tourists watch them work; contact the tourist office for a list.

▨ **HIKING.** The **Rothorn** (2350m) is the most accessible peak near Brienz thanks to the **Brienz Rothorn Bahn.** At 108 years, it is the oldest cog steam railway in Switzerland. (☎952 22 22; www.brienz-rothorn-bahn.ch. Runs June-Oct. 1hr., every hr. 7:39am-4:10pm, last descent 5:30pm; 44SFr, round-trip 68SFr. Bernese Oberland pass 22SFr/34SFr; with SwissPass 33SFr/57SFr.) Getting off at **Planalp,** halfway up the mountain, allows medium-range hikes back down. Follow the railway down, turning left below Planalp to head through Baalen and Schwanden (3½hr.). From the summit, head east toward the lake and turn right at the Eiseesaltel, continuing down to Hofstetten, Schwanden, and Brienz (4hr.). Shelter is available at the **Hotel Rothorn** on the summit. (☎951 12 21; fax 12 51. Breakfast included. Reception 8-11am and 2-5:30pm. Dorms 34SFr, 200m from hotel and bathrooms; singles 90SFr; doubles 140SFr.)

A bus from the station climbs to **Axalp** (8:15am-4:15pm, 9.20SFr) where you can hike to the **Axalphorn** (2321m) on the opposite side of the lake from Brienz, by walking along either the east or west ridge (800m, half-day). Bring a map (check the tourist office at Brienz) and be aware, as both paths are indistinct in places.

Boat service gives access to the Brienzersee's south shore. **Giessbach Falls,** with 14 cascades, is a 10min. ride from Brienz (6.60SFr) and a 1hr. ride from Interlaken. The walk to the falls passes a palatial hotel (15min.), also accessible by cable car from the dock (4.50SFr, round-trip 6SFr). From the hotel, a bridge traverses the river to the falls. A path to the left, along the streams, offers a view of all the waterfalls. At the top, a ridge walk leads to the right over the lake, and then down to the breezy lakeside village **Iseltwald** where a ferry travels to Brienz. (Mid-June to mid-Sept. every hr. 9:09am-6:12pm; mid-Sept.-Oct. 4 per day 11:40am-4:40pm; 9.20SFr.)

For a low-key walk turn right from the train station and take the footpath to the left toward the **Wildpark** and discover where the wood-carvers get their inspiration. Always open and free.

INTERLAKEN   ☎ 0 3 3

In AD 1130, two literal-minded Augustinian monks named the land between the **Thunersee** and the **Brienzersee** "Interlaken," or "between lakes." That land has grown from a collection of small medieval villages to a booming modern city. Geographically, Interlaken lies at the foot of some of the largest and most famous mountains in Switzerland: the **Eiger, Mönch,** and **Jungfrau,** providing easy access to several natural playgrounds. Beneath the enchanting sight of the Jungfrau (4158m), the town spreads out around a large central green, the **Höhematte,** a popular landing pad for the hundreds of paragliders that drift down from the skies each day. Thanks to its mild climate and natural wonders, Interlaken has earned its rightful place as one of Switzerland's prime tourist attractions and as its top outdoor adventure spot.

▄ TRANSPORTATION

By **car,** Interlaken lies on A6. The city has 2 train stations. The **Westbahnhof** stands in the center of town bordering the Thunersee, near most shops and hotels; trains to Bern, Basel, and other western towns stop here. The **Ostbahnhof,** on the Brienzersee 1km from the town center, is slightly cheaper for connecting to eastern towns. Both stations post hotel prices and offer courtesy phones for reservations.

Trains: The **Westbahnhof** (☎826 47 50) and **Ostbahnhof** (☎828 73 19) have trains every hour to: **Bern** (6:39am-10:34pm, 24SFr); **Basel** (5:33am-10:34pm, 56SFr); **Geneva** (5:33am-9:35pm, 63SFr); **Lucerne** (5:33am-8:39pm, 26SFr); **Lugano/ Locarno** (5:33am-4:37pm, 87SFr/76SFr); and **Zurich** (5:33am-10:34pm, 62SFr). **Jungfraubahnen,** Harderstr. 14 (☎828 72 33; fax 72 60; www.jungfraubahn.ch) runs all trains to the small towns on the way up to the Jungfrau. SwissPass valid for Wengen, Mürren, and Grindelwald, 25% discount at higher stops. Eurail 25% discount on the Jungfraubahnen. Trains leave every 30min. June-Sept., and every hr. Sept.-May. from the Ostbahnhof to: **Grindelwald** (6:35am-10:35pm, 9.80SFr) and **Lauterbrunnen** (6:35am-10:35pm, 6.60SFr); with connections to **Kleine Scheidegg** (6:35am-4:35pm, 36.40SFr), **Mürren** (6:35am-7:35pm, 16.40SFr), **Wengen** (6:35am-10:35pm, 12.40SFr), and the **Jungfraujoch** (6:35am-3:35pm, 163.80SFr round-trip, or 125.80SFr with Good Morning Ticket; see **The Jungfraujoch,** p. 354).

Taxis: Interlaken Ost, ☎822 80 80. **West,** ☎822 50 50.

Luggage: Lockers at train station 3SFr.

Parking: Parking is 7SFr per day at the train stations, behind the casino on Centralstr.

BERNESE OBERLAND

Bike Rental: At either **train station,** 30SFr per day; 23SFr per half-day. Open 6am-7pm. **Intersport Oberland,** Postg. 16 (☎822 06 61; fax 73 07) rents mountain bikes. 30SFr, 20SFr per half-day; in-line skates 20SFr per day. Open M-F 8am-noon and 1:30-6:30pm, Sa 8am-noon and 1-4pm. AmEx/DC/MC/V. Some hostels also rent bikes or motor scooters.

Post Office: Marktg. 1 (☎224 89 50). From the Westbahnhof, go left on Bahnhofpl. Open M-F 8am-noon and 1:45-6pm, Sa 8:30-11am. **Postal Code:** CH-3800.

▶ PRACTICAL INFORMATION

Tourist Office: Höheweg 37 (☎826 53 00; fax 53 75), in the **Hotel Metropole,** has free maps and info. Open July-Aug. M-F 8am-6:30pm, Sa 8am-5pm, Su 10am-noon and 4-6pm; Sept.-June M-F 8am-noon and 1:30-6pm, Sa 9am-noon.

Currency Exchange: UBS Bank near the Westbahnhof and **Raiffeisen Bank** near the Ostbahnhof have **ATMs,** as do both train stations. Available in the **train station** (☎826 47 36), though rates are 1% better in town. Open 8am-6pm.

Bookstore: Buchhandlweg Haupt, Höheweg 11 (☎822 35 16). Bestsellers, translation dictionaries, and travel books. Open M-F 8:30am-6:30pm, Sa 8:30am-4pm.

Library: Marktpl. 4 (☎822 02 12). Novels in English. Open M-Tu 3-6pm, W 9-11am and 3-7pm, Th 3-6pm, F 3-7pm, Sa 10am-noon.

Laundromat: Self-Service Wash & Dry, Beatenbergstr. 5 (☎822 15 66). Cross the bridge to the left of the Westbahnhof and take the 2nd right onto Hauptstr. The manager will do laundry for 12SFr per load. Open M-Sa 8am-noon and 1:30-6pm; Sa closes at 4pm. Self-service 6-8SFr; open daily 7am-10pm. **Backpacker's Villa** (see p. 346) has self-service laundry (10SFr; soap included), as does **Balmers,** 8SFr (see p. 348).

Snow and Weather Info: For the Jungfrau, ☎828 79 31.

Emergencies: Police, ☎117. **Hospital,** ☎826 26 26. **Doctor,** ☎823 23 23.

Pharmacy: Grosse Apotheke, Bahnhofstr. 5A (☎822 72 62) and **Pharmacie Internationale,** Höheweg 4 (☎828 34 34), both open M-Sa 7:30am-6:30pm, until 7pm in summer. AmEx/MC/V.

Internet Access: Many hotels, restaurants, and both train stations have quick access terminals. **YESS** on Centralstr. houses 5 terminals (4SFr per 20min.), while **Dolcevita,** Marktpl. behind the post office, offers 7 stations in an ice cream cafe (12SFr per hr.). Both open 11am-11pm. The **Backpacker's Villa** has 4 computers and **Balmers** 2 (10SFr per hr.).

▶ ACCOMMODATIONS

Interlaken guest accommodations have a wide range of atmospheres. Those at Balmers and Funny Farm tend to party as late as the city will allow, while Backpackers provides a more low-key but lively social scene. Further away from the city, Boltigen's Swiss Adventure Hostel creates its own community and offers guests a respite from the wild "spring break" crowds.

▨ **Backpackers Villa Sonnenhof,** Alpenstr. 16 (☎826 71 71; fax 71 72; backpackers@villa.ch; www.villa.ch) diagonally across the Höhenmatte from the tourist office. This central but secluded, remodeled villa is friendly and low-key—perfect after a tough day of backpacking. Spacious rooms have wooden balconies with views of the Jungfrau and Harder Mann. Services include TV with CNN, movies, mountain bike rental (28SFr per day; 18SFr per half day), laundry (10SFr per load, soap included), free phone for taxis, and **Internet** access (10SFr per hr.). Includes breakfast, kitchen, showers, lockers, towels, sheets, and recreation and meditation rooms. Reception 7:30-11am and 4-10pm. Check-out 7-9:30am, but guests can leave luggage for a 2SFr deposit. No cur-

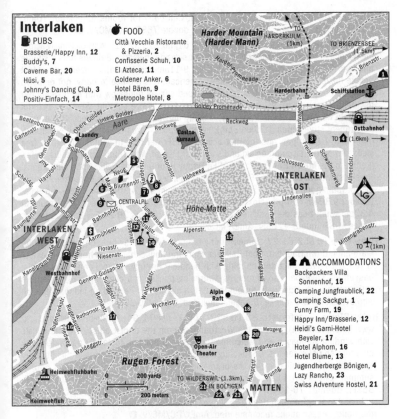

Interlaken

🍺 PUBS

Brasserie/Happy Inn, **12**
Buddy's, **7**
Caverne Bar, **20**
Hüsi, **5**
Johnny's Dancing Club, **3**
Positiv-Einfach, **14**

🍗 FOOD

Città Vecchia Ristorante
& Pizzeria, **2**
Confisserie Schuh, **10**
El Azteca, **11**
Goldener Anker, **6**
Hotel Bären, **9**
Metropole Hotel, **8**

▲ ⛺ ACCOMMODATIONS

Backpackers Villa
Sonnenhof, **15**
Camping Jungfraublick, **22**
Camping Sackgut, **1**
Funny Farm, **19**
Happy Inn/Brasserie, **12**
Heidi's Garni-Hotel
Beyeler, **17**
Hotel Alphorn, **16**
Hotel Blume, **13**
Jugendherberge Bönigen, **4**
Lazy Rancho, **23**
Swiss Adventure Hostel, **21**

few. Call or arrive early in the morning to have a chance at a room. 4- to 7-bed dorms 29-32SFr; doubles 82-88SFr; triples 111-120SFr. 5SFr per person extra for Jungfrau view, balcony, and in-suite bathroom. AmEx/MC/V. ❷

🏅 **Swiss Adventure Hostel,** is in the tiny town of Boltigen (☎773 73 73; fax 73 74; info@swissadventures.ch). A free shuttle runs to and from Interlaken each day (40min.); call for times and availability. The Adventure Hostel has staked its place in this quiet valley as a sporty alternative to the party scene in Interlaken. A small adventure company run out of this hostel offers the same activities as Interlaken companies but with a more personal touch: after your canyoning trip, you eat dinner with your trip leader. **Internet access** (15SFr per hr.), **mountain bike rental** (25SFr per day), a cellar bar and small dance floor (open 9pm-2am), TV, and restaurant (breakfast buffet 7SFr, dinner 12-18SFr) with accomplished chef. Check-in 10am-11pm. 4- to 10-bed dorms 20SFr; double with shower 70SFr; quad with shower 100SFr. Special deals if you do a few adventure sports with them. AmEx/MC/V. ❷

Happy Inn, Rosenstr. 17 (☎822 32 25; fax 32 68; info@happy-inn.com; www.happy-inn.com) lives up to its name with a friendly staff and simple style. From Westbahnhof, go left toward the tourist office and right onto Rosenstr. at the Centralpl. This multi-level building houses clean and spacious 4- to 8-person dorms with metal bunks and lockers.

Free **parking** in back. Reception 7am-6pm. Call early for rooms. Check-out 10am. Breakfast 8SFr. Dorms 22SFr; singles 38SFr; double 76SFr. DC/MC/V. ❷

Balmers Herberge, Hauptstr. 23-25 (☎822 19 61; fax 823 32 61). Walk diagonally across the Höhenmatte from the tourist office and follow signs down Parkstr. Balmers runs a shuttle bus June-August from both stations (every hr. 9-11am and 1-6pm). Switzerland's oldest private hostel (since 1945) is thoroughly American. It is a place to party, not relax. To enjoy the dorms or Balmers tent (a huge striped canvas bungalow with no insulation a few blocks from town), you must value camaraderie above comfort. Services include: **mountain bike rental** (35SFr per day), nightly movies, TV with CNN and MTV, a mini-department store (open 7:30am-8pm), safety deposit boxes (2SFr) available 6:30am-noon and 4-10:30pm, and **Internet access** (20SFr per hr.). In winter, they offer **free sleds** and a 20% discount on ski and snowboard rental. After 9pm, activity shifts underground to the **Metro Bar** (beers 4.50SFr; Happy Hour 9-10pm, 3SFr. Open until 2am.). Breakfast included. Kitchen 1SFr per 20min. Laundry 8SFr per load. Reception in summer 6:30am-noon and 4-10pm; in winter 6:30-10am and 4:30-10pm. Check-out 9am. Lockout 9:30am-4:30pm. No curfew. Sign in early, drop off your pack, and return at 4:30pm when beds are assigned (no reservations). Dorms 20-24SFr; doubles 68SFr; triples 90SFr; quads 120SFr. AmEx/MC/V. ❷

Funny Farm (☎652 61 27; James@funny-farm.ch; www.funny-farm.ch), behind Hotel Mattenhof, down Hauptstr. from Balmers. More frat house than youth hostel, this estate is very accommodating and hopping with people. Currently, Funny Farm offers tennis, basketball, volleyball, an enormous swimming pool with a climbing wall, adventure activities through Alpin Raft, an outdoor bar, a nightly bonfire, and an indoor nightclub with occasional live reggae. Breakfast included. Dorms 20-25SFr. ❷

Hotel Blume, Jungfraustr. 30 (☎822 71 31; fax 71 94; hotel-blume@tcnet.ch; www.hotel-blume.ch), toward the Westbahnhof from the tourist office, attracts guests with winding staircases and welcoming rooms in a building tastefully decorated with blue trim and Mexican art. Connecting doors and a central location make this hotel an ideal option for families or groups of travelers. Reception 7am-midnight; from 6am in summer. Check-out 11am. Breakfast included. Singles 50-75SFr, with shower 75-85SFr; doubles 70-100SFr/110-150SFr; family room 150-200SFr. Ask about the unbeatable **Jungfraujoch** deal–165SFr per person for a double and ticket to the "top of the world." Reservations recommended. AmEx/DC/MC/V. ❸

Hotel Alphorn, Rugenstr. 8 (☎822 30 51; fax 823 30 69; www.hotel-alphorn.ch; accommodation@Hotel-Alphorn.ch). Turn right onto Bahnhofstr., left onto Rugenstr. and right again onto Rothornstr.; it's behind Hotel Eiger. The Alphorn boasts newly remodeled doubles with clean beds, sparkling bathrooms with showers, and TVs with CNN. Breakfast included. 100-150SFr. For slightly more, the three-star **Hotel Eiger** in front has antique rooms with the same amenities, intricate wooden floors, and in-room tea and coffee. Singles 90-120SFr, doubles 130-180SFr. Large 3-person room available (210SFr.) Reception for both 6:30am-10:30pm. Check-out 11am. AmEx/MC/V. ❹

Heidi's Garni-Hotel Beyeler, Bernastr. 37 (☎/fax 822 90 30). Turn right from the Westbahnhof, go left on Bernastr. and walk straight for 300m (5min). Eccentric owners preside over a rambling old house decorated with sleds, bells, old photographs, carousel horses, and old furniture. Private rooms are available with bath and balcony. Common room with TV, kitchen, and laundry (7SFr). **Bikes** 29SFr per day; tours 39SFr. Reception 7am-1am. Check-out 10am. Dorms 23SFr; 2- to 4-bed room 60-140SFr. Doubles 80-90SFr; quad 135-160SFr; 8-person room 250SFr. MC/V. ❷

Jugendherberge Bönigen (HI), Aareweg 21 (☎822 43 53; fax 823 20 58). Take route #3 or #4 (dir: Bönigen) to "Lütschinenbrücke" (5min.), or a 25min. walk. Caters to a younger crowd. This hostel is far removed from the adventure scene in Interlaken. Try to snag a 6-bed room instead of the 25-bed "Good Morning" dorm on the top floor. Breakfast, kitchen, showers, and sheets included. Dinner 12.50SFr. Lockers 2SFr deposit. Laundry 8SFr. **Bike rental** 15SFr per day. Reception 7-10am and 2-11pm. Reserve at least 2 days in advance June-Aug. Closed from mid-Nov. to mid-Dec. 6- and 25-bed dorms 27.70SFr; 4-bed dorms 31.70SFr; doubles 81.40SFr. Additional 6SFr for non-members. ❷

CAMPING

Camping Sackgut (☎079 656 89 58) is closest to town. Head toward town from the Ost-bahnhof, turn right across the 1st bridge, and take another right onto the footpath or road. A few choice spots are available by the river, but most of the campground lies in an exposed grassy parking lot. Laundry 4SFr. Reception 5-7pm. Apr.-June and Sept. Oct. 4.40SFr per person, 6-10SFr per tent, tent bungalow 65SFr, parking 2SFr, electricity 2SFr; July-Aug. 6SFr. per person, 6.50-15SFr per tent, tent bungalow 95SFr, parking 3SFr; electricity 3SFr. Trash 1SFr. ❶

Camping Jungfraublick (☎822 44 14; fax 16 19). Take bus #5 from the Westbahnhof toward Widerswil, and continue 5min. past Balmer's on Gsteigstr. This peaceful location has splendid mountain views. Open May-Sept. 6.50SFr per person, off-season 5.80SFr; tent 8SFr. Reception 8-10am and 4-6pm; summer 7-11am and 2-8pm. ❶

Lazy Rancho (☎822 87 16; fax 823 19 20; www.lazyrancho.ch; info@lazyrancho.ch). Head past Jungfrau Camping and left onto Lehnweg. This spacious, clean campground is equipped with a swimming pool, store, playground, kitchen, and laundry facilities (4-6SFr). Open mid-Apr. until mid-Oct. 5.50-6.90SFr per person, 3-4SFr per child, 7-10SFr per tent site, electricity 4SFr. MC/V. ❶

FOOD

Interlaken has a wide range of restaurants, but generally, the Balmers crowd eats at Balmers (bratwurst and burgers under 10SFr), the hostel crowd eats at the *Jugendherberge* (12.50SFr), and the Funny Farm folks eat from their renovated cable car (wraps 10SFr; burgers and fries 12-15SFr). Most of the restaurants listed here are on Marktg. Head up Aareckstr., the tiny street left from Westbahnhof, and turn left on Spielmatte. **Co-op,** across from the Ostbahnhof or behind the Westbahnhof, also houses a restaurant. (Open M-Th 8am-7pm, F 8am-9pm, Sa 7:30am-5pm; restaurant additionally Su 9am-5pm.)

Restaurant Goldener Anker, Marktg. 57 (☎822 16 72). This family-run restaurant has many traditional specialties and vegetarian dishes. The California salad (grilled turkey strips on lettuce and fresh fruit, 16.50SFr) is delicious. For dessert try Crepe Normandy—stuffed with apples and vanilla ice cream (8SFr). Frequently hosts live bands. Billiards available. Open M-W and F-Su 10am-12:30am. ❸

Confiserie Schuh (☎822 94 41), across from the tourist office, has been an Interlaken landmark since the 19th century. Among a wide array of scrumptious goodies, chocolate medallions (1SFr) and strawberry tarts (5SFr) sell like mad in the summer. Open daily 8am-9pm. ❶

El Azteca (☎822 71 31), downstairs from Hotel Blume, serves up some of the best Mexican food outside of Mexico. Select from a large variety of Mexican delights (12-20SFr) or choose from the four daily lunch *Menüs:* Mexican (16.50SFr), international (15SFr), Swiss (14SFr), and vegetarian (14.50SFr), served noon-1:45pm. June-Sept. open daily M-Tu and Th-Su 7am-11:30pm; Oct.-May 8am-2pm and 6-11:30pm; closed Jan. AmEx/MC/V. ❷

Metropole Hotel (☎ 828 66 66), next to the tourist office, offers two fine dining opportunities. The panoramic restaurant **Top o' Met ❸** offers classics such as *Rösti* (17.50-19.50SFr) and a Sunday brunch with a variety of meat, salad, and dessert buffets (11am-2pm, 42SFr) along with an overview of the city and surrounding mountains. Open 11am-11pm; food until 10pm. **Ristorante Bellini ❹**, the hotel's signature restaurant, serves fine cuisine overlooking the spacious green Höhematte. Try calf liver on *Rösti* with apple slices (30SFr) and tiramisu (10.50SFr) for dessert or choose from a selection of pastas in two sizes (14.50-29.50SFr). Open 11:30am-2:30pm and 6:30pm-midnight. AmEx/DC/MC/V.

Città Vecchia Ristorante and Pizzeria (☎ 822 17 54), Untere G. 5. From Marktpl., follow Spielmattestr. across the river and turn left onto Untere G. Set off from the hustle of the main street, this upscale restaurant offers Italian specialties at reasonable prices. Pizzas (13-19.50SFr) and pastas (13-22SFr) both include a number of vegetarian options. Select from the seasonal menus (22-40SFr) and variety of fine Italian wines (3.50-6SFr per glass). Open 10am-midnight. Closed Sept. 20-Oct. 15 and Tu from Oct. 16-Mar. AmEx/DC/MC/V. ❸

Hotel Bären, Marktg. 19 (☎ 822 76 76). *Rösti* platters (16.50-21.50SFr), seasonal specialties and other hearty Swiss dishes in a warm wood dining room. Open M-Sa 8:30am-11:30pm, also Su July-Aug. ❸

OUTDOORS NEAR INTERLAKEN

> Interlaken's adventure sports industry is thrilling and usually death-defying, but accidents do happen. On July 27, 1999, 19 adventure-seeking tourists were killed by a flash flood while canyoning on the Saxeten river. Be aware that you participate in all adventure sports at your own risk.

ADVENTURE SPORTS. Interlaken's steep precipices, raging rivers, and wide-open spaces serve as prime spots for such adrenaline-pumping activities as paragliding, white-water rafting, bungee jumping, and canyoning (a sport in which wet-suited thrill-seekers rappel, dive, and swim through a canyon). **Alpin Raft** (☎ 823 41 00 or 334 62 02; fax 41 01; mail@alpinraft.ch; www.alpinraft.com), the most established company in Interlaken, has qualified, personable guides, and promises "unlike some first time experiences, this one will be great." All prices include transportation to and from any hostel in Interlaken: **paragliding** (150SFr), **canyoning** (110-195SFr), **river rafting** (95-109SFr), **skydiving** (380SFr), **bungee jumping** (125-165SFr), and **hang gliding** (180SFr). **Outdoor Interlaken** (☎ 826 77 19; fax 77 18; www.outdoor-interlaken.ch) offers **rock-climbing** lessons (89SFr per half-day) and **white-water kayaking** tours (155SFr per half-day). **Swissraft** in Boltingen offers similar adventures, **hydro-speeding** (aided body-surfing down the river; 110SFr), and all-day combinations of multiple activities. (☎ 823 02 10; www.swissraft.ch.) **Skydiving Xdream** charges 380SFr per tandem jump. Stefan Heuser, the owner, has been a member of the Swiss skydiving team for 17 years, including two years as a coach. (☎ (079) 759 34 834; info@justjump.ch; www.justjump.ch. Open Apr.-Oct.)

The independent **Swiss Alpine Guides** (☎ 822 60 00; fax 61 51; mail@swissalpineguides.ch; www.swissalpineguides.ch) lead full-day **ice-climbing** clinics (May-Oct., 150SFr), as well as full-day **glacier treks,** which journey to the other side of the Jungfrau (June-Oct. 120SFr). Interlaken's winter activities include skiing, snowboarding, ice canyoning, snow rafting, and glacier skiing. Contact the **tourist office** (☎ 826 53 00) or any of the adventure companies for information.

HIKES FROM INTERLAKEN. The towns closer to the mountains offer longer, more strenuous treks, but Interlaken has a few good hikes of its own. The most traversed trail climbs to the **Harder Kulm** (1310m, or Harder Mann). Only the Jungfrau can be seen from Interlaken itself, but from the top of this half-day hike, the Eiger and Mönch are also visible. This view is a striking mountainscape, with the black, triangular face of the Eiger framed by the other two snowy behemoths. The easiest starting point is near the Ostbahnhof. From the Ostbahnhof, head toward town, take the first road bridge across the river, and follow yellow signs to "Harderkulm" that later give way to white-red-white *Bergweg* flashes on the rocks. From the top, signs lead back down to the Westbahnhof. A funicular runs from the trailhead near the Ostbahnhof to the top. (2½hr. up, 1½hr. down; May-Oct. 13.40SFr, round-trip 21SFr; 25% discount with Eurail/SwissPass.)

Flatter trails lead along the lakes that flank the city. Turn left from the train station, then left before the bridge and follow the canal over to the nature reserve on the shore of the Thunersee. The trail winds up the Lombach river, then through pastures at the base of the Harder Kulm back towards town (3hr.).

◧ NIGHTLIFE

If you still have energy at the end of the day, Interlaken provides plenty of options for its release. **Balmer's** (p. 348) offers live music on most nights, most often reggae (beer 4.50SFr; bar open 9pm-1am). The **Caverne Bar,** in the basement of the Mattenhof Hotel, in front of the Funny Farm, serves 3.50SFr beer and alternates between live music and techno. (☎821 61 21. Open W-Su 10pm-2:30am.)

If you're feeling adventurous, head beyond the hostel confines to one of the local hangouts. **Buddy's,** Höheweg 33, is a small, crowded English-style pub where the beer is only 3.50-5SFr. (☎822 76 12. Open daily 10am-12:30am.) **Johnny's Dancing Club,** Höheweg 92, located in the basement of the Hotel Carlton, is Interlaken's oldest disco and serves drinks from 6SFr. (☎822 38 21. Open Tu-Su 9:30pm-3am.) For smoky blues try **Brasserie,** Rosenstr. 17. (☎822 32 25. No cover. Beer from 3.20SFr. Open M-Sa 8:30am-12:30am, Su 3pm-12:30am.) **Positiv Einfach,** Centralstr. 11, is a dark cocktail bar complete with a mood room in the back. Mixed drinks 11.50-12.50SFr, but check for theme days, like Tuesdays when almost everything is 6SFr. (☎823 40 44; www.positive-einfach.ch. Open 5pm-12:30am; F-Sa until 1:30am.) For a local taste of this touristed city, check out **Hüsi,** Postg. 3. Beers are 3-4.50SFr and pizzas, ordered specially from a neighboring pizzeria, 14-20SFr. (☎822 33 34; www.huesi.ch. Open Tu-Su 4pm-12:30am; F-Sa until 1:30am.)

The apex of Interlaken's cultural life is the summer production of Friedrich Schiller's **Wilhelm Tell** (in German; English synopsis 2SFr). Lasses with flowing locks and 250 bushy-bearded local men wearing heavy rouge ham up the tale of the Swiss escape from under the Habsburg thumb. The showmanship is complete—20 horses gallop by in every scene, and a vaudeville-like stage around the corner from Balmer's allows the cast to make real bonfires. (Shows from late June to mid-July Th 8pm; mid-July to early Sept. Th and Sa 8pm.) Tickets (22-38SFr) are available at Tellbüro at the tourist office. (☎822 37 22; fax 57 33; open during run M-F 8am-noon and 1:30-5pm), or at the theater on show nights. Children under six not admitted. **Casino Kursaal,** between the Ostbahnhof and the tourist office, houses a newly opened casino and a stage for the **Swiss Folklore Show** in summer. (☎827 61 00; www.casino-kursaal.ch. Open daily from noon-2am; Th-Sa until 3am. Shows May-Sept. daily and Oct. M and Th at 7:30pm; 20SFr. Include dinner at 7pm for 19-39.50SFr more.)

⚑ DAYTRIP FROM INTERLAKEN: ST. BEATUS'S CAVES

To get to the caves, walk 15min. uphill from the Sundlauenen Schiffstation, a 30min. boat ride from Interlaken (every hr. 10:30am-5pm), or take bus #21 (9SFr round-trip from Interlaken Westbahnhof). You can also walk from Interlaken (2hr.) or Beatenberg (1hr.).

At the **Beatushöhlen** (St. Beatus's Caves) in Beatenberg village, it is possible to spelunk through 100m of glistening stalactites, waterfalls, and grottoes. At the entrance, a wax St. Beatus (the Irish hermit and dragon-slayer) stares down some (also wax) cavemen; at the exit, a sarcastic little dragon bids guests "Auf Wiedersehen." Even on hot summer days, the cave stays a cool 8 to 10° C. One-hour tours leave every 30min. from the entrance. Admission includes entry to the **Caving Museum,** 5min. downhill. This tiny room chronicles the discovery and mapping of Swiss grottoes. (☎841 16 43; fax 10 64. Caves and museum open Apr.-Oct. daily 10:30am-5pm. 16SFr, children 8SFr.)

THE JUNGFRAU REGION

A few miles south of Interlaken, the hitherto middling mountains rear up and become hulking white monsters. Welcome to the Jungfrau Region, home to Europe's largest glacier and many of its steepest crags and highest waterfalls. In summer, the region's hundreds of kilometers of hiking consistently stun tourists with astounding mountain views, wildflower meadows, roaring waterfalls, and pristine forests. The three most famous peaks in the Oberland are the **Jungfrau,** the the **Mönch** and the **Eigerr.** In English, that's the Maiden, the Monk, and the Ogre. Natives say that the monk protects the maiden by standing between her and the ogre. (Actually, the Jungfrau is 4158m high, so could probably take care of the puny, 3970m Eiger herself.) On the other side of these giants, a vast glacial region stretches southward, where six major glaciers, including the **Grosser Aletschgletscher,** at 45km long the largest in Europe, converge at **Konkordiaplatz.**

⬛ ORIENTATION. The region is split into two valleys; the first gives access to the glaciers through the town of Grindelwald, while the second, the Lauterbrunnen, holds many smaller towns, including Wengen, Gimmelwald, and Mürren. The valleys are divided by an easily hikeable ridge; on the end closer to Interlaken is the Männlichen Peak. At the other end of the ridge, near the Jungfrau, is the train town of Kleine Scheidegg. Up above, and on either side of Lauterbrunnen, are cliff ledges on which the small towns of Wengen, Mürren, and Gimmelwald are perched; none are accessible by car.

🚠 TRANSPORTATION AND OUTDOOR ACTIVITIES. The **Jungfraubahn** runs throughout the region and includes the cog-railways to the towns above Lauterbrunnen. Because of their proximity, hikes in different towns can frequently be combined, so check out hiking suggestions from other towns regardless of where you're staying. If you plan on doing any serious hiking, be sure to get a copy of the *Lauterbrunnen/Jungfrau Region Wanderkarte* (15SFr at any tourist office), which gives an overview of all of the hikes.

There are three main ski areas in the Jungfrau region: the Mürren-Schilthorn area, the Kleine Scheidegg-Männlichen area, and the Grindelwald-First area, with over 213km of downhill runs between them. The Mürren-Schilthorn area is much smaller than the other two. Day passes for the individual areas are 55SFr. Multi-day passes, which include transport on the Jungfraubahn, are only available for the whole region (all 3 areas). (☎828 72 33; fax 72 604; www.jungfraubahn.ch. Adults 2 days 118SFr, 7 days 312SFr, ages 16-19 94SFr/250SFr, children 6-15 50% discount.) Most towns have separate ski schools. For **snow information** and a **weather report,** dial ☎828 79 31.

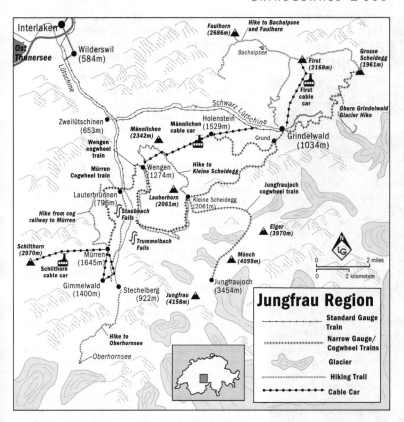

Jungfrau Region

——————— Standard Gauge Train

+++++++++++ Narrow Gauge/ Cogwheel Trains

Glacier

.... Hiking Trail

•—•—•—•—• Cable Car

GRINDELWALD ☎ 033

Grindelwald, launching point to the only glaciers in the Bernese Oberland accessible by foot, crouches beneath the north face of the Eiger—a difficult-to-conquer milestone in any climber's career. (Check out www.eiger-live.ch to experience a local Eiger ascent that was broadcast live in 1999.) It is a cold-weather Shangri-La for the outdoorsy, though the tourism can become overwhelming.

▐ ▌ TRANSPORT AND PRACTICAL INFORMATION

The Jungfraubahn runs from **Interlaken's** Ostbahnhof (40min., 6:35am-10:30pm; 9.80SFr). Trains to the **Jungfraujoch** (see **The Jungfraujoch,** feature) and **Kleine Scheidegg** (27SFr, 45SFr round-trip; Eurail or SwissPass 25% discount) leave from the Grindelwald station (every hr. 7:19am-5:19pm, 6:19pm in summer). There is also a bus from Balmers (round-trip 15SFr). The **tourist office,** in the Sport-Zentrum 200m to the right of the station, provides a kiosk for hotel reservations, chairlift information and a list of free guided excursions. (☎ 854 12 12; fax 12 10; www.grindelwald.ch. Open July-Aug. M-F 8am-7pm, Sa 8am-6pm, Su 9-11am and 3-5pm; Sept.-June M-F 8am-noon and 2-6pm, Sa 8am-noon and 2-5pm.) Services include: **laundry** at **Wash & Dry** next to Da Salvi Pizzeria on Haupstr. (☎ 853 11 68; wash 4SFr,

BERNESE OBERLAND

THE BIG SPLURGE

THE JUNGFRAUJOCH

The most arresting ascent in the Jungfrau region is up the Jungfraujoch, a head-spinning, breath-shortening, 3454m adventure on **Europe's highest railway.** Chiseled into solid rock, the track tunnels through the Eiger and Mönch mountains. Its construction was one of the greatest engineering feats of all time, requiring 16 years and 300 men. The line was to have gone even higher to the Jungfrau summit itself (4158m), but by 1912 the project was so over budget that the final 700m were left to hard-core mountaineers.

Thanks to the air's lack of pollution, the top now shelters Europe's highest manned meteorology station and the **Sphinx Laboratory** for the study of cosmic radiation. Each year, half a million visitors explore the **Ice Palace** (free), a smooth maze cut into the ice. Enjoy the ice sculpture, but watch your footing on ice floors and don't sit too long on the ice bench!

Outside, Siberian huskies pull lazy mountaineers across the snow on **sleds** for 10SFr. Budget sportsmen opt for free **"snow-hurtling,"** i.e. sledding down bunny-level slopes on garbage bags (bring your own bag). If the weather is perfect, try the 30min., snowy trek to the Mönchsjoch climbing hut. For more passive entertainment, gaze out at the frozen expanse of the Jungfraufirm glacier gripping the backside of the mountain.

Trains start at Interlaken's Ostbahnhof and travel to either Grindelwald or Lauterbrunnen, continuing to Kleine Scheidegg and to the peak itself. The entire trip is expensive, but **"Good**

dry 1SFr per 10min. of drying; open 24hr.); **weather forecast,** ☎162; **medical assistance,** ☎853 11 53; **police,** ☎117; **emergency,** ☎144. **Pharmacy Eiger** is right on the main street 100m (☎853 44 66; emergency also ☎425 68 84. Open M-F 8am-noon and 2-6:30pm; Sa 8am-noon and 2-5pm). Access the **Internet** (15SFr per hr.) at the tourist office or **Ernst Schudel's Photo Shop,** across the street. (Open M-F 9am-noon and 2-6:30pm, Sa 9am-noon and 2-6pm.) The **post office** is opposite the station. (Open M-F 8am-noon and 1:45-6pm, Sa 8-11am.) **Postal code:** CH-3818.

ACCOMMODATIONS AND CAMPING

Hotel Hirschen (☎854 84 84; fax 84 80; hirschen.grindelwald@bluewin.ch; www.hirschen-grindelwald.ch), in the center of town. Turn right from the tourist office. Offers clean, bright rooms with comfortable beds and a bowling alley. All rooms have toilet and shower, TV, telephone, and safe. Breakfast and entrance to sports center swimming pool and ice-skating rink included. Reception 8am-10pm. Singles 90-135SFr; doubles 150-220SFr. ❹

Mountain Hostel (☎853 39 00; fax 47 30; mhostel@grindelwald.ch; www.mountainhostel.ch) is a short train ride to Grund (3.80SFr) or a long walk from town. Turn right out of the Grindelwald train station, then immediately right on small trail towards "Grund." Go downhill; bear right at the Glacier Hotel. The bright blue hostel sits at the bottom of the valley. Renovated in 1996, the hostel has gleaming 4- and 6-bed dorms and a plush reception area with **Internet** (15SFr per hour), TVs, foosball, and billiards. Breakfast buffet included. Sleep sack 5SFr. Laundry 12SFr. Outdoor cooking facilities 0.50SFr. Reception 8-11am and 3:30-9:30pm. Dorms 34SFr; doubles 88SFr. ❷

Jugendherberge (HI) (☎853 10 09; fax 50 29; grindelwald@youthhostel.ch; www.youthhostel.ch/grindelwald). Exit the train station and turn left. Go straight for 400m, then cut uphill to the right just before "Chalet Alpenblume" and follow the steep trail all the way up the hill (400m). It's a hike from town, but the enormous wooden chalet is beautiful. Wood-paneled living rooms have fireplaces and many rooms have balconies facing the Eiger. Other amenities include laundry (5SFr), **Internet** (15SFr per hr.), TV and games room, and reduced entrance fees to nearby attractions. Breakfast included, lunch 8.50-11.50SFr, dinner 12.50SFr, vegetarian meals available on request. Lockers and sheets included. Reception 7:30-10am and 3pm-midnight. No lockout. Open May-Oct. and mid-Dec. until Apr. Dorms 27.50-29.50SFr; 4-bed rooms 29.50-34.50SFr; doubles 34.50SFr per person, with toilet and shower 50.50SFr. Non-members add 6SFr per person. AmEx/DC/MC. ❷

Lehmann's Herberge (☎853 31 41). Follow the main street past the tourist office and take the first right. Verena and Fritz run the only hostel in the town proper. Enjoy the comfort of their renovated home as well as their hearty homemade breakfasts (included). Reception 7am-10pm. Dorms and doubles 45SFr per person, after 1st night dorms 40SFr. ❸

Naturfreundehaus (☎853 13 33; fax 43 33; nfhostel@grindelwald.ch; www.naturfreunde.ch), just past Hotel Sonnenberg (20min. from station), offers a cozier alternative to the Jugendherberge. Wood-panelled walls and ceilings, large fluffy pillows and wooden closets add to the chalet-like atmosphere of the hostel. Laundry (4SFr; dry 3SFr), **Internet** (5SFr for 15min.), kitchen (2SFr.) and parking (5SFr) all available. Breakfast 5SFr. Check-in until 10pm. Dorms 28SFr per person. ❷

Gletscherdorf Camping (☎853 14 29; fax 31 29; info@gletscherdorf.ch; www.gletscherdorf.ch). From the station, take a right; at the ski school, turn right downhill. Follow the road through a residential neighborhood toward the RV-filled field below. The small grounds are the closest campground, and have a phenomenal view. Open May-Oct. Reception 8-10am and 5-8pm; come anytime. 6.90SFr per person, 3.50SFr per child, 6-12SFr per tent, electricity 4SFr. Showers included. ❶

 FOOD

Hotel Eiger (☎854 31 31; fax 31 30; hotel@eiger-grindelwald.ch; www.eiger-grindelwald.ch), past the tourist office on the left, offers a variety of eateries. **Memory Bistro** ❷ (open 8:30am-11:30pm) and **Barry's Restaurant** ❷ upstairs (open 6pm-12:30am) offer cheap burgers (9SFr) and veggie *Rösti* (13SFr). Barry's hosts yodelers and hand-organists for Swiss music night W. Later at night head across the hallway for the **Gepsi Bar.** (Beers from 3.50SFr. Open 5:30pm-1:30am.) At **Ye Olde Spotted Cat** (☎853 12 34), on Hauptstr. just past Hotel Hirschen, scratch a few wooden cats' heads while sipping cheap beer (3.80SFr) at this old haunt of Winston Churchill's. Open 11am-12:30am, summer F-Sa until 1:30am. Closed M and Su after 5pm.

Japan Restaurant Kabuki (☎853 60 91), on Hauptstr. past the tourist office under Hotel Grindelwalderhof, stands as a testament to the number of tourists who have made their way to tiny Grindelwald. Although the menu consists mostly of expensive sushi meals, a serving of *maki* (6 pieces 8.50-11.50SFr) or chicken curry

Morning" tickets make things cheaper (available for departures May-Oct. 6:30am, Nov.-Apr. 6:35 and 7:35am, returning before noon). All tickets are round-trip, and there is no way down from the top except by train. (Eurail or SwissPass 25% off. From Interlaken Ostbahnhof 162.80SFr, "Good Morning" ticket 125.80SFr; Lauterbrunnen 145.60SFr/108.60SFr; Grindelwald 145SFr/108SFr; Wengen 134SFr/97SFr; Mürren 165.20SFr/128.20SFr.)

Call ☎828 79 31 for a **weather forecast** or use the cable TV broadcast live from the Jungfraujoch and other high-altitude spots (in all tourist offices and big hotels). Bring **winter clothing** and food—it can be 10°C (50°F) on a July day, and in winter alcohol thermometers crack and antifreeze freezes.

(25SFr) may come as a welcome respite from the usual pounds of *Rösti* and wurst. Open M-Sa 11:30am-10:30pm. DC/MC/V. ❹

Pizzeria Da Salvi (☎853 89 99), located in Hotel Steinbock at the base of the First Bahn (see **Hiking,** below), offers a hearty meal in an Italian atmosphere. Large pizzas (14-19SFr) and a gamut of pastas (16-18.50SFr) don't overshadow the variety of unique entrees (24-41SFr). Try the oven baked lamb (31SFr) and select from a number of delectable ice cream creations for dessert (8-9.50SFr). Open 11:30am-11:30pm. ❸

Restaurant Schmitte (☎853 22 02; 853 20 04; schwizerhof@grindelwald.ch; www.hotel-schweizerhof.com.) Turn left from the train station on the main road (100m). A quiet setting for a luxurious meal. Enjoy risotto with truffles and tomatoes (25SFr; smaller portion 17SFr) or grilled sirloin tips (41SFr/30SFr) in one of the differently themed dining areas or among the fountains on the garden terrace. Open 8am-10pm. AmEx/DC/MC/V. ❺

Tea Room Riggenburg (☎853 10 59), past the tourist office away from the station, offers soups, salads, lasagnas, pastas, and fresh-baked desserts. Drink a huge hot cocoa (3.40SFr) or have a hearty *Birchermüsli* (7SFr) on the heated terrace. Open Tu-Sa 7am-10pm, Su 8am-6pm. ❶

Co-op, on Hauptstr. across from the tourist office, provides easy access to cheap groceries. Open M-F 8am-6:30pm, Sa 8am-4pm.

⚡ HIKING

Hiking possibilities in Grindelwald run the gamut from easy valley walks to challenges for top climbers. The greatest allure for the hiker is the proximity of glaciers. While most hikes are possible without the aid of expensive trains and cable cars, these means of transportation allow access to some fantastic hikes. The **First Bahn** leaves from the center of town and climbs the eastern side of the valley. (☎854 50 51; fax 50 55; firstbahnen@grindelwald.ch; www.gofirst.ch. Runs 8:30am-4:30pm; 29SFr, round-trip 46SFr.) The **Männlichen Gondelbahn, the longest cable car route in Europe,** is on the other side of the valley. (☎854 80 80. Runs 8am-4pm, until 5:15pm in summer; 32.80SFr, round-trip 52.40SFr; 25% discount with SwissPass, 50% with Eurail.) The **Bergführerbüro** (Mountain Guides Office), located in the sports center next to the tourist office, sells hiking maps and coordinates rugged activities like glacier walks, ice climbing, and mountaineering. (☎853 12 00; fax 12 22; gomountain@bluewin.ch; www.gomountain.ch. Open June-Oct. M-F 9am-noon and 2-5pm. 1-day activities 100-600SFr. Reserve ahead for multi-day expeditions.)

Lower Glacier (*Untere Grindelwaldgletscher,* 5hr. circular hike without funicular). This hike is moderately steep, becoming steeper the farther the trail proceeds, although it is conquerable in sneakers. To find the trailhead, walk up the main street away from station until signs point downhill to "Pfinstegg." Hikers can either walk the first forested section of the trail (1hr.), following signs up to Pfinstegg, or take a funicular to the Pfinstegg hut. (8am-4pm, July to mid-Sept. until 7pm. 9.80SFr.) From the hut, signs lead up the glacier-filled valley to "Stieregg," a hut that offers food.

The Faulhorn via the Bachalpsee (7hr.; shorter options available with cable cars). This is the most dramatic strenuous hike away from the glaciers. The HI hostel is the easiest starting point. Head uphill on the road (left at the Y) until signs lead upwards to Allflue, which provides clear views down into town. From Allflue, the trail leads uphill for more than 1hr. to Waldspitz. The final hike from Waldspitz to Bachsee and the Faulhorn travels through highland meadows (5hr.). On the way down, go to **Bussalp** (2hr.), where a bus goes back to Grindelwald. For those with a little less stamina and a bit more money, the **First Bahn** goes straight from town to a station only 1hr. away from the Bachsee, knocking 2-3hr. off the hike. Another level, easy 1hr. hike offering great views of the glaciers runs from the top of the First Bahn to Grosse Scheidegg, where it is possible to catch a bus to Grindelwald.

The Männlichen (1hr.). Access another easy (though more expensive) hike on the other side of the valley by taking the **Männlichen Gondalbahn.** From the Männlichen station, a quick circular hike scales the **Männlichen** peak, which divides Grindelwald from the Lauterbrunnen Valley, before continuing as a flat, 1hr. hike to Kleine Scheidegg and its intimate views of the Eiger, Mönch, and Jungfrau. Hop a train back to Grindelwald from here. This hike is easier (and free or at least with cheaper mechanical access) as part of the hike from **Wengen** (see p. 359).

LAUTERBRUNNEN ☎033

The 72 waterfalls that plummet down the sheer walls of the narrow, glacier-cut valley give Lauterbrunnen its name, "loud springs." The town of Lauterbrunnen, which lies in the middle of the valley of the same name, adjoins Switzerland's highest waterfall, **Staubbach Falls** (280m), which inspired Goethe's poem "Song of the Spirit over the Waterfall" (later set to music by Franz Schubert). Mendelssohn composed some of his "Songs without Words" in Lauterbrunnen as well. Lauterbrunnen's abundant accommodations and easy accessibility by car and train make the town an ideal base for those hiking and skiing throughout the Jungfrau region, as well as exploring the mountain villages.

🖪🔰 TRANSPORTATION AND PRACTICAL INFORMATION

Trains connect every 30min. with: Interlaken Ost (20min., 6:05am-10:05pm, 6.60SFr); Jungfraujoch (1¾hr.; 7:08am-4:10pm; round-trip 145.60SFr, "Good Morning" ticket 108.20SFr); Kleine Scheidegg (45min., 6:10am-5pm, in summer until 6:05pm, 26.80SFr); Mürren (20min., 6:42am-8pm, in summer until 9pm, 9.80SFr); and Wengen (6:10am-midnight, 5.80SFr). The **tourist office** 200m to the left of the train station provides binders of information about activities and large tables to plan your stay. (☎856 85 68; fax 85 69; info@wengen-muerren.ch; www.wengenmuerren.ch. Open Jan.-May and Oct.-Dec. M-F 8am-12:30pm and 1:30-5pm; Oct. also Sa 9am-12:30pm and 1:30-4pm; June and Sept. M-F 8am-6pm, Sa-Su 9am-12:30pm and 1:30-4pm; July-Aug. M-F 8am-7pm, Sa-Su 9am-12:30pm and 1:30-4pm, Sa until 5pm.) Services include: **currency exchange** and small **lockers** and **luggage** storage (3SFr) at the station; **bike rental** at Bike Imboden (☎855 21 14) and **ski rental** at Crystal Sports (☎856 90 90). For **medical assistance** call ☎856 26 26; for **Internet access** visit the tourist office (15SFr per hr.) or the Horner Pub (1SFr per 5min.). The **post office** is across from the station. (Open M-F 7:45-11:45am and 2-6pm, Sa 7:45-11am.) **Postal code:** CH-3822.

⌐ ACCOMMODATIONS

▧ **Valley Hostel** (☎855 20 08; info@valleyhostel.ch; www.valleyhostel.ch). Head left on the main street, past the Co-op on the right. The hostel is down a driveway on the left side of the street. Martha, the friendly owner, offers a pristine environment and a big kitchen. The large windows allow breezes to blow over the comfortable wooden bunks (with fuzzy, cow-patterned sheets) and give views of Staubbach Falls. Showers and sheets included. Laundry (10SFr) and **Internet** (5SFr per 20min) open 8am-10pm. You can request a fondue (in advance) for 16SFr. Reception 8am-noon and 2-9pm. Dorms 22SFr; doubles 52-60SFr. ❷

▧ **Hotel Staubbach** (☎855 54 54; fax 54 84; hotel@staubbach.ch; www.staubbach.ch). Turn left on the main street (400m from the station). This was one of the oldest hotels in town until it was lovingly converted by Craig and Corinne Rochin-Müller into a pleasant and affordable bed and breakfast. Worn oriental rugs lead the way to multiple rooms—each is a little different but all are clean and comfortable with running water. The dark-paneled parlor comes equipped with games, comfortable couches, cable TV, and a kids' corner. Parking and breakfast buffet included. Reception 8am-10:30pm. Check-in 3-10pm. Check-out 11am. Call early to reserve a room. Singles 55SFr, with shower 60SFr; doubles 80SFr/110SFr; 3- to 6-bed family suites 30-50SFr per person. Children in parents' bed 20SFr. 10SFr surcharge for 1-night stays. MC/V. ❸

Hotel-Restaurant Schützen (☎855 30 26; fax 29 50; info@hotelschuetzen.com; www.hotelschuetzen.com). Turn left on the main street, it's to the right. This slightly more expensive option provides comfortable beds with shiny wooden headboards. The spacious rooms come fully equipped with showers, telephones and couches. Breakfast included. Reception 7am-midnight. Check-out 11am. Singles 60-100SFr; doubles 120-170SFr; triples 150-225SFr; quads 180-240SFr. ❹

Camping Schützenbach (☎855 12 68; fax 12 75; info@schutzenbach-retreat.ch; www.schutzenbach-retreat.ch). Take a left on the main road, a left over the river by the church, and keep going down the street as it curves sharply to the right (15min.; follow the signs). This large camping complex has a variety of lodging options as well as a small restaurant and convenient store. Reception 7:30am-noon and 2-7pm. 7SFr, tents 4SFr. Dorms 16.50SFr; doubles with sink 64SFr; 4-bed "tourist rooms" in barracks-like huts 28SFr per person. MC. ❶

⚫ FOOD

Crystal Restaurant ❸ has a short menu but lots of Swiss classics. Try *Älpler-Rösti* for 15SFr, cheese fondue for 20.50SFr, or a daily *Menü* for 15-29SFr that includes salad and an entree. (☎856 90 90. Open daily 8-11am and 5:30-9pm.) **Horner Bar ❶**, farther down the street, has cheap beer (3.20SFr), pizza (8SFr), and **Internet** access for 12SFr per hr. (☎855 16 73. Open 9am-12:30am.) The disco upstairs is open until 2:30am. **Co-op** is near the hostel on the main road. (Open M-F 8am-noon and 2-6:30pm, Sa 8am-noon and 1:30-4pm.)

⚫ OUTDOORS

Lauterbrunnen's greatest hike is the flat trail that leads up the valley (about 7km). The trail below leads to a number of hiking destinations. To reach the trailhead, follow the right branch of the main road as it leaves town (toward Camping Jungfrau). It dwindles slowly to a narrow path before becoming a dirt trail through the woods. **Crystal Sport** (☎856 90 90; fax 90 99; info@crystal-lauterbrunnen.ch; www.crystal-lauterbrunnen.ch) rents hiking boots for 15SFr per day. (Open M-Sa 8am-noon and 2-6:30pm; Su 9am-noon and 4-6pm.)

HIKE DOWN THE LAUTERBRUNNEN VALLEY. The first, and hence most touristed, segment of the trail leads to the **Trümmelbach Falls**. These 10 glacier-bed chutes are the only drains for the glacial run-off of the Eiger, Mönch, and Jungfrau glaciers and pour up to 20,000L of water per second (45min.). Explore tunnels and an **underground elevator**. (Open July-Aug. daily 9am-5pm; May-June and Sept.-Oct. 10am-4pm. 10SFr; with Jungfrau region visitor's card 9SFr.) The falls can also be reached by **bus** from Lauterbrunnen (every hr., 3SFr; Trümmelbach stop).

The flat and relaxing trail leading to the Trümmelbach Falls passes the Staubbach Falls, Spissbach Falls, Agertenbach Falls, and Mümenbach Falls. After the turn-off for the Trümmelbach Falls, the trail becomes less trafficked as it makes its way toward **Stechelberg**, passing even more waterfalls (1½hr.). Stechelberg, a tiny village with a small grocery store, is the last place to catch a bus back to Lauter-

SONGS OF THE WATERFALL From its most famous visitor, J.W. Goethe—who immortalized the valley's Staubbach Falls in his "Gesang der Geisten über den Wassern"—to lesser-known but fiercely loved painters, the Lauterbrunnen Valley has inspired poet and artist alike with its silvery cascades where "in comely waves of foam/It powders white/The smooth rock,/And lightly taken/Simmers in a haze." The last verse of Goethe's poem, possibly the most famous lines in German verse, "O mortal soul,/Thou are like water's image,/O human fate,/Thou resemblest the wind!" was set to music by Schubert when he visited the falls.

brunnen (4.40SFr). From Stechelberg, the trail climbs, entering the end of the valley, accessible only by dirt road. To stay on the trail, enter Stechelberg and follow its one road to the end. The **Schilthorn Bahn cable car** runs from Stechelberg to Birg (35.40SFr), Gimmelwald (7.40SFr), Mürren (14.40SFr), and the Schilthorn (52SFr). The trips to Gimmelwald and Mürren are free with SwissPass; Eurail offers a 25% reduction on all destinations. Gimmelwald and Mürren are carless by law. Leave cars at the parking lot near the cable car (day 5SFr, week 21SFr, month 30SFr).

Trachsellauenen, a two-building enclave 50min. from Stechelberg, is the next destination on the trail. This is the departure point for the trail leading into the **nature reserve.** A 2½hr. mountainous hike leads to the tiny Oberhornsee, a lake which lies beneath the Tschingel glacier.

BICYCLING. Imboden Bike Adventures, on Lauterbrunnen's main street, rents mountain bikes for 20-30SFr per day. (☎855 21 14. Open daily May-Oct. 8:30am-6:30pm; Nov.-Apr. 9am-noon and 2-6:30pm. AmEx/DC/MC/V.) On the Mürren Loop, take a bike via funicular to Grütschalp (7.80SFr), pedal to Mürren and Gimmelwald, and roll downhill to Stechelberg and Lauterbrunnen.

WENGEN ☎033

Wengen (pop. 1,100) occupies a ledge on the cliff-curtained Lauterbrunnental. Accessible only by train, hotel golf carts and a few taxis provide all the transportation around the peaceful town. Despite its seclusion and emptiness in summer, Wengen retains a modern feel and attracts crowds of out-of-town skiers to its top resorts during the peak winter months. Because Eurail does not cover the train ride to Wengen, it is an ideal destination for summer travelers looking for a quiet break from the backpacker social scene of many nearby towns.

⌐? TRANSPORTATION AND PRACTICAL INFORMATION

Wengen is accessible by **train** from Interlaken Ost (45min., every hr. 6:35am-10:35pm, 12.40SFr) and from Lauterbrunnen (15min., every 25min. 6:10am-midnight, 5.80SFr). After stopping in Wengen, the train continues toward Kleine Scheidegg (7:25am-5:20pm, until 6:25pm in summer; 21SFr) and the Jungfraujoch (7:25am-4:30pm; only until 2:30pm in winter; 134SFr, morning ticket 97SFr). Cars can be parked in the Lauterbrunnen **parking garage** (8-16SFr per day depending on season and day of the week). The **tourist office,** to the left and up the hill from the station, doles out information on local hikes and sells maps for 4SFr or 15SFr. (☎855 14 14; fax 30 60. Open June-Sept. and Dec.-Apr. daily 9am-6pm. Other months vary, but generally closed on weekends.) Services include: **currency exchange, lockers** (3-5SFr), and hotel reservations at the train station; **pharmacy** (☎855 12 46; emergency also ☎280 55 40), to the left out of the station and 2min. past the tourist office (open M-F 8am-noon and 2-6:30pm, Sa 8am-noon and 2-5pm in the summer, later in the winter); **hospital** in Interlaken (☎826

26 26); **doctor** (☎856 28 28); and **Internet** at the station, tourist office, or **Hot Chili Peppers** (5SFr per 15min.). The **post office** is next to the tourist office. (Open M-F 8am-noon and 2-6pm, Sa 8:30-11am.) **Postal code:** CH-3823.

ACCOMMODATIONS AND FOOD

Although not one of Switzerland's more glamorous ski resorts, lodging in Wengen does not cater to the budget traveler. Visitors get the best deal by staying in one of the hostels or hotels in Lauterbrunnen. The sole budget option in Wengen, **Mittaghorn** ❷ lies down the hill on the outer edges of town. Follow the road past the Coop under the railroad tracks as it makes switchbacks toward the large yellow building withe green shutters (10min.). Once a hotel and then a schoolhouse, this building has fallen into a peeling apartment building with a mixture of rooms available from May-November. (☎745 58 50, 422 97 05, or 855 15 73; angelainthealps@hotmail.com. Kitchen, cable TV, BBQ and table tennis available. Beds or mattresses 28SFr.) On the way down the hill, turn right at the bakery for more luxurious accommodations at **Hotel Edelweiss** ❹. This chalet-style hotel has pristine and bright wooden accommodations. Each spacious room comes equipped with shower and either a balcony or TV. Breakfast included. Reception all day. (☎855 23 88; fax 855 42 8; edelweiss@vch.ch; www.vch.ch/edelweiss. June-Oct. 65-75SFr per person; mid-Dec. until Apr. 60-85SFr per person. V.)

Hot Chili Peppers ❶, left from the station past the tourist office, is centrally located and one of Wengen's main social highlights. This huge bar offers beer (3.50SFr) and snacks (mostly sandwiches; 7-9.50SFr) as well as **Internet** access (5SFr per 15min), billiards, and darts. (☎855 50 20; chilis@wengen.com. Open 8:30am-2am.) ▓**Ristorante da Sina** ❹, with its intimate, candle-lit tables and extensive wine selection (from 6SFr per glass), sits up the hill from Chili Peppers. Although most menu items are quite pricey (22-49SFr), there are affordable options. Large pizza margherita is 14SFr.; with added goodies like asparagus, artichokes, and spinach, it's 19SFr. Take-out and smaller portions (11-19SFr) available. (Open 11:30am-2pm and 6-11:30pm. AmEx/DC/MC/V.) Next door is **da Sina's Pub,** which hosts a variety of discos, live music, and karaoke. (Beer 4SFr; 0.5L 6.50SFr. Happy Hour 9-10pm and 12-1am offers 2 beers for 4.50SFr. Open 6pm-2:30am.) A **Co-op** supermarket sits opposite the station. (Open M-F 8am-12:15pm and 1:30-6:30pm, Sa 8am-4pm.)

OUTDOOR ACTIVITIES

Wengen's elevation above the valley floor puts it close to the treeline and provides spectacular views. The following 7hr. **hike** from Wengen traverses the ridge dividing the two valleys of the Jungfrau Region, above the tree line almost the entire time. Several cable car stops along the way can shorten the journey.

HIKE TO MÄNNLICHEN AND KLEINE SCHEIDEGG. (7hr.). The hike begins with an ascent of **Männlichen.** Walk up the main street, away from the tourist office, and towards the end of town; follow signs upward to "Männlichen" (red-and-white marked trail). The trail wanders upwards through a meadowed lane cleared by cows. As is true for the whole ascent of Männlichen, there are views of the glacier-laden side of the Jungfrau and the cliff-curtained Lauterbrunnen valley. Toward the top, be sure to turn left when another unmarked trail merges in. The climb to the Männlichen saddle steeply zigzags upwards for about 3hr. The cable car from Grindelwald stops at the saddle, a 15min. stroll from the peak, a vertical promontory with a 360° view of the Bernese Oberland. Walk back down to the Männlichen cable car station and restaurant, then follow the signs to **Kleine Scheidegg.** This highly populated trail curves, without climbing, around the contour of the ridge, all the while looking down on the Grindelwald valley and up to the towering Eiger, Mönch, and Jungfrau. It is possible to take the train from Kleine Scheidegg down to Wengen (21SFr) or Grindelwald (28SFr), or hike back to Wengen on a trail alongside the tracks (2hr). For a quieter hiking option cross over the train tracks and follow the red-and-white trail. The trail passes the Mönch and Jungfrau as closely as is possible on foot, then swings toward Wengen (2½hr. downhill).

SKIING. The **Swiss Ski School** (☎/fax 855 20 22; ski.school@wengen.com; www.wengen.com/sss), beside the Co-op, is the cheaper of the town's two schools. (48SFr for a 3hr. lesson; 5 lessons for 199SFr. Open from late Dec. to early Apr. Su-F 8:30am-1:30pm and 3:30-6:30pm; Sa 8:45-11am and 4:30-7pm.) **Privat Ski and Snowboard School** (☎/fax 855 50 05 or ☎448 71 24; privat@wengen.com; www.wengen.com/privat), as its name suggests, offers lessons to smaller groups. (1-2 people 65SFr per hour; 3-4 70SFr per hr. Office open 5-6:30pm.) Every January, Wengen hosts the skiing World Cup's longest and most dangerous downhill race, the **Lauberhorn.** Hotels generally won't allow tourists to book rooms until about a week in advance so that they can guarantee a room for all the racers and support crews. The downhill course starts 2315m above Kleine Scheidegg, curls around Wegenalp, and ends at Ziel (1287m) at the eastern end of the village, a drop of nearly 1200m in 2½min. This year the town will celebrate with two back-to-back downhill races and slalom on the 3rd day (Jan. 17-19, 2003).

MÜRREN
☎033

The quiet, car-free streets of Mürren (pop. 430) are frequented mostly by tractors and tourists. This gem of a town is lined primarily with hotels and guest houses that sprouted up when Mürren invented slalom skiing. Mürren's most popular sight is the Schilthorn, which Hans Castorp scaled in *The Magic Mountain,* a novel by Thomas Mann. The multitude of hikes, the quiet, friendly atmosphere, and the stunning landscape make Mürren and nearby Gimmelwald destinations in which travelers stay much longer than expected.

▐▀ ▐▌ TRANSPORTATION AND PRACTICAL INFORMATION

Mürren can be reached by cogwheel **train** from **Lauterbrunnen** (every 30min. 6:25am-8:30pm, 9.80SFr), or by **cable car** from Gimmelwald (7.40SFr) or Stechelberg (14.40SFr). Alternatively, **hike** from Gimmelwald (30min. uphill). From the station, the road leading into town forks in two; nearly everything, except the tourist office, is on the lower, left fork. The cable car is at the opposite end of town from the train station. The **tourist office,** in the sports center 100m from the station, off the right fork, has information about private rooms, hiking trails, and skiing prices. (☎856 86 86; fax 86 96. Open July-Aug. M-F 9am-noon and 1-6:30pm, Sa 1-6:30pm, Su 1-5:30pm; Sept.-May M-F 9am-noon and 2-5pm; June M-F 9am-noon and 2-6:30pm.) There are **lockers** (2SFr) at the train and cable car stations. **Stäger Sport** across from the tourist office rents **hiking boots** for 12SFr and mountain **bikes** for 35SFr. (☎855 23 55. Open 9am-noon and 1:30-5pm. Closed May and November.) For **police,** call ☎855 76 11; for **Medical assistance,** call ☎855 17 10. The Eiger Guest House provides **Internet** access (12SFr per hr.) all day, or try the **Feuz** souvenir shop down the main road (10SFr per hr. Open daily 11am-6pm). The **post office** is on the station side of the main street. (Open M-F 8:15-11:30am and 2:30-5pm, Sa 8:15-10:15am.) **Postal code:** CH-3825.

ACCOMMODATIONS AND FOOD

Mürren's accommodations are quiet and comfortable in comparison to the alternatives down the hill in Gimmelwald (see p. 353), but they're also less fun. An enthusiastic British woman at the **Chalet Fontana ❸** offers traditional Swiss lodging in seven private rooms with tea and coffee. (☎855 26 86 or (078) 642 34 85; chaletfontana@muerren.ch. Breakfast included. Reservations recommended. 35-45SFr per person.) The **Eiger Guesthouse ❸**, across the street from the train station, is pristine and comfortable. (☎856 54 60; fax 54 61; eigerguesthouse@muerren.ch.; www.muerren.ch/eigerguesthouse. Breakfast included. Free access to pool and skating rink at Sports Zentrum and **Internet** access for 12SFr per hr. Reception M-F 8am-11:30pm, Sa-Su 8am-12:30am. Dorms 39-44SFr in summer, 45-60SFr in winter; doubles 100-110SFr/110-140SFr, with shower 130-140SFr/140-170SFr. 1-night stays 5SFr extra per person in summer. AmEx/DC/MC/V.) **Alpina Hotel ❹**, down the left fork in the main road, provides chalet-style rooms with showers, balconies and fluffy comforters. Ask for a view of the Eiger, Monch and Jungfrau. Breakfast included. (☎855 13 61; fax 10 49; alpina@muerren.ch; www.muerren.ch/alpina. Singles 75-100SFr; doubles 130-170SFr. AmEx/DC/MC/V.)

Eating out in Mürren is reasonably cheap. *Raclette* and an unobstructed view of the snow-capped mountains are available for 14.50SFr at **Hotel Alpina ❸.** Try the house *Rösti* for 17SFr. The **Eiger Guesthouse ❸** also offers specialties such as fondue (20.50SFr; min. 2 people) or burgers (10.50-17.50SFr) and beer (5.20SFr for 0.5L). **Tham Chinese Restaurant ❷**, down the left fork from the train station, serves Asian food with cheap pan-fried noodles. Wonton noodles are 11.50SFr; vegetable fried rice is 12.50SFr. (☎856 01 10. Open June-Oct. daily 11:30am-9:30pm; Dec. 15-Apr. noon-11pm. Closed May and Oct. 20-Dec.15.) Mürren's **Co-op,** which comes in handy for trips to Gimmelwald, is 15min. down the right fork of the main walkway. (Open M-F 8am-noon and 1:45-6:30pm, Sa 8am-noon and 1:45-4pm.)

HIKING

Mürren's location on the ledge above Lauterbrunnen makes it the ideal starting point for numerous higher-elevation hikes around the Lauterbrunnen Valley. From Mürren (1645m) the trails leading to Gimmelwald, Stechelberg, and the Trümmelbach Falls provide unparalleled views of the Eiger, Mönch, and Jungfrau. Ask at the tourist office for maps and suggestions.

Grütschalp (top of funicular from Lauterbrunnen) to Mürren (1-2hr.). A flat, 1hr. hike follows the train tracks to Mürren. A more isolated mountain route takes twice as long, but has better views. Both trails start across the tracks from the station balcony. A yellow sign to Mürren marks the easier trail, while the red-white-red "Mürren Höhenweg" sign marks the mountainous hike. After an initially steep ascent, the trail wanders through buttercup meadows that stretch before the rising peaks of the Eiger, Mönch, and Jungfrau. When the trail splits, head to "Allmenhubel," then down to Mürren.

Stechelberg and Obersteinberg (1½-5hr.). This hike is a steep descent from the Mountain Hostel in Gimmelwald that gives continual views of the sheer rock slabs lining the Lauterbrunnen Valley. It's a grand approach to **Trümmelbach Falls** (1½hr.), with a return possible by cable car. Or, 5min. after the river crossing on the Stechelberg path, hikers may take a trail that forks right and climbs along the flank of the unsettled Lauterbrunnen valley head. The trail reaches the **Obersteinberg hut** (1½hr. more), which offers overnight lodging, before continuing to the **Oberhornsee** (2hr.).

Northface Trail (2-3hr.) requires sturdy shoes, but offers a comfortable hike from the Allmendhubel (accessible by cograil) to Mürren with breathtaking views of the snow-covered north faces of the Bernese Alps. Follow the multiple signs marking this trail and explaining the history of the mountains.

Schilthorn descent (3-4hr.). For fit and experienced hikers. Head downhill along the secured ridge to **Roter Herd.** At the signpost, backtrack on the left towards the Schilthorn, then take the steep descent to the Rotstock Hut on **Poganggenalp.** Continue to **Bryndli** where a steep narrow trail connects to **Spielbodenalp.** From there a mountain road descends gently to Mürren.

⚠ OTHER OUTDOOR ACTIVITIES

UP THE SCHILTORN. The most popular journey this side of the Lauterbrunnen Valley is the short, albeit expensive, cable car trip to the Schilthorn (2970m) made famous by the exploits of 007 in *On Her Majesty's Secret Service.* (☎823 14 44; fax 24 49; info@schilthorn.ch; www.schilthorn.ch. From Mürren 37.60SFr, round-trip 62.20SFr; morning ticket 46.80SFr round-trip.) The **Piz Gloria Restaurant ❸** spins at its apex. Settle down for a meal (entrees around 20SFr) and take in the 360° panorama from the Schilthorn station's deck. Bear in mind that there is very little to do at the top when it's cloudy.

The ski school has classes for downhill, slalom, and snowboarding. (☎/fax 855 12 47. Six half-day group lessons run 135SFr. For ski pass information see the **Jungfrau Region** introduction, p. 352.) The Inferno Run seeks volunteers every January (usually for 3 days from the 20th) for the Inferno downhill ski, which descends 2170m. The Inferno Triathlon is in August; the Mürren-Schilthorn stretch is last.

NEAR MÜRREN: ▓ GIMMELWALD   ☎033

Gimmelwald is a farming town of slightly over 100 people that was stopped in its tracks over 50 years ago when it was labeled an avalanche zone. The warning has not frightened away backpackers, who often outnumber the locals and inhabit the lower end of town. It retains the most secluded, rustic feel of any town in the Jungfrau. The lack of late-night hangouts has fostered a lively communal atmosphere at the hostel. The lower road in Mürren leads downhill (30min.) to Gimmelwald, as does the **cable car** (7.40SFr) from either Mürren or Stechelberg (just up the valley from Lauterbrunnen). Gimmelwald has **no supermarket,** so stock up in Mürren. Fresh-baked bread (2.50-4.50SFr), fresh milk, and yogurt (both 1.20SFr) are available at Esther's Bed and Breakfast and the Mountain Hostel (see below).

All the beds in Gimmelwald lie along the small trail that rises from the cable car station. At the bottom of the trail, the social **Mountain Hostel ❷** is run by a laid-back couple, Petra and Walter, who offer a communal kitchen and access to life's essentials—fresh bread (3SFr), milk (2SFr), chocolate (2SFr), **Internet** (12SFr per hr.), billiards, and guitars. (☎855 17 04; mountainhostel@tcnet.ch. Showers 1SFr. Reception 8:30-11am and 5:30-10:30pm. Lockout 9:30-11am. Dorms 17SFr.)

At **Hotel Mittaghorn ❹,** at the trail's summit, Walter makes *Glühwein* (mulled wine) and Heidi cocoa (with peppermint schnapps). He also cooks a three-course dinner for guests (15SFr) in Edelweiss suspenders. (☎855 16 58. Breakfast 12SFr. Showers 1SFr for 5min. Order meals in advance. Open Apr.-Nov. Old, wooden beds in the attic 25SFr; doubles 70-80SFr; triples 100SFr; quads 125SFr. Add 3SFr for a 1-night stay.) At **Esther's Bed and Breakfast ❷,** travelers can sleep in the hay in a barn or in a guest house with more comfortable rooms. (☎855 54 88. Breakfast, shower, and kitchen access included. Place in the hay 20SFr; singles 30SFr; doubles 70-85SFr; triples 90SFr; quads 140SFr.) The **Gimmelwald Guest House ❸** provides the only conventional restaurant, serving bratwurst with *Rösti* for 16.50SFr. (Breakfast 12:30-2:30pm. Dinner served after 6:30pm; reserve early.)

BERNESE OBERLAND

WESTERN BERNESE OBERLAND

KANDERSTEG   ☎ 033

Kandersteg sits at the head of the green Kander valley, which extends north to
Spiez, against the imposing peaks of the Doldenhorn (3643m) to the southeast, and
to Bonderspitz (2546m) to the west. It is also the northern terminus of the Lötschberg tunnel, the only connection between the Valais and Bern that doesn't make a
large detour to the east or west. Short day-hikes lead to isolated glacial lakes,
mountain passes with views of the Bernese Alps, and some of Europe's largest glaciers. Slightly out of the way, and noticeably devoid of crowds of English-speaking
backpackers, Kandersteg seems to have been overshadowed by towns nearer the
Jungfrau, but as far as hiking goes, it can compete with them all.

▐▐ TRANSPORTATION AND PRACTICAL INFORMATION

Trains connect Kandersteg north to Spiez (30min., every hr. 5:23am-10:39pm,
16.20SFr) and then Interlaken Ost (1hr., 22SFr), or south to Brig (35min., every
hr. 6:46am-12:38am, 18.80SFr). To reach the center of town, follow the road perpendicular to and right of the train station 75m until it meets the main road. The
tourist office, left along the main road, offers **Internet** access (10SFr per hr.) and
hiking information. (☎ 675 80 80; fax 80 81; info@kandersteg.ch; www.kander-
steg.ch. Open July-Sept. and Jan.-Mar. M-F 8am-noon and 1:30-6pm, Sa 8:30am-
noon and 1:30-4:30pm; Oct.-Dec. and Apr.-June M-F 8am-noon and 2-5pm.) The
Kandersteg Wanderkarte (hiking map; 16.80SFr), an invaluable resource for any
hike, is sold at the tourist office and most stores. The tourist office also offers
an online description of several hikes or a paper version on location. Services
include: **currency exchange, lockers** (4-5SFr), **luggage storage** (5SFr), and **bike
rentals** (30SFr per day; 23SFr per half-day) at one counter of the train station
(open daily 7:10am-7:30pm); **taxis** (☎ 671 23 77 or (079) 333 39 33); **medical assistance** ☎ 675 14 24; **helicopter rescue** ☎ 1414; and **weather report** ☎ 162. A **post office**
is next to the Co-op. (Open M-F 8-11:30am and 2:30-6pm, Sa 8-11am.) **Postal
code:** CH-3718.

▐ ACCOMMODATIONS

Kandersteg International Scout Center (☎ 675 82 82; fax 82 89; reception@kander-
steg.sout.org). Bus from the train station (5min., every hr. 7:20am-6:40pm, 2SFr) to
"Pfadfinderzentrum," or head right on the main road until it goes under the railroad
tracks and it's on the right (20min.). The Center's cheerful, multilingual volunteer staff
prepares beds in the institutional chalet and places at the campsite. The area can be
overrun with groups of scouts and the train runs audibly nearby, but it does provide a
wide range of amenities. The Center organizes a comprehensive array of outdoor activities, including **mountain biking** (35SFr per person), **canyoning** (86-110SFr), **rock
climbing** (23-25SFr per person for a group lesson), and **river rafting** (46-69SFr), and
offers discounts on train rides and nearby tourist attractions. Breakfast 6SFr, lunch
11SFr, dinner 13SFr; order in advance. Kitchen included. Bread, milk, and other staples
available at the reception. Sheets 3SFr. Laundry 6SFr. **Internet** access 2SFr per 15min.
Finnish sauna 9SFr. Reception M-Sa 8:15-11:45am and 2-5:30pm, Su 9:15-11:45am
and 2-5:30pm; longer hours in summer. Call at least a week in advance for reservations. Bed in the chalet 21SFr, 16SFr for scouts; campsite 10.50/8.50SFr. ❷

Hotel National (☎675 10 85; fax 22 85), right on the main road (1km). Has a number of rooms branching from a small common space and filled with wood bunk beds; also offers themed private rooms with a common bathroom. Breakfast included. Kitchen 5SFr. Dorms 32SFr (22SFr without breakfast); singles 60SFr; doubles 100SFr; triples 120SFr. No credit cards. ❸

Hotel Garni Alpenblick (☎675 11 29; fax 21 29; hotel.alpenblick.kandersteg@bluewin.ch), left on the main road, welcomes guests with clean rooms complete with balconies, fluffy comforters, and night stands. TV and game room. Reception 8am-midnight; check-out by noon. Reservations recommended. Rooms 48-58SFr per person; with shower 55-65SFr. Buffet breakfast included. AmEx/DC/MC/V. ❸

Hotel Alpina (☎675 12 46; fax 675 12 33; alpinakandersteg@bluewin.ch, www.alpina-online.com), left on the main road at the north end of town, is great for families, despite the medieval weaponry on the walls of the TV lounge. Multiple sized rooms, some with extra beds, all with shower, toilet, and TV; play room (open 9am-9pm); and a large backyard with a swingset add to the friendly atmosphere. Breakfast included. Reception 8am-11pm; check-in after 2pm; check-out by 11am. Reservations recommended. Closed Apr. to mid-May and Oct. 20-Dec. 20. Singles 67-77SFr, doubles 52-62SFr per person, family rooms (2-5 beds) 57-67SFr per person. AmEx/DC/MC/V. ❹

FOOD

Most restaurants in Kandersteg are in hotels, so don't be shy, but consider removing your hiking boots before dining. **◼Hotel Schweizerhof** ❸ (☎675 22 00), on the riverfront in the town's center, is a gastronomic gem. The wooden-shingled pagoda on the edge of a manicured garden is an ideal place to enjoy a variety of meals. Pastas 12.50-17.50SFr, salads 7-18SFr, and traditional *Käseschnitte* 13-17.50SFr. Follow any meal with a crepe (7-15.50SFr) or one of the delectable ice cream options for 8-9.50SFr. Open daily 9am-7pm, until 10pm in good weather. MC.) The **Hotel Victoria Ritter** ❸ serves elaborate Swiss specialties (18-33SFr) as well as different "Fitness" menus (23-28SFr). Try the Bärner Gnusch, a hearty one-pot mix of meats and vegetables (27SFr) or order from a variety of sandwiches for 8-17.50SFr. (Open daily 9am-midnight. Food served until 10:30pm. Closed May and late Oct. until mid-Dec. AmEx/DC/MC/V.) **Pizzeria Antico** ❷ (☎675 13 13), to the right on the main street past Hotel zur Post, has 18 pizza varieties (11.50-20SFr) and pastas (11-18SFr). (Open 12-2pm and 6-9pm.) The **Co-op** is between the station and town. (Open M-F 8am-6:30pm, Sa 8am-5pm.)

◼ HIKING

You'll pant up the mountain, then lose you breath again when you catch the views that await hikers in the Kandersteg region. Some of the longest glaciers in Europe, most notably the **Kanderfirm,** are east of town, while the **Öschinensee** is surrounded by steep cliffs that rise to jagged peaks. The **Bergsteigschule,** a climbing school, also offers guides into the mountains. (☎675 80 89; www.bs-k.ch.)

Öschinensee (20min.-1½hr.). The most easily accessible trails in Kandersteg traverse the area around the spectacular Öschinensee. The **Öschinenseebahn** departs from near the tourist office and runs to trail heads. (May 8-June 15 and Sept. 16-Oct. 20 8:45am-5pm; June 16-Sept. 1 7:30am-6:30pm; Sept. 2-Sept. 15 7:30am-5pm; 12.60SFr, 17.10SFr round-trip, children 6.30/8.60SFr.) From the top, a 20min. trail rolls to the edge of the blue lake bordered on all sides by sheer rock walls. The low pass that the trail crosses separates the Öschinensee from civilization. The **Öschinensee hut**

❷, is a perfect base for exploration on the lake's shore. Its army camp beds adjoin a living room and TV room. (May 8-June 15 and Sept. 16-Oct. 20 8:45am-5pm; June 16-Sept. 1 7:30am-6:30pm; Sept. 2-Sept. 15 7:30am-5pm; 12.60SFr, 17.10SFr round-trip, children 6.30/8.60SFr. Breakfast included. Dorms 35-40SFr; doubles 120-160SFr.) A small dock with paddleboats and rowboats allows excursions on the perfect calm of the lake. Open May-Oct. and Jan.-Apr. Paddleboats 22SFr per hr., rowboats 16SFr per hr.

Blümlisalp Glacier from the Öschinensee (3-4hr.). A steep, rocky trail—to be attempted only with hefty boots—shoots upwards from the cabin to **Fründenhorn hut** ❷ (3hr.). (☎675 14 33. Open June-Oct. 25SFr per night; children 16SFr.) A longer, more gradual trail probes the glacial region between the Kandersteg Valley and the Jungfrau Region. A trail connects the Öschinensee to the **Blümlisalp hut** ❷, a veritable stone fortress which cowers beneath the Blümlisalp glacier (4hr., open late June until mid-Oct. 27SFr, children 15SFr).

Blausee Hike (1-2hr.). Two trails lead from Kandersteg to the Blausee: one is a challenging series of steep uphills and downhills that passes through a forest (2hr.); the other is a flat passage past mountain streams, fields of flowers, and giant moss-covered boulders (1hr.). Both trails begin as 1 path, to the left of the train station (note signs). This route splits into 2 trails 20min. later. A bus also plies the route (10min., every hr. 5:23am-9:45pm) to and from the strikingly blue-green Blausee. It's surrounded by a tranquil and well-maintained nature park. The restaurant on the lake (☎672 33 33) serves fish from the on-site trout farm. Entrees run about 35SFr. (Lake open daily 9am-4:30pm. Admission 4.50SFr, children 2.40SFr.)

Kanderfirm Glacier Hike (4hr.). Take the morning bus to Selden (☎671 11 72, reservations required at the tourist office, 12SFr) and continue along the road until it turns into a trail which arrives after 2hr. at the western edge of the Kanderfirm's icy tongue.

GSTAAD AND SAANEN   ☎033

At the juncture of four alpine valleys, Gstaad and its earthier sister, Saanen (combined pop. 6,500), are at the heart of Swiss skiing country. Only a few kilometers apart, these two towns share little aside from their similar dark wood structures and chalet roofs. Saanen inhabits the mountainous scenery with contented ease. Gstaad, however, trades in goats for Gucci—its 5-star hotels and cardigan-draped tourists make it a glamorous gem in the placid farmland.

▐ TRANSPORTATION

Gstaad is accessible by **train** from Interlaken (1¾hr.; every hr. 7:22am-8:40pm; 32SFr, round-trip 64SFr) or Montreux (1½hr.; every hr. 7:05am-7:05pm and 9:32pm; 22SFr, round-trip 44SFr). Saanen can be reached from Gstaad by **train** (5min., every hr., 2.60SFr), **Post Bus** (10min.; almost every hr. M-Sa 6:35am-7:33pm, Su 7:50am-7:33pm; 3SFr) or a pleasant 40min. walk along the Yehudi Menuhin Philosophy Path (signs to Saanen lead the way from the station). **Buses** also run to Les Diablerets (50min.; 8:33, 9:50am, 12:03, 1:33pm; 12.40SFr).

◼✱◪ ORIENTATION AND PRACTICAL INFORMATION

Turn right from the train station to reach Gstaad's **tourist office,** and take the main road just past the railway bridge. Pick up a useful area map. (☎748 81 81;

room reservations and package deals ☎748 81 84; fax 81 83; gst@gstaad.ch; www.gstaad.ch. Open mid-June to Aug. and mid-Dec. to mid-Mar., M-F 8:30am-6:30pm, Sa 9am-6pm, Su 10am-5pm; other times M-F 8:30am-noon and 1:30-6pm, Sa 10am-noon and 1:30-5pm.) Saanen's **tourist office** is on its main street. (☎748 81 60; fax 81 69; saanen@gstaad.ch. Open in high season M-F 8:30am-noon and 2-5pm, Sa 9am-noon and 2-5pm.) Gstaad train station services include: **currency exchange, lockers** (3-5SFr), and **bike rental** (30SFr per day, 23SFr per half-day). **Taxis,** (☎744 80 80.) **Note:** since March 2002, you must dial the **area code** (033) at the beginning of local calls. **Webmania** (☎744 29 65; open M-Su 10am-8pm; 2SFr per 10min., more in evening) and **Cafe Pernet** in Gstaad provide **Internet** access. In an **emergency,** call ☎117. For **medical assistance,** call ☎744 86 86. Gstaad's **post office** is by the train station. (Open M-F 8am-noon and 2-6pm, Sa 8:30-11am.) **Postal code:** CH-3780.

⌐ ACCOMMODATIONS AND CAMPING

Gstaad proper has few hotels for the smaller-budgeted, but the tourist office publishes a list of all the hotels and the cheaper option, *Privatzimmer*, which are far from town. If you're looking to stay closer by and don't mind splurging, a couple hotels on the outskirts of town offer reasonable rates. From the tourist office, head right down the Promenade and toward Gsteig. About a 10min. walk from Gstaad's center lie two comparable hotels. **Sport-Hotel Rütti ❹** offers bright, spacious rooms right above a pizzeria. (☎744 29 21; fax 89 42; info@sporthotel-ruetti.ch; www.sporthotel-ruetti.ch. 80-118SFr. AmEx/DC/MC/V.) Across the street, **Hotel Alphorn ❹** provides slightly smaller rooms with TV, minibar, and a clean and family-friendly atmosphere. (☎748 45 45; fax 45 46; office@gstaad-alphorn.ch; www.gstaad-alphorn.ch. 84-110SFr. MC.)

The cheapest option in Saanen is the **Jugendherberge ❷**. From Saanen's station, go straight about 100m, turn right on the main street, head for the end of the street and follow hostel signs past the hospital. Rustic rooms upstairs contrast the brightly colored kitchen, but it is full of amenities: **bike rental** (15SFr per day, 10SFr per half-day), TV and game room, and library. Reservations recommended. (☎744 13 43; fax 55 42; www.youthhostel.ch/saanen. Breakfast and sheets included. Dinner 12.50SFr. Laundry 11SFr. Reception 8-10am and 5-9pm, though you can obtain the access code if you'll be out late. Check-out 8-10am. Closed in November. Dorms 29SFr (ask for a balcony); doubles 77SFr; triples and quads available. Prices do not include tax. Children under 5 free. Non-HI members 6SFr extra. AmEx/DC/MC/V.) **Camping Bellerive ❶** lies just off the road between Gstaad and Saanen, a 15min. walk from both. From the Saanen train station, walk past the tourist office to the intersection and follow the camping signs. (☎744 63 30; fax 744 63 45; bellerive.camping@bluewin.ch. Check-in 9-10am and 6-7pm, but you can arrive at any time. In summer 8.80SFr per adult, 4.40SFr per child, 5.30SFr per tent. In winter 9.90SFr/4.40SFr/5.30SFr.) The **Saanen campsite ❶,** "Beim Kappeli," is on the edge of town. Cross the tracks behind the station and head left along the river. (☎744 61 91; fax 60 42. 5SFr per person, 7SFr per tent, 12SFr per car. MC/V.)

◖ FOOD

To get to **Richi's Pub ❷,** turn right from the Gstaad station. Savor a burger and a beer (14-18SFr), an omelette (12-18SFr), or soup and a salad (14SFr) on leather chair in a no-frills environment (☎744 57 87; fax 99 87. 18+. Open noon-12:30am).

Meanwhile, the front of the building houses **Cafe Pernet ❷**, which offers the same fare to all ages and provides a computer for internet access at 5SFr per 20min (Open 8am-11pm). **Apple-Pie ❸**, at the intersection past the tourist office, serves tasty pizzas (14-21SFr) large enough for two. (☎744 46 48; apple-pie@gstaad.ch. Open 9am-10pm.) In Saanen, try Swiss specialties like a cold meat plate, cheese fondue for two or sauteed veal with *Rösti* (15-30SFr) at the **Saanerhof Restaurant ❸**, across from the train station. (☎744 15 15; fax 13 23; saanerhof@gstaad.ch; www.gstaad.ch/saanerhof. Open M-F 7:30am-11:30pm, Sa-Su 7:30am-12:30am.) The **Co-op,** straight ahead from the station and left on the main road, sells cafeteria meals (2.60SFr per 100g of salad) and cheap groceries. (Open M-Th 8am-6:30pm, F 8am-8pm, Sa 8am-4:30pm, cafeteria only Su 9am-5pm.)

◪ OUTDOOR ACTIVITIES

ADVENTURE SPORTS. Three main adventure companies, **Alpinzentrum** (☎748 41 61) in Gstaad and **Swissraft** (☎744 50 80) and **Absolut Activ** (☎748 14 14) in Saanen, arrange adventure activities in the area. All three companies, in addition to **H₂O Experience** (☎026 928 19 35) in Gstaad, lead **rafting** trips. (Alpinzentrum: 98SFr for 4hr., children 8yrs. or older 78SFr. H$_2$O Experience: 90SFr for 3hr., ages 10-15 70SFr. Swissraft: 105SFr for 3hr. Absolut Activ: 98SFr for 4hr.) Absolut Activ also offers **paragliding,** Swissraft offers **ballooning,** and both have **canyoning and mountain biking** trips (60-370SFr). Alpinzentrum expands its horizons by offering **climbing, glacier tours,** and **jeep safari** (98-150SFr). **CAST Balloonfahrten** (☎062 394 12 35; 380-700SFr) and Hans Büker's **Ballonhafen Gstaad** (☎026 924 54 85; 285-485SFr) launch balloon excursions. **Paragliding Gstaad** (☎079 224 42 70; 190SFr for a tandem flight) and **Mountain Skydive Fallschirmschule** (☎031 819 37 56) can also send you into the stratosphere.

The tourist office publishes a guide of **mountain-bike** trails. One trip runs from Saanen to Rougemount and back. This 8km route travels a flat course along the Saane River through brisk Saanenland meadows. **Horse-trekking** (☎744 24 60; 40SFr per 30min. lesson) or riding in a **horse-drawn cart** (☎765 30 34; 1hr. ride 25SFr per person) offer another avenue into the region. Ask about the "Easy Access" card at overnight accommodations or the tourist office. A two-night stay in the area makes you eligible for a cheap three-day pass to excursions into the mountains via gondolas, admittance to pools, and discounts off guided adventures.

HIKING. The tourist offices have free hiking maps and descriptions of local hikes. A challenging panoramic hike up the **Giferspitz horseshoe** will take your breath away. From Gstaad station, turn right on the main road, left on the main road just before the river, and take the second big road on the right over the river (signs to "Bissen"; the turn is 1km from Gstaad). Follow the yellow *Wanderweg* signs for "Wasserngrat" up the hill to the top cable car station (1936m). The more fit and adventurous might continue to the Lauenehorn (2477m) and, after a rocky scramble, farther to the Giferspitz (2541m), Gstaad's tallest peak. The path circles down to Bissen, but a bus can ease the descent. (1800m ascent. Perfect weather only. Allow 1 day.) A shorter, more accessible hike starts with a cable car ascent to Wispile and a 2-3hr. hike to Lauenensee, a lake, and waterfall nature reserve.

SKIING. In winter, Gstaad offers 250km of ski runs and 69 lifts. Experts will not be challenged but intermediates will find the runs ideal. The **Top Card ski pass** (☎748 82 82; fax 82 60; info@ski.gstaad.ch; www.skigstaad.ch) costs 50SFr a day for one sector. A 2-day pass for 95SFr covers all sectors. A week of skiing costs between 167SFr and 278SFr, depending on age. **Season ski passes** (790SFr) from the Gstaad region allow skiing in Oberengadin/St. Moritz, Kitzbühel/Tirol, Adelboden-Lenk, Alpes Vaudoises, Ordino-Arcalis, and Pal Arinsal (Andorra). Consult the tourist office for details on heliskiing, snowboarding, curling, and skating. Three snowboarding parks and a glacier offer year-round skiing.

SPECIAL EVENTS. The **FIVB Beach Volleyball World Tour** rolls through town at the end of June (free). During the second week of July, the **Allianz Suisse Open Tennis Tournament** brings clay-court action to Gstaad. (Tickets 40-100SFr.) Combining high culture and grit, the **Gstaad Polo Club** hosts the Silver Cup polo tournament in mid-August. Gstaad's **Country Night** festival is an orgy of country music in late September (Concert tickets 55-125SFr), while the **Menuhin Festival Gstaad,** a late-summer event created by Gstaad resident and violinist Yehudi Menuhin, is a bit more refined. (☎ 748 83 33; fax 748 83 39; www.menuhinfestivalgstaad.com.)

CENTRAL SWITZERLAND

With more hospitable, though less dramatic, terrain, Central Switzerland is considerably more populated than the mountainous cantons to the south. The greater population density and diversity brings a greater mass of cultural artifacts, as evidenced by innovative museums, enchanting castles, and medieval Altstädte in Zurich, Lucerne, and other towns along the shores of the region's lakes.

HIGHLIGHTS OF CENTRAL SWITZERLAND

Shock your aesthetics at Zurich's unconventional **Kunsthaus** (p. 381).

Bathe in multicolored light from the incredible stained-glass windows in Zurich's cathedrals, the **Fraumünster** and the **Großmünster** (p. 379).

Confront your mortality on the 660-year-old **Kapellbrücke,** Lucerne's famed, wooden-roofed bridge (p. 391).

Cruise the **Vierwaldstättersee** from Lucerne to Alpnachstad, where you can ascend the world's steepest cog railway to blue-shadowed **Mt. Pilatus** (p. 394).

ZURICH (ZÜRICH) ☎ 01

Battalions of briefcase-toting, Armani-suited executives charge daily through the world's largest gold exchange and fourth-largest stock exchange, pumping enough money into the economy to keep Zurich's upper-crust boutiques and posh restaurants thriving. But there is more to Zurich than money; the city was once the focal point of the Reformation in German Switzerland, led by the anti-Catholic firebrand Ulrich Zwingli. The 20th century brought an avant-garde artistic and philosophical radicalism that usurped Zurich's Protestant asceticism, attracting diverse and progressive thinkers. While James Joyce toiled away at *Ulysses* in one corner of the city, Russian exile Vladimir Lenin read Marx and dreamt of revolution in another. Meanwhile, a group of raucous young artists calling themselves the Dadaists founded a proto-performance art collective, the Cabaret Voltaire, promoting art that challenged the traditional aesthetics. A walk through Zurich's Altstadt and student quarter will immerse you in the energetic youth counter-culture that spawned subversive thinkers, only footsteps away from the rabid capitalism of the famous Bahnhofstr. shopping district.

✈ INTERCITY TRANSPORTATION

Because PTT buses cannot go into Zurich proper, the easiest way into the city is by plane, train, or car.

Flights: Kloten Airport (☎816 25 00) is a major stop for **Swiss International Airlines** (☎084 885 20 00), which emerged from the merger between Swissair and Crossair. Daily connections to **Frankfurt, Paris, London,** and **New York.** Trains to the Hauptbahnhof in the city center (every 10-20min., 5:02am-12:15am, 5.40SFr; Eurail and Swiss-Pass valid), where trains arrive from all over Europe.

Central Switzerland

By car: A1 connects **Bern, Austria,** and southern Switzerland to **Zurich.** From **Basel,** A2 connects directly to Zurich. From **Geneva,** take A1 to Lausanne, A9 to Vevey, and A12 to Zurich.

Trains: Bahnhofpl. To: Basel (1¼hr., 1-3 per hr. 4:46am-1am, 30SFr); **Bern** (1¼hr., 1-2 per hr. 4:46am-1:04am, 45SFr); **Geneva via Bern** (3hr., every hr. 5:26am-10:04pm, 76SFr); **Lucerne** (1hr., 2 per hr. 6:01am-12:07am, 19.80SFr); **Lugano** (3hr., 1-3 per hr. 6:30am-10:07pm, 60SFr); **Milan** (4½hr., every hr. 6:30am-10:07pm, 72SFr); **Munich** (4hr., 4 per day 7:33am-5:33pm, 86SFr); **Paris** (6-8hr., 2 per day 7:13am-3:44pm, 133SFr); **Salzburg** (6hr., 5 per day 7:10am-10:33pm, 97SFr); **Vienna** (9hr., 4 per day 7:10am-10:33pm, 124SFr); and **Winterthur** (25min., every 15min. 5:02 am-12:15am, 10.60SFr). Under age 26 discount on international trains.

Ferries: Boats on the **Zürichsee** leave from Bürklipl. and range from a 1½hr. cruise between isolated villages (every 30min. 11am-6:30pm, 5.40SFr, children 2.90SFr) to a "grand tour" (4-5hr., every hr. 9:30am-5:30pm, 20SFr, 10SFr for children). Ferries also leave from the top of the Bahnhofstr. harbor (every 30min. 10:05am-9:05pm, 3.60SFr) for a cruise of the Limmat River. The Zürichsee authorities (☎487 13 33) offer themed tours—there's even a chance for an "Oldies Night" on the Zürichsee with 50s, 60s, and 70s hits (July-Aug. F 7:30pm, 22SFr) or a ride on the "Salsa/Merengue" boat (June-Aug. Su 7:30pm, 22SFr). Eurail and *Tageskarte* valid on all boats.

■ ORIENTATION

Zurich sits in the middle of north-central Switzerland, close to the German border, on some of the lowest land in Switzerland. Most of the activity within Zurich is confined to a relatively small, walkable area. The **Limmat River** splits the city down the middle on its way to the **Zürichsee.** On the west side of the river are the **Haupt-bahnhof** and **Bahnhofstraße.** Bahnhofstr. begins just outside the Hauptbahnhof and runs parallel to the Limmat River to the head of the Zürichsee. Two-thirds of the way down Bahnhofstr. lies **Paradeplatz,** the town center, under which Zurich's banks reputedly keep their gold reserves. **Bürkliplatz** is at the Zürichsee end of Bahnhofstr., and many grassy quais surrounding the lake provide a spot for sun-bathers to relax and runners to make them feel lazy. On the east side of the river lies the University district, which stretches above the narrow **Niederdorfstraße** and pulses with bars, hip restaurants, and hostels. Grand bridges, offering elegant views of the stately old buildings that line the river, bind the two sectors together.

■ LOCAL TRANSPORTATION

Public Transportation: Trams criss-cross the city, originating at the Hauptbahnhof. Rides longer than 5 stops cost 3.60SFr (press the blue button on automatic ticket machines), and rides less than 5 cost 2.10SFr (yellow button)—the city is small enough to avoid long rides for the most part. Purchase a ticket before boarding and validate it by insert-ing it into the ticket machine. Policemen won't hesitate to fine you (50SFr) if you try to ride for free. Buy a 24hr. **Tageskarte** (7.20SFr), valid on trams, buses, and ferries, if you plan to ride several times. *Tageskarten* are available at the tourist office, hotels, hostels, the automatic ticket machines, or the **Ticketeria** under the train station in Shop-Ville. (Open M-Sa 6:30am-7pm, Su 7:30am-7pm.) The Ticketeria also offers 6-day cards (36SFr, under 25 27SFr). All public buses, trams, and trolleys run 5:30am-midnight. Night buses run from city center to outlying areas F-Sa at 1, 1:30, 2, and 3am.

Taxis: Hail a cab or call ☎777 77 77, 444 44 44, or 222 22 22. **Taxi for the Disabled** ☎272 42 42. 6SFr plus 3.20SFr per km, no tipping.

Car Rental: The best place to rent cars is at the tourist office. They have special deals with agencies: with **Europcar,** get a car with unlimited mileage and insurance for 159SFr per day, 117SFr for 3 or more days. **Branches** at the airport (☎813 20 44; fax 813 49 00); Josefstr. 53 (☎271 56 56); Lindenstr. 33 (☎383 17 47). Try to rent in the city as the airport charges a 40% tax.

Parking: Metropolitan Zurich has many public parking garages, but police advise parking in the suburbs and taking a tram or train for maximum safety and minimum traffic con-gestion. **Universität Irchel,** near the large park on Winterthurstr. 181, and **Engi-Märt,** Seestr. 25, are suburban lots. In the city, try parking at major department stores: **Jel-moli,** Steinmühlepl., **Migros Limmatplatz,** Limmatstr. 152, and **Globus** at Löwenstr. (All open M-F 8am-8pm, Sa 8am-5pm; 1hr. 3SFr, 2hr. 7SFr.) City parking 2SFr for 1st hr.; "Blue-Zone" 24hr. parking 10SFr; suburbs 0.50SFr per hr.

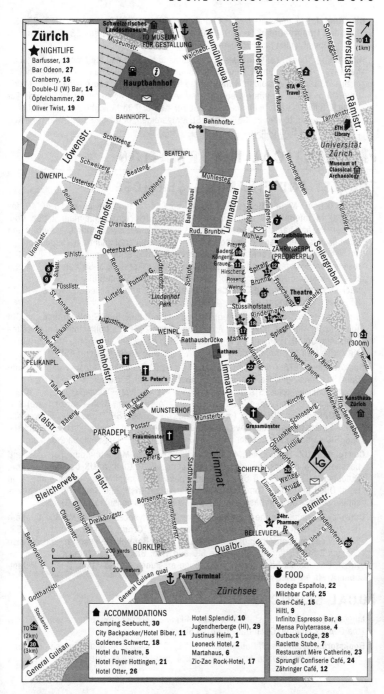

Zürich

NIGHTLIFE
Barfusser, 13
Bar Odeon, 27
Cranberry, 16
Double-U (W) Bar, 14
Öpfelchammer, 20
Oliver Twist, 19

FOOD
Bodega Española, 22
Milchbar Café, 25
Gran-Café, 15
Hiltl, 9
Infinito Espresso Bar, 8
Mensa Polyterrasse, 4
Outback Lodge, 28
Raclette Stube, 7
Restaurant Mère Catherine, 23
Sprungli Confiserie Café, 24
Zähringer Café, 12

ACCOMMODATIONS
Camping Seebucht, 30
City Backpacker/Hotel Biber, 11
Goldenes Schwertz, 18
Hotel du Theatre, 5
Hotel Foyer Hottingen, 21
Hotel Otter, 26
Hotel Splendid, 10
Jugendherberge (HI), 29
Justinus Heim, 1
Leoneck Hotel, 2
Martahaus, 6
Zic-Zac Rock-Hotel, 17

CENTRAL SWITZERLAND

Bike Rental: Bike loans are free at **Globus** (☎(079) 336 36 10); **Enge** (☎(079) 336 36 12); and **Hauptbahnhof** (☎210 13 88), at the very end of track 18. Passport and 20SFr deposit. ()pen daily 7:30am-9:30pm.)

Hitchhiking: Though *Let's Go* does not recommend hitching and the practice is illegal on freeways, hitchers to Basel, Geneva, Paris, or Bonn often take tram #4 to "Werdhölzli" or bus #33 to Pfingstweidstr. Those bound for Lucerne, Italy, and Austria report taking tram #9 or 14 to "Bahnhof Wiedikon" and walking down Schimmelstr. to Silhölzli. For Munich, hitchers have been seen taking tram #14 or 7 to "Milchbuck" and walking to Schaffhauserstr. toward St. Gallen and St. Margarethen, or taking S1 or S8 to Wiedikon and hitching at Seebahnstr.

◪ PRACTICAL INFORMATION

TOURIST AND FINANCIAL SERVICES

Tourist Offices: Main office (☎215 40 00; hotel reservation service ☎215 40 40; fax 215 40 44; information@zurichtourism.ch; www.zuerich.com), in the main station. Concert, movie, and bar information and copies of *Zürich News*, which prints restaurant and hotel listings. Decipher the German *ZüriTipp*, a free entertainment newspaper, for tips on nightlife. The **electronic hotel reservation board** is at the front of the station. The reservation desk finds rooms after 10:30am. Open Apr.-Oct. M-Sa 8am-8:30pm, Su 8:30am-6:30pm; Nov.-Mar. M-F 8:30am-7pm, Sa-Su 8:30am-6:30pm. For bikers and backpackers, the **Touring Club des Schweiz (TCS),** Alfred-Escher-Str. 38 (☎286 86 86), offers maps and travel info.

Tours: The tourist office leads frequent, expensive tours: the "Stroll through the Old Town" (2hr.; May-Oct. daily 3pm; Apr. 11am, 3pm; 20SFr); a trolley tour of major sites (2hr.; Apr.-Oct. 9:45am, noon, and 2pm; 32SFr); and a 3hr. tour of the area surrounding Zurich (3hr.; year round daily 1pm; July-Sept. also Sa-Su 4:30pm; 45SFr).

Budget Travel: STA Travel, Leonhardstr. 10 (☎261 29 55). Open M-W and F 10am-6pm, Th 10am-8pm, Sa 10am-1pm. **Branch** offices at Bäckerstr. 40 (☎297 17 17). Student package tours, STA travel help, ISIC cards. Open M-F 10am-6:30pm, Sa 10am-1pm. Also at Örlikon, open M-F 9am-6:30pm, Sa 9am-1pm. **Globe-Trotter Travel Service AG,** Rennweg 35, 4th fl. (☎213 80 80; fax 213 80 88), specializes in overseas travel. Caters to individual travelers and arranges transport. Student discounts, tickets, and ISIC cards available. Open M-W and F 9am-6pm, Th 10am-6pm, Sa 9am-2pm.

Consulates: UK, Hetibachstr. 47 (☎383 65 60). Open M-F 9am-noon. For visas and passports, UK citizens should contact the consulate in Geneva. **US Consulary Office,** Dufourstr. 101 (☎422 25 66). Visas and passports available only at the embassy in Bern. Open M-F 10am-1pm. **Australian, Canadian, Irish,** and **South African** citizens should contact their embassies in Bern. **New Zealand's** consulate is in Geneva.

Currency Exchange: At the main train station. Cash advances with DC/MC/V with photo ID, 200SFr minimum. Open daily 6:30am-10pm. **Credit Suisse,** Bahnhofstr. 53, 2.50SFr commission. Open daily 6am-10pm. **Swiss Bank,** Bahnhofstr. 45 and 70, also charges 2.50SFr, and its ATMs take MC and Visa. Branches at Paradepl. and Bellevuepl. Both banks have currency exchange machines next to ATMs. Open M-F 9am-5pm. **ATMs** are everywhere.

LOCAL SERVICES

Luggage Storage: At the station. Lockers 5SFr and 8SFr per day. Luggage watch 5SFr at the *Gepäck* counter. Open daily 6am-10:50pm.

Bookstores: Orelli Fussli, Bahnhofstr. 70 (211 04 44), has an entire English bookstore right on busy Bahnhofstr. Also at Fusslistr. 4 (☎884 98 48). Open M-F 9am-8pm, Sa

9am-5pm. **Travel Bookshop,** Rindermarkt 20 (☎252 38 83; fax 252 38 32; info@travelbookshop.ch; www.travelbookshop.ch), has a wide assortment of travel guides (including *Let's Go*) and maps. Open M 1-6:30pm, Tu-F 9am-6:30pm, Sa 9am-4pm.

Libraries: Zentralbibliothek, Zähringerpl. 6 (☎268 31 00). Open M-F 8am-8pm, Sa 8am-4pm. **Pestalozzi Bibliothek,** Zähringerstr. 17 (☎261 78 11), has foreign magazines and newspapers. Open M-F 10am-7pm, Sa 10am-4pm. **Internet** 1SFr per 10min.

Bi-Gay-Lesbian Organizations: Homosexuelle Arbeitsgruppe Zürich (HAZ), Sihlquai 67, (☎271 22 50), P.O. Box 7088, CH-8023, offers a library, meetings, and the free newsletter *InfoSchwül.* Open Tu-F 7:30-11pm, Su noon-2pm and 6-11pm. **Frauenzentrum Zürich,** Matteng. 27 (☎272 85 03), provides information for lesbians and a library of magazines and other resources.

Laundromat: Speed Wash Self Service Wascherei, Müllerstr. 55 (☎(079) 677 71 73). Wash and dry 5kg for 10.20SFr. Open M-Sa 7am-10pm, Su 10:30am-10pm.

Public Showers and Toilets: At the train station. Toilets 1-2SFr. Showers 12SFr. Open 6am-midnight. Clean enough to eat off the floor, though *Let's Go* does not recommend doing so.

Camping Supplies: TrottoMundo, Rindermarkt 6 (☎252 80 00; fax 252 01 82), located on the 2nd fl. above Oliver Twist Pub. Sells hiking, trekking, and camping gear and travel books. Tents from 340SFr. Open M-F 9am-6:30pm, Sa 11am-4pm.

EMERGENCY AND COMMUNICATIONS SERVICES

Emergencies: Police, ☎117. **Fire,** ☎118. **Ambulance,** ☎144.

Medical Emergency: ☎269 69 69. **First Aid,** ☎361 61 61.

24-Hour Pharmacy: Theaterstr. 14 (☎252 56 00; fax 261 02 10; www.bellevue-apotheke.ch), on Bellevuepl.

General Crisis Line: Help-o-Fon, ☎157 00 57

Rape Crisis Line: ☎291 46 46.

Internet Access: The **ETH Library,** Ramistr. 101, in the *Hauptgebäude,* has three **free** computers. Take tram #6, 9, or 10 to "ETH," enter the large main building, and take the elevator to floor H. Open M-F 8:30am-9pm, Sa 9am-2pm. Internet and more at **Quanta Virtual Fun Space,** Limmatquai 94 (☎260 72 66), at the corner of Mühlg. and the busy Neiderdorfstr. Open daily 9am-midnight. **Internet Café,** Uraniastr. 3 (☎210 33 11), in the Urania Parkhaus. 5SFr per 20min. Open M-Sa 9am-midnight, Su 11am-11pm. **Cybergate,** at STARS (opposite the Bahnhofpl. tourist office within the station). 15SFr per hr. Open daily 11am-11pm. **Telefon Corner,** downstairs in the station next to Marché Mövenpick, has 15 PCs. 6SFr per hr. Open daily 8am-10pm.

Post Office: Main office, Sihlpost, Kasernestr. 97, just behind the station. Open M-F 6:30am-10:30pm, Sa 6am-8pm, Su 11am-10:30pm. *Poste Restante:* Sihlpost, Postlagernde Briefe, CH-8021 Zurich. **Branches** throughout the city. **Postal code:** CH-8021.

⌐ ACCOMMODATIONS AND CAMPING

The few budget accommodations in Zurich are easily accessible via public transportation. Reserve at least a day in advance, especially during the summer.

Martahaus, Zähringerstr. 36 (☎251 45 50; fax 251 45 40; www.martahaus.ch). Turn left out of the station, cross Bahnhofbr., and take the 2nd (sharp) right after Limmatquai at the Seilgraben sign. Semi-private, partitioned dorms have clean beds, lockers, night-lights, and towels. The dorms share a large balcony. Airport shuttle every hr. after 6:20am, 20SFr. Breakfast, towels, sheets, showers, and **Internet** access included.

Laundry 10SFr. Lockers 5SFr deposit. Reception 24hr. Dorms 37SFr; singles 75-80SFr; street-side doubles 98SFR, quiet-side doubles 110SFr; triples 129SFr. AmEx/DC/MC/V. ❸ The owners of Martahaus also run the nearby **Luther pension**, a **women-only** residence that shares reception with Martahaus and is slightly cheaper (singles 50SFr). ❸

Hotel Foyer Hottingen, Hottingenstr. 31 (☎256 19 19; fax 256 19 00; info@foyer-hottingen.ch; www.foyer-hottingen.ch). Take tram #3 (dir: Kluspl.) to "Hottingerpl." It's at the corner of Hottingenstr. and Cäcilianstr. A block from the Kunsthaus, this newly renovated house has modern facilities, an in-house chapel, and a multilingual staff. Only women are allowed in the partitioned dorms during summer, but both sexes can rent other rooms. The dorm room has a balcony overlooking the city. Breakfast, lockers, showers, and kitchen included. Laundry 5SFr. Reception 7am-11pm. Breakfast 7-9:30am. 11-bed dorm 35SFr; singles 70SFr, with bath 105SFr; doubles 110SFr/150SFr; triples 140SFr/190SFr; quads 180SFr. MC/V. ❷

Justinus Heim Zürich, Freudenbergstr. 146 (☎361 38 06; fax 362 29 82). Take tram #9 or 10 to "Seilbahn Rigiblick," then take the hillside funicular (by the Migros) uphill to the end. Quiet, cheap, and relatively spacious private rooms in a residence hall with views of Zurich below. Breakfast and kitchen included. Laundry available; you pay for cost of electricity (0.50-1SFr). Reception 8am-noon and 5-9pm. Checkout 10am. Singles 50SFr, with shower 60SFr; doubles 80SFr/100SFr; triples 135SFr/165SFr; all rates reduced for multiple week stays. V. ❸

The City Backpacker-Hotel Biber, Niederdorfstr. 5 (☎251 90 15; fax 251 90 24; backpacker@access.ch; www.backpacker.ch/city-backpacker). Cross Bahnhofbr. in front of station, then turn right onto Niederdorfstr. A spiral stairwell leads up to this high traffic hostel, popular among those looking for a cheap place to crash. With Niederdorf nightlife just outside the window, you may not even need to use your bed. Pick up a free copy of *Swiss Backpacker News.* Kitchen included. Lockers available but bring a lock. Sheets 3SFr, towels 3SFr. Laundry 10SFr. **Internet** 12SFr per hr. Key deposit 20SFr or passport. Reception 8am-noon and 3-10pm. Checkout 10am and is strictly enforced. 4- to 6-bed dorms 29SFr; singles 65-66SFr; doubles 88-92SFr. MC/V. ❷

Hotel Otter, Oberdorfstr. 7 (251 22 07; fax 251 22 75; info@wueste.ch; www.wueste.ch), and the swanky **Wuste Bar** below it attract an eclectic and artsy student crowd. Hip and slightly unconventional, as evidenced by the creative decor of the rooms, Otter is an oasis for those not-so-starving artists. Floor bathrooms. Breakfast served from 9:15am (11am on weekends) until there is no more bread. Reception 8am-5pm. Check-out noon. All rooms have TV and phone. Singles 100SFr; doubles 130-160SFr; apartment with shower and kitchen 180SFr. AmEx/MC/V. ❹

Jugendherberge Zürich (HI), Mutschellenstr. 114 (☎482 35 44; fax 480 17 27; www.youthhostel.ch/zuerich). Take tram #7 (dir: Wollishofen) to "Morgental" and walk 5min. back toward the Migros along Mutschellenstr. The giant hostel (think high school gymnasium) greets travelers day and night, which may account for the long lines at breakfast, close quarters, and dirty bathrooms. Watch CNN or a free nightly movie. Dinner 12.50SFr. Breakfast, showers, and sheets included. Lockers available, but bring your own lock. Laundry 8SFr. **Internet** 1SFr per 4min. Reception 24hr., except noon-1pm. Check-in after 2pm. Check-out 10am. Dorms 32SFr; doubles with bath 90SFr. Non-members add 6SFr. AmEx/MC/V. ❷

Zic-Zac Rock-Hotel, Marktg. 17 (☎261 21 81; fax 21 75; rockhotel@ziczac.ch; www.ziczac.ch). Wake up to the sight of Bryan Adams or Queen? It's possible only at Switzerland's rock 'n' roll hotel. Funky furniture and rock 'n' roll superstar names distinguish each room, with TV, phone, and sink. Light breakfast 5SFr. Laundry 12SFr. Reception 24hr. Singles 75SFr, with shower 90SFr; doubles 120-135SFr/160SFr; triples 156SFr/168SFr; quads with shower 260SFr. AmEx/DC/MC/V. ❹

Leoneck Hotel, Leonhardstr. 1 (☎254 22 22; fax 2200; info@leoneck.ch; www.leoneck.ch). An obsession for cows and paint must have started up this divinely bovine hotel, which sits above the appropriately named restaurant, Crazy Cow. All rooms include bath, phone, TV, hair drying, and of course, plenty of cows. **Internet** (5SFr for 15min.) and **currency exchange** available. Reception open 24hr. Singles 100-140SFr; doubles 150-185SFr; 4-bed family room 240-290SFr. AmEx/DC/MC/V. ❹

Hotel du Theatre, Seilergraben 69 (267 26 70; fax 267 26 71; info@hotel-du-theatre.ch; www.hotel-du-theatre.com). Mainly geared toward businesspeople, this elegant and recently renovated hotel within view of the train station offers discounted rates on weekends. Modern facilities, including keycard access, and high cleaning standards result in highly desirable rooms. All rooms include bathroom, TV, phone, hair dryer, minibar, safe, and modem connection. Breakfast 15SFr. Singles 150-220SFr, F-Su 135-180SFr; doubles 240-260SFr/195-210SFr. AmEx/DC/MC/V. ❺

Goldenes Schwertz, Marktg. 14 (☎266 18 18; fax 266 18 88; hotel@rainbox.ch; www.gayhotel.ch). With rainbow flags proudly hanging out its windows, this gay-friendly hotel prides itself on comfort and well-decorated rooms. Distance from the two busy discos downstairs accounts for gradually higher prices on higher floors. All rooms include sheets, towels, private bathroom, hairdryer, TV, minbar, safe, and telephone. Breakfast (14.50SFr) served in room. Reception 6:30am-11pm. Singles 130-150; doubles 155-180. AmEx/DC/MC/V. ❺

Hotel Splendid, Roseng. 5 (☎252 58 50; fax 262 61 40), off Niederdorfstr., is a small hotel atop a popular piano bar. Newly renovated rooms are small, with eclectic furniture. Doesn't quite live up to its name, but convenient for Niederdorfstr. nightlife. Breakfast 9.50SFr. Hall showers included. Reception 5:30am-2am. Check-out 11am. Singles 56-70SFr; doubles 93-110SFr. AmEx/DC/MC/V. ❸

Camping Seebucht, Seestr. 559 (☎482 16 12; fax 482 16 60). Take tram #11 to Bürklipl.; catch bus #161 or 165 to "Stadtgrenze" and it will be across from the Esso station. Lakeside location makes up for the trek. Market, terrace, cafe, and restaurant on premises. Reception M-Sa 7:30am-noon and 3-10pm, Su 8am-noon. Open May-Sept. 8SFr per person, 5SFr per child aged 4-16. 1.50SFr for tax. 12SFr per small tent, 14SFr per caravan. Showers 2SFr. ❶

🗗 FOOD

Zurich's 1300+ restaurants cover every imaginable dietary preference. The cheapest meals in Zurich are available at *Würstli* stands for about 5SFr. For heartier appetites, Zurich prides itself on *Geschnetzeltes mit Rösti*, slivered veal in cream sauce with hash-brown potatoes. Check out the *Swiss Backpacker News* (at the tourist office and Hotel Biber) for info on budget meals in Zurich. Cheap kebab stands and take-out burger joints on Niederdorfstr. offer meals around 6SFr. The **Manor** department store off Bahnhofstr. 75 (corner of Uraniastr.) has a self-service restaurant on the 5th floor. (Open M-F 9am-8pm, Sa 9am-4pm.)

▧ **Bodega Española,** Münsterg. 15 (☎251 23 10). Catalan delights served by charismatic waiters since 1892. The delicate but filling egg-and-potato tortilla dishes go for 15.50SFr, yummy *tapas* served all day for 4.80SFr. Open daily 10am-12:30am. Kitchen open noon-1:30pm and 6-10pm. AmEx/DC/MC/V. ❷

▧ **Gran-Café,** Limmatquai 66 (☎252 31 19). Separated from the rushing Limmat river only by the street, the outdoor seating for this popular restaurant is often filled on warm days. Enjoy the inexpensive menus (from around 13.80SFr) or try one of their tasty dishes (from 12.80SFr) while admiring the *Great Gatsby*-esque decor. Save room for the cheap sundaes (6-8SFr). Open M-Th 6am-11:30pm, F 6am-midnight, Sa 7am-midnight, Su 7:30am-11:30pm. AmEx/MC/V. ❷

Restaurant Mère Catherine, Nägelihof 3 (☎250 59 40; fax 59 41). Hordes of locals find their way to this yuppie restaurant even though it is hidden away in a small street near the Großmünster. Serving mainly provençal French dishes (starting at 21SFr) with a lot of wine, this bustling place exudes ambience—even a live violinist—with your meal. Seafood lovers will find the bouillabaisse (19.50SFr) quite satisfying. Open daily 11am-midnight. AmEx/DC/MC/V. ❸

Hiltl, Sihlstr. 28 (☎227 70 00; fax 70 07; www.hitl.ch). Trade carrot sticks with the vegetarian elite at this swank restaurant, where the lack of meat makes things surprisingly cheap, though don't let the waitress bully you into ordering more than you want. Highlights include the all-day salad buffet, 4.60SFr per 100g (15SFr for large salad), and the Indian buffet at night (same price). Open M-Sa 7am-11pm, Su 11am-11pm. ❷

Raclette Stube, Zähringerstr. 16 (☎251 41 30). Serving a limited but high-quality menu of classic Swiss fare, this quaint, family-oriented restaurant opens onto the street and offers a good opportunity to lounge for an extended period of time surrounded by English-speakers. Large raclette appetizer 12.50SFr; fondue 39.50SFr per person; all-you-can-eat raclette 32.50SFr per person. Open daily from 6pm. ❹

Outback Lodge, Stadelhoferstr. 18 (☎252 15 75; fax 252 15 85; outback-lodge.ch). Take a walk down under without wearing down your soles at this Aussie-themed restaurant. Dishes like Kangaroo Island (29.50SFr) and Crocodile Dundee (34.50SFr) made from the real thing will make Vegemite lovers feel right at home. Open Su-Th 8:30am-1am, F-Sa 8:30-2am. ❹

Mensa Polyterrasse, behind Rämistr. 101. Take streetcar #6 to "ETH Zentrum" from Bahnhofpl. or take the red Polybahn uphill from Central Station. Eat on the open terrace with the city's church steeples at eye level (flat rate 10.50SFr with ISIC). Open M-F 6:45am-7:45pm and every other Sa 11:30am-1pm. Closed during winter recess. ❷

CAFES

▨ **Sprüngli Confiserie Café,** Paradepl. (☎224 47 11), is a Zurich landmark, founded by one of the original Lindt chocolate makers who sold his shares to his brother. A chocolate heaven, the *Confiserie-Konditorei* concocts peerless confections and delicious desserts, including an awakening mocha sundae (10.50SFr) with homemade ice cream and sherbet, served on the Bahnhofstr. patio. Pick up a handful of the bite-size Luxemburgerli for 7.90SFr per 100g. Lunch *Menüs* 20.50-25.50SFr. Confectionery open M-F 7:30am-8pm, Sa 8am-4pm. Cafe open M-F 7:30am-6:30pm, Sa 7:30am-5pm, Su 10am-5pm. AmEx/DC/MC/V.

Zähringer Café, Zähringerpl. 11 (☎252 05 00; www.cafe-zaehringer.com), across the square from the library, at the end of Spitalg., above the Altstadt. Sip coffee, tea, or Italian soda with a hip young crowd and fill your stomach with greasy goodness (*Rösti* topped with a fried egg 13.50SFr) or a variety of stir-fries (from 15.50SFr). Open M 6pm-midnight, Tu-Th and Su 8am-midnight, F-Sa 8am-12:30am.

Milchbar Café, Kappelerg. 16 (211 90 13), right behind the Fraumünster. A cheap and highly frequented lunch stop among nearby business people. Simple *Menüs* (from 15.50-19.50SFr), inexpensive soups (4.80SFr), and a popular salad bar (3.30SFr per 100g) make it a convenient and pleasant bite to eat between shopping and sightseeing. Open M-F 5am-6pm, Sa 6am-5pm.

Infinito Espresso Bar, Sihlstr. 20, is a chic and minimalist venue, serving a wide coffee selection and other yuppie drinks. Espresso from 4SFr, beers from 6SFr, sandwiches and snacks 4.50-9SFr. Open M-F 7am-10pm, Sa 8am-7pm. Prices for drinks increase about 1SFr after 8pm.

MARKETS AND BAKERIES

Two bakery chains, **Kleiner** and **Buchmann,** are everywhere in Zurich, offering freshly baked bread, sweets (whole apricot pies around 10SFr), and *Kuchen* (*Bürli* rolls 0.85SFr, *Chäschüchli* 2SFr) for reasonable prices. (Open M-F 6:30am-6:30pm.) The 24hr. **vending machine** in the Shop-Ville beneath the train station has pasta, juice, and other staples, but you may feel uncomfortable heading over there alone at night.

> **Farmer's Market,** at Burklipl. Fruit, flowers, and veggies. Tu and F 6am-11am.

> **Co-op Super-Center,** right on Bahnhofbr., is the Co-op to end all Co-ops, visible from almost everywhere. Open M-F 7am-8pm, Sa 7am-4pm.

> **Migros,** Stadelhoferpl. 16, right off Theaterstr. Open M-F 7am-8pm, Sa 8am-5pm. The adjoining restaurant has the same hours.

◎ SIGHTS

It's virtually inconceivable to start your tour of Zurich anywhere except the stately **Bahnhofstraße.** The famous causeway of capitalism has shoppers peering into the windows of Cartier, Rolex, Chanel, and Armani during the day but falls dead quiet when the shops and banks close at 6pm. At the Zürichsee end of Bahnhofstr., **Bürkliplatz** is a good place to begin exploration of the lake shore. The *Platz* itself hosts a colorful Saturday **flea market** (May-Oct. 6am-3pm). On the other side of the river, the pedestrian zone continues on Niederdorfstr. and Münsterg. with a wider range of shops from the ritzy to the erotic. From Niederdorfstr. turn right onto **Spiegelgasse,** Zurich's memory lane. Goethe, Buchner, and Lenin, who once lived on this street, are honored with commemorative plaques. A view of Zurich from overhead points to its three largest sights, **Fraumünster, Grossmünster,** and **St. Peterskirche,** all tightly packed and straddling the Limmat river.

FRAUMÜNSTER. This 13th-century cathedral stands on the site of a church founded in the 9th century by the daughters of the local sovereign, meant to be a convent for noblewomen. Its classic Gothic style juxtaposed with **Marc Chagall**'s not-so-classic stained-glass windows attracts numerous admirers, religious and not. The five choir windows depict Chagall's personal interpretations of stories from the Old and New Testament. The red window on the far left is the Prophet window, next to the blue window depicting Jacob's Ladder. Jesus Christ stands in the top of the green central window, with the yellow Zion window to the right. The blue window on the far right symbolizes the Law, crowned by Moses and the Ten Commandments. A more subdued window called "the heavenly Paradise," designed by Augusto Giacometti in 1930, is hidden in the northern transept. Outside the church on Fraumünsterstr., a mural decorating the courtyard's Gothic archway pictures Felix and Regula, the decapitated patron saints of Zurich, with their heads in their hands. If you get the feeling you're being watched, it's because floating sculptured heads peer from the corners and columns. *(Right off Paradepl. Open daily May-Sept. 9am-6pm; Oct. and Mar.-Apr. 10am-5pm; Nov.-Feb. 10am-4pm.)*

GROSSMÜNSTER. The twin Neo-Gothic towers of this mainly Romanesque church can best be viewed on the bridge near the Fraumünster. Considered to be the mother church of Zwingli's Reformation of German-speaking Switzerland, it has come to be a symbol of Zurich. The choir is ablaze in color from the blood-red and cobalt-blue stained-glass windows, depicting the Christmas story, designed in 1933 by Augusto Giacometti. Below the windows, one of Zwingli's Bibles lies in a pro-

FROM THE ROAD

A WRINKLE IN TIME

I'm the sort of person who prides herself on punctuality, and this obsession with time makes me absolutely despise getting off track. Armed with my assumptions of "the Swiss way," I couldn't wait to experience firsthand the public transportation system heralded worldwide as a model of modern scheduling. But even precision-quartz Switzerland can't make up for a lone traveler's confusion, and a tiny glitch in Swiss scheduling was enough to throw me for a loop.

On my way to Einsiedeln from Zurich, I found myself on a train that left the station (shockingly!) an entire 5 minutes late. So I mentally readjusted the time of arrival at Wadenswil by 5 minutes, and, having had a little too much fun the night before, promptly dozed off. I awoke at about 4 minutes past the original arrival time. I told myself rationally that since it had left a little late, it was therefore running a little late. I convinced myself to stay on the train until the next stop. But the next stop came and passed and so did two others. Finally I admitted to myself that I had missed my stop.

I should have known that the trusty Swiss trains would arrive on time regardless of their time of departure. If the train had left 3 years late, it probably still would have gotten there on time. I realized, seasoned traveler or not, one was bound to be impressed (and sometimes mystified) by Swiss railways.

tected case near his pulpit. One of the Romanesque columns presents a legend concerning Charlemagne's horse, in which it supposedly stumbled over the graves of Felix and Regula, 3rd-century Christian martyrs, and prompted the Holy Roman Emperor to found *Großmünster*. Venture downstairs to the cavernous 12th-century crypt to see the forbidding statue of Charlemagne and his 2m-long sword. If you're feeling active, head up the many twisting stairs to the top of one of the towers for a panoramic view of Zurich. *(Follow Niederdorfstr., which becomes Münsterg., to the end. Church open daily Mar. 15-Oct. daily 9am-6pm; Nov.-Mar. 14 10am-5pm. Tower open Mar.-Oct. daily 1:30-5pm; Nov.-Feb. Sa-Su 9:15am-5pm. 2SFr for entrance to the tower.)* In the same building is the small **Zwingli museum** and monastery. *(Open M-F 9am-4:30pm.)*

ST. PETERSKIRCHE. St. Peterskirche stakes its claim as the largest clock face in Europe. Find it near the Fraumünster, or just look up. *(Open M-F 8am-6pm, Sa 8am-4pm, Su 10-11am.)* Recently excavated Roman baths dating from the first century are visible beneath the iron stairway *(down Thermeng. from St. Peter's).*

LINDENHOF. The original site of **Turricum,** namesake and birthplace of Zurich, the park provides refuge from the daily grind. It has a giant chess board and sweeping views of the river and the Altstadt, but no grass. It attracts both locals and tourists to lounge and admire the vistas. *(Follow Strehlg., Rennweg, or Glockeng. uphill to the intersection of the three streets.)*

GARDENS AND PARKS. The lush, perfect-for-a-picnic **Rieter-Park,** overlooking the city, creates a romantic backdrop for the Museum Rietberg. *(Take tram #7 to "Museum Rietberg.")* The **Stadtgärtnerei** attracts botanists and ornithologists alike to the moist Palmhouse/Aviary, which has artificial streams running through it. The Aviary houses 17 species of tropical birds, including two fantastically plumed green parrots and a mime bird, all of which whiz freely around the building, past your shoulder, and over your head. See art students sketching in their native habitat. *(Sackzeig 25-27. Take tram #3 to "Hubertus" and head down Gutstr. ☎ 492 14 23. Open daily 9-11:30am and 1:30-4:30pm. Free.)* When the weather heats up, visit the bathing parks along the Zürichsee. Strandbad Mythenquai lies along the western shore. *(Take tram #7 to "Brunaustr." and walk in the same direction, cross to the left side of the street, and continue 2min. until you see a set of stairs. Signs hidden by the foliage lead the way. ☎ 201 00 00. Open June to mid-Aug. daily 9am-8pm; mid-Aug. to early Sept. daily 9am-7pm. 6SFr.)*

ÜTLIBERG. The "top of Zurich," this is the king of picnic spots, with a view of Zurich's urban sprawl on one side and pristine countryside on the other. The flat walk from Ütliberg to Felsenegg is a peaceful escape from the city's bustle. From Zurich's Hauptbahnhof, take the train to "Ütliberg" (15min., every 10-30min., 14.40SFr discount with *Tageskarte*), then follow the yellow signs to Felsenegg (1½hr.). A cable car runs from Felsenegg to Adliswil, where a train returns to Zurich. *(Buy tickets at any train or cable car station or at most hotels; free with Eurail.)*

OTHER SITES. The **Fluntern Cemetery** contains the graves of **James Joyce** and **Elias Canetti.** The **Zürich Zoo,** beside the cemetery, has over 250 animal species. Boasting one of the best bear enclosures around, the zoo is a much-frequented cultural treasure. Look for the opening of its gigantic living rainforest exhibit in 2003. *(Zürichbergstr. 221. Take tram #6 uphill to "Zoo." ☎ 254 25 05. Open Mar.-Oct. daily 8am-6pm; Nov.-Feb. 8am-5pm. 16SFr, ages 6-16 and students 8SFr, ages 6 and under free.)*

🏛 MUSEUMS

Zurich has channelled much of its banking wealth into universities and museums, fostering outstanding collections. The larger institutions hold the core of the city's artistic and historical wealth, but many smaller museums are equally spectacular.

ART MUSEUMS

KUNSTHAUS ZÜRICH. The Kunsthaus, which covers Western art from the 15th century on with an obvious bias in favor of the 20th century, is in itself a compelling reason to come to Zurich. The museum does a wonderful job of mixing famous locals—Segantini, Hodler, and the Giacometti family—with the international set, so that no element of the exhibition ever grows stale. The Alberto Giacometti loft is particularly well done, juxtaposing the spindly sculptures he became famous for with the not-so-spindly paintings he created at the same time. Don't miss his self-portrait. *(Heimpl. 1. Take tram #3, 5, 8, or 9 to "Kunsthaus." ☎ 253 84 84; fax 253 84 33. Open Tu-Th 10am-9pm, F-Su 10am-5pm. Multilingual audio tours available. 10SFr, students, seniors, and disabled 6SFr. W free. Added charge for special exhibits.)*

MUSEUM RIETBERG. In confident contrast to the Kunsthaus, Rietberg presents an exquisite collection of Asian, African, and other non-European art, housed in two spectacular mansions in the Rieter-Park (see **Gardens and Parks,** p. 380). Sprung from the

And that I'd been riding the train illegally for the past 3 stops.

At this point, utterly stressed, I hopped off the train and into the station. I was convinced that the lady at the ticket counter was either going to arrest me for fare avoidance or laugh in my face for my ineptitude. She didn't do either (which further confirmed that I didn't understand the Swiss way at all). She sold me a ticket back to Wadenswil and even printed out a schedule, gesturing as she sent me on my way.

When I finally got back on the right train, I made a mental note to stay awake on trains, read the schedule, and have utmost faith in the power of train schedules. As the train pulled out of the station, I realized that the computerized voice announcing the stations was off by one stop.

It felt like a small victory.

—Alinna Chung

well-known collection of Baron von der Heyt, the 50-year-old museum has firmly established itself as one of the best museums in Zurich. Park-Villa Rieter features internationally acclaimed exhibits of Chinese, Japanese, and Indian drawings and paintings. Villa Wesendonck stores most of the permanent collection of non-Western sculpture, with Bodhisattvas from India, China, Japan, Tibet, and Nepal. *(Gablerstr. 15. Take tram #7 to "Museum Rietberg." ☎ 202 45 28; www.rietberg.ch. Villa Wesendonck open Tu and Th-Su 10am-5pm, W 10am-8pm. Park-Villa Rieter open Tu-Sa 1-5pm, Su 10am-5pm. 6SFr, students 3SFr. Special exhibits and permanent collections 12SFr, students 6SFr.)*

OTHER MUSEUMS

SCHWEIZERISCHES LANDESMUSEUM. Housed in a castle right next to the Hauptbahnhof, the Landesmuseum provides fascinating insights into Swiss history with its careful reconstructions and preservation of Swiss artifacts. The generic first floor contains medieval artifacts, but the castle rooms have 16th-century astrological instruments, Ulrich Zwingli's weapons from the Battle of Kappel in which he died (1531), and a tiny bejeweled clock with a golden skeleton morbidly indicating the hour. *(Museumstr. 2, next to the main train station. ☎ 218 65 65. Open Tu-Su 10:30am-5pm and public holidays. Entrance 5SFr, students and seniors 3SFr, under 14 free. Special exhibits around 10SFr.)*

MUSEUM OF CLASSICAL ARCHAEOLOGY. As impressive as the collection of Greek and Roman vases and busts filling the first floor lecture hall is, it seems little more than a foil for the astonishing basement, which houses replicas of nearly every great statue of the ancient world from 800 BC on. *(Rämistr. 73. Take tram #6, 9, or 10 to "ETH." ☎ 257 28 20. Open Tu-F 1-6pm, Sa-Su 11am-5pm. Free.)*

MUSEUM FÜR GESTALTUNG (DESIGN MUSEUM). This museum's enormous spaces, adjoined to the School of Design, display student work, a collection of vintage advertisement posters, and temporary exhibits on subjects such as steam shovel art, female power stations, or giant corn. *(Ausstellungsstr. 60. Take tram #4 or 13 to "Museum für Gestaltung" or walk (5min.) from the main station. ☎ 446 22 11. Open Tu-Th 10am-8pm, F-Su 11am-6pm; graphics, poster, and design collections by appointment. Hall and gallery 10SFr, students 6SFr.)*

LINDT AND SPRÜNGLI CHOCOLATE FACTORY. Visitors are welcomed with an open box of Lindt chocolate and a multilingual movie about chocolate machines. The chocolate spree ends appropriately with free pieces of—what else?—Lindt

---

DA, DA, DA The silent walls of Spiegalg. 3 in Zurich's Altstadt witnessed one of the most rebellious movements in the history of art and theater. The years between the World Wars offered no lull for the city's citizens, as a group of angry young artists spilled their creativity into the craziest forms of art. The result was Dadaism, an art that refused to be art, a style whose guiding principle was confusion and paradoxical humor. Dada's aim was to provoke a rude awakening from standardized thought and bourgeois preconceptions. Dada is said to have taken its name either from the French word for "hobby-horse," which Hugo Ball selected by sticking a pen-knife into a German-French dictionary, or from the refrain of two Romanian founders of the movement, who used to mutter, "Da, da" ("yes, yes" in Romanian). Distinguished painter/sculptor Alberto Giacometti entered the fray during a sojourn in Zurich—it is said that one day, he opened the door of Cabaret Voltaire, stepped out, shouted, "Viva Dada!" at the top of his lungs, and disappeared as promenadeurs on the Limmatquai stopped in their tracks. Lenin was also reputedly a fan of Cabaret Voltaire. Today Cabaret Voltaire is preserved in the entrails of the disco/bar Castel Dada.

chocolate. Get bundles of chocolate at bargain prices at the end of the tour. All exhibits in German. (Seestr. 204. Take train S1 or S8 to "Kilburn." ☎716 22 33. Open W-F 10am-noon and 1-4pm. Free.)

MUSEUM BELLERIVE. Museum Bellerive specializes in constantly changing "out-of-the-ordinary" exhibits. The displays may sound tame, but the museum takes them in unexpected directions—one past exhibition included "Made in Japan" (a room full of plastic Japanese meals). (Höschg. #3. Take tram #2 or 4 (dir: Tiefenbrunnen) or bus #33 to "Höschg." and walk right; it's opposite the Zurich Ballet Academy. ☎383 43 76. Open Tu-Th 10am-8pm, F 10am-5pm, Sa-Su 11am-5pm. 6SFr, students and children 3SFr. Closed between exhibits, so call ahead.)

🎭 🎵 ENTERTAINMENT AND NIGHTLIFE

For information on after-dark goings-on, check **ZüriTipp** (www.zueritipp.ch) or the posters that decorate the streets and cinemas at Bellevuepl. or Hirschenpl. **Niederdorfstraße** rocks as the epicenter of Zurich's nightlife. Beware the deceptive and ubiquitous "night club"—it's a euphemism for strip club. Because of this, **women may not want to walk alone in this area at night.** On Friday and Saturday nights during the summer, Hirschenpl. on Niederdorfstr. hosts sword-swallowers and other daredevil street performers from around the world. Other hot spots include Münsterg. and Limmatquai, both lined with cafes and bars that overflow with people into the wee hours of the morning. Beer in Zurich is pricey (from 6SFr), but a number of cheap bars have established themselves on Niederdorfstr. near Muhleg. If all else fails, go to the cinema. Most movies are screened in English with German and French subtitles (marked E/d/f). Films generally cost 15SFr and up, less on Mondays. After July 18, the **Orange Cinema**, an open-air cinema at Zürichhorn (take tram #4 or 2 to "Fröhlichstr.") attracts huge crowds to its lakefront screenings. To ensure a seat, arrive at least 1hr. before the 9pm showing (15SFr) or reserve a seat at the open-air ticket counter at the Bellevue tram station. Every August, the *Street Parade* brings together ravers from all over the world for a giant techno party (see **Festival Fever**, p. 328).

🍺 **Double-U (W) Bar,** Niederdorfstr. 21 (☎251 41 44), on the 1st floor of Hotel Schafli. A hub of activity, this spot is popular even by the high standards of Niederdorfstr. Comes complete with palm trees and inflatable beer bottles straddled by iguanas. Locals and students crowd the terrace, drinking beer and causing a ruckus (10SFr and up). Open M-Th 4pm-2am, F-Su 4pm-4am.

Cranberry, Metzgerg. 3 (☎/fax 261 27 72), is a gay-friendly bar right off Limmatquai. Popular for pre-partying, it serves an endless selection of mixed drinks (from 9SFr). Pros can opt to create their own concoctions; the indecisive or inexperienced can use the Drink Navigator to ease the ever-important process. Open Su-Tu 5pm-midnight, W-Th 5pm-1am, F-Sa 5pm-2am.

Bar Odeon, Limmatquai 2 (☎251 16 50), Bellevuepl. This posh, artsy joint has served the likes of Vladimir Lenin, but more commonly, a relaxed, gay-friendly crowd. Great street-side seating. Beers from 6SFr. During the day, an ebullient crowd sips espresso. Open 7:30am-2am, F-Sa 8:30am-4am.

Oliver Twist, Rindermarkt 6 (☎252 47 10), welcomes soccer fans in a pub atmosphere that's only somewhat contrived. Beers 6.50SFr and up; wine from 3.80SFr. Pub grub available noon-10pm. English breakfast (15.50SFr) available during major sporting events. Open M-Th 11:30am-midnight, F-Sa 11:30am-2am, Su 4pm-midnight.

Öpfelchammer, Rindermarkt 12 (☎351 23 36). This popular Swiss wine bar (3-5SFr per glass) has low ceilings and wooden crossbeams covered with initials and messages from 200 years of merry-making. Those who climb the rafters and drink a free glass of wine from the beams get to engrave their names on the furniture. It's harder than it looks. Open Tu-Sa 11am-12:30am; closed for a month in summer.

Barfusser, Spitalg. 14 (☎251 40 64), off Zähringerpl., Europe's oldest gay bar, offers outdoor seating during the day and drinking into the night (open daily until 2am).

⚡ DAYTRIP FROM ZURICH

EINSIEDELN   ☎055

Trains leave Zurich for Wädenswil (toward Chur, 1-2 per hour, every 20min. 6:10am-10:16pm, 16.20SFr), where trains run to Einsiedeln (30min.).

Just an hour by train from Zwingli's Protestant pulpit in Zurich, the tiny town of Einsiedeln attracts pilgrims from all over Europe to its spectacular, massive cathedral and legendary Black Madonna. To find the Klosterkirche (cathedral), exit the station, cross the street, turn right on the small lane behind "Doc Holliday's" restaurant, and turn left on Hauptstr. Consecrated in 1735, the cathedral's Milanese exterior with twin lemon-shaped domes dominates the surrounding hills. Endless frescoes by the Asam brothers line the interior; its ornate Baroque ceilings overflows with plump, blushing cherubs floating along an overwhelming pastel background of lavender, green, gold, and pink. After Vespers, around 4pm each day (except Sunday), the monks sing their Gregorian chant. The 1m-high **Black Madonna**, resplendent in Royal Spanish attire against a glowing backdrop of golden clouds, is the cathedral's centerpiece. Years of smoky candlelight and underground storage during the French invasion have darkened the figure. An Austrian craftsman once restored her natural color, but locals, refusing to accept the change, had painted her black again (Klosterkirche open 5:30am-8:30pm.) The **monastery** that stretches back from the cathedral offers 1.5 hour tours of its horse stables and renowned library every Saturday at 2pm. (18SFr; reserve and buy tickets at the tourist office. Conducted in German. Tours in other languages available by appointment.)

The town's **tourist office** sits below the cathedral at Hauptstr. 85, Klosterpl. ((055) 418 44 88; fax (055)418 44 80; info@einsiedeln.ch). Helpful staff can book tours for you and advise you on hiking opportunities in the lush hills surrounding the cathedral. (Open M-F 10am-noon and 1:30-5pm, Sa 9am-12pm and 1:30-4pm, Su 9am-noon.) The gates are usually open, and the pastoral grounds, protected by the crumbling walls of the monastery, are worth a stroll any day. Behind the monastery, short trails lead into the hills where the monastery horses graze.

WINTERTHUR   ☎052

Once the country home of eastern Switzerland's wealthy industrialists, Winterthur (VIN-ter-tur) today houses the fruits of their labor. The incredible array of museums—mostly endowed by those deceased wealthy industrialists—make it an excellent daytrip from Zurich.

◨⚡ TRANSPORT AND PRACTICAL INFORMATION

Trains run to **Zurich** (8 per hr., 10.60SFr) and connect there to Basel, Geneva, and **St. Gallen** (2 per hr., 18.80SFr). Almost all buses to the museums leave from just right of the station. Winterthur's museums are closed Mondays. The **tourist office**, within the train station, overflows with excursion ideas and museum information. It offers a free hotel reservation service and a free but busy **Internet** terminal. (☎267 67 00; fax 267 68 58; tourist-service@win.ch; www.stadt-winterthur.ch.

Open M-F 8:30am-6:30pm, Sa 8:30am-4pm.) On the left side of the station, you'll find **currency exchange** (open daily 6:10am-8:15pm), **bike rental** (30SFr per day; add 6SFr if returning to another station; open M-F 7:30am-7:50pm, Sa 7:30am-7pm, Su 8:30am-12:30pm and 2:30-6:50pm), and **luggage storage** (7SFr; same hours as bike rental). **Lockers** with 24hr. access are also available in the train station (4-6SFr). **Post office** opposite the train station. (Open M-F 7:30am-7pm, Sa 8am-4pm.) 24 hour **ATM** available in the lobby. **Postal code**: CH-8401.

⌂ 🍴 ACCOMMODATIONS AND FOOD

Budget accommodations are hard to find in Winterthur. The only youth hostel is **Jugendunterkunft Winterthur ❷**, 18 Wildbach Str. From the train station, walk 5min. down Tecknikumstr. and turn right onto Zeughaus Str. After that turn, you'll immediately see a fork in the road; take the right fork (Wildbachstr.) and the hostel will be on the left at the next intersection. Simple, clean, and private rooms coupled with its ideal location makes this hostel a good value. Call ahead, because the hostel had plans of moving in the summer of 2002. (☎267 48 48; fax 267 48 49. Breakfast 7SFr. Kitchen, TV room, sheets, towels, and **Internet** access included. Reception 7-10:30am and 4-9:30pm. Open May-Oct. 3-5 bed rooms 25SFr; singles and doubles 33SFr.)

Food stands serve quick and cheap sandwiches throughout the downtown, particularly on Marktg. Locals on their lunch break congregate at **Manta Sandwich-Bar ❷**, Untertor 17, near the train station. Filling gourmet sandwiches (like tomato, mozzarella, and eggplant) go for 5-12SFr. (☎212 43 23. Open M-W and F 6am-6:30pm, Th 6am-9pm, and Sa 6am-5:30pm.) **Restaurant-Pizzeria Pulcinella ❸**, right off Marktg. on Metzg., is another local favorite. Eat in (pizza 14-20.50SFr) or, for 3SFr less, take out. (☎212 98 62. Open M-F 11:30am-2pm and 6-11pm, Sa 6-11pm.) Fruit and vegetable **markets** invade the streets of the Altstadt on Tuesdays and Fridays from about 10am-4pm. **Migros** supermarket sits on the corner of Marktg. and Unt. Graben, right in the Altstadt.

🄶 SIGHTS

Since museums are Winterthur's biggest draw, upon arrival you should get a Tageskarte (7.20SFr), which will get you to the museums via public transportation (biking is also a popular option), and a museum pass (20SFr for 1 day), which will get you into the museums and save you money if you plan on visiting at least 3 of Winterthur's fifteen museums.

OSKAR REINHART COLLECTION. Winterthur's most generous art patron was Oskar Reinhart, as the two museums housing his collection demonstrate. The smaller but more impressive branch of the collection is preserved just outside of town in the ▨**Sammlung Oskar Reinhart am Römerholz**. The collection, valued at about 3 billion Swiss francs, includes works by those who Reinhart considered the "fathers of modern art," like Cranach, El Greco, Goya, Holbein, and Rubens. The museum also showcases 19th-century masterpieces by Cézanne, Daumier, Manet, Van Gogh, and Picasso, including paintings of Arles by Van Gogh, the year before he passed away. Stop to gaze into the soft eyes of the lady in Manet's *At the Café*. *(Haldenstr. 95. Take bus #10 to "Haldengut" (departs every hr. from the station); turn left off the bus and head up Haldenstr. for a steep 10min. walk. The museum also sponsors a shuttle service, which runs from the train station to the villa (every hr. Tu-Sa 9:45am-4:45pm, 5SFr). ☎269 27 40. Open Tu-Su 10am-5pm, Easter Monday, and Whit Monday. 8SFr, students 6SFr. Audio guides available in German, French, and English for 5SFr. Parking is available right outside the museum. Wheelchair accessible.)*

The larger collection is housed in the center of town at ▨**Museum Oskar Reinhart am Stadtgarten.** The museum focuses on the work of Swiss, German, and Austrian painters, particularly portraits. Glass steps lead to the remodeled fourth floor, which houses temporary exhibits. *(Stadthausstr. 6. Turn right out of the station, then go left on Stadthausstr. for 2 blocks. ☎ 267 51 72. Open W-Su 10am-5pm, Tu 10am-8pm. 8SFr, students 6SFr.)*

TECHNORAMA. The **Swiss Technology Museum** houses a day's worth of interactive science experiments for kids from six to 60. Explore the amazing properties of water, the power of magnetism, or the magic behind optical illusions. Train lovers will appreciate the tin toy train collection of Dr. Bommer, considered one of the world's most impressive. All displays are printed in German, French, Italian and English. Try your hand at textile production or water music, or test your hand-eye coordination in the jumbo-jet flight simulator. *(Technoramastr. 1. Take bus #5 (dir: Technorama) to the last stop. ☎ 243 05 05; info@technorama.ch; www.technorama.ch. Open Tu-Su and public holidays 10am-5pm. 17SFr, seniors 15SFr, students 11SFr, ages 6-15 9SFr. Prices subject to change.)*

KUNSTMUSEUM. Winterthur's large Kunstmuseum houses some renowned Impressionist pieces, but its specialty is Modernist art by Arp, Kandinsky, Klee, Léger, and Mondrian. In the summer, the museum features temporary exhibits of contemporary art. *(Museumstr. 52. Turn left from the station, right on Museumstr., and left on Lindstr. ☎ 267 51 62; automated information 267 58 00; info@kmw.ch; www.kmw.ch. Open Tu 10am-8pm, W-Su 10am-5pm. Prices hover around 10SFr, students 6SFr.)* The **city library** and the **Museum of Natural Science** are in the same building. Internet access available at the library. 2SFr for 15min, first 15min free. *(☎ 267 51 66. Library open M 10am-6pm, Tu-F 8am-6pm, Sa 8am-4pm. Museum of Natural Science open Tu-Su 10am-5pm. Free.)*

FOTOMUSEUM. Among Winterthur's smaller museums is the unique Fotomuseum, housed in a former factory. The museum, which serves as the center of the counter-culture crowd in Winterthur, features exhibitions of photography, lectures, and discussions. *(Grüzenstr. 44. Take bus #2 (dir: Seen) to "Schleife." Follow the signs to the museum; at the fork in the road, stay right. ☎ 233 60 86; www.fotomuseum.ch. Open Tu-F noon-6pm, every 2nd W noon-7:30pm, Sa-Su 11am-5pm. 8SFr, students 5SFr.)*

STADTKIRCHE. While wandering around the Altstadt, visit the nearly hidden **Stadtkirche** (city church) on Kirchpl. The church was built in 1180, renovated in the late Gothic style between 1501 and 1515, and now blazes with Alberto Giacometti's stained-glass windows and Paul Zehnder's 1925 murals of brightly colored Bible stories. *(Turn right off of Marktg. onto Unt. Kirchg. Open 10am-4pm.)*

CENTRAL SWITZERLAND

LUCERNE (LUZERN) ☎ 041

Nestled among the foothills of the Alps, Lucerne (pop. 60,000) lies at the end of a lake that has been eternalized by poets and composers. An incredible panorama streching from Mount Rigi to Mount Pilatus sets dramatically different moods for the city's skyline depending on weather, season, and time of day. This inherent interplay of art and nature feeds into the city, guaranteeing something for everyone from sophisticates to outdoor enthusiasts. Tours through one of the most engaging Altstädte in Switzerland, cruises on the placid **Vierwaldstättersee,** and hikes up the regal peaks of Mt. Pilatus and Rigi Kulm keep visitors enthralled for days. With so many opportunities for tourists, Lucerne easily asserts itself as not only the capital of the canton, but one of the most important cities in Central Switzerland. After just a few days, though, the local charm and small size leave travellers feeling at home abroad.

Vierwaldstätter See
(Lake Lucerne)

Inselipark

Hofkirche St. Leodegar
und Mauritius

BAHNHOFPL.

Hauptbahnhof

Migros Markt

Library

TO LION OF
LUCERNE (150m)
& 11 (1.5km)

SCHWANENPL.

Seebr.

Kapellbrücke

STERNENPL.

KAPELLPL.

Rathaus-Steg

Picasso
WEINMARKT.-Museum
KORNMARKT.
HIRSCHENPL.

Jesuiten-
kirche

Kramg.   Reussbr.   Krong.

Münzg.

Franziskaner-
kirche

Bürgerstr.

KASERNENPL.

Jet Wasch
Laundry

Sonnenberg
Tunnel

DÄCHLITURM
ALLENWINDENTURM
PULVERTURM
SCHIRMERTURM
ZEITTURM   WACHTTURM
LUGISLANDTURM
MÄNNLITURM
NÖLLITURM

Reuss

200 yards
200 meters

Lucerne
▲ ACCOMMODATIONS
Backpackers, 26
Camping Lido, 5
Hotel Alpha, 19
Hotel Goldener Stern, 20
Hotel Löwengraben, 9
Hotel Pickwick, 13
Jugendherberge, 1
Linde, 14
Privatpension Panorama, 2
Tourist Hotel Luzern, 8

◆ FOOD
Cafeteria Emilio, 12
Heini Bakery, 11
Kam Tong Take Away, 25
Nölliturm, 7
Ristorante La Gondola, 15
Traffic, 24
Wilden Mann, 17

■ NIGHTLIFE/PUBS
Club 57, 6
Cucaracha, 22
Grand Casino Luzern, 4
Heaven, 18
Jazz Cantine, 10
The Loft, 3
Mr. Pickwick Pub, 13
Pravda, 21
Schüür, 23

CENTRAL SWITZERLAND

✦ 🛈 ORIENTATION AND PRACTICAL INFORMATION

The **Reuss River,** draining from the Vierwaldstättersee (Lake Lucerne), narrows steadily through the center of Lucerne. The train station, tourist office, and post office line the edges of Bahnhofpl. on the bank south of the Reuss, while the streets of the Altstadt twist through the northern bank. The **Kapellbrücke** in the east and the **Spreuerbrücke** in the west are the two ancient wooden bridges that span the Reuss, with three bridges between them.

TOURIST AND FINANCIAL SERVICES

Tourist Office: In the train station (☎227 17 17; fax 17 18; luzern@luzern.org; www.luzern.org). Free city guide (with unwieldy map) and hotel reservation service. Ask about the **Visitor's Card,** which, in conjunction with a hotel or hostel stamp, provides discounts at museums, bars, car rental, stores and more. Open May-Oct. M-F 8:30am-7:30pm (mid-June through mid-Sept. until 8:30pm), Sa-Su 9am-7:30pm; Nov.-Apr. M-F 8:30am-6pm, Sa-Su 9am-6pm.

Budget Travel: STA Travel, Grabenstr. 8 (☎412 23 23; fax 23 26; www.statravel.ch), offers ISICs, student travel deals, and discount flights. Open M-W and F 10am-6pm, Th 10am-8pm, Sa 10am-1pm.

Currency Exchange: At the station. Open May-Oct. M-F 7:30am-8pm, Sa-Su 7:30am-7pm; Nov.-Apr. M-F 8am-7pm, Sa-Su 9am-6pm. **Migros bank,** Seidenhofstr. 6, off Bahnhofstr., has an exchange machine. Open M-W and F 9am-5:15pm, Th 9am-6:30pm, Sa 8:15am-noon.

American Express: Schweizerhofquai 4, P.O. Box 2067, CH-6002 (☎419 99 00). Members' mail held and checks cashed. Travel services open M-F 8:30am-6pm, Apr.-Oct. also Sa 8:30am-noon. **Currency exchange** open M-F 8:30am-noon and 1:30-5pm, Sa 8:30am-noon.

LOCAL SERVICES

Luggage Storage: Downstairs at the station, window 24. **Luggage watch** 5SFr per item. Open 6am-9pm. **Lockers** 3-5SFr.

English-language bookstores: Bücher Brocky, Güterstr.1. From the station take a right onto Iselquai, bear left on Werfstr., then right onto Güterstr. This massive warehouse of books has only a few English shelves, but the selection is unique and the price is right (1SFr for paperbacks). **Raebes,** (☎229 60 20), on Frankenstr. off Zentralstr. Sophisticated selection of English literature, travel books, and maps. **Free Internet** access for customers. Open M 1-6:30pm, Tu-F 8am-6:30pm, Sa 8am-4pm. For English magazines, check out the kiosk in the basement of the train station.

Bi-Gay-Lesbian Organizations: Homosexualle Arbeitsgruppen Luzern (HALU; ☎360 14 60) publishes a monthly calender of events, available at the tourist office. HALU also runs **Why Not,** a discussion group for young gays, W at 8 and 11:30pm.

Laundromat: Jet Wasch, Bruchstr. 28 (☎240 01 51), right off Pilatusstr. past Pilatuspl. from the station. Wash and dry 16SFr. Open May-Oct. M-F 8:30am-12:30pm and 2:30-6:30pm, Sa 9am-1pm; Oct.-Feb. M-F 8:30am-12:30pm, Sa 9am-1pm.

EMERGENCY AND COMMUNICATIONS

Emergency: Police, ☎117. **Fire,** ☎118. **Ambulance,** ☎144. **Medical Emergency,** ☎111. For the **24hr. pharmacy** on duty, call ☎211 33 33.

Internet Access: C+A Clothing on Hertensteinstr. at the top of the Altstadt has 2 **free,** terminals on its lower floor. 20min. time limit. M-W 9am-6:30pm, Th-F 9am-9pm, Sa 8:30am-4pm. Across from the train station, **Voice Communications** has 4 terminals (5SFr for 30min. Open 9am-9:30pm). At the junction of Bruchstr. and Baselstr. the drink bar **Daily** offers **free Internet** with purchase of a drink. (Beer 4SFr, coffee 3.50SFr. Open 7am-midnight.) The best deal, **Stadtbibliothek** (City Library) in the Bourbaki Panorama by the Glacier Garden provides access for 4SFr per hr. (Open M 1:30-6:30pm; Tu-F 10am-6:30pm; Th until 9pm; Sa 10am-4pm. 10SFr deposit required.)

Post Office: Main branch on the corner of Bahnhofstr. and Bahnhofpl. Address *Poste Restante* to: Postlagernde Briefe, Hauptpost; CH-6000 Luzern 1. Open M-F 7:30am-6:30pm, Sa 8-noon. **Postal code:** CH-6000.

■ ACCOMMODATIONS AND CAMPING

Relatively inexpensive beds are available only in limited numbers in Lucerne, so call ahead in order to ensure a roof over your head.

Backpackers, Alpenquai 42 (☎360 04 20; fax 04 42). Turn right from the station onto Inseliquai and follow it through the small industrial area along the lake until it turns into Alpenquai; the hostel is on the right (15min.). Dorm rooms with large balconies, a comfortable dining room, and hundreds of issues of *National Geographic* make this hostel a pleasant spot. The long walk tends to keep away those pursuing night life, but the path is lit. The store sells "survival kits" of pasta, sauce, and wine for 9SFr, and many use the 2 kitchens. Tickets sold for cable cars on local mountains. **Bike rental** 16SFr per day. The staff will wash, dry, and fold laundry for 8SFr. Sheets included. **Internet** 10SFr per hour. Reception 7:30-10am and 4-11pm. No lockout. You can store bags here after check out. 4-bed dorms 27SFr; 2-bed dorms 33; 2SFr cheaper in winter. ❷

Hotel Löwengraben, Löwengraben 18 (☎417 12 12; fax 12 11; hotel@loewengraben.ch; www.loewengraben.ch). Until November 1998, Hotel Löwengraben was a prison providing full services to the miscreants of Lucerne. In only seven months the building was converted into a trendy hostel, dressed in black. The ground floor hosts a bar and restaurant with **Internet** access (15SFr per hr.). Ask about daily events and tours. Löwengraben hosts all-night dance parties (for guests only) every Sa during the summer. Breakfast 11SFr. Dinner 18SFr. Sheets included. 3- and 4-bed dorms (most with private showers and towels) 30SFr; double with shower 140-165SFr. ❷

Tourist Hotel Luzern, St. Karliquai 12 (☎410 24 74; fax 84 14; info@touristhotel.ch, www.touristhotel.ch), on the Altstadt side of Spreuerbrücke. Cheap, clean rooms with views of the river and Mt. Pilatus. Very close to the Altstadt's center. **Internet** access 12SFr per hr. Breakfast included. Free luggage storage. Laundry 10SFr. Reception 7am-10pm. Dorms 40SFr, students 35SFr; doubles 112SFr/98SFr; quads 180SFr/156SFr. Dec.-May dorms 33SFr and rooms 10-20SFr less. Add 10-25SFr per person for private shower. AmEx/MC/V. ❸

Hotel Goldener Stern, Burgerstr. 35 (☎227 50 60; fax 50 61; hotel@goldener-stern.ch; www.goldener-stern.ch), offers simple rooms with large windows and wood finish. From the station head left on Pilatusstr., turn right onto Hirschengr. and veer right onto Burgerstr. Public parking lot across from hotel. Breakfast included. Reception 7am-midnight; Su until 10pm. Check-out 10am. Check-in after noon. Rooms have shower, toilet, TV, and telephone. Singles 95SFr; doubles 140SFr (without shower 100SFr); triples 180SFr; quads 200SFr. Reduced rates in winter. AmEx/DC/MC/V. ❹

Jugendherberge (HI), Sedelstr. 12 (☎420 88 00; fax 56 16). During the day, take bus #18 (only one dir.) to "Jugendherberge." After 7:30pm, take bus #19 to "Rosenberg" and walk in the direction of the bus route, but turn right at the fork (5min; follow signs). White concrete building, near the Rotsee, with a beautiful valley view. Beds have fresh sheets and night lights. Buffet breakfast, showers, lockers, and sheets included. Dinner 12.50SFr. Laundry service 15SFr. Reception Apr.-Oct. daily 7-10am and 2pm-midnight; Nov.-Mar. 7-10am and 4pm-midnight. Call ahead in summer. Dorms 31.50SFr, doubles 78SFr, with shower 108SFr. 6SFr extra for non-members. AmEx/DC/MC/V. ❷

Linde, Metzgerrainie 3 (☎410 31 93; fax 32 05), located centrally on Weinmarkt in the Altstadt, sits above an Italian restaurant. Owner Alberino offers a handful of basic rooms with communal showers and toilet Apr.-Sept. Reception 11am-2pm and 6-10pm. Singles 44SFr; doubles 88SFr. ❸

Privatpension Panorama, Kapuzinerweg 9 (☎420 67 01; www.dos32.com/panorama.htm). Take bus #7 (dir: Wesemlin) to "Felsberg" and follow the perpendicular path downhill. For 8SFr, the owner will pick up travelers at the station. Quiet rooms on a hill are dingy but spacious and offer unbeatable sunset views of Mt. Pilatus and the Altstadt. Breakfast, kitchen facilities, and limited parking included. Laundry 5SF. Singles 45SFr; doubles 70-90SFr; "family room" for 4 140SFr. All without shower. Apartment for 2 with shower 120SFr. Reserve ahead. AmEx/MC/V. ❸

Hotel Pickwick, Rathausquai 6 (☎410 59 27; fax 410 51 08; hotelpickwick@gastrag.ch; www.hotelpickwick.ch), centrally located in the Altstadt between the Kapellbrücke and Rathaus Steg bridge, welcomes guests with bright orange carpets and comfortable rooms. No breakfast, but bar and restaurant downstairs (see **Food**). Reception in bar 11:30am-12:30am. Check-out 11am. Singles 75SFr, with shower 85SFr; doubles 95-105SFr/105-135SFr. Winter prices reduced. AmEx/MC/V. ❹

Hotel Alpha (☎240 42 80; fax 91 31; infor@hotelalpha.ch; www.hotelalpha.ch), at the corner of Pilatusstr. and Zähringerstr., lies in a residential area just outside the city. The airy rooms are bright and spotless. Breakfast included. Reception daily 7:30am-midnight; shorter hours in winter. Singles 65SFr; doubles 98SFr, with shower 120-130SFr; triples without shower 129SFr; quads without shower 164SFr. 2-5SFr cheaper Nov.-March. AmEx/DC/MC/V. ❹

Camping: Lido, Lidostr. 8 (☎370 21 46; fax 21 45; luzern@camping-international.ch; www.camping-international.ch), 35min. along Nationalquai, or take bus #6 or 8 (dir: Würzenbach) to "Verkehrshaus." This campsite near the lake has all the amenities, including laundry (2SFr; 1SFr for 24min. drying), snack bar, and a variety of fresh baked breads on request (2.60-5.60SFr). Showers 0.50SFr per 3min. Reception and snack bar daily 8:30-11:30am and 3-8pm. Open Mar. 15-Oct. 7.70SFr, children 3.50SFr, tent and car 5SFr each. ❶

◖ FOOD

Markets along the river sell cheap fresh goods on Tuesday and Saturday mornings. Supermarkets and department stores offer the cheapest restaurant meals.

Traffic, the train station cafeteria, provides a large selection in a quick cafeteria atmosphere. *Rösti* with egg, chicken, ham, bacon, or cheese 7.90-8.20SFr; half a roasted chicken to go 9.20SFr. Open 6:30am-9:15pm. ❶

Kam Tong Chinese Take Away, Inseliquai 10 (☎218 58 50 or 532 31 54). Turn right in front of the station and right on Inselquai to reach this dim, red-papered eatery that serves large portions of cheap, tasty Asian fare and snacks to go. Most meals cost 12-17SFr. Chicken with cashews 16SFr, vegetable lo mein 12SFr. Open M-W 9am-6:30pm, Th-F 9am-9pm, Sa 9am-4pm. ❷

Mr. Pickwick Pub, Rathausquai 6 (☎410 59 27), in Altstadt between the Kapellbrücke and Rathaus Steg bridge, offers some of the cheapest fare of the restaurants lining the Reuss. Order fish 'n' chips (15.50SFr) or an English chicken curry sandwich (6.50SFr) at the bar. BBC sports on the television. Hotel upstairs. Entrees 15.50-17.50SFr, sandwiches 5.50-7.50SFr. Large selection of beer on tap and in bottles starting at 4.50SFr. (Guinness 5SFr.) Open 11:30am-12:30am. ❷

Ristorante La Gondola, Weinmarkt 3 (☎410 61 15), offers fine Italian cuisine in the heart of Lucerne's Altstadt. Large pizzas run 13.50-26SFr and pastas 14.50-29.50SFr. Try a simple margarita or load it up with ham, mushrooms, artichokes, and tuna for only 18SFr. Open M-Sa 11am-2:30pm and 6pm-midnight. ❸

Wilden Mann, Bahnhofstr. 30 (☎210 16 66; fax 16 29; mail@wilden-mann.ch; www.wilden-mann.ch). Head left from the station on Bahnhofstr. just past the Reussbr. For a luxury night on the town, the "Wild Man" can't be beat. Savor specialities like roasted red snapper (19-44SFr) or raw milk cheese with homemade fruit cake in the wine-bottle decor of the main restaurant. Daily *Menüs* 22-26SFr. Alternately, move next door to the **Burgerstübe** for a traditional Swiss meal in a wood-panelled den. Roasted pork sausage with *Rösti* 21SFr. (Wilden Mann open 11:30am-2:30pm and 6-11pm; Burgerstube 10:30am-11pm.) AmEx/DC/MC/V. ❹

Nölliturm, St. Karlistr. 2 (☎240 28 66), on the Altstadt side of the Geissmatt bridge. Cheap, hearty Swiss specialties with bowling (20SFr per hr.). *Rösti Bernois* (with bacon and onions) 15.50SFr. *Nölliteller* (selection of meats and cheeses) 13.50SFr. Open Su-F 8am-12:30am. ❷

Heini Bakery, Falkenpl. (☎412 20 20), is locally famous for the 20 types of dense, flaky-crusted tarts it prepares each day (4.10-4.90SFr) which are good for meals or desserts. Also try the *Älplermakkronen* (Swiss mac 'n' cheese,13.30SFr) or the Heini plate with vegetable strudel and salad (13.90SFr). Open M-W and F 7am-6:30pm, Th 7am-10pm, Sa 7am-5pm, Su 9am-6pm. ❷

Cafeteria Emilio, Grendelstr. 10 (☎410 28 10), in the Altstadt off Schwanenpl. Locals eat wholesome yogurt and *Müesli* (9.30SFr), while tourists munch daily *Menüs* (13SFr). The terrace on Lederg. provides a refreshing breeze and good people-watching opportunities. Open M-F 6:30am-8pm; Th until 10pm; Sa 7am-6pm, Su 9am-6pm. ❷

MARKETS

Migros, at the station, is open M-W and Sa 6:30am-8pm, Th-F 6:30am-9pm, Su 8am-8pm. Also at Hertensteinstr. 44. Restaurant has the same hours.

Reformhaus Müller, Weinmarkt 1, sells organic foods. Open M and W-F 9am-6:30pm, Tu 8:30am-6:30pm, Sa 8:30am-4pm.

❻ ▥ SIGHTS AND MUSEUMS

THE OLD CITY. The Altstadt is famous for its frescoed houses, especially those of Hirschenpl. and Weinmarkt. The **Kapellbrücke**, a 660-year-old wooden roofed bridge, connects the Altstadt to Bahnhofstr. It was accidentally set on fire by a barge in 1993, but proud citizens restored it within a few months. Further down the river, the **Spreuerbrücke** portrays an image of what the Kapellbrücke looked like before the fire. Both bridges have painted triangle ceiling supports; those on the Spreuer allow you to confront your mortality in Kaspar Meglinger's eerie *Totentanz* (Dance of Death) paintings. On the hills above the river, the **Museg-gmauer** and its towers are all that remain of the medieval city's ramparts. They still define the city skyline, especially when illuminated at night. The Schirmerturm, Männliturm, and Zeitturm, are accessible to visitors. *(Open 8am-7pm in summer.)* The **Zeitturm** (clock tower) provides a particularly pleasing panorama of the city, although closed windows and graffiti preclude photo-ops. *(From the station head left along the river and cross the Spreuerbrücke, the second wooden bridge. Walk left along St. Karli-Quai, turn right (uphill), and follow the brown castle signs.)*

■ **PICASSO MUSEUM.** Two hundred intimate photographs of Picasso on display present the personal side of the great artist's life. Close friend David Duncan captured him delicately sucking the last pieces of fish from a skeleton, trying his foot at ballet, and creating some of his finest works. A large collection of unpublished Picasso lithographs, drawings, and paintings are also on display. *(Am Rhyn Haus, Furreng. 21. From Schwanenpl., take Rathausquai to Furreng. ☎ 410 17 73 or 410 35 33. Open Apr.-Oct. daily 10am-6pm; Nov.-Mar. 11am-4pm. 8SFr, with guest card 7SFr, students 5SFr.)*

■ **VERKEHRSHAUS DER SCHWEIZ (TRANSPORT MUSEUM).** Climb into big-rigs and jet planes or go for a virtual reality ride, but don't miss the museum's real highlight: the trains. Even the children's train chugging around the floor is an authentic steam engine. Learn about balloon flight and get a view of the city on the *Hiflyer*, or plan your next day in Switzerland on the largest aerial photograph of the country right at your feet. The museum also has a planetarium and Switzerland's only IMAX theater. *(Lidostr. 5. ☎ 370 44 44; fax 61 68; www.verkehrshaus.org; IMAX reservations ☎ 375 75 75; www.imax.ch. Take bus #6, 8, or 24 to "Verkershaus" or walk along the Nationalquai for 20min. Open Apr.-Oct. daily 10am-6pm; Nov.-Mar. 10am-5pm. 21SFr, guest card holders and students 19SFr, with SwissPass 16SFr, with Eurail 14SFr. IMAX 16SFr. Both 31SFr. Hiflyer daily 11am-5pm and night flights June-Aug. F-Sa 7-10pm. 20SFr, children 15SFr, family 50SFr. Dial ☎ 370 20 20 for weather updates.)*

LÖWENDENKMAL AND GLACIER GARDEN. Danish sculptor Bertel Thorvaldesen carved the magnificent Löwendenkmal (Lion Monument), the dying lion of Lucerne, out of a cliff on Denkmalstr. The 9m monument honors the Swiss Guard who defended Marie Antoinette to the death at the Tuileries in 1792. Mark Twain described it as "the saddest and most moving piece of rock in the world." From the station, cross Seebrücke to Schwanenpl., follow Schweizerhofquai to the right, and turn left on Denkmalstr. The Glacier Garden, a lunar landscape of smooth sculpture-like rocks, lies up the stairs from the monument. A kitschy but interesting museum takes you through a mishmash of history of Lucerne and leads to the disorienting *Spiegellabyrinth* (mirror maze) next door. *(Open Apr.-Oct. daily 9am-6pm; Nov.-Mar. daily 10am-5pm; 9SFr, with guest card 7.50SFr, students 7SFr.)*

WAGNER MUSEUM. Wagner's once-secluded lakeside home now exhibits original letters, scores, and instruments. His years in Lucerne, the "Tribschen years" (1866-1872), were marked by productivity and personal happiness—it was here that he wed Cosima von Bülow. *(Wagnerweg. 27. Take bus #6, 7, or 8 to "Wartegg." or turn right from the station and walk 25min. along the lake. ☎ 360 23 70. Open mid-Mar. to Nov. Tu-Su 10am-noon and 2-5pm. 5SFr, students and guest card holders 4SFr.)*

KUNSTMUSEUM LUZERN. Housed within the futuristic Lucerne Culture and Conference Center, the Lucerne Museum of Art is home to temporary modern art exhibits. 2002 saw an array of unique creations exploring illness, love, and the "myth of awakening," centered around the bedroom. *(Europapl. 1, next to the train station. ☎ 226 78 00; fax 78 01; info@kunstmuseumluzem.ch; www.kunstmuseumluzern.ch. Open Tu-Su 10am-5pm, W and Th until 8pm. 10SFr, students and guest card holders 8SFr.)*

SAMMLUNG ROSENGART LUZERN. The Rosengart Collection is the newest addition to Lucerne's cultural offerings. This 3-story collection displays works of 20th century artists Miró, Renoir, Kandinsky, Chagall, and Matisse. Bottom floors are dedicated to Picasso and Klee. *(Pilatusstr. 10, left from the train station. ☎ 220 16 60; fax 16 63; stiftung.rosengart@bluewin.ch. Open Apr.-Oct. daily 10am-6pm; Nov.-Mar. daily 11am-4pm. 14SFr, students 9SFr, children 5SFr. Prices reduced by 2SFr with guest card.)*

⚠ OUTDOOR ACTIVITIES

The cheapest option for getting out on the **Vierwald-stättersee** (Lake Lucerne) is to take one of the **ferries** that serve the tiny villages around the lake. Not only can you enjoy the magnificent scenery without exerting yourself, but you can also disembark at any one of the lakeside villages to explore further. There are glass-blowing demonstrations at **Hergiswil** and a short scenic hike at **Bürgenstock** via **Kehrsiten** (round-trip 44SFr), where visitors will find five of central Switzerland's lakes at their feet. For an easy walk along the lake, get off the ferry at **Weggis** (round-trip 2hr., 23SFr). **SGV** boats depart from the piers in front of the train station (☎367 67 67; fax 68 68; info@lake-lucerne.ch; www.lakelucerne.ch; SwissPass and Eurail valid). Catch one of five steam ships, the internal workings of which are displayed.

Lucerne's adventure provider **Outventure** (☎611 14 41; fax 14 42; info@outventure.ch; www.outventure.ch) provides outdoor thrills with local flair. This mid-sized company has grown from the original Mountain Guides Office to a full-service adventure company with **paragliding** (150SFr), **canyoning** (170SFr), **glacier hiking** (170SFr), and **bungee jumping** (160SFr). Outventure is a member of the Swiss Outdoors Association, a group which maintains safety and training standards. Daily shuttle from the tourist office at 8:30am. Book in advance.

🎭 ENTERTAINMENT

Lucerne attracts big names for its summer **Blue Balls Festival** (third week in July, and yes, that's *really* the name) and fall **Blues Festival** (second week in Nov.). In 2002, B.B. King, George Clinton, and Van Morrison performed at Blue Balls. Contact the tourist office, or call/fax Blue Balls ☎227 10 58, or try www.blueballs.ch. The **Lucerne Festival** runs mid-August to mid-September. The festival celebrates classical music but also features contemporary world music. (☎226 44 80. For tickets (20-220SFr) or further info, contact: Lucerne Festival, P.O. Box, CH-6002 Luzern.) The **Nationalquai** is the scene for free summertime **Pavillon Musik** concerts, featuring brass and jazz bands playing Hollywood tunes, Gershwin, and Duke Ellington most Tu, F, and Su nights May-Sept. **Open Air Kino Luzern** (www.open-air-kino.ch), at the outdoor theater in the Seepark near Backpackers Luzern, shows movies (15SFr) every night mid-July to mid-August—most in English. Every July, elite crews worldwide row to Lucerne for the **Rowing Regattas** on the Rotsee. On Saturdays from 8am to noon, catch the **flea market** (May-Oct.) along Burgerstr. and Reussteg.

IN RECENT NEWS

TAKING CHANCES

It's happening all over Switzerland: the cards are flying, the dice are rolling, and guests are arriving with hopes of hearing the coins hit the bucket. In 2001 the Swiss Games Commission (Eidgenössichen Spielbankenkommission; ESBK) granted 21 licenses for casinos to cities all over the country including Basel, Bern, Lucerne, Interlaken, Zermatt, and St. Moritz. This move has resulted in the highest casino density in Europe.

On June 27, 2002, Lucerne opened the first of 7 grand casinos (13 games tables and unlimited slots). An additional 14 regular casinos (3 games tables and up to 150 slots) appeared throughout the year. Visitors flock with dreams of good luck and enjoy the casual gambling scene (there is no dress code in many of the casinos).

The real winners in this game, however, are the government and cantons, who expect to receive around 456 billion SFr from the anticipated 897 billion SFr earnings. Of course, every coin always has a flipside, and this one is no exception. Investigations into suspected Mafia involvement are already underway.

◙ NIGHTLIFE

Club 57, Haldenstr. 57, a 15min. walk down Haldenstr. from the Schweizerhofquai under the Carlton Tivoli Hotel, is replete with candle light and Moroccan red fabric pillows. During the week, 57 plays a hip mixture of jazz and funk; on weekends, DJs spin. (☎262 06 06. Open 8pm-2:30am, F-Sa until 4am. Beer 4-6SFr.) **The Loft,** Haldenstr. 21, is a trendy new club with hip-hop in a cloud of smoke. (☎410 92 44. Open W-Th 10pm-3am and F-Su 9pm-4am. No cover W and Su; Th 10SFr; F 12SFr; Sa 15SFr. Free cover until 11:30pm. Beer from 6SFr.) Across the street the new **Grand Casino Luzern** offers poker, craps, and 217 slot machines. Minimum age 20. Bring a passport. (Haldenstr. 6. ☎418 56 56; www.casinoluzern.ch. Open daily noon-3am; F-Sa until 4am.)

For a more mellow crowd, try the **Jazz Cantine** on Grabenstr. (☎410 73 73. Sandwiches 6-8SFr, Thai noodles 15SFr. Coffee 3.20SFr, beer 3.70SFr. Open M-Sa 7am-12:30am, Su 4pm-12:30am. Food served from 11:30am-2pm and 6:30-10pm.) On the west side of town, **Heaven** is Lucerne's only self-proclaimed gay bar. The small locale offers drinks to jazz-like sounds. (☎210 41 43; www.werbeecke.ch. Beers 4SFr. Open Tu-Th 6pm-12:30am, F-Su 6pm-2am.)

Pravda, Pilatusstr. 29, hosts a crowd similar to that at The Loft with a pop music edge. Beer is 10SFr, wide selections of vodka are 7.50-8SFr. (☎226 88 88; www.pravda.ch. Open W-Th 10pm-2:30am, F-Sa 10pm-4am.) **Cucaracha,** Pilatusstr. 15, has a daily Happy Hour (5-7:30pm) and free Tex-Mex snacks with a drink. (☎226 87 87. Coronas 8SFr. Open daily 5pm-12:15am.) From "Salsa Fest" to "Dive Party" to a "Pleasure HEADbangerparty," **Schüür,** Tribschenstr. 1, hosts a variety of themed nights and concerts. Follow Zentralstr. alongside the train tracks and turn left onto Lagensandbr. The club is on the left side, on the other end of the bridge. (www.schuur.ch. Open Th 8:30pm-2:30am, F-Sa 8:30pm-3:30am. Beer 5SFr.)

◪ DAYTRIPS FROM LUCERNE

Lucerne's most renowned daytrips are excursions to the mountains that haunt the city's skyline. The trip up is as memorable as the view from the top. Don't expect true Swiss countryside on these trips—you'll see few cows—but routes are well-touristed for good reason. Pilatus has the highest vista, but views from Rigi are almost as rewarding.

MOUNT PILATUS

*The most memorable travel route begins with the 1½hr. boat ride from Lucerne to Alpnachstad, ascends with the steepest **cogwheel train** in the world (48° gradient), descends by cable car to Krienz, and takes the bus back to Lucerne (entire trip 3hr.; 78.40SFr, with Eurail 43SFR, with SwissPass 40.60SFr). It is slightly cheaper if riding the cable car both ways. It is possible to cut down on the price by hiking: take the train or boat to Hegiswil and **hike** 3hr. up the hillside to Fräkmüntegg, a half-way point on the cable car (23SFr to Hergiswill, SwissPass and Eurail valid. 22SFr round-trip from Fräkmuntegg to the top). The hike offers constant views of the lake and Lucerne. For more information contact the Pilatus Railway (☎329 11 11; fax 11 12; info@pilatus.com; www.pilatus.com).*

As hulking as the enormous dragons supposedly spotted here in the 15th century, **Mt. Pilatus** stretches 2132m to the top of Lucerne's southern sky. Numerous quick jaunts to the various craggy promontories are possible from the station and restaurant at the top. The trip up the mountain—which, depending on your route, uses 4 different types of transportation—is at least half the fun.

I SPY The imposing facade of Mt. Pilatus has spawned numerous myths. The most oft-told, and the source of the mountain's name, says that the infamous Pontius Pilate was buried on the mountain. Each year on Good Friday, Pilate would emerge from the grave to wash his bloodied hands in the lake below. Any attempts to challenge Pilate's dominion brought storms of fury, so climbing the mountain was prohibited. In 1585, a priest and a few townsmen decided to test the story by going into the foothills and creating a ruckus. When there was no retribution, the spell was declared broken. Since then, there have been numerous Pilate sightings, so go at your own risk.

RIGI KULM

Start your trip on a ferry to Vitznau (round-trip 87SFr, with Eurail and SwissPass 29SFr). Then hike up (5hr.) or take a cogwheel train ride to the top. For a less strenuous hike, take the train partway to Rigi Kaltbad and hike from there (1½hr.). To descend, take the train down, ride to cable car from Grigi Kaltbad to Weggis, and return to Lucerne by ferry.

Rigi Kulm, with a view of Lake Lucerne, rises across the water from Mt. Pilatus. Watching the sunrise from the summit is a Lucerne must; sunsets get top reviews, too (see Mark Twain's 1879 travelogue *A Tramp Abroad*). Staying at **Massenlager Rigi Kulm ❷** on the summit facilitates early morning viewing. Part of Hotel Rigi Kulm, this dormitory has 28 simple bunks. (☎855 03 03; fax 00 55. Reception daily 8am-10pm. Dorms 18SFr; breakfast 14SFr, but money is better spent at a bakery.)

ENGELBERG AND MOUNT TITLIS   ☎041

Take the train from Lucerne to Engelberg (1hr., 6:30am-11:32pm, 15.40SFr) and the cable car from Engelberg to Titlis. (First ascent from Engelberg 8:30am, last ascent from Engelberg 3:40pm, last descent from Titlis 4:50pm; 76SFr, 60.80SFr with Eurail, 68.40SFr with Engelberg guest card, 57SFr with SwissPass; round-trip special 88SFr, 60.80SFr with Eurail, 57SFr with SwissPass.) Guided tours available from Lucerne (including round-trip rail and Titlis fares 95SFr, same discounts).

Near the small town of **Engelberg,** south of Lucerne, the world's first revolving cable car climbs to the crest of **Mount Titlis** (3020m), the highest outlook-point in central Switzerland. The ride gives views of the crevasses below and peaks above. The summit has an active glacial outpost, with observation deck and restaurant, glacial grotto, free tube rides down an ice slide, and free guided **glacier hikes** to the peak of the mountain. (3hr. Late June to mid-Oct. Tu 9am. Reserve at the tourist office.) Wear layers and appropriate footwear.

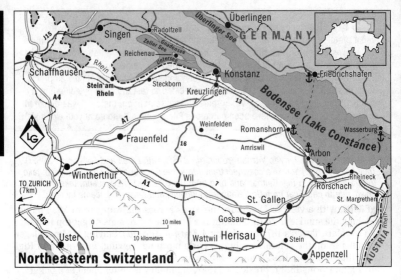

Northeastern Switzerland

NORTHEASTERN SWITZERLAND

Encompassing the cantons of Schaffhausen, St. Gallen, Thurgau, Glarus, and Appenzell, Northeastern Switzerland contains some of the country's best-preserved towns. Stein am Rhein invites visitors to its well-preserved medieval Altstadt while Appenzell maintains the farmhouses and agricultural lifestyle that made Switzerland. The region is also geographically diverse, home to magnificent waterfalls near Schaffhausen and lofty mountains surrounding Appenzell.

SCHAFFHAUSEN ☎ 052

During WWII, the United States accidentally bombed Schaffhausen due to cartographers' gaffes, making it one of the only Swiss cities to be harmed in the war. Remarkably, Schaffhausen managed to retain an expansive and authentic medieval Altstadt. Gilded bay windows, handmade shopkeepers' signs, and fountains decorate the pedestrian streets and offer glimpses into Switzerland's past. The **Munot Fortress,** built in the 1500s, stands tall and valiant above the city. A complete absence of attacks proved it rather unnecessary, and the citizens apparently used the time spared from military operations to kick back—the local *Falkenbier* is reputedly the best in the canton. A mug or two of the bold brew will put you in a prime mood to enjoy Schaffhausen's ambience.

GETTING THERE. If you're in the mood for exploration, consider a **Tageskarte** (29SFr), which allows one day of unlimited travel on Bodensee area railways, waterways, and roadways. **Trains** depart from Schaffhausen for Kreuzlingen (50min., 1-2 per hour 6am-11:05pm, 16.20SFr), St. Gallen (1½hr., 1-3 per hour 5:45am-10:45pm, 26SFr), Winterthur (30min., 1-3 per hour 5:45am-10:45pm, 10.40SFr), and Zurich (25min., 1-3 per hour 5:27am-12:18am, 17.20SFr). Numerous **ferries** traverse the Bodensee, departing from Schaffhausen (from Freiepl., below Festung Munot) to Konstanz (3-4 per day (1 on Su) 9:10am-3:35am; 24SFr) and Stein am Rhein (3 per day, 4 from July 7-Sept. 8, 1 on Su; 19.60SFr). **Parking** is in the garage off Rheinstr., in lots near the cathedral, off Moeratz, and behind the station.

◪ PRACTICAL INFORMATION. The **tourist office,** Fronwagpl. 4, looks out onto the lively Fronwagpl. at the head of Vordenstr., to the right. From the station, head down Schwertstr. (the narrow street to the right), and turn right at the fountain in the main square. The office gives city tours in German, French, or English. (☎ 625 51 41; fax 625 51 43; info@schaffhausen-tourismus.ch; www.schaffhausen-touris-mus.ch. Open Oct.-May M-F 9:30am-12:30pm and 1:30-5pm, Sa 9:30am-1:30pm; June-Sept. M-F 9:30am-6pm, Sa 9:30am-4pm, Su 9:30am-3:30pm. Tours Apr.-Oct. Tu, Th, and Sa 2:30pm; 1hr. 12SFr, children 6SFr.) At the station, are **currency exchange** (open daily 5:45am-8:10pm), **bike rental** (from 30SFr per day with photo ID, 25SFr with SwissPass; 6SFr extra to return bike at another station) and **luggage storage** (open M-F 6:30am-7:30pm, Sa-Su 8am-7:30pm; 5SFr) on the far left side. **Lockers** cost 4-6SFr, with 24hr. access. **Energie Punkt** (Muhlenstr. 19; ☎ 635 11 00), right across from St. Johannkirche, offers two **free Internet** terminals. (Open M-F 9am-6pm, Sa 10am-2pm.) The **post office** faces the station on Bahnhofstr. (Open M-W and F 7:30am-6:30pm, Th 7:30am-9pm, Sa 8am-12:30pm.) **Postal code:** CH-8200.

▐▐ ACCOMMODATIONS AND FOOD. Jugendherberge Belair (HI) ❷, Randen-str. 65, lies in the newer (i.e. early 19th-century) section of Schaffhausen. Take bus #6 (dir: Neuhasen SBB) to "Hallenbad" and find the hostel across the street from the bus stop. The huge hostel is surrounded by shady birch paths. (☎ 625 88 00; fax 624 59 54; schaffhausen@youthhostel.ch; www.youthhostel.ch/schaffhausen. Breakfast, showers, and sheets included. Kitchen available. Reception 8-10am and 5-9pm. Check-out 9:30am. Curfew 10pm; keys available. Dorms 24SFr; singles 30.50SFr; doubles 61SFr; non-members add 6SFr.) Alternatively, head to the **Rhein-falls** (see p. 399). Those seeking a restful night away from town should head to **Lowen ❹,** a small guesthouse just outside of Schaffhausen. Take bus #5 to the last stop, "Herblingen Hirschen" (dir: Herblingen.) Facing the same direction, turn right and head uphill for 3min. The hotel is on your right. (☎ 643 22 08; call ahead to book one of the seven rooms or have the tourist office do it for you. Singles 65SFr, with shower 80 SFr; doubles 110/130 SFr). **Camping Rheinwiesen ❶** stands at the edge of the Rhine, 2.5km from Schaffhausen. Take the train (dir: Kreuzlingen) to "Langwiesen," and you'll be able to see the campground on the far left along the waterfront; it's about a 20min. walk from there. (☎ 659 33 00; fax 33 55; www.camp-ingtcs.ch. Apr. 27-Sept. 29 adults 4.40SFr, children 2.20SFr, tents 5.50SFr; June 30-Aug. 31 6.40SFr, 3.20SFr, 7.50SFr.)

The Fronwagpl. comes alive during the day with outdoor cafes, inexpensive food vendors, restaurants, and live entertainment ranging from mimes to fire-breathers. **Restaurant Thiergarten ❸,** on Münsterpl. across from the Allerheiligen Monastery, spices up its already diverse international menu with different ethnic themes every year while continuing to support local farmers. Past influences include South Africa, the Caribbean, Greece, and Mexico. Bratwurst and *Rösti* for 15.50SFr are among the permanent (and cheaper) Swiss classics. (☎ 625 32 88.

Open daily 9am-11pm.) Health- and environmentally-conscious locals meet at **Zur Flamme ❷**, Vorstadt 9, a purely vegetarian and non-GMO establishment. (Open Tu-F 11am-2:30pm and 6-11pm, and Sa evening.) For take-out, try **Chinatown ❸**, Vorstadt 36, ideal for those itching to picnic out in the sun or to enjoy the pleasant sidewalk seating. Add 1-2SFr. for dining in. Dishes 17.50SFr and under. (☎624 46 77; fax 47 44. Open daily 11am-10:30pm.) **Migros,** Vorstadt 39, has a restaurant as well. (Open M-W and F 8:15am-6:30pm, Th 8:15am-8pm, Sa 8am-4pm.) Stock up on produce at the **open market** (Tu and Sa 7-11am outside the Johannkirche) and at the farmer's market (F 9am-6pm and Sa 8-11am). There's also **Aperto,** in the station, for basic conveniences. (Open M-Sa 6am-9:30pm, Su 7am-9:30pm.)

◙ **SIGHTS.** Throughout the Altstadt, colorful frescoes, fountains, intricate clocks, and woodcarvings transport you into an age of knights, heraldry, and Teutonic bravery. While wandering through the tight streets, keep your eyes trained upwards to see the decorated oriel windows (designed as status symbols) and colorful medieval murals. The murals decorating the **Haus zum Ritter,** on Vorderg., have been called "the most significant Renaissance frescoes north of the Alps."

MUNOT FORTRESS. The 10th-century Festung Munot presides over the grandiose Schaffhausen, offering the most convincing proof of the town's medieval past. After climbing the narrow steps leading through the vineyards that carpet the hill below the fortress, you'll enter the cavernous, dimly lit interior. Skylights cast yellow circles onto the cold stone floor, conjuring visions of townsfolk huddled around fires under the thunder of catapults. Escape the student-filled observation deck at lunchtime, and exit through the door opposite the spiral ramp to admire the deer colony in the moat. You will also find a peaceful garden terrace behind the fortress. (*Turn right at the head of Schwertstr., then left onto Vorderg., continuing until you see signs to the fortress. Open daily May-Sept. 8am-8pm; Oct-Apr. 9am-5pm. Free.*)

ALLERHEILIGEN MONASTERY. The medieval wonders continue on the outskirts of the Altstadt in the labyrinthine **Kloster Allerheiligen** (All Saints Monastery) complex. The monastery, with its herb garden, enclosed courtyard, and Schiller Bell (the inspiration for Schiller's poem "Song of the Bell"), is a peaceful refuge from the bustling city. Within the cloister, you'll find the **Museum zum Allerheiligen,** which encompasses a **Natural History Museum** and exhibits by the **Kunstverein Schaffhausen** (Art Museum). This museum exhibits everything from stuffed boars to modern art, plus a display of Roman and German artifacts. It also houses memorabilia from the 11th-century abbey that stood on the same site. In another recess lies thousand-year-old illuminated manuscripts. The highlight is the onyx, a bedazzling hunk of gold, jewels, and a priceless cameo styled in the first century AD in Augustan Rome. (*From the station, take Schwertstr. up to Vorderg., then turn right onto Münsterg.* ☎633 07 77; fax 633 07 88; www.allerheiligen.ch. *Open Tu-Sa noon-5pm, Th noon-8pm, Su 11am-5pm. Signs in German only. Free.*)

Stop in at the **Münsterkirche** attached to the cloister, a combination of medieval architecture and 20th-century furnishings, with simple wooden pews set against Cubist stained-glass windows. During the Reformation, Protestants stripped the 11th-century church of ornamentation, leaving the interior cool and white.

HALLEN FÜR NEUE KUNST (HALL FOR MODERN ART). This old warehouse has been converted into four floors of permanent gallery space for 12 avant-garde artists. Each floor is littered with massive, seemingly indecipherable shapes, colors, and even sounds. (*Baumgartenstr. 23, across the street from Kloster Allerheiligen.* ☎625 25 15; fax 625 8474; www.modern-art.ch. *Open May-Oct. Tu-Sa 3-5pm, Su 11-5pm; tours Su at 11:30am. 14SFr, students 8SFr.*)

🏔 DAYTRIP FROM SCHAFFHAUSEN

RHEINFALLS

The Rheinfalls are just a 5min. train ride from Schaffhaussen. Take the train headed for Winterthur to Schloß Laufen am Rheinfall. From the train stop, walk up the stairs and follow the signs to the falls.

The **Rheinfalls** are one of Europe's largest sets of waterfalls, though their scope isn't nearly as grand as that designation might lead you to expect. The falls are a mere 23m in height but are known to have a flow of up to 1250 cubic meters per second. Paths around the falls can take you within an arm's length of the gushing water. For a different perspective, boats, operated by **Rhyfall Mändli** (☎672 48 11), leave from both the Neuhausen and Schloß Laufen, but on the Neuhausen side, you can choose from four routes. One route will drop you off on the middle island that appears ready to keel over in the falls. (Apr.-Oct. 11am-5pm; May-Sept. 10am-6pm; Jun.-Aug. 9:30am-6:30pm. 2.50-11SFr, children 1.50-5.50SFr.) A bridge over the falls leads to Schloß Laufen, where for 1SFr you can follow winding, and often slippery, stairs down the steep face of the hill to the foot of the falls.

In the turrets of Schloß Laufen, **Jugendherberge Schloß Laufen am Rheinfalls (HI)** ❷ shelters weary backpackers. Follow the same directions to the Rheinfalls. At the top of the stairs, there will be signs pointing to the hostel, which will be on your left. Simple rooms recall the castle's 15th-century origins and offer splendid views of the Rhine. Reserve a bed in advance because the hostel often fills up with school groups. (☎659 61 52; fax 60 39. Breakfast included for dorms. Kitchen facilities 2SFr. Reception 8-9:30am and 5-9pm. Closed Nov.-Feb. Dorms 23SFr; quads 136SFr. Non-members add 6SFr.) The **Bannerstube** ❷, in the same building as the hostel, serves a number of reasonably priced dishes, including salads and the acclaimed *Füürtopf à discretion*, and has a fantastic view of the falls. Soups are 5.50-7.50SFr and pasta dishes start at 13SFr. (☎659 67 67; fax 659 61 95. Children's menu available. Open Mar.-Dec. daily 11:30am-11:30pm.)

STEIN AM RHEIN   ☎052

The tiny medieval Altstadt of Stein am Rhein will put your camera to good use. All the houses of the square date back to the 15th century. You'll be mesmerized by the detailed facade paintings that depict the animal or scene after which each house was named. One of the most picturesque Altstädte in all of Switzerland, Stein am Rhein attracts flocks of tourists every summer, but if you only have one day in town, make sure it isn't Sunday, as everything is closed. Beyond the town center, visitors enjoy brightly colored ferries and friendly of local proprietors. As of late, Stein am Rhein has sacrificed some of its quiet and charm by allowing cars to course through the Altstadt.

🚍🚆 **TRANSPORT AND PRACTICAL INFORMATION. Trains** connect Stein am Rhein to: Konstanz via Kreuzlingen (1 per hr. 6:24am-midnight, 9.80SFr), Schaffhausen (2 per hr. 5:28am-10:30pm, 7.20SFr), St. Gallen (1 per hr. 6:56am-5:56pm, 22-27SFr), and Winterthur (1 per hr. 5:07am-11:07pm, 12.4SFr). **Buses** connect the city to small towns in the area and Germany. **Boats** depart three times per day (once on Su) for Schaffhausen (1¼hr., 19.60SFr), Konstanz (2½hr., 24SFr), and other Bodensee towns. (☎052 634 08 88; www.riverticket.ch.) An hour-long cruise on the river (☎741 23 93) costs 12SFr, ages 6-16 6SFr.

To reach the city from the station, head straight out of the station onto Bahnhofstr., bear right on Wagenhauserstr., and left on Charreg., which will lead over a bridge and into the Rathauspl. in the Altstadt's center. Once you turn left and continue walking, Rathauspl. becomes Understadt, the town's main drag. **Parking** is available on all streets skirting the Altstadt, and along Hemishoferstr., off Untertor. (Open 10am-6pm. 0.50SFr per hour.) Stein am Rhein's **tourist office**, Oberstadt. 9, lies on the other side of the *Rathaus*. (☎742 20 90; fax 20 91. Open M-F 9:30am-noon and 1:30-5:30pm.) The station has **currency exchange** and **bike rental** (30SFr per day. Open Apr. 1-Oct. 15 M-F 6:15am-7:35pm, Sa 6:15am-6:35pm, Su 7:15am-7:35pm; Oct. 16-Mar. 31 M-F 6:15am-7:10pm, Sa 6:50am-12:10pm and 12:50-5:10pm, Su 8:15-11:35am and 12:50-6:35pm). Lockers 3SFr. **Internet** is in **Kiosk Charregass** (which also serves cheap pizza), Oberstadt 16, past the tourist office, coming from Rathauspl. (Open Tu-Su 9am-6:30pm. 6SFr per 30min.) The **post office** is at the station. (Open M-F 8am-noon and 2-5:30pm, Sa 8am-noon.) **Postal code:** CH-8260.

⌂🔵 ACCOMMODATIONS AND FOOD. The family-oriented **Jugendherberge (HI) ❷** is at Hemishoferstr. 87. From the train station, take the infrequently scheduled bus (dir: Singen; every 1-2 hours) to "Strandbad" and walk about 5min. farther in the same direction. If the bus does not arrive, follow the directions to the Altstadt; once you cross the bridge, turn left and follow the river for 20min. The hostel fills up quickly, so call ahead. Though not ideally located, it has clean, if sometimes small, rooms (many of which overlook the Rhine), a game room, and a friendly and helpful staff. Get up early to avoid crowds and clogged showers in the camp-style bathrooms. (☎741 12 55; fax 741 51 40. Breakfast, showers, and sheets included. Reception 8-10am and 5-10pm. Curfew 10:30pm; keys available. Open Mar. 1-Nov. Dorms 24SFr; doubles 60SFr; family rooms 30SFr per person. Ages 6-16 accompanied by an adult half price. Kitchen access 2SFr. 3SFr off-season discount. Nonmembers add 6SFr. AmEx/DC/MC/V.)

The two young owners of **Rothen Ochsen Wine Bar ❶**, Rathauspl. 9, are dedicated to preserving the tradition connected with their wooden hall, the oldest public house in the town, built in 1466. Though full meals are not available, their soups, appetizers, and wines provide plenty of sustenance. (☎741 23 28; weinstube@rothenochsen.ch; Open Tu-Sa 11am-11:30pm, Su 11am-6pm.) **The Spaghetteria ❷**, Schifflände 8, sits directly on the Rhine and serves cheap and tasty Italian fare, with pasta dishes from 13SFr. The restaurant also displays the **world's longest piece of spaghetti** at 188.8m. (☎741 22 36. Open mid-Mar. to 2nd Su in Nov. daily 9am-around midnight.) Flash your *Let's Go* and get a free large beer when you order a spaghetti plate for lunch. English menu available.) **Café "Zur Hoffnung," ❶** Rathauspl. 21, satisfies a sugar craving with chocolate, fresh-baked pastries, two dozen cakes, and luck-bringing Steiner Scherben. (☎741 21 82. Open Tu-Sa 8am-6pm, Su 9am-6pm.) For wonderfully smooth ice cream (1.50SFr per scoop), visit **Il Gelato ❶**, at Understadt 12, next to the Rathauspl. (☎741 47 48. Open Mar.-Oct. daily 10am-9pm.) Picnickers fill their baskets at the **Co-op**, Rathauspl. 17, at the corner of Rathauspl. and Schwarzhorng. (Open M-F 8:30am-6:30pm, Sa 8am-5pm.)

◼🔷 SIGHTS AND ENTERTAINMENT. The 12th-century establishment of the **Kloster St. George** first made Stein am Rhein prominent. You can reach the Benedictine monastery by heading up Chirchhofpl. from the Rathauspl. The rooms are preserved in their 16th-century state, just as the five-foot-tall monks (judging by the doors) left them, and the cloister exudes a perfect, ascetic peace. Among the ornate wooden engravings, try to find St. George. Less austere is the vibrant *Festsaal*, whose yellow-and-green-tiled floor is off-limits to feet. As lights are few and dim, try to go when it is bright outside for the best view of delicate paintings and engravings. (☎741 21 42. Open Mar.-Oct. Tu-Su 10am-5pm. 3SFr, students 1.50SFr.) Admire the stately **Rathaus** at the corner of Rhig. and Rathauspl.

Museum Lindwurm, Understadt 18, reconstructs 19th-century bourgeois domestic life with careful attention. Details like soil-covered boots in the farmhouse, a scratched chalkboard in the children's room, and live roosters in the farmhouse provide a snapshot of daily living; you can actually try out the playroom. (☎741 25 12. Open Mar.-Oct. W-M 10am-5pm. 5SFr, students 3SFr. Group tours available in English and French with prior reservation.)

A 30min. hike will take you up the mountain to a vantage point from the castle on **Hohenklingen.** To reach this trail, follow Brodlaubeg. out of town; signs point the rest of the way. When the trail meets the road near the top, the castle is to the left. On a clear day, the snowcapped mountains of the Alps are visible.

ST. GALLEN ☎071

Though it lacks the medieval charm of Schaffhausen, St. Gallen's easy access to Zurich, Germany, Austria, the Bodensee, and small mountain villages makes it a popular stopover for travelers. The relatively modern Altstadt livens on weekends when students from St. Gallen University descend from the hill. During the day, the upscale Altstadt is a window shopper's dream but a spender's nightmare. St. Gallen has a few cultural gems to share—most notably the venerable *Stiftsbibliothek*, the Baroque library named a World Heritage Treasure by UNESCO.

▣ TRANSPORTATION

Trains: To: Appenzell (30min., 1-3 per hr. 5:42am-11:40pm, 10.40SFr); Bern (2½hr., 5:10am-10:43pm, 63-65SFr); Geneva (4½hr., 5:10am-8:43pm, 94SFr); Lugano (4hr., 5:10am-8:43pm, 72-76SFr); Munich (3hr.; 4 per day 8:37am-6:37pm; 62SFr, under 26 51SFr); Zurich (1hr., 5:10am-10:43pm, 26-34SFr).

Buses: 2.20SFr, ages 6-16 1.30SFr; *Tageskarte* (day pass) 7SFr, ages 6-16 5SFr; 12 rides 22SFr. Buy tickets at each stop or on some buses; passes and *Tageskarten* available at large kiosks or **VBSG Transit Authority** across from train station.

Taxis: Sprenger AG, Rohrschacherstr. 281 (☎080 055 10 30).

Herold Taxi AG, Poststr. 11 (☎080 082 27 77).

Car Rental: Herold Autovermietung AG, Molkenstr. 7 (☎228 64 28; fax 64 25). 77SFr per day, 195SFr per weekend (3 days). **Europcar,** Neumarkt 1, St.-Leonhardstr. 35 (☎222 11 14; fax 01 57). From 78SFr per day.

Parking: Neumarkt Parking Garage, near the Neumarkt Supermarket on St. Leonhardstr. 5am-9pm 2SFr per hr., 9pm-5am 1SFr per hr. Open M-Sa 5am-12:30am.(☎222 11 14.) Park in one of the city's **blue zones** M-F for 5.50SFr per day, free Sa-Su.

▣ PRACTICAL INFORMATION

Tourist Office: Bahnhofpl. 1a (☎227 37 37; fax 37 67; www.st.gallen-bodensee.ch; info@st.gallen-bodensee.ch). From the train station, cross the bus stop and pass the fountain on the left; the tourist office is on the right. Maps, brochures, and **city tours** available (June 3-Sept. 30 M, W, F 2-4pm; 15SFr, museum admissions and juice included). Special night tour around Christmas. Open M-F 9am-6pm, Sa 9am-noon.

Currency Exchange: At the station. Open M-F 8am-7pm, Sa 8am-5pm, Su 1-5pm. Services include **Western Union.**

Luggage Storage: At the station. Lockers 4-7SFr. Luggage watch 7SFr. Open M-F 7:30am-7:45pm, Sa-Su 9am-noon and 1-6:45pm. A few cheaper lockers (3SFr) stand at the Appenzeller/Trogen station, across from luggage watch.

Laundromat: Quick Wash, Rorschacherstr. 57 (☎245 94 18). Take bus #1 to "Stadttheater" and walk in the same direction for 5min. Wash 6-7.90SFr, dry 1.80-3.80SFr. Open M-Sa 8am-10pm.

Internet Access: Media Lounge, Katherineng. 10 (☎244 30 90; fax 244 30 91). Facing away from the bus stop at Marktpl., cross at far right into Katerineng. This hip lounge with pop music offers cheap Internet access. 2SFr minimum; after 10min. 1SFr per 5min., 12SFr per 1hr. Open M-F 9am-9pm, sporadic hours Sa-Su.

Post Office: St. Leonhardstr. 45, across the street, to the right of the train station. Open M-W and F 7:30am-6:30pm, Th 7:30am-8pm, Sa 7:30am-4pm. **Postal Code:** CH-9001.

▞ ACCOMMODATIONS

▨ **Jugendherberge St. Gallen (HI),** Jüchstr. 25 (☎245 47 77; fax 245 49 83; stgallen@youthhostel.ch). Next to the train station, you'll find the small Appenzeller/Trogener station with 2 tracks (#12 and 13). Take the orange train from track #12 (dir: Trogen) to "Schülerhaus" (2-4 per hr., 5:32-11:32am, 2.60SFr). From the stop, walk uphill 3min. on the right, turn left across the train tracks at the sign for the hostel, and walk downhill 2min. This friendly hostel on a hill attracts an international student crowd. Though it's a bit of a hike to get here, the relaxing atmosphere and superb view make up for it. Extra perks include a breakfast room, terrace, barbecue pit, grassy lawn, library, board games, and TV room. Breakfast, sheets, and shower included. Dinner 12.50SFr. **Internet** access 1SFr for 4min. Lockers 2SFr deposit. Laundry 6SFr to wash, 4SFr to dry. Parking available. Reception 7-10am and 5-10:30pm. Check-out 10am. No lockout. Quiet hours 10pm-7am. Closed Dec. 1 to end of Feb. Dorms 26SFr; 6-bed "family room" with toilet and shower 34SFr per person; singles 46SF; doubles 72SFr. Non-members add 6SFr. AmEx/DC/MC/V. ❷

Hotel Elite, Metzgerg. 9-11 (☎227 99 33; fax 227 99 30; www.hotel-elite-sg.com; hotel-elite@swissonline.ch), on the street opposite the bus station. Exit station and turn left, staying on the road closest to the train tracks. This road will become Bahnhofst. and then Marktpl. Turn left onto Metzgerg. directly opposite the bus stop. Centrally located near the Altstadt, Marktpl., and within walking distance from Museumstr., this hotel offers simple rooms and chocolates on the pillows. Breakfast included. Doors lock and reception closes at 11pm. Check-out 11am. **Internet** available (10SFr. per hr.). Singles 65-69SFr, with toilet and shower 75-93SFr; doubles with shower 124-132SFr, with toilet and shower 144SFr. AmEx/MC/V. ❹

Hotel Weisses Kreuz, Engelg. 9 (☎/fax 223 28 43). Follow directions to Hotel Elite; Engelg. is one street left from Metzgerg. Weisses Kreuz sits atop a lively and smoky bar run by a cheerful staff. Although rooms are simple (and some cramped), the location makes this hotel ideal for late-night pub crawlers in the Altstadt. Breakfast and hall showers included. Reception M-Sa 6:30am-2pm and 5-11pm, Su 9-11am. Singles 56-68SFr, with toilet and shower 78SFr; doubles 108/128SFr. AmEx/MC/V. ❸

Hotel am Ring, Unterer Graben 9, (☎/fax 223 27 47; hotelamring@bluemail.ch) lies in a centrally located historic building, above an extravagantly decorated cafe. Rooms are equally ornate. Singles 85SFr (90SFr with breakfast); doubles 110SFr (130SFr with breakfast) ❹.

🍴 FOOD

Migros, St. Leonhardstr., 1 block behind the train station (open M-W and F 8am-6:30pm, Th 8am-9pm, Sa 8am-5pm), has a buffet restaurant in a separate building behind the market (open M-W and F 6:30am-6:30pm, Th 6:30am-9pm, Sa 6:30am-5pm). A **public market,** on Marktpl., bustles with fresh produce, bread, and meat. (Open 7am-7pm daily.)

▨ Restaurant Scheitlinsbüchel, Scheitlinsbüchelweg 10 (☎244 68 21). Instead of turning left to the youth hostel from the main road, turn right into a small parking lot; as the road enters the woods, turn left onto the uphill trail; when you reach the road again, go left to reach the farmhouse restaurant. Charming because of the green pastures surrounding it, this restaurant provides a panoramic view of St. Gallen with your traditional Swiss meal. Open Tu-Su from 9am until when everyone leaves. MC/V. ❸

Christina's, Weberg. 9 (☎223 88 08). Wooden tables and colorful walls define this bright, modern eatery. Vegetarian and meat dishes from 18.50SFr. Fish lovers should try the homemade *salmontatar.* Open M-Th 9:30am-11:30pm, F-Sa 9:30am-12:30am. AmEx/MC/V. ❸

Weinstube zum Bäumli, Schmiedg. 18 (☎222 11 74), offers Swiss dishes in an intimate setting where many locals sit for hours. Set in one of the oldest buildings in St. Gallen, this quaint restaurant serves all the schnitzel and wurst you could want, or try the traditional *Rösti* (36.50SFr) with fried potatoes, rice, or salad. Don't be shocked if the waiter puts down another plate when you're done with your main course—the restaurant offers two servings of their dishes to its patrons. Open Tu-Sa 9am-12:30am. MC/V. ❹

Barolo Restaurant and Bar, Schmiedg. 1 (☎220 10 72; fax 220 10 73), right across from the Church of St. Lawrence, serves a light menu of Italian flavor. Soups 8.50SFr and pasta dishes from 14.50SFr. Funky, art nouveau light fixtures (which are for sale) and a leopard-print stairwell stand out from the cream-colored interior. Open Tu-Sa 10am-midnight. ❷

Pizzeria Testarossa, Metzgerg. 20 (☎222 03 30; www.testarossa.ch). A short distance up the small street off Marktpl. directly across from the Marktpl. bus stop. Secluded on a rooftop patio, choose from delicious veggie pizzas (from 12.50SFr) and "make-your-own" options. Open M-Sa 11am-2pm and 5pm-midnight, Su 11am-2pm. MC/V. ❷

👁 SIGHTS

Aside from the aptly named Museumstraße, where St. Gallen's four museums are located, the city's main attractions are found within the grounds of the St. Gallen Abbey Precinct. Most noteworthy of these attractions are the magnificent *Stiftsbibliothek* and the Kathedrale St. Gallen. From the far left of the station, walk up Bahnhofstr. to Marktpl., then left on Marktg. to reach the abbey.

STIFTSBIBLIOTHEK. Anyone who loves books and medieval culture will marvel at St. Gallen's main attraction, the *Stiftsbibliothek,* the library of the Benedictine abbey at St. Gallen. You'll glide in on huge fuzzy gray slippers (provided by the library to protect the beautiful floors) to a chorus of oohs and aahs at the library's lavishly carved and polished exotic wood shelves, filled with rows of centuries-old, gilt-spined books. The library maintains a collection of 140,000 volumes and 2000 manuscripts, 500 of which date from before AD 1200, including 3rd- and 5th-century texts from Virgil and early Bibles. Although the appearance of the resident death-blackened mummy might indicate otherwise, the *Stiftsbibliothek* is a living, lending library serving scholars from around the globe. (☎227 34 16; fax 27 34 18; stibi@stibi.ch; www.stibi.ch. Open Apr. 1 to Nov., 2002 M-Sa 10am-5pm, Su 10am-4pm; closed Nov. 11-Dec.1, 2002 for maintenance and renovations. Tours (in German only) Apr., May, Oct.

daily 2pm; June, Sept. 10:30am, 2pm; July-Aug. 10:30am, 2, 3pm. English tours can be arranged through the tourist office. 7SFr, students 5SFr.)

Other attractions of the abbey include the **Kathedrale St. Gallen,** a part of the abbey founded in the 8th century and renovated in the mid-18th. The cathedral has enormous stained glass windows that cast little light on the intricate carvings of the confessionals and the details of the impressive murals. *(☎227 33 88. Open daily 7am-6pm except during Mass.)* The abbey's bright courtyard is ideal for a picnic or sun-bath. On the far side of the abbey from the library sits the less impressive **Evangelical Church of St. Lawrence,** founded in the 9th century. Its smaller interior showcases organ pipes and Easter egg-type wall patterns. Its ornate rooftop is worth a gaze. *(Open M-F 9:30-11:30am and 2-4pm.)*

MUSEUMSTRAßE. Two buildings side by side hold most of St. Gallen's museumworthy relics. Though all the information is in German, impressive displays and varied themes make a trip to Museumstr. perfect for kids and adults on a rainy day. The minute **Natural History Museum** (☎242 06 70; fax 06 72) rotates thoughtful and interactive exhibits of Mother Nature's creations. Housed in the same building, the four-room **Kunstmuseum** (☎242 06 71; fax 06 72) has a small collection that juxtaposes modern and traditional art. St. Gallen's enormous **Historisches Museum** (☎242 06 42; fax 06 44) explores traditional Swiss culture. Displays include ancient kitchens, an old barber shop, and children's toys. The **Ethnology Collection** (☎242 06 43; fax 06 44) has a tour of various foreign cultures, carefully avoiding over-interpretation and allowing authentic artifacts to speak for themselves. *(Museumstr. 32-50. From Marktpl., with your back to the bus stop, walk right on Bohl to get to Museumstr. All museums open Tu-F 10am-noon and 2-5pm, Sa-Su 10am-5pm. 6SFr, students 2SFr. One ticket grants admission to all 4 museums, except special exhibits in the Kunstmuseum.)*

OTHER SIGHTS. For a view of the St. Gallen valley (and perhaps a glimpse of a few endangered species), visit the **Peter and Paul Wildpark,** on Kirchlistr. in Rotmonten. Take bus #5 (dir: Rotmonten) to "Sonne." Walk in the opposite direction of the bus, turn left at the first intersection onto Kirchlistr. and walk uphill 30min. A well-tended trail leads through the park, ensuring that you don't miss the ibex, which have made a comeback from near extinction. *(☎222 67 92 or 241 51 13. Open 24hr. Free.)* For a tamer excursion, explore the campus of the **St. Gallen University.**

🎵 🎭 ENTERTAINMENT AND NIGHTLIFE

St. Gallen's Altstadt resonates with techno beats and the heavy clink of beer mugs. Head for the streets radiating out from Marktpl., which feature cheap and authentic bars and home-grown clientele. Clubs tend to be clustered together, particularly around Goliathg. and Brühlg. Beers are always expensive in dance clubs.

Birreria, Brühlg. 45 (☎223 25 33). Homesick travelers longing for familiar alcohol will definitely find it here. With 240 types of beer from a plain American Budweiser to the African Castle Lager, Birreria lets you take a barley trip around the globe without moving your lazy gut. Drink them at the bar or take them with you for half price. Open M-Sa noon-late, Su 5pm-late.

Ozon, Goliathg. 28 (☎244 81 24). Non-stop chrome and mirrors lend the illusion of size to this compact club. If the flashing lights and smoke don't blind you, the prices will (beer from 9SFr). The music selection changes each night, with hip-hop and soul W-Th and 70s and 80s dance music on the weekend. Cover 10SFr. Open W-Sa 10pm-4pm.

Filou, Schwertg. (☎244 24 98). Follow Goliathg. from Marktpl. to the end, then curve around 200 ft. to the right onto Schwertg. This smoky bar pumps 80s rock and cheap beer (3.5-7SFr) for a 20-something crowd. Beer guzzlers overflow into the picnic tables outside. Dance floor is packed on the weekend. Open daily 5pm-2am.

Trischli Dancing, Brühlg. 18 (☎226 09 00; fax 226 09 50), attracts an unlikely mix of clubgoers. The circular dance floor gives exhibitionists a chance to show off. The club features local bands, karaoke, and other theme nights (foxtrot, anyone?). Make this your last stop, because things get hopping late. Su-Th no cover, F-Sa 7-17SFr. Open July-Aug. Th-Tu 10pm-5:30am; Sept.-June from 9pm to whenever.

For a cultured evening, the **Stadttheater,** Museumstr. 24 (☎242 06 66; www.theaterstgallen.ch), in a fancy Art Nouveau building, hosts over 200 concerts and dramatic works by renowned artists and musicians a year. There are several **movie theaters** at Marktpl. The largest is the **Scala Kinocenter and Bar** (☎228 08 60), on the corner of Marktpl. and Goliathg., with five screens. Every year in late July and early August, the **Open-Air Kino** at Kantonschulpark on Burggraben (www.open-air-kino.ch) screens mostly American films (15SFr).

For real party animals, St. Gallen's celebration of music and debauchery dominates the fields surrounding the town at the end of June. The **Open Air St. Gallen Music Festival** (see **Festival Fever,** p. 328) features over 20 live bands in late June or July. Past headliners have included Metallica, Garbage, Red Hot Chili Peppers, Cypress Hill, the legendary B.B. King, and the Godfather of Soul, James Brown. Tickets sell for 134SFr for all three days or 104SFr. for Saturday and Sunday. Bring a tent (showers and toilets available), or stay in St. Gallen and take the shuttle bus to the concert grounds. (☎0848 800 800; www.openairsg.ch.)

APPENZELL   ☎071

Appenzell, Switzerland's smallest canton, is world-renowned for its *Appenzeller Käse* (cheese) and its highly conservative people; women weren't allowed to vote until 1971. Its inhabitants maintain the traditional agrarian lifestyle—favorite occupations in the region include herding animals and hiking. The canton is dotted with tiny villages, but the town of Appenzell is the gathering place for cantonal meetings and agricultural shows. Appenzell is best explored on foot. Over centuries, local herdsmen have developed an extensive and dense network of trails in the hills and mountains for shepherding their flocks. These trails are frequented by herders in traditional garb and are sprinkled with *Gasthäuser* (guest houses) that provide a night's rest and a luxurious respite from alpine hikes.

THE LOCAL STORY

A SLICE OF HEAVEN

Adolf Fässler is a cheese-maker on the Alp Großhütten (1200m).

Q: Can you describe a normal day of cheese-making?
A: Well, wake-up is 5am. The cows and goats are milked, the pigs are fed, and the cheese is made. In the afternoon, the cheese is stirred; then, after coffee, the animals are milked again and the dishware is cleaned.
Q: Do you do this all alone?
A: With my wife. This is my 51st summer making cheese: 21 years with my father, and now 30 with my wife. Always on the same mountain.
Q: How long does it take to make cheese?
A: For small ones, 5-6 weeks; for large ones, 6-8 weeks. The milk has to be heated and culture and salt added. It is stirred and then poured in a mold. Then it is turned several times. The next day it gets a salt water bath in the cellar and is placed on a wooden plank to dry. Then it is turned every day until it's ripe for sale. We do everything by hand, and use machines only for milking.
Q: Do you sell all your cheese?
A: Yes, mostly to tourists. We also have local clientele who come here every day to buy. It's word-of-mouth business.
Q: Do you make enough money?
A: Well, you can't figure out a per hour wage. The hours are extremely long and it's hard to find time to rest. But I don't need the money; I get more pleasure from nature and work.
Q: You like your job, then?
A: Yes, it's heaven on earth.

▐ TRANSPORTATION. The rattling *Appenzellerbahn* chugs between Appenzell and St. Gallen (45min., 2 per hr. 6:11am-10:46pm, 10.40SFr). From St. Gallen and Gossau (an easier connection), there is a regular train to Zurich (1hr. 32SFr). The train from St. Gallen continues from Appenzell to Wasserauen, a tiny hamlet that serves as a gateway to the Alpenteil valley and its hikes (10min., 3.80SFr).

▐ PRACTICAL INFORMATION. The Appenzell **tourist office**, Hauptg. 4, down Poststr. from the station and right at the intersection with Hauptg., makes hotel reservations, sells detailed hiking maps, and lists happenings around town. (☎788 96 41; fax 96 49; infotourismus@ai.ch; www.myappenzellerland.ch. Open May to mid-Oct. M-F 9am-noon and 1:30-6pm, Sa-Su 10am-noon and 2-5pm; mid-Oct. to Apr. M-F 9am-noon and 2-5pm, Sa 2-5pm.) The tourist office arranges a **free tour** of the **Appenzeller Alpenbitter** factory, in which the region's unique and delicious anise-flavored alcoholic drink is made (1½hr. tour starts at Weißbadstr. 27, mid-June to mid-Oct. W 10am). The tourist office has information about Herr Fässler, a Swiss farmer and cheese maker in Grosshütter (mid-June to mid-Sept.). For all tourist-office-sponsored events, register the day prior by 5pm. **Internet** access is available at the library, or at the tourist office when the library is closed. (5SFr per 30min. Library open Tu-W 2-5pm, Th 2-4pm, F 5-8pm and Sa 9:30-11:30am.) The train station offers **lockers** (3SFr) and **luggage storage** (5SFr). The **post office** is across the street from the train station. (Open M-F 7:30am-noon and 1:30-6pm, Sa 8am-noon.) **Postal code:** CH-9050.

▐◐ ACCOMMODATIONS AND FOOD. The ever-present aroma of Appenzeller cheese lingers around **Gasthaus Hof ❹,** on Landsgemeindepl. in the center of town. This bustling family-run hotel and restaurant provides guests with comfortable beds and crisp comforters in cozy, low-ceilinged rooms. (☎787 22 10; fax 58 83; hotel_hof@hotmail.com. Restaurant and reception open 8am-10pm. Reserve one week in advance from Aug.-Oct. 15. Singles 65SFr, with shower 85-95SFr; doubles with shower 130SFr; triples with shower 180SFr; quads with shower 220SFr. MC/V.) Picturesque lodgings await at **Haus Lydia ❸,** Eggerstrandenstr. 53. From the tourist office turn left onto Hauptg. and again onto Gaiserstr. across the bridge, and turn right onto Eggerstrandenstr. (15min). Alternately take the train one stop toward St. Gallen to Hirschberg, turn right onto Hirschbergstr., again under the bridge and once more onto Eggerstrandenstr. (3min.). Run by a friendly, English-speaking family, Haus Lydia has large rooms with views and an elegant sitting room. When the weather's good, the owners' sons provide musical entertainment. (☎787 42 33; fax 367 21 70; contact@hauslydia.ch; www.haus-lydia.ch. Breakfast included. Reserve 2 weeks in advance. Singles 59SFr; doubles 88SFr.) The tourist office also provides a list of **Privatzimmer.** The **Gasthöfe** (guest houses) that line the trail are comfortable overnight stops (see **Hiking,** below).

◪**Restaurant Traube ❸,** Marktg. 7, near the Landsgemeindepl. in Hotel Traube, serves Appenzeller specialties by candlelight upon traditional hand embroidered placemats. *Appenzeller Chäshörnli* (macaroni and cheese) or *Käseschnitte* with ham, egg, or pineapple run 13-14SFr, while meat entrees cost 21-37SFr. Appenzeller beer is 2.60SFr. (☎787 14 07; www.hotel-traube.ch. Open Mar.-Jan. Tu-Su 9am-midnight. AmEx/DC/MC/V.) The **Co-op** and **Migros,** both with restaurants, are across from one another on Zielstr. off Landsgemeindepl. (Both open M-Th 8am-6:30pm, F 8am-8pm, Sa 8am-4pm.)

◪ SIGHTS. The **Rathaus** houses the museum, town hall, cantonal library, and tourist office. The Großratssaal, with intricately carved wooden walls and 16th-century frescoes of giants supporting the central beam, is particularly remarkable. (Open on special request at the tourist office or district office.) Inside the *Rathaus* and the adjoining Haus Buherre Hanisefs, the **Museum Appenzell**, Hauptg. 4, chronicles local culture in displays of clothing and tools that weave throughout the wooden-raftered house, as well as an old wooden prison cell. A video on hand embroidery (in English and German) is surprisingly captivating and exposes the harsh realities of idealized traditional Swiss life. (☎ 788 96 31. Open Apr.-Oct. daily 10am-noon and 2-5pm; Nov.-Mar. Tu-Su 2-5pm. 5SFr, students 3SFr.) Next door, the stately, asymmetrical **Pfarrkirche St. Mauritius** shows off its Rococo stained-glass windows, gold-filigreed altars, and a magnificent golden chandelier from the Baroque interior. (Open daily 7:30am-7pm.)

HIKES IN THE APPENZELL REGION

Deep in the heart of the Alpstein, Appenzell offers great hiking without the temperature extremes of Zermatt or Ticino regions. The tourist office offers the *Wandervorschläge: Appenzellerland*, whose detailed map shows all rest areas. A comprehensive topographical map is available at the bookstores. Hiking options range from easy strolls through pastures to strenuous overnight treks.

EASIER HIKES

Gonterbad (2hr.). A relaxing walk begins in the nearby town of Gonten (10min. by train from Appenzell; 3SFr). Stroll along a special trail over the meadows to Gonterbad (45min.), where you can rest and wash your feet (towels 2SFr) in the garden of the Bad Gonton Hotel and Restaurant before heading back to Appenzell (45min.).

Kapellenweg Hike (5hr. round-trip). The Kapellenweg provides a close look at local rural life. Cross under the train tracks, take a left, then a right at the major intersection to get to the trailhead; from there, brown "Kapellenweg" signs point the way. For the first 45min., the flat trail winds through local farms. For the adventurous, the trail randomly veers off from the paved road at times, leading through sheep and cow pastures. (Be prepared to hop several wooden fences and shimmy under some barbed wire enclosures.) The trail splits in several places, but all paths eventually lead to the **Kapelle Maria** (1½hr.) and the larger and more ornate **Ahornkapelle** (2½hr.). The paved road is the easiest route to follow, passing a series of small paintings depicting Christ's crucifixion and resurrection. For a more challenging version of the hike (*sans* paintings, but with chapels), follow the "Kapellenweg" signs that lead uphill into the surrounding woods. Both trails lead back to Appenzell.

DIFFICULT HIKES

Hiking around Appenzell can be strenuous, as the trails wind steeply up and down the mountains. Upper regions of this area tend to stay snow-covered late in the year and some parts are covered year-round. Do not hike into snowy areas when there is low visibility. It is safest to hike in pairs or groups. If you hike alone, always make sure to let someone know where you're going and when you're planning on coming back. See **Wilderness Safety**, p. 29, for more information.

For more difficult hikes, start from tiny Wasserauen, the last stop on the Appenzellerbahn (10min. from Appenzell; 3.80SFr). The best way to experience the area is to hike between guest houses, which typically consist of a restaurant and dorm rooms with mattresses side by side on the floor. The first hikes listed leave from the top of **Ebenalp Cable Car**, across the street from the small train station in Wasserauen. (Cable car runs 7:40am-7pm. 18SFr, 24SFr round-trip; students 14SFr/18.50SFr; SwissPass or Eurail holders half-price. Reduced times due to renovations Nov. 5-Dec. 7 and Apr. 2-30; call ☎ 799 12 12 for schedules.) For those

MEADOW MEN Some local farmers spend the entire summer tending the livestock among the alpine meadows. Far from friends and family, these men look forward to the annual *Alpstobete* as a time to reunite with loved ones and celebrate the middle of summer. Originally held the Sunday after St. Jakob's Day (July 25), the patron saint of the Alps, locals don traditional garb of embroidered suspenders and brightly colored dresses to perform age-old courtship dances to folk music. Audiences of locals and tourists alike cheer on performers throughout the end of July, but in some locales festivals extend into mid-August. Ask at the tourist office for local festival dates.

looking to travel and use cable cars daily, consider the *Appenzell Card*, which provides free access to three of the area's four cable cars (Säntis cable car not included) and bus and train lines as far as St. Gallen (31SFr, 3 days 52SFr, 5 days 84SFr; with SwissPass 22SFr/42SFr/68SFr). The **Berggasthaus Ebenalp**, 100m uphill from the top of the cable car, is a good base from which to explore the mountains, with more amenities than other guest houses. (☎799 11 94. Breakfast included. Showers 4SFr. Sleepsack 5SFr. Reception 7am-9pm. Reserve 2-3 months in advance for Sa stays. Open May-Nov. and winter weekends. Dorms 28SFr; singles and doubles with sinks 50SFr per person. AmEx/DC/MC/V.) The last two hikes listed can be done without cable cars.

Wasserauen to Wildkirchli (30min.). This quick and popular hike leads down from the Ebenalp (top station) through caves to the **Wildkirchli**, a 400-year-old chapel built into a cliff face and manned until recently by a hermit priest. **Berggasthaus Äscher ❷** lies just beyond Wildkirchli. At 150 years, Äscher is the oldest *Gasthaus* in the region. Tucked into the sheer cliff face, one interior wall is the rocky mountain. (☎799 11 42; fax 14 49; info@aescher-ai.ch; www.aescher-ai.ch. Breakfast included. No showers. Open May-Nov. 25-35SFr.)

Schäfler to Messmer (1½hr.). This exceedingly steep and rickety downhill trail leads from Berggasthaus Schäfler to **Berggasthhaus Meßmer ❷**. A couple sections of the trail have a metal cable for balance, but this trail still should not be attempted after rain or snow. From Schäfler, follow the signs to "Meßmer," which will leads along a path called the Höheweg (30min.). The trail then turns left and descends even more steeply, for a view of the blue-green Seealpsee below. A steep uphill climb through cow pastures (10min.) leads to the final destination; the braying of livestock and clanging of cowbells signal the end. (☎799 12 55, winter ☎799 10 77; Breakfast included. No running water, but a well outside. Reception 24hr. Reserve 1-2 months ahead for weekends. Open June-Oct. Dorms 24SFr, children under 17 17SFr.)

Wasserauen to Seealpsee (1hr.). For a more strenuous entry into the mountains from Wasserauen, hike uphill to the alpine lake **Seealpsee.** Exit the train station, turn left, and follow the road until it forks. The trail begins at the left fork (just past the Alpenrose). Yellow signs marked "Seealpsee" mark the trail as it rises steeply through spruce forests lined with waterfalls and high alpine meadows of cattle. At the top, the trail passes a few farmhouses and ends at ▨**Berggasthaus Seealpsee ❷**, the 2nd of two guest houses on the trail. The Dörig-Klossner family has run the guest house for generations and knows every detail about the surrounding country. Its pristine location near the waters of the Seealpsee makes it a perfect base to explore surrounding peaks. The restaurant serves homemade spinach *Spätzli*. (☎799 11 40; winter ☎799 14 40; fax 18 20; berggasthaus@seealpsee.ch; www.seealpsee.ch. Breakfast included. Showers 2SFr. Reception 7:30am-midnight. Reserve 1-2 months in advance for weekends. Open Apr.-Nov. Dorms 25SFr; one single 45SFr; doubles 90SFr. MC/V.)

Seealpsee to Säntis (4hr.). The climb to **Säntis** (2503m), the highest mountain in the region, is a good day hike from Seealpsee. From Seealpsee, hike to **Meglisalp** (1hr.), a cozy cluster of 6 farmhouses tucked beneath the peak. **Gasthof Meglisalp ❷** is a great place to stay for a night with the cows and the people who tend to them. A local farmer calls out a prayer with a wooden megaphone every night for the neighbors and their cattle, an old Appenzeller tradition. (☎799 11 28; fax 15 78; info@meglisalp.ch; www.meglisalp.ch. Breakfast included. Reception 24hr. Reserve 1-2 weeks ahead. Open May-Oct. Dorms 31SFr; singles 52SFr; doubles 104SFr.) To get to Säntis from Meglisalp, head either to *Rotsteinpass* (more difficult) or *Wagenlücke* (easier), and then up to Säntis (both trips 3hr.). Two guest houses sit on top of Säntis. **Gasthaus Säntis ❸** is the older and more personalized house. (☎799 11 60, winter 14 11; fax 11 60. Breakfast included. Dorms 37SFr; doubles 114SFr.) There are numerous routes from Säntis back to Wasserauen; the road-weary can take the cable car down to the neighboring town of **Schwägalp** and travel to Appenzell via Urnäsch. (Cable car every 30min. June 10-Oct. 26 7:30am-6:30pm; Oct. 27-Jan. 6 and Jan. 26-June 9 8:30am-5pm. 23SFr, 33SFr round-trip. Bus to Urnäsch and train to Appenzell 13.60SFr.)

GRAUBÜNDEN

The largest, least populous, and most alpine of the Swiss cantons, Graubünden is made up of deep, rugged gorges twisting through snow-clad peaks and forests of larch and fir. The various towns ranging from the capital, Chur, to Portein (pop. 22) are scattered throughout the canton and seem out of place among the overwhelming nature. The Swiss National Park in the Lower Engadine is the most tightly protected alpine landscape in Europe, and many communities, such as Zuoz and Scuol, are equally unspoiled. Glitzy St. Moritz and Davos have sprung up in the snowy midst to host glamorous ski resorts.

As visitors travel from valley to valley, the language slips from German to Romansch to Italian, with a wide range of dialects in between. Travel is not cheap in Graubünden. Invest in the **Graubünden Total Regional Pass** (allows 3, 5, 7, or 10 days of free travel in a 10-day period and a 50% discount on other days; 140SFr, 190SFr, 240SFr, and 290SFr, respectively). The Regional Pass can be issued in

Switzerland only from May to October. It is issued by the **Rhätische Bahn (Viafer Retica** in Romansch), Graubünden's own train company, and is good for trains, buses, and cable cars in the region. SwissPass and Eurail are also valid.

 Plan your trip to Graubünden carefully. In ski season you probably won't be able to get a room if you don't call ahead. There are no rooms available in May and June when the whole valley shuts down for vacation.

HIGHLIGHTS OF GRAUBÜNDEN

Delve into the psychological underworld of Expressionist Ernst Kirchner at his eponymous museum in **Davos** (see p. 419).

Ski in secluded, spectacular, and seductively inexpensive **Arosa** (see p. 414).

Window-shop with the rich and famous in **St. Moritz** (p. 432).

CHUR (COIRA)   ☎ 081

Chur (pop. 32,000), the capital of Graubünden, has been inhabited for over 11,000 years, making it Switzerland's oldest settlement. Despite the area's rich history and diverse culture, Chur attracts few tourists and is a refreshing reality check. It serves as a transportation hub for excursions into Graubünden.

▐ TRANSPORTATION

Chur is the transportation hub for Graubünden. **Trains** connect to: **Arosa** (1hr., every hr. 5:35am-11:02pm, 13.40SFr); **Basel** (2¾hr., 1-2 per hr. 4:48am-10:16pm, 60SFr); **Disentis** (1¼hr., every hr. 6:15am-10:10pm, 25SFr) for the **Furka-Oberalp line; St. Gallen** (1½hr., every hr. 4:48am-10:16pm, 31SFr); **St. Moritz** (2hr., every hr. 5:10am-9:21pm, 38SFr); and **Zurich** (1½hr., 1-2 per hr. 4:48am-10:16pm, 35SFr). **Postal buses** run to **Ticino** through **Bellinzona** (2½hr., 6 per day 8am-6pm, 50SFr).

▐ PRACTICAL INFORMATION

Most directions begin at Postpl., which lies two blocks from the station on Bahnhofstr. Chur's **tourist office,** Grabenstr. 5, left on Grabenstr. off Postpl., makes hotel reservations (2SFr) and distributes guides to the city walking tours. (☎252 18 18; fax 90 76. Open M 1:30-6pm, Tu-F 8:30am-noon and 1:30-6pm, Sa 9am-noon.) Graubünden's **regional tourist office,** Alexanderstr. 24, off Bahnhofstr., stocks city brochures. (☎254 24 24; fax 24 00; contact@graubuenden.ch; www.graubuenden.ch. Open M-F 8am-noon and 1:30-5:30pm.)

Train station services include: **currency exchange, luggage storage** (7SFr), kiosk for **hotel reservations** outside the train station, and **bike rental** (30SFr per day, 23SFr per half-day at baggage check; 6SFr to return bike to another station; open 6am-8pm). **Lockers** are at the station (2SFr); larger ones are at the post bus station above (3-5SFr). **Internet** access is at **The Street Café,** Grabenstr. 47. (☎253 79 14; open M-Th 9am-midnight, F-Sa 9am-2am) or one block farther at the **Flipp-in** video arcade (open M-Sa 11:30am-midnight, Su 1pm-midnight; 15SFr per hr.). **Laundry** is at **Maltesen's Wash Self-Service,** Malteserg. 1. (Open M-Sa 9am-midnight, Su noon-midnight. Wash 6-8SFr, dry 3-5SFr.) The **post office** is just right of the train station in the Post Bus station complex. (Open M-F 7:30am-noon and 1:30-6:30pm, Sa 8am-noon.) At Postpl. a secondary office offers better hours. (Open M-F 7:30am-6:30pm, Sa 8am-2pm.) **Postal code:** CH-7000/7002.

ACCOMMODATIONS

Budget options are hard to come by in Chur and not very luxurious. The nearest hostel is in **Arosa** (see p. 414), and there is a nice hotel nearby in **Bad Ragaz** (see p. 413). **Hotel Drei Könige ❷** has been family-run since 1911. From the tourist office, turn right on Grabenstr. and again on Reichsg. With painted stone archways and poster-lined halls, this hotel seems caught between a castle and a college dorm. (☎ 252 17 25; fax 17 26; dreikoenige@swissonline.ch; www.dreikoenige.ch. **Free Internet** for guests. Breakfast included. Parking 12SFr. Reception 6:30am-10pm. Sheets for dorms 5SFr. Dorms 25SFr; singles 65-70SFr, with shower 85-110SFr; doubles 100-120SFr/140-160SFr.) **Post Hotel ❹**, Poststr. 11 off Postpl., has plant-lined hallways and luxurious rooms. (☎ 252 68 44; fax 01 95; posthotel.chur@bluewin.ch. Breakfast included. Reception 6:30am-midnight. Doors lock at midnight; keys available on request. Singles 75-90SFr, with shower 90-120SFr; doubles 120-150SFr/150-200SFr. AmEx/DC/MC/V.) The high-altitude **Hotel Rosenhügel ❸**, Malixerstr. 32, over the bridge and up the hill, has wooden beds and bureaus and an affable staff. (☎/fax 252 23 88. Breakfast and parking included. Reception 8am-midnight. Singles 50-55SFr; doubles 100SFr, with shower 110SFr; triples 150SFr. AmEx/DC/MC/V.) **Camp Auchur ❶**, Felsensustr. 61, is a green and grassy campsite on the Rhine. Take bus #2 to "Obere Au" past the sports complex; it's on the left, on the gravel path. Equipped with kiosks and restaurant. (☎ 284 22 83. 6.20SFr per person, tents 6.20-14.50SFr. Electricity 3.30SFr. Showers 0.50SFr.)

FOOD AND NIGHTLIFE

Wander around the squares of the old city to find a variety of cuisines, including Spanish, Thai, Greek, and good old *Rösti*.

Valentino's Grill, Untereg. 5 (☎ 252 73 22), the "1st Original Swiss Shwarma," right on Grabenstr. from Postpl. and left under the arches to Unterg. The best budget option. Kebabs 8.90-9.90SFr, falafel in pita 7.50SFr, beer from 3.50SFr. Open M-Th 11:45am-2pm and 5-11:30pm, F 11:45am-2pm and 5pm-2am, Sa noon-2am. ❶

Restaurante Controverse, Steinbruchstr. 2 (☎ 252 99 44), reached by turning left on Grabenstr., which turns into Steinbruchstr. Lives up to its name with artsy decor, Louis XIV drapes, black coffee tables, and neon lights. Pastas 12-22SFr, wine 4-8SFr. Open M-Sa 11am-2:30pm and 5pm-midnight, Su 6-11pm. Closed mid-July to mid-Aug. ❸

La Pasteria Otello, Ottopl. (☎ 250 55 15; fax 55 16; pbarfuss@otello.ch; www.otello.ch). From the station, turn left onto Ottostr. Secluded from the busy town center, this candlelit restaurant is draped in pastel green. Pastas and pizzas are reasonably priced (14.50-26SFr), but fish entrees and specialties (24.50-39.50SFr) are a splurge. Try the award-winning *Pizza al Pescatore* with calamari and half a lobster (39.50SFr). Open M-Su 10am-2pm and 6pm-midnight. AmEx/DC/MC/V. ❹

China Restaurant Han Kung, Rabeng. 6 (☎ 252 24 58; fax 31 98). Follow Poststr. from Postpl. and turn left at St. Martin's Church to find a bit of China in Haus Pestalozza. 3-course lunch specials 14.50SFr. Open Tu-Su 11:30am-1:45pm and 6-9:45pm. ❸

Manor, on Bahnhofstr. 8 floors include a market with fresh, inexpensive breads and sandwiches. Open M-Th 8:30am-7pm, F 8:30am-9pm, Sa 8am-5pm. ❶

Street Café, Grabenstr. 47 (☎ 253 79 14), where classical statues peer down from mirrored, red-draped walls, provides intimate drinking enclaves and a breezy terrace. Beers from 3.90SFr. **Internet** 15SFr per hr. Open M-Th 9am-midnight, F-Sa 9am-2am. ❶

👁 SIGHTS

Footpaths throughout the town lead visitors past Chur's sights. Among the highlights are various churches, museums, and old city buildings. The cavernous 12th-century late-Romanesque **Dom** (cathedral) at the top of the old town displays eight altarpieces in addition to the **Hochaltar**, a flamboyant 15th-century gold-and-wood masterpiece carved by Jakob Russ. The crypt where the Capuchin martyr St. Fidelis is buried houses the **Dom-Museum,** replete with relics. (*Open on request. Call ☎ 252 19 70 between 9am-noon to arrange a visit.*) Downhill, the **Martinskirche** (built in 1491) counters the cathedral's dusky, lurking presence with understated simplicity; aside from the dominating organ and windows of the altar, the church's sole decorations are three stained-glass windows by Augusto Giacometti. The eerie panels depict the birth of a defiant Christ. Clad in blood-red instead of her usual blue, Mary rests with downcast eyes beside a rather bored Joseph.

Chur's **Bündner Kunstmuseum,** Bahnhofstr. 35, at the corner of Bahnhofstr. and Grabenstr., blazes with the art of the Giacomettis: Giovanni, Alberto, and Augusto. Works by Swiss artists Angelika Kauffman and Ferdinand Hodler occupy the ground floor while modern exhibits liven the basement. (*☎ 257 28 68. Open Tu-W and F-Su 10am-noon and 2-5pm, Th 10am-noon and 2-8pm. 7SFr, students 4SFr, under 16 free. During the summer exhibition (usually late June to mid-Sept.) open without afternoon break. 10SFr, students 7SFr.*) The **Rætisches Museum,** Hofstr. 1, houses a collection of tapestries, coins, and archaeological trivia that document the origin of "Rhætia" and its development into current Graubünden. An English guide to the exhibits is available (12SFr). (*☎ 257 28 89. Open Tu-Su 10am-noon and 2-5pm. 5SFr, students 2SFr, seniors and groups 3SFr, under 16 free.*)

NEAR CHUR

BAD RAGAZ   ☎ 081

A massage at Bad Ragaz's thermal baths (34°C) will relax weary muscles at no small expense. Luckily, the laid-back atmosphere of this tree-lined suburb is just as soothing. Bad Ragaz lies in the heart of the region famous as the home of Heidi. Short hikes from the top of mountains, serviced by expensive cable cars, allow exploration of the area immortalized by Johanna Spyri's beloved tale. The 90min. pass to the **Tamina Therma** (thermal baths) grants access to the town spa's three pools, waterfalls, watery lounges, and grottoes. (*☎ 303 27 47. Open daily 7:30am-9pm. 17SFr, solarium extra.*) The **cable car** from Bad Ragaz to Paradiel (26SFr) ascends to the starting point of a 1½hr. round-trip **Heidi hike** with billboards retelling the story. (Wheelchair accessible.) A similar 1½hr. tour from Maienfeld (one stop before Bad Ragaz) passes **Heidi's house.** (*☎ 330 19 12. Open mid-Mar. to mid-Nov. 10am-5pm. 5SFr, children 2SFr.*)

Bad Ragaz is accessible by train from Chur (15min., every 30min. 4:48am-11:16pm, 7.80SFr) and St. Gallen (1¼hr., every hr. 5:59am-10:21pm, 25SFr). The **tourist office,** Maienfelderstr. 5, left off Bahnhofstr., offers hiking and biking suggestions. (*☎ 302 10 61; fax 62 90; info@badragaz-tourismus.ch; www.badragaz-tourismus.ch. Open M-F 8:30am-6pm, Sa 8:30am-noon and 1-4pm.*) **Currency exchange** and **lockers** (2-5SFr) are at the train station. **Bike rental** is at **Bigger & Co.** on Sarganserstr., right from Bahnhofstr. (*☎ 302 15 72; www.biggerzweirad.ch. 14-18SFr per day.*) **Heidi's Backpacker ❷,** Bahnhofstr. 29, has simple rooms, though red velour curtains and framed kitschy paintings add character. **Internet** is available (8SFr per hr.). A kitchen, TV and VCR, BBQ, and large garden are included. (*☎ 302 18 13; heidis-backpacker@bluewin.ch; www.heidis-backpacker.ch. Recep-*

tion 10am-1pm and 3-8pm. 4-bed dorms with private shower 30SFr; singles 35SFr, with shower 40SFr; doubles 70SFr/90SFr. MC.)

AROSA   ☎ 081

A squeaking train ride from Chur (1hr.) twists and turns through rugged peaks and above lush valleys to reach the secluded town of Arosa. Bounded by two main lakes, Obersee by the train station and Untersee below the town, Arosa's landscape is dominated by countless stony peaks including the 2653m Weißhorn. Offered the land for 55,000SFr in 1936, the president of Chur missed his chance, claiming that Arosa's heyday had passed. Today it is a lucrative resort with a network of great skiing in winter and hiking in summer. It remains accessible to budget travelers, thanks to well-equipped dormitories.

◪ ⚡ TRANSPORTATION AND PRACTICAL INFORMATION

Arosa is accessible by scenic **train** from Chur (1hr., every hr. 5:35am-11:02pm, 13.40SFr). A **free shuttle bus** (every hr. in summer, every 20min. in winter) transports visitors in town, between ski lifts, and along the 10min. walk from the train station to the tourist office (stop: "Casino"). The **tourist office,** right out of the station and then right on Poststr., arranges hiking trips and ski lessons. (☎378 70 20; fax 70 21; arosa@arosa.ch; www.arosa.ch. Open Dec. 7-Apr. 13 M-F 9am-6pm, Sa 9am-5:30pm, Su 4-6:30pm; Apr. 14-Dec. 6 M-F 8am-noon and 1:30-6pm, Sa 9am-1pm; June 29-Aug. 17 also open Sa 2-4pm.) **Parking** is free in summer at the **Parking Garage Ochsenbühl** (2SFr for 3hr. in winter; 1SFr per additional hr.). A strict traffic ban is imposed nightly midnight-6am. The **train station** provides **currency exchange** (M-Sa 6am-9pm, Su 6:30am-9pm), **storage** (3SFr), **lockers** (2SFr), and **bike rental** (30SFr per day, 23SFr per half-day; ☎377 14 90). In an **emergency,** call ☎117. **Internet** access is available at Cafe Bar Los, across the street from the tourist office. (15SFr per hour. Open M-F 5pm-2am, Sa-Su 2pm-2am.) The **post office** also offers **Internet** (5SFr per 15min; 8SFr per 30min.) in Arosa's main square, to the right of the train station. (Open M-F 7:45am-noon and 1:45-6:30pm, Sa 8:30am-noon.) **Postal code:** CH-7050.

▐ ACCOMMODATIONS

Most lodgings in Arosa are near the tourist office. Reserve well in advance during prime ski-season.

▨ **Haus Florentinum** (☎377 13 97; fax 378 84 43; flori@arosabergbahnen.ch; www.arosabergbahnen.ch), run by the ski-lift company Arosa Bergbahnen, provides cheap and convenient housing in **winter only** (summer reserved for groups). This enormous former convent in the woods is now a 150-bed party house, complete with large lounges, balconies, and a chapel-turned-disco. Follow the cobblestone path down the hill from the tourist office as it bends left and zigzags up the hill. At the top continue right toward Hotel Hohe Promenade, turn left at the gravel path for Pension Suveran, and right at the dirt path in front of the Pension. Breakfast included. Dinner 15SFr. Parking 7SFr per day. Dec.-Apr. 2-night stay with 2-day ski pass 246SFr, under 19 231SFr; 6-night stay with 6-day ski pass 588SFr/551SFr. ❷

Jugendherberge (HI), Seewaldstr. (☎377 13 97; fax 16 21; jugiarosa@spin.ch), past the tourist office down the hill (follow the signs), has a friendly, multilingual staff. It is a good choice during the summer, when lifts are not necessary for hiking access (it is closer to the bottom of the valley, near the trails). Each dorm has a balcony overlooking the *Untersee* or Engadine slopes. Breakfast and sheets included. Bag lunch 8.50SFr; dinner 12SFr. Showers 0.50SFr per 3min. Reception in summer 7-10am and 5-10pm; winter 7am-noon and 4-10pm. Curfew 10pm, 11pm in winter; key provided. Open June 15-Oct. 15 and Dec. 15-Apr. 15. In summer dorms 29SFr; doubles 70SFr. In winter required half-pension included; dorms 44SFr; doubles 108SFr. ❷

Pension Suveran (☎377 19 69 or 079 640 49 93; fax 377 19 75; info@suveran.ch; www.suveran.ch), on the way to the Haus Florentium above, is a quiet, homey, wood-paneled chalet. Breakfast included. Dinner on request 15SFr. Closed in mid-Oct. May-Oct. singles 46-49SFr; doubles 82-88SFr. Dec.-Apr. singles 57-60SFr; doubles 104-110SFr. Add 10SFr per person in winter for stays shorter than 3 nights. ❸

Camping Arosa (☎377 17 45 or 079 611 30 59; fax 377 30 05; sportanlagen@arosa.ch), is downhill from the hostel. Open year-round. Cooking facilities available. The caretaker is on location 4:45-5:15pm. Pay on the honor system. 7.50-9SFr per person, ages 6-12 4.50SFr, tents 4.50SFr, electricity 3SFr. Showers 0.50SFr per 3min. ❶

Mountain Huts: A number of huts in the area are open during both summer and winter seasons. The **Ramozhütte** (SAC; ☎/fax 252 48 20) is a 2½-3hr. hike up an isolated valley south of Arosa. (Kitchen facilities available. 24SFr per person, 16SFr SAC members.) The **Naturfreundehaus Medergen** (☎374 15 74 or 079 357 20 79) has foam mattresses, a kitchen, and solar-powered lighting. (20SFr per person, ages 13-18 15SFr; reserve in advance.) It is a 2hr. steep uphill hike from the town of Litzirüti, which is 1hr. downhill by foot (northeast) from Arosa. ❷

🍴 FOOD

Le Bistro ❹, in Hotel Cristallo on Poststr., has a French ambiance, with classic posters on the walls, dried flowers covering the ceiling, and high prices. Entrees include Alsacer sauerkraut with ham (34.50SFr); soups are 8.50-9.50SFr. (☎378 68 68. Closed Oct.-Nov. and May-June. Open 12-2pm and 6pm-midnight. Reservations suggested in winter. AmEx/DC/MC/V.) **Hotel Central Arve** ❸, down the hill from the tourist office, has daily *Menüs* for 16.50-20.50SFr in a cozy den. (☎378 52 52. Closed in May. Open 11:30am-2pm and 6-11pm; food served until 10pm. Reservations for summer weekends and in winter. AmEx/DC/MC/V.) At **Orelli's Restaurant** ❷,

IN RECENT NEWS

SO YOU SAY YOU WANT A (BIO)REVOLUTION?

The environmentally conscious Swiss are putting their money where their mouths are when it comes to the fight against abusing and altering Mother Nature's world. It's not just clean air and litter-free streets that the Swiss fight for—it's the very food on their shelves that is the current hot issue for businesses, farmers, and consumers alike.

From the recent boom of vegetarian restaurants to the bio-revolution the Swiss have added many earth friendly characteristics to their diets "Bio" products—ones that are produced without human modification—have invaded supermarkets and restaurants alike. The Swiss even passed a food ordinance law in 2001 that GMOs (food with genetically modified organisms) could not be marketed until they passed government inspection and had proper labeling. Other procedures are underway to prevent GMO imports from crossing the border into Switzerland. Swiss main domestic agricultural products are cereals, vegetables, potatoes, and dairy products. Today, over 10% of farms in Switzerland are organic, which means that GMOs are absent from the seeds and animal feed used.

Currently, the two largest Swiss supermarket chains, Co-op and Migros, dominate the bio market, with over 600 organic products on their shelves. Of course, the decision to move away from GMO products comes at a price. Their environmentally sound counterparts can add up to 10% to the cost of foods.

Poststr., down the hill from the tourist office, hikers eat Swiss cuisine in a family restaurant decorated with Mickey Mouse and stained glass. The thrifty can get the *soup du jour* and bread for 5-8SFr. A vegetarian *Menü* (15SFr), salad buffet (8-12SFr), and warm entrees (15-26.50SFr) like chicken curry or pork with mushrooms and gorgozola round out the options. (☎377 12 08. Open 7:30am-9pm. Closed May and Nov. MC/V.) **Café-Confiserie Kaiser ❷** (☎377 34 54), on Poststr. between the tourist office and Orelli's, concocts killer confections (meringues 7.50SFr). The menu is filled with an equal number of warm meals, such as spaghetti (12SFr) and grilled *Fleischkäse* (slices of liver paste) with *Rösti* for 12.50SFr. (Open 9am-6pm; closed Nov.-Dec. 10 and Easter-June 10.) Get groceries at the **Co-op,** on Poststr. (open M-F 8am-12:30pm and 2-6:30pm, Sa 8am-4pm), or **Denner Superdiscount,** near the station (open M-F 8am-12:15pm and 2:30-6:30pm, Sa 8am-12:15pm and 1:15-4pm).

⚠️ 🎭 OUTDOOR ACTIVITIES AND ENTERTAINMENT

SKIING. Separate passes for the 15 **ski lifts and cableways** that hoist skiers to the 70km network of slopes in the **Arosa-Tschuggen ski area B** are available for tourists not staying in the dorms. The mountains are covered with slopes for all levels although the easier paths are concentrated on the lower Tschuggen area. Ticket offices in Arosa offer a myriad of passes. (Day, morning, afternoon, 1½-day, "choose-your-day" etc. 54SFr per day; 271SFr per week; 410SFr per 2 weeks. AmEx/DC/MC/V.) The smaller Tschuggen-sector day pass is 30SFr. Children under 15 get a 45% discount; ages 16-19 and seniors get a 10-15% discount. Family tickets are available.

HIKING. When the snow melts, it uncovers over 200km of flower-covered hiking paths. An **Alpine guide,** available through the tourist office, leads 8- and 10hr. hikes for fit hikers for only 20SFr. (July to mid-Oct. Tu, Th.) Two cable cars operate in summer. The **Weisserhornbahn cable car,** above the train station, whisks travelers to the top of the Weisserhorn (2653m; every 20min. 9am-5pm, 16SFr, round-trip 28SFr; day pass 32SFr). The summit allows views of the whole Engadine. The **Hörnli-Express** (same prices as Weisserhornbahn), at the other end of town, is accessible by bus. A 1½hr. hike follows the ridge between lifts; longer hikes wind into the valleys opposite the town. Most hikes that do not involve cable cars start from the Untersee (at the very end of the street on which the hostel is located). A number of hiking maps are available from the Arosa tourist office. The "Arosa und Umgebung" map (19.80SFr) comes with a list of suggested trails and lengths. The trail guide booklet "Arosa-Chur-Bündner Herrschaft," published by Kümmerly and Frei, is also available at the tourist office.

> **Alteiner Wasserfällen Hike** (2hr.). This easy-to-medium trail begins at the Untersee and starts out flat, winding in and out of the Hintern Wald and through fields of wildflowers before crossing back and forth over a rushing stream several times. At the end of a climb, the trail splits, leading to the Kleiner Wasserfall or the more impressive Großer Wasserfall. Take the same path to Arosa. To lengthen the hike, climb along the steep trail from the waterfalls to the Atteinsee (5hr. round-trip). This continues to the other side of the ridge and to Davos.

> **Chur hike** (5hr.). This difficult hike begins in front of the train station. The trail leads first along the Eichhörnliweg (Squirrel Walk) past Villa Sonnegg to Maran (1hr.) and then continues to Chur, where the train runs back to Arosa.

OTHER ACTIVITIES. The Untersee's **free beach** is open from 10am to 6pm, while pedal boats are for rent on the Obersee (12-17SFr per hr., 9-12SFr per 30min.

10am-5pm). The **International Jazz Festival** in July grants free admission to local venues. The festival features New Orleans jazz played by American, Swiss, Australian, and English bands. The **Humorfestival** revs up in mid-December with artists worldwide doing comedy shows (tickets 10SFr in afternoon, 35SFr in the evening; available at the tourist office; ask for a schedule of English-speaking performers).

DAVOS ☎ 081

Davos (pop. 12,000) sprawls along the valley floor under seven mountains laced densely with the wires of chair-lifts and cable cars. Originally a health resort for consumptives, the city catered to such *fin de siècle* celebrity guests as Robert Louis Stevenson and Thomas Mann, who, while in Davos, wrote *Treasure Island* and *The Magic Mountain*, respectively. Davos now relies on its world-class skiing to lure visitors. The influx of tourists in recent decades has given the city an impersonal feel, but the thrill of carving turns down the famed run from Weißfluhgipfel to Kublis (a 2000m vertical drop) may make up for that.

◼ TRANSPORTATION

Davos is accessible by **train** from Chur (1½hr., every hr. 5:43am-9:04pm, 27SFr) via Landquart or from Klosters (8.60SFr) on the Rhätische Bahn lines. The town is divided into two areas, Davos-Dorf and Davos-Pl., each with a train station and linked by the 3km **Promenade**. Platz is the site of the tourist office, main post office, and most other places of interest to budget travelers. Dorf is closer to the quiet Davosersee. **Buses** (2.50SFr, SwissPass valid) run between the two train stations and stop near major hotels and the hostel on the Davosersee. **Parking lots** line the Promenade and Talstr. (1-2SFr per hr.). **Rent bikes** at the Dorf station. (☎ 416 24 44. 27SFr per day, 23SFr per half-day.)

◼ PRACTICAL INFORMATION

The high-tech main **tourist office,** Promenade 67, in Platz, up the hill and to the right of the train station, caters mostly to those staying in hotels, but has free **Internet** access at one terminal and an informative brochure about the town. A smaller **branch office** sits across from the Dorf train station. (☎ 415 21 21; fax 21 00; info@davos.ch; www.davos.ch. Both offices open Dec. to mid-Apr. and mid-June to mid-Oct. M-F 8:30am-6pm, Sa 8:30am-4pm (winter until 5pm) and Su 9am-noon. Other times open M-F 8:30am-noon and 1:45-6pm, Platz without break; Sa 8:30am-noon.) The stations **store luggage** (3SFr), rent **lockers** (2-5SFr), and **exchange currency.** (Platz open M-Sa 4:45am-10pm, Su 5:50am-9pm; Dorf open daily 6:50am-8pm.) **Expert Roro,** in Dorf, Promenade 123, across from the blue and pink Hotel Concordia, offers **Internet** access at more terminals than the tourist office. (☎ 420 11 11; 5SFr per 20min., 12SFr per hr. Open M 2-6:30pm, Tu-F 8:30am-noon and 2-6:30pm, Sa 8:30am-noon and 2-5pm.) Closer to the Platz, the Esso gas station below the station houses an Internet cafe. (Open 7am-2am. 16SFr. per hr.) **Laundry** available at self-service **Waschsalon,** Promenade 102. (☎ 416 32 70. Open M-F 8am-8pm, Sa 9am-5pm. 2-4SFr per load; dry 4-5 SFr.) The main **post office** is in Davos-Pl. at Promenade 43. (Open M-F 7:45am-6pm, Sa 8am-noon.) **Postal code:** CH-7270.

◼ ACCOMMODATIONS AND CAMPING

In the summer, or for a more relaxing hostel atmosphere, head to Klosters (see p. 421). Always ask for the Davos **visitor's card,** which grants free unlimited travel on the city's buses and discounts on attractions.

IN RECENT NEWS

BUNA SAIRA!

Switzerland's oft-forgotten fourth national language, Romansch, is spoken only in the province of Graubünden, where it, German, and Italian are the official cantonal languages. Until about 1850, it was the most spoken language in the canton. By 1880, Romansch speakers dropped to 39.8% of the population, a percentage that kept dropping, finally leveling out around 22%. Today, in some small villages like S-chanf, Romansch speakers remain in the majority. Even in larger towns, like Chur, they form as much as a quarter of the population. The language is supported by the Swiss government, but its survival is threatened by the fact that at least four different dialects arose in isolated mountain villages.

Romansch didn't become a written language until the 16th century, when Biblical texts and historical ballads were first translated. In 1985, the Lia Rumantscha, a group dedicated to the preservation and proliferation of the language, succeeded in grounding a common written language drawing on different variants. Now, Romansch has a small literature of its own and translations of everything from the Bible to Asterix comics. Its speakers support five Romansch newspapers, TV news broadcasts, and 100 hours of radio time per week.

Although dependence on the German-speaking economy hinders the progress of Romansch, the Lia Rumantscha continues to fight for the advancement of the language, focusing primarily on the role on the government and schools. Today, many

Jacobshorn Ski Mountain (☎414 90 20; fax 90 21; hotels@jakobshorn.ch; www.fun-mountain.ch). The folks here have made their youth-oriented mountain accessible to budget travelers by opening 4 dorms for winter thrill-seekers, sold as a package with ski passes. All houses have the same furnishings: plain white rooms and down quilts. (Passes good only for Jacobshorn mountain; all 3 open Nov.-May; AmEx/MC/V.) ❷

Snowboarder's Palace, Oberestr. 45-47. Located right above the main tourist office, the Palace has the most authentic ski-lodge appearance with wooden balconies. 2- to 6-bed rooms. Breakfast included. 1-night, 2-day ski pass 135SFr, weekends 195SFr; 6-night, 7-day ski pass 630SFr.

Guest House Bolgenhof, Brämabülstr. 4A, is bland but convenient, right beneath the Davos-Pl. train station and near the ski lifts. Prices same as Snowboarder's Palace.

Snowboardhotel Bolgenschanze, Skistr. 1. The most hopping house, conveniently located over a bar where much of the apres-ski debauchery occurs. 18+. 4-bed dorms with private shower. 1-night, 2-day ski-pass 125SFr, weekend 185SFr; 6-night, 7-day ski pass 570SFr.

Suvretta Guest House, next to the Snowboardhotel, offers 4- and 5-bed rooms with bunks and communal showers for the same price, a little removed from the raucous bar scene. Breakfast in Snowboardhotel Bolgenschanze.

Hotel Edelweiss, Rossweidstr. 9 (☎416 10 33; fax 11 30; edelweiss-davos@gr-net.ch; www.davos-online.ch/edelweiss), situated on the hill between Platz and Dorf, offers great views and a variety of rooms. From the Dorf station take bus #2 (dir: Schiabach), continue toward Platz and turn right onto Bobbahnstr. following signs. Although pale green and yellow hallways give the hotel an institutional feel, the rooms are homey and comfortable. Closed May and Nov. Reception 7am-10pm. Breakfast included. Winter singles 65-80SFr, with showers 102-115SFr; doubles 110-140SFr/164-190SFr; triples with shower 216-255SFr; quads 168-208SFr. Prices drop 15-20SFr per person in summer. AmEx/MC/V. ❹

Hotel Herrmann, Dorfstr. 23, (☎416 17 37; fax 35 73), behind the tourist office in Dorf, provides a peaceful respite for those looking to enjoy the resort town off the slopes. Parking 10SFr per day. Closed May and Nov. Reception 7:30am-10pm. In winter singles with breakfast and dinner 92-110, with shower 105-125SFr; doubles 164-200SFr/190-230SFr. In summer singles with breakfast 60-65SFr/75-80SFr; doubles 100-110SFr/130-140SFr. MC/V. ❹

Camping Färich (☎416 10 43), at "Stilli" on the #1 bus from Dorf (dir: Pischa), is a 4-star facility relatively close to the ski lifts and attractions of the town. The small on-site bar serves pizza in two sizes (8-23SFr). Open May 17-Sept. 29. Reception 8:30-11am and 3-10pm; bar closed noon-2pm. 5-6.80SFr per person,

2.50-3.40SFr per child, 5-6SFr per tent, parking 3SFr, tax 2.90SFr. ❶

⌐ FOOD

Haven't had your *Rösti* fix yet? **Röstizzeria ❸**, in Dorf, Promenade 128, downstairs from the Hotel Dishma, can satisfy a craving with 15 variations (17.50-24.50SFr) and pizza (from 13SFr) in a dining room decorated with carved wood and Japanese fans. (☎416 12 50. Open daily 6am-11pm. AmEx/MC/V.) Grab a Bud and a bar stool, American style, at **Café Carlos ❷**, Promenade 58, fittingly located in a mall opposite the main tourist office. This restaurant offers American standards (burgers and sandwiches from 14SFr; beer from 4SFr) and a pianist from Dallas plays on the leopard-print grand piano after 7pm. (☎413 17 22. Open M-Th and Su 10am-midnight. F-Sa until 1am. AmEx/DC/MC/V.) **Romeo & Juliá Tratorria ❹**, Promenade 89 (500m toward Dorf from Platz), lives up to its name in romance. Enjoy a gourmet meal of sirloin steak (28SFr) or homemade spaghetti with white truffle sauce and jumbo shrimp (31SFr) in this elegant and secluded back room of the Hotel Steigenberger Belvedere. (☎415 60 00; fax 60 01; davos@steigenberger.ch. Reservations suggested in summer; necessary 2-3 days ahead in winter.) A **Migros ❷** is located on the Promenade in both Dorf (open M-F 8:30am-12:30pm and 1:30-6:30pm, Sa 8am-5pm) and Platz (open M-F 8:30am-6:30pm, Sa 8:30am-5pm). An enormous new **Co-op**, with cafeteria-style restaurant (weekly *Menüs* 10SFr), is across from the station. (Open M-Th 8am-6:30pm, F 8:30am-8pm, Sa 8am-5pm; restaurant open M-Th 8am-6:30pm, F 8am-8pm, Sa 8am-5pm, Su 10am-6pm.)

schools in Lower Engandine teach strictly in Romansch until students are 10 years old. At this time, students elect to continue their education in either German or Romansch, with continued study of the other language.

The German majority constantly encroaches on this small linguistic reserve, but the locals remain faithful to their rare heritage, slipping easily between German and Romansch as they move from home to school, books to magazines or even within the same conversation. Travelers can do their part to preserve the language and culture that accompanies it by responding in kind when they hear someone calling out, "Bun di!" (Hello!), "Grazia" (thank you), or even "Tge bel che ti es!" (How beautiful you are!).

🏛 ⚑ MUSEUMS AND OUTDOOR ACTIVITIES

Although surprisingly small for Europe's largest natural **ice rink** (22,000sq. m.), Davos's rink holds the title. By the sports center located between Platz and Dorf, it has figure skating, ice dancing, hockey, speed skating, and curling. (☎415 36 04. Open Dec. 15-Feb. 15. daily 10am-4pm; Th 8-10pm weather permitting. 5SFr, 4SFr with visitor's card; skate rental 6.50SFr with 20SFr deposit.)

KIRCHNER MUSEUM. The frosted glass structure opposite the Hotel Belvedere on the Promenade houses an extensive collection of artwork of Ernst Ludwig Kirchner, whose harsh colors and long figures belie troubled visions. This avatar of 20th-century German Expressionism lived in Davos for 21 years before committing suicide after the Nazis dubbed his art degenerate. Curators oversee an ever-changing exhibition that places Kirchner's work alongside that of related artists. (☎413 22 02. Tu-Su 10am-6pm; Sept.-Dec. 24 and Easter-July 14 2-6pm; students and children under 16 5SFr.)

SKIING. Davos provides direct access to two main mountains—the Parsenn and Jakobshorn—and four **skiing areas,** covering every degree of difficulty. **Parsenn,** with long runs and fearsome vertical drops, is the mountain around which Davos built its reputation. Unfortunately, Parsenn's fame has brought hordes of tourists who can create lines up to 2hr. for the main lift (day pass 57SFr). **Jacobshorn** (www.fun-mountain.ch) has found a niche with the younger crowd since the opening of a snowboarding "fun-park" with two half-pipes (day pass 52SFr). The **Pischa** and **Rinerhorn** are smaller resorts within the Davos area. The **regional ski pass** covers all 6 mountains in the Davos-Klosters area, including unlimited travel on most transport facilities, and doesn't cost much more than individual mountain tickets (2 days 121SFr, 6 days 279SFr). Info and maps are available at the tourist office. In addition to downhill runs, Davos boasts 75km of **cross-country trails** throughout the valley, including a night-lit trail. **The Swiss Ski School of Davos,** Promenade 157 (☎416 24 54; fax 59 51; ssd@bluewin.ch; www.ssd.ch), offers lessons starting at 40SFr per half-day group lesson. **Fullmoons,** Promenade 102 (☎/fax 240 14 77; www.fullmoons.ch), provides telemark lessons and tours (half-day 170SFr).

HIKING. One main ski lift on each mountain is open in summer, and many of the area's trails require these expensive lifts to bring hikers out of the dense valley.

Panoramaweg (2hr.). A relatively flat trail follows the contours of the broad hills above town, following views of the valley and the Swiss Alps. The route stretches from the Gotschnabahn (from Klosters) to Strelapass above Davos (5hr.). The newly renovated Parsennbahn, which leaves from near the Dorf train station, will allow visitors to traverse easily between the "Panoramaweg" stop and Klosters's cable car. Reopening in Dec. 2002; call for prices (☎417 67 67; www.parsenn.ch). Other trails leave from the middle stops of the Parsennbahn.

Davos-Platz to Monstein (5hr.). A more isolated and difficult hike into an adjoining valley that requires no cable car. Take Bus #8 from Platz to the trailhead at Sertig-Dörfli. Signs lead to "Fenezfurgga," which passes waterfalls and a valley that divides the Hoch Duncan and the Alpihorn. A stone wall separates the trail from the resorts beyond. The trek ends in Monstein, where buses connect to Glaris and then Davos.

KLOSTERS ☎081

Davos's sister resort, Klosters, lies across the Gotschna and Parsenn mountains. Though Klosters is 10min. from Davos by train, it is a world removed in atmosphere. While Davos makes an extra effort to be cosmopolitan, Klosters capitalizes on its natural serenity and cozy chalets. Most ski packages include mountains from both towns, and Klosters's main ski lift leads to a mountain pass where one may ski to either town. Klosters also has better access to fantastic biking trails.

◪ TRANSPORTATION. Klosters-Platz and Klosters-Dorf are connected by **train** to Chur through Landquart (1¼hr., every hr. 5:19am-9:31pm, 18.80SFr) and St. Moritz (1½hr., every hr. 34SFr). The same line connects Klosters and Davos (30min., every hr. 5:34am-11:32pm, 9.20SFr). Local buses run between Dorf, Platz, and the major ski lifts (1-6 stops 1SFr, 7-10 stops 2SFr, more than 10 stops 3SFr; guest card holders and children under 16 free).

◪ PRACTICAL INFORMATION. Like Davos, Klosters is divided into Klosters-Platz and Klosters-Dorf, connected by a bus and train; most activity occurs in Platz. Platz and Dorf both provide tourist offices, but the main **tourist office** is in Platz, right from the train station (follow the signs). **Currency exchange** is available on weekends (☎410 20 20; info@klosters.ch; www.klosters.ch. Open May-Nov. M-F 8:30am-noon and 2-6pm, Sa 8:30am-noon and 2-4pm; Dec.-April M-Sa 8:30am-noon and 2:30-6pm, Su 9-11:30am.) Services at the Platz station include: **currency exchange** (open 6am-8:30pm), **lockers** (2SFr), **luggage storage** (open 6am-8pm; pick up until 10:40pm; 3SFr), **scooter rental** (19SFr per day), and **Internet** access (10 SFr per hr; open Tu-F 9am-noon and 2-6:30pm, Sa 9am-noon and 2-4pm.) **Internet** access upstairs in the Park Hotel, Landstr. 190, is also available 24hr. (15SFr per hr.). **Bike rental** is at Andrist Sport on Gotschnastr. (☎410 20 80. 38SFr per day, 130SFr for 6 days. Open Su-Tu and Th-F 8am-noon and 2-6:30pm; Sa 8am-noon and 2-4pm.) The **post office** is to the right of the station. (Open M-F 7:30am-noon and 1:45-6:15pm, Sa 8:30am-noon.) **Postal code:** CH-7250.

◪◪ ACCOMMODATIONS AND FOOD. Jugendherberge Soldanella (HI) ❷, Talstr. 73 (follow the signs from Kirchstr. across from the station; uphill 10min.), is a massive, renovated chalet with wood paneling, a comfortable reading room, and couches on a flagstone terrace. (☎422 13 16; fax 422 52 09; klosters@youthhostel.ch; www.youthhostel.ch/klosters. Breakfast and sheets included. Dinner and lunch on request 12SFr. Reception 7-10am and 5-10pm. No lockout or curfew. Quiet hours 10pm-7am. Closed mid-Apr. to late June and mid-Oct. to mid-Dec. Dorms 27.50SFr; singles 38.50SFr; doubles 69SFr, with sink 77SFr. Family rooms 38.50SFr per person, children 2-6 half-price. Tourist tax 1.90SFr per day June-Sept., 2.20SFr Oct.-May; 6SFr surcharge for non-members. AmEx/MC/DC/V.) **Schweizerhaus ❷**, near the Klosters-Dorf train station, provides remodeled, well-lit rooms close to the Madrisa ski mountain. (☎422 14 81. Breakfast, sheets, and TV included. Closed May-June and Nov. Dorms 35SFr.) Some great deals await in *Privatzimmer* (private rooms) from 25SFr (list at tourist office). The tourist office also has a list of **mountain huts** in the Klosters area. Two of them, the **Silvrettahütte ❷** (☎422 13 06; breakfast 10SFr, breakfast and dinner 28SFr; open Mar.-Apr. and July-Oct.; 26SFr, SAC members 17SFr) and the **Vereina-Berghaus ❸** (☎422 12 16 or 422 11 97; open July to mid-Oct.; breakfast and dinner included; dorms 58SFr; doubles 156SFr), have shuttle buses that transport visitors to and from Klosters. For Silvrettahütte **A-taxi Helmi** provides access to Alp Sardasca, from which the hut is a 2hr. hike. Call ahead for reservations. (☎422 17 13. 60SFr one-way, 26SFr round-trip for 4 people or more.) A shuttle bus for Vereina-Berghaus leaves from the sports store (see **Outdoor Activities** below; 24SFr round-trip).

Gasthaus Casanna ❸, Landstr. 171, offers Italian pasta specialties (16.50-18.50SFr) such as gnocchi with gorgonzola (17SFr) in a smoky den. (☎422 12 29; fax 422 20 29. Open M-F 7am-midnight, Sa 10am-6pm.) **Chesa Grischuna ❸**, Bahnhofstr. 12, right from the station, provides a warm wooden interior decorated with rural antiques. Entrees are expensive, but traditional Swiss specialties are reasonably priced. (*Rösti* with wurst or bacon, egg, and cheese 17SFr. ☎422 22 22; fax 22 25; www.chesagrischuna.ch. Open daily 7am-11pm. Closed Oct. 20-Dec. 15.) **Hotel Rustico ❹**, Landstr. past the Park Hotel, serves fresh entrees (avocado salad with Zanderfilet 25SFr) in a bright interior with colorful paintings of wildlife. (☎422 12 12. Open 11:30am-1:30pm and 6-9:30pm; closed Th.) The **Co-op** has cheap groceries, and the restaurant upstairs has *Menüs* around 10SFr. (Open M-F 8am-12:30pm and 2-6:30pm, Sa 8am-5pm; restaurant M-F 8am-6:30pm, Sa 8am-5pm.)

GRAUBÜNDEN

📶 **OUTDOOR ACTIVITIES. Ski passes** for the Klosters-Davos region run 121SFr for 2 days and 279SFr for 6 days (includes public transportation). The **Madrisabahn** leaves from Klosters-Dorf (1-day pass 46SFr, 6-day pass 249SFr; ages 13-17 82SFr/ 187SFr; children 40SFr/93SFr). The **Grotschnabahn** gives access to Parsenn and Strela in Davos and Madrisa in Klosters (1-day pass 57SFr, 6-day pass 308SFr). The **ski school,** located in Klosters's tourist office, offers ski and snowboard lessons for. (☎410 20 28; fax 20 29; info@ssk.ch; www.ssk.ch. Group lessons from 52SFr per day; call ☎410 20 28 the day before to book private lessons, 310SFr per day.) **Swiss Ski and Snowboard School Saas,** Landstr. 15, has cheaper instruction. (☎420 22 33. Open 8am-8pm. 70SFr per hr.; 285SFr per day.) **Bananas,** operated out of Duty Boardsport, Landstr. 206, gives snowboard lessons. (☎422 66 60; www.bananas.net. 70SFr per 4hr.; private lessons 80SFr per hr.) **Ski rental** is available at **Sport Gotschna** across from the tourist office. (☎422 11 97. Open M-F 8am-noon and 2-6:30pm, Sa 8am-12:30pm and 2-6pm, Su 9am-noon and 3-6pm. Skis and snowboards 38SFr per day plus 10% insurance, 5 days 123SFr; boots 19SFr/69SFr.)

Summer cable car passes (valid on Grotschnaand Madrisabahnen) are also available (6-day pass 120SFr). On the luscious green valley floor, hikers can make a large loop, from Klosters's Protestant church on Monbielstr. to Monbiel. The route continues to an elevation point of 1488m and turns left, passing through **Bödmerwald, Fraschmardintobel,** and **Monbieler Wald** before climbing to its highest elevation of 1634m and returning to Klosters via **Pardels.** Several adventure companies offer a variety of activities including **river rafting, canoeing, horseback riding, paragliding,** and **glacier trekking.**

LOWER ENGADINE VALLEY

The Engadine Valley takes its name from the Romansch name *(En)* for the Inn river that flows through the valley and on through Innsbruck, Austria. The transportation line runs from Maloja at the far west end of the valley to Scuol at the far east, connecting all towns by train or short bus rides. The region is divided into the Upper and Lower Engadine, with the town of Brail, just west of Zernez and the Swiss National Park, on the border.

The Lower Engadine valley represents Graubünden at its purest. Unaltered by the swift torrent of change brought by the ski industry elsewhere, the people maintain a strong connection to their land and culture. The Lower Engadine is a stronghold of the **Romansch language,** and nearly every sign is printed in this Latinate tongue. The region may not be a skier's paradise, but **hikers** revel in the untouched alpine ecosystem of the **Swiss National Park** just south of the valley. Regional travel is easy with the **Lower Engadine Regional Pass,** which covers all trains and post buses (any 3 days in a 7-day period, 50SFr; any 7 days in a 14-day period, 70SFr).

THE SWISS NATIONAL PARK

The Swiss National Park's selling point is its isolation from man-made constructs that allows hikers to experience the undiluted wildness of the natural terrain. Established in 1914, the park became the first national park in the Alps. While its size (only 172sq. km.) pales in comparison to American or Canadian national parks, efforts to protect the ecological balance are far more vigorous. To minimize disturbance, the park has fewer trails than other mountainous areas in Switzerland. The successful conservation movement creates the rare opportunity to hike among marmots, ibexes, eagles, and bearded vultures.

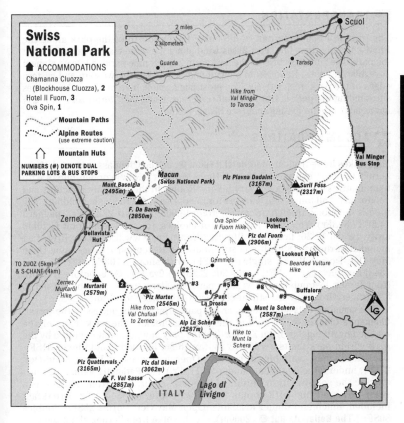

Swiss National Park

ACCOMMODATIONS
Chamanna Cluozza
(Blockhouse Cluozza), **2**
Hotel Il Fuorn, **3**
Ova Spin, **1**

Mountain Paths

Alpine Routes
(use extreme caution)

Mountain Huts

NUMBERS (#) DENOTE DUAL
PARKING LOTS & BUS STOPS

GRAUBÜNDEN

ORIENTATION AND PRACTICAL INFORMATION

The Swiss National Park is a kidney-shaped area of land stretching from S-chanf in the southwest to Scuol in the northeast. The wilderness extends southeast from the towns. The landscape consists of thick pine forests and rocky peaks arrayed around glacial streams. **Munt La Schera** and *Chamanna Cluozza*, the single alpine hut in the park, lie in the center of the park. The grassland of the northern regions is a natural habitat of red deer and marmots.

Camping and campfires are prohibited in the park, as is collecting flowers, plants, or insects. A team of wardens patrols the park at all times, administering fines of up to 500SFr on rule-breakers. The park's central office is in Zernez (see p. 426). Many sights have Romansch names. *Piz* is "mountain," *val* is "valley," *ova* is "stream," *pra* is "meadow," and *chamanna* means "mountain hut." Bird-watching is best mid-June to mid-July; deer, chamois, and ibex are most active in September. The park is closed Nov.-May.

GRAUBÜNDEN

⌐ TRANSPORTATION

The towns of Scuol, Zernez, and S-chanf lie just north of the park along the Rhätische Bahn **train** line. **Post Buses** wind along the three major roads that skirt the park. The Ofenpass bisects the park from Zernez; nine parking lots sit along it at regular intervals. Roads from S-chanf and Scuol skirt the western and eastern edges of the park, respectively. The most manageable hike between the villages surrounding the park is from S-chanf to Zernez, using the *Chamanna Cluozza* hut as an overnight resting spot (see **Hiking,** below).

⌐ ACCOMMODATIONS

Many hikes leave from around **Hotel Il Fuorn ❷,** on the Ofenpass, a bus ride from Zernez (20min., every hr. 7:10am-7:10pm, 8.40SFr). New wooden bunks with foam mattresses welcome weary hikers. Rooms in the hotel are spacious and comfortable (all toilets and showers for the dorms are in the main building). The food is delicious, though pricey (*Spätzle* 19.90SFr, *Rösti* 22.20SFr, spaghetti 14.80-17.80SFr). You don't have a lot of choices; the next restaurant is 10km away. (☎856 12 26; fax 18 01; ilfuorn@ilfuorn.ch; www.ilfuorn.ch. Breakfast included in rooms, 18SFr if you stay in dorms. Reception 7:15am-10pm. Open May-Oct. Dorms 19SFr; singles 72-79SFr, with shower 103-111SFr; doubles 134SFr; triples 171-195SFr; quads 204-232SFr.) **Ova Spin ❷,** is before Il Fuorn from Zernez, just outside the western park boundary. (☎856 10 52 or 079 406 73 33; strimer@frog.ch; www.stimer.ch. Reserve one week in advance. 20SFr.)

The **mountain huts** scattered near the park offer instant access to the forest. **Chamanna Cluozza ❷,** located in the western block of the park, can only be reached by hiking 3hr. from Zernez. It is the only mountain hut operated by the park within park limits. (☎856 12 35; fax 16 86. Breakfast and dinner 31SFr. Packed lunches available on request. Open last week of June to mid-Oct. 27SFr, under 20 and students under 26 11SFr.) The **Parkhütte Varusch ❷,** just outside the southwestern border of the park, a 1hr. hike from S-chanf, is a solar-powered hut with rooms for 2-10 people. (☎854 31 22. Breakfast included, lunch and dinner available. Open May-Oct. Dorms 25SFr; doubles 80SFr.) The **Bellavista hut ❷** (2000m), a 1½hr. hike from Zernez along the trail to the Murtaröl and the Chamanna Chuozza, has five beds, a wood stove, a kitchenette, outhouse, and a clear view of Zernez and Piz Linard from the front porch. (☎856 17 21. Bring drinking water. Call one week in advance for reservations and to get the key from the owner. 20SFr. Sleep sack 5SFr.) **Camping** is not allowed in the park, but Zernez, Scuol, and S-chanf have campsites outside the park boundaries.

▨ HIKING

A network of 20 hiking trails (80km) runs throughout the park, concentrated in the central 100sq. km. Trails are clearly marked, and it is illegal to stray from them. Most hikes in the park involve a lot of climbing, often into snow-covered areas. The **Parkhouse** in Zernez lists which trails are navigable. An extremely helpful park trail map in five languages is available (14SFr), as is a written guide to all 20 park trails (10SFr; 20SFr for both). The Parkhouse also sells a geological map and a vegetation map of the park. Trails that require no mountaineering gear are marked with white-red-white blazes, but as the locals are practically mountain goats, even some of the non-mountaineering routes can be tricky.

▨ Il Fuorn (1794m) to Munt la Schera (2586m) to Buffalora (1968m) (5hr.). Begins at Parking Area 5, a short walk from Il Fuorn. Follow the trail there toward Alp Buffolora and Munt la Schera. A gradual 1hr. ascent through the woods leads above the tree line, where it curves around the side of the mountain. A sign points the way to the summit of **Munt la Schera**, which offers a panoramic view of the Lago di Livigno and Cima Paradiso to the south and the Val da L'Acqua to the east. Signs to "Buffolora" lead through meadows where chamois and red deer often can be found. The trail quickly descends to Munt la Schera, then gently winds down to **Buffolora,** where buses return to Il Fuorn and Zernez.

Ova Spin (1838m) to Alp Grimmels (2050m) (2½hr. round-trip). This trail starts from Parking Area 1, a short bus ride from Zernez (10min., every hr., 4.60SFr), with a short, unimpressive climb, but soon enters into the **Champlönch meadow** (2015m), adorned with spectacular wildflowers. At the end of the meadow, the trail divides. The left fork leads to **Il Fuorn** (see below). The trail off the right fork climbs a short distance through the woods to **Alp Grimmels,** an open meadow that used to be a feeding area for red deer and marmots. Now it is a spectacular picnic area with views of Val Chavagi, Munt La Schera, and Piz Daint. The trail continues down through the forest back to Parking Area 1.

Zernez (1471m) to Chamanna Cluozza (1882m) (3hr.). The trail begins across the wooden bridge, 100m past the Park House. After a flat walk through a meadow, the path enters the forest, where it turns into a steep uphill climb. It turns right at the Fritz Sarasin stone marker. When it splits at Il Pra (1hr.), take the left fork and grab a drink at the freshwater fountain. From here, the trail traverses a grassy field (2100m), where red deer often graze. A descent through the woods leads to **Il Grass** and a view of the Piz Linard from the bridge over the Ova da Cluozza. It is a short climb (80m) to the **Chamanna Cluozza.** With a set of binoculars, you can see tracks of the **Theropod** on the western flank of the Piaz dal Diavel. This 4-5m long herbivorous dinosaur roamed the area over 200 million years ago and left footprints 25-30cm across.

Zernez (1471m) to Murtaröl (2579m) and back (6hr.). This hike begins at the same spot as the Chamanna Cluozza hike and follows the same trail until the path splits at Il Pra (about 1hr.); take the right-hand fork. After passing the Bellavista hut (see **Accommodations,** p. 424), the trail rises above the tree line and offers wide views of Zernez below. The path passes a set of stone walls, built during the 19th century in an effort to prevent avalanches, and curves to a panoramic view of the Val Tantermozza (not accessible to park visitors) and the mountain chain that surrounds it. The **Murtaröl** crest (3½hr.), with simultaneous views of the Engadine, Cluozza, and Tantermozza valleys, is at the end of a short climb. Sometimes herds of chamois and ibexes are visible from the path along the ridge. The route back to Zernez passes bizarre rock formations before plunging into the forest to rejoin the original path at the point where it splits from the Chamanna Cluozza trail.

Val Minger to Tarasp (5hr.). Take the bus from Scuol (dir: Scharl) to "Val Minger" (9.40SFr; with Eurail, SwissPass 4SFr). One of the more difficult hikes. From the bus stop, cross the bridge and turn left on the trail, which begins with a slow and steady climb up rocky stream beds. The excitement lies behind you with views of **Piz Pradatsch.** When the trail moves above the tree line it enters a half-pipe-shaped valley, at the end of which lies the solitary, majestic **Piz Plavna Dadaint.** The **Sur il Foss pass,** with its uniquely intimate view of nearby mountains, lies at the end of the valley. From Sur il Foss, a trail leads around the head of the valley to the **Val dal Botsch pass,** which then leads to Il Fuorn in the center of the park. *This route is only safe in later summer when the snow has melted, and even then should only be attempted with hiking poles and very sturdy boots. Check at the National Park House in Zernez* *for conditions.* An easier route leads right, toward "Tarasp Fontana." The initial descent can be tricky, depending on recent rock slides. The trail moves into a wide rocky plain, bordered by cliffs that create a visual tunnel, towards the mountain range over Scuol, and backward to Piz Nair and the peaks in front of it. The trail heads through the woods to **Tarasp,** where a bus returns to Scuol (every hr. 8:10am-8:10pm, M-F from 6:13am; 4.60SFr).

TOWNS NEAR THE NATIONAL PARK

TRANSPORT HUB: ZERNEZ   ☎081

Zernez (pop. 1100) is the main gateway to the **Swiss National Park** and home to the headquarters of the park, the **National Parkhouse. Trains** depart for **Samedan** (30min., every hr. 6:52am-10:49pm, 12SFr) and **Scuol** (30min., every hr. 5:45am-11:02pm, 13.40SFr) with connections to the rest of Switzerland, including St. Moritz (45min., 16.60SFr). **Currency exchange** is available at the train station (open M-F 5:30-7:10am and 7:40am-8:10pm, Sa 5:30-7:10am and 7:40am-7:10pm, Su 7:40am-12:10pm and 1:40-6:10pm) and **Internet** access at the tourist office (4SFr for 15min., 2SFr every 15min. after). The **post office** is across the street from the train station. (Open M-F 8-11:30am and 2-6pm, Sa 8:30-11am.) **Postal code:** CH-7530.

From the train station, the road to the left that curves through town leads to the **tourist office.** (☎856 13 00; fax 11 55. Open June-Oct. M-F 8:30am-noon and 2-6:30pm, Sa 9-noon and 2-5pm; Nov.-May M-F 8:30am-noon and 2-5:30pm.) The **National Parkhouse,** reached by turning right at the T junction, provides information about trail safety and has an extensive selection of maps and souvenirs. (☎856 13 78; fax 856 17 40; info@nationalpark.ch; www.nationalpark.ch. Open June-Oct. W-Su 8:30am-6pm, Tu 8:30am-10pm.) It also houses a small **museum,** mainly for children, about the park. **Sport Sarsura,** right before the tourist office, provides expensive outdoor gear. (☎856 14 34. Open M-F 8am-noon and 2-6:30pm, Sa 8am-noon and 2-5pm.) The **Co-op,** across the street, and keeps the same hours.

The tourist office lists **private rooms** (from 20SFr). **Hotel Bär-Post ❷,** left from the main intersection, is a classy hotel that offers less classy rooms in a back building. The dorms are small and a bit damp. (☎851 55 00; fax 55 99; baerpost@bluewin.ch; www.forum.ch.baer-postzernez.htm. Breakfast 12SFr. Sleepsack 5SFr. Quiet hours after 10pm. Reception 9am-10pm. Closed Nov. to mid-Dec. Dorms 18SFr. AmEx/DC/MC/V.) Just past the National Parkhouse, **Touristenlager Hummel ❶** offers *lager*-style accommodations with a spice-stocked kitchen and sitting room included. (☎856 18 74. Sheets available on request. Dorms 15SFr; doubles 52-60SFr.) There is camping at **Camping Cul ❶,** across the train tracks from town, on the river. Turn right out of the station and follow the signs. (☎856 14 62. Reception July-Aug. 8am-noon and 1-8pm; Sept.-June times vary. Open May-Oct. 15. 7SFr per person, children 4SFr, tents 6SFr, cars 5SFr; visitor and trash tax not included.) **Grotia Pizzeria Mirta ❸,** at the main intersection, offers some of the best wood-oven pizza (14-18.50SFr) in Graubünden. (☎856 17 35. Open Tu-Su 8am-11pm; closed May and Nov. V.)

S-CHANF   ☎081

The rustic town of S-chanf (pop. 550), with its narrow cobblestone streets and Engadine houses, is a stronghold of local tradition. In most towns Romansch is only a colloquial language; in S-chanf it is the official tongue, spoken in town meetings, schools, and church services. Receiving fewer tourists than most towns in the area, S-chanf is a peaceful and cheap base for exploring the National Park.

■ ❼ **TRANSPORTATION AND PRACTICAL INFORMATION. Trains** stop in S-chanf **only by request** and connect to: Scuol (1hr., every hr. 6:26am-10:30pm, 17.60SFr); St. Moritz (30min., every hr. 6:08am-11:19pm, 10SFr) via Samedan; and Zernez (20min., every hr. 5:20am-10:30pm, 7.40SFr). S-chanf connects to the rest of Switzerland through Samedan. Engadine **Bus** #8 runs from the post office in S-chanf (same stop as Bus #7) into the National Park (10min., M-F 4 per day 8:56am-2:05pm, Sa-Su 5 per day 8:39am-5:05pm, 2.40SFr). Train tickets are sold at the **post office,** down the road to the left of the train station. (Open M-F 8-11:30am and 2:45-5:15pm, Sa 8:30-10:15am.) The **tourist office** is in the **Banca Raffeisen** office, in the same building as the **post office.** (☎854 22 55; fax 850 17 65; infoschanf@datacomm.ch. Open M-F 8:30am-6:15pm.) In an **emergency,** call ☎117.

■ ❐ **ACCOMMODATIONS AND FOOD. Lager Angelini ❷,** in Chasa Rude, has cheap, clean dorms. From the station turn right on the main road past the church and left at the second fountain. (☎854 13 60. Reception 7-10pm. Call ahead. Dorms 26SFr, towel and sheets included; after 5 nights 12SFr, sheets 3SFr.) The friendly folks at the **Hotel Aurora ❹** offer cozy rooms with down comforters and pillows. (☎854 12 64; fax 21 19. Breakfast included. Check-in 7:30am-10pm, right out of the tourist office. Singles 60-82SFr, with shower 65-88SFr, with shower and toilet 75-120SFr; doubles 120-144SFr/130-176SFr/150-250SFr.) Take bus #8 to "Chapella la Resgia" and backtrack along the main road for 20min. to **Camping Chapella ❶.** (☎/fax 854 12 06. Open May-Oct. and Dec. 25-Easter. 7SFr, tent 4SFr, car 2SFr.) **Gasthaus Sternen ❷,** across the street from the tourist office, serves a variety of pizzas (14-20SFr) and huge plates of pasta (10-18.50SFr) in a woodsy interior with a classy touch. (☎854 12 63. Open daily 7:30am-midnight.) **Volg** has groceries down the main street to the right of the tourist office. (Open M-Tu and Th-F 7:30am-noon and 2-6:30pm, W 7:30am-noon, Sa 7:30am-noon and 2-4pm.)

ZUOZ ☎081

Though located in the Upper Engadine, Zuoz's adherence to architectural and linguistic (Romansch) traditions, as well as the warmth of the citizens, mark it as a Lower Engadine town. Its position on the border of both regions makes it a good point from which to explore both sides of the Engadine Valley. Burned to the ground by residents in 1499 to keep it out of Austrian hands, Zuoz (pop. 1,300) was rebuilt in the early 16th century and has changed little since. Ibex, pinwheels, and flowers float on the whitewashed walls of village houses, and a big carved bear defends the fountains from bloodthirsty imperial Habsburg troops.

■ ❼ **TRANSPORTATION AND PRACTICAL INFORMATION.** Zuoz is a **train** ride from St. Moritz (30min., every hr. 6:12am-11:22pm, 9.20SFr) via Samedan (20min., 5.60SFr); and Zernez (20min., every hr. 5:17am-10:26pm, 8.40SFr). The train station provides **luggage storage** (3SFr), **bike rental** (30SFr per day; 23SFr per half day), and **currency exchange** (open M-F 6:40am-6:30pm, Sa 6:40am-6pm, Su 8:10am-12:20pm and 1:40-5:30pm). La Passarella, which extends directly opposite the station (right off the COOP), leads to the main street in town, San Basiaun, which turns into Via Maestra. The **tourist office,** right on Via Maestra, provides keys to the local sights and suggests hikes. (☎854 15 10; fax 33 34; zuoz@spin.ch; www.zuoz.ch. Open July-Aug. and Dec.-Apr. M-F 9am-noon and 3-6pm, Sa 9-11am; May-June and Oct.-Nov. M-F 9am-noon and 3-5pm.) The **Kantonalbank,** past the tourist office, **exchanges currency** and has an **ATM.** (Open M-F 8am-noon and 2-5pm.) The **post office** is in the train station. (Open M-F 8am-noon and 2:15-5:45pm, Sa 8-11am.) **Postal code:** CH-7524.

GRAUBÜNDEN

BOYS WILL BE BOYS Zuoz takes pride in its unique holidays and traditional festivals. On March 1, the **Chalandamarz** engulfs Engadine as young boys wander from house to house, ring huge bells, and sing songs to drive off evil spirits and welcome the spring. Originally a pagan fertility rite, the more peculiar **San Gian's Day** commemorates John the Baptist on July 24, when village boys spritz girls with water from Zuoz's fountains. The Swiss maidens then flee to their houses and pour buckets of water over the boys' heads, with hilarious consequences.

ↂↂ ACCOMMODATIONS AND FOOD. The cheapest lodgings are located in the center of town at **Ferienlager Sonder ❷.** Head down Via Maestra from the tourist office and turn right onto tiny Chanels at the sign for "Ferienlager" for simple rooms in a 16th-century building with kitchen and ping pong. (☎854 14 39; fax 07 73; www.engadina.ch. Dorms 23SFr; after 2 nights 20SFr.) At the 400-year-old **Chesa Walther ❸** opposite the tourist office, comfortable rooms are decorated with gold-tone curtains and bedspreads and simple bureaus. (☎854 13 64. Partial kitchen facilities 5SFr. Rooms with communal bathroom 40SFr). **Hotel Steinbock ❸,** down Via Maestra past the tourist office (150m), offers cozy wood-panelled rooms in a friendly environment. (☎854 13 73; fax 35 60; falco@steinbock-zuoz.ch; www.steinbock-zuoz.ch. Breakfast included. Reception 8-11am and 4:30pm-midnight. Closed Nov. and May. Rooms 60SFr per person. AmEx/DC/MC/V.) **Restaurant Dorta ❸** prepares an impressive menu of Engadine specialties, including *Zuozer Krautpizokel,* a large plate of *Spätzli* (German egg noodles) with ham, bacon, and cream sauce (23SFr). Vegetarians can try the *Maluns,* shredded potatoes with applesauce and plum compote, for the same price. (☎854 20 40; www.dorta.ch. Open Tu 9:30pm, W-Su 11:30am-9:30pm. Closed Nov., Tu, and mornings June and Oct. Reservations recommended.) **Cafe-Restorant Klarer ❹,** in the center of town, offers a variety of pastas for 14-20SFr. Meat entrees (29-45SFr), like grilled Forelle with spinach (29SFr) and roasted duck breast with wild rice (38SFr), are available in the evening. (☎851 34 34; www.klarerconda.ch. Open 7:30am-11pm; May only 7:30am-noon.) The **Co-op** supermarket is opposite the station (open M-F 8am-12:15pm and 2-6:30pm, Sa 8am-5pm); **Primo** is up the hill from the tourist office (open M-F 8am-noon and 2-6:30pm, Sa 8am-noon and 2-4pm).

◪◪ SIGHTS AND HIKING. The small **Church San Luzius** on Via Maestra has sweet-smelling pine pews and Romansch hymnals with brilliantly colored stained glass windows above the altar. The **prison tower** next door is preserved as the last wrongdoer left it—a dark, dank chamber, filled with terrifying implements of torture and chilling dungeon cells. (Descriptions only in German.) Farther from the tourist office on the corner of Via Dorta lies the tiny **San Bastiaun** chapel with fading frescoes. (Ask the tourist office for the keys).

Zuoz woos **bikers** with 37km of marked trails. **Rental** available at the train station or for less across the river at the **Inline Shop** operated by Willi Sport. (Open M-F 10am-12:30pm and 1-6:30pm, Sa 10am-12:30pm and 1-5pm. 25-29SFr per day; 18-20SFr per half day.) For **hikers,** the National Park is right next door, but Zuoz offers a few distinctive hikes of its own. The **Via Segantini** eventually leads to the **Piz Bernina** (4049m). The path begins past the Hotel Engiadina, on Via Maestra. Turn right onto Chröntschet, then walk along the private driveway, which leads to the gravel path labeled "Castell." The shaded path leads to the historic Alpenschloßhotel Castell; from there, follow signs for "Via Segantini." The easy trail, leads from Zuoz to La Punt (2hr.) and Bever (4hr.), where the train runs back to Zuoz.

For a more rugged afternoon, the **Ova d'Arpiglia** leads to a crashing 20m waterfall. To find the trail, turn left from the train station and go through the underpass toward the river. Cross the river on the smaller bridge, head under the road, turn left following the yellow "Wanderweg" sign the dirt road heading into the woods. Stay on the right side of the stream following signs for "Mont Seja," to the waterfall. The path, replete with purple wildflowers, then climbs steeply to a green meadow to the right of the falls; it is known locally as the **"Stairway to Heaven."** Signs point the way from this picnic haven to Zuoz (round-trip 1½hr.).

UPPER ENGADINE VALLEY

350km of ski trails and 60 ski lifts lace the Upper Engadine Valley. Unlike Zermatt and Grindelwald, where Japanese and American tourists abound, the Upper Engadine attracts mostly German, Italian, and Swiss visitors. Connoisseurs rate the downhill skiing in the Upper Engadine a hair's breadth below the Jungfrau and Matterhorn regions. The summer sun clears the snow from the region's ample hiking trails; the most unique hiking skirts the melting glaciers flowing down from **Piz Bernina** (4049m, the highest in the region) and its neighbors.

Ski rental is available in multiple shops throughout the towns. Although not standardized, prices tend to be similar (57-69SFr per day, ages 16-20 30-37SFr, ages 6-16 21-24SFr). **Novices** should head for Zuoz or Corviglia (St. Moritz); **experts** for Diavolezza (Pontresina), Piz Nair (St. Moritz), or Piz Lagalb (Pontresina). One-day passes are available for each town. (St. Moritz and Celerina are sold together.) Prices range according to time in the season from 40-61SFr, ages 16-20 36-55SFr, ages 6-15 20-30SFr; St. Moritz is the most expensive area.) Multiple-day passes are available only for the entire Engadine region—they're not much more expensive and cover most trains and buses as well (5-day pass 225-271SFr, youth 203-244SFr, children 113-136SFr). Cross-country fanatics should glide to **Pontresina,** where hundreds train for the cruel and unusual **Engadine Ski Marathon,** which stretches from Maloja to S-chanf. The race is on the second Sunday in March (March 9, 2003. ☎ 081 850 55 55; fax 55 56 or check online www.engadin-skimarathon.ch for application/registration; entry fee 80SFr. Register by Feb. 1). The weekend before hosts the 17km **Frauenlauf** solely for women. (See above for registration; entrance fee 40SFr.) **Ski schools** in almost every village offer private lessons. For more info call ☎ 081 830 00 00; fax 00 09; info@skiengadin.ch; www.skiengadin.ch.)

PONTRESINA   ☎ 081

Away from the bustle of the rest of the Upper Engadine, Pontresina is nestled in one of the highest wind-sheltered valleys of the region, at the confluence of two major rivers. The resort has glitzy aspirations, with luxury hotels and a modern main street, but the proximity of three towering peaks makes Pontresina a favorite mountaineering destination. Every morning, the famous Diavolezza glacier tour draws hordes of hikers. In winter, Pontresina becomes the cross-country skiing center of the Upper Engadine.

▣ TRANSPORTATION. Trains run to Chur (2hr., every hr. 5:49am-8:04pm, 38SFr) via Samedan and St. Moritz (10min., every hr. 6:52am-7:52pm, 4.60SFr). (Station ☎842 63 37. Open M-F 5:40am-7pm, Sa-Su 6:40am-7pm.) **Post Buses** connect Pontresina to the villages of the Upper Engadine Valley all the way to Maloja. A Post Bus also runs from the left of the train station to the post office, the tourist office, and other important spots in town (every 30min., 6:55am-8:36pm, 2.60SFr).

▨ PRACTICAL INFORMATION. Via de la Staziun winds over two rivers and uphill to the center of town (20min.). The **tourist office,** in the modern "Rondo" building where the Via de la Staziun meets the town, plans free excursions (see p. 431), gives hiking advice, provides information on weekly events, and finds private rooms (from 28SFr). (☎838 83 00; fax 83 10; info@pontresina.com; www.pontresina.com. Open M-F 8:30am-noon and 2-6pm, Sa 8:30am-noon; mid-June to Sept. also Sa 3-6pm and Su 4-6pm; mid-Dec. to Easter also Sa and Su 4-6pm.) The **Ferienregion,** is the regional tourist office (40m uphill from tourist office; follow signs for "Gemeindhaus"). (☎842 65 73. Open M-F 8am-noon and 2-6pm. Dec. 25-Mar. and mid-July to Aug. also Sa 8:30am-noon.) Services include: **currency exchange, luggage storage** (3SFr), **bike rental** (30SFr per day), and **lockers** (2SFr) at the train station (see hours above); **Internet** at the Hotel Walther, 20m past the post office (8SFr per hr.). **Post office** 75m uphill from the tourist office. (Open M-F 7:45am-noon and 1:45-6:15pm, Sa 8:30am-noon.) **Postal code:** CH-7504.

▛ ACCOMMODATIONS. The **Jugendherberge Tolais (HI) ❸**, in the modern, salmon-colored building across from the train station, is convenient for early-morning ski ventures and connections throughout the Engadine Valley. The hostel has a restaurant, ping-pong, swings, and a soccer field. (☎842 72 23; fax 70 31; pontresina@youthhostel.ch; www.youthhostel.ch/pontresina. Breakfast, lockers, sheets, and buffet dinner 6:30pm-8:30pm (later times and vegetarian options on request) included. Laundry 10SFr. Free parking. Reception 7:30-9:30am, 4-6:30pm and 7:30-10pm; June and Oct. until 9pm. Doors lock 11pm; entrance code given. Quiet time from 10pm. Closed May and Nov. 6-bed dorms 43.50SFr; doubles 138SFr; quads 216SFr; non-members add 6SFr. Prices do not include tax (winter 1.85SFr, summer 1.70SFr). AmEx/DC/MC/V.) In the heart of town (5min. uphill from the tourist office, across from Photo Schocher) at **Pension Valtellina ❹**, Mariuccia Della Briotta, a gentle Italian grandmother, furnishes her spartan rooms with warm down comforters. A triple has a balcony overlooking the Piz Bernina and the pink bathrooms are down the hall. (☎842 64 06. Breakfast included. Closed June and early Dec. Doubles 110SFr; triples 150-156SFr.) **Camping Plauns ❶**, in Morteratsch (train dir: Tirano; 3.80SFr), offers laundry (3-4SFr), a basic foods shop, and a grill after 5pm. Campers walk the 3km from the trail head above the train station to the Bernina Pass. (☎842 62 85; fax 834 51 36; a.brueli@bluewin.ch; www.pontresina.com. Open June to mid-Oct. and mid-Dec. to mid-Apr. 8.50SFr per person; ages 12-15 5.50SFr, ages 6-11 4SFr; tents 9SFr; car 4SFr.)

▟ FOOD. The **Puntschella Cafe-Restaurant ❸**, on Via da Mulin off Via Maestra before the post office, is the birthplace of the *Engadiner Torte* (a local delicacy made from candied almonds, raisins, layers of cream and nut puree, and crunchy crust; 4.20SFr). The bakery is filled with a dazzling array of glazed chocolate and fruit delicacies; the restaurant offers local specialties (entrees 13-24.50SFr). Eat on the breezy terrace while gazing at Piz Bernina. (☎838 80 30. Open June-Oct. daily 7:30am-10pm, Nov.-May 7:30am-9pm. MC/V.) **Tea-room Giamotti ❸**, left and across the street from the tourist office, is uninspiring but inexpensive for a hearty meal. Chef's recommendations and *Menüs* start at 15SFr, pastas and omelettes at 9.50SFr. (☎842 62 39. Open daily 8am-10pm; Dec.-Apr. until 9pm. Bratwurst with *Rösti* 14.50SFr.) The **Pizzeria Sportpavillon ❷**, 400m downhill from the tourist office near the bus stop "Sportpavillon," looks out on tennis courts and Piz Bernina. The cheerful waitstaff in red bow ties and matching suspenders serves pizzas (13.50-19.50SFr, from 10-11pm all pizzas 11SFr) and pasta from 14SFr. A family special is enough pizza for 2 adults and 2 children (38SFr); satisfy a sweet tooth with Pizza Ramona (apples, pineapples, and sugar) for 12SFr. (☎842 63 49. Food available daily noon-2pm and 6-10pm; pizzas also 2-4pm and 10-11pm. Reservations suggested 6-8pm.) **Cento ❶**, 20m up the street from Tea-room Giamotti, provides a laid-back setting with wool-covered benches and candle light. (Beers 5-7SFr. ☎839

30 40. House DJ Sat. nights. Open Tu-Su 9pm until whenever. Closed Nov. and May.) The **Co-op** is at the corner of Via Maestra and Via da Mulin. (Open M-F 8am-12:15pm and 2-6:30pm, Sa 8am-5pm.)

◨ **SIGHTS.** In a well-preserved 17th-century farmhouse, the **Museum Alpin, Chesa Delnon,** up the street to the left of the tourist office, presents life in the Engadine as it used to be: devoid of high-tech hikers with wimpy polypropylene and full of bearded, pipe-smoking, wool-clad mountain men with picks and ropes. Sixty varieties of recorded bird calls twitter forth at the touch of a button in the aviary room, also home to 133 stuffed representatives of Engadine fowl. The brilliantly lit mineral collection displays the hidden beauty that forms the bedrock of the valley. (☎842 72 73. Open June-Oct. M-Sa 4-6pm, in bad weather 3-6pm. 5SFr, children 1SFr. A short English description of the displays is free.) At the highest point of the village, the bare exterior of the **Church of Santa Maria** conceals a number of well-preserved frescoes, including the **Mary Magdalene cycle** from 1495. Unfortunately, a tour of the paintings is only available for 40SFr through the tourist office, but look closely at the back wall back to see where the original frescoes from 1230 were painted over. (Open June 10-28 M, W, F and July-Oct. daily 3:30-5:30pm. German tour at 5pm.) For an enchanting hour of music, attend the daily *Kurkonzerte* held in the Taiswald pavilion in the woods. (Mid-June to mid-Sept. daily 11am-noon. Trail by train station; signs point the way.)

◪ **OUTDOOR ACTIVITIES.** In winter, Pontresina is a center for **cross-country skiing.** The youth hostel is the *Langlaufzentrum* (cross-country center); trails are free for guests. The tourist office sells the helpful "Oberengadia Bergell" hiking and mountain biking map, which covers the Upper Engadine (15SFr). A number of trails stretch between the **Muottas Maragl cable car** (☎842 83 08; one-way 18SFr; round-trip 26SFr; base accessible by Post Bus, dir: St. Moritz), the **Piz Languard,** and the cable car below it. The level "Hohenweg" rambles above the valley between the cable cars (4hr.). A more demanding route leads from the Muottas Muragl to the **Alp Segantini,** where the painter Giovanni Segantini spent his last years (1¼hr.). The trail then climbs to Piz Languard, with photographic views up the snaking Morteratsch glacier to the 4049m **Piz Bernina** (3hr.). To reach the Piz Languard more quickly, take the **Alp Languard chairlift** from town (☎842 62 55; 13SFr, round-trip 19SFr). From the top of the lift, follow signs to the steep 2½hr. hike to the peak and restaurant.

For more intimate contact with the **glaciers,** it is possible to take the train (dir: Tirano) to **"Diavolezza"** (6.20SFr) and then the cable car to the top of the **Diavolezza Glacier** (☎842 64 19; 20SFr, round-trip 268SFr), which sits just above the valley between Piz Palu and Bernina. Bring sunglasses; the snow makes the view nearly blinding to the naked eye. The **Mountain Climbing School of Pontresina,** Switzerland's largest, leads a 4hr. hike down the Morteratsch glacier. (☎838 83 33. Hikes daily 11am; meet at the top of the cable car. Meet at the bottom in questionable weather. 30SFr, ages 7-16 15SFr.) Trails also attack the glacier from the bottom, which is significantly cheaper. Take the train from Pontresina (dir: Tirano) to "Morteratsch" (3.80SFr) and walk as far up to and alongside the Morteratsch glacier as desired. From the train stop it is a 30min. walk to the glacier, and a 3hr. hike to the highest hut on the glacier. Signs mark the glacier's recession since the turn of the century. The tourist office has **free** beach volleyball and fishing, **tours,** and **excursions,** including botanical and wildlife observation excursions, and a guided trip to the nearby **Swiss National Park.** For **canyoning** (170SFr), **house running** (rappeling frontwards; prices vary), or **dog sled** rides (winter only, 95SFr), call **Pontresina Events** (☎842 72 57; www.pontresinaevents.ch).

GRAUBÜNDEN

ST. MORITZ   ☎ 081

Chic, elegant, and exclusive, St. Moritz is one of the most famous ski resorts in the world, but offers little of real substance for the average backpacker. Renowned as a playground for the rich and famous, this "Resort at the Top of the World" will convert almost anyone into a window-shopper. As host to the Winter Olympics in 1928 and 1948, St. Moritz catapulted into the international spotlight. Today, the town offers a wide selection of winter sports from world-class skiing and bobsledding to golf, polo, greyhound racing, cricket on the frozen lake, and *Skikjöring*—a sport similar to water skiing in which the water is replaced by snow and the motorboat is replaced by a galloping horse.

▐ TRANSPORTATION

Trains run every hr. to: Celerina (5min., 4:56am-11:45pm, 2.60SFr); Chur (2hr., 4:56am-8:02pm, 38SFr); Pontresina (10min., 7:14am-8:20pm, 4.60SFr); and Zuoz (30min., 4:56am-8:02pm, 9.20SFr) via Samedan. **Post Buses** provide similar routes and the only public access to the Engadine Valley west of St. Moritz. Buses depart from the station and run every hr. (6:38am-12:04am; add 5SFr after 9:36pm) to Maloja (40min., 9.80SFr), Sils (20min., 6.60SFr) and Silvaplana (15min., 3.80SFr).

Several scenic train routes originate in St. Moritz. The legendary **Glacier Express** covers the 290km to Zermatt in a leisurely 7½hr. (departs Oct. 13-Dec. 14 daily, 9:02am, June 16-Oct. 12 9:25am; 131SFr; SwissPass valid, Eurail valid until Disentis), crossing 291 bridges and going through 91 tunnels. The **Bernina Express,** the only Swiss train that crosses the Alps without entering any tunnels, journeys to Tirano, Italy (2½hr., every hr. 7:14am-4:45pm, 26SFr, Eurail and SwissPass valid).

▐ PRACTICAL INFORMATION

The **tourist office,** Via Maistra 12 (follow the signs from the top of Truoch Serlas across from the train station and turn right upstairs after last sign), makes hotel reservations. (☎ 837 33 33; fax 33 66; information@stmoritz.ch; www.stmoritz.ch. Open July to mid-Sept. and mid-Dec. to Apr. M-F 9am-6:30pm, Sa 9am-6pm, Su 4-6pm; May-June and Nov. M-F 9am-noon and 2-6pm, Sa 9am-noon.) The **train station** (☎ 833 59 12) has **currency exchange, Western Union services, luggage storage** (3SFr), a kiosk for **hotel reservations,** and **bike rental** (30SFr per day, 6SFr extra to return to a different train station; 23SFr per half-day), at the same counter (open 8am-6:30pm; bike return until 11pm), along with **lockers** (2SFr). Other services include: **taxi** ☎ 833 35 55; **medical emergency** ☎ 144; **police** ☎ 117. **Swisscom,** in the post office, on Via Serlas on the way to the tourist office, offers **Internet** access. (5SFr per 30min. Open M-F 7:45am-noon and 1:45-6:15pm.) **Bobby's American Pub,** past Galerie Apotheke, has more terminals. (15SFr per hr., 18SFr if you don't buy a drink. Open daily noon-8pm.) **Post office** open M-F 7:45am-noon and 1:45-6:15pm, Sa 8:30am-noon. **Postal code:** CH-7500.

▐ ACCOMMODATIONS

With a cappuccino maker in the main lobby, the **Jugendherberge Stille (HI)** ❸, Via Surpunt 60, provides luxury on a backpacker's budget. Follow signs around the lake left of the station (30min.), or take the Post Bus (dir: Maloja) to "Hotel Sonne" (2.60SFr) and go left on Via Surpunt (10min.). Perks include: wall-to-wall carpeting, 4-bed dorms, semi-private showers, a pool table (2SFr), ping-pong, a game room, **Internet** (4SFr per 15min.), children's playroom, and **mountain bike rental** (15SFr per day, 10SFr after 4pm). The hostel can be overrun by sports teams in the summer; call in advance. (☎833 39 69; fax 80 46; st.moritz@youthhostel.ch; www.youthhostel.ch/st.moritz. Breakfast, dinner, showers, lockers, and sheets included. Lunch 5-9.50SFr, order in advance. Laundry 7.60SFr. Reception June-Oct. 7-10am and 4-9:45pm; Dec.-Apr. 7:30-10am and 4-9:45pm; May and Nov. shortened hours. Curfew 11pm; entrance code given. May-Oct. dorms 45.50SFr; doubles 117SFr, with shower 140SFr. Nov.-Apr. dorms 52SFr; doubles 130SFr/170SFr. Nonmembers add 6SFr. AmEx/DC/MC/V.) The **Sporthotel Stille ❹**, next door, provides bare, motel-style rooms with semi-private bathrooms. (☎833 69 48; fax 07 08; hotel.stille.st.moritz@bluewin.ch; www.hostelstille.ch. Breakfast included. Dinner 19SFr. June-Sept. singles 75SFr; doubles 110SFr. Oct.-Dec. 21 65SFr/100SFr. Dec. 22-May 90SFr/142-152SFr. Reduced prices for longer stays. MC/V.) **Hotel Sonne ❹** offers luxury lodgings with spacious clean rooms with private showers, balconies, TVs, and minibars. (☎833 03 63; fax 60 90; hotel@sonne-stmoritz.ch; www.sonne-stmoritz.ch. Reception 7am-11pm. Breakfast included. Apr.-Dec. 20 singles 95-105SFr; doubles 160-190SFr; triples 210-255SFr. Dec. 21-Mar. 120-165SFr/190-230SFr/240-275SFr. MC/V.) For **Camping Olympiaschanze ❶**, catch the Post Bus (dir: Sils-Maloja) to "St. Moritz Campingplatz" (3SFr). This sprawling campground in the woods has a friendly atmosphere with small picnic tables and weekend BBQs. (☎833 40 90; fax 834 40 96; camping.stmoritz@tcs.ch; www.campingtcs.ch. Open mid-May to Sept. Reception 7:45am-noon and 2:30-8pm. 5.20-7.20SFr, children half-price; tent 6-7SFr; car 3SFr.) Camping is also available in nearby Silvaplana.

◘ FOOD

Restaurant Hauser ❸, on Sonnepl., a block downhill from the tourist office, offers a diverse, relatively inexpensive menu (bratwurst and fries 16.50SFr, tofu with Chinese vegetables 20.50SFr) on a terrace. For a culinary adventure select from a number of Aussie specialties cooked right at the table on a hot stone. (☎837 50 50. Open daily 8am-10pm; specialty available 6-9:30pm.) **Acla ❺**, Via dal Bagn 54, in the Schwizerhof Hotel, has an intimate atmosphere for fine dining. Entrees (36-45SFr) include French duck breast with apricots. Pastas are 16-26SFr. (☎837 07 01. Open daily 11:30am-2pm and 6:30-8:30pm.) **Restaurant Engadinia ❸**, p. da Scoula, is known for fondue (28.50SFr per person; extra for champagne) and "*Rösti*-pizza," 18.50-19.50SFr. (☎833 32 65. Open M-F 8:30am-9:30pm, Sa 11am-9:30pm.) Get groceries at the **Co-op Center,** one square up from the tourist office or at Via dal Bagn 20, the main road between Dorf and Bad, en route to the youth hostel. (Open M-F 8am-12:15pm and 2-6:30pm, Sa 8am-5pm. Location on Via dal Bagn open over lunch time.) The **After Hours** grocery store, Via Maistra 2 (☎834 99 00), under the kiosk, is open 24hr. In mid-March, sample the culinary delights of the annual week-long **St. Moritz Gourmet Festival.** (Mar. 11-15. Check www.stmoritz.ch.)

▥ MUSEUMS AND EVENTS

The **Giovanni Segantini Museum,** Via Somplaz 30, consists of two rooms dedicated to the Italian Expressionist painter, who spent the final 12 years of his life in nearby Maloja. The exhibit's highlight, the alpine trilogy "Life, Nature, and Death," (also known as "Becoming, Being, and Passing") is housed in the upstairs *Kuppelsaal*. (☎833 44 54. Open June 1-Oct. 20 and Dec.-Apr. Tu-Su 10am-noon and 3-6pm. 10SFr, students 7SFr, children 3SFr. English guidebook 10SFr.) The **Engadiner Museum,** Via dal Bagn 39, between Bad and Dorf, is a rare example of Engadine *sgraffiti* architecture, where designs are carved into white plaster on the exterior of buildings to reveal a darker base color. The house features tiny doorways, beautiful *Chuchichästli*s (cupboards), and a macabre plague-era four-poster sickbed with a skeleton on the ceiling. The inscription translates, "As you are, I would like to be," i.e., still alive. (☎833 43 33. Open June-Oct. M-F 9:30am-noon and 2-5pm, Su 10am-noon; Dec.-Apr. M-F 10am-noon and 2-5pm, Su 10am-noon. Closed May and Nov. 5SFr, students 4SFr, children 2.50SFr. English guides 1SFr.) July brings the **Opern Festival** to the legendary Badrutt's Palace Hotel in St. Moritz. The 4th annual festival featuring *Mosè in Egitto* by Gioacchino Rossini starts July 5, 2003. (☎833 01 10; fax 830 80 81; www.opernfestival-engadin.ch. Tickets 70-170SFr.)

▚ OUTDOOR ACTIVITIES

St. Moritz's **skiing** is world-famous. Two main sectors, Corviglia and Corvatsch, are packed with easy runs, although tougher runs pepper the sector. The third sector, Diavolezza, offers some more difficult slopes. From Feb. 1-16, 2003, St. Moritz will host the **Alpine Ski World Championships** (p. 429) with several opportunities to watch the greats tear up the slopes. (☎830 00 01; fax 00 09; ferien@skiengadin.ch; www.stmoritz2003.com. Audience day passes 39-66SFr. Skiing day passes 49-61SFr, youth 16-20 45-55SFr, children 6-15 26-30SFr. ☎830 00 00 for regional ski packages; www.skiengadine.ch. Rental available at several shops throughout town.) Each year the 1.6km **bobsled** run from the '28 and '48 Olympics is rebuilt by 14 skilled laborers with 5000 cubic meters of snow and 4000L of water for the **Olympia Bobrun.** (☎830 02 00; www.olympia-bobrun.ch. 210SFr for 1 run, a diploma, and a photo; call ahead as slots fill up quickly. No experience necessary, but some medical conditions preclude participation. Open Dec. 26-Mar. 3, 2003.)

In the summer visitors take advantage of the **hiking,** including several level trails in an alpine setting. A flat trail cuts its way from St. Moritz to **Pontresina** (1½hr.). The trailhead is on the other side of the train station (the "See" exit) across the bridge. For a more demanding trip (3hr.), ride from St. Moritz up to **Piz Nair** for a rooftop view of the Engadine. (3075m. ☎833 43 44. Closed for repairs summer 2002; call for prices and opening times in 2003.) From this point, a train snakes down to **Suvretta Lake** (2580m) in the shadow of majestic **Piz Julier** (3380m). Follow the Ova da Suvretta back down to the Signalbahn or St. Moritz (3½hr.). **The St. Moritz Experience** (☎833 77 14; fax 832 22 93; info@stmoritz-experience.ch; www.stmoritz-experience.ch) provides **canyoning** (W and F, 180SFr) and **glacier adventures** (M and Th, 120SFr) throughout the week. Other summer activities in St. Moritz include **river rafting** (☎861 14 19; fax 14 10; info@engadin-adventure.ch; www.engadin-adventure.ch; 85-95SFr per half-day, 160SFr per day) and **horseback riding** (☎833 57 33; 60SFr per hr., 90SFr per private lesson).

ITALIAN SWITZERLAND (TICINO, TESSIN)

Ticino (Tessin, in German and French), nestled below the Alps, is renowned for its mix of Swiss efficiency and Italian *dolce vita*—no wonder the rest of Switzerland vacations here. Ecologist and philosopher Luigi Ferrari notes, "In Ticino, I have found images straight out of history." It is here that jasmine-laced villas painted bright colors and traditional stone huts replace the charred-wood chalets of northern Switzerland. The landscape charms with its tropical vegetation and emerald-green lakes. Pastel church facades that hide ancient sanctuaries spill out onto the cities' piazzas. Architecture reigns in Bellinzona, where castles loom. Culture-seekers flock to the annual international film festival in Locarno. Far south in the canton, the financial capital of Lugano also serves as a center for budget travelers thanks to its gardened hostels.

HIGHLIGHTS OF TICINO

Marvel at Marianne Werefkin's modern works in the **Museo Comunale d'Arte Moderna** in Ascona (see p. 448).

Make like James Bond and dive off the 220m high Verzasca dam, the **world's highest bungee jump** (see p. 444).

Groove to bass-heavy beats at the **Bellinzona Blues Festival** (see p. 439).

Couldn't crash Cannes? Try the **International Film Festival** in Locarno (see p. 445).

BELLINZONA ☎ 091

The three **medieval castles** that watch over Bellinzona (pop. 18,000), remind visitors that the city was once a strategic Milanese fort for guarding trade routes through the San Bernadino and St. Gotthard passes. As the capital of Ticino, it is still an important crossroads for tourists heading to lake resorts further south. The city has a sharp modernity missing in other Ticinese towns, making it a haven for lovers of art and architecture both old and contemporary. Meanwhile, the villas and vineyards in the surrounding hills cast a pastoral calm over the city, which is disrupted only once a year by the beats of the **Bellinzona Blues Festival.**

TRANSPORTATION

Bellinzona is the main train hub for Ticino, with **trains** to: Basel (4hr., every 30min. 6:05am-8:36pm, 72SFr); Locarno (20min., 2 per hr. 5:38am-12:38am, 7.20SFr); Lucerne (2¼hr., 6:05am-9:06pm, 50SFr); Lugano (30min., every 30min. 5:06am-12:36am, 11.40SFr); Milan (2hr., every hr. 5:06-9:25pm, 29SFr); Rome (7hr., every hr. 6:46am-7:36pm, 90SFr); and Zurich (2½hr., every hr. 6:26-9:25am and every 30min. 10:26am-9:06pm, 54SFr). Travelers under 26 save on Milan (23SFr) and Rome (68SFr). Trains to and from Geneva require a change in Domodossola, Italy (5½hr., 7 per day, 8:07am-6:38pm, 94SFr), Zurich (5¾hr., 1-2 per hr., 6:26am-6:26pm, 111SFr), or Olten (6hr., 1-2 per hr. 6:05am-6:26pm, 101SFr). **Post Buses** leave from the station for Chur (Coira) via Thusis (3hr., every hr. 6:07am-6:07pm, 50SFr), San Bernadino (1¼hr.; every hr. 6:07am-9:07pm; 19.80SFr), and elsewhere in eastern Switzerland. By **car,** arrive from the north on N2/E35 or N13/E43; from Lugano or the south on N2/E35 north; from Locarno or the west on N13.

PRACTICAL INFORMATION

To reach Bellinzona's **tourist office,** Via Stazione 18, turn left from the train station; it's in the **post office** building and makes free hotel reservations. (☎825 21 31; fax 821 41 20; bellinzona.turismo@bluewin.ch; www.tourism-ticino.ch. Open M-F 9am-6:30pm, Sa 9am-noon. Post office open M-F 7:30am-6:30pm, Sa 9am-12pm.) Services include: **currency exchange, luggage storage** (5SFr at baggage check), **lockers** (3-5SFr), and **bike rental** (at baggage check; reserve ahead; 30SFr per day, 23SFr per half-day; additional 6SFr to return at another station) at the train station (open 6:10am-7:40pm); public **parking** at the station (1SFr per 30min.; 8SFr per day) or in the Colletivo at P. del Sole, off Viale Stazione to the right, down Largo Elvetica (open 24hr.; 7am-10pm 1SFr per 45min; 10pm-7am 1SFr per hr.); **taxis,** ☎825 44 44 or 825 11 51; **Internet** at the **Bar Cervo** gets a crowd. (☎825 40 70. Open M-Sa 7:30am-8pm. 6SFr per hr.) **Postal code:** CH-6500.

⌐ ACCOMMODATIONS

Youth Hostel Montebello, Via Nocca 4 (☎825 15 22; fax 835 42 85; bellinzona@youth-hostel.ch; www.youthhostel.ch/bellinzona), occupies the former Instituto Santa Maria just below the Castello di Montebello. Left from the station and again at Piazza Indipendenza. Although institutional in size and right beside the railroad tracks, this hostel offers sparkling accommodations, laundry (5SFr), **Internet** (15SFr per hr.), and museum-like charm. (Reception 8-10:30am and 3-10pm. Check-out by 10am. Dinner 12.50SFr. Breakfast and sheets included. Dorms 30-35SFr; 6-8 bed rooms 35-40SFr; singles 45-50SFr; doubles 80-90SFr. Non-members 6SFr extra. MC/V.) ❷

Albergo Internazionale, P. Stazione (☎825 43 33; fax 826 13 59; hotel-_international@ticino.com; www.ticino.com/hotel-international), across from the train station, offers a luxurious setting for clean and cozy rooms with showers. Breakfast buffet included. (Reception 8am-noon and 2-6pm. Singles 100SFr; doubles 130-170SFr. AmEx/DC/MC/V.) ❹

Hotel Garni Moderno, Viale Stazione 17b (☎/fax 825 13 76), offers rooms with new carpeting, sinks, and large windows. Go left from the station, right on Via Claudio Pellandini, and right on Via Cancelliere Molo. Breakfast included. Reception in hotel cafe M-Sa 6:30am-10:30pm. Singles 55SFr; doubles 90SFr, with shower 120SFr. MC/V. ❸

Hotel San Giovanni, Via San Giovanni 7 (☎/fax 825 19 19; ristorantesangiovanni@bluewin.ch; www.hotelzimmer.ch). Turn left from the station and right down Scilinata Dionigi Resinelli (100m). Tidy rooms and convenient location. (Breakfast included. Parking available. Reception M-Sa 6:30am-midnight, Su 7:30am-noon. Singles 55SFr; doubles 100SFr, with shower 120SFr; triples 150SFr; quads with shower 200SFr. MC/V.) ❸

Camping Bosco de Molinazzo (☎829 11 18; fax 23 55). Take bus #2 (dir: Castione) to "Arbedo Posta Vecchia." (2.20SFr). The campground has laundry services (3-4SFr for washer and dryer) and a pool. (Open Apr. until mid-Oct. Reception 9am-1pm and 4-10pm. 6.20-7.20SFr per person, ages 6-14 half-price; tent 6-7SFr; electricity 4SFr.) ❶

◖ FOOD

Bellinzona is full of cafes that serve hot and cold *panini* (sandwiches) for 5-10SFr, but warm meals are hard to find. Try **Croce Federale** ❸, Viale Stazione 12, for Italian dining on a terrace overlooking the main road, in an ordinary dining room with a stone oven, or in a splendid back room decorated with floral watercolors. Enjoy pastas (13-19SFr), pizzas (11-18SFr), or meat entrees (25-33SFr) with an inexpensive bottle of local wine. (☎825 16 67. Warm food served from 11:30am-2pm and 6-10pm; pizza until 11pm. Closed Sundays.) **Ristorante Corona** ❷, Via Camminata 5, on the far end of town before P. Nosetto, also offers the wares of a full kitchen. Pastas in two sizes (10-16SFr), pizzas (11-16SFr) and daily *Menüs* (20SFr) available from 12-2pm and 6:30-10pm. (☎825 28 44. Open 7am-midnight; F-Sa until 1am. Pizzas available after 10pm. AmEx.) **Ristorante Manora** ❶, Viale Stazione 5 (on the P. Collegiata), in the basement of the Manor, offers a selection of self-serve snacks. *Panini* 2.10-4.80SFr and ice cream 2.40SFr. (☎823 86 99. Restaurant and grocery store open M-W and F 8:30am-6:30pm, Th 8:30am-9pm, Sa 8am-5pm.) **Peverelli Panetteria Tea Room Pasticceria** ❶ in P. Collegiata, off Viale Stazione, serves a large selection of teas (2.40-3.40SFr), *panini* (5-6SFr), large pizza slices (5SFr), and pastas (10-12SFr). (☎825 60 03. Open M-F 7am-7pm, Sa 7am-6pm.) **Migros** is in P. del Sole, across from the Castelgrande entrance. (Supermarket open M-F 8am-6:30pm, Sa 7:30am-5pm; restaurant open M-F 7am-6:30pm, Sa 7am-5pm.) A huge **outdoor market** along Viale Stazione lays out everything from fruits and breads to incense and rugs (Sa 7:30am-noon).

◙ SIGHTS

Originally joined by stone walls, the three castles of Bellinzona became separate entities when the city joined the Swiss Confederation and the three original cantons Uri, Schwyz and Nidwalden each claimed one of the battlements as its own. Today the **Castelgrande, Castello di Montebello,** and **Castello di Sasso Corbaro** remain linked through their membership in the UNESCO World Heritage list and combined tourism. Tourists may buy a "3 Castelli" ticket (8SFr, students 4SFr), available at the castles, or a special excursion ticket from the train station that includes travel to and from various cities, lunch, and admission to the 3 castles. (Train tickets good for 3 days. Chiasso 30.40SFr, Locarno 22SFr, Lugano 25.40SFr.) For history buffs, the tourist office and castle museums also sell a fascinating guide detailing the war-filled history of Bellinzona (9SFr; available in English).

Rising 50m above the P. del Sole on a huge hunk of rock, the oft-renovated **Castelgrande,** accessible by the free elevator near P. del Sole or by the winding uphill paths from P. Collegieta and P. Nosetto, occupies a site inhabited since the Neolithic period (5500-5000 BC) and fortified since the 4th century. Construction on the current fortress began in the 13th century with the Milanese Visconti family; major changes were introduced between 1473 and 1486. The *bianca* (white) and *nera* (black) towers, rising 28 and 27m high respectively, date from the 13th and 14th centuries. The top of the **Tora Bianca** offers panoramic views of Bellinzona. The castle was renovated from 1984 to 1991, with an elevator, expensive courtyard restaurant, and museum designed to make it more hospitable to tourists. The **museum** exhibits unique painted panels from the house of a Bellizonan noble and a Swiss coin collection. (Open 10am-6pm. 4SFr, students 2SFr.)

The smaller but more satisfyingly dank **Castello di Montebello,** on the hill opposite Castelgrande, offers visitors working drawbridges, ramparts, dungeons, and views as far as Lake Maggiore on a clear day. The castle can be reached on foot from P. Collegiata up the slippery steps of Sallita alla Motta or by bus from Viale Stazione. The tower and former residential quarters now house a mildly interesting **archaeological and civic museum** containing vases, jewelry, and ceramics, as well as ancient bric-a-brac and ceremonial and military arms. (☎825 13 42. Open Feb.-Dec. Tu-Su 10am-6pm. Museum 2SFr, students 1SFr.) The **Castello di Corbaro** (230m above city level), the smallest of Bellinzona's castles, is worth the walk only for the truly intrigued. Take the road from Castello di Montebello or Via Ospedale. The Duke of Milan had the place slapped together in six months after the battle of Giornico (1478), when a Swiss force of 600 defeated 10,000 Milanese. Its **Belvedere Museum** hosts temporary art exhibits. (☎825 59 06. Open Apr.-Oct. Tu-Su 10am-6pm. Museum 4SFr, students 2SFr.)

A number of notable churches grace Bellinzona, tucked away among the villas and hotels. The **Chiesa Collegiata dei SS Pietro e Stefano,** on the P. Collegiata, wears an early Renaissance facade flanked by trumpeting heralds. The breathtakingly ornate stone interior features numerous paintings and frescoes (attributed to Simone Peterzano), overhung by a gilded canopy. The pulpit in "scagliola" (a painted plaster imitation of marble) that dates from 1784 and the holy water stoup, named the "Fontana Trivulziana" after a nobleman from Messocco who owned it in the 15th century, are other interesting features.

To reach the 16th-century **Chiesa di San Biagio** from the train station, walk 15min. to the left or take bus #4 to "Cimiterio"; cross under the railroad tracks, turn left up the stairs, turn left again, and follow the tracks 50m. The church exhibits a gigantic painting of St. Christopher on its exterior and a flock of saints on its columned interior. Tombstones and a beautifully carved granite font are displayed on the south and west walls. (Open 9-11am.)

⚡ OUTDOOR ACTIVITIES

The Ticino River is perfect for idle strollers out for breezes and mountain scenery. A 45min. hike with grand views of Sasso Corbaro and the valley starts in Monti di Ravecchia, a short bus ride from Bellinzona. The trail begins at the hospital parking lot and follows an ancient mule path, leading to now-deserted **Prada,** an ancient trading post possibly dating from pre-Roman times.

🎭 ENTERTAINMENT

Opera lovers with a bit of extra cash will relish the blockbuster productions of the Bellinzona **Open Air Opera** (July 25, 26, 29, 31, and Aug. 2, 2003) performed on the temporary stage within the Castelgrande grounds. Past years have featured productions such as *Aida* and *Nabucco.* (Prices range from 70-140SFr; contact the tourist office or **Ticket Corner.** ☎0848 80 08 00; www.ticketcorner.ch.) The annual **Blues Festival** (June 26-28, 2003) draws drawls from across southern America in late June. Past performers include Luther Allison and Joe Louis Walker. Entrance 10SFr per night.

LOCARNO   ☎091

On the shores of **Lago Maggiore,** Locarno's (pop. 30,000) cypress and magnolia bask in warm breezes. This relatively unspoiled town has a tropical presence, perhaps because it gets the most sunlight in Switzerland—over 2200 hours of sunlight per year. During its world-famous **film festival** each August, Locarno swells with people enjoying balmy evenings of *al fresco* dining beneath palm trees. All this worldly languor coexists in relative peace with the piety of worshipers in the churches of the **Città Vecchia** (old city). In addition to its self-contained charms, Locarno serves as an excellent starting point at the foot of the Ticinese hills for mountain hikes along the **Verzasca** and **Maggia valleys** or for regional skiing.

▐ TRANSPORTATION

"Holiday" passes offer free travel along the bus and train lines in the Lago Maggiore region. Available at the tourist office, the Travel Office at the train station, or at **Viaggi Fart** on P. Grand (☎751 87 31; fax 40 77. 3-day pass 46SFr, children 23SFr; one week 66SFr/33SFr).

> **Trains: P. Stazione** (☎743 65 64; rail info ☎0900 300 300). To: **Bellinzona** (25min., every 30min. 5:59am-1:09am, 7.20SFr), connecting north to **Lucerne** (2½hr., every 30min. 6:05am-9:06pm, 54SFr) and **Zurich** (2½hr., every hr. 6:26am-9:06pm, 58SFr). Trains go south to **Lugano** (50min., every 30min. 5:30am-12:05am, 16.60SFr) and **Milan** (2hr., viz Bellinzona, every hr. 5:06am-9:25pm, 34SFr). For **Geneva** (5¾hr., 90SFr), **Montreux** (4¾hr., 76SFr), or **Zermatt** (4hr., 84SFr), change trains in **Domodossola, Italy** (1¾hr., every hr. 7:55am-7:12pm, 28SFr).
>
> **Buses:** Buses leave the train station or P. Grande for **Ascona** (#31, 20 min., every 15min. 6:23am-midnight), **Minusio** (5min., every 15min. 5:04am-11:46pm), and other nearby towns. Buses also run through the **San Bernadino Pass** to eastern Switzerland.
>
> **Ferries: Navigazione Lago Maggiore,** Largo Zorzi 1 (☎0848 81 11 22), conducts tours of the entire lake, all the way into Italy. A full day on the northernmost part of the lake costs 12SFr; for the entire Swiss side 21SFr. Sail to **Ascona** (15-45min., 9 per day 9:10am-5:15pm, day pass 12SFr) or **Brissago** further south (1¼hr., 9 per day, day pass 21SFr). "Holiday" cards offer 50% off on Lago di Lugano (see above).

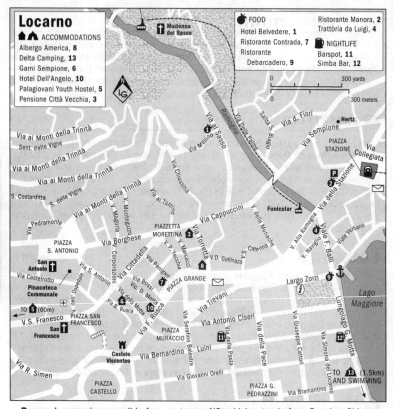

Locarno

▲▲ **ACCOMMODATIONS**

Albergo America, **8**
Delta Camping, **13**
Garni Sempione, **6**
Hotel Dell'Angelo, **10**
Palagiovani Youth Hostel, **5**
Pensione Città Vecchia, **3**

● FOOD
Hotel Belvedere, **1**
Ristorante Contrada, **7**
Ristorante
Debarcadero, **9**

Ristorante Manora, **2**
Trattòria da Luigi, **4**

◗ NIGHTLIFE
Barspot, **11**
Simba Bar, **12**

By car: Locarno is accessible from motorway N2, which extends from Basel to Chiasso (exit: Bellinzona-Süd).

Car Rental: Hertz SA, Garage Starnini SA, Via Sempione 12, Muralto (☎ 743 50 50). Small 4-person car, 141SFr per day. Open M-F 8am-noon and 1:30-5:30pm, Sa 8am-noon. AmEx/DC/MC/V.

Taxi: Ask at the tourist office for a list or look for stations around town. **EcoTaxi** offers some of the best rates in town with hybrid cars (☎ 008 321 321).

Parking: Metered parking on Via della Posta and major streets (1SFr per 30min.; max 90min.). The 24hr. parking garage, **Autosilo Largo SA** (☎ 751 96 13), beneath the *Kursaal*, accessible from Via Cattori, has the same rates 7am-10pm (half-price overnight).

Bike Rental: At the train station. Bikes 30SFr per day, 25SFr per half day. Open 8am-7pm. Call ☎ 743 65 64 to reserve. 6SFr fee for returning a bike to another station.

✦ 🛈 ORIENTATION AND PRACTICAL INFORMATION

Piazza Grande, home of Locarno's International Film Festival, is the city's anchor; the town's social life centers around its arcades. Just above P. Grande, the *Città Vecchia* is home to 16th- and 17th-century architecture, as well as luxurious, yet economical accommodations. **Via Ramogna** connects the P. Grande to the train station. **Via Rusca** extends from its other side to the Castello Visconteo.

Tourist Office: Largo Zorzi (☎791 00 91; fax 785 19 41; buongiorno@maggiore.ch; www.maggiore.ch), on P. Grande in the *Kursaal* (casino). Office makes hotel reservations. Open M-F 9am-6pm, Sa 10am-5pm, Su 3pm-6pm; Nov.-Mar. closed Su.

Currency Exchange: Banks line P. Grande. Banks open M-F 9am-4pm, also, train station open daily 6am-7:30pm. **Western Union** at station open M-Su 9am-6pm.

Luggage Storage: At the train station, 7SFr. Open 6:50am-8:30pm. **Lockers** 4-7SFr.

Bookstore: Libriarte Internationale (☎/fax 743 03 33), P. Stazione 2, around the corner from the train station, houses maps, travel books, and a small selection of English novels. Open M-Sa 9am-6:30pm.

Internet Access: Visitors' Center booth on Viale Balli (☎/fax 751 84 08), across the street and uphill from the dock (12SFr per hr.). Open June-Oct. M, F, Sa-Su 9:30am-6:30pm; W-Th 9:30am-noon and 5-7:30pm. **Rialto** (☎743 11 10) up Via Stazione from the train station (10SFr per hr.) Open M-F 11:30am-1am; Sa-Su 1:30pm-1am.

Emergencies: Police, ☎117. **Fire,** ☎118. **Road information,** ☎021 163. **Weather,** ☎021 162. **Medical Assistance,** ☎111. **Ambulance,** ☎144.

Post Office: P. Grande. Open M-F 7:30am-6:30pm, Sa 8:30am-noon. **Postal Code:** CH-6600.

ACCOMMODATIONS AND CAMPING

A display board outside the train station allows free phone calls to most of the city's hotels and pensions. Reserve everywhere a week in advance March through October; book six months in advance for a bed during the film festival.

Pensione Città Vecchia, Via Toretta 13 (☎/fax 751 45 54; cittavecchia@datacomm.ch; www.cittavecchia.ch). From P. Grande, turn right onto Via Toretta. With the best prices in town and a location to match, it's usually full. The co-ed rooms and bathrooms are simple but clean. Tiny breakfast and sheets (included for singles and doubles) 4.50SFr each. **Bike rental** 15SFr per day. Reception 8am-9pm. Check-in 1-6pm. Call ahead if arriving after 6pm. Dorms 22-33SFr; doubles 128-148SFr; triples 93-102SFr; quads 116-132SFr. ❷

Palagiovani Youth Hostel (HI), Via Varenna 18 (☎756 15 00; fax 15 01; locarno@youthhostel.ch; www.youthhostel.ch/locarno). From P. Grande, turn right on Via della Motta. Take the left fork (Via B. Rusca) past P.S. Francesco, then take V.S. Francesco, which turns into Via Varenna (HI signs point the way from Via Varenna on). High hedges and floral bushes conceal this sterile establishment. Most of the 2- to 6-bed rooms include balconies, sinks, and lockers. Huge buffet breakfast and sheets included. Lunch and dinner 12.50SFr each. Other amenities include laundry (6SFr), towels (2SFr), **Internet** (15SFr per hr.), and **mountain bikes** (15SFr per day, 10SFr per half-day). The hostel can become overrun by families and school groups in July and August, so call ahead. Reception Nov.-Mar. 8-10am and 4-10:30pm; Apr.-Oct. 8-10am and 3-11:30pm. Dorms 32SFr, with shower and bathroom 36-44SFr; doubles 72SFr/88-106SFr. Non-members 6SFr extra. ❷

Garni Sempione, Via Rusca 6 (☎751 30 64; fax 752 38 37). Walk to the end of the P. Grande, turn right onto Via della Motta, and then take the left fork onto Via B. Rusca. This small hotel ventures to take the outside inside with a variety of rooms leading from an enclosed courtyard. Wood panelling and tile along the walls and brightly colored comforters add to the atmosphere. Breakfast included. Reception 8am-9pm. Check-out 11am. Singles 60SFr, with shower 65SFr; doubles 110SFr/120SFr; triples 150SFr/170SFr. Children 6-10 30SFr/35SFr, youths 11-15 40SFr/45SFr. AmEx/DC/MC/V. ❸

Hotel Dell' Angelo, P. Grande (☎751 81 75; fax 751 82 56). On the far side of P. Grande. Winding marble staircases lead guests to clean and simple rooms. All rooms

TERRIBLY EXCITING

I once read that terror and excitement feel exactly the same, with the only difference being the stimulus. On a wild morning in Locarno, I discovered firsthand that this is true.

Canyoning day. I had passed up the opportunity to jump off cliffs and slide down rocks four years ago and had been regretting it ever since. Then, a guide for a local outdoor adventure company offered me a bargain I could hardly refuse, and before I knew what was happening, I was digging through my pack for a swimsuit.

After suiting up in my Neoprene wetsuit uniform, I felt ready for war and wondered how close that was to what my canyoning team and I were about to face. Our first task was a six-foot rock slide at 60 degrees—"Just to get your feet wet," our guide informed us lightly. And they did indeed get wet, along with the rest of me.

Everything else was history. By the end of the morning I had rapelled behind a waterfall, jumped from a 15ft. cliff into a pool of whirling water scarcely 8ft. in diameter, and slid down 20 vertical feet of rock worn smooth by the continuous flow of water. Each challenge was thrust upon me so quickly I had no time to feel fear, which was fortunate. That way, the screams came out as excitement.

—Jocelyn Beh

with shower, TV, and telephone. **Parking** 15SFr. Breakfast included. Reception 7am-1am. Singles 65-135SFr; doubles 100-200SFr; triples 150-250SFr. Add 28SFr per person to include dinner and 42SFr for complete board. AmEx/DC/MC/V. ❸

Albergo America, P. Grande (☎751 76 35; fax 752 36 16). From P. Grande, turn right onto Via Torretta. Centrally located in a historic house, this hotel offers a maze of clean, albeit small, rooms. The white bedspreads and small desks give each room a simple tone. All rooms with showers. Breakfast included. Singles 75SFr; doubles 120-140SFr. AmEx/DC/MC/V. ❹

Delta Camping, Via Respini 7 (☎751 60 81; fax 22 43; info@campingdelta.com; www.campingdelta.com). A 30min. walk along the lakeside to the right from the tourist office (turn left at the info map). Shuttle runs from the campground to Locarno at 11am and 5pm daily, or on request for groups of 3 or more (2SFr). Shaded by birch trees and adjacent to a golf course and rocky beach, this campsite has a restaurant (entrees 9.50-19.50SFr), supermarket, workout room, **Internet** access (5SFr per 30min.) and **bike rental** (20SFr per day, 12SFr per half-day). Reception 8am-8pm; July-Aug. 18 until 10pm. Of the 360 plots on this 5-star site, 72 have a waterside location on the lake or river. 100SFr reservation fee July-Aug., 50SFr of which is returned upon arrival at the site. Open Mar.-Oct. Mar.-May and Oct. 11SFr, tent plot 21SFr, waterfront plot 31SFr; June and August 19-Sept. 12SFr/26SFr/36SFr; July-Aug. 18 18SFr/37-47SFr/47-57SFr. Children 6SFr, electricity 5SFr. ❶

🍴 FOOD

Though most of Locarno's restaurants are pricey, many offer *panini*, pasta, and pizza in the 10-20SFr range, leaving ample funds for that nectar of the gods, gelato. Get your grocery fix at **Aperto,** at the station (open 6am-10pm), or **Co-op** at P. Grande (open M-W and F-Sa 8am-6pm; Th 8am-9pm). A market fills the streets of the *Città Vecchia* every Sa (Apr.-Sept. 9am-1:30pm).

Ristorante Debarcadero (☎751 05 55) on Largo Zorzi by the ferry dock, is one of the very few spots on the lake that's affordable. A crowd of tourists enjoys pizza (11.50-18.50SFr), homemade pastas (12.50-16.50SFr), frappes (8SFr), and beer (3.80SFr), accompanied by pop hits. Open 9am-midnight. ❷

Ristorante Contrada, P. Grande 26 (☎751 48 15). This restaurant is a shrine to felines, which are artistically rendered in every medium on its walls. The covered terrace is ideal for people-watching. Pizza (11.50-19SFr) and pasta (13-22SFr) accompany snacks such as *panini* (7-8SFr) on the menu. Open M-Su 7am-midnight. AmEx/MC/V. ❷

Ristorante Manora, Via della Stazione 1 (☎743 76 76), left of the station, offers quality cafeteria-style food. Breakfast 5.50SFr, salad bar 4.50-10.20SFr, pasta buffet 8.50-9.90SFr, meaty *Menüs* 10.50-16.50SFr. Open M-Sa 7:30am-9pm, Su 8am-9pm. Mar.-Oct. open until 10pm. ❶

Trattoria da Luigi, Via F. Balli 3 (☎751 97 46; fax 42 69), between P. Stazione and Largo Zorzi, offers a romantic dining experience with an arched skylight and flower-accented chandeliers. Although the entrees are pricey (29.50-34SFr), risottos and pastas such as spaghetti with tomatoes, broccoli, olives, and sardines (17.80SFr) are reasonable (16.50-18.50SFr). Open daily 9am-midnight. AmEx/DC/MC/V. ❸

Hotel Belvedere, Via ai Monti Della Trinità 44 (☎751 03 63; fax 52 39; info@belvedere-locarno.com; www.belvedere-locarno.com), off Via al Sasso from Via Cappuccini in the *Città Vecchia*. For a luxurious dining experience, stop at this hillside hotel along the path to the Madonna del Sasso. This pastel restaurant offers traditional pastas (12-15SFr), fish entrees (21-35SFr), and an elaborate Sunday brunch of salads, finger sandwiches, roasted meats, and delectable desserts for 35SFr (noon-2pm). Other days, savor smoked salmon with caviar on traditional *Rösti* (22SFr). Open daily 7-10am, noon-2pm and 6:45-10pm. AmEx/DC/MC/V. ❸

🔵 SIGHTS

For centuries, visitors have journeyed to Locarno solely to see the church of **Madonna del Sasso** (Madonna of the Rock), founded over 500 years ago when a Franciscan monk, Bartholomeo d'Ivrea, had a vision of Mary telling him to build a church high above the city. Its orange-yellow hue renders it immediately recognizable from anywhere in town. The church is accessible by a **funicular** that leaves from a small station just left of the McDonald's (every 15min. 7am-8pm, extended hours in summer; 6.60SFr round-trip, 5SFr with SwissPass, 4.50SFr one-way.) A 20min. walk up the smooth stones of the Via al Sasso (off the Via Cappuccini in the *Città Vecchia*), where capricious lizards scuttle across the path, also leads to the top. Funicular riders will miss the stations of the cross sequencing Christ's passion that lines the trail. A less religious but equally inspiring path heads past the turn-off along a shaded, tropical path to the back of the church. The open courtyard houses a series of life-size wooden niche statues depicting scenes of Christ, including a *Pietà*, a Pentecost, and a 1650 Last Supper. Bramartino's *Fuga in Egitto*, Ciseri's *Trasporto di Cristo al Sepolcro*, and a statue of Mary, sculpted for the church's consecration, adorn the **sanctuary.** Hundreds of silver heart-shaped medallions on the walls commemorate acts of Mary's intervention in the lives of those who have made pilgrimages here. Some of the hearts are accompanied by paintings and embroideries in silk.

The **museum** next door, in the oldest part of the complex, houses a collection of ancient reliquaries and pilgrims' souvenirs. The highlight of the museum is the second-floor collection of disaster paintings—near-drownings, fires, attempted murders, battles, train accidents, and lightning strikes—all commissioned by survivors of the events thanking the Madonna for answering their prayers and intervening to save their lives. Miniature body parts commemorate physical healings. (☎743 62 65; fax 759 13 50; madonnadelsasso@cappuccini.ch; www.cappuccini.ch. Grounds open 6:30am-7pm. Museum open Apr.-Oct. Su-F 2-5pm. 2.50SFr, students 1.50SFr. English guidebooks for the entire complex are available at the devotions shop for 7SFr. Open 9am-7pm.)

To reach the **Chiesa San Francesco** from P. Grande, turn right onto Via B. Rusca and left onto Via S. Francesca. The church was built in the 14th century on top of an older parish founded by the Franciscans shortly after the death of St. Francis of Assisi in 1226. The church displays faded frescoes, added during a 16th-century renovation, beneath its sagging roof. Built of stones scavenged from a demolished castle, the exterior bears incongruous inscriptions from the material's original incarnation. A vanished cemetery, the only remnant of which is a curious skull-and-crossbones from the Orelli family monument, once surrounded the building.

Follow Via Marcacci from the P. Grande and turn left on Via Borghese to reach the cavernous **Chiesa San Antonio,** which presides over the outskirts of the *Città Vecchia.* (San Antonio is one block up from P. San Antonio.) Built between 1668 and 1674, it was renovated in 1863 after the roof and front facade collapsed, killing 45 people. Circular patches of sunlight illuminate a large fresco, *Cristo Morto* (Dead Christ) by G. A. Felice Orelli, which depicts Christ being taken off the cross. Contact the tourist office for the monthly schedule of organ concerts. The small cultural museum in the **Pinacoteca Communale,** across the street, is in a renovated palace, where breezy balconies connect the exhibit rooms surrounding the central atrium. The museum hosts changing exhibitions of lesser-known modern artists. (☎756 31 85, 34 57 or 31 70. Open Tu-Su 10am-5pm when there's an exhibit. 7SFr, students 5SFr.)

A duke of Milan constructed the **Castello Visconteo,** down Via F. Rusca from P. Grande, in the 13th century. Wander through dungeons and towers where soldiers poured boiling oil on attackers. The second floor houses an exhibit on the 1925 Treaty of Locarno, one of many ill-fated attempts to avoid another war. The medieval castle houses the **Museo Civico e Archeologico,** which exhibits Roman artifacts. (☎756 31 61. Open Apr.-Oct. Tu-Su 10am-5pm. 7SFr, students 5SFr; children 1SFr.)

⚲ OUTDOOR ACTIVITIES

ON THE LAKE. The deep blue water of Lago Maggiore is a delight to the eyes. A **ferry** ride to points on both the Swiss and Italian shores offers more intimate contact with the lake (see p. 439). The tropical **Isole di Brissago,** at the lowest point in Switzerland (193m), was cultivated in 1885 by a utopian-minded baroness hoping to create an earthly paradise. Exotic plants from four continents intermingle with delicate stands of bamboo, which conceal splendidly colored exotic birds. An early 20th-century villa occupies one end of the island. (☎791 43 61 or 00 91; fax 07 63; www.isolebrissago.ch. Open Mar.-Oct. daily 9am-5pm. 7SFr.) **Marco Brusa,** along the water towards Delta Camping, rents **boats.** (☎(079) 214 62 57. Pedal boats 15-20SFr per hr., 8-12SFr per 30min.; motor boats 45SFr, 25SFr). **Bagno Spiaggia Lido e Piscine,** near Camping Delta, is an ideal spot for a dip in a pool or the lake. (☎751 44 08; fax 752 16 38. Open 9am-7:30pm. 6SFr, students 4SFr; after 5pm 3SFr/2SFr.) At **Bagno Pubblico La Lanca,** 2min. farther along the lake, it is possible to swim in the lake with swans and ducks for a few francs less. (☎752 12 95. Open 10am-7:30pm; 3SFr, children 6-15 1.50SFr.) Bathe for free at the **Fiume Maggia,** the rock-strewn artery that feeds into the lake.

VAL VERZASCA HIKE. To escape the city, head out on Post Bus #630 to **Sonogno** (1¼hr.; 7:37am-6:15pm;16.60SFr, 33.20SFr round-trip) and hike amid the extraordinary peaks at the end of **Val Verzasca** (valley). From the bus stop, take the first left and follow the yellow signs to **Lavertezzo.** The mostly flat trail is marked by yellow signs with directions and town names, and white-red-white blazes. It passes through cool, shady glens and rocky riverbeds as it follows the Verzasca river through the valley. Close to **Lavertezzo,** the river eases its rapid pace, making swimming possible, but pick a swimming hole carefully, as the water can be quite cold and the undercurrents strong. Climb the **Ponte dei Salti,** a 17th-century, double-arched bridge, and gaze into the clear green ponds. From Sonogno to Lavertezzo is a 6hr. walk, while Lavertezzo to Tenero requires another 5hr., but the Post Bus stops along the trail in the valley.

ADVENTURE SPORTS. The Verzasca Dam has allowed scores of visitors to break speeds of 100kpr., courtesy of its famous **bungee jump,** the highest in the world. The 220m jump, conquered with such panache by James Bond in *Goldeneye*, costs 255SFr the first time (with training, drink, and diploma) and 125SFr for subsequent leaps on the same day (195SFr for other days). Night jumps are possible. **Trekking Team** (☎0848 808 007; www.trekking.ch.), in addition to the Verzasca Dam jump, offers a 70m jump (125SFr first time, 75SFr for a second jump on the same day, then 90SFr), **canyoning** (100-210SFr), **snorkeling** (100SFr), and **cave exploration** (98SFr, children 78SFr, students 48SFr) in **Centovalli.** The **Visitors Center** (☎/fax 751 84 08; www.visitorscenter.ch) on Vaile Bali, across the street and 25m uphill from the ferry dock, books the above activities with Trekking Team, as well as **skydiving** (385SFr for a jump from 3500m with a 30-second free-fall), **paragliding** (165SFr), **windsurfing lessons** (60SFr per hr.), **waterskiing and wake boarding** (45SFr per 10min.), **rock climbing** (250SFr per day), **rafting** (65-105SFr per half-day, 150SFr for full day), and **sailing lessons** (190SFr, 2-4 people). **Bike rentals** 18SFr per half-day and 25SFr per day. (Prices get cheaper with successive days.)

🎵 🎭 ENTERTAINMENT AND NIGHTLIFE

The lakeside ⦿**Simba Bar,** toward Camping Delta, appeals to Locarno's wealthier 20-something crowd, despite its Disney name, with its mesmerizing neon aquarium, sparkly hanging mirrors, and rainbow-hued mosaic bar. (☎752 33 88; www.bar-simb.ticino.ch. Beers for 4.50SFr; drinks 9-14.50SFr. 18+. DJ every night after 8pm. Open Apr.-Sept. daily 5pm-midnight. Oct.-Mar. closed Su-M.) Along Via B. Luini four blocks from the lakeside, **Barsport,** caters to a slightly older local crowd with pool, foosball, and a mix of techno and jazzy world music. (☎751 29 31. Open Su-Th 8pm-1am; F-Sa 10pm-2am. Beers from 3.70SFr; a dip from the Sangria bowl 4SFr.) The **Katjaboat,** a yellow vessel that departs from the Hotel Rosa, down the Via Verbano from the ferry dock, is Locarno's Loveboat. For regular bar prices (mineral water 5SFr, beer 6SFr, gin 11SFr), the young-at-heart can enjoy a 40min. mini-tour of the lake with a sound track of sappy love songs. (☎079 686 39 90. Boat runs 10am-1am, though its schedule tends is as free-spirited as its atmosphere.)

For 11 mid-summer days (Aug. 2-12 2003), everything in Locarno halts for the **International Film Festival,** one of the most important movie premiere events in the world. Unlike Cannes, no invitations are required. Over 150,000 big-screen enthusiasts descend upon the town, so book a room six months to a year ahead. The centerpiece of the festival is a giant 26m by 14m outdoor screen, the largest outdoor screen in Europe, set up in P. Grande for big-name premieres by the likes of Jean-Luc Godard, Woody Allen, Spike Lee, and Bernardo Bertolucci. Smaller screens throughout the city highlight young filmmakers and groundbreaking experimentation. (Unlimited access 270SFr. For daily ticket prices and more info, write to: International Film Festival, Via Luini 3a, CH-6601 Locarno. ☎756 21 21; fax 21 49; info@pardo.ch; www.pardo.ch.)

In the second half of July, Locarno teams up with Ascona to host **Ticino Musica,** a festival of classical music focusing on young musicians and students. It features concerts, operas, and master classes at several venues. Tickets (30SFr) are available at the tourist office and at the door of any event. Free events occur as well. (☎980 09 70; fax 09 71; ticinomusica@bluewin.ch; www.ticinomusica.com.)

AURIGENO
☎ 091

Nestled in Valle Maggia ("magic valley"), Aurigeno offers its own charms with stone-shingled buildings and grapevines galore. An excellent side-trip from Locarno, this out-of-the-way village is a great place to enjoy traditional Swiss-Italian culture and a perfect spot to begin numerous hikes.

▐ TRANSPORTATION AND PRACTICAL INFORMATION

Take **bus** #10 from Locarno (30min., every hr. 7:02am-8:10pm, and 11:35pm, 7.80SFr). The **tourist office** for the valley is in Maggia next to the Co-op. (☎ 753 18 85; fax 22 12. Open M-F 9am-noon and 2-5pm; June-Sept. Sa 9am-noon.) For **taxis,** call ☎ 079 666 12 32, 7am-7pm; **police** ☎ 117; **ambulance** 144; **helicopter rescue** ☎ 1414. The post office, on the main road between the towns, serves Aurigeno and Moghegno. (Open M-F 8-10am and 2:30-5pm, Sa 8-10am.) **Postal code:** CH-6677.

▐ ▌ ACCOMMODATIONS AND FOOD

Accommodations in Aurigeno are scarce, but up the road Maggia offers more hotels. ▨**Baracca Backpacker ❷** (☎ 079 207 15 54) is an ideal starting point in Aurigeno. From the train station in Locarno, take bus #10 (dir: Valle Maggia) to "Ronchini" (25min., every hr. 7:02am-8:10pm and 11:35pm, 7.20SFr). Cross the street and turn right from the bus stop; follow hostel signs through the forest (15min.) and into the town. The hostel is beside the church. Youthful couple Monika and Reto create a homey environment with 10 beds, fresh herbs for cooking and a wood shop for tinkering. The office sells basic groceries (spaghetti 2SFr, tomato sauce 4SFr, wine 9.50SFr, milk 2SFr). Kitchen access included. Look in the games room at the best map in the area and for multiple **hiking, biking,** and **swimming** suggestions. **Bike rental** 10SFr per day. Sleep sack 2SFr per day. (Reception 9-11am and 5-8pm. Open Apr.-Oct. Dorms 25SFr.) At the junction of the main road and the bridge, the Pedroni couple offers the opportunity to **Sleep in the Straw ❷.** (☎ 753 24 62. Open May-Oct. 20SFr including breakfast.)

There are no grocery stores in Aurigeno so stock up in Locarno or head to the **Co-op** in Maggia. (Open M-F 8:30-noon and 2-6:30pm; Sa 8am-12:15pm and 2-5pm; no lunch break from July until mid-August.) **Trattoria Giovanetti ❶,** along the main road (2min.) is the closest thing to a restaurant in town, with cold plates of meats and cheeses (6-15SFr) and minestrone soup (6.50SFr). For warm meals, order ahead. (☎ 753 11 33. Open M-W and F-Sa 8:30am-11pm, Su 9am-11pm.) On the east side of the main bridge, the simple **Osteria del Ponte ❷** serves pastas and lasagna (10-13SFr) and beer (3.20SFr) by the stone hearth inside or on the balcony terrace overlooking the river. (☎ 753 31 95. Open 8:30am-midnight. Closed Tu.) In Maggia, **Restaurant Poncini ❸** (☎ 791 13 96) offers fresh fish (Tu, F, and Sa; 22-38SFr) and pastas (13-22SFr). Enjoy a grilled salmon (28SFr) or just stop in for the tiramisu (8SFr). **Internet** access (4SFr per hr.) also available. (Open M-Tu and Th-F 6am-11pm, Sa-Su 8am-11pm.)

◉ ▌ SIGHTS AND OUTDOOR ACTIVITIES

Just north of the bridge on the east side of the river lies one of Maggia Valley's oldest churches. View the frescos and votive paintings of Giovanni A. Vanoni in the **Sanctuario Madonna delle Grazie.** (Open May-Oct. 15, Tu-Sa 2-4pm.) Vanoni's work is common throughout the valley and can be seen on buildings in Aurigeno as well as in grottoes along several forest paths. In late June and July the valley becomes alive with the sounds of blues during the **Vallemaggia Blues Nights.**

SWIMMING. Aurigeno has its own picturesque waterfall. From Baracca's head left towards town and take the left fork in the main road. Pass a large villa surrounded by a stone wall and go along a small path through the woods (5min.). Alternately, turn right from the hostel and follow brown signs to *Ponte Romana*. This old Roman bridge is a wonder in itself, while the lagoon behind it provides a private swimming hole (20min.).

HIKING. It is easy to get lost—be prepared for long excursions. Maps are available at Baracca (24SFr) or the tourist office in Maggia (21SFr).

Passon della Garina (4-6hr.) Made famous by author Max Frisch, the hike over the Passo della Garina (1076m) into Loco in the neighboring Valle Onsernone offers amazing views for experienced hikers. Head south along the main road (right from the hostel) and follow brown signs toward Chiazza. From this small commune of houses and grape vines, the steep and narrow path follows traditional red-and-white signs to the pass (2hr.). At the pass, hikers have the opportunity to continue upwards along well-marked trails to the summit of Salmone (1559m) and an overview of Lago Maggiore (1hr.). Beyond the pass, the trail continues along steep, narrow paths to Loco (2hr.). To return, take a post bus from Loco to Cavigliano, Bivio Onsernone (4.60SFr), then the train to Ponte Brolla (2.60SFr). From Ponte Brolla bus #10 from Locarno takes travelers back to Aurigeno (5.20SFr). The last bus from Loco runs at 5:05pm. (This hike can also be done in reverse. Morning buses leave Cavigliano for Loco at 7:30 and 10:30am.)

Giro Valle del Salto (1hr. round-trip). An easier hike begins from Maggia's main square (marked with red-and-white painted signs). Climb up the long flight of stairs to the Chapelle della Pioda (476m), which offers vast panoramas of the valley towns. Proceed into Valle del Salto (746m), then descend toward Maggia on the other side of the mountain. Stop in Braià along the way and view a chapel rich with frescos by the painter Giovanni A. Vanoni.

Foroglio-S. Carlo (1½hr.) Above the Maggia Valley, Val Bavona provides some of the most stunning natural beauty in the area. This valley, inhabited only in the summer, produces a large amount of electricity but doesn't have any of its own. Take the bus to Foroglio, where a path along the river leads further to S. Carlo, the northernmost town in the valley. From here visitors can take the cable car to Robiei for more hiking.

BIKING. The 11km village tour through Maggia, Locano, Moghegno, and Aurigeno follows footpaths and side streets throughout the Maggia Valley. Rolling hills make the trip interesting for both athletes and families. Those looking for a more challenging route head toward Prato Sornica (north of Aurigeno). This path starts at the ice rink in **Prato Sornica** and travels through neighboring villages. The moderate route is accented with a 260m technical climb from **Broglio** to **Monti di Rima,** providing a breath-taking panorama (14km).

ASCONA ☎091

In his memoirs of Ascona (pop. 5000), *The First Step into Wonderland*, Jacob Flach effuses, "Here lies a piece of the Mediterranean Sea embedded in rough mountains, a sun-bathed, blooming cape of the Côte d'Azure, a mile of the Riviera beach sprinkled with azaleas and carnations, and a good dose of the blue sky!" In addition to enjoying Ascona's tropical sunshine and sparkling water, history buffs can trace the steps of the leftist thinkers and Bohemian artists who tried, around the turn of the century, to establish a utopian community on the mountain above—humbly dubbed **Monte Verità** (see p. 449).

ITALIAN SWITZERLAND

☎ ⓘ TRANSPORTATION AND PRACTICAL INFORMATION

Travel by **bus** #31 from Locarno (15min., every 15min. 6:23am-midnight, 2.60SFr) or by **ferry** (15-45min., 9 per day 9:10am-5:15pm, day pass 12SFr). The bus stops at "Ascona Posta" on Via Papio. Behind the bus stop the main road of the old city, Via Borgo, stretches to the lake. P. Guiseppe Motta, where the ferry docks, is lined with hotels and restaurants along the waterside. For **currency exchange** and **ATM,** try any of the many banks along Via Papio. (All open M-F 9am-12:30pm and 1:30-4:30pm.) The **tourist office,** in the Casa Serodine behind the Chiesa SS Pietro e Paolo, provides a guide of the area sights and services in four languages and also **exchanges currency** at standard rates. (☎791 00 91; fax 785 19 41; buongiorno@maggiore.ch; www.maggiore.ch. Open Apr.-Oct. M-F 9am-6pm, Sa 10am-5pm; Nov.-Mar. M-F 9am-noon and 1-5pm.) A small train of cars leads **guided tours** of the town from the ferry docks. (☎079 240 18 00 or 859 29 57. 30min.; daily starting at 11am; 7SFr, children 3SFr.) Services include: **taxis,** ☎791 46 46 or 41 41; **parking** at the **Autosilo** at the corner of Via Papio and Via Buonamno (1SFr for 30min., 18SFr per 24hr.) or down Via Papio in **parking garage** (☎751 17 07; 1SFr per hr., 18SFr per 24hr.); and **bike rental** at **Bike Cicli Chiandussi,** Via Circonvallazione 14, down Via Papio and right again before the Migros. (☎780 55 42 or 079 337 11 62. 20-25SFr per day; 15-18SFr per half-day. Open M and W-F 9am-noon and 2:30-6:30pm, Sa 9am-noon and 2-5pm. MC/V.) A kiosk across from the **post office,** 25m down from the bus stop, offers a list of hotels and free phone for reservations. (Open M-F 7:30am-noon and 1:45-6pm, Sa 8:30-noon.) **Postal code:** CH-6612.

🏠 ⌖ ACCOMMODATIONS AND FOOD

Few of the city's beds fall into a budget range; luckily, Ascona makes a good day-trip from Locarno. Those who stay try rooms above the **Ristorante Verbano ❸,** Via Borgo, near the modern art museum. (☎791 12 74. Breakfast included. Closed Su. 45SFr per person.) The tourist office has a list of *affitacamere* (private rooms).

Otello ❸, Via Papio 8, just downhill from the bus stop, offers a taste of Ticino with frescoed stone pillars and Mediterranean scenes along the walls. Choose from Italian pastas (13-22 SFr), or savor selected cheeses (6-9SFr) and a chocolate mousse (7SFr). Wines from 2.80SFr. (☎791 54 10. Open 11:30am-11pm. MC/V.) **Caffé Piazzetta Ascona ❸,** Via Borgo 30, wallows under a white canopy in the heart of the old town. Gnocchi specialities and pizzas run 13-19.80SFr, and pastas are available in two sizes for 9.50-18.50SFr. (☎791 15 44. Open 11am-11pm.) **Ristorante La Torre ❷,** P. Motta 61, offers prime views of the lake, but is famous for its whimsically decorated bowls of homemade gelato (10.50-10.80SFr). Pizza starts at 12.80SFr; daily *Menüs* 19.50SFr. (☎791 54 55; fax 792 27 97. Open daily 10am-12:30am; closed Nov.-Dec. 20.) For groceries, look for the **Co-op**'s orange sign shining down Via Papio from the bus stop. The **Migros** is 200m down the same street. (Both open M-F 8:15am-12:30pm and 2-6:30pm, Sa 8am-5pm; Migros open from 8am.) A **market** spills onto the P.G. Motta every Tuesday (May-Oct. 9am-4pm).

👁 SIGHTS

The Post Bus stop at the corner of Via Borgo and Via Papio, at the edge of the old city, leaves you within walking distance of all the sights and the waterfront. The *Città Vecchia* stretches from the lake to Via Papio with banner-hung streets and wrought-iron balconies. The sole remaining tower of the 13th-century **Castello del Ghiriglion,** 26 P.G. Motto, is at the eastern end of the boardwalk. The **Chiesa SS Pietro e Paolo,** left from where Via Borgo intersects the lake, marks Ascona from

PARADISE LOST Around the turn of the twentieth century, a distinctly left-of-center collection of anarchists, agrarians, artists, philosophers, nudists, writers, and vegetarians attempted to establish Utopia on the banks of the Lago Maggiore. Even political refugees, including Russian anarchist Michail Bakunin, sought refuge in Ascona in the late 1800s. In 1889, the Locarnese philosopher Alfredo Pioda proposed the establishment of a lay convent for international intellectuals to be named "Fraternitas" on La Monescia, the hill behind Ascona. Though his vision never came to fruition, thinkers seeking connections between humankind, nature, the world, and the universe came to La Monescia anyway. The hill was renamed "Monte Verità" ("mount of truth") by Henri Oeden-Koven and Ida Hoffman, a pair of free spirits who founded the "Cooperative Vegetarian Colony" there in 1900. Meanwhile, Ascona's reputation as a cultural center for the elite continued to grow, drawing the likes of D.H. Lawrence, James Joyce, Hermann Hesse, and Karl Jung (and, in the 20s and 30s, members of the German avant-garde and Dadaists like Arp and Segal).

the lake with its slender clock tower. The frescoes inside date from the 15th century; canvas paintings such as the "Crowning of the Virgin" (1617) above the altar date from the 17th century. Banana trees and stone coats-of-arms frame the **Collegio Pontifico Papio**'s 15th-century courtyard. From the tourist office turn right toward Piazzetta S. Pietro, right again onto Contrada Maggiore, left at the Centro Culturale, and right onto Via Cappelle. Presiding over the still-operating Superior private school (est. 1399), the adjacent church of **Santa Maria della Misericordia** hides 15th-century frescoes by Seregnesi and Antonio da Tradate in a dim interior.

Private galleries that line the winding streets promote such artists as Marc Chagall and Georges Braque. **The Museo Comunale d'Arte Moderna,** Via Borgo 34, has an extensive permanent collection of works by Klee, Utrillo, Amiet, and Jawlensky, as well as moving and evocative temperas by Russian Marianne Werefkin that depict haunting mountain scenes and religious pilgrimages of rural Ticino. The museum frequently hosts temporary exhibitions of well-known artists from around the world. (☎780 51 00; fax 51 02; museo@cultura-ascona.ch; www.cultura-ascona.ch. Open Mar.-Dec. Tu-Sa 10am-noon and 3-6pm, Su 4-6pm. 7SFr, students and seniors 5SFr.)

The **Museo Casa Anatta** immortalizes the dashed dreams of Ascona's utopian thinkers (without English labeling). Walk uphill along the winding Strada della Colina from the bus stop or follow the uneven stone stairs of Scalinata della Ruga off Via Borgo for a more direct, although steep, route. This fascinating museum contains photos of a 1930s nudist colony in Brissago, anarchist Ernsy Frick's collection of mystical minerals, and the costumes and crowns worn by members of the "individualistic cooperative" during their ritualistic dances in the woods. One room is dedicated to Otto Gross, a schizophrenic man who started the short-lived University for the Emancipation of Man here at the height of the movement. Don't miss the miniature model of one utopian architect's proposed Temple to the Land of Fidus, in which men would pass from the Room of Ambition to the Room of Love and worship a statue of the Woman of the Earth. (☎791 01 81; fax 780 51 35; reception@csf-mv.ti-edu.ch; www.csf-mv.ethz.ch; www.centro-monte-verita.ch. Open Apr.-June and Sept.-Oct. Tu-Su 2:30-6pm; July-Aug. Tu-Su 3-7pm. 6SFr, students and seniors 4SFr.)

🎵 🎭 ENTERTAINMENT AND NIGHTLIFE

From June 27-July 6, 2003, Ascona will host the annual **New Orleans Jazz Ascona.** Musicians play on the waterfront among sculptures and in local cafes. (www.jazzascona.ch. Tickets 10SFr per night; 25SFr for 3 days; 75SFr for 10; children under

ITALIAN SWITZERLAND

16 free.) The **International Horse Jumping Competition** (late July) and the **Settimane Musicali**, an international festival featuring classical music (late Aug. to mid-Oct.), are other opportunities for revelry. **Bar Lago** hosts live pianists from countries such as Italy and Brazil, and also offers Latino disco music. (☎791 10 65. Drinks from 8SFr. Open 10pm-4am.) On rainy days, catch a flick at the **Cinema Otello,** next to the restaurant of the same name on Via Papio. (☎791 03 23. Afternoon movies in English with German or Italian subtitles 14SFr; students 12SFr.)

LUGANO ☎091

Lugano, Switzerland's third-largest banking center, rests on Lago di Lugano in a valley between San Salvatore and Monte Brè peaks. Shady streets are packed with cobblestone piazzas, and visitors enjoy its seamless blend of religious beauty, artistic flair, and natural spectacle. There are two extraordinary youth hostels, both built from luxury villas, with swimming pools and magnificent gardens.

◪ TRANSPORTATION

Trains: P. della Stazione. Most destinations connect through **Bellinzona** (30min., every 30min. 5:30am-midnight, 11.40SFr). To: **Basel** (4-5hr., every 30min. 5:36am-8:12pm, 79SFr); **Bern** (1-2 per hr.) via **Olten** (5hr., 5:36am-7:47pm, 76SFr), **via Lucerne** (4¾hr., 5:36am-6:57pm, 56SFr), **via Zurich** (4hr., 5:57am-8:38pm, 87SFr); **Geneva** (1-2 per hr.) **via Olten** (7hr., 5:36am-5:36pm, 104SFr), **via Lucerne** (7hr., 5:36am-6:57pm, 104SFr), **via Zurich** (6¼hr., 5:57am-5:30pm, 118SFr); **Locarno** (1hr., every 30min. 5:36am-midnight, 16.60SFr); **Zurich** (3hr., 1-2 per hr. 5:57am-8:38pm, 60SFr); **Zurich Airport** (3¾hr.; 63SFr). Trains connect south through **Chiasso** to **Milan** (45min., every hr. 7:14am-9:48pm, 21SFr; under 26 16SFr).

Public Transportation: Buses run from the neighboring towns to the center of Lugano and also traverse the city. Schedules and ticket machines at each stop. 1.10-1.90SFr per ride, 24hr. "Carta Giorno" (day pass) 5SFr. SwissPass valid.

Taxis: ☎922 88 33 or 922 02 22.

Car Rental: Avis, 8 Via C. Maraini (☎913 41 51). **Hertz,** 13 Via San Gottardo (☎923 46 75). **Europcar,** 24 Via M. Boglia, Garage Cassarate (☎971 01 01).

Parking: Autosilo Comunale Balestra, off Via Pioda, on Via S. Balestra. 7am-noon and 2-7pm. 1SFr per hr., 12SFr for 5hr.; overnight parking (7pm-7am) 6SFr. Open 24hr.

Bike Rental: At the baggage check in the station (☎923 66 91). 30SFr per day; 23SFr per half-day. 6SFr to return at another station. Open 9am-6pm.

✦ ⓘ ORIENTATION AND PRACTICAL INFORMATION

The 15min. downhill walk from the train station to the arcaded Piazza della Riforma, the town's center, winds through Lugano's large pedestrian zone. For those who would rather avoid the walk, a funicular runs between the train station and the waterfront **Piazza Cioccaro** (1.10SFr, 5:20am-11:50pm).

Tourist Office: (☎913 32 32; fax 922 76 53; info@lugano-tourism.ch; www.lugano-tourism.ch) in the Palazzo Civico, Riva Albertolli, at the corner of p. Rezzonico. From the station, cross the "Centro" footbridge; go down Via Cattedrale through p. Cioccaro as it turns into Via Pessina. Turn left on Via dei Pesci and right through p. Riforma toward the Polizei Communale building. The office is across from the ferry. Free city maps and a **guided city walk** in English May-Oct. M 9:30am, from Chiesa degli Angioli (2¼hr.). Open Apr.-May and Sept.-Oct. M-F 9am-7:30pm, Sa 9am-5:30pm, Su 10am-4pm; July-Aug. M-F 9am-7:30pm, Sa 9am-10pm, Su 10am-4pm; Nov.-Mar. M-F 9am-12:30pm and 1:30-5pm.

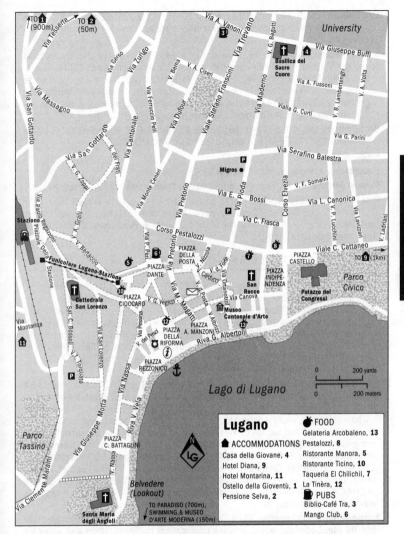

Lugano

♠ ACCOMMODATIONS
Casa della Giovane, **4**
Hotel Diana, **9**
Hotel Montarina, **11**
Ostello della Gioventù, **1**
Pensione Selva, **2**

♦ FOOD
Gelateria Arcobaleno, **13**
Pestalozzi, **8**
Ristorante Manora, **5**
Ristorante Ticino, **10**
Taqueria El Chilichil, **7**
La Tinèra, **12**

▪ PUBS
Biblio-Café Tra, **3**
Mango Club, **6**

Hotel Reservations: Kiosks outside the train station and tourist office list hotels and provide free reservations phones. There's also a counter in the train station. (Open Tu, W, and Su 2-7pm; Th-Sa 11am-7pm; extended hours on request.) The tourist office will make reservations for 4SFr.

Consulates: UK, 22 Via Sarengo (☎950 06 06; fax 06 09). Open M-F 10am-noon.

Currency Exchange: Western Union in the station, ☎923 93 26. Open M-Sa 7:10am-7:45pm, Su 8:30am-noon and 1:30-6:30pm. Banks open M-F 8:30am-4:30pm.

Luggage Storage: Lockers at station. 4-7SFr. Luggage watch 7SFr per piece. Open 24hr.

Lost Property: Check the *Fundbureau* (☎800 80 65) of the Polizei Communale, on the p. Riforma, on the other side of the tourist office building. Open M-F 7:30am-noon and 1:30-5pm.

Internet Access: Biblio-Café Tra, 3 Via A. Vanoni (☎923 23 05). From p. Dante, head down the Via Pretorio (15min.) and turn left onto Via A. Vanoni. Open M-Th 9am-midnight, F 9am-1am, Sa 5pm-1am. 2SFr per 15min. **Manor** in p. Dante has 4 terminals on the 3rd floor. Open M-W and F-Sa 8:15am-6:30pm, Th 8:15am-9pm. 1SFr per 6min. **Burger King,** right from the tourist office, provides 30min. **free** with the purchase of a meal (10.90-12.60SFr). Open Su-Th 9am-midnight, F-Sa 9am-1am.

Bookstore: Melisa, 4 Via Vegezzi (☎923 83 43; fax 73 04). English-language books downstairs. Open M-F 9am-6:30pm, Sa 9am-5pm. AmEx/DC/MC/V.

Police: ☎117.

Emergencies: Ambulance, ☎144. **Fire,** ☎118.

Medical Services: ☎111. **First Aid,** ☎805 61 11. **Pharmacies** are throughout the city.

Post Office: Via della Posta, 2 blocks up from the lake near Via al Forte. Open M-F 7:30am-6:15pm, Sa 8am-12pm. Traveler's checks cashed. Telephones, telegraphs, and faxes at the Via Magatti entrance to the PTT building. **Postal code:** CH-6900; **Postlagerndebriefe** use CH-6901.

ACCOMMODATIONS AND CAMPING

Hotel Montarina, Via Montarina 1 (☎966 72 72; fax 00 17; info@montarina.ch; www.montarina.ch). Walk 200m to the right from the station, cross the tracks, and go 50m uphill. Converted from a luxury villa, this palm-tree-enveloped, independent hostel attracts young families and students with its **swimming pool,** well-groomed grounds, ping-pong table, reading room, tiny kitchen, and terrace. Laundry 4SFr, soap 1.50SFr. Buffet breakfast 12SFr. Sheets 4SFr. Parking available. Reception 8am-10pm. Open Mar.-Oct. In July and Aug. call 2 weeks in advance for reservations. Dorms 25SFr; singles 70-80SFr; doubles 100SFr, with bath 120SFr. ❷

Ostello della Gioventù (HI), Lugano-Savosa, Via Cantonale 13 (☎966 27 28; fax 968 23 63; lugano@youthhostel.ch; www.luganoyouthhostel.ch). Note: there are 2 streets called Via Cantonale, one in downtown Lugano and one in Savosa, by the hostel. Take bus #5 (walk 350m left from the station, past the parking lot, and cross the street to the bus stop) to "Crocifisso," and then backtrack and turn left up Via Cantonale. A former luxury villa, this sprawling hostel has gardens and a **pool** with waterslide. Kitchen access 1SFr (after 7pm only). **Internet** 5SFr for 20min. Breakfast 8SFr. Towels 1.50SFr. Parking available. Laundry 5SFr. Reception 7am-12:30pm and 3-10pm. Curfew 10pm; keys available on request for 20SFr deposit. Reserve ahead. Open mid-Mar. to Oct. Dorms 23SFr; singles 35SFr, with kitchenette 45SFr; doubles 56SFr/70SFr; family rooms for 2-6 people 90-120SFr. Apartments for families (1 week min. stay) 100-170SFr per day. ❷

Pensione Selva, Via Tesserete 36 (☎923 60 17; fax 60 09; villaselva@bluewin.ch). Take bus #9 (dir: Ospedale; leaves opposite train station) to "Sassa," then walk along Via Gottardo for 250m and turn right on Via Tesserete. A path overhung with grapes seals this haven from the city noise and leads to the cozy place with an outdoor **pool** and terrace. Parking available. Breakfast included. Reception 8am-midnight. Closed Nov. Singles 49-58SFr, with shower 69-90SFr; doubles 98-110SFr/118-138SFr. ❸

Casa della Giovane, Corso Elvezia 34 (☎911 66 46; fax 66 40), across the street from Basilica Sacro Cuore. Take bus #9 (dir.: Ospedale; leaves opposite train station) to "Corso Elvezia." This modern peach and blue building provides rooms (most with balconies) for **women only.** The rooftop terrace allows for serious tanning. Breakfast 5SFr. Lunch or dinner 12SFr. Laundry 3SFr (bring soap). Reception 24hr. No curfew, but tell the receptionist when you'll be back. Reserve ahead. 4-bed dorms 20SFr. ❷

Hotel Diana, Via Pico 8 (☎971 41 41; fax 970 17 32; hoteldiana@luganet.ch), offers luxury rooms in a peaceful setting at the base of Mount Bré. Take the funicular to the lake and then bus #1 to "M. Bré" or directly from the station take bus #2 to "Lanchetta." Turn right on Viale Castognola and left on Via Pico after Vialla Catagnola. Polished rooms have balconies with spectacular views of the lake, and come with TVs and **Internet** access. Parking 10SFr. Breakfast included. Reception 8am-10pm. Singles 110-130SFr; doubles 80-190SFr. AmEx/DC/MC/V. ❹

Camping: There are several campsites, 2 of which are in **Agno.** Check with the tourist office for a complete list. For **La Palma ❶** (☎605 25 61; fax 604 54 38) or **Eurocampo ❸** (☎605 21 14; fax 31 87), both lakeside, take the Ferrovia-Lugano-Ponte-Tresa (FLP) train to Agno (4.60SFr). From the station, turn left, then left again onto Via Molinazzo. La Palma open mid-Apr. to mid-Oct. 8.50SFr. Eurocampo open Apr.-Oct. 7.20SFr per person; tents 6-10SFr. All sites have showers.

🍴 FOOD

Outdoor cafes serving similarly priced Italian fare pepper the many lakeside piazzas. **Via Pessina,** off p. della Riforma, livens up at midday with outdoor sandwich and fruit shops. The **Migros,** 15 Via Pretorio, two blocks left from the post office down Via Pretorio, has a food court on the ground floor with huge slices of pizza from 2.90SFr and sandwiches from 2.50SFr. (Open M-W and F 8am-6:30pm, Th 8am-9pm, Sa 7:30am-5pm.) A **public market** on p. della Riforma sells seafood, veggie sandwiches (4SFr) and produce (open Tu and F 7am-noon).

🦐 **La Tinèra,** Via dei Gorini 2 (☎923 52 19), behind Credit Suisse in p. della Riforma, is a romantic, low-lit, underground restaurant, specializing in Lombard cuisine. Daily menu 13-18.50SFr. Try the sausage with *risotto* (14SFr) or a vegetarian goulash (4SFr). Open M-Sa 8:30am-3pm and 5:30-11pm. AmEx/DC/MC/V. ❸

Gelateria Arcobaleno, Via Marconi 2 (☎922 62 18), beside the McDonald's on the waterfront, dishes out the most creative and unusual gelato desserts in town, as well as lowfat yogurt gelato. Menu includes gelato pizza (10SFr), Spiedini (fruit kebabs and yogurt, 2 for 22SFr), and the "Indonesia," a pineapple filled with yogurt gelato, fruit salsa, and whipped cream (11SFr). Scoop of ice cream 3.50SFr; 3 for 7.50SFr. Hot and cold sandwiches 5.50-8.50SFr. Open M-F 8:30am-1am, Sa-Su 9am-1am. ❷

Taqueria El Chilicuil, Corsa Pestalozzi 12 (☎922 82 26), down the Corsa Pestalozzi from the p. Indipendenza. This lively snack bar serves tacos, burritos, and quesadillas (4.50-8SFr), Mexican beer (6SFr), and margaritas (7SFr, pitcher 38SFr). Happy Hour M-F 5-7pm (drinks 1-2SFr less). Open May-Nov. M-Th 11:30am-11pm, F 11:30am-midnight, Sa-Su 7pm-midnight; Dec.-Apr. M-Th closes at 10pm, Sa-Su opens at 5pm. ❶

Ristorante Manora, Manor Department Store in p. Dante, 3rd floor; entrance off Salita Mario e Antonio Chiattone also. Budget eaters can't beat the gourmet self-serve spot. Salad bar (4.50-10.20SFr), pasta (7.90-10.90SFr per plate), and beer (1.20-4.50SFr). Hot daily specials 10-14.90SFr. Open M-Sa 7:30am-10pm, Su 10am-10pm. ❷

Pestalozzi, p. Indipendenza 9 (☎921 46 46), in the hotel. This non-alcoholic restaurant offers well-balanced, veggie-friendly menus (13-16SFr) and the option of a smoke-free dining room. Meat lasagna and mixed salad 12.50SFr. Open 11am-9:30pm, hot food served 11am-2:30pm and 6-9:30pm. MC/V. ❷

Ristorante Ticino, p. Cioccaro 1 (☎922 77 72; fax 923 62 78). This air-conditioned spot in the center of town offers an intimate setting with cozy booths for a special occasion. Choose from a variety of fish and meat entrees (22-38SFr) including chef recommendations such as Norwegian salmon (28SFr). Open M-F 12-2pm and 7-9:30pm; Sa-Su 7-9:30pm. AmEx/DC/MC/V. ❹

⊙ SIGHTS

The frescoes of the 16th-century **Cattedrale San Lorenzo,** just south of the train station, gleam with colors that are still vivid. Bernardio Luini's gargantuan fresco, **Crucifixion,** painted in 1529, rests in the **Chiesa Santa Maria degli Angioli,** right from the tourist office. The small 14th-century **Chiesa San Rocco,** two blocks to the left of the p. della Riforma, in the p. Maghetti, houses an ornate Madonna altarpiece and gruesome Discopli frescoes of saints being flayed alive and pierced with arrows. The national monument **Basilica Sacro Cuore,** on Corso Elevezia across from the Casa della Giovane, is more sparing. See hikers next to disciples in the frescoes ringing the altar. *(Open M-F 7:45am-5:30pm and Sa-Su 10am-6pm.)*

The **Museo Cantonale d'Arte's** permanent collection of 19th- and 20th-century art, including works by Swiss artists Vela, Ciseri, Franzoni, and Klee, is often replaced by temporary contemporary art exhibits. *(10 Via Canova, across from the Chiesa San Rocco. ☎ 910 47 80; fax 47 89; dic-mca@ti.ch; www.museo-cantonale-arte.ch. Open Tu 2-5pm, W-Su 10am-5pm. Special exhibits 10SFr, students 7SFr; permanent collection 7SFr/5SFr. MC/V.)*

An elegant lakeside villa houses the **Museo delle Culture Extraeuropee.** An abundance of wood-carved masks, statues, and shields from distant lands adorn the villa's marble staircases and ornate windows. *(Via Cortivo 24. On the footpath to Gandria in the Villa Heleneum. From the tourist office take bus #1 (dir. Castagnola) to "San Domenica." Make a left U-turn to the street below. The Villa is 700m on the right. ☎ 971 73 53. Open Apr.-Oct. W-Su 10am-5pm. 5SFr, students 3SFr.)*

⚠ OUTDOOR ACTIVITIES

PARKS AND GARDENS. The **Belvedere,** on riva Caccia, is an enormous sculpture garden with an emphasis on modernist metalwork. Chess enthusiasts gather for open-air tournaments. The garden stretches along the lakeside promenade. In the other direction, the serene **Parco Civico** is dotted with flower beds. Small beaches offer direct access to the water. (Open daily Mar.-Oct. 6:30am-11:30p, Nov.-Feb. 7am-9pm.)

BOATING. The dock for the **Societa Navigazione del Lago di Lugano** is across the street from the tourist office. (☎ 923 17 79; fax 971 27 93; info@lakelugano.ch; www.lakelugano.ch.) Tours of Lake Lugano pass tiny, unspoiled towns along the shore, including Gandria (11.60SFr, round-trip 19.20SFr), Morcote (16.60SFr, 27.40SFr), and Paradiso (3SFr, 5SFr). A "grand tour" of the lake in English (3½hr.) costs 32.60SFr, 19.60SFr with SwissPass; 62SFr/52SFr allows a week of unlimited lake travel. SwissPass is valid on all boats. Various points on the lake rent pedal boats (7-8SFr per 30min.). **Boat Saladin** (☎ 923 57 33), across from the Chiesa Santa Maria degli Angioli, provides motor boats. (40SFr per hr., 25SFr per 30min. No license required. Open Apr.-Oct. 9am-midnight.) **Bagno Pubblico,** on riva Caccia toward Paradiso, is good for a swim. (☎ 994 20 35. 4SFr, children 8-16 2SFr. Open May-June 14 and Sept. daily 9:30am-6:30pm, June 15-Aug. 9:30am-8pm.)

HIKING. The tourist office and Ostello della Gioventù have topographical maps and trail guides (15SFr) into the Ticinese mountains. The most rewarding hike is to **Monte Boglio.** The 5hr. round-trip can be extended over two days by staying at the Pairolhütte (ask at hostels or tourist office). Reach the peaks of **Monte Brè** (933m) and **Monte San Salvatore** (912m) by funicular. Monte Brè is down the river to the left of the tourist office. (☎ 971 31 71. 13SFr, round-trip 19SFr; ages 6-16 6.50SFr/9.50SFr.) The San Salvatore funicular is 20min. from the tourist office, down the lake to the right in Paradiso. (☎ 985 28 28; 14-17SFr, round-trip 20-

31.60SFr; ages 6-16 7-8.50SFr/10-15.80SFr.) At Monte San Salvatore, a simple 13th-century church balances on lakeside cliffs. A museum details the history of the Archfraternity of Good Death and Prayer. (Open W-Su 10am-noon and 1-3pm. Free with funicular ticket.) A poorly marked trail descends from the peak through chestnut forests to Morcote (3½hr.), where a ferry connects to Lugano (16.60SFr, Swisspass valid).

ADVENTURE SPORTS. The **ASBEST Adventure Company,** Via Basilea 28, based in the Hotel Continental, provides adventure sport opportunities. Most activities require group interest; lone travelers call ahead for availability. (☎966 11 14; fax 12 13; www.asbest.ch; info@asbest.ch.) In winter, **snowshoe** and **ski** (full-day 90SFr) or **tandem paraglide** over icy crags (170SFr). **Canyoning** (from 90SFr) and **river-diving** (90SFr with appropriate training) are less chilling in Ticino, away from glaciers. In summer, **rock-climb** (90SFr) or **mountain bike** (prices vary; bike not included).

🎵 📷 ENTERTAINMENT AND NIGHTLIFE

During the first two weekends in July, Lugano's **Festival Jazz** fills the p. della Riforma with free music. Past performers include Miles Davis and Bobby McFerrin. The looser **Blues to Bop Festival** (also free) celebrates R&B, blues, and gospel in late August by hosting international singers and local amateurs. The **Wine Harvest Festival,** in mid-October, drowns those fading summer memories. From late June to early August, **Cinema al Lago** shows international films on a large screen installed on the lake, nightly at 9:45pm; after July 15 9:30pm. (☎913 32 32; www.open-air-kino.ch. 15SFr, under 17 12SFr.)

The Latin American **Mango Club,** 8 p. Dante, mixes live salsa and techno. (☎922 94 38. Open W-Su 11pm-5am. 10SFr admission includes beer.) For a change of pace, head down the Via Pretorio from p. Dante and turn left on Via A. Vanoni for the **Biblio-Café Tra,** Via Vanoni 3. This laid-back cafe evokes a bit of leftist Spain with its shaded spot and battered wood tables on which subversives consume 3.60SFr beers. (☎923 23 05. **Internet** 2SFr per 15min. Open M-Th 9am-midnight, F 9am-1am, Sa 5pm-1am.)

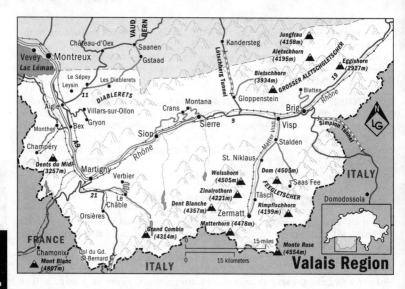

VALAIS (WALLIS)

The Valais occupies the deep, wide, glacial gorge traced by the Rhône river. The clefts of the valley divide the land linguistically: in Martigny and Sion, French is most popular; in Brig and Zermatt, Swiss-German dominates. Whatever the language, the towns share a common penchant for cheese, the secret to good wine, and an industry of shuttling people to the snow-covered peaks on skis or on foot. Though mountain resorts can be over-touristed, the region's spectacular peaks and the skiing, hiking, and climbing make fighting traffic worthwhile. Zermatt has the most to offer skiers and hikers, although some small towns have great appeal. Note: Eurail is not valid on the BVZ train line, which serves many regional towns.

ZERMATT AND THE MATTERHORN ☎ 027

A trick of the valley blocks out the great alpine summits that ring Zermatt, allowing the Matterhorn (4478m) to rise alone above the town. Instantly recognizable and stamped on everything from scarves to pencils, the peak stands as a misshapen monolith that blazes bright orange at dawn and occasionally is clear of clouds long enough for the crowd to snap a picture. The Bahnhofstraße is populated in equal measure by ruddy outdoors-lovers and their shopping-bag-laden counterparts. The town keeps the peace with *Nachtruhe* (quiet hours) after 10pm; raucous noise can result in a fine of 200-300SFr. A short hike or cable car ride best escapes the horde to alpine meadows and splintered icefalls. Hiking, climbing, and skiing—some of Switzerland's best—are top reasons to make the trek to Zermatt.

TRANSPORTATION

To preserve the alpine air, Zermatt has outlawed cars and buses; locals in toy-like electric buggies alternately dodge and target pedestrians. The town of **Täsch,** one stop before Zermatt, has **parking garages** for 7.50SFr per day; the large outdoor lot by the rail station costs 5-6.50SFr per day (and has a reservation board for hotels in Zermatt). Zermatt is accessible only by the **BVZ** (Brig-Visp-Zermatt; www.bvz.ch) rail line (SwissPass valid, **Eurail not valid**).

Trains: (☎921 41 11). The BVZ runs to Zermatt from: **Brig** (1½hr.; 6am-9pm; 34SFr, round-trip 67SFr, if coming from **Lausanne** 73SFr/140SFr or **Sion** 47.20SFr/94SFr) via **Visp; Stalden-Saas** (1hr. 29SFr, round-trip 58SFr; if coming from **Saas Fee** 1hr.; 41.40SFr/82.80SFr); and **Täsch** (10min.; every hr., Sa-Su every 20min; 7.80SFr, round-trip 15.60SFr). The station and tourist office have free phones to Zermatt's hotels and **hotel taxis,** waiting to round up guests after each train arrives.

ORIENTATION AND PRACTICAL INFORMATION

Most shops, services, and restaurants stretch along Bahnhofstr. from the train station to the Hotel Weisshorn and the Cafe du Pont. Halfway between these, Hoffmattstr. heads to the left. Beside the church, Kirchstr. slides down the hill.

Tourist Office: Bahnhofpl. (☎966 81 00; fax 81 01; zermatt@wallis.ch; www.zermatt.ch), in the station complex. Distributes the free booklet *Prato Borni* that provides extremely detailed practical info for getting around the city and the *Wanderkarte* (hiking map, 25.90SFr). Open mid-June to mid-Oct. M-F 8:30am-6pm, Sa 8:30am-6:30pm, Su 9:30am-noon and 4-6:30pm; mid-Oct. to mid-Dec. and May through mid-June M-F 8:30am-noon and 1:30-6pm, Sa 8:30am-noon; mid-Dec.-Apr. M-F 8:30am-noon and 1:30-6:30pm, Sa 8:30am-6:30pm and Su 9:30am-noon and 4-6:30pm.

Bike and Ski Rental: Julen Sport (☎967 43 40), on Hoffmattstr., rents skis and mountain bikes (38-50SFr per day, 28-38SFr per half-day). Open M-Sa 8:30am-noon and 2-6:30pm. AmEx/DC/MC/V. Its companion, **Roc Sport** (☎967 43 40), on Kirchstr., rents the same equipment, but it's best to head straight to Julen. Rental prices for skis and boots are set throughout Zermatt (skis and snowboards 28-50SFr per day, boots 15-19SFr per day; cheaper for longer periods). Try **Glacier Sport** on Bahnhofstr. (☎967 27 19; open daily 8am-noon and 2-6:30pm), **Slalom Sport,** across the river on Kirchstr. (☎966 23 66; open M-Sa 8am-noon and 2-6:30pm), or **Bayard Sports,** directly across from the station (☎966 49 60; open daily 8am-noon and 2-7pm).

Currency Exchange: Free at the train station (5:45am-8pm). **Banks** are generally open M-F 9am-noon and 2:30-6pm.

Luggage: Lockers downstairs in station for ski equipment (15SFr), at end of the tracks (6-8SFr), or storage at the ticket counter (5SFr per bag). Open daily 5:45am-8pm.

Work Opportunities: The North Wall Bar, ☎966 34 12. (See p. 461.)

English-Language Library: In the English Church on the hill behind the post office. Small collection of used novels loaned on the honor system. Open M-Tu and Th-F 4-8pm.

Laundry: Waschsalon Doli (☎967 51 00), behind Swiss Souvenirs and across from the train station. 19SFr per load. Open M-Sa 8am-noon and 2-6pm.

Weather Conditions: ☎162 or check the window of the *Bergführerbüro.* **Winter Avalanche Information,** ☎187.

Emergencies: Police, ☎117. **Fire,** ☎118. **Ambulance/24hr. Alpine Rescue,** ☎144.

VALAIS

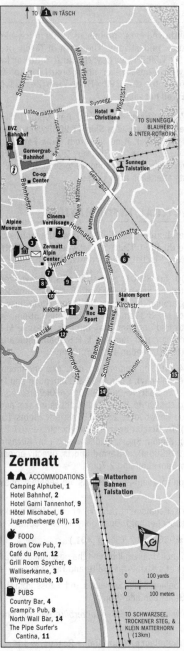

Zermatt

🏠🏕 ACCOMMODATIONS
Camping Alphubel, **1**
Hotel Bahnhof, **2**
Hotel Garni Tannenhof, **9**
Hôtel Mischabel, **5**
Jugendherberge (HI), **15**

🍴 FOOD
Brown Cow Pub, **7**
Café du Pont, **12**
Grill Room Spycher, **6**
Walliserkanne, **3**
Whymperstube, **10**

🍺 PUBS
Country Bar, **4**
Grampi's Pub, **8**
North Wall Bar, **14**
The Pipe Surfer's
  Cantina, **11**

Pharmacy: Pharmacie Internationale Zermatt (☎966 27 27), Bahnhofstr. to right of station. Open M-Sa 8:30am-noon and 2-6:30pm, Su 11am-noon and 5-6pm. Emergency service for 20-30SFr surcharge depending on time.

Internet Access: Ask at the tourist office for a list of public access points. Most cost 15-20SFr per hr. **The Pipe** (☎213 38 07) charges 12SFr per hr.

Post Office: Bahnhofstr., in Arcade Mont-Cervin, 5min. to the right of the station. **ATM.** Open M-F 8:30am-noon and 1:45-6pm, Sa 8:30-11am. **Postal Code:** CH-3920.

🏔 ACCOMMODATIONS AND CAMPING

Climbers, hikers, and snowboarders raise the demand for budget beds in Zermatt. Finding a dorm bed on the spot can be tough in July and August, at Christmas and New Year's, and mid-February through mid-March. Many hotels in winter and all chalets in summer only accept bookings for a week at a time. In desperation, some campers are tempted to sleep illegally in the wide-open spaces above town—this practice can incur fines upwards of 300SFr.

Hotel Bahnhof (☎967 24 06; fax 72 16; welcome@hotelbahnhof.com; www.hotelbahnhof.com), on Bahnhofstr. to the left of the station, is a climber's hangout. Renovated rooms provide hotel housing at hostel rates. Ask for a view of the Matterhorn. No breakfast, but one of the few places with a kitchen and large dining room. Laundry available. Open all year. Dorms 30SFr; 4-bed dorms 172SFr; singles 54-56SFr, with shower 64-68SFr; doubles 84-86/94-96SFr. MC/V. ❸

Hotel Mischabel (☎967 11 31; fax 65 07; mischabel.zermatt@reconline.ch; www.zermatt.ch/mischabel), right off of Hofmattstr. This hotel creaks reassuringly like a rocking chair. Ornate carpets and upholstry decorate the TV room downstairs while the bedrooms allow rustic wood walls to speak for themselves. Breakfast included. Reception 7:30am-10pm. Check-out 11am. Closed Oct. 21-Dec. 15 and May 1-June 15. Singles, doubles, and triples 45-57SFr per person; singles with bath 55-67SFr. MC/V. ❸

Jugendherberge (HI), Winkelmatten (☎967 23 20; fax 53 06; zermatt@youthhostel.ch; www.youthhostel.ch/zermatt). Turn left at the church, cross the river, take the 2nd street to the right (at the Jugendherberge sign) and the left fork in front of Hotel Rhodania. At this fully loaded, if institutional, hostel, tourists get all the goodies and a great deal. Unobstructed views of the Matterhorn from bedroom windows, friendly staff, a giant outdoor chess set, ping-pong, foosball, and **Internet** (5SF per 15min.) await. Breakfast, hearty dinner (including fondue on Su and vegetarian on request), showers, and sleepsack included. Laundry 8SFr. Reception 7-10am and 4-10:30pm. Closed May. Dorms 48SFr; two doubles 116SFr. Non-members add 6SFr. AmEx/DC/MC/V. ❸

Hotel Garni Tannenhof (☎967 31 88; fax 31 73; tannenhof@zermatt.info; www.tannenhof.zermatt.info). Turn right on Bahnhofstr. and left at the Bayard building. Features retro rugs and leather chairs. Breakfast included. Every room has a radio and telephone. Reception 7am-7pm. Reserve at least 1 month in advance in winter, 2-3 weeks in summer. Singles 45-70SFr, with shower 60-80SFr; doubles 90-120SFr/110-140SFr; triples 105-120SFr per person. AmEx/DC/V. ❸

Camping Alphubel (☎967 36 35), in Täsch. Caravaners and motorists can park their vehicles here. From the station, cross the parking lot and turn right in front of the tourist offices past the river, then right across the railroad tracks. Reception 8am-noon and 2-8pm. Open May to mid-Oct. Showers included. 4.50SFr, ages 6-16 2.25SFr; 5SFr per tent, 5SFr per car, caravan 6SFr, electricity 3SFr. Tax not included in price. ❶

Mountain Huts: The tourist office provides a list of private huts in the Zermatt area. A full day's hike from Zermatt, they offer a good deal for serious climbers and hikers. All huts are open July-Aug., are accessible to walkers if there's no snow, and include breakfast unless otherwise noted. Try **Schönbielhütte** (2694m; ☎967 13 54 or 47 62; 35.50SFr), **Rothornhütte** (3198m; ☎967 20 43 or 16 20; fax 16 39; 32SFr; see the Grandchild Hike, p. 463), the crowded **Gandegghütte** (3029m; ☎(079) 607 88 68 or 967 21 12; fax 967 21 49; 26SFr; no breakfast), or **Hörnlihütte,** also called **Berghaus Matterhorn,** (3260m; ☎967 22 64; 43SFr; see Hörnlihütte Hike, p. 462). ❷

FOOD

It's easy to find an inexpensive meal in Zermatt. Revellers flood the streets after dark, sipping whiskey after a day in the snow. The **Co-op** is across from the station. (Open M-F 8:15am-12:15pm and 1:45-6:30pm, Sa 8:15am-12:15pm and 1:45-6pm.)

Walliserkanne (☎966 46 10), Bahnhofstr., next to the post office, looks upscale inside, but offers filling Swiss fare at a reasonable price. They serve *Käseschnitte mit Schinken and Tomate* (toasted cheese with ham and tomato, 18SFr), fondues (23SFr) and *Menüs* (20-23SFr) with vegetarian options. Additionally, Walliserkanne offers take out pizzas (15-18SFr) from 11:30am-11pm. Open 9am-midnight. AmEx/DC/MC/V. ❸

Café du Pont (☎967 43 43), on Kirchpl. Zermatt's oldest restaurant tends to attract a similarly aged clientele. Multilingual menus burnt into slabs of wood hanging on the wall list stick-to-your-ribs Swiss dishes like *Raclette* (7.50SFr), *Rösti* (11-15SFr), and *fondue du Pont* (22SFr). Sandwiches 6.50SFr. Open June-Oct. and Dec.-Apr. daily 9am-11pm; food served 11am-10pm. No credit cards. ❷

Pöstli "Brown Cow" Pub (☎967 19 31), Bahnhofstr., is in the Great Swiss Disaster complex at the Hotel de la Post the Brown Cow. The clientele of lively English-speaking locals comes for the whimsical cow-pattern decor and greasy-spoon food. Try the potato skins (9.50SFr) or sadistically chomp on a burger (11-15SFr). In the summer cool off with a frappe (6.50SFr) or munch on one of the season's special salads (10-18SFr). Heineken 3.40SFr. Open 9am-2am. The rest of the complex offers a 3-story spaghetti factory with evening films and disco, a jazz bar with live music, an underground bar and disco, and a posh hotel. Discos open until 3:30am. No cover. ❷

Whymperstube (☎967 22 96), Bahnhofstr., 200m past the post office, is a quiet escape in the basement of the Monte Rosa hotel. It offers traditional Swiss meals (*Raclette* 7.50SFr and fondue 22-24SFr) among others, like melon with ham (14.50SFr) and pork with vegetables and fries covered in cheese (26SFr). Open daily 6-10pm. Closed May and mid-Oct. until mid-Nov. AmEx/DC/MC/V. ❸

Grill Room Spycher (☎967 77 41 or 20 41), across the river on Kirchstr. and left on Steinmattstr. Those looking to splurge and escape the classic cheese-laden menus should head to the romantic candle-lit setting of Spycher. Wood ceilings and an abundance of greenery provide atmosphere for risotto with mushrooms (25SFr), duck in orange sauce (29SFr), or deer filet with brussel sprouts, chestnuts, and *spätzli* (36SFr). Open daily 6-11pm. Closed May and mid-Oct. until mid-Nov. AmEx/DC/MC/V. ❹

👁 🎵 SIGHTS AND ENTERTAINMENT

The highly recommended **Air Taxi Zermatt** (☎967 76 44) sends tandem-paragliders airborne at starting points from 2,300m to 4,100m (150-190SFr including transportation). The glitzier hotels have **swimming pools;** Hotel Christiania, Wiestistr., has the biggest one. Follow the right bank of the river to the left past the Rothorn/Sunnegga cable railway station. (Hotel ☎967 80 00. 10SFr, children 6SFr. Open M-Su 8-10:30am and 2-8pm; Th until 9pm. Sauna 20SFr.)

The **Alpine Museum,** near the post office, exhibits broken ropes, mangled shoes, and bashed-in lanterns found with the corpses of those who failed to master local peaks, as well as displays of the flora, fauna, and geology of the area. Special attention is given to the first ascent of the Matterhorn on July 14, 1865, when over half the team was killed on the way down. A haunting photograph is all that remains of one victim, Lord Alfred Douglas (the love of Oscar Wilde's life), whose remains were never found. Recovered remains of the Matterhorn's victims are buried in the cemetery next to the church with picks and ropes carved into their graves. (☎967 41 00. Open daily June-Oct. 10am-noon and 4-6pm; July 10-Aug. 20 opens afternoons at 3pm; Dec. 20-May M-F and Su 4:30-6:30pm. 8SFr, children under 16 2SFr.)

The **Cinema Vernissage** (☎967 66 36), next to Julen Sports on Hoffmattstr., screens 2 or 3 nearly new releases per night (M-Sa), usually in English. In winter 2002 a brand new **casino** opened on Bahnhofstr. by Kirchpl. August brings the **Alpine Folklore Parade,** when locals take a break from their mountain chores and dust off their alphorns and lederhosen. The Roman Catholic church hosts **classical music concerts** (25SFr) in July and August.

🅰 NIGHTLIFE

🦑 **The Pipe Surfer's Cantina,** (☎213 38 07; www.gozermatt.com/thepipe), on Kirchstr. before the river on the right, is the nightly site of the craziest beach party in the Alps. Owner Nikk, generous with the free shots (stop by in the afternoon for a 2-for-1 coupon or get one at the HI hostel), keeps customers rolling with his hilarious stories of late-night adventures and sound advice on everything Zermatt (and even Switzerland). The staff are all experts in something, providing a variety of adventure outings and good company (see **Outdoor Activities,** p. 461.) Don't leave without downing a shot of Moo, the made-on-the-premises caramel vodka (6SFr). Frozen margaritas 6SFr, beer 4SFr or

0.5L 6SFr. Food served on request. In winter special Bum's Play plate includes beer and entree. Open daily 3:30pm-2:30am. Happy Hour 7-8pm.

The North Wall Bar (☎966 34 12). Take the 2nd right past the river on Kirchstr., en route to the youth hostel, to this English-speaking climbers' haunt and workman's bar where skiing and mountaineering videos play every evening alongside the dart games. This is the place to scrounge a job in Zermatt—ask the staff, who also give hiking advice. The kitchen will serve you "the hottest pizza in the Alps" (12SFr, plus 1SFr per fancy topping like mussels, corn, broccoli, or egg). Beer, some of the cheapest in town, is 5SFr for 0.5L. Open mid-June to Sept. and mid-Dec. to Apr. 6:30pm-midnight; later in winter. Pizza served until 10pm.

Grampi's Pub (☎967 77 75 or 417 99 85; fax 71 13), Bahnhofstr., across from Pöstli Pub. This centrally located bar thumps with pop dance music. Draft beer 4SFr for 0.25L; bottled beer 6-8SFr; "lady killers" 11-13SFr. Open 8:30am-2am, downstairs bar until 4am (DJ 9pm-3:30am); upstairs Italian restaurant 6pm-2am; food until 1am.

Country Bar (☎967 15 96), on Hofmattstr., next to the Hotel Elite, offers billiards (15SFr per hr.) on large, well-kept tables. Darts also available. Drink beers (6-12SFr) in a subdued atmosphere devoid of tourists. Open 10am-12:30am.

▗ OUTDOOR ACTIVITIES

The Zermatt Alpine Center, which houses both the **Bergführerbüro** (Guide's Office; ☎24 60; fax 966 24 69; alpincenter@zermatt.ch; www.zermatt.ch/alpincenter) and the **Skischulbüro** (Ski School Office; ☎966 24 66; fax 24 65; skischule@zermatt.ch; www.zermatt.ch/skischule), is past the post office from the station. Pick up detailed 4-day weather forecasts, ski passes, and information on guided climbing expeditions. (Bergführerbüro open July-Sept. M-F 8:30am-noon and 3:30-7pm, Sa 3:30-7pm, Su 10am-noon and 3:30-7pm; late Dec. until mid-May daily 5pm-7pm. Ski school office closed in summer but reachable by phone.) Adventure-seekers looking to take home their vacation should contact the **Freeride Film Factory** (☎213 38 07), operated by the Pipe Surfer's Cantina. Skilled guides offer custom hiking, biking, and climbing expeditions for lower prices than the Ski School (160SFr-250SFr), and also give you a 15-20min. videotape of your expedition. See **Pipe Surfer's Cantina** (p. 460).

SKIING. Seventy-three lifts, 14,200m of combined elevation, and 245km of prepared runs make Zermatt one of the world's best-equipped ski centers. Serious skiers will find challenges on **Europe's longest run**—the 13km trail from Klein Matterhorn to Zermatt. The town also has more **summer ski trails** than any other Alpine ski resort—36 sq. km of year-round runs between 2900 and 3900m. In the summer, the **Skischulbüro** (above) offers group 5-day long skiing classes (280SFr) and snowboarding classes (200SFr). Individual, one-day, and summer ski/snowboard lessons available on request. **4Synergies** also offers ski instruction privately or in groups. (☎967 70 20; fax 70 22; info@4synergies.com; www.4synergies.com. Groups 95SFr per day, 410SFr for 5 days.) Meanwhile **Stoked Swiss Snowboard School** provides qualified instructors for down hill rides. (☎967 87 88; fax 79 55; info@stoked.ch; www.stoked.ch. Groups 50SFr for half-day; 200SFr for 5 half-days.) **Ski and boot rental** is standard throughout the area, as is snowboard rental: 28-50SFr per day, 123-215SFr per week. Finding a reliable sports store is easy. (Most shops open daily 8am-noon and 2-6:30pm. See **Orientation and Practical Information,** p. 457.) Zermatt's **ski passes** operate on a regional system during the **summer** (from the end of April to October). Passes are available for any of the regions (Matterhorn, Gornergrat, or Sunnegga complexes). The Matterhorn region costs 60SFr per day. The Klein Matterhorn/Trockener Steg sub-region is now

MONTE ROSA CONQUERS CELEBRITIES The

Monte Rosa (the second highest mountain in Switzerland has a long and illustrious career with glitterati. Leonardo DaVinci, staring up at it from the Italian side, thought it the highest mountain on earth. Among its unlikely conquerors have been Pope Pius XI, who pioneered a new route to the Grenzensattel in 1889 before donning the papal robes. A youthful Winston Churchill climbed the Rosa in 1894 before gaining his fame in more political ventures.

combined with Italy's Mt. Cervinia (1 day 56SFr). From November to the end of April, a combined pass is available for all 3 regions (1 day 72SFr, 7 days 338SFr).

CLIMBING. The only company to lead formal expeditions above Zermatt is the **Bergführerbüro.** Groups go up the Breithorn (135SFr), Pollux (260SFr), and Castor (270SFr) daily in summer (see above for hours). Prices do not include equipment, hut accommodations, or lifts to the departure points. For equipment rental, see **Hiking** below. Climbing the Matterhorn is expensive and requires a guide, perfect physical condition, a 4am start, and extensive rock-climbing experience (at least PD+).

HIKING. Outstanding walks into the world of glaciers and high mountains leave from Zermatt in every direction. Although most paths are well-maintained and marked, a proper **topographic map** (25.90SFr from the tourist office) is essential for safety and enhances the experience. Lifts and railways to the south and east can shorten difficult climbs. (25% discount on many lifts with SwissPass, **Eurail generally not valid.**) Prudent walkers come prepared (see **Health, p. 19**); Zermatt is particularly prone to sudden electrical storms. Check the weather forecast in the Bergführerbüro before departure. Hiking boots can be rented at **Matterhorn Sport,** Bahnhofstr. (☎967 29 56), which also rents out climbing equipment; **Glacier Sport,** Bahnhofstr. (☎967 27 14) across from Walliserkanne; or **Burgener Sport,** Bahnhofstr. (☎967 27 94) next to Grampi's Pub. (1-day rentals 14SFr; 7 days 52SFr; 14 days 80SFr. All stores open 8am-noon and 2-6:30 or 7pm.)

Hörnlihütte Hike (10hr., 5hr. with cable car). The **Hörnlihütte** serves as the base camp for the most popular route up the Matterhorn and is a good platform for watching climbers claw their way up the ridge. The 1600m ascent to the hut is for the fit and well-booted only (a walking stick is recommended); a **cable car** from the far end of town to the **Schwarzsee** via Furi (2584m) saves 900m of climbing. (Schedule varies throughout the year; ask the tourist office. 20.50SFr, return 33SFr). Leave Zermatt along the left bank of the Matter Vispa. Approximately 2km from Zermatt, a wide track marked "Zum See, Schwarzsee und Hörnlihütte" leads down and left across the river. Follow the 3hr. path as it zigzags steeply up to the tiny Schwarzsee, passing gorges on the left. From the Schwarzsee, the path becomes rockier and wilder as it joins the true northeast ridge of the Matterhorn, climbing gently at first but ending in a merciless, exposed *arête* (sharp ridge) by the buildings at Hörnli. **Casual hikers *cannot* continue above the hut.** More than 500 people have died above this point, as a walk around Zermatt's cemeteries attest. For a different descent, bear right at the *Schwarzsee* to the Furgg cable car terminus and follow path to town. It traverses a steep cliff but is stable underfoot and has even closer views of the gorges carved by the **Gornergletscher.**

The Gornergrat (numerous hikes possible). The Gornergrat swarms with as many as 5,000 visitors per day because it provides the best views of the Matterhorn. The train, which departs opposite Zermatt's main station (7am-11pm), ascends to the **Gornergrat** (3090m; 38SFr, round-trip 63SFr) via **Riffelalp** (2211m; 17.20SFr, 32SFr), **Riffelberg** (2582m; 27SFr, 46SF), and **Rotenboden** (2815m; 34SFr, 58SFr), all of which are trail-

OF SKIRTS AND MOUNTAINS In 1867, when most women were concerned with keeping a good house and finding a good man for whom to keep it, 18-year-old Félicité Carrel set her sights on loftier goals. She decided to be the first woman to ascend the infamous Matterhorn. With the help of the Maquignza brothers, who hoped to prove that anyone could climb the mountain, Félicité almost reached her goal. Unfortunately, a change in route along the way forced the climbers up a more difficult path that Félicité, in her required skirts (meant to hold down the wind) was not allowed to attempt. Instead, she waited for her companions 120m below the summit at a landmark that has been known since as Col Félicité.

heads. From the Gornergrat, hikes descend to the wide, flat **Gornergletscher** and along the ridge toward the **Stockhorn** (3532m). A cable car traverses this distance (12SFr each way). Rotenboden is on the other side of Stockhorn. From Rotenboden, hikers can divert to the Monte Rosa hut (5hr. to the hut and back) by following the glacier. Each destination provides a closer encounter with the ice with the cost of losing a fraction of the panorama. Routes from the Riffelalp station descend to Zermatt by following the side of the mountain around to the *Grünsee,* facing the snout of the **Findelngletscher,** then crossing the river and returning to Zermatt by way of the **Moosjesee** and the **Leisee,** 2 small pools that provide a beautiful foreground to the Matterhorn.

Granny Hike; to Zmutt (1hr.). This easy hike offers the most dramatic encounter with the Matterhorn's north face. The path is wide, clear, and well-marked. From Zermatt, follow Bahnhofstr. past the church, then follow the sign to the right. The steady slope climbs through the Arolla pines to the weathered chalets of the hamlet of Zmutt. The path, granting views of the Hörnli ridge and the Matterhorn, levels out as it continues through the meadows above a small reservoir. The Matterhorn's north wall, which drops 200m with an average gradient well over 45°, gradually comes into view above Zmutt.

Grandchild Hike (10hr.). If you want to make the Granny Hike more challenging (well worth the extra effort, since the views get exponentially better as you ascend), the Grandchild hike continues on to the **Schönbielhütte** (2694m, 4hr. from Zmutt). The hike becomes more difficult as it ascends past lakes and waterfalls at the outlet of the rock-strewn **Zmuttgletscher.** The Schönbielhütte is an ideal spot for lunchtime carbo-loading of pasta or *Rösti,* or an overnight stop. On the return journey, the valley frames the Rimpfischhorn (4199m) and Strahlhorn (4190m). The full-day hike is 25km, covering 1050m of gentle elevation.

The Triple-T Hike. This hike of medium difficulty traverses three peaks—from **Tuftern** (2339m) to **Täschalp** (2650m) to **Täsch** (1449m; 6hr.). From Tuftern, the high-mountain trail (under "Unter Gattla") leads to Täschalp. From Täschalp the trail heads upwards to the Täsch hut (2701m, ☎967 53 63, 29SFr including breakfast) and then gradually back down to Täsch. From Täsch, hike back up to Zermatt or take the train (10min.; every hr. 6:32am-9:35pm, Sa-Su every 20min. 6:32am-11:30pm; 7.80SFr).

SAAS FEE ☎027

Saas Fee, the "pearl of the Alps," is one of Switzerland's most dramatic sites. The thirteen 4000m peaks that form a hemisphere above the town peer down ominously. The glacial ice of the **Feegletscher,** "fairy glacier," comes so low that you can visit the frozen giant on a 30min. evening stroll. To protect its alpine glory, this resort town is closed to cars, giving electrically powered mini-vans and trucks free rein over the winding streets. Town officials prohibit disturbing "the fairy-like charm of Saas Fee" after 10pm (noisemakers fined 200SFr). Keep in mind that lifts, restaurants, and hotels shut down for maintenance, renovations, and vacations for townspeople from early May to mid-June.

⌐ TRANSPORTATION

A **post bus** runs (every hr. 5:35am-7:35pm) to Brig (1¼hr.; 17.20SFr; round-trip 34.40SFr) via Saas Grund (10min.; 3SFr/6SFr); Stalden Saas (40min.; 12.40; SFr/ 24.80 SFr), connecting to Zermatt (82.80SFr, reservations required); and Visp (50min., 15.20/30.40SFr), where trains connect to Lausanne, Sion, and the rest of Valais. Reserve a seat on all buses starting at Saas Fee at least 2hr. before departure in the high season. Call ☎958 11 45 or drop by the bus station (open 7:30am-12:35pm and 1:15-6:35pm). **Parking** in the lot across the street to the right of the tourist office. (1 day 11SFr; with guest card after 2nd day 7.50SFr.)

◼◼ ◼ ORIENTATION AND PRACTICAL INFORMATION

The **tourist office,** opposite the bus station, dispenses seasonal information, hiking advice, and useful town maps. Outside, a kiosk provides hotel information and reservations. (☎958 18 58; fax 18 60; reservations ☎958 18 68; fax 18 70; to@saas-fee.ch; www.saas-fee.ch. Open July to mid-Sept. and mid-Dec. to mid-Apr. M-F 8:30am-noon and 2-6:30pm, Sa 8am-7pm, Su 9am-noon and 2-6pm; closed Sundays in May.) The bus depot has small **lockers** (2SFr) and **luggage** storage (2SFr). For a **weather report,** call ☎162. In case of **emergency,** call ☎117. **Vallesia Apotheke** is down the hill from the tourist office at the main street. (☎957 26 18. Open M-Sa 8:30am-noon and 2-6:30pm, Su 4-6pm; for emergencies call ☎079 417 67 18). Call a **taxi** at ☎958 11 35 or 957 33 44. **Cyber Lion** in Haus Waldrain, left past the Migros, offers **Internet access** (☎947 39 61; fax 957 39 62; www.cyberlion.ch; info@cyberlion.ch; 5SFr per 20min.), or ask at Hotel Dom, on the main street past the church (☎957 51 01). There is a **post office** with public **fax** and **ATM** at the bus depot. (Open M-F 8:15am-noon and 2-6pm, Sa 8:15am-noon.) **Postal code:** CH-3906.

◤ ACCOMMODATIONS

Hotel Garni Bergheimat ❸, in the center of town, offers clean mid-sized rooms with showers at a reasonable rate. The rooms aren't exciting, but ask for a south facing window and the glacial views will be. (☎957 20 30; fax 30 82; info@bergheimat.ch; www.bergheimat.ch. Breakfast included. 60SFr per person in summer; 70SFr in winter; 50SFr between seasons.) **Hotel Garni Feehof ❸** is right on the main street. Warm, wooden, and wonderful, nearly all the creaky pine rooms have balconies and beds with enormous marshmallow-like down comforters. (☎957 23 08; fax 23 09. Breakfast and shower included. Reception 9-11am and 3-6:30pm. In winter, reserve 2 weeks in advance. Singles 38-62SFr; doubles 76-142SFr.)

Travelers willing to sacrifice comfort can find bargains in hotel basements. **Hotel Garni Imseng ❷,** across the street from Feehof, has 7 rows of 3-high bunks, with no space in between. However, the hotel is clean, frequently empty, and there is fresh bread in the morning. Doubles upstairs in the hotel have TVs and leather couches but cost three times more. (☎958 12 58; fax 12 55; www.saas-fee.ch/hotel.imseng. Breakfast included. Sheets 5SFr. Reception 8:30am-noon and 2-7pm. Dorms 35SFr, doubles 110SFr per person.) **Mountain huts** are a bold alternative to staying in Saas Fee proper. Breakfast is always included. The **Mischabel ❷** (3329m; ☎957 11 17; 28SFr, dinner available), **Hoh-Saas ❸** (3098m; ☎957 17 13; 36SFr), and **Weissmieshütte** (2726m; ☎957 25 54; 30SFr, dinner included) above Saas Grund are all accessible from July to September. The Saas Fee tourist office (see **Practical Information,** above) and Bergführerbüro (see **Hiking,** below) have more details.

◘ FOOD

Spaghetteria da Rasso ❷, on the main street under the Hotel Britania, has a shady terrace where accordionists occasionally entertain the crowd. Two or more can try the house special with salad, unlimited pasta, and four different sauces for 25SFr per person. (☎957 15 26. Open late June to mid-Oct. 9am-11:30pm; mid-Oct.-Apr. 10am-11:30pm; closed Tu and May-late June. AmEx/MC/V.) Though it's certainly not difficult to find Swiss specialties around town, the **Restaurant Chämi-Stube ❸** (☎957 17 47), a little farther down the hill from the church, is unique in its quiet, candle-lit atmosphere. It serves a variety of *Rösti* for 14-16.50SFr, a Valaisian fondue for 25SFr, and, interestingly, tortillas for 17-28SFr. (Open Dec.-May and mid-June to Oct. 9am-11:30pm. Warm food 11:30am-2pm and 6-9pm. AmEx/MC/V.) Most of Saas Fee's **supermarkets** in the center of town have the same hours. (M-F 8:15am-12:15pm and 2:15-6:30pm, Sa 8:15am-12:15pm and 2:15-5pm.)

◪ OUTDOOR ACTIVITIES

SKIING. During the **summer,** two cable cars to **Felskinn** (3000m; 7:30am-4:15pm; 26SFr, round-trip 34SFr) and an underground funicular, the "Metro Alpin," farther to **Allanin** (3500m; 7:45am-4pm; an additional 26SFr, round-trip 34SFr) enable **skiers** to enjoy 20km of runs and a stupendous alpine view. In the winter, an immense network of lifts opens from Allanin (day ski passes 59SFr, children 35SFr; 6 days 27SFr/167SFr; 13 days 480SFr/288SFr). The **Ski School,** across the street from the church, offers group skiing and snowboarding lessons from mid-Dec. to April. (☎957 23 48; www.saas-fee.ch/skischool. Skiing 46SFr per 3hr., 172SFr per week; snowboarding 43SFr per 2hr., 158SFr per 1 week. Slight reductions available in late Jan. Open M-F 8:30-noon and 2:30-6pm, Sa-Su 4-6pm.) In Saas Fee, many stores **rent skis.** Stores in the **Swiss Rent-A-Sport System** (look for the big red "S" logo) offer 3 grades of equipment (skis and snowboards 28-50SFr per day, 6 days 109-190SFr; boots 15-19SFr/56-80SFr). It is possible to call ahead and have equipment set aside prior to arrival; call or fax the main Swiss Rent-A-Sport outlet in town, **Anthamatten Sport Mode,** located across from the Spaghetteria. (☎958 19 18; fax 957 19 70. Open May-June and Sept.-Nov. daily 9am-noon and 2-6pm; July-Aug. daily 8:30am-noon and 1:30-6:30pm; Dec.-Apr. 8am-7pm. AmEx/DC/MC/V.

HIKING. The **Bergführerbüro** (Mountain Guides' Office), housed in the same building as the ski school, leads climbs of varying difficulty levels to a number of 4000m summits. (☎/fax 957 44 64; mountainlife@rhone.ch; www.rhone.ch/mountainlife. Closed May and June. Open M-Sa 9am-noon and 3-6pm.) Day tours run from 50-200SFr per person. Hikers have 280km of marked trails from which to choose. Maps at the tourist office are 7SFr, or ask for the free brochure with tour description. The **Saas Valley Hiking Pass** (171SFr, family rate 345SFr) provides access for one week to all cable cars and post buses in the valley and entrance to the ice pavilion at **Mittelallanin,** the **Bielen Recreation Center,** and other museums. The pass is available at the tourist office or any cable car station. Most lifts close from May to early June and from mid-October to mid-December.

  Mischabelhütte Hike (full day hike, 1550m ascent). A steep trail leads up to the **Mischabelhütte** (3329m), the best walking-accessible panorama of Saas Fee's natural amphitheater. From the pharmacy on the main street, turn right after the church and take the right fork after 100m. Check for snow cover before departing, as the last part of the hike is rocky and highly unpleasant with any hint of ice.

THE LOCAL STORY

SNOW PLACE LIKE HOME

Jolanda Stettler works at a youth hostel in Sion. She is a ski instructor and avid outdoorswoman.

Q: What kind of work have you done in the mountains?

A: I worked at the Brittainnia Hütte above Saas Fee. It's an SAC (Swiss Alpine Club) Berghütte—they're all over Switzerland. This one was built by the British. With 134 beds, I believe it is one of the biggest in Switzerland.

Q: What was daily life like?

A: We woke up at 4am to cook breakfast for the mountain climbers and skiiers before they left for the day. It was too expensive to have helicopters bring provisions, so we carried everything ourselves or by snowmobile from the ski gondola, 1km away. We even had to bring water.

Q: Did you have a hard time working at such a high altitude?

A: At 3030m, I was lucky that I didn't have altitude sickness, but it was hard for me to sleep, even after working 14hr. days. Also, you feel alcohol much faster. But it is wonderful to be so high up. The sunrises and the natural beauty are so unique.

Q: Who comes to the hut?

A: Many mountain climbers and skiiers, but also tourists. We were often full with 120-130 people who stayed overnight.

Q: That sounds like a great way to experience the Alps!

A: The visitors love it, and I love it too. When you spend time in the mountains, you just want to spend more and more. Is that usual? I think so. They pull you higher and higher.

Glacier Hike (half-day hike). This lovely half-day voyage begins with a cable-car ride to **Plattjen** (2570m). From there a path leads to the right and then left after 5min. to views of the Dom and Lezspitze. From the summit, the trail descends for 15min., then heads left around the amphitheatre, spiraling slowly down below the **Feegletscher.** The view opens up as the path drops to the **Gletschersee** (1910m) at the glacier tip. From there, the trail gently follows the left bank of the outlet stream back to Saas Fee.

Hannig Hike (2½hr.). This easy walk from the church to Hannig follows a trail that begins level (30min.) and gets steeper as it moves into the woods. Follow the "Hannig" signs all the way. On the way up, there are opportunities for close encounters with goats and pigs as the path passes through the small farms on the hill. Stop at the Mannigalp hut for fresh milk and cheese from the cows and goats you saw along the way. After an hour, the path splits into the Hannig trail and the longer, more scenic Hannig Waldweg trail. From the restaurant at the summit, it is possible to continue the trail toward Melchbode and back to Saas Fee or take the **Sonnenbahn Hannig** cable car (15SFr adults, 7.50SFr children, 30% discount with SwissPass) that descends to the Spaghetteria.

OTHER ACTIVITIES. The **Bielen Recreation Center,** next to the bus station, has an expensive but excellent **swimming pool** and **jacuzzi.** (☎957 24 75. Open June daily 1-9pm; July-Oct. 10am-9pm. 13SFr, with guest card 12SFr; children 8.50SFr/7.50SFr.) The Mountain Guide Office organizes outings to a nearby gorge every Monday, Wednesday, and Friday in summer, and every Thursday in winter. Scuttle along water-carved rock faces, aided by safety equipment (95SFr). **Feeblitz,** beside the Alpine-Express, offers a self-controlled rollercoaster ride. Riders control single cars that skate along a winding metal track down the mountain. (☎957 31 11. Open June 15-Oct. 31 daily noon-8pm; July and Aug. and Sa-Su in Sept. and Oct. 10am-6pm; Nov. F-Su 1-5pm; and Dec.-Apr. noon-6pm. 6SFr, under 16 4SFr.)

For two weeks in mid-August, Saas Fee hosts the **Musica Romantica** (www.saas-fee.ch/romantica) classical music festival, which brings artists from all over Europe. (25-65SFr symphony concert tickets, 16-40SFr recital tickets, 130-210SFr weeklong ticket, 50% discount for children under 16.) Contact the tourist office for a list of performers and to purchase tickets. Early August also brings a day of traditional Valaiser cow fighting (www.saas-fee.ch/ringkuhkampf).

BRIG

☎027

A simple town, Brig (pop. 11,500) aptly takes its name from the word for "bridge," providing access to the most famous resorts in Valais. Visitors can enjoy a quiet day visiting Brig's many churches and the Stockalperschloß, but the best reason to come is to catch a train or cable car to a nearby glacier or mountain peak.

▐ TRANSPORTATION AND PRACTICAL INFORMATION

Brig is accessible by **train** from **Interlaken Ost** via **Spiez** (1½-2hr.; every hour 5:33am-11:37pm; 40SFr), **Martigny** (50min.; every hr. 6:54am-12:54am; 23SFr) or **Sion** (45min.; 2 or 3 per hr.; 6:04am-1:09am; 17.20SFr). The **BVZ train** runs between **Brig** and **Zermatt** (1¼hr.; every hr. 5:10am-7:23pm; June-Oct. extra trains and a bus at 8:25pm; 34SFr; Swiss pass valid, no Eurail.) The last return train from **Zermatt** is 7:52pm (June-Oct. 9:10pm). The **Post Bus** leaves for Saas Fee every hour 6:15am-8:15am and returns 5:35am-7:35pm. Reservations required for return trips (1¼hr.; 17.20SFr). The **train station** is open M-Sa 6:30am-8:30pm and Su 7:30am-8pm and offers **bike rentals** (30SFr per day, 21SFr per half-day), **luggage storage** (7SFr per bag), **lockers** (4-6SFr); and **currency exchange** (M-F 7am-7pm, Sa 7am-5pm and Su 8-11:30am and 1-5pm). The **tourist information office** is on the second level of the train station. (☎921 60 30; fax 921 60 31; infor@brig-tourismus.ch; www.brig.ch. Open M-F 8:30am-6:15pm, Sa 8:30am-12:30pm; July-Sept. Sa 9am-6:15pm and Su 9am-12:15pm.) Other services are: **Internet**, at the Good Night Inn across the river from Sebastians Pl., (6SFr per hr.); **police,** ☎922 41 60; **hospital** (emergencies ☎922 33 33); and **taxis,** ☎0800 800 608. A **post office** across the street from the station is open M-F 7:30am-noon and 1:30-6:15pm, Sa 8-11am. **Postal code:** 3900.

▐ ACCOMMODATIONS

For only a bit more than some hostels, **Pension Post ❷,** Furkastr. 23, offers one of the best deals in town. Spacious, high-quality rooms with clean inviting beds come with or without in-room showers. Sheets, towels and breakfast included. (☎924 45 54; fax 45 53. Reception M-F 6am-11pm; Sa 7am-6pm. Dorms 35SFr; singles 40-50SFr; doubles 80-100SFr.) For those with a larger budget, **Hotel Du Pont ❸,** on the far side of Sebastians Pl. has clean though slightly aging rooms in the old building and luxurious doubles with showers in the newer part. (☎923 15 02; fax 95 72; dupont.brig@datacomm.ch. Singles 60SFr, doubles 100SFr; with shower 95/190SFr. AmEx/DC/MC/V.) **Camping Geshina ❶,** just past the local swimming pool, nestled among houses on Geshinaweg, sports lines of trees between wheel-to-wheel RVs and arranges hikes or visits to cheese makers for its guests. (☎923 06 88; geshina@campings.ch. Reception 8-11am and 4-7:30pm; come anytime. Open Apr. 20-Oct. 14. 5.50SFr, children 2.75SFr, tents 5SFr.)

▐ FOOD

The main street is dotted with high-priced hotel restaurants, but try **Walliser Weinstube ❷,** Bahnhofstr. 9, for Swiss classics at a reasonable price, including Käseschnitte for 14-17SFr and *Rösti* for 11-15SFr. (☎923 14 28; fax 67 23; www.walliser-weinstube.ch. Open M-F 6:30am-11pm, Sa-Su 9am-midnight). Past Sebastians Pl. on Alte Simplonstr., **Tea-Room Bistro Viva ❷** offers traditional fare in a non-traditional setting. Try the Älpler macaroni (12SFr) and apple strudel with ice cream (6SFr) in a modern room with that new-car feel. (☎924 56 03. Open Su 8:30am-1pm, M-F 7:30am-6:30pm). **Molino Pizzeria Ristorante ❸** is truly Italian with Romanesque statues decorating the dining area, an ivy-covered terrace, and 14 kinds of pizza (15.20-25.50SFr), soups, and pastas. (☎923 65 56; fax 924 43 13. Open M-Sa 11:15am-2pm and 5:30-11pm, F-Sa until midnight, Su 11:15am-11pm.) **Migros,** left from station and across the street, has a grocery store and restaurant. (Store open M 1:30-6:30pm, Tu-F 8:15am-6:30pm, Sa 7:45am-4pm. Restaurant open M-F 7:30am-6:30pm, Sa 7:30am-4pm.) The **Coop** across the river from Sebastians Pl. on Gilserallee offers cheap groceries and a bistro as well. (Open M 1:30-6:30pm, Tu-F 8am-6:30pm, Su 7:30am-4pm.) There's a **farmer's market** every Saturday from 8am-noon.

🏔 ACTIVITIES

Brig provides easy access by bus or train to major ski areas including **Zermatt, Crans-Montana, Riederalp, Bettmeralp and Piesheralp, Rosswald, Belalp,** and **Saas Fee.** In the summer, head to one of the nearby towns for cable car access to the newly established **Aletsch Nature Reserve** and view 1000m of flowing ice, the longest glacier in Switzerland. Cars aren't allowed beyond the border. Ask at the tourist office for more details about the reserve or for suggested **hikes.** Brig also lies just 2.5km from Brigerbad, home to Europe's first Thermal-Grotto pool and the largest **open-air thermal pools** in Switzerland. (Open May-Sept.) The last weekend in August brings the **Schäferwochenende Belalp,** during which a festival arises around the nearly 2000 sheep that are herded down from the hills. (☎921 60 40; fax 60 41; info@belalp.ch; www.belalp.ch.)

If you're spending the day in the city, visit the 17th century **Stockalperschloß** on Alte Simplonstr. Visit the museum across the street or walk around the rose garden and park on your own. (☎921 60 30. Open May-Oct. Tu-Su 9:15-11:30am and 1:15-4:30pm. Tours in German or by paper every hour. Open 9:30am-3:30pm; also 4:30pm June-Sept. 5SFr, children 2SFr.) It's also nice to visit the **Kollegiumskirche** for a view of the city. Friday evenings in summer bring live music to Sebastians Pl. and occasional open-air movies free of charge.

SION ☎027

Surrounded by the glitz of winter-driven mountain towns, Sion, the capital of Valais canton, is a summer season city. Behind the day-to-day business of the main streets lies the cobblestone-lined old city, including two looming hillside castles and a refreshingly down-to-earth environment. Additionally, Sion's size (large enough for Olympic bids in 2002 and 2006) and accessibility make it an ideal base for exploring all of Valais or for a momentary escape from the touring hordes.

🚆 TRANSPORTATION. Trains pass every 30min. in each direction along the Rhône Valley, going west (4:52am-10:52pm) to: Aigle (35min., 17.20SFr); Lausanne (1¼hr., 27SFr); Martigny (15min., 9.20SFr); and Montreux (50min., 21SFr); and east (6:04am-1:09am) to Sierre (10min., 5.80SFr); and Brig (30-45min., 17.20SFr), where you can connect to Saas Fee (30.40SFr) and Zermatt (47.20SFr). For **rail information,** call ☎0900 300 300; www.cff.ch. The **train station** is open M-Sa 6:30am-8pm; Su 6:50am-8pm. Switzerland's largest **Post Bus station** congests the square in front of the station with a blur of yellow buses. Ask about the Sierre-Sion Regional deal, offering 3 days of unlimited travel in the region over one week for 48SFr, children 38SFr. (☎327 34 34; fax 322 61 26; www.poste.ch.)

◢◤ ORIENTATION AND PRACTICAL INFORMATION. Sion's main artery, Ave. de la Gare, runs north up the hill from the train station, passing ave. du Midi on the right, to form the southwest corner of pl. de la Planta with r. de Lausanne. R. du Grand-Pont, a main thoroughfare of the old town, connects to the end of r. de Lausanne east of the plaza. The **tourist office**, on r. de Lausanne, provides 2hr. **guided tours** (July-Aug. Tu, Th 9:30am, additional group tours on request; 15SFr, children 6SFr, students and seniors 10SFr) and room reservations. (☎327 77 27; fax 77 28; info@siontourism.ch; www.siontourism.ch. Open July-Aug. M-F 8am-6pm, Sa 9am-5pm; Sept.-June M-F 8:30am-noon and 2-5:30pm; Sa 9am-noon.) The train station provides **currency exchange** when station is open (see times above), **lockers** (4-6SFr), and **luggage storage** (7SFr for 24hr.; open 6:45am-8pm). **Internet** access is cheapest at **Quanta**, in the train station. (☎321 10 60. Open M-Th 11am-11pm, F 11am-midnight, Sa 10am-midnight, Su noon-11pm. 4SFr for 30min.) For a **taxi**, call ☎322 32 32. In case of **emergency**, call ☎117. For an **ambulance**, call ☎144. For **pharmacy**, call ☎111. The **post office**, pl. de la Gare, is to the left of the train station. (Open M-F 7:30am-6:15pm, Sa 8:15am-noon.) **Postal code:** CH-1950.

⌂ ACCOMMODATIONS AND CAMPING. Sion's sole budget-friendly accommodation, the **Auberge de Jeunesse (HI) ❷**, ave. de l'Industrie 2, behind the train station, welcomes guests with brightly colored artwork. The building is vast and institutional, with clean bathrooms, little balconies, and lockers in every room. Rooms are often fully booked from June to September, so call ahead. Amenities include **bike rental** (15SFr per day; 10SFr per half-day), ping pong, pool, and foosball. (☎323 74 70; fax 74 38; sion@youthhostel.ch; www.youthhostel.ch/sion. Breakfast included. Lunch on request 12.50SFr. Dinner 12.50SFr, reserve ahead. Kitchen facilities 2.50SFr. Reception 8-10am and 5-9pm. Curfew 10pm; keys on request. 4-bed dorms 28.80SFr; 3-bed dorms 32.80SFr; 2-bed dorms 35.80SFr. 6SFr surcharge for non-members. DC/MC/V.) Staying elsewhere will empty your wallet. Travelers seeking a cheap bed try villages outside Sion; ask at the tourist office. (In **Pont-de-la-Morge**, singles run 40SFr, doubles 80SFr; in **Saint-Léonard** 50-70SFr/70-94SFr. Post Buses run to both towns.) **Camping Les Îles ❶**, rte. d'Aproz, boasts 5-star riverside campsites 4km from town. Take a very short ride on Post Bus #2 to Aproz. (☎346 43 47; fax 68 47. Open Jan.-Oct. and the last two weeks in Dec. 8.40SFr, children 4.20SFr, tents 9SFr; off-season 6.60SFr/3.30SFr, tents 6SFr.)

◖ FOOD. Cafes and restaurants line the cobblestoned streets of the *vieille ville*. Unlike many cafes, the **Café des Châteaux ❸**, r. des Châteaux 3, off r. du Grand Pont, is unpretentious and affordable. Swiss classics like *Raclette* (25SFr) and fondue (19SFr) are served alongside *escargots* (15SFr) and *tripe milanaise* (18SFr). (☎372 13 96. Open M-Tu and Th-Sa 8am-midnight, Su 10am-midnight.) For cheap and filling Turkish delights, head to ave. des Mayennets at ave. du Midi and grab a kebab and drink (7-13SFr) at **Kebab Istanbul ❷**. (☎323 79 05. Open M-Sa 10am-9:30pm, Su noon-9:30pm.) The menu at **Au Vieux Valais ❸**, on r. St. Théodule off r. de Lausanne, is made for two. Try *potence flambée au whisky* (35SFr, with rice and house sauces) or the *fondue bourgnignonne* (32SFr), which comes with salad and potatoes. (☎322 16 74. Open M-F 9:45am-11pm; Sa 6-11:30pm; MC/V.) **Migros** supermarket is in the Centre Commercial on ave. de France, one block left from the station and on ave. Ritz, two blocks right from ave. de la Gare. (De France open: M 1-6:30pm, Tu-Th 8:15am-6:30pm, F 8:15am-7:30pm, Sa 8am-5pm; Ritz open: M 1:30-6:30pm, Tu-F 8:15am-noon and 1:30-6:30pm, Sa 8am-5pm.) The de France location also houses a Migros restaurant.

COWFIGHT For centuries, Valaisian breeders have raised cows in hopes of achieving success at the annual cow fights *(Combats de Reines)*, a regional spectacle that is the source of much pride. The highest bovine reverence has been accorded to the *Heren* strain, valued for its fine milk, meat, and particularly mountain-adapted nature. *Heren* females have an aggressive streak that reveals itself in their violent eyes. When facing off, combatants exhibit a repertoire of well-documented moves and behaviors, from preliminary head movements and *escarpier* (pawing the ground), to head-on and lateral attacks. After a mighty struggle, whichever animal is not lying on the ground recieves an extra-special bell and some salt from her owner, along with the distinction of being *la reine* (the queen), the true honor every virtuous cow is after.

⬛🔲 SIGHTS AND ENTERTAINMENT. Two castles perched upon twin hills offer clear views of Sion. Ave. des Chateaux curves up the hill from r. du Grand-Pont to a cluster of museums and castles. Just past **Château de la Majorie et du Vidomnat** to a fork leads left to **Château de Tourbillon** and right to **Château de Valère**, both of which blaze in floodlamps at night.

The Château de la Majorie et du Vidomnat houses the **Musée des Beaux-Arts.** Fans of Valaisian art will enjoy the *fin de siècle* portraiture and scenes of rural life. (☎606 46 90. Open Oct.-May Tu-Su 1-5pm; June-Sept. 1-6pm; 5SFr, students 2.50SFr; tours 8SFr.) Head up the hill 200m to the old Sion jail where the museum hosts intriguing temporary exhibits. (Open Oct.-May 1-5pm; June-Sept. 1-6pm) Farther up the hill, the **Château de Valère** houses the **Musée Cantonal D'Histoire,** which leads visitors on a tour by numbers through the historic building and Swiss history from early Christian Europe until the present. Beyond the museum, the world's oldest working organ (c. 1390-1430) rests among the faded murals of the **Basilique du Château de Valère** and can be heard at the annual organ festival every Saturday at 4pm in July and August. (Tours in French, English, and German from mid-March until mid-November every hour 10:15am-4:15pm except 3:15pm; also 5:15pm tour June-Sept. Museum 6SFr, children 3SFr, families 12SFr; basilique 3SFr/1.50SFr/6SFr. Combined ticket 7SFr/4.50SFr/15SFr. Museum open Oct.-May 11am-5pm, closed Mondays; June-Sept. 1-6pm. Basilisque open Oct.-May Tu-Sa 10am-5pm, Su 2-5pm; June-Sept. M-Sa 10am-6pm; Su 2-6pm.) The **Château de Tourbillon** offers free admittance to beautiful views and peaceful yards perfect for picnicking. Ask at the tourist office or any museum about the passport to all Swiss museums (2 days within 15, 12SFr).

Summer evenings bring **free concerts** of classical music through the **Academie de Musique** (☎322 66 52) and fusions of rock, funk, and jazz during **Festiv** (second weekend in June), as well as **Open-air Cinema** (last week in June-July).

The Valais canton produces some of Switzerland's finest wines. Most cafes have whitewashed terraces where patrons sip whites *(Fendant* or *Johannisberg)* and reds *(Gamay or Dole)*. Consult the tourist office for organized **wine-tasting excursions** and a list of local cellars. A long-distance path through the vineyards, *le chemin du vignoble*, passes close to Sion and through tasting territory. Always call before arriving at a cellar, and try to organize a group if you want the proprietor to be more welcoming. One *centre de dégustation* is **Le Verre à Pied,** ave. du Grand-Pont 29, which houses 150 wines from multiple sellers throughout the region. (☎/fax 321 13 80. Open 10:30am-1pm and 4-8pm or by reservation.)

MARTIGNY ☎027

French-speaking Martigny (pop. 14,000) serves as one of the major access points to the jagged peak of Mont Blanc (4807m), which straddles the French and Italian borders. The oldest town in Valais, Martigny has long been the center of passages across the Alps, serving Hannibal, Caesar, Charlemagne, and Napoleon, and the architecture displays the resulting multi-cultural influence. A medieval castle towers in the west while a Roman amphitheater stands in the east. Thanks to the **Fondation Pierre Gianadda**, Martigny is a center for modern art and classical music.

▛ TRANSPORTATION. Frequent **trains** west to: Aigle (20min., every 30min. 5am-8pm, every hr. until 11pm, 9.80SFr); Lausanne (45-60min., every 30min. 5am-8am, every hr. until 11pm, 21SFr); and Montreux (30min., every 30min. 5am-8pm, every hr. until 11pm, 15.20SFr); and east to Sion (15-25min., 3 per hr. 6:10am-9:10pm, 2 per hr. until 12:54am, 9.20SFr). A private line travels to Châtelard (45min., every hr. 6:42am-7:48pm, less often Sept. 15-Dec. 16 and Apr. 7-June 16; one-way 16.60SFr), where you change for Chamonix in France (one-way 12SFr, round-trip 15SFr), a starting point for the 10- to 14-day Mont Blanc circuit. The line goes to Orsières (30min., every hr. 7:12am-8:11pm, one-way 9.80SFr), where you change for a bus to Aosta in Italy via the St. Bernard Pass (1½hr., 8:35am and 5pm, one-way 19.80SFr). The **information office** is across the street from the station (☎723 37 01; open M-F 8am-12pm and 1:30-6pm, Sa 8am-12pm). **Buses** run to Champex and the Col de la Forclaz pass, starting points for Mont Blanc, through the **Post Bus** service (☎327 34 34). The station (open M-F 6:15am-8pm, Sa 6:15am-7:15pm, Su 7:45am-12pm and 1:30-7:15pm; call ☎0900 300 300 for schedule information) has a **travel agency.** (Open M-F 9am-noon and 1:30-6pm, Sa 9am-noon and 1:30-5pm.)

▛▟ ORIENTATION AND PRACTICAL INFORMATION. The **tourist office,** pl. Centrale 9, is straight down ave. de la Gare at the far corner of pl. Centrale. (☎721 22 20; fax 22 24. Open May-Sept. M-F 9am-6pm, Sa 8:30am-12:30pm and 1:30-5:30pm, Su 10am-12:30pm and 4-6pm; Oct.-Apr. M-F 8:30am-noon and 1:30-6:30pm, Sa 8:30am-noon.) In the train station, services include: **taxi,** ☎722 22 00 or 21 17; **currency exchange, lockers** (3-5SFr), **luggage storage** (5SFr), and **bike rental** (30SFr per day, 23SFr per half-day). Emergency numbers include: **police,** ☎117; **ambulance** ☎144. The **hospital** (☎603 90 00) has a switchboard that connects you to the late-night doctor and pharmacy. **Internet** access (4SFr per 15min.) at **Cyber Cafe, Casino and Cinema,** on the right halfway between the station and pl. Centrale at r. de la Gare 27. (☎722 13 93. Open M-F 6:00am-midnight, Sa 7am-midnight, Su 9am-11pm.) The **post office,** ave. de la Gare 32, between the station and the tourist office, has a public **fax** and an **ATM.** (☎722 26 72. Open M-F 7:30am-noon and 1:30-6:30pm, Sa 8am-noon.) **Postal code:** CH-1920.

▛ ACCOMMODATIONS AND CAMPING. Budget pickings are slim because travelers in Martigny are mainly business types. About a 5min. walk from the train station stands **Hotel Grand-Quai ❹,** which offers long carpeted hallways of sparse, clean rooms. Reservations suggested for the few single rooms. Breakfast included. (☎722 20 50 or 55 98; fax 723 21 66; info@grandquai.com; www.grandquai.com. From the train station turn left and go to r. du Simplon; the hotel is on the left (5min.). Singles 70SFr; doubles 100SFr.)

Auberge de la Poste ❸ provides lodgings for 5 individuals at the corner of Grand-St. Bernard and r. Du Levant. Rooms are comfortable and relatively clean, once guests get past the tilting floors. (☎722 25 17. Breakfast included. Open Tu-Sa 8am-midnight. Floor bathrooms and showers. Reserve ahead. Singles 45SFr; doubles 80SFr. AmEx/DC/MC/V.)

Camping Les Neuvilles ❶, r. du Levant 68, packs its shaded plot with motor homes. From the station, head straight on ave. de la Gare, take the second left onto ave. des Neuvilles, and turn right onto r. du Levant. Amenities include playgrounds, a store, laundry, a sauna (7SFr), miniature golf (5SFr, children 3SFr), and a solarium. (☎722 45 44; fax 35 44. Reception 8am-noon and 2-8pm. Showers included. 7.60SFr per person, tents 8SFr, 18SFr per car. Additional trash charge 1SFr. AmEx/DC/MC/V.)

FOOD. Cafes crowd Martigny's tree-lined pl. Centrale, some with *Menüs* in the 15-25SFr range. For cheaper fare, **Lords' Sandwiches ❶,** ave. du Grand-St.-Bernard 15, a continuation of r. de la Gare past pl. Centrale, serves 36 kinds of sandwiches (3.80-11.80SFr), including a bacon burger with fries, and the Zeus, an overstuffed roast beef sandwich. Vegetarian options are limited, but try the Socrates with tomatoes, mushrooms, and cheese. (☎723 35 98. Open M-Th 8am-10:30pm, F 8am-11:30pm, Sa 8:30am-11:30pm, Su 3-10:30pm.) **Crêperie Le Rustique ❶,** ave. de la Gare 44, lives up to its name with a dark wood interior and nature scenes painted on stucco. Enjoy savory crepes (9.50-14SFr) or sweet ones (4.50-9.50SFr), washed down with a 3.50SFr mug of cider. (☎722 88 33. Open M-F 8am-11pm, Sa 10:30am-midnight, Su 1:30-11pm.) For straightforward Italian food, try **Pizzeria au Grotto ❷,** r. du Rhône 3, off r. Marc-Morand to the left of pl. Centrale. Follow pizza (8-19SFr) with a monster tirimisu for 5SFr. (☎722 02 46. Open M-Th 8:30am-11pm, F 8:30am-midnight, Sa 10am-midnight, Su 10am-11pm. AmEx/MC/V.) Another Italian option, **Pizzeria d'Octodure ❷,** features a variety of pastas (13-18SFr) and brick-oven pizzas (8-18SFr) made in a semi-open kitchen. Follow ave. de la Gare, turn right on R. Marc-Morand, circle left around the church and three blocks down R. d'Octodure for tasty pizza in a classy setting. (☎722 08 08. Open daily noon-2pm and 7-11pm. MC/V.) The immense **Migros** supermarket at pl. du Manoir 5, just off pl. Centrale, offers all that your picnicking heart desires, while the popular park behind the market can provide the perfect setting. (Open M-Th 8:15am-6:30pm, F 8:15am-8pm, Sa 8am-5pm; Migros restaurant open M-Th 7:30am-6:30pm, F 7:30am-8pm, Sa 7:30am-5pm.) The **public market,** on ave. de la Gare Thursday mornings, sells edible and wearable goods. (Open 8am-noon.)

SIGHTS. The **Fondation Pierre Gianadda,** r. du Forum 59, is Martigny's most engaging attraction. Head down the r. Hôtel-de-Ville behind the tourist office and follow the signs. The foundation displays the mildly interesting **Gallo-Roman Museum** as the permanent collection, while the central atrium and a barn-like building behind host blockbuster international traveling exhibitions. The special exhibits have included artists such as Chagall, Manet, Picasso, Van Gogh, and da Vinci and tend to overshadow the rest of the museum. Downstairs, the entertaining **Automobile Museum** draws a crowd of its own with exhibits of more than 50 vintage cars (1897-1939), including a 1897 Benz, and a Delaunay-Belleville that belonged to Czar Nicholas II. The garden surrounding the foundation contains interesting Gallo-Roman remains and several modern sculptures, including some by Brancusi, Miró, and Rodin. Especially amusing are the bronze sculptures of giant body parts by César. Admission to the illuminated park is free on summer nights. (☎722 39 78; info@gianadda.ch; www.gianadda.ch. Open Nov.-June 10am-6pm and June-Nov. 9am-7pm. Guided tours W 8pm in French or by prior arrangement. Wheelchair accessible. 14SFr, students 12SFr, family ticket 30SFr.) The foundation hosts classical music concerts, many in conjunction with the **Festival Tibor Varga** (see p. 470) and the **Montreux Voice and Music Festival** (see p. 502).

The Fondation also leads 1½hr. **guided tours** of Martigny that include the exhibits. (July 15-Aug. 15 10:30am, 2:30pm; Sept.-June by appointment for groups only. 80SFr plus museum entrance for 2hr.) If you want to explore on your own, the office distributes a brochure detailing a walking tour of Martigny's Roman ruins *(promenade archéologique)*. Past the railroad tracks, remnants of a Roman road point toward Britannia and, through the pass, Roma. Nearby, the grassy 4th-century **Amphithéâtre Romain** is the spectacular setting for the final contest of the Valais **cow fighting** season (see "Cowfight," p. 470). **Le Château de la Bâtiaz,** the ruins of a 13th-century castle, complete with dungeon and tower, once belonged to the bishops of Sion. From the station head along ave. de la Gare and turn right at pl. Centrale along r. Marc-Morand. Climb the massive stone tower extending over an outcropping of bare rock for a bird's-eye perspective of the flat Rhône floodplain. (Open May 16-June 23 and Aug. 26-Oct. 12 F 4pm-midnight, Sa 10am-midnight, Su 10am-6pm; June 24-Aug. 25 opens Th at 4pm. Free.)

FESTIVALS. Martigny hosts the **Foire du Valais,** the trade fair of Valais, in the blue-and-yellow convention center Oct. 3-12 (10-12SFr), where local businessmen and farmers offer everything from shoes to marble sculptures. The first weekend brings two days of all-day **cow fighting,** a must-see event. The **Foire du Lard** (Bacon Fair) has overtaken the pl. Centrale every first Monday in December since the Middle Ages. Traditionally, Valais mountain folk descended on Martigny to stock up on pork products for the winter. Now the festival has expanded to a large open-air market, but the pig still reigns supreme. Also keep an ear out for the **Folklore Festival** in July and August 2004, which will feature international music and displays.

VERBIER ☎ 027

Although it may seem like a typical mountain town, Verbier (pop. 2,500) is a polished resort spanning an altitude of 1500-3330m and serving around one million visitors annually. Multi-star hotels are streamlined, shiny derivations of the classic chalet design. The slopes are the big story in Verbier; its transportation system is designed to move skiers and snowboarder between cable cars. Other sports in the winter and summer thrive as well, casting an athletic glow over this town that's constantly expanding up the mountain. In May and June everything (hotels, shops, restaurants, cable cars, etc.) closes, and the streets are virtually silent.

VALAIS

⬛ TRANSPORTATION. Getting to Verbier is a 2-step process—from Martigny to Le Châble, then from Le Châble to Verbier. It lies on the high-speed train line that connects Montreux and Lausanne to Sion and Brig. The **St. Bernard Express** runs trains to Le Châble (30min., every hr. 8am-6:53pm, 9.80SFr, Eurail and SwissPass valid). Take the **Post Bus** (25min., every hr. 8:32am-7:30pm, 5.20SFr) or the **cable car** (10min., runs nonstop Nov.-Apr. 8:30am-6:45pm, 7SFr, round-trip 13SF) to Verbier. In winter, a **bus** goes directly from Martigny to Verbier; reservations are crucial; there is only 1 bus on Friday evenings and 3 on Saturdays. **Téléverbier** offers **free local bus** service in town (limited between seasons).

⬛ ⬛ ORIENTATION AND PRACTICAL INFORMATION. The **tourist office,** pl. Centrale, publishes the amazingly informative booklet *Le Guide* in 4 languages. (☎775 38 88; fax 38 89; info@verbier.ch; www.verbier.ch. Open M-F 8am-noon and 2-6:30pm, Sa 9am-noon and 4-6:30pm, Su 9am-noon; extended hours in season.) Services include **currency exchange** at the station at Le Châble; **ATM** at the Banque Cantonale du Valais, on pl. Centrale across from and to the right of the tourist office; **luggage** storage at the post office (2SFr); and **bike rental** at several sports shops (see p. 475). **Taxis,** ☎771 77 71 or 34 65. **Police,** ☎117; **hospital,** ☎771 66 77. **Pharmacy** to the right of the tourist office. (☎771 66 22; fax 51 88; emergency ☎771 21 22. Open M-Sa 8:30am-12:15pm and 2:30-6:30pm, Su 10am-12:15pm and 5-6:30pm. AmEx/DC/MC/V.) **Internet** available at **Harold's,** left of the pharmacy (☎771 62 43), or at the **Centre Polysportif** (☎771 66 01). **Weather** report (☎0900 55 21 68). **Post office,** r. de la Poste, just off pl. Centrale (open M-F 9am-noon and 3-6pm, Sa 9-11am) is also the **Post Bus** station. **Postal code:** CH-1936.

> **BOMBS AWAY** Switzerland may be a neutral country, but that doesn't mean its citizens are unprepared for an attack. Every Swiss household must either build its own bomb shelter or pay a yearly fee to reserve one bed per person at a community one. You never know when those shelters will come in handy: in the winter of 1998, hundreds of Verbier residents crowded into the local bomb-shelter (today's hostel, the Bunker) to seek shelter from a deadly avalanche.

ACCOMMODATIONS & CAMPING. The Bunker ❷, under hip new management, caters to young snowboarders during the winter. The hostel is a bomb shelter (see "Bombs Away") beneath the city's Centre Polysportif, a 10min. walk down r. de la Poste from the bus station. Concrete walls and steel vault doors have been painted bright pink, but the place retains a military feel, with no windows and up to 45 cramped beds (3-story bunks separated by fireproof curtains) per room. Services include: shuttle bus to ski lifts, vouchers for ski specials, lounge with cable TV and VCR, **Internet,** and free access to skating rinks, indoor and outdoor pools, sauna, squash courts, and beach volleyball courts at the sports center. (☎771 66 04; fax 66 03; sleep@thebunker.ch; www.thebunker.ch. Breakfast, 3-course dinner, showers, and lockers included. 25SFr deposit for sheets, blanket, and key. Reception 9am-9pm. Open mid-June-April. 35SFr. AmEx/DC/MC/V, min. 50SFr.) For those who prefer the more traditional hostel arrangement, the brand-new **Summer house ❸** next door has sunny rooms that overlook the pool and free access to the sports center. (☎771 66 04; fax 771 66 03. Reservations highly recommended. 4- or 8-bed room including breakfast and showers at the sports center 50SFr. AmEx/DC/MC/V, min. 50SFr.) The classically Swiss **Les Touristes ❸,** is at the bottom of the r. de Verbier in Verbier Village. (☎/fax 771 21 47; www.verbier.ch/les touristes. Singles with or without showers, 60-70SFr; doubles with or without showers, 110-135SFr.) In winter, the **campsite ❶** (☎776 20 51) is outside Le Châble.

FOOD. Though Verbier is on its way to major-ski-resort status, many of its restaurants are budget-friendly; young internationals keep the nightlife jumping and accessible to Anglophones. Restaurants, bars, and clubs pack pl. Centrale and the roads radiating from it. ◧**Le Crok No Name Bar ❶,** named after its previous building, Aux Croquignoles, keeps things short and simple, drawing hip locals and sportsters alike with a tile exterior, terra-cotta bar, and long leather couches. *Panini* sandwiches (8SFr) served, plus frequent rock, funk, or jazz concerts. (☎771 69 34. Open May-June and Sept.-Nov. M, Th-Su 5pm-2am; July and Aug. daily noon-2am; Dec.-Apr. daily 5pm-2am.) **Le Monde des Crêpes ❷** (☎771 28 95), 2min. down r. de la Poste from pl. Centrale, puts an alternative twist on a traditional *crêperie*.

For Italian specialties, hike up the r. des Creux from pl. Centrale to the **Pizzeria Al Capone ❸.** Shorten the walk by taking the Téléverbier bus to "Brunnet" in season. Try pizza (14-19SFr), gnocchi (21SFr), or *plats du jour* (18-20SFr). Diners can eat in the rustic dining room cabin or get an eyeful of snow-capped peaks and neon paragliders on the large terrace. (☎771 67 74. Open daily 8:30am-10pm; food served 11:30am-1:30pm and 6:30-9:30pm. Call in advance for dinner reservations during the high season.) **Le Caveau ❸,** to the right of the tourist office, serves Swiss and local specialties such as *Raclette*, fondue, and *Rösti*. Try the toast smothered in cheese, or the *assiette du jour* for 17SFr. (☎771 22 26. Open noon-2pm and 6:30-10pm.) For picnickers, **Denner superdiscount** is down r. de Verbier from pl. Centrale. (Open M-Tu and Th-F 8:30am-12:15pm and 2:30-6:30pm, Sa 8:30am-12:15pm and 2-5pm.) The **Co-op** is down r. de la Poste. (Open M-W and F 8:30am-12:15pm and 2:30-6:30pm, Th 8:30am-12:15pm, Sa 8:30am-12:15pm and 2:30-5pm.)

⊠ OUTDOOR ACTIVITIES AND ENTERTAINMENT. Verbier has a total of 400km of **ski** runs; its best runs are on the **Mont Fort glacier** (3329m), which offers skiing and snowboarding Nov.-Apr. A behemoth cable car, the **Téléjumbo,** can carry 150 passengers at a time to the glacier via Col des Gentianes (also the site of a snowboard half-pipe). From the Médran cable car station (up the r. de Médran from the tourist office), another cable car runs through Les Ruinettes to **Attelas** (2193m), and farther to **Mont Gelë** (3023m). Those content with a smaller venue can access Verbier's northern slopes with the **Savoleyres** cable car at the end of rte. des Creux. Ski pass prices and cable car schedules are complicated—make sure to pick up the pertinent info at the tourist or Téléverbier offices. (☎775 25 11; www.televerbier.ch; infor@televerbier.ch. 2-day pass to the 4-valley region and Mont Fort 115SFr; for the Verbier slopes only 100SFr. 3-day passes 167/145SFr. Photo ID required. Non-skier day pass 38SFr/21SFr. Ages 16-20 15% off, seniors and ages 6-15 30% off; reduced family rates.) Rental shops in Verbier abound and all offer rentals for the same price, although some stores have deals with certain accommodations. **Medran Sports** down r. de Verbier from the pl. Centrale rents equipment. Skis and snowboards (38SFr). Children 7-12 (18SFr/28SFr). Boots (19SFr for adults and 15SFr for children). Bikes 38SFr per day, 30SFr per half-day. (☎771 60 48). The tourist office makes recommendations to skiers based on skill level; they do the same for the summer **hikers.** For lesson contact **La Maison du Sport** (☎775 33 63; www.maisondusport.com), **La Fantastique** (☎771 41 41; fax 771 42 41; lafantastique@verbier.ch; www.lafantastique.com), or **Adrenaline** (☎771 74 59; fax 74 01; info@adrenaline-verbier.ch; www.adrenaline-verbier.ch).

In summer, La Maison du Sport offers multi-day guided excursions, hikes, adventures in canyoning and rafting, and even a **Kid's Club** for children over 3. There are plenty of opportunities to join the flock of paragliders in Verbier's skies. **Max Biplace** (☎771 55 55 or (079) 219 36 55) offers tandem flights—book at La Fantastique. The **Centre de Parapente,** near the Centre Polysportif (☎771 68 18; www.flyverbier.ch), offers tandem **paragliding** (170SFr). The multi-level **Centre Polysportif** (☎771 66 01, open 8am-11pm.), downhill from pl. Centrale on r. de la Poste, has a **swimming pool** (8SFr, children ages 6-16 5SFr, closes at 9pm), **ice-skating** (6/4SFr; skate rentals 6SFr/5SFr), **squash** (12-14SFr per 30min.), and **tennis** (23SFr per hr.) and houses the Bunker and summer house (see **Accommodations**).

In summer, Verbier draws an array of talented performers to its **classical musical festival** (July 18th-August 3rd 2003), which began in 1994 and has included musicians Kent Nagano, Bobby McFerrin and Björk. In 2000 the main sponsor founded the Verbier Youth Orchestra which performs at the festival under the direction of James Levine. Tickets, 30-120SFr, are available by phone or on location. (☎771 82 82; www.verbierfestival.com.) Free events are posted each day of the festival.

V A L A I S

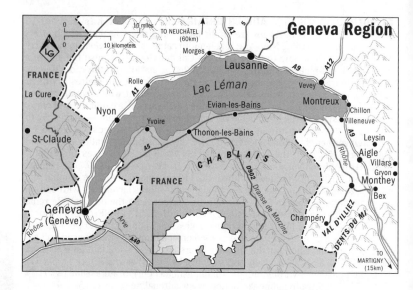

GENEVA AND LAC LÉMAN

All around Lac Léman, hills sprinkled with villas and blanketed by patchwork vineyards sewn with garlands of ripening grapes seem tame and settled...until the haze clears. From behind the hills surge rough-hewn mountain peaks, and in that moment, the lake discards its pretty, cultivated urbanity for the energizing promise of unpopulated wilderness and wide lonely expanses. Many travelers suffer financial anxiety when they consider venturing to the refined Lac Léman region, since high prices are the general rule in tourist-infested Geneva, Lausanne, and Montreux. However, adventurers discover that towns along the lake abound with three of Switzerland's cheapest commodities: tranquility is just a short stroll along a tree-lined quai or into vine-laced hills, chocolate is available for a pittance nearly everywhere, and unforgettable views are, as always, free and plentiful.

HIGHLIGHTS OF LAC LÉMAN

Be moved to humanitarian action at **Geneva's Red Cross Museum** (p. 488).

Find radical inspiration at Lausanne's **Collection de l'Art Brut** (p. 488), then regain peace of mind on a pedal boat.

Tiptoe through the dungeon at Montreux's chilling **Chateau Chillon** (p. 502).

Meet thousands of cool cats in mid-July at the **Montreux Jazz Festival (p. 502)**.

GENEVA (GENÈVE, GENF) ☎ 022

As the most international city in Switzerland, Geneva is a brew of 178,000 unlikely neighbors: wealthy businessmen speed past young artists in the streets, while nuclear families share the sidewalks with dreadlocked skaters. Isolated from the rest of Switzerland both ideologically and geographically, Geneva has a sense of independence that unites the city's proudly eclectic group of citizens.

Genevans have a long tradition of protecting their political and religious independence. As a strategic site, where the Rhône River flows out of Lac Léman, medieval Geneva fended off repeated attacks. In 1536 the city welcomed an unknown 25-year-old, John Calvin, and his version of the Protestant Reformation, voting en masse to convert. His fiery sermons (1536-1564) brought waves of persecuted French and Italian refugees to this "Rome of Protestants." Geneva waged a battle for freedom from the Catholic House of Savoy, whose duke sought to crush both Protestantism and Genevan democracy.

Over the next 150 years, Reformists' zeal occasionally took the form of authoritarian rule, exemplified by the burning of books by Rousseau and Calvin's detractors. Geneva's cosmopolitanism eventually won out, and it became a gathering place for aesthetes and free thinkers. Voltaire lived and worked in the Geneva area, and compatriot Madame de Staël held salons in nearby Coppet. In the early 19th century, mountain-loving romantics Shelley and Byron found inspiration in the city's surroundings. Lenin lived here in the early 1900s before being sent back to Moscow in a sealed train by German leaders hoping to disrupt the Russian government. Under the inspiration of native Henri Dunant, the **International Committee of the Red Cross** established itself in Geneva in 1864, and nations from around the world signed the peace-keeping First Geneva Convention. In 1919, Geneva's selection as the site for the **League of Nations** confirmed the city's reputation as a center for both international organizations and arbitrations. Geneva is still the European office of the **United Nations (UN)** and dozens of other international bodies, from the Center for European Nuclear Research to the World Council of Churches.

⚔ INTERCITY TRANSPORTATION

Flights: **Cointrin Airport** (☎ 717 71 11, flight information 799 31 11; fax 798 43 77) is a hub for **Swiss Airlines** (☎0848 85 20 00). Bus #10 runs to the Gare Cornavin (15min., every 5-10min., 2.20SFr). The ticket dispenser requires exact change—large bills can be broken at the "changeomat" behind the escalator. For a shorter trip to Gare Cornavin, take the train (6min., every 10min., 4.80SFr). There are several flights per day to **Amsterdam, London, Paris, New York,** and **Rome. Air France** (☎827 87 87) has 11 per day to Paris, and **British Airways** (☎0848 80 10 10) has 9 per day to London.

Trains: All trains run approximately 4:30am-1am. There are two stations:

Gare Cornavin, pl. Cornavin, is the main station. To: **Basel** (2¾hr., every hr. 4:44am-8:44pm, 63-71SFr); **Bern** (2hr., every hr. 4:34am-8:34pm, 47SFr); **Interlaken** (3hr., every hr. 4:34am-9:30pm, 63SFr); **Lausanne** (40min., every 30min. 4:34am-12:11am, 18.80SFr); **Milan** (4hr., 8 per day, 82SFr); **Montreux** (1hr., 2 per hr. 5:16am-11:18pm, 29SFr); **Paris** (3¾hr., 10 per day 5:47am-10:23pm, 103SFr); **Vienna** (10-12hr., 4 per day 6:30am-7:30pm, 189SFr); and **Zurich** (3½hr., every 30min., 76SFr). To book a seat on long-distance or international trains, join the throng at the reservation and information counter. Open M-F 8:30am-6:30pm, Sa 9am-5pm. The **24hr. rail information** number is ☎0900 30 03 00 (1.19SFr per min.).

Gare des Eaux-Vives (☎736 16 20), on ave. de la Gare des Eaux-Vives (Tram #12, "Amandoliers SNCF"), connects to France's regional rail lines through **Annecy** (1½hr., 6 per day, 14SFr) or **Chamonix** (2½hr., 4 per day, 24SFr). The ticket machine at the station does not return change. Ticket office open M-F 9am-6pm, Sa 11am-5:45pm.

CGN Ferries: (☎312 52 23) connect Geneva to **Lausanne** and **Montreux,** departing from quai du Mont-Blanc. A round-trip ticket (54-74SFr, ages 16-25 half-price, seniors 20% discount) includes the option of returning to Geneva by train.

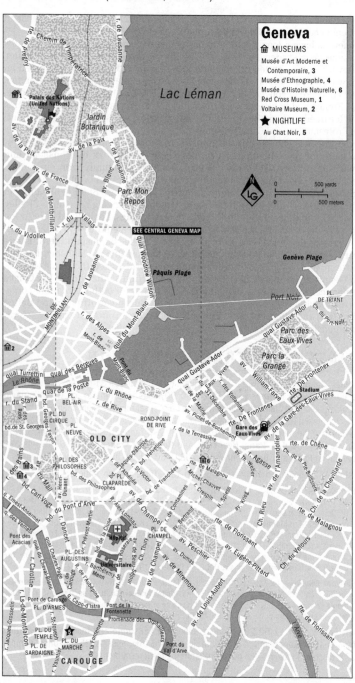

Geneva

🏛 **MUSEUMS**

Musée d'Art Moderne et
Contemporaire, **3**
Musée d'Ethnographie, **4**
Musée d'Histoire Naturelle, **6**
Red Cross Museum, **1**
Voltaire Museum, **2**

⭐ **NIGHTLIFE**

Au Chat Noir, **5**

Lac Léman

rte. de Chemin de l'Impératrice
rte. de pregny
r. de Lausanne

🏛1 Palais des Nations
(United Nations)

*Jardin
Botanique*

av. de la Paix
av. de la Paix
r. de France
r. de Montbrillant

r. Blanc
r. de Lausanne

*Parc Mon
Repos*

r. du Vidollet
r. du Valais

SEE CENTRAL GENEVA MAP

Pâquis Plage

Genève Plage

r. de Lausanne
quai Woodrow Wilson

r. des Alpes
r. de Mont-Blanc
quai du Mont-Blanc

Port Noir

PL.
DE TRIANT

Ch. du Port-Noir

🏛2

PL. DE MONTBRILLANT

quai Turrettini
Le Rhône
quai des Bergues

quai Gustave-Ador

quai Gustave-Ador
*Parc des
Eaux-Vives*

av. William-Favre
*Parc la
Grange*

quai de la Poste
r. du Rhône
PL.
BEL-AIR
r. de Rive
Pont du Mont-Blanc

r. du Stand
bd. Georges Favon
PL. DU
CIRQUE
ROND-POINT
DE RIVE
r. de la Terrassière
av. Pictet-de-Rochemont
r. de Malagnou
rte. De Frontenex

rte. de Chêne
Stadium

r. des Rois
bd. de St. Georges
PL.
NEUVE
OLD CITY
r. du 31 Décembre
r. des Vollandes
r. des Eaux-Vives
av. de la Gare-des-Eaux-Vives
Gare des
Eaux-Vives

r. des Bains
PL. DES
PHILOSOPHES
🏛3
🏛4
bd. du Mail
bd. Carl-Vogt
av. Henri-Dunant
r. des Philosophes
PL.
CLAPARÈDE
bd. des Philosophes
r. St-Victor
av. de Champel
bd. des Tranchées
r. de Contamines
r. Michel-Chauvet
🏛6
av. A. Gasse
av. Th. Weber
av. de l'Amandolier
Ch. de la Pre-Basson
rte. de la Chevillarde

av. Ernest-Ansermet
a. des Vernets
bd. du Pont d'Arve
r. Alex Lombard
r. Crespin
r. Spiess
Ch. Krieg
Ch. Rieu
rte. de Florissant
Ch. du Velours
rte. de Malagnou

Pont des
Acacias
quai du Cheval-Blanc
r. Dancet
r. Prévost-Martin
r. de la Cluse
PL. DE
CHAMPEL
av. Peschier
av. Dumas
av. de Miremont
rte. de Florissant
av. Eugène-Pittard

Hôpital

PL. DES
AUGUSTINS
Universitaire
r. Barthélemy-Menn
r. de l'Athénée
av. de Champel
av. Bertrand

r. Caroline
r. Ls-de-Montfalcon
PL. D'ARMES
Pont de Carouge
PL. DES
AUGUSTINS
Capo-d'Istra
Pont de la
Fontenette
Promenade des Orpailleurs
av. de Louis-Aubert
rte. de Florissant

r. Jacques-Grosselin
PL. DU
TEMPLE
PL. DE
SARDAIGNE
St-Joseph
PL. DU
MARCHÉ
r. Vautier
r. de la Fontenette
Pont du
Val d'Arve

CAROUGE

0   500 yards
0   500 meters

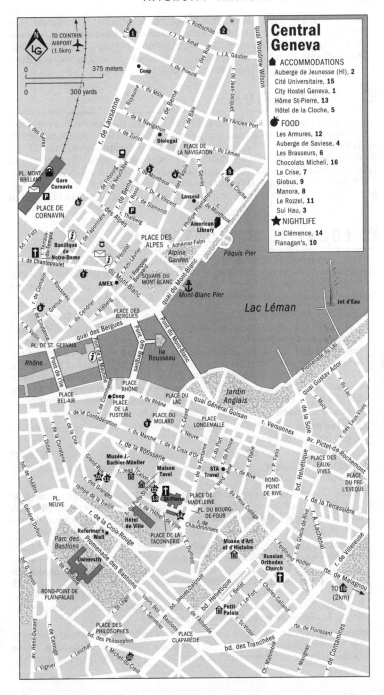

Central Geneva

🏠 **ACCOMMODATIONS**

Auberge de Jeunesse (HI), **2**
Cité Universitaire, **15**
City Hostel Geneva, **1**
Hôme St-Pierre, **13**
Hôtel de la Cloche, **5**

🍴 **FOOD**

Les Armures, **12**
Auberge de Saviese, **4**
Les Brasseurs, **6**
Chocolats Micheli, **16**
La Crise, **7**
Globus, **9**
Manora, **8**
Le Rozzel, **11**
Sui Hau, **3**

⭐ **NIGHTLIFE**

La Clémence, **14**
Flanagan's, **10**

GENEVA AND LAC LÉMAN

By car: Geneva is more accessible from **France** than from the rest of Switzerland. From the **west**, take A40, which continues on to **Lausanne** and **Montreux**. From the **south** take N201 north. From the **north**, take A40 from France or Switzerland. From the **east**, take A40 west. N1 is the best way to reach Geneva from Lausanne or Montreux. Route numbers are not always visible; follow signs for Geneva.

■: ORIENTATION

Geneva began as a fortified city on a hill, and the historic vieille ville's (old city) labyrinthine cobbled streets and quiet squares around John Calvin's **Cathédrale de St-Pierre** still occupy the heart of the urban landscape. Across the Rhône River to the north, billionaires' banks and 5-star hotels gradually give way to lakeside promenades. Farther north, another hill holds the UN, Red Cross, WTO, and rolling green parkland. Across the Arve river to the south lies the village of Carouge, home to many student bars and clubs (take tram #12 or #13 to "pl. du Marché").

▐ LOCAL TRANSPORTATION

Carry your passport at all times; the French border is never more than a few minutes away and buses cross it frequently. Ticket purchasing is largely on the honor system and some backpackers try to get away without paying. *Let's Go* does not recommend fare evasion; fines run 60SFr. Much of the city is walkable.

Public Transportation: Geneva has an efficient bus and tram network. Major hubs are Gare Cornavin, Rd.-Pt. de Plainpalais, and pl. Bel Air (near the ponts de l'Ile). **Transport Publics Genevois** (☎308 34 34), next to the tourist office in Gare Cornavin, provides a free map of local bus routes called *Le Réseau;* the timetables cost a few francs. Open M-Sa 7am-7pm, Su 10am-6pm. Trips that stay within zone 10 (most of the city) cost 2.20SFr; 3 stops or fewer 1.80SFr. Full-day passes 6SFr for 1 zone, 12SFr for 4. Swiss-Pass valid on all buses; Eurail not valid. **Buses** run roughly 5:30am-midnight. **Noctambus** (3SFr) runs 1:30-4:30am. Buy multi-fare and day tickets at the train station, others at automatic vendors at every stop. Stamp multi-use tickets before boarding.

Taxis: Taxi-Phone (☎331 41 33). 6.80SFr plus 2.90SFr per km. Taxi from airport to city around 30SFr, max. 4 passengers (15-20min.).

Car Rental: Avis, r. de Lausanne 44 (☎731 90 00). **Europcar,** r. de Lausanne 37 (☎909 69 90). **Budget,** r. de Zurich 36 (☎900 24 00). All offices at the airport; check for surcharges (around 11%).

Parking: On-street 1SFr per hr. The garage (☎736 66 30) under Cornavin station (enter at pl. Cornavin) is 2SFr for 1hr., 4-6SFr for 2hr. from 7am-7pm; 1SFr per hr. after 7pm. **Garage Les Alpes,** r. Thalberg, is 2SFr per hr. weekdays, 1SFr per hr. nights and weekends. Digital boards on highways list carparks and the number of vacant spaces.

Bike Rental: Geneva is pedal-happy, with well-marked bike paths and special traffic lights for spoked traffic. For routes, get *Itineraires cyclables* or *Tours de ville avec les vélos de location* from the tourist office. Behind the station, **Genèv' Roule,** pl. Montbrillant 17 (☎/fax 740 13 43), has free bikes available. 50SFr deposit and photo ID required; hefty fine if bike is lost or stolen. Slightly nicer neon bikes start at 5SFr per day. Open 7:30am-9:30pm. Genèv' Roule kiosks located at Bain des Paquis, pl. du Rhône, and Plaine de Plainpalais offer the same deals.

Hitchhiking: *Let's Go* does not recommend hitchhiking. Travelers headed to Germany or northern Switzerland have been seen taking bus #4 to "Jardin Botanique." Those headed to France sometimes take bus #4 to "Palettes," then line D to "St. Julien."

⚐ PRACTICAL INFORMATION

TOURIST AND FINANCIAL SERVICES

Tourist Offices: At information offices (marked by a blue lower-case "i" sign), the free must-haves are the city map and the booklet *Info Jeunes/Young People*. The **main office,** r. du Mont-Blanc 18 (☎909 70 00; fax 70 11; info@geneve-tourisme.ch; www.geneve-tourisme.ch), lies 5min. away from Gare Cornavin toward the pont du Mont-Blanc, within the Central Post Office Building. English-speaking staff books hotel rooms (5SFr fee), offers **walking tours,** and provides information on just about everything. The office maintains a free direct phone line to Geneva hotels in Gare Cornavin, as well as a board listing budget accommodations. Open July-Aug. daily 9am-6pm; Sept.-June M-Sa 9am-6pm. During the summer, head for Geneva's **Centre d'Accueil et de Renseignements (CAR;** ☎ 731 46 47), parked in pl. Mont-Blanc, by the Metro Shopping entrance to Cornavin Station. This office-in-a-bus is geared toward young people and posts a list of free musical and theatrical performances, updated daily. Makes hotel reservations free of charge. Open mid-June to mid-Sept. daily 9am-9pm.

Budget Travel: STA, r. de la Rive 10 (☎818 02 00; www.statravel.ch). Student fares. Also home to an extensive travel bookstore. Open M 1-6:30pm, Tu-F 9am-6:30pm, Sa 9am-5pm. AmEx/MC/V.

Consulates: Australia, chemin des Fins 2 (☎799 91 00; fax 91 78); **Canada,** ave. de l'Ariana 5 (☎919 92 00; fax 92 77); **New Zealand,** chemin des Fins 2 (☎929 03 50; fax 03 74); **South Africa,** r. de Rhône 65 (☎849 54 54; fax 54 32); **UK,** r. de Vermont 37 (☎918 24 26; fax 23 22); **US,** R. Versonnex 5 (☎840 51 60; recorded information 51 61; fax 51 62). Call to schedule appointments.

Currency Exchange: ATMs offer the best rates and are easy to find in Geneva. There are a few at Gare Cornavin, at the top of the escalators from the platforms. For traditional service, Gare Cornavin has good rates and doesn't charge commission on traveler's checks. Advances cash on credit cards (min. 200SFr), and arranges **Western Union** transfers. Open M-Sa 6:50am-7:40pm, Su 6:50am-6:40pm. Western Union desk open M-Sa 7am-7:30pm, Su 7am-6:30pm.

American Express: r. du Mont-Blanc 7, P.O. Box 1032, CH-1211 Geneva 01 (☎731 76 00; fax 732 72 11). Mail held 2-3 months. All banking services; reasonable exchange rates. Hotel and train (50SFr) reservations and tickets for tours. Open Nov.-Mar. M-F 8:30am-5:45pm; Apr.-Oct. M-F 8:45am-5:45pm, Sa 9am-noon.

LOCAL SERVICES

Luggage Storage: Gare Cornavin. 6SFr per day. Open M-F 7am-7:40pm, Sa-Su 8am-12:30pm and 1:30-6:45pm. Lockers 4-7SFr. Open 4:30am-12:45am.

Lost Property: with the luggage storage (☎0512 25 14 33). Open M-F 8am-2pm.

Bookstores: ELM (English Language and Media) Video and Books, r. Versonnex 5 (☎736 09 45; fax 786 14 29), has a quality range of new books and a book ordering service. Open M-F 9am-6:30pm, Sa 10am-5pm. AmEx/DC/MC/V. **Librairie des Amateurs,** Grand Rue 15 (☎732 80 97), in the vieille ville. Classy secondhand dealer. Open M 2-6pm, Tu-F 11am-6pm, Sa 2pm-5pm. **Payot Libraire,** r. de Chantepoulet 5 (☎731 89 50), is Geneva's largest chain of bookstores, with an amazingly broad and well-selected stock of English-language books. Open M 2-6:30pm, Tu-W and F 9am-6:30pm, Th 9am-8pm, Sa 9am-5pm. AmEx/DC/MC/V.

Library: American Library, r. de Monthoux 3 (☎732 80 97), at Emmanuel Church. 20,000 titles. 1-month membership (35SFr) allows you to borrow books (6 max.) for 2 weeks. Small but eclectic collection of books on tape (3SFr). Open Tu, Th, and F 12:30-

5pm, W 2-7pm, Sa 10am-4pm, Su 11:30am-1pm. **City Library (Bibliothèque de la Cité),** Pl. des Trois Perdrix 5 (☎418 32 22). Open Tu-F 10am-7pm, Sa 10am-5pm.

Bi-Gay-Lesbian Organizations: Diologai, r. de la Navigation 11-13 (☎906 40 40; www.hivnet.ch/diologai). From Gare Cornavin, turn left and walk 5min. down r. de Lausanne; turn right onto r. de la Navigation. Resource group with programs from support groups to outdoor activities. Publishes *Diologai,* a guide to French-speaking Switzerland's gay scene. Mostly male, but women welcome. Hosts W gatherings for gay men starting at 6pm; call ahead. **360°,** pl. Grenus 2 (☎741 00 70), publishes an eponymous magazine. Walk-in hours Su 4-9pm. **Gay International Group (GIG;** ☎789 18 69; gig@360.ch) is for international gay visitors or semi-permanents in Geneva, including Anglophones. Communal meals every 2-4 weeks. **Centre Femmes Natalie Barney** (women only), Chemin Chateau Bloch 19 (☎797 27 14), offers services similar to those at Diologai, but is smaller and lesbian-oriented. 24hr. answering machine with events listings; live operator W 6-8pm. **Lesbian International Group** is another support group (filozici@hotmail.com).

Laundromat: Lavseul, r. de Monthoux 29 (☎735 90 51 or 732 61 46). 5SFr to wash, 1SFr per 10min. to dry. Open daily 7am-midnight.

Public Showers: Point d'Eau, r. Chandieu 4 (☎734 22 40). Take bus #8 to "Canonnière" and turn right onto r. de Vermont; it's on the left. Free hot showers and personal hygiene center. Open M-F 3-7pm, Sa 10am-2pm. Additional location at r. de Fronteneux 48. Open M-F 9am-noon. **McClean,** at the train station, offers showers for 12SFr and toilets 1-2SFr. Open daily 6am-midnight.

EMERGENCY AND COMMUNICATIONS

Emergencies: Fire, ☎118. **Ambulance,** ☎144.

Police: r. de Berne 6 (☎117, non-emergency ☎715 38 50), next to post office.

Rape Crisis Hotline: Viol-Secours (☎345 20 20). Open M-Tu 2-6pm, W 4-8pm, Th 9am-1pm, F 9am-noon.

Late-Night Pharmacy: A changing set of 4 pharmacies is open late (9 or 11pm) nightly. Consult the closest pharmacy or *Genève Agenda* for addresses and phone numbers.

Medical Assistance: Hôpital Cantonal, r. Micheli-du-Crest 24 (☎372 33 11). Bus #1 or 5 or tram #12. Door #2 is for emergency care, door #3 for consultations. For information on walk-in clinics, call the **Association des Médecins** (☎320 84 20).

Internet Access: Connections Net World, r. de Monthoux 58 (☎715 38 28), offers 20 PCs. 3SFr per 30min., 5SFr per hr. Open M-Sa 9:30am-2:30am, Su 1pm-2am. Copier available. **Point 6,** r. de Vieux-Billard 7a, off r. des Bains (☎800 26 00). 5SFr per hr. Open daily noon-midnight.

Post Office: Poste Centrale, r. de Mont-Blanc 18, a block from Gare Cornavin in the stately Hôtel des Postes. Open M-F 7:30am-6pm, Sa 8:30am-noon. Address *Poste Restante* to: Genève 1 Mont-Blanc, CH-1211, Geneva. Another branch is located behind the train station at r. des Gares 10-16. 24hr. self-service; counters open M-F 7:30am-7pm, Sa 8:30am-noon; urgent mail counter open M-F 7am-10pm, Sa-Su noon-8pm.

▐ ACCOMMODATIONS AND CAMPING

Geneva is a cosmopolitan city, and its 5-star hotel system is geared more toward the international banker than the budget traveler. Luckily, the seasonal influx of university students and interns has created a second network of hostels, pensions, and university dorms moonlighting as summer hotels. The indispensable *Info Jeunes* lists about 50 options; *Let's Go* lists the highlights below. The tourist office publishes *Budget Hotels,* stretching the definition to 120SFr per person.

Even for short stays, make reservations. For longer stays, check *Tribune de Genève*'s weekly supplement of apartment classifieds or the tourist office's board.

City Hostel Geneva, r. Ferrier 2 (☎901 15 00; fax 15 60; info@cityhostel.ch; www.cityhostel.ch). From the station, turn left onto r. de Lausanne, left onto r. de Prieuré, and right onto r. Ferrier. This newly opened hostel's major advantages are its location and the diverse crowd it attracts. The small reception area overflows with friendly backpackers making use of the free nightly movies in the TV room and Heinekens sold at the desk. Kitchen facilities, book exchange, a comprehensive listing of markets in Geneva, and **Internet** access (8SFr per hr.) are available. Sheets 3SFr. Reception 7:30am-noon and 1pm-midnight. Checkout 10am. Single-sex 4-bed dorms 25SFr; singles 55SFr; doubles 80SFr. MC/V. ❷

Hôme St-Pierre, Cour St-Pierre 4 (☎310 37 07; fax 17 27; info@stpierre.ch). Take bus #5 to "pl. Neuve" or walk 15min. from the train station: cross the Rhône at pont du Mont-Blanc, then go up r. de la Fontaine toward pl. du Bourg-de-Four. Take the stairs up Passage des Degres-de-Poules (after Epicerie Pizzo), walk around to the front of the cathedral. It will be diagonally left with your back to the entrance of the cathedral. Mere seconds from the west entrance of the cathedral, this 150-year-old "home" has comfortable beds and a convenient location for exploring the hilly old town area. Enjoy the music of the vieille ville (including a church bell serenade every 15min.) and a convivial atmosphere. Breakfast M-Sa, 7SFr. Lockers 5SFr, showers free. Reception M-Sa 9am-noon and 4-8pm, Su 9am-noon. Popular, so reserve ahead. Dorms 23SFr; singles 36-45SFr; doubles 50-60SFr. MC/V. ❸

Cité Universitaire, ave. Miremont 46 (☎839 22 11; fax 22 23). From the right of the station, take bus #3 (dir: Crets-de-Champel) to the last stop; the Cité Universitaire is directly on your right. Institutional college housing in a modern tower has TV rooms, newspapers, a restaurant, a **disco** (all-night dancing Th and Sa, free to residents), ping-pong, tennis courts, a small grocery shop, and great views. Hall showers included. Reception M-F 8am-noon and 2-10pm, Sa 8am-noon and 6-10pm, Su 9-11am and 6-10pm. Check-out 10am. Lockout 11am-6pm and curfew 11pm; dorms only. 4 dorms (July-Sept. only) 20SFr, lockers included; singles 49SFr; doubles 66SFr; studios with kitchenette and bathroom 75SFr. AmEx/MC/V. ❷

Hôtel de la Cloche, r. de la Cloche 6 (☎732 94 81; fax 738 16 12), off quai du Mont-Blanc across from the Noga Hilton. In this converted mansion, most rooms have a chandelier and TV, and some have antique mirrors and balconies. Ask for a lake view. Breakfast and showers included. Reception 8am-10pm. Reserve a month in advance in summer. Summer singles 70SFr; doubles 95SFr; triples 110SFr, with bath 130SFr; quads with toilet and shower 140SFr. Off-season singles 65SFr; doubles 85SFr; triples 100SFr; quads with toilet and shower 110SFr. AmEx/DC/MC/V. ❹

Auberge de Jeunesse (HI), r. Rothschild 28-30 (☎732 62 60; fax 738 39 87; booking@yh-geneva.ch; www.yh-geneva.ch). Walk 10min. left from the station down r. de Lausanne, then turn right onto r. Rothschild. Take bus #1 from the station (dir: Wilson) to the end of the line. Comfortable last-minute bunks and a ton of people to meet, but not much atmosphere. Check-in lines can be long. Amenities include a sizable lobby, restaurant (dinner 11.50SFr, with dessert and drink 14SFr), kitchen facilities (1SFr per 30min.), TV room with CNN, library, and 3 **Internet** stations (7SFr per hr.). Breakfast, hall showers, lockers, and sheets included. Laundry 6SFr. Special facilities for disabled guests. 6-night max. stay. Reception June-Sept. 6:30-10am and 2pm-1am; Oct.-May 6:30-10am and 4pm-midnight. Lockout in summer 10am-2pm, in winter 10am-4pm. Curfew 1am, in winter midnight. Reservations recommended. Dorms 25SFr; doubles with toilet 70SFr, with toilet and shower 80SFr; quads 110SFr. MC/V. ❷

Camping Pointe-à-la-Bise, Chemin de la Bise (☎752 12 96). Take bus #8 to "Rive" then bus E (north) to "Bise" and walk 10min. down to the lake. The lakefront locale, far from town, will provide a calmer perspective on Geneva. Reception 8am-noon and 2-9pm. Open Apr.-Sept. 6.20SFr per person, 0.50SFr tax per person, 9SFr per tent space. No tents provided, but beds 15SFr. 4-person bungalows 60SFr. ❶

▢ FOOD

It's true that you can find anything from sushi to paella in Geneva, but ethnic foods can break the bank. Many supermarkets have cafeterias with some of the best deals available. *Info Jeunes* lists university cafeterias.

Boulangeries and *pâtisseries* offer gourmet food at budget prices—7SFr goes a long way when you combine a fresh loaf of bread with cheese and tomato from Migros or Co-op. There are extensive dining options in the vieille ville near the cathedral, but you'll pay for the location. In the Les Paquîs area, bordered by the r. de Lausanne and Gare Cornavin on one side and the Quais Mont-Blanc and Wilson on the other, are a variety of ethnic foods. Kebab stands are interspersed with Brazilian cafes, and the colorful neighborhood offers better prices than most. To the south, the village of Carouge is known for its lively student population and funky, chic brasseries. Dining on the waterfront will cost you; enjoy an ice cream cone at a lakeside cafe instead. Around pl. du Cirque and plaine de Plainpalais are cheap, student-oriented "tea rooms," offering bakery fare at good prices.

▨ Chocolats Micheli, r. Micheli-du-Crest 1 (☎329 90 06), produces confectionery works of art. Exquisite Swiss chocolates are perfected in this specialty store *par excellence.* Open Tu-F 8am-7pm, Sa 8am-5pm. MC/V. ❶

Le Rozzel, Grand-Rue 18 (☎312 42 72). Take bus #5 to pl. Neuve, then walk up the hill past the cathedral on r. Jean-Calvin to Grand-Rue. This Breton-style *crêperie* with outdoor seating on the most elegant street in the vieille ville serves large salty crepes (4-18SFr), dessert crepes (4.50-9SFr), and sangria (5SFr). *Menü* available for 21SFr. Open M 7am-4pm, Tu-W 7am-7pm, Th-F 7am-10pm, Sa 9am-10pm. AmEx/MC/V. ❷

Restaurant Manora, r. de Cornavin 4 (☎909 44 10), 3min. from the station on the right, in the Placette department store. This huge self-serve restaurant, with a fresh, large, high-quality selection, offers salads (from 4.50SFr), fruit tarts (3.20SFr), main dishes cooked on the spot (from 7.20SFr), and free water, rarely seen in Geneva. Wheelchair accessible. Open M-Sa 7:30am-9:30pm, Su 9am-9:30pm. ❶

La Crise, r. de Chantepoulet 13 (☎738 02 64). From the station, turn right onto r. de Cornavin and left onto r. de Chantepoulet. Eat in the middle of Mme. LeParc's kitchen for tasty meals at reasonable prices. Quiche and veggies 8.50SFr; soup 3.50SFr; beer or wine 3SFr; *plat du jour* with soup and salad 14SFr. A *Menü* offers great deals. Open M-F 6am-3pm and 5-8pm, Sa 6am-3pm. ❶

Les Brasseurs, pl. Cornavin 20 (☎731 02 06), diagonally left while exiting the station, serves a variety of *flammeküchen,* an Alsatian specialty similar to a thin crust pizza but topped with cream and onions instead of cheese and tomato sauce, and a variety of other toppings (11.20-27.70SFr). The main attractions, however, are the towers of beer brewed on location (starting from 35.50SFr for 3L), made to share. Open M-W 11am-1am, Th-Sa 11am-2am, Su 5pm-1am. Kitchen open 11:30am-2pm and 6-10:45pm but *flammeküchen* available daily until midnight. ❷

Auberge de Saviese, r. des Pâquis 20 (☎732 83 30; fax 784 36 23). Take bus #1 to "Monthoux." Or from Gare Cornavin, turn left onto r. de Lausanne, then right on r. de Zurich, until you hit r. des Pâquis. Sip coffee (2.30SFr) with the other tourists in this English-speaking restaurant. Excellent *fondue au cognac* (20SFr), *Raclette* with all the trimmings (31SFr), and classic regional perch (28SFr). Open M-Sa 10:30am-3pm and 5pm-12:30am, Su 5pm-12:30am. AmEx/DC/MC/V. ❹

Sui Hau, r. de Monthoux 42 (☎731 10 11; fax 69 61). Small Chinese restaurant featuring the elusive lunch and dinner buffet. Lunch buffet 19.50SFr, dinner 25SFr. Open M-F noon-2:30pm and 6-11pm, Sa 6-11pm. MC/V. ❸

Les Armures, r. du Puits-St-Pierre 1 (☎310 34 42; fax 818 71 13), near the main entrance to the cathedral, in Hotel Les Armures. One small step up in price, one giant leap up in atmosphere. A huge plaque announces that President Clinton ate here, and for a small splurge you can too. Good-sized fondue 24-26SFr; pizza 14-17SFr. Open M-F 8am-midnight, Sa 11am-midnight, Su 11am-11pm. AmEx/DC/MC/V. ❸

Globus, r. de Rhône 48, on the pl. du Molard. Self-serve. Inexpensive gourmet delights, including fresh produce, a *fromagerie,* and still-swimming seafood. Daily specials from 11SFr. Open M-W and F 7:30am-6:45pm, Th 7:30am-8pm, Sa 8am-5:45pm. ❷

MARKETS

Co-op, Migros, Grand Passage, and **Orient Express** branches are ubiquitous. On Sundays, the few options include Gare Cornavin's **Aperto** (open daily 6am-10pm) and scattered neighborhood groceries and bakeries.

Public Markets: There are fresh fruits and cheese on **rue de Coutance,** M-Sa 8am-6pm. A produce market is located on **Rd-Pt. de Plainpalais** Tu and F 8am-1pm, Su 8am-6pm. In Carouge, the **pl. du Marché** offers a market W and Sa 8am-1pm. The **pl. de la Navigation** has markets Th and F 8am-1pm. **Marché des Eaux-Vives,** blvd. Helvétique, between cours de Rive and r. du Rhône, is a huge dairy, vegetable, and flower market. Open M and Th 8am-1pm.

⬡ SIGHTS

For centuries, Geneva was tightly constrained by a belt of fortified walls and trenches. By the mid-19th century, when they were finally removed, the city's most interesting historical sites were already established in a dense, easily walkable space. The tourist office offers 2hr. walking tours in the summer on all things *Genevois:* the Reformation, internationalism, the Red Cross, the vieille ville, and the city's museums. Recordings of the tours are available in winter, and a portable cassette player will walk you through 2000 years of Geneva's history. (Mid-June through Sept. M-Sa 10am; Oct. to mid-June Sa 10am. 12SFr, students and seniors 8SFr, children 6SFr. Recording 10SFr plus 50SFr deposit.)

THE INSIDER'S CITY

SHOPPING SURPRISES

It could be antique or the next-best thing, but you won't know unless you poke around some eclectic shops in this decidedly funky neighborhood.

1 Say "Ciao!" to the Italians at the **Société Dante Alighieri.**

2 English writer Mary Ann Evans once lived in this building, before adopting the pseudonym **George Eliot.**

3 Ponder the symbolism of the store sign at 25 Grand Rue—right below the Finnish Consulate.

4 Admire the antique furnishings of **Dorure sur Bois.**

5 Or, shop for newer wares at **Les Héritiers.**

7 Sensuous sculptures and daring decor—find it only at **Desforges Décoration.**

8 Groove to catchy tunes at **Divertimento,** where you can pick up some souvenir music to take home with you.

CATHEDRAL. The vieille ville's **Cathédrale de St-Pierre,** the heart of the early Protestant world, is as austere and pure as on the day Calvin stripped the place of its Catholicism. From its altar, Calvin preached to full houses 1536-1564; his chair from those days still remains. The brightly painted **Maccabean Chapel,** restored in flamboyant style, gives a sample of how the cathedral walls might have looked pre-Reformation. Look out for the stunning organ, a massive silvery construction with a powerful sound. The 157-step **north tower** provides a commanding view of the old town's winding streets and flower-bedecked homes. *(Open June-Sept. daily 9am-7pm; Oct.-May M-Sa 10am-noon and 2-5pm, Su 11am-12:30pm and 1:30-5pm. Closed Su mornings for services. Tower closes 30min. earlier and costs 3SFr. July-Aug. bell-ringing Sa afternoon; June-Sept. free organ recital Sa 6pm.)* The ruins of a Roman sanctuary, a 4th-century basilica, and a 6th-century church rest in an **archaeological site** below the cathedral. *(Open June-Sept. Tu-Sa 11am-5pm, Su 10am-5pm; Oct.-May Tu-Sa 2-5pm, Su 10am-noon and 2-5pm. 5SFr, students 3SFr. Free audioguide available in 6 languages.)*

OLD CITY. Surrounding the cathedral are medieval townhouses and mansions of Geneva's vieille ville. **Maison Tavel,** a fortified urban palace and Geneva's oldest civilian medieval building, is 1min. from the west end. The 14th-century structure now houses a municipal history **museum** by the same name (see p. 489). The **Old Arsenal** a few steps away has five cannons and a mural depicting the arrival of Huguenot refugees—and Julius Caesar. Across the street is the **Hôtel de Ville** (town hall), whose components date from the 15th through 17th centuries. It was here that world leaders met on August 22, 1864, to sign the **Geneva Convention,** governing conduct during war (still in effect today).

Beginning at the *Hôtel de Ville*, the **Grand-Rue** is crammed with medieval workshops and 18th-century mansions, often with hastily added 3rd or 4th floors, the makeshift result of the real estate boom following the influx of French Huguenots after Louis XIV repealed the Edict of Nantes. Plaques commemorating famous residents abound, including one at #40 marking the birthplace of philosopher **Jean-Jacques Rousseau.** Antique shops and art galleries line the Grand-Rue, and nighttime brings live jazz to the restaurants and cafes.

Head away from the vieille ville on r. de Chaudronniers to reach the glittering domes of the **Russian Orthodox Church,** on r. Töpffer, next to the Musée d'Art et d'Histoire. Step inside for the hauntingly lovely icons, stained glass, and heavy incense-weighted air. *(Photography, short skirts, and shorts are not allowed.)*

WATERFRONT. Descending from the cathedral toward the lake is akin to walking forward in time 600 years. The streets widen, buses scuttle back and forth, and every corner sports a chic boutique or watch shop. On the waterfront, the **Jet d'Eau,** down quai Gustave-Ardor, spews a spectacular plume of water 140m high. The sight, a tourist spectacle, was inspired by a faulty piping jet. The world's highest fountain keeps 7 tons of water aloft from March to October.

The floral clock, with over 6500 plants and the world's largest second hand (2.5m), in the nearby **Jardin Anglais** pays homage to Geneva's watch industry. The clock is probably Geneva's most overrated attraction and was once the city's most hazardous. Almost a meter was cut away from the clock because idiot tourists, intent on taking the perfect photo, continually backed into oncoming traffic.

The rose-lined quais lead to two fun-parks. **Pâquis Plage,** quai du Mont-Blanc 30, is popular with the *Genevois*. (☎732 29 74. Open 9am-8:30pm. 2SFr.) Farther from the city center, **Genève Plage,** on quai Gustave Ador, offers a giant waterslide, an Olympic-sized pool, volleyball tournaments, and topless sunbathing. (☎734 26 82. 5SFr.) The source of these waters, the Rhône, was consecrated by the pope during a particularly bad outbreak of the bubonic plague as a "burial" ground.

Ferry tours leaving from quai du Mont-Blanc provide panoramic views of Geneva. **Swiss Boat** (☎732 47 47; 35min. 8SFr, children 5SFr; 1hr. 12SFr/7SFr; 2hr. 20SFr/

ARTAMIS: GUERRILLA ARTIST COLONY
What do you do when you're a young artist in Geneva and have no place to work? If there are 300 others like you, you shut down the tourist industry until the city gives you a place of your own. That's what happened in the summer of 1996 when a group of artists staged a sit-in demonstration at pl. du Bourg-de-Four just below the Cathédrale de St-Pierre. They ripped up pavement, built bonfires, and confused tourists for six days until the city granted them an abandoned industrial park rent-free on the left bank, now called Artamis. (☎320 39 30; www.artamis.org.) You'll find it at quai de Rhône 14, on the #2 and 10 bus lines ("Palladium"). This ten-building complex displays high-quality graffiti and houses thriving art workshops, theaters, and fund-raising facilities. There's an **Internet** cafe (5SFr per hr.), a movie theater (2SFr), and bars. Electronic music enthusiasts should stop by the Database Building, a recording studio where top house and jungle DJs in the area come to experiment. All facilities are open daily 4pm-2am.

15SFr) and **Mouettes Genevoises** (☎732 29 44; 45min. 8SFr, children 5SFr, seniors 6 SFr; 2hr. 20SFr/15SFr/15SFr) narrate cruises in English. **CGN** provides a cruise of the shores of Lake Geneva (55min., 12SFr) and has been sending cruises to lakeside towns, including Lausanne, Montreux, and the stupendous Château de Chillon, for the past 125 years. (☎741 52 31 or 741 52 35. Round-trip 54SFr, Eurail and SwissPass valid). *Les Heures Bleues* provides more details.

PARKS AND GARDENS. Geneva is bedecked with sumptuous gardens scattered strategically throughout the city. Below the cathedral on the r. de la Croix-Rouge, the **Parc des Bastions'** leisurely loveliness stretches from pl. Neuve to the pl. des Philosophes. **Le Mur des Réformateurs** (Reformers' Wall) displays a sprawling collection of bas-relief narrative panels, an array of multilingual inscriptions, and the towering figures of the Reformers themselves. As the largest statues (Knox, Beze, Calvin, and Farel) jostle each other for "leader of the Protestant pack" bragging rights, Cromwell and Rhode Island's Roger Williams trail behind. The imposing campus of **Geneva University** sits opposite the wall, with sunbathers in between.

Strolling north along the river quais brings you to the lush **Parc Mon-Repos** (off ave. de France) and **La Perle du Lac** (off ave. de la Paix), where panting joggers and playful kids stream along curvy paths painted in various floral hues. At the **Jardin Botanique,** opposite the World Trade Organization, basilica-shaped greenhouses grow a collection of rare plants whose aromas waft across r. de Lausanne. (Open Apr.-Sept. daily 8am-7:30pm; Oct.-Mar. 9:30am-5pm. Free.) Venturing farther uphill brings you to **Parc de l'Ariana,** where impressive grounds surround the UN building and the Ariana pottery museum. On the opposite (south) side of the lake, past the Jet d'Eau on quai Gustave-Ador, is **Parc la Grange,** featuring a garden of 40,000 roses, at their peak bloom in June. **Parc des Eaux-Vives,** next to la Grange, is the perfect spot for a picnic or an impromptu frisbee game.

INTERNATIONAL HILL. The garden-parks up the hill behind the train station offer spectacular views of Lac Léman with Mont Blanc in the background (see **Jardin Botanique** and **Parc de l'Ariana,** above). The **Museum of the History of Science** (see p. 489) lies in one park and the **World Trade Organization** lies in another farther north. For even better vistas, climb higher to Geneva's international city, where embassies and multilateral organizations abound. The one to visit is the **International Red Cross,** which contains its own museum (see below). In the Red Cross's shadow stands the European headquarters of the **United Nations,** housed in the building that once sheltered the League of Nations. The guided tour of the UN is quite dull (typical title: "Peace: There is Room for All"), despite some art donated by all the countries of the world and an introductory video recapping the work of the UN in

GENEVA AND LAC LÉMAN

IN RECENT NEWS

DISSOLVING NEUTRALITY

With the UN headquarters already in Geneva and Switzerland's policy toward international relations relaxing, it seemed to some that the Swiss vote on March 3, 2002, to join to the UN was inevitable. However, others, like billionaire leader of the right-wing People's Party (SVP) Christoph Blocher, felt that the decision threatens their position of neutrality. The SVP believes that although joining the UN may be an opportunity to defend their own interests in a larger world body, it may also force the compromise of their position when it comes to international affairs. For similar reasons, the Swiss have remained adamant in their refusal to join the EU, even though it is Switzerland's main trade partner.

Regardless of its new UN status, Switzerland continues to hold a considerable amount of sway in the international area as the holder of the assets of some of the most influential people in the world. The question remains, however, of how neutral Switzerland can be after this big move. Of course, from its role during World War II to the more recent decision to continue the freeze of corrupt Haitian leader Jean-Claude Duvalier's $4.8 million bank accounts, it is difficult to say whether Switzerland's position has ever been truly neutral.

the past year. The constant traffic of international diplomats (often in handsome non-Western dress) provides more excitement than any tour. There's also a not-so-subtle display of Cold War one-upmanship: the armillary sphere depicting the heavens and donated by the US stands next to a monument dedicated to the "conquest of space" donated by the former USSR. (*Visitors' Service* ☎917 48 96 *or* ☎917 45 38, *which also conducts 1hr. tours in any of 15 languages when a sizable group requests them. Enter at the Pregny gate across from the Red Cross. Bring a photo ID. Open July-Aug. daily 10am-5pm; Apr.-June and Sept-Oct. daily 10am-noon and 2-4pm; Nov.-Mar. M-F 10am-noon and 2-4pm. 8.50SFr, seniors and students 6.50SFr, children 4SFr, children under 6 free.*)

🏛 MUSEUMS

Geneva is home to many exceptional museums, usually housed in splendid surroundings, either architectural or natural. A handful of them are free.

RED CROSS MUSEUM. A visit to the ◪**International Red Cross and Red Crescent Museum** will etch the infamous words of Dostoyevsky into your mind: "Each of us is responsible to all others for everything." Built into a hillside and towering over the nearby UN, the museum employs still photographs and wartime film-clip montages, rather than pedantic rhetoric, to drive home its emotional narrative of historic humanitarianism. The stark, unadorned glass and steel building houses a maze of provocative and haunting graphics and audiovisual displays, all through the narrative lens of the life of Henry Dunant, the Red Cross's founder. A startling seven million POW records, including those of de Gaulle from WWI, reside here. Displays in English, French, and German. (*Ave. de la Paix 17. Take bus #8 or F to "Appia" or bus V or Z to "Ariana."* ☎748 95 11 *or* 95 28 *or* 95 25. *Open W-M 10am-5pm. 10SFr, students and seniors 5SFr, under 12 free. Self-guided audio tours 3SFr.*)

ART MUSEUMS. If you visit one art museum in Geneva, the ◪**Petit-Palais** should be it. This beautiful mansion has paintings, sculptures, and drawings by Picasso, Renoir, Gauguin, Cézanne, and Chagall. The inventive basement *salles* (rooms) present themed exhibits: the influence of primitive art on modern aesthetes, the nude female form, and radiant meditations on nature. (*Terrasse St-Victor 2, off blvd. Helvétique. Take bus #36 to "Petit Palais" or #1, 3, or 5 to "Claparède."* ☎346 14 33. *Open M-F 10am-6pm, Sa-Su 10am-5pm. 10SFr, students and seniors 5SFr, children under 12 free. V.*)

The **Musée Barbier-Mueller** has one of the world's most respected collections of African art; artifacts from the collection circulate the globe. Photographs of the objects in their original settings put the frequently changing exhibitions in context. *(R. Jean-Calvin 10. From Grand-rue in the vieille ville, turn onto r. de la Pélisserie and right onto r. Jean-Calvin. ☎312 02 70; musee@barbier-mueller.ch. Open daily 11am-5pm. 5SFr. Children under 12, senior citizens, students, and the unemployed 3SFr.)*

Featuring anything from creative artistry to the just plain weird, the **Musée d'Art Moderne et Contemporaire** displays the most avant-garde art in Geneva. *(R. des Vieux-Grenadiers 10. Take bus #1 to "Bains." ☎320 61 22. Open Tu-F noon-6pm, Sa-Su 11am-6pm. 9SFr; ages 13-18, students, teachers, artists, and retirees 6SFr; children under 12, scholars, students of art, art history, or architecture, the unemployed, and invalids free. Mandatory lockers 2SFr.)* It also houses the **Jean Tua Car and Cycle Museum,** a collection of 70 cars, motorcycles, and bicycles, most pre-WWII. *(R. des Bains 28-30. ☎321 36 37. Open W-Su 2-6pm. 9SFr, students 7SFr, children 4SFr.)*

HISTORICAL MUSEUMS. Maison Tavel, near the Hôtel de Ville, acts as a storehouse for random artifacts typical of daily life in Geneva's past, including the 1799 guillotine from pl. Neuve, a collection of medieval front doors, wallpaper remains, and a vast zinc and copper model of 1850 Geneva that took 18 years to build. Guidebooks in 9 languages available at the entrance. *(R. du Puits-St-Pierre 6. ☎310 29 00. Open Tu-Su 10am-5pm. Free, except for temporary exhibits.)* The **Musée d'Ethnographie** has a tiny but varied collection, which includes Japanese Samurai armor, Australian aboriginal paintings, and a shrunken Bolivian mummy. *(Blvd. Carl-Vogt 65-67. Take bus #1 "Ecole-Médecins." ☎418 45 50. Open Tu-Su 10am-5pm. Permanent exhibits free. Temporary exhibits 4.50SFr, students 2.50SFr, children free.)*

SCIENCE MUSEUMS. Live boa constrictors and Janus, the two-headed turtle, greet you at the **Musée d'Histoire Naturelle.** Overactive children crowd the comprehensive dioramas featuring a range of safari animals while the minerals on the top floor are largely ignored. The display of exotic birds is worth a gander. *(Rte. du Malagnou 1. ☎418 63 00. Take bus #1 to "Museum." Open Tu-Su 9:30am-5pm. Free.)*

OTHER MUSEUMS. Any *Candide* fan should make a pilgrimage to **Musée Voltaire,** located in the former home of the witty writer himself. Statues, paintings, and writing samples in this chandeliered townhouse. *(R. des Delices 25. Take bus #6, 7, 11, 26, or 27 to "Délices" or "Dôle." ☎344 71 33. Open M-F 2-5pm. Free.)*

🔌 🔋 ENTERTAINMENT AND NIGHTLIFE

There is enough to do in Geneva to keep even the most sophisticated traveler happy. *Genève Agenda*, available at the tourist office, is your guide to fun, with listings ranging from festivals to films (be warned—movies run about 16SFr).

FESTIVALS

Summer days bring festivals, **free open-air concerts,** and **free organ music** in Cathédrale de St-Pierre. (June-Sept. Sa 6pm, carillon performances Sa 5pm.) In July and August, the **Cinelac** turns Genève Plage into an open-air cinema that screens mostly American films. (☎840 04 04; www.cinelac.ch. Admission 16SFr.) Check the listings in *Genève Agenda* for indoor cinemas (films marked "v.o." are in their original language with French and sometimes German subtitles, while "st. ang." means that the film has English subtitles).

Geneva hosts the biggest celebration of **American Independence Day** outside the US on July 4, and the **Fêtes de Genève** in early August is filled with international music and artistic celebration, culminating in a spectacular fireworks display. **La Bâtie Festival,** a performing arts festival traditionally held from late August to early September, draws Swiss music lovers for a two-week orgy of cabaret, theater, and concerts by experimental rock and folk acts. (☎908 69 50; batie@world.com.ch.

10-32SFr; many events free; students half-price for the others.) **Free jazz concerts** take place in July and August in Parc de la Grange. Most parks offer free concerts; check at the tourist office for information. The best party in Geneva is **L'Escalade,** commemorating the dramatic repulsion of invading Savoyard troops. The revelry lasts a full weekend and takes place in early December.

BARS AND NIGHTCLUBS

La Jonction, at the junction of the Rhône and Arve rivers, accessible by the #2, 10-20, and the D buses (to "Jonction"), is the home of Artamis (p. 487) and casual bars and concert venues for rockers and ravers. **Pl. Bourg-de-Four,** in the vieille ville below the cathedral, attracts students and professionals to its charming terraces and old-world atmosphere. **Place du Molard,** on the right bank by the pont du Mont-Blanc, has terrace cafes as well as big, loud bars and clubs. **Les Paquis,** near the Gare Cornavin and the pl. de la Navigation, is the red-light district, but also appeals to a less prurient appetite with its wide array of rowdy, low-lit bars, many ethnically themed. **Carouge,** across the river Arve, is a student-friendly locus of nightlife activity, the same place dissidents headed to party during Calvin's purification of the city. Some of Geneva's most popular nightlife is semi-underground. **Squats** have become a popular housing option for counter-cultural youth who don't wish to support The Man by paying rent. The authorities are quite aware of their existence, but rarely break up the parties. Information is generally spread word-of-mouth, but one more official squat is **Le Rhino,** blvd. des Philosophes between Plainpalais and pl. Claparède, unmistakable with its oversized red rhino horn.

■ **La Clémence,** pl. du Bourg-de-Four 20 (☎312 24 98). Generations of students have eaten at this famous chic bar, named after the bell atop the Cathédrale de St-Pierre. It tends to be popular on any given night, but weekend crowds overflow into the square. Teen-idol waiters cater to a chatty clientele of students and young professionals. Come for breakfast (croissant 1.30SFr, coffee 3.10SFr) or beer (3.80-7.20SFr). Open M-Th 7am-12:30am, F-Sa 7am-1:30am.

Flanagan's, r. du Cheval-Blanc 4 (☎310 13 14), off Grand-Rue in the vieille ville. Friendly bartenders pull a good beer in this Irish cellar bar, though you'll be hard-pressed to find an Irish accent among the Anglophones. Pint o' Guinness 8SFr; 6SFr during Happy Hour, daily 5-7pm. Open daily 5pm-2am.

Au Chat Noir, r. Vautier 13, Carouge (☎343 49 98). Take tram #12 to "pl. du Marché," off the far left end of the square. The sensuously curved bar and dark red curtains set the mood in this popular jazz, funk, rock, salsa, and blues venue. Live concerts or DJs every night. (10-15SFr cover.) Beers 5SFr, sangria 6-8SFr. Open M-Th 6pm-4am, F 6pm-5am, Sa 9pm-5am, Su 9pm-4am.

LAUSANNE ☎021

Two thousand years ago, Romans came to the little town of Lausanne on the shores of Lac Léman and found it so enticing that they stayed until the collapse of their empire. Later, the city inspired a different sort of *roman* with the arrival of Dickens and Thackeray. T.S. Eliot managed to create the apotheosis of high Modernist pessimism here, writing *The Wasteland* near the placid Ouchy shoreline and the medieval labyrinth of the vieille ville. Today, Lausanne's unique museums, distinctive neighborhoods, festivals, and magnificent parks make it worth a stay.

▐▀ TRANSPORTATION

Trains: pl. de la Gare 9 (☎157 22 22; 1.19SFr per min.). To: Basel (2½hr., every hr. 5:27am-9:27am, 68SFr); Geneva (50min., every 20min. 4:55am-12:46am, 18.80SFr);

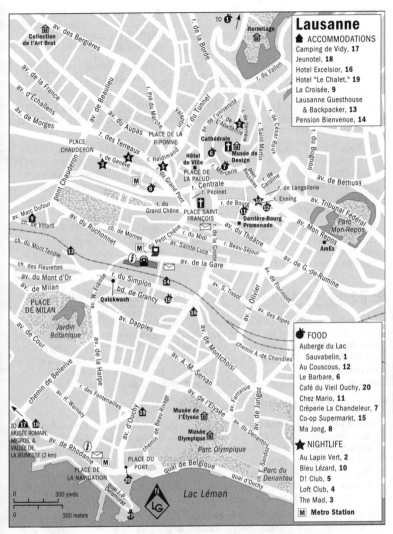

Lausanne

▲ ACCOMMODATIONS
Camping de Vidy, **17**
Jeunotel, **18**
Hotel Excelsior, **16**
Hotel "Le Chalet," **19**
La Croisée, **9**
Lausanne Guesthouse
 & Backpacker, **13**
Pension Bienvenue, **14**

🍴 FOOD
Auberge du Lac
 Sauvabelin, **1**
Au Couscous, **12**
Le Barbare, **6**
Café du Vieil Ouchy, **20**
Chez Mario, **11**
Crêperie La Chandeleur, **7**
Co-op Supermarkt, **15**
Ma Jong, **8**

★ NIGHTLIFE
Au Lapin Vert, **2**
Bleu Lézard, **10**
D! Club, **5**
Loft Club, **4**
The Mad, **3**
Ⓜ Metro Station

GENEVA AND
LAC LÉMAN

Montreux (20min., every 30min. 5:24am-2:29am, 9.80SFr); Paris (4hr., 4 per day
7:36am-5:52pm, 71SFr); and Zurich via Biel (2½hr., 3 per hr. 5:27am-10:27pm,
65SFr).

Public Transportation: The 5-stop **Métro Ouchy** runs from the vieille ville to the Ouchy
waterfront. The **Métro Ouest** runs west to the University of Lausanne and the Federal
Institute of Technology. Both Métros run approximately M-Sa 5am-midnight, Su 6am-
midnight. Buses cross the city roughly 6am-midnight (check bus stops for specific
lines). Exact change needed. 3-stop ticket 1.50SFr; 1hr. pass 2.40SFr; 24hr. pass
7.20SFr; ages 6-16 1.30SFr/4SFr. Métro free with SwissPass or Lausanne Pass.

Ferries: CGN, ave. de Rhodanie 17 (☎614 04 04). To: Evian (4:55am-12:15am, 16SFr, round-trip 27.20SFr); Geneva (3½hr.; 9:15am-5:15pm; 34.80SFr, round-trip 54SFr); and Montreux (1½hr.; 4 per day 9:30am-6:05pm; 20.60SFr, round-trip 35.20SFr). Purchase tickets at dock. Eurail and SwissPass valid. Open M-F 8am-7:30pm.

Taxis: Available at r. Madeleine 1, pl. St. François, pl. de la Navigation, and in front of the station. Or call the **taxibus** (☎0800 080 03 12) or **taxiphone** (☎0800 80 18 02). For 24hr. service call ☎0800 81 08 10.

Car Rental: Avis, ave. de la Gare 50 (☎340 72 00; fax 72 09). **Hertz,** pl. du Tunnel 17 (☎312 53 11). **Europcar,** ave. Ruchonnet 2 (☎323 91 52). **Lococar,** ave. Ruchonnet 30 (☎320 30 80).

Parking: Parking Simplon-Gare, r. du Simplon 2 (☎617 67 44), behind the station (entrance on blvd. de Grancy). 1SFr per 25min., overnight 1SFr per 100min. Open M-F 8am-7pm, Sa 8am-5pm. On city streets, white zones may indicate unlimited parking, rare red zones allow 15hr. parking, blue zones 1½hr. To park on the street, pick up a parking disc from the tourist office. Set the present time and the maximum stay time, and leave the disc displayed on the dashboard.

Bike Rental: (☎0512 24 21 62), at the baggage check in the station. 30SFr per day, 23SFr per half-day. 5SFr off with Eurail or SwissPass. Return bikes at another station for an additional 6SFr. Open 6:40am-7:40pm. Find bike rental starting from 10SFr at pl. du Port 6 (☎606 27 61), next to the Ouchy Métro exit.

■✦ ✌ ORIENTATION AND PRACTICAL INFORMATION

Two-dimensional maps of Lausanne are confusing because the city is on a number of steep hills connected by vaulted bridges. The easiest way to explore the city is on the **Métro Ouchy,** a five-stop subway system which runs from the waterfront up to pl. St. Francois. The Métro's Lausanne-CFF stop is across from the station and goes down to Ouchy (the neighborhood on the waterfront) or up to the vieille ville. Buses #1, 3, and 5 serve the station; most are routed to pl. St. François.

TOURIST AND FINANCIAL SERVICES

Tourist Office: Main office (☎613 73 73 or 73 21; information@lausanne-tourisme.ch; www.lausanne.tourisme.ch), in the main hall of the train station. Open 9am-5pm. **Branch office** across from pl. de la Navigation (M: Ouchy or bus #2: Ouchy). Pick up the *Plan Officiel* (map and public transportation guide) and *Welcome to Lausanne* (booklet listing cheap hotels and private rooms) for free. The staff sells **Lausanne Passes** (p. 491) and makes hotel reservations for 3% commission. Wheelchair-accessible. Open Apr.-Sept. daily 9am-8pm, Oct.-Mar. 9am-6pm. AmEx/DC/MC/V.

Budget Travel: STA Travel, blvd. de Grancy 20 (☎617 56 27; fax 616 50 77; www.statravel.ch), 2 streets downhill from the station past the overpass; turn right off of ave. d'Ouchy. Books student tickets, organizes group travel, and sells ISICs for 15SFr. Open M-F 9:15am-6pm, Sa 9am-noon.

Currency Exchange: At the station (☎312 38 24). Good rates. 2SFr commission. No commission on traveler's checks. Western Union transfers 7am-6:30pm. Cash advances with AmEx/DC/MC/V. Open 6:30am-7:30pm. **24hr. exchange machine** outside offers the same rates for the same commission.

American Express: ave. Mon Répos 14 (☎310 19 00; fax 19 19), across from parking garage. Cashes traveler's cheques, sells airline tickets, and holds mail for 2 months. Travel services open M-F 8:30am-5:30pm; financial office open 2-5:30pm.

LOCAL SERVICES

Luggage Storage: At the train station. (☎0512 24 21 62). 7SFr per day. Open 6:40am-7:40pm. Lockers 5-7SFr per day.

Lost Property: At the train station with the luggage storage. Open M-Sa 6:40am-7:40pm.

Bookstore: Payot Libraire, pl. Pépinet 4 (☎341 31 31; fax 33 45), down r. Pepinet from Pl. St. Francois. Large Anglophone section with contemporary and classic fiction and some nonfiction. Open M 1-6:30pm, Tu-F 8:30am-6:30pm, Sa 8:30am-5pm.

Library: Cantonal and University Palais de Rumine, pl. de la Riponne 6 (☎316 78 80; www.unil.ch/BCU). Open for borrowing M-F 10am-6pm, Sa 9am-noon. Reading room open M-F 8am-10pm, Sa 8am-5pm. Borrowing card free with ID.

Laundromat: Quick Wash, blvd. de Grancy 44 (☎079 449 37 61), 2 streets downhill behind the train station; turn right. Wash and dry around 12-14SFr. Open M and W-Su 9am-8:30pm, Tu noon-8:30pm.

EMERGENCY AND COMMUNICATIONS

Emergency: Police, ☎117. **Fire,** ☎118. **Ambulance,** ☎144. **Crisis Line,** ☎143.

24hr. Pharmacy: Call ☎111 to find out which pharmacy is open all night (they rotate).

24hr. Medical Service, at the hospital (☎314 11 11).

Internet Access: Quanta, ave. de la Gare 4, above the McDonald's and the Métro Lausanne-CFF stop, and across from the train station. 4SFr per 30min. Open M-Th, Su 9am-midnight, F-Sa 9am-1am.

Post Office: Centre Postal, ave. de la Gare 43b (☎344 35 13), on the right as you exit the station. Address *Poste Restante* to: 1000 Lausanne 1 Cases, CH-1001, Lausanne. Open M-F 7:30am-6:30pm, Sa 8am-noon. Express mail M-F 6:30-10pm, Sa noon-4pm, Su 5-9pm. To dispatch your postcard from the site where, from 1783 to 1793, Edward Gibbon wrote his *Decline and Fall of the Roman Empire,* visit **Poste St. François,** pl. St.-François 15 (☎344 38 31). Open M-F 7:30am-6:30pm, Sa 8am-noon. **Postal code:** CH-1002.

▐ ACCOMMODATIONS AND CAMPING

As the home of the world's oldest hotel school, Lausanne has a well-deserved reputation for service-industry excellence. It's a good idea to pick up the tourist office's list of cheap hotels, private boarding houses, and family *Pensionen*, since innumerable festivals, conferences, and congresses can make housing scarce. Owners generally prefer stays of at least three nights and often as long as a month. Travelers looking for apartments to rent can turn to the local paper *24 Heures*, which carries regular listings, or to big department stores' notice boards.

▨ Lausanne Guesthouse & Backpacker, chemin des Epinettes 4 (☎601 80 00; fax 80 01; info@lausanne-guesthouse.ch). From the train station, head left downhill on ave. W. Fraisse. Take first right on Chemin des Epinettes. This newly renovated guesthouse has a convenient location and the comfortable rooms which face the lake. Kitchen, barbecue grill, and lockers included; laundry 5SFr, night car park 10SFr. Key box available for late arrivals/early departures (1SFr). Reception 7am-noon and 3-10pm. At Backpacker: pillow, blanket, and sheets 5SFr. 4-bed dorms 29SFr per person. At Guesthouse: singles 80SFr, with bathroom 88SFr; doubles 86SFr/98SFr. MC/V. ❷

Jeunotel (HI), Chemin du Bois-de-Vaux 36 (☎626 02 22; fax 626 02 26). Take bus #2 (dir: Bourdonnette) to "Bois-de-Vaux." Cross the street and follow the signs. This large hostel is down a long concrete driveway on the right past the *Musée Romain de Lausanne-Vidy*. Courtyards with ping-pong tables, a bowling alley next door, a bar and a restaurant within the complex, and a backpacker crowd enliven it. Breakfast and sheets included. Wheelchair accessible. Parking available. Reception 24hr. Checkout 10am. Reserve in the summer. 8-bed dorms 25SFr; singles 53SFr, with shower 77SFr; doubles 78SFr/94SFr; triples 90SFr; quads 120SFr. Ask about monthly and group rates. AmEx/DC/MC/V. ❶

La Croisée, ave. Marc Dufour 15 (☎321 09 09), 10min. from the train station. Walk up ave. du Ruchonnet and continue as it turns into ave. Marc Dufour. This youth hostel and 2-star hotel offers stunning views of Lac Léman, plus TV room, terrace, and cafeteria space. Breakfast included; dinner around 17SFr. Some hall showers and bathrooms; some are within rooms. Pillow, blanket, and sheets 15SFr. No curfew. Reception open M-F 7:30am-8pm, Sa 7:30am-noon and 4-7pm, Su 8am-noon. Reservations recommended. 4- to 10-bed dorms 40SFr; singles 80-90SFr; doubles 130-150SFr. Children under 6 free, 6-11 50% off, 12-15 30% off. Special rates for extended stays. MC/V. ❸

Pension Bienvenue, r. du Simplon 2 (☎616 29 86), 5min. from the train station. Turn right out of the station, right onto ave. d'Ouchy, and right after the bridge. Or, more quickly, exit out the back entrance of the station, cross the street, turn left onto r. du Simplon, and it's 2 blocks farther on the left side of the street. **Women only.** This well-worn 27-room *Pension* has communal TV rooms and piano. Breakfast included. Kitchen available. Laundry 3SFr. Hall showers and bathrooms only. Reception 9-11:30am and 5-8:30pm. 49SFr. Special rates for extended stays. ❸

Hotel "Le Chalet," ave. d'Ouchy 49 (☎616 52 06). Take Métro Ouchy to "Jordils" or bus #2 (dir: Bourdonnette) to "Jordils." Built in 1877, this chalet has been run by the same eccentric matron since 1940. Travelers enjoy the personal touch and home-like atmosphere in the individualized rooms, each equipped with a sink. Literati occasionally visit the hotel, hoping to commune with the spirit of longtime guest August Strindberg in the evergreen garden. Breakfast 10SFr. Hall showers. Reception 8am-10pm. Singles 55-62SFr; doubles 92SFr. ❸

Hotel Excelsior, chemin du Closelet 6 (☎616 84 51; fax 616 84 58; excelsior@fastnet.ch), 5min. from the train station. Turn right along ave. de la Gare, right on ave. d'Ouchy, and left after bridge on Closelet. Spacious rooms balance the cramped, rundown hallways. Breakfast 8.50SFr. Parking 10SFr. Reception M-Sa 8am-10pm, Su 8-noon and 7-10pm. Singles 70-100SFr; doubles 90-150SFr. AmEx/MC/V. ❹

Camping de Vidy, chemin du Camping 3 (☎622 50 00; fax 50 01; www.campinglausannevidy.ch). Take bus #2 from M: Ouchy (dir: Bourdonnette) to "Bois-de-Vaux." Cross the street and walk down chemin du Bois-de-Vaux past Jeunotel and under the overpass. The office is straight ahead across rte. de Vidy. Restaurant (May-Sept. 7am-11pm), supermarket, and playground. It's near a **swimming pool.** Reception Sept.-June daily 8am-12:30pm and 5-8pm; July-Aug. daily 8am-9pm. Wheelchair accessible. 6.50SFr, students 6SFr, ages 6-15 5SFr; tents 8-12SFr. 1- to 2-person bungalow 54SFr; 3- to 4-person bungalow 86SFr. Electricity 3-4SFr. Showers included. Tax 1.20SFr per tent, 1.30SFr per vehicle. ❶

🍴 FOOD

No visit to Lausanne is complete without a taste of Lac Léman's famous perch or *papet vaudois* (a local delicacy made from leeks, potatoes, cabbage, and sausage). Restaurants, cafes, and bars cluster around pl. St.-François and the vieille ville, while *boulangeries* sell cheap sandwiches on every street. Surprisingly fresh fare and crusty bread await at Métro stations. Numerous grocery stores, frequent markets, and abundant parks make for affordable and pleasant picnics. For crepes, ice cream, and other sweet fare, there are a number of stands on the Ouchy waterfront, which are generally open from the morning well into the evening.

Le Barbare, Escaliers du Marché 27 (☎312 21 32), at the top of steps off the far right of the pl. de la Palud. Stop by this convenient (if oddly located) eatery for lunch or a mid-afternoon treat after trekking to the cathedral. Sandwiches from 5.50SFr, omelettes 7.50-10SFr, and pizzas 12-16SFr. Try the *Chocolate Maison Viennois avec Chantilly,* a rich chocolate drink (5.20SFr), perfect as a reward for the uphill climb. Open M-Sa 8:30am-midnight. DC/MC/V. ❶

Crêperie La Chandeleur, r. Mercerie 9 (☎312 84 19). From pl. St.-François, head down the r. Pépinet to the pl. de la Palud; with your back to the Hôtel de Ville, r. Mercier is off the far right corner of the pl. de la Palud. Enjoy custom-made crepes in a tea-room atmosphere. Try traditional (butter, sugar, or honey around 6SFr), ice cream (7.30-10.30SFr), or gourmet *flambées,* with choice of liqueur (8.30-11SFr). Open Tu-Th 11:30am-10pm, F-Sa 11:30am-11pm. DC/MC/V. ❶

Chez Mario, r. du Bourg 28. Head 5min. up r. du Bourg, which lies behind St.-François. Those who miss their high school hangout should head to Chez Mario, where rambunctious youths convene to eat cheap pizza (from 13SFr) within its graffiti-covered walls. Open daily 11:30am-1am. ❷

Au Couscous, r. Enning 2 (☎321 38 40). From pl. St.-François, head away from the Zurich Bank sign and turn left up r. de la Paix to r. Enning. Inside, a North African theme prevails with red tablecloths, a mosaic-tiled floor, and sequined pillows. Extensive, veggie-friendly menu (13.90-23SFr). Enjoy delicious couscous (23-24SFr) in an appropriate ambience. Open M-Tu 11:30am-2:30pm and 6:30pm-midnight, W-Th 11:30am-2:30pm and 6:30pm-1am, F 11:30am-2:30pm and 6:30pm-2am, Sa 6:30pm-2am, Su 6:30pm-1am. ❸

Cafe du Vieil-Ouchy, pl. du Port 3 (☎616 21 94). This small lakeside cafe provides great view of both the lake and the chateau while you enjoy a *Rösti* platter (9-22.50SFr) or cheese fondue (21SFr). Savor a delectable *coupe maison* (9.50SFr) if you have room for dessert. Open Th-M. ❸

Auberge du Lac de Sauvabelin, at Lac Sauvabelin (☎647 39 29). Try this place if you've got a car, or take the infrequent bus #16 to "Lac Sauvabelin." An oasis far from the bustle of Lausanne, this classy restaurant sits in the middle of a park, next to a deer farm. Traditional Swiss fare (filet of perch 27SFr) served by charismatic waiters. ❸

Ma-Jong, Escalier du Grand Pont 3 (☎329 05 25). From the Lausanne-Flon Métro stop, walk up the incline; Ma-Jong will be on the right. Cafeteria-style, pan-Asian dining in the tradition of Chinese streetside eateries. Specials from pad thai to roast duck are available for 15SFr (with salad and sometimes rice). Try the Japanese fondue, your choice of raw meat to simmer in a pot of heated boullion, for 20SFr. Dim sum and sushi also offered. Take-out or eat-in. Open M-Th 11:30am-10:30pm, F-Sa 11:30am-midnight. ❸

MARKETS

Migros, ave. de Rhodanie 2 (☎613 26 60), right of Métro Ouchy stop or bus #2 stop "Pl. de la Navigation." Locations throughout city. Open M 9am-9:45pm, Tu-Su 8am-9:45pm.

Co-op, (☎616 40 66). From the train station, head downhill past the overpass; turn right onto blvd. de Grancy. Open M-F 8am-7pm, Sa 8am-5pm.

Aperto, at the train station. Open daily 6am-10pm.

Produce markets, at pl. de la Palud and the r. de Bourg behind the pl. St.-François. W and Sa mornings until around noon.

👁 🏛 SIGHTS AND MUSEUMS

"In Lausanne, people are consuming culture as others swallow vitamins," a tourist brochure proclaims. Perhaps something was lost in translation, but nevertheless, 650,000 visitors flock to Lausanne's vieille ville and museums each year. For multi-day visits, the **Lausanne Pass** is a great deal, entitling visitors to museum discounts and free public transportation in and around Lausanne (15SFr for 2 days).

THE OLD CITY AND THE OLD CITY. The medieval town center is known as the vieille ville, but the true old city is on the waterfront, where archaeological digs have unearthed 2000-year-old remains of the *Vicus de Lousonna.* You can stroll through it and see the foundations of a temple, the remains of a basilica, a forum, a few villas, and the traces of a complete Gallo-Roman colony, now overshadowed by gigantic weeds. *(Take bus #2 to "Bois-de-Vaux" and follow signs.)* History buffs can poke around the **Musée Romain de Lausanne-Vidy,** the excavation site of a Roman house whose wall murals still retain their bright colors. Explanations in French. *(Chemin du Bois-de-Vaux 24, next door to the hostel. ☎ 652 10 84. Open Tu-W and F-Su 11am-6pm, Th 11am-8pm. Wheelchair accessible. 4SFr, seniors 2.50SFr, students free.)*

In 1275 the Gothic **Cathédrale** was consecrated under Holy Roman Emperor Rudolph and Pope Gregory X. From pl. de la Palud, with your back to the Hôtel de Ville, head diagonally right and just off the plaza, climb the two series of medieval, covered stairs which lead to the hilltop, where the cathedral's huge wooden doors open up into the hushed, vaulted space illuminated through stained-glass windows. *(Cathedral open July to mid-Sept. M-F 7am-7pm, Sa-Su 8am-7pm; mid-Sept. to June closes 5:30pm. Church services Su 10am, 8:15pm. Free guided tours July to mid-Sept. 10:30, 11:15am, 3, 3:45pm.)*

The Renaissance **Hôtel de Ville** (city hall), with its bronze dragon roof, serves as a meeting point for guided **tours** of the town. *(On the pl. de la Palud, below the cathedral. Tours M-Sa 10am and 3pm. English available. 10SFr, students free.)* Also below the cathedral is the majestic **Palais de Rumine,** which houses the Cantonal and University Library, as well as several small archaeological and zoological museums. *(On pl. de la Riponne. Open M-F 11am-10pm, Sa 7am-5pm, Su 10am-5pm.)*

ART MUSEUMS. The ■**Collection de l'Art Brut** proves to be the most satisfying collection in Lausanne. An utterly original gallery filled with disturbing and beautiful sculptures, drawings, and paintings by artists on the fringe—institutionalized schizophrenics, poor and uneducated peasants, and convicted criminals—started as an odd obsession of Jean Dubuffet, the museum features unconventional masterpieces from a prison cell wall painstakingly carved with a broken spoon to intricate junk and sea-shell masks. Equally fascinating are the biographies of their tortured creators, most displayed in English and French and often accompanied by intense photographic portraits. Don't miss the unforgettable Henry Darger room, portraying the fantasy world of a part-time janitor from Chicago who created an alternate universe on paper. *(Ave. Bergières 11. Take bus #2 or 3 to "Jomini." The museum is across the street. ☎ 647 54 35. Open Sept.-June Tu-F 11am-1pm and 2-6pm, Sa-Su 11am-6pm; July-Aug. open daily 11am-6pm. 6SFr, students and seniors 4SFr, under 16 free.)*

On a more conventional note, the **Musée de l'Elysée** houses an engaging series of diverse exhibits and photographic archives, ranging from 1820 prints to contemporary artistic endeavors in film. *(Ave. de l'Elysée 18. Take bus #2 to "Croix d'Ouchy" and go downhill, then left on ave. de l'Elysée. ☎ 316 99 11; www.elysee.ch. Open daily 11am-6pm. 8SFr, seniors 6SFr, students 4SFr.)* North of the vieille ville, the **Hermitage** is a magnificent house given over to temporary exhibitions that vary from single artists and special themes to individual public and private collections. 2003 will bring works from French painter Derin from March to May and Kupka from June to October. *(Rte. du Signal 2. Bus #16 to "Hermitage" stops infrequently out front. ☎ 320 50 01. Open Tu-W and F-Su 10am-6pm, Th 10am-9pm. 15SFr, seniors 12SFr, students 7SFr, under 18 free. AmEx/MC/V.)*

MUSÉE OLYMPIQUE. This is a high-tech temple to modern Olympians with a smaller exhibit dedicated to the ancient games. An extensive video collection allows visitors to relive any highlight since the games were first filmed, and more recent events can even be seen in the 3-D cinema. The English/French displays of medals, mementos, and equipment arranged around the central spiral ramp are swarmed with kids. The museum is wheelchair-accessible via ave. de l'Elysée. *(Quai d'Ouchy 1. Take bus #2 or Métro: "Ouchy." ☎ 621 65 11. Open May-Sept. M-W and F-Su 9am-6pm, Th 9am-8pm; Oct.-Apr. Tu-W and F-Su 9am-6pm, Th 9am-8pm. 14SFr, students and seniors 9SFr, ages 10-18 7SFr, families 34SFr max. Audioguide available in 7 different languages, 3SFr. MC/V.)*

MUSEUM OF DESIGN AND CONTEMPORARY APPLIED ARTS. This recently opened museum, formerly dedicated to the decorative arts, houses a well-chosen collection of modern, cutting-edge pieces. The basement, with an anachronistic selection of Egyptian and Chinese art, and the collection of glass art on the top floor sandwich the temporary exhibits on the main floors. *(Pl. de la Cathédrale 6, next to the cathedral. ☎ 315 25 30; mu.dac@lausanne.ch. Open Tu 11am-9pm, W-Su 11am-6pm. 6SFr, students and seniors 4SFr.)*

WATERFRONT. A sign along the waterfront declares Ouchy to be "a free and independent community," and indeed its slower tempo, indulgent hotels, and eco-modern sculptures set it strikingly apart from the vieille ville. Ouchy's main promenades, the **quai de Belgique** and **pl. de la Navigation,** are both excellent spots to exercise those calf muscles. The local word is that Lausanne's women have the best-looking legs in Switzerland, the hard-won prize of a life spent hiking the city's hills. *(Let's Go* remains impartial.) Several booths along the water rent out pedal boats (10SFr per 30min.) and offer water skiing or wake boarding on Lac Léman (30SFr per 15min.). See more of Ouchy's inhabitants at the **Bellerive Complex,** a beach park where locals let their children loose on spotless lawns while both genders go topless and take in sun. *(Take bus #2 to "Bellerive" or walk down ave. de Rhodanie from Ouchy. Open mid-May to early Sept. daily from 9:30am until dark or rain. 4.50SFr, students and seniors 3SFr, under 17 2SFr. Discount after 5pm. Lockers 2SFr.)*

PARKS AND GARDENS. The Bellerive Beach is just one of Lausanne's many natural oases. At the **Vallée de la Jeunesse** rose garden, an unassuming path of wildflowers bends to reveal a spectacular display of 1000 bushes arranged in a terraced semi-circle around a fountain, all to the tune of thousands of birds. *(Take Métro-Ouest to Renens.)* More exotic birds trill from the aviaries of the downtown **Parc du Mon-Repos.** Centering around a small chateau where Voltaire wrote in 1755 to 1757, the park includes venerable trees, an orange grove, and a small stone temple. *(Take Bus 17 (dir. Verdeil) to "Mon-Repos.")* The region's propensity to bloom is channeled at the **Derrière-Bourg Promenade,** where flowers depict events from the canton's history. *(Just off pl. St. François.)* The **Botanical Garden of Lausanne** is in one section of pl. de Milan-Montriond Park. Wander past rose bushes, herbs, and signs about local fauna, and visit the observation spot atop a hill next to the gardens for an unobstructed lake panorama. A sign names each peak visible across the water and the date on which it was first conquered. The surrounding neighborhood is charming and untouristed. *(Ave. de Cour 14bis. Just up the hill from the bus #1 stop "Beauregard." ☎ 616 24 09. Park open Mar.-Apr. and Oct. daily 10am-5:30pm; May-Sept. 10am-6:30pm.)*

GENEVA AND LAC LÉMAN

🎵 🎭 ENTERTAINMENT AND NIGHTLIFE

For every exhibit in Lausanne's museums, there are several performances in progress on stage and screen: the **Béjart Ballet, Lausanne Chamber Orchestra, Cinémathèque Suisse, Municipal Theatre, Opera House,** and **Vidy Theatre** reflect Lausanne's thriving cultural life. For information, reservations, and tickets, call Billetel (☎310 16 50). The **Festival de la Cité** (mid-July) brings the vieille ville to life with free theater and dance events. Swiss craftwork fills the **Marché des Artisans** in pl. de la Palud from 6am to 7pm on the first Friday of the month from March to December. **Lunapark** (amusement park) is at Bellerive from mid-May to mid-June.

SWISS GRACE. Founded in 1957 by Maurice Béjart, former dancer and choreographer of the Royal Swedish Ballet, the Béjart Ballet proudly holds a place as one of the world's most famous and innovative dance companies. Renowned for his unconventional style of choreography, Béjart frequently incorporates modern dance and acrobatics into performances by his classically trained ballet dancers. Pieces are known for their element of grand spectacle, and often include literature and multimedia elements. Fortunate to be directed by what some consider to be a living choreographic genius, the Béjart ballet regularly showcases new pieces by Béjart in their repertoire, and performs his dance epochs like *Ninth Symphony of Beethoven, Le Flûte Enchantée,* and *Symphony for a Lonely Man.*

For nightlife, head to pl. St. François and follow your ears. *Lausannois* partygoers inhabit the bars until 1am (2am Sa-Su) and dance at the clubs 'til 4am. The hard-core then head over to the bar in the train station, which opens at 5am.

The Mad, rte. de Genève 23 (☎312 29 19). Exit the Lausanne-Flon Métro stop, go left, and then walk 3min. down rte. de Genève. A 5-floor warehouse discotheque splashed with bright colors and the slogan "Mad But Not Mad" crawling up its side. World-class DJs spin trance W, house Th, and progressive stuff F-Sa. Beer 7.50SFr, mixed drinks 14-25SFr. Open W-Su 10pm-5am. Cover F-Sa before midnight 20SFr, after midnight 25SFr.

Loft Club, pl. Bel-Air 1 (☎311 64 00; www.loftclub.ch). Up the steps off the right hand side of rte. de Genève, heading toward The Mad. While other clubs may just be warming up, the hordes here have already fired up to the sounds of house, hip hop, or techno. So popular that a pat down is required for entry—just make sure you get the security guard. Cover 5-15SFr. W members-only night. Open W-Sa 10:30pm-5am.

Bleu Lézard, r. Enning 10 (☎321 38 30). From pl. St-François turn left to r. de Bourg, then head right past Au Couscous. Suits and students alike crowd this bistro. Decor by local artists. DJs or live music on weekends. Beer 3.50SFr, cocktails 13.50SFr. Vegetarian dishes 15-19SFr. Open Tu and Th 8pm-2am, W and Su 8pm-1am, F-Sa 6:30pm-2am. Kitchen open M-Sa 11:30am-2pm and 6:30-10:30pm, Su 10am-5pm and 6:30-10:30pm. AmEx/MC/V.

Au Lapin Vert (☎312 13 17). On ruelle du Lapin Vert, off r. de l'Académie behind the cathedral, this upscale version of a hole-in-the-wall pub blasts English rock at a crowd of teenagers, college students, and young professionals. Beer 4SFr, mixed drinks 9-10SFr. Open Su-Th 8pm-2am, F-Sa 8pm-3am.

D! Club, ruelle de Grand Pont, entrance at pl. Centrale, attracts Lausanne's mature and well-dressed crowd with its wide range of music. Go left out of the Lausanne-Flon Métro stop, walk under r. de Grand Point bridge, and turn left. Open Th 11pm-4am, F-Sa 11pm-5am. Th Free, F-Sa cover 20SFr.

MONTREUX ☎021

Montreux feels like a resort past its heyday—one that could've been frequented by the elegant, Jazz-Age characters of an F. Scott Fitzgerald novel. The grand hotels and lakefront promenade still emanate wealth and prestige, though decidedly faded. Still, music fans worldwide flock here in early July for the annual **Montreux Jazz Festival.** Not only a celebration of jazz, the festival attracts musicians of all genres and creates an ongoing, city-wide, all-ages party. Luminaries Neil Young, Bob Dylan, Stevie Ray Vaughan, and, most famously, Miles Davis have dropped in. Literary visitors have included Victor Hugo and Fitzgerald himself. Even further back in the area's literary tradition lies the visit of Lord Byron to the disturbingly beautiful **Château de Chillon,** a medieval fortress with a checkered history.

⊟ TRANSPORTATION

Trains: ☎963 45 15, on ave. des Alpes. To: **Bern** (1½hr., 2 per hr. 5:39am-11:05pm, 37SFr); **Geneva** (1hr., 2 per hr. 5:39am-11:39pm, 26SFr); and **Lausanne** (20min., 3-5 per hr. 5:29am-12:09am, 9.80SFr). **Direct trains** also go to **Aigle, Brig, Martigny, Sion,** and (literally) through the mountains to **Gstaad.**

Local Transportation: A very helpful map, available at the tourist office in several languages, divides the area into bus zones; your fare depends on the number of zones you cross. 1 zone 2.20SFr, juniors (ages 6-20) 1.60SFr; 2 zones 2.80SFr/2SFr; 3 zones 3.50SFr/2.50SFr; 4 zones 4.20SFr/3SFr. Day-pass 7SFr/5SFr; available at tourist office. SwissPass valid. Special late-night buses run during the Jazz festival, tickets 2-4SFr (buy at the back of the bus); SwissPass valid. Free buses run from **Vevey** through Montreux to **Villeneuve** M-F 6pm-4am, Sa-Su noon-4am during the Festival.

Boats: CGN, (☎963 46 55), on quai du Débarcadère next to the tourist office. To: **Geneva** (4½hr., 4 per day 9:30am-4:50pm, 40.80SFr/63.40 round-trip); **Lausanne** (1½hr., 5 per day 9:30am-5:55pm, 20.60SFr/35.20SFr); and **Vevey** (25min., 6 per day 9:30am-5:55pm, 9.20SFr/16.60SFr). Rides to **Château de Chillon** (13.80SFr round-trip) and **Villeneuve** (13.80SFr round-trip) available. Buy tickets at the quai, tourist office, or on board. Eurail and SwissPass valid.

Bike Rental: At the baggage check in the station. 30SFr per day, 23SFr per half-day; 6SFr charge to return bikes to other stations (including Aigle, Martigny, and Sion) by prior arrangement. Open 7:30am-8pm. AmEx/MC/V.

◧ ⁊ ORIENTATION AND PRACTICAL INFORMATION

Montreux and its surroundings rise rapidly from the eastern shores of Lac Léman to the edge of the Alps at Les-Roches-de-Naye Jardin. The train station is within walking distance of most sights. Hiking up r. du Marché leads to the vieille ville.

Tourist Office: pl. du Débarcadère (☎962 84 84; fax 84 94; tourism@montreux.ch; www.montreux.ch). Descend the stairs opposite the station and head left on Grand Rue for 5-10min.; the office is on the right, by the water. The harried staff shares the office with desks for festival tickets and bus and train information. Free hotel reservation service within Montreux. They offer 2 free maps. Open mid-June to mid-Sept. M-F 9:30am-6pm, Sa-Su 10am-5pm; late Sept. to early June M-F 8:30am-5pm, Sa-Su 10am-3pm.

Budget Travel: STA Travel, ave. des Alpes 25 (☎965 10 15; fax 10 19). Open M-F 9am-noon and 1:30-6pm. AmEx/MC.

Currency Exchange: No commission at the station. **Western Union** does transfers and credit card advances. Open 6:30am-8:45pm. **Banks** in Montreux are open M-F 8:30am-4:30pm. Some close for lunch, but the one by the station does not.

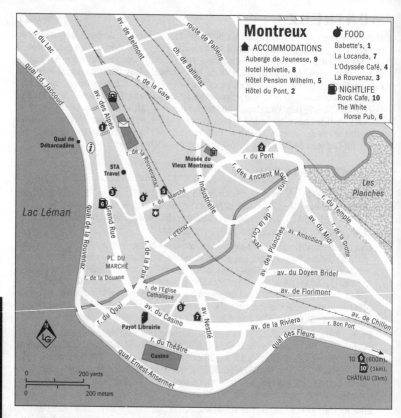

Montreux

ACCOMMODATIONS
Auberge de Jeunesse, **9**
Hotel Helvetie, **8**
Hôtel Pension Wilhelm, **5**
Hôtel du Pont, **2**

🍎 FOOD
Babette's, **1**
La Locanda, **7**
L'Odyssée Café, **4**
La Rouvenaz, **3**

🍸 NIGHTLIFE
Rock Cafe, **10**
The White
Horse Pub, **6**

Luggage Storage: At the station. Lockers 4-7SFr, open 5:50am-8:45pm. Luggage watch 7SFr per bag. Open daily 6:30am-8:15pm.

Bookstore: Payot Libraire, ave. du Casino 42 (☎963 06 07). Friendly staff helps you search a multilingual stock. Open M-F 9am-6:30pm, Sa 9am-5pm. AmEx/DC/MC/V.

Laundromat: Salon-Lavoir, r. Industrielle 30. Open M-Sa 7am-7pm. 5SFr per load.

Emergencies: Police, ☎117. **Fire,** ☎118. **Ambulance,** ☎144. **Hospital,** ☎966 66 66. **Late-Night Pharmacy:** ☎962 77 00.

Internet Access: Internet@Place, Grand Rue 114 (☎966 02 80). 15SFr per hr. includes soft drink. Open M-Sa 10am-8pm.

Post Office: ave. des Alpes 70. Exit the station, turn left. Poste Restante: Montreux 1, CH-1820 Montreux. Open M-F 7:30am-6pm, Sa 8am-noon. **Postal Code:** CH-1820.

🏨 ACCOMMODATIONS AND CAMPING

Cheap rooms are scarce in Montreux and almost nonexistent during the jazz festival. Hotels and hostels are often full before May. Revelers frequently stash their bags in the train station lockers and crash on the lakefront, but the police will move lakeside sleepers out at 7am. Ask at the tourist office for the lists of *Pensions et Petits Hôtels* or studio apartments available during the festival. If you still can't find a room, try the hostel in Vevey (see p. 504; free shuttles to and from the festival) or in Gryon (see p. 511). Otherwise, take bus #1 to "Villeneuve," 5km away, to a handful of budget hotels, or commute from Lausanne or Martigny.

Auberge de Jeunesse Montreux (HI), passage de l'Auberge 8 (☎963 49 34; fax 27 29). Take bus #1 on Grand Rue (dir: Villeneuve) to "Territet." Head up the street, take the 1st right (r. du Bocherex), and go down the stairs (passage de l'Auberge); or walk 20min. along the lake past the Montreux Tennis Club. This modern hostel offers many conveniences, including a dining room, TV, and waterfront location. Light sleepers beware: train tracks run nearby. Wheelchair accessible. Breakfast included. Dinner 12.50SFr. Lockers 2SFr deposit. Sheets included. Free parking nearby. Reception 7:30-10am and 5-10pm. Check-out 10am. Doors lock at 10pm but guests have access. Closed mid-Nov. to mid-Feb. 112 beds in 6- or 8-bed dorms. Dorms 30SFr; doubles 38SFr, with bathroom 42SFr. Non-members add 6SFr. AmEx/DC/MC/V. ❷

Hôtel Pension Wilhelm, r. du Marché 13-15 (☎963 14 31; fax 32 85; hotel.wilhelm@span.ch). From the station, take a left at ave. des Alpes, walk up 3min. and take a left onto r. du Marché, uphill past the police station. Perched high above the nightlife of the waterfront in the vieille ville, you'll find a quiet, clean room and an accommodating staff. Breakfast included. Reception 7am-10pm. Closed Oct.-Feb. Singles 60SFr, 70SFr with shower; doubles 100SFr/120SFr. Cash or traveler's checks only. ❸

Hôtel du Pont, r. du Pont 12 (☎/fax 963 22 49), at the top of the *vieille ville*. From the station, go left on ave. des Alpes (3min.) and then left up r. du Marché. Continue uphill until it becomes r. du Pont; the hotel is on the left (enter through the cafe). Bright, nicely sized rooms with bathrooms and TVs, though it's a far trek to town. Breakfast included. Dinner 18-25SFr. Reception M 7am-3pm, Tu-F 7am-midnight, Sa-Su 8:30am-midnight. Singles 70SFr; doubles 130SFr. Extra bed 40SFr. AmEx/MC/V. ❸

Hotel Helvetie, ave. du Casino 32 (☎966 77 77; fax 77 00; www.montreux.ch/helvetie). From Grand Rue, take bus #1 (dir: Villeneuve) to "Montreux." Rooms with TV, phone, and minibar located only a block from the casino. **Internet** 4SFr per 15min., 12SFr per hr. Breakfast included. Reception 24hr. Check-out noon. Singles 100-120SFr; doubles 150-160SFr. ❹

🍴 FOOD

Montreux is pricey and most establishments are well touristed. Markets with good prices abound on the Grand Rue and ave. de Casino. **Marché de Montreux,** pl. du Marché, is an outdoor food and flea market. (F 7am-1pm.) There's a **Co-op** at Grand Rue 80. (Open M-F 8am-12:15pm and 2-6:30pm, Sa 8am-5pm.)

L'Odyssée Cafe, ave. des Alpes 17bis (961 38 46). Exiting the station, turn left on ave. des Alpes; walk for about 3-5min. Cheap cafe fare. Sandwiches 4.50-6.50SFr, omelettes 7.50-12SFr, daily *Menüs* 14.50SFr. Open M-F 7am-5pm. ❶

La Rouvenaz, r. du Marche, just off Grand Rue. This compact restaurant serves relatively cheap Italian food for a place with a lake view. Pizzas from 14.50SFr. Reasonably priced hotel rooms upstairs. MC/V. ❷

Babette's, Grand Rue 60 (☎963 77 96), downstairs from the station to the left. This casual restaurant serves crepes of all types for lunch (11-14SFr) and dessert (7-10SFr) but offers limited seating. Sandwiches to go 6-15SFr. Open 7am-7pm. ❷

La Locanda, ave. du Casino 44 (☎963 29 33), is a small restaurant with decor that works hard to be cozy. Large pizzas 15-21SFr; salads 7-19SFr. Open M-Tu and Th-Sa 11:30am-3pm and 6:30pm-midnight, W 6:30pm-midnight. AmEx/MC/V. ❸

GENEVA AND LAC LÉMAN

◉ SIGHTS

If you plan to visit more than three area museums, consider purchasing the Montreux-Vevey Museum passport (15SFr), available at the tourist office. The **Château de Chillon** is not only the main sightseeing draw in Montreux, but also one of Switzerland's most visited attractions. Take the CGN ferry from the quai de Débarcadère (13.80SFr round-trip) or bus #1 to "Chillon" from anywhere on Grand Rue or ave. de Casino (2.80SFr, ages 6-20 2SFr). Built on an island in the 13th century, Chillon is a fortress with all the comforts of any happy home: prison cells, a torture chamber, an armory, and boobytraps to fend off attackers who get past the moat. From the dungeon comes the disturbing story of François de Bonivard, a priest who spent four years chained to a dungeon pillar in the 16th century for aiding the Reformation; he was freed in 1536 by Protestant soldiers who seized Montreux from the Catholic Duke of Savoy. Bonivard's captivity inspired Rousseau, Victor Hugo, and most famously, Lord Byron. Byron's poem "The Prisoner of Chillon" tells a romanticized version of Bonivard's plight. In the chateau you can see where Byron etched his name into a pillar, presumably to empathize with poor François. (☎966 89 10; fax 89 12; www.chillon.ch. Open Apr.-Sept. daily 9am-6pm, Mar. and Oct. 9:30am-5pm, Nov.-Feb. 10am-4pm. 8.50SFr, students 6.50SFr, ages 6-16 4SFr, families 21SFr.)

From the museum, the vieille ville is just a few minutes up the r. du Pont. A refreshing world away from the craziness of the waterfront, the r. de Temple offers pure views and a quiet walk to the stone church **Église de Montreux.** The **Musée du Vieux-Montreux**, r. de la Gare 40, on the outskirts of the vieille ville, chronicles Montreux's history from Roman times through its "colonization" by the resort industry in the late 19th century. The two things that make a visit worth its salt are the view from outside and the list of the city's "illustrious guests" from over the years. (☎963 13 53. Open Apr.-Oct. daily 10am-noon and 2-5pm. 6SFr, students and seniors 4SFr, under 17 free.)

🎵 ENTERTAINMENT

The **Montreux Jazz Festival,** world-famous for exceptional musical talent and one of the biggest parties in Europe, pushes everything in town aside for 15 days starting the first Friday in July. Headliners in 2002 included B.B. King and Paul Simon. Demand has sent ticket prices into the stratosphere: individual tickets range from 79-119SFr. Standing room tickets run 49-79SFr. Write to the tourist office well in advance for information and tickets. The easiest way to purchase tickets in advance is at www.montreuxjazz.com. The **jazz hotline** in Montreux, run by the **Jazz Boutique** ticket sellers at Grand Rue 62, is active from mid-March through the summer (☎966 44 36). In Switzerland, buy tickets from **Ticket Corner** (☎848 80 08 00) and at the **Congress Center** in Montreux. Many events sell out before July, some as early as January. If you can find a room but no tickets, come anyway for the **Jazz Off,** 500hr. of free, open-air concerts by new bands and established musicians. The temporary **Jazz Cafe,** is free for fans to spend entire nights partying.

From late August to mid-September, the **Montreux Voice and Music Festival** takes over with operas, symphonies, and classical recitals performed by musicians from as far away as Moscow and Memphis. Tickets to concerts in Montreux and Chillon range from 10SFr (student tickets) to 160 SFr (big names). Contact the **Office of the Classical Music Festival**, left of the Casino, at r. du Théâtre 5, 1st Floor, Case Postale 353, CH-1820 Montreux 2. (☎966 80 25; fax 963 25 06; courrier@montreux-festival.com; www.montreux-festival.com. Office open M-F 10am-1pm and 2-7pm, Sa 10am-1pm. Open for extended hours 2 or 3 weeks before the festival.)

NIGHTLIFE

Montreux caters to all tastes and personalities, from carefree campers to five-star fops. Don't worry about finding "the place to be" in this town—if you're by the water, especially in early July, you're there.

Casino de Montreux, r. du Théâtre 9 (☎962 83 83). From ave. du Casino, turn on r. Igor Stravinsky toward the lake. The casino draws mobs to flashy slot machines. The charm of the 1881 establishment (which helped launch the careers of Stravinsky and fellow composer Ernest Ansemet) is largely gone, but it's worth stopping by to cap off a day with video poker (M-Th 3pm-3am, F 3pm-4am, Sa-Su noon-4am) and *boule* (daily from 8:30pm). Closed for renovations; reopens Jan. 2003. 18+; bring your passport.

Rock Café, r. de l'Auberge 5 (☎963 88 88), up the stairs from the youth hostel. Its name and guitar-art may aspire to imitate the Hard Rock, but this neighborhood bar can't escape its more down-to-earth, grungy style. Loud music, young crowd, billiard room, video games, darts, and pinball. Beer 6SFr per pint; choose among bottles from 8 countries. Open Su-Th 5pm-midnight, F-Sa 5pm-2am. AmEx/DC/V.

The White Horse Pub, Grand Rue 28 (☎963 15 92). A sign on the door declares this an "authentic" English pub, but you won't find anything authentically English (unless *crepes* and *caipirinhas* have become English cuisine). What you'll more likely find is a friendly, Francophone crowd watching sports on the multiple TVs. Sandwiches 7-9.50SFr; fish and chips 15.50SFr; pizza 11SFr; beer 6.20-9.50SFr per pint. Pinball, darts, foosball, and arcade games in back. Open M-F 11am-1am, Sa 11am-2am, Su 3pm-midnight.

VEVEY   ☎021

Vevey experienced its heyday as a resort town back in the 19th century, when hordes of upper-class English made it a virtual colony of the Queen's empire, placing it in countless novels of society. The upside to its 20th-century decline is that Vevey has avoided the 5-star stratification and crowding of nearby Montreux. Charlie Chaplin fled here from McCarthyism in 1953, and Jean-Jacques Rousseau, Victor Hugo, Fyodor Dostoyevsky, Henry James, Le Corbusier, and Graham Greene have all worked within Vevey's borders. The town remains handsome and well preserved, its central location along the shore of Lac Léman making it an ideal base for trips to neighboring Lausanne and Montreux.

TRANSPORTATION AND PRACTICAL INFORMATION

There are three ways to reach Vevey from Montreux: by **bus** #1 to "Vevey" (20min.; every 10min.; 2.80SFr, children 2SFr); **train** (5min., every 15-30min., 3SFr); or **boat** (20min., 5 per day, 9.20SFr). To get to the **tourist office** (Grand-Place 29) from the station, cross pl. de la Gare, go past ave. de la Gare, and turn left onto ave. Paul Cérésole. At the end of the road, cut across the parking lot toward the columned arcade; the office is inside. (☎962 84 74; fax 84 76; veveytourism@vevey.ch; www.montreux-vevey.com. Open from late June to late Aug. M-F 9am-5:30pm, Sa 9am-3:30pm, Su 9am-1pm; from Sept. to mid-June M-F 8:30am-noon and 1:30-6pm, Sa 9:30am-noon.) **Lockers** (4-7SFr) and **bike rental** (open 7:30am-7:30pm; 30SFr, children 25SFr, 23SFr/18SFr per half-day) are available at the train station. **Internet** (12SFr per hr.) is available at **Cyberworld,** r. de Torrent 4/6. (☎923 78 33. Open daily 1pm-midnight.) In an **emergency,** call ☎117; **fire,** ☎118; **ambulance,** ☎144. The **post office** is across pl. de la Gare (open M-F 7:30am-6pm, Sa 8:30am-noon) and has a 24hr. **ATM. Postal code:** CH-1800.

FROM THE ROAD

TRAVELING WHILE CHINESE

I'm undeniably Asian, despite the Boston accent and GAP jeans. Traveling through Switzerland through the final days of the World Cup Soccer tournament, I was frequently identified as Japanese or Korean. People stopped me daily to say *Arigato* or to congratulate me on the success of my team. At first, I was a little surprised, but the Americans had done better than most would expect. Then I realized they meant the Koreans.

I quickly tired of people's assumptions about my ethnicity, which were generally incorrect. There were days when I wanted to announce to the world that there were many countries on the continent of Asia and we're all different. It seemed so obvious to me, especially in Switzerland, a country that seemed to pride itself on tolerance. No one seemed to even contemplate that there might be vast differences between Asian languages and cultures. Or that I wasn't Korean.

But after the World Cup had come and gone and Switzerland had celebrated Brazil's win (or, more importantly, Germany's loss), I found myself alone in a Pan-Asian restaurant, seeking a little comfort food. Maybe I was seeking a comfort in a familiar culture. What I found was something totally different.

At the cashier's desk was a girl whom I heard speaking my native tongue. But when she asked me for my order, she quickly switched to broken English. Slightly disappointed by the lack of recognition, I sat down and waited for my food.

🏠🛏 ACCOMMODATIONS AND FOOD

Overlooking Grand-Place just off the waterfront is the ◼**Riviera Lodge ❷**, pl. du Marché 5. Head straight out of the station on the main road to the open square on the waterfront; the hostel is on the right, with 60 beds in bright, shiny rooms and modern, lavish facilities. The reception desk shares the 4th floor with a terrace and is manned by owner François and his multilingual staff. Several common rooms. Guests receive a pass for discounts and free activities in the Montreux-Vevey region, such as a ride up the Vevey funicular. (☎923 80 40; fax 80 41; rivieralodge@bluewin.ch; www.rivieralodge.ch. Spotless kitchen. **Internet** 3SFr per 15min. Sheets 5SFr. Laundry up to 7SFr. Reception 8am-noon and 5-8pm, extended during summer season. Call if arriving late. 4-, 6-, or 8-bed dorms 24SFr; doubles 80SFr. MC/V.) Many family homes also house travelers; one is **Pension Bürgle ❸**, r. Louis-Meyer 16, off Grand-Place. Take the first right after the hostel; the Pension is on the right. The rooms, though old, are large; many have balconies and TVs. (☎/fax 921 40 23; www.vevey.ch/tourisme/pension-burgle.htm. Breakfast included. Dinner 12SFr. Hallway bathrooms and showers. Reception 7am-11pm. Reserve with 1st-night payment. 42SFr per person. MC/V.)

For cheap, fresh food, check out the comprehensive and bustling **produce** (and **flea**) **market** at Grand-Place (pl. du Marché; Tu and Sa 8:30am-noon.) Do-it-yourself fare at **Migros** (open M 9am-6:30pm, Tu-W and F 8am-6:30pm, Th 8am-8pm, Sa 7:30am-5pm; restaurant opens 30min. earlier M-F) and **Co-op** (same hours), across ave. Paul Cérésole off Grand-Place. Cafe-restaurants with *Menüs* for around 12-15SFr line Grand-Place, but food is cheaper away from the lakefront. An **Aperto** stands next to the train station (open 6am-9:30pm).

🏛 MUSEUMS

Though not as thrilling as Montreux's Château de Chillon, the museums of Vevey are distinctive and well curated. For an excellent deal, pick up a **Montreux-Vevey Museum Passport** (15SFr), which grants entrance to eight museums in the two towns. Many of Vevey's museums can be reached on a stroll by the lake toward the neighboring town of Tour-de-Peilz. **Musée Jenisch,** ave. de la Gare 2, displays well-constructed, temporary exhibits and a room of spontaneous watercolors and pastels by adopted citizen Oskar Kokoschka, who lived in nearby Villeneuve for his last 25 years. (☎921 29 50. Tours available. Open Mar.-Oct. Tu-Su 11am-5:30pm; Nov.-Feb. 2-5:30pm. 15SFr, students 6SFr, seniors 12SFr.) The **Swiss Museum of Games,** at the end of the quai in the 13th-century Savoy Château de la Tour-de-Peilz, is a shrine to the twin ideals of skill and luck. It houses a display of ancient chess pieces, cardboard Cold War games, and Nintendo. Multilingual exhibits wax philosophical on the sociology of games (calling flirtation a game along with cow-tipping in rural America), but it's more fun just to play with the toys. (☎944 40 50. Open Mar.-Oct. 10:30am-noon and 2-5:30pm, Nov.-Feb. Tu-Su 2-5pm. 6SFr, students and seniors 3SFr, under 16 2.50SFr, free when accompanied by an adult. Tours 10SFr, students and seniors 7SFr, under 16 5SFr.)

The **Alimentarium/Food Museum,** on the corner of r. du Léman and quai Perdonnet, tells the story of food, from growth in the sun to processing in the human body. Nestlé advertisements, an interactive kitchen, a 3-D adventure through the digestive tract, and human-sized hamster wheels are some of the highlights of this child-friendly museum. (☎924 41 11. Open Tu-Su 10am-6pm. 10SFr, students and seniors 8SFr, ages 6-16 free.) The **Swiss Camera Museum,** on ruelle des Anciens-Fossés 6, near the tourist office, features five floors filled with historic photographic equipment from daguerreotypes to early spy cameras and modern digital cameras. Though there are several hands-on exhibits, the more technical explanations are hard without good French, and most displays are behind glass. (☎925 21 40. Open Mar.-Oct. Tu-Su 11am-5:30pm; Nov.-Feb. Tu-Su 2-5:30pm. 6SFr, students 4SFr, children free. Group tours 50SFr by appointment.)

🎭🎵 NIGHTLIFE AND ENTERTAINMENT

Nightlife options are slim in Vevey. If you're in the mood for a little craziness, head to nearby Montreux. In Vevey, right behind the Riviera Lodge at r. de Torrent 9, the **National** offers quiet meals (from 19SFr) and beers (from 3SFr) among funky decorations on a romantic candlelit terrace. (Open M-Th 11am-midnight, F-Sa 11am-2am, Su 4pm-midnight.) Across the street from the National at r. de Torrent 4-6 lies **Vertigo,** where drinks are served in a fashionable bar atmosphere.

The **Folklore Market** in pl. du Marché (open July-Aug.) allows sampling of all the local wine you can

Behind the counter, one of the cooks was explaining to another how to prepare noodles in a certain style. He was having trouble because they spoke different languages. Soon, several cooks and waiters joined in to help. I heard the small group switch between at least three different Asian languages laced with bits French and English. When the message finally came through, the whole bunch of them burst out laughing. They started jostling one another, joking about their shared experience of misunderstanding.

I sat there watching their playful interaction, suddenly feeling jealous. It occurred to me that distinguishing different traits between people, as I had sought to do, wasn't nearly as satisfying as finding shared ones.

—Alinna Chung

hold for only the price of the first glass, sometimes as low as 4SFr. Year-round, the **Winetrain** winds its way through 8km of villages and vineyards in Lavaux (every hr. from Vevey station 5:58am-10:08pm; take the "Puidoux-Chexbres" train; round-trip up to 10.40SFr, SwissPass and Eurail valid). The tourist office has a list of tasting venues, a map with directions to the wine centers, and a guide to six nearby hiking tours.

The summertime **International Comedy Film Festival,** dedicated to former resident Charlie Chaplin, features competitions by day and more accessible screenings by night. The **Theatre of Vevey,** r. de Théâtre 4 (☎923 60 55), produces live theater.

LES DIABLERETS   ☎024

Drawing its name from *Quille du Diable*, the tower-shaped rock that looms over the town, Les Diablerets challenges the notion that evil spirits still lurk in the mountains above. Multiple paths throughout the rocky landscape and a skiable glacier (even in summer!) welcome hikers, skiers, snowboarders, and adventure seekers year-round. Come winter, the town (pop. 1,300) emphasizes substance over the snootier stylings of local rivals Gstaad, Crans-Montana, and Verbier. A younger, more sports-driven crowd is the result.

▐ TRANSPORTATION

Three public transport services connect Les Diablerets to the rest of Switzerland: the **train** down to Aigle (50min., every hr. 6:27am-9:28pm, 10.40SFr); the **Post Bus** over the mountains to Gstaad (via the Col du Pillon, summer 5 per day 9:39am-5:09pm, 12.40 SFr) or to Leysin (via train to Le Sepey; summer 7 per day 8:28am-5:28pm, only 2 on weekends; 9SFr); and the **BVB bus** to the mountain town of Villars (via Col de la Croix, July 1-Sept. 16, 35min., 3 per day 10am-5pm, 11.40SFr). Local buses provide access to the Diablerets glacier **cable cars,** which travel to Cabane (one-way 21SFr, round-trip 30SFr) and the glacier (one-way 34SFr, round-trip 49SFr). The first bus leaves at 9:39am and the last returns at 4:46pm. Plan accordingly or be ready for a 45min. walk. Train station attendants will watch your **luggage** in the small ticket room free of charge.

▐ PRACTICAL INFORMATION

The **tourist office,** to the right of the station on r. de la Gare, publishes an impressive range of literature, including a list of activities. (☎/fax 492 33 58; info@diablerets.ch; www.diablerets.ch. Open July 7-Aug. 24 and mid-Dec. to Apr. 8:30am-6:30pm; May-June and Sept.-Nov. M-Sa 8:30am-12:30pm and 2-6pm, Su 9am-12:30pm.) For those looking for an **alternative to tourism,** try contacting the **St. Agnes Refugee Camp** (right from the Grand-Hôtel) for ways to get involved with the community. (☎494 11 71; fax 27 55.) Local services include: **taxis,** ☎079 205 05 55; **emergencies,** ☎144; **ambulance,** ☎494 50 30; **police,** ☎492 24 88. **Internet access** at La Diabletine bar and tea room (☎492 13 55; 3SFr per 15min; open daily 8am-10pm); and **post office,** right of the train station (open M-F 8am-noon and 2:30-6pm, Sa 8-11am). **Postal code:** CH-1865.

▐ ACCOMMODATIONS AND CAMPING

The cheapest accommodations are on the outskirts of town.

WHAT'S IN A NAME? Situated between the beautiful pastures of Anzeindaz and the green Vallée des Ormonts, the summit of Les Diablerets is said to have once hosted comparably lush fields. But according to local legend, the area has been barren and dangerous ever since the fated day a mean-spirited shephard refused the mountain's benevolent aid. As a punishment, the mountain transformed the flowery pastures into the sea of solid glacier that still looms today. The shephards who had brought their cattle to the area left, and the mountain became a playground for evil spirits. The valley people swore they heard spirits playing games, or skittles, with the rocks high above. The rock tower at the southern end of the glacier became known as Quille Du Diable (Devil's Skittle), while the town adopted the name Les Diablerets.

Les Lilas, rte. du Col du Pillon (☎ 492 31 34; fax 31 57), has a dim atmosphere created by the dark wood and low lighting, but the rooms themselves are well-kept and clean. Mid-sized double rooms come with full bathroom and television, and most have balconies that offer beautiful views of the surrounding mountains. Breakfast included. Singles 85-90SFr; small singles without bathroom 45SFr. Doubles 115-150SFr. ❹

Hotel Mon Abri, (☎ 492 34 81; fax 34 82; info@monabri.ch, www.monabri.ch), is on the rte. du Pillon past the Co-op. Under a new young management, Mon Abri continues to be a mecca for hardcore snowboarders and skateboarders. In the summer Mon Abri hosts a massive skateboard camp to which young enthusiasts from all over Europe flock *en masse,* and in the months of October and November it offers snowboard rentals for top-of-the-line test gear. Other amenities include laundry (3SFr per kg), **free Internet,** a weekend bar and **disco,** beach volleyball courts, and **bike** rental in summer. Open all year. Reservations recommended in high season (July-Aug. and Dec.-Apr.). 48SFr per person; children 28SFr. Low season (May-June and Sept-Nov.) 42SFr/20SFr. ❸

Les Diablotins, rte. du Pillon, (☎ 492 36 33; fax 23 55; diablotins@freesurf.ch; www.diablotins.ch) is a big modern block popular with young snowboarding groups. From the station, turn right, bend left around the hairpin turn, and turn left along rte du Pillon at the top of the hill. Avoid the 30min. uphill walk by calling from the station; the hostel will send a minibus. The 2- to 5-bed rooms are in good shape (all have private sinks and most have balconies) in spite of the thousands of schoolkids who tramp through the halls and shared showers each year. This mammoth institution has 4 dining halls, several lounges, a bar, and a **disco**—all segregated by age and noise-tolerance level. Breakfast included. Dinner 16SFr. Reception 8am-8pm. Reserve one week ahead in winter. Jan. 6-Jan. 17 54SFr, under 18 38SFr; Jan. 18-Feb. 7 60SFr/38SFr; Feb. 8-Apr. 3 64SFr/41SFr; Apr. 4-Dec. 25 35SFr/33SFr; Dec. 26-Jan. 5 67SFr/41SFr. Children under 16 30-50% discount. AmEx/MC/V. ❸

Camping La Murée, (☎ 079 401 99 15 camp.lamuree@swissfree.ch). Take the Aigle train one stop to "Vers l'Eglise," go left past the post office and church, and cross the railroad tracks to set up camp among the many RVs at this quiet site in a tiny valley town. Showers included. A newly built lot across the street offers free parking. Reception 6-7pm. 5.80SFr per person in summer, 6.30SFr in winter. Tents 9SFr in summer; 10SFr in winter. ❶

FOOD

Left at the intersection of r. de la Gare and rte. de Colde la Croix, or up the path behind the tourist office, **Pizzeria Locanda Livia** ❷ serves 24 kinds (15-20SFr, 2SFr less for miniature version), including a 4-cheese pizza with gruyère called *rêve de* *souris* (mouse's dream). Chinese food also available in the evening. (☎492 32 80. Open M-Tu and Th-Su 11:30am-2pm and 6:30-10pm. AmEx/DC/MC/V.) At **Le Muguet ❶,** on the right past the tourist office, try a dessert crêpe (5-9.50SFr) with *chocolat viennois* (4SFr), a dish of *chantilly crême* (1.50SFr), or their sandwiches (3.50-8.50SFr) and tea or beer. (☎492 26 42. Open 6:30am-7pm; food until 5pm. MC/V.) For easy access to the good food, ask about renting the apartment upstairs (☎/fax 492 26 43; min. 1 week.) The **Co-op,** left on r. de la Gare from the station, is the perfect place to stock up on cheap cheese, wine, and bread. (Open M-F 8am-12:15pm and 2:30-6:30pm, Sa 8am-12:30pm and 2-5pm.)

🏔 OUTDOOR ACTIVITIES

SKIING. Les Diablerets' year-round skiing got better in 1999 with the completion of a **cable car,** which travels from the Col du Pillon above the village to Cabane, then to the glacier at Scex-Rouge. Diablerets day passes (39SFr), combined Diablerets/Villars passes (46SFr), Alpes Vaudoises transportation and lift passes (52SFr), and other **ski passes** are sold at the cable car's departure point. Book special hotel deals that include stay-and-ski passes, a fondue evening, tobogganing, curling, skating, and babysitting services at the tourist office. **Jacky Sports,** near the tourist office, rents **ski equipment.** (☎492 32 18; www.jackysport.ch. Open June, Oct., and Nov. 9am-12pm and 2-6pm daily; closing times extended 30min. July 1-Sept. 9; Dec.-Apr. 8:30am-6:30pm. Skis and snowboards 28-50SFr per day, boots 15-19SFr; special rates for multi-day rentals. AmEx/DC/MC/V.) **Holiday Sport,** across from the tourist office, is another rental option (☎492 37 17; per day, skis 28-50SFr, boots 9-15SFr; snowboards 38SFr, boots 15-19SFr.) The **ski and snowboard school,** in the tourist office, can prepare you for the slopes. (☎492 20 02; fax 23 48; skischool@diablerets.ch; www.diablerets.ch; 6 half-days 142SFr.) The **New Devil School of Snowboarding** can get the inexperienced ready for the mountains. (☎492 34 31 or 079 412 62 40. Open 8:30am-6:30pm. 2hr. lesson 44SFr.)

HIKING AND BIKING. Jacky Sports and Holiday Sports also rent **mountain bikes.** (Jacky: 35SFr per day, 5 days 110SFr; Holiday: 35-45SFr per day, 5 days 135-145SFr.) A good hike that can be done in several segments, depending on stamina, starts at the tourist office. Turn right across the river at the pharmacy, then right again so that you are facing the Sommet des Diablerets (3209m) and the glacier. The sides of the valley close in as the level riverside walk progresses and deposits you on the stage of a rugged 200m high amphitheater at **Creux de Champ.** (1hr., 160m ascent.) The path starts to climb steeply up the sides to the **Refuge de Pierredar** at 2278m. (3hr. above Les Diablerets, 1110m ascent.) The agile can then push up to **Scex Rouge** (2971m), the cable car terminus on the glacier, which affords an unforgettable alpine view. (1 day, high summer and perfect weather only; guide recommended for later sections of the hike.)

ADVENTURE SPORTS. Les Diablerets' adventure sports awaken the death wish within. **Mountain Evasion** is a misnomer; they organize **canyoning** (80-165SFr), **snowshoeing** (25-70SFr), **rappeling** (85SFr), and **dirt biking** (35-70SFr), not to mention **luging** for 18SFr, or 36SFr for a nighttime descent with fondue. (☎492 12 32; fax 22 67.) Winter office in the Maison du Tourisme, summer office in a little wooden shack along the river. At the pharmacy turn right across the river, then left onto the Chemin de Vernex. (Open 5:30am-6:30pm, but best to call ahead. MC.) Left from the train station and past the post office along r. de la Gare, **Centre ParAdventure** offers **paragliding** (90-150SFr), **canyoning** (80SFr), and the new **Arapaho mud**

bike (40SFr). (☎ 492 23 82 or 079 435 25 82; fax 435 25 82; www.swissaventure.ch. Open 9-9:30am and 5:30-6:30pm.)

LEYSIN ☎ 024

The textured concrete and stucco buildings belie Leysin's French influence in the Swiss Alps. This laid-back town's location, high on the south side of a mountain overlooking the vast Rhone valley, gave it the ideal amount of solar exposure for Dr. August Rollier's tuberculosis treatments in the first years of the 20th century. Patients flocked to Leysin for treatment. By 1930, 3000 of the town's 5,698 inhabitants were working on their tans per order of the good doctor. When World War II brought antibiotics and the end of faith in the treatment of the "sun doctor," the people of Leysin continued the tradition of attracting visitors with irresistible sunny days, wide vistas, and white slopes. Skiers come in droves to get their fix.

TRANSPORTATION AND PRACTICAL INFORMATION

Leysin can be reached in the summer by **bus** from Les Diablerets (via train to Le Sepey, summer 7 per day 8:28am-5:28pm, only 2 on weekends, 9SFr) or year-round by the **cog railway** from Aigle, which chugs passengers up the steep climb at a medium pace. (30min., every hr. 6am-10:38pm; SwissPass valid.) There are 4 stops: Leysin-Village (8.40SFr), Versmont (9.80SFr), Feydey (9.80SFr), and Grand-Hôtel (10.40SFr). A free hourly **shuttle** helps you up and down the hillside, including a stop at the hostel. (June 20-Sept. 14 and mid-Dec. through mid-Apr.) The **tourist office,** located in the Centre Sportif just up the road to the left from pl. du Marché, provides **hiking maps** and general information on the town. (☎ 494 22 44; fax 16 16; info@leysin.ch; www.leysin.ch. Open M-F 8am-9pm, Sa-Su 9am-9pm.) Services include: **ATM** at the **Banque Cantonal Vaudous** just below Hefti Sports; **taxis** (☎ 493 22 93 or 494 25 55); **bike rental** at the station for 27SFr; **snow report** (☎ 494 13 01); **emergency,** ☎ 117; **police,** ☎ 493 45 41. **Pharmacie Leysin** is on pl. du Marché. (☎ 493 45 00. Open M-F 8:30-noon and 2-6:30pm; Sa 9am-12:30pm and 2-5pm.) **Post office** in Leysin-Village on r. du Village. (☎ 494 12 05. Open M-F 8-11am and 2:30-6pm, Sa 8:30-11am.) **Postal code**: CH-1854.

ACCOMMODATIONS AND CAMPING

▩ **Hiking Sheep Guesthouse,** Villa La Joux (☎ 494 35 35; fax 35 37; hikingsheep@leysin.net; www.leysin.net/hikingsheep). From the "Grand Hôtel" turn left on the gravel road, or catch the shuttle in high season. The Sheep has wooden bunks, a convivial dining room, balconies, and pristine kitchen facilities. New owner Paul-Henri goes the extra mile, supplying satellite TV, VCR and video collection, game and meditation rooms, **Internet** access (5SFr per 30min.), **fax** services (2SFr), and **mountain bikes** for rent (30SFr per day, 20SFr per half-day). Buffet breakfast 8SFr. Sheets included. Laundry 10SFr. Only two showers serve the whole house, but renovations and expansions are in the works. Reception open 8-10am and 5-10pm. Check-out 10:30am. No curfew. Dorms 30SFr per person; doubles 80SFr; triples 120SFr. Ask about reduced prices for children, extended stays, and groups. MC/V. ❷

Hotel La Paix, on ave. Rollier, (☎/fax 494 13 75), is opposite the "Versmont" train stop. A doorway decorated with traditional Valais masks open into narrow hallways that connect old-fashioned rooms with fading prints of *belle époque* Leysin. Breakfast included. Lunch or dinner 16SFr. Reception 8am-8pm. Singles 52SFr, with shower 69SFr; doubles with shower 108SFr. AmEx/MC/V. ❸

Hôtel du Soleil (☎494 39 39; fax 21 21; info@hoteldusoleil.ch; www.hoteldusoleil.ch), aptly named, houses several rooms with large windows and terrific views. From Leysin-Village station, walk left on r. de Village, then right on r. du Suchet past the post office. Bathrooms and showers in every room. Breakfast included. (Jan.-Feb, mid-April to July, and Aug. 24-Oct. 20: 3-4 bed dorms, 55SFr; singles 80SFr; doubles 60SFr. Mar., July-Aug. 23 and Dec.: 60SFr/70SFr/90SFr. AmEx/DC/MC/V.) ❸

Camping Semiramis (☎494 39 39; fax 21 21) is a large grassy field near an evergreen forest and in the backyard of Hôtel du Soleil (see directions above). Showers included and a small playground. Summer 6SFr per person, 3SFr per child, 4SFr per tent, electricity 4SFr; winter 6.50SFr/4SFr. 4SFr per tent, electricity 6SFr; between seasons 5SFr/2.50SFr; 3SFr per tent, electricity 4SFr; contact for dates. AmEx/DC/MC/V. ❶

▐ FOOD

La Prafandaz (☎494 26 26), about a 30min. walk from the Hiking Sheep (signs point the way), is a slightly off-the-wall chalet decorated with a ticking-udder cow clock, a handmade aquarium, and evidence of the owner's love of mushrooms—owner/chef Alex makes his own sauce from hand-picked specimens. The menu is short and focuses on the house specialty, *les rosettes*, which consist of meat, vegetables, or salmon rolled into homemade pasta, grilled, and smothered in a rich sauce with a healthy portion of cheese for 10-19SFr. Open Jan.-Apr. 15, May weekends, and June-Oct. 11am-11pm. No credit cards. ❷

La Nonna Restaurant Pizzeria (☎494 21 94), above the Centre Sportif. Feast on hearty Italian pastas (17-22SFr) and risottos (20.50-26.80SFr) or try one of the 29 types of pizza (many vegetarian, 13-20SFr). Daily specials feature soup or salad and a pasta (15-19SFr). Open M-Sa 8am-11:30pm, Su 9am-11:30pm, serves food noon-2pm and 6-10:30pm. ❸

La Grotta (☎494 15 32), down the hill from the Feyday stop, rewards a stroll to the district. This restaurant offers classic pizzas (12-18SFr) as well as omelettes (9-12SFr) and traditional Swiss fondue (34SFr for two). The most outstanding feature is the owner's Swatch collection—a dazzling expo of all editions since 1983, including special music alarm, beeper, and ski-pass versions—which are for sale. Open Tu-Su 9am-11pm. ❷

Co-op, just off the big bend in r. Favez, below pl. du Marché and the Centre Sportif, is ideal for groceries. Open M-F 8am-noon and 2-6:30pm, Sa 8am-12pm and 2-5pm.

▐ OUTDOOR ACTIVITIES

A **Leysin Holiday Card** (distributed after 1 night at any hotel or hostel) grants a 10-50% discount at any of Leysin's sports centers, cable cars, and ski lifts. For guided **hiking** and **adventure sports** contact the **Swiss Climbing Club.** (☎494 18 46; fax 33 75; info@guideservice.ch; www.guideservice.ch.) **Tele-Leysin** (☎494 16 35; fax 16 34; info@teleleysin.ch) offers a relaxed trip to the top of La Berneuse (2331m), where **Restaurant Tournant Panoramique** provides a self-served meal (☎494 31 41). For the more active travelers, a romantic walk begins at the Hiking Sheep, continues past the American School at Leysin and travels to **La Grande Crevasse,** an ideal place to catch the sunset. Head on a rogue path toward the satellite tower for a breath-taking view of the valley below or continue around to the **Prafandaz** to catch a dinner of rosettes at La Prafandaz (see

GENEVA AND LAC LÉMAN

Food, above). The most unusual hike is **La Via Ferrata** (the "iron path"), a series of metal safety cables, steps, and rungs that ascend **La Tour d'Aï** (Leysin's highest peak at 2331m). Not a hike to be undertaken by the inexperienced. Heed the posted warnings and hike properly equipped. Inquire at the tourist office. The 2½hr. hike from the village winds past a cheese farm full of bovine beauties into steep wildflower fields; (small) signs point out the Via Ferrata. The necessary gear (16SFr) is available from **Hefti Sports,** across from the cable car station, or head to the shop, 2min. from the Centre Sportif on pl. du Marché. (Rental ☎ 494 17 44; shop and office 16 77. Open M-Sa 8:30am-noon and 2-6:30pm, Su 10am-noon and 3-6pm.) **Vieceli Sport,** up the road from the Co-op, has rental deals as well. (☎ 494 10 05; open M-Su 8:30am-noon and 1:30-6:30pm. AmEx/DC/MC/V.) **Endless Ride Proshop** (☎ 494 11 31) rents mountain bikes (35SFr/day) and snowboards (35SFr per day, boots 14SFr) near the cable car station. 1-day **ski passes** average 40SFr, children 25SFr; weekly passes are available.

There are two sports centers in the village. **Centre Sportif,** in the pl. Large, has **squash** and **tennis** courts and **pools.** (☎ 494 22 44; infor@leysin.ch; www.leysin.ch. Open M-F 8am-9pm, Sa-Su 9am-9pm; pools have slightly shorter hours.) Visit the **Tobogganing Park** (20SFr for 50min.) or skate at the **Ice Skating Sports Centre** (☎ 494 24 42), downhill near the campsite. (7SFr, students and children 4.50SFr; skate rental 4.50SFr, 3.50SFr.) For **paragliding,** call **Ecole Parapante** (☎ 079 638 26 02; fax 494 26 02), or reach the skies via helicopter (☎ 494 34 34; 50SFr per person, min. 5 people). Horseback riding is available at the **Manège Riding Hall** (☎ 494 17 07).

GRYON   ☎ 024

GENEVA AND LAC LÉMAN

The tiny town of Gryon has experienced a population boom in recent years—from 800 to 1,000. Rather than risk a greater unemployment rate, the proud locals have an ordinance which allows only one child from each family to stay in the town. The kids have a tendency to come back, though, drawn to Gryon's virtually untouched, tranquil mountain setting within reach of the Dents du Midi and the Les Diablerets glacier. Its main draw for world-weary travelers is undoubtedly its popular hostel, the 🗹**Swiss Alps Retreat ❷,** housed in the Chalet Martin. From the station, follow the train tracks uphill; you'll see backpacker signs to your left. A gem even among Swiss hostels, the Swiss Alps Retreat has taken the "hostel" concept back to its roots and improved it with a hipper twist. New arrivals are immediately sucked into a bohemian, barefoot, Anglophone-with-any-accent backpacker community. Owners Bertrand and Robyn (and a super-friendly young staff) provide backpackers a temporary family and activities from hiking to chocolate tasting. Happy to "take a vacation from their vacation," travelers passing through Gryon have been known to stay long and return often. In the nine years it took for the hostel to grow from four beds to 87, ten couples who met at the Chalet Martin have gotten married. Amenities include discounted **ski rentals, Internet** access (10SFr per hr.), **video/DVD rental** (2SFr/4SFr) from a small but entertaining collection, and a pool of possible future spouses. The main chalet has recently been renovated to feature homey common rooms and funky wood-framed showers. Chalet Martin's real attraction, however, is its prime location for taking advantage of the outdoors. The hostel has daily sign-ups for **cheese farm tours, paragliding, thermal baths, guided overnight hikes,** and excursions (like a ski trip to Zermatt). They also lend maps to hikers and provide a 40% discount on ski rentals. (☎ 498 33 21; fax 35 31; info@gryon.com; www.gryon.com. Co-ed dorms and bathrooms. Large kitchen facilities available. Laundry 3-5SFr. Call ahead. For Christmas bookings check the web site. Check-in 9am-9pm. Dorms 18-25SFr; doubles 50-75SFr. Discounted prices for multiple night stays; 110SFr for full week. Cash only.)

Reach Gryon by **cog railway** from Bex (30min.; every hr., last train 8:23pm; 5.80SFr, Eurail and SwissPass valid), which lies on the main rail line connecting the Lac Léman cities (Geneva, Lausanne, Montreux) to Aigle, Martigny, and Sion, or **by foot** from Villars (one stop farther on the cog rail; 45min. walk from the hostel). **Buses** connect to Villars, through Col de la Croix to Les Diablerets (35min., 3 per day 9:02am-4:20pm, 10.40SFr) and from there, a bus runs to Aigle (35min., every 1-2hr. 6:05am-7:45pm, 7.80SFr). The **tourist office,** in neighboring La Barboleuse, is uphill on the route de Villars, about 10min. from the hostel. (☎498 14 22; fax 26 22. Open M-Sa 8am-noon and 2-6pm, Su 9am-noon and 4-6pm.) To reach the **market** from the station, walk downhill on the road on the right instead of uphill (open M-F 7:30am-12:15pm and 2-6:30pm, Sa 7:30am-5pm, Su 8am-noon).

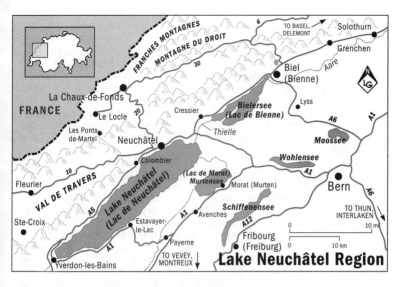

LAKE NEUCHÂTEL REGION

Almost every town in the Lake Neuchâtel region can boast a sandy beach and clear view of the Jura mountains. By-products of this pristine setting are some of the richest Pinot noirs and spritziest Chasselas of the country, a secret well-kept by the Swiss. Perhaps it is this rarely exported nectar that generates the easygoing spirit of locals, who warmly embrace wide-eyed tourists to their dazzling domain.

HIGHLIGHTS OF LAKE NEUCHÂTEL

Stroll through the lush vineyards of **Cressier** and sample the newest wine with fresh local cheese (see p. 518).

Treat yourself to a relaxing soak in the hot springs of **Yverdon-les-Bains** (see p. 518).

Hike from **Biel** along mossy cliffs to legendary **Taubenloch,** and enjoy a 3-course meal at Eau-Berge du Taubenloch (see p. 520).

NEUCHÂTEL   ☎032

Neuchâtel dangles its legs over the edge of its eponymous lake, its glorious edifices looking as if they might melt right into the turquoise water. Alexandre Dumas once said that Neuchâtel appeared to be carved out of butter. Although he was no doubt referring to the unique yellow stone that characterizes the city's architecture, the comment could easily be mistaken for a reference to the calorie-laden treats in local *pâtisseries*. *Neuchâteloise* cuisine prides itself on quality fondue, sausages, and fresh fish from the lake and nearby rivers. The town has winding streets that exude both historical charm and modern, student-oriented flair.

513

▐ TRANSPORTATION

Trains connect Neuchâtel to: **Basel** (1¾hr., every hr. 5:31am-10:24pm, 34SFr); **Bern** (45min., every hr. 5:15am-11:24pm, 17.20SFr); **Fribourg** (1hr., every hr. 5:34am-10:34pm, 18SFr) via **Ins-Murten; Geneva** (1½hr., every hr. 5:57am-11:38pm, 35-40SFr); and **Interlaken** (2hr., every hr. 6am-11:21pm, 38SFr) via **Bern.** An underground **tram** called the Fun'Ambule travels from the bottom floor of the train station to the shore area, where you can catch **bus** #1 to the tourist office and Pl. Pury. **Ferries** provide service to **Biel** (2½hr., 3 per day, 27SFr) and **Murten** (1¾hr., 6 per day, 16.20SFr), departing from the Port de la Ville, just behind the post office (free with Eurail or SwissPass).

■✴▐ ORIENTATION AND PRACTICAL INFORMATION

Neuchâtel centers on **place Pury,** a major square and the hub of every bus line. From pl. Pury, face the lake and walk 2 blocks to the left to find the **tourist office,** Hôtel des Postes (in the same building as the post office). City maps are free. Check out the *Terroir Neuchâtelois* guide for a listing of places that produce local goods. (☎889 68 90; fax 62 96; tourisme.neuchatelois@ne.ch; www.ne.ch/tourism. Open M-F 9am-noon and 1:30-6pm, Sa 9am-noon.) Services include: **lockers** (4-6SFr) and **bike rental** (25SFr per day) at the station; **Internet** at **Shogun,** Faubourg du Lac 31 (☎721 21 01; 7SFr per hr.); **police,** ☎117; **hospital,** ☎722 91 11. The **post office** is open M-F 7:30am-6:30pm, Sa 8:30am-noon. **Postal code:** CH-2001.

▐ ACCOMMODATIONS

Sleep cheaply at **Oasis Neuchâtel ❷,** r. du Suchiez 35, the only hostel in town. From the station, take the underground tram down to the main part of town, then take bus #1 (dir: Cormondrèche) to "Vauseyon." Continue walking on the smaller uphill road and follow it around the large bend. Look up on your left for the yellow happy face affixed to the hostel, about 100m up the hill. Perched far above the center of the city, this quirky house has 38 beds, ping-pong, a BBQ, and an eco-friendly, multilingual atmosphere. However, thin walls let in a lot of noise, and the lack of locks bother some. Beware the long walk after the buses stop running at night, though a nightbus runs to the nearby "Beauregard" stop. (☎731 31 90; fax 730 37 09. Breakfast 7SFr. Shower and sheets included. Reception 8-10am and 5-9pm. No curfew. Reservations recommended. Free on your birthday! 4- to 6-bed dorms 30SFr; doubles 70SFr; 2-person summer teepee 40SFr.) For convenient location near the local nightlife, try **Hôtel des Arts ❹,** r. Pourtalès 3. From the Fun'ambule, walk a block towards the city center on ave. du Premier-Mars and turn left onto r. Pourtalès for reasonably priced citrus-colored rooms filled with modern art. (☎727 61 61; fax 61 62. Breakfast included. Reception 24hr. Check-out noon. Singles 80SFr, with bath 98-130SFr; doubles 100SFr/140-176SFr.) Multi-themed rooms at the **Hotel de L'Ecluse ❺,** r. de L'Ecluse 24 come fully-equipped with clean bathrooms and a kitchenette. Follow ave. de la Gare downhill until the intersection, then follow the signs. The entrance is right by **Globaline,** which offers **Internet** access for 7SFr per hr. (☎729 93 10; fax 93 20. Singles 150SFr; doubles 200SFr; triples 250SFr; quads 290SFr.) There is also the **Paradis Plage campground ❶,** in nearby Colombier, on the lakefront. From pl. Pury, take tram #5 (dir: Boudry) to "Bas des Allées." Cross the tracks at the tram crossing and walk 2min. down the gravel path. (☎841 24 46. Reception 8:30am-9pm. Open Mar.-June and Aug. 11-Oct. 9SFr, children 3SFr, 8SFr per site; July-Aug. 10 9SFr, children 3SFr, 15SFr per site. Electricity 3.50SFr per night.)

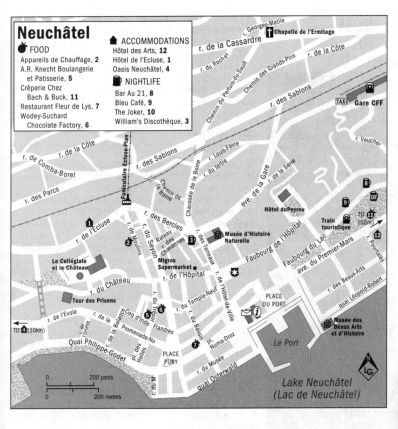

Neuchâtel

🍴 FOOD

Appareils de Chauffage, **2**
A.R. Knecht Boulangerie
  et Patisserie, **5**
Crêperie Chez
  Bach & Buck, **11**
Restaurant Fleur de Lys, **7**
Wodey-Suchard
  Chocolate Factory, **6**

🏠 ACCOMMODATIONS

Hôtel des Arts, **12**
Hôtel de l'Ecluse, **1**
Oasis Neuchâtel, **4**

🎵 NIGHTLIFE

Bar Au 21, **8**
Bleu Café, **9**
The Joker, **10**
William's Discothèque, **3**

🍴 FOOD

Neuchâtel may live off tourists in July and August, but the rest of the year it's a university town, which means there is cheap food aplenty. **Crêperie Chez Bach & Buck ❶**, ave. du Premier-Mars 22, across the street from the Jardin Anglais, near the underground tram exit, counters its friendly, laid-back atmosphere with an intensely detailed list of choices. Enjoy amazing sugar crepes with fruit or ice cream for 3-7.80SFr, or meat or cheese ones for 6-11SFr. (☎ 725 63 53. M-Th 11:30am-2pm and 5:30-10pm, F 11:30am-2pm and 5:30-11:30pm, Sa 11am-11:30pm, Su noon-10pm.) At **A.R. Knecht Boulangerie et Pâtisserie ❶**, on the corner of pl. des Halles and r. du Coq d'Inde, locals munch croissants stuffed with spiced ham (3SFr), fruit tarts (3.20-3.60SFr), and the *pain noix* (3.10SFr). (☎ 725 13 21. Open Tu-Sa 6am-6:30pm.) Further up the pl. des Halles, on r. des Moulins, the unassuming bistro **Appareils de Chauffage et de Cuisine ❸** serves a largely male clientele affordable *plat du jour* for 16.50SFr. (☎ 721 43 96. Open M-Th 7am-1am, F 7am-2am, Sa 8am-2am, Su 7pm-1am.) This cafe is the main source of income for the **Centre d'Art Neuchâtel (CAN)** next door, an experimental art center. (☎ 724 01 60; www.can.ch/can.) Those desperately seeking Italian flavor may be satiated by a visit to **Restaurant Fleur de Lys ❸**. (Pizzas 13.50-30SFr, pastas 16.50-21SFr. AmEx/

FROM THE ROAD

THERE'S NO PLACE LIKE (SOMEBODY ELSE'S) HOME

In a small town with only one hostel, there are bound to be some challenges for the weary budget traveler. I landed in Yverdon-les-Bains with a huge backpack and sore feet, only to learn that the hostel was already fully booked. As a loyal hostel-goer and generally paranoid city girl, I was turned off by the only other option in my price range: the private home. Images of being robbed as I slept in the boiler room passed through my mind as I warily agreed to this alternative accommodation.

When I arrived at a charming house on Rue du College, it occurred to me that I might have overreacted. My hostess greeted me with a warm smile and a bowl of cherries, and showed me to my room, decorated with old French movie posters and fresh flowers on the table. At breakfast the next morning, she served fresh bread with homemade jam and an assortment of fresh fruits and yogurts. I ate while my hostess did the dishes, cheerfully whistling an American rap tune.

After five weeks on the road, it was nice to be home, even if it was somebody else's home. The institutional bunkbeds and line of sinks characteristic of many hostels were nowhere to be found. I was awed at the fact that I was paying little more than a bed in a hostel for this little piece of backpacking heaven. To think that I had ignored this option all along.

—Alinna Chung

DC/MC/V.) Sample chocolates at the **Wodey-Suchard Chocolate Factory ❶**, r. du Seyon 5, directly behind the pl. Pury. (Open M 11am-6:30pm, Tu-F 6:30am-6:30pm, Sa 6:30am-5pm.) In the town center, **Migros**, r. de l'Hôpital 12, has groceries. (Open M-W 8am-7pm, Th 8am-9pm, F 7:30am-7pm, Sa 7:30am-7pm.) There's an **Aperto** in the station. (☎721 20 41. Open daily 6am-10pm.)

👁 SIGHTS

Neuchâtel's cultural offerings are confined to an easily walkable area centering around pl. Pury. You can traverse the town in minutes, unless it happens to be the last weekend of September, when the three-day **Fête des Vendanges** (Wine Festival) occurs and it takes hours to wade through throngs of carousers enjoying parades, jazz concerts, and wine feasts. A Swiss museum passport, available at many museums (30SFr), grants admission to most museums in Neuchâtel, La Chaux-de-Fonds, and neighbor La Locle. Neuchâtel's small but respected archaeological museum re-opened in nearby Hauterive in 2001.

THE OLD TOWN. The heart of town is the vieille ville (old city), which is dominated by a cobblestone marketplace (pl. des Halles, one block to the right of pl. Pury) and home of the thrice-weekly market (T, Th, Sa 6:30am-noon). If you're up for meandering around town in a tourist train, hop aboard at the Jardin Anglais (6SFr, in English, French, and German, every 30min. after 2pm in the summer). Otherwise, explore with the aid of the tourist office map.

CHURCHES, CASTLES, AND DUNGEONS. From the pl. des Halles, turn left onto the r. de Chateau (marked by the red-faced clock, the **Tour de Piesse**) and climb the stairs on your right to reach both the **Collégiale** (a church) and the chateau which gives the town its name. Begun in the 12th century, construction of the church took so long that architectural styles changed from Romanesque to Gothic. The golden stars and blue skies of the vaulted ceiling arch harmoniously over stained-glass windows and faded wall murals that were reinstalled after the fervor of the Reformation died down. The garish **Cenotaph,** a sculptural composition of the Counts of Neuchâtel from 1372 on, all reverently looking skyward, was covered during the Reformation to prevent destruction and was recently restored. *(Open Oct.-Mar. daily 9am-6:30pm, Apr.-Sept. 9am-8pm. Free. Concerts at 6:30 the last F of every month.)* Next door, the

12th-century **chateau** served as the seat of the Count of Neuchâtel during the Middle Ages. Look for splotches of red on the old outside walls, remnants of a fire in 1415 that literally baked the yellow stone. Today the bureaucrats of the cantonal government sit behind the striped shutters and flower boxes. A small garden connects the chateau to the **Tour des Prisons** (Prison Tower). The 125-step ascent allows you to examine the claustraphobia-inducing wooden cells used until 1848 and to enjoy a view from the top. *(On r. Jeanne-de-Hochberg. Open Apr.-Sept. 8am-6pm. 1SFr, coins only.)*

■ MUSÉE D'HISTOIRE NATURELLE. The Musée d'Histoire Naturelle (Museum of Natural History) sits atop the r. des Terreaux, to the left off r. de l'Hôpital. This is the more innovative version of the standard natural history museum, often featuring unconventional exhibits about the Earth and its creatures. A current exhibit, running through May 2003, has sand trickling from the ceiling of the museum constantly since the start of the exhibit in January 2002. *(R. des Terreaux 14. ☎ 717 79 60.) Turn right from the pl. des Halles onto the Croix du Marché, which becomes r. de l'Hôpital. Open Tu-Su 10am-6pm. 6SFr, students 3SFr.)*

MUSÉE D'ART ET D'HISTOIRE. The Musée d'Art et d'Histoire (Museum of Art and History) is an eclectic collection of paintings, weapons, and textiles telling the history of Neuchâtel, mostly in French. The curatorial staff gives presentations (Tu 12:15pm). The uncanny 18th-century automatons created by Jacquet-Droz are the museum's pride and joy; two barefoot boys in velvet coats scribble away while a lady plays the harpsichord. Upstairs, the Art Nouveau cupola includes oil paintings (one of which portrays Neuchâtel as the "Intellectual Life"), stained glass, and sculpted angels that seem to fly out of the walls. *(From pl. des Halles, walk toward the lake and turn left onto esplanade Léopold-Robert 1. ☎ 717 79 20; fax 79 29. Open Tu-Su 10am-6pm. Open M from Easter to June 8. 7SFr, students 4SFr, under 16 and W free. Automaton performances first Su of each month at 2, 3, and 4pm.)*

OTHER SIGHTS. Further along r. de l'Hôpital, elegant gates and 2 alluring sphinxes invite a stroll into **Hotel du Peyrou,** once the home of Jean-Jacques Rousseau's friend and publisher Alexandre du Peyrou. Cheese enthusiasts can make a pilgrimage to the **Fromagerie Les Martel** (cheese factory) in neighboring Les Ponts-de-Martel for a tour and demonstration. *(Major Benoit 25, Les Ponts-de-Martel. 40min. bus ride from train station. ☎ 937 16 66. Open 8am-noon and 5-7pm. Free.)*

■ NIGHTLIFE

A university crowd makes nightlife in Neuchâtel lively; the city is famous for its techno DJs. The **Joker,** Foubourg du Lac 14, has 2 dance clubs specializing in jungle music, with 3-5SFr beers. (☎ 724 48 48. Cover from 10SFr. Open F-Su 10pm-4am.) Just behind Joker is **Bar Au 21,** Faubourg de Lac 23. Nurture beers (2.20-7.80SFr) or long drinks (6-9SFr) under Pink Floyd posters or play foosball with a clientele younger than the bar's name suggests. (☎ 725 81 98. M-Th 7pm-1am, F 7pm-2am, Sa 5pm-2am, Su 5pm-1am.) A few doors down is the popular **Bleu Café.** You can catch a flick while enjoying a sandwich and drink for 20SFr. (Open M-Th 7:15pm-midnight, F 7:45pm-1am, Sa 4pm-1am, Su 4pm-9pm.) **William's Discotheque,** r. des Terreaux 7, across from the Musée d'Histoire, caters to a blue-collar crowd. Medieval stone walls loom over a three-story pit that has a British street lamp as a centerpiece. Beers go for 3.5-6SFr., long drinks for 8-18SFr. Prices increase after 11:30pm. (Open Tu-W and Su 9:30pm-2am, Th-Sa 9:30pm-4am. Free cocktail for ladies on Th. Two free cocktails on your birthday, with ID.)

⚡ DAYTRIPS FROM NEUCHÂTEL

CRESSIER ☎ 032

Trains run from Neuchâtel to Cressier, dir: Biel (10min., every hr. 5:39am-11:22pm, 3.80SFr).

The sleepy medieval wine-making hamlet of Cressier presents a perfect opportunity for a daytrip. Built around a tiny château that houses the local government, the medieval village packs no less than seven **caves** (KAHV; wine cellars) where friendly local vintners offer tours of their facilities and answer questions about grapes. The finale, of course, is *la dégustation*, sampling wines poured by the hands that make them. Choose from *chasselas, pinot noir,* or *l'oeil-de-perdrix,* or leave it to the expert *("Votre choix").*

Caves line the only main street. Of note is the particularly traditional and congenial *cave* of **Jean-Paul Ruedin,** rte. de Troub 4, around the corner from the train station. Jean-Paul is the 14th Ruedin son to operate the family vineyards since the first planted grapes in 1614. The *cave* Ruedin, whose white wine *(vin blanc)* has been honored by the *Gerle d'Or* (Golden Cellar) for several years, expresses a philosophical attitude towards the craft; the door declares, *"Aimer le vin c'est aimer la vie"*—"To love wine is to love life." (☎757 11 51. Open Tu-F 8am-noon and 1:30-5:30pm, Sa 9-11:30am. Call in advance.) For more variety, attend a *dégustation extraordinaire* hosted by the **Maison Vallier,** r. Vallier 1, behind and to the left of the chateau, where many vintners present their wares. (☎/fax 079 669 4854; contact@caveaudesvins.ch. Open Mar.-Nov. F 5-7:30pm, Sa 11am-12:30pm and 4:30-7pm, Su 11am-12:30pm. Group reservations possible. Call in advance.)

Though sampling is encouraged, it is impolite not to buy afterwards. The cheapest bottles start around 9SFr; 4SFr more can buy a fresh baguette, cheese, and chocolate from the **Co-op** next to the church on r. Gustave Jeanneret. (Open M-Tu and Th-F 7:45am-12:15pm and 1:45-6:30pm, W 7:45am-12:15pm, Sa 7:45am-12:15pm and 1:30-4pm.) Take your bounty on a 10min. stroll into the vineyards for panoramic views of the valley by following yellow *tourisme pédestre* signs off r. de Chateau. A little extra effort brings you to tiny **Combe,** where the tinkling of cowbells accompanies the lake view.

YVERDON-LES-BAINS ☎ 024

Trains *to: Basel (2hr., every hr. 5:48am-9:48pm, 45SFr); Geneva (1hr., every hr. 5:51am-12:06am, 30SFr); Lausanne (20min., every hr. 5:51am-12:06am, 13.40SFr); and Neuchâtel (25min., every hr. 5:48am-11:49pm, 12.40SFr). The train station is at ave. de la Gare 1. (☎425 21 15. Open 6am-10pm.) The* **tourist office,** *3min. to the left of the train station past the post office, calls itself the office of "thermalisme." (☎423 62 90; fax 426 11 22; www.yverdon-les-bains.ch/tourisme. Open daily 8am-6pm.)*

What's in a name? In the case of Yverdon-les-Bains, it's the essence of the town: its **thermal baths**. When Roman settlers discovered the source of the hot springs 1500 years ago, they began to use the mineral-rich waters to ease all sorts of ailments. Tourists and locals alike flock to the baths, but the city also offers a charming *vieille ville,* a 13th-century chateau, and some Neolithic ruins attesting to the longevity of the locale's appeal. The ▨**Centre Thermal,** off ave. des Bains, and its glitzy adjoining hotel entice visitors with three pools and therapeutic treatments ranging from electrotherapy to massage. From the train station, head left down ave. de la Gare to ave. Haldimand. Then follow the signs, or take bus #1, 2, or 5 to "Grand Hotel" and cross the parking lot to the entrance. Plug your nose, since the healing powers of the springs come at the price of their sulfurous stench. (☎423 02 32. Open M-F 8am-10pm, Sa-Su 9am-8pm. Last entry 1hr. before closing. Baths 14SFr, ages 3-16 9SFr. Bathing caps required, 3.50SFr. Other facilities charge separately.)

The best way to get close to the southwestern shore of Lake Neuchâtel is to picnic on the narrow strip of beach. Head down r. des Pecheurs behind and to the left of the station. Turn right on ave. des Sports. Follow alongside the stadium. After passing it, take a left and the beach is in front of you. Nearby is a forested area with 47 **standing stones,** a Neolithic mini-Stonehenge dating back to 4000 BC.

Yverdon's aesthetic appeal is concentrated in the *centre ville,* a smallish square flanked by the **Savoy château** to the left and the 18th-century Baroque church on the right, with a charming statue of renowned pedagogue Johann Heinrich Pestalozzi standing between the two. The chateau was built in 1260 by the Dukes of Savoy to protect Yverdon on the east. The square, four-towered edifice houses a museum containing prehistoric artifacts as well as items from Yverdon's days as the Roman camp of **Eburondunum.** Among its prized possessions is the mummy of an Egyptian priest named Nesshou. (☎425 93 10. Museum open Oct.-May Tu-Su 2-5pm; June-Sept. Tu-Su 10am-noon and 2-5pm. 8SFr, students and seniors 7SFr, children 4SFr.) The chateau is also home to the **Musée de la Mode,** featuring temporary exhibits on fashion. (☎425 93 10. Admission included with castle price.) For a total change of pace, visit the inexplicable **Maison d'Ailleurs** (House of Elsewhere), pl. Pestalozzi 14, across pl. Pestalozzi from the chateau entrance. This treasure trove for sci-fi lovers displays otherworldly temporary exhibits as vivid as the artists' imaginations. One floor houses a library devoted to the genre. (☎425 64 38. Open W-F 2-6pm, Sa-Su noon-6pm. 7SFr, students 5SFr.)

BIEL (BIENNE)   ☎032

In 1765, Rousseau spent what he called the happiest moments of his life in Biel. Little of the fortified town remained after the tumultuous years that followed. In 1798, Biel was overrun by Napoleon's armies, laying the foundation for the city's present bilingualism (60% French, 40% German). Industrial Rolex and Omega parks overpower the vestiges of the Altstadt Rousseau loved, but Biel (pop. 50,000) is still attractive for its proximity to Bielersee (Lac Bienne) and the surrounding hills, and because it lacks the hordes of tourists in Interlaken.

█▊ TRANSPORTATION AND PRACTICAL INFORMATION. Trains run to Biel from: Bern (30min., every 30min. 6:18am-12:56am, 13.40SFr); Neuchâtel (20min., 2 per hr. 6:02am-12:33am, 10.40SFr); and Solothurn (20min., every hr. 6am-11:29pm, 9.80SFr). The **tourist office** is outside the train station at Bahnhofpl. (☎322 75 75; fax 323 77 57. Open M-F 8am-12:30pm and 1:30-6pm; May-Oct. also Sa 9am-3pm.) **Currency exchange** and **Western Union** (M-F 6am-8pm, Sa-Su 7am-7pm), **bike rental** (mountain bike 30SFr), **lockers** (open 5am-12:30am; 3-5SFr), and luggage storage (open 7am-9pm; 5SFr per day) are all at the train station. **Internet** access is available at **Migros,** Freierstr. 3, in the Take-Away section, on two coin-operated PCs (1SFr per 5min). The **post office** is left of the train station. (☎321 18 40. Open M-F 7:30am-6:30pm, Sa 7:30am-noon.)

▐▐ ACCOMMODATIONS AND FOOD. Lago Lodge ❷, Uferweg 5, Nidau, bills itself as a "hostel, bistro, and brewery at Lake Biel." It's just steps away from the Bielersee: walk straight out the back entrance of the train station (by track 11), take the first right after crossing the small bridge, and the hostel will be on the left (the entrance after the grafittied wall, 5min.). The Lodge offers a prime location, eclectic Andy Warhol sheets on closely placed beds, a convivial atmosphere, and crowd of young backpackers, and four organic beers brewed on location. (☎331 37 32; fax 37 33; lagolodge@access.ch; www.backpacker.ch/lagolodge. Breakfast 7SFr. Kitchen. Linens 5SFr. Laundry 4-6SFr. **Internet** access 2SFr per 15min. Reception 7am-10pm. Check-out by noon. Dorms 20SFr; 4- to 6-bed rooms 25SFr; doubles 70SFr.)

For picnic supplies, there's always the station's **Aperto** (open daily 6am-10pm), but it's more expensive than the **Co-op City Centre,** on Nidaug. (open M-W and F 8am-8pm, Th 8am-9pm, Sa 7:30am-6pm), or **Migros,** Freierstr. 3, one block straight ahead from the station (open M-F 7:30am-7pm, Sa 7:30am-4pm). In front of Migros, numerous cafes and restaurants in Zentralpl. satisfy those post-hike munchies.

◪ HIKING. The two best **hikes** from Biel pass through magnificent gorges. The walk to **Twannbachschlucht** leads to mountaintop fields ripe for picnics and the trek to **Taubenloch** threads through a rugged canyon and its canopy forest.

Twannbachschlucht (4hr.). To get to Twannbachschlucht, take bus #11 from the train station to "Magglingen/FuniMacolin," then take the rail car from Biel to Magglingen (every 20min. 6:05am-11:45pm, 4.20SFr, SwissPass valid.) From this vantage point, 3 different paths lead to Twannberg, the trailhead of the Twannbachschlucht hike. The paths follow a ridge above Lake Biel and passes through dense forest and flower-filled meadows, ending in the picture-book town of **Twann** at the bottom of the gorge. Return to Biel by train (10min., every hr. 5:53am-11:37pm, 3.80SFr) or lake ferry (7 per day, 7.80SFr, Eurail not valid), or move on to Neuchâtel.

Taubenloch (40min.). Taubenloch is a less ambitious hike, though its dynamic terrain may make it more rewarding. Buses #1, 2, and 3N run to "Taubenloch," where you can enter the canyon through the **Zum Wilden Mann** restaurant's garden (2SFr suggested donation). Legend has it that a beautiful maiden nicknamed "Die Taube" ("The Dove") threw herself to her death to escape an enamored tyrant. The well-cleared trail hugs the edges of 30m drops of sheer rock walls carved eons ago by the rushing rapids below. Waterfalls plunge past mossy cliffs, illuminated by the sunlit green canopy above. Signs warn not to walk on the riverbeds, but subversive locals like to fish in the river. Many hikers turn back at the water treatment plant, but hungrier souls press on for a few minutes to the **Eau-Berge du Taubenloch ❷** restaurant at Frinvillier 2535. Fill up on a delicious 3-course *Menü* for around 15SFr while the owner's animals frolic about. (☎/fax 358 11 32. Open May-Oct. M 11:30am-11pm, Tu-Sa 9am-11pm, Su 9am-7pm; Nov.-Apr. Tu-Sa 9am-11pm, Su 9am-7pm.) Follow the same path back to find Biel again.

◪ ENTERTAINMENT. A **boat tour** of the lake provides a leisurely introduction to the city. To reach the harbor and beach from the train station, turn left at Bahnhofpl., follow the road around to the left, and look for the brown-and-white signs for *Schifflände* and *Débarcadère*. Boat tours range from 15.60SFr (Biel-Twann, 30min.) to 72SFr (Biel-Murten, 3hr.) round-trip. In early July, an **open-air cinema** called "Yellow Movie Nights" runs mostly American recent releases in **Schloßpark Nidau.** Tickets (16SFr) are on sale at the tourist and post offices.

FRIBOURG (FREIBURG)   ☎ 026

Modern Fribourg stretches in front of the train station with a mix of stores and concrete apartment buildings, while its charming vieille ville, established on the banks of the Sarine by the Zähringen dynasty in 1157, stretches down the wooded hills of the gorge to the river. The contrast is stark, but is only one of the divides that describe Fribourg's personality. Young Swiss are drawn to Fribourg by both the university and the siren call of lakes and mountains. The town has a penchant for modern art, open-air shopping, and fine dining, but its most distinctive attractions stem from the quiet remnant of medieval religious fervor. Fribourg was an isolated bastion of Catholicism during the Reformation; even the local brew, Cardinal beer, celebrates a 19th-century bishop. Meanwhile, Fribourg bridges the Swiss linguistic divide: 30% of the population firmly count themselves *Freiburger;* the remaining 70% are *Fribourgeois.*

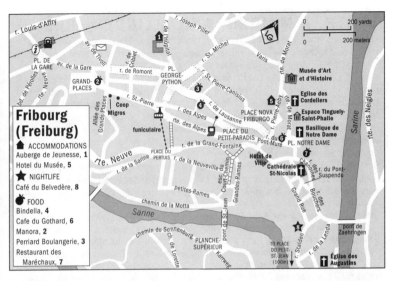

Fribourg (Freiburg)

🏠 ACCOMMODATIONS
Auberge de Jeunesse, 1
Hotel du Musée, 5

⭐ NIGHTLIFE
Café du Belvédère, 8

🍎 FOOD
Bindella, 4
Cafe du Gothard, 6
Manora, 2
Perriard Boulangerie, 3
Restaurant des
   Maréchaux, 7

�"📖 TRANSPORTATION AND PRACTICAL INFORMATION

Fribourg sits on the main rail line between Zurich and Geneva. **Trains** leave for: **Basel** (1¾hr., every 30min. 5:50am-11:16pm, 45SFr); **Bern** (25min., every 30min. 5:16am-12:16am, 12.40SFr); **Interlaken** (1½hr., every hr. 6:42am-9:46pm, 32SFr); **Lausanne** (50min., every 30min. 4:48am-11:47pm, 21SFr); and **Neuchâtel** (1hr., every hr. 4:33am-9:33pm, 18SFr). Fribourg's **tourist office** is at ave. de la Gare 1, 100m to the right of the station door. (☎321 31 75; fax 322 35 27; info@Fribourg-Tourism.ch; www.FribourgTourism.ch. Open M-F 9am-6pm, Sa 9am-3pm, closed Sa afternoons Oct.-May.) **Exchange currency** at the train station (open 6am-8pm) or at one of many banks lining r. du Romont. Services at the station include: **lockers** (4-6SFr; open 5:10am-12:45am); **luggage watch** (7SFr per item; open M-F 7:30am-7:40pm, Sa-Su 8am-7:40pm); and **bike rental** (30SFr per day, ID deposit). For a **taxi**, call ☎(079) 219 46 10. **Internet** access is available at **Cyber Atlantis**, r. de Lausanne 18. (8SFr per hr. Open M-Th 11am-6:30pm, F 11am-11pm, Sa 10am-11pm, Su 1-6pm.) The **post office**, ave. de Tivoli, is the skyscraper to the left of the station. (Open M-F 7:30am-6:30pm, Sa 8am-noon.) **Postal code:** CH-1700.

⌂ ACCOMMODATIONS

Auberge de Jeunesse, r. de l'Hôpital 2 (☎323 19 16; fax 19 40.) Head left out the train station on ave. de la Gare, which becomes r. de Romont; turn left onto r. de l'Hôpital. The entrance is at the far end of the building marked #2. If reception is closed, enter through the 2nd door and leave your bags in the basement lockers (5SFr deposit). This converted hospital has long corridors with rooms in the basement. Bring earplugs—trains run nearby and the hallways echo. Breakfast, showers, and sheets included. Lunch and dinner (with early notice) 12.50SFr. TV room, laundry (3-5SFr), kitchen, and ping pong available. Reception 7:30-10am and 5-10pm. Checkout 10am. Doors are locked when reception is closed; 10SFr key deposit. Open mid-Feb. to late-Nov. Reservations recommended. Dorms 30.65SFr. Non-members add 6SFr. ❷

DEATH, A MAIDEN, AND A LINDEN TREE

Once upon a time (June 22, 1476) in a land far, far away (Fribourg), there lived an old man named Nicholas who declared that he would give his daughter Beatrice's hand in marriage to the man who proved himself most valiant on the battlefield. As the knights went off to fight Charles the Bold in Murten, Beatrice waved a linden branch at Rudolphe, her childhood love. Determined to win her hand, Rudolphe proved himself the bravest knight on the battlefield—at the cost of a mortal wound. Undaunted, he ran back to Fribourg, waving a linden branch and shouting "Victory!" When he finally reached Beatrice's balcony in pl. Hôtel de Ville, he collapsed. Beatrice ran to her love, who could say only "Homeland! Love! To Heaven!" before dying in her arms. The town planted the linden branch as a relic of the victory in the square. In 1984, a traffic accident uprooted the tree, but the town salvaged a shoot and replanted it in the original spot, where it flourishes today. In memory of the battle and of Rudolphe's plight, runners from Murten and Fribourg race between the two cities every October.

Hotel du Musée, r. Pierre Aeby 11 (☎/fax 322 32 09), is above a Chinese restaurant. The reception is in the dining room. From the station, follow ave. de la Gare to r. de Romont to r. de Lausanne. Turn left up r. Pierre Aeby at the end of r. de Lausanne, by pl. Nova-Friburgo. The carpeted, well-furnished rooms are located near most major sights. Breakfast 10SFr. Reception 10am-2:30pm and 5-11:30pm. Reserve ahead. Singles 60SFr, with shower 70SFr; doubles 120SFr/130SFr. AmEx/DC/MC/V. ❸

Camping La Follaz (☎ 436 24 95). From the station, catch a GFM bus to "Marly-Gérines" (2.80SFr). From the stop, backtrack across the bridge, take the 1st right, and follow the signs for 7min. Lakeside plots and showers. Reception 9am-10pm, but call ahead. Open Apr.-Oct. 5.30SFr per person; tents for 1-2 people 5.50SFr, for 4-6 7.50SFr. ❶

🔳 FOOD

Small cafes selling quasi-Italian or Swiss-German dishes populate almost every main street in the vieille ville, as well as r. de Romont. For kebab places, check out blvd. des Pérolles and other streets around the station. A **produce market** stands in pl. Georges Python between r. de Romont and r. de Lausanne (Tu-W 7am-noon) or in pl. Hôtel de Ville (Sa 7am-noon). The virtually inseparable supermarket twins, **Co-op** and **Migros,** share the same street (r. St.-Pierre 6a and 2, respectively, by Grand-Places) and the same hours (M-W and F 8am-7pm, Th 8am-9pm, Sa 8am-4pm). This Co-op also has a restaurant. Head to the **Migros** at Pérolles Centre, blvd. de Pérolles 21 (near the station), for their second-floor restaurant and large grocery with the same hours as above.

Cafe du Gothard, r. du Pont Muré 16 (☎ 322 32 85), by the Tilleul bus stop between the Hôtel de Ville and St. Nicolas. A friendly Francophone staff serves typical Swiss fare within the memorabilia-covered walls of this quirky restaurant. Veal sausage with *Rösti* and salad 14SFr; filet of perch 22SFr. ❸

Bindella Ristorante Bar, r. de Lausanne 38 (☎ 322 49 05). Inventive, high-quality pasta made in-house (from 12.50SFr) and other Italian dishes served by ponytailed waiters. A small splurge to people-watch along the popular r. de Lausanne. Live jazz last Th of the month 8:30pm. Open M-Sa 9am-11:30pm, kitchen noon-2pm and 6:30-10pm. ❷

Restaurant des Marechaux, r. des Chanoines 9 (☎ 322 33 33), next to the cathedral, will satisfy Greek *gourmands* with large veggie-friendly plates. Feast on Greek *spanako-*

pita with *tzatziki* (9.50SFr) or *souvlaki* (26SFr) in a bright and airy dining room over-looking the gorge. Food served 6-11pm. Open 5pm-midnight. ❸

Perriard Boulangerie, r. de Lausanne 61 (☎322 34 89), will satisfy a sweet-tooth with pastries and confectionery delights, such as *noisettines* for 5SFr per 100g and fresh breads for 1.50-3.20SFr. Open Tu-F 7:30am-7pm, Sa 7:30am-6pm, Su 8am-6pm. ❶

Manora, in front of Grand-Places, is a self-service restaurant with meat, fruit, salad, and dessert kiosks that make a fine meal for 8-15SFr. Open M-Sa 8am-7pm, Su 9am-7pm. ❷

◪ SIGHTS

THE OLD TOWN. From the station, head down r. de Romont, past pl. Georges Python, and along r. de Lausanne and its pink-bannered open-air shopping galleries. R. de Lausanne empties into pl. Nova-Friburgo, a busy intersection with a fine view of the **Hôtel de Ville** and its fanciful clock tower. Pantaloon-clad Renaissance automatons chime the hours. A fountain of St. George dominates the courtyard below, giving unexpected showers to visitors and the commemorative **Morat Linden Tree** in heavy winds (see **Death, a Maiden, and a Linden Tree,** p. 522).

MUSÉE D'ART ET D'HISTOIRE. Off pl. Nova-Friburgo, r. Pierre Aeby leads to the Museum of Art and History. Skip the 18th-century portraiture—the haunting historical artifacts are the meat of the collection. Look for a number of the wood carvings of Hans, but most notably Geiler and Roditzer. The gleefully macabre, bejeweled skeleton of St. Felix, ca. 1755, is in itself a worthwhile reason to visit. *(R. de Morat 12. ☎305 51 40. Open Tu-W and F-Su 11am-6pm, Th 11am-8pm. 6-12SFr, depending on special exhibits. Students from 4SFr.)*

JEAN TINGUELY-NIKI DE SAINT PHALLE MUSEUM. On the other side of the Église des Cordeliers from the Musée d'Art et d'Histoire, the museum showcases the work of avant-garde Fribourg native Tinguely and his wife, Saint-Phalle. Tinguely's work features bizarre, massive machines made out of rusty metal, while Saint-Phalle's work uses brilliant colors in curvaceous sculpture. A joint work proves to be less impressive than the work of either. *(R. de Morat 2. ☎305 51 70. Open W and F-Su 11am-6pm, Th 11am-8pm. 5SFr, students 3SFr, children under 16 free.)*

MONASTERY AND CHURCHES. At the **Église des Cordeliers,** part of a Franciscan monastery, the unassuming facade masks a colorful interior, featuring vividly animated paintings framed by multicolored marble, and an elaborate altar that lies in star-studded darkness. *(From the Tinguely museum, backtrack on r. de Morat. Open Apr.-Sept. daily 7:30am-7pm, Oct.-Mar. 7:30am-6pm.)* Down the road is the **Basilique de Notre-Dame,** whose dim, incense-laden atmosphere contrasts sharply with the bright, ornate Église des Cordeliers. Across pl. Notre-Dame rises the bell tower of the **Cathédrale St.-Nicolas,** which shoots above the Fribourg skyline. It took over 200 years to erect the Gothic columns, now smoke-blackened, that shoot upwards into pointed arches and elegant stained-glass windows. View the town from the 76m, 368-step **tower.** *(Cathedral open M-Sa 7:30am-7pm, Su 8:30am-9:30pm. Free. Tower open June-Oct. M-Sa 10am-noon and 2-5:15pm, Su 2-5:15pm. 3SFr, students 2SFr, children 1SFr.)* Although only order members have complete access to the 13th-century **Église des Augustins,** visitors can examine the monastery's huge, eagle-topped altarpiece. *(From the cathedral, head downhill from r. des Chanoines to r. des Bouchers; take a right onto r. de Zähringen and a left onto Stalden. Take the steps of Stalden down to passage des Augustins and turn left.)* Peering from the hills above the town are two tiny chapels.

NEUCHÂTEL REGION

🎵 📷 ENTERTAINMENT AND NIGHTLIFE

Fribourg's university, music conservatory, art groups, and civic institutions host several festivals throughout the year, including a **Carnival** (a Mardi Gras type party in the vieille ville, March 2003), an **International Film Festival** (March 16-23, 2003), an **International Guitar Festival** (late April), an **International Jazz Parade** (mid-July), and the **Belluard Bollwerk International** festival (late June to mid-July), a gathering of musicians, dancers, critics, scholars, and just about anyone else involved in the arts (☎469 09 00; www.belluard.ch). **Open-air cinema** runs from mid-July to mid-August, screening many American films (get advance tickets from the tourist office). The above is just a primer; the tourist office can provide more information on festival-laden Fribourg.

For a relaxed evening, try ▧**Café Belvedere,** Grand Rue 36, at the top of Stalden, which resembles an M.C. Escher drawing with comfortably worn couches perfect for intimate conversation. Alterna-intellectuals lounge on terraces overlooking the gorge, sampling the wine or beer of the month (3.50-5SFr) while listening to the pleasantly dippy music. *Menüs* feature salads, pasta, and various fowl for 12-14SFr. (☎323 44 07. Open M-Tu 11:30am-11:30pm, W-Th 11:30am-12:30am, F 11:30am-3am, Sa 10:30am-3am, Su noon-midnight. Terrace closes at 11pm.)

🔲 DAYTRIP FROM FRIBOURG

GRUYÈRES   ☎026

> To get to Gruyères, buy a ticket (16.60SFr, 33.20SFR round-trip) at the train station in Fribourg and catch a bus from behind the station to Bulle. A 20min. bus ride will land you in Bulle, where you can catch a train to Gruyères (10min.). The last departure from Gruyères is at 8:17pm, though a bus departs at 9:25pm. Buses and trains run approx. every hr.

Tiny Gruyères (pop. 1,412) carries a weighty reputation for its cheese, and it's unlikely that you'll find a cheesier town. The local tourist industry goes to absurd extremes (excessive flower boxes, hostesses in dubiously medieval garb, and suspiciously artificial-smelling smoke permeating a castle whose hearths have been bare and unlit for years), but the towering beauty of the surrounding mountains overcomes the kitsch. A chateau filled with contemporary art and the milky calm of working cheese dairies make this eccentric town well worth a daytrip. Follow the signs from the station to the **tourist office,** which offers currency exchange, but at poor rates. (☎921 10 30; fax 38 50; www.gruyeres.ch. Open M, W-F 9:30am-noon and 1-5pm, Sa-Su 9:30am-5:30pm.)

La Maison du Gruyère, the cheese factory *par excellence*, is located directly across from the train station. Newly renovated, it draws crowds with a souvenir market, cheese-making demonstrations, and its own classic Swiss restaurant. (☎921 84 00; www.lamaisondugruyere.ch. Open Apr.-Sept. daily 9am-7pm, Oct.-Mar. 9am-6pm. Cheese-making daily 9am-3pm. 5SFr, students and seniors 4SFr, family rate 10SFr. Audioguides available in 6 languages.) The truly lactose-devoted can take a GFM bus to "Moléson-sur-Gruyères" to the **Fromagerie d'Alpage.** An anachronistic phenomenon, this 17th-century factory makes cheese the old-fashioned way, over a huge cauldron on the fireplace. (☎921 10 44. Open mid-May-mid-Oct. daily 9:30am-10pm, with demonstrations at 10am and 3pm.)

Gruyères's only major street, lined by flowerbox-adorned old houses, leads even farther uphill to the absolutely beautiful and bizarre **Château de Gruyères.** The castle was home to a series of earls from the 12th through the 16th centuries, but don't expect to be taken back to its earliest days when you walk in—the mismatched decor of each room reflects many different eras: medieval tapestries are

GOT MILK? Before most kids hear of watchmaking or political neutrality, they know about Swiss cheese. But the 84,000 tons of cheese Switzerland produces annually don't only consist of the familiar, hole-ridden variety. While most of it (56,500 tons) is the recognizable Emmental, 22,000 tons is Gruyère, a nutty-tasting cousin without any holes to speak of. The region has been making cheese since the 12th century. Two varieties of cows contribute their milk to the effort: *tachettée rouge* (red) and *noir* (black). Workers process 3 million kg a year by pouring it into large vats, where it is centrifuged, matured with bacteria, congealed with natural enzymes into a yogurt-like consistency, and heated to get rid of excess liquid. Each cheese round is then pressed into shape for 18hr. before it is stamped for quality and authenticity.

juxtaposed with Louis XV chairs, and one room houses **Franz Lizst's** pianoforte (yup, he lived here too). Only the dungeons remain of the original feudal castle; the living quarters burned to the ground in 1493 and were rebuilt as the first Renaissance castle in the Northern Alps. Adding to the anachronistic confusion, the castle is also now home to the **International Center of Fantastic Art,** a varied sci-fi art collection scattered throughout the castle, including a tower of works by artist Patrick Woodroffe. Many rooms offer spectacular views of the **Jardin à la francaise** and the surrounding hills. (☎ 921 21 02. Open Apr.-Oct. daily 9am-6pm, Nov.-Mar. 10am-4:30pm. Last admission 30min. before closing. 6SFr, students 54SFr, ages 6-16 2SFr. Signs in German, French, and English.)

If you're certain there's other life out there, further feed your obsession on the way back to town from the chateau at the eerie **H.R. Giger museum.** This out-of-this-world homage to the Academy Award-winning designer for the alien in Ridley Scott's *Alien* features many models of the chilling creature and items from Giger's private collection. Dark curtains hide a glowing red room filled with erotic aliens in compromising positions. (☎ 921 22 00. Open Nov.-Apr. 11am-5pm, May-Oct. 10am-6pm. 10SFr, students 7SFr.)

NEUCHÂTEL REGION

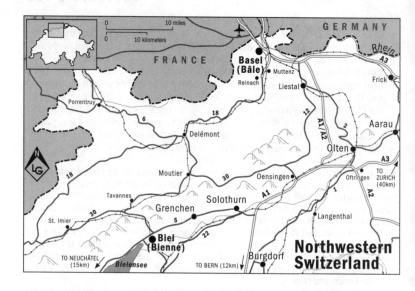

The cantons of Basel-Stadt and Basel-Land, Solothurn, and Aargau inspire peaceful contentment. Odds are, you'll be passing through anyway (Basel is a transportation hub for Germany and France) so why not slow down to enjoy subtle charms, excellent museums with a rich Humanist tradition, and charming Altstädte? Despite their proximity to France, the cantons of northwestern Switzerland are German-speaking. Most towns have French variants of their names, but don't let that confuse you.

NORTHWESTERN SWITZERLAND

HIGHLIGHTS OF NORTHWEST SWITZERLAND

Climb back to the future at the Museum Jean Tinguely in Basel (see p. 532).
Forget Mardi Gras—catch **Fasnacht** fever in Basel (see p. 533).
Sip the *Hell Spezial* with your pretzel in a Solothurn biergarten (see p. 533).

BASEL (BÂLE)   ☎ 061

Situated on the Rhine near France and Germany, Switzerland's third-largest city is home to a large medieval quarter and one of the oldest universities in Switzerland—which numbers Erasmus of Rotterdam, Bernoulli, and Nietzsche among its graduates. Basel takes great pride in its cultural heritage; as you wan-

N.W. SWITZERLAND

Basel (Bâle), Muttenz, Reinach, Liestal, Frick, GERMANY, Rhein, A3, Porrentruy, 18, Delémont, 12, A1/A2, Aarau, A3, Olten, 2, TO ZURICH (40km), Moutier, 30, Oensingen, Oftringen, A2, Tavannes, Solothurn, A1, 1, Grenchen, 5, Langenthal, St. Imier, 30, Biel (Bienne), 22, Burgdorf, Bielersee, TO NEUCHÂTEL (15km), TO BERN (12km), Northwestern Switzerland, FRANCE, 6, 18

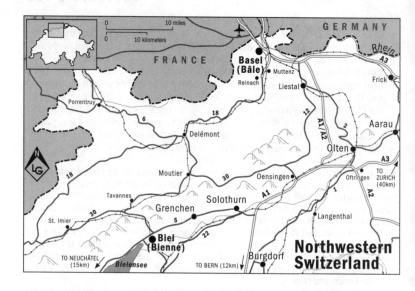

NORTHWESTERN SWITZERLAND

The cantons of Basel-Stadt and Basel-Land, Solothurn, and Aargau inspire peaceful contentment. Odds are, you'll be passing through anyway (Basel is a transportation hub for Germany and France) so why not slow down to enjoy subtle charms, excellent museums with a rich Humanist tradition, and charming Altstädte? Despite their proximity to France, the cantons of northwestern Switzerland are German-speaking. Most towns have French variants of their names, but don't let that confuse you.

HIGHLIGHTS OF NORTHWEST SWITZERLAND

Climb back to the future at the Museum Jean Tinguely in Basel (see p. 532).
Forget Mardi Gras—catch **Fasnacht** fever in Basel (see p. 533).
Sip the *Hell Spezial* with your pretzel in a Solothurn biergarten (see p. 533).

BASEL (BÂLE)   ☎ 061

Situated on the Rhine near France and Germany, Switzerland's third-largest city is home to a large medieval quarter and one of the oldest universities in Switzerland—which numbers Erasmus of Rotterdam, Bernoulli, and Nietzsche among its graduates. Basel takes great pride in its cultural heritage; as you wan-

N.W. SWITZERLAND

526

der the streets you'll encounter art dating from Roman times to the 20th century. On the left bank, the Münster presides over the Altstadt in a towering conglomeration of red sandstone, stained glass, and sprouting spires. The most outstanding attractions of Basel are the 30 museums in the hilly streets of the elegant St. Alban district. Endless art fairs and festivals bring a lively party scene, but the biggest party of them all is Basel's **Fasnacht**, which rivals New Orleans' Mardi Gras.

TRANSPORTATION

The **Euroairport** (☎267 90 25) serves continental Europe, though most trans-continental flights are routed through Zurich. Shuttle buses run passengers between the airport and the SBB train station on the #50 line (daily 4:55am-11:30pm).

Basel is the crossroads of Switzerland, France, and Germany and accordingly has three **train stations:** the French **SNCF** station is next door to the Swiss **SBB station** in Centralbahnpl.; trains from Germany arrive at the **DB station** (Badische Bahnhof, ☎690 11 11), across the Rhine down Greifeng. City trams to town depart the SBB station (every 5min. M-F, every 15min. Sa-Su.). **Buses** to Swiss, French, and German cities depart from respective stations. **Driving** from France, take A35, E25, or E60; from Germany, E35 or A5; from within Switzerland, Rte. 2 north.

Trains: SBB station (☎157 22 22; 1.19SFr per min.), on Centralbahnpl. To: **Bern** (1¼hr., every hr. 5:50am-11:52pm, 34SFr); **Geneva** (3hr., every hr. 6:24am-8:44pm, 71SFr); **Lausanne** (2½hr., every hr. 5:50am-10:26pm, 60SFr); **Milan** (4½-6hr., every hr. 7:10am-3:10pm, 91SFr) via **Lucerne** or **Bern; Munich** (5¼hr., every hr. 7am-8:13pm, 116SFr) via **Zurich** or **Karlsruhe; Paris** (5-6hr., 12 per day 5:51am-12:28am, 69SFr); **Salzburg** (7hr., 5 per day 5:51am-9pm, 122SFr) via Zurich; **Vienna** (10-12hr., 5 per day 5:51am-9pm, 149SFr) via Zurich; and **Zurich** (1hr., every 15-30min. 4:42am-midnight, 30SFr). Make international connections at the French (SNCF) or German (DB) stations. 25% discount on international trips for travelers ages 16-25.

Ferries: 4 ferries cross the Rhine: the **Üli** at St. Johann; the **Vogel Gryff** at Klingental; the **Leu** below the Münster terrace; and the **Wild Maa** at St. Alban (all at M-F 7am-7pm, Sa-Su 9am-7pm; 1.20SFr, children 0.60SFr). Rhine **cruises** depart from the *Schiffstation* next to the tourist office. (☎639 95 00. 2-4 per day Mar.-Oct. 20. Station open M-F 9am-12:15pm and 1-6pm, Sa 10am-4pm, Su 8am-3pm.) Enjoy "Samba Night" or another special Rhine cruise (varying times and prices; check at the station). Round-trip to Rheinfelden 45SFr, to Waldhaus 23SFr. Tickets available 30min. before departure.

Public Transportation: Trams and buses run 5:30am-12:30am. Most sights are within zone #10. 1-zone tickets 2.80SFr, day ticket 8SFr; ages 6-16 half-price. Ticket machines at all stops sell tram tickets. Maps at tourist office or train station.

Taxis: In front of the train station, or ☎271 11 11, 633 33 33, or 271 22 22.

Parking: Jelmoli, Rebg. 20. **Bahnhof SBB,** Güterstr. 2.50SFr per hr.

Bike Rental: At train stations. 30SFr per day. Open daily 6am-9:40pm.

ORIENTATION AND PRACTICAL INFORMATION

Basel sits in the northwest corner of Switzerland, so close to France that the Tour de France sometimes traverses the city. Groß-Basel (Greater Basel), where most sights are located, lies on the left bank of the Rhine; Klein-Basel (Lesser Basel) occupies the right bank. Pick up a city map (0.50SFr) at either tourist office, but Basel's easy-to-use pedestrian tourist signs will help you navigate. To reach **Marktplatz** on foot from the SBB and SNCF stations, cross the Centralbahnpl., go left on Elisabethenanlage, right down Elisabethenstr., and left on Freiestr. (20min.) From

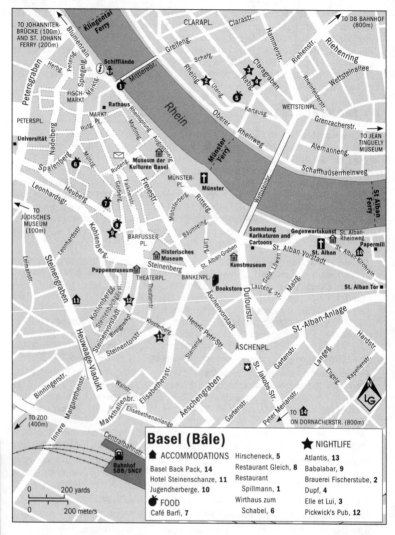

Basel (Bâle)

⚓ ACCOMMODATIONS
Basel Back Pack, 14
Hotel Steinenschanze, 11
Jugendherberge, 10

🍴 FOOD
Café Barfi, 7

Hirscheneck, 5
Restaurant Gleich, 8
Restaurant
  Spillmann, 1
Wirthaus zum
  Schabel, 6

★ NIGHTLIFE
Atlantis, 13
Babalabar, 9
Brauerei Fischerstube, 2
Dupf, 4
Elle et Lui, 3
Pickwick's Pub, 12

the DB station, follow Rosentalstr. (which becomes Clarastr., then Greifeng.) over Mittlere Rheinbrücke and around to the left on Eiseng. (15min.).

Tourist Office: Basel Tourismus, Schifflände 5 (☎268 68 68; fax 68 70; info@basel-tourismus.ch; www.baseltourismus.ch). From the SBB station, take tram #1 to "Schifflände." The office is on the river, near the Mittlere Rheinbr. Guided walking tours are available (2hr., May-Oct. M-Sa 2:30, 15SFr). Hotel reservations 10SFr. Buy a **Basel Card** and get the guided walking tour, admission to all Basel museums, and discounts for some restaurants and taxis. Available at tourist office (24hr. card 25SFr, 48hr.

33SFr, 72hr. 45SFr). Open M-F 8:30am-6pm, Sa-Su 10am-4pm. **Branch office** (☎271 36 84; fax 272 93 42; hotel@messebasel.ch) at the SBB station.

Currency Exchange: The SBB station bureau, including a **Western Union,** offers currency exchange (2SFr fee) and cash advance with MC/V (min. 200SFr). Open daily 6am-9pm.

Luggage Storage: At all stations. Lockers 5SFr, 24hr. access. Storage 7SFr per day, open 6am-9:40pm.

Travel Agency: STA Travel, Freiestr. 15 (☎269 83 00; fax 83 19; sta-basel@statravel.ch). Open M-F 10am-6:30pm, Sa 10am-4pm.

Bookstores: Buchhandlung Bider und Tanner, Bankenpl., Äschenvorstadt 2 (☎206 99 99), is Basel's travel bookshop, with a room of well-selected English-language books. Open M-W and F 8:15am-6:30pm, Th 8:15am-9pm, Sa 8:15am-5pm.

Bi-Gay-Lesbian Organizations: Arcados, Rheing. 69 (☎681 31 32; fax 66 56; info@arcados.com; www.arcados.com), at Clarapl. has lots of information on bars, restaurants, and hangouts. Open Tu-F noon-7pm, Sa 11am-4pm.

Emergencies: Police, ☎117. **Medical,** ☎144. **Hospital,** ☎265 25 25.

Hotlines: Helping Hand, ☎143, for any crisis situation.

Internet Access: Domino, Steinenvorstadt 54. Arcade with an Internet coffee-bar upstairs. 10SFr per hr., after 6pm 12SFr per hr. Open M-Th 9:30am-midnight, F-Sa 9am-1am (in summer Sa 10am-1am), Su 1pm-midnight. 18+.

Post Office: Rüdeng 1. Take tram #1 or 8 to "Marktpl." and walk 1 block back from the river. Open M-W and F 7:30am-6:30pm, Th 7:30am-8pm, Sa 8am-noon. **Poste Restante address:** *Postlagernde Briefe*, Rüdeng., CH-4001 Basel 1. **Postal Codes:** CH-4000 to CH-4059.

ACCOMMODATIONS & CAMPING

All accommodations in Basel offer a complimentary **Mobility ticket.** The ticket offers free use of public transport in zones 10 and 11, where most sights are located, and even the shuttle bus to the airport (normally 6.60SFr).

Jugendherberge (HI), St. Alban-Kirchrain 10 (☎272 05 72; fax 08 33; www.youthhostel.ch/basel). Tram #2 to "Kunstmuseum." Turn right on St.-Alban-Vorstadt, then follow the signs, or walk 15min. from the SBB station down Aeschengraben to St.-Alban-Anlage. At the tower, follow the signs down the hill. This hostel is a mecca for weary travelers, particularly those who don't mind cobwebs. The institutional setup has lockers for every bunk, wheelchair access, TV, and phones, but expect long waits for services. Breakfast, showers, and sheets included. Dinner and lunch 11.50-12.50SFr. **Internet** 10SFr per hr. Laundry 7SFr. **Currency exchange.** Reception Mar.-Oct. 7-10am and 2-11:30pm; Nov.-Feb. 2pm-11pm. Check-out 7-10am. Reservations wise. Dorms 29-31SFr; singles 79SFr; doubles 98SFr. Reduced by 2.50SFr Jan. 1-Feb. 19 and Nov.-Dec. Non-members add 6SFr. AmEx/DC/MC/V. ❷

Basel Back Pack, Dornacherstr. 192 (☎333 00 37 or 076 538 37 19); www.baselbackpack.ch). Exit the rear of the SBB station, go up the stairs, and turn right onto the gallery that leads to Hochstr. Walk straight down Hochstr., then turn right on Bruderholzstr. Follow Bruderholzstr. until it intersects with Dornacherstr. Enter the gate at number 192 and walk all the way to the back of the building. Though removed from the city center, Basel's newest (and only independent) hostel, a renovated factory, offers brand new facilities. Color-coded rooms include matching lockers and extra-high IKEA bunk beds. **Wheelchair accessible.** Breakfast 8SFr. Sheets, showers, kitchen, and locker included. Laundry 10SFr. Reception 8-12am and 4-10pm. Checkout 11am. Dorms 29SFr; singles 80SFr; doubles 90SFr; triples 100SFr; quads 110SFr. ❷

Hotel Steinenschanze, Steinengraben 69 (☎272 53 53; fax 45 73). From the SBB station, turn left on Centralbahnstr. and follow signs for "Heuwaage." Under the bridge, climb the ramp to Steinengraben and turn left. Phone, TV, and balconies. Breakfast included. 24hr. reception. Singles 110-180SFr, under 25 with ISIC 60SFr per night for up to 3 nights; doubles with shower 160-250SFr/100SFr. AmEx/DC/MC/V. ❹

Camping: Camp Waldhort, Heideweg 16 (☎71 64 29), in Reinach. Take tram #11 to "Landhof." Backtrack 200m toward Basel, cross the main street, and follow the signs for a 10min. walk. Beautiful location—in the middle of the woods—but far from Basel. Reception 8am-noon and 2-8pm. Open Mar.-Oct. 7SFr per person, 10SFr per tent. ❶

FOOD

Barfüßerpl., Marktpl., and the streets connecting them are full of cheap eats.

RESTAURANTS

Restaurant Spillman, Eiseng. 1 (☎261 17 60; fax 16 72), at the foot of Mittlere Rheinbr., near Schifflände. An upscale but unpretentious crowd sits above the rushing Rhine in this conveniently located restaurant with a pleasant terrace. Daily lunch *Menüs* starting at 17.80SFr, while most entrees are around 25SFr. If you feel like going all-out, try the Mediterranean-style king prawns (38.50SFr). Open M-Sa 7:30am-midnight. Kitchen open until 9:30pm. ❹

Wirtshaus zum Schnabel, Trillengässlein 2 (☎261 49 09; 49 92). From Marktpl., walk 1 block on Hutg. (by EPA) to Spalenberg.; turn left onto Schnabelg. In this corner terrace, Italian-speakers serve well-prepared German dishes. Daily vegetarian *Menü* available. Pasta 12.80-19.80SFr, other entrees mid-20SFr. Open M-Sa 9am-midnight. AmEx/DC/MC/V. ❸

Restaurant Gleich, Leonhardsberg 1 (☎281 82 86). This casual restaurant serves an array of vegetarian dishes popular with locals, including a large salad buffet. Colorful, healthful dishes 13.50-23.50SFr. Open M-F 9am-9:30pm. ❸

Hirscheneck, Lindenberg 23 (☎692 73 33). Cross Wettsteinbr. and turn left onto Kartansg. An unabashedly left-of-center restaurant-bar where dreadlocks, piercings, and the hammer and sickle prevail. Features two vegetarian and organically grown dishes every day. *Menü* 12-18.50SFr. Open M-F 11am-midnight, Sa 2pm-1am, Su 10am-midnight. Kitchen open M-F noon-2pm and 6-10pm, Sa 6-10pm, Su 10am-4pm. ❷

Café Barfi, Leonhardsberg 4 (☎261 70 38), to the right of Gerberg. from Marktpl. Mostly Italian pizzas and pastas with the unexpected *samosas* (6.50SFr) thrown in. Outdoor diners enjoy accordion serenades. Pasta 15.50-19.50SFr, pizzas 16.50-20.50SFr, homemade lasagna 19.50SFr. Open daily M-Sa 10am-11pm, Su 5-10pm. MC/V. ❸

Manor, Greifeng. 22, and **Pfauen,** Freiestr. 75, are both good, inexpensive self-service restaurants. Both open M-W and F 8:30am-6:30pm, Th 8:30am-9pm, Sa 8am-5pm. ❷

MARKETS

Migros, SBB station. Open M-F 6am-10pm, Sa-Su 7:30am-10pm.

Coop, at Schifflände tram stop. Open M-W, F 7am-7pm, Th 7am-9pm, Sa 7:30am-5pm.

Public market, on Marktpl. Fresh fruits, vegetables, cheeses, and baked goods every weekday morning. Open until 5:30pm M-W, until 1:30pm Th-F.

👁 SIGHTS

Marktplatz, which sits near the river at the culminating point of Freiestr. and other major shopping avenues, is the center of the Altstadt.

THE OLD TOWN. Erected in the early 1500s to celebrate Basel's entry into the Swiss Confederation, the very red **Rathaus** brightens Marktpl. with its blinding facade adorned with gold and green statues. Behind the Marktpl., cross the **Mittlere Rheinbrücke** and see life on the other side. Built in 1225, the bridge connects Groß-Basel to Klein-Basel. A block away from Marktpl. in the heart of the Altstadt, a colorful Gothic fountain livens up the **Fischmarkt.** Leading off of the Fischmarkt, the tiny **Elftausendjungfern-Gässlein** (Lane of 11,000 Virgins) is famous for St. Ursula's pilgrimage of girls to the Holy Land during the Children's Crusade. The medieval practice of walking this lane to recoup indulgences is now defunct, but people still stagger through after overindulging at nearby bars. For a contrasting aesthetic, walk from Marktpl. toward Barfüßerpl. onto Theaterpl. Here, the spectacular **Jean Tinguely Fountain,** also known as the **Fasnachtsbrunnen,** captures a moment of modern chaos as iron sculptures spew water.

MÜNSTER (CATHEDRAL). Behind Marktpl. along the Rhine, the **Münster,** Basel's medieval treasure, stands on the site of an ancient Celtic settlement and a Roman fort. The red sandstone facade features hundreds of figures in various acts of piety ranging from trumpet-playing to dragon-slaying. Behind the altar, guilded Latin inscriptions memorialize the life of Erasmus, the renowned scholar and staunch Catholic who remained loyal to his faith even after his beloved Basel joined the Reformation in 1529. When he died, the city gave him a proper Catholic burial in its Protestant cathedral. Bernoulli, the mathematician who discovered the science behind flight, rests in the cloister among prominent Basler families. Also see the collection of bibles in different languages. The **tower** holds the city's best view of the Rhine, Klein-Basel, and Black Forest. *(Open Easter-Oct.15 M-F 10am-5pm, Sa 10am-4pm, Su 1-5pm; Oct. 16-Easter M-Sa 11am-4pm, Su 2-4pm. Free. Tower closes 30min. before the church. 3SFr. Due to church policy (and past suicides), you must go up with another person.)*

UNIVERSITY QUARTER. The **University of Basel,** founded in 1406, is Switzerland's oldest university. Its library houses rare volumes by Erasmus, Luther, and Zwingli. The grounds are ideal for picnicking, napping, and tanning. Bargain-hunters flock here every Saturday morning for the **flea market,** which starts at 7:30am and lasts until early afternoon. Around the corner from the university library, the 700-year-old **Spalentor** (gate tower), one of the original city wall's three remaining towers and one of the most impressive gates in Switzerland, marks the edge of the Altstadt. *(Head down one of the tiny alleys off Fischmarkt to reach Petersgraben, which leads to Peterspl. and the University quarter.)*

ZOO. The Zoologischer Garten serves well as an excursion for the kids after a day of museum browsing, though animal enclosures are small and uninspired. Restaurants, picnic areas, and ice cream vendors abound. *(Binningerstr. 40, a 10min. walk down Steinenvorstadt from Barfüßerpl. Follow signs along the wooden path, or take tram #1 or 8 to "Zoo Bachletten." ☎ 295 35 35. Open May-Aug. daily 8am-6:30pm; Sept.-Oct. and Mar.-Apr. 8am-6pm; Nov.-Feb. 8am-5:30pm. 14SFr, students and seniors 12SFr, ages 6-16 5SFr.)*

HIKING. Over 1200km of yellow Wanderweg marked trails crisscross the countryside around Basel. Take bus #70 to "Reigoldswil" where the **Gondelbahn** goes to the Jura mountain peak, "Wasserfallen" (937m). From the peak you can hike to Waldenburg (2½-3hr.), or to Jägerwegli (1½-2hr.). A steam engine will take you from Waldenburg back to Liestal where you can connect to Basel (1-3 per hr.).

🏛 MUSEUMS

Basel's 30 museums may seem overwhelming, but they are worth the time it takes to explore them. The **Kunstmuseum** is deservedly the most famous, but many esoteric galleries are also fascinating. Subjects range from medieval medicine to mechanized mannequins. Pick up the comprehensive museum guide at the tourist office, or visit the web site, www.museenbasel.ch. A **Swiss Museum Pass**, valid for one month (all over Switzerland at participating museums) costs 32SFr. A **Basel Card** is good for all museums (see Tourist Office).

🏛 MUSEUM JEAN TINGUELY. Noise and motion are the preferred modes of expression of the intriguing Swiss sculptor; the pink sandstone facade of this improbable homage to him hides endless amounts of interaction and chaotic entertainment. Tinguely's massive "Grosse Méta Maxi-Maxi Utopia" allows visitors to climb over and experience his crazy futuristic vision. (*Paul-Sacher Anlage 1. Take tram #2 or 15 to "Wettsteinpl." and bus #31 or 36 to "Museum Tinguely." ☎ 681 93 20; www.tinguely.ch. Open W- Su 11am-7pm. 7SFr, students 5SFr.*)

KUNSTMUSEUM (MUSEUM OF FINE ARTS). Despite being the first independent public gallery in Switzerland (opened in 1661!), the Kunstmuseum of Basel has not lost its fresh perspective on art. A formidable marble structure, it houses extensive, outstanding compilations of old and new masters and temporary exhibits. The Picasso collection was begun when a resoundingly affirmative electoral referendum persuaded the city government to grant the museum money to buy two. Touched by such enthusiasm, the artist himself donated four more. (*St. Alban-Graben 16. Accessible by tram #2 or 15. ☎ 206 62 62; www.kunstmuseumbasel.ch. Tu and Th-Su 10am-5pm, W 10am-7pm. Combined ticket with Museum für Gegenwartskunst 10SFr, students 8SFr. Special exhibition rates. Free first Su of the month.*)

FONDATION BEYELER. As one of Europe's finest private art collections, the Fondation Beyeler includes works from dozens of major artists in its architecturally dynamic building. Picasso, Matisse, and Cézanne begin the list. The outdoor lily pond is only matched by a Monet version within. (*Baselstr. 101, Riehen. Take tram #6 (dir: Riechen Girenze) to "Fondation Beyeler." ☎ 645 97 00; www.beyeler.com. Open daily 9am-8pm. M-F 16SFr, Sa-Su 20SFr; students 5SFr; after 6pm 12SFr.*)

MUSEUM DER KULTUREN BASEL. A mansion topped by neoclassical friezes houses elements of non-Western cultures that strongly contrast its architecture. Vaguely stereotypical exhibits—check out the "American" kitchen. Particularly notable is the New Guinea geisterhern that stands 3 floors high. In the same building, you'll find the **Naturhistorisches Museum.** (*Augustinerg. 2. ☎ 266 55 00. Both museums open Tu-Su 10am-5pm. 7SFr, students under 30 5SFr, under 16 free. Special rates for temporary exhibitions. Free first Su of the month and 1 hour before closing Tu-Sa.*)

MUSEUM FÜR GEGENWARTSKUNST (MODERN ART). Find most of Basel's really modern art at this museum, which is largely composed of temporary exhibition spaces, between the youth hostel and the Rhine. (*St. Alban-Rheinweg 60. ☎ 206 62 62, www.mgkbasel.ch. Open Tu-Su 11am-5pm. Combined ticket with Kunstmuseum 10SFr, students 8SFr. Special exhibition rates. Free first Su of every month.*)

HISTORICAL MUSEUM (BARFÜßERKIRCHE). The church collection includes stained-glass windows emblazoned with cantonal coats-of-arms, stunning iconography, fine goldsmithing and the oldest crosier city banner. The early Gothic church, with its pink stone columns and huge windows veiled in transparent linen, was converted into a museum in 1894. Downstairs, recreated rooms showcase medieval and Renaissance furnishings. *(Steinenberg 4, on Barfüßerpl. ☎205 86 00; www.historischesmuseumbasel.ch. Open M and W-Su 10am-5pm. 7SFr, students and seniors 5SFr, free on the 1st of the month and for under age 16.)*

OTHER MUSEUMS. The **Puppenhausmuseum (Toy Museum) Basel** holds four floors of toys (including over 2000 toy bears) and miniature model towns packed into display cases. *(Steinenvorstadt 1. ☎225 95 95. Open M-W and F-Su 11am-5pm, Th 11am-8pm. 7SFr, students 5SFr, under 16 free.)* Learn the art of paper making at the **Papiermühle (Paper Mill)** and try your hand at the printing press. *(St. Alban-Tal 37. ☎272 96 52. Open Tu-Su 2-5pm. 9SFr, students 6SFr. Family ticket 22SFr.)* The **Jüdisches Museum der Schweiz** (Jewish Museum) contains small, well-organized exhibits on law, the observation of Jewish holidays, and other aspects of Jewish daily life. *(Kornhausg. 8. Take tram #3 to "Lyss." ☎261 95 14. Open M and W 2-5pm, Su 11am-5pm. Free.)*

ENTERTAINMENT AND NIGHTLIFE

FESTIVALS. In a year-round party town, Basel's carnival, or **Fasnacht,** still manages to distinguish itself. The festivities commence the Monday before Lent (March 5, 2003) with the **Morgestraich,** which has occurred annually for the last 600 years, a not-to-be-missed 4am parade that ends precisely 72 hours later with the **Gässle parade** (March 12 in 2003). Fife and drum music plays to revelers in brilliant masks that lampoon the year's local scandals. Children wander the streets in costumes on Tuesday, and at night there is an exhibition of the lanterns (a feature of the parades) on Münsterpl., as well as concerts of the "Gugge" music. All spectators should purchase a carnival badge. The tourist office provides lists of Basel's other cultural offerings, including concerts, ballets, gallery exhibits, fairs, and the 333rd annual modern ART fair.

Many Swiss youth have been spotted unabashedly blurring the lines between private and public. Couples passionately embrace everywhere—in restaurants, on park benches, and in the middle of a busy street—and often abruptly enough to cause a pedestrian collision. While the older generation may look down on it, the young Swiss continue to enjoy their makeout fest, while tourists gawk at this street entertainment—free of charge.

BARS AND NIGHTCLUBS. A university town through and through, Basel's nightlife reflects the influence of student patrons. Start bar-hopping at **Barfüßerplatz,** where students sit at outdoor tables and drink wine on the steps of the Barfüßerkirche. When the bars close, kids in black often head for after-hours clubs, where things get rolling around 3-4am. Most places are 21+, but the crowds get younger on weekends. The two most popular local beers are **Warteck** and **Cardinal.**

☒ **Atlantis,** Klosterberg 10 (☎228 96 96). From Bankenpl., it's off Elisabethenstr. to the right. One of the older bars in Basel's Altstadt, though you wouldn't know it by the crowd that lines up to get in on weekends. This multi-level, sophisticated bar sways to reggae, jazz, and funk. Bands or DJs play every night the Italian soccer team does not. Concerts around 35SFr. Club nights F-Sa, cover 15-25SFr. Open T-Th 11am-midnight, F 11:30am-4am, Sa 6pm-4am. Kitchen open 11am-2pm and 6pm-2am.

Brauerei Fischerstube, Rheing. 45 (☎692 66 35). Cross Mittlere Rheinbr. and take the 1st right. This old-school *Biergarten* is adjacent to Basel's only brewery, crafting 4 of the best beers in town. The delectably sharp ☒ *Hell Spezial* goes well with the homemade pretzels. Stop by for an early evening *Bier,* 2.90-6SFr. Open M-Th 10am-midnight, F-Sa 10am-1am, Su 5pm-midnight. Full dinner menu from 6pm. MC/V.

Babalabar, Gerberg. 74 (☎261 48 49), to the left off Gerberg. from Barfüßerpl. Flashing lights and a smoky cloud serve to cover up the hot bodies at this trendy dance club. Go for techno nights or samba rhythms from the Latin-crazy DJ, and make sure to dress up. Cover Su-Th 7SFr, F-Sa 10SFr. Open in the summer M and W 9pm-1:30am, Th 10pm-2am, F-Sa 9pm-morning.

Pickwick Pub, Steinenvorstadt 13 (☎281 86 87), near Barfüßerpl. This English-style pub, draped in football memorabilia, hosts a salt-of-the-earth crowd of students and adults alike. Friendly bartenders are happy to go the extra mile. Beers from 3.90SFr. Open Su-W 11am-midnight, Th 11am-1am, F-Sa 11am-3am.

Dupf, Rebg. 43 (☎692 00 11). Cross Weittsteinbr. and turn left onto Rebg. This chic gay and lesbian bar welcomes a mixed crowd. Beers from 4.50SFr. Open daily 5pm-whenever.

Elle et Lui, Rebg. 39 (☎691 54 79). Dupf's bohemian next-door neighbor caters to a gay and lesbian clientele of all ages and tastes. Try the Caipirinha (14.50SFr) if you brought a friend—it's 40% alcohol. Open M 4pm-3am, Tu-Su 6pm-3am.

SOLOTHURN ☎032

Sandwiched snugly between the Jura mountains and the Aare River, Solothurn's charm rubs off on its inhabitants—the friendliness of shopkeepers and restaurateurs is tangible. Annual film, classical music, and literature festivals attest to the town's love affair with culture. Citizens of Solothurn unleash their rambunctious side during the rowdy Winter Carnival. Although Solothurn lacks the major museums and historical sights that would attract tourists for long visits, the Jura mountains offer endless biking and hiking prospects.

⊏⊐ TRANSPORTATION AND PRACTICAL INFORMATION. Trains depart from Solothurn's main station at Hauptbahnhof for: Basel (1hr., every hr. 5:50am-11pm, 23SFr); Bern (40min., every 30min. 5:18am-11:20pm, 14SFr); and Neuchâtel (45min., every hr. 5:58am-11:11pm, 17.60SFr). For a map, or free room reservations, head to the **tourist office,** Hauptg. 69. From the train station, take the underpass toward the Zentrum and follow Hauptbahnhofstr. across Kreuzackerbr. up Kroneng. (☎626 46 46; fax 46 47; info@solothurn-city.ch; www.solothurn-city.ch. Open M-F 8:30am-noon and 1:30-6pm, Sa 9am-noon.) At the **train station,** services include: **currency exchange** and **bike rental** (30SFr per day, 36SFr if returned to another station; both open M-F 6:10am-8:50pm, Sa-Su 6:30am-8:50pm); **taxis,** ☎622 66 66 or 22 22; **lockers** (3-5SFr, 24hr.) and **luggage storage** (7SFr; 6:10am-8:50pm). For **police,** call ☎117; **fire,** ☎118; **hospital,** ☎627 31 21. The **post office,** is past the hostel on Postpl.; turn left off Kreuzackerbr., and onto Landhausquai. (☎625 29 29. Open M-F 7:30am-6pm, Sa 8-noon). **Postal code:** CH-45000.

⬛⬛ ACCOMMODATIONS AND FOOD. Overlooking the Aare River on the edge of the Altstadt, the **Jugendherberge "Am Land" (HI) ❷,** Landhausquai 23, is a slick, high-tech vision of glass and steel incongruously framed by the exterior of a 1642 schoolhouse. From the train station, walk over Kreuzackerbrücke and take the first left onto Landhausquai. Amenities include a pool table, roof terrace, and music room. Beds can be close together in dorms. **Bike rental** is 10SFr per half day, 15SFr per full day. (☎623 17 06; fax 16 39. Breakfast and sheets included. Lunch and dinner 12.50SFr. Lockers 2SFr deposit. Reception 7:30-10am and 4:30-10:30pm. Check-out 10am. 9-bed dorms 26.50SFr; 6-bed dorms 27.50SFr; 5-bed dorms with sink 30SFr; doubles 85SFr; triples with toilet and shower 114SFr. Surtax 2SFr, 1SFr if under 16. Non-members add 6SFr. Wheelchair accessible. AmEx/DC/MC/V.) The **Hotel Kreuz ❸,** Kreuzg. 4, offers more privacy but less modernity. Go left off Kreuzackerbr. before the hostel. (☎622 20 20; fax 621 52 32;

kreuz@soluet.ch. Breakfast and hall showers included. Reception M-F from 11am, Sa from 9am. Spartan singles 50SFr; doubles 90SFr. Prices drop for multiple nights.) Higher prices at the **Zunfthaus zu Wirthen ❹**, Hauptg. 41, are worth it for comforts like private bathrooms, TV, and central location across from the Red Tower (☎ 626 28 48; fax 28 58. Breakfast included). Singles from 103SFr, doubles from 138SFr.

The **Taverna Amphorea ❸**, Hauptg. 51, serves large vegetarian-friendly Greek and Middle Eastern specialties for 13.50-26.50SFr. (☎ 623 67 63. Open Tu and Th 11am-11:30pm, W 9am-11:30pm, F 11am-12:30am, Sa 9am-12:30am.) From Marktpl., turn left onto Hauptg., then left onto Stalden to find the **Sandwich House ❷**, Stalden 9, which puts a techno twist on the friendly neighborhood deli. Sandwiches (4.50-16SFr) have anything from ham and cheese to shrimp and Camembert. (☎/fax 623 33 78. Open M-F 9am-6:30pm, Sa 9am-5pm.) **Restaurant-Bar Lowen ❸**, at the corner of Loweng. and Schaalg., offers meaty meals for reasonable prices. (Open M and W-Th 11am-11:30pm, F 11am-12:30am, Sa 10am-12:30am, Su 2-11:30pm). The **Manor** grocery store/self-service restaurant is at Gurzelng. 18 to the left off Marktpl. (open M-W and F 9am-6:30pm, Th 9am-9pm, Sa 8am-5pm; AmEx/DC/MC/V), or try the **farmer's market** at Marktpl. (W and Sa 8am-noon). There is an **Aperto** at the train station. (Open M-Sa 6am-10pm, Su 7am-10pm. V.)

◙ SIGHTS. Solothurn's well-preserved Baroque architecture alone justifies a visit to the city. The **Red Tower** on the Marktpl. sports several clock faces and a macabre little skeleton. Built between 1762 and 1773 by a Ticino architect, the cheerful Italianate Baroque architecture of the **Kathedrale St. Ursen** greets visitors with streaming fountains as they cross the Kreuzackerbr. The cathedral is dedicated to St. Ursus, the patron saint of Solothurn, who lost his head here for refusing to worship Roman gods. Its **tower** provides the Altstadt's best view. (☎ 622 37 53. Church open Easter-Oct. daily 8am-noon and 2-7pm; Oct.-Easter 2-6pm. Tower 2.50SFr.) The enormous **Museum Altes Zeughaus,** housed in a 1609 arsenal, holds row after row of gory instruments of death, from medieval daggers to WWII artillery. (Zeughauspl. 1, to the left of the cathedral. ☎ 623 35 28. Open May-Oct. Tu-Su 10am-noon and 2-5pm; Nov.-Apr. Tu-F 2-5pm, Sa-Su 10am-noon and 2-5pm. 6SFr, students 4SFr.) On the fringes of town, the staid **Kunstmuseum**, Werkhofstr. 30, has an extensive collection of post-1850 Swiss works. The temporary exhibits (recently, elegant Indonesian statues) tend to be more stimulating than the permanent collection. (☎ 622 23 07. Open Tu-F 10am-noon and 2-5pm, Sa-Su 10am-5pm. Free, but it is worth a donation to see the Jean Tinguely collection box in action.) **Schloß Waldegg**, the local castle, is surrounded by wheat fields that contrast its French gardens. (Take bus #4 to "St. Niklaus" and walk 10min. up Riedholzstr. Open Mar.-Oct. T-Th and Sa 2-5pm, Su 10am-5pm; Nov.-Dec. Su 10am-5pm. Wheelchair accessible. Parking available. 6SFr, students 4SFr.)

Ⓡ OUTDOOR ACTIVITIES. Marked **hiking** and **biking** trails lead through the Jura to nearby Altreu, site of the oldest and best-known stork colony in Switzerland (2hr., trail head at the corner of Kroneng. and Ritterquai). The trek to the **Weißenstein Alpine Center** is more challenging and rewarding. (2hr., rail head at the corner of Wengisteinstr. and Verenawegstr.; follow the yellow signs to Weißenstein.) Take the chairlift (13SFr) down from Weißenstein and hop on a train (4.60SFr) in Oberdorf to return. **Boat tours** leave Solothurn for Biel and from there run to Murten or Neuchâtel. (2½hr.; 27SFr, round-trip 46SFr. SwissPass valid. Ferries run early May to mid-Oct.) In the winter, **cross-country skiing** dominates the athletic scene. Weißenstein (1280m) has 7km of trails and chairlifts for downhill skiing on two small slopes best suited to beginners.

BROUGHT TO YOU BY THE NUMBER 11

Take a closer look while wandering through Solothurn's Altstadt and you'll notice a recurring numerical theme. The number of churches, fountains, and towers is eleven...as is the number of altars, bells, and steps in each flight of stairs in the St. Ours Cathedral! Even the two fountains outside the cathedral have 11 streams of water falling from one level to the next. It was in 1481 that Solothurn became the 11th canton to join the Swiss Confederation, and the town has made sure that its place in Swiss Confederate history is never forgotten...11th!

ENTERTAINMENT. Various **festivals** enliven Solothurn. In 2003, the **Swiss Film Festival** will bring celluloid lovers to the city January 20-25. The **Chesslete** (starts Feb. 27, 2003)—festivities intended to drive away winter—is a week-long topsy-turvy carnival. The party involves fantastical masks, raucous Guggenmusik, and re-naming the town (temporarily) "Honolulu." Swiss writers gather to read, drink, and sit on panels during the annual **literature festival** in May. Solothurn fans of opera enjoy the **Classic: Open Air Fest** in July (www.classic-openair.ch). The city's other big event is the **Jazz am Märetplatz** festival, in late August. Concerts fill the Marktpl. for three days, attracting jazz aficionados from far and wide.

MUNICH (MÜNCHEN)

Perhaps the only place in the world where Lederhosen and Gucci peacefully coexist, the city of Munich is both the sleek, modern capital of the province of Bavaria and a bastion of antiquated regional ritual. Birthplace of the beer garden, Munich's traditional merriment is in sharp contrast with the fragmented avant-garde attitude of Berlin, its long-time alter ego to the north. World-class museums, handsome parks and architecture, a rambunctious arts scene, and an urbane population conspire to create a city of astonishing vitality. Müncheners party zealously during *Fasching* (Jan. 7-Mar. 4, 2003)—Germany's Mardi Gras—and imbibe unbelievable quantities of beer during **Oktoberfest** (Sept. 20-Oct. 5, 2003).

PHONE CODES	The city code for Munich is 089. If calling Austria or Switzerland, dial 01149 (int'l dialing prefix); then dial 43 (Austria) or 41 (Switzerland) before dialing the number.

⚔ TRANSPORTATION

Flights: Flughafen München (☎97 52 13 13 for flight information). S8 makes the 40min. trip between the airport and the Hauptbahnhof every 10min. €8 or 8 stripes on the *Streifenkarte* for one; two to five adults can take a group rate for €15 (available at EurAide). Or, a **Lufthansa shuttle bus** runs between the Hauptbahnhof and the airport (45min.), with a pickup at the "Nordfriedhof" U-Bahn stop in Schwabing. Buses leave from Arnulfstr., on the northern side of the train station, every 20min. 5:10am-7:50pm. Buses return from Terminal A *(Zentralbereich)* and Terminal D every 20min. 7:55am-8:55pm. One-way €9, round-trip €14.

Trains: Munich's **Hauptbahnhof** (☎22 33 12 56) is the transportation hub of southern Germany, with connections to: **Berlin** (8hr., 1 per hr., €141, or €103 via Leipzig); **Innsbruck** (2hr., every 2 hr., €29); **Prague** (7hr., 2 per day, €60); **Salzburg** (1¾hr., 1 per hr., €25); **Vienna** (5hr., 1 per hr., €59); **Zürich** (5hr., 4 per day, €61). For 24hr. schedules, fare information, and reservations (in German), call ☎(01805) 99 66 33. As of December 2002 the Deutsche Bahn will be instituting a new price scale, so expect changes to existing fares.

Hitchhiking: *Let's Go* does not recommend hitchhiking as a safe mode of transportation. Those looking to share rides scan the bulletin boards in the **Mensa,** Leopoldstr. 13. Otherwise, hitchers try Autobahn on-ramps; those who stand behind (on the Autobahn side of) the blue sign with the white auto may be fined. Hitchers going to Salzburg take U1 or 2 to "Karl-Preis-pl."

Public Transportation: MVV, Munich's public transport system, runs Su-Th 5am-12:30am, F-Sa 5am-2am. S-Bahn to the airport runs starting at 3:30am. Eurail, Inter-Rail, and German railpasses are valid on the S-Bahn (S) but *not* on the U-Bahn (U), streetcars, or buses. Buy tickets at the blue *MVV-Fahrausweise* vending machines and **validate them** in the blue boxes marked with an "E" *before entering the platform.* Payment is made on an honor system, but disguised agents check for tickets sporadically; if you jump the fare or don't validate correctly, you risk a €30 fine. Single ride tickets (€2, valid for 3hr.). **Kurzstrecke** (short trip) tickets (€1, 2 stops on the U- or S-Bahn, or 4 stops on a streetcar or bus). A **Streifenkarte** (10-strip ticket) costs €9 and can be used by more than 1 person. Cancel 2 strips per person for a normal ride, or 1 strip per person for a *Kurzstrecke.* Beyond the city center, cancel 2 strips per additional zone. A

Munich

♦ ACCOMMODATIONS
4 You München, 2
Campingplatz Thalkirchen, 14
Euro Youth Hotel, 9
Hotel Helvetia, 8
Jugendherberge München
Neuhaus, 1
Pension Locarno, 6
Pension Schillerhof, 13

● FOOD
Goller, 12
Marché, 10
Schwimmkrabbe, 15

♦ PUBS & NIGHTLIFE
Augustinerkeller, 4
Backstage, 3
Ballhaus, 7
Hirschgarten, 5
Hofbräuhaus, 11
Kunstpark Ost, 16

Ⓢ S-BAHN   Ⓤ U-BAHN

MUNICH

Bayerischer
Landtag

Gasteig

ROSENHEIMER PL. Ⓢ

Müllersches
Volksbad

Forum der Technik
Deutsches Museum

TO ⑯ (in museum) →

Haus der Kunst
Englischer
Garten

Prinzregentenstr.
Seitzstr.
Liebigstr.
LEHEL Ⓤ
Pfarrstr.

St.-Anna-Str.
ST.-ANNA-PL.

Maximilianstr.
MAXI-
DENKMAL

Völkerkundemuseum

Thomas-Wimmer-Ring

ISARTOR Ⓢ
■MAXX

Valentin-Museum
Zentrum für
Aussergewöhnliche
Museen

ISARTORPL.

TO ⑯ (50m) →

← TO AIRPORT (20km) & ⑦ (3km)
■ United States
Franz-Josef-Strauss-Ring
Karl-Scharnagl-Ring

Hofgarten
ODEONSPL. Ⓤ
Residenz
MAX-
JOSEPH-
PLATZ
Nationaltheater
(Staats Oper)

Am
Kosttor
Hofbräuhaus

Hildegardstr.
Tal
Altes
Rathaus

Heilig
Geistkirche
Zwingerstr.

Staatstheater

Theatiner-
kirche

Spielzeug-
museum
Neues
Rathaus
Ⓢ MARIENPL. Ⓤ
MARIENPL.
Peterskirche
Münchener
Stadtmuseum

Viktualienmarkt
GÄRTNER-
PLATZ

TO ⑯ (50m) →

Frauenkirche
FRAUENPL.
PROMENADEPL.
AmEx

ST. JAKOBS PL.

Michaelskirche
Kaufingerstr.

Asamkirche
Sendlinger
Tor
The
■Bookshop

SENDLINGER
TOR Ⓤ

TO ⑯ (5km)
& TIERPARK HELLABRUN ZOO →

Matthäus-
kirche

Deutsches
Theater

KARLSPL.
KARLSPL. Ⓤ
Ⓢ KARLSPL.
Justizpalast
Alter
Botanischer
Garten

Obelisk
KAROLINENPL.
Amerika Haus
LENBACHPL.
MAXIMILIANSPL.
SALVATORPL.
PROMENADEPL.

HAUPTBHF.
Ⓢ HAUPTBHF.
BAHNHOFPL.
Ⓤ HAUPTBHF.

⑥
Ⓤ ⑧

Pharmacy
ℹ
Hauptbahnhof

⑨

Schillerstr.

← TO THERESIENWIESE (250m)

TO ⑯ (2km) →

← TO SCHLOSS
NYMPHENBURG,
BOTANISCHER
GARTEN (4.5km),
& ① (2km)

② ← TO ⑯ (250m) & ⑤ (4.5km)

0   250 yards
0   250 meters

Single-Tageskarte (single-day ticket) is valid for unlimited travel until 6am the next day (€4.50). A **Partner-Tageskarte** (€7.50) can be used by up to 5 adults and a dog.

Taxis: Taxi-Zentrale (☎216 11 or 194 10) has large stands in front of the train station.

Car Rental: Swing, Schellingstr. 139 (☎523 20 05), rents from €43 per day. **Avis** (☎550 12 12), **Europcar/National** (☎620 80 80), **Hertz** (☎533 35 35), and **Sixt** (☎52 52 525) have offices upstairs in the Hauptbahnhof.

Bike Rental: Radius Bikes (☎59 61 13), at the far end of the Hauptbahnhof, behind the lockers opposite tracks 30-36. €3 per hr., €14 per day, €43 per week. Mountain bikes 20% more. Deposit €50, passport, or credit card. 10% discount for students and Eurail-holders, 20% with Munich Welcome Card. Open May to mid-Oct. (Apr. and late-Oct. if good weather) daily 10am-6pm (in July-Aug., Sa-Su 9am-8pm).

▨ ORIENTATION

Munich's center is encircled by the main **Ring** and quartered by two thoroughfares which cross at the **Marienplatz** and meet the traffic rings at **Karlsplatz** (a.k.a. **Stachus**) in the west, **Isartorplatz** in the east, **Odeonsplatz** in the north, and **Sendlinger Tor** in the south. The Hauptbahnhof is west of Karlspl. East of the Isartor, the **Isar** flows south-north by the city center. To get to Marienpl. from the station, go straight on Bayerstr. to Karlspl. and continue through Karlstor to Neuhauser Str., which becomes Kaufingerstr. before it reaches Marienpl. Alternately, take S1-8 (two stops from the Hauptbahnhof, dir.: Ostbahnhof) to Marienpl.

▨ PRACTICAL INFORMATION

▨ **EurAide in English** (☎59 38 89; fax 550 39 65; euraide@compuserve.com; www.euraide.de), along track 11 (room 3) of the Hauptbahnhof, near the Bayerstr. exit. EurAide is an English-speaking office of the Deutsche Bahn and books train tickets for anywhere in Europe at no extra charge. Tickets for the public transit system (at standard prices), maps of Munich (€1), and tickets for a variety of English walking, bus, and bike tours are also available. Pick up a free copy of their brochure *Inside Track*. Open daily June-Sept. 7:45am-12:45pm and 2-6pm; Oct. 7:45am-12:45pm and 2-4pm; Nov.-Apr. 8am-noon and 1-4pm; May 7:45am-12:45pm and 2-4:30pm.

DER Reisebüro (☎55 14 02 00; www.der.de) is in the main hall of the train station and sells train tickets and railpasses. Open M-F 9:30am-6pm and Sa 10am-1pm.

Currency Exchange: ReiseBank (☎551 08 37; www.reisebank.de). In front of the train station on Bahnhofpl. Open daily 7am-10pm. Or around the corner from EurAide at track 11. Open M-Sa 7:30am-7:15pm, Su 9:30am-12:30pm and 1-4:45pm.

American Express: Promenadepl. 6 (☎228 014 65; 24hr. hotline (08001) 85 31 00), to the left of the Hotel Bayerischer Hof. Holds mail and cashes Traveler's Cheques. Open M-F 9am-6pm, Sa 9:30am-12:30pm.

Luggage Storage: At the **train station** (☎13 08 34 68) and **airport** (☎97 52 13 75). Staffed storage room (*Gepäckaufbewahrung*) in the main hall of the train station. Open daily 6am-10pm. €2.05 per piece per day. Lockers in main hall and opposite tracks #16, 24, and 28-36. Open 4am-12:30am. €1-2 per 24hr.

Gay and Lesbian Resources: Gay services information (☎260 30 56). **Lesbian information** and the **LeTra Lesbentraum,** Angertorstr. 3 (☎725 42 72). Telephone times M, W 2:30-5pm, Tu 10:30am-1pm, Th 7-9pm.

Ticket Agencies: To order tickets by phone call **München Ticket** (☎54 81 81 81).

Emergency: Police ☎110. **Ambulance** and **Fire** ☎112.

Pharmacy: Bahnhofpl. 2 (☎59 41 19 or 59 81 19), on the corner outside the train station. Open M-F 8am-6:30pm, Sa 8am-2pm.

Medical Assistance: Klinikum Rechts der Isar, across the river on Ismaninger Str. U4 or 5 to "Max-Weber-Pl." STD/AIDS tests are free and anonymous at the **Münchener AIDS-Hilfe,** Lindwurmstr. 71 (☎544 64 70). Open M-Th 9:30am-6pm, F 9:30am-2pm. UK and US consulates carry lists of English-speaking doctors.

Internet Access: Easy Everything, on Bahnhofspl. next to the post office. Open 24hr. Prices depend on demand, but are always less than €3 per hr. Unlimited passes can be purchased for periods of 24hr. (€4), 7 days (€7), or 20 days (€10).

Post Office: Bahnhofpl., 80335 Munich (☎59 90 87 16). Walk out of the main train station exit and it's the yellow building across the street. Open M-F 7am-8pm, Sa 9am-4pm, Su 10am-3pm.

▐ ACCOMMODATIONS AND CAMPING

Munich accommodations are usually seedy, expensive, or booked; during Oktoberfest, they're just booked. In summer, call before noon or reserve a few weeks ahead. Never sleep in public areas, including the Hauptbahnhof; police patrol all night long.

▓ **Euro Youth Hotel,** Senefelderstr. 5 (☎59 90 88 11; fax 59 90 88 77; info@euro-youth-hotel.de; www.euro-youth-hotel.de). From the Bayerstr. exit of the Hauptbahnhof, make a left on Bayerstr. and a right on Senefelderstr.; the hotel will be on the left. Offers an outlandishly friendly and well-informed English-speaking staff loaded with brochures and spotless, spiffy rooms. Sleek bar open daily 8pm-2am. Breakfast buffet €4.90. Wash €2.80. Dry €1.30. Reception 24hr. No curfew or lockout. Dorms €17.50; singles €45; doubles €48, with private shower, telephone and breakfast €72; triples €63; quads €84. ❸

▓ **Hotel Helvetia,** Schillerstr. 6 (☎590 68 50; fax 59 06 85 70; info@Hotel-Helvetia.de; www.Hotel-Helvetia.de), at the corner of Bahnhofspl., just beyond the Vereinsbank, to the right as you exit the station. The friendliest hotel in Munich. Over half of their beautiful rooms were newly renovated last year and outfitted with wood floors and oriental rugs. Free **Internet** access. Laundry service €6. Breakfast included. Reception 24hr. Singles €30-35; doubles €40-55, with shower €50-65; triples €55-69; quads €72-90; 5-bed room separable into 2 rooms €90-112. Rates rise 10-15% during Oktoberfest. ❸

Jugendherberge München Neuhausen (HI), Wendl-Dietrich-Str. 20 (☎13 11 56; fax 167 87 45; jhmuenchen@djh-bayern.de). U1 (dir: Westfriedhof) to "Rotkreuzpl." Go down Wendl-Dietrich-Str past the Galeria Kaufhof; the entrance is about 2 blocks ahead on the right. The most "central" of the HI hostels (3km from the city center). Free safes in the reception area. Breakfast buffet and sheets included. Sit-down dinner €5.10. Bike rental. €15 key deposit. Reception 24hr. Check-in starts at 11:30am. No curfew. If you have a reservation, arrive by 6pm or call ahead. Big dorm (37 beds) for men only €17.80; 4- to 6-bed co-ed dorms €20.80; doubles €46. ❸

4 You München, Hirtenstr. 18 (☎552 16 60; fax 55 21 66 66; info@the4you.de; www.the4you.de), 200m from the Hauptbahnhof. Exit at Arnulfstr., go left, quickly turn right onto Pfefferstr., then hang a left onto Hirtenstr. Hostel is a block and a half ahead on the right. Ecological youth hostel with restaurant and bar, hang-out areas, a playroom, and wheelchair-accessible everything. Breakfast buffet €4,35. Sheets included. Reception 24hr. 12-bed dorms €17.50; 4-, 6- or 8-bed dorms €20-22; singles €35; doubles €52. ❷ Hotel rooms are also available for those who prefer their own bathroom and telephone. Singles €43.50; doubles €68.50; triples €92. Breakfast included; all prices per room. Reserve in advance. ❷

Pension Locarno, Bahnhofspl. 5 (☎55 51 64 or 55 51 65; fax 59 50 45; www.deut-schland-hotel.de/muc/locarno.htm). From the "Bahnhofsplatz" exit of the train station walk left across Bahnhofspl. and look for the building with the large "Pension" sign. Cozy and newly furnished rooms, all with cable TV and phone. Reception 7:30am-5am. Make reservations online. Singles €38; doubles €57; triples €69; quads €81. ❹

Pension Schillerhof, Schillerstr. 21 (☎59 42 70; fax 550 18 35; hotel-schillerhof@az-online.net; www.hotel-schillerhof.de). Exit onto Bahnhofpl. from the train station, turn right, and go 2 blocks down Schillerstr. Tidy rooms with TV. Breakfast included. Reception 6am-10pm. Online reservation. All rooms will be newly renovated by spring 2003; expect a corresponding increase in prices. Singles €30-40; doubles €45-61. Extra bed €10. Oktoberfest surcharge €13-20 per person. ❸

Campingplatz Thalkirchen, Zentralländstr. 49 (☎723 17 07; fax 724 31 77). U1 or 2 to "Sendlinger Tor," then U3 to "Thalkirchen," and change to bus #57 (20min.). From the bus stop, cross the busy street on the left and take a right onto the footpath next to the road. The entrance is down the path on the left. Well-run assembly of 550 sites on lush grounds on the banks of the river Isor. Jogging and bike paths. TV lounge, groceries, and a restaurant. Tent rental €8 per night. Oktoberfest surcharge €3.60. Showers €1. Wash €4, dry €0.25 per 6min. Curfew 11pm. €4.40 per person, €1.30 per child under 14. €3-4 per tent; €4.30 per car. ❶

🍴 FOOD

The **Viktualienmarkt,** south of Marienpl., is Munich's gastronomic center. (Open M-F 10am-8pm, Sa 8am-4pm.) For an authentic Bavarian lunch, grab a *Brez'n* (pretzel) spread with *Leberwurst* or cheese. Many reasonably-priced restaurants and cafes cluster on **Schellingstr., Amalienstr.,** and **Türkenstr.** Ride U3 or 6 to "Universität." Fruit and vegetable **markets,** many on Bayerstr., are common.

🍽 **Marché,** Neuhauser Str., between Karlspl. and Marienpl. (☎230 879 11). The top floor of this monstrous eatery offers cafeteria-style food displays and a Mövenpick ice cream stand. Downstairs, customers are given food cards before entering the area, which is decorated as a mini-Munich and filled with buffet and food stations where chefs prepare every food imaginable. Great vegetarian selections. You'll get a stamp for each item you take; pay on the way out. Entrees and desserts €2-10 apiece. But don't lose your card! If you do, you'll either throw down €50 or spend the day washing dishes. Bottom floor open 11am-10pm, top floor open 8am-10pm, 11pm in the summer. ❷

🍽 **Schwimmkrabbe,** Ickstattstr. 13 (☎201 00 80). U1 or 2 to "Fraunhoferstr.," then walk 1 block down Klenzestr. and turn left on Ickstattstr. Locals flock to this family-run Turkish restaurant. Try the delicious *Etli Pide* (lamb and veggies wrapped in foot-long bread with salad; €8.70). Filling appetizers €4-9. Hearty dishes €8-18. Open daily 5pm-1am. ❸

Gollier, Gollierstr. 83 (☎50 16 73). U4 or 5 or S7 or 27 to "Heimeranpl.," take a left, and walk 2 blocks north on Garmischer Str. and turn left on Gollierstr. Serves delicious pizzas, casseroles, and crepes (€6-11). Lunch buffet Tu-F 11:30am-2:30pm. Offers many summer specials such as reduced lunch buffet prices and early-bird dinner deals. Open Tu-F 11:30am-3pm and 5pm-midnight, Sa 5pm-midnight, Su 10am-midnight. ❷

🔆 🏛 SIGHTS AND MUSEUMS

MARIENPLATZ. Sacred stone spires tower above the Marienpl., a major S-Bahn and U-Bahn junction as well as the social nexus of the city. At the neo-Gothic **Neues Rathaus,** the **Glockenspiel** chimes with a display of jousting knights and dancing coopers. *(Daily 11am, noon; also 5pm in the summer.)* At bedtime *(9pm),* a mechanical watchman marches out and the Guardian Angel escorts the *Münchner Kindl* (Munich Child, a symbol of the city) to bed. On the face of the **Altes Rathaus** tower, are all of Munich's coats of arms since its inception as a city—with one notable gap. When the tower was rebuilt after its destruction in WWII, the local government decided to exclude the swastika-bearing coat of arms from the Nazi era. *(Tower open M-F 9am-7pm, Sa-Su 10am-7pm. €1.50, 18 and under €0.75, under 6 free.)* Walk one block toward the Hauptbahnhof on Kaufingerstr. to find the onion-domed towers of the 15th-century **Frauenkirche**—now the symbol of the city. Its towers (topped with their characteristic domes in the mid-16th century) offer travelers an elevator-accessible view of the old city. See the final resting place of Kaiser Ludwig der Bayer and a free German language tour Apr.-Oct. at 2pm. *(Towers open Apr.-Oct. M-Sa 10am-5pm. €3, students €1.50, under 6 free.)*

RESIDENZ. Down the pedestrian zone from Odeonspl., the richly decorated rooms of the Residenz, built from the 14th to 19th centuries, form the material vestiges of the Wittelsbach dynasty. The grounds now house several museums. The beautifully landscaped **Hofgarten** behind the Residenz shelters the lovely temple of Diana. The **Schatzkammer** (treasury) contains jeweled baubles, crowns, swords, china, ivory work, and other trinkets from the 10th century on. *(Open daily from Apr. to mid-Oct. 9am-6pm, Th 9am-8pm; in winter 10am-4pm. Last admission 30min. before closing time. €4; students, seniors, and group members €3; children under 18 free with adult.)* The **Residenzmuseum** comprises the former Wittelsbach apartments and State Rooms, a collection of European porcelain, and a 17th-century court chapel. *(German language tours meet just outside the museum entrance Sa 2pm, Su 11am. €6. Max-Joseph-pl. 3. ☎ 29 06 71. Take U3-6 to "Odeonspl." Open same hours as Schatzkammer. €4; students and children €3. Combination ticket to Schatzkammer and Residenzmuseum €7; students and seniors €5.50.)* Across Max-Joseph Pl. gleams the golden-yellow high Baroque **Theatinerkirche,** constructed by Ferdinand Maria between to thank God for the birth of his son.

SCHLOẞ NYMPHENBURG. Wittelsbach elector Ferdinand Maria and his wife, Henriette Adelaide of Savoy, celebrated the birth of their son Max Emanuel in 1662 by erecting an elaborate summer playground. Of particular interest within the palace is also King Ludwig I's **Gallery of Beauties,** a series of paintings commissioned by the king of women who caught his fancy. Beyond the palace walls, stroll through the gardens to the intimate manors housed on the grounds: the Amalienburg, Badenburg, Pagodenburg, and the Magdalen hermitage. Finally, visit the **Marstallmuseum** (carriage museum) to see how 17th century royalty rode in style. *(☎ 17 90 80. Streetcar #17 (dir: Amalienburgstr.) to "Schloẞ Ndymphenburg." All attractions open Apr. to mid-Oct. daily 9am-6pm, Th 9am-8pm; late Oct. to Mar. daily 10am-4pm. Museum and Schloẞ open Tu-Su 9am-noon and 1-5pm. Badenburg, Pagodenburg, and Magdalen hermitage closed in winter. Schloẞ €3.50, students €2.50. Manors €3, students €2. Marstallmuseum €2.50, students €2. Entire complex €7.50; students €6; children under 15 free with adult.)*

BOTANISCHER GARTEN. Next door to Schloẞ Nymphenburg, the greenhouses of the immense Botanischer Garten shelter rare and wonderful flora from around the world. Beyond the greenhouses, revel in the manicured gardens and stroll through the collection of unique and exotic rosebushes. *(Streetcar #17 (dir: Amalienburgstr.) to "Botanischer Garten." ☎ 17 86 13 10. Open May-Aug. daily 9am-7pm; Apr. and Sept. 9am-6pm; Feb., Mar. and Oct. 9am-5pm; Nov.-Jan. 9am-4:30pm. €2.50, students €1.50.)*

MUSEUMS

Munich is a supreme museum city, and many of the city's offerings would require days for exhaustive perusal. A day pass (€15) to all of Munich's museums is sold at the tourist office and at many larger museums.

⬛ALTE PINAKOTHEK. Contains Munich's most precious art. Commissioned in 1826 by King Ludwig I, the last of the passionate Wittelsbach art collectors, this world-renowned hall houses works by Titian, da Vinci, Raphael, Dürer, Rembrandt, Rubens, and other European painters of the 14th through the 18th centuries. *(Barerstr. 27. U2 to "Königspl." Take a right at Konigspl., and a left after 1 block onto Meiserstr. Walk a block and a half to the museum. ☎ 23 80 52 16; www.stmukwk.bayern.de/ kunst/museen. Open Tu-Su 10am-5pm, Th until 10pm. €5, students €3.50; a combination ticket for the Alte and the Neue Pinakotheken €8, €5.)*

DEUTSCHES MUSEUM. One of the world's largest and best museums of science and technology. Fascinating exhibits of original models include the first telephone and the work bench upon which Otto Hahn split his first atom. Don't miss the mining exhibit, which winds through a labyrinth of recreated subterranean tunnels. A walk through the museum's 50+ departments covers over 17km; grab an English guidebook (€4). They've also got a planetarium. *(Museuminsel 1. S1-8 to "Isartor" or streetcar #18 to "Deutsches Museum." ☎ 217 91; www.deutsches-museum.de. Open daily 9am-5pm. €6, students €2.50, children under 6 free.)*

NEUE PINAKOTHEK. A sleek space for paintings and sculptures of the 19th to 20th centuries: Van Gogh, Klimt, Cézanne, Manet, and more. *(Barerstr. 29. ☎ 23 80 51 95; www.stmukwk.bayern.de/kunst/museen. Next to and with the same prices as the Alte Pinakothek. Tour M noon. Open W-M 10am-5pm and Th until 10pm.)*

GLYPTOTHEK. Assembled by Ludwig I in 1825 in pursuit of his dream to turn Munich into a "cultural work of such sheer perfection as only few Germans have experienced," this museum features 2400-year-old pediment figures from the Temple of Aphaea as well as Etruscan and Roman sculptures. *(Königspl. 3. Across Luisenstr. from the Lenbachhaus. U2 to "Königspl." ☎ 28 61 00. Open W and F-Su 10am-5pm, Tu and Th until 8pm. €3, students €2; free tour Tu and Th at 6pm.)*

BMW-MUSEUM. The ultimate driving museum features a fetching display of past, present, and future products of Bavaria's second-favorite export. Headphone stations (in English, German, French and Spanish) and the brochure *Horizons in Time* (available in 10 languages) guide you to the top of the museum. *(Petuelring 130. U3 to "Olympiazentrum." Take the "Olympiaturm" exit and walk a block up Lerchenauer Str.; the museum will be on your left. ☎ 38 22 33 07. Open daily 9am-5pm. €3, students €2.)*

🎭 🎟 ENTERTAINMENT AND NIGHTLIFE

Munich's theater offerings range from dramatic classics at the **Residenztheater** and **Volkstheater** to comic opera at the **Staatstheater am Gärtnerplatz** to experimental works at the **Theater im Marstall** in **Nymphenburg** (standing tickets around €8). Scores of small fringe theaters, cabaret stages, art cinemas, and artsy pubs cluster in Schwabing. Munich's July **opera festival** is held in the ⬛**Bayerische Staatsoper,** Max-Joseph-pl. 2 (☎ 21 85 19 30 or ☎ 21 85 19 19); take U3-6 to "Odeonspl." or streetcar #19 to "Nationaltheater." Standing and student tickets (€4-10) to the numerous operas and ballets are sold at Maximilianstr. 11, behind the opera house, or 1hr. before performances at the side entrance on Maximilianstr. (Box office open M-F 10am-6pm, Sa 10am-1pm. No performances from Aug. to mid-Sept.) The opera festival is accompanied by a concert series in the Nymphenburg and Schleißheim palaces. The *Monatsprogramm* (€1.50) lists schedules for all of Munich's stages, museums, and festivals.

A nighttime odyssey begins at one of Munich's beer gardens or beer halls; the alcohol keeps flowing at cafes and bars, which, except for Friday and Saturday nights, shut off their taps at 1am. Then the discos and dance clubs suddenly spark and throb relentlessly until 4am. The trendy bars, cafes, cabarets, and discos plugged into **Leopoldstr.** in **Schwabing** attract tourists from all over Europe. **Münchener Freiheit** (on the U3/6 line) is the most famous (and most touristy) bar/cafe district. Pick up *Munich Found, in München,* or *Prinz* at any newsstand to find out what's up. Munich's homosexual scene centers in the **Glockenbachviertel,** stretching from south of the Sendlinger Tor through the Viktualienmarkt/Gärtnerpl. to the Isartor. Pick up *Rosa Seiten* at **Max&Milian Bookstore,** Ickstattstr. 2 (☎260 33 20. Open M-F 10:30am-2pm and 3:30-8pm, Sa 11am-4pm), or at any other gay establishment for listings of gay nightlife and services.

■ **Kunstpark Ost,** Grafinger Str. 6 (☎49 00 29 28; www.kunstpark.de). U5 or S1-8 to "Ostbahnhof"; follow signs for the "Kunstpark Ost" exit, turn right onto Friedenstr. and then left onto Grafinger Str.; the Park is half a block down on the right. The newest and biggest addition to the Munich nightlife scene, this huge complex with 40 different venues swarms with young people hitting clubs, concerts, and bars—but most of all, dancing the night away. In 2003 the entire venue will be relocating to Fröttmaning, outside the city center. Visitors should call or check online for additional information abut the move.

Backstage, Wilhelm-Hale Str./Birketweg (☎12 66 100; fax 12 37 370; www.backstage089.de). Streetcar #16 or 17 to "Stubenplatz" or #18 or 19 to "Elsenheimerstr." "Underground" scene, playing hard core, indie rock, electronica, soul, and funk. Primarily local crowd, with lots of tattoos and green hair. Check online or call for live concert listings. Open Su-Th 7pm-3am, F-Sa 7pm-5am.

Ballhaus, Domagkstr. 33 (☎450 800 75), in the Alabamahalle. U6 to "Alte Heide." There's a free shuttle from there to the club. Situated along with three other discos on a former military base in Schwabing. Start out in the beer garden, which opens at 8pm. Try **Alabama** for German oldies on F (9pm-4am, drinks free until 1am) and hits from the 60s to the 80s on Sa (10pm-5am, free drinks all night). **Tempel Club** has typical pop music. (Open Sa 10pm-4am. Drinks from €1.) **Schwabinger Ballhouse** plays international jams. (Open F-Sa 10pm-5am. Cover €8, drinks €1.50-3.)

BEER, BEER, AND MORE BEER

The six great Munich labels are *Augustiner, Hacker-Pschorr, Hofbräu, Löwenbräu, Paulaner,* and *Spaten-Franziskaner;* most restaurants will serve only one. The longest beer festival in the world is Munich's **Oktoberfest** (Sept. 20-Oct. 5, 2003) at Theresienwiese (U4 or 5).

■ **Augustinerkeller,** Arnulfstr. 52 (☎59 43 93), at Zirkus-Krone-Str. S1-8 to "Hackerbrücke." Walk left out of the station on the bridge and take a right on Arulfstr. Founded in 1824, Augustiner is viewed by most Müncheners as the finest beer garden in town. The delicious, sharp Augustiner beer (*Maß* €5.70), entices locals, smart tourists, and students. Food €2-14. Open daily 10am-1am; hot food until 10pm. Beer garden open daily 10:30am-midnight or 1am, depending on weather.

■ **Hirschgarten,** Hirschgarten 1 (☎17 25 91). Streetcar 17 (dir.: Amalienburgstr.) to "Romanpl." Walk south to the end of Guntherstr. and enter the Hirschgarten. The largest beer garden in Europe (seating 9000 people) is boisterous and pleasant, but somewhat remote near Schloß Nymphenburg. Entrees €5-15. *Maß* €5.30. Open daily 9am-midnight, kitchen open until 10pm.

Hofbräuhaus, Platzl 9 (☎290 13 60; www.hofbraeuhaus.de), 2 blocks from Marienpl. Walk past the *Altes Rathaus* and take an immediate left onto Sparkassenstr. Turn right right away onto Lederstr., and then take your first left on Orlandostr.; the Hofbräuhaus is ahead on your right. Although the Hofbräuhaus was originally reserved for royalty and invited guests, a 19th-century proclamation lowered the price of its beer to "offer the Military and working classes a healthy and good tasting drink." *Maß* €6. *Weißwürste* €3.70. Open daily 9am-midnight with live Blasmusik every day.

PRAGUE (PRAHA)

According to legend, Countess Libuše stood above the Vltava and declared, "I see a city whose glory will touch the stars." On that spot, medieval kings built soaring cathedrals and lavish palaces that reflected Prague's status as capital of the Holy Roman Empire. Yet legends of demons and a maze of alleys lent this city a dark side that inspired Franz Kafka's tales of paranoia. Since the fall of the Iron Curtain, foreigners have stormed the city, but walk a few blocks from any major attraction and you'll be lost among cobblestone alleys, without a backpack in sight.

 CITY SUBMERGED. When this book went to print, Prague was in a state of emergency, devastated by the flooding of August 2002. Waters have since receded, but there is lasting damage to parts of the city. The Malá Strana and Kampa Island suffered especially under several meters of water. Call ahead to sights and accommodations to verify openings and hours.

PHONE CODE	**Country code: 420. International dialing prefix:** 00. From outside the Czech Republic, dial int'l dialing prefix (see inside back cover) + 420 + city code + local number.

✈ TRANSPORTATION

Flights: Ruzyně Airport (☎20 11 32 59), 20km northwest of the city. Take bus #119 to Metro A: Dejvická (daily 5am-midnight; 12Kč, luggage 6Kč); buy tickets from kiosks or machines. **Airport buses** (☎20 11 42 96) leave every 30min. from outside Metro stops at Nám. Republiky (90Kč) and Dejvická (60Kč).

Trains: ☎24 22 42 00; international ☎24 61 52 49; www.cdrail.cz. 4 terminals: **Hlavní station** (Metro C: Hlavní nádraží) is the largest. Most international service from **Holešovice station** (☎24 61 32 49; Metro C: Nádraží Holešovice). To: **Berlin** (5hr., 5 per day, 1400Kč); **Budapest** (10hr., 5 per day, 1300Kč); **Munich** (6hr., 3 per day, 1700Kč); **Vienna** (4½hr., 3 per day, 750Kč). Domestic trains: **Masarykovo station** at the corner of Hybernská and Havlíčkova (☎24 61 51 54; Metro B: Nám. Republiky).

Public Transportation: Buy tickets for the **Metro, tram,** or **bus** from *tabák* kiosks, machines in stations, or **DP** (*Dopravní Podnik;* transport authority) kiosks. The basic 8Kč ticket is good for 15min. on a tram (or 4 stops on the Metro); 12Kč is valid for 1hr. during the day, with connections between bus, tram, and Metro. Large bags and bikes require 6Kč ticket. Validate tickets in machines above escalators. 3 **Metro** lines run daily 5am-midnight. **Night trams** #51-58 and **buses** run all night after the last Metro. The tourist office in Old Town Hall sells **multi-day passes** valid for the entire network (24hr. 70Kč, 3-day 200Kč, 7-day 250Kč; student 30-day pass 210Kč).

Taxis: RadioTaxi (☎24 91 66 66) or **AAA** (☎140 14). Both open 24hr. Set rates are a 30Kč flat rate plus 22Kč per km, but taxi drivers are notorious scam artists.

🕮🛈 ORIENTATION AND PRACTICAL INFORMATION

The river Vltava separates the **Staré Město** (Old Town) and the **Nové Město** (New Town) from **Malá Strana** (Lesser Side). On the river's right bank, the **Staroměstské Náměstí** (Old Town Square) is the focal point of the city. From the square, the elegant **Pařížská ulice** (Paris Street) leads north into **Josefov**, the old Jewish ghetto. In

PRAGUE

the opposite direction from Pařížská lies **Nové Město**, which houses **Václavské Náměstí** (Wenceslas Square), the administrative and commercial heart of the city. West of Staroměstské nám., **Karlův Most** (Charles Bridge) traverses the Vltava and connects the Old Town with **Malostranské Náměstí** (Lesser Town Square). **Pražský Hrad** (Prague Castle) sits on the **Hradčany** hilltop above Malostranské nám. Prague's main train station, **Hlavní Nádraží**, and Florenc bus station sit in the northeastern corner of **Václavské nám.** To get to Staroměstské nám., take the Metro A line to Staroměstská and walk down Kaprova away from the river.

Tourist Offices: Pražská Informační Služba (Prague Info Service) is in the Old Town Hall (☎24 48 20 18; English ☎54 44 44). Open in summer M-F 9am-7pm, Sa-Su 9am-6pm; off-season M-F 9am-6pm, Sa-Su 9am-5pm.

Budget Travel: CKM, Manesove 77 (☎22 72 15 95; www.ckm-praha.cz). Metro A: Jiřího z Poděbrad. Budget air tickets for those under 26. Also books lodgings in Prague from 250Kč. Open M-Th 10am-6pm, F 10am-4pm.

Embassies: Australia (☎51 01 83 50) and **New Zealand** (☎22 51 46 72) have consuls, but citizens should contact the UK embassy in an emergency. **Canada,** Mickiewiczova 6 (☎72 10 18 00; http://217.11.254.44/ca/). Metro A: Hradčanská. Open M-F 8:30am-12:30pm. **Ireland,** Tržiště 13 (☎57 53 00 61). Metro A: Malostranská. Open M-F 9:30am-12:30pm and 2:30-4:30pm. **South Africa,** Ruská 65 (☎67 31 11 14). Metro A: Flora. Open M-F 9am-noon. **UK,** Thunovská 14 (☎57 53 02 78; www.britain.cz). Metro A: Malostranská. Open M-F 9am-noon. **US,** Tržiště 15 (☎57 53 06 63; emergency ☎53 12 00; www.usis.cz). Metro A: Malostranská. Open M-F 9am-4pm.

Currency Exchange: Exchange counters are everywhere with wildly varying rates. **Chequepoints** charge commission. **Komerční banka,** Na příkopě 33 (☎24 43 21 11), buys notes and checks for 2% commission. Open M-F 8am-5pm. **ATMs** ("Bankomats") offer the best rates, but sometimes charge large fees.

American Express: Václavské Nám. 56 (☎22 80 02 37; fax 22 21 11 31). Metro A, C: Muzeum. The **ATM** outside takes AmEx cards. Grants MC/V **cash advances** for 3% commission. Open daily 9am-7pm.

Luggage Storage: Lockers in all train and bus stations take two 5Kč coins. Or, use the luggage offices to the left in the basement of **Hlavní station** (15-30Kč per day; open 24hr.) or halfway up the stairs at **Florenc** (10-25Kč per day; open daily 5am-11pm).

Medical Assistance: Na Homolce (Hospital for Foreigners), Roentgenova 2 (☎57 27 11 11; after-hours ☎57 77 20 25). Open M-F 8am-4pm. 24hr. emergency service. **American Medical Center,** Janovského 48 (☎87 79 73). Major foreign insurance accepted. On call 24hr. Appointments M-F 9am-4pm. Average consultation 50-200Kč.

24hr. Pharmacy: U Anděla, Štefánikova 6 (☎57 32 09 18). Metro B: Anděl.

Internet Access: Prague is an Internet nirvana. **Bohemia Bagel,** Masna 2 (www.bohemiabagel.cz). 1.5Kč per min. Open M-F 7am-midnight, Sa-Su 8am-midnight. **Cafe Electra,** Rašínovo nábřeží 62 (☎24 92 28 87). Metro B: Karlovo Nám. Exit on the Palackého Nám. side. 80Kč per hr. Open M-F 9am-midnight, Sa-Su 11am-midnight.

Telephones: Phone cards sell for 175Kč per 50 units at kiosks and post offices.

Post Office: Jindřišská 14. Metro A, B: Můstek (☎21 13 14 45). Airmail to the US takes 7-10 days. *Poste Restante* available. Open daily 2am-midnight. **Postal Code:** 110 00.

ACCOMMODATIONS

Hostel Boathouse, Lodnická 1 (☎41 77 00 57; www.aa.cz/boathouse), south of the city center. Take tram #21 from Nářodni south toward Sídliště. Get off at Černý Kůň

(20min.) and follow the signs. As Věra the owner says, "This isn't a hostel, it's a crazyhouse." Summer camp vibe. Hot breakfast or dinner 70Kč. Dorms 300-320Kč. ❶

Hostel U Melounu, Ke Karlovu 7 (☎/fax 24 91 83 22; pus.praha@worldline.cz.), in Nové Město. Metro C: I.P. Pavlova; follow Sokolská to Na Bojišti; continue and turn left onto Ke Karlovu. A historic building with great facilities. Breakfast included. Reservations accepted. Dorms 380Kč; singles 500Kč; doubles 840Kč. 30Kč ISIC discount. ❷

Traveller's Hostels, in Staré Město (☎24 82 66 62; www.travellers.cz). These summertime big-dorm specialists round up travelers at bus and train stations and shuttle herds to one of their central hostels for lots of beds and beer. Breakfast included.

> **Dlouhá 33** (☎24 82 66 62). Metro B: Nám. Republiky. Follow Revoluční toward the river, turn left on Dlouhá. Unbeatable location; in the same building as the Roxy, but soundproof. Open yearround. Dorms 370-430Kč; doubles 1240Kč; triples 1440Kč. ❷

> **Husova 3** (☎22 22 00 78). Metro B: Národní třída; turn right on Spálená (which becomes Na Perštýně after Národní), and again on Husova. Open July-Aug. Classy dorms 400Kč. ❷

> **Střelecký ostrov** (☎24 91 01 88), on an island off Most Legií. Metro B: Národní třída. Open midJune to mid-Sept. Spacious dorms 300Kč. ❶

> **Ujezd** (☎57 31 24 03), across Most Legií bridge. Metro B: Národní třída. Sports facilities and park. Open June-Sept. Dorms 220Kč. ❶

Dům krále Jiřího, Liliová 10 (☎22 22 09 25; www.kinggeorge.cz), in Staré Město. Metro A: Staroměstská. Exit onto Nám. Jana Palacha, walk down Křížovnická toward the Charles Bridge, turn left onto Karlova; Liliová is the first right. Gorgeous rooms with private baths. Breakfast included. Singles 1500-2000Kč; doubles 2700-3350Kč. ❺

Pension Unitas/Cloister Inn, Bartolomějská 9 (☎232 77 00; fax 232 77 09; cloister@cloister-inn.cz), in Staré Město. Metro B: Národní třída. Cross Národní, head up Na Perštýně away from Tesco, and turn left on Bartolomějská. Renovated rooms in the cells of a former Communist prison where Václav Havel was incarcerated. Breakfast included. Singles 1100Kč; doubles 1400Kč; triples 1750Kč. ❹

Na Vlachovce, Zenklova 217 (☎/fax 688 02 14). Take bus #102 or 175 from Nádraží Holešovice toward Okrouhlická, then walk up the hill. Reserve a week ahead. Beds in romantic 2-person beer barrels 400Kč; doubles with bath 975Kč. ❶

Sokol Troja, Trojská 171 (☎/fax 33 54 29 08), north of the center in the Troja district. Metro C: Nádraží Holešovice. Take bus #112 to Kazanka. Similar places line the road. 130Kč per person, 90-180Kč per tent. Dorms 270Kč; bungalow 230Kč per person. ❶

🍴 FOOD

Tesco, Národní třída 26, has **groceries** right next to Metro B: Národní třída. (Open M-F 7am-8pm, Sa 8am-7pm, Su 9am-7pm.) Look for the **daily market** where Havelská and Melantrichova meet in Staré Město. Most restaurants are cash-only.

▨ **U Sádlů,** Klimentskà 2 (☎24 81 38 74). Metro B: Nám. Republiky. From the square, walk down Revoluční toward the river, then go right on Klimentskà. Medieval theme restaurant with bountiful portions; call ahead. Czech-only menu lists traditional meals (115-230Kč). Open daily 11am-midnight and 1-2am. ❷

▨ **Klub architektů,** Betlémské Nám. 52, in Staré Město. Metro B: Národní třída. A 12th-century cellar thrust into the 20th century. Veggie options 90-100Kč; meat dishes 140-150Kč. Open daily 11:30am-midnight. ❷

U Špirků, ul. Kožná 12, in Staré Město. Metro A: Staroměstská. Authentic Czech decor and the city's cheapest food. Main dishes about 100Kč. Open daily 11am-midnight. ❶

Velryba (The Whale), Opatovická 24, in Nové Město. Metro B: Národní třída. Cross the tram tracks and follow Ostrovní, then go left onto Opatovická. Relaxed cafe-restaurant

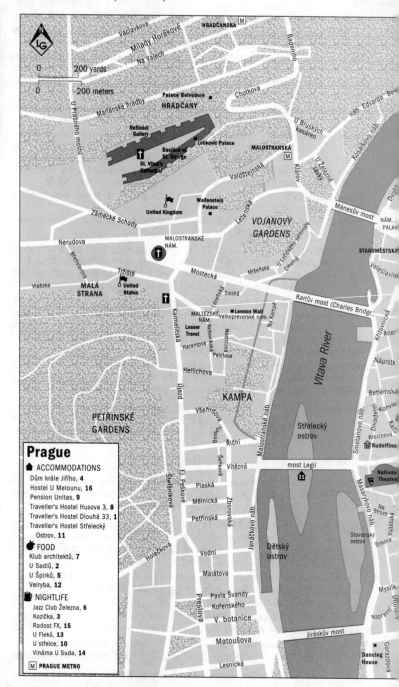

Prague

♦ **ACCOMMODATIONS**
Dům krále Jiřího, **4**
Hostel U Melounu, **16**
Pension Unitas, **9**
Traveller's Hostel Husova 3, **8**
Traveller's Hostel Dlouhá 33, **1**
Traveller's Hostel Střelecký
Ostrov, **11**

🍴 **FOOD**
Klub architektů, **7**
U Sadlů, **2**
U Špirků, **5**
Velryba, **12**

🛏 **NIGHTLIFE**
Jazz Club Železna, **6**
Kozička, **3**
Radost FX, **15**
U Fleků, **13**
U střelce, **10**
Vinárna U Suda, **14**

Ⓜ **PRAGUE METRO**

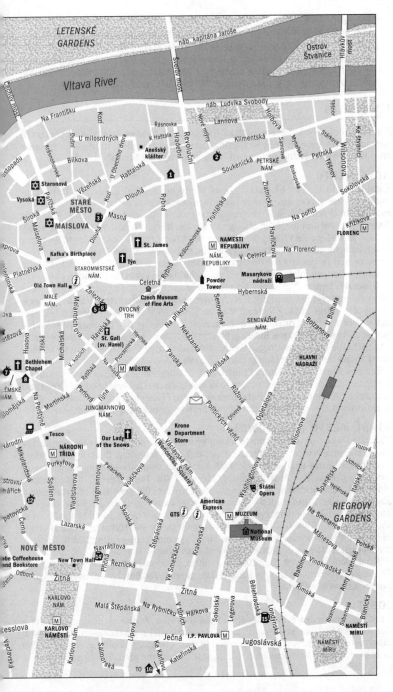

with a gallery downstairs. Main dishes 80-140Kč. Open M-Th 11am-midnight, F 11am-2am. Cafe and gallery open M-F noon-midnight, Sa 5pm-midnight, Su 3-10pm. ❶

Kajetanka, Hradcanské Nám., in Malá Strana. Metro A: Malostranská. Walk down Letenská through Malostranské Nám.; climb Nerudova until it curves to Ke Hradu, continue up the hill. Terrace cafe with a spectacular view. Meat dishes 129-289Kč, salads 49-69Kč. Open winter daily 10am-6pm; spring and summer daily 10am-9pm. ❸

🅖 SIGHTS

Tourist flock toward **Staromwstské Náměstí**, the **Charles Bridge**, and **Václavské Náměstí.** Don't leave without wandering though the back alleys of **Josefov**, exploring the hills of **Vyšehrad**, and getting lost in the maze of **Malá Strana's** streets.

NOVÉ MĚSTO

Established in 1348 by Charles IV, Nové Město has aged well. Today it forms Prague's commercial center. Somehow the monks manage to preserve the immaculate **rose garden** (Františkánská zahrada) in the heart of the district. *(Metro A, B: Můstek. Enter through the arch to the left of Jungmannova and Národní, behind the statue. Open daily mid-Apr. to mid-Sept. 7am-10pm; mid-Sept. to mid-Oct. 8am-8pm; mid-Oct. to mid-Apr. 8am-7pm. Free.)* A plaque under the arcades of Národní třída memorializes the hundreds of citizens beaten by police on November 17, 1989, when a wave of protests led to the collapse of communism in Czechoslovakia during the **Velvet Revolution.**

Wenceslas Square (Václavské Náměstí), a broad boulevard running through Nové Město's center, memorializes Czech ruler and saint **Wenceslas** (Václav), whose statue sits in front of the **National Museum** (Národní Muzeum). Wenceslas has presided over a century of turmoil and triumph, witnessing five revolutions from his pedestal. The **Radio Prague Building,** behind the National Museum, was the scene of a tense battle during the Prague Spring, as citizens tried to protect the radio studios from Soviet tanks with a human barricade. *(Metro A, C: Muzeum.)*

Built by American architect Frank Gehry of Guggenheim-Bilbao fame, the undulating building at the corner of Resslova and Rašínovo nábřeží is called "Fred and Ginger" by Anglophones, and the **Dancing House** (Taneční Dům) by Czechs. *(Metro B: Karlovo nám. Walking down Resslova toward the river, the building is on the left.)*

STARÉ MĚSTO (OLD TOWN)

Thronged with tourists and the hawkers who prey on them, **Charles Bridge** (Karlův Most) is Prague's most recognizable landmark. Five years ago, the bridge's vendors peddled Red Army gear and black market currency deals; today, they sell watercolors of the bridge. The heart of Staré Město is **Old Town Square** (Staroměstské Náměstí), surrounded by eight magnificent towers. **Old Town Hall** (Staroměstská Radnice) is the multi-facaded building with a bit blown off the front. Receiving Prague's only visible war damage, the building was partially demolished by the Nazis in the final week of WWII. Crowds mob to watch the wonderful astronomical clock chime with its procession of apostles and a skeleton representing death. *(Metro A: Staroměstská; Metro A, B: Můstek. Town hall open summer M 11am-5:30pm, Tu-Su 9am-5:30pm. Clock tower open daily 10am-6pm. 30Kč, students 20Kč. Last chime 9pm.)* The Czech Republic's most famous martyred theologian, **Jan Hus,** hovers over Old Town Square in bronze effigy.

JOSEFOV

Prague's historic Jewish neighborhood and the oldest Jewish settlement in Europe lies north of Staromětstské nám., along Maiselova and several sidestreets. *(Metro A: Staroměstská.)* In 1179, the Pope decreed that all Christians should avoid Jews. The next year, Prague's citizens built a 12 ft. wall around the area. The closed city bred legends, many focusing on **Rabbi Loew ben Bezalel** (1512-1609) and his legendary *golem*—a mud creature that supposedly came to life to protect Prague's Jews. For the next 500 years, the city's Jews were exiled to this ghetto, which was vacated during WWII when its residents were deported to death camps. Though it's only a fraction of its former size, a Jewish community still exists in Prague today.

The **Maisel Synagogue** (Maiselova Synagoga) has artifacts from the Jewish Museum's extensive collections. *(On Maiselova, between Široká and Jáchymova.)* Turn left down Široká to reach the **Pinkas Synagogue** (Pinkasova Synagoga), converted in 1958 into a sobering memorial to the 80,000 Czech Jews killed in the Holocaust. Backtrack up Široká and go left on Maiselova to see the oldest operating synagogue in Europe, the 700-year-old **Old-New Synagogue** (Staronová Synagoga). Further up Široká on Dušní is the ornate **Spanish Synagogue** (Španělská Synagoga).

The **Old Jewish Cemetery** (Starý Židovský Hřbitov) remains Josefov's most popular attraction. Between the 14th and 18th centuries, 20,000 graves were laid in 12 layers. The striking clusters of tombstones result from a process by which the older stones were lifted from underneath. Rabbi Loew is buried by the wall directly opposite the entrance. *(At the corner of Široká and Žatecká.)*

MALÁ STRANA

The hangout of criminals and counterrevolutionaries for nearly a century, the Malá Strana is the most prized real estate in Prague. It centers around **Malostranské náměstí** and the Baroque **St. Nicholas's Cathedral** (Chrám sv. Mikuláš), whose dome is a Prague landmark. *(Metro A: Malostranská; follow Letenská to Malostranské Nám. Open daily 9am-4pm. 50Kč, students 25Kč.)* Along Letenská, a wooden gate opens through a wall into the beautiful **Wallenstein Garden** (Valdštejnská Zahrada), one of the city's best-kept secrets. *(Letenská 10. Metro A: Malostranská. Open Apr.-Oct. daily 10am-6pm.)*

PRAGUE CASTLE (PRAŽSKÝ HRAD)

Prague Castle has been the seat of the Bohemian government since its founding 1000 years ago. From the Metro, cross the tram tracks and turn left onto Tychonova to the newly renovated **Royal Summer Palace** (Královský Letohrádek). The main castle entrance is at the other end of the **Royal Garden** (Královská Zahrada), across the **Powder Bridge** (Prašný Most). Before exploring, pass the main gate to see the **Šternberský Palace.** *(Metro A: Malostranská. Take trams #22 or 23 to Pražský Hrad and go down U Prašného Mostu. Open Apr.-Oct. daily 9am-5pm; Nov.-Mar. 9am-4pm. Buy tickets opposite St. Vitus's Cathedral, inside castle walls. 3-day ticket valid at Royal Crypt, Cathedral/ Powder Tower, Old Royal Palace, and Basilica. 220Kč, students 110Kč.)*

Inside the castle walls stands its centerpiece, **St. Vitus's Cathedral** (Katedrála sv. Víta), which may look Gothic but in fact was only finished in 1929—600 years after construction began. Right of the high altar is the **tomb of St. Jan Nepomucký**, 3m of solid silver. The walls of **St. Wenceslas's Chapel** (Svatováclavská Kaple) are lined with gems and a painting cycle depicting the saint's legend. Climb the 287 steps of the **Cathedral Tower** for the best view of Prague. Go downstairs to Charles IV's tomb.

The Old Royal Palace (Starý Královský Palác), right of the cathedral behind the Old Provost's House and the statue of St. George, houses the **Vladislav Hall.** Upstairs is the **Chancellery of Bohemia,** where on May 23, 1618, angry Protestants flung two Habsburg officials out the window, triggering the Thirty Years' War.

Behind the cathedral and across the courtyard from the Old Royal Palace stand the Romanesque **St. George's Basilica** (Bazilika sv. Jiří) and its adjacent convent. The convent houses the **National Gallery of Bohemian Art,** with art ranging from Gothic to Baroque. *(Open Tu-Su 9am-5pm. 40Kč, students 20Kč.)*

MUSEUMS

The ▓**Mucha Museum** is devoted to Alfons Mucha, the Czech Republic's most celebrated artist, who composed some of the pioneering strokes of the Art Nouveau Movement. *(Panská 7. Metro A, B: Můstek. Walk up Václavské Nám. toward the St. Wenceslas statue. Go left onto Jindřišská and again onto Panská.* ☎*62 84 162; www.mucha.cz. Open daily 10am-6pm. 120Kč, students 60Kč.)* The massive **National Gallery** (Národní Galerie) is spread around nine different locations; the Šternberský palác and Klášter sv. Jiří are in the **Prague Castle** (see p. 551). St. Agnes's Cloister (Klášter sv. Anežky) is the other major branch, with a collection of 19th-century Czech art, but is undergoing renovation and has been moved to the **Trade Fair Palace and the Gallery of Modern Art** (Veletržní palác a Galerie moderního umwní). *(Dukelských hrinů 47. Metro C: Vltavská. All open Tu-Su 10am-6pm. 150Kč, students 70Kč.)* The new **Communism Museum** is committed to exposing the flaws of the Communist system that suppressed the Czechs from 1948-1989. It features a model factory and interrogation office. *(Na Příkopě 10. Metro A: Můstek. Open daily 9am-9pm. 180Kč, students 90Kč.)*

🎵 ENTERTAINMENT

Consult *Threshold* or *Do města-Downtown*, both free, or *The Prague Post.* Most performances start at 7pm and offer standby tickets 30min. beforehand. Between mid-May and early June, the **Prague Spring Festival** draws musicians from around the world. For tickets, try **Bohemia Ticket International,** Malé Nám. 13, next to Čedok. (☎24 22 78 32; www.ticketsbti.cz. Open M-F 9am-5pm, Sa 9am-2pm.) The **National Theater** (Národní divadlo), Národní 2/4, stages drama, opera, and ballet. (☎24 92 15 28. Metro B: Národní třída. Box office open M-F 10am-6pm, Sa-Su 10am-12:30pm and 3-6pm.) **Estates Theater** (Stavovské divadlo), Ovocný trh 1, is to the left of the pedestrian Na Příkopě. (Metro A, B: Můstek.) Mozart's *Don Giovanni* premiered here; shows today are mostly classic theater. Use the National Theater box office, or show up 30min. before showtime.

🏙 NIGHTLIFE

The best way to experience Prague at night is in an alcoholic fog. With some of the best beers in the world on tap, pubs and beer halls are understandably the city's favorite form of nighttime entertainment. Prague is not a clubbing city; more popular are the city's excellent jazz and rock clubs.

🍷 **Vinárna U Sudu,** Vodičkova 10. Metro A: Můstek. Cross Václavské Nám. to Vodičkova and follow the curve left. Infinite labyrinth of cavernous cellars. Red wine 120Kč per 1L. Open M-F noon-midnight, Sa-Su 2pm-midnight.

🍷 **Radost FX,** Bělehradská 120 (www.radostfx.cz). Metro C: I.P. Pavlova. Plays intense techno, jungle, and house. Creative drinks. Cover 80-150Kč. Also a late-night cafe. Open M-Sa 10pm-late.

🍷 **Jazz Club Železná,** Železná 16. Metro A, B: Staroměstská. Vaulted cellar bar showcases live jazz nightly. Beer 30Kč. Cover 80-150Kč. Shows 9-11:30pm. Open daily 3pm-1am.

U Fleků, Křemencova 11. Metro B: Národní třída. Turn right on Spálená away from Národní, right on Myslíkova, and then right again on Křemencova. The oldest brewhouse in Prague. Home-brewed beer 49Kč. Open daily 9am-11pm.

Kozička (The Little Goat), Kozí 1. Metro A: Staroměstská. This giant cellar bar is always packed; you'll know why after your first 0.5L of *Krušovice* (18Kč). Czech 20-somethings stay all night. Open M-F noon-4am, Sa-Su 6pm-4am.

U střelce, Karolíny Světlé 12. Metro B: Národní třída. Under the archway on the right, this gay club draws a diverse crowd for its cabarets. Cover 80Kč. Open W-Sa 9:30pm-5am, with shows after midnight.

APPENDIX

CLIMATE

Average Temperature	January		April		July		October	
	°C	°F	°C	°F	°C	°F	°C	°F
Geneva	0	32	9.5	49	19.5	67	10	50
Interlaken	0	32	10	50	19.5	67	11	51
Zurich	-1	30	8	47	18	64	8	47
Innsbruck	-2.5	28	9.5	49	18	64	9.5	49
Salzburg	-1.5	29	8	47	18	64	9	48
Vienna	-1	30	10	50	20	68	11	51
Munich	0.5	33	9	48	19	66	11	51

Although Austria and Switzerland are at about the same latitude as Newfoundland, their climates are considerably milder. In general, winters are cold and snowy enough for skiing, while summers are warm enough for outdoor cafés. July is usually the hottest month, with temperatures reaching 38°C (100°F) for brief periods, with generally cool evenings. February is the coldest, with temperatures down to -10°C (5°F). Mountainous areas of Austria and Switzerland are cooler and wetter the higher you get; as a rule, temperatures decrease about 1.7°C (3°F) with each additional 300m elevation. Snow cover lasts from late December to March in the valleys, from November to May at about 1800m, and year-round above 2500m. Switzerland's lake areas, in the temperate swath of plain that extends across from Lake Constance in the northeast through Zurich and Bern down to Geneva, are wet all year—don't forget your umbrella. For weather information on a particular city, check www.weatherlabs.com.

TIME ZONES

Switzerland and Austria both use Central European time (abbreviated MEZ in German), which is 6 hours later than Eastern Standard Time in the US and 1 hour later than Greenwich Mean Time. It is 9 hours earlier than Eastern Australia Time and 11 hours earlier than New Zealand Time. Austria and Switzerland use the 24-hour clock for all official purposes, so 19:30pm is the same as 7.30pm.

HOLIDAYS AND FESTIVALS

The *International Herald Tribune* lists national holidays in each daily edition, though the listing on www.holidayfestival.com is more complete and useful. If you plan your itinerary around these dates, you can encounter the festivals that entice you and circumvent the ones that don't. Many services shut down on holidays and could leave you strapped for food and money in the event of an ill-timed arrival. Note also that in Austria, the first Saturday of every month is *Langer Samstag* (long Saturday); most stores stay open until 5pm. In small towns, stores are often closed from noon Saturday until 8am Monday; remember this when stocking up on food for weekends. Check the individual town listings and the index for information on the festivals below.

BOTH COUNTRIES

DATE	FESTIVAL	REGION
January 1	New Year's	National
April 13	Good Friday	National
April 16	Easter Monday	National
May 24	Ascension	National
June 4	Whit Monday	National
December 25	Christmas	National

AUSTRIA

DATE	FESTIVAL	REGION
January 6	Epiphany	National
June 14	Corpus Christi Day	National
May 1	Labor Day	National
Late July to Late August	Salzburg Music Festival	Salzburg
August 15	Feast of the Assumption	National
October 26	Austrian National Day	National
November 1	All Saints' Day	National
December 8	Feast of the Immaculate Conception	National
December 26	Boxing Day	National

SWITZERLAND

DATE	FESTIVAL	REGION
January 2	Berchtold's Day	National
Early March	Fasnacht (Carnival)	Basel, Lucerne
Mid-July	International Jazz Festival	Montreux
August 1	Swiss National Day	National
December 26	St. Stephen's Day	National

MEASUREMENTS

Austria and Switzerland use the metric system. Unconventional local units for measuring wine or beer are explained in the text when necessary. Note that gallons in the U.S. are not identical to those across the Atlantic; one US gallon equals 0.83 Imperial gallons.

MEASUREMENT CONVERSIONS

1 inch (in.) = 25.4 mm	1 millimeter (mm) = 0.039 in.
1 foot (ft.) = 0.30 m	1 meter (m) = 3.28 ft.
1 yard (yd.) = 0.914m	1 meter (m) = 1.09 yd.
1 mi. = 1.61km	1 kilometer (km) = 0.62 mi.
1 ounce (oz.) = 28.35g	1 gram (g) = 0.035 oz.
1 pound (lb.) = 0.454kg	1 kilogram (kg) = 2.202 lb.
1 fluid ounce (fl. oz.) = 29.57ml	1 milliliter (ml) = 0.034 fl. oz.
1 gallon (gal.) = 3.785L	1 liter (L) = 0.264 gal.
1 acre (ac.) = 0.405ha	1 hectare (ha) = 2.47 ac.
1 square mile (sq. mi.) = 2.59km²	1 square kilometer (km²) = 0.386 sq. mi.

DISTANCE (IN KM)

Distances may vary depending on the type of transportation used and the route traveled. In certain cases, traveling through a neighboring country such as Germany or Italy can be the fastest route.

	Basel											
Basel		Bern										
Bern	71		Geneva									
Geneva	187	129		Graz								
Graz	597	610	718		Innsbruck							
Innsbruck	290	303	418	307		Interlaken						
Interlaken	98	43	230	581	278		Linz					
Linz	509	536	658	158	245	517		Locarno				
Locarno	180	135	204	520	235	92	478		Lugano			
Lugano	201	158	219	512	233	114	476	21		Salzburg		
Salzburg	410	433	554	200	137	412	108	370	369		Vienna	
Vienna	658	684	801	138	383	661	151	615	608	249		Zermatt
Zermatt	169	105	126	602	311	72	555	82	95	447	694	
Zurich	76	98	224	525	216	92	443	135	153	102	591	159

CITY PHONE CODES

CITY TELEPHONE CODES			
Basel	061	Liechtenstein	075
Bern	031	Locarno	091
Bregenz	05574	Lucerne	041
Geneva	022	Lugano	091
Graz	0316	Salzburg	0662
Innsbruck	0512	Vienna	0222
Interlaken	033	Zermatt	027
Lausanne	021	Zurich	01

LANGUAGE

Confronted with Switzerland's four official languages and the countless dialects of German spoken throughout Austria and Switzerland, many travelers feel somewhat intimidated by the thought of communicating. Each of the following phrasebooks is designed to help you master your most urgent communication needs in each of the major languages spoken in Austria and Switzerland. Each phrasebook is preceded by a pronunciation guide. Don't be afraid to attempt to use the phrases listed; with a little practice, they'll roll off your tongue.

The first, perhaps most helpful phrase a traveler should learn is "Sprechen Sie Englisch?," "Parlez-vous anglais?," or "Lei parla inglese?" (for use in the appropriate regions). Even if the person you ask doesn't speak English, he/she will appreciate your attempt to speak their language. Most younger Austrian and Swiss urbanites speak at least a smattering of English—usually much more—thanks to the establishment of English as a requirement for high school diplomas. Outside of cities and among older residents, however, the English proficiency becomes less reliable and you may have to rely on phrasebooks or an impromptu translation by the local tourist office.

If you're unsure in a foreign vocabulary, it's best to err on the side of formality. For example, it never hurts to use titles like *Herr* (Mr.) or *Frau* (Mrs.), the Italian *Signore* and *Signora*, or the French *Monsieur* (Mr.) and *Madame* (Mrs.). When in doubt, use the formal pronoun "you" (*Sie* in German, *Vous* in French, *Lei* in Italian) with the plural form of the verb. People will let you know when it's time to switch to more familiar language.

GERMAN PRONUNCIATION

Once you learn a few rules of German pronunciation, you should be able to sound out even the longest compound noun. Consonants are the same as in English, with the exceptions of C (pronounced *K*); J (pronounced *Y*); K (always pronounced, even before N); P (nearly always pronounced, even before F); QU (pronounced *KV*); S (pronounced *Z* at the beginning of a word); V (pronounced *F*); W (pronounced *V*); Z (pronounced *TS*). The ß, or *ess-tsett*, is simply a double S. Pronounce SCH as *SH*. In Austria, R is rolled in the front of the mouth, while CH is pronounced in Switzerland with the hoarse, throat-clearing sound that people often erroneously associate with German. Vowels are as follows: A as in "father"; E as the *a* in "hay" or the indistinct vowel sound in "uh"; I as the *ee* in "cheese"; O as in "oh"; U as in "fondue"; Y as the *oo* in "boot"; AU as in "sauerkraut"; EU as the *oi* in "boil." With EI and IE, pronounce the last letter as a long English vowel—*heisse* is HY-ssuh; *viele* is FEEL-uh.

FRENCH PRONUNCIATION

French pronunciation is more difficult than German, as many of the letters in a word are silent. Do not pronounce any final consonants except L, F, or C; an E on the end of the word, however, means that you should pronounce the final consonant sound, e.g., *muet* is mew-AY but *muette* is mew-ET. This rule also applies to plural nouns—don't pronounce the final S. J is like the S in "pleasure." R is rolled in the front of the mouth even more than in Austria. C sounds like *K* before A, O, and U; like *S* before E and I. A ç always sounds like *S*. Vowels are short and precise: A as the *O* in "mom"; E as in "help" (é becomes the a in "hay"); I as the *ee* in "creep"; O as in "oh." UI sounds like the word "whee." U is a short, clipped *oo* sound; hold your lips as if you were about to say "ooh," but say *ee* instead. OU is a straight *oo* sound. With few exceptions, all syllables receive equal emphasis.

ITALIAN PRONUNCIATION

Italian pronunciation isn't too complicated. There are 7 vowel sounds in standard Italian: A as in "father," I as the *ee* in "cheese," U as the *oo* in "droop," E either as *ay* in "bay" or *eh* in "set," and O both as *oh* in "bone" and *o* as in "off." Save for a few quirks, Italian consonants are easy. H is always silent, R is always rolled. C and G are hard before A, O, or U, as in "cat" and "goose," but they soften into CH and j sounds, respectively, when followed by I or E, as in English "cheese" and "jeep" or Italian *ciao* (chow), "goodbye," and *gelato* (jeh-LAH-toh), "ice cream." CH and GH are pronounced like K and G before I and E, as in *chianti* (ky-AHN-tee), the Tuscan wine, and *spaghetti* (spah-GEHT-tee), the pasta. Pronounce GN like the NI in "onion," as in *bagno* (BAHN-yoh), the bathroom. GLI is like the LLI in *million*, so *sbagliato* ("wrong") is said "zbal-YAH-toh." When followed by A, O, or U, SC is pronounced as *SK*. *Scusi* ("excuse me") yields "SKOO-zee." When followed by an E or I, SC is pronounced SH as in *sciopero* (SHOH-pair-oh), "strike."

USEFUL PHRASES

ENGLISH	GERMAN	FRENCH	ITALIAN
Hello	Hallo	Bonjour	Ciao
Excuse me/sorry	Entschuldigung	Excusez-moi	Scusi/Mi dispiace
Could you please help me?	Können Sie mir bitte helfen?	Est-ce que vous pouvez m'aider?	Potrebbe aiutarmi?
Good day	Guten Tag/Grüß Gott (Gruezi/Gruessach)	Bonjour	Buongiorno
Good morning	Guten Morgen	Bonjour	Buonagiorno
Good evening	Guten Abend	Bonsoir	Buona sera
Good night	Gute Nacht	Bonne nuit	Buona notte
Good-bye	Tschüß! (informal); Auf Wiedersehen! (formal)	Au revoir	Arrivederci/ Arrivederla
yes/no/maybe	ja/nein/vielleicht	oui/non/peut-être	si/no/forse
Please	Bitte	S'il vous plaît	Per favore/Per piacere
Thank you	Danke	Merci	Grazie
You're welcome	Bitte	De rien	Prego
Who?	Wer?	Qui?	Chi?
What?	Was?	Comment?	Cosa?
Where?	Wo?	Où?	Dovè?
When (what time)?	Wann?	Quand?	Quando?
Why?	Warum?	Pourquoi?	Perche?
My name is...	Ich heiße...	Je m'appelle...	Mi chiamo...
What is your name?	Wie heißen Sie?	Comment vous appelez-vous?	Come ti chiami?
Where are you from?	Woher kommen Sie?	Vous venez-d'où?	Di dove sei?
I'm from ...	Ich komme aus...	Je viens de...	Sono di...
How are you?	Wie geht's?	Comment ça va?	Come sta (formal)/stai?
I'm fine.	Es geht mir gut.	Ça va bien.	Sto bene.
I'm not feeling well.	Mir ist schlecht.	J'ai mal.	Sto male.
I have a headache.	Ich habe Kopfweh.	J'ai mal à la tête.	Ho un mal di testa.
I need a doctor.	Ich brauche einen Arzt.	J'ai besoin d'un médecin.	Ho bisogno di un medico.
Leave me alone.	Lass mich in Ruhe.	Laissez-moi tranquille.	Lasciame in pace!
I'll call the police.	Ich rufe die Polizei an.	J'appelle la police.	Telefono alla polizia!
Help!	Hilfe!	Au secours!/Aidez-moi, s'il vous plaît.	Aiuto!
Stop/Enough!	Halt!/Genug!	Arrête!	Ferma!/Basta!
Do you speak English?	Sprechen Sie Englisch?	Parlez-vous anglais?	Lei parla inglese?
I can't speak ...	Ich kann kein Deutsch.	Je ne parle pas français.	Non parlo italiano.
I don't understand.	Ich verstehe nicht.	Je ne comprends pas.	Non capisco.
I understand	Ich verstehe.	Je comprends.	Ho capito.
Please speak slowly.	Sprechen Sie bitte langsam.	S'il vous plaît, parlez moins vite.	Parla più lentamente, per favore.
Excuse me?	Wie, bitte?	Pardon?	Come?
Please repeat.	Bitte widerholen sie.	Répétez, s'il vous plaît.	Potrebbe ripetere?
I would like...	Ich möchte...	Je voudrais...	Vorrei...
I'm looking for...	Ich suche...	Je cherche...	Cerco...
How much does that cost?	Wieviel kostet das?	Ça coûte combien?	Quanto costa?

ENGLISH	GERMAN	FRENCH	ITALIAN
Where can I buy something to eat/to drink?	Wo kann ich etwas zu essen kaufen/zu trinken kaufen?	Où est-ce que je peux acheter quelque chose à manger/à boire?	Dove posso comprare qualcosa da bere o mangiare?
OK.	Alles klar.	D'accord.	D'accordo.
I don't know.	Ich weiss nicht.	Je ne sais pas.	Boh./Non lo so.
Where is the toilet?	Wo ist die Toilette?	Où sont les toilettes?	Dov'è il gabinetto?
Please	Bitte	S'il vous plait	Per favore
How do you say that in German?/French?...	Wie sagt man das auf Deutsch?	Comment ça se dit en français?	Come si dice...?
What does this mean?	Was bedeutet das?	Qu'est-ce que ça veut dire?	Cosa vuol dire questo?
Where is the phone?	Wo ist das Telefon?	Où est le téléphone?	Dov'è il telefono?
I am a student (male/female).	Ich bin Student/Studentin.	Je suis étudiant(e).	Sono studente/studentessa.
student discounts	Studentenermässigungen	tarifs réduits pour les étudiants	sconto per gli studenti
No problem	Kein Proble	Ce n'est pas grave	Va bene

DIRECTIONS AND TRANSPORTATION

(to the) right	rechts	à droite	a destra
(to the) left	links	à gauche	a sinistra
straight ahead	geradeaus	tout droite	sempre diritto
here	hier	ici	qui/qua
there	da	lá-bas	lì/là
far	fern	loin	lontano
near	nah	près de	vicino
east/west	Ost/West	est/ouest	ovest/este
north/south	Nord/Süd	nord/sud	nord/sud
I would like a ticket to...	Ich möchte eine Fahrkarte nach...	Je voudrais un billet à...	Vorrei un biglietto per...
Where is this train going?	Wohin fährt dieser Zug?	Quelle est la destination de la train?	Dove va questo treno?
Which bus goes to...	Welcher Bus fährt nach...?	Quel bus va â...?	Qual' autobus va a...?
When does the train leave?	Wann fährt der Zug ab?	Quand est-ce que le train part?	A che ora parte il treno?
Please stop.	Bitte halten Sie.	Arretez, s'il vous plait.	Ferma, per favore.
Where is...?	Wo ist...?	Où est...?	Dov'è...?
the train station?	der Bahnhof?	la gare?	la stazione?
the tourist office?	das Touristbüro?	le bureau de tourisme?	l'ufficio turistico?
the post office?	die Post?	la poste?	l'ufficio postale?
the old town?	die Altstadt?	la vieille ville?	il centro storico?
the hostel?	die Jugendherberge?	l'auberge de jeunesse?	il ostello?
a grocery store?	ein Supermarkt?	le supermarché?	il supermercato?
the bus stop?	die Haltestelle?	l'arrêt d'autobus?	la fermata dell'autobus?
one-way	einfache Fahrt	un billet aller-simple	solo andata
round-trip	hin- und zurück	aller-retour	andata e ritorno

TIMES AND HOURS

At what time...?	Um wie viel Uhr...?	À quelle heure?	A che ora...?
What time is it?	Wie spät ist es?	Quelle heure est-il?	Che ore sono?
It is 5 o'clock.	Es ist fünf (5) Uhr.	Il est cinq (5) heures.	Sono le cinque (5).
It's early.	Es ist früh.	Il est tôt.	in anticipo/presto
It's late.	Es ist spät.	Il est tard.	in ritardo/tardi
opening hours	die Öffnungszeiten	Les heures d'ouverture	orari
daily	täglich	chaque jour	quotidiano
weekly	wochentlich	chaque semaine	settimanale
monthly	monatlich	chaque mois	mensile
today	heute	aujourd'hui	oggi
tomorrow	morgen	demain	domani
yesterday	gestern	hier	ieri
now	jetzt	maintenant	adesso/ora
immediately	sofort	tout-de-suite	subito
always	immer	toujours	sempre
except	ohne	sauf	ecceto
January	Januar	janvier	gennaio
February	Februar	février	febbraio
March	März	mars	marzo
April	April	avril	aprile
May	Mai	mai	maggio
June	Juni	juin	guigno
July	Juli	juillet	luglio
August	August	août	agosto
September	September	septembre	settembre
October	October	octobre	ottobre
November	November	novembre	novembre
December	December	decembre	dicembre
open	geöffnet	ouvert	aperto
closed	geschlossen	fermé	chiuso
morning	der Morgen	le matin	mattina
afternoon	der Nachmittag	l'après-midi	pomeriggio
evening	der Abend	le soir	sera
night	die Nacht	la nuit	notte
break time, rest day	die Ruhepause, der Ruhetag	fermeture	riposo
Monday	Montag	lundi	lunedì
Tuesday	Dienstag	mardi	martedì
Wednesday	Mittwoch	mercredi	mercoledì
Thursday	Donnerstag	jeudi	giovedì
Friday	Freitag	vendredi	venerdì
Saturday	Samstag	samedi	sabato
Sunday	Sonntag	dimanche	domenica
holidays	ferien	vacances	giorni festivi

NUMBERS

No.	German	French	Italian
0	null	zéro	zero
1	eins	un	uno
2	zwei or zwoh	deux	due
3	drei	trois	tre
4	vier	quatre	quattro
5	fünf	cinq	cinque
6	sechs	six	sei
7	sieben	sept	sette
8	acht	huit	otto
9	neun	neuf	nove
10	zehn	dix	dieci
11	elf	onze	undici
12	zwölf	douze	dodici
13	dreizehn	treize	tredici
14	vierzehn	quatorze	quattordici
15	fünfzehn	quinze	quindici
16	sechzehn	seize	sedici
17	siebzehn	dix-sept	diciasette
18	achtzehn	dix-huit	diciotto
19	neunzehn	dix-neuf	dicianove
20	zwanzig	vingt	venti
21	ein-und-zwanzig	vingt et un	ventuno
30	dreißig	trente	trenta
40	vierzig	quarante	quaranta
50	fünfzig	cinquante	cinquanta
60	sechzig	soixante	sessanta
70	siebzig	soixante-dix	settanta
80	achtzig	quatre-vingt	ottanta
90	neunzig	quatre-vingt-dix	novanta
100	(ein)hundert	cent	cento
101	hunderteins	cent-et-un	centuno
1000	(ein)tausend	mille	mille

FOOD AND RESTAURANTS

restaurant	das Restaurant	un restaurant	il ristorante
bar	die Bar	un Bar	il Bar
meal	das Mahl	un repas	pasto

water	das Wasser	l'eau	l'acqua
breakfast	das Frühstück	le petit déjeuner	la (prima) colazione
lunch	das Mittagessen	le déjeuner	il pranzo
dinner/supper	das Abendessen	le dîner	la cena
I am thirsty/hungry.	Ich habe Durst/Hunger.	J'ai soif/faim.	Ho sed/fame.
waiter(ess)	Kellner(in)/Herr Ober	serveur/euse	cameriere/a
Check, please.	Die Rechnung, bitte.	L'addition, s'il vous plaît.	Il conto, per favore.
Service included.	Bedienung inklusiv.	Service compris.	Servizio compresso.
I would like...	Ich hätte gern...	Je voudrais...	Vorrei
It tastes good.	Es schmeckt gut.	C'est bon.	Tutto bene.
Do you have vegetarian food?	Haben Sie vegetarisches Essen?	Avez-vous de la nourriture vegetarienne?	Hai qualcosa vegeteriana da mangiare?
I am diabetic.	Ich bin Diabetiker.	Je suis diabétique.	Sono diabetico.
milk	das Milch	le lait	la latte
coffee	das Kaffee	le café	il caffè
beer/wine	das Bier/der Wein	la bière/le vin	la bierra/il vino
tap water	das Leitungswasser	de l'eau de robinet	acqua di rubinetto
bread	das Brot	le pain	il pane
vegetables	die Gemüse	le légume	le verdure
meat	das Fleisch	la viande	le carne
sausage	die Wurst	le saucisson	la salsiccia
chicken	das Huhn	le poulet	il pollo
pork	das Schweinfleisch	le porc	il maiale
cheese	der Käse	le fromage	il formagio
pasta	die Nudeln	les pâtes	pasta
dessert	der Nachtisch	le dessert	il dolce

MISCELLANEOUS WORDS

a single room	ein Einzelzimmer	une chambre simple	una camera singola
money	das Geld	l'argent	gli soldi
hospital	das Krankenhaus	un hôpital	ospedale
sick	krank	malade	malato/a
smoking	rauchen	fumer	fumare
good/bad	gut/schlecht	bon/mauvais	buono/cattivo
happy/sad	glücklich/traurig	heureux/triste	felice/triste
hot/cold	heiß/kalt	chaud/froid	caldo/freddo
big/small	groß/klein	grand/petit	piccolo/grande
full/empty	voll/ leer	plein/vide	pieno/vuoto
dangerous/safe	gefährlich/ungefährlich	dangereux/sûr	pericoloso/sicuro
Caution!	Achtung!/Vorsicht!	Attention!	Attenzione!
Fire!	Feuer!	Feu!	Fuoco!
You're cute.	Du bist süß.	Tu es mignon/ne.	Sei bellino/a
May I buy you a drink?	Darf ich dir ein Getränk kaufen?	Je peux t'offrir quelque chose?	Posso offrirti qualcosa da bere?
My father is a policeman.	Mein Vater ist Polizist.	Mon père est policier.	Il mio padre è polizia.

INDEX

I N D E X

WHO WE ARE

A NEW LET'S GO FOR 2003

With a sleeker look and innovative new content, we have revamped the entire series to reflect more than ever the needs and interests of the independent traveler. Here are just some of the improvements you will notice when traveling with the new *Let's Go*.

MORE PRICE OPTIONS

Still the best resource for budget travelers, *Let's Go* recognizes that everyone needs the occasional indulgence. Our "Big Splurges" indicate establishments that are actually worth those extra pennies (pulas, pesos, or pounds), and price-level symbols (❶ ❷ ❸ ❹ ❺) allow you to quickly determine whether an accommodation or restaurant will break the bank. We may have diversified, but we'll never lose our budget focus—"Hidden Deals" reveal the best-kept travel secrets.

BEYOND THE TOURIST EXPERIENCE

Our Alternatives to Touism chapter offers ideas on immersing yourself in a new community through study, work, or volunteering.

AN INSIDER'S PERSPECTIVE

As always, every item is written and researched by our on-site writers. This year we have highlighted more viewpoints to help you gain an even more thorough understanding of the places you are visiting.

IN RECENT NEWS. *Let's Go* correspondents around the globe report back on current regional issues that may affect you as a traveler.

CONTRIBUTING WRITERS. Respected scholars and former *Let's Go* writers discuss topics on society and culture, going into greater depth than the usual guidebook summary.

THE LOCAL STORY. From the Parisian monk toting a cell phone to the Russian *babushka* confronting capitalism, *Let's Go* shares its revealing conversations with local personalities—a unique glimpse of what matters to real people.

FROM THE ROAD. Always helpful and sometimes downright hilarious, our researchers share useful insights on the typical (and atypical) travel experience.

SLIMMER SIZE

Don't be fooled by our new, smaller size. *Let's Go* is still packed with invaluable travel advice, but now it's easier to carry with a more compact design.

FORTY-THREE YEARS OF WISDOM

For over four decades *Let's Go* has provided the most up-to-date information on the hippest cafes, the most pristine beaches, and the best routes from border to border. It all started in 1960 when a few well-traveled students at Harvard University handed out a 20-page mimeographed pamphlet of their tips on budget travel to passengers on student charter flights to Europe. From humble beginnings, *Let's Go* has grown to cover six continents and *Let's Go: Europe* still reigns as the world's best-selling travel guide. This year we've beefed up our coverage of Latin America with *Let's Go: Costa Rica* and *Let's Go: Chile;* on the other side of the globe, we've added *Let's Go: Thailand* and *Let's Go: Hawaii.* Our new guides bring the total number of titles to 61, each infused with the spirit of adventure that travelers around the world have come to count on.

Your
travel makes
a difference

Give something back to the communities you visit. Log on to
www.sustainabletravel.org to learn more about:

- ▶ Community-operated lodging, tours other offerings
- ▶ Innovative travel companies
- ▶ Global internship opportunities

BEST is a non-profit initiative that helps travelers, communities, and
businesses protect and restore the natural and cultural
integrity of destinations, while enhancing the livelihoods and
overall well-being of local residents.

THE CONFERENCE BOARD

Business Enterprises for Sustainable Travel • 845 Third Avenue • New York, NY 10022 • 212-339-0227

MAP INDEX

MAP LEGEND

✚ Hospital	🏛 Museum	♠ Hotel/Hostel
♣ Police	✈ Airport	⛺ Camping
✉ Post Office	🚌 Bus Station	Food & Drink
ⓘ Tourist Office	🚆 Train Station	☕ Coffee House
$ Bank	Ⓤ1 U-BAHN STATION	★ Nightlife/Clubs
℞ Pharmacy	⚓ Ferry Landing	Pubs
● Service	TAXI Taxi Stand	Theatre
■ Site or Point of Interest	Funicular/Cable Car	Mountain Pass
Embassy or Consulate	Church	⌂ Mountain Hut
Library	P Parking	Castle
Internet Café	⊓ Gate or Entrance	Ski Resort

Cave
Waterfall
Mountain Peaks
Mountains
Glacier
Cliffs
Tunnel
Ferry Route
Funicular/Cable Car
Pedestrian Zone
Stairs
Footpaths/Trails
Railroads